The Technology of
Wine Making

Third Edition

other AVI books

The Technology of
Wine Making

Third Edition

by M. A. Amerine, Ph.D.

*Professor of Enology and Enologist in the
Agricultural Experiment Station, University
of California, Davis, California*

H. W. Berg, M.S.

*Professor of Enology and Enologist in the
Agricultural Experiment Station, University
of California, Davis, California*

and W. V. Cruess, Ph.D. (Deceased)

*Professor of Food Technology, Emeritus, and Chemist
Emeritus in the Agricultural Experiment Station,
University of California, Berkeley, California*

WESTPORT, CONNECTICUT

THE AVI PUBLISHING COMPANY, INC.

1972

Library of Congress Catalog Card Number: 78-188033

ISBN-0-87055-116-7

Printed in the United States of America

Preface to the Third Edition

We have taken the opportunity of correcting a number of errors in the second edition and also of eliminating some material and adding new. Because of the new classification of yeasts Chapter 5 has been extensively revised. Recent changes in state and Federal regulations required major alterations in Chapter 20.

We are indebted to Mr. Charles Crawford and Mr. Paul Frei of the California wine industry for their advice on the text. Mr. W. Allmendinger and Mr. James Seff of the Wine Institute have also been most generous in supplying statistical and legal information.

M. A. AMERINE
H. W. BERG
Davis, California

September 1, 1971

Preface to the Second Edition

Research in enology has been extensive in many countries since the first edition. This has been especially true in studies on the composition of grapes and wines, wine stability, yeasts and bacteria, and sparkling wines. We have taken advantage of the need of a new edition to make extensive changes in the text on these subjects. In Chapter 6, for example, more than 100 new references have been added. We have also minutely examined the whole book to correct errors, to reflect the latest information and to clarify the meaning.

Professor Cruess asked to be relieved of formal responsibility in this revision. Many parts of the text, however, reflect his extensive research and opinions so it is entirely proper that his authorship be continued.

We are grateful to Professor Ralph E. Kunkee who has read and corrected portions of the revised text. We also thank the Wine Institute, and especially Mr. J. R. Lazarus and Mr. W. Allmendinger for their assistance in supplying legal and statistical information. The errors that remain are the responsibility of the authors. We would be grateful to know of those found by our readers.

M. A. AMERINE
H. W. BERG
W. V. CRUESS
Davis, California

November 1, 1966

Preface to the First Edition

Pasteur's *Études sur le vin* was first published in 1866.[1] The revolution in the fermentation industries that began with Pasteur over a hundred years ago continues still. The essence of this revolution was the application of scientific principles to the fermentation industries. Pasteur, himself a chemist, utilized his knowledge of chemistry. He became a microbiologist. His studies on heat are those of a chemical engineer. In the evaluation of his results by groups of tasters he approached recent techniques for the sensory evaluation of foods.

Today, no one can deny that fermentation industries, of which wine making is a part, have become to a high degree scientific. Applications of nearly all of the modern physical and biological scientific disciplines may be found in them and the results (in antibiotic production, for example) are ample proof of the value of the scientific approach.

However, we cannot explain wine making in a completely scientific manner. Neither the chemical composition of the grape nor of the wine is fully known. The influence of the biological and physical processes during fermentation and aging on each of these constituents has not been clearly elucidated. Finally, the subjective nature of the evaluation of wine makes the interpretation of these extremely complex interrelationships very difficult. Thus, there remains in wine making much that is empirical, for which we have, as yet, no complete explanation.

In this edition we have attempted to apply scientific principles in-so-far as possible. We have included descriptive material of regions, varieties, and processes where it seems to us that these influence the quality of the product, even though we are unable to delineate exactly the exact mechanism of their influence.

It may be pertinent here to point out that whereas processing is paramount for one type of wine—for example, California sherry—variety may be the critical factor for another—New York-Delaware.

This is not a text in European wine making. However, nearly three-fourths of the world's wine is produced in that area and their experience can be of use to us. We hasten to add that this does not mean that Cali-

---

[1] Actually Pasteur began his studies on wine in September, 1858, and the results finally incorporated in his text were largely published as scientific papers prior to 1866.

fornia or American wines—the types primarily discussed—should be slavish imitations of European types. Both of the authors have previously noted that a new and better nomenclature for American wines, without European antecedents, would be of great utility. However, with some exceptions, which we shall note, there has been too little commercial interest in new type names. Some suggestions for others will be made in the text.

In many respects this is the third edition of The Principles and Practices of Wine Making by W. V. Cruess which was published in 1947. However, we have concluded that the text has been changed so much that it would be better to give it a new title. This is still the principles and practices because we believe principles should and must precede practice.

We have received help from many of our colleagues within the University and the industry. We express here our thanks to all of them. Especially thanks are due to Mr. Theodore Carl who prepared certain sections on wine making in Eastern United States and Canada, and to Professors H. W. Berg, J. F. Guymon, J. L. Ingraham, G. L. Marsh, H. J. Pfaff, R. H. Vaughn, and A. D. Webb of the College of Agriculture, and to our colleagues in the California and Mexican wine industry, R. C. Auerbach, J. H. Fessler, M. Ibarra, M. Nightingale, F. J. Pilone, and A. Pirrone.

M. A. AMERINE
Davis, California
W. V. CRUESS
Berkeley, California

September 1, 1960

Contents

CHAPTER 1

Wines and Wine Regions of the World

Wine has been a part of the diet of man since he settled in the Tigris-Euphrates basin and in Egypt several thousand years before our era. From these regions the vine was carried to all the Mediterranean countries by pre-Christian traders. According to Vogt (1963) grape culture for wine production was known to the Assyrians and Egyptians by 3500 B.C. Greek traders brought grapes to Marseille by 600 B.C. and grape culture had spread far down the Rhine by 200 A.D. and reached its widest extension in Europe in the 15th century.

Wine represented a safe and healthful beverage. It also provided calories and vitamins. At a time when food was not the best, wine was an important food adjunct. During periods when life was often strenuous it offered relaxation and a very real surcease from pain. Wine thus became the normal table beverage of the Mediterranean countries, except for those where religion forbade its use. Even non-wine producing countries, such as England, the Benelux, and Scandinavian countries, imported large amounts of wine. Wherever Europeans have settled they have attempted the culture of the vine, or, failing this, they have imported European wines for their needs.

The literature contains many references to the importance of wine from Homer to Hemingway. The first miracle, Cana, of the New Testament has to do with wine. Roman historians and poets have left us eloquent testimony in praise of wine. The vine was cultivated and wines made throughout Europe during the post-Roman and pre-modern period. For a general history of wines, see Allen (1961), Amerine and Singleton (1965), and Younger (1966).

PRINCIPAL WINE REGIONS

Species of *Vitis,* the grape vine, are found widely distributed throughout the world. The fruit of most of these species is unsuited to the production of wine because of deficiencies in composition or production or possibly in some cases to an undesirable flavor.

The most important species, *Vitis vinifera,* is believed to have been brought by man from southern Russia to Asia Minor. From there Phoenecians, Greeks, and later Romans, spread its culture around the Mediterranean and as far north as England, Germany, Czechoslovakia, and Hungary. *Vitis vinifera* also followed European explorers to the temperate

1

TABLE 1

WORLD ACREAGE, WINE PRODUCTION, AND PER CAPITA CONSUMPTION 1956, 1960 and 1969

Country	Vineyards (Thousand Acres)			Production (Thousand Gallons)			Consumption (Gallons Per Capita)		
	1956	1960	1969	1956	1960	1969	1956	1960	1969
Europe									
Albania	8.3[1]	12.0	30.2[1]	924[1]	924[1]	810[7]	...	...	...
Austria	85.5	84.1	112.5	10,306	23,694	59,803	3.7	...	8.8
Bulgaria	351.1	396.3	481.8	30,009[2]	71,914	125,645	1.9	...	5.8
Czechoslovakia	44.1[4]	58.6	78.9	10,824[1]	8,724	19,706	...	...	2.4
France	3,500.0	3,479.0	3,220.9	1,331,923	1,615,487	1,314,720	38.3	37.0	29.6
Germany	164.9	187.5	205.0	24,517	196,237	157,010	2.4	3.0	4.2
Greece	552.0	528.5	530.0[7]	108,868	104,404	145,200[1]	12.4	10.8	7.4
Hungary	465.1	488.5	560.2	62,503	78,038	152,143	30.4	28.3	9.9
Italy	4,080.0	4,195.0	3,715.5	1,680,413	1,460,395	1,886,808	8.1	9.6	29.3
Luxembourg	3.0	3.0	2.9	1,663	3,247	3,221	...	...	8.5
Malta	3.3[3]	3.3	2.9[1]	1,055[5]	1,055[1]	528[1]	...	...	...
Portugal	748.1	774.9	835.6	291,328	316,246	218,364	33.0	22.2	21.5
Rumania	569.9	577.0	819.1	72,598	158,400[1]	164,588	4.1	4.1	6.1
Spain	3,869.1	3,963.6	3,877.3	558,200	561,172	664,667	17.7	13.4	18.3
Switzerland	27.6	29.5	29.0	9,898	25,466	19,775	9.8	12.9	11.0
U.S.S.R.	1,200.0	2,287.2	2,597.0	115,944	172,392	650,865	...	...	1.8[9]
Yugoslavia	655.9	655.2	651.3	84,954	88,440	186,375	7.4	5.8	6.9
South America									
Argentina	536.1	582.1	706.0	351,666[2]	416,466	472,986	20.0	...	23.1
Bolivia	4.5[1]	4.4	4.6[8]	158[1]	158[1]	158[1]	...	...	...
Brazil	121.1	147.2	174.7	36,336[2]	33,199[2]	44,230	...	...	0.5
Chile	264.5	269.8	274.0[7]	104,369	97,944	106,221	15.9	...	13.3
Peru	16.1[1]	15.6	20.0[8]	2,540	1,580[1]	6,602[9]	...	...	0.4[9]
Uruguay	44.7	44.7	44.9[8]	23,074	21,371	22,090[1]	...	6.9	6.9[8]
Africa									
Algeria	951.6	882.6	734.1	491,855	418,461	230,610	...	...	0.3
Egypt	19.2[1]	19.2	26.1[1]	770[5]	792[1]	1,347[10]	...	...	...
Morocco	155.0	164.6	142.8	55,777	60,905	18,658	...	1.0	0.4
South Africa	153.6	159.5	238.0	85,511	83,961	129,418	4.5	...	2.7
Tunisia	113.5	119.1	110.5[7]	33,542	40,572	13,562	...	...	...

North America									
Canada	20.8	20.3	20.2[1]	6,600[1]	9,974	11,383[10]	0.5	...	0.7
Mexico	23.7[5]	24.9	40.8	1,584[1]	1,584[1]	3,014[9]	...	...	0.1
United States	564.0[1]	448.6[3]	463.9[7]	153,648	166,410	224,400[1]	0.9	0.9	1.0
Asia									
Cyprus	71.9[1]	90.4	92.6	5,280[1]	7,392	30,571	...	0.3	3.0[10]
Iran	180.0[1]	180.0[1]	180.0[1]	92[1]	48[1]	951	1.0	1.1	1.1
Israel	24.4	24.0	22.1	2,133	4,379	10,502	0.1	...	0.1
Japan	17.6[6]	25.8	55.9	6,376	12,904	4,467	...	...	...
Jordan	38.9	45.0	43.7[8]	633[1]	660[1]	4,388[1]	...	...	0.7
Lebanon	53.3	55.2	43.4[4]	760	924	1,003[1]	...	...	0.1
Syria	172.8[1]	172.9	206.4	528[1]	528[1]	181[10]	...	...	0.1
Turkey	1,747.5	1,911.6	2,011.2	5,934	4,459	13,620	0.1	...	0.4
Oceania									
Australia	131.1	126.5	139.0	27,559	37,074	63,271	1.3	1.4	2.2
New Zealand	1.0[1]	1.1	2.5[7]	610	1,112[1]	3,564[10]	...	...	1.0
Total	21,755.3	23,258.3	23,547.5	5,793,262	6,309,092	7,182,569			

Source: Bulletin Office international vin 31 (331), 37–44; (332), 37–62; (333), 10–49; 32 (337), 3; 33 (347), 6–52; (348), 13–64; 349, 23–65; 34 (359), 49–83; 43 (477), 1190–97. 1958, 1959, 1960, 1961, 1970. La Journée Vinicole 33 (9725), 4, 6; (9726), 2, 4. 1959.

[1] Estimated.
[2] Includes wine for distilling.
[3] California only.
[4] 1954.
[6] 1955.
[7] 1965.
[8] 1966.
[9] 1967.
[10] 1968.

zones of the New World, South Africa, and Australia. Present acreage and wine production of the various countries are given in Table 1.

Europe is obviously the most important wine-producing area with more than 75 per cent of the acreage and wine production. If the Mediterranean regions of Africa are added the percentages are 80 and 81, respectively. Except for limited areas, in France, Rumania, Russia, and Italy, nearly all of the European production is from V. vinifera. As much as 15 to 20 per cent of French wine is made from "direct producers." These are hybrids of V. vinifera and of some species of Vitis resistant to downy or powdery mildew, black rot, or phylloxera.

The only other regions where species other than V. vinifera are used extensively for wine making are Canada, Eastern United States and Brazil. Many attempts to grow V. vinifera in Eastern United States have been made from Colonial times to the present. No extensive commercial success has resulted from these, although with better rootstocks more favorable results have been obtained. The warm humid growing period of this region (and of Brazil also) favors cryptogamic diseases, insect pests, and probably virus infection. Species other than V. vinifera have been domesticated to provide fruit for wine making and for table purposes. These include V. labrusca, V. rotundifolia, related species, and hybrids of these with each other. More recently the hybrids of these with V. vinifera, the "direct producers" mentioned above, have also been extensively planted.

Romanticists often claim that European wines are superior because the vineyards have low yields and the wineries use century-old barrels. As a matter of fact, European vineyardists have been surprisingly fast in improving production and in changing production methods. At Schloss Johannisberg, according to Alleweldt (1959A) from 1900 to 1927 production averaged only 146 gallons per acre! By the use of high-yielding clones this has been increased to 498 gallons per acre in 1964 without decreasing quality. Similar results have been obtained in Alsace. Most German wines are now fermented in pressure tanks.

France[1]

Climate is obviously one of the critical factors influencing the cultivation of the vine in France. The heat summation of various regions of

---

[1] In the discussion of regions which follows, no attempt has been made to give a comprehensive listing of all the wine types. Our objective has been rather to describe briefly the wine of the region and to evaluate the factors which contribute to its quality. For a more complete discussion of French regions see Amerine and Singleton (1965), Dion (1959), Healy (1963), Jeffs (1971), Lichine (1969), Jacquelin and Poulain (1962), Pestel (1959), Poulain and Jacquelin (1960), Roger (1960), or older treatises by Allen (1924, 1951, 1952B), Marres (1950), Schmutz (1936), Schoonmaker and Marvel (1934), Shand (1960), Simon (1957), and Thudichum and Dupré (1872).

western Europe and California are given in Table 14 on p. 119. See also Winkler (1936, 1962).

The north of France and of certain other regions are too cold for the vine. Even very early ripening varieties, such as Pinot noir, do not ripen sufficiently every year in Burgundy, for example, and sugar must be added to make up the deficiency.

Soil temperature is not only a function of surface temperature but of soil drainage. This in turn depends partially on soil composition and texture. The successful culture of the vine on well-drained slopes in Alsace, Burgundy, and Champagne is partially related to soil temperature.

The nice adaptation of varieties to climatic and soil conditions is the second factor with a demonstrable influence on the quality of French wines. In some regions, Burgundy and Champagne, it is an early-ripening variety, such as Pinot noir, which is important. In others a *mélange* of varieties is necessary in order to secure the best balanced musts from year to year. Châteauneuf-du-Pape and Bordeaux (red and white) are examples of this practice. An excellent survey of the varieties used in the various regions of France is that of Galet (1957–1964). The standard treatise on French enology is Ribéreau-Gayon and Peynaud (1960–1961).

Finally, the fermentation procedure, especially the low-temperature of fermentation of white musts, and the method of aging influence quality. The aging of many Bordeaux red wines in new oak casks gives them a distinct character.

The application of government regulations to regional wine types, commonly known as *appellations contrôlées,* is of increasing importance to the French wine industry but they cover a much wider field. As applied to quality wines they are administered by the *Institut National des Appellations d'Origine des Vins et Eaux-de-Vie* (1952). Essentially these regulations delimit the region, specify the varieties which may be employed, limit the minimum per cent alcohol and the maximum yield per hectare. For a discussion of these French laws and their interpretation see Capus in Lafforgue (1947). The history and philosophy of protected place names in French law were reviewed by Quittanson (1965). It is of interest to note that sensory examination of such wines is provided for. He makes the useful point that the right to a noble name carries obligations with respect to quality. For a description of the social and economic importance of wine *appellations d'origine* to France see Pestel (1959). A quality factor which we believe is particularly important in certain regions is that the wine maker is an artist. This has been expressed by Pestel (1959) as follows:

Mais, et ceci est encore tres particulier, dans les régions de vins fins le vigneron se transforme en artiste . . . Esprit d'observation, patience, courage, discipline, sens artistique, ce ne sont pas des qualités à dédaigner chez les hommes, et la profession qui les fait naître ou les développe doit être considérée comme bien utile pour le pays tout entier.

Even given fine varieties and perfect soil and climate, the slovenly workman may make only an ordinary rather than a great wine. The artist attempts to handle the wine in such a way as to develop and emphasize its individuality. If the treatment destroys the nuances of quality which the wine might have achieved, it loses quality. The artist may use modern tools but he has a clear picture in his mind of the kind of wine which he wishes to produce and then so handles the wine as to obtain the desired quality and character.

Burgundy.—The *vins de Bourgogne* have been famous for centuries. The *borgoñas* of Chile and the burgundies of Australia and California are evidence of the fact that it represents a popular appellation for wines.

The region is approximately thirty-five miles long on a slope generally facing east and south east, called the Côte d'Or. A smaller region to the northwest, is called Chablis. South from the Côte d'Or is a third region which is technically Burgundy. Its wines are commonly sold as Beaujolais, Mâconnais, or Chalonnais. The soil is calcareous in the Côte d'Or, clay in Chablis, and granitic in the southern Burgundy regions.

Chablis is a greatly imitated name throughout the world. Less than 600 acres are now planted in the best part of the region. The variety is

Courtesy of Institut National des Appellations d'Origine des Vins et Eaux-de-Vie

FIG. 1.   VINEYARD IN BEAUJOLAIS

Chardonnay. The wine is tart—the acidity usually exceeds 0.80 per cent (as tartaric) with a pH of no more than 3.1—and light yellow in color. The alcohol content is seldom over 11 per cent (by volume). Variety, climate, exposure and soil conditions have some importance to their quality, but the cool climate is obviously critical.

In the Côte d'Or both red and white wines are produced. For the whites the variety is Chardonnay but here the alcohol content is higher, up to 13 per cent (or more) in the warm years, the acidity a little lower, the pH slightly higher, the color more golden and the flavor richer and more expansive. The greatest whites are Montrachet, Puligny-Montrachet, Chassagne-Montrachet, Corton-Charlemagne, and Meursault.

The reds are mainly produced from Pinot noir. The northern, Côte de Nuits, wines are usually more flavorful and distinctive than the southern, Côte de Beaune, wines but there are many exceptions. Famous vineyards in the former region are Chambertin, Clos de Vougeot, Échézeaux, Musigny, Nuits-Saint Georges, Richebourg, etc., and in the latter Corton, Pommard, Volnay, Beaune, etc. Exposure, soil conditions and temperature differences explain some of the variations in character and quality

Courtesy of Institut National des Appellations d'Origine des Vins et Eaux-de-Vie

FIG. 2. PARTIAL CRUSHING OF THE GRAPES IN A BEAUJOLAIS VINEYARD

between the wines of these vineyards. Low lying cooler areas produce lesser quality wines. Michel (1953) considers the most important problems in producing high quality Burgundy to be control of maturity and temperature of fermentation. He recommends frequent field sampling and different maturity standards for each variety and location to insure proper harvesting. Too rapid a fermentation is the most important negative quality factor. The fermentation temperature should be near 77°F. for maximum quality. Harvesting during the coolest periods of the day and cooling or warming the musts, if necessary, are recommended.

A malo-lactic fermentation is employed to reduce excessive acidity. Some bottled wines may become gassy and have an excessive malo-lactic smell. The variety, however, appears to be the most critical factor. Burgundy is first of all Pinot noir or Chardonnay. Where and when the temperature is favorable and the production practices carefully controlled they produce great wines. Owing to the malo-lactic fermentation the pH varies from 3.3 to 3.5 with acidities usually about 0.6 per cent (as tartaric).

In the southern Burgundy region, Pouilly-Fuissé is a famous white wine (from Chardonnay). Brouilly, Fleurie and Moulin-à-Vent are well-known reds (mainly from Gamay), sold as Beaujolais, Figs. 1 and 2. Throughout the region the seasonal influence is very important. In many years, the grapes do not ripen sufficiently to produce a balanced wine and addition of sugar is resorted to. Recent years of high quality include 1952, 1953, 1957, 1959, 1961, 1962, 1964, 1966, 1967, 1969, and 1970.[2]

The custom of aging Burgundy 2 to 3 years before bottling in relatively small casks (60 to 300 gallons) in cool cellars may also be a factor in their character. Aeration is undesirable and often filtration is avoided. White Burgundies age rapidly and should normally not be kept more than 4 or 5 years. Red Burgundies also age relatively rapidly and most of them should be drunk within 10 years. Beaujolais and other southern Burgundy wines are normally drunk within 3 or 4 years. Many shippers do not own the vineyards from which they sell wine. A few estate-bottled wines are shipped to the American market. The reputation and distinctiveness of these famous small vineyards is carefully maintained—partially because of strict governmental controls and partially because their world-wide fame makes them very valuable and the owners wish to maintain this reputation by producing quality wines.

The best technical discussion of wines of Burgundy is to be found in Ferré's (1958) treatise. Lichine (1969), Poupon and Forgeot (1959),

---

[2] This does not mean that all wines of other years are inferior. Often very good wines may be made in "off" years by careful producers. This applies to other regions as well. Not all wines of "vintage" years are superior.

Gadille (1967), Rodier (1948), and Yoxall (1970) are descriptive. Orizet (1959) on Beaujolais is authoritative.

Bordeaux.—The region is large, producing both white and red wines. It lies along the Garonne, Dordogne, and Gironde rivers east and west of Bordeaux. Exposure and soil conditions are of relatively small importance. Grapes are grown on sandy gravelly, loam, and clay soils and a calcareous subsoil is common. The exposure is generally to the northeast in the Médoc and to the southwest in St. Émilion, i.e., is unimportant.

The important quality factors are the climate, the mixtures of grapes, the method of aging, and, in the case of Sauternes, the mold *Botrytis cinerea*. Large vineyards, commonly called *châteaux*, have been preserved more or less intact for many centuries through the English law of inheritance. Bordeaux, in effect, has had an *appellation contrôlée* for centuries. More than a hundred years ago some of the better vineyards of the Médoc were officially classified into a series of five *"growths"* by the Bordeaux wine trade, see Cocks and Féret (1969) and Roger (1956). Recently, the wines of St. Emilion have been officially classified. The owners of classified vineyards are, of course, proud of their wine and jealous in protecting its reputation. This classification and its emphasis on quality has had a salutary influence on maintaining the quality of all wines of the region. However, the 1855 classification of the Médoc is now often misleading as to relative quality.

The large wine trade with England and Scotland has also been an important factor in developing quality. Finally, bottling at the vineyard has been practiced at Bordeaux for more than a century. Chateau-bottling undoubtedly stimulated consumer interest. The chateau should not chateau-bottle wine of inferior years, but not all *chateaux* can be said to apply this high standard at present.

The most important vineyards producing red wines are in the Médoc, Graves, St. Émilion, and Pomerol, but large amounts entitled to the appellation Bordeaux are produced in adjacent regions. The varieties used vary. Cabernet Sauvignon is generally agreed to be the finest variety for red wines but its wines age slowly and varieties of similar flavor—Malbec, Cabernet franc, Carménère, Merlot, and Petit Verdot—are also widely planted. In St. Émilion Cabernet franc predominates.

This mixture of varieties is based on balancing the acidity of the wine. The acidity of Cabernet Sauvignon is mainly tartaric. Malic acid predominates in Malbec. In warm years malic acid tends to respire during ripening so Malbec musts are too low in acidity for a balanced wine. Little tartaric acid respires during ripening, thus Cabernet Sauvignon musts tend to maintain their acidity. A mixture of the two varieties thus gives a better balance. In cool years both the Malbec and Cabernet Sauvignon maintain their acidity but the wine maker depends on the malo-lactic fermentation (p. 284) to reduce the acidity of the wine. Unlike Burgundy this fermentation is seldom employed to excess in Bordeaux.

The fermentation procedure is not unusual, although since 1950 there has been a tendency to remove the wine from the skins after only 3 or 4 days instead of 8 to 15. This shorter period produces wines of lower tannin and earlier maturity. Whether it gives wines of maximum keeping quality is doubtful.

The aging of Bordeaux red wines in oak barrels (about 60 gallons) for 2 or 3 years is generally considered to be a most important factor in their character—particularly where new cooperage is employed. Aging in the bottle is also necessary for the finest red wines. The best wines may improve in quality in the bottle for 10 to 30 or more years.[3]

Climate has, finally, an over-all control over the quality of the wines. In the colder years the alcohol content is low and the wines tend to be thin and hard. In warmer years, 1952, 1953, 1955, 1959, 1961, 1962, 1966, and 1970 the alcohol content is higher and the wines softer. The wine maker who gambles with the weather may harvest late and produce a good wine in a cold year while his neighbors are producing only ordinary wine. He may also be unfortunate and produce a poor wine from rain-damaged, moldy fruit. Some vineyards were harvested too late in 1964.

There are thousands of named vineyards producing red wines in the Bordeaux region and hundreds of them bottle their wine. It would be invidious to mention only a few. Generally the wines of the classed growths are best, but with increasing application of technology other vineyards can be expected to produce excellent wines. Bordeaux shippers blend district wines of communes (Paullaic, St. Julien, St. Estèphe) or of larger regions (Médoc, St. Émilion, Graves) and even of the whole region (Bordeaux) which can be quite good, or, at times, disappointing.

The Bordeaux region produces dry or nearly dry white wines in Graves and elsewhere; sweet white wines are produced in Sauternes and to a lesser extent in neighboring regions. The white wines of Graves are produced from about three-fourths Sauvignon blanc and one-fourth Sémillon, though the percentage varies between vineyards. The wines are aged 2 or 3 years in barrels before bottling. The wines are high in sulfur dioxide —sometimes to the extent of reducing the quality.

---

[3] Bottles of the same wine vary in their rate of aging depending on the level-of-fill of the bottle, the porosity of the cork, etc. When a case of wine has reached its normal maturity some bottles in the case may be "over-the-hill" while others may still have years of goodness remaining. Wines stored under very even and low temperature conditions may last many years longer than wines of the same vintage which have been stored in cellars with variable or warm temperatures. Excessive vibration of the cellar will also hasten the rate of aging.

Sauternes is one of the most imitated wines in the world. With rare exceptions the imitations bear little resemblance to the Bordeaux product, since Sauternes is one of the most difficult wines to produce. The varietal complement is simple—about two-thirds Sémillon and one-third Sauvignon blanc. Little Muscadelle remains. As the Sémillon variety ripens it is attacked during periods of warm humid weather by the mold *Botrytis cinerea*. When conditions are unfavorable the attack is slow and covers only a few berries of each cluster. The effect of the mold is to

FIG. 3. DELIVERY OF BOTRYTISED GRAPES AT CHÂTEAU
D'YQUEM

loosen the skin so that moisture loss from the berry occurs rapidly. As the berry shrivels its sugar content increases proportionately. The botrytised fruit cannot be left on the vine indefinitely lest undesirable molds invade the fruit which is very susceptible to such attack. It is necessary, therefore, to harvest the botrytised berries by cutting them out from the cluster. If conditions are favorable more berries will become infected and further pickings are necessary. Depending on the rate of infection and drying and the wishes of the vintner as to sugar content 1 or 2 pickings are made, few, if any, chateaux now make more.

The fermentation is slow, because of the high sugar content and because

Courtesy of Institut National des Appellations d'Origine des Vins et
Eaux-de-Vie

FIG. 4. CRUSHING OF BOTRYTISED GRAPES DIRECTLY INTO THE
PRESS AT CHÂTEAU D'YQUEM

of the use of sulfur dioxide, but the alcohol content may exceed 14 per
cent. The finished wine is aged 2 to 4 years in barrels. Bottled wines
may improve in quality for many years. They contain 5 to 15 per cent
sugar. Obviously the *Botrytis* attack must have raised the initial sugar
content of the fruit to 30 or 40 per cent sugar. Since the volume has been
reduced proportionately the cost of production is high.

The *Botrytis* attack not only increases the sugar content but it reduces
the skin-to-volume relationship so that there is an increase in aroma, Figs.
3 and 4. Furthermore, the *Botrytis* itself contributes a distinct aroma to
the wine. The reduction in volume would increase the acidity unduly
were it not that the mold perferentially utilizes acids in its metabolism.
Hence increase in acidity is never so great as increase in sugar. Glycerol
is a by-product of the mold's metabolism but just how important this is
to the quality of wine is not known.

Obviously climate is of great importance to the quality of Sauternes wines. Chateau-bottling is practiced here and the vineyards of the region have been classified, Fig. 5. While Sauternes is the best known district, the appellation, Barsac, is a part of the general region of Sauternes.

The best recent technical books on Bordeaux wines are those of Laf-¹ forgue (1947) and Peynaud (1971). See also Kressmann (1968), Laborde (1907), Penning-Rowsell (1969), and Yoxall (1970).

Champagne.—There is no wine better known than Champagne—the

Courtesy of Institut National des Appellations d'Origine des Vins et Eaux-de-Vie

FIG. 5.   CHÂTEAU LAFAURIE-PEYRAGUEY, SAUTERNES

Showing a typical Bordeaux Chateau in the midst of its vines. Note the nearly flat country

sparkling wine from the region of the same name. The main quality factors are climate, soil, varietal components, pressing procedure, blending, temperature of fermentation, and aging.

The soil is a modified chalk. Drainage is good and this is important in a cold region. Generally the vineyards are on the slopes (Fig. 6) which also helps drainage and soil temperature (and probably protection from frosts). Vineyards extend into the plain if the proper chalk soil is present.

The climate is also important. In the coolest years the grapes do not ripen sufficiently to produce a well-balanced base for a sparkling wine. This is the basic reason for non-vintage Champagne. It is simply low-

Courtesy of Collection C.I.V.C.

FIG. 6.   AERIAL VIEW OF CHAMPAGNE VINEYARDS AT BOUZY

alcohol, high-acid wine of a cold year to which some wine of higher alcohol and lower acidity from a warmer year is added to secure the proper balance. The warmer years, which produce well-balanced wines, are also used for vintage Champagnes. French law permits vintage Champagne to contain a small per cent of wines of a year other than that stated on the label.

The cold climate has also influenced the varietal planting. Normally, only white grapes are employed for making white wines. However, the Chardonnay does not ripen as well as is desired and the earlier-ripening Pinot noir is used. Many clonal selections and subvarieties of Pinot noir are planted (Chappaz 1951). About two-thirds of the grapes are Pinot noir and one-third Chardonnay. Great care is needed in harvesting the Pinot noir so that all diseased fruit is removed, usually done by hand at the vineyard (Fig. 7). Rotten fruit has colored juice which is undesirable since the objective is to produce a white wine.

No crushing is done in order to reduce the time the juice is in contact with the skins. The whole fruit is placed in large, shallow, flat presses and pressed directly. Several pressings are made, of which the earlier ones are the best. The fermentation is usually made at a temperature below 68°F. According to Chappaz (1951) a better quality in respect to bouquet is obtained at a fermentation temperature slightly below 60°F; low-temperature acclimatized yeasts are used. The musts are usually settled before fermentation.

Courtesy of Collection C.I.V.C.

FIG. 7. CUTTING OUT MOLDY BERRIES OF PINOT NOIR FOR
CHAMPAGNE MAKING

Wines of Pinot noir and Chardonnay after two rackings and close filtration are blended in the spring. The Chardonnay adds tartness and finesse
to the blend. Wines of various vineyards are also blended to secure the
desired balance in composition and flavor. A clean, fresh wine of about
10.5 to 11 per cent alcohol is required. Different firms secure a slightly
different character to their wine by appropriate blending.

The secondary fermentation is always made in bottles. The fermentation is made at a relatively low temperature 50° to 59°F. Chappaz (1951)
stresses the importance of this low temperature for the bottle fermentation.

Disgorging is legally delayed for at least one year for non-vintage Champagne. Vintage Champagne must remain in the cellar for 3 years before
disgorging. Amerine and Monaghan (1950) have given some confirmatory evidence and it is generally agreed by the Champagne trade that a
delay of 2 or 3 years is desirable for the best vintage wines. In addition
to Chappaz (1951) useful data on Champagne are given by Manceau
(1929), Moreau-Berillon (1925), Pacottet and Guittonneau (1930), Rosa
(1964), and Simon (1962).

Many other sparkling wines produced outside the Champagne region
and not entitled to the appellation Champagne are produced in France.

Courtesy of Institut National des Appellations d'Origine des Vins et Eaux-de-Vie

FIG. 8. PARTIAL CRUSHING OF WHITE GRAPES AT THE VINEYARD IN ALSACE

Some of these are fermented in the bottle as for Champagne, while others are fermented in closed tanks (p. 475). These are both sold as *mousseux*. Some carbonated wine, sold as much, is also made.

Other Districts.—Many other wines of above-average quality are produced in France and some have very distinctive factors influencing their quality.

In Alsace, the district which in many respects most closely resembles California with respect to nomenclature, variety is the most important quality factor, see Sittler (1956) and Hallgarten (1970). This is reflected in the varietal nomenclature of the wines. Climate and exposure are also important since the region is a cool one. Sylvaner, Chasselas doré, White Riesling, Gewürztraminer, and several other early-ripening varieties are planted (Fig. 8). For a popular account see Layton (1970).

Along the Rhône from Lyon south many different wine types are made but the reds are the most interesting. Climate and exposure are less critical than in Burgundy, since the climate is warmer and sugaring is not

FIG. 9.   CRUSHING IN THE VINEYARD AT VERNON, NEAR VOUVRAY

necessary.   The varietal complement does not appear to be a decisive factor.   More than one variety is used in Côte Rôtie and Châteauneuf-du-Pape.   Hermitage, however, is largely produced from Petite Sirah.   The common characteristic of these wines is their relatively slow rate of aging, and their good color, tannin, and alcohol.   In the bottle they may remain good and even improve in quality for 20 to 30 years.   Even the few white wines produced are rather sturdy, full-bodied wines, which can be kept in the bottle for many years.   A pink Rhône wine, Tavel, is produced mainly from the Grenache variety.   Grenache is subject to oxidation and many Tavels contain excessive sulfur dioxide.

The Loire has vines along much of its length, Fig. 9, mainly producing white still and dry, or sweet, or sparkling wines: from Chasselas doré and Sauvignon at Pouilly-Fumé, Chenin blanc at Vouvray and Angers-Saumur, and Muscadet (Melon) near Nantes. The sweet table wines from Vouvray and Angers-Saumur are produced only in the warmer years from botrytised grapes by procedures comparable to those of Sauternes (p. 11).   Some of these wines are long-lived and of high quality.   Two types of sparkling wines are produced.   Musts of non-botrytised grapes, particularly in the Vouvray region, may not ferment entirely dry.   Later, after bottling, the wines may undergo a very slight fermentation of their residual sugar and the wines become gassy (*pétillant*). The process is tricky since deposits may form if too much yeast growth occurs. Bottle-fermented sparkling wines, *mousseux*, are produced by procedures comparable to those of Champagne. Generally the sparkling wines are not so long-lived as those of Champagne.

A few red wines are produced from Cabernet franc in the vicinity of Bourgeuil and Chinon. They are pleasant but rather light wines, sometimes almost a rosé. For a good description of Loire wines, see Brejoux (1956).

In the south of France a number of fortified wines are made—Banyuls, Muscat de Frontignan, etc. The grapes are left on the vines as long as possible to get the maximum sweetness. The fermentation is slow. The final alcohol is brought to about 15 or 16 per cent. Many of the lesser wines are sold young for blending. Others are bottled after a few years' aging and reach the market as muscatels or red dessert wines. Some reds are aged for a number of years in the wood, or, in glass in the sun, until they lose their red color and their aldehyde content increases. The particular *rancio* flavor of these wines is very distinctive.

Most of the wine produced in France is made in the Midi and is of very low alcohol content, 7 to 10 per cent. The variety Aramon is widely planted and heavily cropped and is responsible for many of the low alcohol wines which are used primarily for blending or bulk sale. The average worker in Paris and the northern departments drinks Midi wine (blended with Algerian wine in many cases). Since the quality is low, little attention to positive quality factors is given except to soundness and alcohol content (which establishes the price). See Galtier (1961).

There are other French wines: rosés from Provence, whites of Monbazillac, Got (1949), and Jurançon, reds and whites of Gaillac, various Arbois types (including the rare film yeast wine of Château Châlon), Seyssel from Savoy, and many local sparkling wines, etc. Some of these owe their character to indigenous varieties and to unique methods of production.

Switzerland

The miracle is that Switzerland produces as much wine as it does in the very cool and limited areas available. In western Switzerland near Neuchâtel and Lausanne the early-ripening Chasselas doré is planted and rather neutral white wines are produced. In eastern Switzerland near Zürich the Pinot noir predominates and pleasant but very light red wines are made. In both regions the acidity of the new wines is often excessive and a malo-lactic fermentation is very common. Following the primary fermentation the wines are lightly racked and the cellar temperature maintained. Yeast autolysis occurs, releasing amino acids, and *Lactobacilli* growth ensues. The total acidity is watched until it reaches the desired level (usually by January or February). The cellars are then opened up and the temperature allowed to drop to near freezing. Natural clarification occurs, the wines are filtered, and sulfur dioxide added. Many of the wines are sold immediately and few are aged more than two or three years. Some wines are bottled under carbon dioxide. The gas acts to prevent oxygen absorption and hence oxidasic casse and also gives the wines a slight but pleasant gassiness. Admirable texts on the production of white and red wines in Switzerland are those of Benvegnin *et al.* (1951), Peyer and Eggenberger (1965), Schellenberg (1962), and Schellenberg and Peyer (1951).

Germany

Germany has been producing wines since Roman times. The climate is relatively poor for grapes and only on well-drained soils with favorable exposures can grapes be brought to maturity, and even there only in the warmer seasons. It is no accident that the slopes along the rivers are the favored areas for vines.

Recently Bocker (1959) has presented some evidence of a direct soil effect on the composition of German musts and wines. Grapes grown on more alkaline chalk (40 to 57 per cent soluble calcium) soils were higher in potassium and magnesium than from neutral or slightly acid soils (5 to 17 per cent soluble calcium). They also underwent a more complete malo-lactic fermentation; in fact, there was direct relationship between potassium content and decrease in malic acid.

The Rhine.—From the falls of the Rhine where it leaves Switzerland nearly to Bonn, grapes are grown along this river and many of its tributaries. Three of these areas are particularly important for the production of quality wine: Rheinpfalz (Palatinate), Rheinhessen, and Rheingau. Many wines are produced in Baden and Württemberg but these are seldom exported and even in Germany are mainly drunk locally. The tall brown bottle is used for all Rhine wines.

Most of the vineyards in Pfalz and the Rheinhessen are on the west bank facing east so that they are warmed by the morning sun. In the Rheingau the exposure is to the south. Thus here the vines receive the sun's rays the maximum period and this is a most important and decisive factor differentiating this district from other Rhine vineyard areas. The vineyards on the tributaries of the Rhine in Württemberg with less favorable exposure also produce lesser quality wines. Drainage, soil, temperature, and exposure are also important to the proper ripening of the grapes. White Riesling, Sylvaner, Müller-Thurgau, and Gerwürztraminer are the main varieties. The vinification is normal but sugaring is often necessary to secure the desired per cent of alcohol. Even in a year as warm as 1959 some musts required sugaring.

Local variations in quality exist. These are due to use of various varieties, differences in climate, and to a unique system of nomenclature. The lesser wines are given regional or proprietary names but most of the wines are sold by the village name often associated with a vineyard name and that of the particular variety. German law also permits labeling of the best wines as to bottling by the producer, time of harvest, year, etc. One aspect of German regulations is seldom mentioned. Wines with a vineyard appellation need only be two-thirds from the vineyard named. For example, a 1959er Geisenheimer Mäuerchen need contain only two-thirds wine of the Mäuerchen vineyard. The remainder may come from any of the other vineyards in the Geisenheim region.

Because of the cold climate and attack by *Botrytis* the harvest may take place over a period of time in order to secure the maximum quality. These designations of times of harvest may also be placed on the label (often with the variety and always with the vintage). The grapes of the later pickings may have considerable *Botrytis cinerea* infection (p. 12) and wines of more or less residual sugar can then be produced. A *Spätlese* means a wine made from late-picked grapes but it may or may not have a noticeable *Botrytis cinerea* infection. In any case, it is a natural wine— i.e., no sugar has been added to the must—and it is probably slightly sweet. An *Auslese* is always produced from selected grapes which normally have had an attack of *Botrytis cinerea*. If very small botrytised parts of the cluster have been separately harvested, the wine may be even sweeter and labeled a *Beerenauslese*. If the grapes have been allowed to shrivel (literally to dry up) on the vine, their wine may be labeled a *Trockenbeerenauslese*. This occurs only in exceptional years, the yield is always very small, and the price of the resulting wines high.

Thus a high quality Pfalz wine might be labeled Deidesheimer (village), Hohenmorgen (vineyard), Riesling (variety), 1953 (year), *Spätlese* (late harvesting), *Original Abfüllung* (bottled by the producer and not sugared). In some cases the bottles from each cask may be kept separate and be so labeled. This requires extra care and the best German wines are expensive. There are moreover other sub-categories (*Kabinett, Gewächs, Edel, etc.*). For a more complete explanation see Simon and Hallgarten (1963), Schoonmaker (1956), Hallgarten (1965), and Langenbach (1951, 1962).

Because high quality German wines are associated with residual sugar and because the sugar tends to mask the very high natural-acidity of the wines (in spite of rather general use of the malo-lactic fermentation), there is a strong tendency for lesser quality German wines, such as district wines like Zeltinger (no vineyard name affixed) and wines of no geographical significance such as Liebfraumilch) to be sold with residual sugar. This is achieved in two ways: by fermentation under pressure so that the fermentation "sticks" before all the sugar is fermented and by addition of sugar. Kielhöfer (1955) reported a sugar content of 0.18 to 2.9 per cent—two-thirds of the tasters preferred the sugar content in the range 2.0 to 2.9 per cent. The remainder marked wines from 1.0 to 2.4 per cent as too sweet or wines from 0.4 to 0.98 per cent as too dry (unbalanced). Some tasters found the whole range from 0.4 to 2.4 per cent pleasing!

Sylvaner is the predominant variety of the Rheinpfalz and Rheinhessen. In the cooler areas near the river the wines are frequently sugared and their flavor less pleasant. A few vineyards are planted to White Riesling and, in the best years, produce very good wines. The negative quality factors are excessive sugaring, use of non-German musts, and too high a sulfur dioxide content.

The Rheingau is one of the great vineyard areas of the world. Exposure, well-drained, terraced, south-sloping sunny slopes, is the revealing quality factor, Fig. 10, since vines not so favorably exposed fail to

Courtesy of Presse- und Informationsamt der Bundesregierung

Fig. 10.   Cellars at Schloss Johannisberg on the Rhine

Fig. 11.   The Vineyard of Bernkasteler Doktor on the Moselle Rising Above the Town of Bernkastel

achieve such maturity and quality. The method of late harvesting of the predominant White Riesling variety has a major influence. The individual practices of the producers are important. There is a soil-climate-producer-time-of-harvest factor which differentiates these wines from each other and which, particularly, distinguishes the Rheingau as one of the world's great wine-producing areas. At their best the wines have a very fullsome aroma of the grape. They are rich even when dry. They ma-

Courtesy of Mainpost, Würzburg

FIG. 12.   CASTLE AND INNERE LEISTE VINEYARD AT WÜRZBURG

ture rapidly. And when they are sweet they are very luscious and remain sound for many years. Famous villages in the Rheingau include Hatten-heim, Rüdesheim, Geisenheim, and Hochheim (actually a few miles off the Main but closer to Rheingau wines in character than to any other district). The word "hock" as a generic name for German wines may have originated from here.

Joining the Rhine at Bingen is the Nahe river. The particular flavor of Nahe wines emphasizes again that soil effect may be important, though it may be due also to fermentation practices.

Moselle.—Even though the Moselle runs generally in a northerly direction it twists and turns so that some of the vineyards along its banks are exposed to the east and south. On well-drained slate soils these produce very distinctive wines in the best years. Some prefer the more grandiose Rheingau wines and others the rather sparse but often magnificent wines of the Moselle-Ruwer-Saar. The greenish-blue tall bottle is used for Moselle wines. Famous villages along the Moselle and Saar include Wehlen, Piesport, Trittenheim, Bernkastel, Fig. 11, Wiltingen, etc.

Franconia.—Starting at Mainz the Main River runs first east and finally south. Near Würzburg a number of distinctive wines are produced on its banks in finely terraced vineyards where the exposure is suitable (Fig. 12). The river bends so that favorable exposure is possible—usually south. The predominant variety is the Sylvaner. Red marl, limestone, or mixed soil types appear to give the wine a muted flavor. There is less late harvesting here. The malo-lactic fermentation is used and with early bottling constitutes the main quality factor. The wines are bottled in the squat green *Bocksbeutel*. It is reputed to be a long-lived wine, but post-World War II vintages have not all borne this out. For extensive descriptions see Kittel and Breider (1958) and Kraemer (1956).

There is one rather unique quality factor which pervades the German wine industry—the very high degree of technical skill which is utilized. German cellars are among the cleanest and most efficiently managed in the world. Pressure fermentation which gives a better utilization of sugar is widely practiced. It also yields wines with a slightly higher residual sugar than non-pressure fermentations. Germ-proof filtration which permits safe bottling of sweet low alcohol wines is regularly practiced. A wine high in volatile acid is never encountered commercially. There are more enological stations and schools in Germany than in any other country. The safe use of ferrocyanide for removal of copper and iron and the use of a malo-lactic fermentation is a tribute to their skill.

The negative quality factors in German wines are (1) the excessive use of sulfur dioxide and (2) the occasional excessive use of potassium ferrocyanide to remove copper and iron (p. 558). The former is far more prevalent and disagreeable than the latter. In line with their degree of technical skill there are a number of first rate technical books on German enology. Among these are Geiss (1960), Goldschmidt (1951), Troost (1961), and Vogt (1963, 1968). Of general interest are the less technical recent books of Cornelssen (1970), Hallgarten (1965), Keller (1953), Langenbach (1951, 1962), Leonhardt (1963), Schoonmaker (1956), Simon and Hallgarten (1963), and Wilhem (1956).

Italy

Italy produces about 1¹/₂ billion gallons of wine per year, from low alcohol table wines to very sweet fortified dessert wines, from the Alps to Pantelleria below Sicily. Vines are grown on every kind of soil, exposure, elevation and along fences, in fields, or on trees. Most of the wine is a sound beverage, much of no particular character.

The factors influencing quality are not so clear for Italy as for France or Germany. In the first place, with exceptions, the types are not so well standardized. The failure to standardize types is due to complex political and economic factors. For centuries Italy had little national character but consisted of city states, Papal dominions, or was under foreign control. It had no important and lucrative export trade to a non-wine producing country (such as France possessed in England, Belgium, and elsewhere), except for Marsala.

The overpopulation of the country was, and remains, very great. This results in polyculture—the cultivation of more than one crop on the same plot of ground. More than 70 per cent of the grapes of Italy are grown in conjunction with other crops. This leads to reduced production and quality for all the crops, and especially to grapes, where pruning, disease, and pest control, and proper timing of the harvest—all critical factors to wine quality—may be interfered with by the culture and harvesting of the other crops.

Courtesy of Prof. Cosmo

FIG. 13.   SYSTEM OF TRAINING VINES IN NORTHERN ITALY

Also the quality wine tradition with exceptions in the Brenner Pass region, Piedmont and Tuscany, does not seem strong. It is worth noting, Bode (1956), that there is comparatively little shipment of bottled wine from one district to another in Italy, and even within a district very few wines are bottled and permitted to reach their maximum quality.

Finally, the producers are too small to care about "commercial" quality or so large that production of standard wines is more important than of quality wines. It is significant that there are few vineyard-bottled wines in Italy. Most of the very considerable attempts to differentiate regions and limit varieties and production and to control quality under the corporative state have come to naught. However, the European Common Market has stimulated classification and standardization of Italian wines.

As with Spain and California the warm climatic conditions often lead to high sugar (aggravated in many cases by late harvesting because of attention to other crops).[4] There is the lack of an export market and of a critical internal market. To summarize: there is a need of critical standards for Italian wines. With so many uninteresting and unstandardized wines it is difficult to make any general summary of quality factors for Italian wines.

Mazzei (1959) has made an admirable summary of defects and how the Italian wine industry might be improved. He suggests wines of 10 to 13 per cent alcohol (12 is recommended), 0.6 to 0.9 per cent total acidity (as tartaric), and no more than 0.06 per cent volatile acidity. The use of good varieties, clean fruit, and better wine making procedures (including cold fermentation and sulfur dioxide) are recommended. Central aging and bottling cellars are considered desirable. The sensory characteristics of each type should be kept as constant as possible. These suggestions also apply to producing areas other than Italy. Cosmo and De Rosa (1960).

In Piedmont, where polyculture is the exception, a number of distinctive varietal types of wines are produced: Barbera, Freisa, Nebbiolo, Bonarda, Grignolino, etc. Barolo is a superior (when well-aged) red wine produced from the Nebbiolo variety. While the variety and site are important, the care in vinification and aging is probably more important. This is partially substantiated by the fact that none of the other Piedmont wines produced from Nebbiolo (Barbaresco, etc.) achieves such high quality.

---

[4] In the Middle Ages and earlier, high alcohol wines were the only ones which could be kept without turning to vinegar. Late harvesting, addition of raisins or mixture with reduced must (p. 452) were methods of achieving high sugar and hence of high alcohol. The caramel flavors were readily excused as being better than half-vinegar low-alcohol products. Old customs die hard. Post-Pasteur technology makes such procedures unnecessary. Yet we still find, even in California, wine makers obsessed with the idea of picking so late that the wines will have 13 or more per cent alcohol!

A negative quality factor for many Piedmont red wines is their gassiness (*frizzante*), due in most cases to a persistent malo-lactic fermentation. Sweet table wines produced from overripe Muscat Canelli (Muscat Frontignan or White Muscat) are often very good in this region. This is also the center of the *spumante* (sparkling and sparkling muscat) and vermouth industries. The quality factors of Piedmont are thus superior viticulture (Fig. 13) varietal selection, time of harvesting, and method of processing.

Some exceedingly good varietal wines are produced north and east of Verona (Fig. 14). Here one finds labeled wines of Merlot, Sylvaner, Traminer, Pinot, Riesling, (not White Riesling but the Italian Riesling or Walschriesling). Variety, the cool climatic conditions, and Teutonic thoroughness in the cellar are the dominant quality factors.

The red wines from near Verona—Valpolicella, Valtellina, and Bardolino — have a reputation as fresh, fruity, easy-to-drink beverages, and occasionally a nicely-aged one may be found. The wines of nearby Soave are standard white wines, pleasant but not memorable.

Chianti.—Although Chianti is probably the best-known Italian wine there are certainly no general taste descriptions which will apply to all Chianti wines. Sangioveto is, indeed, the predominant variety but it is not very distinctive. The *governo* process (in which 10 to 20 per cent of crushed semi-dried grapes are added to the newly-fermented wines) is

Courtesy of Prof. Cosmo

FIG. 14.   HILLSIDE VINEYARDS IN NORTHERN ITALY

used by only a portion of the producers. Many of the *governo* wines are slightly gassy (*frizzante*) and this seems to be appreciated by many consumers. It is a difficult process to control, however, and undesirable bacterial activity is not uncommon. Garino-Canina (1950) found that when the *governo* process is properly controlled it produced wines of better alcohol, color, and flavor. The *governo* wines had undergone considerable malo-lactic fermentation—higher in lactic acid and pH and lower in titratable acidity and malic acid. Cantarelli (1958) showed that the explanation of the higher alcohol lies in the beneficial effect on the efficiency of fermentation of the first lees, i.e., in more alcohol being produced per gram of sugar fermented. Individual producers do make and age excellent wines but the chief attraction of many is the picturesque *fiasci*.

Thousands of other wines are produced in Italy—Castelli Romani, Est! Est!!Est!!!, Lacryma Christi, Falerno, Orvieto, San Severo, etc. It is a rare village that does not have a wine named after it. Yet it is a rare wine which is worth a second taste. In our opinion this is a question of lack of quality standards.

Production techniques account for the other characteristic Italian wines. Many of these depend on very late harvesting of the grapes or to drying the grapes after harvesting in trays, in boxes or by tying on strings and hanging up. Some of these are muscats of 15 or 16 per cent alcohol. Others are the white alcoholic wines of Tuscany or Sardinia—Aleatico, *vino santo*, Malvasia, Vernaccia, Orvieto, etc. Similar types are produced on a small scale elsewhere, such as muscatels in Syracuse and Noto and in many other regions. Except for the *vino santo* they are often fortified. For a description of Sicilian vines and wines see Rossi (1955) and Veronelli (1964).

Marsala.—Processing is responsible for the character of this well-known type. The wines of Marsala were "created" during the 19th century by British wine merchants for export. Conditions in western Sicily were not favorable for the production of a quality table wine. The climate is warm, the grapes are all white (Inzolia, Catarratto, and Grillo predominate), and the vineyards are small and wine production very crude. The taste-wise English merchants were able to create a unique type of wine from such unfavorable raw products. The process finally evolved consists of blending dry wine, high-proof, grape concentrate, *muté* and reduced must to the desired flavor, sugar, and alcohol. The wines are then aged and a modified fractional blending system (p. 415) employed to standardize the types. Whether one appreciates the caramel-like flavor or not, Marsala represents a distinctive type of wine and is the classic example of the manufactured wine.

Vermouth.—The sweet Italian vermouth which originated in the Turin region is one of the world's classic wines and the type is produced in most of the wine-producing countries of the world. The custom of adding herbs to wine is a very ancient one. The presence of so many native herbs in northern Italy, particularly wormwood, probably helped its development. Essentially, Italian vermouth consists of a muscat base wine plus an infusion of herbs, sugar, reduced must and alcohol. Besides the regular amber-colored type, red and white vermouth are produced. The quality of the base wine, the skillfulness of the mixing of herbs (as well as the quality of the herbs), and the aging and finishing procedures are the primary quality factors.

The classical technical texts on Italian wines are those of Carpentieri (1948) and Garoglio (1965). Technical information is also given in the Atti of the Accademia Italiana della Vite e del Vino (1949–1965), Bruni (1964), Ferrarese (1951), Gianformaggio (1955), Marescalchi (1957), Montanari and Ceccarelli (1950), Paronetto and Dal Cin (1954), Tarantola (1954), Tarantola *et al.* (1954), and Verona and Florenzano (1956). Less technical but enthusiastic descriptions of Italian wines in English are those of Anon. (1957), Bode (1956), Dettori (1953), Layton (1961), Rau (1960), Ray (1966), and Veronelli (1964).

Spain

The third largest wine-producing country in the world, but with the largest acreage, offers a wide variety of wines—from light table wines to some of the richest dessert wines produced in Europe. The quality factors, depending on the type of wine produced, include variety, climate, secondary fermentation, and process of manufacture. Table wines are produced from La Mancha to the Pyrenees. Dessert wines are produced from New Castile to the south. Only a few of the wines are produced from delimited areas.

In the north the best table wines are produced. Since the invasion of phylloxera in France, an influx of French vineyardists has obviously had an influence, particularly in the Rioja. There has, however, been little change in the varietal complement—Grenache and Tempranilla are the predominant varieties. The method of fermentation is variable—some crush and press quite normally while others use an old system where the whole grapes are placed in the fermenter. Whole grapes held under a blanket of carbon dioxide apparently result in death (asphyxiation) of the skin cells, which then lose their semi-permeability. The pigments of the skin (and flavor?) are then released into the surrounding liquid. Experimental evidence of this has been given by Amerine and De Mattei (1940). French investigators, chiefly Flanzy (1935) have claimed enhanced quality for wines so produced. The best explanation is that such procedures

FIG. 15.   BARREL AGING IN A BODEGA IN NORTHERN SPAIN

do result in greater flavor and with varieties of low flavor, such as the Grenache, this is probably important.   Others crush but keep the fermenters under a tight cover of carbon dioxide.   The finished Rioja red wines are of normal red color and this might be difficult to achieve with fermentation of only Grenache grapes.

The French influence is obvious in their method of aging: small oak cooperage, Fig. 15, and bottle aging, Fig. 16.   Fractional blending of the older wines also appears in some of the northern Spanish wines (see p. 415).   Vintage dates on Rioja wines should therefore be accepted with caution.   Other table wines are produced throughout northern Spain.

Most of the La Mancha wines of central Spain are white, are sold young, and constitute the great bulk of the wines drunk.   The well-known Valdepeñas wine of La Mancha is seldom of more than very ordinary quality.

Dessert Wines.—The other important Spanish wines are dessert wines. They owe their quality to the climate and to the method of production. Some of these wines are little changed in character from those produced in Roman times.   Priorato, for example, is a mountainous district near Tarrogona.   The Grenache is picked late at a high per cent sugar.   The wines are aged for a number of years in the cask and achieve a *rancio* (high-aldehyde) flavor similar to those of the south of France (p. 18).

Courtesy of Casa Codornia

FIG. 16. BOTTLE AGING IN A BODEGA IN NORTHERN SPAIN

At Málaga, the Muscat of Alexandria variety, partially dried as for raisins, Fig. 17, is used for producing wines. Málaga is one of the sweetest wines produced in the world. Fermentation is never complete. Partial fortification stops the fermentation. The finished wines are 15 to 18 per cent in alcohol and 12 to 20 or more per cent in sugar content. The finished wines are of a dark amber color and have a strong caramel odor.

In central and southern Spain, and in the Jura of France, the native yeast flora is such that if the new wines are left exposed the wine usually does not spoil but a film of yeast forms on the surface. Instead of developing acetic acid, the aldehyde content increases and the wines acquire a special flavor. The main centers in Spain for the commercial production

Courtesy of José Mata

Fig. 17.   Transportation of Musts and Drying Grapes Before Crushing
in the South of Spain

of these wines is in Montilla (south of Cordoba) and at Jerez de la Frontera (near Cadiz).

Montilla is one of the less well known sherry-like wines of Spain. Several varieties are grown in this region of which Pedro Ximenez is the most important. Dry wines of 14 or 15 per cent alcohol "flower" only a year or two to produce cheap aperitif · vines. With longer aging under the *flor* the intensity of odor increases. The dry cellars also lead to the interesting phenomena (also found in the Jerez area) of the alcohol content *increasing* with age.[6] Eventually the alcohol content becomes high enough to inhibit yeast growth. Some of these wines accumulate exceedingly intense and complicated odors—almost too intense for more than sipping.

Sherry.—The wines of Jerez de la Frontera, and of the surrounding district as far as Puerta Santa Maria in one direction and Sanlúcar de Barrameda in another, are among the world's great wines. They form a family of related but diverse types. Their characteristic quality is almost entirely derived from the method of production and aging.

The word "sherry" is undoubtedly derived from the name of the princi-

---

[6] The smaller water molecule moves more rapidly than the larger alcohol molecule through the wood. Evaporation of moisture from the surface is, however, a function of the humidity of the air. In normal cellars alcohol is lost more rapidly than water because of the high humidity of the air. In the dry, above-ground, dirt-floored, airy *bodegas* of southern Spain the humidity is very low and the opposite effect is observed.

FIG. 18. METHOD OF TRANSPORTING GRAPES IN THE SHERRY
DISTRICT

pal city in the sherry district, Jerez. According to Gonzalez (1948)
Spanish sherry in Spain may be designed by any one of the following
words: "Jerez," "Xerez," "Scheris" and "sherry."

Soil is considered an important quality factor but it is difficult to find
objective evidence. The local belief that the highly calcareous (*albariza*)
soils produce the best wines *may* be related to degree of ripening. One of
the important objectives in sherry making is to produce a sound wine of 14
to 15 per cent alcohol. The Palomino grapes normally do not achieve a
sufficiently high degree of sugar to produce this per cent of alcohol.
Drying the fruit in the sun for a day or two, Fig. 17, helps to shrivel the
grapes slightly and thus raise the sugar content . Possibly the low production on the more highly calcareous soils and the unique method of pruning
leads to higher sugar. The Pedro Ximenez and a number of other varieties are also grown.

Variety is, however, not the controlling factor in sherry quality. As a
matter of fact the highly-praised Palomino may be grown for its thick skin
and disease-resistance more than for any real quality of its own. The need
of high sugar favors fairly late harvesting—a factor in favor of the Palomino. However, the musts are low in acid, high in pH, and have a distinct
tendency to darken quickly.

The lack of acidity is the worst defect of this and of other varieties
grown in this district. This is ameliorated by plastering—an ancient practice by which gypsum is added to the grape musts to lower their pH (p.
410). The gypsum-treatment of the crushed grapes also gives higher
yields of juice during pressing—important with the pulpy Palomino. The

Courtesy of Wine Institute

Fig. 19.   Flor Film Growing on Surface of Wine

"treading" of grapes also has for its purpose better disintegration of the grape and hence greater yields of juice.   Not only gypsum but tartaric acid and sulfur dioxide are employed.   The fermentation is conducted in casks of about 130 gallons' capacity.   Following fermentation the wines are racked once or not at all but are left in the partially full containers.   The wines are carefully tasted and classified, p. 414, into potential flor wines and into the *oloroso* type.   The latter are fortified to 16 or more per cent alcohol and do not undergo a secondary film yeast stage.

By early spring a film stage of the yeast begins to develop on the unfortified wines rapidly covering the surface, Fig. 19.   In the above-ground bodegas the film may "drop" during the summer, "flower" again in the fall, and "drop" a second time in the winter.   Obviously temperature control would be an advantage for maintaining continuous film growth and speeding up the process.

Sooner or later the wines, now classified into several types and grades, find their way into a fractional blending system of aging. For about one year the wines are held without blending. At that time a proportion is transferred to older casks of the same type in order to replenish wine which has been used to fill still older casks from which wine has been taken. The "depth" or number of steps in the fractional blending system varies from 3 to 6 or more. It is obvious that the wine withdrawn from the bottom or *solera* cask is a very complicated blend of wines of varying age. Baker *et al.* (1952) have shown that after a certain period of operation the average age of the wine withdrawn from the oldest cask reaches a constant age. This is important because it clearly establishes one of its functions—namely to supply uniform wine from a production system which is notoriously fickle in producing wines of variable quality.

There are many *fino* and *oloroso* soleras in all sherry bodegas, Fig. 20. Generally, however, wine from a single solera is not used directly for bottling, but wines from several soleras may be employed to produce the commercial types. Much of the younger drier *fino*-type sold in Spain is only 14.5 per cent in alcohol. The *manzanilla*, a *fino*-type wine produced at Sanlúcar de Barrameda, is likewise largely unfortified even when shipped outside of Spain. For export to the United States, except for true manzanillas, most sherry, *fino* or *oloroso*, is raised to 18 to 20 per cent alcohol. Adjustments of color are made by adding very small amounts of *vino de color*—reduced must which has been fortified and aged.

Courtesy of Gonzalez, Byass

FIG. 20.   SHERRY BODEGA

It should be emphasized that a sherry firm may produce several qualities of *finos,* one or more aged *finos* (called amontillados), several *olorosos,* and finally at least one dark *oloroso* (Brown or East India sherry). Basically, however, there are two types of sherry—one which owes its character to the effect of a film stage and the other which does not. The other quality factor is the aging system which yields wines of a consistent quality for both types. The soft oak casks employed may be a third quality factor and certainly the concentration effect produced by evaporation is important in the older wines. The flavor produced by autolysis in the deposit of yeasts has not been measured but is believed to be of some importance.

The classic text on Spanish wines is that of Marcilla (1946). The recent studies of Larrea (1957, 1965), Maestro (1952), Mareca (1957), Navas (1950), Rainbird (1966), and Vega (1958) are also useful.

On sherry González (1948) is the best. Marcilla *et al.* (1936) is indispensable. Bobadilla (1956), Bobadilla *et al.* (1954), and Bobadilla and Navarro (1949) should also be consulted. Descriptions in English of the production of sherry may be found in Allen (1933), Croft-Cooke (1956), Cruess (1948), Jeffs (1970), and Joslyn and Amerine (1964).

Portugal

For its size Portugal is one of the most important viticultural areas of Europe. Per capita consumption is over 30 gallons per year and the per cent of total cultivated land devoted to grape growing is high. Under the corporative state the grape and wine industry are largely controlled by the state. In most districts the Junta Nacional do Vinho (JNV) has functioned efficiently to (1) improve the quality of the product and (2) remove excess wines for distillation to hold the market price steady.

The main factors for quality improvement in the areas controlled by the JNV appear to be (1) planting of better varieties and (2) better methods of vinification. The JNV has vigorously attacked both these problems, by competitions, awards of medals for quality of wine or cleanliness of cellar, extension activities, etc. The JNV has constructed a number of important installations of their own where the enological discipline is exemplary but where the quality of the grapes employed still limits the quality of the wine. Their monumental study (1942) of the soils and composition of the grapes should be especially mentioned.

There are a number of local regions of quality wine production (aside from the Douro). Two of importance may be noted. In Sétubal, just south of Lisbon, the Muscat of Alexandria is used to produce a sweet and luscious muscatel.

The second local region of importance is that of the *vinho verde* wines of the Minho district, north of Opôrto. The quality factors here are different from those existing elsewhere in the world. In fact, they may constitute a prime example of "making a virtue of a necessity." In this region vines are largely grown on trees, as in parts of Italy. Under these circumstances the vines overproduce and the fruit cannot reach full maturity. The musts therefore often attain no more than 16 per cent sugar with more than one per cent acidity. The resulting wines would be undrinkable were it not for the malo-lactic fermentation (p. 285).

Courtesy of Instituto do Vinho do Pôrto

FIG. 21. FINE VIEW OF VINEYARDS ON BOTH SIDES OF THE DOURO AT PINHÃO

Note the old style terracing to the right and the new style opposite bridge to left. Unplanted terraces are vineyard areas not replanted after phylloxera

The new wines are left unracked until yeast autolysis induces the malo-lactic fermentation. The wines are often bottled before or during this fermentation and the commercial wines are very gassy. The only other wines which resemble these are some of the *frizzante* northern Italian red table wines, but even there it is seldom that such a high degree of uniformity and gassiness is achieved.

Two small delimited regions should be mentioned. Colares is a red wine produced near Lisbon on slopes facing the Atlantic. The high chloride content of the wine has an effect on the flavor of the wine. Dão is one of the best red table wines of Portugal. It is produced in a delimited district just south of the Douro.

Port.—The quality factors responsible for the red sweet wine called port are not entirely clear, in spite of the very important studies of Baron de Forrester (a 19th century British wine merchant), the Instituto do Vinho do Porto (IVP), the Casa do Douro, and, most important, the technological practices that the port wine shippers have developed over the past one hundred years. The Douro wine region is a small delimited area mainly bordering the Douro river from Régua some distance eastward. No more unfavorable locale for vine growth can be imagined. Vines are grown on the terraced slopes on both sides of the river or its tributaries, Figs. 21 and 22. In spite of the rocky nature of the soil vines flourish. The sub-soil is a slate which is tilted up 90°. The vines' roots thus are believed to penetrate deeply and to find a source of moisture which shallow-rooted vines would not have. Granted that this is correct it can hardly constitute an important quality factor compared to vines which do not suffer moisture deficiency.

Climate appears to have a critical importance. Some years are too warm, resulting in excessive sugar or deficient color for some varieties. However, because of the mixed plantings of varieties this may not be a necessarily critical factor. In a mixed planting it is obviously impossible to pick each variety at its optimum maturity. Therefore, only in the most favorable years may the optimum maturity for all varieties be secured or over- and under-maturity cancel out.

The whole grapes are dumped into stone crushing vats (*lagares*, Fig. 23) and trodden before and during the early stages of fermentation. The treading gives a thorough physical disintegration of the berries and aids color extraction—an important factor considering the limited period of fermentation on the skins. Mechanical crushing and other means of management of the cap have recently been introduced. They apparently produce equal color extraction to treading. Cheap labor appears to be the main factor in favor of treading. The fermenting juice is run directly into tanks containing the fortifying brandy. The spirits used have a proof not greater than 160°. Many ports thus have a noticeable fusel oil odor which the port shippers do not consider a negative quality factor. The initial fortification may be to only about 18 per cent. One reason for the variabil-

Courtesy of Instituto do Vinho do Pôrto

FIG. 22. CLOSE-UP OF TERRACED VINEYARD

Courtesy of Instituto do Vinho do Pôrto

FIG. 23.   STONE LAGARES IN THE DOURO

Courtesy of Guirmaraens

FIG. 24.   PORT LODGE AT VILA NOVA DE GAIA

ity of port is the inherent difficulty of controlling color and flavor extraction with such a primitive system.

The new partially-fortified wines are transferred, usually within a year, to the lodges of the port shippers at Vila Nova de Gaia, opposite Opôrto. A little more spirits may be added before shipment. Storage conditions, even in the above-ground lodges of Vila Nova de Gaia, Fig. 24, are cooler than in the Douro. The wines are aged in oak casks of about 126 gallons' capacity. There is a clear preference for casks of hard oak which contribute the least possible woody flavor to the wine. Further fortification can occur during aging.

The classification, aging, and blending system is a critical quality factor. The new wines are classified by color, sugar content, and quality. The lesser-colored wines are aged 3 to 8 years and blended to produce tawny ports. The moderately-colored wines are blended, bottled, or shipped earlier as ruby ports. The wines of highest color, flavor, and alcohol of a given vintage are shipped within a year to London where before two years they are bottled as vintage ports. Only a small percentage of the finest wine of the best years is so shipped. Recently, some vintage port has been bottled at Vila Nova de Gaia.

Madeira.—The Portuguese island some 600 miles off the north coast of Africa produces a number of white dessert wines. While once a most important wine type, it can no longer be considered a wine of outstanding quality. Negative quality factors are responsible. Prior to the introduction of oïdium, black rot, and phylloxera, grapes apparently ripened better. The higher alcohol permitted long aging, resulting in wines of superior quality. Following the invasion of the cryptogamic diseases, bunch rot and defective fermentations were common. Heating the new wines to 130° to 140°F. saved them from spoilage, but has not resulted in wines of high quality. High volatile acidity is the most common defect. Unless this can be controlled, there appears to be little future in the Madeira export trade except to the Scandinavian countries where their high sugar content recommends them. Pato and Amerine (1959) reported high volatile acidity to reduce consumer acceptance of Madeira wines. They believed their high aldehyde contents may favor consumer acceptance.

The present procedure is to ferment most of the wines dry, partially fortify and bake at not over 140°F. for 3 or 4 months in concrete tanks. The wine is then refortified. Some musts are fortified but are not heated. The producer blends the two types of wine to secure the desired sweetness. The wines are blended from a sort of fractional blending system to produce several types called Sercial, Boal (or Bual) and Malmsey in order of increasing sugar content. These types do not (except for Sercial) represent varietal types as they once did.

On Sétubal see Soares Franco (1938). Gahano's (1951) book on *vinhos verdes* is authentic. General texts on Portuguese table wines by Allen (1957, 1964) are on the popular side. Many articles of general enological interest are found in the Anais of the Junta Nacional do Vinho (1949–1961). On port there is a rich literature, much of which is not technical or critical. The treatise of Cockburn (n.d.) and the Anais of the Instituto de Viho do Pôrto (1940–1958) are most important from the technical point of view. Simon (1934) and Valente-Perfeito (1948) give the contrasting English and Portuguese points of view. Allen (1952A, 1957, 1964) and Croft-Cooke (1957) bring the popular side up to date. A general, and generous, view of Madeira is given by Croft-Cooke (1961).

OTHER EUROPEAN COUNTRIES

Austria

According to Schmidt (1965) there were wines made from wild grapes in Austria before Roman times. He stresses the role of the church in carrying on viticulture during the Middle Ages. Austria has nearly 100,-000 acres of vines. There has been a slow increase since 1931 but the present (1964) acreage is only 80 per cent of that in 1900. There has been an increase in yield per acre so that production reached a modern record in 1964 with over 75 million gallons. Over 80 per cent of the wine is white.

The best vineyards are near bodies of water (the Danube or Neusiedler Sea) or on especially good hillside exposures. The most popular variety is Green Veltliner (21 per cent), followed by Walschriesling (11), Müller-Thurgau (7), Neuburger (5.3), White Portuguese, Blue Franken, and Gray and Green Portuguese. All the other varieties (including White Riesling, Sylvaner, Rotgipfler, Zierfahndler, Ruländer, etc.) amount to less than three per cent of the total. Consumption has increased since W.W. I and is now slightly over 20 liters per capita. A unique feature of the distribution of wine in Austria is the amount sold in bulk directly by *Gastwirte* (wine restaurants, etc.): 46 per cent in 1939, according to Schmidt (1965).

About two-thirds of the Austrian vines grow in the northern part along both sides of the Danube. Krems, Langenlois, Retz, and Dürnstein are important production centers. Baden, Vöslau, Pfaffstätten, Gumpoldskirchen, and Traiskirchen are well-known vineyards just south of Vienna. The wines mature early. Many are drunk in the famous wine restaurants in the Grinzing district of Vienna as an after-dinner beverage, much as we would beer. Füger (1957) has reported wines of late-harvested grapes with 7.7 to 16.4 per cent alcohol and 0.2 to 26.0 per cent sugar.

Both viticulture and enology are very astutely practiced. Cool fermentations, particularly, are favored. Other positive quality factors are the varietal and regional labeling, and the rapid distribution of white table wines in cask. However, Moser (1959) notes the trend toward mechanization of the vineyards and wines of better keeping qualities. He also believes wines with regional or company (producer) labels are more successful than those with varietal appellations. Arthold (1950) is the standard technical work on Austrian wines. Leonhardt (1963) and Rau (1961) give popular discussions.

Hungary

Hungary is one of the important viticultural areas in Europe with nearly 500,000 acres of grapes. Their first vineyards were planted by the Romans.[7] Because of its geographical isolation and the fact that its wines are barely sufficient for home consumption they are not today often exported. However, 300 years ago Hungarian wines enjoyed a thriving export trade and, for Tokay, at least, a world-wide reputation for quality.

No less than 14 regions have been classified and produce wines of distinctive quality (Anon. 1958C). Certain areas are too cold for grape culture. Their quality and distinctiveness are due primarily to two sets of factors: temperature (climate, rainfall, exposure, soil conditions, drainage, etc.) and varietal complement. Leonhardt (1963), especially, emphasizes the extreme variation in temperature that may be expected. The varietal complement, he notes, includes no less than 50 white and 15 red varieties. Western European varieties such as Sylvaner, Traminer, Müller-Thurgau, and Chardonnay are grown beside native varieties such as Furmint, Ezerjó, Hárslevelü, Kéknyelü, Zierfahndler (white), and Kadarka (red), Gamza (Bulgarian), etc. According to Halász (1962) the Furmint variety was introduced in the thirteenth century by Walloons and derived its name from its yellow-brown color which resembles that of ripe wheat (froment). Neubeller (1965), on the other hand, believes it was introduced from Italy and is derived from fiori monti (flowery mountains). Most of the wine is white (about 60 per cent). Rosés constitute nearly one-quarter of the production and red table wine, about 15 per cent. Some sparkling and sweet dessert wines, and even vermouths, are produced. The table wines might deserve wider distribution if the home market did not absorb them: Mori, Badacsonyi, Debröi, Villányi-Pécsi, Egri, and Somlyöi, to mention a few. Kobel (1947) mentions particularly the quality of Walschriesling, Ezerjó, Sylvaner, and other white Hungarian wines. He found the red wines less interesting, particularly those of the widely-planted Kadarka. Egri Bikavér, partially from Kadarka, is considered the best red.

The one exception to the lack of fame of Hungarian wines was Tokay (Tokaj in Hungarian). The past tense is used advisedly because post W. W. II conditions have not been favorable to this district (about 10,000 acres). Tokay is one of the more expensive types of wines to produce and

---

[7] It is of interest to note that the word for wine in Hungarian is *bor*. Thus it is almost unique among European languages in not being derived from the Sanskrit *vena*. The Hungarians must have learned much from their Turkish conquerors.

in a socialist state few are able to afford the price that its classic production demands. Attempts to collectivise the vineyards have also discouraged many growers.

About half of Tokay is the product of a temperamental grape, the Furmint. It ripens late, has a low acidity, and dries on the vine if allowed to hang until October or later. The other Tokay grape is Hárslevelü. The long warm fall, early rains followed by dry weather, well-drained soils, the mixture of varieties and *Botrytis cinerea* are considered the major quality

Courtesy of Prof. Blaha

FIG. 25. HILLSIDE AND VALLEY VINEYARDS IN CZECHOSLOVAKIA

Note modern equipment

factors by Halász (1962). The best conditions—warm summer rains in early October followed by sunny days and cold nights—favor *Botrytis*. The vintage traditionally starts on October 28. In the best years, the juice of these shriveled grapes is used for the sweeter types—Aszu and essence. The finest grapes contain 40 or more per cent sugar. Obviously the short cut of using grape concentrate to produce a sweet table wine tends to reduce the quality. Szamorodni is the lesser quality drier type of Tokay, up to 2.7 per cent sugar according to Neubeller (1965). Aszus had 4.2 to 17.6 per cent sugar and 9.9 to 15.9 per cent alcohol.

The great fame of Tokay probably lies in the care with which the sweetest juice is added to ordinary juice (from 10 to 50 per cent for Aszu) or in its occasional use straight (as *eszencia*). The traditional wines were strong in aroma without the least caramel odor. Post-war Tokays with an amber color and a strong caramel odor may be suspected of containing concentrate.

The other Hungarian wines are sold with a district name plus often a varietal appellation. The standard text is that of Teleki (1937). Recent information on regions and varieties are given in Csepregi (1955), Halász (1962), and Anon. (1958C, 1959). The immediate post W.W. II problems were summarized by Kobel (1947). For technical data see Soós (1955), Rakcsányi (1963) and Neubeller (1965).

Czechoslovakia

The climate here is generally unfavorable and only early-ripening varieties, producing light wines, can be grown. Yet several vineyards with favorable exposures have achieved a good reputation by planting the best varieties and carefully vinifying them (Fig. 25). The wines are almost never exported since all are needed for local consumption. Melnik and Brno are centers of production. Blaha (1952, 1961) noted the search for better varieties that is going on. Hulač (1949) is a modern text on wine making and the treatise of Laho (1962) is admirable.

Rumania

This was a large viticultural country before W.W. II. About 40 per cent of the area of pre-war production is now in Russia but more than 500,000 acres remain. The best are white wines again indicating rather cool climatic conditions. Leonhardt (1963) reports that soil and climatic conditions are generally favorable. Direct producers are still widely planted owing to phylloxera and the quality is thus not so high as it once was. The area on resistant stocks is increasing rapidly. Good western European varieties are now often used: Pinot gris, Aligoté, Traminer, Walschriesling, Pinot noir, Cabernet Sauvignon, Cabernet franc, etc. A few wines are fortified to 18 per cent alcohol. Sparkling wines and brandy are also made.

Climate, varieties and special processing procedure thus appear to be the most important quality factors. Leonhardt (1963) reports place names plus varietal names. A sweet table wine is produced from late-harvested, botrytised grapes in Grasa, and slightly sweet rosé wines are made at Nicoresti. Table-grape varieties are often used to prepare dessert wines. For further information on Rumanian wines see Bernaz (1962), Constantinescu (1958, 1959–1962), and Prisnea (1964).

Courtesy of Prof. N. Nedeltchev

Fig. 26.   a.   Vintage Scene in Bulgaria.   b.   Interior of Winery at
Raulikene, Bulgaria

Bulgaria

There were over 350,000 acres of grapes in Bulgaria at the end of W.W. II, according to Kondarew (1965). This is expected to expand to over 750,000 acres in 1980 of which at least 100,000 acres will be in high quality varieties: Cabernet Sauvignon, Saperavi, Rkatsiteli, Muscat blanc, Aligoté, White Riesling, etc. About one-sixth of the acreage is in table grapes. The most important native wine grape varieties are Pamid, Mavrud, Gamsa, and Sartschin. The climate of Bulgaria is very favorable for grape growing. The temperature summation for the period after the average temperature reaches 50°F. is 3700 to 4000 day degrees. Lack of a critical home or export market has been a handicap. In lieu of wine exports they have developed an active table grape export market. According to Nedelchev (1959) they are trying to increase their wine exports and the industry is being modernized to accomplish this, Fig. 26. Vineyards are being consolidated and expanded into larger units, new and better varieties planted, and the wine types standardized. The following types of wine are now produced: red, pink, and white table wines, red and white dessert wines of 16 to 16.5 per cent alcohol and an equal sugar content, or of 18 to 18.5 per cent alcohol with 10 to 11 per cent sugar. The muscatels are especially appreciated. Bulgarian brandy, over two and a half million gallons per year, is called *rakia*. Leonhardt (1963) reports some wines of low acidity (due to the use of table grape varieties?). This is not typical. See also Georgiev (1949), Dalmasso (1958) and Kondarew (1965).

Albania

According to Nasse and Zigori (1968) the best Albanian wine varieties are Debine (noir and blanche), Kallmet, Mereshnik, Mjaltez, Serine (rouge and blanche), Shesh blanc and Vlosh. Varieties such as Barbera and Merlot have recently been planted. The industry is being modernized. Mainly tables wines are produced.

Yugoslavia

Grapes—about 630,000 acres producing over 150 million gallons—are grown throughout the country. Many of the wines are produced to western standards. However, the dark red, high tannin, alcoholic wines of Dalmatia and elsewhere are almost undrinkable by western standards. A short description of the Yugoslavian industry has been given by Cerletti (1958). The predilection for high tannin wines may date to the Slavic invasion from the fat-lamb-eating viticultural Caucasian areas (p. 49). Some of the types of wine produced clearly reflect western European varieties—Burgundac, Traminac, Rizling, Refoško, Merlot, Sémillon, Veltlenac, Slankamenka (here called Plavina), Rulandec, etc., and some reflect Hungarian or local origin—Kadarka, Furmint, Smederevka, Žilavka, Plavina, Prokupats, etc. The Walschriesling (Italian Riesling) is especially favored. The importance of varieties and their uses for standardizing types in Yugoslavia is fully explained by Bulič (1949) and Turcovič (1950A, 1950B, 1952, 1962).

Serbia produces Župa red wines and Prokupats (a variety) pink wines. The former is a wine of high color and tannin. Other Serbian wine regions are Krajina, Šumadija, Metohia, Vlasotinci, Venčac-Oplenac, and Smederevo (Smederevka is the vine).

Macedonian wines resemble those of Dalmatia—many are high in color and tannin. The Tikveš and Ohred are important regions and Vranats the native variety. Bosnia and Herzegovina produce few wines. A white Žilavka, mainly from the variety of the same name, and a red Blatina, of a deep red color and often high in tannin, may be noted.

Croatia includes Dalmatia, Istria, and Croatia proper. Dalmatian wines are often of relatively high alcohol and dry or sweet with a very high tannin content. Well-known types are Dingač, Prošek (sweet), Opol (pink, red, and dark red), Maraština (white table and dessert), Vugava (white table), and Benkovak (a region). Plavac mali is the important native variety. Istrian wines are lower in alcohol than those of Dalmatia. Western European varieties such as Refosco, Barbera, Cabernet Sauvignon, and Sémillon are widely planted in Istria. In Croatia, 75 per cent of the wine is white. Besides western European varieties a red Fruška Gora, Banat (Vršac is a well-known white and Merlot a high quality red), Subotica-Horgoš (a sandy region with dessert as well as table wines), and Graševina may be noted. Plješevac and Ilok (from a state vineyard) are also well known.

Slovenia is a northern region of high quality wines. Teran is a red wine with a pronounced lactic acid flavor. Ljutomer (formerly Luttenberger) is a region of many wine types—mainly labeled under varietal appellations: Silvanac, Rizling, Sauvignon (also Sovinjon), Traminac, Merlot, etc.

While the climate is favorable for the growth of vines in Yugoslavia, it sometimes leads to excessive sugar and alcohol, and to slightly sweet wines. The high tannin content of some of the red wines is a negative quality factor by our standards. For further information see Pogrimilovic (1969) and Radenković (1962).

Russia

No viticultural area, except possibly Bulgaria, is expanding its grape acreage as rapidly as Russia. See Dalmasso and Tyndalo (1957), Gerasimov (1957), Levy (1958), and Leonhardt (1963) for a fuller discussion of modern Russian viticulture and enology in Italian, English, French, and German. The standard texts in Russian include Azarashvili (1959), Beridze (1965), Davitaya (1948), Egorov (1955), Frolov-Bagreev and Agabal'yants (1951), Gerasimov (1964), Kalugina et al. (1957), Mogilyanskii (1954), and Prostoserdov (1955). The important technical publications of the Biochemical Institute of the Akademiya Nauk S.S.S.R. (1947–1964) should also be consulted as well as the reports of the "Magarach" grape and wine experiment station at Yalta in the Crimea and of various other experiment stations. According to Levy there are at least ten institutes devoted to the study of grapes and wine in Russia. The immediate post-war acreage of about 800,000 acres has now (1964) reached approximately 2.5 million acres and plans are announced for further expansion.

While there are only a few unbiased appraisals of the quality of post W.W. II wines these are sufficient to indicate that even in a socialist state quality has been taken into account. The best indication of this is the price of wine which on the retail market varies from 30 cents to $1.75 per bottle in Moscow, according to Levy (1958). The Russians are today the world's greatest authorities on ampelography—the classification and evolution of grape varieties. The new Russian ampelography edited by Frolov-Bagreev (1946–1965) is a model of its kind. Levy (1958) reported the ampelographical collection at the Institute Taïrov near Odessa occupied 46 acres and included 700 varieties. For a detailed evaluation of the Soviet industry and a slightly less optimistic view of the prospects for quality, see Amerine (1963, 1965).

Scientific research is being developed with exemplary speed. This includes development of grapes for cold climates, new procedures for production of several types of wines, including continuous fermentation of sparkling wines (Amerine 1959B, 1963) and training of technologists capable of utilizing the most modern laboratory and control procedures. See, for example, Durmishidze (1955). The production of sparkling wines, Fig. 27, is especially favored.

There are some negative quality factors. Hot climatic conditions in some areas may lead to excessively alcoholic wines. The traditional method of fermenting for long periods on the skins is certainly inimical to quality but is disappearing. Most important, perhaps, is the absence of a critical clientele capable of influencing the development of the wine industry.

The main areas for grape growing in the Soviet Union are in Moldavia, the Ukraine (including Crimea and the Transcarpathian region), R. S. F. R. (Rostov, Krasnodar, Daghestan), Georgia, Azerbaidzhan, Uzbekistan

Courtesy S.S.S.R. Embassy

FIG. 27.   SPARKLING WINE PLANT IN TBILISI

and Armenia.   Georgia (over 200,000 acres), is one of the oldest, if not the oldest, viticultural region and has the best reputation (Beridze, 1965).

As for brandy, Armenia and Georgia are the centers of the industry. Considerable attention has been given to standardizing a series of qualities of brandy based mainly on time of aging according to Dshanpoladyan (1958).   Thus, "Otborny" brandy had an average age of 6 to 7 years, and "Jubeleyny" of 10 years, and "Prasditshchny" 14 years.   The technical advance of the Russian wine and brandy industry is particularly noted in Anon. (1958A), Maltabar *et al.* (1959), and Nilov and Skurikhin (1960). The rapid rise in sparkling wine production is especially noticeable.   Interesting advances are the draining tanks (for white musts), lined aluminum tanks, continuous sparkling wine production, and a central tasting commission.

Greece—Cyprus

Grapes were grown in Greece for many centuries before our era.   But the problems of producing wines in a warm climate were no less in Homer's time than today.   Thus perfumes, spices, and honey were added to many if not most ancient wines to mask or reduce the development of spoilage in wines stored in warm climates and to give the wines a special character.   About one-third of the wines produced in Greece today contain one or more per cent of sandarac resin.   These wines, *retsinas*, have a distinct turpentine odor which is most disagreeable to the uninitiated. Producers must keep separate equipment for handling them.   Surprisingly a taste for such wines can be achieved.   The non-retsina wines are of no more than average interest. Some production of fortified very sweet muscat wines for export occurs, particularly from the island of Samos. Mavrodaphne is a sort of tawny port type, often with a distinct caramel flavor. The cooperative wineries and the development of trained enologists are decidedly hopeful signs for the future. However, here again, the lack of a critical local clientele and the unstandardized practices of the small producers are discouraging.

There are over 90,000 acres under cultivation in Cyprus, but the average yield is very low—about one ton per acre. Under the Ottoman Empire from 1571 until 1878 wine making was discouraged. The predominant grape (77 per cent) is a red variety called Mavro. It is used for dry red, rosé, and sherry as well as for concentrate. Xinisteri (20 per cent) is the main white variety. Both these grapes when dried to about 45° Balling are crushed together and slowly fermented to produce the sweet tawny Commandaria wine. Improvement in varieties is considered to be one of the necessary steps for improving the wines. Since Cyprus is still free of phylloxera this presents important quarantine problems for introduction of new varieties. Zivania is the native brandy, about 100° proof according to Kuchel (1959). It is produced in small stills (less than 50-gallon).

ASIA

Few wines are made in Asia and the less said of most of these the better. The hot climate leads to high-sugar, low-acid grapes. The fermentations are often defective. Storage conditions are poor. Many of the resulting wines are sweet and acetic or dry and alcoholic. Islam religion prevents consumption of wines and many of the varieties of grapes available for wine are more suitable for eating or drying than for wine production.

Israel

In Israel the wines show the best chance of improvement. The modern wine industry dates from the importations in 1880's of French varieties by Baron Rothschild. The most important wineries are at Rishon-le-Zion and Zicron-Jacob where modern equipment has been installed. While European type names, such as sauterne, port, sherry, etc., have been employed, Israel as a recent signatory to the Madrid pact announced the intention of abandoning these European-type names by 1960. This will be a real sacrifice and may constitute a step towards revision of wine nomenclature in other countries. However, as of mid-1965 Israeli wines with names such as "burgundy" were still on the market. Because of the warm climatic conditions the best wines are of the dessert types. A recent text in grape growing in Israel is that of Hochberg (1954–1955). Concerning the problems of the Israeli wine industry today see Ostashinsky (1958), Rappaport (1959) and Ough (1965). According to Ough (1965) the 1964 acreages of wine grape varieties in Israel were 39 per cent Carignane, 37 Alicante Grenache (Grenache?), 11 Muscat of Alexandria, 6 Sémillon, 5 Clairette (Boorbaulenc), 1.5 Alicante Bouschet, and only 0.5 other varieties. It appears that much of the white wine is produced from Grenache.

The wines of Lebanon, Syria, Iran, and Pakistan need little comment. They could be improved if the vinification were improved (cooling, etc.) and if the dessert wines were properly fortified. In 1960 Alleweldt (1965B) reported over 1,875,000 acres of grapes in Turkey with an average yield of $2^1/_2$ tons per acre. Grape culture certainly dates to 2000 B.C. Today 37 per cent of the grapes are used for raisins and another 37 per cent for making *Pekmez*, a concentrated grape juice of 50 to 65 per cent sugar. Only about 2 to 3 per cent of the total grapes, 40,000 to 50,000 tons, go to wine production. Sultanina (Thompson Seedless) is, of course, the predominant variety. A number of native wine grape varieties were listed by Alleweldt (1965B): Dimrit (also used as a table grape), Misket Bornova, Papas Karasi, etc. Some European grapes are grown, i.e. Cinsaut. The wines are sold with type and district names, usually at a standard price through a governmental monopoly. Alleweldt considered the following as quality red wines: Trakya, Buzbag (a blend of wines of the varieties Öküz Gözü and Buzbag), Horzkarasi, Kalecik and Kavaklideres. The best white wines were labeled Kalecik, Navince, Misket (or Musket of Bornova), Vinikol, Kavaklideres and Trakya. Other reds and whites include Cabuk, Güzelbag, Yeni Marmara, Mutuk and Taris. Turkey is an example of what can be done by technicians working for the government or a monopoly. Biron (1950), Akman (1949, 1951) and Akman and Yazicioglu (1953), have done much to modernize the industry. The very hot climate is a handicap.

Japan

There is a small but progressive wine industry in Japan. The high humidity makes growing of V. *vinifera* varieties difficult but some are produced plus a number of non-vinifera varieties and hybrids. The use of sugar is very general and many of the wines are sweet and fortified with non-vinous alcohol. Yokotsuka (1955) reported wine production of 25 million gallons in Japan in 1952, produced from about 30,000 acres.[8] This was compared to sake production of about 100 million gallons. The two main Japanese grape growing regions are the Kofu and Osaka valleys.

[8] Both these figures are larger than those given in Table 1. The difference is the basis of reporting. Over 43,000 acres were reported in 1964.

The native varieties in these districts, Koshu and Jaraku respectively, appear to have been introduced from the continent. A number of V. *labrusca* varieties have been imported from this country—Delaware and Campbell Early being widely grown. Yokotsuka admits that the unfavorable climatic conditions make the bulk of the Japanese wines unbalanced, astringent, and of poor quality. Wine making procedures are also primitive in many cases. For a more optimistic view see Amerine (1964).

AUSTRALIA

Vines were first brought to Australia in 1788. Several small vineyards were planted at once and were later considerably expanded. Wine was shipped to England in 1822 where it received a silver medal. The dominant man in the industry after 1824 was James Busby. He wrote three books on grape culture and imported over 600 varieties from Europe into Australia, according to Laffer (1949). Many wineries in existence today started over one hundred years ago: Reynell in 1834, Gramps in 1847, "Yalumba" in 1849, and Seppelts in 1851. The pride which these firms have in their product has been emphasized by Webb (1959). For further information see James (1966) and Simon (1966).

The most important wine region today is in South Australia, followed by New South Wales and Victoria. There is a small but growing industry in Western Australia and a few vines in Queensland. There are about 130,-000 acres in wine grapes and annual wine production is around 45 million gallons. A limited number of varieties are planted, especially in South Australia which is free of phylloxera. Until recently it prohibited vine importations. Increasing attention is being given to planting of the best varieties. The climate is rather humid in the Hunter River valley though the district has a good reputation. Elsewhere climate does not appear to be a dominant factor.

The wineries are generally large with modern equipment (Fig. 28). Adequate facilities for aging are available and there is much interest in producing high quality bottle-aged wines, particularly by certain firms. These include a variety of white and red table wines as well as flor sherries and red dessert wines of the port type. Anon. (1959) reports that 1957–1958 sales in Australia were divided among types of wine as follows: dry sherry (11 per cent), sweet sherry (31 per cent), white dessert (14 per cent), red dessert (17 per cent), table (22 per cent), and sparkling (5 per cent). There is also a thriving brandy industry.

AFRICA

The wine industry of this continent in the north is in Morocco, Algeria, Tunisia, and Egypt and in the far south in the Union of South Africa.

FIG. 28. LARGE SOUTH AUSTRALIAN WINERY IN VINEYARD AREA

North Africa

The French developed Algeria as an adjunct of their low-alcohol Midi wines. Their intent was to produce wines of 12 per cent alcohol which would be suitable for blending with their thin Midi wines. They were eminently successful. Red, rosé, and white table wines and some dessert wines are produced. The warm climatic conditions insure good ripening and wines of 11 to 14 per cent alcohol. Heavy-yielding varieties are employed—Carignane, Alicante Bouschet, Clairette blanche, etc. In the cooler mountainous areas some wines of better quality are produced—a few have achieved consumer recognition. The vinification is generally very modern—sulfur dioxide, concrete tanks, improved systems of color extraction, etc. Most of the wine is shipped to France in tank ships, for blending purposes and early sale. The classic textbook on Algerian wines is that of Fabre (1946–1947), now somewhat out of date. A recent and admirable modern study, with many points of interest to California producers is that of Brémond (1957). See also Chedeville (1945), Isnard (1951–1954), and Peyronnet (1950). The future of the Algerian wine industry is somewhat in doubt since the independence of that country and the reduction in exports to France.

Morocco has a very ancient wine history, going back to the Roman period. Joppien (1960) notes that grapes are grown in many parts of Morocco, many of them native table grapes. The modern period begins with the French occupation of 1912. This resulted in the introduction of typical European wine grapes and construction of modern wineries. Important vineyards were planted near Meknes, Marrakesch, Casablanca, Rabat, Kenitra, and Oujda. Varieties such as Clairette (blanche?), Maccabeo, (Pedro?) Ximenes, Grenache, Cinsaut, Carignane and Alicante Bouschet are widely planted. The vintage follows the Algerian pattern, starting in August during the hottest period. Joppien (1960) states that the fermentations are very rapid and that the new wines are cooled and centrifuged so that wine is ready to export in September! The vintage amounts to over 50 million gallons óf which two-thirds is exported, most of it red. The analyses published by Joppien show that the alcohol content of the table wines are around 12 per cent. By American standards the volatile acidity was high—0.066 to 0.143 per cent.

Tunisia also produces wines, largely intended for export. The cellars may not be quite so modern as in Algeria and the local trade is less. It is not a very hopeful viticultural region for the future under present political conditions. There is also a very small wine industry in Egypt. The climate is warm for table wine grapes.

South Africa

The vine was introduced at Capetown in 1652. A sweet muscatel, Constantia, achieved considerable fame in Europe in the 18th century. The climate is favorable (though rather warm in some areas) and about 240,000 acres are planted to vines. Total wine production ranges up to 100 million gallons. In the cooler Coastal Belt, Cinsaut, Palomino (erroneously named White French), Stein (a bud sport of high acid), and Green grape are the important varieties. In the warmer Little Karroo region Cinsaut, Palomino, Muscat of Alexandria, Thompson Seedless, and Muscadel (Muscat blanc) are the predominant varieties planted, Fig. 29. Soil types are very variable—from sandy to heavy loams of a range in fertility. The vinification is generally modern (with exceptions, of course). About half the crush is distilled for high proof or brandy. Much of the wine is intended for export to England and elsewhere. These are mainly of the dessert type: ports of 18 to 20 per cent alcohol or muscatels of about 17.7 per cent. The ports are made in the tawny and ruby types but they also produce some bottle-aged vintage port. Flor sherry of 17 to 20 per cent is

Courtesy of K.W.V.

Fig. 29.   South African Harvest Scene

one of the most distinctive and high quality products of the Cape.   The musts are plastered to raise the acidity and the traditional film-yeast is used as is the fractional blending solera system.

South Africa makes a distinction between the light-bodied claret type (12.6 per cent alcohol) and the heavier-bodied burgundy types (13.2 per cent).   Besides Cinsaut some Cabernet, Petite Sirah, and Gamay are used. Much attention has been given to cool and pressure-tank fermentation of white table wines—particularly of the Riesling type.   Many of these are slightly sweet.   Some of the white wines are estate (winery) bottled and have distinctive vineyard names (some of obvious German derivation).

Both bottle- and tank-fermented sparkling (Fonkelwyn) wines are produced.   (They are not called champagne.)   Perlwine (wines of about 0.6 atmospheres pressure at 80.6° with not over 3.2 gm. per liter of carbon dioxide) are also made by the tank process.   They would prefer a higher carbon dioxide level than this, according to Ambrosi (1959).

South Africa produces a native liqueur called Van der Hum which has a wine alcohol base and a tangerine flavor.   Brandy of several qualities and ages is also available.   For brandy pot stills are preferred and a special board controls the quality.

For an account of Cape wines see De Bosdari (1955) and Ambrosi (1959).

The KWV (Ko-operative Wynbouwers Vereniging) has stabilized the industry by establishing minimum prices, by distilling surpluses, etc., by standardizing the types for export, and by encouraging the production of high-quality properly-aged flor sherry and port. Ambrosi (1959) reports over eight million gallons of port in KWV storage cellars, Fig. 30. It has also sponsored the production of better brandy by introducing double distillation in pot stills, harvesting the grapes on the green side, and aging the brandy. South African red table wines are also often praised, particularly those from the Cabernet Sauvignon.

Technical and historical information regarding the production of wine in South Africa has been given by Anon. (1969), De Bosdari (1955), Leipoldt (1952), and Theron and Niehaus (1948).

SOUTH AMERICA

There are vineyards in Peru, Chile, Argentina, Bolivia, Uraguay, Paraguay, and Brazil. For a discussion of these wines see Marrison (1971) and Amerine (1959C).

Peru

Vines wére planted here near Cuczo in the colonial period about 1550 and at one time wine and brandy were exported, particularly to California.

Courtesy of K.W.V.

FIG. 30.   WINERY OF K.W.V. AT PAARL, SOUTH AFRICA

Less than 20,000 acres are now planted. Varieties similar to the Mission variety of California were planted and some are still grown there. They represent a serious negative quality factor because of their low acidity and color and relatively high sugar content. The climate is warm and usually very dry so that vine growth is not good. Years of excessive rainfall at vintage time may further reduce crop and quality. Marrison (1971) reports the methods of vinification are often crude though sulfur dioxide is employed in the better wineries. The wines, he says, are naturally high in alcohol and may be further fortified and then diluted with water. Pisco brandy was a colorless muscat brandy which achieved a certain fame in California, particularly as an ingredient of Pisco punch, in the pre-Prohibition period. It is still produced but the samples tasted have not been notable for quality.

Chile

Vines were introduced from Peru at a very early date—some of them worthless seedlings similar to the Mission variety. However, in contrast to Peru the climate is quite favorable and vines were much more successfully cultivated. The French influence on grape growing and wine making may be seen. French varieties were extensively imported, starting in 1851, and varieties such as Sauvignon blanc, Sémillon, Malbec, Merlot, and Cabernet Sauvignon are widely planted. The vinification is not yet the best. The whites, for example, are almost universally fermented on the skins too long and are often kept in the wood past their prime. The reds are much better, though some are overaged.

Chilean viticulture is free of phylloxera and mildew. While most of the production is of table wines some red sweet wine is produced in the southern vineyards. Chile has the largest export trade of any American country. This is partially due to the very modest price of their wine. While the quality of selected wines is good, much of the white wine is too dark and tannic. A description of Chilean wines is given by Léon (1947) and Dalmasso (1956). The best are labeled *Reservado* or *Gran Vino*.

Argentina

Grapes were introduced from Chile about 1557. It is by far the largest producer of wine in the New World, about 300 million gallons annually. The main center of production is in Mendoza but there is considerable production in the south near Neuquén where some quite good wines are produced. The climate and soil are very favorable and the vineyards are well cared for. While some seedling (Criolla) varieties from the colonial period remain many European varieties are widely planted—particularly the Malbec and Merlot for red wines and Pedro Ximenes, Trebbiano, Riesling, and Sauvignon blanc for whites. There are many very large vineyards of high production. The wineries are also very large and generally very modern. The background of the producers is largely Italian. The wines resemble those of that country in being sound ordinary products. Argentina has the largest per capita consumption of wine in the Americas. Some aged superior wines are produced. One should note that much of the wine (*chica*) is of low alcohol content (up to 8 per cent). There is also an important production of vermouth and anise-flavored brandy. Dalmasso (1956) gives a good description of the total industry, noting particularly the low cost of production. For technical information see Magistocchi (1955), Maveroff (1949), and Oreglia (1964).

Brazil

It is surprising that grapes can be grown in this tropical country. However, in the province of São Paulo there are grapes and further south in Rio Grande do Sul more extensive vineyards. From these about 30 million gallons of wine are produced annually. Because of the tropical humidity American *V. labrusca*, etc. varieties such as Isabella and Herbemont and the direct producers predominate. The wines are ordinary and Italian influences are dominant. Both table and dessert wines are produced.

Other Countries

Very few grapes can be grown successfully in the high plateau country of Bolivia. But some wine is produced for local consumption, about 150,-000 gallons annually.

Near Montevideo in Uruguay there are extensive vineyards. The climate is not always favorable because of drought. A few wines of quality are produced but more are ordinary. Annual production amounts to over 20 million gallons.

There have been vineyards in Paraguay since the earliest settlements, particularly at the missions. The climate is not favorable, the varieties are poor, and the production and quality are small. For a more complete description of these wines see Amerine (1959C) and Hyams (1965).

NORTH AMERICA

The vineyards of North America may be classified into four regions: Canada, Eastern United States, California, and Mexico.

Canada

The Canadian industry is largely restricted to the Niagara peninsula where Lake Ontario protects it from the north winds and Lake Erie lies on the west and further moderates the temperature. About 75 per cent of the grape acreage is planted to Concord, 15 per cent to Niagara, and the remainder to native varieties such as Agawam, Delaware, and Catawba, plus considerable direct-producing hybrids and a small amount of V. *vinifera*, According to Benson (1959) prices range from $85 per ton for the ordinary varieties to $125 per ton for the low-yielding higher-quality grapes. These are high by 1959 California standards when one considers that the sugar content was only 12 to 18 per cent. Considerable water is used to reduce the total acidity—indicated by the statutory limitation of 250 gallons per ton. Since the Canadian tax on dessert wines is on the spirits used in fortification there is considerable use of syruped fermentation (p. 451). Some wines of 17 per cent alcohol are produced in this way. The more expensive dessert wines are produced by fortification with high-proof spirits. Both baked (Tressler process) and flor sherry are made in Canada. Table wines are produced by the use of sugar and water in the usual way (p. 493). Rosé and sparkling wines in addition to the usual red and white table wines are produced.

There is a small grape industry in British Columbia (about 2000 acres) but the winter temperatures are low and grape growing difficult. Bowen *et al.* (1965) recommended direct producers. They reported sugar contents of 11.4 to 19.5 per cent and very high acidity.

Eastern United States

During the Colonial period numerous attempts were made to introduce the European grape to the colonies along the Atlantic seaboard. Winter killing, high summer humidity, phylloxera, and perhaps virus diseases defeated all of these efforts. It was not until about the end of the 18th century that serious attention was turned to domesticating varieties of the numerous local species. Gradually a number of varieties which were suited to cultivation were developed. These included Concord, Catawba, Niagara, Delaware, Ives Seedling, and a host of others.

These all resemble each other with a more or less strong and distinctive aroma, believed to be partially due to methyl anthranilate. The odor is commonly said to be "foxy" both in this country and abroad. They are generally of insufficient sugar to produce a balanced table wine and sugaring is permitted. The industry is most important in upper New York state in what is known as the Finger Lakes region. The moderating influence of these deep lakes helps prevent winter killing and possibly late spring frosts. At any rate, the vineyards are mainly on the slopes facing the lakes. There is a small wine industry in Ohio. Especially near Sandusky where Lake Erie exerts a moderating influence on the temperature, there are many vineyards. Other vineyards and wineries are found in Michigan, Pennsylvania, Illinois, Arkansas, Missouri, and elsewhere.

The native varieties are used to produce varietal types and also are often labeled with European appellations. Thus we have New York Delaware, and New York rhine. A considerable amount of sparkling wine is also produced (p. 498). There is also an extensive shipment of wines (particularly of dessert wines) from California to eastern producers for blending. Thus eastern muscatels, ports, and some sherries may contain considerable California wine.

In Maryland a small wine industry, mainly based on the direct producers, has developed. Small quantities of wines are produced in the South Atlantic states from varieties of *Vitis rotundifolia*—the so-called Scuppernong grapes. These have a quite different aroma from *V. labrusca* type grapes, due to phenethyl alcohol (p. 113).

While the summer temperatures of eastern United States are frequently very desirable for vine culture, no extensive plantings of *V. vinifera* varieties have yet been acclimatized there. In the meantime the eastern wines because of their obvious and strong aromas have an appeal for many consumers. Recently Concord wines and concentrate have been blended with California red wines and sugar to produce sweet kosher-type wines. A large clientele for these wines has developed. More detailed information on methods of production of eastern U.S. wines are given later in Chapter 12. See also Schoonmaker and Marvel (1941).

MEXICO

Seeds of Spanish grapes were introduced into Mexico shortly after the Conquest. For a history see Heliodoro and Valle (1958) and Hyams (1965). Later, seeds and cuttings of these were carried south (to Peru) and north (to Baja California) by missionaries and explorers. The seedling variety, Mission, is supposed to have originated at Parras. It was, unfortunately, low in acid and color. It, or its near seedling relations, were also taken to Peru, Chile, Argentina, and, from Baja California to California.

Most of the Mexican vineyards are located in regions of excessively warm climatic conditions. This, coupled with the low acidity and low color of the "Mission" seedlings accounts for the lack of consumer acceptance of some of their wines. Recently Mexican viticulture has begun to introduce new and better varieties and procedures (Anon. 1958B and Amerine, 1959C) and, with suitable fermentation and aging controls, standard wines should be produced. The best Mexican wines currently produced appear to be dessert types—particularly of the muscatel and related types. Many of the brandies appear to be artificially flavored.

California

Many of the factors influencing the quality of California wines are considered elsewhere in the text—particularly climate (p. 116), varieties (p. 125), and production techniques. Since this book will probably be used most extensively in this state the other quality factors will be considered in greater detail for this region than for others. Production of wines and brandy in California since 1909 is given in Table 2.

TABLE 2

PRODUCTION OF WINES AND BRANDIES IN CALIFORNIA, 1909–1970 AVERAGES

Calendar Years	Total All Wines[1]	Dessert and Appetizer Wines	Vermouth and Special Natural Wines	Table Wines	Beverage Brandy[2]
		Thousands of Gallons			
1909–1913	43,950	19,161	. . .	24,434	.. . .
1933–1937	54,081	38,199	. . .	16,482	1,854
1938–1942	81,721	56,455	. . .	25,266	3,971
1943–1947	113,878	78,204	1,242[3]	35,674	4,350
1948–1952	130,091	96,237	818	33,853	2,615
1953–1957	126,559	92,027	2,116[4]	34,532	3,650
1958–1962	148,704	96,343	14,210	52,361	5,380
1963–1967	172,582	94,900	18,835	77,682	12,865
1968	172,640	75,263	19,543	97,377	13,299
1969	215,568	77,737	23,313	137,831	12,961
1970	183,590	59,232	30,810	124,358	. . .

Source of data: Wine Institute Bulletins and first and second editions.
[1] The total is not obtained as a sum of the other entries since table and dessert wines are diverted to production of sparkling and flavored wines. For table and dessert wines the production is only for July to December.
[2] In proof gallons and on fiscal year basis. Estimates before 1963.
[3] 1944–1947.
[4] Beginning of production of special natural wines.

The historical development of any region has an obvious influence on its present and future status. The historical influences are particularly important for California. The original vineyards were planted at the Missions, primarily of the Mission grape from Baja California, in order to produce wines for religious and domestic use. It is, as indicated previously, a late-ripening grape of low color and acid and generally of high sugar. Its table wines are flat and spoil easily. The Mission grape is still grown in California to the extent of several thousand acres. It was partially responsible for the generally low quality of California table wines in the pre-1880 period and when used for table wines is still a negative quality factor. It can be used for white dessert wines of above average quality.

There is one positive factor that remains from the Mission period—the development of the wine type angelica, Amerine and Winkler (1938). While the exact origin of this wine type remains in doubt it seems to have been made originally during the Mission period from musts of the Mission grape.

The next historical influence was the emphasis on varieties which arose from three separate sources: the work of Agoston Haraszthy, the research of Eugene Waldemar Hilgard and the propaganda efforts of the State Board of Viticultural Commissioners.

Haraszthy's importation of varieties from Europe was of great potential importance. Regrettably the political situation on his return was such that the vines could not be properly distributed and some misnaming of varieties probably occurred during their haphazard distribution; see Fredericksen (1947). Hilgard of the University of California published a series of masterful studies on the adaption of grape varieties to California conditions between 1880 and 1892. He clearly noted the critical importance of climate, variety, and time of harvesting in a region as warm as California. The State Board of Viticultural Commissioners was also keenly interested in the question of varieties and did a great deal of useful propaganda in favor of planting better varieties. Their varying influences are discussed by Amerine (1959A, 1960).

The next important factor was, and is, the very diversified European origin of our California vineyardists and wine makers. Almost from the start French, German, Italian, British, Spanish, and other nationalities of grape growers and wine makers were active in the state. They brought their various varieties of vines, and wine making procedures, techniques and type nomenclature into California. Much of their influence was highly desirable. The climatic conditions of California, however, were quite different from those of the European regions from which they came. Thus, the time of harvest in Europe was 2 to 6 weeks *too late* for California conditions. The temperature of fermentation and storage were also higher and led to problems of bacterial spoilage. The wonder is that so many sound wines were produced in the pre-1900 period.

Another negative influence was the free use of the only wine type names which they knew—claret (for the British), champagne, chablis, and burgundy (for the French), chianti (for the Italians), etc. In some cases this extended to use of private or local place names—Château d'Yquem, Johannisberg, etc. The ethics of the time and place should, of course be considered. Their use may have helped distribution but it gave an imitative character to the industry. Often attention was given to producing wines which resembled foreign types rather than to creation of unique native types. This influence continues today.

Since Repeal, the emphasis has been on rapid turnover and large-scale operations. This has changed normal aging.[9] The small producer found

---

[9] Aging in large containers, of course, reduces the rate of aging.

the competition too great. The decreasing number of wineries in California (about one-third as many as immediately after repeal) is both a positive and negative quality factor. Large, modern, well-equipped and -staffed wineries are obviously advantageous in the economical production of standard wines. It would be too bad for the future of the California wine industry if they absorbed the smaller quality-minded wineries and converted all their products to standard, sound, and, alas, often rather uninteresting wines. The "differences" between wines is a good part of their aesthetic interest. We think the industry may underestimate the great potential of the American market for wines of special character. Also the reputation of these fine wines helps build the confidence of the public in all California wines. The large importations in foreign wines into this country should convince us that there is a demand for special wines of distinctive quality, even though most imported wines are *not* of high quality.

The negative influence of using European names for native wines has often been noted in the new wine areas of the world. James (1955) stressed this for Australia. There is no doubt in our minds that the continued use of foreign appellations for California wines is not in the best interest of the proper image of our wine industry. Furthermore, use of these names simply advertises the wines of the original region. Possibly some of the recent success of natural flavored wines and of various varietal wines in California is an indication of where the future may lie. One point may be important: If the varietal approach is made too "pure" there can be no progress. The regulations should be made flexible enough to include clonal selections and similarly-flavored hybrids. As further support may we note the wide variety of strains of Pinot noir permitted in Burgundy and use of clonal selections of Rieslings in Germany.

The continuing pattern of the California grape and wine industry has been one of years of high production and low prices followed by years of lower production but higher prices. This has had a very restraining influence on the industry. It has encouraged, certainly, high production by the vineyardists and attitudes of short term profit by the wine makers. Under these circumstances the development of an acceptance of quality is difficult. As to which is the "egg and which the chicken" we leave the decision to the agricultural economists. Certainly the complex interrelation of the table, raisin, and wine industry has had a potent effect on the industry and may have aided the up and down pattern. It has also tended to encourage the planting of dual- or triple-purpose grapes which in some cases are not suited to the production of high quality wines. The widespread planting of Thompson Seedless is a negative quality factor. Recent plantings of varietal grapes and higher prices should correct this.

One result of this uncertain economic status was the development of the California Wine Association (CWA) in the late 19th century (Peninou and Greenleaf, 1954). It certainly stabilized the trade, and what is more important, succeeded in standardizing types. Better varieties began to be extensively planted about the turn of the century. The CWA blending and finishing cellar at Richmond plus the undoubted tasting ability of Henry Lachman resulted in the first large-scale standardization of California wine types. In the post-Prohibition period this uncertain economic position has given birth to two other organizations—the Wine Institute and the Wine Advisory Board.

The Wine Institute is a non-profit trade organization which includes most of the California producers. Its influences have been manifold. Trade and legal assistance to its members have been most important. It has also constituted a sounding board for industry opinion. The industry has thus been enabled to speak singly in many important cases. The Wine Advisory Board (WAB) is a governmental agency whose revenue is derived from a tax on sales of wine and whose efforts are largely devoted to trade promotion. This has fortunately been generously interpreted so that it includes allotments for research.

Another historical factor was the development of the vineyard-winery company with an emphasis on quality. A number of these survive. Their historical stature is certainly of considerable value to them commercially and to the industry as a whole. Prohibition eliminated most of these. Some have had a second life under new owners.

Prohibition also had other effects—the influence of which is difficult to evaluate. Sales of dessert wines were greatly stimulated by Prohibition. Whereas in the pre-World War I period (1900–1910) dessert wines accounted for about 40 per cent of the production, it has accounted for up to 75 per cent of the production in the post-W.W. II period. The reasons for this change in taste are not known. Recently the percentage of dessert wine consumption has been decreasing. Prohibition also brought in a producer-wholesaler-retailer relationship which eventually did away with the retail sale of wine in bulk. While this may have increased the profits of the California producers it is by no means as certain that it favorably influenced per-capita consumption since it markedly increased the cost of wine to the consumer. Some doubt exists that "winery bottling" of standard wines has markedly improved quality.

Prohibition brought the winery under close control of the government. In the post-Prohibition period many regulations have thus been easily (possibly not all desirable) introduced into the industry. Analytical standards for volatile acidity, alcohol content, and even for sugar content for types were easily established in this atmosphere of permissiveness. The effect continues with the current campaign to control the sanitary practices of the industry.

The impact of industrialization was gradually felt by the California wine industry in the post-Prohibition period. These various influences are too recent for complete evaluation but they have led to much centralization, a trend which will probably continue.

Gallo (1958) in an analysis of the future of the California wine industry predicted development of new wine types. He particularly noted the need for changes in laws and regulations to permit development of low-carbonation wines. Among the advances of the first 25 years after repeal he noted development of slightly sweet, red table wines, creation of the rosé market, cold fermentation, early bottling of white wines, sterile filtration, flor sherry, ion-exchange, better maturity standards, production of wine vinegar, a successful berry wine industry, introduction of special natural wines, etc.

The technological information provided by the College of Agriculture of the University of California and its students was (and continues to be) of considerable value. The highest standards of viticulture and enology were emphasized. The importance of variety, an extension of Hilgard's work, was stressed. The importance of the newer techniques of food handling were brought to the attention of the industry and the responsible governmental agencies. Their recommendations have been promulgated by numerous conferences, circulars, bulletins and books, in addition to regular University classes and extension courses (Amerine 1959A). The wine judgings of the California State Fair and the meetings of the Technical Advisory Committee of the Wine Institute, and of the American Society of Enologists have been of importance in improving quality. The latter and Wine Institute have provided scholarships for students.

BIBLIOGRAPHY[1]

ACCADEMIA ITALIANA DELLA VITE E DEL VINO. 1949–1965. Atti. Tipografia S.T.I.A.V., Siena. 17 vols.

AKADEMIYA NAUK S.S.S.R., INSTITUT BIOKHIMII. 1947–1964. Biokhimiya Vinodeliya (Biochemistry of Wine Making). Izdatel'stvo Akademii Nauk S.S.S.R., Moscow. 8 vols.

AKMAN, A. V. 1949. Sarap, Sirke ve Dayanikle Sira (Equipment for Juice and Wine Cellars). Üniversitesi Basimevi, Ankara.

AKMAN, A. V. 1951. Sarap Analiz Metodlar (Methods of Wine Analyses). Üniversitesi Basimevi, Ankara.

AKMAN, A. V., and YAZICIOGLU, T. 1953. Technology of Fermentation. Ankara. University Fac. Agr. Pub. No. 51.

ALLEN, H. W. 1924. The Wines of France. T. Fisher Unwin Ltd., London.

ALLEN, H. W. 1933. Sherry. Constable and Co., London.

[1] Titles have been translated only for non-western European languages.

ALLEN, H. W. 1951. Natural Red Wines. Constable and Co., London.
ALLEN, H. W. 1952A. Sherry and Port. Constable and Co., London.
ALLEN, H. W. 1952B. White Wines and Cognac. Constable and Co., London.
ALLEN, H. W. 1957. Good Wine from Portugal. Sylvan Press, London.
ALLEN, H. W. 1961. A History of Wine: Great Vintage Wines from the Homeric Age to the Present Day. Faber and Faber, London.
ALLEN, H. W. 1964. The Wines of Portugal. McGraw-Hill Book Co., New York.
ALLEWELDT, G. 1965A. Die Qualitätsweinproduktion aus rebphysiologischer Sicht. Deut. Weinbau 20, 1231–1232.
ALLEWELDT, G. 1965B. Der Rebenanbau in der Türkei. Wein-Wissen. 20, 109–126.
AMBROSI, H. 1959. Die Weine Südafrikas. Deut. Wein-Ztg. 95, 482, 484, 498, 500, 502.
AMERINE, M. A. 1959A. Chemists and the California wine industry. Am. J. Enol. Vitic. 10, 124–129.
AMERINE, M. A. 1959B. Continuous flow production of still and sparkling wine. Wines and Vines 40, No. 6, 41–42.
AMERINE, M. A. 1959C. The romance of Pan-American wines. Pan American Medical Assoc., San Francisco Chapter, Annual Bulletin 1958, 21–27.
AMERINE, M. A. 1960. Hilgard and California viticulture. Hilgardia 33, 1–23.
AMERINE, M. A. 1963. Viticulture and enology in the Soviet Union. Wines and Vines 44, No. 10, 29–34, 36; No. 11, 57–62, 64; No. 12, 25–26, 28–30.
AMERINE, M. A. 1964. Der Weinbau in Japan. Wein-Wissen. 19, 225–231.
AMERINE, M. A. 1965. Research on viticulture and enology in the Soviet Union. Food Technol. 19, 179–182.
AMERINE, M. A., and DEMATTEI, W. 1940. Color in California wines. III. Methods of removing color from the skins. Food Research 5, 509–519.
AMERINE, M. A., and JOSLYN, M. A. 1970. Table Wines; the Technology of Their Production. 2 ed. University of California Press, Berkeley and Los Angeles.
AMERINE, M. A., and MONAGHAN, M. W. 1950. California sparkling wines. Wines and Vines 31, No. 8, 25–27; No. 9, 52–54.
AMERINE, M. A., and SINGLETON, V. L. 1965. Wine: An Introduction for Americans. University of California Press, Berkeley and Los Angeles.
AMERINE, M. A., and WINKLER, A. J. 1938. Angelica. Wines and Vines 19, No. 9, 5.
ANON. 1957. Wines of Italy. Istituto Nazionale per il Commercio Estero, Rome.
ANON. 1958A. The development of viticulture and wine making in Soviet Russia. Am. J. Enol. 9, 86–91.
ANON. 1958B. Grape and wine industry of Mexico. Am. J. Enol. 9, 92–93.
ANON. 1958C. Vignobles et vins hongrois. La Journée Vinicole 32 (9338), 1, 4. (Translation by M. A. A. in Am. J. Enol. and Vitic. 10, 142–146, 1959).
ANON. 1959. Wine grape varieties for new plantings. J. Agr. South Australia 62, 428–435.
ANON. 1961. Wine-producing in Yugoslavia. Federal Chamber of Foreign Trade, Belgrade.
ANON. 1969. A Survey of Wine Growing in South Africa 1968–1969. Public Relations Department of the KWV, Paarl.

68   THE TECHNOLOGY OF WINE MAKING

ARTHOLD, M. 1950. Handbuch der Kellerwirtschaft. 5 ed. Scholle-Verlag, Wien.

AZARASHVILI, P. B. 1959. Vinogradnye Vina i Kon'iaki Gruzii (Vineyards, Wines and Brandies of Georgia). Pishchepromizdat, Moscow.

BAKER, G. A., AMERINE, M. A., and ROESSLER, E. B. 1952. Theory and application of fractional blending systems. Hilgardia 21, 383–409.

BENSON, C. T. 1959. The Canadian wine industry. Wines and Vines 40, No. 9, 23.

BENVEGNIN, L., CAPT, E., and PIGUET, G. 1951. Traité de Vinification. 2 ed. Librairie Payot, Lausanne.

BERIDZE, G. I. 1965. Vino i Kon'iaki Gruzii; les Vins et les Cognacs de la Georgie. Izdatel'stvo "Sabchota Sakartvelo," Tbilisi.

BERNAZ, D. 1962. Tehnologia vinului. Editura Agro-Silvică, Bucharest.

BIRON, M. 1950. Vignes et Vins de Turquie, Thrace-Marmara. Istanbul.

BLAHA, J. 1952. Ceskoslovenská Ampelografia. "Orac," Bratislava.

BLAHA, J. 1961. Réva Vinná (Grape Growing). Nakladatelství Ceskoslovenské Akademie Věd, Prague.

BOBADILLA, G. F. DE. 1956. Viniferas Jerezanas y 'de Andalucia Occidental. Instituto Nacional de Investigaciones Agronómicas, Madrid.

BOBADILLA, G. F. DE, and NAVARRO, E. 1949. Vinos de Jerez. Estudios de sus Ácidos, desde el Período de Madurez de la Uva Hasta el Envejecimiento del Vino. Instituto Nacional de Investigaciones Agronómicas, Madrid. pp. 474–519.

BOBADILLA, G. F. DE, QUIROS, J. M., and SERRANO, J. J. 1954. Vinos de Jerez. El Enyesado de los Mostos. Instituto Nacional de Investigaciones Agronómicas, Madrid. pp. 411–446.

BOCKER, H. 1959. Untersuchungen über den Einfluss von Mineralstoffen auf den bakteriellen Säurerückgang in Trauben- und Fruchtweinen. Zentr. Bakteriol. Parasitenk. Abt. II 112, 337–350.

BODE, C. 1956. Wines of Italy. The McBride Company, Inc., New York.

BOWEN, J. F., FISHER, D. V., and MacGREGOR, D. R. 1965. Grape and wine production in British Columbia. Am. J. Enol. Vitic. 16, 241–244.

BREJOUX, P. 1956. Les Vins de Loire. Compagnie Parisienne d'Éditions Techniques et Commerciales, Paris.

BRÉMOND, E. 1957. Techniques Modernes de Vinification et de Conservation des Vins dans les Pays Chauds. Librairie de la Maison Rustique, Paris.

BRUNI, B. 1964. Vini Italiani Portanti Una Denominazione di Origine. Edizioni Calderini, Bologna.

BULIČ, S. 1949. Dalmatinska Ampelografija (Dalmatian Ampelography). Poljoprovredni Nakladni Zavod, Zagreb.

CANTARELLI, C. 1958. The increase of the fermentation speed in wine making. Rev. ferm. et indust. aliment. 13, 59–71.

CARPENTIERI, F. 1948. Enologia Teorico-Pratica. 14 ed. Editrice Fratelli Ottavi, Casale Monferrato. 2 vols.

CERLETTI, B. 1958. Aspetti della enologia Jugoslava. Atti accad. ital. vite e vino 10, 228–240.

CHAPPAZ, G. 1951. Le Vignoble et le Vin de Champagne. L. Larmat, Paris.

CHEDEVILLE, C. 1945. Manuel d'Oenologie. Bascone and Muscat, Tunis.

COCKS, C., and FÉRET, E. 1969. Bordeaux et Ses Vins, Classés par Ordre de Mérite. 12 ed. Féret et Fils, Bordeaux.

COCKBURN, E.. n.d. Port Wine and Oporto. Wine and Spirit Publications Ltd., London.

CONSTANTINESCU, G. 1958. Raionarea Viticulturi. Editura Accademiei Republicii Populare Romîne, Bucharest.

CONSTANTINESCU, G. 1959–1967. Ampelografia Republicii Populare Romine. 8 vol. Editura Academiei Republicii Populare Romîne, Bucharest.

CORNELSSEN, F. A. 1970. Die deutschen Weine. Seewald Verlag, Stuttgart.

COSMO, I., and DeROSA, T. 1960. Manuale di Enologia, Guida del Buon Cantiniere. Edizioni Agricole, Bologna.

CROFT-COOKE, R. 1956. Sherry. Alfred A. Knopf, New York.

CROFT-COOKE, R. 1957. Port. Putnam, London.

CROFT-COOKE, R. 1961. Madeira. Putnam, London.

CRUESS, W. V. 1948. Investigations of the flor sherry process. Calif. Agr. Expt. Sta. Bull. 710.

CSEPREGI, P. 1955. Szölöfajtáink; Ampelográfia (Grape Growing, Ampelography). Mezögazdasági Kiadó, Budapest.

DALMASSO, G. 1956. La viticoltura in Europa e nel Sud-America. Riv. inter. agr. 1, No. 5, 38–47.

DALMASSO, G. 1958. Viticoltura ed enologia nella Bulgaria d'oggi. Atti accad. ital. vite e vino 10, 70–124.

DALMASSO, G., and TYNDALO, V. 1957. Viticoltura e ampelografia dell' U.R.-S.S. Atti accad. ital. vite e vino 9, 446–548.

DAVITAYA, F. F. 1948. Klimaticheskie Zony Vinograda SSSR (Grape Climatic Zones in Russia). Pishchepromizdat, Moscow.

DE BOSDARI, C. 1955. Wines of the Cape. A. A. Balkema, Cape Town, Amsterdam.

DETTORI, R.. G. 1953. Italian Wines and Liqueurs. Federazione Italiana Produttori ed Esportatori di Vini, Liquori ed Affini, Rome.

DION, R. 1959. Histoire de la Vigne et du Vin en France des Origines au XIXᵉ Siècle. Paris.

DSHANPOLADYAN, L. 1958. Die Weinbrände Armeniens. Die Branntweinwirt. 80, 177–179.

DURMISHIDZE, S. V. 1955. Dubil'nie Veshchestva i Antots'yani Vinogradvoĭ Lozi i Vina. (Tannins and Anthocyanins of Grapes and Wine.) Izdatel'stvo Akademii Nauk SSSR, Moscow.

EGOROV, A. A. 1955. Voprosy Vinodeliya (Enological Principles). Pishchepromizdat, Moscow.

FABRE, J.-H. 1946–1947. Traité Encyclopédique des Vins. Chez l'Auteur, Alger. Tome I. Procedes Modernes de Vinification. 5 ed. 1946. tome II. Analyse des Vins et Interpretation des Resultats Analytiques. 3 ed. 1947. tome III. Maladies des Vins; Vinifications Speciales. 4 ed. 1947.

FERRARESE, M. 1951. Enologia Pratica Moderna. 3 ed. Editore Ulrico Hoepli, Milan.

FERRÉ, L. 1958. Traité d'Oenologie Bourguignonne. Institut National des Appellations d'Origine des Vins et Eaux-de-Vie, Paris.

FLANZY, M. 1935. Nouvelle méthode de vinification. Rev. viticult. 83, 315–319, 325–329, 341–347.

FREDERICKSEN, P. 1947. The authentic Haraszthy story. Wines and Vines 28, No. 6, 25–26, 42; No. 7, 15–16, 30; No. 8, 17–18, 37–38; No. 9, 17–18, 34; No. 11, 21–22, 41–42.

70 THE TECHNOLOGY OF WINE MAKING

FROLOV-BAGREEV, A. M. 1946–65. Ampelografiya S.S.S.R. (Russian Ampelography). Gos. Pishchepromizdat, Moscow. 8 vols.

FROLOV-BAGREEV, A. M., and AGABAL'YANTS, G. G. 1951. Khimya Vina (Chemistry of Wine). Pishchepromizdat, Moscow.

FÜGER, A. 1957. Österreichische Spätleseweine. Mitt Rebe u. Wein. Serie A (Klosterneuburg) 7, 67–70.

GADILLE, R. 1967. Le vignoble de la Côte Bourguignonne. Paris.

GAHANO, A. B. 1951. A Região dos Vinhos Verdes. Comissão de Viticultura da Região dos Vinhos Verdes, Porto. (Also published in French as Le Vin "Verde.")

GALET, P. 1957–1964. Cépages et Vignobles de France. I. Les Vignes Américaines. II. Les Cépages de Cuve. III. Les Cépages de Table. IV. Le Raisins de Table. La Production Viticole Française. Paul Déhan, Montpellier.

GALTIER, G. 1961. Le Vignoble du Languedoc Mediterraneen et du Roussillon. Editions Causse, Graille & Castelnau, Montpellier.

GALLO, E. 1958. Outlook for a mature industry. Wines and Vines 39, No. 6, 27–28, 30

GARINO-CANINA, E. 1950. La Pratica Enologica del "Governo" nel Quadro delle Transformazion Chimico-Biologiche della Rifermentazione. Scuola Tipografica San Giuseppe, Asti. (From Atti VIII Congresso Internazionale Industria Agraria, Bruxelles. 1950).

GAROGLIO, P. G. 1965. La Nuova Enologia. Libreria LI. CO/SA, Florence.

GEISS, W. 1960. Lehrbuch für Weinbereitung und Kellerwirtschaft. Bad Kreuznach.

GEORGIEV, IV. 1949. Vinarstvo. (Wine Making). Zemizdat, Sofia.

GERASIMOV, M. A. 1957. Viticulture and enology in Russia (translation by M. A.A.). Wines and Vines 38, No. 3, 26–27. (From Vignes & Vins No. 48, 14–16; No. 49, 12. 1956.)

GERASIMOV, M. A. 1964. Tekhnologiya Vinodeliya (Technology of wine making). Pishchepromizdat, Moscow.

GIANFORMAGGIO, F. 1955. Manuale Pratico di Enologia Moderna. 3 ed. U. Hoepli, Milan.

GOLD, A. H. 1968. Wines of the World. Virtue, London.

GOLDSCHMIDT, E. 1951. Deutschlands Weinbauorte and Weinbergslagen. 6 ed. Verlag der Deutschen Wein-Zeitung, Mainz.

GONZÁLEZ GORDON, M. M. 1948 (i.e. 1949). Jerez, Xerez, Scheris. Jerez Industrial, Jerez de la Frontera.

GOT, A. 1949. Monbazillac. Éditions d'Aquitaine, Bordeaux.

HALÁSZ, Z. 1962. Hungarian Wine Through the Ages. Corvina, Budapest.

HALLGARTEN, S. F. 1965. Rhineland; Wineland. Withy Grove Press, Manchester.

HALLGARTEN, S. F. 1970. Alsace and its Wine Gardens. 2 ed. Wine and Spirit Publications, Ltd., London.

HEALY, M. 1963. Stay Me with Flagons. Michael Joseph Ltd., London.

HELIODORO VALLE, R. 1958. The history of wine in Mexico. Am. J. Enol. 9, 146–154.

HOCHBERG, M. 1954–1955. Gidul Ha-Gefen (Grape Growing). Tel-Aviv. 2 vols.

HULAČ, V. 1949. Príručka Sklepniho Hospodárství (Manual of Cellar Management). Nákladem Ústredního Svazu Československých Vinařú, Brno.

HYAMS, E. S. 1965. Dionysus; a Social History of the Wine Vine. Macmillan, New York.

INSTITUTO DE VINHO DO PÔRTO. 1940–1958. Anais de Instituto do Porto. Porto. 17 vols.

INSTITUT NATIONAL DES APPELLATIONS D'ORIGINE DES VINS ET EAUX-DE-VIE 1952. L'Oeuvre de l'Institut National des Appellations d'Origine des Vins et Eaux-de-Vie. Paris.

ISNARD, H. 1951–1954. La Vigne en Algérie. Ophrys, Gap. 2 vols.

JACQUELIN, L., and POULAIN, R. 1962. The Wines & Vineyards of France. G. P. Putnam's Sons, New York.

JAMES, W. 1966. Wine in Australia. 4 ed. Georgian House, Melbourne.

JEFFS, J. 1970. Sherry. 2 ed. Faber and Faber, London.

JEFFS, J. 1971. The Wines of Europe. Faber and Faber Ltd., London.

JOHNSON, H. 1968. Wine. Sphere, London.

JOPPIEN, P. H. 1960. Zur Kenntnis der Weine Morokkos. Deut. Wein-Ztg. 96, 518, 520, 522, 524.

JOSLYN, M. A. and AMERINE, M. A. 1964. Dessert, Appetizer and Related Flavored Wines; The Technology of Their Production. University of California, Division of Agricultural Sciences, Berkeley.

JUNTA NACIONAL DO VINHO. 1942. Contribuição para o Cadastro dos Vinhos Portugueses de Área de Influència da J. N. V. Tipografia Ramos, Lisbon. 2 vols.

JUNTA NACIONAL DO VINHO. 1949–1961. Anais da Junta Nacional do Vinho. Tip. Alcobacense, Lim., Lisbon. 13 vols.

KALUGINA, G. I., SAMARSKIĬ, A. T., and RUDNEV, N. M. 1957. Vinodelie i Vina Moldavii (Wines and Vines of Moldavia). Pishchepromizdat, Moscow.

KELLER, D. J. 1953. Pfalzwein Almanach. Neustadter Druckerei, Neustadt a.d. Weinstrasse.

KIELHÖFER, E. 1955. Die Restsüsse beim Moselwein. Deut. Weinbau 10, 240–241.

KITTEL, J. B., and BREIDER, H. 1958. Das Buch vom Frankenweine. Universitätsdruckerei H. Stürz AG, Würzburg.

KOBEL, F. 1947. Der Obst- und Weinbau in Ungarn. Schweiz. Z. Obst- u. Weinbau 56, 413–417, 429–436, 445–449.

KONDAREW, M. 1965. Die Entwicklung des Weinbaues in Bulgarien. Wein-Wissen. 20, 428–432.

KRAEMER, A. 1956. Im Lande des Bocksbeutels. Druck und Verlag Pius Halbig, Würzburg.

KRESSMANN, E. 1968. The Wonder of Wine. Hastings House, New York.

KUCHEL, R. H. 1959. Vine and wine industry of Cyprus. Australian Wine, Brew. and Spirit Rev. 78, 72, 74, 78.

LABORDE, J. 1907. Cours d'Oenologie. Tome I. L. Mulo, Paris; Féret and Fils, Bordeaux.

LAFFER, H. E. 1949. The Wine Industry of Australia. Australian Wine Board, Adelaide.

LAFFORGUE, G. 1947. Le Vignoble Girondin. Louis Larmat, Paris.

LAHO, L. 1962. Vinohradnictvo (Wine Making) Slovenské Vydavateľstvo Pôdohospodárskej Literatúry, Bratislava.

LANGENBACH, A. 1951. The Wines of Germany. Harper and Co., London.
LANGENBACH, A. 1962. German Wines and Vines. Vista Books, London.
LARREA, R. A. 1957. Arte y Ciencia de los Vinos Espanoles. Siler, Madrid.
LARREA, A. 1965. Tratado Practico de Viticultura y Enologia; Manual para Capataces Bodegueros. Editorial Aedos, Barcelona.
LAYTON, T. A. 1961. Wines of Italy. Harper Trade Journals Ltd., London.
LAYTON, T. A. 1970. Wines and People of Alsace. Cassell, London.
LEIPOLDT, C. L. 1952. Three Hundred Years of Cape Wine. Stewart, Cape Town.
LÉON, V. F. 1947. Uvas y Vinos de Chile. Sindicato Nacional Vitivinícola, Santiago de Chile.
LEONHARDT, G. 1963. Das Weinbuch; Werden des Weines von der Rebe bis zum Glase. VEB Fachbuchverlag, Leipzig.
LEVY, J. F. 1958. Vignes et vins d'URSS. Vignes et Vins No. 65, 24–26; No. 66, 17–19; No. 67, 27–28; No. 68, 15–16, (Translation by M.A.A. in Wines and Vines, 40, No. 11, 45–46, 48; No. 12, 27–28, 1959.)
LICHINE, A. 1969. Wines of France. 7 ed. Knopf, New York.
MAESTRO PALO, F. 1952. Defectos y Enfermendades de los Vinos. Tip. "La Académica," Zarogoza.
MAGISTOCCHI, G. 1955. Tratado de Enología Adaptado a la República Argentina. Ed. El Ateneo, Buenos Aires.
MALTABAR, V. M., NUTOV, L. O., and FERTMAN, G. I. 1959. Tekhnologiia Kon'yaka (Technology of brandy production). Pishchepromizdat, Moscow.
MANCEAU, E. 1929. Vinification Champenoise. Chez l'Auteur, Épernay.
MARCILLA ARRAZOLA, J. 1946. Tratado Práctico de Viticultura y Enología Españoles. 2 ed. SAETA, Madrid. 2 vols.
MARCILLA ARRAZOLA, J., ALAS, G., and FEDUCHY, E. 1936 (i.e., 1939). Contribución al estudio de los levaduras que forman velo sobre ciertos vinos de elevado grado alcohólico. Anales Centro Invest. Vinícolas 1, 1–230.
MARECA CORTÉS, I. 1957. Orientaciones Enológicas para el Bodeguero. Semana Gráfica, Valencia.
MARESCALCHI, C. 1957. Manuale dell'Enologo. 12 ed. Casa Editrice Fratelli Marescalchi, Casale Monferrato.
MARRES, P. 1950. La Vigne et le Vin en France. Librairie Armand Colin, Paris.
MARRISON, L. W. 1971. Wines for Everyone. St. Martin's Press, New York.
MAVEROFF PIAGGIO, A. 1949. Enología. J. Best, Mendoza.
MAXWELL, K. 1966. Fairest Vineyards. Keartland, Johannesburg.
MAZZEI, A. M. 1959. Buoni vini da pasto. Italia agricola 96, 757–788.
MICHEL, A. 1953. Le problème de la qualité des grands vins de Bourgogne. Prog. agr. et vitic. 140, 84–91, 116–121.
MOGILYANSKII, N. K. 1954. Plodovoe i Yagodnoe Vinodelie (Fruit and Berry Wine Making). Pishchepromizdat, Moscow.
MONTANARI, V., and CECCARELLI, G. 1950. La Viticoltura e l'Enologia nelle Tre Venezie. Arti Grafiche Longo e Zoppelli, Treviso. Supplemento Aggiornnato Sino all'Anno 1950. 1952.
MOREAU-BERILLON, C. 1925. Au Pays du Champagne. Le Vignoble-le Vin. Librairie L. Michaud, Reims.

MOSER, L. 1959. Die österreichischen Weine, ihre Art und die Absatzmöglichkeiten. Weinberg u. Keller 6, 342–343.

NASSE, T., and ZIGORI, V. 1968. Disa të dhëna mbi·karakteristikat e verërave të prodhuara nga vinifikimi i varieteteve të rrushit të kiltivuar në vëndin tonë. Bul. Univ. Shtet. Tiranës, Seria Shkencat Natypore 2, 95–105.

NAVAS ROMANO, E. 1950. La Bodega Moderna. 2 ed. Editorial Gustavo Gili, S.A., Barcelona.

NEDELCHEV, N. 1959. The grapes and wines of Bulgaria. World Crops 11, 111–113.

NEUBELLER, J. 1965. Der Tokajerwein und seine Heimat. Mitt. Rebe u. Wein, Serie A (Klosterneuburg) 18, 304–306.

NILOV, V. I., and SKURIKHIN, I. M. 1960. Khimiya Vinodeliya i Kon'yachnogo Proizvodstva (Chemistry of Wine and Brandy Production). Pishchepromizdat, Moscow.

OREGLIA, F. 1964. Enologia Téorico- Practica. Rodeo del Medio, Mendoza.

ORIZET, L. 1959. Mon Beaujolais. Jean Guillermet, Editions du Cuvier, Villefranche-en-Beaujolais.

OSTASHINSKY, E. 1958. Wine industry. Israel Economic Forum 9, 27–30.

OUGH, C. S. 1965. Wine production and development of the research winery. Report to the government of Israel. FAO Rept. 2025, 1–73.

PACOTTET, P., and GUITTONNEAU, L. 1930. Vins de Champagne et Vins Mousseux. Librairie J.-B. Baillière et Fils, Paris.

PARONETTO, L., and DAL CIN, G. 1954. I Prodotti Chimici nella Tecnica Enologica. Scuola d'Arte Tipografia D. Bosco, Verona.

PATO, C. M., and AMERINE, M. A. 1959. Analysis of some typical Madeira wines. Am. J. Enol Vitic. 10, 110–113.

PENINOU, E., and GREENLEAF S. 1954. Wine making in California. III. The California Wine Association. The Porpoise Bookshop, San Francisco.

PENNING-ROWSELL, E. 1969. The International Wine and Food Society's Guide to the Wines of Bordeaux. London.

PESTEL, H. 1959. Les Vins et Eaux-de-Vie à Appellations d'Origine Contrôlées en France. Imprimerie Buguet-Comptour, Mâcon.

PEYER, E., and EGGENBERGER, W. 1965. Weinbuch. 5 ed. Verlag Schweizerischer Wirteverein, Zürich.

PEYNAUD, E. 1971. Connaissance et Travail du Vin. Dunod, Paris.

PEYRONNET, F. R. 1950. Le Vignoble Nord-Africain. J. Peyronnet, Paris.

POGRMILOVIC, B. 1969. Wines and Wine-growing Districts of Yugoslavia. "Zadruzna Stampa," Zagreb.

POULAIN, R., and JACQUELIN, L. 1960. Vignes et Vins de France. Flammarion, Paris.

POUPON, P., and FORGEOT, P. 1959. Les Vins de Bourgogne. 2 ed. Presses Universitaires de France, Paris.

PRISNEA, C. 1964. Bacchus in Rumania. Meridiane Publishing House, Bucharest.

PROSTOSERDOV, N. N. 1955. Osnovy Vinodeliya (Fundamentals of Enology). Pishchepromizdat, Moscow.

QUITTANSON, C. 1965. L'appellation d'origine, facteur permanent de recherche de la qualité. Rev. ferm. ind. aliment. 20, 49–61.

74 THE TECHNOLOGY OF WINE MAKING

RADENKOVIĆ, D. G. 1962. Vino, Savremeni Problemi Vinarstva u Svetu i Kod Nas. (Wine, Current Problems of the World and National Wine Industry). Belgrade.

RAINBIRD, G. M. 1966. Sherry and the Wines of Spain. McGraw-Hill, New York.

RAKCSÁNYI, L. 1963. Borászat (Wine Making). Verlag Mezögazdasági Kiadó, Budapest.

RANKOVIĆ, B. Ć. 1955. Vinarstvo (Viticulture). Zadruzhna Kniga, Belgrade.

RAPPAPORT, S. 1959. Wine production in Israel and its future prospects. Israel Economic Forum 9, 79–82.

RAU, K. 1960. Was Trinkt Man in Italien? Albert Müller Verlag, Stuttgart.

RAU, K. 1961. Was Trinkt Man in Oesterreich? Albert Müller Verlag, Stuttgart.

RAY, C. 1966. The Wines of Italy. McGraw-Hill, New York.

RIBÉREAU-GAYON, J., and PEYNAUD, E. 1960–1961. Traité d'Oenologie. 2 vol. Librairie Polytechnique Ch. Béranger, Paris.

RODIER, C. 1948. Le Vin de Bourgogne. 3 cd. Louis Damidot, Dijon.

ROGER, J. R. 1956. Le Vins de Bordeaux. Compagnie Parisienne d'Éditions Techniques et Commerciales, Paris.

ROGER, J. R. 1960. The Wines of Bordeaux. Dutton, New York.

ROSA, T. de. 1964. Tecnica dei Vini Spumanti. Rivista di Viticoltura e di Enologia, Conegliano.

ROSSI, A. 1955. La Viticoltura in Sicilia. Mori, Palermo.

SCHELLENBERG, A. 1962. Weinbau. Verlag Huber & Co., Frauenfeld.

SCHELLENBERG, A., and PEYER, E. 1951. Weinbuch für die Schweizer Wirte 3 ed. Schweizerischer Wirteverein, Zürich.

SCHMIDT, H. C. 1965. Der Weinbau in Österreich. Wein- Wissen. 20, 525–536.

SCHMUTZ, C. 1936. Le Vin. Librairie Delagrave, Paris.

SCHOONMAKER, F. 1956. The Wines of Germany. Hastings House, New York.

SCHOONMAKER, F., and MARVEL, T. 1934. The Complete Wine Book. Simon and Schuster, New York.

SCHOONMAKER, F., and MARVEL, T. 1941. American Wines. Duell, Sloan and Pearce, New York.

SHAND, P. M. 1960. A Book of French Wines. 2 ed. Alfred A. Knopf, New York.

SIMON, A. L. 1934. Port. Constable and Co., London.

SIMON, A. L. 1957. The Noble Grapes and the Great Wines of France. McGraw-Hill Book Company, Inc., New York.

SIMON, A. L. 1962. Champagne; with a Chapter on American Champagne by Robert J. Misch. McGraw-Hill Book Co., Inc., New York.

SIMON, A. L. 1966. The Wines, Vineyards and Vignerons of Australia. Lansdowne House, Melbourne.

SIMON, A. L., and HALLGARTEN, S. F. 1963. The Great Wines of Germany and Its Famed Vineyards. McGraw-Hill Book Co., New York.

SITTLER, L. 1956. La Viticulture et le Vin de Colmar à Travers les Siècles. Éditions Alsatia, Paris.

SOARES FRANCO, A. P. 1938. O Moscatel de Setúbal. Editorial Império, Lisboa.

Soós, I. A. B. 1955. Borászati Kémia (Enological Chemistry). Mezögazd. Kiadó, Budapest.

TARANTOLA, C. 1954. Enologia. Unione Tipografico- Editrice Torinese, Torino.

TARANTOLA, C., CAMPISI, C., BOTTINI, E., and EMANUELE, F. 1954. Industrie Agrarie. Unione Tipografico-Editrice Torinese, Torino.

TELEKI, S. 1937. Weinbau und Weinwirtschaft in Ungarn. Payer and Co., Berlin.

THERON, C. J., and NIEHAUS, C. J. G. 1948. Wine making. 3 ed. Union South Africa Dept. Agr. Bull. 191.

THUDICHUM, J. L. W., and DUPRÉ, A. 1872. A Treatise on the Origin, Nature and Varieties of Wine. Macmillan and Co., London.

TROOST, G. 1961. Die Technologie des Weines. 3 ed. Eugen Ulmer, Stuttgart.

TURCOVIĆ, Z. 1950A. Gospodarska Vrijednost Sorata Vinove Loze (Economic Value of Wine Grape Varieties). Poljoprivredni Nakladni Zavod, Zagreb.

TURCOVIĆ, Z. 1950B. Savremeni Uzgoj Vinove Loze (Modern Wine Grape Culture). Poljoprivredni Nakladni Zavod, Zagreb.

TURCOVIĆ, Z., and TURCOVIĆ, G. 1952–1962. Ampelografski Atlas (Ampelographical Atlas). Poljoprivredni Nakladni Zavod, Zagreb. 2 vols.

VALENTE-PERFEITO, J. C. 1948. Let's Talk About Port. Instituto do Vinho do Porto, Porto.

VEGA, L. A. de. 1958. Guía Vinícola de España. Editora Nacional, Madrid.

VERONA, O., and FLORENZANO, G. 1956. Microbiologia Applicata all'Industria Enologica. Edizione Agricole, Bologna.

VERONELLI, L. 1964. The Wines of Italy. McGraw-Hill Book Co., New York.

VOGT, E. 1963. Der Wein, seine Bereitung, Behandlung und Untersuchung. 4 ed. Verlag Eugen Ulmer, Stuttgart.

VOGT, E. 1968. Weinbau and Weinbereitung. In Diemair, W. ed. Alkoholische Genussmittel. Berlin, Springer Verlag (See pp. 172–310.)

WEBB, A. D. 1959. The Australian wine industry. Wines and Vines 40, No. 7, 29–30.

WILHEM, C. F. 1956. In- und Auslandsweine; ABC der Internationalen Weinkarte. C. Knoppke, Grüner Verlag, Berlin.

WINKLER, A. J. 1936. Temperature and varietal interrelations in Central-Western Europe and Algeria. Wine and Vines 17, No. 2, 4–5.

WINKLER, A. J. 1962. General Viticulture. University of California Press, Berkeley and Los Angeles.

YOKOTSUKA, I. 1955. The grape growing and wine industry of Japan. Am. J. Enol. 6, 16–22.

YOUNGER, W. 1966. Gods, Men and Wine. World Publishing Co., Cleveland.

YOXALL, H. W. 1970. The International Wine and Food Society's Guide to the Wines of Burgundy. Stein and Day, New York.

CHAPTER 2

The Composition of Grapes

The character and quality of a wine is determined by (1) the composition of the raw materials from which it is made, (2) the nature of the fermentation process, and (3) the changes which occur naturally, or are made to occur, during the post-fermentation period. This chapter considers the composition of grapes and the factors influencing it.

HOW GRAPES RIPEN

Amerine (1956) distinguishes physical and chemical changes which occur during ripening. Obviously, however, there is an intimate interrelationship between the two if changes in volume occur, as they do.

Physical Changes

The grape berry in its early weeks is a tiny, green-colored, very acid pellet. Cell division and a very slow berry enlargement continue for some time. Cell division ceases about the time noticeable changes in berry size, color, and texture occur.

The rate of increase in volume of the berry may show a slight decrease during the period of seed development, Fig. 31. Following this a very rapid increase in berry size occurs so that in a few weeks the tiny berry becomes a plump, sweet, colored fruit. The period of most rapid increase in volume does not exactly coincide with the start of ripening. Fig. 31 indicates that the increase in soluble solids precedes this period by about two weeks.

The fruit does not continue to increase in size indefinitely. When the fruit has reached normal maturity there is a rather abrupt cessation of cell enlargement and under very warm conditions there may be a decrease in volume. Peynaud and Maurié (1956) suggest harvesting one week·after the fruit reaches its maximum weight. The decrease in weight occurs mainly by withdrawal of water from the fruit to the leaves—especially during periods of soil moisture deficiency. Poux (1950) also noted that increase in sugar content paralleled increase in berry weight. The ratio grams sugar per gram/total weight in grams was a constant for a given variety when the fresh weight was at its maximum.

Within the berry there are changes in the relative amounts of skins, seeds, and pulp during maturation. The changes on a per cent basis and on the basis of grams per 100 berries are shown in Fig. 32. On a per cent

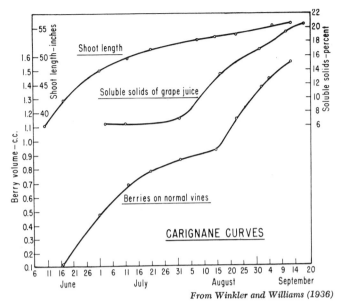

From Winkler and Williams (1936)

FIG. 31. BERRY SHOOT GROWTH AND RIPENING

basis the pulp increases from about 73 to 89 per cent of the weight while the per cent seeds and skins decrease from about 13 to 4 and 8, respectively. On a per berry basis the increase in the weight of pulp is more striking and a slight increase in skin weight occurs. It should be noted that separation of the pulp from the skin and seeds is difficult and subject to manipulative and evaporation errors.

Another physical change which is of practical importance is that in turgidity. Unripe berries are hard and difficult to crush. As the fruit ripens there is an increase in turgidity. During overripening the fruit shrivels and there is a loss in turgidity—making the fruit again difficult to crush.

Another physical change occurs when the grape is attacked by *Botrytis cinerea*. This weakens the attachment of the skin to the flesh and makes the fruit easier to crush, Nelson and Amerine (1957).

A summary of the physiology of *Botrytis cinerea* in its attack on grapes has been given by Charpentié (1954). Besides the increase in glycerol and sugar there is a net decrease in malic and tartaric acids, especially in tartaric. The effect on the acidity and its intensity depends on the climate following botrytis attack. Gluconic acid is a constant product of botrytis attack. Amounts of 0.50 to 2.50 gm. per liter were reported in wines made from botrytised Bordeaux grapes. Normal wines had only about 0.29 to 0.92 gm. per liter. Charpentié suggested a minimum gluconic acid as a measure of the authenticity of botrytised wines. Galacturonic and glucu-

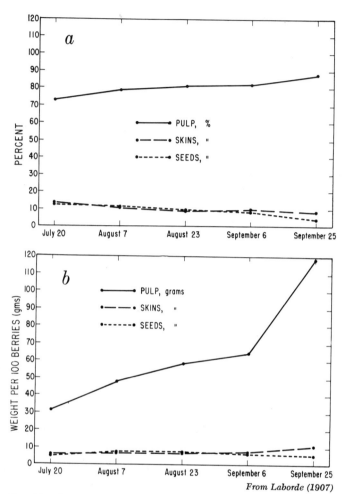

From Laborde (1907)

FIG. 32. CHANGES IN (a) PER CENT AND (b) IN WEIGHT PER 100
BERRIES OF PULP, SKINS AND SEEDS DURING RIPENING

ronic acids have both long been considered to be present in small amounts
in musts and in larger amounts in musts or wines of grapes attacked by
Botrytis cinerea. Rentschler and Tanner (1955) reported little glucuronic
acid in normal or botrytised musts but considerable galacturonic acid.
Dimotaki-Kourakou (1964) was unable to detect glucuronic. The constant presence of glucuronic and galacturonic acids in musts and wines
help to explain, according to Blouin and Peynaud (1963), the deficit of anions in the acid balance, the high dextro-rotatory condition of certain
wines and some of the unknown compounds that combine with sulfur

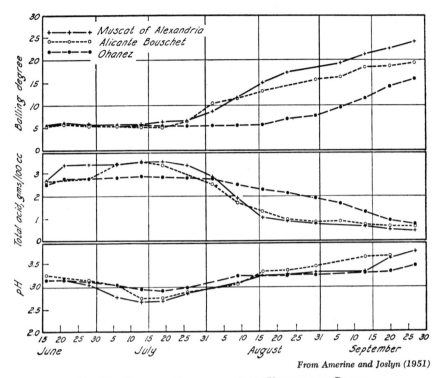

From Amerine and Joslyn (1951)

FIG. 33. RIPENING CHANGES IN THREE VARIETIES OF GRAPES

dioxide. For 100 mg. of free sulfur dioxide, 1 milliequivalent of glucuronic acid will combine with 2 to 3 mg. of sulfur dioxide and 1 milliequivalent of galacturonic acid will combine with 5 to 6 mg. of sulfur dioxide. It is difficult to control field conditions to secure the optimum botrytis growth. Attack by other molds or rains may cause some sugar loss. Even under the best conditions considerable net sugar is lost by respiration—up to 30 per cent. Dextrose is attacked more by the mold than levulose so the dextrose/levulose ratio decreases.

Chemical Changes

The grape consists of a seed (except for a few varieties), surrounding pulp and an enclosing skin. The relative proportion of each of these and their composition changes during maturation (p. 75). The present concept is that the grape ripens from the exterior to the interior, but there may be varietal differences in this. The pulp near the skin is thus, throughout the season, lower in acid and higher in sugar than that near the seed. Because of the increasing proportion of the fruit in the intermediate

TABLE 3

COMPOSITION OF MUST AND RESULTING WINE OF EIGHT SUCCESSIVE FRACTIONS[1]

(From the same grapes in a Champagne press)

Pressing No.	Amount Hl.	Alcohol, by Volume in Wine Per cent	Titratable Acidity, as Tartaric Gm./100 Ml.[2]	pH Must	pH Wine	Tartaric Acid Wine Gm./100 Ml.	Potassium Acid Tartrate Wine KHT Gm./100 Ml.	Calcium Wine Gm./Liter
1	2	11.8	0.79	2.98	3.01	0.470	0.358	0.094
2	2	11.75	0.85	2.94	2.98	0.542	0.363	0.094
3	6	11.8	0.96	2.87	2.85	0.584	0.373	0.094
4	6	11.7	0.93	2.94	2.94	0.565	0.387	0.094
5	4	11.8	0.82	2.96	2.94	0.462	0.368	
6	4	11.8	0.66	3.12	3.16	0.415	0.462	0.086
7	2.7	11.7	0.51	3.43	3.43	0.288	0.537	0.062
8	2	11.4	0.45	3.69	3.84	0.152	0.725	0.082

[1] Source of data: Francot (1950).   [2] In original must.

pulp zone, its composition dominates that of the total juice more and more as the season advances. This is of some importance in measuring ripening changes. In partially ripe or ripe fruit when the berries are turgid the free-run juice is mainly from the pulp near the skin and will be higher in sugar and lower in acid than the juice from the press. In overripe fruit where both turgid and nonturgid fruit are present the free-run may be lower in sugar and higher in acids than the press juice. This is due to the lesser proportion of juice from near the skin—and from the non-turgid riper fruit—in the press juice.

When whole grapes are pressed, as in the Champagne region of France, Françot (1950) found the first juice to be higher in sugar and lower in pH *and* in titratable acidity than that of later pressings. This is summarized in Table 3. Intermediate pressings were higher in acidity and lower in pH than the first juice, apparently because more tartrate-buffered material was present. Certainly few non-turgid berries are present so this represents the first case noted above. In California where shriveling is common the second case is more common.

The over-all changes in sugar, total acidity, and pH are shown for two varieties which ripen in mid-season and one which ripens very late (Ohanez) in Fig. 33. During the more rapid stages of ripening in the warmer parts of California the Balling may increase 0.1° to 0.4° per day and for each increase of a degree Balling the acidity may drop 0.05 to 0.15 per cent. When ripening starts there is a continuous increase in per cent sugar in the fruit. The two sugars present, levulose and dextrose, do not increase at the same rate, as shown in Table 4. Dextrose is the predominant sugar in unripe fruit while levulose is at least equal and often higher in ripe and overripe fruit, p. 96. Very little sucrose has been found in V. *vinifera* grapes; more is found in V. *labrusca* and other native species.

TABLE 4

CHANGES IN TOTAL SUGAR, DEXTROSE, LEVULOSE, AND THE LEVULOSE-DEXTROSE RATIO DURING MATURATION[1]

	Chasselas Doré				Furmint			
Date	Total Sugar	Dex-trose	Levu-lose	L/D	Total Sugar	Dex-trose	Levu-lose	L/D
	Per Cent	Per Cent	Per Cent		Per Cent	Per Cent	Per Cent	
August 22	11.3	6.1	5.2	0.85	...	...	...	...
August 27	12.9	7.3	5.6	0.77	2.7	1.8	0.9	0.50
September 11	18.1	9.0	9.1	1.01	14.4	7.2	7.2	1.00
September 24	15.2	7.5	7.7	1.03	15.2	7.4	7.8	1.05
October 9	19.2	9.2	10.0	1.09	19.5	9.3	10.2	1.10
October 29	22.7	10.4	12.3	1.18	22.3	9.9	12.4	1.25
November 22	20.0	8.8	11.2	1.27	20.3	8.9	11.4	1.28

[1] Source of data: Szabó and Rakcsányi (1937).

The titratable acidity decreases during ripening, whether expressed on a per berry or on a per cent basis. Since the acids are translocated into the fruit from the leaves the changes in acids occurring in the leaves during ripening are noteworthy. Amerine and Winkler (1958) and Peynaud and Maurié (1953B) both report a continuous increase in malates in the leaves. The tartrate content of the leaves, generally decreases slightly during maturation. As Vitte and Guichard (1955) noted there are significant differences between varieties. The changes in malates and tartrates in the fruit have been extensively studied by Peynaud (1947), Peynaud and Maurié (1956) and Amerine (1956). The method of expressing the results is particularly important. For earlier studies see Gerber (1897), Girard and Lindet (1898), Laborde (1907), Moreau and Vinet (1932), Genevois (1938), Gatet and Genevois (1940), Ferré (1947), Tsuchiya (1951), Ournac (1952), and Ribéreau-Gayon (1955).

On a per cent basis malates and tartrates both decrease during ripening, but there are differences between varieties, On a per berry basis the tartrate content generally remains relatively constant while the malate decreases, though less markedly than on a per cent basis.

There are several possible explanations of these changes. The most rational is that malates are respired during the later stages of ripening. Under very warm conditions tartrates also may be respired. The de-

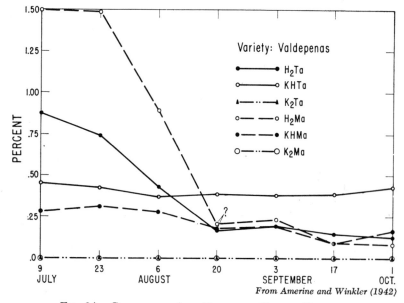

From Amerine and Winkler (1942)

FIG. 34. CHANGES IN ACID FRACTIONS DURING RIPENING

creases on a per cent basis obviously partially reflect the continuous increase in volume of the fruit, i.e., they are simply diluted.

It is also important to consider the changes in relative amounts of free acids, acid salts, and salts during ripening. These are directly related to the changes in pH. During ripening the pH increases continuously from about 2.8 to 3.1 or higher, depending on variety (p. 99) and season (p. 118). This means that the per cent free acid decreases. The pK_1 of tartaric acid is 2.98 and of malic acid 3.41. This means that at a pH of 2.98 50 per cent of the tartrate is present as the free acid and at a pH of 3.41 50 per cent of the malate is present as the free acid. These changes are summarized for the Valdepeñas variety in Fig. 34 (the per cent potassium tartrate and potassium malate are essentially zero).

This change in pH is due to the translocation of potassium and other cations into the fruit. The alkalinity of the ash is a measure of cation content and this steadily increases during maturation. Table 5 also shows that the potassium and sodium contents increase. Calcium remains relatively constant on a per cent basis. On a per berry basis all increase in an even more striking fashion.

There is considerable interest in the changes in nitrogen during ripening because of their importance to the growth of yeasts and bacteria. The changes in the juice of one variety, on a per cent basis, are shown in Fig. 35. A slight decrease in total nitrogen, a more marked decrease in ammonia, no change in amine nitrogen, and an increase in polypeptide and protein nitrogen may be noted. On a per berry basis the decreases are less marked and the increases greater. Differences between varieties have been noted by Peynaud and Maurié (1953A). During grape maturation there is a significant increase in proline, serine, and threonine and a decrease in arginine, ammonia and amine nitrogen in musts of Cabernet Sauvignon and Merlot grapes, according to Lafon-Lafourcade and Guimberteau (1962). In general, as grapes ripen there is an increase in the forms of nitrogen which are less easily utilized by yeasts. This may explain why musts of overripe grapes sometimes ferment slowly.

TABLE 5

ALKALINITY OF THE ASH, CALCIUM, POTASSIUM, AND SODIUM CHANGES DURING MATURATION OF SÉMILLON[1]

Date	Balling	Alkalinity of the Ash	Calcium	Potassium	Sodium
		Ml. 0.01 N	Mg./Liter	Mg./Liter	Mg./Liter
August 26	18.1	23.4	26	825	34
September 1	18.7	29.7	18	1395	93
September 21	21.9	. . .	20	1400	158
October 12	24.3	38.9	20	1240	120

[1] Source of data: Amerine (1956).

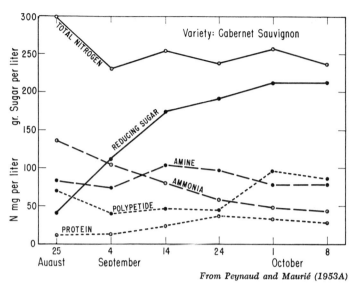

From Peynaud and Maurié (1953A)

FIG. 35. CHANGES IN NITROGEN FRACTIONS DURING RIPENING

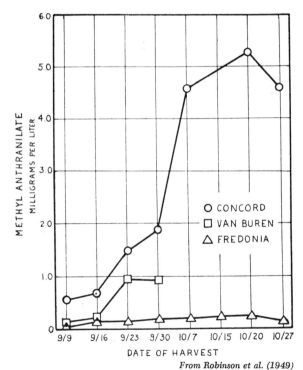

From Robinson et al. (1949)

FIG. 36. METHYL ANTHRANILATE DEVELOPMENT DURING RIPENING

The ease of separation of the juice from the solid matter is apparently a function of the pectin content. Present evidence is that the total pectic substances increase during maturation.

It is qualitatively known that the amount of odorous materials increase during ripening. Thus, an unripe muscat berry has little of the muscat aroma. Our lack of knowledge of the nature of the odorous substances of *Vitis vinifera* grapes has prevented obtaining quantitative data. For *V. labrusca* varieties, however, where methyl anthranilate is the most important odorous constituent, a marked increase during ripening has been noted for Concord (Fig. 36).

Ethyl alcohol constitutes the most important part of the volatile material. Procedures for distillation of the volatile materials into chromic acid can, therefore, give us little information. The results of Deibner *et al.* (1965) show that there is an increase in oxidizable volatile materials (probably largely ethyl alcohol) until the sugar content reaches its maximum and thereafter a decrease.

The changes in color during maturation are qualitatively very obvious. The chlorophyll content gradually decreases in both white and red varieties though some chlorophyll appears to remain in all varieties. An increase in flavone pigments in white varieties and in anthocyan pigments in red may also be observed. P. Ribéreau-Gayon (1958B) followed the formation of delphinidin, petunidin, malvidin, and peonidin during ripening of Merlot grapes. The increase in malvidin during ripening appears to be greater than that of the other pigments but the differences were not large.

Durmishidze (1955) reported *l*-gallocatechin increased during ripening while *d*-catechin decreased. There is an over-all decrease of tannins of over 50 per cent in the fruit during ripening. For a detailed summary of the changes in polyphenolic compounds during ripening, see Singleton and Esau (1969).

Cantarelli and Peri (1964) showed that total phenolics and the leucoanthocyanins decreased during ripening of white grapes. There was considerable variation between varieties in the content of both. During fermentation, probably by enzymatic action, there is a decrease in phenolics. Settling, centrifugation and filtration of musts are recommended as methods for reducing their amount.

The redox-potential decreases during ripening from about 400 mV to 350 mV according to Diebner (1955). V. A. Berg (1953) reported a decrease from 560 to 331 mV. This may be related to the decrease in ascorbic acid (vitamin C) which occurs during ripening.

Peynaud and Lafourcade (1958) showed the following changes in B vitamins in Bordeaux grapes during ripening (thiamin and riboflavin in μ, others in mg.):

		Days after Start of Ripening					
		0	10	20	30	40	50
Thiamin	Per liter	237	284	277	371	419	354
	Per 1000 berries	152	212	214	306	357	253
Riboflavin	Per liter	7.0	8.0	9.3	7.5	7.0	6.6
	Per 1000 berries	3.8	5.2	7.5	5.6	4.5	3.6
Pantothenic	Per liter	0.72	0.84	0.84	0.92	0.92	0.95
acid	Per 1000 berries	0.34	0.46	0.58	0.63	0.61	0.66
Nicotinamide	Per liter	0.77	0.80	0.82	0.86	0.74	0.78
	Per 1000 berries	0.39	0.46	0.59	0.63	0.66	0.70
Pyridoxine	Per liter	0.24	0.33	0.38	0.39	0.32	0.37
	Per 1000 berries	0.14	0.23	0.29	0.30	0.26	0.26
Biotin	Per liter	5.0	4.0	2.3	2.8	2.7	3.2
	Per 1000 berries	3.1	3.0	1.8	2.3	2.2	2.2
Mesoinositol	Per liter	286	311	351	380	398	388
	Per 1000 berries	118	184	212	247	238	297

Decreases in thiamin and riboflavin may be noted. Mesoinositol, nicotinamide and pantothenic acid appear to increase. Others increase on a per berry basis, owing no doubt to the decrease in size of the fruit after full maturity (p. 76). Biotin appears to decrease during the ripening period.

MEASUREMENT OF MATURITY

Berries from the same cluster do not all have the same composition: those from the extremities (from the ends of the cluster or its subdivisions) are frequently greener in color, higher in acid and lower in sugar than are the berries from the main body of the cluster. Clusters from different parts of the vine are of varying composition. Some varieties have an appreciable second crop (Zinfandel, for example) which ripens later than the first crop. Grapes on vines in different parts of the same vineyard are sometimes of markedly different composition owing to differences in soil moisture, soil fertility or exposure. These variations are especially noticeable under cool climatic conditions (see p. 119). Maturity is also affected by vineyard practices. Poor control of leaf hoppers or red spider, resulting in loss of chlorophyll or foliage, will delay maturity. Grapes on vines of a single variety but of different ages will also mature at different times. Furthermore maturation is not an even and regular process. Cold rainy weather may reduce the rate of ripening while very hot dry weather will increase it. For these and other reasons measurement of field maturity is not easy as has been noted by Amerine (1956), Amerine and Roessler (1958A, 1958B), Benvegnin and Capt (1955), Berg and Marsh (1954), and Roessler and Amerine (1958).

Importance

The determination of the field maturity of grapes is important because only when the grapes are harvested at their optimum maturity can wines of the maximum quality be produced. This is the basis for the banns of Europe. The vintage could not begin until the village elders, nobleman, or abbot so decreed and this decision was based on some primitive method of field determination of maturity. The objective was always the same—to harvest at optimum maturity in order to achieve maximum quality. Where the field determination of maturity is neglected the wines are always of lesser and more variable quality. Some Italian wines, for example, suffer from being made from overripe grapes. Closer control of harvesting would also be advantageous in other regions including California.

Proper timing of the harvest is particularly important when governmental control of fruit sanitation is introduced, as is currently being done in California. It is then often of critical importance to pick the fruit at the earliest moment so as to get the crop harvested before the rainy season begins.

A further reason for determining field maturity is that the varieties do not ripen at the same time each year nor at the same time relative to each other. The sugar content (one measure of maturity) at the beginning of the ripening period is not always directly related to that at the time of harvest. Unverzagt (1954) measured the degree Oechsle (essentially the specific gravity) of three German varieties on September 1, October 1, and at harvest for the period 1943 to 1953. The results with Sylvaner were as listed on the following table.

Thus in 1951 the grapes were greenest on September 1. The largest increase in sugar between September 1 and harvest was in 1944 and the least in 1950, when there was no increase in sugar content after October 1. The largest increase between September 1 and October 1 was in 1947 and 1951 and the least in 1950. The highest sugar was attained in 1945 and 1947.

Year	September 1	October 1	Harvest	Date of Harvest
1943	52	85	88	Oct. 4
1944	32	67	80	Oct. 28
1945	60	86	94	Oct. 13
1946	44	72	82	Oct. 28
1947	66	95	110	Oct. 22
1948	45	75	81	Oct. 19
1949	48	81	87	Oct. 19
1950	53	72	72	Oct. 7
1951	29	58	73	Nov. 9
1952	57	81	82	Oct. 22
1953	61	85	90	Oct. 25

With White Riesling, Sylvaner, and Müller-Thurgau the results were generally similar. These data emphasize the fact that the date of harvest varies from year to year.

How to Sample

In view of the variability of the fruit some sort of statistically satisfactory system of field sampling is required.   The studies of Amerine and Roessler (1958A, 1958B) and Roessler and Amerine (1958) are applicable to this problem.   They compared three methods of sampling: lots of 100 berries, 10 clusters, or single vines.   The berries were randomly selected— from both sides of the vine in the row and from both sides of the row and from the bottom, middle and top of the clusters one berry from each of 100 vines.   For the ten clusters the same block of 100 vines was used and a single cluster taken from every tenth vine.   Again clusters from the middle and sides of the vine and from both sides of the row were picked.   In their studies 10-berry, 10-cluster, and 10-vine samples were taken simultaneously from the same field.

They concluded that berry sampling was the simplest and most effective method of collecting maturity information.   It is the least wasteful of fruit but is slower than cluster sampling.   The advantages of berry sampling are summarized in Table 6.

TABLE 6

APPROXIMATE EQUIVALENT NUMBERS OF LOTS FOR EQUAL RELIABILITY[1]

Standard Error of Means	No. of Lots of		
	100 Berries	10 Clusters	Vines
Balling and Abbé			
0.39	2	4	11
0.32	3	5	17
0.28	4	7	22
0.25	5	9	27
Total acid			
0.028	2	4	8
0.023	3	6	10
0.020	4	8	14
0.018	5	10	18
pH			
0.028	2	2	8
0.023	3	3	10
0.020	4	4	14
0.018	5	5	18

[1] Source of data: Roessler and Amerine (1958).

This simply means that there is more variability in cluster and vine lots than there is in berry lots and hence for an equal standard error of the means more 10-cluster lots or vine lots than 100-berry lots must be harvested.   If one uses twice the standard error it will give the approximate deviation from the population mean that will be exceeded by the mean of a sample once in 20 times. Therefore, if one wishes to be within 1° Balling 95 per cent of the time two 100-berry, four 10-cluster, or eleven vine lots should be harvested. To reduce this to 0.5° Balling 5 berry, 9 cluster, or 27 vine lots would have to be harvested.

Therefore, in field sampling to be within 0.5° Balling one should harvest 5 lots of 100 (or 200 for small-berried varieties) berries from 500 vines or 9 lots of 10 clusters each from the same area. It would be impractical and wasteful to harvest 27 vine lots. These data indicate why direct field measurement with a hand refractometer is not likely to be popular or satisfactory. One would have to sample, record, and average 500 individual berry readings!

Field sampling should begin for each variety and each field about 3 or 4 weeks before the probable date of harvest. Samples should be taken weekly or, in event of very warm weather, twice weekly. This will give the grower a picture of the relative degree of ripeness of each variety and, depending on the acreage of each, the probable size of the picking crew which will be necessary. In a later paper Roessler and Amerine (1963) again reiterate their faith in the reliability of berry sampling. Similar results were obtained by Rankine et al. (1962). Baker et al. (1965) also showed that sequential measurements on grape juice of refractometer, pH and total acidity gave distributions which were non-normal. Vineyard heterogeneity was considered to be the cause and the variations were more subtle than could be handled by the usual statistical trial designs.

Preparation of Sample

A variety of methods are employed for crushing samples of fruit. The least desirable is the use of a piece of cheese cloth into which the grapes are placed and then macerated by pounding. Only the turgid fruit is thus crushed and the high sugar of the shriveled berries is not represented in the sample.

Small roller crushers, Fig. 37, do a fair job if the rollers are set close together and the fruit placed in the crusher in small portions (not as whole clusters). Waring Blendors (or similar equipment) are not satisfactory as they grind the seeds and also because it is hard to strain the mushy mixture.

Probably the best procedure is the use of screw-type (or meat grinder) crushers, Fig. 38. These crush all the fruit and if not operated too tightly do not grind up the stems and seeds. With this type of crusher raisined fruit is only slightly broken up and little of its sugar has time to dissolve in the juice. The problem is an important one with varieties which ripen unevenly, such as Zinfandel. The alternatives of fermenting the sample or of extracting with water are slow and do not give the immediate results

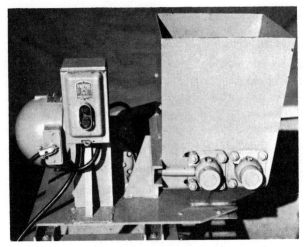

FIG. 37.   ROLLER CRUSHER FOR SMALL SAMPLES OF GRAPES

FIG. 38.   SCREW-TYPE CRUSHER FOR SMALL SAMPLES OF
GRAPES

which are desired by growers at the time of delivery of their fruit.   See
California Department of Agriculture (1955).

Whichever method of crushing is used the juice which is obtained will
contain more or less suspended material, particularly with certain varieties and late in the season.   The juice can be allowed to settle and the
clear supernatant liquid used but this may require several hours.   Cen-

trifuging an aliquot is the best procedure. This requires expensive equipment but if the most accurate results are desired it may be worth while. If a hand or Abbé refractometer is employed centrifuging is unnecessary according to Cooke (1964).

Methods of Measurement

The first, and often the only measure taken is that of the soluble solids using a Brix or Balling hydrometer. The clear juice is poured into a hydrometer cylinder so as to incorporate as little air as possible. A clean hydrometer, preferably one calibrated to 0.1° at 68°F. or 77°F., should be used. Very good hydrometers calibrated for the range 16° to 24° are available, Fig. 141. The hydrometer should float freely in the cylinder. The reading should be made with the eye at the level of the surface of the liquid. Unless the temperature of the sample is the same as the calibration temperature of the hydrometer a correction will have to be applied. Some hydrometers have self-contained thermometers and correction scales. These should always be checked for accuracy. In other cases a thermometer is used to determine the temperature of the contents of the hydrometer cylinder and Table 65 for making the correction in Balling.

To determine the soluble solids with an Abbé refractometer is somewhat less satisfactory because of the cost of the equipment and the need for close temperature control. The hand refractometer is cheaper and temperature-compensated models are available and quite satisfactory. See Goldberg (1965). Hand refractometers can be read to ±0.05°.

For determining the total acidity a 5 ml. sample is pipetted into a clean 200 ml. wide-mouthed Erlenmeyer and 50 ml. of boiling distilled water added. The titration should be made with 0.1 N sodium hydroxide to a phenolphthalein end point (p. 693) or better in a pH meter to a pH of 8.4. For wineries with many maturity samples per day automatic titrimeters will prove useful and economical.

Interpretation of Results

From the measurements made above one will have available a degree Balling, per cent titratable acidity (as tartaric acid), and the pH. The recommended ranges for these in musts for making the various types of wines are as follows:

Type of Wine	Balling	Titratable Acidity	pH
White table	19.5–23.0	>0.70	<3.3
Red table	20.5–23.5	>0.65	<3.4
Sweet table	22.0–25.0	>0.65	<3.4
Dessert	23.0–26.0	>0.50	<3.6

These recommendations have to be interpreted for special conditions. In a very warm, early-ripening season, especially if the crop is light, the acidity may be too low and harvesting should start at the lower end of the Balling range. The opposite will be true in cool, late ripening years. For sparkling wine stock the winery may want very tart wines of no more than eleven per cent alcohol. This per cent alcohol will be produced from grapes of approximately 20° Balling.

No one of these measures of maturity alone is adequate. Amerine and Winkler (1940) studied the use of the Balling/acid ratio as a basis for determining the best date of harvest. They harvested grapes periodically during the ripening period. From these data a curve was drawn of degree Balling versus titratable acidity. The acidity at degree Ballings of 20°, 22°, and 24° was read off the curve and the Balling/acid ratio at these Ballings for each variety calculated. If the standard is established that 0.65 is the minimum acceptable acidity for table wines then a maximum Balling/acid ratio of 31 at 20° Balling, 34 at 22°, and 37 at 24° results. Varieties with Balling/acid ratios of below these may be classified as true table wine varieties and those with ratios above as dessert wine varieties. A few varieties have a ratio below 31 at 20° but are above the limiting ratio at 22° or 24°. Such varieties require very careful harvesting if they are to be used for table wines. Amerine (1956) suggested maximum and minimum ratios be established for musts for dessert wines. Poulton (1970) recommended a ratio of 32 to 38 for table wines in South Africa. Ough and Alley (1970) found 30 to 32 best for Thompson Seedless.

Berg (1960) established minimum acid requirements in the various Balling ranges for each of four grades as a measure of grape quality. Since his tables are based on the analysis of nearly 47,000 loads of grapes delivered to wineries during the period 1950 to 1960 they may be used to measure the effect of seasonal variations and viticultural practices (such as overcropping) on the Balling/acid ratio.

Amerine (1956) notes that French experts have recommended Balling/acid ratios of 28 to 35 for varieties of the Burgundy district which compares favorably with the recommended ratios of 31, 34, and 37 mentioned above. Other measures of maturity may be used—maximum weight, etc.

Garino-Canina (1959) has proposed a vinous index for wine grapes. This would include the following ratios: (a) sugar/acid (or some modification of it), (b) tartaric acid/malic acid, (c) tannin/non-tannin polyphenol, and (d), amino acid/total nitrogen. Furthermore, a chemical determination of the unique aromatic constituents of each variety may be used. The finest table wines also seem to be made from varieties of small berries, and, for reds, of not too much color. The juice/solid ratio should apparently be high. The ratios may vary with the type of wine.

FIG. 39. PICKING KNIFE USED FOR PICKING MOST CALIFORNIA WINE GRAPES

For region V conditions LaRosa (1955) and LaRosa and Nielsen (1956), recommended lower pH requirements for harvesting grapes, whether for table or dessert wines. While we do not agree that pH is an adequate measure for harvesting grapes, we applaud LaRosa's insistence that greater attention should be paid to harvesting grapes at the proper stage of maturity. We believe this is related to the sugar/acid ratio, to the absolute sugar and pH contents, to the variety of grape, and perhaps to the season and relative time of the season. Doubtless, amount of crop is a crucial factor. Overcropping makes rational measures for harvesting meaningless. We can find no significant measures of maturity for Palomino grapes at Madera, cropped to 16 tons per acre and with 17° Brix on October 1. Such grapes had better be consigned to producing distilling material.

HARVESTING AND TRANSPORTATION

Grapes for winery use are usually harvested with a curved knife in California (Fig. 73). However, picking shears, such as are used in table grape harvesting, would allow better cutting out of defective fruit. When botrytised fruit is being harvested, as in Sauternes, shears are useful.

A variety of containers are employed to receive the harvested fruit.

Courtesy of Wine Institute

Fig. 40.   Picking Grapes into Boxes in California Vineyard

Where women harvest the grapes, which is common in Europe, small baskets or buckets are used. The picker then dumps this into a larger container, usually carried on a man's back. In the Douro district of Portugal the men may carry these directly to the winery. In Alsace and Germany the man may dump the grapes into a large wooden tank on a wagon at the edge of the vineyard, see Fig. 8. In Champagne the grapes are placed in large baskets for sorting before being crushed, Fig. 7.

In California the traditional method was to cut the clusters from the vines with picking knives, Fig. 39, and place them directly into boxes holding 40 or 50 lbs. of grapes, Fig. 40. These were then loaded onto trucks and moved to the winery. This system is expensive and it is difficult to keep the boxes clean, especially in rainy weather. In some cases the boxes are dumped into gondola trucks for transportation to the winery.

At present there is a tendency to pick into buckets and dump these directly into the two, four, or six-ton gondola trucks. In one case the pickers harvest into 50-gallon metal drums which are then picked up and emptied into a gondola truck by a special machine.

The less the grapes are handled prior to crushing the better. Therefore, systems where the pickers harvest into small gondolas which are moved directly to the crusher are probably best, Fig. 41. The shorter the delay

Courtesy of Wine Institute

FIG. 41. PICKING GONDOLA BEING LOADED ON TRUCK FOR TRANSFER TO WINERY

from harvesting to crushing the better. On arrival at the winery the fruit is weighed and sampled for sugar, acidity, and defects.

A California firm has devised a special sampling tube for use with gondola trucks. A voluntary grape inspection program was used in 13 California wineries during the 1959 season. Grape quality inspection of grapes for winery use will probably be a permanent part of the California industry. A limit of about 10 to 20 per cent defective grapes appears a reasonable one for San Joaquin valley grapes. For North Coast grapes where botrytis infection, which is less objectionable flavor-wise than other fungal defects, may be prevalent in years of early rainfall, a somewhat higher maximum limitation may be desirable, perhaps 20 to 25 per cent.

Gondola trucks should be washed before being returned to the vineyard. Boxes should also be washed before being reused.

COMPOSITION OF MUSTS

Water

Ripe grapes contain 70 to 80 per cent water. Amerine (1956) has suggested that grams of water per fruit and in per cent could be measured as a criterium of maturity.

Sugars and Related Compounds

As the source of ethyl alcohol in the wine the sugars of the fruit are of paramount importance. They are also, of course, important for their taste. Dextrose and levulose are the primary sugars. While they normally are present at full maturity in a 1/1 ratio this ratio may fluctuate considerably. Thus Amerine and Thoukis (1958) found for 57 samples of the 1955 vintage levulose/dextrose ratios of from 0.71 to 1.45. In a wide variety of grapes Sisakyan and Marutyan (1948) reported decreasing dextrose/levulose ratios during ripening. Sucrose generally increased.

These ratios may have some importance to the wine maker. Levulose is nearly twice as sweet as dextrose. For making sweet table wines it would obviously be desirable to have high levulose varieties available. Also, to retain residual sugar it would be desirable to use strains of yeast which ferment levulose as slowly as possible. The so-called Sauternes strain of yeast apparently is such a yeast.

Little sucrose has been found in varieties of V. vinifera. However, in non-V. vinifera grapes as much as ten per cent sucrose may be present. Most of this will be hydrolyzed during fermentation. Hence very little or no sucrose remains in dry wines even when sucrose is used for amelioration before fermentation. Tests for residual sucrose are therefore not reliable as indicators of amelioration. Amerine and Bailey (1959) found that

TABLE 7

PECTIN CONTENT OF GRAPES[1]

| Species and Authority | Locality | Pectin Content, Per cent | | |
		Minimum	Maximum	Average
Vitis vinifera:				
von der Heide and Schmitthenner (1922)	Germany	0.11	0.33	...
Marsh and Pitman (1930)	California	0.03	0.17	0.12
Besone (1940)	Davis, Calif.	0.02	0.21	0.13
		0.05	0.11	0.08
Ventre (1930)	France	0.14	0.39	0.26
		0.03	0.07	0.05[2]
Françot and Geoffroy (1951)	France	0.05	0.08	0.06[3]
		0.04	0.53	0.20[4]
Garina-Canina (1938)	Italy	0.08	0.39	...
Vitis labrusca:				
Willaman and Kertez (1931)	New York	...	0.60	...
Besone (1940)	Davis, Calif.	0.11	0.29	0.18

[1] Source of data: Amerine and Joslyn (1951).   [2] First press.   [3] Second press.   [4] Last press.

there is more sucrose and starch in the main stem compared to the lateral branches of the fruit cluster. There was more reducing sugar in the lateral branches, particularly in the brush. They reported 1 to 2 lbs. of fermentable sugar in the stems per ton of grapes. Later, Amerine and Root (1960) in other varieties reported 2.3 to 4.8 lbs. per ton of fermentable sugar. Small amounts of sucrose (0.019 to 0.18 per cent) were found in musts of California grapes by Kliewer (1965). About 0.5 to 2.0 per cent sucrose (by acid hydrolysis or invertase) was reported in a variety of grapes by Sisakyan and Marutyan (1948). Kliewer also detected raffinose (0.01 to 0.32 per cent), melibiose, stachyose and maltose but no pentoses in the musts of the varieties examined. Others have reported small amounts of pentoses in wines.

The pectin content of the ripe fruit varies from 0.02 to 0.6 per cent (see Table 7). The pectin content of "eastern" grapes is generally higher than that of *V. vinifera* varieties. This includes alcohol-precipitable material and most of this is gums and arabans according to Peynaud (1951) as the following data illustrate (gm. per liter):

| Variety | Total Pectin Material | Pectic Acid | | Gums or Arabans |
		Free	Esterified	
Merlot	1.77	0.07	0.19	1.51
Sémillon	4.43	0.02	0.14	4.27
Cabernet franc	1.22	0.08	0.37	0.77

These values are lower than those reported by Solms *et al.* (1952) but the per cent esterified is higher. They found only an average of 31.4 per cent esterified in Swiss musts. Peynaud (1952) also reported that musts from grapes attacked by *Botrytis cinerea* were lower in pectic acid but nearly three times as high in gums. Also when heat is applied to musts to hasten color extraction high pectin content results. During fermentation from 30 to 90 per cent of the pectins are precipitated, apparently due to the pectolytic activity of the yeasts and to precipitation at the alcohol content of the wine; see Usseglio-Tomasset (1959).

Marteau *et al.* (1961) showed that demethoxylation of pectins occurs rapidly in musts due to PE and that the level of methanol depends on the level of pectinic acids in the must. Naturally-occurring PE can affect the demethoxylation but added pectolytic enzymes act more rapidly. The final level of methanol is the same. This natural PE activity explains the low pectin content of wines.

The presence of colloidal materials in musts and wines has been known since Pasteur. Besides pectins, these have been attributed to gums, mucilaginous materials (dextrans?), coloring matter, tannins, proteins and protein degradation products, and to certain inorganic salts. In some cases, an equilibrium between a compound in the colloidal and non-colloidal state appears to exist. Deibner *et al.* (1958) have summarized data on the colloidal constituents of musts and wines. The colloidal content of musts is reduced by drying the grapes, by tannin fining, by pasteurization, by storage, and by oxidation.

The cuticular waxes from the surfaces of various varieties of grapes were extracted with chloroform and re-extracted into petrol-ether insoluble "hard" wax and petrol-ether soluble "soft" wax by Radler (1965). About two-thirds of the cuticular wax consists of oleanolic acid. The amount of this triterpene acid seems to be less in grapes grown on unirrigated vineyards. The main (40–60 per cent) constituents of the "soft" wax were free alcohols. In *Vitis vinifera* varieties only a small amount of hydrocarbon is present but in Isabella (*V. labrusca*) 23 per cent of the "soft" wax was hydrocarbon. The chain length of the hydrocarbons varied from C_{18} to C_{35} with C_{25}, C_{27}, C_{29}, and C_{31} being most prevalent. The alcohol fractions varied in chain length from C_{20} to C_{34}, with C_{26} and C_{28} predominating. The results with the hydrocarbons of Isabella are similar to the earlier data of Markley *et al.* (1938) with Concord. They reported 30 per cent C_{29} and 70 per cent C_{31} compared to 27 and 50 per cent in this paper.

Acids

The two principal acids of the grape are tartaric (*d*-tartaric) and malic (*l*-malic). Tartaric is a relatively strong acid and one of the reasons for the biological stability of wine is that it is buffered to a relatively low pH.

The total acidity, calculated as tartaric acid, may vary from as low as 0.3 to as high as 1.5 per cent. The amount varies with the season and variety. Tartaric acid does not appear to be formed from malic acid. Rather it appears to be a by-product of photosynthesis with carbon atoms 2 and 3 of tartaric acid being the same as atoms 3 and 4 of dextrose. So far as is known tartaric acid is not a part of the Krebs cycle.

The malate content, as malic acid, of ripe California grapes is reported by Amerine (1956) to vary from 0.08 to 0.84 per cent. Amerine (1951) suggested that for California conditions low-malate varieties were to be preferred since the high-tartrate varieties were more likely to have a lower pH. He noted (1956), however, that a low potassium content was necessary if the pH was to be buffered to a low pH. The tartrate/malate ratio varies from 0.75 to 6.1.

Very little citric acid (l-citric) is found in mature grapes, about 0.01 to 0.03 per cent. Musts of low total acidity are also likely to be lower in citric. Hennig and Lay (1965) reported 0.03 to 0.04 gm. per liter of oxalic acid in three German musts and 0.0 to 0.06 in 20 wines. Kliewer (1966) found small amounts of isocitric, cis-aconitic, glutaric, fumaric, pyrrolidone carboxylic and α-ketoglutaric acids in musts. In musts of diseased grapes glucuronic and gluconic acids are found. A very small amount of phosphoric acid, less than 0.05 per cent as phosphate, is found in normal musts and up to 20 per cent of this is found in the organic form. The significance of different forms of phosphate to fermentation and wine quality needs study.

pH and Buffer Coefficient

The pH of California musts at maturity varies from about 3.1 to 3.9 depending on the variety, region and season. Northern European musts may not reach 3.0 even in good seasons. The buffer capacity of grape musts, $\Delta pH/\Delta NaOH$ where $\Delta NaOH$ is the milliliters of 0.1 N sodium hydroxide added per liter, is very low, indicating a high buffer capacity, i.e., more dibasic acids (see Amerine and Winkler 1958 and Françot 1945).

Nitrogenous Components

The total nitrogen contents of musts varies between 100 and 1100 mg. per liter, the usual amount being about 600. Expressed as protein pre-Prohibition data for California musts showed a range from 0.01 to 0.2 per cent. The amount present varies markedly with soil conditions. Musts from insect-injured grapes are also reported to be high in total nitrogen. Ammonia nitrogen in musts varies from 5 to 150 mg. per liter. Here soil nitrogen will have an especially notable effect.

Only small amounts of amine nitrogen are found in musts—usually less than 100 mg. per liter, though up to 400 has been reported. Polypeptide nitrogen likewise seldom exceeds 100 mg. per liter in ripe fruit. Again reports of up to 350 have been made. Protein nitrogen amounts to less than 50 mg. per liter. Hennig (1944) has made a more complete fractionation of the nitrogenous material in musts of the 1941 and 1942 vintages (as mg. per liter):

Nitrogen Fraction	1941	1942
Total	1075	748
Ammonia	112	15
Amino	408	319
Amide	34	16
Humin	20	17
Phospho-tungstic	349	231
Protein	40	18
Residue	112	132

The phospho-tungstic nitrogen fraction includes the tri- and tetrapeptides, diamino acids, such as arginine and lysine, and heterocyclic acids, such as histidine and proline, as well as purines. The amino fraction includes dipeptides; the humin nitrogen, tyrosine, and tryptophane; and the amides, asparagine, and glutamine. The residues are compounds of unknown composition. Lafon-Lafourcade and Peynaud (1959) reported the following average nitrogen content of Bordeaux musts and wines (mg. per liter):

	Total	Ammonia	Amine[1]	Amine[2]
Musts	454	70	129	141
Red wines	320	11.5	96	90
White wines	184	6.3	36	95

[1] By formol titration.
[2] By microbiological assay.

The amino acids which have been reported are given in Table 8. Castor (1953) reported 26.5 to 160.7 mg. per liter of glutamic acid and 7.0 to 113 of arginine. The amounts of 14 other amino acids were usually below 10 mg. and lysine, methionine, glycine, and cystine were present at 2 mg. per liter or less. In a later study (1956) he reported 349 mg. per 100 ml. of proline, 48 mg. of serine and 21 of threonine. Flanzy and Poux (1965) reported a much higher content of proline in musts of 1962, a warm year, compared to 1963, a cool year. Most of the other amino acids were present in larger amounts in 1963 compared to 1962. However, the total was greater in the 1962 musts. Generally, the per cent utilization of amino

TABLE 8

FREE AMINO ACIDS OF MUSTS AND WINES

Amino Acid	Investigators											
	1	2	3	4	5	6	7	8	9	10	11	12
α-Alanine	+	+	−	−	+	+	+	+	+	+	+	+
β-Alanine	−	−	−	−	−	−	−	−	−	−	−	+
α-Aminobutyric acid	−	−	−	−	+	+	+	+	−	−	+	+
Arginine	−	−	−	+	+	+	+	+	−	+	+	+
Asparagine	−	−	+	−	−	+	−	−	−	+	+	+
Aspartic acid	+	+	−	+	+	+	+	+	+	−	+	+
Cysteine	−	−	−	−	−	−	−	−	−	−	+	+
Cystine	−	−	−	+	−	+	−	+	+	+	+	+
Glutamic acid	+	+	+	+	+	+	+	+	+	+	+	+
Glutamine	−	−	−	−	−	−	−	−	−	−	+	+
Glycine	+	+	−	+	+	+	+	+	+	+	+	+
Histamine	−	−	−	−	−	+	−	−	−	−	−	+
Histidine	−	+	−	+	+	+	−	+	−	+	−	+
Hydroxyleucine	−	−	−	−	−	−	−	−	−	−	−	+
Hydroxypipecolic acid	−	−	−	−	−	−	−	−	+	−	−	+
Hydroxyproline	−	−	−	−	−	−	−	−	−	−	−	+
Isoleucine	+	−	−	+	+	+	+	−	−	−	−	+
Leucine	+	−	−	+	−	+	+	+	+	−	+	+
Lysine	−	−	−	+	+	+	+	+	−	+	−	+
Methionine	−	−	−	+	+	−	−	+	−	−	−	+
Methionine sulfone	−	−	−	−	−	−	−	+	−	−	−	−
Norvaline	−	−	−	−	−	+	−	−	−	−	−	+
Ornithine	−	−	−	−	−	−	−	−	−	−	−	+
2-Oxyproline	−	−	−	−	−	−	−	−	−	−	+	+
Phenylalanine	+	+	−	+	+	−	−	−	−	−	−	+
Pipecolic acid	−	−	−	−	−	−	−	−	−	−	−	+
Proline	+	+	+	+	-	+	+	+	+	+	+	+
Serine	+	+	+	+	+	+	+	−	+	+	+	+
Threonine	+	+	+	+	+	+	−	−	+	−	−	+
Tryptophane	−	−	+	+	−	−	−	+	−	−	−	+
Tyrosine	+	−	−	+	+	+	−	−	−	+	+	+
Valine	+	+	+	+	+	+	+	+	+	+	+	+

Source of data: Lafon-Lafourcade and Peynaud (1959).

acids during fermentation was greater in 1963 (except for arginine and threonine which were utilized about the same in both years).

Hennig (1955) appears to be the only investigator who has reported the amino acid citrulline in wines and Koch and Bretthauer (1957) the only ones to find ornithine.

A summary of the average values in musts and wines is given in Table 9 (p. 102).

Koch and Sajak (1959) summarize their studies in the proteins of grapes and wines by noting how complex the grape proteins are. The water-soluble nitrogenous constituents are believed to be low molecular-weight polypeptides and proteids. The complete list of amino acids involved and their peptide linkage is still unknown. They note that heat treatment gives protein stability and that bentonite treatment results in an essentially protein-free wine.

TABLE 9

AMOUNT OF FREE AMINO ACIDS IN MUSTS AND WINES[1]

(Mg. per liter)

| Amino Acid | Musts | | | Wines | | | |
| | Castor (1953) | Lafon-Lafourcade and Peynaud (1959) | Lüthi and Vetsch (1953) | Bourdet and Herard (1958) | | Lafon-Lafourcade and Peynaud (1959) | |
				Red	White	Red	White
Alanine	...	...	50–100	67	70	...	...
Aminobutyric	...	...	...	31	24	...	...
Arginine	403	327	...	84	91	47	46
Asparagine	...	...	...	56	41	...	...
Aspartic acid	52	2	6	76	72	31	38
Cystine	4	0	...	106	47	17	25
Glutamic acid	687	173	3–15	334	315	221	200
Glutamine	...	...	...	46	27	...	...
Glycine	7	22	5–8	12	16	28	26
Histidine	92	11	...	34	13	14	14
Isoleucine	66	7	... ⎫	36	24	⎧ 26	29
Leucine	62	20	... ⎭			⎩ 19	19
Lysine	16	16	...	43	37	47	40
Methionine	14	1	...	28	49	5	4
Phenylalanine	51	5	...	22	15	19	16
Proline	...	266	...	531	770	72	201
Serine	...	69	1–3	9	11	49	54
Threonine	...	258	20–25	27	32	187	111
Tryptophane	47	0.6	...	0	0	2.5	0
Tyrosine	20	0	...	32	37	11	13
Valine	60	6	...	19	16	45	36

[1] Source of data: Lafon-Lafourcade and Peynaud (1959).

Koch (1963) finds soluble proteins in grapes, the nature of which differ somewhat between varieties. The amounts increase during ripening and more appears to be formed in warm seasons. For the White Riesling and Müller-Thurgau varieties it appears to be a glucoprotein with some 18 amino acids. The isoelectric point of the proteins of different varieties varies from 3.3 to 4.0.

Nucleotides and nucleosides identified in wine by Tercelj (1965) included: guanine, adenine, cytosine, hypoxanthine, xanthine, thymine uraciles, cytidine, thymidine, adenoside, uridine, guanosine, GMP, CMP, AMP, TMP, and IMP.

A more sophisticated study of the nitrogenous compounds of musts and wines is that of Tercelj (1965). He confirms the spectacular decrease in amino acids during fermentation, noting, however, the wide variation between amino acids. Filtration also results in a very large reduction in amino acids, again varying widely between the various amino acids. He considers this a practical means of stabilizing sweet table wines.

Peynaud and Maurié (1953A) have observed a possible relationship between titratable acidity and amine nitrogen content which might indicate a parallelism between the formation of amino and other organic acids. Further work needs to be done.

Variety	Titratable Acidity	Amine Nitrogen
	Per cent Tartaric	Mg. per L.
Merlot	0.60	52
Cabernet Sauvignon	0.66	59
Sémillon	0.69	73
Malbec	0.72	82
Cabernet franc	0.78	92
Sauvignon blanc	0.84	98
Petit Verdot	0.87	104

The colloidal material of grape juice contains 10 to 13 per cent protein according to Markh and Boneva (1952). They noted only 4 to 21 per cent of the total colloids irreversibly precipitated by heating and chilling.

Pigments

Little quantitative data on the amounts of the pigments of musts are available. Traces of chlorophyll, carotene, and xanthophyll are found in most musts. A summary of our present knowledge of grape anthocyanins has been given by Webb (1964). While paper chromatographic techniques have been of great value, he notes correctly that the isolated and purified pigment may differ from that actually present in the grape skin or in wine.

The path for biosynthesis of anthocyans suggested by Durmishidze (1959) was: catechin → cyanidin → quercetin → gallocatechin → delphinidin → malvidin.

Quercetin (a flavone) is relatively insoluble and present in only traces. Its glycoside, isoquercitrin (a flavanol) occurs in amounts of from 1 to 30 mg. per liter. Genevois (1934) attributed the slight fluorescence of white wines to be due to 0.04 to 0.1 mg. per liter of flavine and lumiflavine. Hennig and Burkhardt (1957) also demonstrated rutin in white wines. Filter pad clogging by a dry red wine was found to be due to quercetin (71%), kempferol (24%) and myricetin (5%) by Ziemelis and Pickering (1969).

Very active research on the anthocyan pigments of red wines is currently under way in a number of laboratories using the newer techniques of paper chromatography. The main pigment of V. vinifera varieties is the monoglucoside of malvidin (oenidin) according to P. Ribéreau-Gayon and Sudraud (1957).

In V. labrusca delphinidin monoglucoside and monomethoxydelphinidin monoglucoside were reported by Brown (1940). Sastry and Tischer (1952) identified malvidin 3-monoglucoside in the skins of Concord grapes. In general, American species contain diglucosides and *V. vinifera* varieties do not. Interspecific hybrids may or may not contain diglucosides, but most do.

No diglucosides of malvidin were found in the varieties of *V. vinifera* examined by Biol and Michel (1961, 1962). However, 29 of the 37 direct-producer hybrids tested contained the diglucoside. Among the hybrids without the diglucoside of malvidin were Burdin 7,705, Landot 244 and 4411, Seibel 5,455, 10,878, 11,803 and 14,596 and Seyve-Villard 23,353. Biol and Foulonneau (1961) did find the diglucoside of peonidin in *V. vinifera* varieties and also some acylated diglucoside of malvidin. Cappelleri (1965) reported malvidin diglucoside in 2 varieties of *V. vinifera* (of 109 tested): Negrara veronese and Negronza. Liuni *et al.* (1965) found diglucoside in Merlot, Cabernet franc and Raboso Piave. The oxidation product of malvin is malvon (Visintine-Roumanin, 1967).

The report of Smith and Luh (1965) indicates that Rubired has a different pigment complex from *V. vinifera* varieties, having a predominant diglucoside pattern. The decreasing order of pigments was: malvidin 3,5-diglucoside, peonidin 3,5-diglucoside, malvidin 3-monoglucoside, peonidin 3-monoglucoside, delphinidin 3-monoglucoside, petunidin 3-monoglucoside, an unidentified pigment, petunidin 3,5-diglucoside, malvidin 3,5-diglucoside acylated with *p*-coumaric acid, another unidentified pigment, malvidin 3-monoglucoside acylated with *p*-coumaric acid, and delphinidin 3,5-diglucoside. Anderson *et al.* (1970) identified acetic acid as a major acylating acid in acylated anthocyanin-3-monoglucosides.

In Merlot (*V. vinifera*), Zamorani and Pifferi (1964) reported 43 per cent malvidin monoglucoside, 32 of delphinidin monoglucoside, 10 of petunidin monoglucoside, and 5 of peonidin monoglucoside. Traces of diglucosides were detected. Considerably more diglucoside was present when 100 mg. per liter of sulfur dioxide was used for the fermentation.

Precise determination of diglucosides is difficult. The official French procedure is that of Jaulmes and Ney (1960). Further precision appears to be possible with the procedure of Deibner and Bourzeix (1964) and Deibner *et al.* (1964). Bouschet hybrids have been shown to contain diglucosides by Deibner and Bourzeix (1960, 1964). A review of the work on differentiating wines of *V. vinifera* from those of other species has been given by P. Ribéreau-Gayon (1964). The presence of diglucosides of malvidin is presumptive evidence of non-*V. vinifera* wine. Ribéreau-Gayon and Ribéreau-Gayon (1958) reported easy preparation of the paper chromatograms with young wines. Later, little coloring material moves from the origin. This they attribute to transformation of some of the soluble anthocyans to a colloidal condition.

Hrazdina *et al.* (1970) determined the relative stability of the principal diglucoside pigments and found them most stable at pH 5.0 where they are rapidly converted to the colorless base form.

Table 10 gives some of the relationships between species. The important differences between species may be summarized as follows according to P. Ribéreau-Gayon (1958A): in *V. lincecumii, V. aestivalis* and *V. coriaceae* cyanidin and peonidin predominate (2 OH groups on the side ring); in *V. riparia* and *V. rupestris* diglucosides are the main pigments; and in other species, including *V. vinifera,* monoglucosides are present in the largest amounts, see Table 10. However, P. Ribéreau-Gayon (1958B) has also noted a regional variation. California-grown *V. vinifera* varieties contained a much higher percentage of malvidin than did French-grown.

The importance of leucoanthocyanin in red wines has been emphasized by Bate-Smith and Ribéreau-Gayon (1959). The principal source (up to two-thirds) of the leucoanthocyanins has been identified as the seeds. These are desirable, up to a point, as a source of astringency. They also aid fining by organic fining agents. P. Ribéreau-Gayon (1957) reported considerable leucocyanidin in a young red wine. He believed it important from the sensory point of view as well as for its possible vitamin-like activity. Four leucoanthocyanins were identified in Cabernet Sauvignon grapes by Somaatmadja *et al.* (1965). Two were leucocyanidins, one was leucodelphinidin and one was not characterized. While they all had some inhibitory effects on growth of bacteria, they differed from each other in their effect on specific bacteria. This is similar to the report of Masquelier (1958) and of Powers *et al.* (1960).

Grohmann and Gilbert (1959) have given a simple procedure for determining if non-*Vitis vinifera* wine is present in a sample. The test is based on the absence of diglucoside pigments that fluoresce in ultra-violet light.

In *V. rotundifolia* Brown (1940) reported the red pigment was probably a 3,5-diglucoside of 3',0-methyldelphinidin, which he named muscadine. In *V. hypoglauca* F.U.M., the Australian wild grape, Cornforth (1939) found malvidin monoglucoside but little or no delphinidin glycoside or its methyl esters.

In most grapes the red pigments occur only in the skins but in Teinturier grapes and in some of their hybrids, such as Alicante Bouschet, Grand noir, etc., and in some direct-producer hybrids, such as Salvador, the color pigments are also present in the pulp.

Besides the pigments grapes contain other polyphenolic compounds. Hennig and Burkhardt (1957, 1958, 1960) in White Riesling grapes or young wines reported chlorogenic acid, isochlorogenic acid, caffeic acid (either the cis or trans form), a lactone of *p*-coumaric acid, quinic acid, and shikimic acid. The latter two acids are, of course, components of

TABLE 10

ANTHOCYANS OF THE SPECIES *Vitis*[1]

Constituents	Ri-paria	Rupes-tris	Lince-cumii	Aesti-valis	Coria-cea	La-brusca	Arizo-nica	Berlan-dieri	Rubra	Monti-cola	Cordi-folia	Vini-fera
Total number of constituents	14	12	17	9	7	10	12	9	12	6	11	9
					Per cent of each							
Cyanidin												
Monoglucoside	2	:	29	30	58	5	8	8	5	3	10	3
Diglucoside	5	2	2	3	4	:	1	:	1	:	:	:
Peonidin												
Monoglucoside	:	:	7	11	6	10	14	16	20	5	11	15
Diglucoside	2	8	3	4	4	1	10	2	1	:	2	:
Delphinidin												
Monoglucoside	14	9	17	30	20	21	13	23	30	36	15	12
Diglucoside	12	34	1	:	:	:	:	:	1	:	:	:
Petunidin												
Monoglucoside	10	3	8	10	4	15	10	20	20	26	18	12
Diglucoside	17	22	1	:	:	1	:	1	2	:	2	:
Malvidin												
Monoglucoside	6	2	4	6	:	33	29	26	16	27	30	35
Diglucoside	21	8	1	2	:	2	10	2	2	:	5	:
Constituents not identified	11	12	27	4	4	12	5	2	2	3	7	23

[1] Source of data: P. Ribéreau-Gayon and Sudraud (1957). See also J. and P. Ribéreau-Gayon (1958a).

chlorogenic acid. Esculetin, umbelliferone, myricitrin and several unknown compounds were also reported. Weurman and de Rooij (1958) did find chlorogenic acid isomers in grapes (possibly *neo*-chlorogenic and *p*-coumarylquinic acids). Tanner and Rentschler (1956) found *only* chlorogenic acid when the stems of Chasselas doré were crushed and fermented with the fruit. The stems of two other varieties, however, contained no chlorogenic acid. They, therefore, believe that this acid and caffeic and quinic acids are not present in grape juice or wine. Burkhardt (1965) reported *p*-coumarylquinic acid and its calcium salt in musts and wines.

Tannin

The tannins occur in the skins, stems and seeds. The free-run juice of white grapes usually contains less than 0.02 per cent tannin. Benvegnin *et al.* (1951) report the following in a white and red variety:

Part of Grape	Tannin, Per cent		Tannin, Kg. per 100 Kg. of Fruit	
	Chasselas doré	Pinot noir	Chasselas doré	Pinot noir
Seed	5.2	6.4	0.17	0.26
Stem	3.2	3.1	0.12	0.11
Skin	0.6	1.7	0.05	0.10

The tannins of grapes are classified as hydrolyzable (those which are like esters in character and can be broken down by hydrolysis) and condensed (where the nuclei are held together by carbon linkages). The tannins isolated by Durmishidze (1955) and Hennig and Burkhardt (1957, 1958) include *d*-catechin, *l*-epicatechin, *l*-epigallocatechin, *dl*-gallocatechin, and *d*-epicatechingallate. Except for the latter these are condensed tannins. Su and Singleton (1969) have further clarified this problem. The skins are lower than the seeds in *l*-epigallocatechin. The Russian worker did not find free gallic acid. The Germans found both gallic and ellagic acids as well as protocatechuic acid. Gallic and ellagic acids are very bitter but are largely removed by gelatin fining. Durmishidze (1959) suggested that the biosynthesis of tannins might proceed as follows: sugars → mesoinositol → phloroglucin → tannins. See Fig. 42 for the close relationships between tannins, flavanols, and anthocyanidins. For a complete review of the phenolic substances in grapes and wines and their significance see Singleton and Esau (1969).

Vitamins

The vitamins of grapes are primarily important as accessory growth factors for micro-organisms although some of them are present in sufficient

Compounds Identified	Amount		Nature of Compounds
	Reds	White	
Benzoic acids			
R=R'=H p-hydroxybenzoic acid R=OH, R'=H protocatechuic acid R=OCH₃, R'=H vanillic acid R=R'=OH gallic acid R=R'=OCH₃ syringic acid	50–100	1–5	Esters
R=H salicylic acid R=OH gentisic acid			
Cinnamic acids			
R=H p-coumaric acid R=OH caffeic acid R=OCH₃ ferulic acid	50–100	2–10	Esters with anthocyans and tartaric acid
Flavonols			
R=R'=H kempferol R=OH, R'=H quercetin R=R'=OH myricetin	15	0	2 or 3 glucosides and 1 glucuronoside in musts; 3 aglycones in wines

Benzoic acids structure: R'—C₆H₄(HO)—COOH, and R—C₆H₄(OH)—COOH

Cinnamic acids structure: R—C₆H₄(HO)—CH=CH—COOH

Flavonols structure: benzopyran-4-one ring system with substituents R, R', and OH groups.

Anthocyanidins

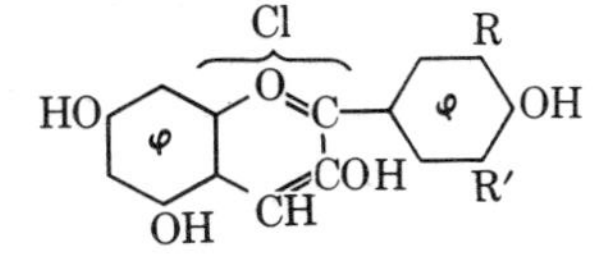

20–500   0   Glucosides and acylated glucosides (to p-coumaric acid); varies for different species of *Vitis*

R=OH, R'=H cyanidin
R=OCH₃, R'=H peonidin
R=R'=OH delphinidin
R=OCH₃, R'=OH petunidin
R=R'=OCH₃ malvidin

Tannins-flavan-3-ols

1500–5000   0–100   X[1]
50–100   0

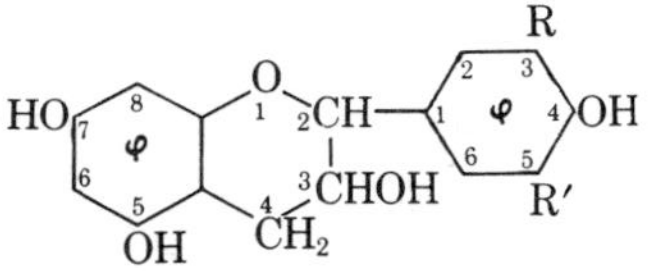

R=OH, R'=H catechin
R=R'=OH gallocatechin

Tannins-flavan-3,4-diols

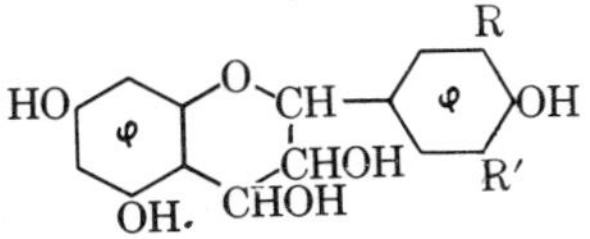

Traces   0

R=OH, R'=H leucocyanidin
R=R'=OH leucodelphinidin

Fig. 42. Structure of Polyphenolic Compounds

[1] X = Polymers of flavans, principally of 3,4 flavan-diols; as monomers small amounts of the flavans are found in red wine. Source of data: P. Ribéreau-Gayon (1964).

amounts to be of importance in human nutrition.

Ascorbic acid is present in *fresh* grapes in amounts of 1 to 18 mg. per 100 gm. with most values below 8, according to the summary of Amerine and Joslyn (1951). Dehydroascorbic acid is also present. Little therapeutic value is likely since the amounts are small and decrease rapidly after crushing. In Canada, Zubeckis (1964) reported fresh grapes contained 1.1 to 11.7 mg. per 100 ml. of juice of ascorbic acid, except for the Veerport variety which contained 18.5 to 33.8 mg. per 100 ml. There was a slight increase during ripening. The amounts decreased steadily during crushing and fermenting and little or none was present in the wine. Pasteurized grape juice retained about one-third the original ascorbic acid. Even in grapes stored at 0°C. (32°F.) there is a slow decrease in ascorbic acid, more in white than in red grapes according to Ournac (1958). Some doubt on the possible presence of ascorbic acid in wines is given by the inability of Baraud (1951, 1953) to find any color reaction with tartrazine.

Vitamin A is present in very small amounts in fresh grapes, which is not strange in view of their small carotene content.

Thiamin is a normal constituent of grapes and most of the available data are summarized in Table 11. Fresh grapes usually contain less than 600 μ per kg. Sulfiting, pasteurization, or filtering grape juice through bentonite all markedly reduce the thiamin content of grape juice. Thus Schanderl (1959) found 120 to 128 μ per liter in fresh German grape juice but only 27 to 135 in commercial grape juice. Mathews (1958) reported traces to 250 μ per liter in four Swiss commercial grape juices. Riboflavin occurs in musts up to 1.45 mg. per kg. according to Table 11, but the usual

TABLE 11

VITAMIN CONTENT OF VARIOUS MUSTS[1]

Vitamin	Minimum	Maximum	Source[2]
Thiamin (B₁)	0.1	1.2	1, 5, 8, 10, 11
Riboflavin (B₂)	T	1.5	1, 4, 5, 6, 7, 8, 10, 11
Pyridoxine (B₆)	0.1	2.9	1, 6, 9, 10, 11
Pantothenic acid	0.25	10.5	1, 2, 3, 6, 7, 8, 9, 10, 11
Nicotinic acid	0.3	8.8	4, 5, 6, 8, 9
Biotin	0.001	0.06	3, 6, 9, 10
Inositol	3.4	4.8	6, 10
p-Aminobenzoic acid	0.00	0.04	6, 10
Choline	0.5	4.01	6, 10
Folic acid	T	0.05	8, 10, 11

[1] Mg./liter except mg./100 ml. for inositol.
[2] Source of data: (1) Perlman and Morgan (1945), (2) Peynaud and Lafourcade (1955), (3) Peynaud and LaFourcade (1956), (4) Cailleau and Chevillard (1949), (5) Flanzy and Causeret (1954), (6) Castor (1953), (7) Smith and Olmo (1944), (8) Hall *et al.* (1956), and (9) Radler (1957), (10) Mathews (1958), (11) Burger *et al.* (1956).

amount is about 0.4 mg. or less, especially in commercial grape juice according to Mathews (1958). Riboflavin is easily destroyed by light.

About 50 per cent is lost by sulfiting or by fining with bentonite. If added to unsulfited grape juices in colored bottles it is well retained.

Pyridoxine is present up to 2.9 mg. per kg. in musts (Table 11). Added pyridoxine is retained well by grape juice. Pantothenic acid may occur in musts in amounts up to 15 mg. per kg. (Table 11). It is retained during storage. Smith and Olmo (1944) found significantly higher amounts of pantothenic acid in the juice of tetraploid compared to diploid varieties. *Labrusca x vinifera* interspecific hybrids were also higher in this vitamin than hybrids of *vinifera* varieties. Wines may have up to 1.9 mg. per liter as calcium pantothenate.

For musts, Lafon-Lafourcade and Peynaud (1958) showed a marked increase during maturation of p-aminobenzoic acid and a slight increase in pterolglutamic acid and choline. Musts of Bordeaux grapes contained 15 to 92 μ per liter (average 47 of p-aminobenzoic acid, 0.9 to 1.5 μ (average 1.2) of pterolglutamic acid and 24 to 39 μ per liter (average 33) of choline. They state, however, that the extremes found in a large number of determinations were 15 to 93, 0.9 to 1.8 and 13 to 39 and they give averages of 51, 1.2 and 26 respectively.

Nicotinic acid has been reported in amounts up to 2.8 mg. per kg. of Thompson seedless grapes by Teply *et al.* (1942). Other vitamins present are B_6, biotin, p-aminobenzoic acid, and inositol according to Castor (1953). Other data are given in Table 12. Russian investigators have re-

TABLE 12
VITAMIN CONTENT OF MUSTS AND WINES[1,2]

Vitamin	Musts			White Wines			Red Wines		
	Mini-mum	Maxi-mum	Aver-age	Mini-mum	Maxi-mum	Aver-age	Mini-mum	Maxi-mum	Aver-age
Biotin	1.5	4.2	2.6	1.0	3.6	2.0	0.6	4.6	2.1
Choline	...	...	...	17	27	21	17	41	2
Mesoinositol	380	710	500	220	730	497	290	510	334
Nicotinic acid	1650	4200	3260	990	2190	1570	1320	2180	1890
Pantothenic acid	500	1380	820	550	1240	810	470	1870	980
Pyridoxine	310	920	420	220	820	440	250	780	470
Riboflavin	3	60	21	8	133	32	103	245	177
Thiamin	160	450	333	2	58	10	...	...	7.5
Cobalamine (B12)	0	0.13	0.05	0	0.16	0.07	0.04	0.10	0.06

[1] Mg./liter for mesoinositol and choline; μ/liter for the others.
[2] Source of data: Peynaud and Lafourcade (1957).

ported a vitamin P factor in wines. Durmishidze (1955, 1958) has repeatedly stressed the relation of d-catechin, l-gallocatechin, etc., to the socalled capillary fragility vitamin. See also Lavollay and Sevestre (1944) and DeEds (1949).

Enzymes

A variety of enzymes are found in musts. Bayer *et al.* (1957) studied the polyphenoloxidase of grapes and reported it to contain copper. Its activity was rapidly and completely inhibited by sulfur dioxide. Centrifuging musts greatly reduced their enzyme activity, most of which is localized in or on the skins. A highly purified extract was prepared by acetone extraction, dialysis, and centrifuging. Enzyme activity was measured colorimetrically using purpurgallin. Durmishidze (1955) also showed that peroxidase and polyphenoloxidase were observed in all phases of vegetative growth of vines. Enzymatic oxidation is important for many wines, particularly when made from moldy grapes.

The o-phenol groups react with oxygen in the presence of polyphenoloxidase to produce yellow- or red-colored quinones. These in turn react with more oxygen to produce brown-colored condensation products.

Other enzymes noted by Amerine (1954) included: tannase, invertase, pectinase, ascorbase, catalase, dehydrase, esterase, and a proteolytic enzyme.

Odorous Constituents

Recently more studies of the odor constituents have been made. Holley *et al.* (1955) confirmed that methyl anthranilate is the predominant aroma-producing constituent of Concord grapes. In addition they found (mg. per ml. of essence): ethanol (35), methanol (1.5), ethyl acetate (3.5), methyl acetate (0.15), acetone (0.3), acetaldehyde (0.03), methyl anthranilate (0.033), and acetic acid. They also reported an unidentified chloroform-extractable constituent. These authors note that since about 90 per cent of the volatile organic material is ethanol that procedures for testing juice quality based on the quantitative determination of volatile material by dichromate or permanganate oxidation do little more than determine the alcohol. Haagen-Smit *et al.* (1949) used fresh Zinfandel grapes from the volatile oil of which they isolated (gm. per 100 kg. fruit in each case): ethyl alcohol (244), acetaldehyde (1.8), acetic acid (0.0053) *n*-butyric acid (0.003), *n*-caproic acid (0.0015), glyoxylic acid (0.118), *n*-butyl phthalate (2.25), leaf aldehyde (0.327), waxy substance (0.024), and a carbonyl compound (0.024).

In Muscat of Alexandria grapes Webb and Kepner (1957) isolated (mg. per kg. of fruit): methanol (3.7), ethanol (111.0), *n*-butanol (0.03), 3-methylbutanol (0.01), *n*-hexanol (0.49), cis-3-hexenol (0.26), acetaldehyde (0.85), *n*-hexanal (0.03), 2-butanone (0.01), 2-pentanone (0.01), 2-hexenal (0.05), methyl acetate (0.08), ethyl caproate (0.04), a butyrate ester, a valerate ester, another caproate ester, a caprylate ester, a caprate ester, a laurate ester, ethyl esters (all esters, 0.16), and acetals. They did not find any terpene alcohols which Cordonnier (1956) had reported, possibly they believe because of decomposition in their pot stills. Cordonnier found about 2 mg. per liter of geraniol, terpineol, limonene, and linaloöl in muscat essences. Bayonove and Cordonnier (1970) and others have confirmed that linaloöl is the main muscaty component of ripe grapes.

Using paper chromatography Cordonnier (1956) found four clear spots at R_f 0.48, 0.60, 0.74, and 0.94 for Muscat blanc (Muscat Canelli or Muscat Frontignan in California) and at 0.44, 0.58, 0.72, and 0.93 for Muscat of Alexandria. The intensity of the spots was positively correlated with the amount of muscat aroma. He suggested linaloöl or a compound containing linaloöl as the revealing aromatic constituent of these two muscat varieties. For Grenache there was a slight spot at 0.45 and a clear spot at 0.93. By simple chromatography Cordonnier was not able to establish elder flowers as a sophisticant of non-muscat wines. Coriander gave a clear spot at R_f 0.75 so by his technique wines sophisticated with coriander could not be differentiated from true muscat wines.

Kepner and Webb (1956) reported the following composition of V. rotundifolia: ethyl, n-butyl, n-hexyl, β-phenethyl alcohols and acetate, laurate and isopropyl esters. Methyl alcohol, n-hexanal, 2-hexenal, and acetal were also probably present. No nitrogen or sulfur containing compounds were found. V. vinifera also shows no nitrogen compounds. Kepner and Webb therefore note that the presence of nitrogen compounds in the volatile constituents is presumptive evidence of labrusca varieties many of which contain anthranilic acid esters. β-Phenylethyl alcohol is obviously the revealing aromatic compound of V. rotundifolia.

The components and relative amounts of the compounds isolated from a volatile extract of Sauvignon blanc were reported by Chaudary et al. (1964) as follows (L = large, M = medium, S = small): ethanol (L), 1-propanol (S), 2-methyl-1-propanol (S), 1-butanol (T), 3-methyl-1-butanol (M), 1-pentanol (T), 1-hexanol (L), 2-phenethyl alcohol (L), ethyl formate (T), ethyl acetate (S), ethyl propionate (T), isoamyl acetate (M), act.-amyl acetate (S), n-amyl acetate (T), n-hexyl acetate (L), ethyl caproate (L), ethyl heptanoate (S), ethyl caprylate (T), ethyl caprate (M), isoamyl caprylate (S), hexyl heptanoate (S), hexyl caprylate (L), 2-hexenal (L). The following compounds were probably present: methyl acetate, n-propyl acetate, n-propyl propionate, isobutyl propionate, ethyl valerate, n-amyl propionate, isoamyl butyrate, isobutyl caproate, hexyl valerate, isobutyrate ester, and 3-hexenoate ester.

Stevens et al. (1965) reported the higher boiling extract of Concord grapes was largely methyl anthranilate. The low-boiling constituents were ethyl acetate, iso-propyl acetate, ethanol, 2-propanol, ethyl propionate, propyl acetate, 1-propanol, 2-methyl-3-buten-2-ol, ethyl butyrate, 2-

TABLE 13

COMPOSITION OF MUSTS AND WINES[1]

	Must	Wine
	Per cent	Per cent
1. Water	70–85	80–90
2. Carbohydrates	15–25	0.1–0.3
Dextrose	8–13	0.5–0.1
Levulose	7–12	0.05–0.1
Pentoses	0.08–0.20	0.08–0.20
Arabinose	0.05–0.15	0.05–0.10
Rhamnose	0.02–0.04	0.02–0.04
Xylose	T	T
Pectin	0.01–0.10	T
Inositol	0.02–0.08	0.03–0.05
3. Alcohols and related compounds		
Ethyl	T	8.0–15.0
Methyl	0.0	0.01–0.02
Higher	0.0	0.008–0.012
2,3-Butylene glycol	0.0	0.01–0.15
Acetoin	0.0	0.000–0.003
Glycerol[2]	0[2]	0.30–1.40
Sorbitol	T	T
Diacetyl	0.0	T–0.0006
4. Aldehyde	T	0.001–0.050
5. Organic acids	0.3–1.5	0.3–1.1
Tartaric	0.2–1.0	0.1–0.6
Malic	0.1–0.8	0.0–0.6
Citric	0.01–0.05	0.0–0.05
Succinic	0	0.05–0.15
Lactic	0	0.1–0.5
Acetic	0.00–0.02	0.03–0.05
Formic	0	T
Propionic	0	In spoiled wines
Butyric	0	In spoiled wines
Gluconic		From botrytised grapes only
Glucuronic		From botrytised grapes only
Glyoxylic	?	0.00012
Mesoxalic	?	0.0001–0.0003
Glyceric	...	T
Saccharic	...	T
Amino	0.01–0.08	0.01–0.20
Pantothenic	...	T
Quinic	0	T
p-Coumaric	T	?
Shikimic	T	?
Sulfurous	0	0.00–0.05
Carbonic	T	Various

methyl-1-propanol, 1-butanol, 2-methyl-1-butanol, 3-methyl-1-butanol, and ethyl hexanoate.

Metals

For the metal content of musts, see Table 13 and Amerine (1958).

According to Jaulmes et al. (1960), musts contain 0.025 to 0.4 mg. per liter of lead with most samples with 0.1 to 0.25. In their studies there was

TABLE 13 (*Contd.*)

COMPOSITION OF MUSTS AND WINES

	Must	Wine
6. Polyphenol and related compounds		
Anthocyans	T	T
Chlorophyll	T	0–T
Xanthophyl	T	?
Carotene	T	?
Flavonol		
Quercetin	T	T
Quercetrin	T	T
Rutin	?	?
Tannins	0.01–0.10	0.01–0.30
Catechin	T	T
Gallocatechin	T	T
Epicatechin gallate	T	T
Gallic acid	T	T
Ellagic acid	T	T
Chlorogenic acid	T	T
Isochlorogenic acid	T	T
Caffeic acid	T	T
p-Coumarylquinic acid	T	T
7. Nitrogenous compounds		
Total	0.03–0.17	0.01–0.09
Protein	0.001–0.01	0.001–0.003
Amino	0.017–0.110	0.010–0.200
Humin	0.001–0.002	0.001–0.002
Amide	0.001–0.004	0.001–0.008
Ammonia	0.001–0.012	0.00–0.071
Residual	0.01–0.02	0.005–0.020
8. Mineral compounds	0.3–0.5	0.15–0.40
Potassium	0.15–0.25	0.045–0.175
Magnesium	0.01–0.025	0.01–0.020
Calcium	0.004–0.025	0.001–0.021
Sodium	T–0.020	T–0.044
Iron	T–0.003	T–0.005
Aluminum	T–0.003	T–0.07
Manganese	T–0.0051	T–0.05
Copper	T–0.0003	T–0.0005
Boron	T–0.007	T–0.004
Rubidium	T–0.0001	T–0.0004
Phosphate	0.02–0.05	0.003–0.090
Sulfate	0.003–0.035	0.003–0.22
Silicic acid	0.0002–0.005	0.0002–0.005
Chloride	0.001–0.010	0.001–0.060
Fluoride	T	0.0001–0.001
Iodide	T	T–0.001
Carbon dioxide	0	0.01–0.05[3]
Oxygen	T	T–0.00006

[1] Source of data: Hennig (1958), Amerine (1954, 1958), Ribéreau-Gayon and Peynaud (1958), Eschnauer (1959).   [2] Except for botrytised grapes.   [3] In normal still wine.   About 0.1 is the beginning of gasiness.

generally, but not always, a decrease in lead content during fermentation. The manganese content of Sicilian wines ranged from 0.25 to 2.20 mg. per liter according to Corrao (1963).

Boron fertilization markedly delays grape maturity (in fact, prevented satisfactory ripening) in France, according to Decau and Lamazou-Betbeder (1964). There are various unconfirmed reports that potassium fertilization hastens maturity and increases sugar content. Dupuy *et al.* (1955) found that soils high in phosphorus often produced wines with higher iron contents. Much of the iron appeared to have been dissolved from soil adhering to the fruit. The enrichment was not due to simple dissolving of iron from the soil but to reductive biological processes during fermentation. This was confirmed by Flanzy and Deibner (1956). They also found iron pickup from crushers and presses. This was also emphasized by Cordonnier (1953) and Nègre and Cordonnier (1953).

Table 13 summarizes data from a variety of sources for the composition of table wines. Special wines may have a composition somewhat outside the limits given. Also musts of raisined or botrytised fruit and their wines will not fit these limits.

ENVIRONMENTAL FACTORS

While the composition of most fruits reflects the environmental conditions under which they are grown there is no doubt that this is more critical for the grape than for other fruits. The primary environmental factor is temperature. Secondary factors are rainfall and humidity, wind, soil (*per se*), and combinations of these.

Temperature

This is the primary environmental factor influencing the distribution of *V. vinifera* grapes within the various climatic regions in the temperate zones. The rather narrow limits within which grapes are or can be grown

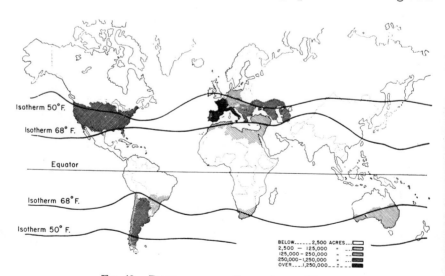

FIG. 43. DISTRIBUTION OF GRAPES IN THE WORLD

are shown in Fig. 43. Outside of these limits the winter temperatures are so low that vines cannot survive (as in most of Canada, etc.); or, the summer temperatures are not warm enough to ripen grapes (as in England, etc.); or, late spring frosts may kill new growth (as in Idaho or the Sierra Nevada foothills of California); or, high summer humidity may prevent growth of V. *vinifera* varieties owing to virus and other diseases, etc. (as in southern United States or Central America); or, summer temperatures may be too high (as in most desert regions).

Aside from these adverse temperature conditions, it is the temperature received during the growing season which is most important. Vines nor-

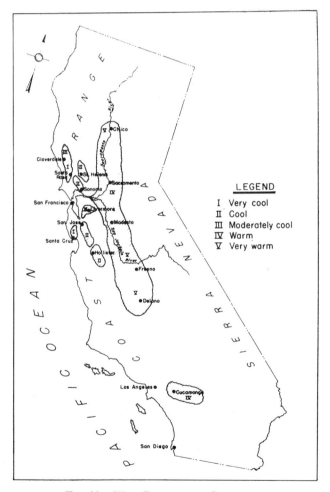

FIG. 44. WINE DISTRICTS OF CALIFORNIA

mally start to grow in the spring when the average daily temperature reaches 50°F. The summation of temperature above 50°F. is then the effective temperature influencing vine growth and the composition of the fruit. Winkler (1936) has calculated the summation (as day-degrees) for the principal grape growing regions, Table 14 and Fig. 44. It may be seen that grapes are successfully grown when the summation of temperature is as low as 2000 day degrees and as high as 5000.

In the warmer regions grapes mature earlier, and at the same per cent sugar have a lower titratable acidity, less color, and a higher pH. For example, in southern Spain the harvest normally begins in September, in southern France in late September or early October, and in Germany in October or November. In California grapes are picked for winery use in the south San Joaquin valley in August. The harvest at Lodi begins in September. The main picking at Napa, Fig. 45, is in early October. Grapes in the cool Santa Cruz mountains ripen in late October.

The main effects on total acidity and pH are shown in Table 15. It can be seen that in the cooler districts, even though the grapes were not harvested at the same stage of maturity, the acidity was usually higher and the pH lower. The effect of region on sugar content is not obvious from this table and in fact in practice is often suppressed by the overcropping which occurs in the warmer regions. Overcropped vines show delayed

Courtesy of Wine Institute

FIG. 45.   NAPA VALLEY WINERY WITH VINEYARD

TABLE 14

TEMPERATURE SUMMATION DURING THE GROWING SEASON IN ALGERIA, EUROPE, AND CALIFORNIA[1]

Place	Day Degrees Above 50 °F	Winkler Region[2]
Algiers, Algeria	5200	V
Bakersfield	5030	V
Fresno	4680	V
Merced	4620	V
Palermo, Italy (Marsala)	4140	V
Naples, Italy (Lacrima Christi)	4010	V
Davis	3618	IV
Lodi-Stockton	3590	IV
Florence, Italy (Chianti)	3530	IV
Calistoga	3281	III
Livermore	3260	III
Asti, Italy (Barbera, etc.)	2980	II
Ukiah	2970	II
St. Helena	2900	II
San Jose	2590	II
Bordeaux, France (Claret)	2519	II
Beaune, France (Burgundy)	2400	I
Sonoma	2360	I
Oakville	2300	I
Aptos	2110	I
Chalon-sur-Marne, France (Champagne)	2060	I
Auxerre, France (Chablis)	1850	I
Trier, Germany (Moselle)	1730	I
Geisenheim, Germany (Rheingau)	1709	I

[1] Source of data: Winkler (1936).
[2] I, 2500 day-degrees or less; II, 2501 to 3000; III, 3001 to 3500; IV, 3501 to 4000; and V, over 40JJ.

TABLE 15

INFLUENCE OF REGION ON THE COMPOSITION OF GRAPES PICKED AT APPROXIMATELY THE SAME STATE OF MATURITY[1]

Variety	Balling			Total Acid			pH		
	Fresno[2]	Davis[3]	Bonny[4] Doon	Fresno	Davis	Bonny Doon	Fresno	Davis	Bonny Doon
	De- grees	De- grees	De- grees	Per cent	Per cent	Per cent	pH	pH	pH
Alicante Bouschet	...	18.8	18.9	...	0.78	1.20	...	3.47	3.10
Burger	...	17.8	17.6	0.55	0.81	...	...	3.46	3.15
Cabernet Sauvignon	22.9	22.4	20.7	0.65	0.67	1.10	3.48	3.63	3.41
Carignane	21.8	21.8	...	0.62	0.70	...	3.67	3.58	...
Sauvignon vert	23.3	...	20.3	0.50	...	0.67	3.81	...	3.24
Sémillon	...	19.0	18.0	...	0.67	0.97	...	3.45	3.10
Zinfandel	...	22.4	21.3	...	0.61	0.86	...	3.58	3.28

[1] Source of data: Amerine and Joslyn (1951).
[2] Fresno—4680 day-degrees of temperature above 50°F. during the growing season.
[3] Davis—3618 day-degrees of temperature above 50°F. during the growing season.
[4] Bonny Doon—2400 day-degrees of temperature above 50°F. during the growing season.

maturity or may not ripen. Amerine (1956) has also indicated possible differences in the tartrate/malate ratio due to temperature. This results from the fact that malic acid is respired at lower temperatures than tartaric acid. Generally, therefore, one reason for the lower acidity of warm regions is their lower malic acid content. However, if the harvest is made very late in a cool region and very early in a warm region this difference may not show up. Amerine (1956) also noted that exceptions to the rule would occur when (1) there is no very hot period during ripening in a warm region or (2) there is a very hot period during ripening in a cool region.

The effect of temperature on color is very well known. The well-known Tokay variety at Lodi (region IV) has a bright orange-red color. At Fresno and south (region V) it rarely has more than a pink blush. In the coast counties (region II) it may develop a slight purple-red color. The wine grape Grenache is another example. In the cooler regions it has a full red color. At Davis (region IV) it is barely suited to making a rosé. At Delano (region V) it can be crushed and white free-run juice easily obtained. Typical data are given in Table 16.

TABLE 16

INFLUENCE OF REGIONAL CONDITIONS ON COLOR OF GRAPES[1]

		Regions and Averaged Color Value[2]			
Variety	Delano	Lodi, Guasti, Davis	Livermore Valley, Asti, Ukiah	Napa Valley, Santa Clara Valley	South Sonoma County, Santa Cruz Mts.
Alicante Bouschet	74	85	92	143	235
Carignane	45	49	57	83	100
Mataro	8	14	20	55	65
Petite Sirah	70	80	89	143	200
Zinfandel	27	44	52	62	200

[1] Source of data: Winkler and Amerine (1937).
[2] These figures represent the relative intensity of color expressed on an arbitrary scale; the higher the figure the greater is the concentration of pigment.

The seasonal effect is also primarily due to differences in temperature. The seasons of 1935 and 1936 were ideal for observing this difference in California. The 1935 season at St. Helena, for example, was cool (2276 day-degrees) and the harvest fairly late. In 1936 very hot (2664 day-degrees) weather (plus a small crop) led to much earlier ripening, higher sugar content (and hence more alcohol), less color, and lower total acidity. Typical data are given in Table 17. Under plant conditions the expected lower color in wines of warm seasons does not always develop. This is because fermentation of high sugar musts develops more alcohol

TABLE 17

EFFECT OF SEASON AND VARIETY ON THE COMPOSITION OF MUST AND WINE[1]

Variety	Average Date Collected		Must				Wine			
	1935	1936	Balling		Alcohol		Total Acid		Color Intensity[2]	
			1935	1936	1935	1936	1935	1936	1935	1936
			Degrees	Degrees	Per cent[3]	Per cent[3]	Per cent	Per cent		
Alicante Bouschet	Oct. 1	Sept. 23	21.7	22.9	10.9	12.3	0.61	0.57	64	63
Burger	Sept. 30	Sept. 19	19.8	19.5	9.6	11.0	0.66	0.55	..	..
Carignane	Sept. 30	Sept. 19	22.3	23.3	10.9	12.4	0.70	0.50	27	22
Palomino	Sept. 24	Sept. 30	21.5	22.9	11.0	12.5	0.38	0.36	..	..
Petite Sirah	Sept. 28	Sept. 22	23.2	25.6	11.3	13.9	0.67	0.56	77	59
Zinfandel	Oct. 1	Sept. 19	24.7	23.9	12.8	13.5	0.71	0.58	31	19
Average of 6 varieties	Sept. 29	Sept. 19	22.2	23.1	11.1	12.6	0.62	0.52	50	41
Average of 240 samples[4]	Sept. 30	Sept. 21	22.1	23.0	11.0	12.2	0.61	0.50	39	33

[1] Source of data; Winkler and Amerine (1938).
[2] These figures represent the relative intensity of color expressed on an arbitrary scale; the higher the figure, the greater is the consumption of pigment.
[3] Per cent by volume.
[4] Represents about 49 varieties from several districts of California.

and thus may extract a greater percentage of the color than the lower alcohol wines of cool years. The shriveling of the grapes in warm seasons may also decrease this difference between seasons.

While temperature differences as great as these are uncommon in California they are very common in Europe. Many of the vineyards of Europe and eastern United States and Canada do not receive enough heat to mature their grapes every year. Their wines are thus very unbalanced in the cooler years—low in alcohol and pH and high in titratable acidity, even when sugar is used to ameliorate the musts.

Favorable exposure results in temperature differences which can produce very marked differences in maturity and hence in quality in cool regions. It is not important in California except in the coolest seasons.

Soil

It is universally believed in Europe that calcareous soils produce the best wines. This may well be correct, but probably not because of the calcium content of the soil *per se.* Calcareous soils are usually well-drained. Well-drained soils are warmer,[1] hence there is better vine growth and better ripening. The slate soils of the Moselle are believed to retain the day-time heat and thus help warm the vine at night. The effect of soil structure on root growth in the Douro region has already been mentioned (p. 39). Also the high calcium sulfate content of the soil and its presence on the grapes constitute a sort of natural plastering in the sherry district of Spain (p. 32). One of the clearest bits of evidence on the importance of soil is the Cognac region of France where the more highly calcareous the zone the higher the price of the musts and wines. This may be a direct soil effect.

Rainfall

There is no evidence that rainfall or irrigation has any direct deleterious effect. But there is plenty of evidence that summer rainfall markedly increases the humidity and thus the susceptibility of the vine to fungus diseases. Control of the fungus diseases necessitate vineyard spraying with copper sulfate, etc. It also reduces sugar content according to Ferenczi (1955).

Rainfall also may reduce the temperature. In Hungary, Ferenczi (1955) showed a high positive correlation ($r = +0.8459$) between titratable acidity and amount of precipitation for the period May through September. The correlation for the period July through September was less ($r = +0.6680$). We believe that sunshine and temperature rather than the rainfall itself can account for these effects.

---

[1] And the air above them is also warmer.

Occasionally the soil may become so dry that vine growth ceases and maturation is delayed or never attained. Also where vines are over-cropped, if a severe moisture deficiency occurs during the latter stages of ripening, when the leaves are still functional, the leaves may withdraw water from the fruit and cause severe shriveling. Such grapes produce very poor wines.

Other Factors

Dehydrating winds off the Sahara early in the season may prevent normal ripening of grapes in Madeira, Spain, and Sicily. Late in the season the grapes may shrivel and raisin on the vine. Hail not only reduces or damages the crop but may defoliate the vine and thus delay maturity of the remaining fruit. Late spring frosts reduce the crop and, if the season is otherwise good, may result in better ripening and enhanced quality. There have been various reports that the rootstock might influence the composition (and hence the quality) of the fruit of the scion. Bénard *et al.* (1963) used nine stocks for Grenache. The analytical differences on the musts and wines were small except that musts of fruit on Couderc 161–49 and Teléki 5BB seemed to be less in ash, alkalinity of ash and potassium and higher in iron. We are not convinced of the statistical significance of the results.

VARIETY

There are perhaps 5000 named varieties of *V. vinifera* and 2000 of *V. labrusca* and other native species. In addition there are a very large number of hybrids between *V. vinifera* and American species—the so-called "direct producers."

Grapes may be white, green, pink, red, or purple in color when ripe. They may have small or large fruit and clusters. The shape of their berries, clusters, and leaves vary. They may ripen very early to very late. The texture may be pulpy and solid or soft and liquid. When mature their sugar content may be low or high and likewise the titratable acidity may normally be small or large—even under favorable climatic conditions. The effect of temperature and other environmental factors on the composition of these many varieties is also marked. They are, moreover, subject to insect and disease to varying degrees. They respond differently to pruning. And there are complex interrelations between these various influences.

Except for California the main varieties planted in the vineyard districts of the world have been mentioned elsewhere in the text. California grape acreages are given in Table 18. This discussion will therefore be primarily concerned with varietal recommendations for California conditions. The

TABLE 18

CALIFORNIA GRAPE ACREAGE BY•CLASSES AND VARIETIES 1944, 1959, AND 1969[1]
Total Acreage

Class and Variety	1944	1959	1969	1971
Raisin varieties	253,553	242,297	253,683	247,513
Thompson Seedless	182,194	215,054	235,543	232,146
Table varieties	82,619	86,565	75,867	71,109
Wine varieties	174,194	125,671	147,400	179,854
Alicante Bouschet	25,606	10,299	7,413	6,745
Barbera	...	...	2,112	7,529
Burger	2,987	2,992	2,310	2,208
Burgundy[2]	...	707	...	...
Cabernet Sauvignon	...	660	5,098	7,616
Carignane	32,051	25,257	26,963	27,241
Chardonnay	...	...	2,457	3,057
Chenin blanc[3]	...	621	3,868	8,689
Colombar	1,480	617	...	...
Early Burgundy	...	...	801	736
Emerald Riesling	...	...	...	1,262
French Colombard	...	1,422	8,574	18,660
Gamay	...	757	1,640	1,627
Gamay Beaujolais	...	...	969	2,046
Gewürztraminer	...	...	591	732
Gray Riesling	...	...	754	949
Grenache	4,229	11,761	12,995	13,530
Mataro	7,692	3,777	2,003	1,855
Mission	10,906	8,388	6,991	6,490
Palomino	5,072	9,171	7,079	6,504
Pedro Ximenes	...	652	513	501
Petite Sirah	7,721	4,710	4,332	5,604
Pinot blanc	...	...	385	726
Pinot noir	...	...	2,715	3,446
Royalty	...	...	2,007	2,158
Rubired	...	...	2,033	2,438
Ruby Cabernet	...	...	1,656	4,753
St. Émilion	...	...	...	964
Salvador	...	2,177	2,002	2,067
Sauvignon blanc[4]	...	2,011	1,130	1,594
Sauvignon vert	...	...	1,120	909
Sémillon	...	1,272	1,224	1,828
Sylvaner[5]	574	1,331	1,195	1,248
Tinta Madeira	...	...	486	644
Valdepenas	...	919	1,853	2,006
White Riesling	...	...	1,586	1,856
Zinfandel	50,349	25,572	21,704	21,424
Other whites	8,780	2,051	2,611	}8,212
Other reds	16,747	7,016	5,737	

[1] Source: California Crop and Livestock Reporting Service (1945, 1960, 1970, 1971).
[2] Includes Early Burgundy, Crabb's Black Burgundy, Mondeuse, Portuguese Blue and Refosco, except Early Burgundy listed separately in 1969 and 1971.
[3] Includes Pinot blanc, White Pinot, Pinot de la Loire, White Zinfandel and Pinot vrai, except Pinot blanc listed separately in 1969 and 1971.
[4] Includes Sauvignon vert, except in 1969 and 1971.
[5] Includes White and other Rieslings, except White Riesling listed separately in 1969 and 1971.

recommendations generally follow those of the California Agricultural Experiment Station with some modifications based on the authors' personal predilections. While these recommendations apply primarily to California conditions they have some validity for other regions of similar climatic conditions.

The difficulties of estimating the grape acreage by varieties are emphasized by the reports of Winkler (1964) and Henderson et al. (1965). Winkler's estimates were made on the basis of a special survey while those of Henderson and his colleagues are from the official planting records of the California Crop Reporting Service. In 1964 Winkler estimated 879 bearing acres of Cabernet Sauvignon and 538 non-bearing in the central coast counties. The "official" figures of Henderson et al. showed 834 bearing acres of Cabernet Sauvignon in the same plus other counties of California in 1964.

Statewide the largest increases in bearing wine grape varieties for the period 1952–1963 according to Winkler were for Chardonnay (1070 per cent), Chenin blanc (258), Emerald Riesling (190), Pinot blanc (107), Sauvignon blanc (35), Sylvaner (148), White Riesling (77), Cabernet Sauvignon (133), Gamay (244), Grignolino (11), and Pinot noir (245). These figures indicate the increasing interest in the planting of fine wine grapes during this period. The only losses were for Folle Blnache (32 per cent, because of its susceptibility to fungus attack?), Ruby Cabernet (6) and Sémillon (9). See Table 18 for other changes.

The change in prospects for varietal plantings between 1952 and 1965 are well illustrated by Olmo's (1955) prediction. Burger and Sauvignon vert were both predicted to increase in acreage. Neither has fulfilled this promise.

White Table Wines

At the present time it is believed that the following considerations should be particularly considered in the selection of varieties for these types of wines. First is the varietal character. Varieties with distinctive varietal character are needed for wines which are to be named after the variety. However, more neutral flavored wines may be needed for sparkling wine stock.

Second is the composition under the climatic conditions of the region. Varieties which regularly ripen with sufficient titratable acidity and a fairly low pH are to be preferred; see page 91. Resistance to sunburn and insects and disease is also important.

Third is production. No variety which is incapable of high production should be grown in the regions where standard wines are produced (regions IV and V particularly) and all other factors being equal production is an important economic factor in the selection of a suitable variety for all regions.

Minor factors such as convenience of pruning and harvesting, ease of training, rootstock compatibility, etc. also need to be considered.

Resistance to darkening of color, both of the must and of the wine is also desired. Berg and Akiyoshi (1956) have noted this deficiency in a number of varieties. Ease of separation of the juice from the skins is, of course, important.

The recommendations by region are given in Table 19. The production

TABLE 19

RECOMMENDED VARIETIES FOR WHITE TABLE WINE PRODUCTION IN CALIFORNIA

Variety	Produc-tion[1]	Ripens[2]	Flavor[3]	Region[4]		
				I and II	III and IV	V
	Tons/ Acre					
Aligoté	M	M	S	QR	QR	NR
Chardonnay	L	E	D	HR	NR	NR
Chenin blanc	M+	M−	N+	R	QR	NR
Emerald Riesling	H	M−	D−	NR	QR	QR
Folle blanche	M−	L	S	QR	QR	NR
Flora	M+	M	D−	QR	NR	NR
French Colombard	H	E+	D−	QR	R	HR
Gewürztraminer	L	E	D+	R	NR	NR
Red Veltliner	M	L	N	QR	QR	NR
Sauvignon blanc	M	M	D	HR	QR	NR
Sémillon	M+	M	D−	HR	R	NR
Sylvaner	M	E	S	R	QR	NR
White Riesling	M−	M−	D−	HR	NR	NR

[1] L for 1 to 3; M for 4 to 6; H for over 6.
[2] E for early, M for mid-season, L for late.
[3] N for neutral, S for slightly distinctive, and D for distinctive.
[4] HR is highly recommended, R for recommended, QR for qualified recommendation, and NR for not recommended.
Adapted from Amerine and Winkler (1963).

estimates are for good soil and climatic conditions but are only approximate. Lower production can be anticipated on shallow soils, particularly on hillside vineyards.

A new hybrid for white table wine production has been released for trial by Olmo (1959). The Flora is the result of a Sémillon-Gewürztraminer cross. The production is better than that of Gewürztraminer and it is said to have a similar if less aromatic aroma.

Red Table Wines

For these wines varietal character, composition and production are likewise important. The color should not only be adequate but stable. Salvador and Alicante Bouschet are examples of varieties of high but unstable color. Resistance to sunburn and mold is also important. Petite Sirah is an example of a variety which fails in some regions owing to excessive sunburn. It and Pinot St. George are varieties which mold easily when the humidity is high owing to early rains.

A new variety produced by Olmo (1959) is the Calzin, a cross between Zinfandel and Refosco. It is intended as a substitute for the irregular-ripening, mold-sensitive Zinfandel. Production is good. The main problem is its excessively high tannin and only moderate color.

TABLE 20

RECOMMENDED VARIETIES FOR RED AND PINK TABLE WINE PRODUCTION IN CALIFORNIA

Variety	Production[1]	Ripens[2]	Flavor[3]	Region[4]		
				I and II	III and IV	V
	Tons/Acre					
Barbera	L+	E	S	NR	QR	QR
Cabernet Sauvignon[5]	M−	L	D	HR	QR	NR
Carignane	H	L	S	NR	R	QR
Gamay[6]	H	L	N+	QR	NR	NR
Grenache	M[7]	M	N+	QR	QR	NR
Petite Sirah	M+	M	S	R	NR	NR
Pinot noir	L	E	D	R	NR	NR
Ruby Cabernet	M[7]	M	D	NR	R	QR
Refosco (Mondeuse)	M	M−	N	QR	QR	NR
Zinfandel	M	M	D	R	NR	NR

[1] L for 1 to 3, M for 4 to 6, H for over 6.
[2] E for early, M for mid-season, L for late.
[3] N for neutral, S for slightly distinctive, and D for distinctive.
[4] HR for highly recommended, R for recommended, QR for qualified recommendation, and NR for not recommended.
[5] In spite of statements of various amateurs there is an abundance of evidence that the Cabernet Sauvignon should be preferred to the Cabernet franc.
[6] The Gamay, of the Napa Valley; the Gamay Beujolais now appears to us to be a Pinot as far as aroma is concerned.
[7] Production is very variable (from M to H depending on region, season, clone, etc.).
Adapted from Amerine and Winkler (1963).

The recommendations by region are given in Table 20. Again the production estimates are only approximate.

Pink or Rosé Wines

Many of the varieties recommended for red table wines can also be used for pink wines if pressed off the skins soon enough. Thus both Cabernet and Pinot noir rosé wines have been produced. The early pressing reduces their varietal character. However, a strong varietal character is not at present considered an important requirement for this type of wine. Zinfandel has been recommended for rosé production in order to reduce its tendency to high alcohol (from its shrivelled berries). Petite Sirah might also be so used were it not that its orange-pink color is not desirable.

Aleatico has been used for producing muscat-flavored sweet table wines. It must be carefully handled since it ripens early and sunburns easily. Furthermore, its acidity is low. The most important rosé wines produced in the state are Grenache and Gamay. The Grenache rosé is very popular but we find some of its wines too flat and others to have a bitter aftertaste. The Gamay in the Napa Valley does very well in most years but may not ripen in the cooler seasons. It has a fruity character which is what a rosé should have.

Dessert Wines

The requirements listed on p. 91 should be carefully considered in selecting varieties for dessert wines. The varietal flavor is particularly important for muscat-flavored wines. Production is also essential for the competitive standard wines. Freedom from mold is likely to be considered more and more important as sanitation inspection systems are used. The selection of varieties with a higher natural acidity would do much to improve the quality of our California dessert wines.

Two new hybrids for dessert wines have been developed and released for trial by Olmo (1959). Rubired is a variety of high color, a good producer, is partially mildew tolerant and is recommended for blending. Royalty is a variety of good color and flavor. If the colors prove stable these varieties should be of considerable utility to the California dessert wine industry. The recommendations by regions are given in Table 21.

TABLE 21

RECOMMENDED VARIETIES FOR DESSERT WINE PRODUCTION IN CALIFORNIA

				Region[4]		
Variety	Production[1]	Ripens[2]	Flavor[3]	I and II	III and IV	V
	Tons/Acre					
Carignane	H	L	S⁻	NR	R	R
Grenache	M[5]	M	S⁻	NR	QR	R
Grillo	H	M⁻	N	NR	QR	R
Mission	H	L	N	NR	NR	R
Muscat Canelli[5]	L⁺	E	D	QR	QR	QR
Muscat of Alexandria	M	L	D	NR	NR	R
Palomino	H⁻	L	N	NR	NR	R
Royalty	H	M	S	NR	QR	QR
Rubired	H	M	S	NR	QR	QR
Souzão	M	M	S	NR	QR	R
Tinta Madeira	M	M⁻	D⁻	NR	QR	R

[1] L for 1 to 3, M for 4 to 6, H for over 6.
[2] E for early, M for mid-season, L for late.
[3] N for neutral, S for slightly distinctive, and D for distinctive.
[4] HR for highly recommended, R for recommended, QR for qualified recommendation, and NR for no recommended.
[5] Production variable (depending on region, season, clone, etc.).
Adapted from Amerine and Winkler (1963).

Many table or raisin grapes, particularly the Thompson Seedless, are delivered to California wineries each year. Much of this fruit is used for the production of distilling material. When used for wine certain precautions should be employed. If intended for table wines the fruit should be harvested early in the season while the sugar-acid relationship is as favorable as possible. Also when intended as a base for light-colored flavored wines early harvesting is desirable. For dessert wines later harvesting is permissible but not so late as to allow the acidity to fall too low. Another aspect of selection of varieties has been emphasized by Anon (1959), namely that of the present and prospective types of sales. As applied to California the demand for dessert wines has been slipping.

If urban development in rural vineyard areas continues in the coast counties future grape plantings will have to be made in new areas in the coast counties or in the central valley. Since these grapes are mainly varieties for table wines this means that new varieties suitable for the production of such wines will have to be developed for central valley planting.

BIBLIOGRAPHY

AMERINE, M. A. 1951. The acids of California grapes and wines. II. Malic acid. Food Technol. 5, 13–16.

AMERINE, M. A. 1954. Composition of wines. I. Organic constituents. Advances in Food Research 5, 353–510.

AMERINE, M. A. 1956. The maturation of wine grapes. Wines and Vines 37, No. 10, 27–30, 32, 34–36; No. 11, 53–55.

AMERINE, M. A. 1958. Composition of wines. II. Inorganic constituents. Advances in Food Research 8, 133–224.

AMERINE, M. A., and BAILEY, C. B. 1959. Carbohydrate content of various parts of the grape cluster. Am. J. Enol. Vitic. 10, 196–198.

AMERINE, M. A., and JOSLYN, M. A. 1951. Table Wines. The Technology of Their Production in California. University of California Press, Berkeley and Los Angeles.

AMERINE, M. A. and ROESSLER, E. B. 1958A. Methods of determining field maturity of grapes. Am. J. Enol. 9, 37–40.

AMERINE, M. A. and ROESSLER, E. B. 1958B. Field testing of grape maturity. Hilgardia 28, 93–114.

AMERINE, M. A., and ROOT, G. A. 1960. Carbohydrate content of various parts of the grape cluster. II. Am. J. Enol. Vitic. 11, 137–139.

AMERINE, M. A., and THOUKIS, G. 1958. The glucose-fructose ratio of California grapes. Vitis 1, 224–229.

AMERINE, M. A., and WINKLER, A. J. 1940. Maturity studies with California grapes. I. The Balling-acid ratio of wine grapes. Proc. Am. Soc. Hort. Sci. 38, 379–387.

AMERINE, M. A., and WINKLER, A. J. 1942. ibid. II. The titratable acidity, pH, and organic acid content. Proc. Am. Soc. Hort. Sci. 40, 313–324.

AMERINE, M. A., and WINKLER, A. J. 1958. ibid. III. The acid content of grapes, leaves and stems. Proc. Am. Soc. Hort. Sci. 71, 199–206.

AMERINE, M. A., and WINKLER, A. J. 1963. California wine grapes: composition and quality of their musts and wines. Calif. Agr. Expt. Sta. Bull. 794.

ANDERSON, D. W., GUEFFROY, D. E., WEBB, A. D., and KEPNER, R. E. 1970. Identification of acetic acid as an acylating agent of anthocyanin pigments in grapes. Phytochem. 9, 1579–1583.

ANON. 1959. Wine grape varieties for new plantings. J. Agr. South Australia 62, 428–435.

BAKER, G. A., AMERINE, M. A., and ROESSLER, E. B. 1965. Characteristics of sequential measurements on grape juice must. Am. J. Enol. Vitic. 16, 21–28.

BARAUD, J. 1951. Une nouvelle méthode de dosage de l'acide ascorbique. Bull. soc. chim. France 18, 837–843.

BARAUD, J. 1953. Dosages simultanés de l'acide ascorbique, de l'acide dihydroxymaléique et de la réductone. Bull soc. chim. France 20, 521–525.

BATE-SMITH, E. C., and RIBÉREAU-GAYON, P. 1959. Leuco-anthocyanins in seeds. Qual. Plant. et Mat. Veg. 5, 189–199.

BAYER, E., BORN, F., and REUTHER, K. H. 1957. Über die Polyphenoloxydase der Trauben. Z. Lebensm.-Untersuch. u.-Forsch. 105, 77–81.

BAYONOVE, C., and CORDONNIER, R. 1970. Recherches sur l'arôme du muscat. I. II. Ann. Technol. Agr. 19, 72–93, 95–105.

BÉNARD, P., JOURET, C., and FLANZY, M. 1963. Influence des porte-greffes sur la composition minérale des vins. Ann. technol. agr. 12, 277–285.

BENVEGNIN, L., and CAPT, E. 1955. L'échantillonnage à la vigne pour l'évaluation de la maturité du raisin sur cep. Rev. romande agr., viticult. et arboricult. 11, 13–14.

BENVEGNIN, L., CAPT, E., and PIGUET, G. 1951. Traité de Vinification. Librairie Payot, Lausanne.

BERG, H. W. 1960. Grape classification by total soluble solids and total acidity. Wine Institute, San Francisco. Mimeo.

BERG, H. W., and AKIYOSHI, M. 1956. Some factors involved in browning of white wines. Am. J. Enol. 7, 1–7.

BERG, H. W., and MARSH, G. L. 1954. Sampling deliveries of grapes on a representative basis. Food Technol. 8, 104–108.

BERG, V. A. 1953. Redox potential in grapes during ripening (transl.) Vinodelie i Vinogradarstvo S.S.S.R. 13, No. 8, 13–15.

BIOL, H., and FOULONNEAU, C. 1961. Le paeonidol 3.5 diglucoside dans le genre Vitis. Ann. technol. agr. 10, 345–350.

BIOL, H., and MICHEL, A. 1961. Étude chromatographique des vins rouges issus de cépages réglementés. Ann. technol. agr. 10, 339–344.

BIOL, H., and MICHEL, A. 1962. Étude chromatographique des vins rouges issus de cépages reglémentés. Ann. technol. agr. 11, 245–247.

BLOUIN, J., and PEYNAUD, E. 1963. Présence constante des acides glucuronique et galacturonique dans les moûts de raisins et les vins. Comp. rend. 256, 4774–4775.

BOURDET, A., and HÉRARD, J. 1958. Influence de l'autolyse des levures sur la composition phosphorée et azotée des vins. Ann. technol. agr. 7, 177–202.

BROWN, W. L. 1940. The anthocyanin pigment of the Hunt Muscadine grape. J. Am. Chem. Soc. 62, 2808–2810.

BURGER, M., HEIN, L. W., TEPLY, L. J., DERSE, P. H. and DRIEGLER, C. H. 1956. Vitamin, mineral, and proximate composition of frozen fruits, juices, and vegetables. J. Agr. Food Chem. 4, 418–425.

BURKHARDT, R. 1965. Nachweis der p-Cumarylchinasäure in Weinen und das Verhalten der Depside bei der Kellerbehandlung. Rebe u. Wein, Serie A (Klosterneuberg) 15, 80–86.

CAILLEAU, R., and CHEVILLARD, L. 1949. Teneur de quelques vins français en aneurin, riboflavin, acid nicotinique et acid pantothenique. Ann. agron. N.S. 19, 277–281.

CALIFORNIA CROP AND LIVESTOCK REPORTING SERVICE. 1945. Acreage estimates California fruit and nut crops as of 1944. Sacramento.

CALIFORNIA CROP AND LIVESTOCK REPORTING SERVICE. 1960. California fruit and nut acreage . . . as of 1959. Sacramento.

CALIFORNIA CROP AND LIVESTOCK REPORTING SERVICE. 1971. California grape acreage . . . as of 1970, Sacramento. Also Special Survey, 1971.

CALIFORNIA DEPARTMENT OF AGRICULTURE. 1955. Order adopting regulations of the Department of Agriculture pertaining to determining average soluble solids of grapes for by-products. Filed June 24, 1955. Sacramento.

CANTARELLI, C., and PERI, C. 1964. The leucoanthocyanins in white grapes: their distribution, amount, fate during fermentation. Am. J. Enol. Vitic. 15, 146–153.

CAPPELLERI, G. 1965. Risultati di un'indiagine sulla ricerca della malvina in una serie di vini di Vitis vinifera. Atti accad. ital. vite e vino 17, 153–159.

CASTOR, J. G. B. 1953. The free amino acids of musts and wines. I and II. Food Research 18, 139–145, 146–151.

CASTOR, J. G. B. 1956. Amino acids in musts and wines, proline, serine and threonine. Am. J. Enol. 7, 19–25.

CHARPENTIÉ, Y. 1954. Contribution à l'Étude Biochimique des Facteurs de l'Acidité des Vins. Institut National de la Recherche Agronomique, Paris.

CHAUDARY, S. S., KEPNER, R. E., and WEBB, A. D. 1964. Identification of some volatile compounds in an extract of the grape, Vitis vinifera var. Sauvignon blanc. Am. J. Enol. Vitic. 15, 190–198.

COOKE, G. M. 1964. Effect of grape pulp upon soluble solids determination. Am. J. Enol. Vitic. 15, 11–16.

CORDONNIER, R. 1953. Le fer et ses origines dans le vin. Ann. technol. agr. 2, 1–14.

CORDONNIER, R. 1956. Recherches sur l'aromatisation et le parfum des vins doux naturels et des vins de liqueur. Ann. technol. agr. 5, 75–110.

CORNFORTH, J. W. 1939. The anthocyanin of Vitis hypoglauca F.v.M. J. Proc. Roy. Soc. N. S. Wales 72, 325–328.

CORRAO, A. 1963. Sul contenuto in manganese dei vini siciliani. Riv. viticolt. e enol. (Conegliano) 16, 343–349.

DECAU, J., and LAMAZOU-BETBEDER, M. 1964. Étude des effets de la fertilisation boratée des vignes carencées en bore sur la vinification et sur la composition minérale des vins. Ann. technol. agr. 13, 19–29.

DEEDS, F. 1949. Vitamin P properties in grapes and grape residue. Proc. Wine Technol. Conf., Davis 1949, 48–50.

DEIBNER, L. 1955. Évolution du potentiel d'oxydo-réduction au cours de la maturation des raisins. Ann. technol. agr. 4, 133–139.

DEIBNER, L., and BOURZEIX, M. 1960. Sur les incertitudes dans la différenciation des cépages Vitis vinifera et hybrides rouges par chromatographie sur papier de leurs substances colorantes. Comp. rend. acad. agr. France *46*, 968–971.

DEIBNER, L., and BOURZEIX, M. 1964. Recherches sur la détection des anthocyannes diglucosides dans les vins et les jus de raisin (par chromatographie sur papier et fluoriscopie de taches obtenues). Ann technol. agr. *13*, 263–282.

DEIBNER, L., BOURZEIX, M., and CABIBEL-HUGUES, M. 1964. La separation des anthocyannes diglucosides par chromatographie sur couche mince et leur dosage spectrophotometrique. Ann. technol. agr. *13*, 359–378.

DEIBNER, L., RIFAI, H. and FLANZY M. 1958. Substances colloïdales des jus de raisin; influence des différents modes de conservation sur leur stabilité. Ann. technol. agr. 7, 5–19.

DIMOTAKI-KOURAKOU, V. 1964. Absence d'acide glycuronique dans les vins. Ann. technol. agr. *13*, 301–308.

DUPUY, P., NORTZ, M., and PUISAIS, J. 1955. Le vin et queleques causes de son enrichissement en fer. Ann. technol. agr. *4*, 101–112.

DURMISHIDZE, S. V. 1955. Tannin Compounds and Anthocyanins of Grape Vines and Wines (transl.). Izd. Akad. Nauk S.S.S.R., Moscow.

DURMISHIDZE, S. V. 1958. Vitamin P in grapes and wine (transl.) Vinodelie i Vinogradarstvo S.S.S.R. *18*, No. 2, 15.

DURMISHIDZE, S. B. 1959. Tannins and anthocyans in the grape vine and wine. Am. J. Enol. Vitic. *10*, 20–28.

ESCHNAUER, H. 1959. Spurenelemente im Wein. Angew. Chem. *71*, 667–671.

FERENCZI, S. 1955. Effect of the amount of summer rainfall on the titratable acidity of wines (transl.) Növénytermelés *4*, 323–332.

FERRÉ, L. 1947. Sur maturation des raisins par la chaleur artificielle. Bull. office intern. vin. *20*, No. 196, 30–37.

FLANZY, M., and CAUSERET, J. 1954. Les vitamines du vin. Bull. office intern. vin *27*, No. 282, 20–24.

FLANZY, M., and DEIBNER, L. 1956. Sur la variation des teneurs en fer dans les vins, obtenus en présence ou en absence d'une terre ferrugineuse. Ann. technol. agr. *5*, 69–73.

FLANZY, C., and POUX, C. 1965. Les levures alcooliques dans les vins. Protéolyse, protéogénèse (III). Ann. technol. agr. *14*, 35–48.

FRANÇOT, P. 1945. Acide total et acidité réele des moûts et des vins de Champagne. Bull. office intern. vin *18*, No. 167/170, 114–118.

FRANÇOT, P. 1950. Champagne et qualité par le pressurage. Vigneron Champenois *71*, 250–255, 273–283, 342–351, 371–382, 406–416.

GARINO-CANINA, E. 1959. Italie. Bull. office intern. vin *32* (344), 3–15.

GATET, L., and GENEVOIS, L. 1940. Formation et évolution biologique des acides organiques dans le raisin Saint-Émilion à Cognac. Rev. viticult. *92*, 243–247, 259–263.

GENEVOIS, L. 1934. Recherche de la flavine dans les vins blancs. Bull. soc. chim. France *1*, 1503–1504.

GENEVOIS, L. 1938. Formation and évolution biologique des acides organiques dans les raisins. Rev. viticult. *88*, 103–110, 121–125, 382–386, 447–452.

GERBER, C. 1897. Recherches sur la maturation des fruits charnus. Ann. sci. nat. bot. 8 série *4*, 1–6.

GIRARD, A., and LINDET, L. 1898. Recherches sur le développement progresif de la grappe des raisin. Compt. rend. *126*, 1310–1315. (See also Bull. Min. Agr. *14*, 694–782. 1895).

GOLDBERG, H. E. 1965. Principles of refractometry. Wine Institute. Tech. Advis. Committee, Dec. 10. 1965.

GROHMANN, H., and GILBERT, E. 1959. Zum papierchromatographischen Nachwies von roten Hybridenfarbstoffen. Deut. Wein-Ztg. *95*, 346, 348.

HAAGEN-SMIT, A. J., HIROSAWA, F. N., and WANG, T. H. 1949. Chemical studies on grapes and wines. I. Volatile constituents of Zinfandel grapes (*Vitis vinifera*). Food Research *14*, 472–480.

HALL, A. P., BRINNER, L., AMERINE, M. A., and MORGAN, A. F. 1956. The B vitamin content of grapes, musts and wines. Food Research *21*, 362–371.

HENDERSON, W. W., KITTERMAN, J. M., and VANCE, F. H. 1965. California Grape Acreage by Varieties and Principal Counties as of 1964. Crop and Livestock Reporting Service, Sacramento.

HENNIG, K. 1944. Einige Fragen zur Bilanz der Sticksoffverbindungen im Most und Wein. Z. Lebensm.-Untersuch. u.-Forsch. *87*, 40–48. (*See also* Bull. office intern. vin *16*, No. 159, 82–86. 1943.)

HENNIG, K. 1955. Der Einfluss der Eiweiss- und Stickstoffbestandteile auf Wein. Deut. Wein- Ztg. *91*, 377–378, 380, 394, 396.

HENNIG, K. 1958. Das Chemische Bild des Mostes und Weines. Weinfach Kalender *1958*, 194–209.

HENNIG, K., and BURKHARDT, R. 1957. Über die Farb- und Gerbstoffe, sowie Polyphenole und ihre Veränderungen im Wein. Weinberg u. Keller *4*, 374–387.

HENNIG, K., and BURKHARDT, R. 1958. Der Nachweis phenolartiger Verbindungen und hydroaromatischer Oxycarbonsäuren in Traubenbestandteilen, Wein und weinähnlichen Getränken. Weinberg u. Keller *5*, 542–552, 593–600.

HENNIG, K., and BURKHARDT, R. 1960. Vorkommen und Nachweis von Quercitrin und Myricitrin in Trauben und Wein. Weinberg u. Keller *7*, 1–3.

HENNIG, K., and LAY, A. 1965. Die gewichtsanalytische Bestimmung der Oxalsäure im Most und Wein. Weinberg u. Keller *12*, 425–427.

HOLLEY, R. W., STOYLA, B., and HOLLEY, A. D. 1955. The identification of some volatile constituents of Concord grape juice. Food Research *20*, 326–331.

HRAZDINA, G., BORZELL, A. J., and ROBINSON, W. B. 1970. Studies on the stability of the anthocyanidin-3,5-diglucosides. Am. J. Enol. Viticult. *21*, No. 4, 201–204.

JAULMES, P., and NEY, M. 1960. Recherche des vins d'hybrides producteurs directs par chromatographie. Ann. fals. et fraudes *53*, 180–192.

JAULMES, P., HAMELLE, G., and ROQUES, J. 1960. Le plomb dans les moûts et les vins. Ann. technol. agr. *9*, 189–245.

KEPNER, R. E., and WEBB, A. D. 1956. Volatile aroma constituents of *Vitis rotundifolia* grapes. Am. J. Enol. *7*, 8–18.

KLIEWER, W. M. 1965. The sugars of grapevines. II. Identification and seasonal changes in the concentration of several trace sugars in *Vitis vinifera*. Am. J. Enol. Vitic. *16*, 168–178.

KLIEWER, W. M. 1966. The sugars and the organic acids of *Vitis vinifera*. Plant Physiol. *41*, 923–931.

Koch, J. 1963. Protéines des vins blancs. Traitements des précipitations protéiques par chauffage et à l'aide de la bentonite. Ann. technol. agr. *12* (numéro hors série 1), 297–311.

Koch, J. and Bretthauer, J. 1957. Zur Kenntnis der Eiweissstoffe des Weines. I. Chemische Zusammensetzung des Wärmetrubes kurzzeiterhitzter Weissweine und seine Beziehung zur Eiweisstrübung und zum Weineiweiss. II. Einfluss der Mosterhitzung auf die Eiweissstabilität der Weissweine. Z. Lebensm.-Untersuch. u.-Forsch. *106*, 272–280, 361–367.

Koch, J., and Sajak, E. 1959. A review and some studies on grape protein. Am. J. Enol. *10*, 114–123.

Laborde, J. 1907. Cours d'Oenologie. I. L. Mulo, Paris; Féret & Fils, Bordeaux.

Lafon-Lafourcade, S., and Guimberteau, G. 1962. Évolution des aminoacides au cours de la maturation des raisins. Vitis *3*, 130–135.

Lafon-Lafourcade, S., and Peynaud, E. 1958. L'acide *p*-aminobenzoïque, l'acide ptérolglutamique et la choline (vitamines du group B) dans les vins. Ann. technol. agr. *7*, 303–309.

Lafon-Lafourcade, S., and Peynaud, E. 1959. Dosage microbiologique des acids aminés des moûts de raisins et des vins. Vitis *2*, 45–56.

LaRosa, W. V. 1955. Maturity of grapes as related to pH at harvest. Am. J. Enol. *6*, 42–46.

LaRosa, W. V., and Nielsen, U. 1956. Effect of delay in harvesting on the composition of grapes. Am. J. Enol. *7*, 105–111.

Lavollay, J. and Sevestre, J. 1944. Le vin, considéré comme un alimente riche en vitamin P. Comp. rend. acad. agr. France *30*, 259–261.

Liuni, C. S., Calo, A., and Cappelleri, G. 1965. Contributo allo studio sui pigmenti antocianici de alcune specie del genere *Vitis* e di loro ibridi. Atti. accad. ital. vite e vino *17*, 161–167.

Lüthi, H., and Vetsch, U. 1953. Papierchromatographische Bestimmung von aminosäuren in Traubenmost and Wein. Deut. Weinbau Wissensch. Beihefte 7 (1), 3–6; (2), 33–54.

Markh, A. T., and Boneva, L. A. 1952. Investigation of the colloids of grape juice (transl.) Vinodelie i Vinogradarstvo S.S.S.R. *12*, No. 9, 14–17.

Markley, K. S., Sando, C. E., and Hendricks, S. B. 1938. Petroleum ether-soluble and ether-soluble constituents of grape pomace. J. Biol. Chem. *123*, 641–654.

Marteau, G., Scheur, J., and Olivieri, C. 1961. Cínétique de la libération enzymatique du méthanol au cours des transformations pectolytiques du raisin. Ann. technol. agr. *10*, 161–183.

Masquelier, J. 1958. The bactericidal action of certain phenolics of grapes and wine. *In* J. W. Fairbairn (Editor), The Pharmacology of Plant Phenolics, Academic Press, New York.

Mathews, J. 1958. The vitamin B complex content of bottled Swiss grape juices. Vitis *2*, 57–64.

Moreau, L., and Vinet, E. 1932. Rôle des matières de réserves de la vigne dans la mise en fruit du cépages et dans la véraison des raisins. Ann. agron. [N.S.] *2*, 363–374.

Nègre, E., and Cordonnier, R. 1953. Les origines du fer des vins. Comp. rend. acad. agr. France *39*, 52–56 (*See also* Prog. agr. et vitic. *139*, 160–164. 1953).

NELSON, K. E., and AMERINE, M. A. 1957. The use of *Botrytis cinerea* Pers. in the production of sweet table wines. Hilgardia *26*, 521–563.

OLMO, H. P. 1955. Our principal wine grape varieties present and future. Am. J. Enol. *5*, 18–20.

OLMO, H. P. 1959. New University of California wine grape varieties released in 1958. Wines and Vines *40*, No. 2, 28–29.

OUGH, C. S., and ALLEY, C. J. 1970. Effect of 'Thompson Seedless' grape maturity on wine composition and quality. Am. J. Enol. Viticult. *21*, 78–84.

OURNAC, A. 1952. Recherches sur la maturation artificielle du raisin. Ann. technol. agr. *1*, 85–105.

OURNAC, A. 1958. Évolution de la vitamine C dans le raisin conservé en frigorifique. Ann. technol. agr. *7*, 167–175.

PERLMAN, L., and MORGAN, A. F. 1945. Stability of B vitamins in grape juices and wines. Food Research *10*, 334–341.

PEYNAUD, E. 1947. Contribution à l'Étude Biochimique de la Maturation du Raisin et de la Composition des Vins. Imp. G. Sautai & Fils, Lille.

PEYNAUD, E. 1951. Sur les matières pectiques des fruits. Ind. agr. aliment. (Paris) *68*, 609–615.

PEYNAUD, E. 1952. Sur les matières pectiques des moûts de raisin et des vins. Ann. fals et fraudes *45*, 11–20.

PEYNAUD, E., and LAFOURCADE, S. 1955. L'acide pantothenique dans les raisins et dans les vins de Bordeaux. Ind. agr. aliment. (Paris) *72*, 575–580, 665–670.

PEYNAUD, E., and LAFOURCADE, S. 1956. Sur la teneur en biotine des raisins et des vins. Comp. rend. *234*, 1800–1803.

PEYNAUD, E., and LAFOURCADE, S. 1957. Les vitamines "B" dans le raisin et dans le vin. Congrès International Étude Scientifique Vin et Raisin, Bordeaux *1957*, 65–70.

PEYNAUD, E., and LAFOURCADE, S. 1958. Évolution des vitamines B dans le raisin. Qual. Plant. et Mat. Veg. *3/4*, 405–414.

PEYNAUD, E., and MAURIÉ, A. 1953A. Sur l'évolution de azote dans les différentes partes du raisin au cours de la maturation. Ann. technol. agr. *2*, 15–25.

PEYNAUD, E., and MAURIÉ, A. 1953B. Évolution des acides organiques dans le grain de raisin au cours de la maturation en 1951. Ann. technol. agr. *2*, 83–94.

PEYNAUD, E., and MAURIÉ, A. 1956. Nouvelles recherches sur la maturation du raisin dans le Bordelais, années 1952, 1953 et 1954. Ann. technol. agr. *4*, 111–139.

POULTON, J. 1970. Harvesting grapes for maximum profit. Wynboer *38*, 22–26.

POUX, C. 1950. Relation entre le poids des sucres et le poids de matière fraiche dans les raisins de différentes variétes de *Vitis vinifera* au moment de la maturité. Compt. rend. acad. agr. France *36*, 605–607.

POWERS, J. J., SOMAATMADJA, D., PRATT, D. E., and HAMDY, M. K. 1960. Anthocyanins. II. Action of anthocyanin pigments and related compounds on the growth of certain microorganisms. Food Technol. *14*, 626–632.

RADLER, F. 1957. Untersuchungen über den Gehalt der Moste einiger Rebensorten und -arten an den Vitaminen Pyridoxin, Pantothensäure, Nicotinsäure und Biotin. Vitis *1*, 96–108.

RADLER, F. 1965. The main constituents of the surface waxes of varieties and species of the genus *Vitis*. Am. J. Enol. Vitic. *16*, 159–167.

RANKINE, B. C., CELLIER, K. M., and BOEHM, E. W. 1962. Studies on grape variability and field sampling. Am. J. Enol Vitic. *13*, 58–72.

RENTSCHLER, H., and TANNER, H. 1955. Über den Nachweis von Gluconsäure in Weinen aus edelfaulen Trauben. Mitt. Gebiete Lebensm. u. Hyg. *46*, 200–208.

RIBÉREAU-GAYON, J. 1955. Maturation du raisin en fonction du climat et du cépage. Ann. nut. et aliment. *9*, A95–A112.

RIBÉREAU-GAYON, J., and PEYNAUD, E. 1958. Analyse et Contrôle des Vins. 2 ed. Béranger, Paris and Liège.

RIBÉREAU-GAYON, J., and RIBÉREAU-GAYON, P. 1958. The anthocyans and leucoanthocyans of grapes and wines. Am. J. Enol. Vitic. *9*, 1–9.

RIBÉREAU-GAYON, P. 1957. Le leucocyanidol dans les vins rouges. Compt. rend. acad. agr. France *43*, 197–199, 596–598.

RIBÉREAU-GAYON, P. 1958A. Les anthocyannes des raisins. Qual. Plant. et Mat. Veg. *3/4*, 491–499.

RIBÉREAU-GAYON, P. 1958B. Formation et évolution des anthocyannes au cours de la maturation du raisin. Compt. rend. *246*, 1271–1273.

RIBÉREAU-GAYON, P. 1964. Les composés phénoliques du raisin et du vin. I. II. III. Ann. physiol. veg. *6*, 119–147, 211–242, 259–282.

RIBÉREAU-GAYON, P., and SUDRAUD, P. 1957. Les anthocyannes de la baie dans le genre *Vitis*. Compt. rend. *244*, 233–235.

RICE, A. D. 1965. Identification of grape varieties. J. Assoc. Offic. Agr. Chem. *48*, 525–530.

ROBINSON, W. B. SHAULIS, N. J., and PEDERSON, C. S. 1949. Ripening studies of grapes grown in 1948 for juice manufacture. Fruit Prods. J. *29*, No. 2, 36–37, 54, 62.

ROESSLER, E. B., and AMERINE, M. A. 1958. Studies on grape sampling. Am. J. Enol. *9*, 139–145.

ROESSLER, E. B., and AMERINE, M. A. 1963. Further studies on field sampling of wine grapes. Am. J. Enol. Vitic. *14*, 144–147.

SASTRY, L. V. I., and TISCHER, R. G. 1952. Behavior of the anthocyanin pigments in Concord grapes during heat processing and storage. Food Technol. *6*, 82–86. (*See also ibid 6*, 264–268.)

SCHANDERL, H. 1959. Die Mikrobiologie des Mostes und Weines. Eugen Ulmer, Stuttgart.

SINGLETON, V. L. and ESAU P. 1969. Phenolic Substances in Grapes and Wine, and Their Significance. Supplement 1, Advan. Food Res. Academic Press, New York and London.

SISAKYAN, N. M., and MARUTYAN, S. A. 1948. Sakhara vinogradnoi yagody (Sugars of grape berries). Biokhemiya Vinodeliya *2*, 56–68.

SMITH, M. B., and OLMO, H. P. 1944. The pantothenic acid and riboflavin in the fresh juice of diploid and tetraploid grapes. Am. J. Bot. *31*, 240–241.

SMITH, R. M., and LUH, B. S. 1965. Anthocyanin pigments of the hybrid grape variety Rubired. J. Food Sci. *30*, 995–1005.

SOLMS, J., BÜCKI, W., and DEUEL, H. 1952. Untersuchungen über den Pektingehalt einiger Traubenmoste. Mitt. Gebiete Lebensm. u. Hyg. *43*, 303–307.

SOMAATMADJA, D., POWERS, J. J., and WHEELER, R. 1965. Action of leucoanthocyanins of Cabernet grapes on reproduction and respiration of certain bacteria. Am. J. Enol. Vitic. *16*, 54–61.

STEVENS, K. L., LEE, A. MCFADDEN, W. H., and TERANISHI, R. 1965. Volatiles from grapes. I. Some volatiles from Concord grapes. J. Food Sci. *30*, 1006–1007.

SU, C. T., and SINGLETON, V. L. 1969. Identification of three flavan-3-ols from grapes. Phytochem. *8*, 1553–1558.

SZABO, J., and RAKCSÁNYI, L. 1937. Das Mengenverhältnis der Dextrose und der Lävulose in Weintrauben, im Mosten und im Wein. 5th Cong. intern. tech. chem. agr. *1*, 936–939. (*See also* Magyar Ampelol. Evkonyv. *9*, 346–361. 1935.) .

TANNER, H. and RENTSCHLER. A. H. 1956. Über Polyphenole der Kernobst- und Traubensäfte. Fruchsaftind. *1*, 231–245.

TEPLY, L. J., STRONG, F. M., and ELVEHJEM, C. A. 1942. Distribution of nicotinic acid in foods. J. Nutrition *32*, 417–423.

TERCELJ, F. 1965. Étude des composés azotés du vin. Ann. technol. agr. *14*. 307–319.

TSUCHIYA, K. 1951. Changes in the chemical composition of grapes during maturation for several leading varieties (transl.). J. Hort. Assoc. Japan *20*, 120–125.

UNVERZAGT. 1954. Reifemessungen bei verschiedenen Traubenmosten. Deut. Wein-Ztg. *90*, 374–376.

USSEGLIO-TOMASSET, L. 1959. L'evoluzione delle sostanze colloidali dal mosto al vino. Ann. sper. agrar. (Rome) *13*, 375–404.

VISINTINI-ROUMANIN, M. 1967. Richerche sui pigmenti antocianici nella vite e nel vino. IV. L'ossidazione della malvina. Riv. viticolt. e enol. (Conegliano) *20*, 79–88.

VITTE, G., and GUICHARD, G. 1955. Évolution des acides organiques de la vigne. Rev. gen. bot. *62*, 622–628.

WEBB, A. D. 1964. Anthocyanins of grapes. *In* Runeckles, V.C. Phenolics in Normal and Diseased Fruits and Vegetables. Plant Phenolics Group of North America, Montreal.

WEBB, A. D., and KEPNER, R. E. 1957. Some volatile aroma constituents of *Vitis vinifera* var. Muscat of Alexandria. Food Research *22*, 384–395.

WEURMAN, C., and DE ROOIJ, C. 1958. Chlorogenic acid isomers in "Black Alicante" grapes. Chem. and Ind. *1958*, 72.

WINKLER, A. J. 1936. Temperature and varietal interrelations in Central Western Europe and Algeria. Wines and Vines *17*, No. 2, 4–5.

WINKLER, A. J. 1954. Effects of overcropping. Am. J. Enol. *5*, 4–12.

WINKLER, A. J. 1964. Varietal wine grapes in the Central Coast Counties of California. Am. J. Enol. Vitic. *15*, 204–205.

WINKLER, A. J., and AMERINE, M. A. 1937. What climate does. Wine Review *5*, No. 6, 9–11; No. 7, 9–11, 16.

WINKLER, A. J., and AMERINE, M. A. 1938. Color in California wines. I and II. Food Research *3*, 429–447.

WINKLER, A. J., and WILLIAMS, W. O. 1936. The effect of seed development on the growth of grapes. Proc. Am. Soc. Hort. Sci. *33*, 430–434

ZAMORANI, A., and PIFFERI, P. G. 1964. Contributo alla conoscenza della sostanza colorante dei vini. Riv. viticolt. e enol. (Conegliano) *17*, 85–93.

ZIEMELIS, G., and PICKERING, J. 1969. Precipitation of flavanols in dry red table wine. Chem. Ind. *1969*, 1781–1782.

ZUBECKIS, E. 1964. Ascorbic acid in Veerport grape during ripening and processing. Rept. Hort. Expt. Sta. and Prod. Lab. Ontario *1964*, 114–116.

CHAPTER 3

American Wine Types and Their Composition

The nomenclature of American wine types is far from standardized. This is not surprising. The industry is comparatively young. For the most part traditional European wine type names have been adopted as a guide for consumers. In the pre-Prohibition era specific type names such as Margaux or even Château Yquem (seldom correctly as d'Yquem) were used. The Federal Alcohol Administration Act of 1925 (U. S. FAA 1937) and particularly its Regulations No. 4 (U. S. Treasury Department 1961) define four types of wines which may be produced in this country for interstate commerce: grape types (i.e., varietal), generic (sake and vermouth), semigeneric (see p. 738), and non-generic, i.e., geographic (see pp. 738–739).

GENERIC TYPES

Only sake and vermouth have been so classed. Sake is defined as a product "produced from rice in accordance with the commonly accepted method of manufacture of such product."

Vermouth

Vermouth production is described in Chapter 13. It is defined in the regulations simply as a "type of aperitif wine compounded from grape wine, having the taste, aroma, and characteristics generally attributed to vermouth." Three types are commonly produced in this country: dry, light dry, and sweet. California dry vermouth is described by the recommended specifications of the Wine Institute (1971) as a herb-flavored, straw to light golden colored wine of less than 4 per cent sugar and with an alcohol content of over 15 per cent. No single herb odor should be easily recognizable and excessive bitterness is said to be objectionable. In our experience there has been a tendency to reduce the vermouth character too much in many American dry vermouths. This is undoubtedly due to the extensive use of dry vermouth as an ingredient of the Martini cocktail. Bartenders naturally demand a vermouth with a gin color so that as much as possible of the cheaper vermouth can be used in the mixture. As a result the type is often barely recognizable as vermouth and loses its desirability as a "straight" drink. It would be better to keep "dry" vermouth as an aged beverage type with adequate vermouth character and a light amber color and allow the light dry type to fill cocktail needs.

Light dry vermouth has been recognized for some years now as a herb-flavored appetizer wine, though the amount of herb character is very small in some. It was developed specifically for the cocktail trade and most of those on the market are very light in color. Some are stronger than others in vermouth character. In line with the suggestion made above this type should have only a slight vermouth character and very moderate bitterness. The sugar content should not be over four per cent.

Sweet vermouth is defined by the Wine Institute (1971) as an appetizer wine and, in spite of its high sugar content much sweet vermouth is used as an appetizer, especially in Europe. It should be amber to dark amber in color (many have a slight-reddish hue) and a muscat aroma is desirable, but a baked character is not. The recommended Balling is 8° to 14°. This indicates a sugar content of about 12 to 18 per cent. The herb character must be pronounced but the characteristics of no single herb should predominate.

SEMIGENERIC TYPES

These include the 16 specific examples given in federal regulations (see p. 738). These can be classified as white or red table, sparkling, or dessert types.

White Table

Chablis, moselle, rhine (syn. hock), sauterne and white chianti[1] are geographical names that are now considered semigeneric types in this country. They must, however, be used on the label only in conjunction with an appropriate appellation of origin disclosing the actual place of production of the wine. Thus in practice these wines must be labeled "American" chablis, "California" moselle, "Napa" sauterne, etc.

The Wine Institute (1971) recommendations are that California chablis be light- to medium-straw in color, light to medium in body, medium acidity, fruity, well-balanced, and have a good bottle bouquet. These specifications cover a wide range of wine types and do not, in our opinion describe a type which can be distinguished from California sauterne, rhine, or white chianti. This could be rectified by abandoning all three type names and selling the wines as California dry white table wine. The industry is obviously economically and psychologically fearful of such a development. If California chablis is to be different from the other dry white semigeneric types, we would recommend that the industry consider keeping it low in pH (below 3.21), high in acidity (0.65 per cent minimum), very dry (below 0.2 per cent sugar), very light in color, and fresh

---

[1] The regulations list only chianti but this may, presumably, mean white or red.

and fruity, with not over 11.5 per cent alcohol. A maximum free sulfur dioxide content should be set at a low figure—perhaps 15 to 25 p.p.m. The requirement of good bottle age was obviously used to insure that the sulfur dioxide content was not too high. A very low sulfur dioxide content requirement would be more rational and, in fact, more in line with the desire to make this a fresh and fruity type. The crux of this and later similar suggestions is the low maximum alcohol content. This is partially to insure that the wine would be as fresh and fruity as possible but also to make a distinguishable difference between one type and another.

California rhine or Riesling is defined as a pale to medium straw colored wine of medium body and medium to tart acidity. It should be fresh and fruity and have good bottle age. Again the recommendations cover a wide range and overlap those of other types. Frankly, we believe rhine should replace the varietal appellation Riesling unless Riesling clearly represents a varietal type. Moreover, we see no easy method for producing a non-varietal rhine type in between California chablis and California sauterne.

California Riesling could be similar to chablis in color, acidity and pH but be in a more reduced condition (minimum free sulfur dioxide of 25 p.p.m. as against a maximum of 25 p.p.m. for chablis). It might also be slightly sweet (0.5 to 3 per cent sugar as against not more than 0.2 per cent for chablis).

Sauterne, and medium sauterne are defined in the Wine Institute (1971) specifications. The Federal Alcohol Administration Act specifies only sauterne and haut sauterne (a miserable appellation with no legal status in France and which, fortunately, has been little used here).

California sauterne is defined as a straw to light golden colored wine of full body and without noticeable high acidity. It should have balance and softness on the palate and a good bottle bouquet. Again there is a considerable area of overlapping with other semigeneric types.

Here we would recommend that color, acidity, and alcohol content be used to differentiate the type from California chablis. The color should be a full yellow, the acidity moderate (maximum 0.65 per cent), the alcohol not *less* than 11.5 per cent and the sugar below 0.2 per cent.

The Wine Institute recommendation for California medium sauterne is the same as for dry sauterne except that the sugar content must be between 0.5 and 3 per cent and a slight muscat aroma is permitted. If the modifications above of color, acidity and alcohol content are employed, this would appear to us to be a useful and distinctive type of wine.

California white chianti is no longer defined in the Wine Institute (1971) recommendations and certainly there is little justification or place for the type.

Red Table

Burgundy and chianti are geographical names that are now considered semigeneric in this country. As sold in the American market the eastern wines all have a pronounced labrusca character which is entirely foreign to the original wine types. We have no suggestions therefore for defining these semigeneric types when they have a labrusca character, except that they be abandoned.

However, it is no secret that California claret, burgundy, and chianti as sold on the American market, are not distinguishable types of wines. Possibly for a given firm there may be such a distinction, but as between wineries one man's claret is likely to be another man's burgundy. This is immediately obvious from the recommendations of the Wine Institute (1971). California claret is a tart, light to medium red-colored wine of light or medium body. California burgundy is a full-bodied, medium to deep red-colored wine of balance and softness on the palate derived from proper aging. California chianti is a full-bodied, medium-red colored wine of medium tartness, fruity flavor and a moderately aged, well-balanced character. Certainly the prescribed body, color, or tartness are not sufficiently different for the average or even expert consumer to differentiate the types.

Many suggestions have been made for distinguishing between these types. The most rational one of making them conform to some varietal origin has not been accepted by the California wine industry. Among the varietal suggestions have been those to include some Cabernet in claret and some Pinot noir in the burgundy. Lack of these varieties has undoubtedly led to rejection of this proposal. In only a few cases did producers follow this procedure. The alternative varietal suggestion that California claret contain some Zinfandel character and our burgundy some Petite Sirah has likewise been rejected, although individual producers again have followed this concept more or less closely. Pre-prohibition practice apparently was to include some Zinfandel in many clarets but never in burgundy.

In our opinion a color, alcohol, acidity differentiation is the only one that appears practicable at present. California claret would then have a light red color and contain at least 0.65 per cent acidity and *not over* 11.5 per cent alcohol. California burgundy would be a medium to dark red colored wine of less than 0.65 per cent acidity and *over* 11.5 per cent alcohol. We see no need for the type name California chianti and, fortunately, it is seldom employed. The concept of chianti as a rough high-tannin wine has long since disappeared both here and in Italy. We have seen no indication since the first edition of this book that this suggestion has met with any more favor than the previous suggestions.

Sparkling

Champagne is the only sparkling type recognized as being a semigeneric appellation of geographical region. Owing to the production of sparkling wines by two procedures (see Chapter 11), two specifications are given by Wine Institute (1971). California champagne (bottle fermented) is defined as a pale to straw-colored sparkling wine of good acidity and body with a fresh, fruity, well-balanced flavor and a distinctive bottle bouquet. We suggest a minimum acidity of 0.75 per cent to insure the fresh fruity flavor.

There are no generally accepted industry standards for sugar content. To fill this need we recommend that *brut* or *nature* champagnes contain less than 1.5 per cent sugar, that *extra dry* or *extra sec* wines have 1.5 to 3.5 per cent sugar, that *dry* or *sec* wines have 3.5 to 5.0 per cent, and *sweet* or *doux* wines have over 5 per cent. The same limits would apply to tank-fermented sparkling wines. For judgings, the Wine Institute (1971) classifies wines as group 1 (less than 1.5 per cent sugar), group 2 (1.5 to 2.5 per cent), and group 3 (over 2.5 per cent).

The requirement that bottle-fermented sparkling wines have a distinctive bottle bouquet is a good one but with the introduction of the transfer system (p. 470) it will be more and more difficult to attain. The requirement that bottle-fermented wines be kept in the bottle for at least nine months to one year *before* disgorging, as presently required in France, is a plausible restriction. To improve these types some limitation in maximum sulfur dioxide content should be imposed. Bottle-fermented champagne should be essentially free of free sulfur dioxide and tank-fermented should not contain over 10 p.p.m. free, in our opinion. The federal requirement that American (California) champagne should possess the taste, aroma, and other characteristics attributed to Champagne as made in the Champagne district of France is interesting as it would imply some sort of varietal limitation on the grapes to be used for champagne in this country. When applied to labrusca-flavored eastern United States sparkling wines, the requirement is even less rational or enforceable.

Pink champagne is not mentioned in the semigeneric terms of the federal regulations but presumably is approved with the word champagne. California pink champagne is defined as a wine of "true" pink color, fruity, fresh, tart, well-balanced, and light-bodied and with over 1.5 per cent reducing sugar. How a wine of over 1.5 per cent reducing sugar can be light-bodied is not clear to us. The tart requirement might be strengthened by setting a minimum per cent total acidity, perhaps as high as 0.75 per cent. The "true" pink color is apparently designed to prevent blending of red and white wines which often gives a purplish pink color. It eliminates, however, Petite Sirah, Pinot noir and Grenache rosé wines—all of which have an orange hue. This we think undesirable. A specific color specification which would include orange-pink (p. 711) might prove more useful.

Sparkling burgundy (synonym champagne rouge) legally includes both bottle- and tank-fermented wine. The Wine Institute (1971) recommendation is that these shall include both light and heavy bodied and light and dark colored wines. They should have a good acidity and be fruity, smooth, well-balanced, and have a distinctive bottle bouquet and over 1.5 per cent sugar. The requirement that tank-fermented wine have a distinctive bottle bouquet is surely wishful thinking.

Dessert

Geographical appellations which are considered to be semigeneric in this country include angelica, malaga, marsala, madeira, port, sherry, and tokay.

If angelica is a wine of geographical origin, it apparently originated in this state and hence should have been classified as a wine entitled to an appellation of origin. The California wine industry has never acted to protect this appellation—the only typical American generic appellation for a wine of widespread consumer acceptance. At any rate, it is a smooth, fruity-flavored wine of full body[2] and light to dark amber. A minimum Balling of 7° is prescribed by the Wine Institute (1971) specifications and California regulations fix the minimum total acidity at 0.25 per cent and an alcohol content in the range 18.0 to 21.0 per cent. Muscat aroma or a baked character are considered undesirable. In sum this should be a very sweet, unbaked non-muscat dessert wine.

Malaga, madeira, and marsala are seldom produced in this country and so rarely in California that no Wine Institute specifications have been written for them. Should distinctive types resembling these be produced it would, in our opinion, be very desirable to develop unique California or American type names for them.

California port is defined as a medium to deep ruby red wine with a rich, fruity, and full-bodied taste. The minimum Balling is 6° and it should have a moderate acidity (0.25 per cent fixed in the minimum legal limit but this is far too low). The intention is that California port should be a younger wine than California tawny port.

California tawny port should have a reddish-brown or tawny color and should show considerable aging. Since a baked character is undesirable this presumably means that hydroxymethylfurfural (p. 207) should not be present in more than traces. A legal minimum for this compound would

---

[2] All dessert wines are "full bodied" if they contain sugar, in our opinion.

prevent baked sherry-like ports being sold as tawny port. Otherwise tawny port has the same sugar and acid limitations as port. Neither should contain a recognizable muscat character.

California white port is described as a neutral flavored, light-straw to pale-gold colored wine which is smooth and medium- to full-bodied and with a Balling of 6 °or more. It should also be fresh and mellow. This conglomeration of requirements may be meaningful for a specific wine but many California white ports are not fresh and, as previously noted, medium- and full-bodied are inappropriate for wines of 6° Balling. Fortunately the time when water-white charcoaled wines were sold as white port has passed. There has developed, with the advent of lined steel tanks, however, the possibility of fermenting light colored Thompson Seedless musts out of contact of the air and thus producing a very light colored wine without the use of charcoal. We would be more in favor of keeping angelica as the sole very sweet non-muscat white wine and allowing white port to develop into a less sweet appetizer type. A maximum Balling of about 4° would differentiate the types. As long as sales managers determine what shall or shall not be sold this is not likely to develop and some overlapping of the two types is inevitable.

California sherry is the type produced by baking (p. 397) whereas California flor sherry is a type produced by the use of an aldehyde-producing yeast (p. 418). The former must have a baked character while Wine Institute (1971) specifications specifically provide that a baked character be absent from the latter. This should prevent blending of the first into the second but not the reverse. Neither type may have a recognizable muscat aroma. It may now have an alcohol content of 17.0 to 21.0 per cent.

California dry or cocktail sherry should be golden to a pale amber color, have a nutty, well developed "sherry" (i.e., baked) character without any burnt taste and should be light in body but mellow. A maximum reducing sugar content of 2.5 per cent is provided. This is, in our opinion, too high for a genuinely "dry" type and 1.5 would be a better maximum. Also a minimum total acidity of perhaps 0.5 per cent or more should be established to prevent flat-tasting wines reaching the market.

California medium sherry (usually sold simply as California sherry) should be medium amber in color, full-bodied, rich, nutty with a well-developed "sherry" (i.e., baked) character. There are further requirements that they be well-balanced, smooth, without any burnt taste, and have 2.5 to 4.0 per cent sugar. This is too small a range and if dry sherry had a maximum sugar of 1.5 the range 1.5 to 4.0 would be more enforceable.

Finally California sweet sherry (often called cream or mellow sherry) is defined as a medium to dark amber-colored wine of full body and a rich and nutty flavor with well-developed "sherry" (i.e., baked) character. It must be well-balanced and smooth without any burnt taste. A sugar range of 4.0 to 12.0 per cent is provided and this should certainly be adequate. The rather dark color limitation may be too stringent. Light colored cream sherry might be developed by baking in the absence of air.

For California dry flor, medium flor, and sweet flor sherry the same general characteristics and sugar limitations apply as to the above three types, except, of course, the baked (or nutty) character must be absent and a flor character present. In addition medium flor sherry may be light to medium amber in color rather than medium to dark amber as with California medium sherry. Certainly, however, a genuine dry flor sherry might be lighter than golden in color. Also the light body requirement for both dry types does not seem rational to us. The restriction of the dry type to 1.5 per cent maximum sugar should also apply here.

California tokay is defined by the Wine Institute (1971) recommendations as a blended wine, meaning that port, sherry, and angelica are used in its production (p. 452). It must be an amber-colored wine with a pinkish tinge though light red wines with an amber hue are permitted. This latter requirement is not likely to be confused with tawny port since California tokay must have a slight nutty sherry (i.e., baked) "taste" (sic) and tawny port may not have such an odor. A "light fruitness" is said to be desirable but we are unable to define this desideratum. The wine type must be mellow and well balanced and have a Balling of 4° to 6°. This is a rather narrow range and might better be 3° to 7° since the California type does not in any way resemble its Hungarian prototype.

GEOGRAPHICAL TYPES

The only specific American geographical *type* specifically mentioned in regulations is "Central Coast Counties Dry Wine" but this has not been used in so far as we are aware. San Joaquin (Fig. 46), Napa Valley Wine, Alameda County Wine, and the like are *not* adequate descriptions since they do not represent a recognizable type. In order to use American geographical type names it is necessary to combine them with some generic, semigeneric, or grape type name, i.e., "American" vermouth, "California" port, or "Napa Valley" Sémillon. Most newly-developed viticultural regions do not use geographical names. Note particularly that Alsace has not developed regional names since its liberation in 1918 although it appears to be moving in this direction.

Geographical appellations of origin have many advantages from the point of view of the consumer. They identify the wine with something he already knows—a region. They also differentiate the wine from all other wines since they are obviously not imitations. This appears to give the consumer confidence and adds to his appreciation. The French and Germans have been most active in delimiting and capitalizing on geographical appellations (pp. 5 and 20).

At present "dry red table" and "dry white table" are available for developing into regional appellations, such as "Livermore" dry white table wine, etc. However, if every producer made his Livermore dry white table

Courtesy of Wine Institute

FIG. 46.   SAN JOAQUIN VALLEY VINEYARD

wine from different varieties, harvested them at different degrees of maturity and vinified them by varying procedures the wines would have little resemblance to each other. They would therefore not represent a unique type. Further controls appear necessary other than the 75 per cent from the region requirement.

GRAPE TYPES

When a wine is produced from at least 51 per cent by volume of a given variety of grape and derives its predominant taste, aroma and characteristics from this variety it is entitled to be labeled by a varietal name. These are widely used in Germany, Alsace, Switzerland, Austria, Yugoslavia, northern Italy, and, since repeal, in California. They represent at present most of the premium wines produced in California and are likely to continue to do so for some time.

White Table

The following are presently in production by one or more California producers: Sauvignon blanc, Sémillon, light muscat, light sweet muscat, Grey Riesling, White (Johannisberger) Riesling, Sylvaner (Franken Riesling), Traminer (Gewürztraminer), Pinot Chardonnay (better just Chardonnay), Pinot blanc,[3] Folle blanche, and French Colombard. These 12 varietal types are not all that may be produced in the future but they represent the most important ones of our present industry.

In each case they should have a distinguishable varietal aroma. Except for muscat it is difficult to describe in words what this varietal aroma is. Some attempts in this direction are given in Table 22.

TABLE 22

RECOMMENDED DEFINITIONS OF CALIFORNIA VARIETAL WHITE TABLE WINES

Type	Sugar	Total Acidity	Color	Aroma
	Per cent	Per cent		
Sauvignon blanc	<1.5	>0.6	L–M yellow[1]	Spicy, aromatic
Sweet Sauvignon blanc	>1.5	>0.6	L gold	Spicy, aromatic
Sémillon	<1.5	>0.6	L–M gold	Aromatic, fig-like
Sweet Sémillon	>1.5	>0.6	L gold	Aromatic, fig-like
Light Sweet Muscat	>6	>0.5	L gold	Muscat
Grey Riesling	<0.2	>0.5	L yellow	Slightly aromatic
White Riesling	<0.2	>0.7	L yellow	Slightly aromatic, yeast-like
Sylvaner	<0.2	>0.6	L yellow	Slightly aromatic, yeast-like
Gewürztraminer	<0.2	>0.6	L yellow	Spicy, very aromatic
Chardonnay	<0.2	>0.6	L–M yellow	Aromatic, ripe-grape
Pinot blanc	<0.2	>0.6	L yellow	Slightly aromatic
Chenin blanc	<0.2	>0.7	L yellow	Very slightly aromatic
Folle blanche	<0.2	>0.7	V L yellow	Fruit-like
French Colombard	<0.2	>0.7	V L yellow	Very slightly aromatic, pungent

[1] L for low, M for medium, VL for very low.

The recent approval in California of Malaga and Tokay as "varietal" table wines is a serious blow to the rational labeling of California wines. Neither variety produces a wine with a distinctive varietal character. These are typical table grape varieties with a very bland flavor in the fruit and in the wines. Furthermore, these appellations are already used for well-established dessert wine types.

---

[3] This is commonly considered synonymous with White Pinot but this is not necessarily so. Most California White Pinot comes from Chenin blanc (Pineau de la Loire). There is, however, a true Pinot blanc which is grown by a few growers. The name White Pinot should be reserved for wines of this variety and most of the present White Pinot wines be sold as Chenin blanc.

Red Table

Cabernet, Zinfandel, Pinot noir, Red or Black Pinot,[4] Barbera, Gamay, Grignolino, and Concord are listed in the Wine Institute (1971) specifications. Again each wine should have a distinguishable varietal aroma. Some suggested definitions are given in Table 23. We confess that dis-

TABLE 23

RECOMMENDED DEFINITIONS OF CALIFORNIA VARIETAL RED TABLE WINES

Type	Total Acidity	Color	Aroma
	Per cent		
Cabernet	>0.55	M red[1]	Musty, aromatic
Zinfandel	>0.65	M red	Berry-like
Pinot noir	>0.6	L–M red	Ripe grape, aromatic
Red Pinot	>0.6	L–M red	Moderately aromatic
Barbera	>0.7	M red	Slightly aromatic
Gamay	>0.65	L–M red	Fruit-like
Grignolino	>0.6	Orange red to M-red	Aged to reduce astringency
Concord[2]	>0.65	M red	Methyl anthranilate (foxy)

[1] M for medium, L for low.
[2] In California 12° to 14° Balling but elsewhere in this country may be a dry or nearly dry wine.

tinctive definitions between types are not yet possible for many varietal wines. However, this does not mean that such definitions will not be devised.

Sparkling Types

The only California varietal sparkling type presently defined is sparkling muscat. This should be pale to straw in color, "have a good acidity and body. It should be fresh, fruity, well-balanced and have the unmistakable flavor and aroma of muscat grapes. The reducing sugar should be above four per cent" (Wine Institute 1971). With this description we have no disagreement except that fresh and fruity may mean the same thing and thus a simple minimum total acidity of 0.6 per cent may suffice.

Dessert Types

Several varietal dessert types are in production and many more may be produced in the future. These include muscatel, Muscat de Frontignan (or Muscat Canelli), and black or red muscatel.

Muscatel should, according to the industry recommendations, be rich (in muscat aroma?), fruity, and full-bodied with the unmistakable aroma of muscat grapes. It may range in color from straw (light yellow) to

---

[4] This is the so-called Pinot St. George and does not appear from its pigment complex to be a Pinot variety. See Rankine et al. (1958) and Albach et al. (1959).

amber. A moderate acidity and a minimum Balling of 6° is prescribed. The intention of the regulations is apparently that Muscat of Alexandria grapes should be used. A baked character is specifically considered undesirable. The present California minimum fixed acidity of 0.25 per cent is certainly too low to be considered "moderate" in acidity—0.50 would be better. Muscat de Frontignan, Muscat Frontignan and Muscat Canelli are all dessert types produced from a very ancient variety correctly known as Muscat blanc which is the predominant variety in the region of Frontignan in France and of Canelli in Italy. The geographical implications of "de Frontignan" and "Canelli" are apt to prove confusing to the consumer. Whether White Muscat or Muscat blanc would differentiate this wine from the muscatel from Muscat of Alexandria is, on the other hand, doubtful. The present requirement that the wine be fruity and possess the unmistakable muscat character of the variety is generally satisfactory.

Black or red muscatel should be medium to deep red in color. A rich, fruity and full-bodied wine with a pronounced muscat aroma is required. The specific notice that the muscat aroma be derived from Muscat Hamburg or Aleatico grapes is interesting in that it rules out blends of Muscat of Alexandria (51 per cent) and some red dessert wine. The minimum Balling is again 6° and the requirement that the wine be fruity and show balance (of what?), derived from proper aging (how long?) is at least confusing.

Other Types

So far not defined by us are several miscellaneous types—rosé, sweet rosé, dry red table wine, red table wine, sweet red table wine, dry white table wine, sweet white table wine, and aperitif wines.

California rosé is a wine of a fruity, light, and tart flavor. The color is specified as being "pink with or without an orange modifying tint and should not have an amber tint." The color specifications appear to be sufficiently broad but the type should be qualified to limit the sugar content to 0.2 per cent. The fruity tart flavor might be qualified by a minimum total acidity of at least 0.60 per cent.

California sweet rosé is a relatively recent type which has been added to provide a rosé wine of over 0.5 per cent sugar. The other requirements are as for California rosé and the same qualifications are applicable, e.g., a minimum total acidity.

California red table and sweet red table wines provide for non-varietal, non-generic, or semigeneric wines. The sugar limits are respectively <1.5, and > 1.5 per cent. A variety of proprietary types are included in these classes. For example, most kosher-type wines would presumably be classified in the sweet, red, table-wine class.

Only two white table wine classes are presently defined: dry white table wine and sweet white table wine. The first has a maximum of 0.5 per cent sugar and the latter must be of more than 0.5 per cent sugar.

No specific specifications for the new categories of special natural wines or of various flavored dessert wines have yet been devised. In many respects these are flavored wines which resemble vermouth and other flavored wines. Since they are all, so far, proprietary wines the specifications of the individual producers must suffice for their identification. The main limitation is that they cannot be made to resemble a natural fruit wine. Since no natural lemon wine exists lemons can be used to flavor grape wine to make a special natural wine.

For other information on California wine types see Adams (1964), Balzer (1970), Blumberg and Hannum (1971), Cook (1966), Melville (1968), and Morgan (1971).

BIBLIOGRAPHY

ADAMS, L. D. 1964. The Commonsense Book of Wine. David McKay Company, Inc., New York.

ALBACH, R., KEPNER, R. E., and WEBB, A. D. 1959. Comparison of anthocyan pigments of vinifera grapes. II. Am. J. Enol. Vitic. 10, 164–172.

BALZER, R. L. 1970. This Uncommon Heritage. The Ward Ritchie Press, Los Angeles.

BLUMBERG, R. S. and HANNUM, H. 1971. The Fine Wines of California. Doubleday & Company, Garden City, New York.

COOK, F. S. 1966. The Wines and Wineries of California. Mother Lode Pub. Co., Jackson, Calif.

MELVILLE, J. 1968. Guide to California Wines. 3 ed. revised by J. Morgan. Nourse Publishing Co., San Carlos, Calif.

MORGAN, J. 1971. Adventures in the Wine Country. Chronicle Books, San Francisco.

RANKINE, B., KEPNER, R. E., and WEBB, A. D. 1958. Comparison of anthocyan pigments of vinifera grapes. Am. J. Enol. 9, 105–110.

U. S. FEDERAL ALCOHOL ADMINISTRATION. 1937. Federal Alcohol Administration Act as in Effect on May 15, 1937. U. S. Govt. Print. Office, Washington. (Modified in 1942, 1948, and 1958.)

U. S. INTERNAL REVENUE SERVICE. 1970. Wine. Part 240 of Title 26 (1954), Code of Federal Regulations. U. S. Govt. Print. Office, Washington. IRS 146. Also published in Commerce Clearing House Reports.

U. S. TREASURY DEPARTMENT. 1961. Regulations No. 4 Relating to Labeling and Advertising of Wine. U. S. Govt. Print. Office, Washington. IRS 449.

WINE INSTITUTE. 1971. California wine type specifications, recommended as desirable for California wine and brandy types for guidance of judges at fairs. Wine Institute, San Francisco. June 14, 1971.

CHAPTER 4

The Molds and Yeasts of Grapes and Wine

MOLDS

Molds are of importance in wine making, first, because of the damage they may do to the grapes before or after picking and, second, because they often grow in empty wooden cooperage imparting a moldy odor and flavor to the wine. They do not grow in wine because of the inhibitory effect of the alcohol.

Yeasts of the genus *Saccharomyces* are necessary in the fermentation of the must, but they and other yeasts may cause the clouding of bottled table wines. The flor yeasts, which represent a special group, are used in the making of Spanish sherries and certain Jura French wines (*vins jaunes*). Wild yeasts, such as the apiculate yeasts and others, may be harmful to wine quality when they develop during fermentation, although in some cases they may produce flavors which give a distinct or unique character to the wines.

GENERAL CLASSIFICATION OF MICROORGANISMS

The complete classification and description of the microorganisms of importance and interest to the wine maker would be beyond the scope of this book. A brief discussion of the more important forms only will be given. See Lodder and Kreger-van Rij (1952), Henneberg (1926), Lodder (1970), and other references for further information. The present chapter considers only yeasts and molds; the bacteria that are of concern to the enologist are discussed in Chapter 16.

Some of the fungi are saprophytes and can utilize only non-living substances for growth; others are parasitic and can attack living tissues. Examples of the former are *Penicillium* mold and wine yeast, *Saccharomyces cerevisiae*. Typical fungal parasites are *Botrytis cinerea* ("noble mold") and *oïdium* of the vine (powdery mildew).

Fungi may be unicellular or multicellular. Yeasts are higher fungi whose dominant form of growth is unicellular. Certain other fungi are always multicellular in growth. Still others may under certain conditions grow as one-celled organisms and later on under changed conditions become multicellular.

This chapter deals with the occurrence, morphology, and some other general properties of the yeasts and molds of importance in wine production. The chemistry of fermentation and certain other chemical aspects of

151

yeast activity are presented in Chapter 5. See also Prescott and Dunn (1960) and Underkofler and Hickey (1954).

MOLDS

Molds are distinguished by the formation of a mycelium. They differ from each other principally in their methods of producing spores and conidia, but there are also easily recognizable differences in the appearance of the mycelium and in the nature of the chemical changes which they induce in media suited to their growth. Variations in external and microscopical appearance, however, are not always reliable for identification and classification as the appearance is often affected profoundly by conditions of growth. Primitive fungi form a mycelium without cross walls (non-septate), and the mycelium is termed "non-septate" or "coenocytic." These molds are also termed *Phycomycetes*. The other molds, or higher fungi, possess a septate mycelium.

Some molds form yeast-like cells under certain conditions and may even induce feeble alcoholic fermentation, as do some of the *Monilia* and *Mucor* molds.

Many genera, species, and varieties or sub-species of molds have been described in the literature. They are usually aerobic, although they have been encountered as a feeble growth in bottled juices that have not been thoroughly pasteurized.

Penicillium

Molds of the penicillium group are most troublesome to the California wine maker. Raper and Thom (1949) published a comprehensive treatise on these molds. In the initial stages of growth *Penicillium* is white in appearance. Later, spores or conidia are formed in enormous numbers and give a powdery appearance to the growth, which is blue, green, or pink, according to the color and age of the conidia and the age of the culture.

P. expansum, (formerly *P. glaucum*) is the best known of the penicillium molds and the one responsible for very great losses to fresh fruit shippers and fruit product manufacturers. The asexual spores of conidia are spherical in shape and are formed in great abundance upon upright hyphae or conidiophores. The conidia are light and are carried by air currents. They are universally distributed on surfaces and in the air.

This mold will grow on practically all food materials exposed to the air, if the conditions of moisture content and freedom from antiseptics permit the growth of any microorganism. It prefers sugar-containing substances such as fruits, fruit juices, jams, etc., but will also develop on such material as moist leather or the moist inner surface of empty wooden barrels or tanks. Any acid material affords a more favorable medium for growth than does an alkaline or neutral medium. After early fall rains it often grows in great abundance on cracked grapes rendering them unfit for wine making. The taste of these wines is very unpleasant, and on the basis of our experience in 1957 very little is required to taint the wine. "Corked" wines may also have *Penicillium* sp. in the cork.

Growth is more abundant at temperatures ranging from 59° to 75°F. but will occur at temperatures near freezing and slowly at temperatures of 95° to 98°F. It is known as a "cold weather" mold.

Aspergillus

The members of this group are recognized by their peculiar method of conidia formation. The conidia are borne upon upright conidiophores which terminate in abrupt enlargements or "knobs." From these enlargements known as "vesicles," spring numerous spike-like projections—the sterigmata—bearing chains of conidia, Fig. 47. For a key to the aspergillus molds see Raper (1945).

A. niger.—This species is also very common in California vineyards and orchards. Growth at first resembles that of the *Penicillium* molds, being white and cottony. After conidia are formed in abundance, the growth becomes black in color. Unlike *P. expansum* it produces very little moldy flavor or odor in grapes but may lead to secondary infection by yeasts and bacteria. If often grows abundantly on grapes damaged by rain, particularly in the San Joaquin Valley. It is recognized by its black dustlike conidia. It is sometimes termed a hot weather mold, Fig. 48.

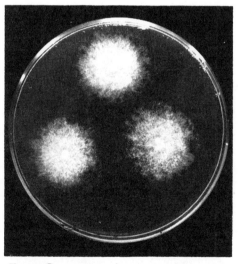

Fig. 47. Young Colonies of Aspergillis Mold from Grapes

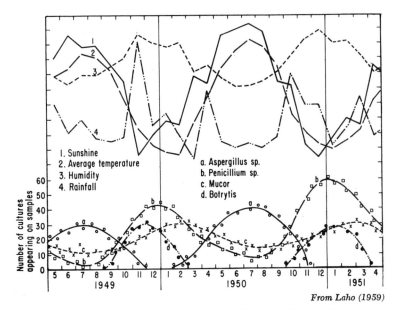

From Laho (1959)

FIG. 48.   CHANGES IN MOLD COUNT IN VINEYARD DURING YEAR

Mucor and Rhizopus.—The *Mucor and Rhizopus* molds are widely distributed. A general characteristic of these "pin molds" is the possession of
a unicellular mycelium in which hyphae are not divided by cross walls or
septa. This type of mycelium is designated as "syphonaceous" or coenocytic. The conidia or spores are borne in spherical sacs known as sporangia,
which are usually visible to the unaided eye. Each is carried upon an
upright fruiting thread or sporangiophore, hence the name "pin molds."

The *Mucor* molds, Fig. 49, occur very frequently upon fresh fruit, especially during shipment. Grapes often develop a hairy, grayish cottony
growth of this mold which prevents their fresh sale. Most members of this
group are capable of converting starch into sugar. In sugary liquids
under anaerobic conditions, yeast-like cells are formed which convert the
sugar into alcohol and carbon dioxide. The species *Rhizopus* is closely related to *Mucor, R. nigricans* being encountered frequently on damaged
grapes. Again it is the secondary infection which follows the mold attack
which may seriously reduce the value of the grapes.

Rhizopus sp., *Aspergillus* sp., and *Acetobacter* sp. are the main organisms involved in summer bunch rot in grapes grown in the southern San
Joaquin Valley. Hewitt *et al.* (1962) showed that the fungus *Diplodia
viticola* was responsible for initiation of summer bunch rot.

Botrytis.—This mold develops upon grapes in rainy and foggy weather as a short, grayish, hair-like growth. The mycelial threads penetrate the grape skin. Under the microscope the conidia are seen to occur in grape like clusters. It causes rapid evaporation of the water from the fruit, which results in a marked concentration of sugar. As much as two per cent glycerol may be found in musts of botrytized grapes. Botrytis also metabolizes organic acids in the fruit. The Sauternes wines of France owe their quality to these facts, pp. 11–13. Nelson (1951) and Nelson and Amerine (1956, 1957) have used this mold successfully on grapes after picking for the production of natural sweet table wines. Because of the low relative humidity of the air in California vineyards during the picking season, botrytis seldom grows abundantly on grapes on the vine except in years of early rainfall and high humidity such as 1957 (see p. 389).

Fig. 49.   Mucor Mold from Grapes ($\times$ 80)

The question of whether botrytis is beneficial or not under field conditions depends entirely on the weather after its first attack. If it is fortuitously dry and warm the botrytised grapes will lose water and produce high sugar musts of superior quality, as for example in the best years in Sauternes and Germany. But if, and this should be emphasized, cold humid conditions ensue after the initial attack *Botrytis cinerea* is not a beneficial mold. When this occurs the skin cracks, secondary yeast, bacterial and mold infections occur and the grapes lose sugar and quality. Under these conditions rapid and immediate harvesting is advisable.

The favorable and unfavorable effects of *Botrytis cinerea* on the quality of musts has been emphasized by Charpentié (1954). Malic and tartaric acids are attacked about equally at low pH's by the fungus. At higher pH's citric acid is formed but *in vivo* this was not observed. Charpentié views botrytis as a biological means of deacidifying musts and of increasing the sugar content of grapes. The experiments of Dittrich (1964) do not substantiate the claim that botrytised musts ferment slowly because of the presence of an antibiotic, botryticin. The slow fermentation of botrytised musts appeared to be due to their higher sugar contents. Musts of botrytised grapes do have a high dextran content.

Brown Rot.—*Sclerotinia functigena* causes brown rot of various fruits and attacks fruit on the tree (or in boxes). It is one of the most widely distributed and destructive of the fungus parasites, and although of minor importance in grape or grape wine production it may greatly damage other fruits used for making wines.

Oïdium.—The "powdery mildew" is a very destructive fungus on California grapes and grape vines. It is commonly termed *oïdium*. It is controlled by dusting the vines with sulfur. When it attacks grapes early in the season it causes the grapes to crack and in severe cases prevents ripening.

It forms a pure white, felt-like mycelium on culture media. Under the microscope, mycelial threads as well as the characteristic barrel-shaped oidia will be found.

Downy Mildew (*Plasmopara*).—This is the mildew that almost destroyed the grape industry of Europe in the 1870's. It is a *Phycomyces* and is controlled by Bordeaux spray. However, it is still a serious disease of grapes in Europe and eastern United States, but seldom occurs in California because of the usual dry weather and low humidity during the ripening period.

Alternaria and Dematium.—*Alternaria* species and *Dematium pullulans* are frequently found on fruits, especially on grapes that have been left on the vine until after the fall rains. *Alternaria* appears as a brownish-green or often black growth similar in appearance to *Penicillium*. Under the microscope the conidia resemble Indian clubs divided by walls.

Actinomyces.—So far as the authors know growth of *Actinomyces* does not occur in normal wines. However, it may grow in empty casks or on equipment. It is reported to produce an earthy odor. Since earthiness is found in some wines, *Actinomyces* have been suggested as a source. We know of no proof. For data on these microorganisms see Nonomura and Ohara (1959).

YEASTS

Yeasts are distinguished from the molds in that they usually maintain an unicellular growth, although many of them may form mycelium or pseudomycelium under special conditions. Furthermore, many molds form yeast-like cells under suitable conditions, and such cells often induce alcoholic fermentation. The ascospores of some species of yeasts closely resemble those of certain molds.

Botanical Classification of Yeasts

Lodder (1970) classified the ascosporogenous yeasts as *Endomycetales* with four families: *Dipodascaceae, Endomycetaceae, Saccharomycetaceae*, and *Spermophthoraceae*. The family *Saccharomycetaceae* has four subfamilies: *Schizosaccharomycoideae* (*Schizosaccharomyces*), *Nadsonioideae* (*Nadsonia, Saccharomycodes, Hanseniaspora*, and *Wickerhamia*), *Saccharomycoideae* (*Saccharomyces, Kluyveromyces, Lodderomyces, Wingea, Endomycopsis* (?), *Pichia, Hansenula, Pachysolen, Citeromyces, Debaryomyces, Schwanniomyces, Dekkera*, and *Saccharomycopsis*) and *Lipomycetoideae* (*Lipomyces*).

The flor yeast of Spain was classified by Prostoserdov and Afrikian (1933) as *S. cheresiensis*, but Mrak and Phaff point out that Marcilla *et al.* (1936) in Spain have given it the name *S. beticus*, a term also used by Castor (1957), by Amerine (1958), and by Joslyn and Amerine (1964). Lodder and Kreger-van Rij state that this yeast should probably be designated as *Saccharomyces oviformis* Osterwalder. It differs from typical strains of wine yeast, *S. cerevisiae* by its ability to form a pellicle on wines of 12 to 16 per cent alcohol. For its use in wine production see p. 414. A similar yeast is used in France in the Château Châlon area in the production of the well-known *vin jaune* of the Arbois district. It resembles *S. cerevisiae* in its fermentation characteristics and generally morphology. Scheffer and Mrak (1951) called a flor yeast isolated from California wines *S. chevalieri*. It closely resembles the Spanish flor yeasts used experimentally in California by Cruess (1948), pp. 421–422.

See also Feduchy (1956) and Yokotsuka (1954) for further information on these yeasts. Lodder (1970) now classifies *S. oviformis* as *S. bayanus* and *S. beticus* as *S. capensis* or *S. bayanus*.

The yeasts forming ballistospores (i.e., yeasts corresponding to the *Basidiomycetes* fungi) are non-fermentative and are not of general importance to the wine maker. The non-sporulating yeasts (which correspond to the *Fungi imperfecti*) belong in the family *Cryptococcaceae*. Those of importance in wine making are discussed later in this chapter.

For the properties of the spore-forming and non-sporulating yeasts see Cook (1958), Lodder and Kreger-van Rij (1952), Mrak and Phaff (1948), Stelling-Dekker (1931), and especially Lodder (1970).

Isolation and Purification of Yeasts

It is not possible in a book of this scope to give detailed directions for the isolation and purification of yeast cultures. In our laboratories an agar medium is made as follows: grape juice is diluted with three times its volume of water and 20 gm. of purified agar agar is dissolved in one liter of the diluted juice by heating and stirring.

This agar after sterilization in tubes is poured into sterile petri dishes. Isolation of yeast cultures is made by streaking the juice or other source material on the solidified agar, incubating, usually at room temperature, and picking isolated colonies by sterile inoculating wire. For detailed instructions see Tanner (1944), Guilliermond and Tanner (1920) or Rose and Harrison (1968–1970).

Spore Formation

Under favorable conditions of temperature and moisture supply, the true yeasts (sporogenous yeasts) form ascospores. These vary in number per cell and in shape according to the species concerned. Those of wine yeast are spherical, and usually 2, 3, or 4 spores are formed per ascus. They are somewhat more resistant to environmental conditions than the vegetative cells. Sporulation is the beginning of the sexual stage of reproduction of yeast.

The classical medium for demonstrating spore formation is the moist gypsum block. Other spore media are sterilized carrot slices, potato slices, Gorodkowa's medium, and V-8 juice agar (see Mrak and Phaff 1948). The sporulating cells may be fixed on the microscope slide by heating in the usual manner and staining. See Tanner (1944) or other books on yeast for details. The authors find staining usually unnecessary for wine yeasts.

Identification of Yeast Cultures

Pure cultures of yeasts are identified on (a) morphological and (b) physiological characteristics, particularly the fermentation of various sugars. For details of procedure see Cook (1958), Lodder and Kreger-van Rij (1952), Mrak and Phaff (1948), Tanner (1944), Henrici (1930), Guillermond and Tanner (1920), Stelling-Dekker (1931), Roman et al. (1957), and Lodder (1970).

Yeasts of Grapes and Wine

Many studies have been made of the yeasts naturally occurring on grapes. As Amerine and Joslyn (1970) have stated, these investigations, for the most part, have been incomplete because they have not included the role, if any, of the yeasts in wine making. See also Kunkee and Amerine (1970).

Cruess (1918) isolated and studied nineteen different organisms occurring on California grapes grown in five districts. In all cases the undesirable organisms greatly outnumbered the desirable wine yeasts. Grape samples from vines grown in three districts in which wine had never been made commercially contained no *S. cerevisiae*, Fig. 50, indicating that

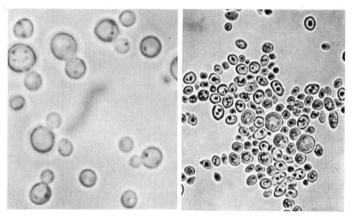

FIG. 50. YOUNG AND OLD CELLS OF *Saccharomyces cerevisiae*

wine yeasts are apt to be rare in regions where wine making is not carried on. In these cases mainly molds were found on green grapes. As the grapes ripened "wild" yeasts appeared. The true wine yeasts were the last to appear, but in all cases they were greatly outnumbered by undesirable microorganisms. There was a great increase in all types of microorganisms when the grapes were allowed to stand in the boxes after picking.

Holm (1908) isolated several yeasts from grapes grown in regions in California remote from wineries. No true wine yeasts were found. Mrak and McClung (1940) made an extensive study of the yeasts naturally occurring on grapes and in grape products from the principal grape-growing regions of California. Of the 241 pure cultures studied 159 formed spores and included *S. cerevisiae* (Hansen); *S. bayanus* (Saccardo) (probably a flor yeast); *Zygosaccharomyces*, (now called *Saccharomyces*), two species; *Pichia*, three species; *Zygopichia* (now obsolete), one species; *Debaryomyces*, two species; *Hansenula*, one species; *Torulospora* (now obsolete), one species; *Hanseniaspora*, one species; and *Kloeckeraspora*, one species. The 82 cultures of imperfect, non-spore forming yeasts include *Torulopsis*, *Candida*, *Kloeckera*, *Schizoblastosporion*, *Rhodotorula* and several species of *Candida*. Several new species were found and described. They also studied yeasts occurring on grapes in musts and new wines, in cloudy bottled wine, in pomace, on leaves, and in vineyard soil.

For a survey of the species of yeasts found in grapes and wines see Kunkee and Amerine (1970) and Galzy (1956). Galzy lists *Brettanomyces bruxellensis* and *B. lambicus; Candida albicans, C. brumptii, C. guilliermondii, C. krusei, C. rugosa, C. tropicalis, C. valida*[1a], and *C. vini*[1a]; *Cryptococcus albidus; Debaryomyces hansenii*[1b]; *Hanseniaspora valbyensis; Hansenula anomala* and *H. saturnus; Kloeckera africana, K. apiculata, K. corticis*[1c], and *K. javanica*[1d]; *Metschnikowia pulcherrima*[1e]; *Kluyveromyces veronae*[1f]; *Pichia farinosa, P. fermentans,* and *P. membranaefaciens; Rhodotorula aurantica, R. glutinis, R. pallida,* and *R. rubra*[1g]; *Saccharomyces bailii*[1h], *S. bayanus*[1i], *S. bisporus, S. cerevisiae*[1j], *S. chevalieri, S. debrueckii* var. *monogolicus, S. exiguus, S. fermentati, S. florentinus, S. fructuum, S. heterogenicus, S. italicus*[1k], *S. pastorianus, S. rosei, S. rouxii, S. rouxii* var. *polymorphus,* and *S. uvarum*[1l]; *Saccharomycodes ludwigii*[1m]; *Schizosaccharomyces octosporus* and *Sch. pombe; Torulopsis candida*[1n] and *T. stellata*[1o]; and *Trichosporon pullulans*.

Ohara *et al.* (1959) have studied and identified many of the yeasts occurring in the fermentation of grape musts in Japan. They identified many of the above and *S. cerevisiae, S. rosei, S. bayanus, K. apiculata, Pichia fermentans, C. vini* or *C. valida, Hansenula anomala* var. *anomala*[1p], *Torulopsis stellata, T. glabrata,* and *T. colliculosa*. These workers also observed that the apiculate yeasts and *Torulopsis* disappeared immediately after the addition of 150 mg. per l. sulfur dioxide whereas at 75 there was little effect on these yeasts. The effect was less on *S. cerevisiae*, although appreciable at 125 and 150 mg. per l. They made experiments in which mixed cultures of *S. cerevisiae* and various "wild" yeasts were used, and on the fermentation of blends of orange and grape juices. See Van der Walt and Van Kerken (1958*b*) and Van Kerken (1963) for a discussion of the species of yeasts of South African grapes and wines.

Domercq (1957) reported on the yeasts of Bordeaux grapes, identifying

---

[1] Formerly classified as: *a C. mycoderma, b D. kloeckeri, c* partially *K. magna, d K. jensenii, e C. pulcherrima, f S. veronae, g* partially *R. mucilaginosa, h* partially *S. acidifaciens, i* partially *S. oviformis, j* partially *S. willianus,* and var. *ellipsoideus, k* partially *S. steineri, l S. carlsbergensis, m* partially *Sacch. bisporus, n T. famata, o* partially *T. bacillaris,* and *p C. pelliculosa.*

many of those listed above and *Brettanomyces vini* (now *B. intermedius*), *Rhodotorula vini* (?) and *S. elegans* (now *S. bailii* var. *bailii*). The general picture of Italian and Bordeaux fermentations is that they start with non-spore forming yeasts. At Bordeaux it starts with *Kloeckera apiculata* for the reds and *K. apiculata* and *T. stellata* for the whites. These are rapidly succeeded by spore-forming yeasts of *S. rosei*. *S. bayanus* predominated in fermenting high sugar musts. It was found in only about 2 per cent of red musts and in 8 of white. *S. bayanus* appears to be particularly important in Bordeaux wines, especially as a cause of spoilage of sweet table wines. *Sacch. ludwigii* and *S. bailii* were rarely found in musts but are common in white wines where they appear to be a cause of spoilage (cloudiness).

Bréchot *et al.* (1962) found only 13.4 per cent *Kloeckera* sp. in fermenting musts of Beaujolais in contrast to 58.2 per cent in Bordeaux wines in Domercq's (1957) study and the 76.4 per cent in Italian wines reported by Castelli (1954). *S. cerevisiae* was the dominant yeast followed by *S. italicus*. In contrast to Domercq's (1957) studies, *S. bayanus* was rare in Beaujolais. The microflora was relatively rich in *Hansenula* sp., *Brettanomyces* sp., *Candida* sp., *Endomyces* sp., *Rhodotorula* sp., and *Torulopsis* sp.

Minárik (1964) reported the predominant yeasts in new Czechoslovakian wines to be *Saccharomyces cerevisiae* and *S. bayanus*. Also present was *S. chevalieri* which caused clouding of wines. The main surface yeast was *Candida vini* or *C. valida*. Some surface films were due to *C. zeylanoides* and *Pichia* sp. A yeast which fermented in 60 per cent sugar solutions was isolated by Barre and Galzy (1960) and was named by them *S. osmophilus* (now *S. rouxii*). Schanderl and Staudenmayer (1964) point out that in contrast to other yeasts *Brettanomyces* are little affected by sulfur dioxide.

Domercq (1957) reported *T. stellata* only from botrytised grapes. *S. heterogenicus*, *S. bailii*, and *Sacch. ludwigii* were not found in red grapes but are common on white. Yeast from white grapes were generally capable of fermenting to higher alcohol.

In general the types of yeasts found in grapes and wines throughout the world are remarkably similar. There are, however, distinct differences in the proportion of each yeast in different regions. The yeasts found under almost all conditions are *S. cerevisiae* and *K. apiculata*.

Where rapid fermentation to dryness is desired, probably *S. bayanus* is the yeast of choice. It (or *S. bailii*) should not be used where sweet table wines are being produced. It is also useful in restarting "stuck" wines. Peynaud and Domercq (1959) also praised the "flinty" odor of wines fermented with it. The winery has a microflora of its own, as the following data of Peynaud and Domercq (1959) indicate (number of isolates in parenthesis): outside of tanks, S. bayanus (6), S. cerevisiae (3), C. vini or C. valida (13) Pichia (1); at bungs, S. bailii (7), S. bailii (2), C. vini or C. valida (2); bottling equipment, S. bayanus (4), S. bailii (4), C. vini or C. valida (10), Brettanomyces sp. (5); and floors of cellars, S. cereviseae (1), Pichia sp. (7), and C. vini or C. valida (7). For other studies see Ciferri and Verona (1941), Castelli (1941, 1948, 1954, 1955, 1960), Capriotti (1954), and Florenzano (1949).

Saccharomyces cerevisiae.—This yeast is used for the fermentation of grape juice and other fruit juices. The shape of the cells varies from almost spherical to plump sausage shape, but the typical outline under the high power of the microscope is short ellipsoidal. The usual size of the cells is about 8×7 μ. Spores are formed in abundance on moist gypsum blocks, 2 or 3 spherical spores per cell, 1 or 4 less commonly.

A vinous or wine-like flavor is produced in fruit juices. Different strains do not differ greatly in their effect on flavor. In other words, one should not expect a strain of this yeast to impart a Pinot noir or Chardonnay or Sémillon flavor when isolated from these varieties of grapes because the principal flavor in these cases is that of the grape. Some vendors of yeasts have made extravagant claims in this regard.

Most cultures of S. cerevisiae form high amounts of alcohol in suitable media containing an excess of fermentable sugar, 16 per cent alcohol by volume by unsyruped fermentation being fairly common and 18 per cent or more by syruped fermentation (p. 451).

In grape must or other fermentable liquid the first evidence of growth is a slight haziness and formation of a white or grayish-white sediment. As growth proceeds gas is formed, rises through the liquid, and during active fermentation froth or foam forms on the surface. The gas carries the yeast cells through the liquid causing it to be cloudy. At the same time a strong odor of alcoholic fermentation develops. The grape juice fermented to a very low sugar content, 0.2 per cent or less, is spoken of as being dry. After fermentation ceases the yeast cells sink and form a sediment called lees or yeast lees. Most juices at a favorable temperature, become completely fermented within 2 to 3 weeks.

Saccharomyces rouxii.—S. rouxii is the representative species of osmophilic yeasts. Conjugation of two cells precedes spore formation and the spores are round to slightly oval. Mrak and McClung (1940) isolated two species from California grapes.

Several related species have been isolated from food products of the Far East; for example, from fermenting sugary liquids used for distillation of brandy, from soy bean sauce, and from raw sugar. A similar yeast has been found by Phaff and Douglas (1938) in cloudy, bottled wines. These yeasts are rapid fermenters of liquids low in sugar.

Saccharomyces sp. yeast is used in the Orient in the fermentation of rice wort for sake. The starch of the rice is converted to sugar by *Aspergillus oryzae*. The mixed culture of yeast and mold is known as *koji*. Possibly because of the gradual furnishing of sugar to the yeast by slow hydrolysis of the starch by the mold conditions are similar to those in syruped fermentation. Very high amounts of alcohol are formed, 17 per cent by volume or more, according to Roman *et al.* (1957). *S. cerevisiae* has been considered by some microbiologists as the name to be applied to most beer yeasts, bread yeasts, and distillery yeasts. Hansen is credited with giving the first description of *Saccharomyces*. His first culture came from beer. He also described several subspecies or varieties, such as *ellipsoideus, alpinus, turbidans, orasti,* and others. They are now (Lodder, 1970) classified as *S. cerevisiae*.

The beer yeast cultures that we have encountered form larger cells than does wine yeast, and the cells are usually spherical or egg shaped. In grape must they form less alcohol than does wine yeast. Bread yeasts that we have used experimentally have been characterized by rapid fermentation of grape must and the formation of amounts of alcohol that compare favorably with those produced by wine yeast. Distillery yeasts are classified as *S. cerevisiae* strains and produce rapid fermentations and high alcohol content in suitable media. *S. uvarum* (a bottom yeast) of Hansen is similar to other beer yeasts of the top yeast, *S. cerevisiae,* group, except that it ferments melibiose.

Other Genera of True Yeasts.—*Sacch. ludwigii,* sometimes erroneously classified as *S. ludwigii,* is occasionally found in grapes and other fruits. It was described by Hansen in 1889. The cells are large and often lemon shaped. Spores are spherical and smooth, 4 per cell. The spores conjugate before germinating. A strain of this yeast formed 9.2 per cent alcohol by volume in experiments made by Wahab *et al.* (1949).

Other spore-forming yeasts were isolated by Mrak and McClung (1940) (see p. 592).

Fission Yeasts.—These yeasts multiply in the same manner as bacteria by formation of a transverse wall or septum in the cell and the splitting of the cell into two new cells along the line of the septum. A species of this genus was described in 1893 by Lindner, who was the first to use the term *Schizosaccharomyces*. The yeast described by him was isolated from African beer. Lodder (1970) states that the genus contains four species; namely *Sch. japonicus, Sch. malidevorans, Sch. pombe,* and *Sch. octosporus*.

Sch. pombe ferments dextrose, sucrose, and maltose, but not lactose or galactose and ferments only the dextrose portion of raffinose. Spores, as in other species of this genus, are formed after conjugation of two mother cells. Usually four oval to spherical spores are formed per cell. *Sch. octosporus* forms 4 to 8 spores per ascus, 8 being more common than 4. Dittrich (1963A, 1963B) and Peynaud and Sudraud (1964) have attempted to utilize the ability of *Sch. pombe* to ferment malic acid to alcohol and other compounds but not to lactic acid. Both found it a slow fermenter and showed that it was difficult to prevent other yeasts from over-growing *Sch. pombe*.

In experiments on grape must fermentation with *Sch. octosporus* was quite rapid and a pleasing aromatic odor was developed. *Sch. octosporus* was isolated by Beijerinck from Greek currants in 1894. Presumably, therefore, it occurs on grapes although insofar as we are aware, this genus has not been isolated from California grapes. It has been encountered in spoiled home-canned fruits by W.V. Cruess. It is osmophilic and is fairly common on dried fruits. *Sch. japonicus* var. *versatilis* was isolated by Wickerham and Duprat (1945) from spoiled home-canned grape juice in 1945.

Hansenula.—This genus is quite widely distributed and is common in natural fermentations. Cruess (1918) described a pure culture isolated from wine grapes. Mrak and McClung (1940) reported on four cultures of *Hansenula* from grapes. Bedford (1942) made a thorough study of the taxonomy of this genus. Wickerham (1951) listed 15 species and Lodder (1970) 25.

Most species of *Hansenula* form films on liquid culture media and on wines of low alcohol content such as distilling material. They differ from most other yeasts in their ability to use nitrate as a source of nitrogen, and in the shape of its spores, usually hat shaped or "saturn" shaped. Also, it forms in grape must large amounts of esters, chiefly ethyl acetate. Wahab *et al.* (1949) conducted experimental fermentations of grape must and orange juice with ten cultures of *Hansenula* in comparison with eight other yeasts including champagne "Ay" yeast, a *Kloeckera*, a *Nadsonia*, two *Hanseniaspora*, *Saccharomycodes ludwigii* and one of *Schizosaccharomyces octosporus*. In most cases the wines fermented with *Hansenula* possessed too much odor of ethyl acetate to be palatable but after aging ten weeks, several of the wines had developed pleasing flavors and bouquets which were more pronounced and more aromatic than those of wines made with champagne "Ay" yeast alone. Alcohol production ranged from 6.1 to 10.2 per cent by volume and volatile esters from 0.252 to 0.439 g. per 100 ml. Surprisingly, several of the strains were quite resistant to sulfur dioxide. Several grew on wines of 12 per cent alcohol but not on those of

13 per cent. It is possible that one or more strains of *Hansenula* might be useful for increasing the ester content, flavor, and bouquet of wines. See also the discussion of mixed cultures (p. 167).

In the standard description of the most important member, *H. anomala,* the size of the cells is given as 2.5 μ $\times$ 5–10 μ and the outline of the cells oval to long oval. It forms a wrinkled, chalky white pellicle and moderate to heavy sediment. Spores are formed in abundance and are hat-shaped.

Candida.—*Candida vini* and *C. valida* are non-sporulating film yeasts that grow on wines of low alcohol content. They form a chalky-white film. They are frequently found on distilling material and on pickle brines. They were first described by Persoon in 1822. His description, according to Lodder and Kreger-van Rij (1952), was very inadequate. *Mycoderma* is a name that has been used in connection with yeasts, molds, and bacteria. Thus in the early French literature one finds the terms "*Mycoderma aceti*" for vinegar bacteria and "*Mycoderma vini*" for the yeast film occurring on wines. *Mycoderma* has also been used to designate the yeast film that develops on pickle brine, although this film or "scum" contains many species of yeast. Ciferri and Verona (1941) after a study of 54 cultures from wine suggested that the film yeast commonly known as *Mycoderma vini* can be named *Mycokluyveria.* Lodder and Kreger-van Rij (1952) classified it as *C. mycoderma.* Lodder (1970) split the species into *C. vini* and *C. valida.* For more information on *Candida* see Verona and Rambelli (1961). The term "wine flowers" is often used to designate the yeast film that develops on wines of low alcohol content, but this is a loose term that includes several genera.

It can utilize ethyl alcohol as a source of carbon, as it forms a film on synthetic media containing alcohol as the only carbon source. It is strongly oxidative, oxidizing alcohol and fruit acids to carbon dioxide and water. Its cells are variable in shape and size, but long, cylindrical cells up to 13 μ length are typical. An extensive mycelium is formed on slide cultures. It produces little or no fermentation in dextrose media, and none in those containing galactose, sucrose, maltose, or lactose. It does not utilize nitrate. *C. tropicalis* is frequently found on fruits, forms a pellicle on fruit juice and ferments dextrose, levulose, maltose, and sucrose.

Apiculate Yeasts.—These small yeasts, Fig. 51, often lemon shaped, occur in abundance during the early stages of natural fermentation of grape must and apple juice. Lodder and Kreger-van Rij (1952) state that Rees first gave the name of *S. apiculatus* to these yeasts in 1870. Lindner (1903) later divided them into a sporulating genus that he termed *Hanseniaspora* and non-sporulating genus, *Hansenia.* Zikes (1911) and Niehaus (1932) also wrote on the classification of these yeasts. The term *Hanseniaspora* is still used for spore-forming apiculate yeasts, but the term *Han-*

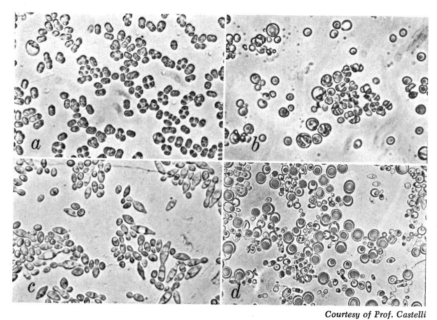

Courtesy of Prof. Castelli

FIG. 51.   Saccharomyces (a), Hansenula (b), Kloeckera (c) AND Candida (d)

senia for the non-sporulating apiculate yeasts has been replaced by the term *Kloeckera* suggested by Janke (1924). The species K. *apiculata* is one most frequently encountered in the natural fermentation of grape must and apple juice. The cells of this species vary from oval to lemon shaped.

A comparative study of the apiculate yeasts was made by Miller and Phaff (1958). They state that three species of *Hanseniaspora* are now recognized, i.e., *Hans. valbyensis*, *Hans. uvarum*, and *Hans. osmophila* and that the life cycles of those that form hat-shaped spores and those that form spherical spores are similar. The vegetative cell is diploid. Four hat-shaped or one or rarely two spherical spores are formed per ascus, depending on the species. The spores are uninucleate and conjugation between spores does not occur. Vegetative cells of *Hans. valbyensis* and *Hans. uvarum* are diploid while those of K. *apiculata* are haploid.

Non-spore forming (asporogenous) forms may arise by mutation or selection, or may result from possible changes in nutritional and environmental conditions. Four species and two varieties of *Kloeckera* are recognized, i.e., K. *apiculata*, K. *africana*, K. *corticis*, K. *javanica*, and its var.

lafari and var. *javanica*. For a study of *Hans. uvarum* and its rapid disappearance during fermentation, except in continuous procedures, see Sapis-Domercq (1969).

Variation in Yeast Sedimentation.—Some wine yeasts, particularly the native strains of *S. cerevisiae* from California grapes, give a "powdery" or fine-grained sediment after fermentation. This sediment is easily disturbed during racking and on that account it is difficult to draw off the new wine close to the lees. Other varieties, notably Champagne yeasts of France, give a very coarse or granular and heavy sediment. The yeast settles quickly after fermentation and in racking there is little tendency for the yeast lees to rise and mix with the wine. Consequently, the racked wine is apt to be clearer and less of it is lost in the lees.

The clouding of bottle wines by various yeasts is a very important problem and is discussed in Chapter 16. (See also Van der Walt and Van Kerken 1958A).

Single Strains Versus Mixed Cultures.—There is a difference of opinion among European enologists concerning the use of a single strain of yeast in the fermentation of must. Some believe that better flavor and bouquet are obtained by the use of natural mixed cultures. Florenzano (1949) found several species, other than *S. cerevisiae* in the refermentation of new wine by the "governo" technique (pp. 27–28), used in Tuscany and concludes that they are of importance in the development of the quality of these wines. Mestre and Mestre (1946) found that selected pure cultures of *S. cerevisiae* produced more alcohol and gave a faster fermentation than the native yeasts, but that they did not convey the characteristic flavor of their region of origin.

Malan and Lovisolo (1958) found that in botrytised musts of high sugar content the initial fermentation is carried out by *K. apiculata*. Tarantola (1946) reported that his strains of *K. apiculata* were objectionable because of their low alcohol-forming power and production of excessive amounts of acetic acid and aldehyde. Bioletti and Cruess (1912) and Cruess (1918) came to a similar conclusion.

Castelli (1955, 1960) reviewed the past research conducted on this problem at the University of Perugia giving the results of 1301 cultures. He states that the effects produced by yeasts other than *S. cerevisiae* in the natural fermentation of Italian musts cannot be neglected. In this regard he lists six genera and species including *K. apiculata*, two species of *Torulopsis, S. bayanus* and *S. uvarum*.

Rankine (1955) in Australia compared 98 strains of wine yeast from various sources. The final alcohol content of the fermented musts varied from 8 to 15 per cent at 77°F. Most strains produced more volatile acid at 77°F. that at 59°F. Glycerol production varied considerably, and more was produced at 77°F. than at 59°F. The production of aldehyde was investigated for 11 strains, two of which produced exceptionally large amounts at 59°F. Castor and Amerine (1942) used 32 different strains of wine yeast in the fermentation of Trebbiano musts and observed minor differences, particularly in bouquet. Castor (1954) compared the products of fermentation and flavors produced by different yeasts. He found considerable variation, particularly in the flavor.

A large (8-fold) influence of yeast strain on hydrogen sulfide formation was emphasized by Rankine (1963). Not only do strains of wine yeast differ remarkably in their ability to produce hydrogen sulfide, but Zambonelli (1964) was able to show that hybridization of positive and negative strains was possible. The F_1 progency were positive producers.

Mestre and Mestre (1946) in studies on spontaneous fermentations and those conducted with pure cultures of S. cerevisiae from various regions found that the wine yeasts did not differ greatly in their effect on the character of the wine. The pure cultures gave more consistent and more satisfactory results than did the spontaneous fermentations with natural mixed cultures.

Saller (1957) concludes from his investigations that wines of better quality are obtained by use of fermentations with pure cultures of S. cerevisiae than by spontaneous fermentation with the natural, mixed yeast flora of grapes. He found that in addition to elimination or inhibition of the undesirable yeasts by pasteurization or sulfur dioxide, low temperature during fermentation was successful in securing a dominant fermentation by the true wine yeast. However, there is a rather marked belief among wine makers of certain European countries that the mixed cultures of spontaneous fermentation often give wines of superior flavor and bouquet. We found this belief held especially by some wine producers of the Bordeaux district in France. While the investigations of Peynaud and Domercq (1953, 1955) do not verify this belief, nevertheless, they state that it is difficult to say whether or not certain yeasts impart special characteristics to the wine. See also Peynaud and Ribéreau-Gayon (1947), Gomes (1969), Renaud (1939–1940), and Rankine (1968).

Wahab et al. (1949) found that wines of different flavors and bouquets could be made by fermenting sterilized musts with pure cultures of ester-forming yeasts and completing the fermentations with S. cerevisiae. Their observations tend to confirm those of Castelli (1955) and of other Italian investigators, that the effects of yeasts other than S. cerevisiae cannot be disregarded.

Toledo and Teixera (1955) in experiments on the effect of kind of yeast starter on production of volatile acid obtained the best results when the must was inoculated initially with S. *rosei* and 48 to 96 hours later with S. *cerevisiae.* They also (1957) compared 25 strains of S. *cerevisiae* isolated from Brazilian grape musts and found that these gave similiar results except in production of volatile acidity. They concluded that the strains that produced the least volatile acidity might be useful in making wine in Brazil.

Schulle (1953A) found that the addition of a *Saccharomyces (rouxii?)* culture with S. *cerevisiae* to a must rich in sugar resulted in an increased yield of alcohol in comparison with fermentation of the same must with a culture of the latter yeast alone. He also (1935B) obtained similar results by use of *Hanseniaspora* sp. with S. *cerevisiae.*

It is possible that wines of distinctive flavor and bouquet can be made with mixed cultures under carefully controlled conditions, but because of the difficulty in selecting and securing the special microflora required and because of the danger of spoilage in uncontrolled natural fermentations, it is recommended, for the present at least, that only selected, proven strains of wine yeast be used in the commercial production of wine. See Jorgensen (1936).

Exogenous Vitamin Requirements.—Wikén and Richard (1951) found that the wine yeasts known as Fendant, Herrliberg, and Salenegg used in commercial wine making in Switzerland showed excellent growth in synthetic media devoid of vitamins, whereas the Dezaley strain required at least three vitamins for normal growth. Work with other yeasts indicated that the sporogenous wine yeasts are a highly heterogeneous group as regards the need for an exogenous supply of vitamins. See Joslyn (1951) and Thorne (1946) for further information.

Steinberg (1952) found that certain yeasts grew as well in a special synthetic medium as in grape must. He proposes that yeast cultures for use in wineries be grown in such a medium as it can always be duplicated and in Switzerland is less costly than grape juice. Also, compared with grape must it is less viscous, develops less sediment and foam and has less color. See p. 261 for present commercial use in California.

Effect of Climate.—Castelli (1955) has studied the apiculate yeasts of Italy and other countries and has concluded that the locality where the grapes are grown has an important effect on the kinds of yeast found upon them. Other investigations on the effect of climate on the kinds of yeasts found on grapes have been reported by Castelli in 1941, 1948, 1955, and 1960. See p. 170.

Peynaud and Domercq (1953, 1955) found eight different species of asporogenous and 22 species of sporogenous yeasts in the musts of the Bordeaux region of southern France. They observed that grapes attacked severely by *Botrytis cinerea* contained a somewhat different yeast flora than grapes that had not been attacked by botrytis. Catalano (1957) has reported that 50 per cent of the yeast cultures isolated by him from musts of Apulia region of southern Italy were *S. cerevisiae* strains. Also found in appreciable numbers were *K. apiculata, S. rosei,* and *Hans. valbyensis.*

Capriotti (1954) in a study of the yeasts occurring on grapes grown in Italy and Holland found that climate had a very marked effect on the prevalence of various species. For example, *Hansenula* species seldom occurred in the cool northern provinces of Italy but were very common in the warm provinces of southern Italy and of Sicily. On the other hand, *K. apiculata* was very common in northern Italy and was found less frequently in southern Italy and in Sicily. *S. cerevisiae* was found in almost all Italian samples regardless of where grown. *S. italicus* on the other hand, was found much more frequently in southern than in northern Italy. *Saccharomyces rosei,* a species favored by Castelli (1948) for use in wine making, was quite evenly distributed. In the musts of grapes grown in Holland he found that *K. apiculata* predominated during the initial stages of fermentation. It was followed by *C. guilliermondii* and *Pichia* sp. *H. anomala* developed during the intermediate phase and *S. cerevisiae* did not appear until later, but completed the fermentation very successfully. Domercq (1957) believes this is due to adaptation of different yeasts to various levels of sugar.

Cantarelli (1955) states that *Kloeckera* (Janke) (apiculate yeast) is responsible for the initial stage of the natural fermentation of musts in the cold-temperature zone of Italy and *Hanseniaspora* (Zikes) carries on the initial stage in the warm hot zone of southern Italy. In this respect his observations agree with those of Capriotti. Both species markedly retarded the activity of *S. cerevisiae.*

Growth at Low Temperatures.—Strains of *S. cerevisiae* vary considerably in their ability to carry on fermentation at low temperatures. For example, Castelli (1941) in fermentation at six different temperatures by ten strains of wine yeast isolated from Italian musts and wines found that one strain gave 12.3 per cent of alcohol at 41° to 43°F. while another gave only six per cent. At 50° to 54°F. and 59° to 63°F. all cultures gave high yields of alcohol; but at 77°F. the yeast that gave the highest alcohol yields at 41° to 43°F. produced only nine per cent of alcohol. Several other strains were also retarded slightly to moderately at this temperature. At 86°F. all strains were greatly retarded and still more so at 98.6°F. Porchet (1938) in Switzerland isolated two varieties of wine yeast that fermented must at temperatures below 32°F. Osterwalder (1934A, 1934B) found that wine yeast can be acclimatized to low temperatures.

The research of Porchet and of Osterwalder is of considerable importance in Switzerland where the temperature often becomes low during the vintage season.

Tchelistcheff (1948) found that white musts fermented between 45° and 60°F. with a finishing temperature of 66° to 68°F. gave wines of greater freshness of flavor and fruitiness, low volatile acidity, higher glycerol and less lees than musts fermented at 78° to 88°F. Fermentation of white musts at low temperature (60°F. or lower) is now common practice in the production of dry table wines of high quality in California. Hohl and Cruess (1936) using syruped fermentations of must with champagne yeast and a temperature range of 44.6° to 98.6°F. obtained 16.5 per cent alcohol at 44.6°F., 16.4 at 50°F., 16.7 at 60.8°F., 16.5 at 68° to 71.6°F., 13.9 at 77°F., 13.3 at 82.4°F., 12.2 at 87.8°F., 8.6 per cent at 93.2°F., and 6.3 per cent at 98.6°F. Pederson *et al.* (1959) found that grape juice stored commercially at 22° to 28°F. in tanks occasionally developed large numbers of yeast cells. It was found that several species were represented, although strains of *Saccharomyces Torulopsis, Hanseniaspora,* and *Candida* predominated.

Thermal Death Time.—Using specially-designed capillary tubes Jacob *et. al.* (1964) reported thermal death times of *Saccharomyces cerevisiae* of one minute at 135.5°F. and 0.1 minute at 143.6°F. for one strain and about 1.8° lower for another. Synergistic effects were noted due to alcohol but the yeast death time was not lowered sufficiently to account for the results of Yang *et al.* (1947).

BIBLIOGRAPHY

AMERINE, M. A. 1958. Personal communication.

AMERINE, M. A., and JOSLYN, M. A. 1940. Commercial production of table wines. Calif. Agr. Expt. Sta. Bull. 639.

AMERINE, M. A., and JOSLYN, M. A. 1970. Table Wines: the Technology of Their Production. 2 ed. University of California Press, Berkeley and Los Angeles.

BARRE, P., and GALZY, P. 1960. Étude et détermination d'une levure osmophile. Ann. technol. agr. 9, 345–348.

BEDFORD, C. L. 1942. A taxonomic study of the genus *Hansenula.* Mycologia 34, 628–649.

BIOLETTI, F. T., and CRUESS, W. V. 1912. Enological investigations. Calif. Agr. Expt. Sta. Bull. 230, 23–118.

BRÉCHOT, P., CHAUVET, J., and GIRARD, H. 1962. Identification des levures d'un moût de Beaujolais au cours de sa fermentation. Ann. technol. agr. *11,* 235–244.

BREED, R. S., MURRAY, E. G. D., and HITCHENS, P. 1957. Bergey's Manual of Determinative Bacteriology. 7th edition., Williams and Wilkins Co., Baltimore.

CANTARELLI, A. 1955. Studio comparativo dei lieveti apiculati dei generi *Kloeckera* (Janke) ed *Hanseniaspora* (Zikes). Ann. Microbiol. *6*, 86–129.

CAPRIOTTI, A. 1954. Recherches sur les levures de la fermentation vinaire en Italie. Antonie van Leeuwenhoek J. Microbiol. Serol. *20* 374–384.

CASTELLI, T. 1941. Temperatura e chimismo dei blastomiceti. Ann. Microbiol. *2*, 8–22,

CASTELLI T. 1948. I lieveti della fermentazione vinaria nelle regione Pugliese. Ricera Sci. *18*, 66–94.

CASTELLI, T. 1954. Fermentazione e rifermentazione nei paesi caldi. Xe Congrès Inter Ind. Agr. *2*, 1891–1909.

CASTELLI, T. 1955. Yeasts of wine fermentations from various regions in Italy. Am. J. Enol. *6*, 18–20. (*See also* Riv. Vitic. e Enol. (Conegliano) *1*, 258–264, 1948.)

CASTELLI, T. 1960. Lieviti e Fermentazioni in Enologia. Luigi Scialpi Editore, Rome.

CASTOR, J. G. B. 1954. Fermentation products and flavor profiles of yeasts. Wines and Vines *35*, No. 8, 29–31.

CASTOR, J. G. B. 1957. Nutrient requirements for growth of sherry flor yeast, *Saccharomyces beticus*. Appl. Microbiol. *6*, 51–60.

CASTOR, J. G. B., and AMERINE, M. A. 1942. Unpublished data. Dept. of Viticulture and Enology, Univ. Calif., Davis.

CATALANO, M. 1957. La flora blastomicetica dei mosti pugliesi prove di fermentazione su scala semi-industriale con ceppi selezionati. Ann. fac. agr. univ. Bari *11*, 395–425.

CHARPENTIÉ, Y. 1954. Contribution à l'étude biochimique des facteurs de l'acidité des vins. Ann. technol. agr. *3*, 89–167.

CIFERRI, R., and VERONA, O. 1941. Descrizione dei lieviti della uve, dei mosti e dei vini. In: Garoglio, P. G. Trattato di Enologia. *2*, 275–309. Il Progresso Vinicolo ed Oleario, Florence, 1941.

COOK, A. H. 1958. The Chemistry and Biology of Yeasts. Academic Press, New York.

CRUESS, W. V. 1918. The fermentation organisms from California grapes. Univ. Calif. Publ. Agr. Sci. *4*, No. 1, 1–66.

CRUESS, W. V. 1948. Investigations of the flor sherry process. Calif. Agr. Expt. Sta. Bull. *710*.

DITTRICH, H. H. 1963A. Versuche zum Apfelsäureabbau mit einer Hefe der Gattung *Schizosaccharomyces*. Wein-Wissen. 18, 392–405.

DITTRICH, H. H. 1963B. Zum Chemismus des Apfelsäureabbaues mit einer Hefe der Gattung *Schizosaccharomyces*. Ibid. *18*, 406–410.

DITTRICH, H. H. 1964. Über die Glycerinbildung von *Botrytis cinerea* auf Traubenbeeren und Traubenmosten sowie über der Glyceringehalt von Beeren- und Trockenbeerenausleseweinen. Ibid. *19*, 12–20.

DOMERCO, S. 1957. Étude et classification des levures de vin de la Gironde. Ann. technol. agr. *6*, 5–58, 139–183.

FEDUCHY MARINO, E. 1956. Contribución al estudio y relación de la "Flor" española de levadura perteneciente a las principales regiones vinícolas. Bol. Inst. nac. invest. agron. (Madrid) *35*, 211–237.

FLORENZANO, G. 1949. La microflora blastomiceta dei mosti e dei vini di alcune zona Toscane. Ann. sper. agrar. (Rome) [N.S.] *3*, No. 4, 887–918.

GALZY, P.   1956.   Nomenclature des levures du vin.   Ann. technol. agr. 5, 473–491.
GOMES, J. V. M.   1969.   Emprego de leveduras seleccionadas em vinificação. Anais Inst. Vinho Porto 23, 41–70.
GUILLIERMOND, A., and TANNER, F.   1920.   The Yeasts.   John Wiley and Sons, New York.
HENNEBERG, W.   1926.   Handbuch der Gärungsbakteriologie.   2 vols.   Parey, Berlin.
HENRICI, A. T.   1930.   The Yeasts, Molds and Actinomycetes.   John Wiley and Sons, New York.
HEWITT, W. B., GOODING, JR., G. V., CHIARAPPA, L., and BUTLER, E. E.   1962. Etiology of summer bunch rot of grapes in California.   (Abstr.) Phytopath. 52, 13.
HOHL, L. A., and CRUESS, W. V.   1936.   Effect of temperature, variety of juice and method of increasing sugar content on maximum alcohol production by Saccharomyces ellipsoideus.   Food Research 1, 405–411.
HOLM, H. C.   1908.   A study of yeasts from California grapes.   California Agr. Expt. Sta. Bull. 197, 169–175.
JACOB, F. S., ARCHER, T. E., and CASTOR, J. G. B.   1964.   Thermal death time of yeast.   Am. J. Enol. Vitic. 15, 69–74.
JANKE, A.   1924.   Allgemeine Technische Microbiologie.   Steinkopff, Dresden.
JORGENSEN, A.   1936.   Practical Management of Pure Yeast.   3 ed. rev. by A. Hansen.   Lippincott Co., Philadelphia.
JOSLYN, M. A.   1951.   Nutrient requirements of yeast.   Mycopath. et Mycol. Appl. 5, 260–276.
JOSLYN, M. A., and AMERINE, M. A.   1964.   Dessert, Appetizer and Related Flavored Wines.   University of California, Division of Agricultural Sciences, Berkeley.
KUNKEE, R. E. and AMERINE, M. A.   1970.   Yeasts in winemaking.   In Rose, A. H., and Harrison, J. S., eds.   The Yeasts, Vol. 3, Academic Press, New York.
LINDNER, P.   1893.   Schizosaccharomyces pombe, n. spec., ein neuer Gärungserreger.   Wochschr. Brau. 10, 1298:
LINDNER, P.   1903.   Sporenbildung bei Saccharomyces apiculatus.   Ibid. 20, 505.
LODDER, J.   1970.   The Yeasts.   North-Holland Publishing Co., Amsterdam, London.
LODDER, J., and KREGER-VAN RIJ, N. J. W.   1952.   The Yeasts—A Taxonomic Study.   North Holland Publishing Co., Amsterdam, and Interscience Publishers, New York.
MALAN, C. E., and LOVISOLO R.   1958.   I lieviti della fermentazione vinaria in Piedmont.   Atti accad. ital. vite e vino 10, 124–146.
MARCILLA ARRAZOLA, J., ALAS, G., and FEDUCHY, E.   1963.   (i.e. 1939) Contribución al estudio de las levaduras que forman velo sobre ciertos vinos de elevado grado alcohólico.   Anales. Centro Invest. Vinícolas 1, 1–230.
MESTRE, ARTIGAS, C., and MESTRE, JANE, A.   1946.   Fermentaciones comparativos con diferentes levaduras.   Min. agr. inst. nac. invest. agron, Estación Vitíc. y Enol., Villafranca del Panadés, Cuaderno 68, 1–28.
MILLER, M. W., and PHAFF, H. J.   1958.   A comparative study of the apiculate yeasts.   Mycopath. et Mycol. Appl. 10, 113–141.

MINÁRIK, E. 1964. Die Hefeflora von Jungweinen in der Tschechoslowake. Mitt. Rebe u. Wein, Serie A (Klosterneuburg) *14*, 306–315.

MRAK, E. M., and McCLUNG, L. S. 1940. Yeasts occurring on grapes and grape products in California. J. Bact. *40*, 395–407.

MRAK, E. M., and PHAFF, H. J. 1948. Yeasts. Ann. Rev. Microbiol. 1948, *17*, 1–46.

NELSON, K. E. 1951. Factors influencing the infection of table grapes by *Botrytis cinerea*. Phytopathology *41*, 319–326.

NELSON, K. E., and AMERINE, M. A. 1957. Use of *Botrytis cinerea* for the production of sweet table wines. Am. J. Enol. *7*, 131–136.

NELSON, K. E., and AMERINE, M. A. 1957. Use of *Botrytis cinerea* for the production of natural sweet wines from botrytised grapes. Am. J. Enol. *8*, 127–134.

NIEHAUS, C. J. G. 1932. Untersuchung über Apiculatishefen. Zentr. Bakt. Parasitenk. III. Abt. *87*, 97–150.

NONOMURA, H., and OHARA, Y. 1959. Distribution of *Actinomycetes* in the soil. Bull. Research Institute of Fermentation, Yamanashi Univ. 77–88.

OHARA, Y., NONOMURA, H., and YUNOME, H. 1959. Dynamic aspect of yeast flora during vinous fermentation. Bull. Research Institute of Fermentation, Yamanashi Univ. 7–12, 13–18.

OSTERWALDER, A. 1934A. Die verkannten Kaltgärhefen. Schweiz. Z. Obst- u. Weinbau *50*, 487–490.

OSTERWALDER, A. 1934B. Von Kaltgärhefen und Kaltgärung. Zentr. Bakteriol. Parasitenk. II. Abt. *90*, 226–249.

PEDERSON, C. S., ALBURY, M. N., WILSON, D. C., and LAWRENCE, N. L. 1959. The growth of yeasts in grape juice at low temperatures. Appl. Microbiol. 7, 1–6; 7–11; 12–16.

PEYNAUD, E., and DOMERCQ, S. 1953. Étude des levures de la Gironde. Ann. technol. agr. 4, 265–300.

PEYNAUD, E., and DOMERCQ, S. 1955. Étude de la microflore des moûts et des vins de Bordeaux. Compt. rend. acad. agr. France *41*, 103–106.

PEYNAUD, E., and DOMERCQ, S. 1959. A review of microbiological problems in wine-making in France. Am. J. Enol. Vitic. *10*, 69–77.

PEYNAUD, E., and RIBÉREAU-GAYON, J. 1947. Sur les divers de fermentation alcoolique détermines par diverses races de levures elliptiques. Comp. rend. *224*, 1388–1390.

PEYNAUD, E., and SUDRAUD, P. 1964. Utilisation de l'effet désacidifiant des *Schizosaccharomyces* en vinification de raisins acides. Am. Technol. Agr. *13*, 309–328.

PHAFF, H. J., and DOUGLAS, H. C. 1938. A note on yeasts occurring in dessert wines. Fruit Prods. J. *23*, 317–321.

PORCHET, B. 1938. Biologie des levures provoquant la fermentation alcoolique à basse température. Ann. ferment. *4*, 578–600.

PRESCOTT, S. C., and DUNN, C. C. 1960. Industrial Microbiology. McGraw-Hill Book Co., New York.

PROSTOSERDOV, N. N., and AFRIKIAN, R. 1933. Jerezwein in Armenien. Das Weinland *5*, 389–391.

RANKINE, B. C. 1955. Quantitative differences in products of fermentation by different strains of wine yeasts. Am. J. Enol. *6*, 1–10.

RANKINE, B. C. 1963. Nature, origin, and prevention of hydrogen sulfide aroma in wine. J. Sci. Food Agr. *14*, 79–91.

RANKINE, B. C. 1968. The importance of yeasts in determining the composition and quality of wines. Vitis 7, 22–49.

RAPER, K. B. 1945. A Manual of the Aspergilli. Williams and Wilkins, Baltimore.

RAPER, K. B., and THOM, C. C. 1949. A Manual of the Penicilla. Williams and Wilkins, Baltimore.

RENAUD, J. 1939–40. La microflore des levures du vin. Son role dans la vinification. Ann. ferment. 5, 410–417.

ROMAN, W., ARIMA, I. T., NICKERSON, W. J., PYKE, M., SCHANDERL, H., SCHULTZ, A. S., THAYSEN, A. C., and THORNE, R. S. 1957. Yeasts. The Academic Press, New York.

ROSE, A. H., and HARRISON, J. S. 1968–70. The Yeasts. Academic Press, New York. 3 v.

SALLER, W. 1957. Die Spontane-Sprosspilzflora frisch gepresster Traubensäfte und die Reinhefegärung. Mitt. Rebe u. Wein, Serie A (Klosterneuburg), 7, 130–138.

SAPIS-DOMERCQ, S. 1969. Comportement des levures apiculées au cours de la vinification. Connaiss. Vigne Vin 4, 379–392.

SCHANDERL, H., and STAUDENMAYER, T. 1964. Über den Einfluss der schwefligen Säure auf die Acetaldehydbildung verschiedener Hefen bei Most- und Schaumweingärungen. Mitt. Rebe u. Wein, Serie A (Klosterneuburg) 14, 267–281.

SCHEFFER, W. R., and MRAK, E. M. 1951. Characteristics of yeast causing clouding of dry white wines. Mycopath. et Mycol. Appl. 5, 236–249.

SCHULLE, H. 1953A. Die Bedeutung der Apiculatus–Hefen für die Gärtätigkeit der echten Weinhefen in zuckerreichen Mosten. Archiv. Microbiol. 18, 342–348.

SCHULLE, H. 1953B. Über das Zasammenwirken von Hefen der Gattung Saccharomyces und der Untergattung Zygosaccharomyces bei der Vergärung von zuckerreichen Mosten. Archiv. Mikrobiol. 18, 133–148.

STEINBERG, B. 1952. Justification de l'emploi d'un milieu synthetique pour la multiplication des levures destinées à la vinification. Mitt. Gebiete Lebensm. u. Hyg. 43, 219–235.

STELLUNG-DEKKER, N. M. 1931. Die Sporogenen Hefen. Die Hefesammlung des "Central-bureau voor Schimmelcultures," I Teil, Amsterdam.

TANNER, F. W. 1944. The Microbiology of Foods. Garrard Press, Champaign, Ill.

TARANTOLA, C. 1946. Nuovo contributo allo studio dei lieviti apiculati. Ann. Accad. Agr. Turino 88, 115–133. (See also Bull. off. intern. vin 21, No. 208, 70–72. 1948).

TCHELISTCHEFF, A. 1948. Comments on cold fermentation. Univ. California College Agr. Wine. Technol. Conf., Davis, 98–101.

THORNE, R. S. 1946. The nitrogen nutrition of yeast. Wallerstein Lab. Commun. 9, 97–114.

TOLEDO, O., and TEIXERA, C. G. 1955. Vantaggi della associazone di lieviti nella fermentazione vinaria: riduzione dell acidita volatile nei vini. Agricoltura Italiana 55, 155–164.

TOLEDO, O. and TEIXERA, C. G. 1957. O emprego de leveduras selectionadas na fermentação do vinho. Boletin Tecnico Instituto Agronomico Estado São-Paulo 16, 251–260.

UNDERKOFLER, L. A., and HICKEY, R. J. 1954. Industrial Fermentations. 2 vols. Chem. Pub. Co., New York.

VAN DER WALT, J. P., and VAN KERKEN, A. E. 1958A. Survey of yeasts causing turbidity in South African wines. Bull. of the Wine Industry Research Group. Stellenbosch.

VAN DER WALT, J. P., and VAN KERKEN, A. E. 1958B. The wine yeasts of the Cape. Part I. Antonie van Leeuwenhoek J. Microbiol. Serol. 24, 239–252.

VAN KERKEN, A. E. 1963. Contribution to the ecology of yeasts occurring in Wine. University of the Orange Free State, Pretoria. Mimeo.

VERONA, O., and RAMBELLI, A. 1961. Notizie, ricerche e considerazioni relative Candida pulcherrima ed altri lieviti ad analoga fisionomia. Ann Fac. Agr. Pisa 22, 91–121.

WAHAB, A., WITZKE, W., and CRUESS, W. V. 1949. Experiments with ester forming yeasts. Fruit Prod. J. 28, 198–200, 202–219.

WICKERHAM, L. J. 1951. Taxonomy of Yeasts. U.S. Dept. Agr., Tech. Bull. 1029, 1–56.

WICKERHAM, L. J., and DUPRAT, E. 1945. A remarkable fission yeast, Schizosaccharomyces versatilis nov. sp. J. Bact. 50, 597–607.

WIKÉN, T., and RICHARD, O. 1951. Untersuchungen über die Physiologie der Weinhefen I. Mitteilung zur Kenntnis der Wachstumsbedingungen einer auxoautotrophen schweizerischen Kulturweinhefe. Antonie van Leeuwenhoek J. Microbiol. Serol. 17, 209–226; 18, 31–34, 293–315.

YANG, H. Y., JOHNSON, J. H., and WEIGAND, E. H. 1947. Electronic pasteurization of wine. Fruit Prod. J. 26, 295–299.

YOKOTSUKA, I. 1954. Studies on Japanese Wine Yeasts. Research Institute of Fermentation, Yamanashi University, Kofu.

ZAMBONELLI, C. 1964. Ricerche genetiche sulla produzione di idrogeno solforato in Saccharomyces cerevisiae var. ellipsoideus. Ann. Microbiol. 14, 143–153.

ZIKES, H. 1911. Zur Nomenklaturfrage der Apiculatushefen. Zentr. Bakteriol. Parasitenk. II. Abt. 30, 145–153.

CHAPTER 5

Chemistry of Fermentation and Composition of Wines

FERMENTATION

Fermentation originally indicated the conversion of grape juice into wine. It is now applied to a variety of processes of anaerobic dissimilation of organic compounds by microorganisms, by living cells, or by extracts prepared from them. It is also used for certain aerobic microbial processes. Alcoholic fermentation is but one of the many chemical processes which may be classified as fermentation. Other industrial fermentations of importance produce antibiotics, acetic acid (vinegar), citric acid, butyl alcohol, etc.

In any dissimilation process organic compounds of higher energy are converted to products of lesser energy with the subsequent release of energy in the form of heat. Dissimilation processes are therefore oxidation-reduction reactions including: (1) addition of oxygen, (2) removal of hydrogen, or (3) loss of an electron. In the usual process hydrogen from the donor is transferred by a series of enzymes and respiratory pigments to a reducible substance, the hydrogen acceptor. Atmospheric oxygen, reducible compounds in the substrate or intermediate compounds may act as acceptors. Aerobic processes involve atmospheric oxygen while the other two types are anaerobic in nature. An important difference between aerobic and anaerobic processes is that the former release much larger amounts of energy.

History

The famous French chemist, Lavoisier, in 1789 made quantitative studies on alcoholic fermentation—one of the first such studies of a natural phenomena. In 1810 Gay-Lussac correctly reported the over-all reaction in the famous equation which bears his name:

$$C_6H_{12}O_6 = 2C_2H_5OH + 2CO_2$$

It became clear in the late 19th century that the Gay-Lussac equation represented only the over-all process of alcoholic fermentation.

The relation of yeasts to the process of alcoholic fermentation had been noted by many early investigators. In fact the species name *Saccharomyces* comes from the Greek *sakcharos,* sugar, and *mykos,* fungus. However, Liebig, the great German organic chemist, considered the yeasts to be without significance in fermentation and the weight of his authority

177

halted progress in understanding the process until Pasteur's definitive studies.[1,2]

Chemistry

Pasteur's work, even though he did not clearly understand the nature of the process, established the essential validity of the Gay-Lussac equation but also showed that a variety of by-products were present which were not accounted for by the equation. Among the common by-products are glycerol, acetic and lactic acids, and acetaldehyde. Since Pasteur's time many biochemists have devoted their time to tracing the complex process from sugar to alcohol, carbon dioxide and by-products. Fig. 52 indicates the general scheme and accounts for glycerol as one of the by-products.

Even though the variety of by-products and the importance of the enzyme system were established before 1900 it was not until 1913 that Neuberg developed the first tenable scheme of alcoholic fermentation. Progress was rapid thereafter leading to the present generally-accepted series of reactions, Fig. 52.

During the initial induction stage the hexose phosphate is converted to α-glycerophosphate and 3-phosphoglycerate, since at first the entire sequence of reactions is delayed because no acetaldehyde is present. Glycerol is produced directly from the α-glycerophosphate. The 3-phosphoglycerate is transformed to pyruvate which is decarboxylated to acetaldehyde. As acetaldehyde accumulates it becomes the hydrogen acceptor (in place of dehydroxyacetone phosphate) and reacts with reduced coenzyme I (NADH) to produce ethyl alcohol. During the stationary phase this process predominates and little glycerol is formed. If acetaldehyde is not available (when removed by sulfite, for example) the induction phase continues and glycerol is produced. Most of the reactions are reversible.

In the presence of a high concentration of sulfur dioxide in acid solution acetaldehyde, carbon dioxide, and glycerol are the primary products and alcohol a by-product. If the sulfite solution is alkaline acetaldehyde, glycerol, alcohol, and carbon dioxide are all produced. Other types of fermentation have been reported. See Amerine (1965A). The glycolytic sequence clearly shows the complexity of the system. It also shows how glycerol, lactic acid, and acetaldehyde may accumulate as by-products.

---

[1] Pasteur himself did not work with pure cultures. Christian Emil Hansen introduced this technique and successfully applied it to brewing. Müller-Thurgau in Germany was the first to make pure yeast cultures with grape must fermentations. His pupil at Geisenheim, Wortmann, was distributing pure cultures in 1894, according to Schanderl (1959).

[2] Büchner, of course, actually clarified the conflict when he was able to induce cell-free fermentation by using ground-up yeast cells shortly before 1900.

1. glucose[1] $\xrightarrow[(\text{Mg}^{++}, \text{ATP} \rightarrow \text{ADP})]{(\text{hexokinase})}$ glucose-6-phosphate

2a. glucose-6-phosphate $\xrightarrow[(\text{NADP} \rightarrow \text{NADPH} + \text{H}^+)]{(\text{glucose-6-phosphate dehydrogenase})}$ 6-phosphogluconate $\rightarrow$ hexose
monophosphate shunt system

2. glucose-6-phosphate $\xrightleftharpoons[]{(\text{phosphohexoisomerase})}$ fructose-6-phosphate

2b. fructose $\xrightarrow[(\text{Mg}^{++}, \text{ATP} \rightarrow \text{ADP})]{(\text{hexokinase})}$ fructose-6-phosphate

3. fructose-6-phosphate $\xrightarrow[(\text{Mg}^{++}, \text{ATP} \rightarrow \text{ADP})]{(\text{phosphofructokinase})}$ fructose-1,6-diphosphate[2]
   (Neuberg ester)

4. fructose-1,6-diphosphate[2] $\xrightleftharpoons[(\text{Zn}^{++}, \text{Co}^{++}, \text{Fe}^{++} \text{ or Ca}^{++})]{(\text{aldolase})}$ D-glyceraldehyde-3-phosphate +
   (Harden-Young ester)
   dihydroxyacetone phosphate

5. D-glyceraldehyde-3-phosphate $\xrightleftharpoons[]{(\text{triosphosphate isomerase})}$ dihydroxyacetone-phosphate
   (Fischer-Baer ester)

5a. dihydroxyacetone-phosphate $\xrightleftharpoons[(\text{H}^+ + \text{NADH} \rightarrow \text{NAD})]{(\alpha\text{-glycerolphosphate dehydrogenase})}$ L-α-glycerol phosphoric
   acid

5b. L-α-glycerol phosphoric acid $\xrightleftharpoons[]{(\text{phosphatase})}$ glycerol

6. D-glyceraldehyde-3-phosphate + H_3PO_4 $\xrightleftharpoons[(\text{NAD} \rightarrow \text{NADH} \rightarrow + \text{H}^+)]{(\text{triosphosphate dehydrogenase})}$ 1,3-diphos-
   phoryl-D-glycerate

7. 1,3-diphosphoryl-D-glycerate $\xrightleftharpoons[(\text{Mg}^{++}, \text{ADP} \rightarrow \text{ATP})]{(\text{phosphorylglyceryl kinase})}$ 3-diphosphoryl-D-glycerate

8. 3-diphosphoryl-D-glycerate $\xrightleftharpoons[(2,3\text{-diphosphoryl-D-glycerate})]{(\text{phosphyrylglyceryl mutase})}$ 2-phosphoryl-D-glycerate

9. 2-phosphoryl-D-glycerate $\xrightleftharpoons[(\text{Mg}^{++})]{(\text{phosphoenolpyruvic transphorylase})}$ phosphorylenolpyruvate[3]

10. phosphorylenolpyruvate $\xrightleftharpoons[(\text{Mg}^{++}, \text{K}^+, \text{ADP} \rightarrow \text{ATP})]{(\text{phosphoenolpyruvic transphosphorylase})}$ pyruvate

11. pyruvate $\xrightleftharpoons[\text{TPP}]{(\text{carboxylase})}$ acetaldehyde + CO_2

11a. pyruvate $\xrightleftharpoons[(\text{NADH} + \text{H}^+ \rightarrow \text{NAD})]{(\text{lactic dehydrogenase})}$ lactic acid

12. acetaldehyde $\xrightleftharpoons[(\text{NADH} + \text{H}^+ \rightarrow \text{NAD})]{(\text{alcohol dehydrogenase})}$ ethanol

ADP, ATP. Di- and triphosphates of adenosine.

NAD$^+$, NADH. Oxidized and reduced nicotinamide adenine dinucleotide. (NAD is also called coenzyme I or DPN).

NADP, NADPH. Oxidized and reduced nicotinamide adenine dinucleotide phosphate. (NADP is also called coenzyme II or TPN).

TPP. Thiamine pyrophosphate.

---

[1] Starch is converted to glucose-1-phosphate (the Cremer-Cori ester) with phosphoric acid and phosphorylase. Glucose-1-phosphate plus the enzyme phosphoglucomutase and magnesium ions is converted to glucose-1,6-diphosphate.
[2] Fructose-1,6-diphosphate is also converted to fructose-6-phosphate in the presence of fructose diphosphatase, magnesium ions, and water.
[3] Phosphorylenolpyruvate plus phosphorylenolpyruvate enolase and ITP and TTP (Inosine di- and triphosphates) may also produce oxaloacetate.

FIG. 52. CHEMICAL REACTIONS IN ALCOHOLIC FERMENTATION

The tricarboxylic acid cycle (Krebs) which starts with pyruvate can explain by-products such as succinic acid. For the glycolytic cycle note that no less than 22 enzymes are required plus both magnesium and potassium ions and six or more coenzymes.

Yield

The yield of alcohol is of great practical importance to the wine maker. According to the Gay-Lussac equation theoretical yields of 51.1 per cent alcohol and 48.9 per cent carbon dioxide are possible. It is obvious that this is biologically unobtainable and in practice will depend on a variety of factors—amount of by-products, amount of sugar used by yeasts, sugars used by other microorganisms, alcohol lost by evaporation or entrainment (which in turn partially depends on the temperature and the rate of fermentation), presence of air, stirring or other movement of fermenting mass, and other factors.

The yield is therefore not a fixed quantity but will vary depending on the variables mentioned above. The best practical yardstick for yield is therefore empirical studies made under carefully controlled conditions. The following experiments are suggestive.

The experiments of Gvaladze (1936) found yields of alcohol varying from 47.86 to 48.12 per cent and of carbon dioxide of from 47.02 to 47.68 per cent of the weight of sugar fermented. Various practical experiments in Europe indicate that one per cent alcohol can be obtained from 16 to 17 gm. of sugar whereas the stoichiometric yield is 1 per cent from 15.65 gm. of sugar. In other words, in practice yields are about 90 to 95 per cent of the theoretical. The loss is partially due to use of sugar by yeasts and partially from losses due to entrainment.

Warkentin and Nury (1963) note the varying reports of alcohol losses during fermentation that have been reported in the literature. The high losses reported by Banolas (1948) they attribute to using the vapor pressures of pure compounds in his calculations. The low results of Stradelli (1951) they believe is due to the assumption that the alcohol-water-sugar system follows Raoult's law. Marsh (1958) has summarized the systems of estimating the sugar content of musts and alcohol yields as shown in Table 24.

Marsh (1951) notes that a rough approximation of proof gallons per ton is obtained from the formula (Brix—3.0) $\times$ 284.5 $\times$ (100—% pomace). The number of proof gallons of dry table wines is simply per cent alcohol $\times$ 2 $\times$ volume of wine at 60°F. For dessert and sweet wines the proof gallon equivalent may be obtained from Table 25 which has been abbreviated from the original.

In practical terms the wine maker wishes to calculate yields in terms of

TABLE 24

YIELD OF ALCOHOL FROM MUST

Must		Brix—3.0			Gm./Liter—30	
Brix	Sp. Gr.	Sp. Gr.	Sugar[1]	Alcohol[2]	Sugar[3]	Alcohol[2]
	20°/20°	20°/20°	gm./100 ml.	%/vol.	gm./100 ml.	%/vol.
15	1.061	1.048	12.56	7.4	12.89	7.6
20	1.083	1.070	18.15	10.7	18.62	11.0
25	1.106	1.092	23.98	14 1	24.59	14.5
30	1.129	1.115	30.05	17.8	30.81	18.2

[1] (°Brix—3.0) × sp. gr. = gm./100 ml. of sugar.   The 3.0 is an average, it may be as low as 2.5 or as high as 3.5.
[2] Gm./100 ml. of sugar × 0.59 = %/vol. of alcohol.
[3] (°Brix of must × sp. gr. of must) − 3.0 = gm./100 ml. of sugar.

gallons of alcohol per ton of grapes. Obviously here the sugar content of the grapes must be specified. Furthermore, the per cent unfermentable material varies from variety to variety. Even for the same variety it varies during the season depending on the degree of dehydration of the stems, ratio of skins to pulp (which also varies with the size of the fruit), the per cent raisins present, and on other factors. For grapes of about 21° to 23° Balling yields of 20 to 25 gallons of alcohol per ton of grapes may be expected. The wine makers should, of course, strive to get the maximum yield but so many variables affect the yield that except for very large operations no single factor is likely to prove valid. This is particularly true when there are marked differences in the composition of grapes between seasons. It should be particularly emphasized that delivery or tank Ballings are very unreliable for establishing yield. They seldom include a proportionate amount of juice from shriveled or raisined berries. However, during fermentation the sugar of such fruit is dissolved and markedly increases the fermentable sugar. Deceptively high alcohol yields, based on the original load or tank Ballings, are then obtained.

Berti (1951) and Marsh (1958) have both studied this for California conditions. Berti's results on the theoretical yields of wine for different must Ballings and losses are shown below:

The effect of strain of yeast on alcohol yield has been extensively studied. The problem is complicated, as Amerine (1954) has noted, by the

		Must Balling					
Alcohol	Sugar	18°	20°	20°	20°	22°	24°
Per cent	°Balling			Per cent Loss			
		10	8	10	12	10	10
				Gallons per ton			
20	No sugar	98	112	110	108	123	136
20	6	76	87	86	83	96	105
20	7	74	85	83	81	93	103
21	6	72	83	81	79	91	101

TABLE 25

PROOF GALLON EQUIVALENTS PER GALLON OF WINE

Per Cent Alcohol by Volume

Brix of Wine	14.0	15.0	16.0	17.0	18.0	18.5	19.0	19.5	20.0	20.5	21.0	21.5
−4.0	...	...	...	...	...	...	0.38166	0.39315	0.40464	0.41623	0.42782	0.43938
−3.5	...	...	...	0.34072	0.36418	0.37573	0.38730	0.39887	0.41044	0.42205	0.43366	0.44526
−3.0	...	...	0.32324	0.34648	0.36974	0.38128	0.39282	0.40434	0.41586	0.42750	0.43916	0.45077
−2.5	...	0.30574	0.32910	0.35232	0.37552	0.38709	0.39866	0.40923	0.42180	0.43338	0.44496	0.45657
−2.0	0.28804	0.31140	0.33472	0.35802	0.38116	0.39271	0.40426	0.41583	0.42740	0.43898	0.45056	0.46217
−1.5	0.29392	0.31724	0.34054	0.36380	0.38700	0.39855	0.41010	0.42166	0.43322	0.44481	0.45640	0.46800
−1.0	0.29964	0.32298	0.34624	0.36952	0.39272	0.40426	0.41580	0.42734	0.43892	0.45052	0.46212	0.47472
−0.5	0.30542	0.32882	0.35214	0.37536	0.39856	0.41010	0.42164	0.43320	0.44476	0.45635	0.46794	0.47906
0.0	0.31132	0.33464	0.35796	0.38120	0.40440	0.41593	0.42746	0.43902	0.45058	0.46216	0.47374	0.48534
0.5	0.31720	0.34050	0.36372	0.38704	0.41020	0.42177	0.43334	0.44488	0.45642	0.46800	0.47958	0.49117
1.0	0.32314	0.34644	0.36974	0.39296	0.41612	0.42767	0.43922	0.45077	0.46232	0.47390	0.48548	0.49706
1.5	0.32904	0.35234	0.37564	0.39886	0.42202	0.43356	0.44510	0.45664	0.46818	0.47976	0.49134	0.50293
2.0	0.33494	0.35824	0.38154	0.40472	0.42790	0.43945	0.45100	0.46254	0.47408	0.48566	0.49722	0.50880
2.5	0.34090	0.36420	0.38748	0.41070	0.43380	0.44536	0.45692	0.46846	0.48000	0.49158	0.50316	0.51475
3.0	0.34686	0.37016	0.39344	0.41662	0.43976	0.45130	0.46284	0.47439	0.48594	0.49750	0.50906	0.52064
3.5	0.35286	0.37614	0.39942	0.42262	0.44578	0.45730	0.46882	0.48137	0.49192	0.50349	0.51506	0.52663
4.0	0.35886	0.38214	0.40544	0.42862	0.45178	0.46330	0.47482	0.48636	0.49790	0.90946	0.52102	0.53200
4.5	0.36490	0.38820	0.41148	0.43464	0.45778	0.46931	0.48084	0.49237	0.50390	0.51547	0.52704	0.53861
5.0	0.37098	0.39426	0.41752	0.44070	0.46384	0.47537	0.48690	0.49843	0.50996	0.52152	0.53308	0.54466
5.5	0.37702	0.40034	0.42360	0.44678	0.46992	0.48143	0.49294	0.50448	0.51602	0.52757	0.53912	0.55070
6.0	0.38318	0.40644	0.42972	0.45286	0.47600	0.48752	0.49904	0.51057	0.52208	0.53365	0.54522	0.55679
6.5	0.38932	0.41258	0.43584	0.45900	0.48206	0.49361	0.50516	0.51669	0.52822	0.53977	0.55132	0.56289
7.0	0.39548	0.41872	0.44198	0.46512	0.48826	0.49977	0.51128	0.52280	0.53432	0.54588	0.55744	0.56901
7.5	0.40166	0.42490	0.44816	0.47130	0.49442	0.50593	0.51744	0.52897	0.54050	0.55204	0.56358	0.57515
8.0	0.40786	0.43112	0.45438	0.47750	0.50062	0.51212	0.52362	0.53514	0.54666	0.55823	0.56978	0.58133
8.5	0.41412	0.43736	0.46058	0.48372	0.50684	0.51837	0.52990	0.54139	0.55288	0.56444	0.57600	0.58755
9.0	0.42038	0.44360	0.46684	0.48996	0.51308	0.52458	0.53608	0.54760	0.55912	0.57066	0.58220	0.59376

Source of data: Marsh (1951).

fact that total soluble solids, not fermentable sugar, has been measured in most studies. Since actual reducing sugar is seldom measured it appears useless to try to establish an exact relationship between sugar and alcohol yield. Possibly under conditions of a given region and a limited number of grape varieties a useful factor can be found. But as Amerine (1954) has pointed out such a factor varies from season to season.

FACTORS INFLUENCING FERMENTATION

Only the most important factors which affect the process of alcoholic fermentation of grapes will be considered here. For more detail see books on the physiology of yeasts such as White (1954), Cook (1958), Ingram (1955), and Schanderl (1959).

Carbon Sources

Most strains of wine yeasts (*S. cerevisiae*) can generally grow on a medium which provides a utilizable source of energy and carbon, a source of nitrogen, and contains inorganic salts. While monosaccharides are the normal and perhaps preferred substrate for yeasts they can grow on a variety of other carbon sources. Acetic acid, for example, can be utilized by yeasts and during the early stages of fermentation appreciable amounts of acetic acid will disappear. Wine yeasts also oxidize ethyl alcohol but only certain strains will grow on it. Most wine yeasts ferment dextrose more rapidly than levulose even though fructofuranose has an affinity for hexokinase twice that of any form of dextrose. The Sauternes' strain *S. bailli*, ferments levulose more rapidly. Gottschalk (1946) believes this is because the cell walls of this strain are more permeable to levulose. The work of Szabó and Rakcsányi (1937) is illustrative of the complicated nature of the general problem. They found dextrose to ferment more rapidly when the musts contained 17 to 20 per cent reducing sugar. Between 20 and 25 per cent both sugars fermented at the same rate, while at higher concentrations levulose fermented more rapidly.

Levulose is much sweeter than dextrose. According to Koch and Bretthauer (1960), the dextrose/levulose ratio can be increased by sugaring with partially-fermented wine, sucrose, or grape juice. This gives the wine a less sweet taste. Use of selected yeasts could result in sweeter wines at the same total sugar content.

As a matter of fact, above about 25 per cent sugar retards fermentation and at even higher levels (about 70 per cent) most wine yeasts will not ferment the sugar. The inhibiting effect of high sugar is partially owing to the osmotic effect. The length of the fermentation of German *Trockenbeerenauslese* musts of 40 to 67 per cent sugar is as much as 5 to 7 years according to Schanderl (1959) with a final alcohol content of only 5 to 9 per cent. He notes also that alcohol-tolerant yeasts have been known to ferment *Auslese* wines up to 16 per cent alcohol. Note at higher sugar content there is also an increase in volatile acid production. This is shown in Fig. 53. The optimum sugar concentration for maximum speed of fer-

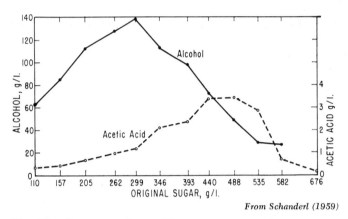

From Schanderl (1959)

FIG. 53.   EFFECT OF SUGAR CONCENTRATION ON ALCOHOL AND
VOLATILE ACID PRODUCTION

mentation is fairly low, perhaps only 1 or 2 per cent. For maximum yield of alcohol per gram of sugar fermented the optimum sugar concentration is higher but has not been established for grape musts. It certainly varies depending on the other constituents of the must, the temperature, and the strain of yeast (p. 196). The maximum alcohol content in a single fermentation is obtained with musts of from 25 to 35 per cent sugar. Gray (1945) for distillers' yeast reported diminished yields of alcohol per gram of sugar fermented at above 5 per cent dextrose. The maximum alcohol content obtainable in normal winery practice is about 16 per cent; however, this varies with strain of yeast (p. 167), temperature, conditions of aeration, and the method of conducting the fermentation. For syruped fermentations it is considerably higher. See p. 451 for experiments on syruped fermentations. Yeasts can also be acclimatized to ferment at higher sugar concentrations though alcohol tolerance may be reduced by such acclimatization. According to Delle (1911), 4.8 per cent sugar has the same repressing influence on alcohol fermentation as 1 per cent by volume of alcohol. Amerine and Kunkee (1965) have reviewed the literature and their experiments show that the repressing influence of sugar is greater when the fortification is made in the early stages of fermentation compared to later stages. There was a small effect of variety and yeast strain. The practical implication is that wines of lower alcohol could be safely marketed at higher sugar contents.

Alcohol

Alcohol itself has an inhibiting effect on fermentation which increases with temperature. This effect is, of course, related to the maximum yield of alcohol which can be expected from various sugar concentrations. The direct effect of alcohol and its dependence on temperature has been demonstrated in this simple experiment by Schanderl (1959). A wine was dealcoholized to various percentages of alcohol. Then yeasts were introduced into each and the wine held at 122°F. for 1 to 5 minutes. The yeast surviving, as per cent, were as follows:

Duration of Heating	Per Cent Alcohol					
	0	3	6	9	12	15
Minutes						
1	15.0	1.5	0.28	0.20	0.009	0.05
2	5.3	0.28	0.30	0.03	0.00	0.00
3	1.0	0.20	0.18	0.03	0.00	0.00
4	0.25	0.28	0.09	0.02	0.00	0.00
5	0.22	0.04	0.02	0.002	0.00	0.00

Carbon Dioxide

The effect of carbon dioxide in alcoholic fermentation is too often neglected. Schmitthenner (1950) showed that a carbon dioxide content of 15 gm. per liter (about 7.2 atmospheres) essentially stopped yeast growth. The carbon dioxide effect on yeast growth did not prevent alcoholic fermentation. A much higher carbon dioxide pressure, up to 30 atm. was necessary to prevent alcoholic fermentation. Especially important is his observation that *Lactobacilli* can grow at high carbon dioxide pressures (see p. 386). This may explain the difference in pressure fermentation by various experimenters according to the amount and nature of microflora present and their varying effects on the character and quality of the product. Schanderl (1959) reports *Lactobacilli* and *Mucor racemosus* in pressure tanks. Also present were *Torulopsis sp.* and *Kloeckera sp.* both of which produced acetic acid under carbon dioxide pressure. We have no easy explanation as to why Australian, German, and South African experimenters generally favor pressure fermentations.

Acids

Very little attention has been paid to the effects of fixed organic acids on the alcoholic fermentation of musts. It is known that if the pH is very low, 3.0 or lower, fermentation is somewhat reduced. Yeasts are, however, not very sensitive to the amounts of fixed organic acids present in normal musts. There may be some effect of organic acids on the by-products of alcoholic fermentation. The acids are, however, important in maintaining the pH low enough so as to inhibit the growth of many undesirable bacteria.

Fatty acids such as acetic, butyric, and propionic, do have a decided inhibitory effect on yeasts. Fortunately the amounts present in normal fermenting musts are far below the critical concentration. However, sticking of acetified musts has been noted and there they may be important (pp. 267 and 597).

Nitrogen

Although most yeasts have no absolute requirements for amino acids the amino acids of musts are important as nitrogen sources and do stimulate the rate of yeast growth. Most grape musts contain adequate nitrogen for four or five fermentations. Except in very unusual cases nitrogen addition to fermenting grape musts is not necessary. Sparkling wines for the secondary fermentation can profit by nitrogen addition in particular circumstances according to Schanderl (1959). He recommended addition of ammonium salts in such cases. Fruit musts are often deficient in nitrogen and urea or ammonium phosphate must be added. Yeasts also utilize the small amounts of ammonia present in musts. The changes in total nitrogen during fermentation are indicated in Fig. 54.

Nilov and Valuĭko (1958) reported less nitrogen loss during fermentation in the absence of air. This was true for total nitrogen, amino nitrogen, and protein nitrogen. There was a temperature effect so that with aeration more nitrogen was lost at 59°F. and less at 77°F. The order of loss for total nitrogen without aeration at different temperature was 59°F. (most), 77°, 41°. With aeration the order of loss was 59°, 41°, 77°F. For amino nitrogen, no aeration, it was 59°, 77°, 41°F. and with aeration 59°, 41°, 77°F. For protein nitrogen without aeration it was 59°, 77°, 41°F. and with aeration 41°, 59°, 77°F. In other words, aeration seemed to cause more loss at the lower temperatures. The familiar decrease in nitrogen in the must and increase in the yeast is shown in Fig. 54.

Since each generation of yeasts reduces the nitrogen content of the must it has frequently been suggested that stable sweet table wines be produced by growing successive generations of yeasts in musts and filtering off the yeasts before alcoholic fermentation started. This is actually practiced in Italy for the production of very sweet, low alcohol sparkling *moscato spumante*. According to Schanderl (1959) the total nitrogen content is reduced to 30 to 50 p.p.m. with no ammonia and the wine is sta-

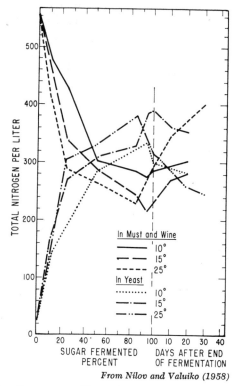

From Nilov and Valuiko (1958)

FIG. 54.   CHANGES IN TOTAL NITROGEN DURING AND AFTER
FERMENTATION IN MUSTS AND IN YEASTS FERMENTING THEM

ble as far as alcoholic fermentation is concerned.   However, in California
the desired stability has not been reached when this has been tried.   A
more rational approach would be to develop yeast strains which had a
very large and specific demand for one or two of the critical amino acids.
Upon depletion of these required amino acids yeast growth would be
greatly inhibited.

Minerals

The normal course of alcoholic fermentation requires magnesium, potassium, zinc, cobalt, iodine, iron, calcium, copper, and anions of phosphorus and sulfur.   For growth alone yeasts require copper, iron, magnesium,
potassium, phosphorus, and sulfur.   Adequate amounts are supplied by
grape and fruit juices.   The presence of excessive iron (over 6 p.p.m.) or
copper as factors in hindering the fermentation of sparkling wines has
been noted by Schanderl (1959).   The amounts of copper which he noted

as inhibitory were far above those normally encountered in practice, at least in this state. Aluminum is also an inhibitor of fermentation, if 25 or more p.p.m. are present. He has also demonstrated that elemental sulfur has a strong inhibitory effect and recommends close filtration to remove it from sparkling wine cuvees. The possible changes in sulfur-containing compounds during fermentation are shown in Fig. 55.

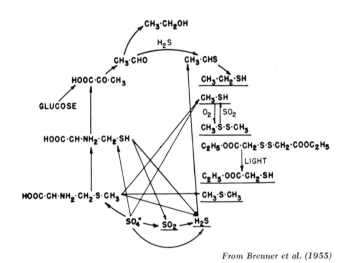

From Brenner et al. (1955)

FIG. 55. INTERRELATIONSHIPS OF SULFUR COMPOUNDS

Antiseptics

The use of sulfur dioxide in wines was known in the Middle Ages. It is now universally employed to protect containers as well as wine. When sulfur dioxide is dissolved in an aqueous solution an equilibrium between various forms is set up:

$$SO_2 \text{ (gas)} \rightleftharpoons SO_2 \text{ (aq.)}$$
$$SO_2 \text{ (aq.)} + H_2O \rightleftharpoons H_2SO_3$$
$$H_2SO_3 \rightleftharpoons H^+ + HSO_3^- \qquad K_1 = 1.7 \times 10^{-2}$$
$$HSO_3^- \rightleftharpoons H^+ + SO_3^= \qquad K_2 = 5 \times 10^{-6}$$
$$2HSO_3^- \rightleftharpoons S_2O_5^= + H_2O$$

All forms of sulfur dioxide in this equilibrium are known as free sulfur dioxide. The bisulfite ion (HSO_3^-) can react with aldehydes, dextrins, pectic substances, proteins, ketones and certain sugars to form bisulfite addition compounds:

$$\underset{\substack{\| \\ O}}{\overset{\substack{H \\ \;}}{RCO}} + HOSO^- \rightarrow \underset{\substack{R \\ \|\, \\ O}}{\overset{\substack{O \\ \| \\ H}}{HOC{-}SO^-}}$$

This is the form known as fixed or bound sulfur dioxide. Acetaldehyde reacts preferentially with the bisulfite but as more sulfur dioxide is added, or in musts, some will react with the sugars—more with dextrose than levulose. Joslyn (1952) reported that it is rare to find a wine with sufficient sulfurous acid in excess of acetaldehyde to combine with sugars. Braverman (1953) noted that sulfur dioxide only combines with sugars with a free aldehyde group. The amount fixed and the speed of binding is lower and slower the lower the pH. He found no levulose-sulfite compound. Similar results were obtained by Gehman and Osman (1954). The antiseptic property of sulfur dioxide is due mainly to the free form. The results of Fornachon (1963) indicated that the level of sulfur dioxide bound to acetaldehyde was important in determining whether lactic acid bacteria will grow in wines. He reported that this varied with the strain of bacteria. Finally, when sulfur dioxide and excess acetaldehyde were present, certain strains of lactic acid bacteria rapidly attacked the aldehyde and liberated sufficient sulfur dioxide to prevent further growth.

The ratio of free to bound in a given wine depends on the temperature, the amounts of sugar and aldehyde and the pH. The effect of pH on the relative amounts of the various forms of sulfur dioxide is shown in Fig. 56. The dissociation constants and the per cent sulfur dioxide fixed at 20°C. (68°F.) at pH 3–4 with 50 mg. per liter of free sulfur dioxide in cider was determined for various compounds by Burroughs and Whiting (1960) as follows: acetaldehyde, 1.5×10^{-6}, 100; pyruvic acid, 4.0×10^{-4}, 66; α-ketoglutaric acid, 8.8×10^{-4}, 47; L-xylosone, 2.1×10^{-3}, 27; monogalacturonic acid, 3.0×10^{-2}, 2.5; trigalacturonic acid, 3.7×10^{-2}, 2.1; xylose, 6.9×10^{-2}, 1.1; and dextrose, 6.4×10^{-1}, 0.12. Kielhöfer (1958) obtained similar results.

Kielhöfer (1963) showed that the antiseptic effect of sulfur dioxide is less in the presence of yeasts. In wines, its most beneficial effects have to do with its ability to combine with various constituents, particularly with acetaldehyde. After fermentation, sulfur dioxide should be added in sufficient quantities to completely combine with acetaldehyde. It also combines with other undefined constituents, especially in wines produced from botrytised grapes. In the white sweet table wines of Bordeaux from 40 to 80 per cent of the total sulfur dioxide appears to be combined to these undefined components, according to Blouin (1963). He believes the most important compounds are glucuronic, galacturonic, pyruvic, and

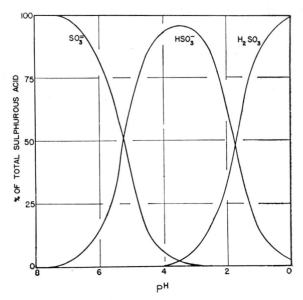

FIG. 56.   EFFECT OF pH ON FORM OF SULFUROUS ACID IN WATER
AT 77°F.

α-ketoglutaric acids.   Sulfur dioxide gives lasting protection against enzymatic oxidation but little against non-enzymatic oxidation due to slow exposure to air during aging.   Hennig and Burkhardt (1960) also found caffeic and p-coumaric acids to bind bisulfite.

Amerine and Ough (1964) showed that the sulfur dioxide content during fermentation significantly influences the final total aldehyde content but does not influence the amount of free aldehyde present.   The accumulation of aldehydes during fermentation appears to be dependent on the [NADH]/[NAD] ratio.   A smaller ratio seems to be favorable for aldehyde accumulation.

Not only does the antiseptic power of sulfur dioxide depend on the forms present but on the kind and activity of the microorganisms.   Yeasts can be acclimated to grow and ferment in the presence of high amounts of sulfur dioxide.   Schanderl (1959) has shown, moreover, that a sulfite-tolerant yeast is more sensitive to sulfur dioxide at high concentrations than a non-acclimatized strain of the same yeast.   He reported yeasts which fermented in the presence of 1000 p.p.m. of sulfur dioxide at pH 3.18.   Yeasts are also more sensitive to sulfur dioxide in the presence of alcohol, at the same pH, than in its absence.   Since sulfur dioxide reduces the oxidation-reduction potential of musts Schanderl believes this may have an effect in slowing down fermentation—aside from any antiseptic property.

Musts with an rH value of 20.2 ferment more rapidly than those at rH 18.2. Some bacteria are sensitive to very small amounts of sulfur dioxide. Molds and many yeasts are very sensitive to sulfur dioxide and most microorganisms are repressed with no more than 100 p.p.m. of sulfur dioxide. Some effects of sulfur dioxide in preventing volatile acid formation by bacteria are shown in Table 26.

TABLE 26

EFFECT OF SULFUR DIOXIDE IN PREVENTING HIGH VOLATILE ACIDITY IN WINES[1]

Year	Method of Fermentation			Number of Samples	Percentage of Samples Containing Viable Lactic Acid Bacteria	Composition of Wine, Per Cent			
	Metabisulfite Added	Cooling	Pure Yeast			Alcohol	Volatile Acid	Total Acid	Sugar
	No	No	No	101	100	11.5	0.118	0.66	0.49
1913	Yes	No	No	6	0	12.6	0.048	0.50	0.42
	Yes	No	Yes	67	0	12.1	0.066	0.57	0.21
	No	No	No	81	81	12.7	0.173	0.80	0.52
1934	Yes	No	No	64	20	11.6	0.064	0.71	0.21
	Yes	No	Yes	21	80	13.4	0.087	0.62	0.36
	Yes	Yes	Yes	69	14	12.4	0.060	0.50	0.17

[1] Sources of data: Cruess (1935A, 1935B).

Schanderl (1959) believes that the fungicidal action of sulfur dioxide on wild yeasts has been exaggerated. The concentration of sulfur dioxide is small in must and its effect better explained on the basis of antioxidative action—wine yeasts growing better under anaerobic conditions.

Some strains of yeast form sulfur dioxide (Würdig, 1969, Würdig and Schlotter, 1969, 1971, and Dittrich and Staudenmayer, 1970). Such strains do not produce hydrogen sulfide but result in high fixed sulfur dioxide.

Sulfur dioxide is less effective when the yeasts are in full fermentation. This is probably because some of the sulfur dioxide is fixed by the acetaldehyde as it is produced. This is one reason why a single addition of sulfur dioxide is more effective than the same total amount added in smaller doses during fermentation. The latter procedure also results in a high fixed sulfur dioxide content. There are also losses by entrainment.

Sulfur dioxide not only results in accumulation of acetaldehyde but may increase glycerol production. It prevents the malo-lactic fermentation which may be desirable in some cases but not in others. For other properties of sulfur dioxide see pp. 257–258. There is a long controversy as to the toxicity of sulfites. Causert et al. (1964) reported no anatomical or physiological problems due to ingestion of sulfite but there was a marked and significant decrease in excretion of thiamin and an increase in urinary excretion of calcium when sulfites were ingested. They recommend caution in consumption of wines approaching 450 p.p.m. of sulfur dioxide. The data of DeEds (1961) and Lanteaume *et al.* (1969) also indicated little danger of toxicity since few wines approach the 450 p.p.m. limit.

Substitutes for Sulfur Dioxide

While sulfur dioxide is universally used for its antiseptic and antioxidative properties there is general agreement that the odor of free sulfur dioxide is undesirable. There has been, therefore, a long search for a substitute. Because of their toxicity salicylic acid, monobromoacetic and monochloroacetic acids, ethylene oxide and numerous other antiseptics have been prohibited. Benzoic acid has not been used because of its low yeast toxicity and also because public health regulations frequently require a statement in the label of the amount used.

Recently ascorbic acid has been widely used in Germany as an antioxidant. The most detailed study of its effectiveness is that of Kielhöfer (1959). He found that small amounts of free sulfur dioxide could not be replaced completely by ascorbic acid because ascorbic acid does not bind acetaldehyde as sulfur dioxide does. However, the differences in sensory tests were small. Wines with ascorbic acid (25 and 50 mg. per liter) retained a low redox potential (or ITT value) for periods of 10 and 20 months. The free sulfur dioxide in the wine was 38 mg. per liter which is rather high by California standards. Also only a small amount of ascorbic acid was oxidized to dehydroascorbic acid (not more than 18 mg. per liter). Nevertheless, the fact that ascorbic acid does not combine with free acetaldehyde, means that in practice determination of the redox potential or the ITT is valueless and that for most white table wines there is presently no substitute for some free sulfur dioxide.

Applications of fungicides which remain in the grapes can also cause inhibition of alcoholic fermentation. Captan has been found by Castor *et al.* (1957) to interfere with yeast growth.

Sorbic acid appears to be an effective antiseptic for yeasts, see Auerbach (1959) and p. 258. However, adequate information on the amounts needed for various types of wine is not yet available. Saller and Kolewa (1957) reported 200 mg. per liter is sufficient to prevent yeast growth. Control of yeast growth in sweet table wines was obtained at 80 mg. per liter of sorbic acid and 30 mg. per liter of sulfur dioxide by Ough and Ingraham (1960). Control of refermentation was better at 53°F. compared to 72°F. The sensory threshold for sorbic acid was 135 mg. per liter, but some members of the panel were very sensitive to sorbic acid (as low as 50 mg. per liter). They concluded that its use in high quality wines was contraindicated. Peynaud (1963) found sorbic acid in amounts up to 200 mg. per liter in the presence of 30 to 40 mg. per liter of free sulfur dioxide to be useful in the conservation of sweet Bordeaux wines. At a pH of 3.1 150 mg. per liter was sufficient but at pH 3.5 more than 200 mg. per liter was required. The per cent undissociated sorbic acid is 98 at pH 3.1 and 94 at pH 3.5. The undesirable odor associated with the use of sorbic acid appears to be due to the formation of crotonic aldehyde ($CH_3CH=$ $CHCHO$) and unsaturated compounds of the type $-CH=CO-C=O$. Geraniol may be the undesirable compound. They recommend freshly-prepared pure sorbic acid, storage of treated wines in the absence of oxygen and sufficient sulfur dioxide to prevent a malo-lactic fermentation. The sorbic acid should be introduced into the wine slowly to prevent its precipitation by the acids of the wine. While sorbic acid may reduce the amounts of sulfur dioxide required for stability of sweet table wines, the possibility of development of off-odors remains.

Diethylpyrocarbonate (DEPC) was first used as an antiseptic in wines by Hennig (1960). The recommended level was 100 to 200 mg. per liter. Hennig (1963) summarized his experiments on the use of DEPC for German sweet table wines. He recommended 50 to 100 mg. per liter with 10 to 15 mg. per liter of free sulfur dioxide and emphasized the necessity of immediate dissolution of the DEPC in the wine. He correctly recommends that DEPC be added just before bottling and that the bottles, fillers, and corks be sterilized with sulfur dioxide. Hennig believed that 0.5 gm. per liter of DEPC would be needed before sensory detection of residual ethyl carbonate would be obvious. The amount may be considerably less. Cooke et al. (1964) reported a sensory difference when 280 mg. per liter of DEPC was used. The problem of accurate addition of DEPC has been solved by electronically coupling a turbine-type flow meter to a specially designed linear variable orifice control valve which continuously controls a set mg. per liter blending rate. Kielhofer and Würdig (1964) reported that carbon dioxide, nitrogen, helium, or oxygen did not remove the odor of ethyl carbonate but storage in the presence of air did. Pure DEPC does not form ethyl carbonate during storage. Garoglio and Stella (1964) claim non-toxicity of DEPC 20 hours after being added to a wine. They also recommended that the DEPC be pure and be used with a small amount (60–100 mg. per liter) of sulfur dioxide (ascorbic acid cannot replace the sulfur dioxide). The most recent rulings of the Food and Drug Administration should be consulted before DEPC is used.

Antibiotics

Antibiotics have been recommended for the beer industry and may find a place in wine making. The public health aspects of their use deserve, however, careful consideration. Actidione, mycosubtilin and other antibiotics have been tested by Ribéreau-Gayon et al. (1952A), by Kielhöfer

(1953), and others. Vitamin K_5 has been tested by Yang et al. (1958). Yang and Orser (1962) used 10 p.p.m. plus 100 p.p.m. of sulfur dioxide to stabilize sweet table wines. The odor threshold is 50 p.p.m. Some darkening of white wines was noted. There is no doubt that many antibiotics are effective for short periods of time. None is presently permitted by federal regulations. An antibiotic in musts infected with *Botrytis cinerea* was reported by Ribéreau-Gayon et al. (1952B). This may be partially responsible for the slow fermentation of botrytised grapes. (See, however, p. 156.)

While antibiotics appear attractive there are definite limitations to their use. Gillissen (1954) has summarized these as follows: must not be toxic in large amounts in a short period, man must not be sensitive to them, they should not cause the resistance of microorganisms to increase, the normal bacterial flora of man should not be harmed, they must not be toxic to man when used in small amounts over a long period, they should be specific for undesirable microorganisms in wines, in wine they should be odorless and tasteless, and the constituents of wine should not affect their activity. To these requirements we would add that any antiseptic added to wine should be easy to detect and to determine quantitatively.

Growth Factors

It has been known for many years that yeasts respond to accessory growth factors. Among those found desirable or necessary are biotin, inositol, nicotinic acid, pantothenic acid, p-aminobenzoic acid, pyridoxine, and thiamin. However, under winery conditions conclusive results as to the value of adding growth factors to musts have not been obtained. This is undoubtedly due to the fact that several of these are present in appreciable quantities in musts (pp. 107, 110–111) and also to the fact that yeasts can themselves produce some in sufficient quantities.

Silva (1953) found thiamin (B_1) to decrease the alcohol yield of fermentation slightly (0.1 to 0.4 per cent). Riboflavin increased the yield and ascorbic acid caused no change. In plant trials riboflavin increased the yield 0.1 to 0.3 per cent. Giudice (1955), however, found 50 to 100 mg. of thiamin per hectoliter resulted in a slight increase in alcohol production. Others have found increased alcohol, glycerol and reduced volatile acidity with 50 to 133 mg. hectoliter of thiamin. Ribéreau-Gayon and Peynaud (1952) also believed thiamin of some use in Bordeaux wineries. Wikén and Richard (1951–1952) did not find addition of vitamins necessary. Although sulfur dioxide destroys thiamin, addition of this vitamin to desulfited grape juice did not activate fermentation in the experiments of Flanzy and Ournac (1963). Lafon-Lafourcade and Peynaud (1965) believe that the liberation of pyruvic acid indicates that alcoholic fermentations progress with deficiency of thiamin.

Joslyn (1951) has summarized the studies on the nutrilite requirements of yeasts, noting especially that yeasts during a long incubation period may grow in the absence of most nutrilites except one whereas during rapid growth several may be required.

Tannins

There is some evidence that tannins may inhibit yeast growth. Schanderl (1959) has shown that natural tannins vary greatly in their antiseptic value but that wine yeasts are much more resistant than wild yeasts. The amounts used in his tests were large. Turbovsky et al. (1934) and Nègre (1939) both considered tannins of some value to a wine's resistance to bacterial spoilage. The evidence is minimal.

Šikovec (1966) found considerable variation in the effect of various polyphenolic compounds on the course of alcoholic fermentation. Chlorogenic and isochlorogenic acid stimulated fermentation while gallic, ellagic, and caffeic acids inhibited it. During aging chlorogenic acid is hydrolyzed producing caffeic. This is one reason bottle-fermented wines sometimes ferment slowly. Another reason is that wines high in tannin lead to the formation of involution forms and at higher alcohol contents to death. Possibly this is the origin of the practice of adding tannin to sparkling wine cuvees. Šikovec also noted that some strains of yeast were more inhibited by polyphenols than others. Yeast cells adsorb polyphenols and partly assimilate them.

Temperature

The optimum temperature for fermentation by most wine yeasts is between 71.6°F. and 80.6°F. according to Schanderl (1959). However, temperature has many other effects besides its direct effect on yeast growth and activity. These are due to losses of alcohol and aromatic constituents at higher temperatures and to the by-products formed as well as to direct effects on the efficiency of fermentation. For a more complete discussion see Amerine and Joslyn (1951) and Chapter 4.

European enologists generally believe that considerable evaporation and entrainment of alcohol by carbon dioxide occurs at the higher fermentation temperatures. Their early results were generally for temperatures above 90°F. More recent studies summarized by Saller (1955) showed losses of about 0.65 per cent of the alcohol occurred with a fermentation temperature of 68°F. The loss was only 0.18 per cent at 41°F. While 90°F. temperatures occur in California fermenters it is believed that the loss amounts to less than 1.5 per cent of the alcohol produced and probably to much less under optimum conditions. Closed fermenters and cooling which are now generally used in the industry would reduce the loss somewhat. Nevertheless there is certainly some reduction in the alcohol yield at higher temperatures of fermentation. Dietrich (1954) reported loss of 1.4 per cent of the alcohol produced in fermentations at 77°F. In fruit wine fermentations to 18 per cent alcohol the loss was 1.7 per cent.

The loss of alcohol by entrainment during alcoholic fermentation of laboratory-scale fermentations was demonstrated by Zimmermann et al. (1964) to increase with the temperature of fermentation, alcohol level of the winè being fermented, agitation of the fermenting liquid, and the presence of the pomace cap. The rate of loss is at a maximum during the middle of fermentation, i.e., during the period of maximum rate of fermentation. The evaporation and entrainment losses were 0.65 per cent at 79.7°F. for grape juice with an initial Brix of 21° and 0.84 per cent for crushed grapes. In plant-scale operations the maximum loss is toward the end of the fermentation and does not differ between open and closed fermenters. The losses in plant operations were 0.7 per cent for a juice of 16° Brix at 77.9°F. This result is not in conflict with the 0.83 per cent loss reported by Warkentin and Nury (1963) with a higher Brix juice.

Castelli (1941), also using small fermenters, found that the optimum temperature for alcoholic fermentation was about 60°F. At the higher temperatures the yield was not only less but greater amounts of volatile acidity were produced. Acetoin was also always present in the wines fermented at the higher temperatures.

Yeasts can be acclimated to ferment at rather low temperatures. Some of the differences in results obtained are undoubtedly due to this. Beraud and Millet (1949), for example, found that yeasts grown at 44.6°F. produced more alcohol per cell than those grown at 77°F. They reported that increased alcohol production of low temperature-acclimatized yeasts lasted through several fermentations.

Schanderl (1959) indicates another disadvantage of high fermentation temperature—the slowing down of the fermentation and the invasion of undesirable thermophilic organisms. The effect of temperature (122°F.) and of alcohol content on the survival of yeast cells is indicated in Table 27. This shows that yeasts are much more sensitive to heat at 12 and 15 per cent alcohol.

In practice high temperatures (above 80°F.) for white table wine fermentations give lesser quality wines. For California conditions Jordan's (1911) results are very clear and still timely. Milder wines of greater aroma and keeping qualities resulted from cool fermentations. Saller (1955) discussed this aspect of temperature. He recommended cold-re-

TABLE 27

EFFECT OF TEMPERATURE AND ALCOHOL ON YEAST SURVIVAL[1]

Duration of Heating at 122°F.	Alcohol Content, Per Cent					
	0	3	6	9	12	15
	Yeast Cells Remaining After Four Days					
Minutes	Cells per 0.5 Ml.					
0	50,000	50,000	50,000	50,000	10,900	4,200
1	7,500	755	140	100	1	2
2	2,640	140	150	14	0	0
3	520	100	70	14	0	0
4	120	147	47	11	0	0
5	110	19	10	1	0	0

[1] Source of data: Schanderl (1959).

sistant yeasts and temperatures of not over about 50°F. The temperature is adjusted to about 35.6°F. automatically during fermentation in order to keep the rate of fermentation constant. An example of such a cooled fermentation is given in Fig. 57. He reported enhanced quality in the cooled fermentation wines. Similar results were obtained by Tchelistcheff (1948) in the Napa Valley of California using cellar temperatures of 45° to 60°F. and a finishing temperature of not over 68°F. His observation that cold-fermented wines are cloudy and yeasty at the end of fermentation is a general one. He noted particularly the greater freshness and fruitness of flavor, together with a lower volatile acidity. The amount of alcohol loss was also less, the alcohol yield higher and the tartrate content lower. Low fermentation temperatures for white table wines are now in wide use in this State, South Africa, and elsewhere.

Various explanations for the enhanced quality of low temperature fermentations have been given. There appears to be a retention of aromatic constituents of the grape and from the fermentation. The effect on

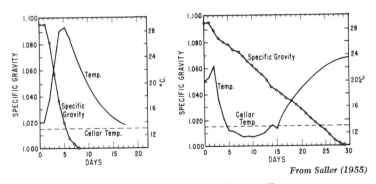

From Saller (1955)

FIG. 57. EFFECT OF COOLING ON THE RATE OF FERMENTATION

glycerol content is not so clear. Some investigators have found more glycerol (Tchelistcheff 1948; Hickinbothan and Ryan 1948; and Brockmann and Stier 1948; etc.) while others have found less (Uchimoto and Cruess 1952; etc.). Reduced phosphatase activity, which would reduce hydrolysis of glycerol-1-phosphate at high temperature, has been suggested as a reason for the first result and a larger number of yeast cells at the higher temperature for the latter. The results of Hickinbotham and Ryan (1948) may help to explain some of the divergent results. They found less glycerol in laboratory-scale fermentations and suggest that carbon dioxide content may have an effect. The lower acidity and extract content of cold-fermented wines do not appear to be important quality factors. Their lower volatile acidity is, of course desirable.

The advantages of cool fermentations for white table wine may be summarized as follows: less activity of bacteria and wild yeasts, less loss of volatile aromatic principles, greater alcohol yield, more residual carbon dioxide, and less residual bitartrate.

For red wines the effect of temperature is not so clear since color extraction is necessary. Amerine and Ough (1957) found better flavor and color for Pinot noir fermentations at 75° to 80°F. than at 50° to 60°F. and this is probably true for most red grape fermentations.

Pressure

In the last ten years pressure tanks for controlling the rate of fermentation have been widely employed in Germany and elsewhere. The basic text of the process of pressure fermentation is that of Geiss (1952). The fermentations are conducted in pressure tanks in which the fermentation is allowed to build up to 2 to 4 atm. depending on the stage of fermentation in order to keep the rate of fermentation essentially constant. The main advantage of the procedure is that there is a greater yield of alcohol per gram of sugar fermented (owing to less growth of yeast). Moreover, pressure fermentations often do not go to completion and this is considered an advantage for the high acid German musts. Higher ester contents are also reported. While the process appears to be useful for sugared German musts the results have not all been favorable and Amerine and Ough (1957) could not recommend it for California conditions on the basis of the higher volatile acid production. A large Australian installation of 10,-000 gallon pressure tanks is shown in Fig. 58.

Use of pressure to aid in color extraction does not appear to be necessary in this state but may prove useful in cold regions where musts have low color. The use of carbon dioxide pressures of 7 to 10 atm. to prevent fermentation should be noted (see also p. 673).

Oxygen

Oxygen is, of course, necessary for the maximum growth of yeasts, though some yeasts will grow with little oxygen. The aeration provided by oxygen may be not only for the oxygen requirements of the yeast but also to remove fermentation products from the surface of the cells and to supply fresh nutrients; see Joslyn (1951). He notes that agitation as well as aeration influences yeast growth. Associated with this is the engineering problem of the rate at which oxygen dissolves. Rate of stirring, pitch of stirrer blade, composition of feed gas, size of fermenter, and other factors influence the effective oxygen supply to the culture.

Fig. 58.   Refrigerated Pressure Tanks (10,000 Gallons) in Australia

Courtesy of G. Gramp and Sons. Ltd.

Alcoholic fermentation takes place best in the absence of air. Less of the sugar is used by the yeast in respiration and there is no oxygen to interfere with enzyme activity. Aeration also involves losses in alcohol by entrainment and evaporation. Many wine makers have noted that aeration during normal fermentation results in wines with higher aldehyde and darker color.

Nevertheless, it is possible that some fermentations may be slow to start because there is inadequate oxygen for yeast growth. Jordan (1911) recommended aeration during fermentation more often than modern enologists would think desirable. Schanderl (1959) has shown that yeasts from aerated cultures generally produce more alcohol than those from non-aerated cultures but the effect varies according to strain of yeast.

Surface Effect

The naturally cloudy must or one which has been made cloudy ferments much more rapidly than the same must which has been clarified or fined. This is demonstrated in Fig. 59. Settling musts have this effect and whether settling is desirable or not must be determined in each case.

Fermentation Rate

Though temperature has the greatest influence on fermentation rate, Ough and Amerine (1961) showed that musts of different varieties had

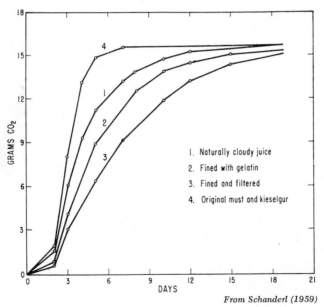

1. Naturally cloudy juice
2. Fined with gelatin
3. Fined and filtered
4. Original must and kieselgur

From Schanderl (1959)

FIG. 59.   EFFECT OF SURFACE ON RATE OF FERMENTATION

different fermentation rates at the same fermentation temperature. Ough (1964) found the principal variables (outside of temperature) to be degree Brix, pH and ammonia content of the juice. From these he was able to calculate rate prediction equations at 70°F. which give both maximum and average rates of fermentation over the range of 20°–0° Brix.

COMPOSITION OF WINE

The information given in Chapter 2 and previously in the chapter is pertinent to a discussion of the composition of wines. Mainly points of legal, biochemical, and sensory importance will be briefly summarized here.

Wine is a very complex mixture of organic and inorganic compounds. For a more complete discussion of wine composition see von der Heide and Schmitthenner (1922), Ribéreau-Gayon and Peynaud (1958, 1960–1961), Amerine (1954, 1958B), and Vogt (1958).

Ethyl Alcohol

The biochemical aspects of alcohol have been considered in other sections. The importance of ethyl alcohol to the sensory quality of the wine has not been adequately studied. At low concentrations alcohol has only a slight odor. It is, however, an excellent solvent for odorous materials. It has a slight sweet taste and moderates the taste of acids. A dealcoholized wine is much more tart than the same wine with its alcohol. The odor threshold, according to Berg et al. (1955B) is 0.004 to 0.0052 gm. per 100 ml. Hinreiner et al. (1955B) have demonstrated that sugar increases the threshold for alcohol and also the minimum-detectable-difference concentration—the effects increasing with sugar and alcohol concentration. The following data are typical:

Ethyl Alcohol	Sucrose			
	0	5	10	15
Per cent	Per cent	Per cent	Per cent	Per cent
0	0.005	0.15	0.35	0.45
10	2.0	3.0	4.0	4.0
15	3.0	4.0	4.2	4.2

These were with sugar-water-alcohol solutions. With wine Hinreiner et al. (1955A) did not find that addition of sugar increased the difference threshold.

Although most of the alcohol in wines results from fermentation during prolonged aging a little may result from hydrolysis of glucosides.

The legal limits for alcohol vary markedly for different countries and are usually related to the tax structure. See p. 748, for example, for the taxes in the United States on wines of below or above 14 per cent alcohol. In some countries the higher alcohol wines are not only subject to a higher tax but also to much closer governmental supervision.

Methyl Alcohol

It is generally agreed that methanol is not produced by alcoholic fermentation, from glycine for example, but is primarily derived from hydrolysis of naturally-occurring pectins. Thus more methyl alcohol has been reported when pectolytic enzymes were added to musts or pomace. More is also produced when must is fermented on the skins, hence there is generally more in red wines than rosé or white. Fruit wines are especially high in methyl alcohol. Flanzy and Loisel (1958) noted higher methanol in wines from macerated grapes than from non-macerated fruit. From this it appeared that free methanol was present in the fruit. Flanzy and Bouzigues (1959) found no change in the methanol content during the fermentation of a white must. There was an increase with a red must during fermentation. The higher content in the red must they attributed to the higher methyl esterase content of the solid part of the fruit. They concluded that the methanol content was not related to the pectin content and that fermentation did not change the methanol content. They also reported that distillation did not produce methanol, nor did heating *per se*. Even addition of formic acid did not produce methanol. See Bertrand and Silberstein (1950) for a different view.

The amount of methyl alcohol in wines, Amerine (1954), ranges from traces to 0.635 gm. per liter, average about 0.1. Ribéreau-Gayon and Peynaud (1958) give a range of 0.036 to 0.350 gm. per liter. Feduchy *et al.* (1964) reported 0.039 to 0.624 gm. per liter in 220 Spanish wines. A polemic has developed in France as to whether wines made from non-*Vitis vinifera* have more methyl alcohol than those from *V. vinifera*. See Flanzy (1934). Data from our laboratory (M.A.A.) indicate that they normally do not. The sensory importance of methyl alcohol has not been studied. Certainly many methyl esters are very fruity in odor.

Higher Alcohols

Usseglio-Tomasset (1964) concluded that the higher alcohols always present are 1-propanol, 1-butanol, 2-butanol, 2-methyl-1-propanol, 2-methyl-1-butanol, 3-methyl-1-butanol, 1-pentanol, and 1-hexanol. Some interrelationship exists between the formation of 1-butanol and 1-hexanol. Higher alcohols which are not present or only in trace (T) amounts include 2-propanol (T), 2-methyl-2-propanol, 3-methyl-2-butanol (T), 2-pentanol, 3-pentanol, and 2-hexanol (T). According to Peynaud and Guimberteau (1956) about 90 per cent or more of the higher alcohols of wines are represented by isoamyl (a mixture of 3-methyl-1-butanol, 2-methyl-1-butanol) and 2-methyl-1-propanol (150 to 600 mg. per liter). In red wines about one-fourth the higher alcohol was 2-methyl-1-propanol, in whites one-third.

The problem of the higher alcohol content of fusel oils and brandies is discussed in Chapter 16. The amount of higher alcohols produced is less when ammonium phosphate is added prior to fermentation. Certainly, however, not all of the higher alcohols are derived from deamination of amino acids. Castor and Guymon (1952) showed that their formation paralleled that of ethyl alcohol. Thoukis (1959) suggested sugars as the source of the higher alcohols not accounted for from deamination.

It is not generally recognized that the higher alcohols of wines are of sensory importance as Guymon and Heitz (1952) noted. The amounts in table wines varied from about 0.14 to 0.42 gr. per liter and in dessert wines from about 0.16 to 0.90—the higher amount undoubtedly arising from the use of fortifying spirits of high fusel oil content.

At very low concentrations the higher alcohols may play a desirable role in sensory quality. Even at rather high concentrations the port industry of Portugal seems to accept and appreciate their odor. (This may be an acquired taste, not a real preference.) In this country dessert wines of high fusel oil are considered undesirable. Filipello (1951) found a negative correlation between higher alcohol content and sensory quality.

Pisarnitskiĭ (1964) attributed the flowery character of Riesling wines to phenethyl alcohol. He found 1-propanol in Cabernet but not in Riesling wines. Rankine and Pocock (1969) found few tasters who could identify normal amounts of phenethyl alcohol or n-hexanol.

Guymon and Heitz (1952) and Villforth and Schmidt (1953–1954) showed that red wines contain slightly more higher alcohols than white. The latter also demonstrated that wines of some varieties contained more than others and that less was produced in pressure-tank fermentations and more in wines of sugared musts. Guymon et al. (1961) showed that oxidative conditions during fermentation favor higher alcohol production. The presence of pomace, as in red wine production, aerates the wine and this leads to greater amounts of higher alcohols. Even yeasts which are very poor fermenters (*Hansenula qnomala and Debaryomyces hansenii*) produce high amounts of higher alcohols. Crowell and Guymon (1963) demonstrated that vigorous aeration during fermentation greatly increased formation of higher alcohols (up to seven-fold) and of acetoin and diacetyl. They also show that naturally-occurring suspended materials also resulted in larger production of higher alcohols, particularly of isobutyl and isoamyl alcohols. The amounts of 1-propanol and 2-methyl-1-butanol were little changed by the presence of suspended solids. The wide difference in ability of yeasts to produce higher alcohols was also noted by Webb and Kepner (1961) (data in weight per cent based on these four alcohols only):

Yeast	1-propanol	2-methyl-1-propanol (isobutanol)	2-methyl-1-butanol (act.-amyl)	3-methyl-1-butanol
Burgundy	18.2	12.4	12.0	57.4
Jerez	20.2	8.4	4.5	66.9
Montrachet	2.6	2.7	16.5	78.2

Amerine *et al.* (1959) suggested that the higher alcohols may not only be important because of their own odor but because of their solvent action towards other odorous substances and the volatility of these in such mixtures.

Glycerol

Pasteur reported glycerol as a by-product of alcoholic fermentation just one hundred years ago. No constant ratio of alcohol to glycerol has been established. There are a variety of reasons for this. Thus according to Gentilini and Cappelleri (1959), glycerol production is favored by lower temperatures, higher tartaric acid content, and by addition of sulfur dioxide (see p. 257). Increase in sugar content decreases glycerol yield relative to alcohol. Vitamins and other growth factors did not change the glycerol content. Most of the glycerol develops in the early stages of fermentation. Yeasts differ markedly in their glycerol yield. Finally, moldy grapes, particularly from *Botrytis cinerea,* contain glycerol and hence wines made from such fruit are higher in glycerol.

Amerine (1954) has summarized a large number of glycerol analyses. Most enologists consider that glycerol is of considerable sensory importance because of its sweet taste and its oiliness. A threshold of 0.38 to 0.44 per cent in water was established by Berg *et al.* (1955A). Hinreiner *et al.* (1955B) reported acidifying to pH 3.4 raised the threshold to 1.5 gm. per 100 ml. and that a 10 per cent alcohol solution had a threshold of 1.0 gm. per 100 ml. Hinreiner *et al.* (1955A) found a difference threshold of 0.9 gm. per 100 ml. in a dry white table wine (of 0.3 gm. per 100 ml. of glycerol) and 1.3 for a red table wine (of 0.8 gm. per 100 ml. of glycerol). These results do not indicate that glycerol is of importance in the quality of wines, and certainly not in the case of sweet wines.

Ribéreau-Gayon *et al.* (1959) have shown that arginine and ammonia increase the production of 2,3-butylene glycol and that cysteine and a full complement of amino acids resulted in higher succinic acid production. High amino acid content and ammonia also increases acetic acid production. Application of these studies to practical conditions would be particularly interesting, since California musts are generally high in nitrogen but acetic acid formation is low. There is little interest in the determination of glycerol or 2,3-butylene glycol except in research work. In Europe where sugaring is used it has been suggested by Rebelein (1957B, 1958) that the K value (the ratio of glycerin $\times$ 2,3-butylene glycol divided by (alcohol)^3) might give an indication of sugaring, fortification, or use of green grapes if the value fell below 7×10^{-6}. Hennig (1959) did not find this to be so using wines of known origin. He did report that the analytical methods used by Rebelein (1957A, 1958) were accurate.

2,3-Butylene Glycol, Acetoin, Diacetyl, etc.

The origin of these three compounds during alcoholic fermentation has not been clearly established. Some biochemists believe that certain yeasts form only 2,3-butylene glycol and other yeasts only acetoin. Others find both produced during active fermentation. Lafon (1956) on the basis that the amount of acetoin formed was independent of the degree of respiratory intensity considers that it is not produced by oxidation of 2,3-butylene glycol. Amerine (1954) suggested that the varying results may be due to differences in experimental technique—age of cultures, oxidation-reduction potential, etc. He has also summarized the data on the amounts present in various wines. For 2,3-butylene glycol this ranges from about 0.1 to 1.6 gm. per liter, with the average generally being in the range 0.4 to 0.9. The amounts present do not appear to be related to quality (it has practically no odor and a slight bitter-sweet taste which would be masked by the 10 to 20 times greater amounts of glycerol present). There is more in wines which have fermented more sugar. This is the basis for suggestions that the alcohol to 2,3-butylene glycol relationship be used to establish that a wine has been fortified or not. It is curious that Armagnac brandy should have eight times as much as Cognac. Peynaud and Lafon (1951A, 1951B) suggested that this might be useful in distinguishing different brandies.

Acetoin does have an odor but the amounts present are small—2 to 84 mg. per liter; 3 to 32 in normal German wines according to Dittrich and Kerner (1964). During alcoholic fermentation there is an increase up to the middle of the fermentation to a maximum of 25 to 100 mg. per liter after which it almost disappears, according to Guymon and Crowell (1965). This accounts for the higher amounts in fortified dessert wines where the fermentation is stopped about midway. In submerged-culture flor sherries very high amounts are reported. Its apparent source in this case is ethanol via acetaldehyde. Diacetyl is present in normal amounts in these sherries. (This is in contrast with a previous report but the method then used did not distinguish diacetyl and acetoin.) More acetoin is reported in wines fermented with added acetaldehyde and in wines attacked by *Acetobacter*.

Diacetyl has a pronounced buttery odor and in a few cases may be of sensory importance. Normal wines average about 0.2 mg. per liter according to Dittrich and Kerner (1964). Above 0.89 wines have a sour milk odor. It is curious that Cognac brandy contains more diacetyl than pomace brandy. For typical analysis see Table 28.

TABLE 28

2,3-BUTYLENE GLYCOL, ACETOIN AND DIACETYL IN WINES[1]

2,3-Butylene Glycol	Acetoin	Diacetyl
Mg./Liter	Mg./Liter	Mg./Liter
492	2.0	0.4
513	9.6	0.7
535	7.6	0.4
612	7.8	0.5
628	4.6	0.1
653	3.0	0.6
720	10.7	0.3
750	5.4	0.1
763	14.8	0.3
783	3.6	0.3
828	5.2	0.1
1260	15.2	1.6
1298	30.3	1.6
1485	84.0	1.8

[1] Source of data: Ribéreau-Gayon and Peynaud (1958).

Inositol, $(CHOH)_6$ (or better mesoinositol), is another alcohol found in wines. It is present in musts. Mannitol, $CH_2OH(CHOH)_4CH_2OH$, is always a bacterial spoilage product (p. 589), from the reduction of levulose. Sorbitol is an indication of addition of fruits, particularly of apples.

Acetaldehyde

Acetaldehyde is a normal by-product of alcoholic fermentation (p. 178). Kielhöfer and Würdig (1960B) have also shown that aldehyde retention is much greater when sulfur dioxide is added before the fermentation, and especially high when sulfur dioxide is added during fermentation. They also confirmed the high production of aldehyde when incompletely fermented wines were aerated in the presence of actively-growing yeast cells, for example, by centrifuging cloudy wines. Non-enzymatic production of aldehyde in white wines is very small, especially in the absence of iron, according to Kielhöfer and Würdig (1960A). They did report non-enzymatic aldehyde formation in the light was greater than in the dark. They conclude that the primary source of aldehydes is from enzymatic processes, i.e., in the presence of yeast.

In the amounts found in newly-fermented wines, below about 75 mg. per liter, it has little sensory importance, especially so since most of our wines have sulfur dioxide added which fixes most of the aldehyde. However, it has a pronounced odor and Berg et al. (1955A) reported a threshold of only 1.3 to 1.5 mg. per liter in water. But in table wines Hinreiner et al. (1955A) found difference thresholds of 100 to 125 p.p.m.

During aging, owing to oxidation of ethyl alcohol or to the activity of film yeasts, the amounts present in wines is greatly increased. Thus Spanish sherries may have up to 500 p.p.m. and average over 200. Amerine (1958A) and Ough and Amerine (1958) have reported accumulations of up to 1000 p.p.m. when the flor yeast, Saccharomyces bayanus is grown under aerobic conditions with a slight pressure and occasional stirring (see pp. 426–427). The "faded" odor of newly bottled, low sulfur dioxide wines is apparently due to temporary accumulation of acetaldehyde.

While an aldehyde tone is desirable in sherry the quality of sherry cannot be entirely attributable to acetaldehyde. However, a minimum acetaldehyde content must be established for flor sherry in order to prevent overly blended wines reaching the market. Other aldehydes occur and are important, see p. 432.

Acetal

Acetaldehyde reacts with ethyl alcohol to form acetal, a substance with a strong aldehyde-like odor. Very little is found in wines, usually less than 5 mg. per liter because the acetalisation reaction is slow. It is catalyzed by low pH. Russian investigators believe a high acetal to acetaldehyde ratio to be an important measure of quality in flor sherry.

Hydroxymethylfurfural

When levulose is heated in acid solutions it is dehydrated to produce hydroxymethylfurfural as follows:

$$
\begin{array}{cc}
\overset{\text{H}}{\text{HOC}}\!\!-\!\!-\!\!-\!\!\overset{\text{H}}{\text{COH}} \\
\text{HOH}_2\text{C}\!\!-\!\!\text{CH} \quad \text{HOC}\!\!-\!\!\text{CH}_2\text{OH} \\
\diagdown \text{O} \diagup
\end{array}
\longrightarrow
\begin{array}{cc}
\text{HC}\!\!-\!\!-\!\!-\!\!\text{CH} \\
\text{HOH}_2\text{C}\!\!-\!\!\text{C} \quad \text{CCHO} \\
\diagdown \text{O} \diagup \\
+\ 3\text{H}_2\text{O}
\end{array}
$$

Its presence in wines is therefore a good check on whether they have been heated during processing or have been prepared from concentrate. Since heating of port to give it a tawny character is prohibited in Portugal a low legal limit has been placed on the presence of hydroxymethylfurfural. It has a caramel-like odor. Amerine (1954) found two-thirds of the 154 California dessert wines which he tested showed its presence, indicating rather general heating of these wines during processing. California sweet sherrys and tokays and Madeiras can, of course, be expected to have a large concentration of this substance—up to 300 mg. per liter. Malaga, which is partly made from raisined fruit, contains hydroxymethylfurfural.

Esters

It is commonly believed that the esters are an important part of the odor of wines and brandies. For normal wines this appears to be an exaggeration since the esters normally present have little odor, particularly in the amounts present. Only ethyl acetate seems to be important—below about 200 mg. per liter it may be a desirable odor but above this it appears to give a spoiled character to the wine.

Both neutral and acid esters are found in wine. The total esters in various wines as summarized by Amerine (1954) varied between about 200 and 400 mg. per liter (as ethyl acetate). Ports and sherries were higher. The volatile neutral esters averaged 70 to 200 (344 for sherry) mg. per liter as ethyl acetate.

As to the mechanism of ester formation equilibrium is seldom attained, even for very old wines as the following data of Peynaud (1937) indicate:

Year	Age	Ratio[1]		
		Minimum	Maximum	Average
1893–1914	22–43	0.73	0.79	0.75
1926–1930	6–10	0.57	0.71	0.66
1931–1932	4–5	0.59	0.73	0.64
1933	3	0.49	0.67	0.62
1934	2	0.50	0.65	0.56
1935	0.75	0.28	0.38	0.34

[1] Actual/theoretical (from Berthelot formula).

Citric acid, for example, is only very slightly esterified at the pH of wine, lactic, and succinic acids approach the limit of esterification most nearly and rapidly. Yeasts and bacteria produce esters. The esterase activity of wines is slight. Esters of caffeic acid and tartaric acid (dicaffeiltartaric, monocaffeiltartaric and monoferulytartaric acids) were isolated from grape leaves and wines by P. Ribéreau-Gayon (1965).

Peynaud (1937) suggested amount of ethyl acetate rather than per cent acetic acid as the legal limit, because: (1) addition of *pure* acetic acid to a wine does not give it a spoiled character, (2) applying a vacuum to a moderately spoiled wine improves its odor but only ethyl acetate is removed, (3) adding pure ethyl acetate to a wine gives it a spoiled character, and (4) heating a clean wine with acetic acid in a sealed tube will give it a spoiled character. New wines of high spoiled character and a low volatile acidity and wines of high volatile acidity and low spoiled character are occasionally observed. Peynaud suggested a maximum volatile neutral ester content of 220 mg. per liter (as ethyl acetate) in lieu of a limit on volatile acidity. However, in most cases ethyl acetate and acetic acid are produced in proportionate amounts so that if one is high so is the other. Furthermore, with time, the esterification equilibrium should bring them into a predictable relation to each other. The slightly more laborious procedure for determining the volatile neutral ester content probably prevents adoption of Peynaud's suggestion. Pisarnitškii (1964) found more esters of the fatty acids caproic and caprylic in old Riesling and Cabernet compared to young.

Volatile Acidity

The term volatile acidity is a rather loose one. It refers to the volatility with steam of the fatty acids. Besides acetic and lactic which are normal by-products of alcoholic fermentation formic, butyric, propionic, and traces of other fatty acids are present.

Lactic acid is not only a normal by-product of alcoholic fermentation but is a product of the malo-lactic fermentation. In some red wines it may be the predominant acid present. It is not very volatile and Jaulmes (1951) has devised a special rectification column so that little or no lactic acid distills over during the distillation. This is justified since lactic acid is not a "normal" spoilage product in wines. The volatile acidity thus includes the fatty acids in the series starting with acetic but excludes lactic, succinic, carbonic and sulfurous acids.

The determination of volatile acidity as an indication of spoilage is one of the standard procedures of modern enology and has become a part of the legal requirements for wine standardization. The amounts of acetic acid produced during alcoholic fermentation are small—usually less than 0.030 gm. per 100 ml. Bacterial action before, during, and after fermentation may lead to much higher quantities by oxidation of alcohol or occasionally to bacterial attack on citric acid, sugars, tartrates, glycerol, etc. The spoiled vinegary character of such wines is the reason for the adoption of legal standards.

Acetic acid is not only a by-product of alcoholic fermentation but during the course of fermentation an appreciable amount may be utilized by the yeast. As indicated elsewhere more is produced at higher sugar than at low. Also it is produced mainly during the initial stages of alcoholic fermentation. Peynaud (1939–1940) envisages the following scheme:

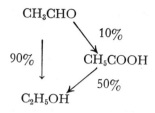

The particular pathway followed depends on the rH, phosphate content, temperature, and the acidity of the media. More is formed in the presence of oxygen than in its absence. Activity of yeasts other than the true wine yeasts and association or competitive activity are also important.

Reduction of a high volatile acidity by neutralization is not practicable because the fixed acids are also diminished. Film yeasts will reduce the volatile acidity as will addition of the high volatile acid wine to a must in vigorous fermentation. However, the legal aspects of converting a food product that is over the legal limits to one which is below the limits needs to be considered. Furthermore, the addition of high volatile acid wines to sound fermenting musts does run the risk of contaminating the whole product, see Amerine (1954).

Little formic acid is present in normal wines—possibly more in raisin wines than other wines (Vogt, 1958). Whether or not a high pH and formic acid are associated with the mousy flavor in wines has not been clearly established. Butyric acid is present in very small amounts in normal wines (10 to 20 p.p.m.) but much more is found in wine vinegar (290 p.p.m.) and in wine to which St. John's bread, *Ceratonia siliqua*, has been added (80 to 250 p.p.m.). It is rare in wines in this country. Propionic acid is probably not found in unspoiled wine.

The amount of volatile acidity in commerical wines naturally varies very markedly with their source and condition of fermentation. Experience indicates that careful wine makers can produce wine with less than 0.030 mg. per 100 ml. of volatile acidity (as acetic) and that during aging this should not exceed 0.100. No detailed studies of volatile acidity-ester relationships in old dessert wines appear to have been made but the amounts in Madeira and other aged dessert wines seem to indicate that a high volatile acidity is less objectionable when desirable volatile products of aging are present. The legal limits in this country are given in Chapter 19. According to Jaulmes (1951) the French limit for wines at wholesale is 0.15 gm. per 100 ml. (as acetic) and 0.187 for wines at retail.

Fixed Acids

The tartaric, malic, and citric acids of the musts are found in the resulting wines, but in decreased amounts. They are important constituents of wine not only for their acid taste but also because they protect the wine from spoilage, maintain the color, and are themselves sometimes attacked by microorganisms.

In trials with a variety of species of yeasts, Iñigo and Bravo (1963) reported significant differences in the per cent fixed acidity of new wines. *Metschnikowia pulcherrima* forms fumaric acid. They found important differences in the rate of formation of volatile acids during fermentation by the different species of yeasts. Rankine (1965) found 1 to 128 mg. per liter of pyruvic acid (ave. 20) in 67 Australian wines. Variety, region, and year did not influence the pyruvic acid content. Yeast strain and fermentation temperature (more pyruvic acid at 86°F. than at 59°F.) did have an effect.

The acid taste is due to the hydrogen ion content but there is no direct relationship between pH and acid taste. The buffer capacity of the wine, the relative amounts of the various acids, the sugar content and other factors influence the apparent acid taste. The thresholds for the various acids tested by Berg *et al.* (1955A) were as follows:

Acid	pKa_1	pKa_2	Threshold	Difference Threshold[1]
			Gm. per 100 Ml.	Gm. per 100 Ml.
Citric	3.09	4.39[2]	0.0023–0.0025	0.07
Lactic	3.81	...	0.0038–0.0040	...
Malic	3.46	5.05	0.0026–0.0030	0.05
Succinic	4.18	5.23	0.0034–0.0035	...
Sulfurous	1.77	7.00	0.0011	...
Tartaric	3.01	4.05	0.0024–0.0027	0.05
Bitartrate[3]	...	...	0.0075–0.0090	0.10

[1] At 0.25 per cent for d-tartaric, at 0.30 per cent for potassium acid tartrate, at 0.21 per cent for malic, and a 0.23 per cent for l-malic.
[2] pKa_3 5.74.
[3] Potassium acid tartrate.

Münz (1963) notes that the acid taste of wines is primarily due to the acid salts since most of the acids are partially neutralized. Wines in which an appreciable part of the acids are not bound to minerals are generally too acid in taste. Soluble salts appear to reduce the acid taste. The buffering capacity of musts and wines is expressed in terms of potassium equivalent: 1 gm. per liter of potassium versus 0.31 gm. of magnesium and 0.59 gm. of sodium. Münz prefers adjusting the acidity of musts in preference to that of wines. If the acid taste of wines needs to be adjusted (as is frequently the case in Germany), he prefers to do this by blending. Amerine *et al.* (1965) reported that, at the same titratable acidity, the order of sourness was malic, tartaric, citric, and lactic. At the same pH, the order was malic, lactic, citric, and tartaric. A noteworthy feature of this report was the relatively small differences in pH (0.05 pH unit) and titratable acidity (0.02 to 0.05 per cent) which could be detected by the panel. They concluded that both pH and titratable acidity were important in determining sensory response to sourness.

Hinreiner et al. (1955B) did not find up to 10 per cent sucrose to influence the acid threshold. Ethyl alcohol, however, did increase the acid threshold and the effect was greater if sucrose was present. Tannin also seemed to increase the minimum detectable difference for acid in the absence of sugar. Sugar in the absence of tannin did not have this effect. However, the presence of sugar tends to minimize the effect of tannin on the minimum detectable-difference concentration of acid. Hinreiner et al. (1955A) also reported a difference threshold of 0.15 gm. per 100 ml. in a white table wine. One per cent sucrose did not change the difference threshold. Ough (1963) and Pangborn et al. (1964) found similar difference thresholds.

The decrease in tartrates is caused primarily by the deposition of potassium acid tartrate. Potassium acid tartrate occurs in grapes as a supersaturated solution. Since it is less soluble in alcoholic solution it precipitates during and after fermentation. Too low a temperature in which the wine is no longer liquid decreases the amount and rate of tartrate deposition. Cambitzi (1947) found optically inactive racemic calcium tartrate in old wine deposits. Since wines contain only dextrotartaric acid this indicates autoracemization. The calcium salt of racemic tartaric acid is only about one-eighth as soluble as the dextro salt. Calcium tartrate is less soluble at higher pHs. Therefore, DeSoto and Warkentin (1955) recommended that the pH of California dessert wines be kept below 3.70. The pH of wines is conditioned largely by the tartrate. It is relatively difficult for bacteria to attack but under proper conditions certain lactic acid bacteria do. It is one of the acids authorized for addition to wines.

Genevois (1951) considers that tartaric acid catalyzed by ferrous ion yields dihydroxymaleic, and by oxidation-reduction and decarboxylation finally results in glyoxal. Baraud (1953) was unable to find dihydroxymaleic. Rodopulo (1951) also studied possible iron-catalyzed changes in tartaric acid. He reported glyoxylic and oxalic acids to be oxidation products. During bottle storage diketosuccinic and dihydroxymaleic acids were believed to be formed. Dihydroxymaleic acid accelerated the oxidation of tartaric acid. The exact mechanism is not clear and some enologists question the presence and importance of dihydroxymaleic acid.

Tartaric acid appears to give rise to oxalic via dihydroxyfumaric and diketosuccinic acids. Little dihydroxyfumaric or diketosuccinic acid accumulates, according to Dupuy (1960). Another possible source of oxalic acid is l-ascorbic acid. Ascorbic acid is oxidized to dehydroascorbic acid which is degraded by further oxidation to oxalic and l-threonic acids. Both copper and iron act as catalysts. The oxidation is greater at low pH. Polyphenoloxidase catalyses oxidative degradation of ascorbic acid.

Malic acid disappears during alcoholic fermentation to the extent of 10 to 30 per cent. Peynaud (1947) considers this due to splitting off of two hydrogen atoms and decarboxylation of the resulting oxaloacetic acid to acetaldehyde which in turn acts as a hydrogen acceptor and is reduced to alcohol. The influence of the malo-lactic fermentation on malic acid has been discussed elsewhere (pp. 284–287). Münz (1967) notes that the acid taste depends not only on the concentration of acid but also on its buffer capacity and on sugars and other compounds. The most important buffering is due to potassium, with lesser effects of calcium, magnesium, and sodium.

Citric acid from the grapes is attacked by various bacteria (there is less in reds than in whites) to produce acetic acid. Action of yeasts on sugars produces small amounts. Citric acid complexes with iron so it is frequently added as preventative against casse (p. 553). A number of countries limit the amount of citric acid which can be added (usually to 0.05 gm. per 100 ml.). However, as Ribéreau-Gayon and Peynaud (1958) note Sauternes have far more than this so that it is impossible to say that a wine of over 0.08 gm. per 100 ml. has had more than 0.05 gm. added or not. In normal wines it is rare that more than 0.05 gm. are present. Amerine (1954) indicates averages for various types of wines of 0.01 to 0.03.

Citric acid is slowly decarboxylated during aging. Citramalic (or α-methylmalic) acid is one product. Carles (1959) did not find citramalic acid in musts and believes its presence in wines is from decarboxylation of citric acid. However, Dimotaki-Kourakou (1962) believed citramalic acid was only a product of alcoholic fermentation.

Succinic acid is a product of alcoholic fermentation. As a general rule in table wines about one per cent as much succinic acid is present as alcohol by volume, but the range of succinic acid as per cent of the weight of alcohol produced varies from 0.68 to 2.25. More is formed at the beginning of fermentation than later and the amount formed per gram of sugar fermented varies with the must and yeast. It originates from sugars rather than from amino acids, but there may be other mechanisms.

Succinic acid is very resistant to bacterial attack. Thus under flor sherry it has been shown not to change. It has a salt-bitter-acid taste which is vinous in character. Its ethyl ester may be an important component of the odor of some wines.

Lactic acid has a slight odor and is a weak acid. It is a constant by-product of alcoholic fermentation, 0.04 to 0.75 gm. per liter. Its relation to the malo-lactic fermentation and spoilage organism has been mentioned elsewhere (pp. 8 and 286). In flor sherry aging there is a slow increase. It is increased by a malo-lactic fermentation and more so by excessive bacterial activity. More is produced in red wines than white.

The other fixed acids are of less importance. Glyoxylic acid is found in wines and in grapes. In diseased grapes up to 0.13 per cent glucuronic and 1.0 per cent gluconic may be formed whereas normal fruit contained only 0.03 per cent of the former. Botrytised grapes in Peynaud and Charpentié's (1953) studies had 0.29 to 2.46 gm. per liter, average 1.02.

Gluconic acid is therefore a good test for wines made from botrytised grapes. Würdig *et al.* (1969) reported 2- and 3-methyl-2,3,-dihydroxybutyric acids and 2-hydroxy-glutaric acid (and its lactone). They found 33 to 144 mg. per liter (average 68) of 2-methyl-2,3-dihydroxybutyric acid. Möhler and Pires (1969A, 1969B, 1969C) found 2-methyl-2,3-dihydroxybutyric acid in wines (60 to 525 mg. per liter, average 220). The large variation may be due to the method used or to differences in processing. Castino (1969) found 52 to 144 mg. per liter (average 92).

A new method for removing excess acidity was developed by Kielhöfer and Würdig (1963). Addition of calcium carbonate removes all of the tartrate. They raised the pH to above 5 with calcium carbonate and then added fresh untreated must to reduce the pH to 4.5. Under these conditions a double salt is formed and some tartrate remains in solution.

Carbonic acid constitutes a very special case for both still and sparkling wines. It has no odor and very little taste. But it does have a feel and disengagement of the bubbles from the wine probably brings more odors to the surface. Carbon dioxide probably also plays a protective role by keeping oxygen away from the surface of wines.

New wines are saturated with carbon dioxide. Thereafter carbon dioxide is gradually lost. The state of carbon dioxide in wine has not been adequately studied. It is not the same as in a water-alcohol solution of the same composition. Wine retains carbon dioxide much longer than water-alcohol solutions. The time the wine is kept under pressure influences the rate at which carbon dioxide is given off. Some sort of fixation appears to take place. For beer Anderson (1959) states that carbon dioxide is dissolved and in equilibrium with carbonic acid, small amounts form basic salts and carbamino compounds, and some may be fixed by colloids. From the fact that carbon dioxide is easily lost from beer he rejects chemical forces and believes that the carbon dioxide-protein relationship is one of electrostatic attraction. Anderson inspects and rejects various possibilities accepting that it is adsorbed, the negative pole of the carbonic acid being adsorbed to the positively charged beer proteins. This was supported by electrolysis experiments. Differences in the holding ability of different beers would be due to fundamental changes in the carbon dioxide fixing power of the proteins. More carbon dioxide is adsorbed at a lower pH. Miller's (1959) concept of the liquid gas system being a kind of emulsion—the dispersed phase being the gas phase and the liquid the enclosing phase might be adapted to Anderson's theory. Carbon dioxide may be present in a supersaturated condition in new wines, according to the data summarized in Amerine (1958B). The data of Ettienne and Mathers (1956) are given in Table 39 for low carbon dioxide pressures. For the relation of pressure, carbon dioxide and temperature see Fig. 104.

The amount of carbon dioxide varies according to the alcohol and sugar content, the viscosity, the pressure of gas and perhaps on other factors. Vogt (1958) reports 0.282 gm. at 50°F. which corresponds to 143.0 ml. per 100 ml. At 41°F. this becomes 0.329 gm. or 167.0 ml.

Miller (1959) finds that deaerating the wine before carbonation gives a better impregnation and a slower evolution of gas when the bottle is opened.

The forms in which carbon dioxide is present have stimulated much Russian work which has been summarized by Amerine (1954, 1958B). A physical adsorption or an esterification reaction is indicated. Diethylpyrocarbonate, $(C_2H_5OOC)_2O$, is not normally present.

Sugar

The importance of dextrose and levulose in alcoholic fermentation has been discussed (p. 183). Their importance to taste should be emphasized. Glycerol and 2,3-butylene glycol are also sweet. Berg et al. (1955A) reported thresholds in water of 0.13 to 0.15 gm. per 100 ml. for levulose, 0.40 to 0.44 for dextrose and 0.38 to 0.44 for glycerol. For dextrose in water the difference concentrations were: at 1 per cent, 0.4 to 0.7 gm. per 100 ml.; at 5 per cent, 0.6 to 0.8; at 10 per cent, 0.8; and at 15 per cent 1.0 to 1.1. The influence of alcohol, acids and tannins on sucrose thresholds was also studied by Berg et al. (1955B). Ethyl alcohol enhances the sweetness of sugar solutions over a range of 1 to 15 per cent sucrose as determined by sugar threshold or by minimum detectable difference. In the range 2.55 to 3.40 pH had a negligible effect on sugar thresholds. Tannin increased the threshold level for sugar detection and the minimum detectable difference.

Hinreiner et al. (1955A) reported the following difference thresholds:

Sucrose Level	Minimum Detectable Sucrose Increment in	
	White Wine	Red Wine
G./100 Ml.	G./100 Ml.	G./100 Ml.
0	0.9	0.8
1	0.8	0.7
5	1.1	1.0
10	1.7	1.6

These differences are greater than for aqueous solutions but are similar to those for water-alcohol-acid solutions. During aging there may be a slight increasing in reducing sugar due to hydrolysis of glucosides.

Pentoses

There are reports of arabinose, xylose, methyl pentose, rhamnose and of pentosans and methyl pentosans in wines. The non-fermentable residual reducing material is largely pentoses and amounts to from 0.01 to 0.20 gm. per 100 ml. The best data indicate 0.04 to 0.13 gm. per 100 ml. of arabinose. Arabinose is one possible source of furfural during distillation or pasteurization of wines. Rhamnose is reported at less than 0.05 gm. per 100 ml. Xylose is absent from most wines, less than 0.005 gm. per 100 ml. according to Guichard (quoted by Ribéreau-Gayon and Peynaud (1958)). Pentosans are slowly hydrolyzed during aging. Arabinose is attacked by *Lactobacilli*. Recently Esau and Amerine (1964) identified *altro*-heptulose, *D-glycero-D-manno*-octulose, and *manno*-heptulose. These are seven- and eight-carbon atom sugars.

Little sucrose is found in wines. A sensitive procedure for sucrose is given by Guimberteau and Peynaud (1965). However, sucrose is rapidly hydrolyzed in wines and the test must be carried out a few days after addition of the sucrose. Amerine (1954) summarized various data showing an average sucrose in wines of 0.01 to 0.06 gm. per 100 ml.

Caramel may not be added to California wines. Its detection in wines is therefore of some importance. Amerine (1954) indicates several tests should be used before stating that caramel has been added. Wucherpfennig and Lay (1965) found a slow increase in hydroxymethylfurfural (hmf) when wines of 0.4 to 3.4 per cent sugar were heated at 122°F. for 120 hours and more at 158°F. Reducing the pH increased the hmf produced; adding amino acids had little effect. Old German white wines had higher amounts than young. The threshold is 100 to 200 mg. per liter.

Pectins

If a clear must is slightly acidified and 4 or 5 volumes of alcohol added a haze will develop and eventually settle as a gelatinous deposit. This is pectin. This precipitation occurs naturally during alcoholic fermentation so that the amount of pectin materials in finished wines is only 10 to 70 per cent that of the musts. Finished wines have 0.3 to 0.5 gm. per 100 ml. of pectins and gums. The gums of wines are generally arabans, anhydrates of arabinose and galactans. The mucilaginous materials are classified as glucosans, anhydrides of dextrose, or as dextrans. Wines with oily disease (*graisse*) contain considerable mucilaginous material. Grapes attacked by *Botrytis cinerea* also have considerable dextran. Dextrans act as protective colloids in wines and thus hinder natural clarification or clarification by fining. They also make filtration difficult. Wines have from 14 to 30 per cent of the colloid content of musts according to Tarantola and Usseglio-Tomasset (1936). For 3 varieties, the total colloids in the wine was composed of (in per cent):

Variety	Araban	Galactan	Pectin	Protein
Dolcetto	22.1	28.1	43.5	6.6
Cortese	35.6	47.4	5.8	10.3
Barbera	35.4	29.6	23.6	11.7

To remove pectins pectolytic enzymes are frequently used—either before or after fermentation. They do aid filtration and reduce the pectin content. They also raise the galacturonic acid content and slightly increase the methyl alcohol content.

Nitrogen

The over-all importance of the nitrogenous constituents of wines cannot be overemphasized. They play a role in clarification, in bacterial development, and possibly, either directly or indirectly, in odor development.

Paparelli and Colby (1890) reported that California musts were very high in total nitrogen and protein nitrogen compared to European wines. They reported total nitrogen of 0.011 to 0.090 per cent (average 0.041) and of proteins of 0.071 to 0.560 per cent (average 0.262) in 16 young wines. European data summarized by Amerine (1954) gave averages of 0.10 to 0.77 gm. per liter for total nitrogen.

There are many different kinds of nitrogenous material in wine: proteins, peptones, polypeptides, amides, amino acids, and ammonia. Only very small amounts of ammonia are found in wine—it is nearly or completely utilized in alcoholic fermentation. Finished wines summarized by Amerine (1954) had none to 0.071 gm. per liter (averages 0.05 to 0.027). Diemair and Maier (1962) reported protein contents of white German wines to range from 60 to 411 mg. per liter. A number of reports on the nature of the proteins in German table wines have been made: Koch *et al.* (1956), Koch and Bretthauer (1957), Koch (1957, 1963), Koch and Sajak (1959, 1963), Diemair *et al.* (1961A, 1961B, 1961C). These reports show higher proteins in the wines of warmer seasons. Varieties differ considerably in the amounts present. The isoelectric point is very close to the pH of the wine.

The amount of different forms of nitrogen reported in wines also depends on the methods used for their determination. Amine nitrogen by formol titration is low because it does not include proline, the most abundant amino acid of wines. The microbiological procedure for amino acids often gives high results because the microorganisms may utilize some small size peptides in their nutrition.   Only the free amino acids will be detected by chromatography.   This is shown by the data of Lafon-Lafourcade and Peynaud (1961).

Lafon-Lafourcade and Peynaud (1961) found threonine, lysine, glutamic acid, and serine next abundant after proline; then—alanine, glutamic acid, aspartic acid, histidine, leucine, etc.   In general, proline and threonine constituted about 70 per cent of the total amino acid content.   The average total amino nitrogen, as nitrogen per liter, for the four years was 207, 126, 144, and 115.   There was some difference in the response of the different amino acids to season: the mg. per liter of proline was 700, 560, 560, and 395 but for threonine 148, 138, 283, and 205.   They also reported considerable differences in total amino nitrogen as well as between amino acids for different varieties.   The malo-lactic fermentation of white wines generally resulted in slight variations in the amino acid content of wines; for red wines there were slight decreases in arginine, α-alanine, phenylalanine and serine and increases in glutamic acid, methionine, threonine (sometimes) and tryptophane.   Clearly there are complicated bacterial effects on amino acids.

Heating the must to 176°F., then pressing and fermenting, resulted in lower total nitrogen and less amino acids compared to not heating.   There was little difference between closed and open tanks except there was less histidine and lysine and more threonine in wines fermented in open tanks.

Tarantola (1954) observed marked increases in valine, leucine, and tyrosine in wines stored on the lees.   This was not observed by Bidan and André (1958).   The study of Bourdet and Hérard (1958) showed markedly large increases in aspartic acid, glutamic acid, lysine α-alanine, glycine, serine, threonine, valine, leucine, isoleucine, γ-aminobutyric acid, phenylalanine, tyrosine, asparagine, and glutamine in red wines stored seven days on the lees (in small containers, stirred once each day), compared to new wine separated before the seven days' storage.   There was, however, a decrease in arginine, proline, histidine, and cystine and little change in methionine and α-aminobutyric acid.   In contrast, in a flor yeast wine there were spectacular increases in arginine, lysine, histidine and methionine compared to those present in a white wine of another source.   In two young wines 90 to 91 per cent of the nitrogen was present as free amino acids, 6 to 9 per cent as amides and only 0.4 to 3.3 per cent as ammonia and non-protein nitrogen.

The wide variation in qualitative and quantitative data on the amino acid contents of musts and wines is attributed by Bidan and André (1958) to be due to differences in the methods employed, to the heterogenity of samples (particularly as to the age and treatment of wines), to the differences in methods of fermenting the wines, and to the presence or absence of a malo-lactic fermentation. The legal limit for ammonia in wines in France is 20 mg. per liter which is probably too low for some red wines. Ammonia has been shown to stimulate flor film growth.

The amino acids present in musts and wines have been given in Tables 8 and 9. There have been reports that there was a relation between amino acid content and the bouquet of the wine. Bidan and André (1958) did not find any such correlation with eight French white wines.

Flanzy et al. (1964) confirmed that new wines have less total nitrogen than the musts from which they were derived. They also showed that when the wine was left in contact with the lees for 1 to 3 months that the nitrogen content of the wine increased, reaching a maximum in about 2 months. Most (87 per cent) of the increase was in amine nitrogen and the rest in amide and protein nitrogen. During this period obviously yeast autolysis is occurring. They classified the amino acids in four groups: 1. used during fermentation and not restored by autolysis: arginine, phenylalanine and histidine; 2. used during fermentation and restored by autolysis: proline; 3. used during fermentation and present in increased quantities after autolysis: glutamic acid, aspartic acid, leucine, isoleucine, valine, serine, lysine, tyrosine and tryptophane; and 4. increased by fermentation and by autolysis: cystine, methionine and glycine.

The results are somewhat complicated by the fact that the wines underwent a malo-lactic fermentation during storage. Sensory examination showed improvement in the quality up to a month on the lees, but no specific data are presented. Alanine is especially important in the nutrition of certain lactic acid bacteria. The formation of the "malic" enzyme by *Lactobacillus arabinosus* (now *L. plantarum*) requires 11 amino acids according to Bocks (1961): arginine, cysteine, histidine, isoleucine, leucine, lysine, methionine, phenylalanine, tryptophane, tyrosine, and valine. Also necessary were adenine sulfate, guanine, thiamine, and uracil.

When ammonia was added to musts there was a spectacular increase (10 to 30 times) in certain amino acids in the resulting wines according to Flanzy et al. (1964). This was especially marked for arginine, histidine, lysine, valine, tyrosine, isoleucine, methionine, aspartic acid, and alanine, and less marked for glutamic acid, tryptophane, cystine, serine and proline. There were, however, marked differences in the increases for certain amino acids between the musts of the two varieties studied and with those of a later study, Flanzy and Poux (1965). Aeration during fermentation influenced these changes differently for various amino acids—naturally being less favorable for the amino acids such as glutamic acid and aspartic acid which are involved in the respiratory cycle. When ammonium tartrate was the source of the ammonia, the resulting wines were lighter in color. In general addition of ammonia improved the quality and Flanzy and Poux (1965) confirmed this for wines of another season. However, no statistical analysis of the sensory data are given.

Tyrosol, 15 to 45 mg. per liter, was reported in Bordeaux red and white wines by Ribéreau-Gayon and Sapis (1965). They also found 0 to 0.8 mg. per liter of tryptophol but rarely in white wines. Further, they reported 10 to 75 mg. per liter of phenethyl alcohol and 0 to 5 mg. per liter of γ-butyrolactone. These compounds were formed during fermentation from the corresponding amino acids. Ough (1971) reported an average of 1.8 mg. per liter of histamine in 253 California table wines and slightly more in dessert wines and less in fruit wines.

Amide nitrogen is present in very small amounts—0.001 to 0.008 gm. per liter. Asparagine and glutamine are examples. The polypeptides—usually determined by precipitation with phosphomolybdic acid—represent the most important part of the organic nitrogen of wines, from 60 to 90 per cent according to Ribéreau-Gayon and Peynaud (1958). In 41 white Spanish wines Cabezudo et al. (1963) reported 2 to 13μg of biotin per liter compared to 2 to 18 in 46 red wines. The averages tended to be higher in red wines aged in the wood. According to Peynaud and Lafourcade (1957) the free pyridoxine content of 31 Bordeaux white wines was 0.12 to 0.67 mg. per liter (average 0.31) and the total 0.22 to 0.82 (average 0.44); for 58 reds the free ranged from 0.13 to 0.68 (average 0.35) and the total from 0.25 to 0.78 (average 0.47).

In 15 Bordeaux white wines, Lafon-Lafourcade and Peynaud (1958) reported 15 to 133 μg per liter (average 69) of p-aminobenzoic acid, 0.4 to 4.5 μg (average 2.4) of pterolglutamic acid and 19 to 27 μg per liter (average 21) of choline (12 wines). The averages of the first two were similar in red wines but choline was higher (29). Wines are as high or higher in these three vitamins as their musts. See Chapter 2 for additional data.

Tannins

For a discussion of the tannins of the fruit see Chapter 2. Ribéreau-Gayon and Peynaud (1958) have correctly noted that our concepts of the polyphenolic compounds of wines are undergoing a rapid change as new techniques are developed. Using permanganate oxidation, red wines contain 0.10 to 0.3 gm. per 100 ml. but this includes coloring matter.

During aging the tannin content decreases. This is due to combination with aldehydes, to precipitation with added or natural proteins, and to other reactions. Tannins have an inhibitory effect on certain enzyme systems but do not have marked bactericidal properties. (See, however, p. 195.)

There is little bitter or astringent taste in white wines since they contain 0.05 per cent or less tannin. Berg et al. (1955A) found a threshold for grape-seed tannin of 0.02 gm. per 100 ml. Hinreiner et al. (1955A) obtained a difference threshold of 0.10 gm. per 100 ml. for a white table wine and 0.15 in a red (natural tannin contents 0.02 and 0.20 gm. per 100 ml.). Sucrose did not change the difference threshold. Experienced tasters are more sensitive than inexperienced but also apparently like wines of higher tannin content. It has been suggested that bitter-tasting foods may increase the appetite (or postpone a feeling of satiety). The relation of tannins to the body and bitterness of wines needs further study.

Catechin and leucoanthocyans are colorless phenolic derivatives of flavans (i.e., of 2-phenyl-benzo-dihydropyrans). The relationship of the flavan, the anthocyans, catechin and leucoanthocyans is shown in Fig. 42.

Leucoanthocyans are colorless but are transformed into anthocyans when heated at 100°C. in an acid medium. Ribéreau-Gayon and Stonestreet (1964) reported the per cent leucoanthocyans to increase with the age of red wines as follows: 1962, 0.15; 1961, 0.19; 1960, 0.15; 1958, 0.23; 1953, 0.23; 1947, 0.37; 1938, 0.27 and 1921, 0.44. The tannin content, as determined by permanganate oxidation, also tended to increase in the same wines: 34, 37, 34, 48, 48, 64, 54, and 68 respectively. Berg (1963) however, found the leucoanthocyan content to decrease with age. The increase reported by Ribéreau-Gayon and Stonestreet more likely reflects seasonal and vinification practice variations rather than a real increase as the values were obtained from different wines. The leucoanthocyans of the seeds and skins appear to be different from those of the stems. Through enzymatic oxidations flavonols, catechins and leucoanthocyanins are converted to their corresponding quinoids. Further reaction causes the quinoids to polymerize and darken in color. To detect leucoanthocyanins Wucherpfennig and Bretthauer (1962) treated wine with butanol-hydrochloric acid. A rapid darkening of the color (measured at 550 nm) indicates their presence.

The properties of the catechins have been summarized recently by Herrmann (1959). (±)-Catechin, (−)-epicatechin, 3-galloylepicatechin, and (±)-gallocatechin are all reported in the wines and grapes of *Vitis vinifera*. One unappreciated property of the catechins is their importance in the enzymatic oxidative browning of fruit juices and their wines. They also change color to grey or blue-black with traces of iron. Both catechins and leucoanthocyans can also influence the taste—producing a bitter taste. This is more apparent in fruits such as apples and pears than in grapes. Herrmann (1959) even feels the catechins may, in the proper amounts, play a quality role in wines. This is undoubtedly the basis for the recommendation that tannins be added to musts or new wines. Unfortunately, the commercially available grape-seed tannins are apparently not of the same composition as the tannins of the grape. However, when the *o*-polyphenoloxidase content is high (as in botrytised grapes) they can only constitute a negative quality factor by causing browning. In red wines, of course, excess iron causes dark colored polyphenol-iron compounds to precipitate. Wines in which glycerol has been converted to acrolein turn bitter. This has been attributed to acrolein-catechin and acrolein-anthocyan compounds. See Chapter 2 for related compounds in grapes.

Among the phenolic compounds isolated from wines by Hennig and Burkhardt (1960) were: d-catechin, l-epicatechin, l-epigallocatechin, gallic acid, protocatechuic acid and ellagic acid. They also reported the polyphenols: chlorogenic, isochlorogenic, cis- and $trans$-caffeic acids and probably esculetin. Corse $et\ al.$ (1965) have since shown isochlorogenic acid to be a complex mixture of closely related compounds. Among the phenolic compounds were cis- and $trans$-coumaric acid and probably umbelliferone. Green grapes and young wines contained shikimic acid. Quinic acid is found in musts and young and old wines. They reported chlorogenic acid generally present in table wines. Caffeic acid is liberated later in the maturation process. Gallic and protocatechuic acid are found in small amounts in wines. Gallic acid tended to disappear during aging. Old wines seldom contain appreciable amounts of hydrolyzable tannins. Pomace wines are high in free-gallic and ellagic acids.

Burkhardt (1965) reported p-coumarylquinic acid or its calcium salt in grapes and wines. It does not lead to browning.

Rebelein (1965) found wines with low catechin and low methanol (normal), others with high catechin and high methanol (evidence of pomace wines), some with high catechin and low methanol (evidence of use of red grapes pressed early), and others with low catechin and high methanol (high methanol fortifying spirits). Where both catechin and methanol were low and there was a red color, artificial coloring is suspected.

Color

The pigments present in musts and hence in wines have been discussed in Chapter 2. It is sometimes observed that an increase in color occurs in red wines some months after production. Sambelyan (1959) believes this is due to two phenomena—conversion of malvidin to malvin and mainly to transformation of leucoanthocyans to colored forms. Ribéreau-Gayon and Stonestreet (1964) consider the aging of red wines to gradually result in anthocyan pigments passing to a colloidal state and precipitating. This allows the yellow-brown color of the tannins to be seen. This yellow-brown color increases with aging as the tannins condense. Oxidation of pigments also contributes materially to the increase in the brown color. Color changes in red wines can take place as a result of changes in the amounts present or of shifts in the equilibrium between colored and colorless forms of the pigments. Decrease of color, for example, can occur due to oxidation or polymerization of colored forms or might take place as a result of a shift in equilibrium from the colored to the colorless form. An example of the shift from colorless to colored forms occurs, Berg and Akiyoshi (1962), during early aging. During longer aging, the color loss was less in wines containing sulfur dioxide or with higher alcohol contents. Due to the shift from colorless to colored forms old wines have a much higher percentage of their total anthocyans in the colored form. Bieber (1967) found up to 275 mg. per liter of malvin in labrusca hybrids. Fermentation reduced this by 50 per cent or more. Valuĭko and Germanova (1968) showed that iron and copper ions strongly catalyze the oxidation of anthocyans.

The browning of white wines is largely due to the oxidation of phenolic compounds such as catechins and leucoanthocyanins. The velocity of the color change depends on the amount of phenolic compounds, the temperature, and the amount of dissolved oxygen in the wine. A light pressing of the crushed grapes reduces the leucoanthocyanin content.

Oxygen

In spite of its very great importance in wine handling there is little data on the oxygen content of wines, the factors which influence its absorption, and the exact sequence of reactions which it produces in different types of wines and at different temperatures. The first potentiometric curves on the variation in oxidation-reduction potential in the presence of reducing or oxidizing agents appear to be those of Geloso (1931). They were, however, done at pH 9 and their application to normal wine aging is doubtful. A general summary of the changes in the oxidation-reduction potential during fermentation and processing has been given by Deibner (1957A). See also Garino-Canina (1935), Joslyn (1938, 1949), Joslyn and Dunn (1938), and Schanderl (1948). The studies of Ribéreau-Gayon and Gardrat (1957) were done at the normal pH of wines. Ascorbic acid does not appear to be a factor in determining the oxidation or reduction titration curves of wines. The minimum potential found by reduction was lower in old than in young wines. The polyphenolic constituents begin to be reduced at relatively high potentials. However, if the polyphenols are first reduced they begin to be oxidized at relatively low potentials. The polyphenolic compounds thus appear to be important in the oxidation and reduction of wines. The inflection point for the curve for the reduction of red wines is 0.26 mv. at pH 3. For malvidin the normal potential at pH 2.5 is 0.3 mv. Ribéreau-Gayon and Gardrat were careful not to claim that the polyphenolic compounds, the anthocyans in particular, constitute the oxidation-reduction system of wine. But they do state that they may at least have an influence on such a system. It is claimed that the condensation of anthocyans during aging markedly modifies the oxidation-reduction potential of the wine. In studies on oxidation-reduction potentials it is important to distinguish those due to genuine reversible thermodynamic systems and those due to non-thermodynamic systems. Ribéreau-Gayon (1963) emphasized the complicated nature of the redox system of wines. Copper complexes are much more active as catalyzers of oxidation than iron or iron complexes. Traces of sulfhydryl derivatives (glutathione, for example) inhibit their activity. The main thing to remember is that wine is not a poised system. This means that the oxidation-reduction potential of a wine is primarily dependent upon the state of oxidation of the iron and copper present and on the amount of sulfur dioxide. In other words, it is easily shifted and, therefore, of little utility.

During fermentation, there is a rapid decrease in potential from about +0.4 to 0.1 v (with considerable variation among musts). Deibner believes this decrease is associated with the reduction of quinones during fermentation due to glutathione. The decrease depends on the conditions of culture of the pure yeasts according to Schanderl (1948). The redox potential is higher when the yeasts used are grown in the presence of air. The changes in the oxidation-reduction potential during fermentation are due to complex factors: composition of media, method of fermentation, temperature and degree of aeration, presence of sulfur dioxide, ascorbic acid, etc. In sparkling wines there is also a reduction in potential during the secondary fermentation, whether in bottle or tank. After final dosage there was a small decrease during bottle aging.

Following fermentation, wines stored in wood and racked frequently show a rapid increase in potential but in the absence of oxygen the potential may decrease. Wines stored in the bottle several years also show a decrease in potential. Joslyn (1949) showed that California red table wines generally had a lower potential while aging in the wood than white wines. Garino-Canina (1935) and Schanderl (1950–51) reported marked decreases in potential of wines exposed to direct sunlight. Deibner (1957B) noted potentials of up to 0.5 v when wines were aerated. But as Joslyn (1949) stated, the relation does not seem to be direct. Lower potentials occur in wines stored several weeks in the bottle. There is an especially large increase in potential at the time of the first racking, unless it is made in the absence of air. Gelatin or charcoal fining or pasteurization raise the potential.

The simple and rapid potentiometric procedure of Ough and Amerine (1960) should facilitate more accurate data. According to Ribéreau-Gayon (1947) the maximum oxygen which table wines can absorb is 5.6 to

6 ml. per liter at 68°F. However, wine can absorb a relatively large amount of oxygen over a period of time. Frolov-Bagreev and Agabal'-yants (1951) demonstrated that wines in small casks (250-liter) absorbed 40 ml. of oxygen the first year—20 by diffusion, four from around the bung and 16 during four rackings. The second year about 30 ml. were absorbed.

Minerals

The inorganic constituents of wines are of considerable biochemical, technological and physiological importance. Many are needed in alcoholic fermentation. Some are a part of the oxidation-reduction system. Others affect the clarity and flavor. Many are significant in human nutrition—usually desirably so but in a few cases from the toxic point of view so that legal maxima are prescribed. Except for the most recent publications, references to original papers will be found in Amerine (1958B).

Anions

The boric acid (H_3BO_3) content of wines is usually less than 50 mg. per liter, usually 15 to 30 (Bionda and Ciurlo 1959; Jaulmes et al. 1960). Film yeasts are believed to grow better in wines of high boron.

Bromide occurs in very small amounts (Jaulmes et al. 1961, Bergner and Lang 1970). The recommended maximum is 1 mg. per liter. Higher amounts probably indicate use of monobromacetic acid as an antiseptic. This compound is illegal in the United States and many other countries. Chloride is present in appreciable quantities—up to 0.4 gm. per liter. The French and Swiss limit is 0.607 gm. per liter (as chloride), which is certainly high enough. The limit is of some importance because of the possible contamination of wines from improperly cleaned ion-exchangers and also to detect use of monochloracetic acid as an antiseptic. Cabanis (1962) reported that when the chloride content was less than 60 mg. per liter, the bromide content was less than 0.6 mg. per liter. When the chloride content was 60 to 80 mg. per liter, the bromide could be as high as 1 mg. per liter; for more than 80 mg. per liter of chloride, bromides up to 3 mg. per liter were found. Since no organic bromine compounds are naturally present in wines, detection of addition of bromine-containing organic agents is simple: extraction wth ether. Even should organic bromine compounds hydrolyze (as they do), one can still use the chloride:bromide relationship as an indication of sophistication.

Normal musts and wines contain less than 5 mg. per liter of fluoride, and most wines contain considerably less than this—below one. Wines with more than five may have gotten it from late applications of fluosilicate insecticides or from illicit use of fluoride antiseptics. Sudraud and Cassignard (1959) also report that concrete tanks lined with magnesium fluosilicate are a potential source. Not only were the wines high, up to 50 mg. per liter, in fluorine but the musts fermented more slowly. Above 25 mg. per liter fermentation is more and more delayed and above 50 will seldom start. Iodide is present only in traces in wines, seldom over 0.3 mg. per liter.

The importance of phosphates in alcoholic fermentation does not need to be stressed (p. 178). Ferric phosphate casse is a recurrent and troublesome problem of wines. Fermentation on the skins increases the phosphate content of the resulting wine. Archer and Castor (1956) reported a phosphate uptake of 0.00128 to 0.00167 mg. per 10^6 cells. In new wines there are about 50 to 900 mg. per liter of which only a small amount, about 10 to 20 per cent, is present as organic phosphate (glycerophosphates, etc.). Many of the older enology texts claim a relationship between phosphate content and sensory quality. However, there is very little critical data which would substantiate this claim.

Silicate is found in very small amounts—20 to 60 mg. per liter.

Sulfate is of technological, sensory and legal importance. Sulfates have a slight salty-bitter taste. The plastering (p. 411) of musts leads to very high sulfate values. Furthermore, the oxidation of sulfurous acid may lead to high wine-sulfate contents. Finally there are legal limits on the maximum sulfate content of wines in various countries, usually 2 or 3 gm. per liter (as potassium sulfate). It has been reported by Schanderl (1959) that sulfate could be reduced to sulfurous acid during alcoholic fermentation. Zang (1963) and Zang and Franze (1966) also claimed that sulfur dioxide was produced in fermenting musts that had not been treated with sulfur dioxide. Amerine (1956B) failed to substantiate this clearly. Rankine (1963) likewise was unable to verify this.

Hydrogen sulfide and methyl (and possibly ethyl) mercaptan are occasionally found in young wines. The former usually arises from reduction of elemental sulfur (remaining in the grapes from mildew control). Thoukis and Stern (1962) showed that the presence of even 1 mg. per liter of free sulfur would result in the formation of detectable amounts of hydrogen sulfide during alcoholic fermentation. This amount of hydrogen sulfide was easily removed by aeration. When as much as 5 mg. per liter of free sulfur were present, sufficient hydrogen sulfide and probably mercaptans were formed to make removal by aeration difficult. In their studies sulfur dioxide was a minor source of hydrogen sulfide. Accumulation of hydrogen sulfide is greater with cold anaerobic fermentations. The primary source of free sulfur is from vineyard spraying for mildew. Therefore, late spraying for mildew should be avoided. The problem is not as simple as this as Fig. 55 illustrates. Ricketts and Coutts (1951) demonstrated that hydrogen sulfide was liberated during fermentation by 6 of the 8 yeasts studied. Macher (1952) also showed that the amount produced differed markedly between yeasts. Rankine (1963) has also shown differences in the hydrogen-sulfide producing tendency of different yeasts and recommends selection of special yeasts. He reported more sulfide produced at lower must pH, higher fermentation temperatures (in contrast to the results of Thoukis and Stern) and with greater depth of fermentation. Reduction of sulfur dioxide is one source, sulfur-containing nitrogen compounds is another. Methyl mercaptan may be the most objectionable compound. As Fig. 55 shows, this could arise from reduction of systeine. Cysteine is formed from cystine by reduction with sulfites.

The detection threshold for hydrogen sulfide in wines is given as 1 mg. per liter by Rankine (1963). Free sulfur dioxide removed 97 per cent of 10 mg. per liter of hydrogen sulfide in five days. He reported ethanethiol, presumably formed by the reaction of acetaldehyde and hydrogen sulfide, as having an objectionable odor. Prompt removal of hydrogen sulfide from young wines is recommended. Tanner and Rentschler (1965) noted that ethyl mercaptan has a relatively low boiling point and can be removed by aeration. Ethyl disulfide, on the other hand, has a high boiling point. It is best reduced to ethyl mercaptan with ascorbic acid and then removed by aeration. In practice we have not found this to be effective.

Cations.—Aluminum is a normal constituent of wines. While Jaulmes (1951) has proposed a maximum limit of 50 mg. per liter the amounts found in normal wines do not exceed about 15 and most wines have no more than 1 to 3 mg. per liter. Aluminum containers and pipes and fining agents are the usual source of higher amounts. Red wines are higher in aluminum than whites.

Arsenic is present in wines in amounts of no more than 0.01 to 0.02 mg. per liter. The recommended maximum is 0.02. Arsenical insecticides are the source of higher amounts but these are not used in California and seldom elsewhere. Most of the arsenical which reaches the fermenter is removed during fermentation. Lead arsenate is nearly insoluble at the alcoholic concentration of wine.

Cadmium is slightly soluble in wine hence cadmium-lined containers should not be used for storage of wines.

The calcium present in wines is derived from the fruit, from soil or plastering, calcium-containing filter-aids, and fining agents, concrete tanks, filter pads and possibly from the careless use of calcium hypochlorite. Concrete tanks should be treated to avoid calcium pick-up so far as possible. Filter pads, as presently produced, contain little calcium. They should, however, occasionally be checked and properly washed (p. 562). The amount of calcium pick-up from filter aids and fining agents such as bentonite is not known. Probably less is extracted by low acid wines than by high. On the other hand, once the calcium is present in the wine calcium tartrate deposition is less in wines with a pH of below 3.7 than in wines above this pH. DeSoto and Warkentin (1955), therefore, recommended acidifying high pH wines so that the pH is below this level. The insidious nature of excess calcium tartrate is the long delay in its deposition.

Copper is an important constituent of musts and wines as a necessary element for fermentation, as a part of the oxidation-reduction system (particularly as leading to copper casse, p. 557), and as a factor in taste. Very small amounts of copper are normally present in new wines. The data of Amerine and Joslyn (1951) for newly fermented California wines are pertinent in this regard (mg. per liter):

Source of Wine	No. of Samples	Minimum	Maximum	Average
Commercial	46	0.16	0.39	0.25
Experimental white	39	0.04	0.43	0.12
Experimental red	33	0.04	0.28	0.09

Vasconcellos (1947) reported that only 3.1 per cent of the must copper remained in the new wine. Amerine and Thoukis (1956) found in small scale fermentations that 41 to 89 per cent was lost during fermentation. Benvegnin and Capt (1934) also showed that 90 per cent of the must copper was removed with the pomace and lees. Françot and Geoffroy (1956) reported that 25 to 83 per cent of the must copper was lost during fermentation.

For information on the theories of copper clouding of wines see p. 556. Yeast poisoning from copper seldom, if ever, occurs in California musts because copper sprays for the control of mildew are not used in this state. Flavor may be affected by as little as 5 mg. per liter. Wines seldom contain over 0.5 to 1 mg. per liter unless (a), the must had a very high copper content or (b), the wine had been in contact with copper. The recommended legal maximum is one mg. per liter. Excessive copper in wine is primarily due to contamination. For this reason modern wineries have eliminated copper equipment which might come in contact with must or wine. For methods of removal of copper see pp. 558–562.

Iron is of interest to enologists for the same reasons as copper—cloud formation, oxidation-reduction reactions, effect on yeast, and flavor impairment. Iron from the surface of the grapes far exceeds that from the interior of the fruit. Some, but by no means all, of the must iron is lost during fermentation, the percentage loss depending on the oxidation-reduction conditions during and after fermentation and on the length of time the new wine remains on the skins. It is not possible at present to say how much is lost during commercial fermentations. The data of Schanderl (1959), which were obtained under winery conditions, suggest that from one-third to one-half is lost during fermentation and that essentially all of this is in or on yeast cells. See p. 554.

The primary source of excessive iron in wine appears to be from contact with iron equipment. Ferric phosphate is less soluble in lactic or tartaric acids than in malic. Consequently, during the malo-lactic fermentation precipitation of ferric phosphate may occur. For methods of removal of excessive iron see p. 558. The importance of iron in an oxidation-reduction system is recognized by most enologists. Whether or not some minimum amount is necessary for normal aging has not been established. While the range in iron content is wide, 0.0 to 50 or more mg. per liter, most California wines contain less than 10.

Little or no lead is found in normal musts. Even where lead sprays are used little is reported in wine, and this rapidly decreases during racking and storage as lead tartrate is very insoluble. Settling the must also helps eliminate lead. The legal limit varies from 0.2 mg. per liter in Great Britain, to 0.35 in Germany, to 3.5 in Switzerland. Jaulmes et al. (1960) reported that for French wines 29 per cent exceeded the 0.2 limit and 0.6 would be a more practical maximum. The sources are lead capsules, unlined cement tanks, lead-based paints, rubber hoses, lead-containing metals in pumps, filters, fillers, faucets, gaskets, etc., and even lead in filter pads, bentonite, and glass. See Rankine (1957) and Gentilini (1961). Of course, no lead sprays should be used in the vineyard. In 29 Italian table wines, Tarantola and Libero (1958) reported lead contents of 0.08 to 0.66 mg. per liter (average 0.17). In 6 vermouths the lead ranged from 0.11 to 0.22 mg. per liter (average 0.17). They reported 29 to 67 per cent of the lead content of musts was lost during fermentation. Other reports showed: Algeria (67) 0.02–1.78, average 0.25 (Bremond and Roubert 1956), Australia (55), 0.04–0.86, average 0.23 (Rankine 1955), Germany (7), 0.00–0.16 (Gilbert and Grohmann 1959), Portugal (54), trace–2.6 (De Almeida 1947), Portugal (162), 0.20–1.00, average 0.33 (Pereira (1959), and Russia (44) 0.24–0.90 (Bolotov 1939). Amati and Rastelli (1967) found 1 to 92 mg. per liter of lithium in 112 Italian wines with most samples between 5 and 60.

Magnesium is found in very small quantities in wines, 50 to 165 mg. per liter. There is more in the musts than in the wine. The magnesium/calcium ratio increases during fermentation from about one to two to four.

Manganese is found in all wines in very small amounts—more in wines made of grapes grown in high manganese soils. There is more in red than white wines. The range reported in various wines is from 0.5 to 15 mg. per liter but wines of over about 2.5 mg. are believed to be sophisticated—

either from potassium permanganate (added to reduce excessive sulfur dioxide?) or from manganese-containing charcoal. Würziger (1954) found 0.5 to 3.2 mg. per liter in 70 wines. In 66 German musts, Gärtel (1956) reported 0.29–2.30 mg. per liter (average 0.70). Wines of hybrids (direct producers) are slightly higher in manganese according to Tuzson (1964). In 842 Hungarian wines, the average was about 1.5 mg. per liter. Deibner and Bénard (1956) found additions of 5 to 15 mg. per liter of manganese plus heating improved the sensory quality of sweet wines. They believed that 1 to 5 mg. per liter of molybdenum, with or without manganese, enhanced quality. Gärtel (1960) reported 0.001 to 0.0358 mg. per liter in 41 wines. Russian enologists reported wines high in manganese, molybdenum, vanadium, titanium, and boron of better sensory quality. Amerine (1958B) found these claims difficult to evaluate. The amounts of trace elements were summarized by Eschnauer (1961).

Potassium constitutes about three-fourths of the total cation content of wines. Its importance in alcoholic fermentation and in bitartrate stability may be noted. Reports that it favorably affects sensory quality have not been documented adequately. Possibly the effect is mainly one of reducing the acidity. Amerine (1958B) reported potassium values from 0.1 to 1.76 g. per liter with the average varying from 0.36 to 1.1. Use of tartrate-potassium solubility-product calculations to predict tartrate stability have been proposed by Nègre (1954) and Wiseman (1955). The actual values of the latter varied from 8.2 to 21.8 $\times$ 10^{-5} compared to calculated values of 1.40 to 2.85 $\times$ 10^{-5}. Berg and Kieffer (1958–1959) have made similar calculations which are a useful guide. (See pp. 563–565.)

Rubidium is present in amounts of 0.2 to 4.2 mg. per liter, average about 0.5. More rubidium in the skins and stems make reds higher than whites.

Sodium is of particular interest to wine makers today because of the increasing use of ion exchangers. Other sources of high sodium are from ocean spray (for vineyards near the sea), sodium bisulfite or metabisulfite, and possible from fining agents. Sodium bitartrate is much more soluble than potassium bitartrate. There may be undesirable flavor effects from high sodium. High sodium wines are undesirable for people on restricted sodium intake due to hypertension. The amounts in wines vary very widely. From 5 to 443 mg. per liter were noted by Amerine (1958B) but most wines had less than 100. Jouret and Poux (1961C) reported about 4 times as much sodium and 5 to 6 times as much chloride in wines produced from vines grown on saline soils compared to those on non-saline soils. Surprisingly, there is also more potassium but a lower alkalinity of the ash. Jouret and Bénard (1965) have demonstrated wide variations in chloride/sodium and potassium/sodium ratios in wines from different rootstocks. Cultural and climatic conditions were also important. It has been suggested that the sodium content (as sodium chloride) not be higher than 50 mg. per liter. Tamborini and Magro (1970) recommended for Italian wines that the potassium/sodium ratio not be under 10.

Tin is seldom found in wines—usually from contact with tin utensils. Small amounts of tin result in cloudiness and hydrogen sulfide formation. Tin-plated equipment is reported by Eschnauer (1963) to be the source of tin in wines (0.1 to 0.9 mg. per liter). Tin pickup should be avoided since at about 1 mg. per liter it may lead to tin-albumin cloudiness.

Zinc has been determined more often because of the use of zinc-containing insecticides and fungicides. Normal wines usually contain less than 5 mg. per liter though reports as high as 19 have been made. The recommended limit is 5–6 mg. per liter (Vogel and Deshusses 1962; Tanner 1963). As much as half of the tin in musts is lost during fermentation. The use of zinc to prevent over-blue fining is illegal. More than about 5 mg. per liter of zinc gives a slight metallic taste to wines. In German musts, Gärtel (1957) reported 0.5 to 2.0 mg. per liter.

Balance of Products

Based on the various reactions occurring during alcoholic fermentation Genevois (1936) proposed a balance of by-products as follows: $5s + 2a + b + 2m + h = 0.9$ g. where s is succinic acid, a is acetic acid, b is 2,3-butylene glycol, m is acetoin, h is acetaldehyde, and g is glycerol con-

TABLE 29

BALANCE OF BY-PRODUCTS OF ALCOHOLIC FERMENTATION[1]
(1–6 red, 7–12 white)

	Glycerol (g)		Acetic Acid	Succinic Acid	2,3-Butylene Glycol	Acetaldehyde		
			(a)	(s)	(b)	(h)	Σ^2	Σ/g
	Gm./l.	Milli-mol	Milli-mol	Milli-mol	Milli-mol	Milli-mol		
1	8.55	93	22.1	9.1	7.0	0.6	97.3	1.05
2	8.00	87	15.0	8.4	7.8	0.6	80.4	0.92
3	7.64	83	20.6	9.0	8.4	1.2	96.8	1.17
4	8.36	91	15.0	8.9	8.7	1.2	84.4	0.93
5	8.28	90	14.4	9.9	7.9	0.8	87.0	0.97
6	7.17	78	15.6	8.3	6.9	0.5	80.1	1.03
7	7.92	86	11.5	9.1	4.9	1.9	75.3	0.88
8	12.3	133[3]	16.2	10.1	11.0	1.2	95.1	...
9	15.1	164[3]	19.7	7.6	10.1	1.8	89.3	...
10	15.4	168[3]	16.2	8.1	8.1	1.7	82.7	...
11	24.4	262[3]	27.9	10.8	12.3	1.7	124	...
12	26.0	283[3]	23.1	11.0	10.9	1.0	113	...

[1] Source of data: Peynaud (1950).
[2] $\Sigma = 2a = 5s + b + h$.
[3] Amount calculated as produced from botrytis on grapes is 28, 66, 77, 126, and 159 millimo s, respectively (using the Σ/g factor of 0.9).

tent. For a variety of wines and yeasts the Bordeaux school of enologists has found this to give a good balance of the by-products of alcoholic fermentation. Table 29 summarizes the results on six red and six white Bordeaux wines. The balance applied to yeasts which produced quite different amounts of acetic acid, succinic acid, and 2,3-butylene glycol. It was also satisfactory for fortified wines. Nevertheless, further studies on by-product inter-relations could be profitably undertaken.

The cation and anion balance of wines has successfully been made on a number of wines. Ribéreau-Gayon and Peynaud (1958) have summarized much of these data. The following is the balance of 47 Bordeaux red wines (average pH 3.40) by Peynaud (1947) (in milliequivalents):

Cations
Titratable acidity **75.00**
Alkalinity of the ash **23.50**
Ammonia **1.20**

Sum of Cations **99.70**
Anions (acids)
Tartaric **26.9**
Malic **2.8**
Citric **1.4**
Acetic **17.4**
Succinic **15.5**
Lactic **25.5**
Acid esters **3.1**
Phosphoric **4.5**
Sulfurous **0.8**

Sum of Anions **97.9**

More data is needed using improved methods of analyses.

BIBLIOGRAPHY

AMATI, A., and RASTELLI, R. 1967. Sul contenuto in litio di vini italiani. Ind. agr. 5, 233–237.
AMERINE, M. A. 1954. Composition of wines. I. Organic constituents. Adv. Food Research 5, 353–510.
AMERINE, M. A. 1958A. Acetaldehyde formation in submerged cultures of Saccharomyces beticus. App. Microbiol. 6, 160–168.
AMERINE, M. A. 1958B. Composition of wines. II. Inorganic constituents. Adv. Food Research 8, 133–224.
AMERINE, M. A. 1965A. The fermentation industries after Pasteur. Food Technol. 19, 75–80, 82.
AMERINE, M. A. 1965B. Personal communication.
AMERINE, M. A., and JOSLYN, M. A. 1951. Table Wines. The Technology of Their Production in California. Univ. Calif. Press, Berkeley and Los Angeles.
AMERINE, M. A., and KUNKEE, R. E. 1965. Yeast stability tests on dessert wines. Vitis 5, 187–194.

AMERINE, M. A., and OUGH, C. S. 1957. Studies on controlled fermentation. III. Am. J. Enol. 8, 18–30.

AMERINE, M. A., and OUGH, C. S. 1964. Studies with controlled fermentation. VIII. Factors affecting aldehyde accumulation. Am. J. Enol. Vitic. 15, 23–33.

AMERINE, M. A., and THOUKIS, G. 1956. The fate of copper and iron during fermentation of grape musts. Am. J. Enol. 7, 45–52.

AMERINE, M. A., ROESSLER, E. B., and FILIPELLO, F. 1959. Modern sensory n.ethods of evaluating wine. Hilgardia 28, 477–567.

AMERINE, M. A., ROESSLER, E. B., and OUGH, C. S. 1965. Acids and the acid taste. I. The effect of pH and titratable acidity. Am J. Enol. Vitic. 16, 29–37.

ANDERSON, J. H. 1959. CO_2 retention and an academic theory. Comm. Masters Brewers Assoc. America 20, Nos. 1–2, 3–7, 15; Nos. 3–4, 6–12; Nos. 5–6, 12–14.

ARCHER, T. E., and CASTOR, J. G. B. 1956. Phosphate changes in fermenting must in relation to yeast growth and ethanol production. Am. J. Enol. 7, 45–52.

AUERBACH, R. C. 1959. Sorbic acid as a preservative agent in wine. Wines and Vines 40, No. 8, 26–28.

BANOLAS, E. 1948. On the new apparatus for the rational equipment of wine making cellars. Inter. Inst. Refrig. Bull., Annex. 2, 9–23.

BARAUD, J. 1953. La réaction de la tartrazine appliquée à l'étude des vins. Bull. soc. chim. France 20, 525–527.

BENVEGNIN, L., and CAPT, E. 1934. Contribution à l'étude du cuivre dans les moûts et vins. Mitt. Gebiete Lebensm. u. Hyg. 25, 124–138.

BERAUD, P., and MILLET, J. 1949. Observations sur le pouvoir alcoogéne des levures cultivées à basse température. Ann Inst. Pasteur 77, 581–587.

BERG, H. W. 1963. Stabilisation des anthocyannes, comportement de la couleur dans les vins rouges. Ann. technol. agr. (numéro hors série 12, 247–261.

BERG, H. W., and AKIYOSHI, M. 1962. Color behavior during fermentation and aging of wines. Am. J. Enol. Vitic. 13, 126–132.

BERG, H. W., and KEEFER, R. M. 1958–1959. Analytical determination of tartrate stability in wine. Am. J. Enol. 9, 180–193; 10, 105–109.

BERG, H. W., FILIPELLO, F., HINREINER, E., and WEBB, A. D. 1955A. Evaluation of thresholds and minimum differences concentrations for various constituents of wines. I. Water solutions of pure substances. Food Technol. 9, 23–26.

BERG, H. W., FILIPELLO, F., HINREINER, E., and WEBB, A. D. 1955B. Evaluation of thresholds and minimum difference concentrations for various constituents of wines. II. Sweetness: the effect of ethyl alcohol, organic acids and tannin. Food Technol. 9, 138–140.

BERGNER, K. G., and LANG, B. 1970. Zum Bromgehalt deutscher Wein. Mitt. Rebe u. Wein, Obstbau u. Früchteverw. 20, 189–201.

BERTI, L. A. 1951. Production factors. Proc. Am. Soc. Enol. 1951, 186–190.

BERTRAND, G., and SILBERSTEIN, L. 1950. La fermentation du sucre par la levure produit-elle normalement du méthanol? Compt. rend. 230, 800–803. See also Ibid. 229, 1281–1284, 1949; 234, 491–494, 1952.

BIDAN, P., and ANDRÉ, L. 1958. Sur la composition en acides aminés de quelques vins. Ann. technol. agr. 7, 403–432.

BIEBER, H. 1967. Die fluorimetrische Bestimmung von Malvin in Traubenmost und Wein. Deut. Lebensm.-Rdsch. 63, 44–46.

BIONDA, G., and CIURLO, R. 1959. Sur la teneur en bore de quelques vins de la Ligurie. Ann. fals. et fraudes 52, 369–72.

BLOUIN, J. 1963. Constituants du vin combinant de l'acide sulfureux. Ann. technol. agr. 12 (numéro hors série 1), 97–98.

BOCKS, S. M. 1961. Nutritional requirements for the induced formation of malic enzyme in Lactobacillus arabinosus. Nature 192, 89–90.

BOLOTOV, M. P. 1939. O soderzhanii i istochnikakh svintsa i medi v vinakh (The content and source of lead and copper in wines). Voprosy pitan. 8, No. 2, 100–108.

BOURDET, A., and HÉRARD, J. 1958. Influence de l'autolyse des levures sur la composition phosphorée et azotée des vins. Ann. technol. agr. 7, 177–202.

BRAVERMAN, J. B. S. 1953. Le mécanisme de l'action de l'anhydride sulfureux sur certains sucres. Conf. Comm. Sci. Féderation Internationale des Producteurs de Jus de Fruits.

BRENNER, M. W., OWADES, J. L., and FAZIO, T. 1955. Determination of volatile sulfur compounds. IV. Further notes on mercaptans. Am. Soc. Brewing Chemists Proc. 1955, 125–132.

BROCKMANN, M. C., and STIER, T. J. B. 1948. Influence of temperature on the production of glycerol during alcoholic fermentation. J. Am. Chem. Soc. 70, 413–414.

BURKHARDT, R. 1965. Nachweis der p-Cumarylchinasäure in Weinen und das Verhalten der Depside bei der Kellerbehandlung. Mitt. Rebe u. Wein, Serie A (Klosterneuburg) 15, 80–86.

BURROUGHS, L., and WHITING, G. 1960. The sulphur dioxide combining power of cider. Ann. Rept. Agr. Hort. Expr. Sta., Long Ashton 1960, 144–147.

CABANIS, J. E. 1962. Le brome dans les vins. Montpellier.

CABEZUDO, D., LLAGUNO, C., and GARRIDO, J. M. 1963. Contentido en biotina y otros componentes fundamentales en vinos de las principales zonas vinícolas de España. Agroquim. technol. alim. 3, 369–375.

CAMBITZI, A. 1947. Formation of racemic calcium tartrate in wines. Analyst 72, 542–543.

CARLES, J. 1959. Sur les décarboxylations dans les vins et l'apparition de l'acide citramalique. Rev. esp. fisiol. 15, 193–200.

CASTELLI, T. 1941. Temperatura e chimismo dei blastomiceti. Ann. microb. 2, No. 1, 8–22.

CASTINO, M. 1969. Gli acidi 2-metilmalico, 2,3-diidrossilisovalerianico e 2,3-diidrossi-2-metilbutirico nei vini. Riv. viticolt. e enol. (Conegliano) 22, 197–207.

CASTOR, J. G. B., and GUYMON, J. F. 1952. On the mechanism of formation of higher alcohols during alcoholic fermentation. Science 115, 147–149.

CASTOR, J. G. B., NELSON, K. E., and HARVEY, J. M. 1957. Effect of captan residues on fermentation of grapes. Am. J. Enol. 8, 50–57.

CAUSERT, J., HUGOT, D., THUISSIER, M., BIETTE, E., and LECLERC, J. 1964. L'utilisation des sulfites en technologie alimentaire: quelques aspects toxicologiques et nutritionnels. IV Congrès d'Expertise Chimique, Athens, special no., 215–224.

COOK, A. H.   1958.   The Chemistry and Biology of Yeasts. Academic Press, New York.

COOKE, G. N., KUNKEE, R. E., and OUGH, C. S.   1964.   Continuous addition of diethylpyrocarbonate into wine. Wine Institute, Tech. Advis. Committee, Dec. 11, 1964.

CORSE, J., LUNDIN, R. E., and WAISS, JR., A. C.   1965.   Identification of several components of isochlorogenic acid. Phytochem. *4*, 527–529.

CROWELL, E. A., and GUYMON, J. F.   1963.   Influence of aeration and suspended material on higher alcohol, acetoin, and diacetyl during fermentation. Am. J. Enol. Vitic. *14*, 214–22.

CRUESS, W. V.   1935A.   Further data on the effect of SO_2 in preventing high volatile acidity in wines. Fruit Prods. J. *15*, 324–327, 345.

CRUESS, W. V.   1935B.   Notes on producing and keeping wines low in volatile acidity. Fruit Prods. J. *15*, 76–77, 108–109.

DE ALMEIDA, H.   1947.   Investigação acerca das causas da possível presença do chumbo. Anais Inst. Vinho Porto *8*, 13–28.

DEEDS, F.   1961.   Summary of toxicity data on sulfur dioxide. Food Technol. *15*, 28, 33.

DEIBNER, L.   1957A.   Modifications du potentiel oxydoreducteur au cours de l'élaboration des vins de différents types. Ann. technol. agr. *6*, 313–345.

DEIBNER, L.   1957B.   Effet de différents traitements sur le potentiel oxydoréducteur des vins au cours de leur conservation. *Ibid. 6*, 363–372.

DEIBNER, L., and BÉNARD, P.   1956.   Recherches sur la maturation des vins doux naturels. II. Essai de catalyseurs métalliques. *Ibid. 5*, 377–397.

DELLE, P. N.   1911.   The influence of must concentration on the fermentation and composition of wine and its stability (transl.) Odessa, Otchet- vinodeiel'cheskoi stantsii russkikh" vinogradarei i venodielov" za 1908 i 1909g, 118–160.

DESOTO, R., and WARKENTIN, H.   1965.   Influence of pH and total acidity on calcium tolerance of sherry wine. Food Research *20*, 301–309. (*Also in* Am. J. Enol. 7, 91–97. 1956.)

DIEMAIR, W., and MAIER, G.   1962.   Bestimmung des Eiweissgehaltes. Z. Lebensm. -Untersuch, u. -Forsch. *118*, 148–152.

DIEMAIR, W., KOCH, J., and SAJAK, E.   1961A.   Zur Bestimmung des "löslichen" Proteins in Most und Wein. *Ibid. 116*, 5–7.

DIEMAIR, W., KOCH, J., and SAJAK, E.   1961B.   Zur Kenntnis der Eiweissstoffe des Weines. V. Allgemeine Eigenschaften des löslichen Traubenproteins. *Ibid. 116*, 7–13.

DIEMAIR, W., KOCH, J., and SAJAK, E.   1961C.   *Ibid.* VIII. Die Eiweisstrübung. *Ibid. 116*, 327–335.

DIETRICH, K. R.   1954.   Die Vermeidung von Schwundverlusten an Alkohol bei der Gärung. Deut. Wein-Ztg. *90*, 448.

DIMOTAKI-KOURAKOU, V.   1962.   Le présence de l'acide α-methyl-malique dans le vins. Ann. fals. et expert. chim. *55*, 149–158.

DITTRICH, H. H., and KERNER, E.   1964.   Diacetyl als Weinfehler; Ursache und Beseitigung des "Milchsäuretones." Wein-Wissen. *19*, 528–538.

DITTRICH, H. H., and STAUDENMAYER, T.   1970.   Ueber die Zusammenhänge zwischen der Sulfit-Bildung und der Schwefelwasserstoff-Bildung bei *Saccharomyces cerevisiae*. Zent. Bakt., Parasit., Infekt., Hyg. Abt. II. *125*, 113–118. (See also Deut Wein-Ztg. *104*, 707–709. 1969)

DUPUY, P. 1960. Le métabolisme de l'acide tartrique. Ann. technol. agr. 9, 139–184.

ESAU, P., and AMERINE, M. A. 1964. Residual sugars in wine. Am. J. Enol. Vitic. 15, 187–189.

ESCHNAUER, H. 1961. Spurenelemente im Wein und im Weinbau. Mitt. Rebe u. Wein, Serie A (Klosterneuburg) 11, 123–130.

ESCHNAUER, H. 1963. Zinntrübungen im Wein. Weinberg u. Keller 10, 523–528.

ETTIENNE, A. D., and MATHERS, A. P. 1956. Laboratory carbonation of wine. J. Assoc. Offic. Agr. Chem. 39, 844–848.

FEDUCHY MARIÑO, E., SANDOVAL PUERTA, J. A., HIDALGO ZABALLOS, T., RODRÍGUEZ MATÍA, E., and HORCHE DÍEZ, T. 1964. Contribución al estudio analítico de las dosis de metanol existentes en productos procedentes de la fermentatión vínica. Bol. Inst. Nac. Invest. Agron. 51, 453–484.

FILIPELLO, F. 1951. Correlation of fortifying brandy with wine quality. Proc. Am. Soc. Enol. 1951, 154–156.

FLANZY, C., and POUX, C. 1965. Les levures alcooliques dans les vins, protéolyse, protéogenèse (III). Ann. technol. agr. 14, 35–48.

FLANZY, C., POUX, C., and FLANZY, M. 1964. Les levures alcooliques dans les vins. Protéolyse et protéogenèse. Ibid. 13, 283–300.

FLANZY, M. 1934. L'Alcool Méthylique dans les Liquides Alcooliques Naturels. Imprimerie Regionale, Toulouse.

FLANZY, M., and BOUZIGUES, L. 1959. Pectines et méthanol dans les moûts de raisin et les vins. Ann. technol. agr. 8, 59–68.

FLANZY, M., and LOISEL, Y. 1958. Évolution des pectines dans les boissons et production de méthanol. Ibid. 7, 311–321.

FLANZY, M., and OURNAC, A. 1963. Fermentation des jus de raisins frais et désulfités. Influence d'additions de levures et de thiamine. Ibid. 12, 65–84.

FORNACHON, J. C. M. 1963. Inhibition of certain lactic acid bacteria by free and bound sulphur dioxide. J. Sci. Food Agr. 12, 857–862.

FRANÇOT, P., and GEOFFROY, P. 1956. Repartition du cuivre dans les moûts et vins au cours du pressurage Champenois. Vigneron Champenois 77, 451–459.

FROLOV-BAGREEV, A. M., and AGABAL'YANTS, G. G. 1951. Kkimiya Vina. (Chemistry of Wine). Pishchepromizdat, Moscow.

GÄRTEL, W. 1956. Untersuchungen über den Mangangehalt von Rebteilen und Most. Weinberg u. Keller 3, 554–560.

GÄRTEL, W. 1957. Untersuchungen über den Zinkgehalt von Rebteilen und Most. Ibid. 4, 419–424.

GÄRTEL, W. 1960. Molybdänbestimmung in Most und Wein. Ibid. 7, 373–379.

GARINO-CANINA, E. 1935. Il potenziale di ossidoriduzione e la tecnica enologica. Ann. chim. appl. 25, 209–217.

GAROGLIO, P. G., and STELLA, C. 1964. Ricerche sull'impiego in enologia dell'estere dietilico dell'acido pirocarbonico (DEPC) allo stato puro. Riv. viticolt. e enol. (Conegliano) 17, 422–453.

GEHMAN, H. and OSMAN, E. M. 1954. The chemistry of the sugar sulfite-reaction and its relationship to food problems. Adv. Food Research 5, 53–96.

GELOSO, J. 1931. Relation entre le vieillissement des vins et leur potentiel d'oxydo-réduction. Ann. brass. distil. 29, 177–181, 193–197, 257–261, 273–279.

GEISS, W. 1952. Gezügelte Gärung. Sigurd Horn Verlag, Frankfurt.

GENEVOIS, L. 1936. Acide succinique et glycérine dans la fermentation alcoolique. Bull. soc. chim. biol. 18, 295–300.

GENEVOIS, L. 1951. Les produits secondaries de la fermentation; acids organiques des vins; matières colorantes et vieillessement des vins. Rev. ferment. ind. aliment. 6, 18–25, 43–47, 88–96, 111–115.

GENTILINI, L. 1961. Il piombo in enologia. Riv. viticolt. e enol. (Conegliano) 14, 307–311.

GENTILINI, L., and CAPPELLERI, G. 1959. Variazioni del contenuto in glicerina del vino in funzione di fattori che influenzano il decorso dell'atto fermentativo. Ann. sper. agrar. (Rome) [N.S.] 13, 289–306.

GILBERT, E., and GROHMANN, H. 1959. Eine einfache quantitative polarographische Bleibestimmung in Traubenmost und Wein. Deut. Lebensm.-Rdsch. 55, 300–303.

GILLISSEN, G. 1954. Über die Verwendung antibiotischer Stoffe anstelle von schwefliger Säure in der Oenologie. Deut. Wein-Ztg. 90, 195–196.

GIUDICE, E. del. 1955. Intorno all'azione dell'aneurina sul processo di fermentazione vinaria. Riv. viticolt. e enol. (Conegliano) 8, 311–315.

GOTTSCHALK, A. 1946. Mechanism of selective fermentation of d-fructose from invert sugar by Sauternes yeast. Biochem. J. 40, 621–626.

GRAY, P. P., and STONE, I. 1939. Oxidation in beers. I. A. simplified method for measurement. Wallerstein Lab. Comm. 2, No. 5, 5–16.

GRAY, W. D. 1945. The sugar tolerance of four strains of distillers' yeast. J. Bact. 49, 445–452.

GUIMBERTEAU, G., and PEYNAUD, E. 1965. Recherche et estimation du saccharose ajouté aux moûts et aux vins à l'aide de la chromatographie sur papier. Ann. fals. et expert. chim. 58, 32–38.

GUYMON, J. F., and CROWELL, E. A. 1965. The formation of acetoin and diacetyl during fermentation, and the levels found in wines. Am. J. Enol. Vitic. 16, 85–91.

GUYMON, J. F., and HEITZ, J. E. 1952. The fusel oil content of California wines. Food Technol. 6, 359–362.

GUYMON, J. F., INGRAHAM, J. L., and CROWELL, E. A. 1961. Influence of aeration upon the formation of higher alcohols by yeasts. Am. J. Enol. Vitic. 12, 60–66.

GVALADZE, V. 1936. Relation Between the Products in Alcoholic Fermentation (transl.) Lenin Agr. Acad. U.S.S.R., Moscow.

HEIDE, C. VON DER, and SCHMITTHENNER, F. 1922. Der Wein. F. Vieweg und Sohn, Braunschweig, Germany.

HENNIG, K. 1959. Erfahrungen beim Nachweis gezuckerter und gespriteter Wein nach Rebelein. Bericht Hessische Lehr.-u. Forsch. Wein-, Obst- u. Gartenbau, Geisenheim 1957/58, 28–29.

HENNIG, K. 1960. Der Pyrokohlensäurediäthylester, ein neues, rückstandloses, gärhemmendes Mittel. Weinberg u. Keller 7, 351–360.

HENNIG, K. 1963. Emploi du pyrocarbonate d'éthyle dans le traitement des vins. Ann. technol. agr. 12 (numéro hors série 1), 115–124.

HENNIG, K., and BURKHARDT, R. 1960. Detection of phenolic compounds and hydroxy acids in grapes, wines, and similar beverages. Am. J. Enol. Vitic. 11, 64–79.

HERRMANN, K. 1959. Über Katechine and Katechin-Gerbstoffe und ihre Bedeutung in Lebensmitteln. Z. Lebensm.-Untersuch. u. -Forsch. 109, 487–507.

HICKINBOTHAM, A. R., and RYAN, V. J.   1948.   Glycerol in wine.   Australian Chem. Inst., J. and Proc. 15, 89–100.

HINREINER, E., FILIPELLO, F., BERG, H. W., and WEBB, A. D.   1955A.   Evaluation of thresholds and minimum difference concentrations for various constituents of wines.   IV. Detectable differences in wines.   Food Technol. 9, 489–490.

HINREINER, E., FILIPELLO, F., WEBB, A. D., and BERG, H. W.   1955B.   Evaluation of thresholds and a minimum difference concentrations for various constituents of wines.   III. Ethyl alcohol, glycerol and acidity in aqueous solutions.   Ibid. 9, 351–353.

INGRAM, M.   1955.   An Introduction to the Biology of Yeasts.   Pitman Publishing Corp., New York.

INIGO LEAL, B., and BRAVO ABAD, F.   1963.   Acidez y levaduras vínicas. II. Evolución de la acidez fija del mosto por la acción de distintas especies de levaduras vínicas.   III. Curso cinético de la acidez volátil en fermentados de mosto originados por distintas especies de levaduras vínicas.   Rev. cienc. apl. 17, 40–43, 132–135.

JAULMES, P.   1951.   Analyse des Vins.   2 ed.   Librarie Coulet, Dubois et Poulain, Montpellier.

JAULMES, P., BRUN-CORDIER, S., and BASCOU, P.   1961.   La teneur naturelle des vins en acide borique.   Ann fals. et expert. chim. 53, 70–82.

JAULMES, P., BRUN-CORDIER, S., and CABANIS.   1961.   Teneur naturelle des vins en brome.   Trav. soc. pharm. Montpellier 20, 84–92.

JAULMES, P., HAMELLE, G., and ROQUES, J.   1960.   Le plomb dans les moûts et les vins.   Ann. tecnol. agr. 9, 189–245.

JORDAN, J. R.   1911.   Quality in Dry Wines Through Adequate Fermentations.   San Francisco.

JOSLYN, M. A.   1938.   Electrolytic production of rancio flavor in sherries.   Ind. Eng. Chem. 30, 568–577.

JOSLYN, M. A.   1949.   California wines.   Oxidation-reduction potentials at various stages of production and aging.   Ind. Eng. Chem. 41, 587–592.

JOSLYN, M. A.   1951.   Nutrient requirements of yeast.   Mycopath. et mycol. appl. 5, 260–276.

JOSLYN, M. A.   1952.   Chemistry of sulfite addition products.   Proc. Am. Soc. Enol. 1952, 59–68.

JOSLYN, M. A., and DUNN, R.   1938.   Acid metabolism of wine yeast.   I. The relation of volatile acid formation to alcoholic fermentation.   J. Am. Chem. Soc. 60, 1137–1141.

JOURET, C., and BÉNARD, P.   1965.   Influence des porte-greffes sur la composition minérale des vins des vignes de terrains salés.   Ann. technol. agr. 14, 349–355.

JOURET, C., and POUX, C.   1961C.   Note sur les teneurs en potassium, sodium et chlore des vignes des terrains salés.   Ibid. 10, 369–374.

KIELHÖFER, E.   1953.   Die Wirkung antibiotischen Stoffe auf die Weingärung.   Deut. Wein-Ztg. 89, 638, 640, 642.   (For translation see Am. J. Enol. 5, 13–17, 1954.)

KIELHÖFER, E.   1958.   Die Bindung der schwefligen Säure an Weinbestandteile.   Weinberg u. Keller 5, 461–476.

KIELHÖFER, E.   1959.   Neue Erkenntnisse über die Wirkung der Schwefligen Säure in Wein und die Möglichkeit ihres Ersatzes durch Ascorbinsäure.   Verlag Sigurd Horn, Frankfurt.

KIELHÖFER, E. 1963. État et action de l'acide sulfureux dans les vins; règles de son emploi. Ann. technol. agr. 12 (numéro hors série 1), 77–89.

KIELHÖFER, E., and WÜRDIG, G. 1960A. Die an Aldehyd gebundene schweflige Säure im Wein. I. Acetaldehydbildung durch enzymatische und nicht enzymatische Alkohol-Oxydation. Weinberg u. Keller 7, 16–22.

KIELHÖFER, E., and WÜRDIG, G. 1960B. Ibid. II. Acetaldehydbildung bei der Gärung. Ibid. 7, 50–61.

KIELHÖFER, E., and WÜRDIG, G. 1963. Die Entsäuerung sehr saurer Traubenmoste durch Ausfällung der Weinsäure und Apfelsäure als Kalkdoppelsalz. Deut. Wein-Ztg. 99, 1022, 1024, 1026, 1028.

KIELHÖFER, E., and WÜRDIG, G. 1964. Einige bei der Anwendung von Pyrokohlensäurediäthylester zu biologischen Weinstabilisierung auftretende Probleme. I. Weinberg u. Keller 11, 495–504.

KOCH, J. 1957. Die Eiweissstoffe des Weines und ihre Veränderungen bei verschiedenen kellertechnischen Behandlungsmethoden. Ibid. 4, 521–526.

KOCH, J. 1963. Protéines des vins blancs. Traitements des précipitations protéiques par chauffage et al l'aide de la bentonite. Ann. technol. agr. 12 (numéro hors série 1) 297–313.

KOCH, J., and BRETTHAUER, G. 1957. Zur Kenntnis der Eiweissstoffe des Weines. I. Chemische Zusammensetzung des Wärmetrubes kurzzeiterhitzter Weissweine und seine Beziehung zur Eiweisstrübung und zum Weineiweiss. Z. Lebensm.-Untersuch. u. -Forsch. 106, 272–280.

KOCH, J., and BRETTHAUER, G. 1960. Das Glucose-Fructose Verhältnis der Konsumweine in Abhängigkeit von verschiedenen kellertechnischen Massnahmen. Ibid. 112, 97–105.

KOCH, J., and SAJAK, E. 1959. A review and some studies on grape protein. Am. J. Enol. Vitic. 10, 114–123.

KOCH, J., and SAJAK, E. 1963. Zur Frage der Eiweisstrübung der Weine. Weinberg u. Keller 10, 35–51.

KOCH, J., BRETTHAUER, G., and SCHWAHN, H. 1956. Über die chemische Zusammensetzung des Wärmetrubes kurzzeiterhitzer Weine und seine Beziehung zu der sogenannten "Eiweisstrübung." Naturwissen. 43, 421–422.

LAFON, M. 1956. Sur quelques caractères physiologiques et biochimiques des levures de vin. Ann. Inst. Pasteur 91, 91–99.

LAFON-LAFOURCADE, S., and PEYNAUD, E. 1958. L'acide p-aminobenzoïque, l'acide ptéroylglutamique et la choline (vitamines du groupe B) dans les vins. Ann. technol. agr. 7, 303–309.

LAFON-LAFOURCADE, S., and PEYNAUD, E. 1961. Composition azotée des vins en fonction des conditions de vinification. Ibid. 10, 143–160.

LAFON-LAFOURCADE, S., and PEYNAUD, E. 1965. Sur l'évolution des acides pyruvique et α-cétoglutamique au cours de la fermentation alcoolique. Compt. rend. 261, 1778–1780.

LANTEAUME, M. T., RAMEL, P., GIRARD, P., JAULMES, P., GASQ, M., and RANNAUD, J. 1969. Détermination et comparaison des DL 50 du métabisulfite de potassium, de l'éthanal et de leur combinaison (hydroxy-éthane-sulfonate de potassium) par voie orale sur le rat de souche Wistar. Ann. fals. et expert. chim. 62, 231–241.

MACHER, L. 1952. Hefegärung und Schwefelwasserstoffbildung. Deut. Lebensm.-Rdsch. 48, 183–189.

MARSH, G. L. 1951. Calculation of Proof Gallon Equivalent Per Ton of Grapes. Wine Institute, Tech. Advis. Committee, July 20, 1951.

240 THE TECHNOLOGY OF WINE MAKING

MARSH, G. L. 1958. Alcohol yield: factors and methods. Am. J. Enol. 9, 53–58.
MILLER, F. J. 1959. Carbon dioxide in wine. Wines and Vines 40, No. 8, 32. See also Carbon Dioxide in Water, in Wine, in Beer and in Other Beverages. Oakland, California. 1958.
MÖHLER, K., and PIRES, R. 1969A. Verteilungschromatographie organischer Säuren. Z. Lebensm.-Untersuch. u. -Forsch. 139, 337–345.
MÖHLER, K., and PIRES, R. 1969B. Bestimmung von organischer Säuren in Wein durch Verteilungschromatographie. Ibid. 140, 3–12.
MÖHLER, K., and PIRES, R. 1969C. Nachweis und Bestimmung von Anglicerinsäure (2-Methyl-2,3-dihydroxybuttersäure) in Wein. Ibid. 140, 88–93.
MÜNZ, T. 1963. Die Kalium-Pufferung im Most und Wein. Wein-Wissen. 18, 496–502.
MÜNZ, T. 1967. Die geschmackliche Wandlungs fähigkeit der Apfelsaure. Wein-Wissen. 22, 266–272.
NEGRE E. 1939. Sur le collage des vins. Ann Ecole Natl. Agr. Montpellier n.s. 25, 279–94.
NEGRE, E. 1954. Les facteurs de solubilité de l'acide tartique en présence de potassium. Application au cas du vin. Compt. rend. acad. agr. France 40, 705–709.
NILOV, V. I., and VALUĬKO, G. G. 1958. Izmenenie soderzhaniya azotistykh veshchestvo pri brozhenii vinogradnogo susla (Changes in nitrogen during fermentation). Vinodelie i Vinogradarstvo S.S.S.R. 18, No. 8, 4–7.
OUGH, C. S. 1963. Sensory examination of four organic acids added to wine. J. Food Sci. 28, 101–106.
OUGH, C. S. 1964. Fermentation rates of grape juice. 1. Effects of temperature and composition on white juice fermentation rates. Am. J. Enol. Vitic. 15, 167–177.
OUGH, C. S. 1971. Measurement of histamine in California wines. J. Agr. Food Chem. 19, 241–244.
OUGH, C. S., and AMERINE, M. A. 1958. Studies on aldehyde production under pressure, oxygen, and agitation. Am. J. Enol. 9, 111–122.
OUGH, C. S., and AMERINE, M. A. 1960. Dissolved oxygen determination in wine. Food Research 24 744–748.
OUGH, C. S., and AMERINE, M. A. 1961. Studies with controlled fermentation. VI. Effects of temperature and handling on rates, composition and quality of wines. Am. J. Enol. Vitic. 12, 117–128.
OUGH, C. S., and INGRAHAM, J. L. 1960. Use of sorbic acid and sulfur dioxide in sweet table wines. Am. J. Enol. Vitic. 11, 117–122.
PANGBORN, R. M., OUGH, C. S., and CHRISP, R. B. 1964. Taste interrelationship of sucrose, tartaric acid, and caffeine in white table wine. Am. J. Enol. Vitic. 15, 154–161.
PAPARELLI, L., and COLBY, G. E. 1890. On the quantities of nitrogenous matters contained in California wines. Soc. Prom. Agr. Sci. 7 p. See also Univ. California. Report of the Vitic. Work. 1887–1893, part II, p. 422–446.
PEREIRA, J. 1959. Pesquisa do chumbo no vinho do Porto. Anais Inst. Vinho Porto 18, No. 4, 1–29.
PEYNAUD, E. 1937. Études sur les phénomènes d'estérification. Rev. viticult. 86, 209–215, 227–231, 248–253, 299–301, 394–396, 420–423, 440–444; 87, 49–52, 113–116, 185–188, 242–249, 278–295, 297–301, 344–350, 362–364, 383–385. See also Ann. ferment. 3, 242–252. 1937.

PEYNAUD, E. 1939–1940. Sur la formation et la diminution des acides volatils pendant la fermentation alcoolique en anaèrobiose. Ann. ferment. 5, 321–337, 385–401.

PEYNAUD, E. 1947. Contribution à l'étude biochimique de la maturation du raisin et de la composition des vins. Inds. agr. et aliment. 64, 87–95, 167–188, 301–317, 399–414. Printed as a book by Imprimerie G. Santai et Fils, Lille. 1948. Summarized in Rev. viticult. 92, 177–180, 271–272 (1946) and Bull. office intern. vin 20 (191), 34–51. 1947.

PEYNAUD, E. 1950. Analyses complétes de . . . vins. Ann. technol. agr. 1, 252–266, 383–388.

PEYNAUD, E. 1963. Emploi de l'acide sorbique dans la conservation des vins. Ann. technol. agr. 12 (numéro hors série 1), 99–114.

PEYNAUD, E., and CHARPENTIÉ, Y. 1953. Dosage de l'acide gluconique dans les moûts et les vins provenant de raisins attaques par le Botrytis cinerea. Ann. fals. et fraudes 46, 14–21.

PEYNAUD, E., and GUIMBERTEAU, G. 1956. Sur la teneur des vins en alcools supérieurs. Estimation séparée des alcools isobutylique et isoamylique. Ibid. 51, 70–80.

PEYNAUD, E., and LAFON, M. 1951A. Note complémentaire sur les corps acéto-ïniques des eaux-de-vie. Ibid. 44, 399–402.

PEYNAUD, E., and LAFON, M. 1951B. Présence et signification du diacétyle, de l'acétoine et du 2,3-butanediol dans les eaux-de-vie. Ibid. 44, 264–283.

PEYNAUD, E., and LAFOURCADE, S. 1957. Teneurs en pyridoxine des vins de Bordeaux. Ann. technol. agr. 6, 301–312.

PISARNITSKIĬ, A. F. 1964. O nekotorykh buketistykh veshchestvakh vin Risling i Kaberne (Some flavors of Riesling and Cabernet wines.) Vinodelie i Vinogradarstvo S.S.S.R. 24, No. 7, 23–25.

RANKINE, B. C. 1955. The lead content of some Australian wines. J. Sci. Food Agr. 6, 576–579.

RANKINE, B. C. 1957. Factors influencing the lead content of wine. Ibid. 8, 458–466.

RANKINE, B. C. 1963. Nature, origin and prevention of hydrogen sulphide aroma in wines. Ibid. 14, 79–91.

RANKINE, B. C. 1965. Factors influencing the pyruvic acid content of wines. Ibid. 16, 394–398.

RANKINE, B. C., and POCOCK, K. F. 1969. β-phenethanol and n-hexanol in wines: influence of yeast strain, grape varieties and other factors; and taste thresholds. Vitis 8, 23–37.

REBELEIN, H. 1957A. Unterscheidung naturreiner von gezuckerten Weinen und Bestimmung des natürlichen Alkoholgehaltes. Z. Lebensm.-Untersuch. u. -Forsch. 106, 403–420.

REBELEIN, H. 1957B. Vereinfachtes Verfahren zur Bestimmung des Glycerins und Butylenglykols in Wein. Ibid. 105, 296–311.

REBELEIN, H. 1958. Zur Erkennung naturreiner Weine mittels des K-Werts. Deut. Lebensm-Rdsch. 54, 297–307.

REBELEIN, H. 1965. Beitrag zum Catechin- und Methanolgehalt von Weinen. Ibid. 61, 239–240.

RIBÉREAU-GAYON, J. 1947. Traité d'Oenologie. Librairie Polytechnique Ch. Béranger, Paris et Liège.

RIBÉREAU-GAYON, J. 1963. Phenomena of oxidation and reduction of wines and applications. Am. J. Enol. Vitic. 14, 139–143.

Ribéreau-Gayon, J., and Gardrat, J. 1957. Application du titrage potentiométrique à l'étude du vin. Ann. technol. agr. 6, 185–216.

Ribéreau-Gayon, J., and Peynaud, E. 1952. Sur l'emploi en vinification de quelques activeurs vitaminiques de la fermentation. Compt. rend. acad. agr. France 34, 444–448.

Ribéreau-Gayon, J., and Peynaud, E. 1958. Analyses et Contrôle des Vins. 2 ed. Librairie Polytechnique Ch. Béranger. Paris and Liège.

Ribéreau-Gayon, J., and Peynaud, E. 1960–1961. Traité d'Oenologie. 2 vol. Librairie Polytechnique Ch. Béranger, Paris.

Ribéreau-Gayon, J., Peynaud, E., and Lafourcade, S. 1952A. Action inhibitrice sur les levures de la vitamine K_5 et de quelques antibiotiques. Compt. rend. acad. agr. France 39, 479–481. (See also Compt. rend. 235, 1163–1165.)

Ribéreau-Gayon, J., Peynaud, E., and Lafourcade, S. 1952B. Sur la formation de substances inhibitrices de la fermentation par Botrytis cinerea. Compt. rend. 234, 478–480.

Ribéreau-Gayon, J., Peynaud, E., and Guimberteau, G. 1959. Formation des produits secondaires de la fermentation alcoolique en fonction de l'alimentation azotées des levures. Ibid. 248, 749–751.

Ribéreau-Gayon, P. 1965. Identification d'esters des acides cinnamiques et de l'acide tartrique dans les limbes et les baies de V. vinifera. Ibid. 260, 341–343.

Ribéreau-Gayon, P., and Sapis, J. C. 1965. Sur la présence dans le vin de tyrosol, de tryptophol, d'alcool phényléthylique et de γ-butyrolactone, produits secondaires de la fermentation alcoolique. Ibid. 261, 1915–1916.

Ribéreau-Gayon, P., and Stonestreet, E. 1964. La constitution des tanins du raisin et du vin. Compt. rend. acad. agr. France 50, 662–670.

Ricketts, J., and Coutts, M. W. 1951. Hydrogen sulfide in fermentation gas. Amer. Brewer 84, No. 8, 27–30; No. 9, 27–30 74–75; No. 10, 33–36, 100–101.

Rodopulo, A. K. 1951. Okislenie vinnoĭ kisloty v vine v prisutstvii soleĭ tyazhelykh metallov (aktivirovanie kisloroda zhelezom) (Oxidation of tartaric acid in wine in the presence of salts of heavy metals (activation by iron)). Izvest. Akad. Nauk. S.S.S.R., Ser. Biol. 1951, No. 3, 115–128.

Saller, W. 1955. Die Qualitätsverbesserung der Weine und Süssmoste durch Kälte. Sigurd Horn Verlag, Frankfurt.

Saller, W., and Kolewa, S. R. 1957. Die Möglichkeit der Verwendung von Sorbinsäure zur Weinkonservierung. Mitt. Rebe u. Wein, Serie A (Klosterneuburg) 7, 21–26.

Sambelyan, A. M. 1959. Izmenenie krasyshchikh veshchestv pri vyderzhke vina (Changes in coloring matter during the aging of wine). Vinodelie i Vinogradarstvo S.S.S.R. 19, No. 4, 6–8.

Schanderl, H. 1948. Die Reduktions-Oxydations-Potentiale während der Entwicklungsphasen des Weines. Der Weinbau, Wiss. Beih. 2, 191–198, 209–229. (See also Wines and Vines 29, No. 10, 27–28. 1948.)

Schanderl, H. 1950–51. Über den Einfluss des Entsäuerns verschiedener Schönungen und des Lichtes auf das rH und pH der Weine. Wein u. Rebe 1950–1951, 118–128.

SCHANDERL, H. 1959. Die Mikrobiologie des Mostes und Weins. 2 ed. Eugen Ulmer, Stuttgart.

SCHMITTHENNER, F. 1950. Die Wirkung der Kohlensäure auf Hefen und Bakterien. Seitz-Werke, Bad Kreuznach.

ŠIKOVEC, S. 1966. Der Einfluss einiger Polyphenole auf die Physiologie von Weinhefen. I. Der Einfluss von Polyphenolen auf den Verlauf der alkoholischen Gärung, insbesondere von Umgärungen. Mitt. Rebe u. Wein, Serie A (Klosterneuburg) 16, 127–138.

SILVA, H. B. DA. 1953. Breve nota sobre a influência das vitaminas no rendimento da força alcoólica resultante da fermentação do mosto. Anais Junta Nacional Vinho 5, 69–76.

STRADELLI, A. 1951. Evaporazione di alcool durante la fermentazione dei mosti. Riv. viticolt. e enol. (Conegliano) 4, 50–53.

SUDRAUD, P., and CASSIGNARD, R. 1959. Enrichessement des vins en fluor par les enduits de cuves à base de fluosilicates. Vignes et Vins No. 77 (feuillets techniques), 2–4.

SZABÓ, J., and RAKCSÁNYI, L. 1937. Das Mengenverhältnis der Dextrose und der Lävulose in Weintrauben, im Mosten und im Wein. 5th Congr. intern. tech. chim. agr. 1, 936–949. (See also Magyar Ampelol. Evkonyv. 9, 346–361. 1935.)

TAMBORINI, A., and MAGRO, A. 1970. Il trattamento dei vini con resine scambiatrici e il rapporto potassio:sodio. Riv. viticolt. e enol. (Conegliano) 23, 87–94.

TANNER, H. 1963. Der Zinkgehalt von Weinen und Obstweinen. Mitt. Rebe u. Wein, Serie A (Klosterneuburg) 13, 120–123.

TANNER, H., and RENTSCHLER, H. 1965. Weine mit Böckser; Ursachen das Böcksers und Wiederherstellung davon befallener Weine. Schweiz. Z. Obst. und Weinbau 74, No. 1, 11–14.

TARANTOLA, C. 1954. Separazione e identificazione cromatografia degli amino acidi nei vini. Atti accad. Ital. vite e vino 6, 146–157.

TARANTOLA, C., and LIBERO, A. 1958. I microelementi nei vini. II. Il piombo. Riv. viticolt. e enol. (Conegliano) 11, 47–60.

TARANTALO, C., and USSEGLIO-TOMASSET, L. 1963. I colloidi delle uve nei vini. Ibid. 16, 449–463.

TCHELISTCHEFF, A. 1948. Comments on cold fermentation. Univ. of Calif. Wine Technol. Conf., August 11–13, 1948, Davis.

THOUKIS, G. 1959. The mechanism of isoamyl alcohol formation using tracer techniques. Am. J. Enol. 9, 161–167.

THOUKIS, G., and STERN, L. A. 1962. A review and some studies of the effect of sulfur on the formation of off-odors in wine. Am. J. Enol. Vitic. 13, 133–140.

TURBOVSKY, M. W., FILIPELLO, F., CRUESS, W. V., and ESAU, P. 1934. Observations on the use of tannins in wine making. Fruit Prods. J. 14, 106, 121, 123.

TUZSON, I. 1964. Mangangehalt ungarischer Weine. Mitt. Rebe u. Wein, Serie A (Klosterneuburg) 14, 299–305.

UCHIMOTO, D., and CRUESS, W. V. 1952. Effect of temperature on certain products of vinous fermentation. Food Research 17, 361–366.

USSEGLIO-TOMASSET, L. 1964. Gli alcoli superiori nei fermentati alcolici. Riv. viticolt. e enol. (Conegliano) 17, 497–530.

VALUĬKO, G. G., and GERMANOVA, L. M. 1968. Issledovanie protsessa obests-vechivaniĩa krasnykh vin (Study of the discoloration process of red wines). Prikl. Biokh. Microb. 4, 464–467.

VASCONCELLOS A LANCASTRE, A. de Q. 1947. O cobre no vinho do Pôrto. Anais Inst. Vinho Pôrto 8, 55–103.

VILLFORTH, FR., and SCHMIDT, W. 1953–1954. Über höhere Alkohole im Wein. Deut. Weinbau, Wissen. Beih. 7, 161–170; 8, 107–121.

VOGEL, J., and DESHUSSES, J. 1962. Sur la teneur des vins en zinc. Mitt. Gebiete Lebensm. Hyg. 53, 269–271.

VOGT, E. 1958. Weinchemie und Weinanalyse. 2 ed. E. Ulmer, Stuttgart.

WARKENTIN, H., and NURY, M. S. 1963. Alcohol losses during fermentation of grape juice in closed containers. Am. J. Enol. Vitic. 14, 68–74.

WEBB, A. D., and KEPNER, R. E. 1961. Fusel oil analysis by means of gas-liquid partition chromatography. Ibid. 12, 51–59.

WHITE, J. 1954. Yeast Technology. John Wiley and Sons, New York.

WIKÉN, T., and RICHARD, O. 1951–1952. Untersuchungen über die Physiologie der Weinhefen. Antonie van Leeuwenhoek J. Microbiol. Serol. 17, 209–226; 18, 31–44.

WISEMAN, W. A. 1955. Potassium and cream of tartar in wines. Chem. and Ind. (London) 1955, 612–617.

WUCHERPFENNIG, K., and BRETTHAUER, G. 1962. Versuche zur Stabilisierung von Wein gegen oxydative Einflusse durch Behandlung mit Polyamidpulver. Weinberg u. Keller 9, 37–55. (See also Fruchtsaft-Ind. 7, 40–54, 1962.)

WUCHERPFENNIG, L., and LAY, A. 1965. Zur Bildung und zum Vorkommen von Hydroxymethylfurfurol in Weinen. Weinberg, u. Keller 12, 209–216.

WÜRDIG, G. 1969. Möglichkeiten zur Einsparung von schwefliger Säure bei der Weinbereitung. Deut. Wein-Ztg. 105, 857.

WÜRDIG, G., and SCHLOTTER, H. A. 1965. Untersuchung zur Aufstellung einer SO_2-Bilanz im Wein. Deut. Wein-Ztg. 105, 634–642.

WÜRDIG, G., and SCHLOTTER, H. A. 1971. Ueber das Vorkommen SO_2-bildender Hefen im naturlichen Hefegemisch des Traubenmostes. Deut. Lebensm.-Rundsch. 67, 86–91.

WÜRDIG, G., SCHLOTTER, H. A., and BEDESSEM, G. 1969. Vorkommen, Nachweis und Bestimmung von 2- und 3-Methyl-2,3-dihydroxybuttersäure und 2-Hydroxyglutarsäure im Wein. Vitis 8, 216–230.

WÜRZIGER, J. 1954. Beitrag zur Kenntnis des Mangangehaltes im Wein. Deut. Lebensm.-Rdsch. 50, 49–51. (See also Wein u. Rebe 21, 364–368. 1954.)

YANG, H. Y., and ORSER, R. E. 1962. Preservative effect of vitamin K_5 and sulfur dioxide on sweet table wines. Am. J. Enol. Vitic. 13, 152–158.

YANG, N. Y., STEELE, W. F., STEIN, R. W., CAIN, R. F., and SINNHUBER, R. O. 1958. Vitamin K_5 as a good preservative. Food Technol. 12, 501–504. (See also Ibid. 11, 536–540. 1957.)

ZANG, K. 1963. Schweflige Säure im ungeschwefelten Most. Deut. Wein-Ztg. 99, 214.

ZANG, K., and FRANZE, K. 1966. Schweflige-Säure-Bildung im Verlauf der Traubenmost-Gärung. Ibid. 102, 128, 130.

ZIMMERMANN, H. W., ROSSI, E. A. JR., and WICK, E. 1964. Alcohol losses from entrainment in carbon dioxide evolved during fermentation. Am. J. Enol. Vitic. 15, 63–68.

CHAPTER 6

Winery Design, Equipment, Operation, and Sanitation

The equipment used in winery operations, the principles of their operation, and the over-all operation of the winery from crushing to bottling will be considered in this chapter. However, since the crushing and fermentation aspects differ so much from one type to another some will be considered only briefly here and in more detail in the appropriate succeeding chapters. The finishing operations, which are somewhat similar for all types, will be considered more fully.

LOCATION

The type of winery should be considered in its location. There is considerable logic in separating the crushing and fermenting functions of the winery from the storage and finishing operations. This, of course, is only possible for very large operations. The justification for this separation is obvious. The crushing and fermenting processes can logically be considered in close relation to the production of grapes. With the present technological improvement in wine aging and finishing these operations can be separated from the crushing and fermenting operations and concentrated in central plants with appropriate equipment and facilities. These operations can be conducted separately for all except the small winery. Many large scale combined operations exist in the industry already and are not likely for economic reasons to be changed in the near future. The most obvious reason for such a separation is that the crushing and fermentation facilities should be as near to the source of grapes as possible. The best grapes for wine production are those which are crushed as soon as possible after harvesting.

It is also obvious that finishing operations for standard wines can be conducted on a large scale. Since highly skilled technicians are required, it is desirable that these operations be on a scale which justifies their employment. This has long been practiced in France and is becoming the practice in Russia, in Yugoslavia, and in this and other countries.

The problems of operating large wineries in the hot interior valley of California, particularly for the production of table wines, have been emphasized by La Rosa (1963). He noted the critical importance of control of harvesting and fermentation (especially cooling), development of new and simpler methods for achieving stability, reduction of sugar and pigment losses, purity of water, waste disposal, and quality control.

245

Factors Influencing

Close proximity of vineyard and crusher facilitates operations and reduces costs of transportation. Among the other factors which should be considered are drainage and sewage facilities. This has become one of the most critical problems of California wineries and will be considered in greater detail later, p. 342. Because of the problem of waste disposal wineries should not normally be located near cities. However, since some cities provide sewage facilities this may prove advantageous. Large wineries with many employees may also find it easier to secure labor when located in or near cities. Also, if the winery has a public relations program for visitors, cities or a location on a main highway may be desirable. Wineries with retail departments should also consider ease of access and parking for the motorist.

The location should be such that the prevailing wind is away from the populated area. For fruit fly control it is desirable that the winery not be near orchards or vineyards.

DESIGN

Few California wineries have been functionally and artistically designed. This is unfortunate because winery operation is more expensive when the functions are not properly considered. Also by proper architectural design the winery can be a credit to the community and a tourist attraction.

By functional design, we mean that each department of the winery should be designed with its particular operation clearly in mind. This means that the architect and the technical staff should study each operation together so that there is a clear understanding of what are the essential operations and how each should be carried out. Many wineries could profitably examine their operations for more rational arrangements.

Departments

The crushing operations are normally separated from the winery proper, yet they should be arranged for easy transfer of the must to the fermenting room or pressing area with a minimum of piping. The aging or storage area should be air conditioned. A centralized and well arranged processing department will be necessary. This should be convenient to the control laboratory. Adjacent bottling and shipping departments are desirable. The machinery room must be well separated from the wine storage because of possible undesirable odor arising from it. The distillery department is, for underwriter reasons, separated from the winery usually outdoors. Brandy storage is usually placed in a separate building. The sparkling wine, vermouth, and other specialized departments logically require separate storage facilities, though near the aging, processing, and bottling departments.

A well-designed winery will not only be functionally arranged with respect to different departments, but each department will be designed for efficient operation and ease of cleaning. This means waterproof concrete-surfaced floors with adequate drainage and sufficient high pressure hot and cold water and steam throughout the plant. Adequate lighting and electrical outlets for equipment must be installed. Special protection for electrical fixtures near sherry heaters and in brandy dumping areas and near stills is required.

CRUSHING

This department is now usually located outside the winery for two reasons: to facilitate delivery of the grapes and for ease of cleaning. Also by keeping the crusher outside the winery, fruit flies are not introduced into the winery. The crushing area should be carefully designed for ease of unloading (hoists, conveyors, etc.) and for ease of cleaning (well-drained concrete pavement, water supply, etc.), Figs. 60 and 61. The must pump should be adequate to handle the capacity of the crusher. The must line should be lined or corrosion-resistant.

Three types of crushers are in use—namely, the roller type, the disintegrator, and the Garolla type. The latter predominate in California. Machinery producers offer improved crusher-stemmers.

Courtesy of Wine Institute

FIG. 60.   UNLOADING GRAPES FROM GONDOLA

Courtesy of Wine Institute
Photo by Max Yavno

FIG. 61. A BOX OF FRESHLY PICKED WINE GRAPES IS
BEING EMPTIED ONTO A CONVEYOR WHICH WILL CARRY
THE GRAPES TO BE STEMMED AND CRUSHED

The roller crusher consists of two fluted, horizontal rolls of bronze, steel or stainless steel, operated by gears and turning toward each other during operation. The rolls are adjustable, and should be set so that the berries are thoroughly crushed without breaking the seeds or grinding the stems. The crushed grapes and stems fall through the rolls into the stemmer, consisting of a stationary horizontal cylinder perforated with holes large enough to allow the crushed grapes to fall through and small enough to retain most of the stems. Rapidly revolving metal paddles hammer the grapes through the holes and the stems are carried out of the end of the cylinder. Both stems and leaves should be removed as they contain undesirable compounds. Crushers that operate at variable speeds for different varieties are needed. After removal of the stems the crushed grapes are pumped by must pumps to the fermenter.

The Garolla crusher (Fig. 62) was introduced from Italy to California after repeal and is now made by machinery manufacturers in this state. It

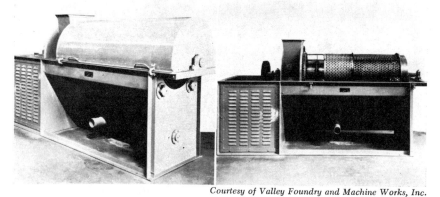

Courtesy of Valley Foundry and Machine Works, Inc.

FIG. 62.   LARGE CRUSHER STEMMER

Left, covered, right, open.   Rated capacity 25 tons per hour

consists of a large horizontal, coarsely perforated cylinder. Revolving blades inside the cylinder move the stems toward the exit, and hammer the bunches of grapes. The combined effects of the moving parts does a thorough job of crushing and stemming. One objection to this type of crusher-stemmer is the excessive amount of stems left in the must, particularly if the paddles are operated at high speed as they usually are. This may be corrected by adjusting the pitch of the blades. The Garolla crusher should be made of stainless steel, although copper has been used. Little of the copper dissolved at this stage of wine making remains in the wine but it would be better to avoid its presence.

While most of the older crushers in California wineries are made of steel, the later models are usually of bronze. Considerable iron may be dissolved from a steel crusher and stemmer. Most of the iron dissolved during these operations is precipitated during fermentation and storage; nevertheless, if the dissolving of iron by the juice or wine can be avoided at any stage of winemaking, it is good practice, since excessive iron is an enemy of good quality and stability.

The stems should be washed or ground for fermenting and distilling. Other wineries remove them to the fields daily. Centrifugal crushers have, so far, not been used here, but they are widely employed in Europe.

Recently large disintegrators which entirely break up the skins and stems, Fig. 63, have been used by a number of wineries. These have been employed in three ways: for crushing fresh grapes, for disintegrating fermented pomace, and for tearing up stems. When used for the low tannin red grapes of the San Joaquin Valley the additional tannin from disintegrated grapes seems to be beneficial. However, the wines are inclined to

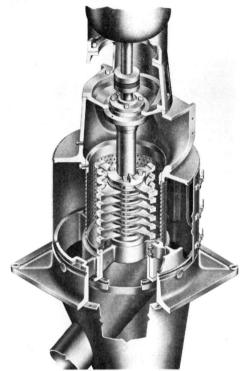

Courtesy of Carl Rietz

FIG. 63.   RIETZ VERTICAL DISINTEGRATOR

have a stemmy taste. There is also an apparent increase in gallons of wine per ton. For white wines, however, too much color is commonly obtained. As used with fermented pomace or with stems, particularly when raisins are present, the disintegrator does give a higher alcohol yield. For distilling material, the disintegrator is of great utility. No detailed cost studies compared to the traditional crusher-stemmer are known to us.

Better methods of crushing could undoubtedly be developed if sufficient engineering skill was directed to the problem. The apparatus of Graham (1959) for fresh juice appears useful. The Serpentine press of Coffelt and Berg (1965) is promising. The study of Zhdanovich *et al.* (1967) on effect of pressing depth and perforation area should be extended.

THE FERMENTING ROOM

The fermenting room includes fermenters, juice separators, presses, pomace conveyors, sumps, yeast propagators, and cooling equipment.

Fermenters

Until recently, the fermenters were usually of concrete in this state. However, lined iron and stainless steel tanks are replacing concrete. Smaller wineries still use oak or redwood fermenters. One problem of concrete fermenters is their proper lining. Treatment with oxalic acid has been recommended. Use of silicates or fluosilicates for coating cement tanks is not recommended. They react incompletely with calcium and they may get into the wine which would be illegal. Use of tartaric acid still appears to be the best all-around treatment for new cement containers for ordinary wines. In addition, some coating is needed. There is still no unanimity of opinion as to the best coating. Some use asphalt-base paints. These often "peel" and expose the surface. Various plastic paints are employed. These appear to us to be the best when properly applied. Microcrystalline wax is also used by a number of wineries. This must be carefully applied and with time wears away. Glass lining of concrete tanks is not done in this country because of its high cost. Manholes are provided on top of the tanks in many cases so the fermenters can also be used for storage, though some open fermenters are still used. The size of the fermenter depends on the size of the lots to be produced and on the amount of cooling equipment available. Small wineries should use small fermenters because they are easier to keep cool and because they make it easier to separate lots of different varieties, fields, qualities of fruit, etc.

Drag screens, horizontal rotating cylinders, and flat rotating screens are used to separate juice from pomace prior to pressing. The latter are preferred because they contribute less solids to the juice.

Pressing

The amount of free-run juice varies slightly from variety to variety and with degree of maturity. From 60 to 70 per cent of the extractable juice is usually obtained as free-run. With one pressing in the usual basket press an additional 25 to 35 per cent is obtained. A second pressing gives 5 to 10 per cent more.

Special settling tanks for white musts are used in some wineries in order to separate as much as possible of the free-run juice before placing the pomace in the press. Roller juice extractors have been used by several wineries but generally they are found to yield wines with an excessive amount of sediment.

The effect of pressing on the composition of musts and of their resulting wines is very complex. Carles *et al.* (1963), for example, reported a decrease in tartrate but an increase in malate in musts during pressing. The potassium and phosphate contents increased during pressing. Those of

Courtesy of L. M. Martini

FIG. 64. HYDRAULICALLY-OPERATED BASKET PRESSES

Courtesy of Widmer Wine Co.

FIG. 65. WILLMES PRESSES IN NEW YORK WINERY

calcium, magnesium, iron and copper at first decreased and then increased; so did the pH. These results were obtained with one variety with two types of hydraulic presses in one region.

Basket-type presses are less and less used in California, Fig. 64. They are slow, expensive to operate, and difficult to keep clean. But they give a good yield of clear juice. They should have a pressure gauge to control

Courtesy of Valley Foundry and Machine Works, Inc.

FIG. 66.   LARGE DOUBLE CONTINUOUS PRESS

the rate of application of pressure and the amount of pressure. They are being replaced with the Willmes, Vaslin and similar types of cylindrical presses which are easy to fill and to operate, (Fig. 65, p. 252).

Continuous "straight" screw presses, Fig. 66, operate well on washed or fermented pomace but not on unfermented musts. "Tapered" screw presses work well on unfermented musts and produce less cloudy juice. "Straight" screw presses are used mainly to press the pomace from a Metzner-type still, Fig. 135 (p. 630), from washers, or from fermenters. Coffelt and Berg (1965) reported on a new type of press, called the Serpentine, which expresses juice by passing must between two perforated belts over a series of pulleys.

Wineries with large distilling material requirements may simply drain off the free-run, add water to the residue, and ferment for distilling material. The pomace may then be ground in a hammer mill, the fermentation completed, and distilled in a pomace still. Or, they may use a continuous washing system to remove the sugar from the pomace.

Recovery of alcohol from fermented pomace is a major problem of California wineries. Various procedures are used: grinding the pomace in a hammer mill or disintegrator and distilling in a special still, passing through a Metzner-type still, and water extraction. In washing the single-contact batch operation is the simplest. It produces a relatively dilute wash solution. By dividing the total amount of water to be used into several fractions the recovery is improved but the extract is still dilute.

Berg and Guymon (1951) have studied countercurrent extraction as a means of improving recovery and increasing the alcohol content of the wash. This may be done batch-wise or in a continuous system. The water moves countercurrent to the pomace. They conclude that reasonable recoveries cannot be obtained with less than three stages. To secure the highest alcohol content in the wash with a three stage system three pressings should be used. Coffelt *et al.* (1965) devised a 3-stage countercurrent system. They showed that it is more satisfactory than a washing system since it provides good sugar levels in the product. The main defect of washing is that it produces dilute solutions and involves handling and disposal problems.

Pomace Conveyors

For red wine production some method of removing the pomace from the fermenter is necessary. So far this problem has not been solved. The usual solution is to place the pomace conveyor at the floor level so that the pomace can be sluiced out of the fermenter. This assumes that the winery has a distillery. If water is used in place of wine the cost of distillation will be materially increased. Sloping the floors of the fermenters will help. Manual removal of pomace from the fermenter with or without an elevator is still practiced in many wineries which have no distillery. This is expensive and because of the carbon dioxide uncomfortable and even dangerous. An automatic mechanical means of removing the drained pomace would be very desirable. The pomace conveyor should be covered yet easily opened for repair or cleaning. Continuous chain conveyors and screw conveyors are commonly used.

Fermentation of Uncrushed Grapes

There have been many reports of placing uncrushed grapes in tanks and allowing them to ferment. The theory appears to be that the fermentation of the free-run juice will produce carbon dioxide in sufficient quantities to asphyxiate the cells of the uncrushed grapes—resulting in greater color and flavor release. An example of this type of research is that of Bénard and Jouret (1963). Peynaud and Guimberteau (1962) showed that three types of reactions occur when grapes are placed under carbon dioxide or nitrogen for several days: (1) alcoholic fermentation, (2) reduction in malic acid, and (3) internal movement of constituents into solution, particularly of nitrogenous compounds, polyphenols and aroma materials. Hydrolysis of pectins with liberation of methanol and some increase in free amino acids also occurs.

USE OF SULFUR DIOXIDE

The forms present and the antiseptic value of sulfur dioxide have already been considered in connection with yeasts, pp. 188–190. The practical aspects of its use will be considered here.

Sources

Sulfur dioxide is most conveniently and cheaply available to the wine maker in cylinders as the liquid under a pressure of about 50 lbs. per sq. in. The specific gravity is about 1.4. For large operations this may be metered directly into the must lines. It can also be weighed out of tanks or volumetric dispensers are available. Many smaller wineries use liquid sulfur dioxide to prepare a solution of sulfurous acid. The gas is slowly added to ice cold water. It can be weighed in from the cylinder so as to prepare an approximately 6 per cent solution.

The exact concentration of sulfurous acid in the solution can be determined by titration of an aliquot as follows: pipette 10 ml. into a 100 ml. volumetric flask. Fill to the mark with distilled water and mix. Pipette 10 ml. of this solution into 50 ml. of distilled water. Titrate at once with 0.1 N iodine solution to near the end point. Add 0.5 ml. of one per cent starch solution and titrate to a light blue end point. From the normality of the iodine and the amount of iodine used one can calculate the sulfur dioxide content. If a solution of bisulfite or metabisulfite is to be titrated, acidify the final diluted aliquot with 5 ml. of 10 per cent sulfuric acid before titration.

The sulfur dioxide content can also be determined from the specific gravity of the solution. The following table from Willson et al. (1943) is useful in this connection:

Concentration of Sulfur Dioxide	Specific Gravity At		
	59 °F.	68 °F.	86 °F.
Per cent			
1.0	1.004	1.003	1.000
2.0	1.009	1.008	1.005
3.0	1.014	1.013	1.010
4.0	1.020	1.018	1.014
5.0	1.025	1.023	1.019
6.0	1.030	1.028	1.024
7.0	1.035	1.032	1.028
8.0	1.040	1.037	...

These solutions lose strength in storage so their concentration should be redetermined frequently. They should be stored in glass.

Some use potassium metabisulfite. The sodium salt, though cheaper, is not recommended. Both have slightly more than 50 per cent available sulfur dioxide when dissolved in musts or wines but the 50 per cent value is used in practice. The salts lose strength in storage. They may also be used to prepare a 6 per cent solution—this also loses strength in storage.

Sulfur wicks are employed by small wineries. These are easy to use and have the advantage of exhausting the oxygen in the container in which they are burned. Unless the sulfur dioxide is removed by repeated rinsings, wine subsequently placed in the cask will pick up sulfur dioxide—up to 60 p.p.m. from small barrels. Sulfur wicks are a simple method of disinfecting casks during storage. The disadvantage of sulfur wicks is that sulfur may sublime into the walls of the container or pieces of elemental sulfur from the wick may fall to the bottom of the cask. If used for fermentation, this elemental sulfur will be reduced to hydrogen sulfide.

Whatever form is employed it must be distributed evenly throughout the must or wine. Even when the sulfur dioxide is added continuously during the filling of the tank it is wise to pump the liquid over to mix it thoroughly. Much of the effectiveness of sulfur dioxide is lost in many cases because it is unevenly distributed.

Amounts to Add

Very little sulfur dioxide is needed for musts when the grapes are in perfect condition, cool, and have a large microflora of desirable wine yeast. In practice 100 to 200 p.p.m. of sulfur dioxide are added. The amount to be used depends on the condition of the musts as indicated in Table 30.

The amounts to add to wines differ with the type of wine, its composition and condition, size of container, and temperature of storage and other factors. See pp. 363, 384, 393 and 441. It may be added automatically at the crusher.

TABLE 30

AMOUNT OF SULFUR DIOXIDE TO ADD TO MUSTS[1]

Maturity	Condition	Temperature	Concentration	Liquid Sulfur Dioxide		Sulfurous Acid 6 Per cent		Potassium Metabisulfite	
				Per 1000 Gal.	Per Ton	Per 1000 Gal.	Per Ton	Per 1000 Gal.	Per Ton
			P.p.m.	Oz.	Oz.	Gals.	Pints	Oz.	Oz.
Underripe	Clean, sound	Cool	75	10	2	$1^1/_4$	2	20	$3^1/_2$
Mature	Clean, sound	Cool	112	15	$2^1/_2$	2	3	31	5
Overripe	Moldy, low acid	Hot	270	36	6	$3^1/_4$	$4^1/_4$	56	9

[1] Source of data: Amerine and Joslyn (1951).

Effects of Sulfur Dioxide

Besides its effective antiseptic action (p. 189) sulfur dioxide has a number of other desirable properties in musts and wines.

Its clarifying action in musts is due to the fact that it neutralizes the negatively charged colloids and thus aids in their settling. By preventing fermentation sulfur dioxide allows natural settling to take place. This effect is particularly used for settling white musts, p. 385.

Sulfurous acid is a strong acid and thus has an acidifying action of its own. It also prevents growth of the malo-lactic organisms and thus helps to maintain the acidity.

Sulfur dioxide (70 p.p.m.) in the presence of an excess of acetaldehyde does not inhibit growth of the homofermentative *Lactobacillus plantarum* but completely inhibits the heterofermentative *L. hilgardii* and *Leuconostoc mesenteroides*. In the latter cases the bacteria reduce the aldehyde content so that the resulting wine contains sufficient free sulfur dioxide to inhibit growth. Finally, there is its dissolving activity as a strong acid, because of its solvent effect on potassium acid tartrate. Sulfur dioxide also has a solvent effect on anthocyan pigments. Berg and Akiyoshi (1962) also showed that treated wines retained their color better than untreated. Pifferi and Zamorani (1964) showed that fermentation of Merlot with high amounts of sulfur dioxide resulted in wines with more diglucoside pigments. Confirmation is needed of this result.

The antioxidative property of sulfur dioxide prevents direct effects of oxygen on musts and wines and inhibits some enzyme systems. The antioxidative effect of a given amount of sulfur dioxide varies markedly from one wine to another. Schanderl (1959) has shown that the rH value is markedly reduced with a small amount of sulfur dioxide in some wines and very little in others, but that generally the reduction was greater with young wines.

Wines made from sulfited musts are of higher alkalinity of ash, fixed acidity, glycerol and extract and of lower volatile acidity. The hue of red wines is also better. The wines also keep better in storage.

If too much sulfur dioxide is added to musts, fermentation will be delayed, may be incomplete, and the resulting wines will have a high fixed sulfur dioxide content. If too much is added to wines the color will be bleached, the odor will be objectionable and the consumer may reject the wine.

Fessler (1961) noted that ascorbic acid (or erythorbic acid, its optical isomer) should not be used on wines of high sulfur dioxide content. His observations would seem to indicate that if 0.5 to 1.5 lbs of ascorbic or erythorbic acids are to be added per 1000 gallons then the sulfur dioxide content should not be greater than about 100 mg. per liter. Addition of 2 lbs. of either acid raised the free sulfur dioxide from 18 to about 90 mg. per liter. Trial bottlings with different amounts of sulfur dioxide and ascorbic or erythorbic acid should be made on each wine. Kielhöfer (1960) showed that ascorbic acid does not function as an antioxidant but rather as a catalyst for the oxidation of certain constituents of the wine, particularly of sulfurous acid. For example, without ascorbic acid the sulfurous acid content of a wine decreased from 128 to 106 mg. per liter in 15 days; with ascorbic acid it decreased in the same time to 29 mg. per liter. The redox potential attains very low values in the presence of ascorbic acid, sufficient to dissolve, at least partially, precipitated ferric complexes. For best results, ascorbic acid should be added to wines just before they are to undergo aeration, as in racking or filtration. In some cases wines treated with ascorbic acid undergo greater oxidation than untreated wines, probably because ascorbic acid catalyzes the oxidation of certain constituents that are not oxidized in its absence.

Chapon and Urion (1960) in their work on beer have provided the probable explanation for the action of ascorbic acid in wine. By following the rate of disappearance of added ascorbic acid, they found that the oxidation of ascorbic acid was accompanied by the oxidation of an equivalent amount of various organic substances, and that the rate was directly proportional to the sum of the copper ions and iron complexes. This is the phenomenon known as coupled oxidation in which the system acts as a powerful oxidant, oxidizing an equal amount of other substances present which molecular oxygen does not touch. As long as free sulfur dioxide is present the reaction is markedly inhibited, but in its absence is greatly accelerated.

OTHER ANTISEPTICS

Sorbic acid or its potassium or sodium salts have been approved for use in wines providing that not more than 0.1 per cent remains in the wine. A number of wineries experimented with it particularly for preventing yeast activity in sweet table wines, but the undesirable odor which develops during storage has reduced interest.

Hennig (1959) reported 50 to 100 p.p.m. of diethylpyrocarbonate (DEPC) were sufficient to prevent secondary fermentation and it is now in use in Germany and this country, especially during the bottling of tank-fermented or transfer-system sparkling wines and sweet table wines. One of the problems of using DEPC is to secure rapid and uniform distribution through the wine. Various kinds of pumps and mixing were tested by Kielhöfer and Würdig (1964). When 100 p.p.m. of DEPC is added to wine from 5.9 to 8.3 p.p.m. of diethylcarbonate are formed. This is a stable compound which can be removed from the wine with difficulty. Kielhöfer (1963) noted that the amount of DEPC for control of different yeast strains varied. In practice 50–250 mg. per liter is normally sufficient. *Saccharomyces bailii* is more resistant. Kielhöfer reports 40 to 50 mg. per liter are necessary in this case. Kielhöfer (1963) agrees with Ough and Ingraham that DEPC is effective within 10 to 30 minutes with 25 to 100 p.p.m. of DEPC. Despite Russian claims that diethyl pyrocarbonate (DEPC) is present in sparkling wines, Kielhöfer (1963) was unable to detect its presence. In fact, DEPC hydrolyzes rapidly—in a few hours. It is not recommended for cloudy wines. On thermodynamic grounds it can be present in very small amounts.

With the increasing use of new antiseptics it is desirable to determine whether a wine contains an unknown antiseptic. Various procedures have been proposed. Most of these are necessarily biological methods involving inhibition of growth of a standard organism. The procedures of Carafa (1959) and Lüthi and Bezzegh (1963) appear useful. Use of gas-liquid chromatography should also facilitate their detection.

PURE YEAST STARTERS

In some small wineries it is customary to allow the crushed grapes or the juice to ferment spontaneously, that is, without the addition of a starter of yeast. However, the true wine yeast (p. 159) are greatly outnumbered on the skins and stems of sound grapes by the wild yeasts. These latter may interfere with the fermentation. Grapes that arrive at the winery in partially crushed condition or badly molded, as is often the case after early fall rains, may also have large numbers of acetic bacteria. On the other hand, grapes early in the season may have on their surface very few yeast cells of any kind and molds will predominate, Cruess (1918). At this time of the season also, the crusher, pumps, pipe lines, vats, and tanks are probably relatively free of yeasts. Hence, early in the crushing season, it is desirable to inoculate the crushed grapes or juice with a pure yeast starter.

In midseason, and from that period to the end of the season, true wine yeasts are very abundant. Open fermentation vats, after one successful fermentation has been conducted in them, are heavily impregnated with yeast cells. Under such a condition fermentation begins promptly after the vats are filled and, if other conditions are favorable, satisfactory fermentations generally ensue. However, certain wild yeasts may also get a foothold in the fermentation vats and contaminate succeeding vats of crushed grapes. For this reason we recommend use of yeast starters throughout the season. See also Fornachon (1950), Jorgensen (1936), Lüthi (1955), Moreau and Vinet (1936), Rankine (1955), Schulle (1954), Sémichon (1929), and Ventre (1935).

Sources

Since the time of Pasteur, microbiologists have given much attention to the naturally-occurring yeasts of grapes. Among these earlier investigators should be mentioned Pacottet (1926), Guilliermond (1912), and Kayser (1924) of France, Wortmann (1892) of Germany, and Müller-Thurgau (1889) of Switzerland. Pure cultures of many different strains of wine yeast have been studied as to their suitability for wine making.

Among the most desirable strains are those of Pacottet, among them the well-known burgundy and champagne wine yeasts in the University of California's collection. These two yeasts have been supplied to wineries and vinegar factories for the past 60 years. They, and several other yeasts, form a heavy granular and compact sediment at the end of the fermentation period. They are known as agglomerating, or agglutinating yeasts (p. 167). During the violent period of the fermentation, the yeast often comes to the surface where it forms a gray covering, which breaks up and falls to the bottom of the tank or cask as fermentation progresses. Wines made with these yeasts clear rapidly after fermentation is complete.[1] The volume of the lees or yeast sediment is small and, being compact and granular, the yeast does not tend to rise in the wine during racking. The usual California wine yeast naturally occurring on our grapes is fine grained, and during fermentation forms a finely divided cloud throughout the fermenting liquid. When the fermentation period is complete, and the yeast has settled it is easily disturbed, causing cloudiness. However, the granular and the fine-grained type of yeast do not appear to differ materially in respect to rate of fermentation, alcohol-forming power, and effect on flavor of the wine.

Beer yeast has proven unsatisfactory for fermentation of crushed grape musts as it imparts an undesirable flavor and forms too little alcohol. Distillery yeasts, dry bread yeasts, and Japanese sake yeasts, on the other hand, resemble true wine yeasts closely and give high yields of alcohol. The dry bread yeast is suitable for use in making wine in the home. Commercially used wine yeasts in California, in addition to burgundy and champagne, are Montrachet,[2] Tokay,[3] and Steinberg.[4] In European wine making countries many other strains of wine yeasts are utilized by wine makers. A number of these are in the collections of the University of California at Davis; others can be secured from fermentation laboratories,

---

[1] The "champagne" and "burgundy" yeasts were brought to California by Professor F. T. Bioletti, who introduced their use in California wineries and who encouraged the application of pure yeast in wine making for many years.

[2] A burgundy strain introduced by Professor J. G. B. Castor.

[3] Introduced by Fruit Industries Ltd.

[4] A popular wine yeast of Germany.

such as those in the American Type Culture Collection, 2112 M Street, N.W., Washington, D. C., the Institut National Agronomique of Paris, the Botanische Institut at Geisenheim, Germany, the Versuchsanstalt für Obst-, Wein- und Gartenbau at Wädenswil, Switzerland, the Centraalbureau voor Schimmelcultures, Delft, Holland, or the Northern Regional Research Laboratory, U. S. Dept. of Agriculture, Peoria, Illinois.

The University of California's cultures were at one time carried in 10 per cent sucrose solution in Steinberg flasks and in some cases yeasts have remained alive in this solution for more than 30 years. At present the pure cultures are carried on agar slants under sterile oil. The cultures should be obtained well in advance of the vintage season as it usually requires about two to four weeks to revive and increase them sufficiently for use in the winery.

Pure wine yeast in compressed cake and in dry granular form has been prepared experimentally by Castor (1953). Thoukis et al. (1963) described the large scale commercial production of *Saccharomyces cerevisiae*. The wet compressed yeast cake was found to be suitable for use in wineries. By means of mass pitching, little grape sugar was used for growth of yeast. The rapid establishment of anaerobic conditions permitted lower levels of sulfur dioxide in the musts. The yeast cakes were also much simpler to use than the traditional winery procedures and are less expensive since the sugars of grapes are not used for yeast multiplication. Goldman (1963) recommended the use of wet compressed yeast cake for sparkling wine production because the yeast population for the tirage bottling could be more accurately calculated and controlled. Wine yeast in such forms was made on a large pilot scale about 1954 by a plant in Oakland, Calif.

Brémond (1957) reports that lyophilized yeasts were successfully used in Algeria in 1954. The Pasteur Institute in Paris prepares these by freezing at a temperature of solid carbon dioxide and alcohol, then evaporating at a low temperature under vacuum. A dry powder of yeast cells was produced and on being placed in the proper media rapidly remultiplied. Fell (1961) was able to freeze-dry (lyophilize) mixtures of yeast and lactic acid bacteria. He used the samples to successfully ferment grape musts with a simultaneous malo-lactic fermentation. However, in plant experiments even wines which had no added bacteria underwent a malo-lactic fermentation. This is not surprising since the winery equipment probably contained many lactic acid bacteria. At present most of the yeast used in the larger California wineries is obtained as dry pressed yeast. It is added in large amounts to reduce use of sugar for yeast multiplication.

For fermentation at low temperatures, yeasts especially acclimated to cold should be used; see Osterwalder (1934).

Propagating Equipment

Pure wine yeast propagating installations, Fig. 67, are of several types. Such equipment may consist of two or more covered tanks, each holding 50 to 100 gallons of juice. One is placed above the other. The upper tank is fitted with a steam coil of stainless steel or other resistant metal (never ordinary steel, iron, copper, tin, or zinc). The juice in this tank can be sterilized by heating it with the steam coil and can then be cooled by passing cold water through the coil. The lower tank is fitted with a small coil or cross of stainless steel pipe with small holes in it to permit passage of compressed air through the juice to aerate it. Such aeration increases the rate of yeast growth. The compressed air should be filtered by passage through cotton or several layers of cloth in the air supply line to remove dust, oil droplets, and other materials that might contaminate the juice.

Other pure yeast propagating devices such as those made for breweries or distilleries are available or satisfactory installations can be made on the winery premises. The tanks may be constructed of concrete, lined steel, wood, or stainless steel. Stainless steel is to be preferred as it is corrosion

Courtesy of Wine Institute

FIG. 67. PURE YEAST TANKS BEING USED TO INOCULATE FREE-RUN RED JUICE

resistant, easily cleaned and durable. Two or more sets of tanks may be set up and equipped as outlined above. Also, the size suggested may be much larger, e.g., 500 to 1000 gallons.

Propagating Procedure.—The following directions may be followed for increasing the pure yeast culture for use in the winery: (1) Purchase a quart bottle of grape juice, or heat a quart of fresh juice to boiling and scald a quart bottle in boiling water. Pour the boiling hot juice into the scalded bottle. Plug the bottle with clean, sterile, absorbent cotton. Set bottle aside to cool overnight. (2) Take the test tube slant of pure yeast and fill it about three-fourths full with the sterile grape juice and replace the cotton plug. Set aside overnight. Transfer to the bottle of juice. Set aside in a warm place, between 70 and 80°F. Shake bottle occasionally to aerate the juice.

(3) In the meantime prepare a five-gallon bottle of sterile juice. This is done by boiling 4½ gallons of juice in a large aluminum or agate ware pot, and pouring it into a five-gallon bottle. Or sterilize the five-gallon bottle containing 4½ gallons of juice in an autoclave or in live steam in an enclosed space (steamer) until the juice is about 165°F. Plug it with sterile absorbent cotton. Allow the juice to cool 24 hours or until a thermometer sterilized in alcohol or 180 proof brandy shows that the temperature is below 90°F.

(4) When the quart bottle of yeast is in active fermentation, 3 to 4 days, pour into the five-gallon container. Shake or roll the five-gallon container several times a day to aerate the juice. Keep the mouth of the bottle well plugged with sterile cotton. In about 4 or 5 days this juice should be actively fermenting.

(5) After the five-gallon bottle of juice is in fermentation, sterilize fresh juice in the upper pure yeast tank by heating it to 160°F. and cooling to below 90°F. Sterilize the lower tank of the pure yeast apparatus with live steam and allow it to cool.

Draw off the cooled, sterile juice from the upper tank into the lower, but do not fill it more than three-fourths full. About 3 or 4 hours before adding the fermenting juice from the five-gallon bottle, add 100 to 125 p.p.m. of sulfur dioxide in the form of bisulfite or metabisulfite to the sterile juice in the tank. The purpose is to acclimate the yeast to sulfur dioxide. Then pour the fermenting contents of the five-gallon bottle into the tank of sterile juice. Aerate the juice by passing filtered compressed air through it for a few minutes.

(6) In 3 or 4 days the juice in the lower tank should be fermenting vigorously. About two-thirds to three-fourths of its liquid may be drawn off and used to inoculate a vat of crushed red grapes or tank of white must. About 2 to 3 gallons of the yeast culture are used to inoculate each 100 gallons of crushed grapes or must.

(7) More juice is then sterilized and cooled in the upper tank to replace that used in the winery. The lower tank should be equipped with a large fermentation bung to allow escape of carbon dioxide gas and to protect the juice against contamination from the surrounding air. The upper tank is protected against contamination by a cotton bung or an air filter. Filtered air should be used for aeration of the culture in the lower tank.

In other wineries the juice in the two upper tanks is treated with about 150 p.p.m. of sulfur dioxide and allowed to settle overnight. The settled juice is drawn off the sediment into two lower tanks where it is heavily in-oculated with a pure yeast culture. When actively fermenting this juice is used in the winery, leaving one-fourth to one-third of the culture in the lower vats to inoculate the next lot of settled juice. In practice the cul-tures in the two lower vats are generally used on alternate days, so that each culture when used in the plant is 48 hours old and at maximum vigor. The propagation and use of pure yeasts in a large California winery has been described by De Soto (1955). Other useful publications are given in the list of references at the end of this chapter. After one or more tanks of juice or vats of crushed grapes have been heavily inoculated with pure yeast and are in full fermentation their contents may be used to inoculate other tanks, though pure yeast cultures are preferred.

Caution.—If at any time in either method of propagating the yeast start-er for winery use in the pure yeast apparatus, there is reason to believe that the culture is no longer reasonably pure, empty and sterilize the appa-ratus and begin all over again with a pure culture from a yeast laboratory. Do not run the risk of spoiling a large proportion of your vintage with con-taminated yeast.

FERMENTATION

The specific fermentation requirements for each type of wine are con-sidered in the succeeding chapters.

Continuous Fermentation

Systems in which the raw material is continuously introduced into the fermenter and removed continuously from the same or another fermenter are now in wide use by the fermentation industries.

Such systems make possible considerable saving in space and labor. The process can be instrumented for automatic control. The product is thus of uniform composition. The primary problem is in sterilizing the raw material and in preventing contamination during operation. There may also be occasional problems with development of mutant yeasts. Am-erine (1959) has reviewed the problem and noted especially the successful use of a continuous process for production of sparkling wines in Russia. A recent report of Konovalov (1958) shows that in continuous fermentation at 7.6 per cent alcohol yeast cells continue to grow and to fix P^{32} while in the batch process the yeast cells stop dividing or fixing phosphorus at an early stage of the fermentation. Kunkee and Ough (1966) found that lack of yeast multiplication was a problem in continuous fermentations under pressure. See also Willig (1950).

Riddell and Nury (1958) describe a semi-continuous fermentation sys-

Courtesy Wine Institute

Fig. 68.   Stainless Steel Fermenting Tanks

Note their location outdoors

tem.   It operated on a ten-day cycle.   The wine in the main fermenter fermented at about 3° Balling and the feed was about 5 per cent per hour.

Cooling

For the theory of this operation, see pp. 195–198.   Alcoholic fermentation liberates much heat.   In a small container, such as a gallon jug, most of the heat is lost by radiation to the surroundings, but in a fermentation vat or tank considerable is retained with consequent rise in temperature in the tank.   Even in a cool cellar, the temperature of the fermenting grapes may rise to the danger point unless artificial cooling is used.   At 95°F. wine yeast is greatly weakened, and at 100° to 105°F. most of it dies or loses its fermenting power with consequent stopping ("sticking") of the fermentation. This is a common occurrence if cooling is not applied. For the best results, the fermentation should not be allowed to rise above 85°F. in a red wine fermentation; at 90°F. the yeast may be injured and the flavor and bouquet of the wine damaged.

Another disadvantage of very high fermentation temperature lies in the fact that heat-tolerant spoilage bacteria may grow, producing volatile acids, mannitol, and off-flavors. They may completely spoil the wine. If the sulfur dioxide content is sufficiently high, the bacteria will not be able to grow. Nevertheless, the damage to the yeast at high temperature is not affected by the sulfur dioxide content and, therefore, even in the presence of sulfur dioxide, high temperatures should be avoided. While Ough and Amerine (1961) reported fermentation of Pinot noir at 70° or 80°F. gave better wines than at 53°F., with Cabernet Sauvignon they found 70°F. was better than 80° or 53°F. Prehoda (1963) reported similar results.

Consequently, as the temperature approaches 85°F. during fermentation, cooling should be instituted and the fermenting must cooled some 10°F. or more. Proportionally, there is less loss of heat by radiation from large than from a small vat. However, for average conditions it is possible, by means of empirical formulas to calculate in advance about how much cooling will be needed for a given set of conditions. For example, Bioletti (1906) gave the following formula: $C = 1.17S + T - M$, in which S is the Balling degree, T the temperature of contents of the vat, M, the maximum temperature desired, and C, the number of degrees F. to be removed by cooling. For example, if $S = 24$, T, 80°F., and M, 85°F., then $C = (1.17 \times 24) + 80 - 85 = 23.1$°F. This means that at some time during the fermentation the must will have to be cooled at least 23°F. in order to prevent the temperature rising above 85°F. This assumes that about 50 per cent of the heat produced is lost from the fermenter.

According to Marsh (1959) the loss of heat during the first half of the fermentation is no more than 33 per cent. Thus the minimum cooling required under average conditions is 150,000 B.t.u. per 1000 gallons of must. For grapes received in a warm condition or with a high sugar content 250,-000 B.t.u. per 1000 gallons or 50,000 B.t.u. per ton should be used in cooling calculations. For dessert wines, with their limited fermentation period, about half the above requirements can be used. Should constant temperature be needed during fermentation of table wines the B.t.u. requirements will be about one-third greater than those indicated. Barrillon et al. (1970) calculated that for 106,000-gallon continuous fermenters 40 per cent of the heat produced had to be removed by cooling.

The two main systems employed for cooling musts in California are internal cooling coils in the fermenters and external shell-and-multitube coolers. In both cases 60°F. water (or cooler) is often used—usually with a cooling tower. However, mechanically refrigerated water coolers may be required to supplement the cooling tower. Marsh estimates that if cooling operations are conducted on a twelve-hour basis 208,000 B.t.u. per hour of refrigeration will be required per 50 tons of grapes crushed for table wine. This means 2500 gallons of water per hour rising 10°F. will be needed for cooling.

In actual plant studies Marsh (1959) reported the mean over-all coefficient of heat transfer was 245 B.t.u. per hour per square foot of heat transfer area per degree Fahrenheit. The range was 111 to 390 B.t.u. The most economical use of cooling water results when wine and water flow through the unit at approximately the same rates.

When red musts have been heated to facilitate color extraction a much greater cooling capacity is required. To reduce the temperature from 120° to 70°F. requires the removal of nearly 100,000 B.t.u. per ton.

One may do all of the needed cooling in one cooling operation; or he may prefer to apply cooling 2 or 3 times during the fermentation, in order not to have to reduce the temperature so low in a single cooling that fermentation is slowed. In most cases, cooling is begun at about 80° to 85°F., and the must is cooled to 70° to 75° F. and, if it again rises to 85°F., is cooled a second time. However at the end of fermentation, cooling must not be so low that the fermentation is arrested. Where stainless steel fermenters are used water may be run over them to cool by exchange and evaporation.

Stuck Wines

When the fermentation stops before all of the desired sugar is fermented the wines are said to have "stuck." Sticking occurs due to over-heating, to infection by various bacteria, to too cold a temperature, and in a few cases because of unbalanced musts. The first is the only type observed nowadays and it is rare. One peculiarity of wines which cease fermentation at a high temperature is the difficulty with which they are refermented and their susceptibility to bacterial spoilage. When a wine sticks the wine maker should immediately determine the cause of the difficulty.

The influence of size of container on the temperature during fermentation was reported by Müller-Thurgau in 1887 as follows:

Cask Size	Maximum Temperature
Liters	°F.
600	66.3–71.6
1200	69.8–77
4800	86
7200	95

If sticking is due to a high temperature cool the must at once to about 70°F. Another fermenter of the same type of must should be brought to vigorous fermentation and about 10 per cent of the stuck wine added each day. If another tank is not available pump a small amount of the cooled stuck wine to another fermenter and add 10 to 20 per cent of an actively fermenting pure yeast starter. When the wine is in fermentation proceed as above by adding portions of the stuck wine. Following fermentation the wine should be carefully checked for composition and condition, the acidity corrected, and sulfur dioxide added as necessary. Addition of ammonium phosphate (7.5 lbs. per 1000 gallons) has proven useful in stimulating stuck fermentations in some cases.

When the sticking is due to low temperatures warming is usually sufficient but addition of a large starter of actively-fermenting pure yeast culture is recommended. Sticking due to excessive growth of microorganisms is now very rare in California. The best use of such wines is to dilute and sulfite them, and gradually add them to an actively-fermenting tank of distilling material. The sooner they are disposed of the better.

FORTIFICATION

Since now about half of the wine made in America is of the dessert type fortification is an important winery operation. Many sherries are not fortified until the fermentation is completed. Some muscatel and angelica are fortified after only a very limited period of fermentation. In order to produce a wine of a given final sugar content the time of fortification will vary depending on the initial sugar content of the grapes. Fig. 69 is very useful in predicting when the fortification should be made. Note that the data in this figure are based on fortifying to 18.0 per cent alcohol.

Flanzy (1959) recommended adding small amounts of alcohol at the start of the fermentation and several times later until the proper total amount has been added. The early addition undoubtedly slowed down the fermentation. Deibner and Bénard (1956) proposed distilling alcohol directly into fermenting wines as a means of improving the quality of dessert wines. Later Bénard et al. (1958), based on aging in bottles in the laboratory, believed the samples where the alcohol was distilled into the wine were superior. Confirmation is needed. Singleton and Guymon (1963) found some enhancement of the quality of white port which was fractionally fortified during fermentation. They attribute this to reduction of the aldehyde content during the continuing fermentation. With red port the quality improvement was less apparent. However, there was an increase in the color of red ports fortified with spirits of higher aldehyde content. This result was confirmed by Singleton et al. (1964).

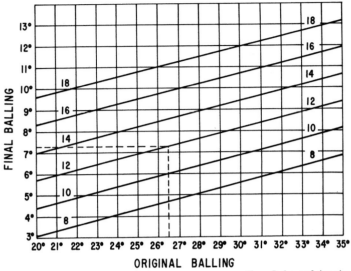

ORIGINAL BALLING

From Joslyn and Amerine

Fig. 69. When to Fortify Musts of Varying Original Balling to Produce Wines of 18.0 Per Cent Alcohol and a Given Balling

In the example: to produce wine with 7.3° Balling and 18.0 per cent alcohol from a must whose original Balling was 26.5°, it is necessary to add the fortifying spirits at 12°. This assumes immediate cessation of fermentation after fortification which may not be strictly correct.

A Baeyer reaction between phenols and aldehydes to produce more adsorbable, less reactive, red products was proposed.

To distinguish between fermented dessert wines and fortified grape juice (*mistelle*) Dimotaki-Kourakou (1964) suggested paper chromatographic detection of citramalic acid. This acid is formed during fermentation, 60 to 180 mg. per liter, and its absence would indicate a beverage prepared from unfermented grape juice. Again confirmation is needed.

Procedure

The actual fortification is under the supervision of an inspector of the Internal Revenue Service. In theory he measures the volume of wine, determines its alcohol content, and supervises the addition of the necessary volume of high proof spirits, and its mixing (usually by compressed air). In practice, the wine maker determines the alcohol concentration, verifies the volume, and carries out the fortification.

TABLE 31

NUMBER OF GALLONS OF WINE SPIRIT TO BE ADDED TO 100 GALLONS OF WINE CONTAINING VARIOUS PERCENTAGES OF ALCOHOL TO PRODUCE A FORTIFIED WINE CONTAINING 18 PER CENT ALCOHOL

Alcohol in Initial Wine (Volume Per cent)	Per Cent of Alcohol in Wine Spirits									
	82	84	86	88	90	91	92	93	94	95
	Gallons of Wine Spirits to be Added to 100 Gallons									
0	28.13	27.27	26.47	25.71	25.00	24.66	24.32	24.00	23.68	23.38
1	26.56	25.76	25.00	24.29	23.61	23.29	22.97	22.67	22.37	22.08
2	25.00	24.24	23.53	22.86	22.22	21.92	21.62	21.33	21.05	20.78
3	23.44	22.73	22.06	21.43	20.83	20.55	20.27	20.00	19.74	19.48
4	21.88	21.21	20.59	20.00	19.44	19.18	18.92	18.67	18.42	18.18
5	20.31	19.70	19.12	18.57	18.06	17.81	17.57	17.33	17.11	16.88
6	18.75	18.18	17.65	17.14	16.67	16.44	16.22	16.00	15.79	15.58
7	17.19	16.67	16.18	15.71	15.28	15.07	14.86	14.67	14.47	14.29
8	15.63	15.15	14.71	14.29	13.89	13.70	13.51	13.33	13.18	12.99
9	14.06	13.64	13.24	12.86	12.50	12.33	12.16	12.00	11.84	11.69
10	12.50	12.12	11.76	11.43	11.11	10.96	10.81	10.67	10.53	10.39
11	10.94	10.61	10.29	10.00	9.72	9.59	9.46	9.33	9.21	9.09
12	9.38	9.09	8.82	8.57	8.33	8.22	8.11	8.00	7.89	7.79
13	7.81	7.58	7.35	7.14	6.94	6.85	6.76	6.67	6.58	6.49
14	6.25	6.06	5.88	5.71	5.56	5.48	5.41	5.33	5.26	5.19
15	4.69	4.55	4.41	4.29	4.17	4.11	4.05	4.00	3.95	3.90

The calculation of the volume of fortifying brandy to add can be made by reference to Table 31 or by calculation from the formula $X = [V(C - A)]/B - C$ where X is the wine gallons of fortifying brandy of B per cent, V the gallons of wine of A per cent alcohol, and C the desired alcohol content of the final wine (usually 20.5 in California). Since there is a contraction when alcohol and water are mixed (Table 32) this will not be exact. There are also discrepancies owing to the alcohol continuing to increase during fermentation and, if the fortifying brandy is not rapidly and thoroughly mixed, after the fortification. This can lead to low sugar and high alcohol. It is therefore customary to pump the wine to the fortifying tanks at a Balling 2° to 3° above that shown in Fig. 69. Furthermore, the wine maker soon acquires experience with his equipment to judge the correct time of fortification. One method of preventing errors is to always fortify the same volume of wine. Following mixing the gauger is required to take samples to verify the actual alcohol content.

A sample calculation of the volume of spirits is as follows: 25,000 gal-

TABLE 32

PER CENT CONTRACTION OF WATER-ALCOHOL-SUGAR MIXTURES WHEN FORTIFIED TO 20.5 PER CENT ALCOHOL WITH 184° PROOF FORTIFYING BRANDY[1,2,3]

	Per cent Contraction				
Original Per cent Alcohol	With 0 Per cent Dextrose[3]	With 5 Per cent Dextrose	With 10 Per cent Dextrose	With 15 Per cent Dextrose	With 20 Per cent Dextrose
	Per cent	Per cent	Per cent	Per cent	Per cent
0	1.347	1.38	1.39	1.41	1.45
5	1.258	1.30	1.34	1.37	1.37
10	0.908	0.87	0.88	0.78	0.80
15	0.595	0.628	0.655	0.754?	0.661

[1] Source of data: Joslyn and Amerine (1964).
[2] The contractions were obtained by adding a measured volume of high-proof to a measured volume of the alcohol-water or alcohol-water-sugar mixture. The volume of the fortified mixture was obtained by dividing the weight of 100 ml. of water-alcohol-sugar mixture plus the fortifying brandy by the weight of 100 ml. of the final fortified solution (by the specific gravity, in other words). The theoretical volume of the mixture is known (by addition of volumes) and the difference between it and the actual volume represents the contraction. The per cent contraction was calculated as per cent of the theoretical volume.
[3] International Critical Tables gives the contraction as 1.50 per cent for fortification from 0 per cent alcohol to 20.5 per cent alcohol at 0 per cent dextrose when 100 per cent alcohol is used to fortify.

lons of wine of 5.5 per cent alcohol are to be fortified to 20.5 per cent alcohol using high proof of 189°. How many gallons of high proof spirits are required? $X = [25,000 (20.5 - 5.5)]/(94.5 - 20.5) = 5067.57$ wine gallons. Regulations require the calculation to the second decimal place though this has little significance in practice.

Quality of Spirits

Neutral spirits are preferred by most California producers. Low fusel oil content is especially desired. This appears to be best for early-maturing dessert wines which are not to be aged in wood. However, there are no extensive commercial experiments showing the quality to be expected when spirits of lower proof and a higher content of congenerics are used and the wine aged.

In a comparison of rectified potato spirits (95.6 per cent), redistilled potato spirit (96.4) and grape high proof spirits (95.5) and commercial brandy (62.3) for fortification of dessert wines Egorov *et al.* (1951) preferred the wines fortified with redistilled potato spirits. The poorest was the sample fortified with commercial brandy. All the samples were examined shortly after finishing so the results are not surprising. Furthermore, the taste results were quite close: 7.2 to 8.0 with no statistical analysis of the differences. Flanzy (1959) preferred high proof spirits to commercial neutral alcohol for fortification but the differences only developed during aging. Bénard *et al.* (1958) reported high proof spirits better than Armagnac or Cognac. Only a few samples were used and no statistical analyses of the sensory results given. Costa (1938), on the other hand, preferred spirits of only 150° to 160° proof for port in Portugal. Observation of Portuguese ports indicates that many are high in fusel oil and that this is not considered a negative quality factor. See also p. 39. Unless a demand for aged highly flavored dessert wines is developed it is doubtful if California producers should or will change their present practice.

STORAGE

Wines are stored in oak, Fig. 70, concrete, Fig. 71, redwood, Fig. 72, lined iron or steel, Fig. 73, and stainless steel containers. All storage areas should be air conditioned, and if wood is employed humidity control is also needed. Caves provide temperature and humidity control. If the tanks are outdoors they should be insulated.

The storage room (except for a very small one) should be arranged with permanent pipes (stainless steel or glass) for transfer of wines. Hoses should be used only for temporary transfer. It is, of course, hardly necessary to add that all equipment must be installed for ease of cleaning.

Containers

The type and size of container used will depend on the quality of wines and the purpose of the aging program. Wineries with a quality wine program may profitably and necessarily use oak cooperage, particularly for their red wines. Lined iron, or stainless steel containers do not permit aging but they offer permanent storage with a minimum of loss or aeration. They can be lagged for better temperature control. Wines stored in smooth lined tanks do not clarify as well as those in smaller tanks with a rough interior.

Courtesy of Wine Institute

FIG. 70.   OAK OVALS, TANKS AND LINED STEEL TANKS IN
CALIFORNIA WINERY

Courtesy of Wine Institute

FIG. 71.   LARGE CONCRETE TANKS FOR STORING WINE IN
CALIFORNIA WINERY

For fine red table wines and for quality dessert wines oak is the preferred material for storage. Not only do the wines clarify better in small containers but they acquire a slight woody character and the necessary air for aging. Very large oak tanks, however, are probably little better than redwood, lined-iron or concrete for storage. The preferable size of oak for wine storage is from 50 to 500 gallons. These are known as barrels for sizes of 50 gallons or smaller. Larger sizes are called ovals, puncheons (round), pipes (for port), butts (for sherry), or simply casks. When properly cared for the thicker staved will last for centuries.

Courtesy of Wine Institute

FIG. 72.   REDWOOD STORAGE TANKS IN CALIFORNIA WINERY

Courtesy of Gallo Wine Co.

FIG. 73.   LINED STEEL WINE STORAGE TANKS

Data on the extraction of material from wood meal and wood chips was given by Singleton and Draper (1961). The composition of the extracts was surprisingly constant. Sensory tests indicated that an extract equivalent to 1 lb. of wood would give a detectably woody character to 200 gallons of port.

Redwood and concrete were commonly used for tank construction in the California industry through the 1940's. Beginning in the 1950's lined steel tanks, because of their many advantages including lower costs in the larger sizes, largely replaced concrete. The estimated cost of coated steel tanks in 1970 was as follows (cents per gallon):

Tank Capacity	Steel and Erection	Foundations, Fittings, Paint	Baked Inside Coating	Total Cost
10,000	28.0	16.7	12.0	56.0
50,000	17.0	4.5	5.5	27.0
100,000	12.0	3.1	4.1	19.2
200,000	8.5	1.9	3.0	13.4
600,000	6.3	0.9	1.8	9.0

The comparative costs of coated steel and redwood tanks in 1970 was as follows (cost in cents per gallon):

Tank Capacity	Steel (Baked)	Redwood
6,250	...	51.7
10,000	56.0	...
12,500	...	35.4
25,000	...	26.1
50,000	27.0	...
100,000	19.2	...
200,000	13.4	...
600,000	9.0	...

Due to improvements in fabricating techniques, the cost of stainless steel tanks has been reduced materially. Peters (1970) estimated their costs as follows (cents per gallon):

Tank Capacity	Tank Erection	Fittings	Total Cost
6,000	42.6	9.4	52.0
12,000	28.8	6.2	35.0
18,000	25.8	4.2	30.0
48,000	22.0	2.0	24.0
60,000	17.6	1.4	19.0
110,000	16.6	0.9	17.5
170,000	14.2	0.8	15.0
225,000	12.0	0.5	12.5

The annual losses from different type tanks in gallons per 1000 gallon capacity was calculated as follows: concrete (60,000 gallons) 7.0, redwood (60,000 gallons) 3.3, steel (60,000 gallons) 0.8, and steel (200,000 gallons) 0.6. Just why the loss from concrete is greater than from redwood is not known. Skofis (1966) gives the losses as 2.16 per cent from concrete and 2.95 from redwood and only 1.8 from oak. (See Brands (1956) and Doon (1958) for data on steel tanks.) He also noted that cleaning and maintenance costs and fire insurance is much greater for redwood than for concrete or steel. Depreciation of concrete is slightly greater than for steel of the same capacity.

Care of Cooperage.—Alkaline solutions are most effective in removing tannins from new barrels. Soaking with 1 per cent sodium carbonate is the usual treatment. Combined with superheated steam (2 or 3 atmospheres pressure) and several rinsings with water they will produce a container with little extractable tannin. Salt solution, dilute sulfuric acid, and lime are not effective.

New redwood tanks should be soaked with a warm dilute solution, about 1 per cent, of soda ash for several days, followed by soaking with water for several days with two or more changes. Storage of clean distilling material before using the tank is also desirable. New oak containers are also soaked out with a warm soda ash solution, followed by several "soakings out" with water and finally thorough steaming. The steaming should be done at very low pressure to prevent warping of the head. Filling with very hot water or running steam into the water until it is nearly boiling is preferable.

Berg (1948) recommends the following cleaning procedure for used cooperage: wash the interior with water and then spray with a hot, about 120°F. 20 per cent solution of "Winery Special," which consists of 90 per cent soda ash and ten per cent caustic soda; then wash thoroughly with hot water and spray with a solution of chlorine compound containing about 440 p.p.m. of available chlorine. Again wash thoroughly with cold water, drain, and mop dry. Burn a sulfur wick in the tank (about 2 ozs. for 1000 gallons). Rewash and inspect visually and by smell before use.

To remove cream of tartar deposits, argols, most wineries use a hot alkaline solution. Berg (1948) suggests a solution containing 80 lbs. each of soda ash and sodium hydroxide per 1000 gallons of water. Three pounds of Oronite D-40 may be included. This solution is used until it contains 12 to 15 per cent tartrates. For recovery of the tartrates see Chapter 18. A jet of steam is sometimes used to remove tartrate deposits from concrete tanks.

Barrels are usually cleaned by hot soda ash solution, rinsing, steaming thoroughly, and final washing. Burning a sulfur wick in the barrel is advisable if it is not to be used immediately. Avoid use of too strong a soda solution or its use for too long a time as softening and disintegration of the wood may occur.

Molding of the *outside* of storage tanks occurs under humid conditions. Amerine and Joslyn (1951) state that washing with a solution of a quaternary ammonium compound may be effective in removing the mold and the residual disinfectant may retard future mold growth. Paints containing copper-8-quinolinolate appear to be the most promising for control of mold growth.

Berg (1948) recommends V.E.X. (trade designation of a proprietary preparation) 4 to 12 ozs. per gallon at 160° to 180°F. to remove mold, grime, varnish, and linseed oil from the outside of containers when such drastic treatment is necessary.

Tank trucks and railroad cars are often returned in unsatisfactory condition and require special treatment. The interior surfaces should first be examined for defects. Chlorinated solutions are usually best for disinfection. Ample supplies of hot and cold water, under good pressure, are especially useful in such cases.

Where casks or tanks leak because of cracked staves they should be recoopered. The staves of redwood sherry cooking tanks (not recommended) often become soft and leaky and require recoopering. This includes scraping of the staves and replacing leaky or moldy staves. It may be necessary in some cases to replace the head also. A single moldy stave may contaminate and damage the flavor of a whole tank of wine. The inside of the tank or cask should be examined carefully for mold, cracks, and other defects. Mold should be scraped off as it cannot be removed by washing. The walls are then washed with a hot alkaline solution such as a strong solution of a mixture of soda ash and caustic. This should be followed by rinsing with water and spraying with a hypochlorite solution containing 500 to 1000 p.p.m. of available chlorine. This treatment should be followed by several washings with hot water. Steaming may be necessary in severe cases. All of the free chlorine must be removed by thorough washing. Inert and impervious plastic or wax have been used to temporarily repair old or badly leaking tanks. See also Berg (1948).

Concrete fermentation tanks are left open and dry when not in use. They should be thoroughly cleaned before being left open in order to prevent mold growth. Spraying detergents and cleaners, using automatic equipment, over the interior surfaces is useful for all kinds of containers. All the residual detergent must be washed out with water before reuse.

Storing empty barrels and tanks during the hot, dry summer months is a serious problem. Amerine and Joslyn (1951) recommend that stored empty barrels be sulfured by sulfur wick or by introducing sulfur dioxide from a cylinder of the gas. The inside of the barrels should be kept wet, and the barrels should be stored indoors or in the shade. Sulfuring is repeated as needed; but over-sulfuring should be avoided.

Until World War II, many California wineries had large inventories of 50-gallon barrels for the shipment of wine. At present, most California wine is bottled on the premises or shipped in tank cars and the storage of empty 50-gallon barrels is no longer a problem. This is fortunate since the care of empty used 50-gallon barrels is difficult. When returned from dealers, they are often moldy or vinegar sour. They should be treated as indicated above.

Open wooden tanks should be thoroughly cleaned and then may be filled with saturated lime water, which is made by mixing about 15 pounds of lime with each 1000 gallons of water. This solution will usually keep the tank sweet. If storage is prolonged it is usually necessary to drain out the lime solution periodically and replace it with freshly prepared solution, particularly during the first months of storage.

Dilute hypochlorite solution (250 p.p.m. of active chlorine) has been used to fill storage tanks but soon loses its strength because of reaction with the wood and other organic matter. Sodium bisulfite in dilute sulfuric acid (0.5 lb. of concentrated sulfuric acid and 1 lb. of bisulfite per 1000 gallons of water) will usually keep tanks or barrels in good condition. It is advisable to inspect the containers occasionally to prevent drying-out of the top. Painting lime on the interior surfaces of open tanks is not recommended.

Filling Up

Tanks of table wine must be kept completely filled and sealed, in order to prevent acetification. This requires that smaller containers of like wine be on hand from which to fill the larger tanks and casks. This is particularly true of vintage wines which must be "topped" by wine of the same vintage. The smaller the container the more frequent the filling up—particularly in warmer cellars and during the warmer periods of the year. For very large containers 10,000 gallons and up, "topping" may be needed every month or six weeks and in the warmer part of the year there may be sufficient expansion in volume that some wine must be removed.

Racking

This simple operation is often neglected as an aid to clarification. Racking, first of all, removes a considerable amount of carbon dioxide. It also raises the redox potential. One of the dangers in leaving the new wine in contact with its yeast sediment is that it may lead to yeast autolysis[5] and, at the low redox potential, formation of hydrogen sulfide. Of course, if residual sugar remains some delay in racking may be desirable to allow the wine to ferment dry. Also, if a malo-lactic fermentation is desired to reduce the total acidity this racking may be delayed. Great care and frequent analyses are suggested in this latter case.

Normally, however, wines should be racked within a month of the end of the fermentation, and sooner is advisable under warm cellar conditions, with small containers, and with low acid table wines.

AGING[6]

Aging is one of the most interesting and important, yet one of the most complex processes in wine making. Newly-fermented wine is cloudy,

---

[5] Yeast autolysis is defined by Joslyn (1955) as "an enzymatic self-destruction of the yeast cell and essentially involves hydrolysis of the protoplasmic constituents and their excretion into the surrounding medium."

[6] The Russian practice of designating changes that occur in the wines before bottling as "maturation" and those that occur in the bottle later as "aging" seems a rational one.

harsh in taste, yeasty in odor, and without the pleasing bouquet that develops later in its history. As it ages properly, the harsh taste and yeasty odor diminish and a smooth, mellow flavor and clean odor are produced. The bouquet also develops during aging in the wood and the bottle. The wine maker's task is to free the wine from its suspended material and yeasty odor and to prepare it for bottling by proper aging practices.

The process of clarification involves reducing the temperature, storage in various types of containers, racking, filtration, fining, centrifugation, pasteurization (or other heat treatments), refrigeration, passage through ion exchange resins, and other processes.

Courtesy of Wine Institute

FIG. 74. OAK CASKS FOR TABLE WINE STORAGE IN CALIFORNIA

The objectives of must and wine treatment have been summarized by Mayer-Oberplan (1956) as follows: (1) removal of suspended material, (2) removal of off-tastes and -odors, (3) removal of off-color, (4) removal of substances which would later cloud the wine, (5) removal of foreign or toxic materials, (6) removal of residual fining agents, (7) to hydrolyze pectins and proteins, (8) to make musts and wines filterable, or (9) as a preventive measure.

Red table wines may improve in bouquet in the wood, Fig. 74, at optimum storage temperatures and in moderate-sized containers for about 1 to 4 years, depending upon the composition of the wines. A light, white wine, such as a Riesling, will age more rapidly than a heavy red wine. Most California dry red wines improve in the wood for 3 to 4 years whereas white wines require little, if any, wood aging and are ready for bottling in only a year or two. When a table wine has attained its optimum quality in the tank (when it has become bottling ripe) it then begins to decrease in quality. New table wines, particularly reds, when placed in completely filled bottles and sealed tightly remain new and harsh in flavor and age very slowly. Properly aged wines placed in bottles, Fig. 75, continue to improve for several years after bottling. This is notably true of red table wines where maximum quality may not be attained for ten or more years, as for our best California Cabernet wines.

Dessert wines continue to improve for many years in wood. However, these fortified wines also undergo a rather rapid initial aging and, within a few months after the vintage, are generally sufficiently aged to be passably pleasing in flavor. However, ports, especially tawny ports, require several years of wood aging and some ports improve with bottle aging.

Fig. 75.   Table Wine Bottle Aging Cellar in California Winery

Courtesy of Wine Institute

Madeira and California sherry are "cooked" for several months at a relatively high temperature in order to hasten aging and develop the desired flavor and color.

Theory

The principal changes in flavor and bouquet during aging in the wood are generally believed to be due to slow oxidation. Wood extractives also have a material affect on flavor. For further information see Joslyn (1934), Amerine (1950), and Singleton (1959). Oxidation may be beneficial or injurious to the quality of the wine. Every wine maker knows that to leave a tank or cask of dry wine exposed to the air, or to leave it partly filled, will result in its rapid accumulation of acetaldehyde and possibly of ethyl acetate and acetic acid. On the other hand, oxygen does play an important role in aging of several types of wines. The average oak cask or redwood wine tank is not air-tight but is rather porous. Air can, and does, enter slowly; the oxygen is absorbed by the wine and brings about a series of oxidation reactions that may change the character of the wine in many respects. Oxygen also enters the wine during pumping, filtering, and racking as well as from the head space in the tank or cask. These sources of oxygen are probably much more important than entry of air by diffusion through the wood.

Pasteur showed that normal aging of certain red wines cannot take place without oxidation. He also proved that the amount of oxygen required is small and that when this amount is exceeded the wine becomes flat and may take on a "madeirized" odor. He also believed that table wines in hermetically-sealed bottles failed to age. There is some doubt that this last conclusion is correct, particularly for white table and red wines of low tannin content.

Table wines exposed to the air rapidly absorb oxygen. In a bottle filled about four-fifths full and sealed, the wine absorbs all the oxygen from the air in 24 hours. The first effect of the oxygen is to make the wine flat in flavor due to formation of aldehyde. This change occurs when a wine is fully exposed to the air for a short time. If the bottle is filled and sealed it will gradually improve in flavor, provided the oxidation has not been too severe.

Oxidation of tannin and coloring matter and precipitation of the oxidation by-product may occur. The reddish brown layer of coloring matter in the bottom or on the sides of bottles of old red wines is well known. In this case the action of the oxygen is evidently slow.

It is well known that exposing partly filled bottles to sunlight very greatly increases the rate of aging. In fact, Pasteur secured a patent on this process of rapid aging more than 80 years ago. Aldehydes and acetals are said to be responsible for much of the "new" taste of immature table wines. There is some evidence that these are desirable for some dessert wines. Some of the higher alcohols of the wine may be converted to acids and these in turn may form esters with the ethyl and other alcohols to give part of the flavor and bouquet of aged wines.

Oxygen is absorbed, not only during storage from the air that penetrates the pores, but also, as stated above, during racking, pumping, filtration, and filling up. Water (and to a less extent alcohol) is lost by evaporation through the pores of the wood, resulting in a head space beneath the bung. Air diffuses in to fill this space and the wine then absorbs the oxygen from this air. Once in every 20 to 30 days the cellarman must open the tank or cask and fill this space with wine. In so doing he unavoidably aerates the added wine thus introducing more oxygen. Oxygen, absorbed during aging from air diffusing through the wood amounts to over 30 ml. per liter and that absorbed during each racking to 5 to 6 ml. per liter; or 20 to 25 ml. per year with four rackings; or during its normal life in wood over 100 ml., sufficient to account for all the oxidative changes occurring during aging.

The saturation level of oxygen in wine is generally considered to be 6 to 7 ml. per liter. Cant (1960) showed that wines being removed from cold stabilization approached oxygen saturation. He used a nitrogen stripping column which on a single pass reduced oxygen to two ml. An in-line nitrogen sparger was less effective for high oxygen wines and equally effective to the column for low oxygen wines. Carbon dioxide was less effective. The cost of stripping was about 50 cents per 1000 gallons. During bottling the greatest oxygen pickup occurred as the wine was discharged into the filling machine bowl. Purging the air from the bottles with carbon dioxide is generally believed desirable. More recently Bielig (1966) reported absorption of 0.6 mg. per liter of oxygen during filling at normal temperatures. This corresponds to 2.4 mg. per liter of sulfur dioxide. Bottling under pressure increases this to 1.5 mg. per liter. Flushing the bottles with nitrogen reduces oxygen absorption to 0.4 mg. per liter. At the time of bottling, the wine may contain 1.2 mg. per liter of dissolved oxygen and as much as 4.8 mg. per liter may be absorbed from the space between the liquid and the closure. He concludes that the two best methods of reducing the effect of oxygen are (1) to reduce contact with air during cellar handling, and (2) to leave as small an air space in the bottle as practicable.

The presence of sulfur dioxide in wines materially retards aging since much of the oxygen is consumed in oxidizing the sulfurous acid. Aldehydes, formed by oxidation of the various alcohols in the wine, affect the flavor and bouquet and may also form insoluble compounds with the tannin and coloring matter or with other aldehydes.

According to the observations of most cellar men, different wines require different amounts of oxygen. Thus a light white table wine requires less than heavy red wine or sherry. Also, as mentioned previously, the presence or absence of sulfur dioxide will greatly affect the oxygen required. Controlled oxidation and reduction of table and dessert wines offers many opportunities for improvement of our wines. Ough and Amerine (1959) have described electrodes for measuring the oxygen content. Continuous control of the redox potential during aging is the next step.

In some wines, particularly those made from moldy grapes, there is an excess of polyphenoloxidase that catalyzes or brings about the union of oxygen with the polyphenolic constituents of the wine. It causes overaging and development of a brown color and an aldehyde odor in low sulfur dioxide wines.

There are a number of alcohols and acids in the wine that may unite to form esters. First, there are fixed acids, namely, tartaric acid, malic acid, succinic acid, and lactic acid (the first two present in the juice, the latter two formed during fermentation). Acetic acid, propionic acid, formic acid, and probably traces of other more or less volatile acids are formed during fermentation. Acetic acid is much the most abundant. The important volatile esters, largely those of acetic acid, are important in spoilage but in small amounts undoubtedly contribute to the fragrance of the wine. The contribution of the non-volatile esters to the odor of a wine has not been established but it must be small when one considers the small quantities present and their relatively indistinctive odors. Further evidence is necessary to establish this. Methyl esters, particularly, may play a part and ethyl laurate and related esters seem to have some role in wine odor (p. 209).

Some varieties of grapes, such as the Muscat, Sémillon, Cabernet, Concord, and Catawba, have pronounced characteristic aromas and flavors (see p. 112). These are carried over to a large degree in the wine and form an important part of the aroma of the aged wine. Aging, however, tends to cause these natural grape aromas and flavors to diminish and become less obvious.

Microorganisms

California enologists are not accustomed to think in terms of an acid-reducing fermentation although it occurs in many wineries, unrecognized by the wine maker. Our warm climate usually gives us sufficiently low acid grapes. It is a capricious fermentation, not occurring with some wines, and it was early recognized as being a dangerous fermentation if allowed to proceed too far—which was common with our high pH California wines. However, in Europe its value was early recognized. Alfred Koch was cultivating the organisms as early as 1897. Austrian, German, and Swiss enologists established the importance of biological acid reduction before the first world war. Ferré did the same for Burgundy in the 20's and Ribéreau-Gayon for Bordeaux in the 30's (Peynaud and Domercq 1961). According to Jerchel et al. (1956) there are two probable reactions in the malo-lactic fermentation. The most likely is:

$$
\begin{array}{c}
\text{CH}_2\text{COOH} \\
| \\
\text{CHOHCOOH} \\
\text{malic acid}
\end{array}
\xrightarrow{\text{NAD}^+,\ \text{Mn}^{++},\ \text{"malic" enzyme}}
\begin{array}{c}
\text{CH}_3 \\
| \\
\text{COCOOH} \\
\text{pyruvic acid}
\end{array}
+ \text{CO}_2 + \text{NADH} + \text{H}^+
$$

$$
\begin{array}{c}
\text{CH}_3 \\
| \\
\text{COCOOH}
\end{array}
\xrightarrow{\text{H}^+,\ \text{NADH}_2,\ \text{lactic dehydrogenase}}
\begin{array}{c}
\text{CH}_3 \\
| \\
\text{CHOHCOOH} \\
\text{lactic acid}
\end{array}
+ \text{NAD}
$$

Flesch and Holbach (1965) have confirmed this.

Sudraud and Cassignard (1959) report that addition of 100 p.p.m. of sulfur dioxide before fermentation delayed the start of the malo-lactic fermentation in the wine for up to 60 days. It was also delayed considerably by storage at 59°F. compared to 77°F. Press wine also showed a delayed malo-lactic fermentation compared to the free-run. They consider the malo-lactic fermentation to be indispensable for the great red wines of Bordeaux and useful for overly acid white wines. There is not only a softening of the taste but there is a change in odor. Air is harmful to the malo-lactic fermentation. At the same pH tartaric acid inhibits growth of lactic acid bacteria much more than malic acid.

The possibility of using selected cultures of lactic acid bacteria was studied by Bidan (1956). The cultures used were from northern (Alsace), central (Loire) and southern (Gaillac) regions of France. Most investigators with lactic acid bacteria have found the cultures isolated were somewhat atypical to those previously identified. Thus Bidan's (1956) *Lactobacillus fermenti* had a different optimum temperature and utilized xylose, in contrast to the type culture. Bidan's *L. fermenti* resembled *L. hilgardii* and the *Bacterium intermedium* of Müller-Thurgau. Another culture resembled *Leuconostoc citrovorum* but differed from it in several physiological characters. The basic *B. gracile* he proposed to call *Leuc. gracile*. Still another culture he found to be a *Pediococcus* for which the name *P. vini* was proposed. This report of *Pediococcus* in wine apparently antedates the report of Gini and Vaughn (1962). He believes it to be the same as the *Micrococcus variococcus* of Müller-Thurgau and Osterwalder (1912, 1918) or the *M malolacticus* of Seifert (1903). A strain of *L. plantarum* isolated by Barre and Galzy (1962) produced little volatile acidity. One can determine whether the lactic acid produced is L (+), D (−) or racemic by using the lactic dehydrogenase properties of yeasts grown under anaerobic or aerobic conditions. Their strain produced both L (+) and D (−) lactic acid.

Of 225 strains of lactic acid bacteria isolated from Piedmont wines by Malan et al. (1965), 132 were Leuc. mesenteroides, 50 Leuc. dextranicum, and 43 Leuc. citrovorum. The first was more valuable in Barbera and the second in other varieties. They noted that the malo-lactic fermentation may profitably be prolonged until spring with high acid varieties but should be stopped earlier, or prevented, for the low acid varieties to prevent spoilage.

Marques Gomes et al. (1954) and Peynaud and Domercq (1959, 1961) believed it practical to supply wine makers with pure cultures of malo-lactic bacteria for winery use—cultures which do not form volatile acidity and which can be rapidly increased to the desired amounts. These they proposed to use on non-sulfited musts or on sulfited musts several days after the fermentation is under way.

Similar results were reported by Webb and Ingraham (1960). Webb (1962) described the original isolation of pure strains. In some cases there was an undue rise in volatile acidity. He noted that it was difficult to induce the malo-lactic fermentation in old wines. Several yeast types also appeared to inhibit a malo-lactic fermentation. Webb felt that some of his strains contributed desirable odors to Pinot noir wines. Kunkee et al. (1964) were able to induce a malo-lactic fermentation at any state of alcoholic fermentation. This was much more rapid with a strain of Leuconostoc than with one of Lactobacillus. Although there was a slight increase in volatile acidity in the treated wines, it did not adversely affect quality. Ingraham et al. (1960) identified three rods L. hilgardii (15 isolates), L. brevis (1), L. delbrueckii (2), and two cocci, Leuconostoc sp. (10) and Pediococcus (?, 12) from California wines. Fornachon (1957) reported L. hilgardii and L. brevis in Australian wines undergoing the malo-lactic fermentation. Later (1964) he identified Leuc. mesenteroides. In general, this strain tolerated a low pH better than species of Lactobacillus. Since these are the wines that most need a malo-lactic fermentation the importance of this bacteria is emphasized. Fornachon (1963) stated that for Australian conditions species of Leuconostoc were the most suitable organisms. Lafon-Lafourcade (1970) induced very rapid (<8 hours) degradation of malic acid using massive (1–5 gr. per liter) amounts of bacterial cells, or more slowly (<12 days) with 100 mg. per liter. Every wine constitutes a different problem as to the desirability or non-desirability of a malo-lactic fermentation.

In Yugoslavia, Milisavljević (1958) has shown that the malo-lactic fermentation is very general—occurring first in wines of low alcohol, low acid, and little free sulfur dioxide, especially when stored at warmer temperatures. Thus a wine of 13 per cent alcohol started the malo-lactic fermentation with 50 mg. per liter of total sulfur dioxide at pH 3.22; 75 mg. was the limit at pH 3.46 and 100 did not prevent it at a pH of 3.85. At 10 per cent alcohol a malo-lactic fermentation can occur at a pH of 2.93. He believed the effect of the malo-lactic fermentation to be generally very desirable in Yugoslavian wines. Later (1964) he reported some strains of yeast inhibited the malo-lactic fermentation more than others.

In 144 California commercial wines, Ingraham and Cooke (1960) reported over half had undergone a malo-lactic fermentation as evidenced by the disappearance of malic acid. The malo-lactic fermentation was much more common in red table wines (75 per cent) compared to white table (32.1 per cent), and rosé (12.5 per cent). They believed there was a causal relationship between the malo-lactic fermentation and the quality of red table wines. However, most of the high quality wines were from the cooler coastal districts and other quality factors were present.

The amino acid requirements of the malo-lactic bacteria have been studied by Radler (1958). Of 22 amino acids studied ten were absolutely essential. They also require nicotinic, folic and pantothenic acids, riboflavin, and possibly thiamin. Silva Babo (1963) found the vitamin B complex especially favorable to the growth of lactic acid bacteria and believes the favorable effects of adding lactic acid bacteria during the alcoholic fermentation were due to the better nutrition provided by the presence of yeasts. More data would be useful. The changes in amino acids in an enriched culture by *Leuconostoc* sp. or *Lactobacillus* sp. appears to be much different than in musts and wines. Peynaud and Domercq (1961) reported marked decreases in all of the amino acids except α-alanine. They also noted much less mesoinositol in wines which had undergone a malo-lactic fermentation. It has long been known that diacetyl and acetoin are by-products of the malo-lactic fermentation. In 41 white wines which had not undergone a malo-lactic fermentation, Radler (1962) reported an average value of acetoin plus diacetyl of 4.3 mg. per liter compared to an average of 9.3 in 101 white wines which had undergone a malo-lactic fermentation. However, the malo-lactic fermentation does not always result in higher acetoin and diacetyl contents. Radler believed that in some red wines small amounts of diacetyl (detection threshold 1 mg. per liter) gave the wine a desirable odor. Kielhöfer and Würdig (1960) also showed that they are produced during alcoholic fermentations.

Peynaud (1955), Lüthi (1957), Radler (1957), Carr (1958), and Tarantola (1959), reviewing the whole problem of the malo-lactic fermentation, believe that its rational control is now possible.

In the sherry district of Jerez de la Frontera film yeasts are active in bringing about the aging of the famous wines of southern Spain. In Japan, it has been found by Takahashi and others that aging of sake can be hastened by the use of certain film yeasts. See Chapter 9 for a further discussion of film yeasts.

Temperature

A temperature of about 52° to 60°F. is best for the aging of table wines. For dessert wines the range may be somewhat higher. It is desirable to have the storage room, for table wines especially, well insulated against fluctuations in temperature. For dessert wines some fluctuation in storage temperature may be desirable because of the improved absorption of oxygen which this aids but so far no critical experiments seem to have been made. In hot climates it appears necessary to refrigerate artificially the storage room, certainly for table wines, to prevent a harmful rise in temperature. While aging of dessert wines is a function of the temperature and such wines will age much more rapidly at 90°F. than at 60° to 70°F. it appears that quality is best preserved and enhanced when the wine is aged in the temperature range of not over 70°F. After the wine is aged it will keep best at low temperatures as further chemical changes are then retarded. For a fuller discussion of the effect of temperature, see Ough and Amerine (1966).

Accelerated Maturation

With repeal of Prohibition there was a desire on the part of many wine makers to age their wines rapidly. Many different treatments were attempted in various wineries. One logical and beneficial treatment consisted in racking the wines as soon as fermentation and settling were complete, followed at once by filtration to render the wine clear. Excess cream of tartar was then removed by cooling the table wines to 23° to 26°F., and the dessert wines to about 18°F. Maturation was accelerated by the oxidation induced by racking and transfer, pasteurization or cooking, or by combinations of two, or all three, of these treatments. The favorable effect of heating dessert wines in the absence of air has been claimed by many investigators, particularly in the Soviet Union. The data are not too convincing, particularly in the absence of an indication of the statistical significance of the sensory evaluation. See, for example, Deibner and Bénard (1957). Heating wines in the wood resulted in no decrease in potential if the container was not tightly sealed. Joslyn (1949) found the potential decreased while heating shermat in large containers. These procedures, which are now very general for standard quality wines in this state and abroad, do result in earlier maturation. They often contribute little to the intrinsic character or quality of the finished wine. This is to be expected since the initial quality is not high and further aging by the traditional methods would not result in a proportionate increase in quality.

Most procedures involve some induced oxidation: exposure to sunlight or ultra-violet light, aeration at low temperature to allow easier oxygen absorption followed by raising the temperature to induce oxidation, use of ozone, hydrogen peroxide, catalysts, etc. Many of the treated wines have a "faded" or "over-aged" character which is unpleasant. Even dessert wines, such as port and muscatel, which have been so treated have not been of notable quality. Addition of oak shavings or chips (with or without aeration) hastens maturation of dessert wines. The results may be disappointing if the amounts are not carefully controlled. We should emphasize that this does not mean that these may not be useful applications of such materials or processes under *controlled* conditions.

In all rapid aging methods it must be borne in mind that, while oxygen and heat are the most useful known agents to hasten aging of wine, either can be overdone very easily, resulting in serious injury or spoiling of the product. Each wine behaves differently; a given treatment may improve one and spoil another. Therefore, rapid aging cannot be applied by rule of thumb, but must be used with intelligence, skill, and care, adapting the severity of the various treatments to the product at hand. Much progress can be expected in this area. See especially Singleton (1959).

Working with a variety of types of wines Singleton and Draper (1963) did not find ultrasonic treatment to give desirable results. Often a "scorched" flavor was imparted to the wine by the treatment. Even when combined with various gas treatments (nitrogen, air, carbon dioxide, oxygen, hydrogen) the results were disappointing.

Use of ionizing radiation has been frequently attempted on wines, with varying claims of success. Paunovic (1963) reported negative results when lethal activity was attempted but recommended further experimentation.

PROCESSING

A central area, temperature-controlled for comfort of workmen, should be provided outside the storage area. This will include pumps, heat exchangers, filters, pasteurizers, fining tanks, centrifuges, ion exchange columns, blending devices, flow meters, in-line strippers to remove oxygen, and other equipment used in the modern winery. These should be arranged with a central control panel so that wine from any part of the winery can be processed without contamination with other wine. For the smaller winery rubber hoses may be used for transfer of wine from one container to another or to and from the processing equipment.

Special rooms for vermouth or flavored wine production may be needed in the larger wineries. The sparkling wine department may require a variety of facilities: bottling room, fermenting room for tanks or bottles, aging room, riddling area, disgorging area, and labeling, storage and shipping rooms. Low temperature rooms, refrigeration equipment, special filters, and other equipment may be needed.

Pumps

A variety of pumps are available for special uses in the winery. All should be made of stainless steel.

Piston pumps are the oldest pumping principle. They need little care, last a long time and are little affected by foreign matter in the wine. They have a good suction and efficiency and can be buffered against irregular operation by an air regulator. They can be used for all kinds of work, especially where there is a considerable difference in height. Piston pumps for wine handling up to 5000 gallons per hour are made. Both single and double action piston pumps are manufactured. Lees are often pumped with single cylinder double-acting reciprocating piston-type pumps.

Centrifugal pumps are the most used pumps and are especially good where there is a large counter pressure and a non-pulsating pressure is required. These are made with a number of modifications—self-priming and non-self-priming and these can be single speed or variable speed. They can be mounted on wheeled trucks or permanently installed, as at sumps. They can be controlled by valves at the inlet or at the outlet by means of a by-pass. They are especially used as must pumps.

Gear and rotary pumps are similar in outward appearance to centrifugal pumps and depend on revolving gears or impellers to force the wine through the line. These have found wide use in modern wineries.

For maintaining a vacuum on the vacuum pan used in concentrating grape must, various types of vacuum pumps are used. Probably the most satisfactory is the steam jet vacuum pump which develops and maintains a high vacuum by the passage of high pressure steam past an orifice connecting to the vacuum line. The old style vacuum pans built before Prohibition were usually equipped with steam driven, large bore, piston vacuum pumps that handle both the condensate, and the air and other gases from the pan. They maintained only a rather poor vacuum, usually about 25 in., and have now been largely replaced. Modern vacuum pans are equipped with a barometric condenser to handle the condenser water and condensate from the pan; while the steam jet handles only the non-condensable gases, air chiefly, from the must and air leakage.

Rotary vacuum pumps are similar in principle and design to the familiar laboratory vacuum pump used for laboratory filtrations, operation of vacuum drying ovens, etc. Special vanes, revolving rapidly in oil in a closely fitting cylindrical housing, maintain a high vacuum although this pump will not handle much water or condensable vapors without excessive wear and loss of vacuum. They are intended to handle dry gases.

All pumps should be operated at the pressure and speed suggested by the manufacturer, or as determined by trial, for best efficiency. Positive-displacement pumps are used in vacuum-type automatic bottling machines. The stainless steel impeller bump type or the rubber impeller type such as are used in canneries are also used in wineries.

Transfer Lines

Musts and wines are transported about the winery through metal pipes, rubber hoses, or glass tubes.

The best metal for pipes is stainless steel. It is expensive and hence is used more for wines than for musts. The large must lines should be lined with an inert material. Glass pipes are practicable and permanent though somewhat expensive. They should be installed so that they can be easily drained. Aluminum pipes have been used satisfactorily with musts.

Rubber hoses are standard equipment in California wineries. They are made in a wide variety of sizes. Only those lined with odorless rubber should be used for wine. Rubber hoses become stained with wine after use and should be cleaned occasionally. A dilute warm solution of citric acid or a mild hot detergent can be used. Trial is sometimes needed to find the proper agent. When not in use rubber hoses should always be placed in racks at an angle so that they will drain dry.

Refrigeration

New wines are supersaturated with respect to potassium acid tartrate. As Marsh and Joslyn (1935) have shown the excess tartrate will usually precipitate if enough time is allowed, or if the temperature is reduced sufficiently for shorter periods of time.

In most northern European countries the cold winters chill the wines sufficiently to cause satisfactory separation of excess cream of tartar; but under Mediterranean or Californian conditions detartration is so slow, especially in the very large tanks in the warm interior valley wineries, that it is customary to resort to artificial refrigeration of the wine to near its freezing point or to use ion-exchangers; (see Skofis 1953). The temperatures employed are 22° to 25°F. for table wines and 15° to 19°F. or slightly lower for fortified dessert wines.

However, at low temperatures, the wine dissolves oxygen to a greater degree than at room temperature, resulting in rapid aging through oxidation when the wine is returned to the warm cellar temperatures. This is a disadvantage for many table wines but may not be harmful for certain dessert wines, and may even be somewhat beneficial for many dessert wines.

Some wineries store the refrigerated wine in tanks located in a cold room. This is the most expensive system. However, if a longer storage period is possible the minimum temperature need not be so low. Others refrigerate the wine to near the freezing point by pumping it from a large tank through a tubular refrigerator, usually direct-cooled with Freon or ammonia, and returning it to the tank until the desired low temperature is attained. The temperature then rises slowly and, when it reaches about 32°F., it is refrigerated again. Some wineries use auxiliary brine cooled coils in the tanks to maintain the desired temperature after attaining it by an outside refrigerating unit. The refrigerating tubes and coils should be of stainless steel. Storage periods of about two weeks at 25°F. are usually employed for table wines and slightly lower temperatures for dessert wines, though Berg and Keefer (1958–1959) have shown that this is often inadequate.

Marsh and Guymon (1959) have given an excellent presentation of the behavior of tartrates in wine and of methods of stabilization of wine against deposition of tartrates after bottling. The two common methods in use for this purpose are refrigeration and the use of ion exchange resins. Three methods are in use for applying refrigeration, namely, (a) the method in which the cooling apparatus is mounted in the chilling tank, (b) that in which it is mounted externally to the tank, and (c) that in which the tanks are located in a refrigerated room. In method (c) the wine is usually refrigerated by external cooler as it flows from storage to the chilling room. The freezing point of table wines is usually between 20° and 22°F. and of dessert wines between 12° and 17°F. Marsh and Guymon (1959) point out that while a period of 15 days storage of the wine at within one degree of its congealing temperature may often be adequate, a rise of only a few degrees markedly prolongs the required time of storage. This is one of the chief disadvantages of the first two. They state also that in these two methods uniform temperature throughout the contents of the tank is seldom attained because of the often large difference in temperature of the wine near the top of the tank and that near the bottom.

Pipes or hollow plates are used in the coolers. There is a tendency for water to separate on the cooling pipes or plates, especially if the difference in temperature between the refrigerant and wine is great, thus reducing their efficiency. The solubility of cream of tartar not only decreases with decrease in temperature but also with increase in alcohol content. However, as Marsh and Guymon (1959) point out, the rate of separation of cream of tartar at low temperatures is more rapid in table than in dessert wines and more rapid in white than in red wines. Precipitation rate at best is slow and the wine should, therefore, be held within one degree of its congealing point for at least 15 days. However, they state that the same result can be attained in 3 or 4 days if the wine is completely congealed throughout the refrigeration period. Storage time can also be shortened by seeding the wine with clean crystals of potassium bitartrate and by mild agitation. Chilling is not so effective in removing excess calcium tartrate as potassium bitartrate.

The response of wines to refrigeration varies greatly not only between types but even between wines of the same type. Berg *et al.* (1968) point out that only with periodic sampling and laboratory analysis is it possible to ascertain the rate of potassium bitartrate deposition and the total amount removable within a given period of refrigeration. Therefore, they suggested that the wine be analyzed for potassium and tartrate content before and after four and six days of refrigeration, and the decrease in values be used to determine whether it is worthwhile to continue refrigerating for potassium bitartrate removal.

The external refrigerating units are usually of the single pass shell-and-multitube type, Fig. 76, the wine flowing through the tubes (or plates) and the refrigerant expanding into the shell. The wine is circulated through the refrigerating unit until it reaches the desired temperature. Marsh and Guymon (1959) state that wine in tanks (not in a refrigerated room) warms more rapidly than usually believed. Therefore, they suggest that the refrigeration load be carried by two units instead of one; one to rapidly cool the wine to refrigeration temperature and a second, smaller unit to maintain that temperature. Approximately ten tons of mechanical refrigeration capacity is required to hold 30,000 gallons of wine at 16°F.

A refrigerant should be used that will not damage the wine in case of a leak in the refrigerating unit. The unit should be made of metal that is not attacked by the wine. The surface of the plates or pipes of the unit may become coated with tartrates, a condition that reduces efficiency, but the coating is easily removed with dilute alkaline solution.

Schreffler (1952) has emphasized the importance of efficient use of mechanical refrigeration equipment in the winery as a means of reducing costs. Under average winery conditions one ton of refrigeration (12,000 B.t.u. per hour) should require 1.0 to 1.3 horsepower applied to the compressor. The actual over-all operating efficiency of a unit can be determined by measuring the temperature drop and the volume of wine being cooled and then calculating the number of B.t.u. being removed per hour. This is checked against the ammeter reading of the motor to find the relative amount of work being done by the compressor. The efficiency of heat exchangers is greatly reduced by deposits of tartrates or other material. Passing wine through the cooler at high velocity reduces the tendency to deposit tartrates. Schreffler also notes that if the velocity of some tubes is less than that of others they may become completely clogged thus reducing the effective capacity of the unit.

Efficient oil separators with baffles and regular draining of the separators are also recommended for ammonia systems to increase efficiency. For water-cooled heat exchangers removal of algae and scale is necessary to prevent reduced capacity. Expansion valves should be sufficiently large so no back pressure is built up. Finally, Schreffler recommends that insulated storage tanks be used to hold the wine being cooled so that when the wine reaches the desired temperature it may be held constant at this temperature by the use of a small refrigerating unit with cooling coils in the tank. The larger unit can then be used for another lot of wine. This procedure obviously increases the processing capacity of the plant.

Plate-type heat exchangers recover some of the refrigeration from wine being removed from cold storage, as much as 50 to 60 per cent. This is usually done by passing the cold wine through the heat exchanger directly from the filter. This, however, may cause back pressure and slow down flow through the filter. In this case a pump may be connected to the discharge side of the heat exchanger to increase flow. Plate-type heat exchangers should be cleaned carefully at frequent intervals to prevent accumulation of deposits in the plates.

The use of a refrigerated room is the most satisfactory and most expensive system. In order to avoid undue fluctuation of temperature in the room the wine is usually passed through a shell- and tube-cooler on entering the room.

When brandy aged at above 101° proof is reduced to 84° proof with water a precipitation of some alcohol-soluble water-insoluble wood extractives occurs. Usually, therefore, the brandies are held at 15° to 25°F. for 1 to 14 days. The insoluble materials are much more soluble at higher temperatures so the precipitate must be filtered off at a low temperature. According to Marsh and Guymon (1959) the only advantage for chilling more than 1 or 2 days is to allow the sediment to settle and thus facilitate filtration.   The high viscosities of water-alcohol mixtures at low temperatures also makes them difficult to filter.

Ion Exchangers.—Since refrigeration is a costly process, at present there is much activity in both Europe and California in the use of ion exchange resins to remove excess potassium and calcium from wines.   It is customary to remove the excess potassium and calcium ions, replacing them with either sodium or hydrogen ions; excess tartrate can also be removed.

The first ion exchange substances used on an industrial scale were the naturally-occurring mineral zeolites.   They were used chiefly in the treatment of water.   They are hydrated silicates.   The formula of a typical

Courtesy of Societé Unicoop and Cognac "Prince de Polignac"

FIG. 76.   MODERN REFRIGERATION EQUIPMENT IN A FRENCH
WINERY

Note sanitary features

zeolite, Thompsonite, is $NaCa_2Al_5(SiO_4)_56H_2O$.   The zeolites have the property of exchanging alkali ions for calcium, magnesium, and other cations in solution.   Eichorn mentioned by Fessler (1958), in 1858 found that the process is reversible, that is, the zeolite that has taken up calcium, magnesium, etc. and given up sodium or potassium can be regenerated by treatment with sodium chloride solution, or mineral acid or alkali.

Certain synthetic resins are also capable of exchanging ions.   High capacity cation exchange resins can be prepared as sulfonic acid resins. Polyamine type resins with anion exchange properties are produced (Kunin and Myers, 1950).   Dorfer (1970) gives practical directions.

If a cation resin is regenerated by treatment with strong sodium chloride solution, the resin is then in the sodium form and will exchange sodium for the potassium, magnesium, and calcium of the wine; if regenerated with an acid, it will be in the hydrogen form and will exchange hydrogen ions for the calcium, magnesium, potassium, and certain other positive ions. The sodium cation resins have little effect on the pH value of the wine, whereas, acid resins (hydrogen resins) lower the pH value appreciably.

The chemical reactions for the action of a sodium-exchange resin are as follows where Z represents the resin:

$$CaSO_4 + Na_2Z \rightarrow CaZ + Na_2SO_4$$
$$2KH(C_4H_4O_6) + Na_2Z \rightarrow K_2Z + 2NaH(C_4H_4O_6)$$

In regenerating the resin, the scheme is as follows:

$$K_2Z + 2NaCl \rightarrow 2KCl + Na_2Z$$

The potassium chloride is leached out and discarded in the sodium chloride brine. The reactions for the cation resin in acid form are similar, with hydrogen replacing the sodium. When the acid form of the resin is used, sodium also is removed from the wine or other liquid and is replaced by hydrogen ions. Thus, wine treated with the acid or hydrogen form of the resin becomes more acid in reaction and lower in pH value. Such wine may then be too tart but might be blended with wine of lower acid content. Or a mixture of the acid and sodium forms of the resin could be used. The use of ion-exchange resins is now permitted by the state and federal wine regulatory agencies.

The resin is generally used in a column (a tall, narrow tank) and the wine is usually allowed to flow downward through the resin. However, the resin may also be added directly to the wine. Only about 30 per cent of the capacity of the resin is realized in this case, according to McGarvey et al. (1958), and the resin is used but once. With the column method the resin is regenerated after use and lasts indefinitely. Thus, it is much more economical in its use of resin than is the batch method. The latter is primarily for use in smaller wineries in which the cost of a permanent installation of stainless steel columns and connections might not be justified. With a column the uppermost portions are continuously receiving fresh wine and on that account the procedure results in a fully exhausted exchanger, starting from the top downward.

Percival et al. (1958), Dickinson and Stoneman (1958), Moser (1956), Rankine and Bond (1955), Ribéreau-Gayon et al. (1956), and McGarvey et al. (1958) have presented the basic principles for the treatment of wines with ion-exchange resins and their practical use in the winery. They generally recommend the columnar method for the reasons previously given.

The tall stainless steel tank is filled with an appropriate cation resin found to be effective by the manufacturer. Water covers the resin in the column and must be displaced by wine. Each cubic foot of resin will introduce about 0.7 gallon of water. This displacement of the water is done by upward flow of the wine to be treated, the flow being at the rate about 0.5 gallon per minute per square foot of cross section area.

After the wine has been introduced in the above manner to displace the water and air in the interstices between the resin beads, the direction of wine flow is reversed, i.e., wine is introduced into the top of the column and flows downward at the rate of 2 to 2.5 gallons per cubic foot of resin. This is continued until the resin no longer removes potassium from the wine satisfactorily (as determined by chemical analysis).

At this point the wine remaining in the column is drained off, the amount remaining in the bed, chiefly in the spaces between the beads, will be about 0.7 gallon per cubic foot of resin. This wine is displaced by a volume of water equal to the volume of resin, the wine being diluted somewhat in this process. The diluted wine may be returned to process or used for distilling material.

As the beads act as a filter, considerable solids may accumulate during a run. Therefore, the bed should be backwashed with water at a flow rate of 4 to 6 gallons per minute until the effluent is quite clear. The time required is usually about 30 minutes. The bed is allowed to settle and is then regenerated.

A brine containing ten per cent of sodium chloride is prepared. About 10 to 15 lbs. of sodium chloride as a 10 per cent solution will be required for each cubic foot of resin. A flow rate of about $1/2$ gallon per minute per cubic foot of resin is recommended by the manufacturer. After regeneration the bed should be rinsed with water to displace all the brine remaining in the column. About 40 gallons of water will be required for each cubic foot of resin. Rinsing is continued until the effluent no longer possesses any taste of salt or until a qualitative test for chloride is very faint or practically negative. The water remaining in the column is displaced with wine in the manner previously described and the cycle started again. If the column is not to be used again at once, the resin should be left in water and sufficient sulfur dioxide added to prevent growth of microorganisms.

The removal of potassium ions by the exchange resin is instantaneous, according to Percival et al. (1958). Almost complete removal of the potassium from the resin is attained during regeneration with sodium chloride and calcium and magnesium are completely removed. The treated wine contains sodium approximately equivalent to the potassium, calcium, and magnesium removed by the resin. Sodium bitartrate is, of course, much more soluble than potassium bitartrate.

Percival *et al.* (1958) list the following advantages of the ion exchange procedure over chill proofing for stabilization of wine: (1) the capital investment is about one-tenth of that required for refrigeration; (2) labor costs are less or not any greater than in chill proofing; (3) operating costs are low, as pumping costs of ion exchange are lower than refrigerant compression cost of chill proofing; (4) low hold-up time 3 to 4 hours per cycle compared to weeks in chill proofing; (5) ion exchange is independent of the type of wine and gives complete stabilization in respect to potassium bitartrate and calcium tartrate.

Fessler (1958) using a small column built to the scale of commercial installations and holding five gallons of wine obtained the following results:

Type of Wine	Potassium before Treatment	Potassium after Treatment	Cold stability Before Treatment	Cold stability After Treatment	Total Acid[1] before Treatment	Total Acid after Treatment
	P.p.m.	P.p.m.			G./100 Ml.	G./100 Ml.
Dry white	801	144	Unstable	Stable	0.603	0.583
Dry red	1310	234	Unstable	Stable	0.522	0.506

[1] The red table wine was of pH 3.73 before and 3.72 after treatment.

He observed that by blending treated and untreated wines, in each case of the same lot, that potassium stability was attained at 500 p.p.m. for the dry white and dry red wines used in the experiments. The sulfur dioxide content was changed very little by the exchanger treatment. The calcium content was reduced to a negligible amount. With a sodium cation resin the iron content of four white table wines before treatment was 3.8, 5.0, 5.0, and 6.0 p.p.m. and after treatment 3.2, 4.0, trace, and 3.8 p.p.m., respectively. With the acid form of the resin a white wine of 6.0 p.p.m. iron was reduced to 1.4 p.p.m. For red table wines the results were similar. The disadvantage of the acid resin is, of course, that it greatly lowers the pH. With two white wines of 0.6 p.p.m. of copper before treatment, the values after treatment with the sodium resin were 0.5 and 0.4 p.p.m.; with the acid resin no copper remained.

Du Plessis (1964) treated two South African musts (pH 3.6 and 3.7) with ion exchange resins in the hydrogen cycle, reducing the pH to 3.2, 3.0 and 2.8. However, the quality was decreased by the treatment probably because of the high tartaric acid in the wine (especially for Riesling). Gerasimov and Kuleshova (1965) and others have observed nearly or complete removal of thiamin by either sodium or hydrogen form cation exchangers or by bentonite fining. From 12 to 40 per cent of the pantothenic acid was removed by the ion exchangers, 17 to 35 per cent of the pyridoxine and 48 to 84 per cent of the nicotinic acid but the inositol and biotin was not affected. Bentonite removed 70 per cent of the pyridoxine and nicotinic acid but did not affect pantothenic acid. Ion exchangers change the content of inositol and biotin only slightly.

Fessler (1958) believed the sodium form of exchange resins would be of definite value in reducing the iron content of wines, but agrees with Joslyn and Lukton (1953) that their value for reducing the copper content is doubtful. A specific resin for copper removal is now available.

With a sodium-cycle ion exchanger, Permutit Q, Mindler et al. (1958) found no change in alcohol, total acidity, fixed acidity, or pH. They also claimed that treated wines resisted oxidation better than non-treated. The claim that there was sufficient reduction in copper, iron and calcium to avoid metal cloudiness is not borne out by commercial practice as usually only a small portion of the iron and copper are removed. Also, in practice, the pH goes up. Anion resins are available that will remove excess oxidized color from wine (see McGarvey et al. 1958).

According to Berg (1957) the ion-exchange treatment of wines was at that time in use in Italy, and under intensive study in France, Germany, Switzerland, Austria, and Portugal. Marsh (1959) believes that ion exchangers will in time be in use in all wine-producing countries. Continuous column exchangers are less expensive than the batch process. Not all the wine is run through the ion exchanger—only enough so that when blended back to the main lot the average potassium content will be below some critical value. Berg and Keefer (1958–1959) have given data on this level (p. 565). One large plant in California is treating all of its wines by the ion-exchange method. It also uses it for reducing the potassium, calcium, and magnesium content of grape juice to be bottled and of juice for grape concentrate. Both anion and cation ion exchangers are being used in the wine industry (Fig. 77), usually after refrigeration. Cation exchanges must be used judiciously so as not to reduce unduly the potassium content and increase the sodium.

Ion exchange is also used in the processing of fruit juices. One of the problems is the regenerant cost. Popper and Nury (1964) used calcium tartrate as the recoverable regenerant. There was little change in pH or flavor. Ion-exchange treated wines frequently fine poorly with bentonite according to Rankine and Emerson (1963). They recommend fining with sodium bentonite prior to ion-exchange treatment. If this is not possible, the bentonite fining should be accompanied by addition of gelatin.

Filtration

With the introduction of large filter presses filtration has become the predominant method of clarifying wines after racking in California. Filtration is a physical process, that is, it mechanically removes suspended

Courtesy of Valley Foundry and Machine Works, Inc.

Fig. 77. Two Resin and One Brine Solution Ion Exchange
Tanks in a California Winery

material through filtration through a small pore size filter pad. Adsorption on the filter aid and filter is also a factor in filtration, particularly with asbestos pad filters. In practice, the deposited material also acts as a filter material as it is deposited on the filter pad. If nothing is done to keep the pad pores open, the filter surface will soon be reduced to a point where pressure builds up and the volume passing through diminishes. In practice this is prevented by continuously adding a filter aid to the wine to be laid down on the pad with the yeast and other suspended material in the wine. Most filter aid materials are diatomaceous earths which, because of their irregular shaped components, are effective in increasing the period of efficient filter operation. For a general discussion of wine filtration see Geiss (1952, 1957) and Ribéreau-Gayon (1935).

While most wines eventually become fairly clear, and some even brilliant by natural settling and clearing, the majority require at least one filtration; usually two or more. The most important variable in filtration is clarity. Use of in-line turbidity measuring devices, such as the LT-150 of Agricultural Control Systems Inc., are therefore recommended. This instrument utilizes a forward scattering system which ratios the forward scattered light from the light source to that of the direct transmitted beam. Because a very thin ribbon of light is used any bubbles that are present pass through it rapidly and the "blip" they cause can be removed electronically.

Pressure-drop and flowrate are both related to filter performance. Recording the pressure differences across the filter is a useful practice since it detects sudden changes in operation which are almost always associated with poor clarity.

The capacity of a filter depends on (1) the size of the filter surface (which depends on the dimensions and the number of plates used) and (2) the porosity of the filter sheets. Filters of very small size with few plates as well as those 4 x 4 feet size and with as many as 200 plates are available. Some are portable, Fig. 78, while others are fixed in position.

Filters can be operated at constant pressure or constant volume of flow. The latter is preferable for rough filtration but to achieve a constant flow a flow-measuring device to regulate a variable speed drive pump is necessary. For adding diatomaceous earth slurry proportionating pumps can be used.

A mixing tank may also be used into which the proper amount of filter aid is added continuously and mixed with the wine, Fig. 79. There are

Courtesy of Valley Foundry and Machine Works, Inc.

FIG. 78.   PORTABLE FILTER PRESS

Note drip pan and vari-speed turbine-type pump

FIG. 79.   MODERN FILTER PRESS WITH FILTER-AID MIXING TANK
(LEFT)

also injection systems which inject the proper amount of filter aid directly
into the line between the pump and the filter.

Filters should be made of stainless steel or other inert material. The
plates are often made of plastic or other light material to facilitate handling.

In order to reduce filtration costs attention should be paid to preclarifi-
cation. Bentonite fining, centrifuging, and reducing the temperature are
means to this end. Also, one should never filter from the bottom of the
tank but the clear wine should be filtered first and the cloudy wine last.

Bulk Filtration.—At one time, pulp filters were commonly used for bulk
filtration of wines but at present most large California wineries use filter
presses or leaf filters for this purpose.

Pulp filters consist essentially of several thick discs of cotton pulp, separated by metal screens, all housed in a metal cylinder. Pulp filters are
now seldom used in California wineries.

Filter presses consist of hollow metal frames and fluted plates attached
to a metal frame. The metal used must be corrosion-resistant so that it
does not affect the wine. Aluminum, or an aluminum alloy, is often used
as it is light and resistant but some metal pickup occurs. Between the
frames and plates special canvas sheets usually protected by a paper sheet
are placed for bulk filtration. The plates and frames are tightened by a
heavy screw so that the filter cloth and plates are leakproof. On its way
to the filter press the wine is mixed continuously with infusorial earth filter aid such as Hyflo Super-Cel or Filter-Cel in a small metal mixing tank.
Too much filter aid should not be used. The amount will vary with the

type and cloudiness of the wine. A filtering surface builds up on the cloth as the filter aid is deposited. The wine is forced through the filter press by a non-pulsating gear pump or centrifugal pump. When filtration becomes slow, the filter press is taken down and the cloths replaced with fresh ones while the used ones are washed. Filter presses are convenient to set up, clean to use, and have great filtering capacity. See Figs. 77 and 79 for illustration of typical filter presses.

Leaf filters consist of several hollow screens inside a metal cylinder. The screens are supported by an inner metal frame. All metal used in the filter is stainless steel or other corrosion-resistant metal or alloy. A pre-coat of filter aid is deposited on the screens by pumping wine or water heavily charged with filter aid through the filter. Then the wine to be filtered is mixed continuously with a little filter aid and is pumped through the filtering layer of filter aid on the screens. These filters are very convenient, have good capacity, and do a satisfactory job of filtration but the screens are expensive and easily injured. They also become dirty and uneven coating and poor filtration results. If not thoroughly cleaned they may become a source of contamination. One advantage of the leaf filters is that the screen can be cleaned by simply reversing the direction of flow of the liquid. Filter presses, however, have become the dominant bulk filter of the industry. For bulk wines, often a final filtration through a filter press or leaf filter will suffice.

Polishing Filtration.—Wine to be bottled should be brilliantly clear, and even if fined brilliantly clear it will usually contain small "flecks" of coagulated fining agent. Therefore, it is customary to give the wine a finishing or polishing filtration shortly before bottling. It is essential in conducting a polishing filtration to avoid undue aeration as it may cause clouding or injure flavor, bouquet, or color; and it is also essential to avoid contamination of the wine with metals that may cause haziness, such as copper, tin, zinc, and iron. The metal parts of the filter should be made of stainless steel or other corrosion-resistant alloy. Also it is necessary to avoid contaminating the wine with calcium salts from the filter pads; or with off-flavors from the new pads. This has been a source of trouble in the past.

The usual polishing filter consists of a series of hollow metal plates mounted on a frame, and between the metal plates are placed thin filter pads, made of asbestos fiber and cotton filter pulp or heavy filter paper. As noted above the pads may become a source of contamination of the wine with calcium salts, with subsequent clouding of the wine or deposition of calcium tartrate crystals. Therefore, in case of doubt, a dilute solution (one per cent) of citric acid should be passed through the pads after the filter is set up, in order to remove calcium and earthy flavors. This is followed by circulating water and draining. The pads are available in various porosities, i.e., degrees of tightness or density. The coarser the texture or density, the more rapid the filtration rate and the less brilliant the appearance of the wine. The wine is pumped through the filter pads by non-pulsating centrifugal pumps. The German Seitz filter was the pioneer pad filter in this field and many are still used. There are now, however, several very good American makes of pad filters.

A polishing filter more generally used in France than in the United States is the porous candle filter. It consists of a number of hollow porous porcelain or carbon tubes attached to a hollow plate and housed in a stainless steel sheet metal cylinder. The wine is pumped through the candles, generally without use of a filter aid. The candles are cleaned by reversing the flow of liquid (water), after use and by treatment with soda ash solution or other detergent to loosen and remove colloidal deposits from the pores. One advantage of the candles is that they may be used repeatedly whereas filter pads can be used only once. These are known as Pasteur filters.

The screen filter, if used with a polishing grade of filter aid at low pressure, can also be employed as a polishing filter for some wines, particularly dessert types, but is not so efficient as the pad filters.

Sterilization Filtration.—The Seitz Co. of Bad Kreuznach, Germany, demonstrated a number of years ago that wine and fruit juices can be rendered sterile, germ- or yeast-free, by filtration through sterile, very tight filter pads such as that company's special EK pads. The most recent Seitz process of sterile filtration includes three stages: sterilizing, filling, and corking (Figs. 80 and 81). Sterilizing of the bottles is accomplished by use of sulfur dioxide gas, by removal of the gas with sterile water, filling under pressure, and corking with sterile corks. When sulfurous acid solutions are employed to sterilize the bottles the bottles must be well drained in order to prevent excessive pickup of sulfur dioxide. Even with a two minute draining cycle a sulfur dioxide pickup of 60 mg. per bottle has been noted. A number of American makers of filters now have sterilizing pads available. The filter plates, pipes, hose lines, etc., beyond the filter to the bottling machine, and the latter, and the bottles and corks, must, of course, be sterilized and kept sterile during filtration and bottling.

Whenever sterile filtration is to be used the following precautions must be taken: (1) the filter and all the lines, bottling equipment and corks and bottles must be sterile and (2) sterilizing agent should not remain in the bottles or filter to contaminate the wine. The filter, pump, and lines can be sterilized with steam but dilute solutions of quaternary ammonium agents are often used. The bottles, corks, and special bottling machine are sterilized by rinsing with a strong sulfur dioxide solution and then with sterile water. In the best installations the entire filtration, bottling and

Courtesy of Seitz-Werke, Kreuznach

FIG. 80.   FULLY AUTOMATIC STERILE BOTTLING ROOM

From left to right sterilizing, filling, and corking.   The sterilizing
is done with sulfur dioxide gas

Courtesy of Seitz-Werke, Kreuznach

FIG. 81.   STERILE BOTTLING ROOM FOR HAND OPERATION

Note rotary table in wall for introduction of bottles.   The machine
in the background is a semi-automatic rotary filter and on the right
is a semi-automatic corking machine, capacity 1400 bottles per hour

corking is done in a small room which can be sterilized. One secret of success is to operate at a low, even filtration pressure. This means that the wine should be as nearly brilliant as possible before sterile filtration.

This method of sterilization of wine is useful in the bottling of sweet table wines to render them yeast-free and thus make it unnecessary to use excessive doses of sulfur dioxide in the wine. However, it is a difficult and painstaking procedure and often impracticable in the average winery because of the danger of recontamination with yeast. However, there is no reason why wine cannot be successfully sterile-filtered if the winery takes adequate precautions. The candle filter can be used for the same purpose but the same problems of operating under sterile conditions arise.

Peynaud and Domercq (1959) reported sterile filtration of fine Bordeaux wines "seems to fatigue the wines."

Membrane (Millipore) filters are the latest innovation in sterile filtration. The filters are porous membranes composed of inert cellulose esters. Because of the uniformity of pore size, absolute sterility can be achieved by choosing a filter of the correct pore size. Since pore volume occupies approximately 80 per cent of the total filter volume, extremely large flow rates are obtained provided the wine is prefiltered.

Pasteurization

Both bulk pasteurization and the hot bottling of wine are being less and less used by wine makers throughout the world, and especially in this country. Improved filtration and fining techniques and the rational use of antiseptic agents have made them normally unnecessary. Fine table wines, particularly, should not be pasteurized. Furthermore, the early-maturing table wines being produced today are relatively free of potentially harmful microorganisms and pasteurization is not only unnecessary but often is harmful to the quality of the wine, particularly the color.

Pasteurization is applied in one of three ways, namely, (a) by flash pasteurizing and returning to the storage tank; (b) flash pasteurizing into the final bottle; and (c) pasteurization by heating the filled and sealed bottle. There is also some bulk pasteurization and hot holding at a temperature of 120°F. for several days to stabilize wines—usually dessert types; see Holden (1955) and Pederson et al. (1935).

Bulk pasteurization is used for three purposes; first, to stabilize the wine chemically and physically by coagulating certain heat-coagulable colloids; second, to stabilize it microbiologically by destroying bacteria and yeasts; and third, to hasten aging, particularly of ordinary dessert wines.

Pasteurizers should be constructed of stainless steel and so designed that they can be easily disassembled and cleaned. Two designs are in use in California wineries. The first consists of a tubular heat interchanger made up of several horizontal metal tubes encased in a metal jacket, in which incoming wine is heated nearly to pasteurizing temperature by the outgoing hot pasteurized wine; and of a similar set of tubes heated by steam. All parts of the pasteurizer coming in contact with the wine should be of some metal not attacked by the wine. Particularly corrosive are wines containing appreciable sulfur dioxide. Another objection to the tubular heat exchanger is the difficulty of controlling the time at a given temperature. However, when these are used for bulk pasteurization for bringing the contents of a tank of wine up to a given temperature, they give satisfactory results. They are often used, for example, to bring the wines in the sherry baking tank up to the desired baking temperature.

Courtesy of Wine Institute

Fig. 82. Plate-Type Heat Exchanger and Holding Tanks

A more recent pasteurizer that is rapidly increasing in favor is of the well-known A.P.V. design, which originated in England; similar types manufactured in this country are now available. The heating section consists of a series of hollow plates that are clamped together in a metal frame. Steam or hot water is on one side of each plate to act as a heating medium, and the liquid to be heated is on the other side. A similar set of plates forms the heat interchanger. Heating and cooling are rapid and efficient, and the plates are easily removed for cleaning. One advantage of the plate pasteurizer is that the temperature of the wine can be raised to the desired figure very quickly and held there for a short but determined time. As for the tubular pasteurizer, all parts coming in contact with the wine should be of stainless steel. The two forms of wine pasteurizers (plate and tubular) are shown in Figs. 82 and 83. While the tubular heat exchanger has been used for pasteurizing at the time of bottling the plate pasteurizer is preferred for this purpose.

A third pasteurizer, not at present used for wines, makes use of the heating effect produced by passage of an alternating current against the resistance of a liquid such as milk, wine, or fruit juice. It consists of a rectan-

Courtesy of Valley Foundry and Machine Works, Inc.

FIG. 83.   HEAT EXCHANGER AND PASTEURIZER

gular chamber of which two sides (opposite each other) are made up of carbon which serves as electrodes and two walls of an insulating material, such as Bakelite. The liquid flows through this box between the two plate electrodes while a 110 volt high frequency A.C. current flows between the electrodes. Ordinary 60 cycle current causes considerable hydrolysis with production of off-flavors. See Glazewski and Cruess (1948) and Tracy (1931, 1932). The rate of flow of the liquid and the amperes of current supplied to the electrodes are adjusted (automatically in the large units) to give the desired temperature. The heated liquid, if desired, can be cooled in a standard heat interchanging unit such as is used for the two pasteurizers previously described. The electrodes are at wine temperature. Therefore, there is less superheating than in steam-heated pasteurizers.

It is possible that megathermic (electronic) heating, by means of passing the wine between the plates of an electronic heating device supplied with very high frequency (about 15,000,000 cycles per second) could be used except for the high cost of equipment and current. It heats liquids almost instantaneously. Yang *et al.* (1947) have studied this method.

In the best method of flash pasteurizing wine in bulk, it is heated for about one minute to 180° to 185°F. and is then cooled continuously against the incoming wine and water or refrigerant cooled pipes.

The time x temperature relationship for pasteurization of wines was considered by Sudraud (1963). Vegetative yeast cells are killed at 113° to 122°F. while yeast spores are only killed at 131° to 140°F. See also p. 171.

To stabilize ordinary white dry table and dessert wines, a common method consists in adding about 100 p.p.m. of sulfur dioxide, heating to about 140° to 145°F., adding bentonite, holding at 130° to 120°F. for 1 to 3 days, racking, cooling, and filtering. It is often very effective for removing heat-sensitive proteins.

Most fruit wine produced in the Pacific Coast states is pasteurized to 145°F. (or higher) and bottled hot. Usually, but not always, the bottled wine is cooled rapidly by water sprays to room temperature. At least one large California winery pasteurizes all table wine on its way to the bottling machine.

Fining

Fining is the clarification of a wine or other liquid by adding a substance or substances in solution or suspension which, when added to the wine, react with the tannin, acid, protein or with some added substance to give heavy, quick-settling coagulums. In most cases the fining agent also adsorbs suspended material. All fining agents also exert some clarifying action mechanically as the precipitated material settles. The usual fining agents for wine are gelatin, casein, tannin, isinglass, and bentonite. White of eggs has also been used, as has blood albumen, fresh blood, and skim milk. Blood and skim milk add bacterial nutrients to the wine that may favor growth of spoilage bacteria and may adversely affect the flavor and protein stability.

For best fining small tanks are desirable. This is possible when labor costs are not high but is becoming less and less common in this country. The wines should be low in carbon dioxide. The fining agent (or the fining agent plus constituents from the wine with which it combines) should be heavier than the wine. High acid wines are easier to fine than low acid and dry than sweet. Since the normal suspended materials in wine are negatively charged a positively charged fining agent is preferred. The smallest possible amount of fining agent should be used. The fining agent should be quickly and thoroughly mixed with the wine. A low and especially a constant temperature is important for successful fining. The fining agent should remain in contact with the wine the shortest possible period.

Laboratory Fining Tests.—In order to determine how much of any given fining agent or agents is required for a given wine, small scale fining tests should be made.

For example, it is desired to know how much tannin and gelatin are needed for a certain wine. Have on hand in the laboratory a 1 per cent solution of the tannin dissolved in 100° proof (50 per cent alcohol) brandy, and 1 per cent solution of gelatin in water made by warming 1 gm. of gelatin in water until dissolved, adding 0.5 gm. of citric acid and 0.1 gm. of sodium benzoate as preservative. Then to 100 ml. portions of the wine in 4 oz. bottles add 0.5, 1.0, 1.5, 2.0, 2.5, and 3.0 ml. of tannin, with shaking, and then the same volumes of the gelatin solution. The samples are shaken and allowed to stand several hours. The one showing brilliancy at the lowest concentrations of fining agents is naturally chosen. If none is clear, try a larger volume of tannin in relation to gelatin, also larger amounts of both until the proper ratio and amounts are found; normally one part of gelatin reacts with one of tannin, but for white wines deficient in tannin it may be necessary to use more of tannin than gelatin.

Suppose 1.5 ml. of tannin and 1.5 ml. of gelatin solutions were found best. This represents 0.015 gm. of each per 100 ml.; or 0.15 gm. of each per liter. Since one gallon equals about 3785.4 ml., then the amount of each per gallon is $3.8 \times 0.15 = 0.57$ gm. and for 100 gallons, 100×0.57 or 57 gm. Since an ounce is 29.8 gm., this is roughly 2 ozs.

Similar calculations and laboratory solutions are used for casein, bentonite, and other fining solutions. Casein may be made up as a 2 per cent solution, and bentonite as a 5 per cent suspension in water; both prepared as described later in this chapter.

Tannin and Gelatin Fining.—In the pre-Prohibition era in California the most common fining agents were tannin and gelatin. Gelatin itself has a positive charge in wine and hence precipitates with the negatively charged tannin. Tannin need not be added to pink and red wines. Certain fruit wines of high tannin content fine very well with gelatin alone.

One of the best tannins is that extracted from grape seeds and skins and known commercially as "oenotannin." If well purified, it is nearly free of objectionable odor and flavor. Other tannins used in treating wines are sumac tannin, oak bark tannin, oak gall tannin and purified quebracho tannin. So-called tannic acid, either synthetic or from oak tannin, is also used. The tannin should be free of off-flavor and odor and should impart as little color as possible to the wine. In addition to its use as a fining agent, tannin is also added to wines occasionally to impart a slight astringency, and should be of high purity, such as is U.S.P. tannin and tannic acid. The legal aspect of using tannin should be determined in each case.

Gelatin is made from bones and other by-products of meat packing. For use in the fining of wines it should be of high purity and free of undesirable odors and flavors. As sold in the wine trade, it is frequently in sheet form (Gold leaf and Silver leaf grades) but it is also packed in granular and in powdered form. Weger (1963) preferred commercial 20 per cent liquid gelatine to powdered gelatine because of its easier use and greater brilliancy. Joslyn (1953) has reviewed the chemistry and method of action of gelatin in wine. He reports that commercial gelatin varies in composition. However, when dissolved in water it absorbs 5 to 9 times its weight of water and forms high viscosity sols. This review also noted the importance of pH, temperature, tannin content, aging of the gelatin solution and other factors to the effectiveness of the agent. To obtain a good clarification, especially with white table wines, the gelatin solution must not be subjected to high temperatures. With red wines the addition of gelatin reduces both the color and the tannin content.

In fining a white wine predetermined amounts of gelatin and tannin are weighed out and dissolved separately in two portions of the wine to give about a 1 to 2 per cent solution of each. The wine is warmed to dissolve the gelatin; or the gelatin is dissolved in hot water and then diluted with some of the wine to a two per cent solution. The tannin solution is added first, by adding it slowly to a tub as the wine flows into the tub and is returned to the tank by pumping. The wine should be allowed to rest for 24 hours. The gelatin solution is then added in similar fashion after the tannin has again been well mixed by pumping over. The wine is allowed to settle until clear; usually 2 or 3 weeks. The temperature throughout the cask should be kept constant during fining with organic fining agents. Therefore, small casks give the best clarification. It is then racked and given a polishing filtration. In fining a white wine care should be taken not to aerate it too vigorously as this may damage the color, flavor, and bouquet. Because of the danger of overfining and the resulting persistent cloudiness which results white wines, either table or dessert, are nowadays seldom fined with gelatin. When used about 1 to 2 ozs. each of tannin and gelatin per 100 gallons are sufficient. According to Kean and Marsh (1956) the addition of gelatin to a wine increases its protein content and hence its susceptibility to copper casse.

Red wines are sometimes fined with this agent, especially where the wine is excessively high in tannin. Addition of gelatin will, however, lighten the color consequently it should be used cautiously. Two ounces per 100 gallons is a common amount but the correct quantity should be determined by laboratory tests.

Casein.—Casein is the principal protein of milk and of cheese. It is sold as a powder or granular product, made from skim milk by precipitation with acid, washing, draining, drying, and grinding. It is insoluble in acids but is soluble in alkaline solutions. Normal casein is insoluble in water, but a water-soluble modified casein (sodium or potassium caseinate) is available. For use in clarifying wines water-insoluble casein may be dissolved in dilute sodium carbonate or dilute ammonium hydroxide. According to the usual theory when the casein solution is added to wine, the acidity of the latter neutralizes the alkali of the solvent or caseinate and precipitates the casein as a flocculent curd. This precipitate adsorbs and mechanically removes material from the wine as it settles. Sodium and potassium caseinate can be used directly.

A casein solution for laboratory tests is made by first dissolving 0.5 gm. of sodium carbonate per 100 ml. of water and then 2 gm. of casein per 100 ml. Or, better, add about 5 ml. of strong ammonia water to each 100 ml. of water and dissolve in this solution 6 gm. of casein per 100 ml. Then boil off the excess ammonia until the vapors have very little odor of ammonia, cool and dilute to 300 ml. This is a 2 per cent solution that is almost neutral and hence neutralizes very little of the acid of the wine. The range needed for fining wine is usually between one part of casein per 1000 of wine to one per 5000.

It is occasionally advisable to first add to the wine about one-half as much tannin as of casein; preferably 24 hours in advance of the casein. The exact amounts to add should be determined by laboratory tests for each wine. For further information on casein fining see O'Neal *et al.* (1951), Ribéreau-Gayon and Peynaud (1934–1935), Ibarra and Cruess (1948), and Amerine and Joslyn (1951). One of the advantages of casein is that it lightens the color.

Bentonite.—Bentonite is a montmorillonite clay with tremendous swelling properties in water. It is mined in a small area in Wyoming. Though deposits in many other regions, within the United States and abroad, are now being mined and used in the clarification of wines, the Wyoming bentonite is consistently superior. For the fining of dessert wines and most table wines of average quality, bentonite has replaced other fining agents in California. As a fining agent it was first used on honey by Lothrop and Paine (1931). Saywell used it for vinegar and wine in 1934. See Mayer-

Oberplan (1956) concerning bentonite fining of various wine types.

While Ough and Amerine (1960) reported 12.5 lbs. of bentonite per 1000 gallons of must did increase clarity and filter speed and lightened the color of new wines, they did not recommend its use in fermenting musts.

The possible advantages of bentonite fining are protein removal, prevention of copper cloudiness, possible prevention of iron clouding, adsorption of growth factors, oxidases and other materials, and mechanical clarification. The disadvantages are possible exchange of sodium, potassium, calcium, magnesium and other ions, adsorption of red colors, removal of vitamins and amino acids, and excessive sediment.

According to Weger (1965), bentonite can be used as needed in Italy but German law limits it to 1.5 gm. per liter and Austria to 2.0 (also requiring low sodium and iron in 10 per cent acid extracts). He also calls attention to the different properties of calcium and sodium bentonites. Sodium bentonite has greater swelling properties, results in a greater volume of precipitate and less product than calcium bentonite. The amount of protein removed may differ by 60 per cent. They also appear to differ in degree of reduction of acidity and amount of ion exchange. The effects varied between wines. Therefore, Weger recommended clear labeling of bentonites and laboratory testing before use. Weger (1965) preferred gelatine-bentonite as the general fining agent for red wines and albumen-tannin-gelatine-bentonite for whites.

Saywell (1934) recommended preparation of a five per cent suspension of the powdered bentonite in water or wine by sifting the bentonite into the water while stirring it vigorously with a mechanical stirrer. It is stirred for several hours and should be allowed to stand 24 hours or longer to undergo further dispersion. A five per cent suspension is about 42.5 lbs. per 100 gallons of water. Present industry practice is to prepare about an 8 per cent suspension in water and achieve the desired swelling by heating to about 120°F. by introducing steam directly into the suspension. The heating is repeated twice at 24 hour intervals. This procedure is better practice than adding powdered bentonite to the wine or preparing a suspension in water without heating.

The range of bentonite required is about 1:500 to 1:2500; for new cloudy dessert wines the dose is usually 3 to 6 lbs. per 1000 gallons. For well-settled, fairly clear dessert wines about 3 to 5 lbs. is often sufficient. Well-settled dry table wines may require less.

Bentonite is also very useful in case of a failure with gelatin and tannin or casein; it will usually clarify the most recalcitrant wine. It also removes considerable protein according to Kean and Marsh (1956) and Berg (1953). Bentonite has a negative charge in wine and is particularly useful in removing heat-sensitive proteins. Some wine makers warm dessert wines to about 110°F. before adding the bentonite. However, others prefer to clarify at refrigerated temperatures. Berg (1960) reports that bentonite-treated Spanish sherries are more tartrate-stable than non-bentonited wines.

Bentonite has the disadvantage that it gives a rather bulky lees. By combining the bentonite lees from several tanks, further settling will take place and more clear wine can be recovered. The final lees are diluted and distilled for recovery of brandy, or sold to another winery for that purpose if a still is not available.

When properly used bentonite has little or no effect on the flavor and bouquet of table or dessert wines. However, it should be used with caution for the best wines. The recommendation of the Bordeaux school of enologists that some activated charcoal should be added to remove the off-odor of bentonite suggests that it can give a flavor to the wine. Bentonite may be added with a tannin and gelatin or casein fining, where it greatly hastens settling of the other finings.

An impure clay, generally called Spanish clay, from Lebrija, Spain, is very generally used in the Jerez de la Frontera district of Spain in fining sherry wines. X-ray data indicate that it contains considerable montmorillonite, the chief constituent of bentonite. In physical behavior, in water, it resembles bentonite somewhat but has much less swelling power. Also it absorbs water more slowly than does bentonite. It was used in California before Prohibition but has been replaced by bentonite, a superior fining agent.

In fining red and rosé wines with gelatin or bentonite, Bergeret (1963) found that the preferred agent depends on the type and age of the wine. Bentonite removes more color from young wines than gelatin; the opposite is true for old wines. Bergeret considers this to be due to the relatively greater activity of bentonite on the colloidal colored material of young wines. Bentonite is also especially effective (often too much so) in removing color from rosé wines. Generally tannins are better removed by gelatin fining.

Isinglass.—This fining agent is not the mineral "isinglass"; but is a product made from sturgeon and is used only for fine white table wines. It is purchased in thin strips, and is prepared for use by soaking the required amount of the sheet isinglass in wine or water overnight, then rubbing it through a fine screen, followed by stirring, rubbing, etc., in the wine until all lumps disappear; a very tedious job. A Waring blender is very useful to save this hand work. It is diluted with wine to about 1 per cent. It is then ready to use. Tannin may be added to the wine as for gelatin, about 24 hours in advance, but less tannin is required than for gelatin and in some cases may be unnecessary. The general procedure is about as for gelatin and tannin in other respects but isinglass is temperamental and should be used with caution. Furthermore, it is expensive. There is some evidence that isinglass gives a sharp permanent clarification for dry white table wines and, therefore, it has found favor for wines that are to be used for production of sparkling wines. In case of failure, a bentonite fining may be used to remove the finely divided isinglass. No critical experiments on the combined use of a variety of combinations of fining agents seem to have been made.

Egg Albumen.—Fresh egg albumen is seldom used in California although mentioned prominently in some European books. About 4 to 8 egg whites per 100 gallons of wine are recommended. They are beaten to a froth and mixed with about ten volumes of wine before being added to the main volume of wine. About 24 hours previously tannin is usually added to the wine. In laboratory scale tests it does not always give a permanent clarification and it should never be used without prior laboratory tests. At least one California winery prefers it to dry egg albumen.

Dry egg albumen in granular or flake form is commercially obtainable. It is made up into a 1 per cent solution by soaking in cold water overnight and then rubbing until all lumps disappear. It is then used, as is gelatin, with a 1 per cent tannin solution. We prefer gelatin as it is less apt to leave a residue of unstable protein in the wine to precipitate later and cloud the wine. Furthermore, it is difficult to prepare for large scale fining operations.

Use of Pectic Enzymes.—Pectin-hydrolyzing enzymes are used to clarify wines, particularly for fruit wines. The variability of results using pectic enzymes is due, according to Berg (1959A), to differences between the enzymes and to differences between musts. In general, the enzymes increased juice yield, clarity and rate of browning. Pectinol and Pektizyme have proven very satisfactory for this purpose. For enzymes of a standard strength a rate of about 1 gm. per liter or about 0.75 lb. per 100 gallons, or about 7.5 lbs. per 1000 gallons has been recommended. For the more concentrated preparations, the proportionate amount is employed. Also it is very effective, even if the juice is not settled and racked before fermentation; that is, it causes rapid clearing of the wine after fermentation, even without preliminary settling. Also, it is effective if added during fermentation or immediately after fermentation. Berg (1959) found evidence that darkening of many wines occurs if a pectic enzyme is employed before pressing. However, purification of the enzyme preparation has materially reduced the problem.

Blue Fining.—While use of potassium ferrocyanide is not legal in the

United States it is widely, successfully, and legally used in Germany and many other countries. Blue fining (perhaps more correctly known as Möslinger blue fining[7]) is used to remove excess copper, iron, manganese, and zinc from wines. When properly used it is rapid, effective, leaves no residue and helps to clarify the wine, particularly of excessive protein. It can be used in combination with other finishing agents. It is reported to remove or reduce frost taste, decrease the rate of aging (especially important with white wines), and reduces the bacterial count and the susceptibility of the wine to bacterial activity.

When wines are stored on the ferrocyanide precipitate at 59°F. for a month, the free and total cyanide content of the wine remains less than 0.01 mg. per liter according to Tarantola and Castino (1964). At 77°F. however, as much as 0.1 mg. per liter will be found after a month's storage. If excess potassium ferrocyanide is used, much more cyanide is formed. Even so, with a greatly exaggerated excess, the amount of cyanide formed is only 1/60 to 1/120 the lethal dose.

Small amounts of hydrogen cyanide occur in untreated wines. Jaulmes and Mestres (1962) fix the maximum at 0.25 mg. per liter. In three wines fined with potassium ferrocyanide and poorly handled (blue deposit), there were 0.006, 0.05, and 0.015 mg. per liter of free hydrogen cyanide and 0.095, 0.55 and 0.62 mg. per liter of total. They give a sensitive method for its determination. A more complicated procedure is given by Deibner and Mourgues (1963). Their technique permits detection of 0.0625 mg. per liter and recovery appears to be 90 per cent. See p. 717.

Other Agents.—In lieu of blue fining Cufex, a proprietary fining agent is used in this country for removal of excess copper. Its properties and use are described in Chapter 15. Aferrin, mainly magnesium phytate, is also approved for removal of excess iron.

Yeast fining has not been used in this country but it offers certain advantages for new wines of excessive color or off-flavor. About ten per cent of fresh yeast are added to the wine. After about 1 or 2 weeks the wine is centrifuged or filtered. The yeasts not only reduce the rH of the wine but absorb appreciable color and off-odors such as those of molds or frost, etc. Simultaneous use of charcoal and bentonite is often useful.

Charcoal may be used in small amounts to remove off-odors. Government permission is required in certain cases. Various types of activated charcoals are available. The agent which laboratory tests prove best should be used. In evaluating efficiency of charcoals for removal of red or brown colored pigments from wine, Singleton and Draper (1962)

---

[7] Named for the chemist, W. Möslinger, who fought a long battle with the German authorities leading to its acceptance in 1923.

found that there was a general positive correlation of efficiency and ability of the carbon to catalyze the air-oxidation of ascorbic acid. The charcoals did differ from each other and specific tests to determine the most efficient are recommended. The oxidizing property of charcoal can be reduced by adding ascorbic acid, without influencing the decolorizing effect.

Sparkolloid, a proprietary fining agent, is approved for use in this country. It appears to be most useful for pre-bottling clarification. PVPP (polyvinyl-polypyrrolidone) has been approved for fining. It is a detannizing agent. It was recommended for fining California red wines by La Rosa (1958) and Clemens and Martinelli (1958). In a comparative test between PVPP and gelatin Ough (1960A) reported PVPP removed more tannin than gelatin and treated wines were easier to filter. PVPP also removed more color, the amount of sediment was greater, and in color stability tests there was a slight difference in favor of gelatin. There was a slight preference for gelatin-treated wines in sensory tests. De Rosa and Biondo (1959) also reported PVPP inferior to gelatin for white wines. Most enologists are reluctant to recommend gelatin for fining white wines except under special conditions. Tannin adsorption by PVP proceeds efficiently at 43°F. according to Mennett and Nakayama (1970).

Berg (1953) showed a clear relation of grape variety to susceptibility to browning. This was confirmed by Berg and Akiyoshi (1956) although iron and copper generally increased the tendency to browning but some browning occurred even in the absence of these minerals or of sulfur dioxide. Enzymatic action did not seem to be a factor. Caputi and Peterson (1965) showed that at room temperatures Palomino wines darkened readily in the presence of dissolved oxygen while French Colombard darkened in the absence of oxygen. Even with dissolved oxygen the darkening was little influenced by the presence of oxygen unless the temperature was raised. To reduce browning, they found nylon (Nylasent 66 of National Polymer Products) was helpful in some cases but harmful in others. PVPP (Polyclar AT of Antara Chemicals) at the rate of 4 to 6 lbs. per 1000 gallons, was more generally beneficial. Even so, the effect was small in some cases. They concluded that browning is strongly influenced by temperature but the effect is not predictable in the light of our present knowledge.

De Villiers (1961) and Cantarelli (1962) recommended use of nylon paste to improve the color of white wines, to remove browning precursors, to increase resistance to browning, and to reduce anthocyanogen and tannin content. Fuller and Berg (1965) recommended nylon in preference to casein because of its greater protection against browning. Because of its cost it should be recovered and regenerated.

Glucose oxidase has been recommended as an agent for removal of oxygen from dry white table wines. Ough (1960B) found treated wines to be darker than untreated on exposure to air. He did not recommend it.

Deibner and Bénard (1958) were unable to show any removal of iron from wines with sodium alginate. It may be noted that the three wines used were exceptionally high in iron, 97 to 187 mg. per liter.

Martini (1965) has proposed using racemic tartaric acid before refrigerating wines as a method of removing excess calcium. Crystallization was encouraged by pumping over. It should be used only on clear wines.

Jaulmes et al. (1963–64) fined wines with ferrocyanide (20 mg. per liter), bentonite (1 gm. per liter or 8 lbs. per 1000 gallons), gelatin-tannin (100 mg. per liter of each), albumen (1 gm. per liter) and kaolin (3 gm. per liter). There were large losses of vitamins and amino acids, and bentonite caused the greatest losses.

Centrifugation

The possibility of using centrifuges to clarify musts or wines has been recognized for many years. Haushofer (1958) believes that the centrifuge offers advantages for the preparation of grape juice, for reducing the speed of fermentation, and for still wine clarification. Generally they are economically justified in large installations where they can be used almost continuously. Because they aerate the wines considerably it is doubtful if they should be employed for high quality table wines and their use in California is likely to be restricted by their high cost of operation. The mechanical problems that need to be solved in the rational use of centrifuges are (1) to prevent undue aeration with loss of carbon dioxide, aroma and bouquet, and alcohol, (2) to reduce metal contamination, and (3) to keep the cost per gallon as low as possible.

Modern centrifuges specifically designed for fruit juices and wine have now been produced. They appear to be particularly useful for fruit and grape juices, especially if the juice is first pasteurized and then passed through the centrifuge. In some cases these clarified juices have been used for producing wines. This appears to be useful when the grape juice has been made from moldy grapes. New wines or newly-fined wines can be clarified rapidly by centrifugation but whether this is economically sound or not is not known.

Fessler and Nasledov (1951) point out one very real advantage of the centrifuge—the small loss of wine. There is little lees wine, no wine is lost in washing filter pads, and there is no bulky filter wash.

Blending

The blending of wines is one of the most important cellar operations, for upon its proper conduct depends the uniformity of quality and character of each of the cellar's principal brands of wine. The proper function of blending is often misunderstood by the public and even by winery personnel. The primary purposes of blending are to (a) develop specific types and (b) to maintain the character and quality of these types. Mixing of the wine of several casks to equalize the vintage is not considered blending in the sense used here.

Blending is normally not employed where the character and type of the wine are established by the regional origin of the wine and its vintage. Thus most of the products of specific vineyards in Germany, Burgundy, and Bordeaux are not blended but represent solely the product of the vineyards or regions named. Moreover, since the quality varies from year to year the vintages are kept separate from each other. To a lesser extent this is true for varietal type wines, but many are blended and not vintaged, particularly in California.

However, in Spain, Portugal, and many other regions the type depends on judicious blending of wines produced by various production and aging techniques. Obviously wine of a single vintage is impossible under these circumstances. Furthermore, the vintage is often of little importance, as for wines of moderate or standard quality. This applies to many California wines where the ultimate bottler does his own blending from a variety of sources. For a discussion and demonstration of the values of blending see Singleton and Ough (1962).

All of the wines in the cellar should be analyzed regularly before blending. The usual determinations are alcohol, volatile acidity, total acidity, extract, sugar, and tannin. See Chapter 19. Careful tasting should also be done on each of the wines which are to be employed in the blend to establish the characteristic sensory qualities of each.

A sample of the previous blend that is to be matched should be available. This sample must be held in a tightly sealed bottle at a cool temperature. The standard is tasted carefully to fix its qualities in mind. There should also be on hand an analysis of this older blend. Then, with the notes and analyses of previous blends before him, the taster makes up several small blends in the laboratory; taking perhaps 50 ml. of one wine, 40 of another, and 70 of another in order to approximate the quality and composition of the standard. After mixing without undue aeration, the blend is tasted and analyzed carefully and compared with the flavor and composition of the standard blend. By several blends of this sort, one can usually closely approximate the old blend provided, of course, the wines are of the proper types.

From the laboratory blends one decides how much of each of the wines to be blended will be needed. A trial blend of a gallon or two is then made and after a week or two retasted for conformity to the standard.

Triangular taste tests (p. 681) are very useful for establishing the success of the new blend. Success in this case is inability to distinguish the quality and character of the standard from that of the new blend. Suppose the cellar has only 30,000 gallons of one of the wines; this will set the size of the blend. This wine is pumped into the scrupulously clean blending tank and the proper volumes of the other wines are added. After pumping over until well mixed, the blend is tasted and, if found satisfactory, is given a polishing filtration and bottled, barreled, or pumped to the shipping tank car.

Blending is often neglected as a means of producing standard wines. It is generally agreed that for mass distribution wines of uniform quality are most important. Careless blending and failure to maintain such uniform quality and type are reprehensible. Attention is also called to the advantages of fractional blending as a means of maintaining a standard quality and type (p. 415).

Blending should not be practiced indiscriminately. The reputation of a winery can be enhanced by keeping especially fine tanks separate and aging and bottling them under premium labels. The public has demonstrated, in many cases, its willingness to pay for such wines if they are truly of exceptional quality.

BOTTLING

Bottling, labeling, and casing are the final operations that the wine receives at the cellar. At present, most of the larger California wineries bottle their wines at the cellar, although considerable of the State's wine is shipped in tank cars or tank ship to bottling plants throughout the United States. World War II price ceilings and scarcity of wine tank cars combined to increase greatly the bottling of wines at the cellar. This change is generally beneficial to both the industry and the consumer, as it protects both against unscrupulous, inexperienced, and careless bottlers or bulk suppliers. In the past some of these have adulterated wines, or allowed them to spoil before bottling, or otherwise mishandled them through intent or ignorance. However, it may have increased the price of wine to the consumer and it is in almost complete contrast to French, Italian, and Spanish practice where much of the wine is sold in bulk directly to the consumer.

The principal objects of bottling are to protect the wine against spoilage or deterioration by microorganisms and oxygen, to present the winery's customers with dependable wines, and to provide bottle-aged wines to critical consumers.

Good wine can be, and is often, spoiled or damaged by extreme aeration during bottling, or by infection with spoilage organisms, or by improper corking or sealing. Cleanliness and sanitation are extremely important in these operations. Corks should be sterilized and the bottles should be scrupulously clean. In this country new bottles are almost always used.

Bottles

Wine bottles are of many forms and sizes, ranging in size from the 5 gallon demijohn to the small "split," holding only enough wine for an individual serving. They vary in form from the Italian balloon-shaped "fiasco" to the elongated, narrow rhine wine bottle. The bottle should be carefully selected for size, strength, shape, and for freedom from defects. Strength is very important to prevent breakage by present high speed bottling, corking, and capping machines. Recently a number of new shapes have been employed for some California wines.

The glass should be clear white, greenish, greenish-brown or brown for white wines; and dark green or greenish-brown for red or pink wines. It should be free of flaws, strains, and bubbles, and uniform in thickness. Abnormalities in the glass can be readily detected by examining the bottle before a lighted surface through spectacles fitted with polarizing lenses. This is especially important with bottles which must withstand heavy pressures, such as those used for sparkling wines. According to Schanderl (1950–1951) greenish-brown bottles screen out most of the wavelengths of light that induce adverse light-sensitive reactions in wines.

A recent Portuguese experiment with port (Anon 1959) gave very interesting results. They bottled the same port in four different colored bottles: clear glass, green, light chestnut, and dark chestnut bottles. Four light conditions were used, two of each bottle being kept in each of the following: complete darkness, room light, directly in the sun, and five minutes per day of ultra-violet. After two months the potentials measured were as follows (in mV):

	Dark Chestnut	Light Chestnut	Green	Clear	pH
Darkness	326	320	314	300	3.66
Room	358	351	314	332	3.65
Sun	294	290	292	290	3.64
Ultra-violet	350	346	343	334	3.64

The green and clear glass bottled wines also lost part of their color when stored in the sun. The author concludes that reducing conditions are delayed in wines stored in amber-colored glass.

When 1.5 mg. per liter of ascorbic acid were added to another series all bottles reached nearly the same low potential in one month, but again the green and clear glass bottles were somewhat lower, particularly in sun light or with ultraviolet. From these results naturally the chestnut colored bottle was preferred. It filters out more light of the wave lengths of the ultraviolet portion of the spectrum that are responsible for the undesirable photochemical reactions in wines. The transmission of light through different colored bottles is indicated in Fig. 84.

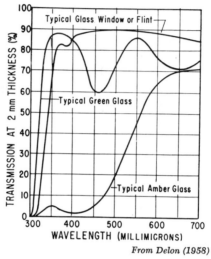

From Delon (1958)

FIG. 84. EFFECT OF COLOR OF GLASS
ON LIGHT TRANSMISSION AT DIFFER-
ENT WAVELENGTHS

The necks of the bottles to be corked should be properly blown to take the corks, that is properly tapered and smooth. The necks of those to be sealed with screw caps should be so threaded that the inner disc of the cap fits tightly on the top of the bottle and the side of the cap is flush with the side of the bottle. Data from our laboratories indicate that screw caps do permit greater access of oxygen and therefore more rapid deterioration of oxygen-sensitive wines, but the harmful effects develop slowly.

Riesling wines are bottled in tall, narrow, long necked, light brown bottles, commonly spoken of as rhine wine bottles. In Germany, Moselle wines are bottled in similar shaped bottles but which are of green or blue-green color. Franconia wines are bottled in squat, broad bottomed flagons (*Bocksbeutel*) of green glass. This bottle is also used in Chile for certain white and even red wines.

The red burgundies of France and California come in greenish bottles similar in outline but less heavy than champagne bottles. However, many French Burgundies are bottled in distinctly brownish-green bottles, which for the reasons previously given, offer the best protection against adverse light effects. These bottles are also used for French Chablis.

The clarets of Bordeaux reach the consumer in straight sided bottles of light to very dark green glass. The shoulder is rather flat and the neck, like the body, is cylindrical rather than tapering. This bottle is used in California for claret, Zinfandel, and some other red wines. The bottle used for French Sauternes and Graves, and for California sauterne is similar in shape to the Bordeaux claret bottle but is made of clear white or light green glass. The color of the glass is less important for these types of wines because of their generally high sulfur dioxide content which reduces the effect of adverse light-induced reactions in the wine.

Sparkling wines are sold in green bottles of very heavy walls and deeply indented bottoms. The tops carry a rather wide flange to hold the wire used in tying down the cork or to catch the crown cap.

One of the most famous of wine bottles is the straw-covered chianti flask or *fiasco* of Tuscany. The fiasco is round-bottomed and, if the woven straw covering is removed, it will not stand up. Some California red wines as well as white are bottled in modifications of these picturesque fiaschi. However, the finest chianti wines of Tuscany are often packed in bottles of conventional Bordeaux shape; nevertheless, American wine consumers have long associated the *fiasco* with chianti or chianti-type wines.

California dessert wines sometimes are packed in bottles similar in outline to whisky bottles, and usually sealed with screw caps. Spanish sherries and Portuguese ports come in dark green or brown glass bottles of straight sides and are somewhat similar to the Bordeaux red wine bottles in outline. They are usually, but not always, sealed with cork rather than screw tops. These, and various special mold bottles, are also employed for California dessert wines. While most are closed with screw caps some have taper corks with wood or plastic tops.

Vermouths are usually marketed in green-colored bottles with a shape somewhat between that of the Bordeaux- and burgundy-type bottle. Many producers have special shaped bottles for their wines.

Second-hand bottles require soaking and washing in hot alkaline solution to thoroughly cleanse the interior. A thorough final rinsing in water is essential. Continuous automatic washers are available for this purpose. No trace of chemical or dirt should remain in the bottle. The bottles should be allowed to drain and dry before use but not to become contaminated with dust. Most European wineries employ used bottles, especially for ordinary wines. Their sterilization is difficult. Halter (1960) showed that even with a 15 to 18 minute period in an antiseptic solution, many yeasts and molds remained in the bottle. Used bottles are seldom employed in this country at present. New bottles usually require only thor-

FIG. 85.   FILLER FOR QUART BOTTLES (LEFT) AND GALLON JUGS

ough rinsing with water.   The rinse water should be potable water completely above suspicion of contamination.   However, Castor (1956), Schanderl (1957), and Halter (1959, 1960) have shown that one should not assume the new bottles are free of undesirable microorganisms unless specially closed at the factory.   While some wineries have used forced air drafts to clean new bottles a better procedure is to rinse and drain the bottles before filling in automatic bottling machines.

Filling

Rossi, Jr. (1963) reported that Westinghouse Sterilamps, which have about 80 per cent of their radiation at 253 mμ, were effective in preventing acetification of low alcohol wines for bottling or of distilling material held in partially-filled containers.   Where exposure was not excessive, less than six weeks, no harmful effects on wine quality were noted.

Fillers are of various types, ranging from the single hand-operated hose and nozzle of the smallest winery to the high-speed bottle filler, which fills 100 or more bottles a minute (Fig. 85).   These latter may be beer or milk bottle fillers modified to take wine bottles.   The filler and bottles revolve during filling.   Filling can be made under vacuum thus reducing oxygen pickup somewhat.

One of the simplest fillers is the syphon filler consisting of a small tank with a float to maintain a constant level of wine, into which the wine flows by gravity.   From this reservoir the wine flows by gravity through metal or hard rubber tubes into the bottles or jugs. The height of fill is readily adjustable. Bottom-filling equipment is now available but there is doubt that some types reduce aeration during filling.

Filling machines must be kept scrupulously clean and should be rinsed out with a little wine before use. Not too much air space should be left in the bottle after filling, as excess air promotes oxidation. Unfortunately, even if the wine is tax-paid prior to bottling, the fill must be regulated by the stated capacity of the bottle. If the actual capacity is greater than the legal stated capacity an excessively large air space will be required by government authorities. This requirement should be modified to permit filling the bottles properly, especially since no evasion of taxes is involved.

The retention of heat in hot-filled bottles is often neglected. Bottles filled at 140°F. and stored at 64°F. did not reach room temperature for 22 hours in the study of Haushofer and Rethaller (1964). Obviously, greater oxidation will occur when wines remain at higher temperatures for longer periods of time. Wucherpfennig and Kleinknecht (1965) reported much less color in cold-filled white wines compared to those bottled and stored for 24 hours at 176°F. However, when the cold-filled wine was bottled in the presence of air and the hot-bottled wine (122°F.) was bottled under carbon dioxide there was little difference in their absorption curves between 380 and 500 mμ. There were greater differences in color among hot-filled bottles than there were between cold-filled bottles. However, no specific changes in color pigments or polyphenolic compounds could be demonstrated as between the two treatments.

They also found hot filling need not unduly reduce the carbon dioxide content of the wine provided carbon dioxide was used as the counter-pressure during filling. Vacuum filling did reduce the carbon dioxide content.

Corks and Corking

Many of those accustomed to use of dry wines on the table prefer that the bottles be closed with straight, untapered corks, in the conventional manner. The corks should be at least 1.5 in. long for choice wines which may remain in the bottle several years and 2 in. or longer corks are preferred for red wines which may remain even longer. They should be fine grained, smooth, and free of serious defects. The necks of the bottles should have the proper straight taper, and be free of bumps, grooves, and other imperfections so that the cork will be sealed throughout its length against the neck of the bottle.

Freshly cut corks contain dust in the pores and substances that may impart a disagreeable taste to the wine. They may also be infected with mold spores, yeasts, etc. Therefore, they should be cleaned and sterilized, and also slightly softened before use. One method consists in soaking for an hour or longer in a dilute (1 per cent) sulfur dioxide solution, containing a little glycerol, and then rinsing in water. The corks are then drained or centrifuged prior to use. Or, they may be soaked in a dilute sulfur dioxide solution and then briefly in a dilute warm glycerol solution. They must be drained before use. The corks should not be soaked too long so that when they are compressed into the neck of the bottle excessive moisture and water-soluble material is pressed out. The old method of merely softening the corks by steaming or by dipping in boiling water is very objectionable because the corks later stick in the bottle neck and may have to be dug out piecemeal. Amerine and Joslyn (1951) described the operation of the corking machine as follows. The corking machine operates in two stages: first, the cork is compressed to a small cylinder by the operation of horizontal movable jaws, or stationary jaws and plunger; and next, the compressed cork is driven into the bottle by a vertical plunger. The best type of corker is one that compresses the cork from all sides by jaws closing uniformly like the iris of a camera lens, although machines, in which the cork is rolled as it is compressed from three sides by movable jaws, are also satisfactory. Stationary-jaw, horizontal-plunger type compression is less desirable because of the danger of pinching or irregularly compressing the cork. As the cork is compressed, if it is not dry, drops of moisture ooze out from the botton; these must be wiped off or blown off by an air stream to prevent contamination of the wine.

The laminated cork (two or more pieces glued together) dates from at least 1895, according to Sharf and Lyon (1958). They are especially useful for making sparkling wine corks. They attribute the "corked" odor to the presence of *Aspergillus glaucus* in the cork.

Stephan (1964) has shown that cork stoppers permit passage of about 0.01 ml. of oxygen per month while polyethylene stoppers allowed 0.16 ml. per month. Even specially treated polyethylene stoppers permitted 0.01 to 0.03 ml. per month to pass. For this reason we do not recommend use of polyethylene stoppers for sparkling or still wines that are to be aged in the bottle for more than a short period of time.

Screw caps are now used as regular-type closures for most ordinary table wines, and for nearly all dessert wines. These are available in a variety of types and patterns. When screw caps are used, particular attention should be paid to the finish on the neck of the bottle. The cap should seat properly on an inert material and seal the bottle completely. Capping machines which form a screw as they screw an aluminum cap onto the bottle are widely employed. Some liners are permeable to oxygen. Pilfer-proof closures are satisfactory and commonly used.

To prevent insect infestation of the top of the exposed cork and to make the seal more air-tight, it was once customary to seal off the top with beeswax. This practice is not common at present. Imported or domestic metal foil caps are placed over the neck of the bottle and crimped into place in a special machine in some wineries but plastic capsules are now used by most. These are placed in a moist condition on the neck of the bottle and are then dried so that they form a tight seal over the closure. Crown caps are used for the bottle fermentation of sparkling wines and for fruit wines. Small bottles of sparkling wines are sometimes distributed with crown caps.

Inspection and Storage Tests

Before labeling and packing, each bottle must be carefully inspected in a strong light for undesirable haze, cloud or sediment. Freshly-bottled wine may be stored for several weeks before the final inspection in order to give it time to recover, show spoilage, or throw down sediment. However, nowadays the bottles move from the larger wineries so rapidly that no such testing is possible. The storage tests, therefore, usually precede bottling since shipment and delivery to retail outlets may follow bottling with a minimum of delay. Changes can be hastened by storing some bottles at 90°F. in an incubator and at 25°F. (for table wine) and 18°F. (for dessert wine). Large bottlers will, therefore, find it very profitable to install such testing equipment and to incubate and refrigerate trial bottling of each lot of wine prior to the final bottling.

Labeling

The labeling requirements of the federal government and the various states are very complicated and frequently require legal interpretation. The general requirements for wines bottled in this country are given in Chapter 21. Wines imported into this country now generally require certificates that they conform to the labeling requirements of the region of origin.

In general the source and type of wine must be stated in a similar size of type. Place of production and of bottling are also given on the label. The per cent alcohol must be stated, but in practice need only approximately state the true per cent alcohol. The size of the bottle must, however, be accurately given.

Hand labeling is messy and expensive. Semi-automatic labelers are better but each bottle must be handled individually. They can take up to 2000 or more bottles per hour. Automatic labelers which will handle 24,-000 or more bottles per hour are manufactured and widely used (Fig. 86).

Both lead and plastic capsules are used. For lead foils none are completely automatic but a so-called three-fourths automatic machine han-

Courtesy of Wine Institute

FIG. 86. MODERN BOTTLING LINE WITH AUTOMATIC CORKING AND LABELING
EQUIPMENT

Note small number of employees

dling up to 7000 bottles per hour is manufactured. Preformed plastic capsules are applied automatically. In another system the plastic capsule is
cut from a tube and applied mechanically.

Casing

For large wineries, automatic casing is necessary. These are constructed so that the bottles are inserted automatically. If a stamp is required it is automatically placed on the case at the same time as the lid is
being glued and sealed shut.

Sources of Information.—The California magazine *Wines and Vines*
each year in September publishes an issue which includes lists of suppliers
of all kinds of winery equipment. A useful reference work on German
equipment is Weinfach-Kalender (1971).

BARRELING

At one time much of California's wine and prior to World War II, most
French wine, was sent to market in barrels. Spanish sherry is exported to
America, England, and elsewhere chiefly in butts of about 130 gallons
each, rather than in bottles, and is bottled at destination; and port from
Portugal is most often exported in casks to England and elsewhere for bot-
tling.

At present, however, most California wine is bottled on the winery
premises and barrels are seldom employed for shipping, except for some

sacramental wines and very occasionally for bond-to-bond shipment. Shipping bungs are driven in over a small piece of heavy duck or other cloth to make a tight seal. To prevent tampering a strip of tin may be placed over the bung and nailed down. The barrels should be stenciled on the head as to type, shipper, addressee, etc.

OTHER DEPARTMENTS

Quality Control

Modern quality control involves interaction between the laboratory, sensory testing and plant operations. An odor-free area for critical sensory evaluation is needed (p. 678 *et seq.*). Quality control charts or permissible limits of variation from the norm can be constructed from these data. See Kramer and Twigg (1970) for use of quality control charts.

Machinery

Refrigerating compressors, boilers, hot water tanks and air conditioning equipment should all be centralized in a single area separated from the other departments. Adequate fire protection equipment should be installed. An adjacent shop area is desirable.

Distillery

The still tower is separated from the winery, often outdoors, to obtain lower insurance rates. Adjacent rooms for receiving the spirits, for fortification and for an office for the government agent are needed. Metal receiving tanks are commonly used. The fortification tanks should be as close to the fermenting room as possible. They should be equipped with compressed air for rapid mixing. The brandy warehouse is usually equipped with wooden or metal racks for holding the 50-gallon barrels in which brandy is stored. Scales for weighing are necessary. If brandy is to be bottled, a dumping area, tanks for mixing and diluting, refrigeration equipment and a special bottling line in a separate room are necessary. The industry prefers "wine spirits addition" to fortification.

Other Facilities

The office may be a single room for the small winery and may serve as a tasting room for visitors. In a large winery a whole complex of offices will be needed. The public relations department may require various types of tasting rooms for visitors with off-sale facilities. One winery is arranged with a special raised walkway through the winery for conducted tours of visitors. This keeps the visitors from interfering with winery operations.

Employees' dressing room and lockers, and sanitary facilities for the public and employees are required. Large wineries provide a dining room for their employees—with or without a cafeteria.

SANITATION

The modern winery must be kept impeccably clean at all times to conform to public health regulations and so as not to offend the aesthetic standards of the consuming public according to Duffy (1958).

The California wine industry for the past 15 years has been engaged in a large scale sanitation program. At first this was largely directed towards in-plant clean up. Truax (1950) emphasized that sanitary measures are not necessarily introduced for public health reasons but more often to increase plant efficiency, protection of equipment, avoidance of off-flavors, satisfaction of consumers' aesthetic values, meeting legal requirements, and improvement of employee working conditions. This was also noted by Amerine and Joslyn (1951) and Doyle (1951, 1952). Davison (1961) summarized the accomplishments of the sanitation program of the California wine industry as follows: voluntary grape inspection, better harvesting and handling of grapes, better in-plant sanitation and better trained personnel. Wine Institute recommendations, Davison (1961–1971), are periodically up-dated, last in 1971. Wine Institute now has an Environmental Studies committee to study methods of preventing pollution.

Effective sanitation is required by State and Federal Food and Drug agencies. In recent years these agencies have become increasingly vigilant and active in respect to sanitary conditions in wineries and the enforcement of legal sanitation regulations. An important provision of these regulations is the famous "may have" clause, which provides that food shall be deemed to be adulterated "if it has been prepared, packed, or held under insanitary conditions whereby it *may have* become contaminated with filth, or whereby it *may have* been rendered injurious to health." This provision permits action to be taken against a product, including wine, solely on the basis of insanitary conditions during production.

The disposal of stillage, pomace, stems, and other winery wastes is an important part of a winery sanitation program. Certain aspects of this problem have been discussed in Chapter 18.

Surveys

The California Department of Public Health has conducted sanitary surveys of all wineries in the state and made recommendations in writing to each plant. These surveys have been continued until the present (1966). Enforcement action is contemplated where conditions warrant it. However, the policy of the Department is one of education rather than drastic police action. The wine producer is given ample time to conform to the recommendations. The Federal Food and Drug officials also take an active interest in the wine industry's sanitation problems.

The wine industry through the Wine Institute has hired a sanitarian whose duties include assistance to wineries in setting up sanitation programs, furnishing information and training to sanitarians employed by wineries, evaluating equipment, materials and production procedures, making surveys upon request of wineries, and establishment of research projects in cooperation with scientists of the University of California and other research agencies on such subjects as picking practices, picking containers for grapes, gondolas, grape loading devices, lug box washing, insect control, etc.

Every winery should have a sanitation program with some competent individual responsible for this very important aspect of production. The winery that is too small to afford a full-time sanitarian can make use of the industry's sanitarian and can also delegate responsibility for sanitation to a key member of the plant's personnel as a part-time duty. Where a State or Federal inspection or survey is made a responsible member of the winery's staff should accompany the one making the survey and seek his advice and recommendations. The same applies to surveys conducted by the industry's sanitarian.

The National Canners Association has an outline for a sanitary survey (available in mimeographed form at the National Canners Association, Washington, D. C., or from the Western Laboratory of the N. C. A. at University Avenue and 6th Street in Berkeley, California). It includes such points as sanitary hazards from adjacent property, plant grounds, buildings, steam and moisture removal, water supply, drainage, floors, waste disposal, clean-up procedures, preparation department, warehousing, packaging department, insect infestation and control, rodent infestation and control, storage of unused equipment and containers, basement, drinking fountains, toilets, washing facilities for plant personnel, dressing rooms and lockers, employee sanitation, first-aid facilities, laboratory, lunch room, and general housekeeping. While the outline is specifically designed for canneries, it contains many very useful suggestions for sanitary surveys of wineries. See also Food Engineering (1954) and Pearson et al. (1955).

The Vinegar Fly Problem

In recent years the vinegar or fruit fly, *Drosophila melanogaster* Meigen, has been recognized as a pest of certain crops, particularly tomatoes, figs, and grapes. According to Siegel (1958) this pest threatens the existence of the tomato canning industry in several Eastern States. In California a great deal of laboratory and field investigations have been conducted on control of the fly in and on tomatoes and on grapes used for wine making. It is primarily a field or vineyard problem and hence control, to be effective, must include measures that will reduce infestation of the raw product before it is harvested. Since it is especially attracted to fermenting musts it creates an important sanitation problem for the California wine industry. The problem is complicated by the huge fruit fly population which builds up in the Central Valley grape regions of California prior to grape ripening. Figs, peaches, melons, and tomatoes are particularly notorious breeders of fruit flies. Since whole or parts of drosophila flies are considered filth by Federal and State agencies it is essential that means be developed to prevent fly and egg contamination.

Much of the fly population in wineries is brought to the wineries from the vineyard. Berg et al. (1958) found the fruit fly content to be greatest in the Fresno area, less in the Lodi-Modesto area, and rather small in the Napa-Sonoma region. Field control measures presently considered desirable include discing in all dropped and cull fruit immediately after harvest, disposing of all organic wastes, use of repellent insecticides in the orchard or vineyard and attractant insecticides on dumps, use of poison bates in and downwind from orchards before and during harvest, and generally following good sanitation practices. These recommendations, Anon. (1958), will also help control dried fruit beetle which is also a problem with grapes.

The Bureau of Food and Drug Inspection of the California State Department of Public Health, has made the following recommendations to the wine industry:

(1) Remove pomace from the winery premises before it becomes a breeding place for vinegar flies and other insects such as dried fruit beetles. Most wineries now remove the pomace daily.

(2) Remove stems, as vinegar flies multiply in stem piles. If not removed, spray the stem piles with a powerful insecticide.

(3) Spread pomace and stems in a thin layer in the field or vineyard in order that they will dry quickly. Stems may be burned when dry.

(4) Eliminate all conditions under which vinegar flies can multiply; such as unclean gutters or hoses, pumps, conveyors, crushers and stemmers, and leakage under storage or sherry baking tanks. Vinegar flies breed prolifically in small pools of wine caused by leakage.

(5) Wash gondola delivery trucks thoroughly after each delivery. Washing and sterilizing lug boxes frequently is another desirable practice.

(6) Do not allow grapes to accumulate in cracks and crevices around the crushing department or elsewhere.

(7) Use concrete instead of dirt or gravel floors as the latter may become a breeding place for the flies if they become and remain wet with wine.

(8) Replace wooden chutes, conveyor flumes, bins, etc. at the crushing

station with metal, preferably stainless steel. Many wineries have replaced wood with stainless steel at crushing stations.

(9) Exclude, insofar as possible, vinegar flies from the winery. A fan placed in the doorway to create a strong outward flow of air is desirable. Many wineries have now installed such fans. Screening of doorways, windows, and other opening of the bottling room is recommended. The screen should be of 20 or finer mesh.

(10) In using insecticide sprays in the plant, only those that are not toxic to humans are permitted. These are the pyrethrins, rotenone, and piperonyl butoxide. Do not use the sprays in locations where the dead flies may drop into the must or wine, as dead flies in the wine are just as objectionable as living ones flying over the wine.

(11) Cooperate in control and research with other industries; such as, those of tomato canning, dried fruit production, and fresh fruit packing.

(12) Arrange daily deliveries so that loads of grapes will be crushed promptly and none allowed to stand overnight.

Berg *et al.* (1958) examined many large samples of grapes taken in the vineyards and from 1534 loads delivered to wineries during the 1957 season. The research was continued during the 1958 season (Berg 1959B). They found that the date of picking before the rains of the 1957 season had occurred had little effect on the vinegar fly population. Following the rains of that season, susceptible varieties developed mold and fermentation and there was a tremendous increase in the vinegar fly population. However, it was found that the per cent of moldy berries was not always a quantitative criterion of infestation with vinegar flies.

The fact that female fruit flies can retain eggs in their bodies, lacking suitable sites for oviposition, means that a new life cycle can be started very soon after a female fly arrives. The summer life cycle varies from 5 to 8 days but is much longer in the winter months, in fact there is little fly activity at temperatures below about 55°F. Maximum fly activity occurs in the range of 75°–80°F. in low light intensity and with low wind velocity.

The forms present in the bunches of uncrushed grapes were the larvae and eggs: the winged insects, of course, had flown before counts were made. There was an increase in flies in the majority of loads allowed to stand overnight. Berg *et al.* (1958), Middlekauff (1957), and Duffy (1958), therefore, recommend that picking and crushing be controlled so that grapes are crushed promptly after picking and loading. Most grapes in the interior valley wine districts are delivered in gondola trucks. Various forms of loaders are used. It was found that cleated conveyor type loaders crushed many of the grapes with the result that vinegar flies swarmed in great numbers around and above such loads. Growers should not be allowed to "tramp" the loads as it crushes many grapes with consequent increase in vinegar flies.

In the 1958 study Berg (1959) established that (1) delay in harvesting, overcropping, and late irrigation increase the amount of rot in the fruit; (2) wine grapes are more susceptible to rot than table or raisin grapes; (3) rain during the picking season increases rot; (4) the degree of insect infestation varies between areas, seasons, and varieties; and (5) although insect infestation increases with increasing amounts of rot up to a maximum there is not sufficient correlation between the two to use one as a predictor of the other.

In cases where loads had to be held overnight spraying with 0.1 per cent or stronger solution of pyrethrin or with a mixture of 0.1 per cent pyrethrin and 1 per cent piperonyl butoxide repelled the insects but did not kill them. Dust impregnated with these insecticides also was effective. Deposition of eggs on the grapes was prevented temporarily by these treatments. In the vineyard Ebeling (1958) and others have stated that more powerful insecticides can be used, provided dangerous residues do not remain on the grapes. For example, malathion disappears from the plant and fruit within a few days after application. Malathion has been used successfully on apples and its use approved for grapes, provided it is applied at least three days prior to harvest. Ebeling (1958) compared the effectiveness of 36 insecticides for control of drosophila. In the laboratory 19 inerts dusts were tested. One of the silica aerogels, SG 77, when applied as a dust in 4 oz. jars containing the flies resulted in 100 per cent kill within 28 minutes; this was less than the time for 100 per cent kill with 2.5 per cent dieldrin dust. The practical application of such dusts is being studied. It is believed that the silica aerogel dusts act by rapid dehydration of the insects.

Factors Influencing.—Middlekauff (1957) states that most eggs are deposited at temperatures above 55°F. and when the light intensity is low. There is little activity when the sun is bright or when a strong breeze is blowing. The insect becomes objectionable about mid-August and increases until cold weather occurs. Michelbacher and Middlekauff (1954) state that the average time required for drosophila eggs to hatch is 24 hours and that one female can lay about 2000 eggs in her lifetime. Middlekauff (1957) has observed hatching of the eggs within 2 hours after laying. These facts account for the sudden appearance of great numbers of the fly. See also Michelbacher et al. (1953) and Yerington (1958).

Berg et al. (1958) found that varieties with tight bunches such as Zinfandel, Grenache, Carignane, and Alicante Bouschet showed more molding and vinegar fly infestation than did the Muscat of Alexandria and the Emperor. The Tokay in spite of its thick skin also showed heavy molding and vinegar fly infestation after the 1957 rains; perhaps because it develops large tight clusters subject to berry rupture.

Overcropping, which is very common in the Fresno area, results in late maturing, weak berries subject to rupture following rain, or late irrigation with consequent increase in mold and drosophila infestation. There was great variation in insect counts among vineyards in the same locality and in loads from a single vineyard. The range in mold and rot ranged from 6.4 to 91.1 per cent and the insect count 90 to 1259 insects per pound of grapes. While leaf folders, dried fruit beetles, and other insects were counted, the drosophila made up 88.8 to 91.0 per cent of the insects found.

There is no doubt that elimination of waste fruit would do much to reduce the fly problem. Such control would be expensive and would have to be done on a community wide basis to be effective. To alleviate the problem vineyard practices which reduce incidence of rot are a first line of control. These include proper pruning so as to prevent over-cropping, withholding irrigation water during ripening, harvesting as soon as the grapes reach maturity (very important), harvesting and transporting the grapes to the winery with a minimum of injury, and very rapid movement from the field to the winery (perferably within one hour). Insecticides that kill fruit flies are available but with the tremendous fly population of adjacent unsprayed areas it is doubtful as to how much value they would be. Where the vineyard is isolated insecticide control may prove effective. In using insecticides the latest Food and Drug tolerances must be very carefully considered and strictly adhered to. In addition, it is highly advisable to consult the latest "Pest and Disease Control Program for Grapes" which is revised annually by the California Agricultural Experiment Station.

Protection of the interior of wineries from drosophila is also an important problem. The first requirement is that no interior breeding spots be available. Leaking tanks are a favorite breeding spot and should be completely eliminated. The second requirement is that no flies be permitted to enter the storage and bottling areas of the plant. Considerable information on fruit fly control is given in Anon. (1958) and California (1959). DeCamargo and Phaff (1957) give information on the yeasts carried by drosophila.

In spite of the intensive and extensive research of the University of California and U.S. Department of Agriculture entomologists, the National Canners Association research staff and many others, there is as yet no very effective means of keeping the vinegar fly population within desirable bounds.

Other Insects and Rodent Control

The housefly may become a pest in and around the winery. It breeds in manure piles, garbage, human excrement, and other refuse. Elimination of such breeding places is the best means of control.

Cockroaches, of which there are five common species, are a frequent pest. Like rats they are omniverous in their food habits. They are very prolific and live for two or three years. They live in cracks, crevices, under moist boards and similar spots and come out at night. Pyrethrin, sodium fluoride, or chlordane applied to cracks, floors near baseboards, and other likely spots will kill them. Care must be taken to prevent contamination of grapes, must, or wine with the insecticide.

Crickets sometimes invade wineries during late summer or early fall. Spraying or dusting the floor or ground area in front of doorways or the other entrances and dusting the floor near the baseboards with four to five per cent malathion dust will kill most of the crickets.

Ants may enter the bottling room or other area. Poisonous ant pastes and malathion placed in runways are commonly used to control them. Destruction of colonies, usually located outside the plant, is an effective control measure. Carbon bisulfide, kerosene, chlordane, and malathion are lethal to ant colonies. Wasps and bees sometimes become numerous at the crush station, but there is no very safe and satisfactory program of control.

The presence of rats or mice in the winery is highly undesirable. Rats are carriers of filth and spread their droppings, hair, and urine about the plant and in this manner may cause contamination of equipment and stored supplies such as fining materials, filter aid, etc. They are always more numerous than the few that are seen in the plant. There are, according to Doyle (1954), twenty hidden rats for each one that is seen. All new construction should be rodent-proof and old buildings made as rodent-proof as possible. Supplies should be stored in a rodent-proof enclosure. Rats may enter through doorways left open at night, through skylights, partly closed windows and through the space beneath the eaves. Great ingenuity and care are required in order to make any exclusion program effective. Mice are even more difficult to exclude. Holsendorff (1937) and Storer (1948) have given methods of rodent-proofing buildings. The bottling room, above all others, should be screened and otherwise made rat proof. Harborages should be eliminated. Rats are wary of traps, although the setting of traps in runways may catch a fair number. Cats and dogs should not be permitted in the winery even for such a desirable objective as rodent control.

Birds and bats may become pests. Their droppings may contaminate equipment, tanks, vats, etc.

Poisoning has proven an effective rodent control measure, although in the winery itself poisons that are toxic to humans cannot be used. The rodenticide, Warfarin, is now used extensively in food establishments for the control of rats and mice. It acts slowly and kills by internal bleeding.

The bait should be put out daily in order to maintain a fresh and fairly constant supply. It is used in a dry, granular bait or in a cereal such as barley or wheat or in water. Red squill, a plant product harmless to humans, is also used as a rodenticide. It is a powerful emetic and is therefore soon eliminated by domestic animals but the rat cannot vomit, hence retains the poison.

In certain locations outside the winery other poisons such as "1080," strychnine, "Antu," zinc phosphide, and others may be used, if proper care is taken to prevent their entry into the winery or the poisoning of humans or domestic animals. See Sampson (1943), Kalmbach (1945), Parker (1948), and Anon. (1952) for further information on rodent control.

Care of Containers

Although gondola trucks chiefly are used for the delivery of grapes to large wineries, lug boxes are still used by many vineyardists and smaller wineries. The boxes may become unsanitary and moldy, and thus a source of contamination. At one winery Skofis (1957) subjects the lugs first to a hot detergent solution, and then to a spray of water. Such equipment may be built on the premises or may be had from cannery equipment manufacturers. Coating the inside of lug boxes with a compound that forms a smooth hard surface on drying will greatly facilitate washing and will discourage mold growth. "Cellu-san" is used extensively for this purpose by the canning industry.

General Sanitation

Very small accumulations of organic material such as partially crushed grapes, wine seepage, must, etc. will support a large population of insects, particularly vinegar flies. Therefore, frequent cleaning of floors, conveyors, floor gutters, flumes, hoses, crushers and crushing stations, pumps, and other equipment is essential. Corners and crevices that can not be reached easily add greatly to the difficulty of effective clean-up operations. Floors should be of concrete, properly sloped and drained, and should be scrubbed and washed down with ample water. It is desirable to occasionally wash them with dilute hypochlorite to disinfect the surface and cracks. Excessive concentrations or too frequent use should, of course be avoided. Industrial vacuum cleaners have proven effective for dry cleaning.

Wine spilled on the floor should be washed away immediately. If the spilled wine has stood on the floor for a considerable time, it is advisable to follow washing by applying lime or strong hypochlorite solution. In general it is best to keep the floors dry between washings.

The tops of tanks, overhead walks, and ramps should be swept and kept clean. Washing may be necessary occasionally, but care must be taken to keep water and washings out of the wine. Skofis (1957) states that plastic bung hole extensions for the openings in the tops of tanks have proven very useful.

When it is necessary a pyrethrin or other permissible spray may be "fogged" into a room or load of grapes. Fogs of oil-based insecticides, although effective for a longer period than water-based, are apt to be inflammable. Unless the fogging is complete some insects will escape, Stafford (1958).

Yerington (1964) reports vapor dispensers of Vapora (also dichlorvos or DDVP which is 0,0-dimethyl 0,2,2-dichlorovinyl phosphate), used in the form of pellets placed in a heating chamber, can assure effective control in a cellar for a full season with one loading.

Equipment after use should be dismantled, thoroughly washed with water, and with a detergent if necessary. It should then be sterilized with live steam or a disinfectant such as hypochlorite solution, rinsed thoroughly with water, and drained. Filter cloths should be thoroughly washed in a washing machine, rinsed, and dried. Hoses should be placed on sloping racks to drain and dry after washing. Special precautions should be taken to clean and sterilize equipment after it has handled spoiled or contaminated wine. This includes hoses, pumps, filters, pipes, fillers, pasteurizers, etc.

As the bottling room is the final possible source of contamination with bacteria or metal, its care and cleanliness must be very thorough. It should be well lighted, well ventilated, and its floors and walls easily cleaned. Ample space between machines is highly desirable to permit easy cleaning. Equipment should be dismantleable in order to permit thorough cleaning.

Receiving bins, chutes, flumes, and other parts of the crushing station should be made of stainless steel and crevices in which grapes or stems may lodge and spoil should be eliminated. The crushers and all equipment, including must lines, must be kept clean. They should be washed and flushed with water frequently, at least twice a day, and should not be allowed to stand with crushed grapes or must in them for more than an hour or two. Stemmers and crushers should be carefully inspected before the crushing season and any badly worn or defective parts replaced. A breakdown during the season may prove very costly and inconvenient.

It is also customary to wash out gondolas thoroughly with a powerful stream of water after each delivery.

Toilets and urinals must be adequate, kept in sanitary condition, and located at a reasonable distance from the bottling department or other operation where the wine or must is handled. Washing of the hands after use of the toilet facilities should be required. Drinking fountains with proper guards to prevent contact of the mouth or nose with the metal of the water outlet should be provided.

Workmen should not be permitted to enter recently emptied tanks unaccompanied, because carbon dioxide or alcohol vapors may be present in dangerous amounts. In the past workmen have been killed by carbon dioxide gas in a covered tank and, violent explosions of alcohol vapors have occurred. If a man enters an empty tank, a second person should remain outside to render aid if necessary. The emptied tank should be thoroughly drained by leaving the bottom and top manholes open for several hours before a workman enters, or forced air ventilation employed.

Detergents and Cleaners

Increasingly wineries are installing cleaning-in-place systems to replace manual cleaning.

A balanced detergent must have the ability to dissolve organic matter, adequate tendency to keep undissolved matter in suspension, and good wetting and rinsing properties. Furthermore, it must have sufficient sequestering ability to prevent the formation of insoluble calcium salts which would otherwise deposit on cleaned surfaces. Since no one compound possesses all of these properties mixtures of a basic cleaner, a dispersing agent, a wetting compound and a sequestering chemical are used.

Basic Cleaning Agents.—Alkalis and alkaline salts are now used, caustic soda (sodium hydroxide) being the most common. It dissolves proteins but has poor dispersing, wetting, and rinsing properties. Sodium metasilicate has good dispersing and wetting properties and is a fair protein dissolver. Moreover, it can be used on aluminum which caustic soda cannot. The alkaline phosphates are the agents of choice for lined tanks. They have poor organic matter-dissolving ability but have excellent dispersing properties.

Dispersing and Wetting Agents.—The purposes of these is to secure an intimate contact of the liquid with the surface being cleaned and to aid rinsing. The alkaline phosphates and sodium metasilicate are satisfactory. Highly surface-active compounds, usually non-ionic organic compounds containing a long polyethylene glycol chain, are very effective at low concentrations (0.2 to 0.5 per cent). For cleaning-in-place systems formulations which do not foam are preferred.

Sequestering Agents.—These agents are used to complex dissolved calcium and magnesium, thus preventing formation of insoluble salts and build-up of surface deposits. At present EDTA (ethylenedi-aminetetraacetic acid) is used. Its complexing properties are good in the pH range 8 to 13 and it is thermally stable. It is also effective in dissolving calcium salt deposits. Use of 0.1 per cent EDTA will prevent deposits with water containing 260 p.p.m. of hardness (expressed as calcium carbonate). When large calcium deposits must be removed, up to 5 per cent EDTA in caustic soda can be sprayed on the surface and recirculated.

Upperton (1965) recommended a mixture of 1.5 per cent caustic soda, 0.25 per cent of a wetting agent, and 0.1 per cent EDTA for general use in the brewery, either for hot soaking or cold recirculation. With a high-pressure system 0.75 per cent caustic soda should be adequate.

Sterilizing Agents.—Hypochlorites are widely used for cold sterilization in wineries; see Griffin (1946), Harris (1947), Mercer and Somers (1957), and Somers (1951). They tend to corrode stainless steel. Quaternary ammonium compounds have been used to sterilize filters, etc. Thorough rinsing is necessary.

It is possible to combine the detergent and the sterilizer according to Upperton (1965). Quaternaries, with proper precautions, can be mixed with caustic soda. EDTA is usually added. One problem is that the sterilant may be exhausted before the detergent because of contact with contaminated surfaces. Such combinations are, therefore, more economical when used after a pre-rinsing. See also Somers (1948, 1949). A good general cleanser is a mixture of sodium hydroxide and a silicate; it is less caustic than hydroxide and is more easily removed by rinsing. "T.S.P.," trisodium phosphate, is a popular cleansing agent; although alkaline it is less caustic than sodium hydroxide, rinses readily, softens water, and prevents calcium deposits in hard waters.

So-called cationic detergents work only in acid solutions and are therefore inactivated by soaps. Roccal and Emulsol are trade preparations of this type and act not only as cleaners but also as germicides. The anionic detergents (such as Dreft, Vel, Drene, etc.) work only in alkaline solutions; soap belongs in this group. There exist also non-ionic detergents. One should make certain that the detergent used does not impart an odor or taste to equipment surfaces. See Anon. (1952) and Lawrence and Block (1968) for further information on the proper use of detergents and disinfectants.

Amerine and Joslyn (1951) have given three lists of materials used for cleaning and disinfecting: one for surfaces in contact with grapes, must or wine; one for walls, floors, and outside surfaces of equipment, and one for outdoor purposes. The lists have been prepared from "Winery Sanitation Guide," Wine Institute (1961–1963). With permission of the authors, the two lists are reproduced here.

LIST NO. 1. FOR SURFACES IN CONTACT WITH GRAPES, MUST, OR WINE

For cleaning wooden or concrete containers:
1. Materials containing sodium carbonate, silicates, and phosphates usually sold under trade names.
2. Trisodium phosphate and other phosphates.
3. Soda ash or sal soda.

For cleaning metal equipment:
4. Any one of the three above.
5. Caustic soda (injures wood and concrete).
6. Carbon abrasive.
7. Citric acid (to remove scale and oxides).

For neutralizing, in the form of a solution or spray:
8. Lime (slaked).
9. Soda ash or sal soda.

For sterilizing:
10. Sodium or calcium hypochlorite.
11. Combinations of sodium or calcium hypochlorite and alkaline materials, sold under trade names.
12. Chloramines.
13. Combinations of chloramines and alkaline materials, sold under trade names.
14. Sulfur dioxide in the form of liquid sulfur dioxide or metabisulfite. Sodium bisulfite is also used.
15. Sulfur wicks or sulfur pots, burned inside of closed wooden cooperage.

LIST NO. 2. FOR WALLS, FLOORS, AND OUTSIDE SURFACES OF EQUIPMENT

For cleaning:
16. Same as Nos. 1 to 3.

For sterilizing:
17. Chlorine compounds mentioned under Nos. 10 and 11.
18. Sulfur dioxide.
19. Quaternary ammonium compounds, sold under trade names: but must be used so that no trace of the compounds can get into the wine.

LIST NO. 3. FOR OUTDOOR PURPOSES

For cleaning and disinfecting wood or concrete platforms or crushing equipment, or for spraying on grounds and pomace piles:
20. Lime (unslaked).
21. Chloride of lime.
22. Sodium bisulfite.

For disinfecting and insect control, usually in the form of spray:
23. Chlorinated benzenes, (do not use near processing equipment or cooperage or anywhere inside the winery).
24. Dichlorvos (DDVP), (do not use near processing equipment, above open tanks or anywhere it could come into contact with wine).
25. Sulfur dioxide.
26. Pyrethrin.

These four materials (Nos. 23, 24, 25, 26), alone or in combinations, are also sold under various trade names.

Chlorination.—In most canneries the entire water supply for the plant is chlorinated and this may often be a desirable practice for wineries. Chlorination beyond the "break point" is termed "in-plant chlorination." Usually 0.5 to 1.0 p.p.m. of free chlorine in the chlorinated water is sufficient. Stronger solutions are used in floor and equipment clean-up operations. The chlorine kills bacteria, yeasts and molds on floors and equipment and thus prevents bacterial slime formation on floors, conveyors, etc.

WASTE DISPOSAL

Pomace and stems, as previously mentioned, are now removed daily by most plants. The recovery of tartrates from pomace and the drying of pomace have been discussed in Chapter 18. The cream of tartar separating in rather important quantities during the refrigeration of wine for stabilization is usually recovered.

The disposal of stillage (still slops), the waste dealcoholized liquid from brandy stills, presents a difficult problem. If it is run into artificial basins or settling ponds to disappear by percolation and evaporation, anaerobic putrefaction with production of very offensive odors may occur. Complaints of nearby residents have forced remedial measures. This method is still in use by some wineries. If the stillage is run into a stream, it may kill the fish and make the water unsuitable for other use. In 1946 and 1947 extensive pilot plant and industrial scale investigations were conducted on disposal of grape stillage by the Coast Laboratories of Fresno in cooperation with Marsh and Vaughn of the University of California. The principal finding was that by running the stillage on to prepared plots of land to a fairly shallow depth and then allowing each plot to dry thoroughly before using it again, offensive odors and the breeding of mosquitoes were prevented, Fig. 87. Such a system of stillage disposal is known as "intermittent irrigation." For each 100,000 gallons of conventional stillage produced per day, seven acres of suitable land should be available. The stillage during a 24-hour period is run on to one of the seven plots for 24 hours and then is allowed to percolate into the soil and dry. Usually, if the stillage is not more than four inches deep on the plot, it will seep into the soil within 48 hours leaving a cake of solids on the surface. In a few days the cake will dry and break up into small pieces that curl up around the edges and expose the soil for an additional run of stillage. Each plot is used once in seven days. If the soil is heavy, a longer drying period and hence more land will be required. If the stillage is from pomace stills, twice as long a drying period is needed. (See Marsh and Vaughn (1944), Mercer (1955), O'Connell and Fitch (1950), Rudolfs and Heukelekian (1954), Vaughn and Marsh (1945, 1953, 1956) and Vaughn et al. 1950).)

Fig. 87. Still Slops on Intermittent Irrigation Plot (Upper). Dried Still Slops Showing Curling

In the present method of heating distilling material in the still by direct steam, the volume of the distilling material (DM) is increased about 15 per cent by condensation of steam. For example, 100,000 gallons of DM will give about 115,000 gallons of stillage.

The "clean" waste water, such as that from cooling fermenting must and for condensing the alcoholic distillate from the still, should be kept separate from the stillage in order not to greatly increase the total volume. It can be disposed of by running into a stream after gaining permission from the proper authorities, or by intermittent irrigation of a vineyard or orchard.

The investigators have recommended that the volume of stillage be held to a minimum by so operating the plant that the DM has at least 8 per cent of alcohol. The effect of the volume of water added to the pomace in extracting it for DM is shown in Table 33.

If settling tanks are installed for pomace stillage much of the suspended solids can be removed and dried on land plots separately from the stillage. About 5000 gallons of sludge per 100,000 gallons of pomace stillage will

TABLE 33

RELATION OF VOLUME OF STILLAGE TO ALCOHOL CONTENT OF DISTILLING MATERIAL[1]

Gallons of Original 12 Per cent DM	Gallons of Water Added	Gallons of Final DM	Per cent Alcohol in Final DM	Proof Gallons of Brandy Produced	Gallons of Stillage Produced[2]
100,000	0	100,000	12	24,000	115,000
100,000	20,000	120,000	10	24,000	138,000
100,000	50,000	150,000	8	24,000	172,500
100,000	100,000	200,000	6	24,000	230,000
100,000	200,000	300,000	4	24,000	345,000
100,000	500,000	600,000	2	24,000	690,000

[1] Source of data: Coast Laboratories (1947).
[2] Because of steam condensate from the still, the stillage volume is approximately 15 per cent greater than the DM volume.

settle out. At least seven sludge drying beds, one for each day's operation, will be required, according to Coast Laboratories (1947). As soon as it is dry the sludge should be removed from the plot before fresh sludge is put on the plot again. For each acre of land used for disposal of the main volume of stillage, about one-tenth of an acre is required for the sludge. Another method consists in passing the drained pomace through a disintegrator and, then over a fine screen. The skins and other coarse material that pass over the screen are pressed. Only the fines that pass through the screen go to the still.

By liming conventional stillage to pH 11 suspended materials and colloids coagulate and settle, giving 20 to 30 per cent by volume of sludge and 50 to 70 per cent clear amber colored liquid. The dried cake from conventional and from pomace stillage, as well as the dried sludge from DM settling tanks, has considerable fertilizing value, equal to 2 to 4 times the fertilizing value of barnyard manure.

Municipalities object to the disposal of stillage in their sewage disposal systems because of its high BOD (biological oxygen demand—a measure of the difficulty of converting the organic matter into nonobjectionable compounds), the low pH value of the stillage, which interferes seriously with bacterial decomposition of the organic matter, and the seasonal rather than year round operation of the stills.

In one plant, according to Marsh and Vaughn (1959), stillage is neutralized with lime to the point of color change, about pH 5, and is then diluted with wash water and other waste water as much as possible. If the DM is lees from racking and from refrigeration, it is centrifuged to remove most of the tartrates before neutralization, as they would cause plugging of the pipe line from the winery to the city sewage line and greatly increase the BOD of the stillage. By neutralizing the stillage to about pH 5.0 its buffering power on the sewage is also greatly reduced. The treated stillage adds a great deal of bacterial food to the sewage; consequently, decomposition in the sewage plant is very rapid with evolution of much gas, largely combustible methane and hydrogen which could be collected from covered digestion tanks and burned under boilers to produce steam.

In another case, mentioned by Marsh and Vaughn (1959), in which disposal by ponding produces objectionable odor, it was planned to pretreat the stillage by passing through a trickle filter in order to reduce the BOD to a reasonable level before it is sent to the municipal sewage plant. Pretreatment will probably also include removal of much of the suspended solids and neutralization or partial neutralization of the stillage.

According to Marsh and Vaughn (1959), at least two wineries use the stillage for vineyard irrigation by the furrow method. Great care must be taken, however, to use it rather sparingly for it is toxic to plants if applied too generously. It is recommended that small scale tests first be made to establish safe practice. Proebsting and Jacob (1938) made a study of the use of stillage for irrigation and found that plants were killed when it was used in amounts equivalent to the water normally used in irrigation. In time the soil poisoned by the stillage recovered. They also pointed out the danger of contaminating the underground water supply.

HEALTH OF WORKERS

Amerine and Joslyn (1951) have made several useful recommendations concerning the health and welfare of workers in the winery. Referring to the survey of Russell *et al.* (1939) it is recommended that all prospective employees be given a physical examination and, if later employed, they be placed in work for which they are physically fitted. Sufficient light and ventilation must be provided. In addition to adequate sanitary facilities, the importance of good personal hygiene should be emphasized.

Use of waterproof boots and clothing is essential for certain workmen. First aid cabinets should be placed at convenient locations and properly maintained. Gas masks should be provided for ammonia fumes in case of leakage of ammonia equipment or pipelines of the refrigeration department where ammonia is used as the refrigerant. Freon because of its non-toxicity is a safer refrigerant than ammonia. Large wineries will provide in-plant facilities for treatment of sick or injured personnel.

An active safety educational program, in charge of a safety-minded member of the staff, is strongly recommended. Wiring should be of the four wire grounded type, and extension cord lights should be adequately protected. Motors should be splash-proof. Electrical outlets for pumps and other equipment operated by electric motors should be covered.

Amerine and Joslyn (1970) also call attention to the toxicity of sulfur dioxide gas and state that its concentration in the air in the plant should not exceed 10 p.p.m. At higher concentrations he should wear eye protectors and an approved respirator. The American Petroleum Institute (1948) has a useful report on its toxicity and on precautionary measures.

BIBLIOGRAPHY

AMERICAN PETROLEUM INSTITUTE. 1948. API Toxicological Review: Sulfur Dioxide. American Petroleum Institute, New York.

AMERINE, M. A. 1950. The response of wine to aging. Wines and Vines *31*, No. 3, 19–22; No. 4, 71–74; No. 5, 28–31.

AMERINE, M. A. 1959. Continuous flow production of still and sparkling wine. Wines and Vines *40*, No. 6, 41–42.

AMERINE, M. A., and JOSLYN, M. A. 1970. Table Wines; the Technology of Their Production. 2 ed. Univ. of Calif. Press, Berkeley and Los Angeles.

ANON. 1952. Sanitation for the Food Preservation Industries. McGraw-Hill Book Co., Inc., New York.

ANON. 1958. Drosophila Conference, Western Regional Research Laboratory, Mimeo. U. S. Dept. Agr., Albany, Calif.

ANON. 1959. Ensaios sobre a influencia da cor do vidro das garrafas no envelhecimento do vinho do porto. Cadernos Instituto Vinho Porto *233*, 244–247.

BARRE, P., and GALZY, P. 1962. Étude d'un lactobacille homofermentatif isolé du vin. Ann. technol. agr. *11*, 121–130.

BARRILLON, D., GAC, A., PIERSON, G., and POUX, C. 1970. Étude du bilan thermique d'un vinificateur continu. Ann. Technol. Agr. *19*, 155–175.

BÉNARD, P., and JOURET, C. 1963. Essais comparitifs de vinification en rouge. *Ibid.* *12*, 85–102.

BÉNARD, P., ANDRÉ, P., and DEIBNER, L. 1958. Influence du mode d'alcoolisation et de la nature des alcools sur la qualité des vins doux naturels. *Ibid.* *7*, 111–125.

BERG, H. W. 1948. Cooperage handling. Univ. Calif., Wine Technol. Conf. *1948*, 38–45.

BERG, H. W. 1953. Varietal susceptibility of white wines to browning. I. II. Food Research *18*, 399–406, 407–410.

BERG, H. W. 1957. Use of ion exchange resins for the stabilization of tartrates. Wine Institute, Tech. Advis. Committee, May 13, 1957.

BERG, H. W. 1959A. The effects of several fungal pectic enzyme preparations on grape musts and wines. Am. J. Enol. Vitic. *10*, 130–134.

BERG, H. W. 1959B. Investigation of defects in grapes delivered to California wineries: 1958. Am. J. Enol. Vitic. *10*, 61–69.

BERG, H. W. 1960. Stabilization studies on Spanish sherry and on factors influencing KHT precipitation. Am. J. Enol. Vitic. *11*, 123–128.

BERG, H. W., and AKIYOSHI, M. 1956. Some factors involved in the browning of white wines. Am. J. Enol. *7*, 1–7.

BERG, H. W., and AKIYOSHI, M. 1962. Color behavior during fermentation and aging of wines. Am. J. Enol. Vitic. *13*, 126–132.

BERG, H. W., ALLEY, C. J., and WINKLER, A. J. 1958. Investigation of defects in grapes delivered to California wineries, 1957. *Ibid.* *9*, 24–31.

BERG, H. W., DE SOTO, R., and AKIYOSHI, M. 1968. The effect of refrigeration, bentonite clarification and ion exchange on potassium behavior in wines. Am. J. Enol. Viticult. *19*, 208–212.

BERG, H. W., and GUYMON, J. F., 1951. Countercurrent water extraction of alcohol from grape pomace. Wines and Vines *32*, No. 10, 27–31.

BERG, H. W., and KEEFER, R. M. 1958–1959. Analytical determination of tartrate stability in wine. Am. J. Enol. *9*, 180–193; *10*, 105–109.

BERGERET, J. 1963. Action de la gélatine et de la bentonite sur la couleur et l'astringence de quelques vins. Ann. technol. agr. *12*, 15–25.

BIDAN, P. 1956. Sur quelques bactéries isolées de vin en fermentation malolactique. *Ibid. 5*, 597–617.

BIELIG, H. J. 1966. Ein Beitrag zur Frage der Sauerstoffaufnahme bei der Abfüllung von Getränken. Weinberg u. Keller *13*, 65–78.

BIOLETTI, F. T. 1906. A new wine-cooling machine. California Agr. Exp. Sta. Bull. *174*, 1–27.

BRADFORD, B. 1958. Modern insecticides. How do they act? What are their effects? Wine Institute, Tech. Advis. Committee, Aug. 15, 1958.

BRANDS, E. R. 1956. Steel tank coatings. *Ibid.* Feb. 20, 1956.

BRÉMOND, E. 1957. Techniques Modernes de Vinification et de Conservation des Vins dans les Pays Chauds. Librairie de la Maison Rustique, Paris.

CALIFORNIA. 1959. California Agricultural Experiment Station research on drosophila flies in fruits and vegetables. Berkeley. Mimeo.

CANT, R. R. 1960. The effect of nitrogen and carbon dioxide treatment of wines on dissolved oxygen levels. Am. J. Enol. Vitic. *11*, 164–169.

CANTARELLI, C. 1962. I trattamenti con resine poliammidiche in enologia. Atti accad. ital. vite e vino *14*, 219–249.

CAPUTI, JR., A., and PETERSON, R. G. 1965. The browning problem in wines. Am. J. Enol. Vitic. *16*, 9–13.

CARAFA, P. 1959. La ricerca aspecifica per via biologica degli antifermentativi nei mosti e nei vini mediante impiego di substrato solidificabile. Riv. viticolt. enol. (Conegliano) *12*, 277–287.

CARLES, J., ALQUIER-BOUFFARD, A., and MAGNY, J. 1963. De quelques variations apparaissant dans le jus de raisin au cours du pressurage. Compt. rend. acad. agr. France *48*, 773–780.

CARR, J. 1958. The vitamin requirements of lactic acid bacteria from eiders. Antonie van Leeuwenhoek, J. Microbiol. Serol. *24*, 63–68.

CASTOR, J. G. B. 1953. Experimental development of compressed yeast us fermentation starters. Wines and Vines *34*, No. 8, 27; No. 9, 33.

CASTOR, J. G. B. 1956. Bacteriological test of the sterility of factory-closed, new wine bottles. Am. J. Enol. *7*, 137–141.

CHAPON, L., and URION, E. 1960. Ascorbic acid and beer. Wallerstein Lab. Comm. *23*, 38–44.

CLEMENS, R. A., and MARTINELLI; A. J. 1958. PVP in clarification of wines and juices. Wines and Vines *39*, No. 4, 55–58.

COAST LABORATORIES. 1947. Grape stillage disposal by intermittent irrigation. Wine Institute, San Francisco. Mimeo.

COAST LABORATORIES. 1948. Improved distilling material production methods as an aid in stillage disposal. Wine Institute, San Francisco. Mimeo.

COFFELT, R. J., and BERG, H. W. 1965. New type of press—the Serpentine. Wines and Vines *46*, No. 4, 69.

COFFELT, R. J., BERG, H. W., FREI, P., and ROSSI, E. A., Jr. 1965. Sugar extraction from grape pomace with a 3-stage countercurrent system. Am. J. Enol. Vitic. *16*, 14–20.

COSTA, L. C. DA. 1938. O problema das aguardentes e dos alcoóis. Influência de sua origem e grau na beneficiação de vinhos. Anais inst. super. agron., Univ. téc. Lisboa *9*, 67–76.

CRUESS, W. V. 1918. Fermentation organisms from California grapes. Univ. Calif. Publ. Agr. Sci. *4*, 1–66.

DAVISON, A. D. 1961. Review of wine industries' sanitation program. Am. J. Enol. Vitic. *12*, 31–36.

DAVISON, A. D. 1961–1971. Wine Institute Sanitation Guide for Wineries. Wine Institute, San Francisco. (Last version edited by H. Cook.)

DECAMARGO, R., and PHAFF, H. J. 1957. Yeasts occurring in drosophila flies and in fermenting tomato fruits in northern California. Food Research *22*, 367–372.

DEIBNER, L., and BÉNARD, P. 1956. Recherches sur la maturation des vins doux naturels. Ann. technol. agr. *5*, 357–377.

DEIBNER, L., and BÉNARD, P. 1957. Effets de traitements thermiques, à l'abri de l'air, sur les qualités des vins doux naturels. *Ibid. 6*, 421–427.

DEIBNER, L., and BÉNARD, P. 1958. Emploi des alginates pour la déferrisation des vins. *Ibid. 7*, 103–109

DEIBNER, L., and MOURGUES, J. 1963. Détection des ferrocyanures et de l'acide cyanhydrique dans les jus de raisin et les vins au moyen de la réaction de Mois. *Ibid. 12*, 177–202.

DE ROSA, T., and BIONDO, V. 1959. Indagine sull'impiego del PVP come chiarificante in un vino bianco. Riv. viticolt. e enol. (Conegliano) *12*, 381–394.

DE SOTO, R. T. 1955. Integration yeast propagation with winery operation. Am. J. Enol. *6*, 26–30.

DE VILLIERS, J. P. 1961. The control of browning of white table wines. Am. J. Enol. Vitic. *12*, 25–30.

DICKINSON, B. N., and STONEMAN, G. F. 1958. Stabilization of wines by ion exchange. Wines and Vines *39*, No. 6, 33, 35.

DILLON, C. L. 1958. Current trends in glass technology. Am. J. Enol. *9*, 59–63.

DIMOTAKI-KOURAKOU, V. 1964. Differenciation des mistelles d'avec les vins doux. IV Congrès d'Expertise Chimique, Athenes special no., 355–359.

DOON, H. R. 1958. Closed steel fermenters. Wine Institute, Tech. Advis. Committee, May 26, 1958.

DORFER, K. 1970. Ionenaustauscher. 3 ed. Verlag Walter de Gruyter, Berlin.

DOYLE, E. S. The role of sanitation in production and quality control. Mod. Sanit. *3*, No. 9, 30–32.

DOYLE, E. S. 1952. Preventive sanitation. Canner *115*, No. 9, 11–12.

DOYLE, E. S. 1954. Plant sanitation. *In* Fruit and Vegetable Juices by D. K. Tressler and M. A. Joslyn. Avi Pub. Co., Westport, Conn. p. 276–293.

DUFFY, M. P. 1958. Sanitation and better housekeeping in the production of wine in California. Wine Institute, Tech. Advis. Committee, May 26, 1958.

DU PLESSIS, C. S. 1964. The ion exchange treatment (H cycle) of white grape juice prior to fermentation. II. The effect upon quality. South Afric. J. Agr. Sci. *7*, 3–16.

EBELING, W. 1958. Vinegar fly control treatments. Calif. Agr. *12*, 12–15.

EGOROV, A. A., KOLTYARENKO, M. R., and PREOBRAZHENSKIĬ, A. A. 1951. Uluchshenie kachestva spirtovannykh (Improvement in wine quality from fortifying spirits). Vinodelie i Vinogradarstvo S.S.S.R. *11*, No. 8, 6–8.

FELL, G. 1961. Étude sur la fermentation malolactique du vin et les possibilités de la provoquer par ensemencement. Land. Jahr. Schweiz. *75*, 249–264.

FESSLER, J. H. 1958. Ion exchange resins for tartrate stabilization. Wine Institute, Tech. Advis. Committee, May 26, 1958.

FESSLER, J. H. 1961. Erythorbic acid and ascorbic acid as antioxidants in bottled wines. Am. J. Enol. Vitic. *12*, 20–24.

FESSLER, J. H., and NASLEDOV, S. N. 1951. The clarification of wines with the centrifuge. Proc. Am. Soc. Enol. *1951*, 201–206.

FLANZY, M. 1959. Élaboration des vins spiritueux doux (vins doux naturels); réglementation et alcoolisation. Ann. technol. agr. *8*, 81–100.

FLESCH, P., and HOLBACH, B. 1965. Zum Abbau der L-Äpfelsäure durch Milchsäurebakterien. I. Über die Malatabbauenden Enzyme des Bakterium "L" unter besonderer Berücksichtigung der Oxalessigsäure-Decarboxylase. Arch. Mikrobiol. *51*, 401–413.

FOOD ENGINEERING. 1954. Food Plant Sanitation and Maintenance. McGraw-Hill Book Co., New York.

FORNACHON, J. C. M. 1950. Yeast cultures. Australian Brewing Wine J. *69*, No. 3, 32.

FORNACHON, J. C. M. 1957. The occurrence of malo-lactic fermentation in Australian wines. Aust. J. Appl. Sci. *8*, 120–129.

FORNACHON, J. C. M. 1963. Travaux récents sur la fermentation malolactique. Ann. technol. agr. *12* (numéro hors série 1), 45–53.

FORNACHON, J. C. M. 1964. A *Leuconostoc* causing malo-lactic fermentation in Australian wines. Am. J. Enol. Vitic. *15*, 184–186.

FULLER, W. L., and BERG, H. W. 1965. Treatment of white wine with Nylon 66. *Ibid. 16*, 212–218.

GEISS, W. 1952. Die Filtration von Wein, Süssmost, Schaumwein und Spirituosen. Joh. Wagner and Söhne K. G., Frankfurt.

GEISS, W. 1957. Kaltsterile Abfüllung von Wein. J. Diemer Verlag der Deutschen Wein-Zeitung, Mainz.

GERASIMOV, M. A., and KULESHOVA, E. S. 1965. Deĭstvie ionitov na vitaminy vin (Effect of ion exchange on the vitamins of wines). Vinodelie i Vinogradarstvo S.S.S.R. *25*, No. 8, 4–8.

GINI, B., and VAUGHN, R. H. 1962. Characteristics of some bacteria associated with spoilage of California dessert wines. Am. J. Enol. Vitic. *13*, 20–31.

GLAZEWSKI, I. G. A., and CRUESS, W. V. 1948. Pasteurization of wine by electricity. Wines and Vines *29*, No. 6, 31, 32.

GOLDMAN, M. 1963. Rate of carbon dioxide formation at low temperatures in bottle-fermented champagne. Am. J. Enol. Vitic. *14*, 155–160.

GRAHAM, R. P. 1959. New type of continuous juice press. Wine Institute, Tech. Advis. Committee, May 25, 1959.

GRIFFIN, A. E. 1946. Break point chlorination practices. Wallace and Tiernan Co., Tech. Bull. 213, Belleville, N. J.

GUILLIERMOND, A. 1912. Les Levures. Doin et Fils, Paris. *See also* The Yeasts by Guilliermond, A., translated and revised by Tanner, F. W. Wiley and Sons, Inc., New York, 1920.

HALTER, P.   1959.   Biologische Untersuchungen fabrikneuer Weinflaschen. Schweiz. Z. Obst- u. Weinbau 68, 211–213, 241–245.
HALTER, P.   1960.   Biological investigations of new wine bottles. Am. J. Enol. Vitic. 11, 15–18.
HARRIS, J. J.   1947.   Chlorination in the food plant. Continental Can Co., Research Dept. Bull. 13.
HAUSHOFER, H.   1958.   Die Zentrifuge als Getränkeklärmachine. Mitt. Rebe u. Wein, Serie A (Klosterneuburg) 8, 227–238.
HAUSHOFER, H., and RETHALLER, A.   1964.   Die Heissabfüllung von Wein unter besonderer Berücksichtigung des Kohlensäuregehaltes und der Reduktionsmittel. Ibid. 14, 1–20.
HENNIG, K.   1959.   Pyrokohlensäure-Diäthylester, ein neues gärhemmendes Mittel. Deut. Lebensm.-Rdsch. 12, 297–298.
HOLDEN, C.   1955.   Combined method for heat and cold stabilization of wine. Am. J. Enol. 6, 47–49. (Also Food Technol. 8, 565–566, 1954.)
HOLSENDORFF, R.   1937.   The rat and rat-proof construction. U. S. Pub. Health Serv. Suppl. 131.
IBARRA, M., and CRUESS, W. V.   1948.   Observations on removal of excess color from wine. Wine Review 16, No. 6, 14–15.
INGRAHAM, J. L., and COOKE, G. M.   1960.   A survey of the incidence of the malo-lactic fermentation in California table wines. Am. J. Enol. Vitic. 11, 160–163.
INGRAHAM, J. L., VAUGHN, R. G., and COOKE, G. M.   1960.   Studies on the malo-lactic organisms isolated from California wines. Ibid. 11, 1–4.
JAULMES, P., and MESTRES, R.   1962.   Le dosage de l'acide cyanhydrique dans les vins. Ann. technol. agr. 11, 249–269.
JAULMES, P., BESSIÈRE, C., FOURCADE, S., and CHAMPEAU, C.   1963–64.   Dosage microbiologique des vitamines et des acides aminés dans les vins après différents traitement. Bull. Société Pharm. Montpellier 23, 361–369; 24, 36–41.
JERCHEL, D., FLESCH, P., and BAUER, E.   1956.   Untersuchungen zum Abbau der 1-Apfelsäure durch Bacterium gracile. Liebigs Ann. Chem. 601, 40–60.
JORGENSEN, A.   1936.   Practical Management of Pure Yeast, 3rd ed., revised by A. Hansen. Chas. Griffin, London.
JOSLYN, M. A.   1934.   Possibilities and limitations of the artificial aging of wines. Fruit Prods. J. 13, 208, 241.
JOSLYN, M. A.   1949.   California wines. Oxidation-reduction potentials at various stages of production and aging. Ind. Eng. Chem. 41, 587–592.
JOSLYN, M. A.   1953.   The theoretical aspects of clarification of wine by gelatin fining. Proc. Amer. Soc. Enol. 1953, 39–68.
JOSLYN, M. A.   1955.   Yeast autolysis. I. Wallerstein Lab. Commun. 18, 107–122.
JOSLYN, M. A., and AMERINE, M. A.   1941.   Commercial Production of Brandies. California Agr. Expt. Sta. Bull. 652.
JOSLYN, M. A., and AMERINE, M. A.   1964.   Dessert, Appetizer and Related Flavored Wines. Univ. Cal., Division of Agricultural Sciences, Berkeley.
JOSLYN, M. A., and LUKTON, A.   1953.   Prevention of copper and iron turbidities in wine. Hilgardia 22, 451–533.
KALMBACH, E. R.   1945.   "Ten-eighty"; a war-produced rodenticide. Science 102, 232–233.

KAYSER, E. 1924. Les races des levures et leur influence sur le bouquet des vins. Chimie et industrie, Sp. No. May, 619–625.

KEAN, C. E., and MARSH, G. L. 1965. Investigation of copper complexes causing cloudiness in wines. I. II. Food Research 21, 441–447; Food Technol. 10, 355–359.

KIELHOFER, E. 1960. Neue Erkenntnisse über die schweflige Säure im Wein und ihren Ersatz durch Ascorbinsäure. Deut. Wein-Ztg. 96, 14, 16, 18, 20, 22, 24.

KIELHÖFER, E. 1963. Emploi du pyrocarbonate d'éthyl dans le traitement des vins. Ann. technol. agr. 12 (numéro hors série 1), 125–126.

KIELHÖFER, E., and WÜRDIG, G. 1960. Die Bestimmung von Acetoin and Diacetyl im Wein und der Gehalt deutscher Weine an diesen Substanzen. Wein-Wissen. 15, 135–146.

KIELHOFER, E., and WÜRDIG, G. 1964. Einige bei der Anwendung von Pyrokohlensäurediäthylester zur biologischen Weinstabilisierung auftretende Probleme. Weinberg u. Keller 11, 495–504.

KONOVALOV, S. A. 1958. Osobennosti zhiznedeyatel'nosti drozhzhei pri nepreryvnom sposobe brozheniya (Characteristics of yeast activity in the continuous method of fermentation). Mikrobiologiya 27, 120–126.

KRAMER, A., and TWIGG, B. A. 1970. Quality Control for the Food Industry. 3 ed. Vol. I. Avi Publishing Co., Westport, Conn.

KUNIN, R., and MYERS, R. J. 1950. Ion-Exchange Resins. John Wiley and Sons, New York.

KUNKEE, R. E., and OUGH, C. S. 1966. Multiplication and fermentation of Saccharomyces cerivisiae under carbon dioxide pressure in wine. Appl. Microbiol. 14, 643–648.

KUNKEE, R. E., OUGH, C. S., and AMERINE, M. A. 1964. Induction of malolactic fermentation by inoculation of must and wine with bacteria. Am. J. Enol. Vitic. 15, 178–183.

LAFON-LAFOURCADE, S. 1970. Étude de la dégradation de l'acide L-malique par les bactéries lactiques non proliférantes isolées des vins. Ann. technol. agr. 19, 141–154.

LA ROSA, W. V. 1958. Observations with the use of PVP on wines. Wine Institute, Tech. Advis. Committee, March 7, 1958.

LA ROSA, W. V. 1963. Enological problems of large-scale wine production in the San Joaquin Valley. Am. J. Enol. Vitic. 14, 75–79.

LATHROP, R. E., and PAINE, H. S. 1931. Some properties of honey colloids and the removal of colloids from honey by bentonite. Ind. Eng. Chem. 23, 328–332.

LAWRENCE, C. A., and BLOCK, S. S. 1968. Disinfection, Sterilization, and Preservation. Lea & Febiger, Philadelphia.

LÜTHI, H. 1955. Reinhefe Anwendung und Qualitäts-Produktion. Schweiz. Weinzeitung 63, 722–725.

LÜTHI, H. 1957. La rétrogradation malolactique dans les vins et les cidres. Rev. ferm. ind. alim. 12, 15–21.

LÜTHI, H., and BEZZEGH, T. 1963. A microbiological method for qualitative determination of a chemical preservative in wines. Am. J. Enol. Vitic. 14, 61–67.

MALAN, C. E., OZINO, O. I., and GANDINI, A. 1965. Gli schizomiceti malo-lattica di alcuni vini del Piemonte ed i blastomiceti predominanti nel corso della loro attivitá. Atti accad. ital. vite e vino 17, 235–280.

MARQUES GOMES, J. V., SILVA BABO, J. V. DA, and GUIMARAIS, A. F. 1954. L'emploi des bactéries sélectionnées dans la fermentation malolactique du vin. Bull. office inter. vin. *29*, No. 299, 349–357.

MARSH, G. L. 1959. Personal communication. Davis, Calif.

MARSH, G. L., and GUYMON, J. F. 1959. Refrigeration in wine making. Am. Soc. Refrig. Eng. Data Book, Vol. I, Chap. 10. (Periodically updated.)

MARSH, G. L., and JOSLYN, M. A. 1935. Precipitation rate of cream of tartar from wine. Ind. Eng. Chem. *27*, 1252–56.

MARSH, G. L., and VAUGHN, R. H. 1944. Slop disposal system based on tartrate recovery. Wines and Vines *25*, No. 6, 15, 17, 28–30, 35.

MARSH, G. L., and VAUGHN, R. H. 1959. Personal communication. Davis, Cal.

MARTINI, M. 1965. L'acido tartarico racemico come decalcificante nei vini. Riv. viticolt. e enol. (Conegliano) *17*, 379–386.

MAYER-OBERPLAN, M. 1956. Das Schönen und Stabilisieren von Wein, Schaumwein und Süssmost. Verlag Sigurd Horn, Frankfurt.

McGARVEY, F. S. PERCIVAL, R. W., and SMITH, A. J. 1958. Ion exchange develops as a process in the wine industry. Am. J. Enol. *9*, 168–179.

MENNETT, R. H., and NAKAYAMA, T. O. M. 1970. Temperature dependence of tannin adsorption by poly-N-vinyl pyrrolidone. Am. J. Enol. Vitic. *21*, 162–167.

MERCER, W. A. 1955. Cannery waste disposal and its problems. I and II. Canning Trade *77*, No. 40, 6–7; No. 41, 6–7.

MERCER, W. A., and SOMERS, I. I. 1957. Chlorine in food plant sanitation. Adv. Food Research *7*, 120–171.

MICHELBACHER, A. E., and MIDDLEKAUFF, W. W. 1954. Vinegar fly investigations in Northern California. J. Econ. Entomol. *47*, 917–922.

MICHELBACHER, A. E., BACON, D. G., and MIDDLEKAUFF, N. W. 1953. Vinegar fly in tomato fields. Calif. Agr. *7*, 19.

MIDDLEKAUFF, W. W. 1957. Biological and control observations on drosophila. Wine Institute, Tech. Advis. Committee, May 13, 1957.

MILISAVLJEVIĆ, D. 1958. Mlečno vrenje jabučne kiseline u vinu (The malolactic fermentation in wines). Arhiv Poljopriv. Nauke Tehniku *11*, 67–81. 67–81.

MILISAVLJEVIĆ, D. 1964. Méthodes d'isolement de culture et de classification des bactéries malolactiques. Bull. office intern. vin, *37*, 374–384.

MINDLER, A. B., GRUNDNER, W. T., and SELTZ, P. 1958. Ion exchange in wine treatment. Wines and Vines *39*, No. 9, 27–28, 30.

MOREAU, L., and VINET, A. 1936. Les levures selectionèes en vinification. Ann. ferment. *1*, 101–107.

MOSER, J. 1956. The ion exchanger in modern cellar practice. Am. J. Enol. *7*, 157–161.

MÜLLER-THURGAU, H. 1889. Über den Ursprung der Weinhefe- und hieran sich knüpsende praktische Folgerungen. Weinbau u. Weinhandel *7*, 427–428, 438–440.

MÜLLER-THURGAU, H., and OSTERWALDER, A. 1912. Die Bakterien im Wein und Obstwein und die dadurch verursachten Veränderungen. Centr. Bakt. Abt. B. *36*, 129–339.

MÜLLER-THURGAU, H., and OSTERWALDER, A. 1918. Weitere Beiträge zur Kenntnis der Mannitbakterien im Wein. *Ibid. 48*, 1–36.

O'CONNELL, W. J., JR., and FITCH, K. A. 1950. Waste disposal. Food Industries *22*, 71–78.

O'NEAL, R., WEIS, L., and CRUESS, W. V.   1951.   Observations on the fining of wine with casein.   Food Technol. 5, 64–68.

OSTERWALDER, A.   1934.   Die verkannten Kaltgärhefen.   Schweiz. Z. Obst- u. Weinbau 50, 487–490.

OUGH, C. S.   1960A.   Gelatin and polyvinylpyrrolidone compared for fining red wines.   Am. J. Enol. Vitic. 11, 170–173.

OUGH, C. S.   1960.   Die Verwendung von Glukose Oxydase in trockenem Weisswein.   Mitt. Rebe u. Wein, Serie A (Klosterneuburg) 10, 14–23.

OUGH, C. S., and AMERINE, M. A.   1959.   Dissolved oxygen determination in wine.   Food Research 24, 744–748.

OUGH, C. S., and AMERINE, M. A.   1960.   Experiments with controlled fermentation.   IV.   Am. J. Enol. Vitic. 11, 5–14.

OUGH, C. S., and AMERINE, M. A.   1961.   Studies with controlled fermentation. VI.   Effects of temperature and handling on rates, composition, and quality of wines.   Ibid. 12, 117–128.

OUGH, C. S., and AMERINE, M. A.   1966.   Effects of Temperature on Wine Making.   Calif. Agr. Expt. Sta. Bull. 827.

PACOTTET, P.   1926.   Vinification.   Librairie J.-B. Baillière et Fils, Paris.

PARKER, M.   1948.   Food Plant Sanitation.   McGraw-Hill Book Co., New York.

PAUNOVIC, R.   1963.   Possibilité d'utilisation des radiations dans la conservation des vins.   Ann. technol. agr. 12 (numéro hors série 1), 143–153.

PEARSON, E. A., FEUERSTEIN, H., and ONODEAN, B.   1955.   Treatment and utilization of winery wastes.   Univ. Calif. Sanitary Engineering Lab., Berkeley.

PEDERSON, C. S. GORESLINE, H. E., and BEAVENS, E. A.   1935.   Pasteurization of New York wines.   Ind. Eng. Chem. 27, 1257–1265.

PERCIVAL, R. W., McGARVEY, F. X., and SONNEMAN, H. O.   1958.   Wine stabilization by columnar ion exchange.   J. Assoc. Offic. Agr. Chemists 38, 144–151.

PETERS, P.   1970.   Personal communication.

PEYNAUD, E.   1955.   Neue Gegebenheiten bezüglich des biologischen Säureabbaues.   Mitt. Rebe u. Wein, Serie A (Klosterneuburg) 5, 183–191.

PEYNAUD, E., and DOMERCO, S.   1959.   Possibilité de provoquer la fermentation malolactique en vinification à l'acide de bactéries cultivées.   Compt. rend. acad. agr. France 45, 355–358.

PEYNAUD, E., and DOMERCQ, S.   1961.   Études sur les bactéries lactiques des vins.   Ann. technol. agr. 10, 43–60.

PEYNAUD, E., and GUIMBERTEAU, G.   1962.   Sur la formation des alcools supérieurs par les levures de vinification.   Ibid. 11, 85–105.

PIFFERI, P. G., and ZAMORANI, A.   1964.   Contributo alla conosenza della sostanza colorante dei vini.   II.   Riv. viticolt. e enol. (Conegliano) 17, 115–121.

POPPER, K., and NURY, F. S.   1964.   Recoverable static regenerant ion exchange treatment of Thompson Seedless grape juice.   Am. J. Enol. Vitic. 15, 82–86.

PREHODA, J.   1963.   Hömérsékletszabályozás a vörös borok erjesztésénél.   (Temperature regulation of the fermentation of red wines.)   Borgazdaság 11, 15–23.

PROEBSTING, E. L., and JACOB, H. E.   1938.   Some effects of winery distillery waste on soil and plants.   Proc. Am. Soc. Hort. Sci. 36, 69–73.

RADLER, F.   1957.   Untersuchungen über die experimentelle Durchführung des biologischen Säureabbaues.   Vitis 1, 42–52.

RADLER, R.   1958.   Der Nähr- und Wuchsstoffbedarf der Apfelsäure-abbauenden Bakterien.   Arch. Mikrobiol. 32, 1–15.

RADLER, F. 1962. Die Bildung von Acetoin und Diacetyl durch die Bakterien des biologischen Säureabbaus. Vitis 3, 136–143.

RANKINE, B. C. 1955. Yeast cultures in Australian wine making. Am. J. Enol. 6, 11–15.

RANKINE, B. C., and BOND, R. D. 1955. Prevention of potassium bitartrate deposition in wine by cation exchange resins. Australian J. Appl. Sci. 6, No. 4, 541–549. (Abstract in Am. J. Enol. 7, 124.)

RANKINE, B. C., and EMERSON, W. W. 1963. Wine clarification and protein removal by bentonite. J. sci. food agr. 14, 685–689.

RIBÉREAU-GAYON, J. 1935. Sur le filtration des vins. Bull. assoc. chimistes, sucr., dist. 54, 212–238.

RIBÉREAU-GAYON, J., and PEYNAUD, E. 1934–1935. Études sur le collage des vins. Rev. viticult. 81, 5–11, 37–44, 53–59, 117, 124, 165, 171, 201–205, 341–346, 361–365, 389–397, 405–411; 82, 8–13.

RIBÉREAU-GAYON, J., PEYNAUD, E., PORTAL, E., BONASTRE, J., and SUDRAUD, P. 1956. La stabilisation des vins par les éxchangeurs d'ions metalliques. Inds. agr. aliment. (Paris) 7, 157–161.

RIDDELL, J. L., and NURY, M. S. 1958. Continuous fermentation of wine at Vie-Del. Wines and Vines 39, No. 5, 35.

ROSSI, E. A., JR. 1963. Ultraviolet light as an aid in winemaking. Am. J. Enol. Vitic. 14, 178–184.

RUDOLFS, W., and HEUKELEKIAN, H. 1954. Sure methods of disposing of food wastes. In Food Engineering, "Food Plant Sanitation and Maintenance," 2nd ed. McGraw-Hill Book Co., New York. (See pp. 1–13.)

RUSSELL, J. P., INGRAM, F. R., and DAKAN, E. W. 1939. Industrial hygiene survey of California wineries. California Dept. Pub. Health, Indus. Hyg. Invest. Rept. 2, 1–36.

SAMPSON, W. W. 1943. Annotated outline of the principles of control of rodents affecting man. Sanitarian 5, 271–274, 299–302; 6, 327–332, 359–361, 379–381.

SAYWELL, L. G. 1934. The clarification of wine. Wine Review 2, No. 5, 16–17. (Also Ind. Eng. Chem. 26, 981–982, 1934.)

SCHANDERL, H. 1950–1951. Über den Einfluss des Entsäuerns, verschiedener Schönungen und Lichtes auf das rH und pH der Weine. Wein u. Rebe 1950–1951, 118–128.

SCHANDERL, H. 1957. Über den Keimgehalt direkt am Kühlkanal der Glashütte verpackter neuer Weinflaschen. Deut. Wein-Ztg. 93, 155–160.

SCHANDERL, H. 1959. Die Mikrobiologie des Mostes und Weines. Eugen Ulmer, Stuttgart.

SCHREFFLER, C. 1952. Heat transfer in winery refrigeration. Proc. Am. Soc. Enol. 1952, 211–217.

SCHULLE, H. 1954. Reinhefezusatz und Gärverlauf. Deut. Wein-Ztg. 90, 736–739.

SEIFERT, W. 1903. Über die Säureabnahme im Wein und dem dabei stattfindenden Gärungsprozess II. Z. landwirtsch. Versuchs. Deut. Oesterr. 6, 567–585.

SÉMICHON, L. 1929. Les fermentations pures en vinification. Compt. rend. acad. agr. France 15, 438–446.

SIEGEL, M. 1958. The tomato menace (vinegar fly). Canning Trade 81, 7, 15.

SHARF, J. M. and LYON, C. A. 1958. Historical development of stoppers for sparkling wines. Am. J. Enol. 9, 74–78.

SILVA BABO, M. 1963. Essais d'application des bactéries malolactiques aux vins verts. Ann. technol. agr. *12* (numéro hors série 1), 57–58.

SINGLETON, V. 1959. Some possibilities of rapid aging. Wines and Vines *40*, No. 7, 26.

SINGLETON, V. L., BERG, H. W., and GUYMON, J. F. 1964. Anthocyanin color level in port-type wines as affected by the use of wine spirits containing aldehydes. Am. J. Enol. Vitic. *15*, 75–81.

SINGLETON, V. L., and DRAPER, D. E. 1961. Wood chips and wine treatment; the nature of aqueous alcohol extracts. *Ibid. 12*, 152–158.

SINGLETON, V. L., and DRAPER, D. E. 1962. Adsorbents and wines. I. Selection of activated charcoals for treatment of wine. *Ibid. 13*, 114–125.

SINGLETON, V. L., and DRAPER, D. E. 1963. Ultrasonic treatment with gas purging as a quick aging treatment for wine. *Ibid. 14*, 23–35.

SINGLETON, V. L., and GUYMON, J. F. 1963. A test of fractional addition of wine spirits to red and white port wines. *Ibid. 14*, 129–136.

SINGLETON, V. L., and OUGH, C. S. 1962. Complexity of flavor and blending of wines. J. Food Science *27*, 189–196.

SKOFIS, E. 1953. The role of refrigeration in the stabilization and clarification of wines. Proc. Am. Soc. Enol. *1953*, 69–77.

SKOFIS, E. 1957. Sanitary progress at Roma. Wine Institute, Tech. Advis. Committee, Dec. 6, 1957.

SKOFIS, E. C. 1966. Personal communication.

SOMERS, I. I. 1948. How to establish a plant cleaning program. Food Industries *20*, 8–12, 166, 199–204, 328–330.

SOMERS, I. I. 1949. How to select detergents for food plant cleaning. *Ibid. 21*, 295–296, 429–431.

SOMERS, I. I. 1951. In-plant chlorination. Food Technol. *5*, 1–7.

STAFFORD, E. M. 1958. Spray program for drosophila in wineries. Wine Institute, Tech. Advis. Committee, May 26, 1958.

STEPHAN, E. 1964. Polyäthylenstopfen für Wein- und Sektflaschen. Weinberg u. Keller *11*, 447–450.

STORER, T. I. 1948. Control of rats and mice. Calif. Agr. Expt. Sta. Circ. *142*.

SUDRAUD, P. 1963. Stabilisation biologique des vins par chauffage. Ann. technol. agr. *12* (numéro hors série 1), 131–140.

SUDRAUD, P., and CASSIGNARD, R. 1959. Travaux récents sur la fermentation malolactique en Bordelais. Vignes et Vins No. *80*, 10–13. (This issue contains other articles on the importance of the malo-lactic fermentation.)

TARANTOLA, C. 1959. Attuali vedute sulla fermentazione malolattica. Riv. viticolt. e enol. (Conegliano) *12*, 191–205.

TARANTOLA, C., and CASTINO, M. 1964. La formazione di acido cianidrico nei vini trattati con ferrocianuro potassico. *Ibid. 17*, 483–493.

THOUKIS, G., REED, G., and BOUTHILET, R. J. 1963. Production and use of compressed yeast for winery fermentation. Am. J. Enol. Vitic. *14*, 148–154. (*See also* Wines and Vines *44*, No. 1, 25–26.)

TRACY, R. L. 1931. Sterilization of fruit juices by electricity. Fruit Prods. J. *10*, 269–271.

TRACY, R. L. 1932. Lethal effects of alternating current on yeast cells. J. Bact. *24*, 423–428.

TRUAX, D. L. 1950. Why sanitation in the food industry. Proc. Am. Soc. Enol. *1950*, 124–128. (*See also Ibid. 1950*, 129–137.)

UPPERTON, A. M. 1965. Some observations on detergents and sterilizing agents in British breweries. Wallerstein Lab. Comm. 28, 137–142.

U. S. INTERNAL REVENUE SERVICE. 1962. Gauging Manual Embracing Instructions and Tables for Determining the Quantity of Distilled Spirits by Proof and Weight. U. S. Govt. Print. Office, Washington (IRS Publ. 455).

VAUGHN, R. H., and MARSH, G. L. 1945. The disposal of dessert winery waste. Wine Review 13, No. 11, 8–11.

VAUGHN, R. H., and MARSH, G. L. 1953. Disposal of California winery wastes. Ind. Eng. Chem. 45, 2686–2688.

VAUGHAN, R. H., and MARSH, G. L. 1956. Problems in disposal of California winery wastes. Am. J. Enol. 7, 26–34.

VAUGHN, R. H., NIGHTINGALE, M. S., PRIDMORE, J. A. BROWN, E. M., and MARSH, G. L. 1950. Disposal of wastes from brandy stills by biological treatment. Wines and Vines 31, No. 2, 24–25.

VENTRE, J. 1935. Les Levures en Vinification. Coulet, Montpellier, France.

WEBB, R. B. 1962. Laboratory studies of the malo-lactic fermentation. Am. J. Enol. Vitic. 13, 189–195.

WEBB, R. B., and INGRAHAM, J. L. 1960. Induced malo-lactic fermentations. Ibid. 11, 59–63.

WEGER, B. 1963. Analisi e prove di chiarificazione con la gelatina liquida. Riv. viticolt. e enol. (Conegliano) 16, 446–448.

WEGER, B. 1965. Calcium- und Natriumbentonite. Wein-Wissen. 20, 545–559.

WEINFACH-KALENDER. 1971. Weinfach-Kalender 1971. 82 Jahrgang. Verlag der Deutschen Wein-Zeitung, Mainz.

WILLIG, R. 1950. Continuous fermentation of wine. Wynboer 19, 14–15.

WILLSON, K. S., WALKER, W. O., MARS, C. V., and RINELLI, W. R. 1943. Liquid sulfur dioxide in the fruit industries. Fruit Prods. J. 23, 72–82. (See also Chem. Indust. 53, 176–186.)

WORTMANN, J. 1892. Untersuchungen über reine Hefen. I. Landwirt. Jahrb. 21, 901–936.

WUCHERPFENNIG, K., and KLEINKNECHT, E. M. 1965. Beitrag zur Veränderung der Farbe und der Polyphenole bei Abfüllung von Weisswein durch Einwirkung von Sauerstoff und Wärme. Wein- Wissen. 20, 489–514.

YANG, H. Y., JOHNSON, J. H., and WIEGAND, E. N. 1947. Electronic pasteurization of wine. Fruit Prod. J. 26, 295–299.

YERINGTON, A. P. 1958. What wineries can do about drosophila. Wine Institute, Tech. Advis. Committee, May 26, 1958.

YERINGTON, A. P. 1964. The use of dichlorvos (DDVP) in wineries for drosophila control. Wine Institute, Tech. Advis. Committee, Dec. 11, 1964.

ZHDANOVICH, G. A., NECHAEV, V. P., and IAKOVLEV, P. M. 1967. Issledovanie protsessa izvlecheniiā susla pervoĭ fraktsii iz vinogradnoĭ mezgi. Trudy Vses. Nauchno. Issledov. Inst. Vinod. Vinograd. "Magarach" 15, 21–26.

CHAPTER 7

Red Table Wine Production

OUTLINE OF RED WINE MAKING

The red, colored pigments of most grapes are localized in the skins. Therefore, in the making of red table wines the juice is fermented on the skins in order to extract this color during fermentation. In the making of white wine, on the other hand, the juice is fermented free of the skins, in order to extract as little color and tannin as possible. As the cellar operations differ somewhat in other respects the two wine types will be considered in separate chapters. For general information see Amerine and Joslyn (1970), Bioletti (1906, 1908, 1911), Bremond (1965), Geiss (1952), Ribéreau-Gayon and Peynaud (1960–1961), and Theron and Niehaus (1938).

VARIETIES

The recommended varieties for red table wine production in the various regions of California have been listed on p. 127. The comments here are on their special wine making characteristics.

There does not seem to be any doubt that Cabernet Sauvignon produces the highest quality red table wines yet made in this state. The grapes normally arrive at the winery in excellent condition and ferment well. If fermented on the skins more than 4 or 5 days, the tannin content may be high and the wines will require longer aging. Both in California and Bordeaux there has been a tendency to press early. This results in wines of less tannin and color but earlier maturity. The best Cabernets may not mature until they have had 10 or more years of bottle aging.

Pinot noir presents special problems in California because it ripens very early in the season. Also, it appears to favor a warm fermentation and in some cases, a malo-lactic fermentation. There are, further, at least two clones—one much less colored than the other. We do not believe the highest possible quality has yet been achieved from Pinot noir in this state. Both cask and bottle aging are recommended.

Zinfandel ripens unevenly and great care in harvesting must be exercised. The best wines appear to come from vineyards on the slopes of hills in regions II and III. In regions IV and V bunch rot is a problem. Contrary to pre-prohibition opinion the best Zinfandels profit by cask and bottle aging. We have tasted excellent Zinfandels of 10 to 15 years of age.

Ruby Cabernet, because of its high total acidity, should be used for red

357

table wines only when grown in regions IV and V. There does not seem to be any more rapid aging for this variety than for Cabernet Sauvignon when produced by the regular procedures from grapes grown in regions II or III. Wines produced from grapes grown in regions IV and V appear to mature more rapidly.

Petite Sirah is highly subject to bunch rot and sunburn. Grapes from regions II and III are most likely to produce the best wines. The same is true of Refosco and Carignane. Grenache produces the best red wines from grapes grown in region I. Elsewhere they should be used for producing rosé wines.

Calzin has been extensively tested for red table wines. It is deficient in color and, suprisingly, exceedingly high in tannin. It is not recommended for planting or wine making in this state. Barbera, because of its high total acidity, is recommended for planting in region IV for use in blending.

TESTING THE GRAPES

As grapes approach maturity, they should be tested frequently in order that they may be picked at the proper stage of ripeness (see pp. 86–94).

As the grapes are received, each load should be tested for Balling degree. If the grapes are found to be excessively high in sugar they should be used for making port wine or for distilling material. The addition of acid is often indicated for table wines. It is best to add the acid early in the history of the wine; for example, at the time of transfer from the fermenting vat to the storage tank. Tartaric acid is preferred in cases of low acidity (below 0.6 per cent).

For this reason, Balling (or Brix) tests on the grapes should always be accompanied by titration of the samples for total acidity. There is evidence to indicate that acidification before fermentation results in better development of bouquet and flavor than if it is delayed until fermentation is complete. In fact, addition to the crushed grapes is probably the best procedure, except for the unavoidable loss of some of the added acid in the pomace. It is also desirable to follow the pH during ripening as musts of high pH are unsuitable for making high quality table wines. A pH meter (p. 91) is used for this determination.

PICKING

In California harvesting is usually done, often by contract, by crews of itinerant pickers who pick several vineyards in succession. Short, curved knives or short-bladed shears are used in cutting the bunches from the vines but picking shears, such as used for table-grape harvesting, are preferable, as they slash the fruit less and also permit easier cutting out of rotten berries. Lug boxes holding from 45 to 55 lbs. of grapes have been

Fig. 88.   Picking by Bucket and Transportation by Gondola

used for picking and for transporting the grapes to the winery in most table-wine vineyards. However, small gondolas which can be moved through the vineyard are becoming increasingly popular. The gondola is taken directly to the winery, Figs. 88 and 89. In some of the large dessert-wine grape vineyards, the grapes, after picking into buckets or lugs, are dumped into large steel-bodied, hopper-like trucks (called gondolas) and transported long distances in bulk to the winery. This is objectionable from the standpoint of sanitation and microbiology, for inevitably many of the grapes are crushed in bulk transfer, with consequent fermentation and contamination with fruit flies (*Drosophila melanogaster*). Fermentation, bacterial growth, and volatile acid formation have then been noted in gondola trucks where crushing was delayed. Less objectionable is the practice of picking into moderate sized bulk containers which are transported directly to the crusher. Economy dictates that as little handling of fruit be employed as possible, consequently direct mechanical harvesting into containers which can be mechanically dumped into the crusher is now common and will undoubtedly generally be used in the future.

Lug boxes or picking buckets or tubs should be clean; not moldy or vinegar sour. Washing and steaming such containers during the vintage, especially after a rain, is necessary.

Courtesy of Wine Institute

FIG. 89. GONDOLA TRUCKS BEING DUMPED INTO CONTINUOUS CONVEYOR

Only sound (not moldy, or mildewed, or vinegar-soured) grapes should be taken by the pickers. Some varieties develop a considerable quantity of second crop bunches that ripen 2 or 3 weeks later than the main crop. If the main crop is overripe, it is often desirable to pick the second crop along with the first in order that the second crop will furnish much needed acidity. On the other hand, if the grapes are not overripe, it is better that the second crop be left on the vine to ripen. The Zinfandel usually sets a good second crop which if picked with the first crop in a cool region will make the must unduly acid. Training pickers is recommended.

In the eastern United States and in European vineyards special baskets are generally used by the pickers. Baskets, however, are difficult to keep clean.

TRANSPORTATION

Many wineries, particularly in the coastal countries of California and in the wine districts of European countries, are located in or adjacent to the vineyards. In such cases, transportation to the winery is quick and convenient. On hilly slopes, it may be necessary to use a tractor-drawn sled; but usually the truck can drive directly to the lugs of grapes stacked at the ends of the rows. In some European vineyards, the freshly picked grapes are crushed in the vineyard into open wooden tanks on wheels. This saves space but is not recommended for the warm California conditions. See Winkler (1935) on the importance of rapid transportation.

In California the truck carries the lugs of grapes directly to the crusher, Fig. 89, the quicker the better. Long distance bulk transportation of wine grapes in large gondola trucks is not recommended for the reasons previously given: crushing may occur during loading and in transit with possible spoilage by wild yeasts, molds, and vinegar bacteria or contamination with fruit flies. Some grapes are shipped 100 miles or more in the manner described. The practice is much more objectionable for thin-skinned wine grapes than for thick-skinned table grapes but it is doubtful if it can be justified on sanitary grounds. Experiments made by Cruess (1918) showed that it would be better to crush the grapes at the point of shipment into suitable tanks, and to add sulfur dioxide in sufficient amount to prevent the growth of wild yeasts, molds, and vinegar bacteria. A still better plan is, of course, to make the grapes into wine in a winery near the vineyards, and then ship the new wines to the purchaser who is too distant to permit shipment of the fresh grapes in the best condition. Crushing at the vineyard into stainless steel or lined closed tanks offers several advantages. Coupled with partial fermentation in small wineries near the vineyard it offers possible savings in transportation to central finishing plants. The residual sugar of the pomace could then be fermented and the alcohol recovered by distillation.

CRUSHING

For a discussion of crushers, see pp. 247–250.

Beneath the crusher is located a sump, of metal, concrete, or wood, into which the crushed grapes fall from the crusher-stemmer. From this sump the crushed grapes are pumped into the fermentation vat, often by a special plunger pump of wide diameter and fitted with a heavy bronze ball which serves as a valve. See pp. 290–291 for a discussion of pumps.

The crushed grapes are pumped through pipes of large diameter to the fermentation vats. These pipes are of steel; copper and aluminum have been used. It would no doubt be better practice to make these must lines of stainless steel or glass-lined steel, although the initial cost would be high. Pyrex glass piping is used in some wineries for transfer of wines; probably they could also be made in large enough diameter to serve as must lines for crushed grapes. Copper is used in some wineries for must lines but should be avoided. Aluminum is not recommended for wines. Plastic pipes are also available but should be watched for flavor pickup.

Pumps and must lines should be flushed out with water, an antiseptic, and water again after the day's crushing is over and again before use the next morning, since, in the presence of air, the juice attacks the metal. Alkali detergents should never be used on aluminum must lines. Must lines, after considerable use, often accumulate a coating of tartrate which protects the must against metallic contamination. If the must lines are steel it is desirable to leave the coating of tartrate undisturbed.

MUST TREATMENT

In some regions, and with certain varieties of grapes, the acidity of the grapes is too high and the sugar content too low for production of palatable wine. In such cases, the addition of both water and sugar may be essential. In Switzerland, where this condition prevails, sugar only is added and no water. After the wine is made, certain bacteria, discussed later, destroy the excess acidity. In Canada and eastern United States both sugar and water are used by some producers, sugar only by others. In the Burgundy region of France, sugar is used in cold years. In Germany sugar is also employed in many seasons. See pp. 8, 20, and 493.

Amelioration

In California grapes ripen very rapidly during hot weather and often become too ripe for the making of wine of normal composition. Diluting slightly with water is permissible within certain limits prescribed in the regulations but, at best, it is a poor and unnecessary practice which the better wine makers avoid by picking at the proper stage of maturity.

If the Balling degree exceeds 25°, it is considered that the grapes are not suitable for dry wine production, even if both acid and water could be added. If the grapes must be reduced more than 2° Balling by the addition of water, the resulting wine is apt to be substandard in quality. Grapes of excessively high sugar content should be used for making dessert wine (fortified wine) or should be mixed with grapes of lower sugar content, or, preferably, should be diverted to distilling material.

In California a state law forbids the addition of sugar to crushed grapes or must. However, grape concentrate may be used for amelioration as it was by a few coast wineries during the cool 1948 season.

Addition of Sulfur Dioxide

As previously stated in Chapter 6 it is essential that a small amount of sulfur dioxide, or one of its salts, be added to the crushed grapes in red wine making in order that wild yeasts and spoilage bacteria be held in check.

For sound grapes about 100 p.p.m. of sulfur dioxide is needed; for moldy or soured grapes, about twice this amount. Sulfur dioxide is preferably automatically added at the crusher. If added in the vat, pumping over should follow the addition to insure even distribution. For general principles on the use of sulfur dioxide see pp. 188–192 and 255–258.

Warming

At the end of the season, when the weather has turned cold, it may be necessary to warm the crushed grapes by drawing off the free-run, heating to about 140°F. and returning it to the vat, continuing until the mass is heated to about 70°F. in order that the yeast will initiate fermentation promptly. In the Burgundy region of France such heating is fairly common. There is evidence also that color and flavor extraction are better at 70° to 85°F. Care must be taken, however, that the fermentation is not started at such a high temperature that it will rise to the sticking point during fermentation.

Addition of Starter

The preparation of a starter of pure wine yeast has been described in Chapter 6. We shall assume that enough starter has been prepared, that is, must fermenting with a pure culture of a desirable strain of wine yeast, such as champagne Ay, burgundy, or Montrachet, or other proven strain.

Within about two hours after addition of the sulfurous acid or bisulfite, add to each 1000 gallons of crushed grapes about 20 gallons of the pure yeast starter. This period of waiting before addition of the yeast allows time for the sulfur dioxide to lose some of its germicidal value through formation of combined sulfur dioxide and also allows time for it to act upon the wild yeasts and spoilage bacteria. After the first fermentations of the season when the fermenters are filled with active yeast a lesser amount of starter may be used. Several hours after addition of the starter when the yeasts have had a chance to multiply, the crushed grapes are thoroughly punched or pumped over to mix the yeast with the entire contents of the vat.

When this vat of grapes is fermenting rapidly, the wine maker may take some of the fermenting must to inoculate another vat of crushed grapes. When it is in fermentation it may be used to start one or more other vats of crushed grapes, and so on through the season. However, it is preferable to have a fresh starter of pure yeast available throughout the season and to inoculate from one vat to the next only when no pure starter is available. This is particularly true at the end of the season when the grapes may be of less desirable quality. If too large a starter is used, the fermentation may become violent too early in the fermentation, making extra cooling necessary.

FERMENTATION

Fermentation converts grape sugars to alcohol and carbon dioxide with the liberation of considerable heat (pp. 195–198).

The carbon dioxide gas escapes from the vat. The sugar in the must is converted to alcohol which is lower in density than water. Hence the specific gravity (or the Balling degree) of the must decreases in proportion to the progress of the fermentation; and the decrease in Balling (or Brix) degree is an approximate measure of the amount of sugar that has been fermented.

Balling and Temperature Records

Most wine makers keep a record of Balling degree and temperature of the fermenting grapes against time. For example, they will usually take the Balling and temperature 2 or 3 times daily and record the data on a sheet tacked to the vat, or by writing it on the side of the tank with white chalk. A permanent record is preferred as one may wish to refer to it to explain the anomalous character of the finished wine.

In making a temperature reading a long-stemmed, metal-cased thermometer, several feet long, is inserted through the cap and readings taken immediately below the cap and also at 1 or 2 feet below the cap, Fig. 90. These thermometers are equipped with a dial scale that is very easily and quickly read. The thermometer should be checked before each season against an accurate chemical thermometer. The practice of scooping out a pailful, or dipper, of the fermenting juice and pomace, and taking its temperature with a small mercury thermometer, is apt to give very erroneous results, as much as 10°F. too low. The temperature must be taken in the vat itself. Larger tanks may have recording thermometers installed at various places in the tank. If only one temperature reading is made it should be taken after the cap has been punched down thoroughly or the contents pumped over.

Temperature observations will indicate when it is necessary to cool the fermenting must. The Balling readings also show the progress of the fermentation, as well as the approximate time to draw the free-run off the pomace and to press the pomace.

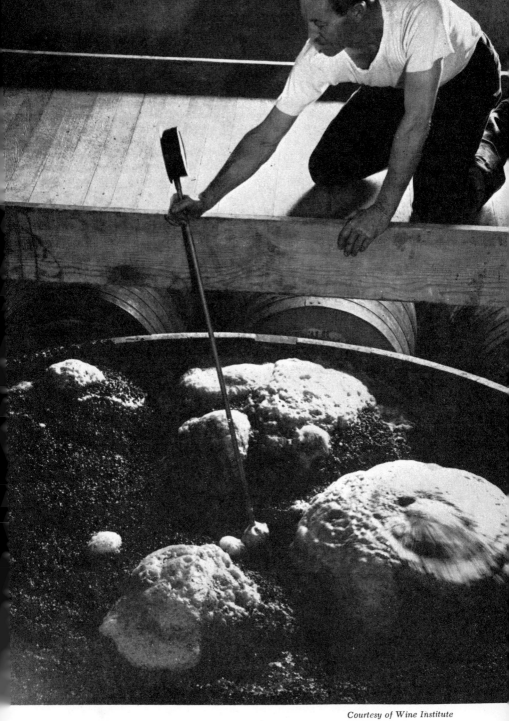

FIG. 90.   TAKING TEMPERATURE OF RED WINE FERMENTATION WITH LONG STEM
THERMOMETER

In taking the Balling degree of small fermenters, a hole is punched in the cap after it has been punched down or the contents pumped over and a dipperful of the fermenting must is taken. If it contains much pulp and skins, it should be strained. A kitchen screen-type strainer will suffice; or a layer of cheesecloth will do. For large fermenters the must is pumped over and a sample taken from the must line. The must is poured into a tall hydrometer cylinder and a hydrometer is floated in the liquid and read at the level of the liquid. Also the temperature of the must in the cylinder is taken. From a temperature correction table, such as that in Chapter 19 (Table 65), suitable temperature correction is made, if so desired. The average wine maker merely takes the Balling degree and does not bother to take the temperature. For practical purposes, this is often sufficient. See also Amerine and Ough (1957).

Glass hydrometer cylinders are too easily broken for routine use; hence the winery usually provides one made of stainless steel, copper or aluminum, or merely of a short section of rubber hose set in a wooden block. The cylinder should be about 1.5 by 15 in.

Punching and Pumping Over

The skins, pulp, and seeds (at least some of the seeds) are brought to the surface during fermentation by the buoyant effect of the carbon dioxide gas, and form a thick layer or cap, from one to several feet in thickness. This cap becomes very dense during the height of the fermentation: in very large fermenters it is so dense that it will almost hold the weight of a man. Fermentation is extremely rapid in the cap, and the temperature therein may be several degrees above that of the must beneath the cap. Consequently, thermophilic (heat-loving) bacteria may grow in the cap and in some cases cause a rapid rise in volatile acid; or the temperature may rise so high that the yeast in the cap is killed or greatly weakened. Ough and Amerine (1960, 1961) have presented data showing cap temperatures 10 to 15°F. higher than that of the main volume of must below the cap.

For these reasons, and also to promote extraction of the color and tannin from the skins and seeds, the pomace of the cap and the fermenting must should be throughly mixed several times a day. This can be done in small plants by punching by hand with a pole, on the end of which is a circular or square piece of 2- or 3-in. redwood, approximately 8 × 10 in. in size. This is hard work, especially in the high carbon dioxide atmosphere. The operation may be continuous in a fermentation room of average size. In large wineries punching by hand is impracticable, and instead of punching, mixing is attained by drawing the must from the bottom and pumping it back over the cap, spraying or spreading it over the entire surface of the cap. This is done several times a day for each vat.

Pumping over was found slightly superior to punching down for color extraction by Ough and Amerine (1961).

The progress of the fermentations, the physical movement of the skins against each other, and enzyme action result in disintegration of the pulp. Extraction of color and tannin from the skins is primarily due to the solvent action of the alcohol produced by the fermentation. Pectic enzymes apparently hydrolyze the pectic substances and hence destroy the slimy nature of freshly crushed grapes. The alcohol produced by fermentation also precipitates pectins and other organic matter. Thus, after fermentation the skins are no longer slippery to the touch and hence may be pressed easily; whereas, freshly crushed grapes are difficult to press.

STUCK WINES

If the fermentation is arrested by too high temperature, with considerable remaining unfermented sugar, the yeast will be so weakened in most cases that it will be unable to complete the fermentation. The wine may contain 1 to 6 per cent of unfermented sugar. It is therefore, neither a dessert wine nor a table wine, and is very liable to spoilage by bacteria. In a dessert winery it may be fortified with high proof brandy and made into a port wine for blending with ports of higher sugar content. In a table wine winery, without a fortifying permit or high-proof brandy, the only alternative is to complete the fermentation. (See p. 267). Closed fermenters may stick unless aerated the first or second day.

DRAWING OFF

When the fermenting must has attained the desired amount of color and tannin, it is drawn off the pomace. In California this is usually at about 4° to 10° Balling. In northern Italy the wine may be allowed to remain with the skins and seeds for a week or more after fermentation is complete, in order to secure wines of very high tannin content. Such practice is not advisable under American conditions, and is dangerous because acetification may occur. In California wineries, the crushed grapes are in the vats usually only about 3 to 4 days and rarely more than five days.

Berg and Akiyoshi (1957) showed that color extraction from Carignane and Zinfandel grapes reach a maximum with only 3 to 6 per cent alcohol. Ough and Amerine (1962) reported color extraction from Cabernet Sauvignon and from Cabernet Sauvignon-Grenache blends was not complete until about 12 per cent alcohol. In order to extract the maximum color from heavily pigmented grapes, such as Cabernet Sauvignon, they recommended prefermentation blending. This recommendation is only when blending is considered desirable. In spite of blending only about 41 per cent of the color available at the start of the fermentation was present 4 months after fermentation. For varieties such as Cabernet Sauvignon the rate of color extraction is relatively independent of the concentration of extracted color or of the amount of pigment present.

The total amount of color extracted is dependent on the amount of pigment present.

In small wineries drawing off usually consists in allowing the free-run wine to flow into a tub through a large bronze spigot and pumping the wine to a storage tank. In larger wineries, the wine usually flows direct to a centrifugal pump and is pumped to a finishing tank. In either of these methods the wine will be aerated and thus invigorate the yeast, so that fermentation will run smoothly to completion in the storage tank. Whether the yeast sediment in the bottom of the vat should be included with the free-run wine has not been determined. It is very desirable to strain out the seeds and particles of pulp that accompany the free-run as the wine flows into the sump, tub, or storage tank. The screen used for the purpose should be of stainless steel, not of galvanized iron.

The free-run wine is less astringent, smoother, and of somewhat lower color content than the press wine and, in making fine wines, should be kept separate from the press wine.

Singleton and Draper (1964) indicate that grape seeds contribute significantly to the tannin content of red wines. Complete extraction of the tannins of the seed could contribute 0.2 to 0.4 per cent tannin to the wine. Half or less actually appears in red wines in normal fermentation. P. Ribéreau-Gayon and Milhé (1970) found 35 to 50 per cent of the tannin of red wines from skins, 15 to 20 from seeds and 20 to 40 from stems. The stems reduced the color intensity of the wine. At higher fermentation temperatures the proportion of tannin from the skins increases.

Pressing

In the pressing of red wine pomace, a vertical or a horizontal basket or a Willmes press should be used in preference to a continuous press, Fig. 91. In modern plants pressure is applied by a pump and hydraulic ram operating against the press bottom. The press rises against a circular head held in a massive steel frame, as the pressure is very great. In some wineries, the pressure is applied by gears which force the cylindrical top of the press downward into the basket of pomace. In very small wineries a hand-operated lever screw furnishes the pressure. Horizontal basket presses in which pressure is exerted from both ends are also used.

In large wineries continuous presses are employed. The continuous

Courtesy of Healdsburg Machine Co.

FIG. 91. BATTERY OF HYDRAULIC PRESSES

press requires much less labor than the basket press and is more or less automatic in operation. However, it grinds the pomace considerably and hence produces a press wine which contains much pulp and sediment. It is very muddy in appearance and of poorer flavor than press wine from a basket or Willmes press. Some wineries return the press wine to a vat of freshly crushed grapes in order that most of the suspended matter will be picked up by the pomace of that vat. This is not recommended. Some wineries also combine the press wine from a basket press with the free-run wine. However, the press wine from a continuous or basket press should be kept separate from the free-run if the highest quality wine is desired. Wineries which have a distillery may use only the free-run must for wine and convert the remaining pomace and wine to distilling material.

For Bordeaux red wines Sudraud and Cassignard (1958) find that low fermentation temperatures decrease color and tannin extraction. Acidifying the musts increases the color but not the tannin and retards the start of the malo-lactic fermentation. Sulfiting delays the malo-lactic fermentation. For early-maturing red wines under Bordeaux conditions they recommend no correction of acidity, *no* sulfur dioxide, complete removal of the stems, and a pumping over, with aeration, on the second day of the fermentation. The free-run and press wines are combined. P. Ribéreau-Gayon *et al.* (1970) obtain maximum color extraction with Bordeaux grapes with 8 to 9 days of fermentation on the skins. Color decreased with longer periods but tannins continued to increase.

Berg and Akiyoshi (1957, 1958) have shown that in non-sulfited musts alcohol is the factor of major importance in color and tannin extraction. Sulfur dioxide increased color extraction but with Zinfandel decreased color stability. Increase in color is obtainable by fermenting red musts under pressure but we do not believe the results justify the expense.

THE AFTER-FERMENTATION

Although the wine from the fermentation vat may show 0° Balling, or even a reading of less than 0°, it may still contain unfermented sugar. The alcohol causes a low Balling reading as it is of lower density than sugar and water. Therefore, it is highly essential that the fermentation run to completion in the storage tank; that is, to 0.20 per cent sugar by chemical analysis or lower. Conduct of this secondary or after-fermentation requires close attention, because dropping temperature may result in sticking. Sticking is not due in this case to high but to low temperature. Supplying oxygen may result in renewed yeast growth and fermentation.

For this reason, the wines in the storage tanks during this period should be sampled every 2 or 3 days and the degree Balling measured. At this stage a —5° to +5° Balling hydrometer can be usefully employed. Temperature corrections should be made. When the degree Balling remains constant for two samplings then the wine should be analyzed chemically for sugar content as described in Chapter 19. The hydrometer is of little value at this stage as it will not reflect the relative sugar content in the presence of a varying per cent alcohol. Taste is a poor index, even if the wine maker is experienced and has a normally acute taste. Chemical analysis is the only sure procedure.

Also, the temperature should be observed occasionally and, if fermentation is arrested by too low a temperature, the wine may require warming by passage through a pasteurizer to bring the contents of the tank up to about 70°F. If fermentation ceases, and the temperature is still sufficiently high, the wine should be aerated by pumping over vigorously or allowing it to splash into a sump. Or air may be pumped into the bottom of the tank to rise vigorously through the wine. The sediment should be well stirred to resuspend the yeast to encourage growth of yeast.

FIRST RACKING, FILLING UP, ETC.

In very obstinate cases it may be necessary to add yeast food: that is, ammonium phosphate or urea. Ammonium phosphate is better as it furnishes both nitrogen and phosphorus. If only nitrogen is needed urea is adequate. The legality of such additions should be checked.

The tank of wine during this period should be protected against vinegar bacteria by means of a fermentation bung. This may be made by boring a small hole in a cellar bung and inserting through it a U-shaped tube. The bung is inserted in the bung hole of the tank and one arm of the U tube is inserted in a jar or bottle of dilute metabisulfite solution. This fermentation bung builds up a slight pressure of carbon dioxide gas in the tank, which prevents the growth of vinegar bacteria or of yeast films. The U tube may be made of block tin or copper or, for that matter, of glass tubing. Winery supply houses usually carry the bungs and tubes in stock. For very large tanks simply loosely covering the manhole of the tank is usually sufficient to maintain an atmosphere of carbon dioxide over the surface of the wine.

After bubbling in the fermentation bung practically ceases, indicating that fermentation is nearly complete, the fermentation bung is replaced by a plain, solid, cellar bung. However, some fermentation is still going on and gas pressure will develop in the tank. Therefore, workmen must loosen the bungs every day or two at first, and less frequently later, to release the gas pressure. They then insert the bung fairly tightly. Also, toward the end of fermentation new wine of the same lot is added to fill the tank completely and, as needed, this addition is repeated to keep the tank full. It is possible to dispense with a fermentation bung by merely inserting a cellar bung loosely in the bung of the storage tank during the secondary fermentation, but vinegar flies may be a problem.

Usually within six weeks at most after crushing, the wine has been completely fermented and we shall assume that it is perfectly dry; that is, that chemical analysis shows that it contains less than 0.20 per cent of the fermentable sugar. Keep the tank completely full by regular (weekly at first and later at intervals not exceeding a month) filling up with new wine of like character from smaller packages and keep the tank tightly bunged.

When a sample drawn from near the bottom of the tank shows that the wine is well settled, it is ready for the first racking. Usually this will be within 4 to 6 weeks after drawing off from the fermentation vat. The first racking in many wineries is made during the month of November or December and, at the latest, in early January in the Northern Hemisphere.

In small wineries the wine is drawn off into a tub and pumped from it to another tank. In large wineries the wine flows by hose to a centrifugal pump which pumps it to another tank. Or it may be drawn into a sump below floor level and pumped from the sump to another storage tank. Sulfur dioxide should be added to give about 100 p.p.m. total. Wines should be tasted at this time and, when necessary, appropriate blends made.

The lees, namely the sediment of yeast, pulp, tartrates, etc., left in the bottom of the tank after racking, contains considerable wine and tartrates. The lees from several tanks may be combined and allowed to settle for recovery of additional clear wine, or the wine recovered by passing through a lees press. Or, the lees may be sold "as is" for brandy production. In racking, great care must be taken not to stir up the lees.

In European countries and to a lesser extent in California, the primary fermentation is followed by the malo-lactic fermentation. This fermentation is due to lactic acid bacteria and converts malic to lactic acid with the release of carbon dioxide. This release of carbon dioxide is why many wine makers have confused the malo-lactic fermentation with a continuation of the primary fermentation. The advantage of this fermentation is that it reduces the titratable acidity and raises the pH. This is desirable for high acid wines and probably useful in the cooler regions of California in certain seasons and with some varieties. However, often the acidity is already too low and the pH too high in California and such a fermentation may lead to actual spoilage of the wine. The greatest use of the fermentation appears to be in eastern United States wines which have not been unduly ameliorated with water and in certain red wine producing areas of Europe. The malo-lactic fermentation may be induced to occur simultaneously with the alcoholic fermentation. Ough and Amerine (1961) preferred a delayed malo-lactic fermentation.

The malo-lactic fermentation can be facilitated by leaving the wine on the lees to facilitate yeast autolysis and release of amino acids, etc., for growth of the bacteria. High temperature storage also favors the autolysis. To prevent the malo-lactic fermentation early racking, cool storage and maintaining 100 p.p.m. or more sulfur dioxide is usually sufficient.

Loss of color during the secondary fermentation of red wines is commonly observed. Vetsch and Lüthi (1964) demonstrated that in some cases this was related to the degradation of citric acid by *Leuconostoc* types of bacteria. The dehydrogenation of citric acid apparently supplies the hydrogen to reduce the anthocyanin pigments.

OTHER METHODS OF RED WINE FERMENTATION

At one time during the pre-Prohibition era in California, the California Wine Association made much of its dry red wine as follows: the grapes were crushed into a vat in the usual manner. The juice was drawn off from the bottom of the vat and heated in a continuous pasteurizer to about 140°F. and pumped back into the vat. The heating was continued until the crushed grapes and must had attained a temperature of about 130°F.

They were allowed to stand, with pumping over occasionally, until sufficient color and tannin were extracted. The free-run was then drawn off and the drained grapes pressed. The two juices were combined, cooled to below 80°F., sulfited, and fermented with a starter of pure yeast. Heating destroys the slipperiness of freshly crushed grapes and renders pressing fairly simple. It also sterilizes the juice. Wines made in this manner were mellow and smooth in character and it was said that they aged more rapidly than wines made without heating. Details may be found in Bioletti (1906). Modern procedures are described by Ferré (1926), Berg (1950), Berg and Marsh (1950) and Marsh and Guymon (1959). While heat-extraction of color has many attractive features the wines often have a purplish tint and usually are difficult to clarify. A procedure for rapid extraction of color without its accompanying disadvantages would be very useful.

Coffelt and Berg (1965) treated whole grapes with steam under pressure. The objective of their study was to produce wines of good color and quality without fermentation on the skins. They reported grapes from Region IV to respond better to the heat treatment than those from I. The most favorable results for dry red wines were obtained with a 4-second heating period in 1961, and, with less favorable results in 1962 and 1963, with heating times of 27 and 10–15 seconds. Rankine (1964) showed that there was little measurable difference between wine made from grapes dipped in boiling water for 30 seconds and then held at 40–50°C. for about one hour and pressed compared to those that were fermented for five days on the skins and then pressed. There was, however, a slight reduction in quality in the wine from the heated grapes.

In some California wineries large, covered concrete fermenters are used. The cover of the vat or tank is of concrete and has a manhole near the center for escape of gas during fermentation. The tank is filled only about three-quarters full or somewhat more, leaving a large headspace. It is impossible to punch the pomace in such a tank, of course, as the tank is usually very large and hence has a very thick cap, and is covered. Hence, it is desirable to pump the must over frequently during fermentation to facilitate color extraction. The pumping over can be made automatic and a permanently installed spray system is preferable to manually operated hoses. In such a tank, the dense atmosphere of carbon dioxide in the headspace prevents acetification in the cap. However, because of its large size and the cover, much cooling is necessary to keep the temperature below the sticking point.

Another method is the Algerian lessivage system in which a special concrete vat is used. The cap is submerged and the rising gas *appears* to cause the liquid to circulate up through the cap. Actually little circulation occurs and in essence the system is a submerged cap type of fermentation.

Other systems, in which an intermittent automatic flow of liquid over the surface controlled by the pressure of the carbon dioxide produced by fermentation, are employed. When combined with temperature control such systems do give adequate color extraction but they are complicated in design, difficult to clean, and it is questionable if they result in any saving in cost.

Recently, procedures by which the crushed grapes are introduced under the cap have been recommended by Cremaschi (1951) and Maveroff (1955). The cap is then pushed to the top from which it is continuously scraped off. The theory is that the low per cent alcohol solution into which the freshly crushed grapes are introduced acts as an antiseptic and insures a clean fermentation. In essence this is a modification of the Sémichon *superquatre* procedure, Quaccia (1935) and Sémichon (1929). In practice it depends on having a continuously clean fermentation. This may be practicable under ideal conditions but it has proven difficult to control in practice. Certainly it has not been tested for the production of premium-quality wines.

The ancient practice of filling the fermentation tank with intact grapes and allowing the fermentation to proceed spontaneously (with or without covering the tank) is still used in many regions: in the Rioja district of Spain, in Italy, Switzerland, the south of France, on the Rhône, and particularly in Beaujolais, according to Chauvet et al. (1963). The persistence of the practice is apparently due to favorable effects on the quality of the resulting wines: a fine bouquet, earlier maturity, slightly more alcohol, and a softer taste. Two processes appear to take place in this procedure: an intracellular fermentation of malic acid (and possibly of some tartaric) and an improved malo-lactic fermentation. The process is not more generally used because of the longer period of fermentation, the high amount of press wine, and the danger of contamination. For previous studies see Flanzy (1935), Gallay and Vuichoud (1938), Garino-Canina (1948), Peynaud and Guimberteau (1962) and Bénard and Jouret (1963). See also p. 254.

Metal pressure tanks were introduced into the German wine industry after World War II. Klenk (1958) has reviewed this trend. He considers them to have been particularly valuable for red table wines. The main advantages of the pressure tanks are their ease of control of temperature, reduced danger of bacterial contamination, and simplicity of cleaning. In California, Ough and Amerine (1961) found pressure fermentation of Pinot noir gave less satisfactory wines than by standard procedures.

CARE OF WINE

Laboratory Examination

At the time of the first racking the composition of all new red wines should be determined by analysis for volatile acid, total acid, pH, sugar, alcohol and tannin. The sulfur dioxide content should also be determined and raised to about 100 p.p.m. — *total*

At regular intervals thereafter during aging, certain of these analyses should be repeated. Also, it is advisable to examine the wines once or twice a year under the high power of a microscope to make certain that spoilage bacteria do not gain a foothold.

On the basis of laboratory examination measures should be taken to halt any deleterious changes that may be indicated. The total sulfur dioxide content should be maintained at or about 75 p.p.m. after any desired malolactic fermentation has been accomplished. See Chapter 16 for methods of controlling wine contamination. It should be emphasized that routine sulfuring of empty casks and subsequent filling with wine results in appreciable pick-up of the sulfur dioxide by the wines placed in them. Thorough washing of sulfured casks is recommended.

Fining and Racking

In the Bordeaux district of France it is customary to fine the new wine with gelatin some time during the first year of aging; not only to clear it but also to remove excess tannin. In California wineries it is customary to fine the new wine after the first racking with bentonite as described in Chapter 6. For common wines this is the desirable procedure and hastens development of the wine. Fine red wines may be fined with gelatin after the second or third racking. Use of fresh egg-white is not recommended (p. 315). During aging the wine should be racked at least twice a year to rid it of sediment and aerate it, thus promoting normal aging.

Aging

The larger the storage container the slower is the aging. Thus, in 30,-000-to 60,000-gallon tanks the aging of dry red wine is very slow unless rackings and aerations are frequent. Aging is hastened by refrigerating, aerating and pasteurizing. In some wineries bulk common wines are subjected to such a cycle several times early in their life in order to hasten aging. Such quick aging may be justifiable for common wines but is ruinous to fine wines. Development of a fine bouquet and flavor is attained only by slow aging.

If large tanks are used for storage and aging of high quality wines it is desirable that final aging be done in much smaller containers such as ovals, puncheons, or other small oak cooperage. Many successful producers of premium quality red table wines age the wine finally for about 6 months in 50-gallon oak barrels. However, it is possible to mature a common California red wine sufficiently in one year or less for the standard wine trade. But for a fine Cabernet one should age for about three years in wood. After bottling such wines should be held at least a year in bins before labeling and casing for sale. They will improve for 5 to 15 years in the bottle.

A red wine of light body and tannin content requires less aging than does a heavy bodied and high tannin Cabernet. It may be at its best after two years in the wood and one year in the bottle. In Italy and France it is customary to drink most of the common red wines within a year after crushing. Many drinkers of common wines prefer the rather "raw" flavor of new wines to the mellow flavor of thoroughly aged wine. Light wines of low alcohol are probably best when drunk young.

Other Cellar Operations

During aging it will be necessary to filter the wine or fine it at least once and to give it a finishing filtration before bottling. Also in most California wineries it is customary to refrigerate table wines to near the freezing point (about 25° to 23°F.) for about three weeks to rid them of excess cream of tartar. Cation exchange resins are also being used (see p. 295). Stabilizing ordinary wines by heating to 140°F. and allowing to cool slowly for 3 to 4 days, followed by racking and fining and filtration has been used but may actually contribute to instability.

Many California red wines are benefited by the addition of citric or tartaric acid as they are often deficient in total acidity. This should be done early in the aging of the wine in order to permit the wine to come to equilibrium before finishing. For details of these and other operations see Chapter 6.

In Europe, where the alcohol is frequently very low, equipment to freeze out water and thus increase the alcohol has been used. The disadvantages of increasing the alcohol content by freezing wines are well known: changing the tartrate/malate ratio, increase in titratable acidity, and browning of white wines. In California, the process is unnecessary. In the occasional year when musts are low in sugar, as in 1948, California wine makers should add grape concentrate to the musts or should blend the wines. Addition of high proof grape spirits to table wines to raise their alcohol content is not recommended. In contrast to other European enologists Jaulmes and Hamelle (1954) see no objection to the use of cold-concentrated wines. The lower costs of transportation, easier storage, and the possibility of producing dessert wines or flavored sparkling wines are cited as possible advantages. We find the concept less desirable, leading to overcropping in the vineyard.

Blending

Usually the wines of a given vintage are blended and the earlier this is done the better. If the wine is to be aged as a "vintage wine" then it is not permitted to blend the wines of two different seasons. Common wines that are not to be labeled "vintage wines" are not restricted as to blending; consequently, their blending should be designed to give the best possible wines.

Also, blending should be used to maintain similarity of character of a given brand of wine from year to year in order that the customer will find the wines of that brand reasonably constant in flavor, color, and bouquet. For further details see Chapter 6.

Rosé

Pink or rosé wines are produced either by fermenting pink varieties of grapes on the skins or by using red grapes and separating the juice from the skins early in the fermentation—usually in 24 to 36 hours.

BIBLIOGRAPHY

AMERINE, M. A., and JOSLYN, M. A. 1970. Table Wines; the Technology of Their Production. 2 ed. University of California Press, Berkeley and Los Angeles.

AMERINE, M. A., and OUGH, C. S. 1957. Studies on controlled fermentation. III. Am. J. Enol. 8, 18–30.

BÉNARD, P., and JOURET, C. 1963. Essais comparatifs de vinification en rouge. Ann. technol. agr. 12, 85–102.

BERG, H. W. 1950. Heat treatment of musts. Wines and Vines 31, No. 6, 24–26.

BERG, H. W., and AKIYOSHI, M. 1957. The effect of various must treatments on the color and tannin content of red grape juices. Food Research 22, 373–383.

BERG, H. W., and AKIYOSHI, M. 1958. Further studies of the factors affecting the extraction of color and tannin from red grapes. Ibid. 23, 511–517.

BERG, H. W., and MARSH, G. L. 1950. Heat treatment of musts. Wines and Vines 31, No. 7, 23–24; No. 8, 29–30.

BIOLETTI, F. T. 1906. A new method of making dry red wine. California Agr. Expt. Sta. Bull. 167.

BIOLETTI, F. T. 1908. Improved methods of wine making. California Agr. Expt. Sta. Bull. 197.

BIOLETTI, F. T. 1911. The principles of wine making. California Agr. Expt. Sta. Bull. 213.

BREMOND, E. 1965. Techniques modernes de vinification et de conservation des vins en pays mediterraneens. La Maison Rustique, Paris.

CHAUVET, J., BRÉCHOT, P., DUPUY, P., CROSON, M., and IRRMANN, R. 1963. Évolution des acides malique et lactique dans la vinification par macération carbonique de la vendange. Ann. technol. agr. 12, 237–246.

COFFELT, R. J., and BERG, H. W. 1965. Color extraction by heating whole grapes. Am. J. Enol. Vitic. 16, 117–128.

CREMASCHI, V. W. 1951. Continuous fermentation process. U.S. Pat. 2,536,-993. June 2.

CRUESS, W. V. 1918. The fermentation organisms of California grapes. Univ. California Pubs. Agr. Sci. 4, 1–66.

FERRÉ, L. 1926. Autolyse de la matière colorante dans les raisins entiers soumis à l'action de la chaleur humide—application à la vinification des vins rouges. Compt. rend. acad. agr. France 12, 370–375.

FLANZY, M. 1935. Nouvelle méthode de vinification. Rev. vitic. 83, 315–319, 325–329, 341–347.

GALLAY, R., and VUICHOUD, A. 1938. Premiers essais de vinification en rouge d'après la méthode Flanzy. Ibid. 88, 238–242.

GARINO-CANINA, E. 1948. Fermentation "vinaire" avec des détails biochimiques du processus de la fermentation. Bull. Off. Inter. Vin. 21 (204), 55–61.

GEISS, W. 1952. Gezügelte Gärung. Joh. Wagner & Söhne K. G., Frankfurt.

JAULMES, P., and HAMELLE, G., 1954. Composition et emploi des vins concentrés per le froid a fort degré alcoolique. Ann. technol. agr. 3, 241–258.

KLENK, E. 1958. Erfahrungen mit Anwendung von Metalltanks zur Rot- und Weissweinbereitung. Deut. Wein-Ztg. 94, 398–406.

MARSH, G. L., and GUYMON, J. F. 1959. Refrigeration in wine making. Am. Soc. Refrig. Eng. Data Book, Vol. I, Chap. 10. (This is periodically updated.)

MAVEROFF, A. 1955. Vinificación continua sistéma Cremaschi. Bol. tec. fac. cien. agr. Univ. Nac. Cuyo 12, 1–32.

OUGH, C. S., and AMERINE, M. A. 1960. Experiments with controlled fermentations. IV. Am. J. Enol. Vitic. 11, 5–14.

OUGH, C. S., and AMERINE, M. A. 1961. Studies on controlled fermentation. V. Effects on color, composition, and quality of red wines, Ibid. 12, 9–19.

OUGH, C. S., and AMERINE, M. A. 1962. Studies with controlled fermentation. VII. Effect of ante-fermentation blending of red must and white juice on color, tannins, and quality of Cabernet Sauvignon wine. Ibid. 13, 181–188.

PEYNAUD, E. 1971. Connaissance et Travail du Vin. Dunod, Paris.

PEYNAUD, E., and GUIMBERTEAU, G. 1962. Modification de la composition des raisins au cours de leur fermentation propre en anaérobiose. Ann. physiol. veget. 4, 161–167.

QUACCIA, L. 1935. The Sémichon process of fermentation. Fruit Prods. J. 14, 169.

RANKINE, B. C. 1964. Heat extraction of colour from red grapes for wine making. Australian Wine, Brewing and Spirit Review 82, No. 6, 40–42.

RIBÉREAU-GAYON, P., and MILHE, J. C. 1970. Recherches technologiques sur les composés phénoliques des vins rouges. I. Influence des differentes parties de la grappe. Connaissance Vigne Vin 4, 63–74.

RIBÉREAU-GAYON, J., and PEYNAUD, E. 1960, 1961. Traité d'Oenologie. 2 vol. Librairie Polytechnique Ch. Béranger, Paris and Liége.

Ribéreau-Gayon, P., Sudraud, P., Milhé, J. C., and Canabas, A. 1970. Recherches technologiques sur les composés phénoliques des vins rouges. II. Les facteurs de dissolution des composés phénoliques. Connaissance Vigne Vin 4, 133–144.

Sémichon, L. 1929. Les fermentations pures en vinification, par le système de sélection dit de "fermentation superquatre". Compt. rend. acad. agr. France 15, 438–446.

Singleton, V. L., and Draper, D. E., 1964. The transfer of polyphenolic compounds from grape seeds into wines. Am. J. Enol. Vitic. 15, 34–40.

Sudraud, P., and Cassignard, R. 1958. Influence de certaines conditions dans la vinification en rouge. Ann. technol. agr. 7, 209–216.

Theron, D. J., and Niehaus, C. J. G. 1938. Wine making. Union of South Africa Dept. Agr. Bull. 191.

Vetsch, U., and Lüthi, H., 1964. Farbstoffverluste während des biologischen Säureabbaues. Schweiz. Z. Obst- u. Weinbau 73, 124–126.

Winkler, A. J. 1935. Making red wines in Algeria. Wine Review 3, No. 7, 14–15, 40.

CHAPTER 8

Production of White Table Wine

White wines are not simply colorless wines. They differ fundamentally from red wines in production, composition, and sensory quality. Since they are not produced by fermentation on the skins the tannin and extract contents are lower. Whereas red table wines are usually dry or nearly so white table wines may be very sweet, as with French Sauternes, the *Auslese* wines of Germany, or with a number of California types.

PROCESS

White wines are usually more delicate in flavor than red and, owing to the lack of tannin and coloring matter, defects in taste and appearance are more apparent in them. Red grapes are usually fermented in open vats, whereas white juice is preferably fermented for dry wine in covered tanks or casks. White wine fermentations are usually allowed to run to completion in tank or cask, and then the casks or tanks kept full until the first racking in November. Clarification and bottling may take place in 6 to 24 months—the lighter (lower-alcohol) types being sold first.

However, in the making of bulk standard wines in California some of the larger wineries ferment the white juice in open vats until the Balling drops to 0° before transferring it to storage tanks for the after-fermentation. The fermentation of white juice in open vats results in loss of bouquet and flavor *if* there is a quality potential in the grapes employed. For general information, see Amerine and Joslyn (1970), Benvegnin *et al.* (1951), Heide and Schmitthenner (1922), Jordan (1911), Moreau and Vinet (1929), Nègre and Fançot (1965), Saller (1955), and Troost (1961).

Varieties

The recommended varieties for planting in California have already been listed (pp. 125–126). Some further comments here regarding their enological characteristics seem desirable.

White Riesling is *the* variety for Riesling wine if one can afford it. It is a shy producer, sunburns easily, and requires a low fermentation temperature. In California it is most often erroneously named Johannisberg (or Johannisberger) Riesling but White Riesling is preferable. Sylvaner (Franken Riesling) and the so-called Grey Riesling have little Riesling character, either in this country or abroad. The Walschriesling (Italian Riesling) is not grown commercially in this country and does not produce a Riesling wine in the countries where it is grown (Italy and Yugoslavia) but its wine is pleasant. The Emerald Riesling has a distinctive aroma, more reminiscent of its muscat than its Riesling parent. Its tendency to darken, as noted by Berg and Akiyoshi (1956) is a serious defect but its high acidity is a more than compensating factor, especially in regions III and IV in California where the warm climatic conditions lead to low acidity in other varieties. The Sylvaner, Grey Riesling, and Emerald Riesling each vinified separately and properly cared for have a place in our wine industry if planted in the correct region. Because of their tendency to darken musts of Grey and Emerald Rieslings should probably be well settled before fermentation.

Chardonnay produces excellent wines but is a poor producer. It should be fully matured before harvesting if the characteristic ripe grape aroma is to be developed. Ballings of 23° are desired. Another low producer is the Gewürztraminer. However, its distinctive aroma makes it useful. Very careful harvesting is necessary to secure sufficient maturity for flavor but one must avoid low acidity and excessive sugar by too late harvesting. Flora, a new release of the California Agricultural Experiment Station is now being extensively tested as a supplement to or replacement of Gewürztraminer.

Sémillon is one of the best all-purpose varieties now available, if it is not overcropped and is not picked too early. Picked in mid-season at Ballings of 22.5 to 23.5, it is the basis of a good standard white table wine. At slightly higher Ballings, even under California conditions, it can produce sweet table wines. In years of early rainfall immediate harvesting is advisable to prevent excessive botrytis rot.

Sauvignon blanc is an excellent variety but must be mature if its wine is to have a characteristic aroma. This means harvesting at a Balling of at least 22.5°. Overcropping is possible and delays maturity. Wines from overcropped vines also have less flavor. Some of the best white table wines of California have been made from this variety.

For standard white wines French Colombard, Folle Blanche, Chenin blanc, and Veltliner are all useful. Some rot may develop in Chenin blanc and Folle Blanche in rainy years. Delay in maturity owing to overcropping is a fault of Veltliner. Still under trial is Helena, a new and promising hybrid of the California Agricultural Experiment Station. Aligoté is probably about as useful as these varieties.

Not recommended for general planting for white table wines are Trebbiano (Ugni blanc or St. Emilion), Palomino (darkens), Sauvignon vert (low acidity), Green Hungarian (thin, neutral wines), and Burger (thin but possibly useful as a sparkling wine stock); or table grape varieties such as Thompson Seedless, etc.

PICKING AND TRANSPORTING

The proper time of harvest varies from variety to variety, region, season, amount of crop, and the prospective use of the fruit. The only way to fix the time accurately is to determine the maturity of the grapes in the vineyard as outlined on p. 86 *et seq.* For early-maturing, fruity, white table wines harvesting can begin at 20° to 21° Balling. For richer more flavorful slower-maturing wines harvesting may be delayed to Ballings of 22° to 23°. The acidity and pH must also be considered. Wines of better flavor and keeping quality and easier clarification are produced from musts with an acidity of over 0.70 per cent (as tartaric) and pH of 3.3 or lower.

In California the white grapes are preferably picked into clean lug boxes or aluminum tubs; carried to the end of the row to be picked up by truck or conveyed into small or large metal containers for transport to the winery, Figs. 92 and 93. If the vineyard is on a steep slope the boxes are

Fig. 92.   Dumping Grapes in a Conveyor to Gondola

moved by tractor-drawn sled which delivers them to the truck. Increasing amounts of grapes are transferred in the vineyard to small or larger gondola trucks. Where the transfer is carefully made, the gondolas clean, excessive crushing of the grapes avoided, and the movement to the winery rapid, the system works well. However, it is difficult to transfer the delicate white grapes long distances in gondola trucks without·considerable crushing. Harvesting directly into large metal containers which can be unloaded by power lifts is also common. Mechanical harvesting is now being widely used in New York and California.

Great care should be exercised in picking in order to avoid moldy bunches, particularly late in the season. In some European vineyards, Champagne, for example, each bunch is inspected and, if necessary, unfit individual berries are removed by small shears. Such extreme care is not necessary or economically possible in California; however, after early rains the bunches which become moldy should not be picked for wine making.

The boxes or baskets should be scrupulously clean and free of all mold.

Courtesy of Valley Foundry and Machine Works, Inc.

Fig. 93.   Grape Harvesting Dump Trailer

PROCESSING

Crushing

The Garolla-type crusher is now commonly used in California for crushing white grapes and is very satisfactory for the purpose. Very few wineries still use the old fashioned steel rolls and the conventional stemmer. Crushing equipment is described in Chapter 6.

The grapes should be more thoroughly crushed than those for red wine making in order to facilitate pressing. The stems are removed by both types of crushers and stemmers; but often some are returned to the crushed grapes as the press is being filled, since they make pressing easier and more effective. Crushed fresh grapes are gelatinous or slimy and very difficult to press.

While most of the copper and iron dissolved before fermentation from metallic equipment is lost in the lees after fermentation, nevertheless, it is good practice to avoid such metallic contamination by using stainless steel crushers, stemmers, pumps, and must lines.

Juice Separation

From 75 to 150 p.p.m. of sulfur dioxide, or its equivalent in bisulfite or metabisulfite, should be added to the must line or to the crushed grapes as the vat is being filled, in order to prevent browning of color and growth of wild yeasts. See pp. 188–192 and 255–258.

A number of different systems of handling the crushed grapes are used in this state. The Willmes press most expeditiously gives the highest yields of clear juice. Basket-type hydraulic presses, Fig. 94, gave relatively clear juice but are slow to operate. Pressure should be gentle at first until a good press cake is established. In some cases hydraulic presses are operated in connection with a roller juice-extractor followed by a final pressing in a continuous press. Juice extractors and continuous presses inevitably grind up the pomace and yield cloudy musts with considerable suspended material. The must from continuous presses should be kept separate from the free-run or basket-press must.

Courtesy of Presse- u. Informationsamt der Bundesregierung

FIG. 94. BASKET PRESS AND PRESSED POMACE

In order to increase yields some wineries place the crushed grapes in false-bottomed tanks or hoppers and allow the free-run juice to drain before pressing. Some hoppers have mechanical arrangements to facilitate draining. Better methods of separating the liquid from the solids with respect to labor and quality would be of great value to the wine industry. Wineries with needs for distilling material may use only the free-run juice and add water to the remaining pomace to produce distilling material. (253–254).

Rack-and-cloth presses are not employed in California. They are often used in eastern United States for the native grapes which are very slippery and hence difficult to press in basket presses (pp. 251–253).

In some wineries the crushed grapes may be allowed to stand in the vat overnight to extract a small amount of tannin and to lose some of their sliminess. However, this treatment can easily be overdone, resulting in browning of the color and extraction of too much tannin and skin flavor. For common wines made in districts of hot summer climate it may be advisable to ferment white grapes on the skins for several hours to extract tannin. This tannin aids in later clarification with gelatin; however, too much color may be extracted.

Settling

As previously recommended, the crushed grapes and must should contain at this stage of the process about 75 to 150 p.p.m. of sulfur dioxide. This will prevent fermentation of sound grapes for 8 to 24 hours, depending on the temperature and the condition of the grapes. It is considered good practice to keep the must as cool as possible and allow it to settle overnight. The settled juice is then drawn off the sediment. This rids it of much suspended material.

The sediment may be combined with that from other lots and fermented separately. Settled musts produce earlier-clarifying wines but some believe they are less flavorful. Settling is particularly desirable with musts for sweet table wines. Musts from grapes infected with *Botrytis* should always be settled.

Amelioration

Acid, if needed, may be added at this time. Addition of acid before fermentation promotes clean fermentations and apparently gives smoother wines than if added later during aging; but losses of acid in the lees are greater if the acid is added before fermentation. Tartaric acid is preferred. Citric should not be used before fermentation. Fumaric acid is cheap and satisfactory for standard wines. U.S.P. grade tannin at the rate of about 0.25 to 0.50 lb. per 100 gallons aids in clearing and stabilization but the wine will usually be slightly darker and the practice is now uncommon. For use of pectic enzymes see Kilbuck *et al.* (1949), Berg (1959) and pp. 97—98 and 315.

Addition of Starter

A starter of pure yeast to the extent of 2 to 3 per cent is advisable. The yeast should be of an agglomerating, i.e., granular type, such as champagne or burgundy strains. Use of fermenting musts as starters is not recommended. They are not as pure as properly prepared yeast starters (see pp. 259–264).

FERMENTATION

White wines for the best results should be fermented at lower temperatures than red wines. The most desirable temperature range under California conditions is about 50° to 60°F. (see Tchelistcheff 1948). At 80°-F. and above, bouquet, aroma, and flavor are damaged. Fermentation is conducted in lined steel, concrete or wooden tanks, ovals, or puncheons. The smaller the container the easier the control of temperature but the greater the problem of controlling oxidation.

During the height of the fermentation cooling will usually be necessary in tanks, but not in barrels. Some wineries ferment in special cold rooms (50°F. or lower). In such rooms carbon dioxide accumulates at the floor level and appropriate safety measures should be taken.

Small containers should be protected with fermentation bungs throughout the fermentation. During the final stages it is also advisable to equip the tanks or large casks with fermentation bungs to prevent acetification. Also, during the last slow stages of fermentation, the containers should be kept full.

Geiss (1952) has advocated controlling the rate of fermentation of white table wines by fermenting in pressure tanks. The pressure is allowed to build up to about eight atmospheres when fermentation nearly ceases. The pressure is then released and allowed to build up again. This procedure seems to give good results in Germany and has been recommended in South Africa and Australia. The results of Amerine and Ough (1957) and of Ough and Amerine (1960) in California have not been favorable—the pressure-fermented wines being higher in volatile acidity and more subject to bacterial spoilage. We believe that control of temperature as a means of maintaining a slow rate of fermentation is more rational. Saller's (1955) results are suggestive.

Ribéreau-Gayon *et al.* (1963) have shown increased quality of white wines prepared from musts heated 149° to 167°F. before fermentation. This may be true of musts more or less infected with *Botrytis* and other molds. We believe this result should be accepted with caution for California conditions—if for no other reason than cost.

AGING AND FINISHING

Racking should be done as soon as fermentation is complete, usually in early December or *sooner* in warm cellars. The total sulfur dioxide content should be maintained at about 100 p.p.m. in California white table wines to prevent darkening of the color, though high acid wines require less. The final sugar content of *dry* white wines should not be above 0.12 per cent. Spoilage of wines with residual sugar may occur unless special attention is given to their keeping. However, modern wineries are able to handle wines with residual sugar without spoilage. Rapid clarification by chilling, fining, and close-filtration are employed. Storage under constant low temperature conditions is also helpful.

The addition of high grade tannin is occasionally advisable early in the aging process in order to stabilize the wine. It should be white U.S.P. tannin. The amount required is small, usually less than 0.05 per cent. Any excess can be removed later by fining with gelatin. Use of Cufex or other approved procedures to remove excess iron and copper is more often advisable (see pp. 315–316 and 558–562).

Aging and cellar operations such as fining, racking, filtration, refrigeration to remove excess tartrates, and other operations are about as previously described for red wines. Stabilization by heating to 140° to 142°F. with bentonite may be useful in clarifying wines of high nitrogen content (p. 552). In some large wineries common white table wines are rapidly aged as previously described for red wines but fine white wines are aged slowly and bottled at 1 to 2 years of age. Fine white wines are usually greatly improved by aging in the bottle for 2 to 3 years, Fig. 95.

Heating of table wines for 15 to 30 days at about (128°F. in the absence of oxygen gave increased odor complexity and greater bottle bouquet in the experiments of Singleton *et al.* (1964). Whether the wines have consumer acceptability has not been determined.

SWEET TABLE WINES

Dry California sauterne is handled in the same manner as dry table wines, i.e., they are the same as California chablis and rhine wines.

Sweet sauterne requires additional treatment. This type may be made from very sweet grapes and the fermentation arrested by racking before fermentation is complete and adding a heavy dose of sulfur dioxide (250 p.p.m. or more). This sulfur dioxide will decrease and be fixed during aging.

One method of sweetening the sauterne in California is to add, after aging, the required amount of grape juice preserved in the unfermented condition with about 1000 p.p.m. or more of sulfur dioxide. This preserved juice is called *muté* from the French. This procedure is not recommended as it results in wines of high sulfur dioxide content.

Another method is by the addition of a white dessert wine. This increases the alcohol content and may give the wine a dessert wine character. Concentrate should not be used for sweetening finished wines as the resulting wines are very difficult to clarify. Sauterne usually requires stabilization as outlined in the next section. Sucrose cannot be used for sweetening California table wines.

Courtesy of Presse- u. Informationsamt der Bundesregierung

FIG. 95. BOTTLE AGING CELLAR FOR WHITE WINES

Amerine and Ough (1960) and Ough and Amerine (1963) have demonstrated that high quality sweet table wines can be produced using grape concentrate. However, their concentrate was produced in a Howard "Lotemp" vacuum concentrator in which the must temperature during concentration is kept between 60° and 70°F. The resulting concentrate (70° Brix) had a greenish color and no caramel odor. The concentrate gave no test for hydroxymethylfurfural. They preferred to add the concentrate to finished dry table wines. One possible disadvantage of adding the concentrate after the fermentation is that the dextrose/levulose ratio is higher. Since levulose is sweeter than dextrose, this would indicate that at the same total sugar content the after-fermentation concentrate wines might taste less sweet. Their sensory tests did not show this to be a significant factor. They reported that DEPC (100 to 200 mg. per liter) plus 100 to 125 mg. per liter of sulfur dioxide was effective in stabilizing the wines. Sterile membrane filtration is also available and is widely used.

Recommendations for commercial production of wines from botrytised grapes in California have been given by Nelson and Nightingale (1959). See Dormontal (1930) for the French process. They stress the importance of humidity control during the infection and desiccation periods. See p. 155 for the process. In order to facilitate commercial operation Nelson et al. (1963) developed a technique for the large scale production of spores of Botrytis cinerea Pers. The mold was grown in liter Roux culture bottles at 20–22°C. in indirect light. The spores could be stored for at least ten months without appreciable reduction in viability.

The use of special yeasts in the production of sweet table wines has not yet been brought to commercial perfection. The results of Peynaud (1957) for Bordeaux musts would indicate preferential use of Saccharomyces bayanus for dry wines and its avoidance (or that of S. bailii) for sweet table wines. Peynaud stresses particularly the danger of contamination with undesirable yeasts from equipment and the surroundings (floors, walls, etc.).

California dry sauterne should contain less than 1 per cent of sugar by chemical analysis; California sauterne, less than 3 per cent and more than 2 per cent; and California chateau type, more than 6 per cent. French Sauternes usually have more than ten per cent of reducing sugar.

STABILIZATION

White table wines in California should become permanently clear, i.e., stable during the first year's aging. If they are to be bottled earlier it may be necessary to stabilize them by flash pasteurization to about 142°F. This may be followed by holding them at about 130°F. for 24 to 48 hours, accompanied by about 100 p.p.m. of freshly added sulfur dioxide. A bentonite fining is then given, followed at 48 hours by racking, cooling, and filtering. Or, the wine is stabilized by flash pasteurization to 160° to 185° F. followed by cooling, refrigeration for several weeks to remove tartrates and colloids (or by ion-exchange treatment), fining, and filtration. Neither of these procedures are desirable from the quality point of view.

The first of the two methods removes colloids and some metals, particularly copper. Check the stability of white wines as directed in Chapter 15.

In stubborn cases, it may be necessary to fine with Cufex or other permissible procedures as described in Chapters 6 and 15, in order to remove heavy metals and certain unstable colloids; in fact, both pasteurization and treatment for metal removal may be necessary with some wines, particularly those of certain years.

BIBLIOGRAPHY

AMERINE, M. A., and JOSLYN, M. A. 1970. Table Wines: the Technology of Their Production. 2 ed. University of California Press, Berkeley and Los Angeles.

AMERINE, M. A., and OUGH, C. S. 1957. Studies on controlled fermentations. III. Am. J. Enol. 8, 18–30.

AMERINE, M. A., and OUGH, C. S. 1960. Methods of producing sweet table wine. Wines and Vines 41, No. 12, 23–29.

BENVEGNIN, L., CAPT, E., and PIGUET, G. 1951. Traité de Vinification. 2 ed. Librarie Payot, Lausanne.

BERG, H. W. 1959. The effects of several fungal pectic enzyme preparations on grape musts and wines. Am. J. Enol. Vitic. 10, 130–134.

BERG, H. W., and AKIYOSHI, M. 1956. Some factors involved in browning of white wines. Am. J. Enol. 7, 1–7.

DORMONTAL, C. 1930. Sauternes. J. Bière, Bordeaux.

GEISS, W. 1952. Gezügelte Gärung. Joh. Wagner und Söhne, Frankfurt.

HEIDE, C. VON DER, and SCHMITTHENNER, F. 1922. Der Wein. F. Vieweg und Sohn, Braunschweig, Germany.

JORDAN, R. 1911. Quality in Dry Wines Through Adequate Fermentations. Privately Published, San Francisco.

KILBUCK, J. H., NUSSENBAUM, F., and CRUESS, W. V. 1949. Pectic enzymes. Investigations on their use in wine making. Wines and Vines 30, No. 8, 23–24.

MOREAU, L., and VINET, E. 1929. Guide de Vinification Rationnelle des Raisins Blanc. 2 ed. Imprimerie des Sciences Agricoles, Paris.

NEGRE, E., and FRANÇOT, P. 1965. Manual Pratique de Vinification et de Conservation des Vins. Flammarion, Paris.

NELSON, K. E., and NIGHTINGALE, M. S. 1959. Studies in the commercial production of natural sweet wines from botrytised grapes. Am. J. Enol. Vitic. 10, 135–141.

NELSON, K. E., KOSUGE, T., and NIGHTINGALE, A. 1963. Large-scale production of spores to botrytise grapes for commercial natural sweet wine production. Ibid. 14, 118–128.

OUGH, C. S., and AMERINE, M. A. 1960. Studies on controlled fermentations. IV. Ibid. 11, 5–14.

OUGH, C. S., and AMERINE, M. A. 1963. Use of grape concentrate to produce sweet table wines. Ibid. 14, 194–204.

PEYNAUD, E. 1956–1957. Les problèmes microbiologiques de la vinification et de la conservation des vins blancs doux. Vignes et Vins 51, 5–7; 52, 11–13; 54, 8–12; 55, 13–15.

RIBÉREAU-GAYON, J., CASSIGNARD, R., SUDRAUD, P., BLOUIN, J., and BARTHE, J. C. 1963. Sur la vinification en blanc sec. Comp. rend. acad. agr. France 49, 509–512.

SALLER, W. 1955. Die Qualitätsverbesserung der Weine und Süssmoste durch Kälte. Verlag Sigurd Horn, Frankfurt.

SINGLETON, V. L., OUGH, C. S., and AMERINE, M. A. 1964. Chemical and sensory effects of heating wines under different gases. Am. J. Enol. Vitic. 15, 134–145.

TCHELISTCHEFF, A. 1948. Comments on cold fermentation. Wine Technol. Conf., Aug. 11–13, Davis 1948, pp. 98–101.

TROOST, G. 1961. Die Technologie des Weines. 3 ed. E. Ulmer, Stuttgart.

CHAPTER 9

Production of Sherry

Sherry is the most important California wine type. Production in 1955 was about 30 million gallons. Joslyn and Amerine (1964) state that sweet white wines of low acidity containing unfermented sugar readily develop on exposure to air a peculiar characteristic flavor known as rancio (*goût de rance* in France). The excessive caramelized odor of some baked sherries is not, according to Joslyn and Amerine, a true rancio flavor.

There are three types of wine sold under the name of sherry. The first is that of the flor sherries of Jerez de la Frontera in Spain which owe their characteristic flavor and bouquet to the growth and action of flor yeasts that develop on the surface of the wine. Similar types are produced in Australia, California, Canada, the Jura region of France, the Soviet Union, and South Africa. The second type is California sherry that owes its flavor and bouquet to baking. This type resembles the wine of the island of Madeira more than any other. The third type is that which is aged in small cooperage for several years without flor yeast or baking. The aged non-flor sherries of Australia and California are of this type, as are some of the wines of Banyuls in the south of France and the Prioratos of northern Spain.

Sherry, particularly if dry, is used traditionally as an appetizer wine or cocktail hour beverage.

CALIFORNIA SHERRY

The origin of the California baked sherry process is not definitely known. One might assume that it began as an attempt by a California wine maker to produce wines similar in flavor and bouquet to certain kinds of Spanish sherry. If so, the attempt failed. It is known that some California sherry in the last century was baked in glass hot houses in barrels or puncheons, heat being furnished by the sun. Later, artificially-produced heat was employed. See Amerine and Twight (1938), Marquis (1936), and Twight (1936).

The principal sherry producing areas in California are located in the San Joaquin Valley, the Lodi district and in southern California.

Grapes

In Spain the Palomino is the principal variety grown for sherry production. It is low in acidity but the sugar content is very acceptable for

391

sherry, when well ripened. It is rather neutral in flavor and aroma and the wines darken in color after production, according to Berg and Aki-yoshi (1956). In California other white varieties available in abundance are also used. These include the Thompson Seedless variety (Sultanina) grown extensively in the San Joaquin Valley for raisin production and for fresh shipment for table use; Malaga, an important white table and shipping variety; Emperor, a shipping grape of light red skin color and white juice; and the Tokay (Flame Tokay), a red grape of white juice grown extensively in the Lodi area. In New York and other eastern states labrusca varieties characterized by their pronounced varietal flavor are used. By the Tressler method the foxy flavor is partially eliminated (p. 499).

In the making of baked sherry, the grape variety is probably of less importance than in the making of any other California wine, because the flavor and bouquet of the final product depend chiefly on the baking process and other cellar operations. However, varieties of marked flavor, such as the Muscat of Alexandria, should not be used, because sherry should not possess a Muscat varietal flavor.

Picking and Delivery

The grapes for sherry making should be well ripened, as the final acidity should not be as high as for table wines and the corresponding pH value may be somewhat higher. Berg (1956) made sherries of various pH values by acidifying new white wine made from Tokay grapes, the adjusted pH values being 4.0, 3.8, 3.6, 3.4, and 3.2. Experienced tasters gave the sherry of pH 3.2 the highest score and those of 3.4 and 3.6 a score that was a close second to that of pH 3.2. The sherry of pH 4.0 was given the lowest rating. The chief defect of the Palomino variety is its relatively high pH.

Some sherry is made from the grapes sorted out at packing houses as unsuitable for shipping fresh for table use. These grapes are usually sound, but early in the shipping season may be lower in Balling degree and higher in acidity than is desired. However, sherries made from such grapes may be useful for blending.

In the principal sherry producing districts of the State the grapes are picked into large pans or lug boxes and transferred to gondola trucks for delivery to the winery, or are first placed in small gondolas which in turn are emptied into large gondola trucks.

Crushing

Sherry making in California is usually a large-scale operation. The grapes are crushed and stemmed in the same manner as for other wines

(p. 247). Garolla-type crushers and stemmers described in an earlier chapter have superseded roller crushers and orthodox stemmers.

To the crushed grapes sulfur dioxide in the form of the gas from a cylinder of the liquid is added, or potassium metabisulfite is used. See Chapter 6 for details of adding sulfur dioxide.

Fermentation

The crushed grapes are allowed to drain and the free-run is pumped to fermenters. They are large, usually of 60,000 gallon capacity or even larger. In smaller plants concrete vats or redwood tanks of 10,000 to 20,000 gallons are used. The drained crushed grapes are generally employed to produce fortifying brandy. A starter of fermenting must from another fermentation or of must fermenting with pure yeast is usually added to the juice.

During fermentation, it is customary to artificially cool the must to maintain the temperature below 85°F. Ten of 19 plants surveyed stated that 80°F. is a more desirable maximum.

Usually the must is fermented dry or to a low sugar content. A small amount of sugar is considered desirable during baking, but is often added later in the form of angelica or fortified sherry material of high sugar content. In a survey of Martini and Cruess (1956) 11 of the 16 cellars fortified at −1° or lower Balling, one at 0° Balling, and two "when dry."

Settling and Racking Before Fortification

It is desirable to allow the wine to settle for a few days after fermentation in order to rid it of the yeast lees before fortification. Some plants allow the wine to settle and rack it before fortification. In the rush of the crushing season it is not always practicable to allow the new wine to settle before fortification; hence, it is in many cases pumped directly from the fermenter to the fortifying room.

Fortification

Government regulations formerly required that wines be placed in a separate room (fortifying room) for fortification. This is no longer necessary, but the producer must designate and properly mark the tank to be used for fortifications. Until 1971 California Department of Public Health required commercially recognized types of dessert or appetizer wines to have a range of 19.5 to 21.0 per cent alcohol by volume. Altar wines are excepted; they may have as little as 17 per cent of alcohol. Some states have different legal requirements in respect to alcohol content. Other wine producing countries have various legal standards. For example, Theron and Niehaus (1947–48) state that in South Africa the alcohol content of fortified wines may be as low as 17 per cent. The United States Federal legal range is 17 to 21 per cent for sherry and 18 to 21 per cent for all other dessert wines. California regulations are now the same as the Federal.

Wines to be consumed rather young are more pleasing (less harsh) at 18 than at 21 per cent alcohol content. Some fermentation, according to Joslyn and Amerine (1964), continues for a short time after fortification of actively fermenting must. Addition of 15 per cent of alcohol to un-fermented juice inhibits yeast development; when added to actively fer-menting juice fermentation is at first arrested but resumes later at a slow rate until the maximum alcohol level tolerated by the yeast, usually 16 to 18 per cent, is reached.

Certain lactic acid spoilage bacteria, particularly the *Lactobacillus tri-chodes* (Fornachon *et al.* 1949) can grow in the absence of sulfur dioxide at 18 to 20 per cent alcohol in dessert wines. However, if the wine con-tains 75 p.p.m. or more of sulfur dioxide, or if the pH value is below 3.4, the growth of *L. trichodes* is prevented. Other Lactobacilli are inhibited by 100 p.p.m. of sulfur dioxide.

As the quality of the wine spirits has a great effect on the flavor of dessert wines only sound, clean spirits free of objectionable flavors and odors should be used. Sherry material should be fortified with spirits of neutral flavor. The higher the alcohol content the more neutral is the fla-vor of the spirits and the lower the content of congenerics (aldehydes, fusel oils, etc.). The majority of California producers prefer wine spirits of 190° proof (95 per cent alcohol by volume) to one of lower alcohol content. The higher the alcohol content of the brandy the less will it dilute the wine.

Guymon (1955) showed conclusively that use of high aldehyde high proof for fortifying shermat did not lead to high quality baked sherry. Even baking wines high in aldehyde did not necessarily result in higher quality.

On the other hand, Joslyn and Amerine (1964) cite Costa (1938), Cas-tella (1909) and Garino-Canina (1934) as reporting that brandies of lower proof (152–156° proof, 76–78 per cent alcohol) are used in fortifying the finest dessert wines of Sicily and Portugal, because they retain a good deal of the flavor and bouquet of the wines from which they are made. Wines fortified with such brandy require longer aging than those fortified with brandy of 180–190° proof. In Australia Castella has stated: "for cheap wines, which are consumed young, or for slightly increasing the strength of old, matured wine, should such prove necessary, silent spirit highly rec-tified is used."

The new wine is pumped into a special tank approved for this purpose, where it is measured and its alcohol content determined by ebullioscope. The Federal inspector, in theory, supervises the actual addition of high proof spirits. He calculates the gallons of high proof spirits to bring the sherry material to the desired alcohol content, usually 17 to 18 per cent by volume. See Chapter 6 for methods of calculating the amount of high proof spirits needed for fortification.

It is very difficult to secure uniform mixing of high proof spirits and wine. The spirits are of lower specific gravity than the wine and tend to float. In some wineries the wine is pumped over vigorously during and after addition of the spirits until it is found by analysis that the fortified wine is of uniform alcohol content throughout the fortifying tank. In most plants compressed air is used to agitate the mixture vigorously; in some plants mixing is done by propeller or by a combination of propeller and

TABLE 34

ALCOHOL AND BALLING BEFORE AND AFTER FORTIFICATION OF SHERRY MATERIAL[1]

	Location of Winery, and Years		
	Sanger, 1906–1913	Lodi, 1938–1940	Fresno, 1938–1940
Number of samples	27	53	32
Initial alcohol content			
Range, per cent	6.2–13.4	9.8–15.5	10.8–14.2
Average, per cent	9.1	12.5	12.2
Initial Balling			
Range, degree	4.0–20.0	....–4.6	−1.7– 3.4
Average, degree	11.5	...	1.1
Final Balling			
Range, degree	...	−4.8––1.4[2]	−4.3––0.5
Average, degree	...	−3.3[2]	−2.3
Final alcohol content			
Range, per cent	18.2–23.6	20.1–23.9	20.4–21.2
Average, per cent	21.1	20.8	20.7

[1] Source of data: Joslyn and Amerine (1964).
[2] Average and range for 22 samples only.

compressed air. Aeration has the advantages, in addition to its speed, of removing excess carbon dioxide from the wine and of aiding subsequent maturation. Before the Prohibition era, Joslyn and Amerine (1964) state, some wine makers preferred to add the spirits to the fortifying tank before the wine and permit natural mixing of the two. Although, as pointed out previously, there is a slight over-all decrease in volume, heat is evolved on mixing of alcohol and wine and consequently there is a temporary increase in volume.

After thoroughly mixing, a sample of the fortified wine is carefully analyzed to see if the actual final alcohol content corresponds to the estimated, and a sealed one pint sample set aside. Two such samples representing fortifications at different periods of the month, are forwarded to the nearest laboratory of the Alcohol, Tobacco and Firearms Division of the Internal Revenue Service for analysis. There are many variations in the details of fortification, such as the type and size of the fortifying tank, the method of adding the spirits, the method of mixing and the period of time the fortified wine is left in the fortifying tank. See Chapter 6 for further information on fortification.

Typical fortification data, after Joslyn and Amerine (1964), are given in Table 34. Of interest are the higher Balling degrees of the Sanger pre-prohibition wines and their low alcohol content before fortification. The newly fortified wine destined to become sherry is known as shermat.

Settling

During fortification there is rapid flocculation of the yeast and colloids. Therefore, it is desirable to leave the newly fortified wine in the fortification tank for about 24 hours before it is racked and pumped to storage. In the rush of the season, however, this is frequently not practicable and often the new sherry material is transferred to the storage cellar immediately and settling is allowed to take place there. In any event, the sooner the newly fortified sherry material is separated from the crude lees (yeast, coagulated colloids, seeds, skins, and other solids) after settling, the better is its flavor and the more rapidly it will mellow during storage. If left on the lees too long autolysis of the yeast is apt to occur, as Fornachon et al. (1949) point out, resulting in an increase in bacterial nutrients and thus making the wine much more susceptible to spoilage by *Lactobacillus trichodes*.

Treatment Before Baking

Usually the shermat is not aged before baking. Most producers of dessert wines would prefer to age it for at least one year before baking, but economic factors prevent this for competitive sherries.

Only one of the plants in the Martini and Cruess (1956) survey refrigerated the sherry material before baking, 30°F. for 72 hours. Such treatment is usually applied to the baked product. None pasteurized the sherry material before baking. About half of the plants surveyed adjust the sulfur dioxide content before baking. Two brought it to 150 p.p.m., three to 100 p.p.m. and two to 75–85 p.p.m. Eleven of the 16 plants did not adjust the pH or total acidity of the wine before baking; one added acid to lower the pH to 3.7, one added acid to give a total acidity of 0.4 gm. per 100 ml., one to give 0.45 to 0.50 per cent and one to give 0.5 per cent total acidity. If the grapes are picked at the proper maturity adjustment of the total acidity or pH should not be necessary.

The majority of the plants surveyed, 11, clarified the sherry material with bentonite and filtered the wine before baking. See Chapter 6 for a discussion of fining operations. Where filtration is employed at this stage it is a rough rather than a polishing filtration. The sugar content of the sherry material during baking is important. The presence of a small amount of reducing sugar is generally considered necessary for satisfactory baking, as it shortens the time required, and caramelization of the sugar improves the flavor. The reducing sugar content actually used in the industry varies from 1.0 to 2.2 per cent for dry sherry, 2.7 to 3.5 for medium, and 7.5 to 10 for sweet (cream sherry). The majority of California sherry producers surveyed bake their sherry material at about 2 per cent reducing sugar, as determined chemically, and add sweeter sherry or angelica after baking to obtain the desired reducing sugar content. (Note that a Balling degree of −1.0 usually indicates in shermat a wine about 2 per cent in reducing sugar.) The alcohol content should be adjusted by blending to about 20 per cent.

Baking

In California, the usual baking practice consists in heating the wine under conditions which result in slight caramelization of the sugar and a certain degree of oxidation, although the importance of oxidation is not known. It is probably of minor importance in view of the fact that very large, relatively impervious concrete and metal tanks are now used for baking. On the other hand, in baking by the Tressler process in eastern states very extensive oxidation probably occurs. The time necessary for the desired changes is dependent upon the temperature of baking and access of air. Contact with iron or copper during baking should be avoided, because they may impart metallic tastes and render the wine unstable in respect to iron or copper casse. Baking also brings about a blending of the brandy used in the fortification and the wine.

Formerly a few wineries baked some of their sherry material in 50 to 200 gallon oak containers stored in a heated room, usually 120°F. for 4 to 6 months. Evaporation loss is heavy in this method, one cellar reporting a loss of 5.7 to 6.6 per cent per year. When sherry is baked in barrels the hoops on the barrels in a baking room tend to become loose from drying out of the staves. If baked too long, the wine acquires too much flavor of the oak. However, this method properly applied is considered by Joslyn and Amerine (1964) to give a better sherry than baking in large containers at a higher temperature.

Because of the high cost of handling small wooden containers most California wineries use large lined steel, concrete, or wood tanks for baking. The concrete tanks are often of 60,000 gallon capacity. In one plant at least, the sherry baking tanks hold 200,000 gallons each, and in another 95,000 gallons each. The redwood sherry baking tanks usually hold 20,-000 to 35,000 gallons each. One cellar reported evaporation losses of only 0.2 per cent in large concrete or large redwood tanks, except in cases where the wooden tanks developed leaks, in which the seepage loss may become 2 to 3 per cent or greater. Lined steel tanks are now used by several wineries for baking. A heat resistant lining is necessary.

The methods of heating the wine vary considerably but fall into two classes, namely internal (in the tank) heaters and outside heaters. Usually the in-tank heaters consist of steam-heated copper or stainless steel coils; but the coils may be heated by circulating hot water. Stainless steel is preferred to iron or copper. If in-tank coils are used, the steam should be admitted below the outlet of the coils in order that the coil is virtually filled with hot water produced by condensation of the steam; otherwise excessive scorching and sticking of baked-on wine solids to the coils is apt to occur. The coils are usually placed near the bottom of the tank and about one foot from the walls. Convection currents are set up by the rising heated wine; but slow circulation of the wine by pump helps to minimize local overheating. An automatic temperature recorder-regulator should be placed on each large tank.

Often the hot sherry after cooking is completed is passed through an outside heat exchanger where it is cooled by a stream of unheated sherry material on its way to a baking tank. In this manner the baked sherry is quickly cooled at little cost and the incoming sherry material is heated to near baking temperature. In some plants the wine is heated continuously in a heat interchanger outside the tank and returned to the tank. Temperature is maintained automatically. In a few plants the maximum cooking temperature is not maintained continuously, the wine being brought to that temperature and heating discontinued until the wine drops during a period of several days to 118°–120°F., when it is again heated. In a few plants the sherry cooking tanks are located in a heated room.

In the sherry plant survey the temperatures used in baking differed considerably at the various plants. Nine of 16 plants used 128° to 135°F.; four used 140°F. One used 140°F. for its competitive sherries and 120°F. for its premium quality dry, medium, and sweet sherries. Another used 130°F. for its competitive sherries and 120°F. for premium quality sherries. The present tendency is to use lower baking temperatures.

The length of baking required varies more or less indirectly with the temperature, that is the higher the baking temperature the shorter the time of baking. For example, in the survey made by Berg (1951) 17 cellars using concrete tanks with in-tank heating coils baked at 130° to 140°F. for 9 to 20 weeks and five that used outside heaters baked at 130° to 140°F. for 9 to 20 weeks. The longer periods were used at 130°F. and the shorter at 140°F. In the survey by Martini and Cruess (1956) the length of baking ranged from 45 to 120 days. Sherry producers interviewed recently (1965) have stated that baking is less severe than in former years; probably because of the present consumer preference for sherries of light color and mild flavor.

As previously mentioned, the character of sherry is usually improved by contact with oak. Six of 16 cellars in the sherry survey used oak chips at the rate of 5 to 10 lbs. per 1000 gallons and 2 aged the sherry in oak barrels. The others used no oak. One large plant in 1958 used about 10 lbs. of oak chips per 1000 gallons in two sevenths of its sherry during the last 30 days of baking. Each two tanks of oak-treated sherry are blended with five tanks of untreated sherry.

Typical analyses before and after baking as reported in the survey previously mentioned showed that a slight loss in alcohol content and practically no loss in volatile acid and total acid content occurred. However, a sharp decrease in sulfur dioxide content was observed. Joslyn and Amerine (1964) state that during baking aldehydes increase initially but decrease as baking is continued, and rise as the sherry cools. Color increases during baking. Mattick and Robinson (1960) noted an especially high amount of formic acid in wines heated in the presence of oxygen (160 mg. per liter). Acetic acid was also comparatively high in the treated wines (at or above the legal limit). Preobrazhenskiï (1963) reported the highest temperature used in the Soviet Union was 171°F. The typical raw material was a wine of 19 or more per cent alcohol and 4 to 6 per cent sugar. The aldehyde content of the finished product was 120 to 160 mg. per liter.

Fremenko et al. (1963) simultaneously heated and aerated shermat to produce what we would call California sherry but which in the Soviet Union is called "Madera." The quality was considered better than that produced without aeration. Heitz et al. (1951) reported baking in the absence of oxygen resulted in wines with a special low-aldehyde flavor.

In most cases reported in the sherry survey of Martini and Cruess (1956) there was very little or no increase in iron content during baking; but the copper content increased considerably in some cases, typical data being: before baking 0.18 p.p.m., after 2.5 p.p.m.; 0.5 and a trace before baking, 0.6 p.p.m. after. Copper pickup probably came from the copper coils used for heating. There is some increase in the calcium content of the wine during baking in concrete tanks, probably greater in new than in old tanks.

Usually taste is the principal criterion of judging when baking is adequate, although color comparison is also used in some plants. In a few wineries baking is done at a certain temperature for a definite period for all sherries. One plant tests the sherry qualitatively for hydroxymethyl-furfural as a check on the taste of the baked product (p. 715).

Cooling and Stabilization

Of sixteen plants surveyed in 1956, ten allowed the sherry to cool naturally after baking; four cooled rapidly by heat interchanger, generally using the ingoing sherry material to cool the outgoing baked sherry. Most sherry producers rely on the baking to stabilize the finished product against hazing or clouding in the bottle by colloids precipitated by heat, although a few plants flash pasteurize the baked sherry at 180° to 185°F. Theoretically, the long heating at baking temperature should precipitate all of the heat-coagulable colloids.

The customary clarification of the new sherry with bentonite has a very definite stabilizing effect as it removes most of the protein, according to Kean and Marsh (1956). In a typical case the total protein content of a wine was reduced from an original of 78 to 2 mg. per liter by addition of 600 mg. per liter of bentonite.

Koch (1957) has reported that all wines heated to 167°F. in his experiments were practically heat stable. All commercial wines treated with bentonite and examined by him were protein-free. Heat-treated wines were also stable, but contained some protein and were fuller bodied to the taste than the same wines clarified with bentonite. Kielhöfer (1951) found that clarification with bentonite reduced the total nitrogen content of the wine 9 to 59 mg. per liter. Holden (1955) states that bentonited dessert wines remain as stable as those that have been heat treated. The general experience of commercial producers of California sherries is that clarification of new sherries with bentonite stabilizes them against clouding by heat-degraded substances.

Clarification

The cooled sherry is racked from any sediment that forms during heating and subsequent settling. The amount of bentonite required varies with the cloudiness of the wine from about 2 lbs. per 1000 gallons of fairly clear wine to 5 or more per 1000 gallons of very cloudy wine. Bentonite is useful in case of failure of attempted clarification with gelatin and tannin or with casein. It will usually clarify the most recalcitrant wine. See Chapter 6 for further information on bentonite.

The sherry after clarification is racked and filtered as described in Chapter 6. Of 16 plants reporting in the survey previously mentioned, 8 filtered twice, 6 three times, and 2 only once. When carbon is used it is customary to filter the treated wine twice in order to completely remove all carbon particles. In addition the sherry is usually given a polishing filtration before bottling.

Aging

Most California sherry is bottled or shipped in bulk after aging for a relatively short time. The majority of the plants in the survey previously mentioned age their competitive sherries less than 6 months and premium quality sherries for 2 to 3 years or longer.

Cooperage for aging in these wineries ranged from 50-gallon oak barrels to concrete tanks of 60,000 gallon capacity. Some plants store sherry in

Courtesy of L. M. Martini

FIG. 96.   SHERRY AGING CELLAR IN CALIFORNIA

concrete tanks of up to 200,000 gallon capacity, others in equally large or larger lined steel tanks. At one time considerable sherry was aged in 50-gallon barrels in the open but, owing to excessive labor cost and loss in volume by evaporation and leakage through small holes made in the staves by borers, this practice is now uncommon. However, sherry aged in this manner is valuable for blending with sherry aged in bulk as it is rich in flavor and bouquet and usually dark in color.

Although sherry is greatly improved by aging in oak, new oak containers should be treated as described elsewhere (see Chapter 6) to remove extractives which give wine a harsh, unpleasant taste. If the oak has been properly prepared and the sherry is not stored too long its aging in 50-gallon barrels or puncheons is commendable.

In order to stabilize the wine, particularly in respect to deposition of cream of tartar, and hazing or clouding on chilling, it is customary to refrigerate it to near the freezing point, about 16° to 18°F. and hold it at or near this temperature until deposition of excess cream of tartar is complete, usually 2 to 3 weeks. The equipment and procedure are discussed in Chapter 6. Treatment of wines including sherry with ion exchange resins in order to replace much of the potassium with sodium is widely practiced. See pp. 295–299.

Color Removal

At present most of the competitive sherries produced in California are very light in color, a condition attained in most cases by partial decolorization with activated carbon. However, the taste and color of sherries that have undergone treatment with activated carbon are less desirable than those of wines not so treated. Many American consumers seem to prefer sherries of very pale color and mild flavor; therefore, the producers of sherry are probably justified in trying to supply this apparent demand. Whether dedicated sherry consumers can be developed with a wine of such low sherry character is another matter. Perhaps the cost and difficulty of producing high quality sherry has been a factor in developing these charcoaled, very light-colored sherries rather than actual consumer preference.

The decolorizing carbon is usually added during refrigeration, although in some plants it is added after and in some before refrigeration. The carbon powder is usually added as a slurry in wine. However, in at least one large plant it is added dry. It is left in the wine from 24 hours to as long as 30 days; in most plants 24 hours only. Filter aid is added before or during filtration; the amount reported varies from 2 to 9 lbs. per 1000 gallons, depending upon the condition of the wine. If filter aid is not added, fine particles of carbon are apt to pass through the filter.

The carbon and the wine are usually mixed by aeration with compressed air, although pumping over is used in some plants. As stated elsewhere, pumping over is the slower method. The amount of carbon used in the various plants varies greatly and in a given plant, according to the result desired. As little as 0.25 lb. per 1000 gallons has been used by one producer largely for reduction of off-flavor, although 2 lbs. or more per 1000 gallons is more often employed, if color reduction is also desired. Another plant adds 1 to 1.5 lbs. of carbon per 1000 gallons toward the end, and another uses 1 to 2 lbs. 1 to 3 days before the end of the refrigeration period. Another plant uses 2 lbs. per 1000 gallons as a routine addition and an additional 8 to 15 lbs. later if severe reduction in color is required. The legal aspects of excessive reduction in color should be considered (p. 747). In one plant a preliminary clarification with caseinate and bentonite, or gelatin and bentonite is given. In this case the clarified wine is racked and filtered before treatment with carbon, and the carbon is used after refrigeration. Usually one filtration is given to remove the carbon and a polishing filtration is applied before bottling or before bulk shipment.

Blending

After the sherry has been baked, stabilized, and cleared, various lots are blended in order to produce final products that will be as uniform in appearance, flavor, and bouquet as possible from year to year. Uniformity is a well known characteristic of Spanish sherries; one can usually depend upon different bottles of Spanish sherry of a given brand to be practically the same in quality and character, regardless of the year of bottling.

One large California producer makes a blend of 500,000 gallons consisting of 7 to 8 parts of dry sherry to one of sweet. A reasonable continuity of character of the final wine is secured by following a fairly rigid program of processing and blending. The wines going into the blend are accurately analyzed and any necessary adjustment made in respect to acidity or other component.

In all plants careful attention should be given to tasting of all major lots of sherry. By careful comparison with samples of previous blends an attempt is made to match the flavor, bouquet, and color by blending. It is advantageous to make up small blends in the laboratory to determine in advance as accurately as possible how much of each wine is required in the final blend. Color may be judged by eye, although use of a colorimeter is very desirable in order to eliminate the personal factor. Composition of the two wines can be matched on the basis of chemical analysis. Taste and bouquet, however, must be matched as nearly as possible by sensory tests made by experienced persons. The plant should not rely entirely upon the judgment of a single person. See p. 681 and Amerine *et al.* (1959).

Mixing of the wines in the blend is usually accomplished by pumping over or by mechanical stirrers or in the case of sherries can also be done by clean compressed air free of off-odor or -flavor and free of any other objectionable material such as rusty droplets of water or oil. Aeration would probably ruin the quality of a delicate table wine but since baked sherry is not damaged by moderate oxidation this method of mixing is permissible.

The blend should be tested for cold and heat stability and analyzed for copper and iron content. In case too much of either metal is present the wine should be treated to remove the excess. See Chapters 6 and 15. Calcium should be determined also if the plant has had difficulty with calcium tartrate deposition.

A fractional blending system is used in a few instances. In this method the sherry is aged in oak puncheons or small tanks and only part of the contents of several different containers is removed for use in a blend. The wine removed is replaced with newer wine of the same type. Usually not more than 50 per cent of the contents of each container should be removed and not more than twice a year. Continuity of character is thereby maintained. A few cellars do follow this practice, particularly in the production of blends of flor sherry. See Amerine *et al.* (1959) and Baker *et al.* (1952) for further discussion of blending and evaluating wines.

Citric acid is the usual acid employed for adjusting the acidity. It also prevents clouding due to iron if sufficient acid is added.

Addition of Sulfur Dioxide or Tannin

As sherry is very susceptible to spoilage by *Lactobacillus trichodes* the sulfur dioxide content of the final blend should be brought to 100 p.p.m. The stability of some sherries against clouding may be improved by addition of a small amount of tannic acid. Joslyn and Amerine (1964) suggest 1 lb. of grape tannin per 1000 gallons of sherry. It should be used before the final filtration. However the necessity or desirability of adding tannin is questioned by many producers and needs further study.

Excess Metals

It is believed by some that sherry will tolerate a much higher content of copper than will other wines and that much of the copper dissolved from copper heating coils is lost in the lees formed during refrigeration. However, Fessler (1952) recommends that no copper be permitted in finished wines. Of the 16 plants reporting in the 1956 survey, three set the desired limit for copper content of sherry at 0 p.p.m.; one at 0.1 p.p.m.; five at 0.2 p.p.m.; two 0.3 p.p.m.; one 0.4 p.p.m.; two 0.5 p.p.m.; and one 1.0 p.p.m.

The limits suggested for iron content were: one plant, 1.5; two, 2.5 to 4.0; two, 4.0; one, 4.5; three, 5.0; one, 7; one, 8; two, 10; and one, less than 3.0 p.p.m.

Copper is usually removed by Cufex or by ion exchange. If the iron content is excessive, citric acid is added in sufficient amount to prevent iron casse. One plant uses 3 lbs. of citric acid per 1000 gallons for this purpose.

Those reporting in the survey set the limit for calcium content of sherry within the range of 60 to 100 p.p.m. Its concentration is reduced during refrigeration or can be brought to any desired level by use of ion exchange resin in the sodium form. For further discussion of calcium instability and removal of excess calcium see pp. 562–564 and Warkentin (1955).

It is of interest that three of the plants in the 1956 survey stabilized sherry for metals just before refrigeration; eleven just before bottling; one before baking and two did not treat the wine for metal stabilization.

The baked and stabilized sherry should be aged at least one year in small cooperage, preferably in oak ovals, puncheons, sherry butts, or barrels to develop flavor and smoothness, Fig. 96. If aging is conducted in large tanks three years' aging is none too much. However, most California sherry is bottled and marketed soon after baking and finishing.

Unbaked Sherry

As indicated in a subsequent section, most of the sherry made in Australia is not baked. The authors have sampled imported Australian sherries of various types and found them of pleasing quality. Before enactment of the prohibition amendment much California sherry was not baked but was aged slowly in oak cooperage until the desired color, flavor and bouquet were obtained. Competition has made the production of unbaked sherry unattractive economically because of its greater cost. It could be used in a few plants for production of premium sherries.

Finishing

A polishing filtration, usually by some form of asbestos pad filter, is given the sherry before bottling or shipment in bulk. Care should be taken to use only filter pads that do not appreciably increase the calcium content of the wine. In the survey previously mentioned, the majority of the wineries reporting filtered their sherry directly into a bottling tank.

Sherry is commonly shipped from one winery to another in California by tank car or by tank truck and to out of state points usually by rail or by tank car. One producer ships in bulk by steamship to eastern and southern United States ports. The bulk shipment of wine in lined tank railway cars is very common, Fig. 97.

FIG. 97.   TANK CARS FOR WINE

Bottling

Bottling of sherry at the winery has become more extensive in recent years than was the case early in the post-repeal period. Bottling equipment and bottling have been discussed in Chapter 6. The bottles are usually closed with screw caps. In some cases, such as for premium sherries, special corks, that may be removed without a cork puller and readily used for reclosure, are employed.

Owing to fortification, sherry, unlike table wines, is not damaged by moderate exposure to air, and therefore may be left in a partly filled bottle for several weeks, as is often customary in the home.

Considerable sherry is made in New York and other states in the Eastern United States. This subject has been presented in Chapter 12.

AUSTRALIA AND SOUTH AFRICA

The production of non-flor sherries in Australia according to Fornachon (1959) of Adelaide, South Australia is as follows:

1. A fortified dry or sweet wine is made in the usual way with fortification to between 19 and 20 per cent of alcohol by volume. The sugar content of these wines varies from less than 1 per cent to over 5 per cent, depending on the type of sherry being made. The titratable acidity is normally between 0.4 and 0.55 gm. per 100 ml. (as tartaric) and the pH is between 3.4 and 3.9.

2. After the gross lees have settled, the wine is racked and is again racked once or twice during the first year and clarified by fining with bentonite if necessary.

3. After clarification the wine is racked into oak "hogsheads" (casks of about 65 imperial gallons, i.e., about 78 U. S. gallons) which are stored in the warmest part of the winery until the wine is considered sufficiently aged. Sometimes a special building of corrugated iron is kept for use as a sherry house, but artificial heating is not used and the temperature is not controlled. Maturation

of the wine may take from 1 or 2 up to 4 or 5 years or more according to the quality of the wine, the conditions of storage and the opinion of the wine maker. During this period the wine is usually racked once a year and in some cases the casks are allowed to become slightly ullaged (not completely full).

4. Sulfur dioxide is used during fermentation and usually again at the first or second racking. Some wine makers continue to determine and adjust the sulfur dioxide content of the wine during maturation while others do not.

5. The matured sherry is racked and blended if necessary to adjust the sugar content and fined or filtered. It is usually refrigerated, racked and filtered cold some time before bottling.

The making of the "brown sherry" in South Africa is similar to that of producing non-flor sherry in Australia except that gypsum is added to the must before fermentation. Theron and Niehaus (1947) state that brown or South African oloroso-type sherry is made about as follows:

Must for brown sherry is drawn off the skins after fermentation has begun and a cap formed. Gypsum is added at the rate of 2 to 4 pounds per leaguer (about 15.75 to 31.50 lbs. per 1000 gallons). The lower amount is used with musts of higher acidity. The gypsum causes a more rapid clarification of the young wine, lowers the pH value by increasing the free, fixed acidity and according to Theron and Niehaus promotes the real sherry flavor. Although a flor yeast is used for fermenting the must the new wine for brown sherry is not aged under flor yeast film. Small casks are preferred and proper attention is given to control of temperature during fermentation. Sulfur dioxide is used in the customary manner, though not to excess. The must is usually fermented completely dry but it may also be fortified with sugar remaining. The fortification is made at the first racking with neutral high proof to 30° to 32° "proof spirit" (17.1 to 18.3 per cent alcohol by volume). It is then matured in a solera, but, of course, without the growth of a flor film. Final finishing of the sherry is done in the large cellars of the cooperative "K.W.V." or other wine merchants. A very sweet wine, Jeripico, is made by fortifying the unfermented, or only slightly fermented, must and aging in the same manner as "brown sherry." It is generally used for blending with drier sherries and appears to be similar to California angelica, at least in composition.

SPANISH SHERRY

Sherry can be produced in Spain in only a delimited area near Cadiz (p. 32). Other information on the sherry industry of Spain is given in Chapter 1.

The sherries of Spain are made in and around Jerez de la Frontera, which lies near the Guadalquivir River between Seville and Cadiz and about ten miles from the ocean. The climate is warm and favorable to the production of well ripened grapes of fairly high sugar content. The word sherry is undoubtedly derived from the name of the principal city in the sherry district, Jerez de la Frontera. According to Gonzalez (1948) Spanish sherry in Spain may be designated by any one of the following words: "Jerez," "Xerez," "Scheris," and "sherry." The Spanish government has defined and given the limits of the area in which wines that are permitted to bear the name of Jerez de la Frontera are produced. Quoting from the act the following statement is of interest: "Article 8. Pursuant to Article 30 of the Statute of Wine, the zone with the right to use the designation 'Jerez–Xerez–Sherry,' shall be within the municipal limits of Jerez de la Frontera, Puerto de Santa Maria and Sanlúcar de Barrameda." See also Anon. (1935, 1941, 1950), Berg (1959), Cruess (1937), Domecq (1940), Goswell (1968), Joslyn and Amerine (1964), Rocques (1903), and Ocheltree (1932).

Besides the Palomino and the Pedro Ximenez (used for production of very sweet wines) the less important varieties Mantuo de Pilas, Mantuo Castellano, Albillo, Perruno, and Cañocazo are grown.

The best soil for growing Palomino grapes on the low rolling hills of the Jerez district is a white, gypsiferous one known as *albariza*. It is very high in calcium content. Vines grown on it give a low yield but produce grapes of high quality for sherry production. *Barros* soils are more extensive and are a mixture of limestone soil and clay. They are said to pro-

Courtesy of Pedro Domecq

FIG. 98. HARVESTING GRAPES IN SHERRY DISTRICT

Note white soil

duce much heavier crops than do the *albariza* soils. *Arenas* soils are very sandy, and prevalent in the Sanlúcar district, where the grapes are used in making *manzanilla* wines.

Vines are planted close together, pruned very low, and are grown without irrigation. Berg (1959) states that the yield is only about two tons per acre.

Harvesting

According to Castella (1909, 1926) the harvest, Fig. 98 usually begins in the Sanlúcar area earlier than in the Jerez de la Frontera district. The soils of Sanlúcar are sandy and the wines usually are lighter in body and alcohol content than those of Jerez. The harvest begins in September at Jerez and continues to mid-October. The grapes are cut at the desired maturity (after the main stems have become brown) with short-bladed knives, rather than with clippers, and are placed in small shallow wooden boxes

Courtesy of Gonzalez, Byass

Fig. 99.   Spreading Grapes to Dry in Sherry Region

with handles, known as *tinetas*, or in small baskets. The *tineta* holds about one *arroba* (about 25 lbs.), Fig. 99.

Approximately 60 *arrobas* of grapes yield sufficent must for one *bota* (butt or cask), the customary container for fermentation of must and aging of wine. The vineyard is picked over more than once if the grapes are not all of the desired maturity. For *fino* wines, the optimum Baumé degree is 14° to 15°, (about 26° to 28° Balling), and for *oloroso* wines, above 15° Bé.

The small boxes or baskets of grapes are transported by mule back in special frames, or by ox cart or by truck to the *almijar*, an open courtyard next to the *casa de lagares* (crushing house). The grapes are spread on small esparto grass mats in the sun, the contents of one or more boxes or baskets to each mat, Fig. 99. At night the grapes are sometimes covered to prevent deposition of dew. Grapes for *fino* wines lose very little of their water content, as they are left in the *almijar* only 24 hours or less. Those for *oloroso* wines are usually left several days. Pedro Ximenez grapes are left up to two weeks, during which time they become partially "raisined." The must often attains 40° Balling, and has a raisin-like flavor and color. Much more hand labor obviously is used than in California wineries.

Crushing

Formerly the grapes were emptied into a shallow rectangular wooden vat, *lagar*, about 12 feet square and 1.5 feet in depth, and elevated above the crushing floor. Each crushing house contained several of these vats. Enough grapes were placed in the *lagar* to furnish free-run and first pressing wine for one butt, about 130 U. S. gallons. Men equipped with special heavy-soled shoes crushed the grapes by treading, Fig. 100.

That crushing in this manner was continued until the early 1960's was at least partially due to the belief by some that less tannin and coarseness was extracted from the stems and skins than by mechanical crushing. This coarseness (*basto* flavor) is to be avoided as the greatest enemy of quality in Spanish sherries, according to Gonzalez (1948). Now treading has been almost entirely replaced by mechanical crushing as modern crushers produce high quality sherries at a very considerable saving in labor costs.

Plastering

Plastering is a customary feature of the crushing process of Jerez de la Frontera. The crushed grapes are sprinkled with *yeso*, a crude plaster of Paris made by heating the naturally-occurring gypsum of this area to a high temperature. The amount of *yeso* added varies according to the dis-

Courtesy of Gonzalez, Byass

Fig. 100. Treading Grapes in Sherry District

This practice is now obsolete

trict, the shipper, and the method of pressing, according to Amerine (1948). Castella (1926) reports that it usually ranges from about 12 to 15 lbs. per ton, or 6 to 7.5 gm. per kg. Gonzalez (1948) has reported that it averages about 1.5 gm. per kg. of crushed grapes, or about 3 lbs. per ton. Marcilla (1946) recommends that not more than 12.5 gm. of *yeso* per kg., 25 lbs. per ton, be used. See also Bobadilla *et al.* (1954) and Hickinbotham (1952).

The principal purpose of plastering is to increase the active acidity of the must, i.e., to lower its pH and to facilitate pressing by reducing viscosity. Thus, cream of tartar plus *yeso* gives calcium tartrate plus potassium acid sulfate:

$$KH(C_4H_4O_6) + CaSO_4 \rightarrow Ca(C_4H_4O_6) + KHSO_4$$

The latter in turn reacts with some of the cream of tartar:

$$KHSO_4 + KH(C_4H_4O_6) \rightarrow K_2SO_4 + H_2(C_4H_4O_6)$$

to give some free tartaric acid. These changes may be written in a single equation:

$$CaSO_4 + 2KH(C_4H_4O_6) \rightarrow K_2SO_4 + H_2(C_4H_4O_6) + Ca(C_4H_4O_6)$$

Plastering is thus a means of converting the weakly acid salt, potassium bitartrate, into an equivalent amount of free tartaric acid. The calcium tartrate formed in the reaction is almost insoluble and the potassium sulfate remains in the wine. By reducing the pH, plastering renders the wine much less susceptible to spoilage by lactic bacteria. Not all of the plaster of Paris spread on the crushed grapes reacts with the bitartrate of the must, as calcium sulfate is only slightly soluble, and the rate of solution is slow. Amerine (1948) states that the addition of tartaric acid to the juice in some cases may entirely replace the use of *yeso*. This is necessary in the making of wines to be shipped to countries that have a low legal limit for sulfate in wines. Baker (1945) in Australia found that the addition of four pounds of plaster of Paris per 100 gallons (about 4.8 gm. per liter) to Palomino must reduced the pH value from 3.88 to 3.41 and of Albillo must from 3.65 to 3.27. In experiments reported by Brajnikoff and Cruess (1948) it was found that calcium sulfate added to dry wine of one year of age had very little effect on the pH. Even a massive dose of 32 gm. per liter reduced the pH value only from 3.60 to 3.45. When added to fresh must, however, the affect was much more marked as shown in the following:

Calcium sulfate, gms. per liter	0	1	2	4	8	16	32
pH of wine	3.8	3.7	3.45	3.35	3.25	3.20	3.20
Total sulfates, per cent[1]	0.023	0.136	0.205	0.279	0.282	0.314	0.33

Source of data: Brajnikoff and Cruess (1948).
[1] As sulfate.

The reason that calcium sulfate has so little effect on the pH value when added to aged wine is that the wine contains much less bitartrate than the fresh juice. Much of the excess bitartrate crystallizes out of the wine during fermentation and subsequent storage. In these experiments the added calcium sulfate had but little effect on the rate of fermentation.

Draining and Pressing

Sherry is made from the juice of the free-run and that from a brief and gentle first pressing.

The free-run juice drains from the *lagar* into a butt. The crushed drained grapes are stacked around a vertical pole in the *lagar* and a long, narrow strip of esparto grass matting is wound tightly around the heap of crushed grapes to completely enclose them, each end of the strip being held by wooden pegs forced into the mass of crushed grapes. Pressure, applied by hand-operated screw and plate, is rather brief, so that the first pressing juice will not contain too much tannin. The free-run and first pressing are combined and constitute the juice out of which sherry is made.

Juice from a second pressing by a more powerful screw or hydraulic press is used for making dry wine for local consumption. The pomace from the second pressing may be mixed with water, pressed and this diluted juice fermented for distilling material; or some of the wine may be used as a pomace wine by the workman.

Amerine (1948) states that when treading is omitted hydraulic presses are used for the first and second pressing, followed by continuous presses for the third pressing. The juice from the first and second pressing is used for making sherry and that from the third pressing for preparing distilling material or pomace wine. Recently, drainage racks have been used to remove as much as possible of the juice before pressing.

Addition of Sulfur Dioxide

At the time of Castella's visit (1909) to Spain neither sulfur dioxide or pure yeast cultures were in use. However, Bobadilla (1938, 1947B) states that sulfur dioxide is often added to the must to insure a clean fermentation and freedom from spoilage bacteria. He states that in his experiments 20 to 30 gm. sulfur dioxide per hectoliter, 200 to 300 p.p.m., were used, according to the maturity of the grapes and weather condition (rainy or dry). He found in new wine containing 180 p.p.m. of total sulfur dioxide of which approximately 20 p.p.m. was free sulfur dioxide that formation of the flor yeast film was delayed only 18 days. The wines from the treated musts cleared more rapidly after fermentation than the untreated; were lighter in color; of about 0.8 per cent higher alcohol content; higher extract content; 0.1 to 0.2 gm. per liter higher in sulfates, and much sounder in respect to bacteria than the untreated. The flavor and bouquet of the treated wines were excellent. On the average about 160 p.p.m. of total and 9.5 of free sulfur dioxide remained in the new wines at the end of fermentation. Amerine (1948) confirms Bobadilla's statement that sulfur dioxide is often added to the must.

Fermentation

According to Berg (1959) pure cultures of yeast are not used, since the grapes apparently carry large numbers of flor yeast cells. Fermentation begins promptly and is usually satisfactory. See, however Bobadilla (1940). Fermentation is conducted in butts of about 130 gallon capacity. They are not completely filled. Earthenware funnels or special tubes are usually inserted in the bung holes to prevent heavy loss of must by frothing during fermentation.

During the fermentation of Jerez de la Frontera musts Iñigo *et al.* (1963), found 13 yeast species but *S. cerevisiae, S. italicus* and *S. chevalieri* were the yeasts primarily responsible for alcoholic fermentation. *S. bayanus* was found in only one of 20 musts compared to its appearance in half the musts from Montilla. *Saccharomycodes ludwigii* and *S. delbrueckii* were reported for the first time in Spanish musts. *Candida utilis* also appeared frequently. It is especially notable that flor films appeared within 10 to 12 days of the completion of alcoholic fermentation. Film formation under aerobic conditions is a characteristic of a number of yeasts. See. p. 157.

As a general rule most of the butts remain at the crushing house during fermentation, although some are moved to the bodegas (large cellars) in Jerez, Sanlúcar de Barrameda, and Puerto Santa Maria for fermentation. The musts are not cooled during fermentation. Probably loss of heat from the butts is sufficient to prevent a dangerous rise in temperature. The butts of new wine usually remain in the open until the first racking in November and December. According to Gonzalez (1948) the second racking may not be made until July or August. See also Bobadilla (1947C).

At the time of the first racking each butt of new wine is carefully tasted, analyzed, and classified into one of three general groups, namely, one, two, and three *rayas*, and the butts marked /, //, and ///. Later, the wines are classified again, this time as *palmas, cortados*, and *rayas*. There are several sub-classes in each of these major groups. This rather complex system of classification will be described only briefly here.

The *palma* wines possess the composition, flavor, bouquet, and color desired for producing *fino* and *amontillado sherries* and, therefore, are the most desirable of the new wines. They are pale in color, completely dry, delicate in flavor and bouquet and resemble a young dry white table wine, although of lower acidity. They should contain 14.5 to 15.5 per cent alcohol and be free of any suggestion of coarseness of flavor and bacterial spoilage. If the alcohol content of the *palma* wine is below 14.5 per cent, neutral high-proof brandy is added to bring it to 14.5 to 15.5 per cent at the time of the first racking.

Next in quality are the *cortado* wines. These are more generous or bigger wines than the *palmas* and are of higher alcohol content, often of darker color, but free of coarseness of flavor and bouquet. They are the wines from which *oloroso* sherries are made. If one of these wines is still fermenting in late November or early December, racking may be delayed until mid-winter. They are usually of 16 per cent or higher alcohol content, or if below 16 per cent and distinctly of *cortado* type may be fortified to 16 per cent or above. Bobadilla (1947A) states that all *cortado* wines are now fortified to about 18 per cent alcohol. A wine between a *palma* and a *cortado* may be classed as a *palo cortado*, which may develop into a *fino* during aging, and hence is not fortified.

The *raya* wines constitute a group of lower grade. At time of classification they are often not as far advanced as the *palmas* and *cortados*, and it is not certain whether or not they may develop into something better. Thus a good, or *una raya* wine may become a *fino* or *aloroso*, although it has not progressed far enough for a *fino* at the time of first classification. A *dos rayas* wine is of lower quality and may be coarse in character, but may develop into an *oloroso* in time. A *tres rayas* wine is of still poorer quality, and may eventually have to be used as distilling material. As with the *palmas* and *cortados*, alcohol may be added to the *rayas* that are too low in this constituent.

After racking, the new wines are usually held several months and examined again before being placed in a solera, and some changes may be made in the previous classification, depending on the development of the wine. During this preliminary storage flor film develops on wine in many of the butts. Wines in this preliminary storage stage are known as *añada* wines.

The Solera System

Strictly speaking, the term solera means only the final stage in the Jerez aging system. In most Spanish literature all other stages of the system are called *criaderas*, and Bobadilla (1947A), calls the entire system a *criaderas-soleras* system. Castella (1909) and Gonzalez (1948) have suggested that solera is derived from the word *suelo*, meaning ground, or floor of the *bodega*, since the butts of the last stage (solera) rest on the floor of the cellar, or on skids a few inches above the floor. However, members of the Spanish sherry trade generally use the term solera to mean the entire system, including all stages, and we so use it in this book.

The following is Castella's (1926) description of a solera:

A solera is a series of butts of sherry in process of maturation or rearing, so arranged as to provide for progressive, fractional blending. It is divided into a varying number of stages; from the final stage is withdrawn the finished wine, whilst young wine is introduced into the earliest stage. Let us suppose for the sake of illustration a solera of 50 butts divided into five stages each containing ten butts is being operated. The butts are of 130 U. S. gallon capacity but as they are a little ullaged their net content would be about 113 U. S. gallons. This solera has been functioning for many years; when first established each stage probably represented a single vintage, but with continual replenishing these have long since lost their original significance.

Stage I contains the oldest wine; from it the finished wine is withdrawn, but in doing so the butts are only partially emptied, not more than one-half being removed in any one year. Withdrawal is usually made twice a year, 25 gallons

Courtesy of Wisdom and Warter

FIG. 101.   SHERRY BODEGA SHOWING OLOROSO SOLERA

being removed on each occasion.   Butts of stage I are immediately replenished from stage II, which in turn is replenished from stage III and so on.   Stage V is replenished with young wine or with wine kept as an *añada* for a year or even longer.   The usual age is a few months.

The wine thus moves steadily forward through the different stages until its final withdrawal, when it is a complex blend, none of it being less than $5^{1}/_{2}$ years old, but containing in varying proportion still older wine, including very small quantities of every wine that has reached stage one since its establishment.

A solera on the above lines would yield only 500 gallons of finished wine each year, from a stock of 5000 gallons.   Interest and loss by evaporation[1] render it impossible for a solera wine to be reared at a low price.   Nor is the above an extreme sample.   Soleras differ in the number of their stages.   For the rapidly developing *manzanillas* of Sanlúcar 3 or 4 stages is the rule.   Five or 6 stages are frequent in *fino* soleras at Jerez, although some consist of 8 or 9, turning out as might be expected very expensive wines.

Though it (the solera system) finds its greatest utility in connection with *fino* wines, it is now generally applied to all types, Fig. 20.   *Oloroso* and the final stage of *amontillado* soleras, owing to their strength, have no flor on the surface of the wine.   With these the merit lies in the automatic blending and uniformity

[1] Gonzalez (1948) reports that the loss in volume by evaporation is about 4 gallons per year for each 100 gallons of wine in the butts, but that it will vary considerably according to ratio of surface exposed to volume, location in the cellar, temperature, and other factors.

of product the system assures. In addition to the above, composite soleras are to be met with, destined for the production of special wines of very high price. One of these might be termed a solera of soleras, the youngest stage being replenished with a blend of finished wines from other soleras; such complex soleras comprise very few stages.

In replenishing one stage from the preceding, the Spanish do not merely add 25 gallons from one butt to another butt in the next stage. A part of each butt in a given stage goes into every butt of the next stage. The amount taken from a butt in stage II, for example, will be divided among all the butts in stage I, in order to insure uniformity throughout the solera. Each butt of stage III will be divided among all butts of stage II, and so on.

To accomplish the transfer wine is drawn off by syphon and special pitchers or directly into pitchers from a small bung hole near the bottom of the butt. It is poured into the butts of the following stage by means of a funnel and a copper tube, with perforations near the bottom, which is inserted into the bung hole. Wine poured through this tube flows out sidewise through the perforations, thus disturbing neither the lees nor the flor film.

The wine is rather freely exposed to the air in the butts, the bung holes being loosely fitted with large corks, according to both Gonzalez (1948) and Castella (1922). This is done in the belief that too abundant an air supply results in flatness of flavor rather than in development of the pungent bouquet and flavor of a *fino*.

Marcilla *et al.* (1963) give the following analysis of a Spanish *fino* wine of high quality before final fortification (per 100 ml.): alcohol 16.5 per cent by volume, glycerol 0.41 gm., aldehydes 0.0294 gm., volatile esters 0.051 gm., total acid as tartaric 0.59 gm., volatile acid as acetic 0.022 gm., total sugars 0.095 gm., total ash 0.584 gm., potassium sulfate 0.478 gm., total extract 2.57 gm., and total sulfur dioxide 0.0058 gm. They found the composition of five wines of a typical solera to be as follows:

Stage	Alcohol	Glycerol	Aldehydes
	Per cent	Gm./100 Ml.	Gm./L.
New wine	15.70	0.76	0.020
Third criadera	15.80	0.64	0.048
Second criadera	15.45	0.63	0.038
First criadera	15.60	0.45	0.189
Solera (oldest)	16.30	0.34	0.310

Bobadilla (1943) states that the following conditions should be observed in establishing and operating a *fino* solera: (1) there should be abundant surface of wine exposed to air in each butt, i.e., the head space should be not less than 20 per cent; (2) the temperature should not exceed 77°F. nor be below 60°F., the optimum being about 68°F.; (3) the alcohol content should not be above 15.5 per cent nor below 14.5 per cent, since above 15.5 per cent flor film growth may be slow or absent and below 14.5 per cent acetification is apt to occur; (4) the sulfur dioxide content should not exceed 180 p.p.m.; above this level growth of the film is difficult; (5) the tannin content must be very low (not above 0.01 per cent), else the color is apt to be dark and the flavor coarse; (6) the iron content should be low as there are indications that excessive amounts interfere with film growth (and may cause clouding); and (7) the pH value should be between 2.8 and 3.5; below pH 2.8 film formation is difficult; above 3.5 there is grave danger of bacterial spoilage. In Spain plastering or addition of tartaric acid usually ensures a pH within this range.

Wines destined for flor sherry should not contain over 110 mg. per liter of total sulfur dioxide nor more than 6 or 7 free, according to Abramov and Potyaka (1965).

The Flor Film

Flor yeasts form a film over the wine in the butts usually within a few weeks after completion of fermentation. However, Berg (1959) states that it may be delayed for a year or more in some cases. It is composed of cells of the same yeast that fermented the must. If the film is slow to develop, transfer is made from a butt of wine covered with a vigorous film. Bobadilla (1943) advises such transfer as regular practice.

At first islands of film form. These grow and coalesce to form a smooth, thin continuous film. Within a few weeks it thickens and becomes wrinkled. With abundant air supply the young film is nearly white in color. Old film is apt to be gray and with scanty air supply may become light brown. As the film thickens and becomes wrinkled portions break away and sink to the bottom of the container, to be replaced by growth of new film. The yeast sediment slowly autolyzes, a process that undoubtedly affects the flavor and bouquet of the wine.

The primary products of the film yeasts from ethyl alcohol are acetaldehyde, 2,3-butylene glycol and acetoin, according to Saavedra and Garrido (1963).

Once a flor solera is established the film is allowed to grow relatively undisturbed on the wines in all stages of the solera. The butts are seldom emptied; hence the sediment, formed of film that has settled to the bottom of the butts, is allowed to accumulate. Amerine (1948) states that butts may be emptied and cleaned after many years' sediment has been allowed to collect.

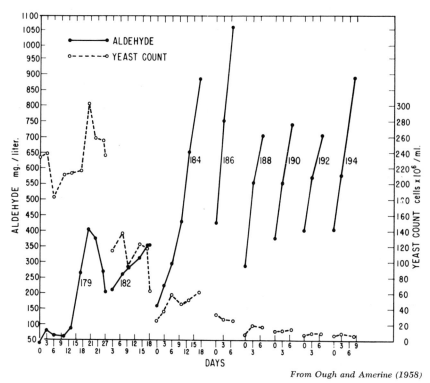

From Ough and Amerine (1958)

FIG. 102. CHANGES IN YEAST COUNT AND ALDEHYDE CONTENT
DURING SUBMERGED CULTURE FERMENTATION

Blending and Finishing

The usual sherry exported from Jerez is a blend, often a rather complex one. The producers of well-known, established brands of sherry attempt to make wines that are uniform in color, bouquet, flavor, and composition regardless of the year of bottling. In addition to the exported brands considerable sherry is blended on order.

The *fino* wines are usually sweetened slightly by the addition of a small amount of sweet wine such as *Pedro Ximenez,* but in cases in which it is desired to retain the full *fino* character, a *fino* wine is usually blended only with other *finos*. For increasing the color of a wine such as an *oloroso, vino de color* may be added.

Requisite amounts of the various wines to be used in the blends are usually drawn from the last stage (often termed the first stage in Spain) of the soleras and blended in a tank of suitable size. However, in periods of heavy demand, wine for bottling may be drawn from preceding stages also. If necessary, the blend is fortified with brandy of very high proof and of smooth, neutral flavor. During aging in the solera, wines increase in alcohol content by more rapid evaporation of water than alcohol, and according to Bobadilla (1943), *olorosos* usually require no fortification at time of final blending for bottling.

The aged wine is clarified and filtered if need be. Berg (1959) states that gelatin, isinglass, and Spanish clay are the usual clarifying agents; Gonzalez and others state that egg whites are also used. After addition of gelatin or isinglass Spanish clay (*tierra de Lebrija*), properly prepared by soaking and agitation in wine, is usually added. Gonzalez (1948) has described its preparation. It resembles bentonite in its clarifying properties. Use of phytates for metal removal was studied by Freyre (1954).

A smaller shipping solera for the more popular types is maintained by the larger firms. From this solera the final blend may be given a polishing filtration. Asbestos pad filters are generally used for this purpose. It is then either bottled in Jerez, or is shipped in butts to New York, London, or some other important sherry-importing port, where it is racked, filtered if necessary and bottled.

Stabilizing

Refrigeration of the wines to stabilize them against deposition of tartrates and clouding of bottled wine at low temperatures is not employed to any great extent for Spanish sherry. Berg (1959) reports that one bodega in the Jerez area has the necessary refrigerating equipment, but that most of the plants are not so equipped. It is possible, he states, that ion exchange resins will be used for stabilization as they are in commerical use in California, South Africa, Italy, and France and there is interest in them in Spain. Berg states that the addition of Pedro Ximenez sweet wine increases the protein content of the blend and its presence often causes the wine to be unstable in respect to clouding. He found some Spanish wines to be unstable as judged by California standards of stability. For tartrate stabilization studies on Spanish sherries see Berg (1960).

Spoilage

If the alcohol content is too low acetification may occur. Bobadilla (1947A) and Cruess (1948) recommended that the alcohol content be at least 15 per cent by volume. Occasionally lactic bacteria develop as 15 to 15.5 per cent alcohol is not sufficient to prevent their activity. However, Fornachon (1943) has found that lactic bacteria cannot grow in wine of pH 3.4 or lower. Plastering often results in lowering the pH to this value or lower. Sulfur dioxide can also be used as a preventive; however, this reduces the free acetaldehyde content.

Classes of Spanish Sherries

The usual classes of Spanish sherry in commerce are the following: *fino*, a very pale, very dry sherry, light in body and of characteristic, slightly pungent bouquet and flavor; *vino de pasto*, similar to *fino* and made from *palma* wine, usually somewhat milder than *fino*; *amontillado*, a *fino* that has aged for a long period in wood and lost much of its original *fino* character darker than a *fino*, very dry to slightly sweet; *manzanilla*, a dry *fino* wine of light color and delicate flavor, produced near Sanlúcar de Barrameda, often not fortified; *oloroso*, wine of deeper color than *fino*, usually fairly sweet, not aged under flor yeast film, sometimes called "golden" or "East India" sherry in commerce; and *amoroso*, a wine which is similar to the *oloroso*, often quite dark in color, and not aged under flor film.

INVESTIGATIONS AND PRACTICE IN CALIFORNIA

The following investigations have been conducted in the laboratories of the Food Technology Department at Berkeley, the enology laboratories at Davis, and in several California wineries. See especially Cruess (1943, 1948), Cruess *et al.* (1938), Joslyn and Amerine (1964), Martini (1950), and Strud (1953).

The Yeasts

Hohl and Cruess (1940) studied 15 distinct strains from more than 50 pure cultures isolated from Spanish sherry and from Château Châlon wine (an Arbois *vin jaune*).

French flor yeasts were included, because in the Arbois district, near Dijon and Beaune in France, they are used in making an unfortified white wine similar to Spanish *fino*. The yeasts have been fully described by Hohl and Cruess (1939) and a condensed description is given by Cruess (1948): Six spore formers were classified as strains of *Saccharomyces cerevisiae* and four non-sporulating cultures were classified, temporarily at least, as *Torulopsis*. However, these yeasts closely resembled the spore-forming strains of *S. cerevisiae* in other respects. Four of the yeasts produced no to very little fermentation, although they formed films on wine of less than 13 per cent alcohol. Marcilla *et al.* (1936) have given the species names of *Saccharomyces beticus* to the Jerez film yeasts. Fornachon (1953B) and Ough and Amerine (1958) have used Marcilla's designation, *S. beticus*. Iñigo and Bravo (1963) reported that *S. cheriensis* differed from *S. beticus* in rate of formation and utilization of volatile acids during fermentation. Lodder (1970) now classfies *S. beticus*, *S. cheriensis* and *S. oviformis* as *S. bayanus* on sound taxonomic grounds.

Both the Jerez and the Arbois flor yeasts imparted the characteristic flor flavor and bouquet to wine, although the Arbois yeasts appeared to be somewhat more active than the Jerez yeasts in this respect. In 30° Balling must the Jerez yeasts formed from 16.0 to 18 per cent alcohol by volume and the Arbois yeasts from 15.9 to 17.4 per cent. For comparison, champagne Ay yeast formed 15.6 per cent alcohol. By syruped fermentation the Jerez flor yeasts formed from 17.6 to 19.1 per cent and the Arbois flor yeasts 18.2 to 18.8 per cent. The Jerez yeasts generally showed slightly higher average alcohol tolerance than the Arbois yeasts and developed films somewhat more rapidly.

At 68° to 71.6°F. all formed films on white wine. At 80.6° to 86°F. film formation was very scant and was absent at 89.6°F. In winery experiments the films in 50-gallon barrels dropped during the warm summer months and reappeared during the cool fall months, confirming the observations of Gonzalez (1948), Fornachon (1953B) and of many others. Fornachon states that film growth is seldom satisfactory above 72°F. under cellar conditions. He states that 68°F. is optimum for film growth, but that production of flor flavor is often more satisfactory at 59°F.

Saenko and Sacharova (1959) and Saenko (1964) have recommended a continuous film process in which the temperature is maintained at 64.4° to 68°F. Small amounts of new wine are introduced daily under the film to replace that which is removed.

Sulfur Dioxide Tolerance

Hohl and Cruess (1939) found that the fermentative strains studied by them possessed the usual tolerance of S. cerevisiae yeasts to sulfur dioxide in wine and must. Marcilla et al. (1936) and Fornachon (1953B) recommend that the sulfur dioxide content be not above 100 p.p.m. total because it interferes with development of the flor flavor and bouquet. Williams (1943) opposed the use of any sulfur dioxide as he believed that it lessens the development of flor character.

Effect of Film on Acids

The observations of Schanderl (1936), Marcilla et al. (1936), Marcilla (1946), Baker (1945), Saenko (1945), Fornachon (1953B), and Bobadilla (1943) that the film stage of flor yeasts rapidly reduces the volatile acidity (acetic acid content) of wines was confirmed by Cruess and Podgorny (1937). Fixed acidity decreased in laboratory and winery scale experiments as shown in the data given in the following table for lots of wine in 50-gallon barrels or in butts.

With small lots of wine in flasks the rate of destruction of fixed acid is

TABLE 35

EFFECT OF JEREZ FLOR YEAST FILM ON TOTAL ACIDITY[1]

Winery	Months Under Film	Original Total Acidity as Tartaric	Final Total Acidity as Tartaric
		Gm./100 Ml.	Gm./100 Ml.
Inglenook	18	0.60	0.38
Italian Swiss Colony	24	0.43	0.37
Solano	23	0.48	0.26

[1] Source of data: Cruess (1948).

much more rapid than in 50-gallon barrels. It is also rapid in tanks when the depth of wine is shallow. The rate is a function of area to volume ratio: the greater the ratio of area exposed to film to volume the more rapid is the oxidation of fixed acid.

In laboratory scale experiments with small lots of wine the alcohol content decreased during the film stage but in winery experiments with 50-gallon barrels the alcohol content gradually increased as shown in Table 36.

TABLE 36

CHANGES IN ALCOHOL CONTENT OF WINE UNDER FLOR FILM IN WINERY EXPERIMENTS[1]

Winery	Months Under Film	Original Alcohol	Final Alcohol
		Per cent	Per cent
Italian Swiss Colony	11	15.80	16.30
Novitiate	20	14.80	15.45
Cresta Blanca	22	14.22	14.70
Cribari	13	15.50	15.90

[1] Source of data: Cruess (1948).

Effect of Sugars and Yeast Nutrients

Fornachon (1953B) states that added sugar is soon fermented by the flor yeast and that such addition is inadvisable as it may delay development of flor character. He recommends that wine to be made into flor sherry have less than 0.20 gm. per 100 ml. See Allan (1939) and Chaffey (1940) for a contrary view which needs to be checked.

Addition of ammonium phosphate stimulated film formation in Hohl and Cruess' experiments (1939). Grape concentrate stimulated growth moderately and dextrose had very little effect. The effects of various other substances were studied by Freiberg and Cruess (1955). Film formation was satisfactory at pH values of 3.1 to 4.0.

Effect of Yeast Lees on Flavor

In laboratory experiments relatively large volumes of flor film sediment were added to unfortified and to fortified wine that had been well aged under flor film. The treated wines were stored in well-filled, tightly sealed glass containers for a year. The effect on flavor was favorable and very pronounced. The treated wines possessed much of the characteristic after-taste of imported Spanish sherries.

At the surface of wines under flor film the condition is strongly oxidative, but in the wine under the film a reducing condition exists as evidenced by the bleaching of the color of the wine and measurement of the redox potential, Nielson (1952).

Winery Experiments

Flor sherries were made experimentally in fifteen different wineries in 40-gallon to 20,000-gallon lots using 50-gallon barrels or sherry butts in most cases, but tanks or ovals of 1500–3000 gallon capacity were also employed. At least two years, and usually three, were necessary to develop sufficient flor character. Aged wine required less time under flor than new wine. In most experiments the entire contents of the container were fortified when sufficient flor flavor and bouquet had developed.

Acetification occurred in one experiment in which the wine under experiment contained 15 per cent of alcohol; but did not occur at 15.5 per cent.

Baking destroyed the flor flavor and bouquet. Aging was found most satisfactory in completely filled, tightly-sealed oak containers. Excess color was removed in some experimental flor sherries by fining with casein. Bentonite proved very effective for fining flor wines of satisfactory color.

Tank and Barrel Process.—In one plant in which flor sherry was produced on a commercial scale for several years, redwood tanks were used. These were filled with dry Palomino wine to within about two feet of the top and inoculated with flor film. Growth of the film was heavy and development of flor character was rapid, Fig. 101. The tanks were equipped with the usual covers fitted with bung holes of customary diameter. The wine was over 15 per cent in alcohol. When the wine had attained sufficient flor character about one-half the wine in each tank was removed and fortified. New dry Palomino wine replaced that drawn off. Drawing off and replacement were repeated at about four-month intervals; in this manner a modified solera was maintained. The cellar temperature was held artificially within the optimum range for growth of the flor film. The fortified wine was aged in well-filled sherry butts and later used for blending with pale dry baked sherry of mild flavor.

In another plant the wine under flor was in sherry butts and a portion drawn off at regular intervals for fortification, aging, and blending with unbaked sherry. The portion drawn off was replaced with new wine of similar composition. Several California wineries have made flor sherry in 50-gallon barrels or sherry butts and fortified portions withdrawn at intervals.

Another winery used tanks in a room in which the temperature was controlled. Only a portion of the wine in each tank was withdrawn for fortification at regular intervals and replaced by dry wine of similar composition. The depth of wine in the tanks is such that development of flor character is rapid, as it was found that at too great depth development of flor bouquet was very slow. In all of these cases a modified solera system was used.

SUBMERGED FLOR PROCESS

Experiments have been made in Canada, Australia, and California on production of flor-type sherry without the customary film stage.

Australia and Canada

Fornachon (1953A) obtained very rapid production of aldehyde by shaking suspensions of active cells of S. bayanus (flor yeast) in a 14 per cent alcohol solution. In pure nitrogen, that is under anaerobic conditions, no aldehyde was formed. In water-alcohol solution of 14 per cent alcohol equilibrium was reached at about 1200 mg. of acetaldehyde per liter. In wine of similar alcohol content 630 mg. of aldehyde per liter was attained at equilibrium. These values are above those reached in wines under films.

Fornachon, according to Rankine (1955), also packed a column with oak chips on which he grew flor yeast. This procedure is similar to the process used for impregnating beechwood chips or coke with vinegar bacteria in a vinegar generator. Wine was passed slowly through the column and acquired considerable flor wine character. The column was difficult to operate and the product was not entirely satisfactory.

Crowther and Truscott (1955–56, 1957) in Canada found that by continuously pumping over new wine fermented with flor yeast the wine developed flor wine flavor and bouquet. In later experiments they obtained maximum flor character in three weeks and a rise in aldehyde content to 250 mg. per liter.

In California

Amerine (1958) and Ough and Amerine (1958) have reported on the rapid production of acetaldehyde in wine by flor yeast under air pressure. The apparatus used was that described by Amerine (1953). It consists of two 90-liter (approximately 23 gallons) stainless steel tanks, capable of withstanding over 100 lbs. per square inch internal pressure. It is equipped with temperature control equipment which can maintain 65°F. within 1°F., stirrers, a source of compressed air, air filters, air regulatory system, and lines to stand a pressure of 100 lbs. per square inch.

In one experiment grape concentrate was diluted to 22.5° Balling and fermented to dryness with S. bayanus (flor yeast). The new wine was fortified to 14.5 per cent alcohol and maintained at 100 lbs per square inch air pressure with the yeast in one of the pressure tanks for three days and then at 15 lbs. per square inch. The wine was stirred mechanically for five minutes each hour. When the wine reached the desired level of acetaldehyde content about half of it was removed and replaced with dry white wine of 14.5 per cent alcohol, and the above process was repeated. During the run air was allowed to escape from the tank at the rate of 100 ml. per minute continuously. The wine was fortified to 17.5 per cent alcohol content at the end of each experiment.

A culture of the film stage of S. bayanus was used very successfully in another experiment. Also air pressures of 5, 7.5, 10, 15, and 20 lbs. per square inch were compared. The rate of aldehyde production was greatest at 15 lbs. per square inch (143 mg. per liter per day) and least rapid at 5 lbs. per square inch (58 mg. per liter per day). In some runs the malic acid decreased and the lactic acid increased, indicating the growth and activity of malo-lactic bacteria.

There was very little change in pH value, volatile acidity, and total acidity during other runs and only a slight decrease in alcohol. Aldehyde content, however, increased rapidly. An interesting observation was that aldehyde production increased as the number of active yeast cells increased. After eleven more days no further increase in aldehyde was observed. In a typical experiment aldehyde production was at the rate of 77 mg. per liter per day; at 1100 to 1200 mg. aldehyde per liter aldehyde production ceased, confirming Guymon and Nakagiri's observation (1955) that at this range of aldehyde content wine yeast cease to ferment.

The intimate and direct relation between yeast count and aldehyde formation is indicated in Fig. 102. These data clearly indicate that continuous submerged culture fermentations are possible. Crowell and Guymon (1963) showed such sherries to be very high in diacetyl and acetoin (1.8 to 160 mg. per liter of diacetyl and 4.3 to 450 mg. per liter of acetoin).

The 1957 experimental wines of Amerine and Ough were aged in 10-gallon oak barrels. After nine months' aging the wines were analyzed. There was very little change in the composition including the aldehyde content and there was no clouding during aging, while flavor and bouquet improved. The experimental wines possessed a marked flor flavor and bouquet. Sugar content was adjusted to a considerable range after fortification; the preferred concentration being 0.5 to 1.5 per cent. Also the flor wine was blended in various proportions with good quality baked sherry. A blend of 75 per cent of the experimental with 25 per cent of baked sherry was considered best by an experienced taste panel. High aldehyde content was preferred to low by the taste panel. In this case blends of experimental flor sherries of 276, 637, and 1002 mg. per liter with 25 per cent of baked sherry were used, although Ough and Amerine point out that this observation may have no special practical significance. Their (1959) recommendations are given below.

1. The process if used should be arranged as a continuous system; tanks, lines, and other accessories must be constructed to stand 15 p.s.i.g. pressure plus a safety factor.
2. A culture from an active flor yeast of good quality can be used to start a submerged culture.
3. Alcohol level must be kept between 14 and 15 per cent during aldehyde formation.
4. The wine used should have a pH between 3.2 and 3.4. Slightly lower pH will yield a better product.
5. Operating pressure should be kept between 10 and 15 p.s.i.g.
6. For high quality, aging in oak barrels is probably necessary.
7. Blending will vary according to the wine used, but indications are that a very good product can result from 25 per cent of baked pale dry sherry blended with a high-aldehyde flor sherry with a final sugar level of 0.5 to 1.5 per cent.

At present, several California wineries produce wines of high aldehyde content by the discontinuous submerged technique. De Soto (1961) reported on the successful commercial application of the submerged flor culture process. Both a 990-gallon Charmat tank and a 5000-gallon glass lined steel tank were successfully used. Approximately six to seven weeks were required in both cases to raise the aldehyde level to about 650 p.p.m. DeSoto indicated that they were quite satisfied with the process as to simplicity, feasibility, and quality of the product. We have heard that tanks of from 20,000 to 100,000 gallons capacity have been used. The submerged culture process was successfully used under plant conditions by Farafontoff (1964). In contrast to the results of Ough and Amerine (1958) they did not use pressure and aldehyde content peaked at the same time as maximum yeast cell count and decreased thereafter. One reason for the pressure in the Ough and Amerine work was to prevent contamination during long continuous fermentation. Singleton *et al.* (1964) heated submerged culture flor sherry of high aldehyde content in the hopes of inducing acetal formation and greater odor complexity. The experiment was unsuccessful.

FLOR SHERRY PROCESS IN AUSTRALIA

According to Rankine (1958) the modified adaptation of the Spanish methods has proven successful in Australia. The first flor cultures were introduced in 1908 by Castella, but the first Australian flor sherry was not marketed until 1930. See Williams (1936) for an early report. The output of this type of wine has steadily increased until over 1,000,000 gallons or about 10 per cent of the fortified wine production is made annually as flor sherry. The full-bodied medium dry flor sherry is more popular than the drier *finos*, as Australians prefer sweeter wines.

Grapes and Yeasts

The varieties of grapes normally used are Pedro Ximenez, Doradillo, and Palomino (also known as Sweetwater). The Sémillon is often used to soften the higher acidity of the Pedro Ximenez. The amount of Palomino is limited although it is considered the best variety for making *fino*-type sherries.

The sherry is made with a selected strain of flor yeast, usually obtained from the Australian Wine Research Institute. In some of the grape growing areas, flor yeast has become indigenous and causes trouble by its unwanted growth on and in unfortified table wine.

Methods of Production

Rankine (1958) has described the Australian method of making flor sherry about as follows: The base wine is made in the same manner as white table wine with use of sulfur dioxide and a selected wine yeast (not flor yeast). The wine is fined and its alcohol content increased to about 15 per cent by light fortification. The wine is put on flor in hogsheads or puncheons or waxed concrete tanks, the latter with wooden covers slanted to prevent dripping of condensate into the wine with consequent breaking of the film. The wine is under flor about two years in casks and 3 to 6 months in tanks. If film formation is delayed because of lack of nitrogenous yeast nutrient, a small amount of an ammonium salt is added. A moderate film growth rather than a heavy film is desired because yeastiness of flavor and slow development of flor character result from the latter.

The wine is fortified to 18 or 19 per cent alcohol and the sulfur dioxide content adjusted to about 100 p.p.m. when it has developed the desired amount of flor character. It is then aged for about two years in wood. A few wineries employ a modified solera system during aging of the fortified wine. Some of the flor sherry is blended with non-flor sherry to improve the flavor and bouquet of the latter.

Fornachon's Investigations

On the basis of his research Fornachon (1953B) recommended that the alcohol content of the wine for flor yeast growth be 14.5 to 15.2 per cent; sugar content less than 0.15 g. per 100 ml.; tannin less than 0.02 gm. per 100 ml.; pH, 3.1 to 3.4; sulfur dioxide concentration about 100 p.p.m.; depth of wine in tanks used for flor growth about 24 inches; cotton "bungs" for casks of wine under flor to provide ventilation and exclude vinegar flies; inoculation by spraying the surface of the wine with a culture of flor yeast in wine; and that the wine be filtered or fined immediately after separation from the flor. He found that the yeast destroyed acetaldehyde under anaerobic conditions with increase in volatile acid, the reaction probably being:

$$2CH_3CHO + H_2O \rightarrow C_2H_5OH + CH_3COOH$$

The higher the oxygen content of the headspace the more rapid was the production of acetaldehyde. As much as 20 per cent of carbon dioxide in the headspace did not retard aldehyde production. The mineral requirements of the flor yeast were found to be adequate in all Australian wines tested. The flor wine was very susceptible to oxidation and he recommended, therefore, that containers be well filled and sealed during aging. Aldehyde production was more rapid and the redox potential was higher at 14.5 per cent alcohol than at higher alcohol concentrations. He suggested that the oxidation of alcohol to acetaldehyde near the surface of the wine under flor and conversion of aldehyde to acetic acid and ethyl alcohol in the depths of the wine go on simultaneously. He particularly emphasized the value of using high quality wines as a base for the flor.

FLOR SHERRY PROCESS IN SOUTH AFRICA

According to Niehaus (1958) considerable flor sherry is produced in South Africa. He also states that flor yeasts occur naturally on the grapes of that region and that it is unnecessary to use cultures from Spain. He recommends the procedure outlined below. The grapes, preferably of the Palomino variety, are harvested at 22 to 23° Balling, crushed and immediately pressed. Gypsum is added to the must at the rate of four pounds per leaguer (153.7 gallons), and the must is inoculated with an active culture of flor yeast (2 to 3 gallons of starter per leaguer). The fermentation is controlled by cooling and by addition of small amounts of potassium metabisulfite from time to time. The must is fermented dry, being completed in closed tanks fitted with fermentation bungs. The young wine is stored for about two weeks and is then drawn off the lees and fortified to 16 to 16.5 per cent of alcohol with sound, clean, neutral fortifying brandy. Pipes or sherry butts are thoroughly steamed. Two gallons of thick lees from recently fermented wine are placed in the cask and the entire inner surface coated by rolling the cask. The fortified wine is then introduced. Some of the yeast floats and an active film of flor soon develops.

Great care is taken not to raise the alcohol content beyond 16.5 per cent and to use only sound lees. The oak containers are then stored in a cool well-ventilated cellar. The bung holes are stoppered with a special ventilated bung. The wines are then allowed to remain under the flor film for 15 to 18 months. When the wine has reached the desired stage under flor it is syphoned off the lees and stored in completely filled, sealed, fresh puncheons or butts for further aging before final fortification and finishing. See also Theron and Niehaus (1947) and Niehaus (1937).

FLOR PROCESS IN FRANCE AND RUSSIA

For the flor-type (Château Chalon) wines of the Jura, Bidan and André (1958) found very little lees after six years' aging, 1 to 1.5 liter for 400 to 600 liters. They report cellar foremen to say that these wines "mangent leur lie." Neither the high aldehyde or acetoin contents of these wines would account for their bitter aftertaste. They were unable to relate the odor or taste of flor wines with their amino acid content. In commerce the wines are very dry, low in alcohol, and high in total acidity. Production is very small. According to Bidan and André, the yeasts are *Saccharomyces bayanus* and *S. bisporus*, var. *bisporus*.

Native flor-type yeasts have been produced in Armenia and Georgia in the Soviet Union for many years according to Prostoserdov and Afrikian (1933) and Saenko (1964). During the period under the film Saenko (1948) showed that the oxidation-reduction potential decreased rapidly as the acetaldehyde and acetal contents increased. In recent years, the process has been industrialized and flor-type sherries are commercially available in the Soviet Union. Experiments on continuous production of flor-type wines are also underway.

Saenko (1964) analyzed 26 Soviet flor-type sherries. The alcohol content varied from 13.9 to 20.5 per cent, sugar from 2.7 to 3.5 per cent, aldehyde from 106 to 656 mg. per liter and acetal from 142 to 555 mg. per liter. Her analysis of 21 Spanish sherries showed 17.3 to 21.6 per cent alcohol, 0.0 to 8.2 per cent sugar, 90 to 233 mg. per liter of aldehyde and 83 to 437 mg. per liter of acetal. The sensory scores for the Soviet wines

TABLE 37

COMPOSITION OF VARIOUS SHERRIES[1]

Type and Source	No. of Samples	Alcohol Per cent	Total Solids (at 212 °F.) Gm./100 Ml.	Ash Gm./100 Ml.	Total Acid as Tartaric Gm./100 Ml.	Volatile Acid Gm./100 Ml.	Alkalinity of H₂O Soluble-Ash as ml. 0.1-N H₂SO₄ to Neutralize Ash Ml. 0.1 N/100 Ml.
California dry, maximum	16	20.64	4.88	0.400	0.497	0.079	18.8
California dry, average	16	20.10	3.80	0.295	0.416	0.063	14.1
California dry, minimum	16	19.56	1.58	0.228	0.332	0.042	10.6
Spanish, fino or amontillado, maximum	38	20.72	4.92	0.490	0.536	0.124	7.6
Spanish, fino or amontillado, average	38	19.88	3.43	0.421	0.454	0.080	5.7
Spanish, fino or amontillado, minimum	38	17.74	1.45	0.374	0.364	0.048	3.4
Spanish, oloroso and amoroso, maximum	23	20.52	12.72	0.520	0.578	0.120	14.9
Spanish, oloroso and amoroso, average	23	19.72	7.82	0.434	0.477	0.102	7.7
Spanish, oloroso and amoroso, minimum	23	18.78	5.32	0.370	0.420	0.073	5.0
Eastern U.S.A., sherry, maximum	10	20.04	7.52	0.305	0.480	0.110	17.0
Eastern U.S.A., sherry, average	10	18.90	4.03	0.245	0.406	0.071	12.4
Eastern U.S.A., sherry, minimum	10	15.66	2.05	0.175	0.315	0.046	8.0

[1] Source of Data: Valaer (1947).

ranged from 8.17 to 9.50, average 8.51 while those of the Spanish wines ranged from 8.61 to 9.48, average 9.22.

Slight decreases or increases in amino acids occurred in sherry wines under a film, according to Saenko and Sakharova (1963). No changes or only slight changes in organic acids occurred under the film up to 180 days.

COMPOSITION OF COMMERCIAL· SHERRIES

Valaer (1945, 1947, 1950) has made many analyses of imported Spanish sherries and of California sherries (Table 37).

The imported and the domestic sherries were of similar alcohol content which is not surprising, owing to the federal regulations in respect to alcohol content of fortified wines. The ash of the imported sherries was higher than the domestic owing to the use of gypsum (plastering) in the production of Spanish sherries; for the same reason the alkalinity of the ash of the Spanish sherries was lower than of the domestic. The Spanish sherries analyzed by Valaer seemed to be somewhat higher in volatile acidity than those made in the U. S. In total acidity the sherries from the three regions represented were similar, although the lowest total acidity was that of an eastern U. S. sherry (0.315 gm. per 100 ml.) and the highest was that of a Spanish sherry (0.578 gm. per 100 ml.). The total solids content of the dry sherries as would be expected was lower than that of the medium sweet to sweet sherries.

Valaer also gave the aldehyde content of 27 typical sherries, some of which were imported and some domestic. The average aldehyde content of the imported Spanish sherries was 141.1 mg. liter; the maximum was 198 mg. and the minimum was 66 mg. For the California sherries the average, maximum, and minimum values were 29.1, 41.8, and 13.2 mg. per liter. For the eastern U. S. samples the values were 66.21, 127.6, and 9.4 mg. per liter. It is of interest that sherries made in the eastern U. S. were of higher aldehyde content than the California sherries. This may be due to use of oxygen during baking by the Tressler process. The Spanish sherries were higher than the domestic American sherries in aldehyde content, owing to the use of flor yeast in the production of many of the imported samples analyzed by Valaer. See also Amerine (1947).

The importance of aldehydes in flor sherry has been re-emphasized by recent studies. Nilov and Furman (1964) reported acetaldehyde, propionaldehyde, iso-butyraldehyde (2-methyl-propanal), iso-valeraldehyde (2-methyl-butanal) and furfural. Rodopulo et al. (1965) and Rodopulo and Egorov (1965) also found formaldehyde, caprylaldehyde, and enanthaldehyde. During aging under the flor film the esters (especially ethyl acetate) and some alcohols (3-methyl-1-butanol and 1-hexanol) increased

TABLE 38

COMPOSITION OF SEVERAL CALIFORNIA AND SPANISH SHERRIES[1]

Sample	Total Acidity as Tartaric	Volatile Acidity as Acetic	Alcohol	pH	Total Sugars	Total Ash	Sulfates as SO$_4$
	Gm./ 100 Ml.	Gm./ 100 Ml.	Per cent		Gm./ 100 Ml.	Gm./ 100 Ml.	Gm./ 100 Ml.
California Sherries							
Solano, dry	0.39	0.064	18.85	3.65	1.40	0.236	0.064
Cresta Blanca, dry	0.42	0.048	19.20	3.58	2.14	0.289	0.082
Concannon, dry	0.58	0.067	18.70	3.55	2.42	0.374	0.144
Calif. Growers, dry	0.45	0.050	18.80	3.45	2.42	0.308	0.107
Spanish Sherries							
Amoroso	0.48	0.085	20.7	3.47	4.93	0.401	0.158
Pinta brand (*fino*)	0.46	0.054	21.0	3.40	1.84	0.462	0.221
Amontillado	0.48	0.066	19.6	3.30	2.38	0.428	0.252
Oloroso	0.53	0.085	20.0	3.40	6.95	0.408	0.202
Apitiv (fino)	0.33	0.048	19.3	3.75	1.08	0.371	0.182

[1] Source of data: Brajnikoff and Cruess (1948).

markedly. Thus, aldehydes, acetals, esters and higher alcohols are all involved in the flor sherry bouquet.

Using gas chromatographic techniques on flor sherries, Webb and Kepner (1962) found relatively large amounts of 2-phenethyl alcohol and diethyl succinate, moderate quantities of 3-methyl-1-butanol, diethyl malate, and 2-phenethyl acetate, small amounts of 2-methyl-1-butanol, 1-hexanol, ethyl isobutyrate, ethyl caproate, ethyl caprylate, ethyl lactate, isoamyl acetate, isoamyl caproate, isoamyl caprylate, γ-butyrolactone, and 2-phenethyl caproate and only traces of 2-methyl-1-propanol, ethyl acetate, isobutyl isobutyrate, isobutyl caproate, isoamyl isovalerate, and hexyl acetate. Several unidentified components were found. (Webb (1965) later identified *act.*-amyl lactate as one of these.) Probably present were *act.*-amyl isovalerate, *act.*-amyl caproate, *act.*-amyl caprylate, and isoamyl 2-methylbutyrate. Webb and Kepner suggested that 2-phenethyl alcohol and its acetate and caproate esters contribute significantly to the over-all odor of flor sherry. Diethyl succinate and diethyl malate have less distinctive odors which they believe contribute to kinesthetic (tactile?) impressions. The ethyl esters of isobutyric, caproic, and caprylic acids do appear to be important to flor sherry odor. Ethyl lactate, they suggest, is responsible for the cheese-like odor of certain flor sherries. The esters of the higher molecular weight acids and alcohols also contribute to the over-all odor. See also Suomalainen and Nykänen (1966).

The nature of the aroma components of the methylene chloride extracts of flor, baked and submerged culture sherries was compared by Webb *et al.* (1964). Since furfural was the only component unique to a single type (baked), they concluded that the differences in odor were due to differences in the ratios of components. They particularly noted the large quantity of ethyl acid succinate in all types of sherry. However, in the flor sherries a number of unidentified components were noted. They held out the hope that it might be possible to define the different types by correlation of subjective and objective results. In a flor sherry wine, Bourdet and Hérard (1958) reported 57 per cent of the nitrogen was present as free amino acids and 35 per cent as peptides. They also noted marked enrichment of wines in inorganic and organic phosphorus in wines stored on the lees. This was especially true of a film yeast wine.

Brajnikoff and Cruess (1948) give the analysis of several California and imported sherries as shown in Table 38. As was the case for the samples analyzed by Valaer the Spanish sherries were higher in ash than the domestic. They were also higher in sulfates owing to plastering. All of the California sherries were dry or medium dry and therefore of low or medium low sugar content. Samples 6, 7, and 9 of the Spanish were dry and samples 5 and 8, sweet. The aldehyde contents of three experimental flor sherries were found by Brajnikoff and Cruess to be 127.2, 130.9, and 153.0 mg. per liter. These values are much lower than obtained by Ough and Amerine by their submerged-oxidation-under-pressure procedure, but comparable to the aldehyde content of imported Spanish sherries as reported by Valaer.

BIBLIOGRAPHY

ABRAMOV, S. A., and POTYAKA, P. K. 1965. Vliyanie sernistoĭ kislosty na razvitie kheresnykh drozhzhie (Influence of sulfur dioxide on the development of the flor yeast). Vinodelie i Vinogradarstvo S.S.S.R. 25, No. 5, 14–17.

ALLEN, H. M. 1939. A study of sherry flor. Australian Brewing Wine J. 58, No. 10, 31–33; No. 11, 70–71.

AMERINE, M. A. 1947. The composition of wines of California at expositions. Wines and Vines 28, No. 1, 21–23, 42–43, 45; No. 2, 24–26; No. 3, 23–25, 42–46.

AMERINE, M. A. 1948. Personal communication.

AMERINE, M. A. 1953. New controlled fermentation equipment at Davis. Wines and Vines 34, No. 9, 27–30.

AMERINE, M. A. 1958. Aldehyde formation in submerged cultures of Saccharomyces beticus. Appl. Microbiol. 6, 160–168.

AMERINE, M. A., ROESSLER, E. B., and FILIPELLO, F. 1959. Sensory evaluation of wine. Hilgardia 28, 477–567.

AMERINE, M. A., and TWIGHT, E. H. 1938. Sherry. Wines and Vines 19, No. 5, 3–4.

ANON. 1935. How sherry is made. Spanish Commercial Office. Mimeo.

ANON. 1941. Designation of origin of Jerez, Xerez, Sherry. Order of Dept. of Agr., Madrid, Spain, Oct. 20, 1941. Translation by D. B. Mattimore, Wine Institute, San Francisco.

ANON. 1950. Jerez, Xerez, Sherry. Bull. off. intern. vin. 23, No. 233, 22–33.

BAKER, R. 1945. A study of base wines for flor sherries. Thesis, Roseworthy College, Australia.

BAKER, G. A., AMERINE, M. A., and ROESSLER, E. B. 1952. Theory and application of fractional blending systems. Hilgardia 21, 383–409.

BERG, H. W. 1951. Stabilization practices in California wineries. Proc. Am. Soc. Enol. 1951, 90–147.

BERG, H. W. 1956. Personal communication. Davis, Calif.

BERG, H. W. 1959. Personal communication on visit to Jerez de la Frontera, Spain.

BERG, H. W. 1960. Stabilization studies on Spanish sherry and on factors influencing KHT precipitation. Am. J. Enol. Vitic. 11, 123–128.

BERG, H. W., and AKIYOSHI, M. 1956. Some factors involved in the browning of white wines. Am. J. Enol. 7, 1–8.

BIDAN, P., and ANDRÉ, L. 1958. Sur la composition en acides aminés de quelques vins. Ann. technol. agr. 7, 403–432.

BOBADILLA, G. F. DE. 1938. L'emploi de l'anhydride sulfureux au point de vue des qualités organoleptiques et hygiéniques des vins. Le point de vue Espagnol. Veme Congrés Intern. Vigne et Vin, Lisbonne 2, 80–83.

BOBADILLA, G. F. DE. 1940. Levaduras seleccionadas típicas de Jerez. Agricultura (Revista Agropecuaria) 9, No. 102, 358–360. (Also Sindicato Vertical de la Vid, Cervezas y Bebidas 3, No. 8, 5–10. 1944.)

BOBADILLA, G. F. DE. 1943. Aplicaciones industriales de las levaduras de flor. Agricultura (Revista Agropecuaria) 12, No. 133, 203–207.

BOBADILLA, G. F. DE. 1947A. Graduaciones alcoholica de los vinos en las soleras. Typed Rept. Estación de Viticultura y Enologia, Jerez de la Frontera.

BOBADILLA, G. F. DE. 1947B. Sobre el empleo del anhidrido sulfuroso en la vinificación del Jerez. Typed Rept. 1. Estación de Viticultura y Enologia, Jerez de la Frontera.

BOBADILLA, G. F. DE. 1947C. Tiempo de crianza del Jerez antes de llegar a las soleras. Typed Rept. Estación de Viticultura y Enologia, Jerez de la Frontera.

BOBADILLA, G. F. DE, QUIROS, J. M., and SERRANO, J. J. 1954. Vinos de Jerez. El enyesado de los mostos. Bol. inst. nac. invest. agron. (Madrid) 14, No. 31, 412–446.

BOURDET, A., and HÉRARD, J. 1958. Influence de l'autolyse des levures sur la composition phosphorée et azotée des vins. Ann. technol. agr. 7, 177–202.

BRAJNIKOFF, I., and CRUESS, W. V. 1948. Observations on Spanish sherry process. Food Research 13, 128–135.

CASTELLA, F. DE. 1909, 1926. Sherry, its making and rearing. Victoria Dept. Agr. J. 7, 442–446, 515–528, 577–583, 621–630, 724–727; Ibid. 24, 690–698.

CASTELLA, F. DE. 1922. Maturation of sherry. Australian Brewing Wine J. 41, 37.

CHAFFEY, W. B. 1940. Some factors influencing the development and the effect of flor yeasts. Ibid. 58, No. 9, 33–34; No. 10, 31–34; No. 11, 31–32.

COSTA, L. CINCINNATO DE. 1938. Le problème des eaux-de-vie et des alcools. Veme Congrés Intern. Vigne et du Vin, Lisbonne 2, 181–189.

CROWELL, E. A., and GUYMON, J. F. 1963. Influence of aeration and suspended material on higher alcohol, acetoin, and diacetyl during fermentation. Am. J. Enol. Vitic. 14, 214–222.

CROWTHER, R. F., and TRUSCOTT, J. H. L. 1955–56. Flor type Canadian sherry wine. Hort. Expt. Sta. and Prod. Lab. Rept., Vineland, Ontario, Canada 1955–56, 75–83.

CROWTHER, R. F., and TRUSCOTT, J. H. L.   1957.   The use of agitation in making of flor sherry.   Am. J. Enol. 7, 11–12.
CRUESS, W. V.   1937.   Lessons from Spanish sherries.   Wine Review 5, No. 1, 14–16, 36–37; No. 2, 12–14, 20; No. 5, 14–16.
CRUESS, W. V.   1943.   Notes on Spanish sherry experiments.   Ibid. 11, No. 9, 8–9.
CRUESS, W. V.   1948.   Investigations of the flor sherry process.   Calif. Agr. Expt. Sta. Bull. 710.
CRUESS, W. V., and PODGORNY, A.   1937.   Destruction of volatile acidity of wine by film yeasts.   Fruit Prods. J. 17, 4–6.
CRUESS, W. V., WEAST, C. A. and GILILAND, R.   1938.   Summary of practical investigations on film yeast.   Ibid. 17, 229–231, 251.
DE SOTO, R. T.   1961.   Commercial production of flor sherry by the submerged method.   Wine Institute, Tech. Advis. Committee, August 11, 1961.
DOMECQ, P.   1940.   Sherry in the Making.   Pedro Domecq Co., New York and Jerez de la Frontera.
FARAFONTOFF, A.   1964.   Studies to determine the feasibility of flor sherry production in California.   Am. J. Enol. Vitic. 15, 130–134.
FESSLER, J. H.   1952.   Development of the Fessler compound.   Wines and Vines 33, No. 7, 15–16.
FORNACHON, J. C. M.   1943.   Bacterial Spoilage of Fortified Wines.   Australian Wine Board, Adelaide.
FORNACHON, J. C. M.   1953A.   The accumulation of acetaldehyde by suspensions of yeast.   Australian J. Biol. Sci. 6, 222–233.
FORNACHON, J. C. M.   1953B.   Studies on the Sherry Flor.   Australian Wine Board, Adelaide.
FORNACHON, J. C. M.   1959.   Personal communication.
FORNACHON, J. C. M., DOUGLAS, H. C., and VAUGHN, R. H.   1949.   Lactobacillus trichodes nov. spec., a bacterium causing spoilage in appetizer and dessert wine.   Hilgardia 19, 129–132.
FREIBERG, K. J., and CRUESS, W. V.   1955.   A study of certain factors affecting the growth of flor yeast.   Appl. Microbiol. 3, 208–213.
FREMENKO, G. G., BOL'SHOI, V. A., and BELOCUROV, D. M.   1963.   Noyvi metod prigotovleniya madery (A new method of making madeira).   Vinodelie i Vinogradarstvo S.S.S.R. 23, No. 5, 21–27.
FREYRE NIETO, E.   1954.   Applicación de fitato de calcio a la clarificación y estabilización de vinos de Jerez.   Bol. Inst. Nac. Invest. Agron. (Madrid) 14, No. 31, 395–409.
GARINO-CANINA, E.   1934.   Sull valorizzazione dell'alcool de vinos sotto il riflesso económico della tecnica vitivinicola.   Annuar. R. staz. enol, sper. Asti 1, 215–221.
GONZALEZ GORDON, M.   1948.   Jerez, Xerez, Scheris, Sherry.   Imprenta A. Padura, Jerez de la Frontera, Spain.
GOSWELL, R. W.   1968.   Sherry manufacture.   Process Biochem. 3 (2): 47–49.
GUYMON, J. F.   1955.   Effect of brandy upon the quality and changes in composition of California-type sherry during baking.   Am. J. Enol. 6, 36–41.
GUYMON, J. F., and NAKAGIRI, J. A.   1955.   Utilization of heads by addition to alcoholic fermentation.   Ibid. 6, 12–25.
HEITZ, J. E., ROESSLER, E. B., AMERINE, M. A., and BAKER, G. A.   1951.   A study of certain factors influencing the composition of California-style sherry during baking.   Food Research 16, 192–200.

HICKINBOTHAM, A. R. 1952. What does plaster do? Australian Brewing Wine J. 70, No. 8, 4, 6, 8, 10.

HOHL, L. A., and CRUESS, W. V. 1939, 1940. Observations on certain film forming yeasts. Zentr. Bakteriol. Parasitenk. Abt. II 101, 65–78. (Also Fruit Prods. J. 20, 72–75, 108–111, 1940.)

HOLDEN, C. 1955. Combined method for heat and cold stabilization. Am. J. Enol. 6, 47–49.

IÑIGO LEAL, B., and BRAVO ABAD, F. 1963. Acidez y levaduras vínicas. III. Curso cinético de la acidez volátil en fermentados de mosto originados por distintas especies de levaduras vínicas. Rev. cienc. apl. 17, 132–135.

IÑIGO LEAL, B., VÁZQUES MARTÍNEZ, D., and ARROYO VARELA, V. 1963. Los agentes de fermentación vínica en la zona de Jerez. Ibid. 17, 296–305.

JOSLYN, M. A. 1948. Personal communication. Berkeley, Calif.

JOSLYN, M. A., and AMERINE, M. A. 1964. Dessert, Appetizer and Related Flavored Wines. University of California, Division of Agricultural Sciences, Berkeley.

KEAN, C. E., and MARSH, G. L. 1956. Investigation of copper complexes causing cloudiness in wines. II. Bentonite treatment of wines. Food Technol. 10, 355–359.

KIELHÖFER, E. 1951. Die Eiweisstrübung des weines. IV. Z. Lebensm.-Unters. u. -Forsch. 92, 1–9.

KOCH, J. 1957. Die Eiweissstoffe des Weines und ihre Veränderungen bei verschiedenden kellerischen Behandlungsmethoden. Weinberg u. Keller 4, 521–526.

MARCILLA ARRAZOLA, J. 1946. Tratado die Viticultura y Enologia Españolas. Vol. II. Sociedad Anónima Española de Traductores y Autores, Madrid.

MARCILLA, J., ALAS, G., and FEDUCHY, E. 1936. Contribución al estudio de las levaduras que forman velo sobre ciertos vinos de elevado grado alcoholico. Anales Centro Invest. Vinícolas 1, 1–230.

MARQUIS, H. H. 1936. California sherry production. Wine Review 4, No. 6, 6–7, 22.

MARTINI, L. P. 1950. Flor sherry experiments. Proc. Am. Sóc. Enol. 1950, 113–118.

MARTINI, L. P., and CRUESS, W. V. 1956. Sherry production practices survey. Wine Institute, Tech. Advis. Committee, Feb. 20, 1956. San Francisco.

MATTICK, L. R., and ROBINSON, W. B. 1960. Changes in the volatile acids during the baking of sherry wine by the Tressler baking process. Am. J. Enol. Vitic. 11, 113–116.

NIEHAUS, C. J. G. 1937. South African sherries. Farming in South Africa 12, 82, 85.

NIEHAUS, C. J. G. 1958. Personal communication.

NIELSON, N. E. 1952. The effect of oxygen on growth and carbon metabolism of flor and related yeasts. Ph.D. Thesis, Dept. of Food Technology, Univ. Calif. Berkeley.

NILOV, V. I., and FURMAN, D. B. 1964. Oveshchestvakh, obuslovlivayuschikh buket vina tipa kheres (Substances causing the bouquet of a wine of the sherry type). Sadovodstvo, Vinogradarstvo i Vinodelie Moldavii 1964, No. 11, 32–34.

OCHELTREE, J. B. 1932. The sherry wine industry (of Spain). American Consular Office, Seville, Spain. Mimeo.

OUGH, C. S., and AMERINE, M. A. 1958. Studies on aldehyde production under pressure, oxygen and agitation. Am. J. Enol. 9, 111–123.

PREOBRAZHENSKIĬ, A. A. 1963. Osobennosti maderizatsii v germetizirovannykh rezervuarakh (Heating wines in closed tanks). Vinodelie i Vinogradarstvo S.S.S.R. 23, No. 6, 4–9.

PROSTOSERDOV, N. N., and AFRIKIAN, R. 1933. Jerez Wein in Armenien. Das Weinland 5, 389–391.

RANKINE, B. C. 1955. Yeast cultures in Australian wine making. Am. J. Enol. 6, 11–15.

RANKINE, B. C. 1958. An outline of flor sherry making in Australia. Mimeo. Rept.

ROCQUES, X. 1903. Les vins de liqueur d'Espagne. Le vin de Jerez. Rev. vitic. 19, 446–53, 501–505, 570–573, 594–598.

RODOPULO, A. K., and EGOROV, I. A. 1965. Karbonil'nye soedineniya kheresa (The carbonyls of sherry). Vinodelie i Vinogradarstvo S.S.S.R. 25, No. 1, 6–9.

RODOPULO, A. K., EGOROV, I. A., and LASHINA, V. E. 1965. O buketistykh veshchestvakh keresa (Bouquet properties of sherry). Prikl. biokh. mikrobiol. 1, 95–101.

SAAVEDRA, I. J., and GARRIDO, J. M. 1963. La levadura de "flor" en la crianza del vino; el etanol en el metabolismo en fase de velo. Rev. cienc. apl. 17, No. 95, 497–501.

SAENKO, N. F. 1945. Improving sick and defective wines by means of a sherry film (transl.). Vinodelie i Vinogradarstvo S.S.S.R. 5, No. 4, 4–10.

SAENKO, N. F. 1948. Izmenenie okislitel'no-vosstanovitel'nogo potentsiala i sostava vina pri vyderzhke ego pod kheresnoĭ plenkoĭ (Modification of the oxidation-reduction potential and of the composition of sherry wine during aging under a film). Biokhim. Vinodeliya 2, 86–100.

SAENKO, N. F. 1964. Kheres (Sherry). Izdatel'stvo "Pishchevaya Promyshlennost'" Moscow.

SAENKO, N. F., and SACHAROVA, T. A. 1959. Vliyanie uslovii kul'tivirovaniya kheresnykh drozhzhei na ikh rost i biokhimicheskuyu aktivnost' (Influence of cultural conditions of sherry yeasts on their development and biochemical activity). Vinodelie i Vinogradarstvo S.S.S.R. 19, No. 2, 19–23.

SAENKO, N. F., and SAKHAROVA, T. A. 1963. Prevrashchenie organicheskikh kislot i aminokislot v protsesse vyderzhki vina pod kheresnoĭ plenkoĭ (Changes in the organic and amino acids in sherries under a film). Ibid. 23, No. 3, 3–6.

SCHANDERL, H. 1936. Untersuchungen über sogenannte Jerez-Héfen. Wein u. Rebe 18, 16–25.

SINGLETON, V. L., OUGH, C. S., and AMERINE, M. A. 1964. Chemical and sensory effects of heating wines under different gases. Am. J. Enol. Vitic. 15, 134–145.

STRUD, S. 1953. Flor sherry production. Wine Institute, Tech. Advis. Committee, July 24, 1953.

SUOMALAINEN, H., and NYKÄNEN, L. 1966. The aroma compounds produced by sherry yeast in grape and berry wines. Suom. Kemist. B 39, 252–256.

THERON, C. J., and NIEHAUS, C. J. G. 1947–48. Wine making. Union of South Africa Dept. Agr. Bull. 191.

TWIGHT, E. H. 1936. California sherry making. Wines and Vines 17, No. 4, 5, 15.

VALAER, P. 1945. Composition of domestic and imported sherries. Alcohol and Tobacco Tax Unit, Internal Revenue Service, Washington, D.C. Mimeo.

VALAER, P. 1947. Sherry wine, methods of its production and the analyses of Spanish and American sherry wine. Alcohol and Tobacco Tax Unit, Internal Revenue Service, Washington, D.C.

VALAER, P. 1950. Wines of the World. Abelard Press, New York.

WARKENTIN, H. 1955. Influence of pH and total acidity on calcium tolerance of sherry wine. Food Research 20, 301–310.

WEBB, A. D. 1965. Personal communication.

WEBB, A. D., and KEPNER, R. E. 1962. The aroma of flor sherry. Am. J. Enol. Vitic, 13, 1–14.

WEBB, A. D., KEPNER, R. E., and GALETTO, W. E. 1964. Comparison of aromas of flor sherry, baked sherry, and submerged-culture sherry. Ibid. 15, 1–10.

WILLIAMS, J. L. 1936. The manufacture of flor sherry. Australian Brewing Wine J. 55, 64. (See also South Australia Dept. Agr. Bull. 46, 267–274, 322–325.)

WILLIAMS, J. L. 1943. The manufacture of flor sherry. J. Dept. Agr. South Australia 46, 267–274, 322–325.

CHAPTER 10

Port and Other Dessert Wines

In the preceding chapter the production of sherry was discussed. The other principal fortified dessert wines are port, angelica, Málaga, Madeira (of the island of Madeira), Marsala, California tokay and muscatel, and similiar types produced in many countries.

PORT

The production of sweet red wines in Portugal has been one of that country's most important industries for more than two centuries. Red sweet wines, often called port, or port-type, are also produced in Australia, California, Chile, South Africa, and the Soviet Union. California is the principal producing region in the United States. See Chapter 1 and Castella (1908), Ottavi and Garino-Canina (1930), Sébastian (1909), Simon (1934), and Vizetelly (1880) for a general discussion, and Lachman (1903) and Twight (1934) for historical data on the California industry.

At present California wine makers must use such red wine varieties as are available. Probably the Alicante Bouschet is the poorest of these, owing to its low sugar musts, the tendency of its wines to lose color, and to its slightly unpleasant aroma. Carignane, Zinfandel, Mataro, and Petite Sirah are satisfactory when picked before raisining occurs; however, Mataro is deficient in color. The Mission and Grenache, grown in the same area, are lacking in acid and color but are of pleasing flavor. Blends with Salvador and Alicante Bouschet often have to be employed in order to bring up the color. It is to be hoped that more suitable grape varieties will be planted in the Fresno area, such as Tinta Madeira, Souzão, Royalty, and Rubired. The latter are two new hybrids released by the University of California. They were created by Prof. H. P. Olmo specifically for red sweet wine production. In the hot interior valleys of California, where most of the sweet dessert wines are made, many varieties of red wine grapes fail to develop sufficient color for production of port of satisfactory tint, unless special methods of vinification are used. There is great need for the planting of varieties of maximum red color in these areas to bring up to a desirable depth the color of ports made from the varieties grown at present. The Salvador is widely used for this purpose but its flavor is poor. The Souzão, Rubired and Royalty should help supply this deficiency without the undesirable flavor. There may be a problem of color stability with the Rubired.

440

Normal Vinification of Port

The principal problem in making port is extraction of sufficient color during a restricted period of fermentation.

The grapes should be well ripened, 23° to 25° Balling and should be picked to eliminate moldy fruit and handled with care to avoid bruising. They should be crushed as soon as possible after picking. Shipping loose in bulk in gondolas with long delays in crushing is not conducive to quality. Use of rain-damaged grapes that have molded on the vines is also undesirable, as such grapes give wines of poor flavor and unstable color.

Crushing and stemming are conducted as for grapes for dry red wine (p. 247). The crushed grapes are pumped into large fermentation vats holding 10,000 gallons or more. Some sulfur dioxide should be added during filling of the vat to give about 100 p.p.m. in the must. This will insure a cleaner fermentation, help to stabilize the color, and assist in extraction of the color.

Early in the season a 1 or 2 per cent starter of pure-yeast is added to the crushed grapes. Later in the season, a similar quantity of fermenting must from a vat in active fermentation will answer the purpose but it is better to continue to use a pure yeast culture. Flanzy (1959) reported better quality dessert wines when the must was fermented at 59° to 68°F. compared to 86°F. He believed sulfur dioxide reduced the quality of the dessert wines. Both these results need confirmation.

Frequent pumping over of must in large vats is essential to extraction of the color. In Portugal color extraction is accomplished by intermittent treading of the fermenting grapes; an effective but not very aesthetic procedure (p. 39).

If the grapes have good color, and the wine maker has been lucky, his must will have attained fair color when it has fermented to the point at which it is ready for fortification to give a standard port of 18 $\times$ 7 composition (18 per cent alcohol and 7° Balling) after fortification. Thus, if the original grapes tested 24° Balling and were fermented and fortified at 12.5° to 18 per cent alcohol, the resulting wine should be about 7°. As a matter of fact, in this case, the fermenting must would be drawn from the vat at about 14.5° Balling, since there may be nearly 2° drop during drawing off, pumping to the fortifying tank, measuring, and wine spirits addition. In warm regions the 14.5° Balling will be reached in 24 to 48 hours after crushing.

The free-run will naturally not be very deep in color. When possible the drained skins and seeds (pomace) should be pressed, preferably in a basket or Willmes press. However, a continuous press is generally used because of its convenience and economy of operation. The press wine is often fortified and is of deeper color. One can readily see the difficulty in

FIG. 103. CONCRETE FERMENTERS FOR FERMENTING WATERED POMACE
Note: These are no longer widely used, mainly being replaced with metal
fermenters. See Fig. 68.

extracting sufficient color in such a short period of fermentation, especially with grapes grown near Fresno, or in other hot localities. Hence, "normal vinification" of port is usually not practicable. Other methods are discussed in the next section.

Most San Joaquin wineries draw the free-run colored fermenting must off at the proper stage and pump it to the fortifying tanks. The residual pomace is then watered and fermented for distilling. It is next passed to a Metzner still, to a hammer mill for grinding in order to use a pomace still, to a continuous press, or to a "scalping" apparatus (a spray of water used to remove the alcohol). Countercurrent extraction has also been used to recover the residual sugar; see Berg and Guymon (1951). In some cases the pomace is transferred to other tanks for completion of fermentation (Fig. 103).

The relation between initial Balling (or Brix) degree of the grapes, Balling of the must, and final Balling after fortification to 18 per cent alcohol, is shown in Fig. 69. Wine makers commonly pay too little attention to fortification at the proper sugar content. The result is that some lots are fortified too soon and more too late. Closer attention to this table would reduce this problem.

Fermenting Dry Before Wine Spirits Addition

A few wine makers ferment much of the must for port on the skins to about 0° Balling, that is, as if they were going to make claret or burgundy.

Then, this more or less dry wine is fortified to give a wine of good color. Pressing of the drained pomace gives a press wine of deep color, which may also be fortified. Another must is fortified after a very short fermentation period to give a wine of high sugar content but of pale color. The dry and sweet ports are later blended to give standard port of 18 × 6 composition. Instead of using a fortified must, red concentrate has been used to give the desired sugar. Only high quality red concentrate should be used. The latter procedure is preferable.

Extraction of Color by Heat

In this procedure the must is drawn off, pumped through a pasteurizer, and returned to the vat of crushed grapes until the temperature reaches about 120°F., at which temperature it is held for perhaps 24 hours. Joslyn and Amerine (1964) suggested heating to 140°F. or higher for a shorter time. At 140°F. the color "flows" (is extracted) rapidly. Amerine and De Mattei (1940) have shown that good color extraction can be attained immediately by dipping the grapes in boiling water for one minute before crushing.

The must is drawn off and the grapes pressed; when color extraction is sufficient at the time of drawing off pressing may be omitted. If still hot, the juice should be cooled. A small amount of wine may be added to bring the alcohol to above the legal minimum of 0.5 to 1.0 per cent and the must fortified to 20 to 21 per cent alcohol. Or it may be cooled, fermented to the proper sugar content, and fortified. In the former case it can be blended later with fortified dry port to give a wine of standard alcohol and Balling degree.

The present tendency is to heat the crushed grapes to 180°F., hold at this temperature for 2 or 3 minutes, and pump through a cooler to a fermenter. The free-run, colored juice is drawn off, cooled, yeasted, fermented and fortified. The pomace is cooled, diluted with water, yeasted, and fermented for distilling material. Unfortunately, the red color of wines made from heated musts is often too blue and of poor stability. It is common experience also that wines from heated musts are difficult to clarify. For further details see Berg (1940), Berg and Marsh (1950), Berg and Akiyoshi 1958), Joslyn and Amerine (1964), and Nury (1957).

Coffelt and Berg (1965) developed equipment for heat treating whole grapes with steam under pressure. Because of the high temperatures obtainable, heating times of only a few seconds were required to give juices which after partial fermentation and fortification produced ports of superior color and equal or better quality than those produced by more conventional procedures.

Color extraction by heat or by fermenting on the skins should not be too long, or the wine may also be too high in tannin. Port should be smooth, not astringent.

Addition of alcohol to the fermenting pomace in order to extract more color has been recommended by Berg and Akiyoshi (1960) and by Nedeltchev (1959). However, Nedeltchev also tried heating the crushed grapes and the pomace only. The best results were obtained by preheating whole grapes in boiling water for 3 or 4 minutes. He reported particularly that heating of the whole grapes avoids the cooked taste. Finally, Nedeltchev reported that addition of tartaric was superior to use of concentrate as a method of increasing the acidity of low acid musts. This result should be checked.

For details of fortification see p. 268. Singleton et al. (1964) reported better color in young ruby ports fortified with high aldehyde wine spirits. They suggested this was due to reaction of acetaldehyde with anthocyanins via an acid-catalyzed Baeyer reaction to produce polymers. See also Costa (1938) and Egorov et al. (1951).

There have been many reports in Europe that fortifying dessert wines in two or more steps resulted in a higher quality product than addition of all of the spirits at one time. Singleton and Guymon (1963) made a test of this with California white and ruby ports. The multiple addition did seem to result in better quality, particularly with white port. They showed that this was probably due to the reduction in aldehydes by fermentation at the relatively low alcohol following the initial partial fortification. Commercial use of multiple additions of wine spirits would seem to be indicated if high aldehyde spirits are used, as they apparently often are in European countries.

Balancing the Port Cellar

The port to be bottled should be of standard composition, often, about 18 × 7—about 18 per cent alcohol and 7° Balling (13 to 15 per cent total extract). Obviously then, if the entire season's ports were all blended into one uniform blend the composition of the components should be such that the average will be about 18 × 7.

If some of the ports are dry, others must be very sweet, in order to even out when the blends are made. Therefore, careful check must be kept on the volume of all lots of port as made during the season. It may be necessary to make up extra gallonage of sweet or dry port, as the case requires, near the end of the season in order that the final blend will be about 18 × 7. It should be reemphasized that closer control of the time of harvesting and of fortification to produce only standard ports is the best practice.

Use of Concentrate

Some of the larger California wineries operate vacuum pans during the grape season in the production of concentrated musts to be used in sweetening fortified wines, including port. In making red concentrate the crushed grapes are heated to 140°F. or higher by drawing off the free-run juice, heating it, and returning it to the vat until the color is extracted. The free-run is drawn off and the grapes pressed in a basket or continuous press. The press and free-run are combined and sent to the vacuum pan. Or, the similar method described by Nury (1957) may be used. In making white concentrate the grapes are not heated and only the free-run is used. The juice is usually concentrated to 70° to 72° Balling. Formerly, some wine makers have fortified the concentrate to 20 to 21 per cent alcohol in order not to reduce the alcohol content of wine to which it was added later. The concentrate may be added to the wine at any time before it is refrigerated and finally filtered.

It has been observed that grape concentrate often develops very resistant cultures of lactic bacteria that can infect and spoil or damage the wine to which the concentrate is added. Use of freshly prepared concentrate of high quality and 75 to 100 p.p.m. of sulfur dioxide should reduce this hazard.

Clarification

In most wineries, the newly fortified port is allowed to settle for 3 to 4 weeks, or longer, to undergo natural clarification. Like other fortified wines port usually clears rather rapidly. When the color has been extracted with heat the addition of a pectic enzyme is essential.

The wine is drawn off the sediment and fined with about 3 to 5 lbs. of bentonite per 1000 gallons in the form of a slurry in water as outlined elsewhere for sherry. It is then allowed to settle about three weeks or until the fining agent settles.

Usually the fined wine settles clear or brilliantly clear, but it will contain a few small flocks of bentonite or pulp, etc. that must be removed by filtration. Also, if insufficient bentonite has been used the wine may be more or less hazy. In either event it must be filtered. Therefore, it is racked from the sediment, Hyflo Super-Cel or other infusorial earth is added continuously, and the wine filtered in a filter press or metal screen filter of the West Coast type. The earlier a dessert wine is fined and filtered, usually the more stable it will be.

The filtered wines are then blended to give a standard port of the desired sugar content. Attention should also be paid to balancing the color and standardizing the flavor and quality.

Stabilization

Ports seldom need to be heat-stabilized either before or after refrigeration, even if intended for early shipment. However, a major problem in the stabilization of port wine is to prevent deposits in the bottle. In one experiment Azevedo (1963) reported storage at −9°C. (16°F.) for 6 to 7 days, filtration and flash pasteurization at 104°C. (219°F.) for 7 seconds gave the best results. Pasteurization before chilling was unsuccessful. Fining with bentonite (0.6 gm. per liter) and then with 0.1 gm. per liter of gelatin gave wines with less cloudiness after aging, irrespective of the treatment.

The filtered blended wine is refrigerated to 16° to 18°F. and either held at that temperature for about three weeks or longer to rid the wine of excess cream of tartar and certain colloids; or it is cooled to that temperature and allowed to rise to about 32°F., when it is again chilled to 16° to 18°F.; this cycle being repeated 3 to 4 times over a 30-day period. Some wine makers store the refrigerated wine in tanks in a cold room maintained at about 26° to 28°F.; others maintain 16° to 18°F. by auxiliary cooling coils in the tank, which is at cellar temperature. If the original stabilization is done at a low enough temperature for a long enough period and no subsequent tartrate pick-up occurs (from tartrate-lined tanks) re-refrigeration should not be necessary. Ion-exchange treatment (p. 295) is also used for tartrate stabilization. We do not approve multiple chilling procedures.

Cooling from cellar temperature to 16° to 18°F. is accomplished by passing the wine through tubular coolers refrigerated with Freon or ammonia. Needless to say, the tubes must be watertight in order that the refrigerant does not contaminate the wine. Ammonia can quickly ruin the wine; Freon is said to do little harm if it comes in contact with wine. Refrigeration reduces the Balling degree slightly, possibly 0.1° to 0.15°, owing chiefly to loss of cream of tartar. Because compressor oil may be present we doubt whether contact with Freon is without harmful effect on wines.

Cream of tartar collects on the walls and in the sediment in the refrigerating tank. After crystallization or separation of cream of tartar is complete, the wine is drawn off and filtered using infusorial earth and a filter press or other suitable filter.

Aging

The previous operations of fining, filtering, and refrigerating, coupled with pasteurizing, bring about marked aging of the wine. In fact, this cycle may be repeated several times to rapidly age the wine; particularly when the demand is very brisk. Occasional aeration between or during these operations still further speeds up aging, of a kind. As stated elsewhere, aging is a very complex process involving oxidative changes, esterification, etc. Quick aging of this type intensifies oxidative changes but not all of the other normal aging processes. Hence, quickly aged wines are usually slightly oxidized and may be low in color owing to losses during treatment. However, the oxidation-reduction potential of dessert wines is surprisingly low from the data presented by Deibner (1957), especially of port-type wine stored in the bottle for 15 to 45 years. This is, of course, atypical data and not applicable to California dessert wines.

Some wine makers bake the port for a few days at 120° to 140°F. if it is needed badly to fill an order. It may also be aerated by pumping over after or before baking. This often gives the port an amber color and oxidized odor. In fact, some trade demand has developed for this rapid-aged tawny port. However, much better quality, from the point of view of many port drinkers, is secured by aging the wine about one year at cellar temperature, racking occasionally, and finally aging another year or two in oak.

Oak shavings produce some of the effect of aging in oak. Port improves for several years in wood. However, some consumers prefer a newer wine of a bright red color and a fruity flavor. Well aged port is, however, smoother, possesses a fine odor and a beautiful tawny color. At present, the prevailing custom is to market most California port rather young—at 1 to 2 years, or even at less than one year. Addition of sweet sherry has also been employed to impart "age" to new port; but it is also apt to give it a caramelized flavor and an undesirable nutty sherry character.

Finishing

Like other dessert wines, port is subject to attack by certain bacteria—particularly by *L. trichodes* (p. 591). As this organism is very sensitive to sulfur dioxide it may be held in check by maintaining a level of 75 to 100 p.p.m. This is particularly important just before bottling or shipping as the infection is most apt to develop in the bottle.

If the wine has not been pasteurized before aging, it may be flash-pasteurized before final polishing filtration in the case of standard wines. This is done by passing the wine through a stainless steel, tubular or plate-type flash pasteurizer with heat interchanger, in which the incoming wine cools the outgoing. Pasteurization is at about 180° to 185°F. with a holding period of about one minute. After cooling, the wine is given a polishing filtration before bottling or shipping. For quality wines we doubt if this is necessary.

RED MUSCATEL

There are several varieties of red or purple muscat grapes that do well in California—Muscat Hamburg and Aleatico being the most common. A

Los Gatos, California, winery made an excellent red muscatel of grapes grown on its hillside vineyards. The wine was aged about five years in small cooperage before bottling. The muscat flavor is pronounced but pleasing; the acidity is somewhat higher than for Fresno white muscatel, and the general flavor and bouquet smooth. The winery uses its regular port technique in making this wine.

The Aleatico is an orange-red variety of muscat flavor extensively grown in Italy (particularly in Tuscany) and, to some extent, in the San Joaquin Valley in California. It can be made into a dessert wine of light or of medium tawny color by port wine techniques. It has also been made into an unfortified sweet wine preserved with a high concentration of sulfur dioxide. Neither type is produced in California at present.

WHITE PORT

In Portugal, white port is made by fortifying the partially-fermented juice of white grapes and aging in the same manner as red port. In California white port was made after Repeal by decolorizing angelica with vegetable decolorizing carbon and filtering to give a water-white fortified sweet wine of neutral flavor. Such flavor as it possessed was that of the carbon. A wine may be decolorized to the equivalent of 0.6 Lovibond providing it had no more than this at the time of production. Precise measurement of this small amount of color is not difficult with the recently developed spectrophotometers. The tendency is to fortify light colored free-run musts and keep the wine in metal tanks out of contact with the air to prevent darkening. Charcoal is thus much less used than formerly.

ANGELICA

This is a unique California product. The origin of the name is not definitely known. Perhaps early California wine makers derived the name from Los Angeles; see Amerine and Winkler (1938).

The process of manufacture is very simple. White grapes are crushed, stemmed, pumped into a vat, and about 100 p.p.m. of sulfur dioxide added as the vat is filled. The free-run juice is drawn off and fermented slightly; or, is allowed to ferment on the skins slightly to give at least 0.5 per cent alcohol before fortification (a legal requirement). Or, a little dry white wine may be added to the drawn-off juice. Use of low-color red grapes, such as Mission and Grenache, is also possible. Only the free-run juice is used and settling of the musts is recommended. The juice (essentially unfermented) is then fortified to 20 to 21 per cent alcohol. Most wine makers allow the fermentation to proceed to several per cent alcohol if the must is very sweet; but the preferred practice is to fortify the slightly fermented juice. Settling of the fortified wine 1 to 30 days, racking, fining with bentonite, settling, filtering, refrigeration, aging, pasteurization and finishing are conducted essentially as described for port.

MUSCATEL

This is one of California's best dessert types; see Twight and Amerine (1938). Since WW II sales have decreased. Some wine connoisseurs disdain the muscat as plebian and of coarse flavor. But its flavor is a distinctive one. One defect of some of the state's muscatel is its low content of muscat juice or wine. The law allows a wine containing as little as 51 per cent of muscat to be labeled muscatel. This ruling is often a mistake. There are plenty of muscat grapes in California; more could be grown if needed. The law might well require muscatel to be made 100 per cent of muscat grapes! We suspect that some muscatel contains less than 51 per cent of muscat wine; how is one to prove that it does or does not? Its taste is often so pale, so weak in muscat flavor, that one can scarcely detect any muscat. In self-protection muscat grape growers should see that the law is revised to require that muscatel shall be 100 per cent muscat.

Varieties

In California the Muscat of Alexandria, the well known raisin grape of Spain, Australia, and California, is used in making most of the muscatel. The berries are large and grow in loosely filled bunches. The flavor and aroma are very pronounced if the vines are not overcropped. The Muscat blanc (called Muscat Frontignan in California and Muscat Canelli in Italy) is grown in small quantities only, as the vines are poor producers and the grapes sunburn easily. However, its wine is of better flavor and aroma than that of the Muscat of Alexandria. The Malvasia bianca is another white variety of muscat flavor suitable for making muscatel. Orange Muscat has also been recommended for producing muscatel. However, the Muscat of Alexandria is the primary source of muscatel in California.

Most of the muscat grapes of California are produced in the San Joaquin Valley in the Fresno and Kings County area. They are grown in sandy loam soil in most cases and always under irrigation. A small quantity is grown in southern California in the Cucamonga region and a few near Escondido. The muscat attains high sugar content and is usually of 23° to 25° Balling or higher when picked. One of its defects is the tendency for raisining of some of the grapes on the vine. The raisined grapes are difficult to crush and, if crushed, may darken the color of the wine and impart a raisin flavor.

The muscat is grown in California and Australia principally for drying for raisins. Often in the past, its use for wine making has served as a balance wheel for the raisin industry, absorbing the surplus grapes in years of poor prices for raisins. Muscat grapes are consumed in the fresh condition in considerable amounts in California but do not ship well, hence are not very plentiful in the fruit markets.

Fermentation

The muscat grapes are crushed and stemmed as described for other varieties and are pumped into open vats. About 100 p.p.m. of sulfur dioxide, or its equivalent of sodium or potassium metabisulfite, should be added at time of crushing in order to prevent spoilage by lactic and acetic bacteria. In case some of the grapes are moldy more sulfur dioxide should be used. A starter of yeast should be added; preferably 2 to 3 per cent of a pure yeast culture, or, less desirably, a similar quantity of fermenting must from another vat.

It is customary to ferment crushed muscat grapes 24 hours or longer before drawing off the fermenting juice or pressing, in order to extract more flavor from the skins. If the must has not dropped to the degree Balling desired for fortification at the time of pressing, fermentation is continued in another tank. Another procedure used for extracting as much muscat flavor as possible has been to heat the crushed grapes for 2 or 3 minutes at 180°F. Others draw off the free-run, heat to about 160°F. and pour back over the pomace. While heating processes do increase the amount of muscat aroma extracted, as well as the yield, they may lead to dark-colored wines which are difficult to clarify and are of lesser quality.

Fortification

The fermenting must is fortified to give a finished wine of about 18 per cent alcohol and 7° Balling. This is over ten per cent sugar as determined chemically. For a must originally 25° Balling, fortification would be made at about 14°. As in the case with port it may not be feasible to make every fortification at the proper sugar content. Some wines will be below 7° after fortification. Therefore, it will be necessary to fortify some wines at higher sugar content in order that the Balling degree of wines of too low degree can be brought to 7° by blending.

The alternative is the sweetening of the wines with muscat grape concentrate. Most wine makers prefer to avoid the expense and trouble of making, storing, and using concentrate. However, without the use of concentrate, the wine maker must see to it that the average degree Balling of his muscatels is close to 7°, and the alcohol per cent about 18. Greater care in timing the fortification is the proper solution of this problem.

For dessert wines, particularly those of the muscatel type, Flanzy (1959) counsels slow fermentation because this preserves the varietal aroma better. He also believes that to be eligible for fortification the fermenting must should be of high original sugar. Contributing factors for the production of quality dessert wines in the south of France are the limitation on varieties planted and on their yield per acre. The latter insures high sugar musts. He also stresses the critical importance of fortifying at the right time. Flanzy distinguishes two types of fortified wines in France. First, *vins doux naturels*, which have not less than 5 per cent and not more than 10 per cent of 90 per cent or over alcohol added. The second category is *vins de liqueur* where there is no limit on how much fortification takes place, with alcohol as low as 46 per cent being used. This is more typical of California dessert wines.

Syruped Fermentations

Cruess *et al.* (1916), Hohl and Cruess (1936), Cruess and Hohl (1937), and Hohl (1938) found it possible to reach high alcohol levels by periodically adding concentrate during fermentation. The legal and tax incentives for their production no longer exist and few are produced.

Finishing

The subsequent operations for muscatel are approximately as described for port; namely, settling after fortification, fining with bentonite, filtration, refrigeration, cold filtration, pasteurization, and a polishing filtration before bottling. Some wine makers hasten aging by giving the wine a short baking at 120° to 140°F. as described for sherry, but such treatment may seriously damage the muscat flavor. Aeration by pumping over, refrigeration, and pasteurization are all aging operations and tend to lessen the rough character of the newly fortified wine but may give it an undesirable oxidized character. Normally muscatel should be aged for 3 to 4 years before finishing and bottling, in order to produce a smooth wine of pleasing flavor. Every precaution should be used to keep the color golden and the flavor fruity.

Spoilage During Fermentation

During the 1935 vintage considerable muscat must was lost by acetification during fermentation. Vaughn (1938) showed that this spoilage could be induced by certain strains of rapidly growing acetic bacteria that developed even during yeast fermentation. Cruess (1937) also reported that lactic bacteria as well were responsible in experimental fermentations. The musts that were lost by acetification in the wineries had not been sulfited. As little as 70 p.p.m. of sulfur dioxide prevented the spoilage by either acetic or lactic bacteria during fermentation.

Proper Aging

Muscatel greatly improves in quality through sufficient aging, that is, aging for about three years. This allows the harsh flavor of the added brandy to ameliorate and the new wine flavor and the yeastiness to completely disappear. The wine becomes mellow and smooth. As Joslyn and Amerine (1964) point out aeration during several years' aging should not be excessive, i.e., the puncheons or casks or tanks should, after the first few months, be kept well filled at least once each 3 to 6 months. Part of the aging period should be in oak. Use of fractional blending systems for aging muscatels appears rational and practicable.

CALIFORNIA TOKAY

As stated elsewhere (p. 44) Tokay wine is made in Hungary from the partially dried (on the vine) grapes of the Furmint and other varieties without fortification. In California tokay wine is usually a blend of about one-third each of port, sherry, and angelica. It must not be too red nor have too strong a baked flavor. The sherry imparts the baked flavor and the port the color. It has *no* relation in character to Hungarian Tokay.

CALIFORNIA MALAGA, MADEIRA, AND MARSALA

Only small quantities of these are produced and the standards vary markedly from winery to winery. It is doubtful if they would continue to be produced if there were not a small local demand for them in various parts of the country.

California malaga is made by baking a very sweet sherry material or by sweetening a sherry with grape concentrate; see Bioletti (1934). In eastern United States kosher-type wines are sometimes labeled as malaga even though more a red sweet table type than a dessert wine.

In California very little madeira is made. It may be a baked angelica, or sweet sherry, or a blend of angelica and sherry. California sherry is much nearer true Madeira than Spanish sherry, both in character and method of production.

In California a marsala type is occasionally made by baking sweet fortified sherry material. Joslyn and Amerine (1964) state that black grapes, such as the Mission and Carignane, are sometimes used in California, the grapes being pressed before fermentation. It may be necessary to remove the color by aeration of the must although most of it disappears in baking if some aeration is given. One wine maker formerly concentrated must by boiling it down in an open copper kettle until well caramelized. This was added to the marsala after baking. This wine did resemble Italian Marsala since a burnt flavor is a characteristic feature of this wine (see p. 28). The process is legal in this country.

BIBLIOGRAPHY

AMERINE, M. A., and DE MATTEI, W. 1940. Color in California wines. III. Methods of removing color from the skins. Food Research 5, 509–519.

AMERINE, M. A., and WINKLER, A. J. 1938. Angelica. Wines and vines 19, No. 9, 5, 24.

AZEVEDO, M. PACHECO DE. 1963. Problèmes de la stabilisation du vin de Porto. Ann. technol. agr. 12 (numéro hors série 1), 379–389.

BERG, H. W. 1940. Color extraction for port-wine manufacture. Wine Review 8, No. 1, 12–14.

BERG, H. W., and AKIYOSHI, M. 1958. Further studies of the factors affecting the extraction of color and tannin from red grapes. Food Research 23, 511–517.

BERG, H. W., and AKIYOSHI, M. 1960. The effect of sulfur dioxide and fermentation on color extraction from red grapes. Ibid. 25, 183–189.

BERG, H. W., and GUYMON, J. F. 1951. Countercurrent water extraction of alcohol from grape pomace. Wines and vines 32, No. 10, 27–31.

BERG, H. W., and MARSH, G. L. 1950. Heat treatment of musts. Ibid. 31, No. 7, 23–24; No. 8, 29–30.

BIOLETTI, F. T. 1934. How Marsala is made. Calif. Grape Grower 15, No. 12, 5, 17.

CASTELLA, F. DE. 1908. Port. Victoria Dept. Agr. J. 6, 176–191.

COFFELT, R. J., and BERG, H. W. 1965. Color extraction by heating whole grapes. Am. J. Enol. Vitic. 16, 117–128.

COSTA, L. C. DA. 1938. O problema das aguardentes e dos alcoóis. Influência da sua origem e grau na beneficiação de vinho. Anais inst. super. agron., Univ. Téc. Lisboa 9, 67–76.

CRUESS, W. V. 1937. Observations on volatile acid formation in muscat fermentations. Fruit Prods. J. 16, 198–200, 219.

CRUESS, W. V., BROWN, E. M., and FLOSSFEDER, F. C. 1916. Unfortified sweet wines of high alcohol content. Ind. Eng. Chem. 8, 1124–1126.

CRUESS, W. V., and HOHL, L. A. 1937. Syruped fermentation of sweet wines. Wine Review 5, No. 11, 12, 24–25.

DEIBNER, L. 1957. Évolution du potentiel oxydoréducteur au cours de la maturation des vins. Ann. technol, agr. 6, 347–362.

EGOROV, A. A., KOTLIARÉNKO, M. R., and PREOBRAZHENSKIĬ, A. A. 1951. U lushenie kachestva spirtovannykh vinogradnykh vin. (Improvement in wine quality from fortifying spirits) Vinodelie i Vinogradarstvo S.S.S.R. 11, No. 8, 6–8.

FLANZY, M. 1959. Élaboration des vins spiritueux doux. Ann. technol. agr. 8, 81–100.

HOHL, L. A. 1938. Further observations on production of alcohol by Saccharomyces ellipsoideus in syruped fermentations. Food Research 3, 453–465.

HOHL, L. A., and CRUESS, W. V. 1936. Effect of temperature, variety of juice, and method of increasing sugar content on maximum alcohol production by Saccharomyces ellipsoideus. Ibid. 1, 405–411.

JOSLYN, M. A., and AMERINE, M. A. 1964. Dessert, Appetizer and Related Flavored Wines. University of California, Division of Agricultural Sciences, Berkeley.

LACHMAN, H. 1903. A monograph on the manufacture of wines in California. U. S. Dept. Agr. Bur. Chem. Bull. 72, 25–40.

NEDELTCHEV, N. J.   1959.   Research on basic technology of dessert wines of the Shiroka Melnishka Loza variety (transl.) Nauch. Trud. Tekh. Inst. Vina i Vino. Promishlenost. *3*, 1–37.

NURY, M. S.   1957.   Continuous color and juice extraction of grapes.   Wine Institute, Tech. Advis. Committee, Dec. 6, 1957.   San Francisco.

OTTAVI, O., and GARINO-CANINA, E.   1930.   Vini di Lusso, Aceti di Lusso.   8 ed.   Casa Editrice Fratelli Ottavi, Casale Monferrato.

SÉBASTIAN, V.   1909.   Traité Pratique de la Préparation des Vins de Luxe. Masson et Cie., Paris.

SIMON, A. L.   1934.   Port.   Constable and Co., Ltd., London.

SINGLETON, V. L., and GUYMON, J. F.   1963.   A test of fractional addition of wine spirits to red and white port wines.   Am. J. Enol. Vitic. *14*, 129–136.

SINGLETON, V. L., BERG, H. W., and GUYMON, J. F.   1964.   Anthocyanin color level in port-type wines as affected by the use of wine spirits containing aldehydes. *Ibid. 15*, 75–81.

TWIGHT, E. H.   1934.   Sweet wine making in California.   Calif. Grape Grower *15*, No. 10, 4–5; No. 11, 4–5, 7.

TWIGHT, E. H., and AMERINE, M. A.   1938.   Wines made from Muscat grapes. Wines and Vines *19*, No. 7, 3–4.

VAUGHN, R. H.   1938.   Some effects of association and competition on *Acetobacter*. J. Bact. *36*, 357–367.

VIZETELLY, H.   1880.   Facts About Port and Madeira.   Ward, Lock and Co., London.

CO_2
$0.277 \text{ gm.} / 100 \text{ ml}$
$\text{Wine} / \text{liter}$
2.77 "

CHAPTER 11

Sparkling Wine Production

Sparkling wines, those which contain a visible excess of carbon dioxide are difficult to define precisely. The present United States maximum for still wines is 0.277 gm. per 100 ml. of carbon dioxide (at 60°F.). See U. S. Internal Revenue Service (1961). This is equivalent to 7 lbs. per sq. in. pressure at 60°F. Protin (1960) notes most countries now distinguish between slightly gassy wines (*pétillants* or *perlants*) from wines with a full pressure. He reports the unofficial position of various countries as follows:

Country	Type	Pressure	Tem- perature
		Pounds/Sq. inch	°F.
Austria	*Pétillant*	1.1 Maximum	68
	Sparkling	10.0 Minimum	68
Chile	Sparkling	10.0 Minimum	59
France	*Pétillant*	3.3 Maximum	59
	Sparkling	10.0 Minimum	59
Germany	*Pétillant*	1.1 Maximum	68
	Sparkling	6.6 Minimum	68
Spain	*Pétillant*	2.2 Maximum	?
	Sparkling	7.7 Minimum	?
Switzerland	*Pétillant*	1.1 Maximum	59
	Sparkling	8.8[1] Minimum	59

[1] Also the minimum is reported as 4 gm. per liter which does not check with the data in Table 39.

The problem is complicated in this country because of the higher taxes on sparkling compared to still wines. Postel (1970) gives 1.8 to 2.0 gr. of carbon dioxide per liter as the limit above which the wine may no longer be considered "still."

DEFINITION

No classification based on method of production is adequate to define the types of sparkling wine. The consumer, however, is not interested in the method of production as much as in the recognizability of the various types of sparkling wines. Therefore, we arbitrarily define as sparkling wines those which have more than 1.5 atmosphere pressure at 50°F. The amount of dissolved carbon dioxide at this pressure and temperature is approximately 3.9 gm. per liter. If the carbon dioxide is kept at this figure the pressure at 60°F. will be about 1.8 atm., at 70°F. 2.1 atm., and at 80°F. 2.4 atm., see Fig. 104. This is about half the minimum suggested by the

TABLE 39

RELATIONSHIP OF PRESSURE AT 60°F. TO AMOUNT OF CARBON DIOXIDE IN WINE[1]

Pounds Pressure	Volume of CO_2	CO_2 Dissolved
Per Sq. Inch		Gm./100 Ml.
0	0.95	0.1866
1	1.00	0.1964
2	1.08	0.2121
3	1.15	0.2259
4	1.23	0.2416
5	1.30	0.2560
6	1.35	0.2652
7	1.40	0.2750
8	1.45	0.2848
9	1.52	0.2986
10	1.65	0.3241

[1] Source of data: U.S. Internal Revenue Service (1956).

Office International de la Vigne et du Vin for sparkling wines, 4 atm. at 68°F., Protin (1960).

The enologist, tax expert, and connoisseur will need a more detailed classification of the many different types on the market. In the classification which follows there are some overlappings in carbon dioxide content. The *source* of the carbon dioxide is thus the basis of this subdivision. In some cases there may be no sensory test which will distinguish between the types!

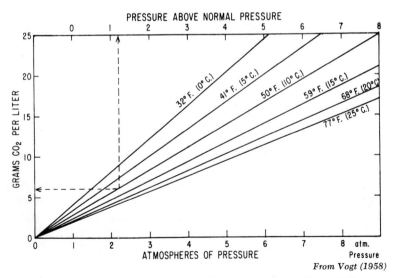

From Vogt (1958)

FIG. 104. EFFECT OF PRESSURE AND TEMPERATURE ON CARBON DIOXIDE CONTENT

Type   I. Excess carbon dioxide produced by fermentation of residual sugar from the primary fermentation. This includes many Alsatian, German, Loire, and Italian wines as well as the muscato amabile in California.

Type II. Excess carbon dioxide from a malo-lactic fermentation. The Vinho Verde wines of northern Portugal are the best representative of this type, but there are many examples in Italy and elsewhere in Europe.

Type III. Excess carbon dioxide from fermentation of sugar added after the process of fermentation. Most of the sparkling wines of the world are produced by this procedure.

Type IV. Excess carbon dioxide added. This includes the so-called carbonated wines and many "crackling" wines.

Carpenè (1959) distinguished four types of fermented sparkling wines: (1) slow bottle fermentation, long aging on yeast, disgorging, (2) same but transferred and filtered, (3) rapid bottle fermentation, no aging on lees, transferred and filtered, and (4) tank fermented. He stresses the importance of aging on the yeast. He agrees with Schanderl (1943, 1959) that while the fermentation is the same in tanks or bottles the products of methods (1) and (3) or (4) are different. See also Amerine and Monaghan (1950).

TYPE I SPARKLING WINES

Almost any wine can be made sparkling by stopping the fermentation before all of the must sugar has fermented and then, later, bottling the wine. If even a few viable yeasts are in the wine at the time of bottling, and if the sulfur dioxide content is not excessive, the sugar will later most likely ferment and the wine will become gassy. If the fermentation is slow at a low even temperature the amount of yeast cells produced may be surprisingly low. In some cases, when the yeast deposit is excessive, the wines are treated as Type III sparkling wines and clarified in the usual way (p. 463). One reason why more wines of this type are not produced in California is that it is most difficult to stop the fermentation with the desired residual sugar content. However, with the increasing technological control of fermentation (temperature, pressure, DEPC, depletion of amino acids, etc.) and with the generally high sugar content of our musts it should not be difficult to produce wines by such procedures. The addition of high quality grape concentrate before fermentation also offers interesting possibilities.

Sparkling wines as we know them probably originated in this manner. It is no accident that the first centers of sparkling wine production were in northern France. It is in such cold regions that the fermentation is slow and incomplete. When the temperature increased the following spring the fermentations restarted and gassy wines resulted.[1]

TYPE II SPARKLING WINES

So far as we know there are no sparkling wines of this type produced in this country. Frequently imported Italian red wines will be found which are distinctly gassy and in some cases this is obviously owing to the growth of lactic acid bacteria. (Some wines are carbonated.) It is unlikely that any regular production of such types can be expected here. To secure an adequate malo-lactic fermentation the wines must be of relatively low alcohol content and have a rather high percentage of malic acid. Grapes grown on vines trained on trees so that they are difficult to prune properly will often overcrop and produce grapes of low sugar and high malic acid. These in turn yield wines with the desired composition—low alcohol and high acid. Just such conditions exist in the Minho district of northern Portugal and in many parts of Italy. The result is that often, but not always, a malo-lactic fermentation takes place after bottling and gassy wines result.

The process is unlikely to be a popular one for two reasons: the wines are of low alcohol and thin and the process is difficult to control as the growth of the bacteria is not easy to predict or even to induce. Poorly finished French red Burgundy wines are sometimes found to be gassy from an unwanted malo-lactic fermentation.

TYPE III SPARKLING WINES

In the early nineteenth century when sugar became more easily available and when a more scientific concept of the process of alcoholic fermentation began to develop, this type of wine began to be produced on a commercial scale. The tradition that it originated somewhat earlier in the 18th century with the Benedictine monk, Dom Pérignon, in the Champagne region of France is a pretty one and is nicely demolished by Chappaz (1951). Chappaz pays tribute to Dom Pérignon as well as a number of other monks for bringing the culture of the vine and the production of wine to such a northern region. Possibly he was responsible for introduction of the heavy tied-in cork. Chappaz (1951) believes his blending of

---

[1] This is as good a place as any to lay to rest the romantic idea that wine is *per se* a living thing which moves in sympathy, i.e., ferments and becomes gassy, with the vines in the spring and fall. Wine is a living thing because of the microorganisms and enzyme systems which it contains and it does move "in sympathy" with the vine for precisely the same reasons that the vine shows seasonal growth—changes in temperature. If the wine is kept at a constant temperature such activity is not restricted to the spring and fall.

wines from different areas of the Champagne region was Dom Pérignon's great contribution to the Champagne industry. Certainly he was not the father of Champagne because it was not until the sugar tables of François were published in 1829 that the *sparkling* wine trade of this district began to be commercially successful.

Champagne

The old province of Champagne in northern France has given its name to the most famous sparkling wine in the world and is one of the most imitated types of wine produced. We have discussed elsewhere (pp. 13–16) the primary factors influencing the quality of this wine type: mixing of white wines from red and white grapes to achieve the necessary balance of alcohol and fruitness,[2] skilled blending of wines of different parts of the district and even of different years, slow cool fermentations, relatively long aging in the bottle and control of the sugar content of the finished product. Even before the Champagne riots of 1910–1911 the district had been delimited (on January 4, 1909, for example) and only wines produced from grapes grown in this district may be sold as Champagne in France. For production details, see Françot (1945, 1950), Françot and Geoffroy (1951), and Weinmann and Telle (1929).

Sparkling wines from other parts of France are legally known as *vins mousseux*, even though they may be fermented in the bottle and otherwise handled by the same procedures as Champagne. Some tank-fermented sparkling wines are produced in France where they are also sold as *mousseux*. See Pacottet and Guittonneau (1930).

Other Regions

German sparkling wine (*Schaumwein*) is commonly sold as Sekt, a coined name which does not refer to the sugar content. Both tank and bottle processes are used. See Herzog (1954), Koch (1923), and Schanderl (1938). In Italy non-muscat sparkling wines are usually sold as *spumante* or *gran spumante* and muscat sparkling wines as *moscato spumante*. Both the tank and bottle process are used in Italy. The muscat-flavored Asti *spumante* is produced by an elaborate system of filtration (Tarantola, 1937). Kishkovshiǐ (1963) not only showed the resulting wine to be low in total nitrogen but that it is also low in most but not all amino acids. Spain and Portugal produce *espumante*.[3]

---

[2] This brilliant idea is also credited to Dom Pérignon.
[3] Recently a Spanish sparkling wine imported into Great Britain as Spanish champagne was granted the right to use this name, much to the annoyance of the French Champagne industry. Court action reversed this decision. See Simon (1962) for an illuminating history of the incident.

In Australia and the United States tank and bottle-fermented wines are sold as champagne. South Africa sells their sparkling wines as such, i.e., not under the name champagne. There is a large sparkling wine industry in the Soviet Union (Agabal'yants, 1954, Rodopulo, 1966).

The sparkling wine industry in the Finger Lakes region of New York dates back to 1860. It was found that some of the light white wines of the area when properly blended produced an excellent sparkling product. Native grapes such as Delaware, Catawba, Dutchess, Elvira, and Isabella, grown in vineyards on the hillsides of the Finger Lakes, produced wines suitable for this purpose. For red champagne, more commonly called sparkling burgundy, varieties such as Ives Seedling, Fredonia, Clinton, and Concord make an acceptable base. Cold Duck is a red sparkling wine, with or without labrusca flavor, made in various states and currently very popular. Some is even imported.

It is the general practice in preparing the base wines for use in New York champagne and sparkling burgundy to use only the free-run juice and the juice obtained while low pressure is exerted. It is imperative that the grapes to be used for sparkling wines should be picked at the peak of maturity and be free of mold or other undesirable contamination. Free-run and low pressure press juice is desirable as such juice will be lower in acidity than if the entire juice from the grape is used. The must of these eastern grapes is usually too low in sugar to produce a wine of 10.5 to 11 per cent alcohol, with the possible exception of Delaware which in some seasons reaches 20° to 22° Balling. Where it is necessary to increase the degree Balling of the juice to this level, dry sugar is usually employed.

In the initial fermentation of the juice to be used subsequently for champagne, it is desirable to conduct the fermentation at a low temperature and in casks of relatively small size: 500- to 5000-gallon casks. In the smaller containers it is simpler to keep the fermentations cool. When the initial fermentation is complete, containers are consolidated so as to fill completely the individual casks and the yeast or lees allowed to settle prior to racking. After several rackings or a filtration the individual varietal wines are examined carefully both analytically and by sensory examination and selection is made of the amount of each to be used for blending into the base wine for the secondary fermentation. Some varietals of previous vintages are generally used for blending with current vintages.

The blended cuvée (or sparkling wine blend) should be about 11.0 to 11.5 per cent alcohol and have an acidity of 0.70 to 0.80 per cent. The wine should be cold stabilized by storing below 26°F. for a period of ten days or longer (or be treated with an ion exchange resin) and should be relatively low in sulfur dioxide. If the free sulfur dioxide content is above 10 p.p.m. some difficulty may be encountered with the secondary fermentation in the bottle or tank. The yeast to be used in secondary fermentation may be acclimated to a higher sulfur dioxide content. It is safer not to have to contend with this inhibiting substance. It is also better from the point of view of the quality of the final product. The iron and copper content of the base wine should be low or later clarification may prove troublesome.

After secondary fermentation in the bottle is completed, the wine is allowed to age in contact with the yeast sediment for a considerable period of time. Some premium quality fermented-in-the-bottle New York sparkling wines are aged for a year or longer in contact with the yeast. It is generally believed that the wine develops a more pleasing "champagne" flavor the longer it is kept in contact with the yeast cells, for several years at least. Periodically, the wine maker will examine bottles in tirage and decide when they are ready for disgorging and final clearing.

Both the traditional method of disgorging (p. 471) and the transfer system (p. 470) are now used in New York.

California

The first important sparkling wine was produced in California in the 1860's by Arpad Haraszthy. It was, of course, made by the traditional bottle-fermentation process, Haraszthy having received his training in France. Prior to Prohibition a number of California producers had very good sparkling wines on the market, all produced by the bottle fermentation process except a few carbonated types.

Following repeal bottle and tank sparkling wine production increased slowly until after World War II. Since then production has increased more sharply as shown in Table 40. Both bottle- and tank-fermented production has increased. Since 1958, a considerable percentage of the bottle production has been handled by the transfer system (p. 470).

TYPE IV SPARKLING WINES

The production of carbonated wines is decreasing in this country. At least three reasons are probably responsible for this decline. Following repeal some over-aged and high sulfur dioxide wines were carbonated in the mistaken belief that the American public would buy any sparkling wine. Secondly, producers, distributors, and retailers generally over-priced carbonated wines so that they had little price differential from other sparkling wines. This was partially due to the discriminatory and excessive taxes which the federal government places on all sparkling wines. Third a combination of these probably caused carbonated wines to lose "status."

The authors believe, however, that carbonated wines have a place on the American market, especially if the tax structure was more realistic. The odious "carbonated" could be avoided by the use of special names. The popularity of some of the imported carbonated "crackling" wines is evidence that this can be accomplished.

PRODUCTION OF THE CUVÉE

The ideal wine for bottle fermentation is also quite appropriate for the tank process.

Varieties

The grapes grown under Californian conditions should not be allowed to become too ripe, since the wine to be used for a sparkling wine should be of good acidity and not too high in alcohol content. In California, grapes suitable for making sparkling wines have been grown successfully in Sonoma and Napa counties which lie near the coast. The Santa Clara valley has also produced good base wines from grapes grown in that area. The hot interior valleys are not suitable for the production of grapes for a high quality sparkling wine. However, if the grapes are picked early in the season when they have just reached 19° to 20° Balling, wines of acceptable quality may be produced.

The best variety of grapes for California sparkling wine is still not established. Amerine and Monaghan (1950) found White Riesling very suitable. Certainly if the grapes are not allowed to become too ripe this variety makes an excellent wine. However, its low productivity makes it expensive to produce. Folle Blanche has produced a number of very pleasant sparkling wines. Wines of Burger have a neutral flavor but are somewhat thin. French Colombard is suitably high in acid but has a rather pronounced aroma which some do not care for. Chenin blanc and Velt-

TABLE 40

SPARKLING WINE ENTERING DISTRIBUTION CHANNELS

In the United States According to Origin, 1949 to 1969 Inclusive[1] (in 1000 gallons)

Year[2]	United States Produced			Foreign produced[3]	Total
	California	Other States	Total		
1949–1950	382	699	1081	512	1593
1951–1955	532	847	1379	627	2006
1956–1960	1311	1331	2642	821	3463
1961–1965	2326	2322	4828	1131	5794
1966	3737	3660	7397	1635	9032
1967	4622	4131	8753	1916	10669
1968	5872	4413	10285	2228	12513
1969[4]	8717	4985	13702	2409	16111

[1] Source: Compiled by Wine Institute from reports of the U. S. Treasury Department, Internal Revenue Service, U. S. Department of Commerce, Bureau of the Census and California State Board of Equalization.
[2] Calendar year.
[3] Imports for consumption.
[4] Preliminary.

liner both produce wines which may be useful. Chardonnay and Pinot noir are seldom available in California and, because of their early ripening, often produce wines of 12.5 per cent alcohol. The importance of the cuvée has been emphasized by Rossi, Jr. (1965): "a sparkling wine can be no better than the base wine used and the base wine in turn can be no better than the grapes originally crushed." He emphasized that not only good varieties but harvesting at the optimum maturity and "cold" fermentations were desirable. Bo (1965) reiterated this.

Processing

Since a light color is desired, only the free-run should be used. Some sulfur dioxide may be necessary to permit settling of the musts. The fermentation should be carried to completion; it is a mistake to leave fermentable sugar in the wine although in pre-Prohibition days it was customary to do so. Use of a good culture of champagne yeast and a cool fermenting temperature (60°F. or less) are desirable practices.

The fermented wine should contain more than 10 per cent of alcohol by volume and less than 12 per cent. If the alcohol content is too high, it will be impossible or difficult to secure satisfactory fermentation in the bottle; if too low, the wine will not keep well and the addition of brandy will be necessary to attain the proper alcohol content in the finished product.

After fermentation is complete and the lees have settled, the wine is racked. Usually two additional rackings are given: at the time of blending (about six weeks later) and after fining.

Tannin may be added after the first racking to aid in clarification and to stabilize the wine when tests show that this is necessary. In our experience this is seldom required or desirable. The amount needed will vary with the composition of the wine, those high in extract may require as much as 0.03 per cent by weight, and the lighter wines of low extract as little as 0.01 per cent. Only the purest tannin of light color should be employed. Later, the wine is fined with bentonite, gelatin or isinglass, as described in Chapter 6. Gelatin fining will remove most of the residual tannin but must be used with care. Close filtration is also needed.

Tartrate stabilization is essential in sparkling wine production. The procedures previously given may be employed (p. 291). Rossi, Jr. (1965) found no adverse effect on fermentation when a portion of the wine was ion-exchanged.

Blending

The four critical stages in the preparation of sparkling wines are (1) the preparation of a well-balanced cuvée, (2) the proper conduct of the fermentation, (3) the aging on the lees, and (4) the clarification.

It is rare that a single wine having all the desired characteristics for the cuvée is available, or is available in sufficient quantities for the winery's needs. It is necessary, therefore, to blend several lots of wine to secure the desired quality and quantity.

The cuvée should first be prepared in the laboratory and tasting room. The primary requisites are a good total acidity (0.70 gm. per 100 ml. or more), a low volatile acidity (below 0.040 gm. per 100 ml.), a moderate alcohol content (between 11 and 11.5 per cent), a light yellow color, a fresh and impeccably clean flavor, a relatively low pH (below 3.3), and a balanced aroma in which no single varietal characteristic predominates. Addition of citric acid to increase the acidity and to inhibit ferric phosphate formation is occasionally necessary but careful producers also balance the acidity by judicious blending of wines of suitable acidity. The policy of the individual producer and the demands of his clientele will determine the proper level of acidity. Rossi, Jr. (1965) preferred blending to balance the acidity. He indicated citric acid was widely used.

Wines intended for sparkling wine production should be low in sulfur dioxide, in our opinion, if the producer wishes to secure the maximum quality. A total sulfur dioxide content of 60 p.p.m. was suggested by Manceau (1929) and we see no reason to raise this limit. It is not that sulfur dioxide may reduce the rate of fermentation as much as the fact that it is a foreign odor in sparkling wines. Schanderl (1965B) found that cuvées made with cation-exchange wine fermented slowly in the bottle.

Paul (1960) analyzed sparkling Austrian wines that had been awarded gold, silver and bronze medals. The total sulfur dioxide content of the six gold medal wines ranged from 53 to 92 p.p.m. (average 70), in the 12 silver medal wines from 18 to 220 (average 112), and in the 5 bronze medal wines 51 to 201 (average 145). In seven French Champagnes the total varied from 23 to 72 p.p.m. (average 55). Only one of the gold medal wines had any free sulfur dioxide and none of the Champagnes had any. Paul recommends that as small an amount of sulfur dioxide as possible be used in the fermentation of the musts and in the preparation of the cuvée. Paul also analyzed the wines for the other constituents none of which appeared to be significantly related to quality. The best sparkling wines had a pH of 3 to 3.2 and a titratable acidity of 0.65 to 0.75 per cent. French Champagnes generally had a lower ash content and, surprisingly, a higher alcohol content, 11.8 to 12.7 per cent (average 12.3).

After the laboratory blend it is desirable to make a somewhat larger blend and make a trial bottling. Under any circumstances the cuvée will have to be cold-stabilized and filtered.

Present United States' regulations require that wines with a vintage label be 100 per cent of the year given. French regulations require that no more than 80 per cent of a given vintage can be used for producing vintage-labeled sparkling wines. This is a recognition of the difficulty of securing a perfectly balanced wine of a single vintage. California producers, moreover, must themselves ferment wines intended for vintage dating, thus preventing them from buying wines, even of the same vintage, to balance their own stocks. This part of the law might well be repealed. We see no need in California for permitting blending in a certain portion of wines of another vintage to balance vintage wines.

Sugaring

At this stage the wine maker will have a brilliant wine of the proper aroma, flavor, and alcohol content. The pressure desired in sparkling wines at the end of the closed fermentation is about 5 to 6 atmospheres at 50°F.; that is, about 75 to 90 lbs. pressure per square inch. For each atmosphere of pressure approximately 0.4 per cent of sugar (4 gm. per liter of wine) are required. Thus to produce six atmospheres' pressure would require 6 × 0.4 or 2.4 per cent, or 24 gm. of sugar per liter, or about 20 lbs. per 100 gallons of wine. In practice 200 lbs. of dry sugar are usually used per 1000 gallons of wine. The wine must be analyzed for its reducing sugar content and the sugar present in the wine allowed for in calculating the amount to be added. Thus, if the wine contains 0.5 per cent of sugar, that is, five gm. per liter, then there would be required 24—(5—1) or 20 gm. per liter to give 6 atmospheres' pressure. Unless this allowance is made, too much sugar may be added, resulting in excessive loss of bottles and wine through bursting of the bottles during fermentation. The 1 takes into account the normal unfermented residual sugar (per liter) in fermented wines.

The sugar is dissolved in wine, preferably aged wine, to give a solution of 500 gm. of sugar per liter, that is, a 50 per cent solution of sugar in wine. There is also added 1.0 to 1.5 per cent of citric acid; which, if the wine is allowed to stand several weeks before use, will invert much of the cane sugar, rendering it more fermentable. Or, if the wine to be bottled has a rather high alcohol content, the sugar may be dissolved in water and the solution heated with the acid to hasten inversion. Invert syrup may be purchased and diluted with wine to 50 per cent sugar content. This invert syrup must be free of iron, or it will cause the wine to cloud in the bottle because of ferric phosphate casse. It was formerly sold in five gallon tin cans and dissolved considerable iron from the tin plate. For wine makers' use, it should be delivered in tanks or drums, as is corn syrup and molasses. The diluted syrup should be filtered to remove pieces of lint, etc.

After addition of one of the above to the wine to be bottle- or tank-fermented the wine should be thoroughly mixed because the syrup tends to settle to the bottom of the mixing tank. A glass-lined tank with mechanical agitator is very useful for mixing the syrup and the wine. If the syrup contains exactly 50 per cent of sugar, the amount to be added to the wine is easily calculated. A laboratory test of the actual reducing sugar content is a useful precaution.

Yeasting

Well in advance of making up the sweetened wine for bottling, a pure culture of fermenting yeast should be prepared in sufficient quantity. This should be of the champagne yeast type; that is, a granulating or agglomerating yeast that forms a coarse, heavy sediment in the bottle and that can be completely and easily removed after fermentation in the bottle is complete.

To prepare a starter of yeast, use wine from the same lot that is to be bottled later. Begin about eight days in advance of bottling with a room temperature of about 70°F. The yeast is received from the supplier in a small bottle or test tube in which the yeast is growing on the surface of agar. To some of the wine to be used in preparing the starter, add enough of the wine syrup (containing 50 per cent sugar) to give about five per cent of sugar. Add to the test tube of yeast culture. Shake gently to aerate. Store in a warm place (70° to 85°F., not higher) until fermenting. Then prepare about two-thirds of a gallon of wine by adding enough of the syrup to give five per cent of sugar. Shake the test tube of fermenting yeast culture, and add the liquid to the wine in the gallon bottle. Plug with cotton and shake well. When in fermentation it may be used to start the fermentation of five gallons or more of wine of five per cent sugar content. When this has fermented to 1 or 2 per cent sugar, it may be used to inoculate the lot of wine. Dried yeast starters are also available.

Enough pure yeast starter is required to allow the addition of 2 or 3 per cent of starter to the wine to be bottle- or tank-fermented. Large sparkling wine producers should maintain a vigorous starter in wine continuously for ready use. Stainless steel tanks are useful for this purpose. Rossi, Jr. (1965) preferred to use sulfur-dioxide acclimated yeasts in preference to yeast cakes.

The starter is added to the sugared wine and the wine stirred to distribute the yeast evenly throughout the wine; during bottling gentle agitation is required to prevent the yeast in the cask or tank from settling to the bottom, thus giving too little yeast in some bottles and too much in others. Occasionally ammonium phosphate (or urea) is a desirable addition to provide yeast food; the amount required will be a matter of experiment, but will probably lie between 0.5 and 1.0 gm. per liter. Even less often should tannin, bentonite, or charcoal be added at this stage.

During bottling, the wine must be well aerated by pumping over or by allowing it to "splash" into a tub or barrel or by direct aeration, since air is necessary for growth of the yeast.

Bottling

Bottles for champagne must withstand relatively high pressure and therefore are of special design and of very thick glass. Careful annealing is necessary to give bottles of sufficient strength. Inspection of a certain number of bottles of each lot for defects under polarized light is good practice. In this country, only the 0.1 and 0.2 gallon bottles are normally used. Larger sizes are filled from the 0.2 gallon bottles. The wine is placed in clean, dry bottles and corked with large "champagne" corks of highest quality. It is usually recommended that these corks be softened by placing them in a basket and moistening them several times a day until soft enough to be used, often 2 to 3 days. They should not be softened by soaking in hot water. The cork is held in place by an iron clamp (agrafe)

Courtesy of Wine Institute

FIG. 105. CHAMPAGNE BOTTLES AWAITING CLARIFICATION

or is wired down. The clamp is applied easily and rapidly by a special machine and may be used repeatedly.

Most wineries now use crown caps during this fermentation. They have been found very satisfactory, giving less "leakers" and being easier to remove for disgorging. They are also lower in cost.

The Second Fermentation

Most wineries neglect the heat produced by the secondary fermentation and the temperature often rises too high, resulting in poorer carbon dioxide absorption and greater bottle breakage. In our opinion 60°F. should be the maximum for the bottle fermentation if the highest quality sparkling wine is to be produced. During the secondary fermentation the producer should periodically examine bottles from the pile to determine the completeness of the fermentation.

In Bottles.—In California the bottles are then stacked in a warm room to undergo fermentation. Two considerations apparently cause California producers to use a rather high temperature for this fermentation. First, there is the desire of some producers for a very rapid turnover. Second, is the fear that at too cool a temperature some of the bottles may not ferment to dryness. Most important is a constant temperature room without drafts. The bottles must be placed horizontally, not upright, in order that the corks are kept wet with the wine, and drying out thus prevented (Fig. 105).

The wine should be left in contact with the yeast at least a year before disgorging, in order that fermentation will be complete, to allow the yeast cells to die, and to permit development of the "champagne" bouquet. The importance of this aging on the yeast cannot be overemphasized if bottle-fermented sparkling wines are to be distinctively different from tank-fermented wines. If the fermentation is not uniform or appears unusually slow, then the stack should be torn down, the contents shaken up, and the bottles restacked in their original position—easily done by placing a chalk mark on the bottom of the bottle to indicate the original position of the sediment in the bottle.

Finishing

The yeast sediment must now be removed from the bottles or the wine from the yeast in the case of the tank process.

From Bottles.—In order to get the yeast onto the cork the bottles are placed *sur point,* that is, upside down in racks with the bottles nearly vertical, necks downward, Fig. 106. The bottles are turned frequently to the right and to the left while they are in this position to loosen the yeast and cause it to settle; the bottle is at the same time "jolted" by dropping it

Courtesy of Wine Institute

FIG. 106.   CHAMPAGNE BOTTLES ON RACKS

Courtesy of Gold Seal Vineyards

FIG. 107.   RIDDLING BOTTLE-FERMENTED NEW YORK SPARKLING
WINE

back into the rack to dislodge the yeast, Fig. 107. · Eventually, the yeast and other sediment rest on the cork. There is an art to getting the light and heavy deposits down onto the cork at the same time. Usually a white brush mark is made on the bottom of the bottle to guide the "turner" as to how much distance to the right or left the bottle should be turned each day.

Usually the bottles are turned one-eighth of a turn per day. The shaking is accomplished by letting the bottles drop back onto the racks after the twirling. At the start the bottles are kept at a less acute angle. Later the angle of the bottles in the racks is increased. A skilled turner can handle up to 30,000 bottles per day unless the clarification is slow. Wines differ greatly in their rate of clarification. A coarse granular sediment may move onto the cork within a week; others need a month or more.

Transfer System.—Because of the problems inherent in clearing a bottle of its deposit the German "transfer" system has recently been introduced into this country. The fermentation in the bottles takes place as above. However, the bottles are not placed in racks but are emptied into a tank under pressure. A special emptying apparatus permits this with a minimum loss of wine or pressure, Fig. 108. From the tank the dosaged wine is then filtered, under pressure, to bottles. While the same bottles may be washed and reused to receive the filtered wine, the best practice is to use new bottles.

Courtesy of Wine Institute

FIG. 108. CHAMPAGNE BOTTLES BEING PLACED IN TRANSFER MACHINE

As Geiss (1959) points out the transfer system is not new—patents were issued as early as 1903, one to Karl Kiefer of Cincinnati. The two main objections to individual disgorging of bottles had already been noted: unaesthetic use of the finger to remove yeast in the neck of the bottle and the loss of wine and pressure.

In the modern "transfer" system an attempt is made to retain certain of the advantages of the bottle system without its disadvantages. The bottle fermentation takes place in the usual manner in bottles (fermentation in magnums would be less costly). The bottles are chilled to near 32°F., with the cork standing upright. The cork is withdrawn and the wine emptied under pressure into a tank. Unless a pump is used to pump the wine into the tank the pressure in the tank must obviously be somewhat less than that in the bottle. In order that the first wine introduced into the tank not lose most of its pressure there must be a counter pressure, slightly higher than that in the bottles being disgorged, in the receiving tank, preferably of nitrogen. In the transfer system, the final dosage liqueur may be added to the empty tank before it is pressurized or by means of a pressure cylinder after it is full. In the latter case, the contents of the full tank are then circulated with a pump to insure thorough mixing. The sparkling wine is then filtered into another pressured tank under refrigeration and isobarometric conditions. Bo (1965) felt the transfer system provided "quality control" but presented no statistical sensory data.

Wines produced by the transfer system have a considerable economic advantage over those produced entirely by the bottle process. The costly riddling step is eliminated. The cost and loss of wine during disgorging is also eliminated. They also enjoy an advantage over the tank system since they can be labeled "champagne" without the *déclassé* statement that they are "bulk-fermented," "fermented in bulk," etc. It is also possible to disgorge wines of different ages into the transfer tank and thus create new blends.

If wineries using the transfer system would age the wine in the bottles for at least a year before transferring, we would find less to criticize in the practice. However, the transfer system is often used on wines which have barely completed their fermentation. Therefore, many viable yeast cells are presented in the bottling tank. Since it is difficult to germ-proof filter a wine under pressure, some viable yeast may get into the final bottle. When these wines contain an appreciable percentage of reducing sugar they will referment unless sulfur dioxide is added. This is the same objection that we have to the tank system as we shall presently point out (p. 475).

Disgorging.—The next operation in the regular bottle process is that of disgorging Fig. 109. This is normally accomplished by freezing a small "plug" of wine in the neck of the bottle next to the cork. The wine in the bottles also should first be cooled to about 45°F. to reduce the pressure. The freezing mixture can be an ice and calcium chloride mixture or various proprietary products. The operation can be mechanized so that bottles enter the cold bath, neck down, at a constant rate and are removed just when the neck is properly frozen.

Now comes the disgorging procedure, when the yeast and other deposits which have been so carefully collected on the cork are removed with minimum loss of pressure from the wine. The bottle is held at a 45° upward angle pointing into an opening cut in the side of a barrel or similar receiver, Fig. 110. The clamp is then removed and the pressure in the bottle allowed to force out the cork and ice plug. If a crown cap is used it is easily pried off and the ice plug ejected as above.

The bottle is now quickly returned to a vertical position. Any yeast adhering to the neck of the bottle is removed with the finger or a special rubber covered stick. The careful disgorger will also occasionally smell the froth from a bottle to be sure that no sulfur bombs have developed. These are bottles where excessive yeast or free sulfur was present during fermentation resulting in the formation of hydrogen sulfide.

Courtesy of Irroy

FIG. 109. CHAMPAGNE DISGORGING

Courtesy of Taylor Wine Co.

FIG. 110.   DISGORGING SPARKLING WINE IN NEW YORK CELLAR

Note freezing unit on left and dosage machine in rear

The bottles can then be placed in a special rack which seals the mouth of the bottle until it can be filled and corked.   Enough wine or liqueur must be added to replace that lost in disgorging.   The wine at this stage is "dry," that is, very low in sugar content.   Most consumers prefer that the champagne contain some to considerable sugar—markets vary in their requirements.

A syrup is prepared of cane sugar, fine brandy (Cognac has been used by some American producers, California brandy by others), and high quality, well-aged, white wine.   Some use a wine of about 20 per cent alcohol to which sugar is added until the wine is about 50 per cent sugar. To prevent refermentation up to 150 p.p.m. of sulfur dioxide are added. The usual syrup contains 60 per cent of sugar or rather 60 grams of sugar per 100 ml. and about 10 to 15 per cent as much brandy as wine.   If a very sweet champagne is desired, the syrup is not diluted; if a dry champagne is to be made, the syrup may be diluted with wine to the necessary extent before addition to the bottle.   A measured amount is added in either case and, if the bottle is then not sufficiently full, sufficient champagne from another bottle is added.   Machines that add the syrup automatically in measured amounts are also available.   In adding the syrup, the liquid must be poured in gently and allowed to flow down the side of the bottle to avoid frothing. The bottle is then corked and the cork wired down in the characteristic manner with a machine designed for the purpose.

As to what the preferred closure may be is not yet established. Single, double, and up to 5-piece corks are found on the market. In this country corks are being replaced by polyethylene closures for the final bottling. These appear to be quite satisfactory and are certainly less costly than cork, however, they are more porous to air than cork stoppers. Consumers generally like polyethylene stoppers for sparkling wines because of their ease of removal and their cleanness. Stephan (1964), however, reported that an appreciable number of consumers thought them "untraditional."

The usual significance of the marks on the labels for sparkling wines is *brut* or *nature* (for the driest), *sec* and *demi-sec* (for the medium sweet) and doux (for the sweetest). Because of the prestige value of *brut* some producers make their *brut* very sweet—up to 2 or even 2.5 per cent sugar. Doubtless this does reach a wider group and hence is good for sales. However, the producer who is trying to make a high quality really dry *brut* will find it hard to compete since a dry *brut* demands a higher quality (and more expensive) raw material than a sweet.

The authors recommend, therefore, that *brut* be restricted to 1.5 per cent reducing sugar, that *secs* contain about 2 to 4 per cent, and that *demi-secs* have about 5 per cent. Should a *doux* be produced, a sugar content of 6 or more is indicated. Similar levels for Austria were given by Paul (1960).

There is considerable breakage during fermentation in bottles, and there is considerable danger also to the operator during disgorging and handling of the sealed bottles. This danger is, of course, greatly reduced if the bottles are refrigerated before handling. *Whenever filled sparkling wine bottles are handled the operator's face should be protected by a face mask.*

Sparkling burgundy can be prepared by the bottle or tank process although red wine may be somewhat more difficult to referment than white. The difference appears to be due to the influence of tannins in red wines and their usually higher alcohol content on the rate of fermentation.

Hemphill (1965) makes the point that bottle-fermented sparkling wines constitute a decreasing percentage of the total American sparkling wine production. He notes, correctly we believe, that this is due to increasing labor costs rather than to any claimed quality advantage of tank-fermented or transfer system wines. To reduce costs, Hemphill recommends plywood bins holding about 500 bottles, use of a forklift, and automated riddling. He claims that an electric vibrator largely eliminated riddling. He used portable electric vibrators with permanently mounted air vibrators connected to solenoid valves and timed to work at night. He claims no manual riddling is necessary and that by new combinations of vibration time and frequency the clarification time will be reduced. We would be more easily convinced if time and economic studies were presented. Most important, none of these recent investigators present any comparative sensory data.

From Tanks.—In California, as well as in Russia and other countries, much of the sparkling wine is now made by the tank or Charmat process (Tschenn 1934). The preparation of the cuvée is exactly the same for tank- and bottle-fermented wines. Since the great economic advantage of the tank process is rapid fermentation, this must be considered in selecting the temperature of fermentation. We know of no controlled tests on this point. Various wineries ferment at temperatures as low as 50°F. and as high as 75°F. Certainly at the higher temperature there is a less satisfactory absorption of the carbon dioxide in the wine and when the bottled wine is opened the wine may rapidly go "flat" in the glass. Cold-acclimatised yeasts should always be used with low-temperature fermentations.

In Italy Carpenè (1959) reported tank fermentations at about 55.4°F. were completed in about two weeks. Rossi, Jr. (1965) also gave two weeks as the fermentation time in California at 50°F. Carpenè stressed that the yeast must be carefully selected. Following the necessary fermentation, the wine is cooled to about 36°F., transferred to another tank and cooled to 24.8°F. to precipitate tartrates, centrifuged and filtered and then bottled. Carpenè also speaks of pasteurizing in the bottle in some cases to insure stability.

Rossi, Jr. (1965) reported that some producers of tank-fermented sparkling wines preferred to add all of the sugar at the start and manipulate the temperature so as to retain the required sugar concentration in the finished wines. Others ferment "dry" and then sweeten. Biologically, the first probably makes "sense" but the second seems to be more practical.

Sparkling wine tanks are normally insulated with cork or, more recently, with urethane foam (which can be sprayed on and, therefore, provides a seamless finish). A thin vapor-proof outer coat is applied to prevent water absorption.

Tank fermentations have several advantages. Excess pressure can be allowed to escape by the use of safety valves. The rate of fermentation can be controlled by changing the temperature. The labor cost is only a fraction of that of the bottle process. They also have disadvantages. The thick yeast sediment in the bottom of the tank must be removed from contact with the wine since, because of its depth, reducing conditions are extreme and hydrogen sulfide production may occur. Another disadvantage is the difficulty of removing all viable yeast cells from a young wine at 5 to 6 atmospheres of pressure.

In order to increase the amino acid content of tank-fermented wines Schanderl (1959) recommends installing high speed stirrers in the tank. When these are used for even a short period of time after the yeast is added there is a striking increase in the amino acid content of the wine and a decrease in the amount of aging required to produce the "champagne" nose. This is the practice in some German sparkling wine plants.

However, Schanderl (1965A) reports formation of fatty substances in yeast cells when free sulfur or sulfites are present. Excessive shaking of bottles or stirring of tank-fermented wines can result in release of the fat and an accumulation of fat particles on the surface. They are not removed by disgorging or filtration.

Continuous sparkling wine production is being used in Russia (Amerine, 1959, 1963). Broussilovski (1959) stressed the importance of conducting the continuous tank fermentation entirely in the absence of air. He shows that there is an enrichment of the wine in amino acids during such an oxygen-free fermentation. However, Kunkee and Ough (1966) were not successful in getting adequate yeast growth and fermentation under pressure.

As originally conceived by Charmat the tank process involved a pretreatment by heating in a closed tank to a temperature of about 140°F. under a pressure of 140 to 160 lbs. pressure. Charmat also envisaged heating the wine with various amounts of air, presumably to improve quality by esterification, but recent Russian work would indicate that this probably did not actually improve the quality of the finished product. The heating period recommended was 8 to 10 hours and internal heaters were used as indicated in Fig. 111 in the maturation tank. Following the heating the wine was cooled by circulating brine through the jacket of the maturation tank. The cooled wine was then transferred to the fermentation tank by connecting valve 1 to valve 3, leaving valve 4 open during the transfer. The requisite amounts of yeast starter and sugar were added to the fermentation tank at the same time. The recommended fermentation temperature in the original studies was about 75°F. At this temperature the fermentation lasted no more than 10 to 15 days. However, the best modern practice indicates that, economic considerations permitting, a better quality product is obtained with a longer fermentation period at a lower temperature. While the amount of sugar added is usually calculated to produce 5 or 6 atmospheres of pressure, should too much sugar be added the excess pressure can be allowed to escape through a safety valve. The most interesting feature of the original Charmat process was the refrigeration tank arrangement. This tank contained an inner, leak-proof plastic bag. The fermented wine plus sweetening desired was transferred from the fermentation tank to the refrigeration tank by connecting valve 3 to valve 6. It is necessary in transfers of this type that a counter pressure be established in the receiving tank prior to the transfer in order to prevent unnecessary loss of carbon dioxide. The wine entering through valve 6 goes outside the plastic bag which collapses against the wall of the tank. Refrigeration is then applied to reduce the temperature of the wine to about 22°F. The wine is left at this temperature for several days and is then filtered under isobarometric pressure by connecting valve 6 through a pump to valve 7 of the filter and from valve 8 of the filter to valve 5 of the

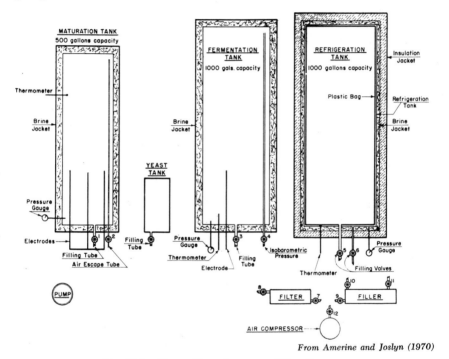

From Amerine and Joslyn (1970)

FIG. 111. THREE-TANK SPARKLING WINE SYSTEM

Note plastic bag in third tank

refrigeration tank, i.e., to the *inside* of the plastic bag. Theoretically, the plastic bag lining permits carbon dioxide to diffuse through. At any rate the filled bag finally fills the tank and thus does not come into contact with air. When it is desired to bottle wine, a new charge of fermented wine is pumped from the fermentation tank into the refrigeration tank into the space outside the plastic bag. As it fills the tank the filtered and clarified wine inside the plastic bag is forced out into the bottling machine by connecting valve 5 to 9, valve 10 of the filler to valve 4, and valve 11 to valve 12 of the air compressor.

In the more common two tank procedure, Fig. 112, used in this country two stainless steel pressure tanks are employed. These are usually 500 or 1000 gallon capacity although 1500 and 2000 gallon tanks are also used. An active yeast culture is prepared, usually 3 to 5 per cent of the volume of the wine to be fermented. The wine itself is sweetened so as to produce six atmospheres' pressure and the desired final residual sugar. The yeast culture and wine are pumped to tank No. 1 through valve 1, leaving valve 3 open during the filling. The fermentation takes place at 50° to 60°F. Usually no more than 2 or 3 weeks are required to produce the requisite pressure. The wine is analyzed and additional sugar added if necessary. The tank is then promptly cooled to about 24°F. in order to stop the fermentation. Some wineries adjust the sulfur content to 200 to 250 p.p.m. but this certainly reduces the quality of the finished product. The wine is held at the low temperature for about a week. Tank No. 2 is then cooled and its pressure adjusted with compressed air or preferably with nitrogen to a pressure slightly greater than that of tank No. 1, by using valve 5. Wine from tank No. 1 is then filtered into tank No. 2 by connecting valves 3 and 6, the pump to valve 2 and to valve 7 of the filter. Valve 8 of the filter is connected to valve 5. When the wine level in tank No. 1 reaches that of the tube attached to valve 2, valves 2, 5, 7, and 8 are closed. The pump is then connected to valve 1, and valves 5, 7, and 8 are opened as be-

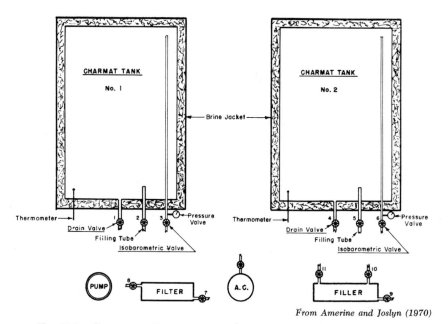

From Amerine and Joslyn (1970)

FIG. 112. CALIFORNIA TWO-TANK SYSTEM OF SPARKLING WINE PRODUCTION

fore. This gives the maximum efficiency to the filtration by filtering the clear wine before the cloudy. The clarified cold wine in tank No. 2 is now ready to bottle. To do this the air compressor (or nitrogen source) is connected to valve 10 of the filler. Connect valves 11 and 6 and 5 and 9. The pressure on valve 10 of the filler is adjusted to be slightly greater than that in tank No. 2. At this time valves 10, 6, 11, and 5 are opened in this order and the bottling is started. When the wine level reaches that of the tube attached to valve 5, valve 9 is then connected to valve 4 and the remainder of the wine bottled.

Two methods of securing proper sugar content are used. In some wineries enough sugar is added at the start so that when the fermentation is "stuck" by the low temperature the wine will contain the requisite amount of sugar. A better procedure is to ferment the wine dry, chill, and then add the necessary sugar solution. However, the tank must be stirred (by pumping over, to secure a uniform mixture). It is then filtered cold under pressure of compressed air or nitrogen. The more rational procedure of using a counter-pressure of carbon dioxide is prohibited by federal regulations. Compressed air is objectionable because some of the air will be dissolved in the wine and may cause undue oxidative darkening of the wine. To prevent this, and also to inhibit the growth of viable yeasts which get through the filter sulfur dioxide must be added. This is objectionable from the point of view of quality since as much as 200 p.p.m. may be required. For isobarometric transfer Carpenè (1959) finds compressed air the worst, carbon dioxide is psychologically wrong, and he, therefore, recommends nitrogen. He recommends that sparkling wine plants should be air conditioned—to avoid day-to-day temperature variations and the differences in pressure which this would cause.

For best filtration the tank should have one take-off above the sediment level so that the filter will not have a large amount of material on the pads until the very end of the filtration—when the lower take-off is used.

In both tank and transfer systems settling of the wine to allow the major part of the sediment to settle before filtration is recommended. Filtration under pressure is a special problem. The large "surface" of the filter pads offers a large area for release of gas. Geiss (1959) recommends a higher pressure than the tank pressure in order to prevent release of carbon dioxide. Figure 113 shows a filtration with and without such a counter pressure. The wine is bottled and corked under pressure. The pressure is low at this temperature and there is little loss of pressure in bottling. All operations by the tank system can be completed in a month or less. Labor cost is greatly reduced and the process is placed on a factory basis.

Drboglav (1940) and others have shown that the low quality of many tank-fermented sparkling wines is due to the introduction of oxygen dur-

Courtesy of Seitz Werke

FIG. 113.   EFFECTS OF FILTERING WITH AND WITHOUT COUNTER PRESSURE

Left, with counter pressure, cross section of pad below filter.   Right, without counter pressure

ing finishing, increasing the aldehyde content and darkening the color. Much better wines are produced when the wine is handled under carbon dioxide and the best under carbon dioxide and with a small amount of sulfur dioxide. Kielhöfer and Würdig (1963) found 5 to 20 mg. per liter of oxygen in newly-bottled tank-fermented wines, but none in bottle-fermented wines. To reduce the oxygen content in the first case, they recommend sulfur dioxide and ascorbic acid. They found transfer system wines must be treated the same as tank-fermented. In German tank-fermented sparkling wines, which have a relatively high sulfur dioxide base, acetaldehyde is produced in considerable amounts during the fermentation. It is thus necessary to add more sulfur dioxide. Schanderl and Staudenmayer (1964) recommend adding fresh yeast to the wine and agitating. This reduces the acetaldehyde content and may remove some metals and tannins by adsorption. Some reduction of the redox potential is obtained by adding ascorbic acid at the time of the tirage bottling. During aging in the bottle, there was usually a decrease in potential. Frolov-Bagreev (1948) reported the potential of Champagne was markedly lower than that of Soviet sparkling wines, probably because the Soviet sparkling wines are largely tank-fermented. The techniques for measuring the potential were criticized by Deibner (1957).

Turbulent-flow transfer of sparkling wines in nonwettable or rough pipes results in large losses of carbon dioxide compared to transfer in smooth wettable pipes, according to Merzhanian (1963). He also reported 20 per cent loss during filtration.

Rossi, Jr. (1965) reported that in California tank-fermented wines the brandy dosage "is only infrequently used today." He believes this reflects industry satisfaction with "natural grape flavors as developed with sound fermentation and aging techniques." Excessive use of brandy dosage is, of course, to be deplored. However, discreet use of a dosage may be useful, especially to some of our more neutral flavored California sparkling wines. Following tank fermentation, Filippov (1963) added 2 to 3 per cent of enzyme concentrate to the wine at the time of bottling. The enzyme concentrate was prepared by storing wine and yeast (1 to 1) for three months at 41° to 50°F., stirring twice monthly with carbon dioxide. Only the clear supernatant material was used.

One of the persistent problems of tank-fermentation production of sparkling wine is their "sweating" following bottling and preceding labeling. Rossi, Jr. (1965) used infra red lamps in the far infrared region. Automatic timer control and various arrangements of the circuits helped to standardize the process and prevent over-heating of the bottles.

Comparison of Tank and Bottle Process.—The differences between bottle fermented and tank fermented wines were studied by Janke and Röhr (1960A). They developed two objective tests: (1) carbon dioxide release ratio (ratio of the amount of carbon dioxide released at 58°F. and 95°F. expressed as per cent), and (2) the amount of nitrogen separated from one liter of wine by ultrafiltration. The first test gives a measure of the relative stability of carbon dioxide in wines and the second may measure the colloidal nitrogen released by yeast autolysis. In 53 commercial wines the carbon dioxide release ratio was 21 to 31 (average 27.8) for 24 bottle-fermented wines and 30 to 46 (average 35.5) for 29 tank-fermented wines. Obviously tank-fermented wines lose their carbon dioxide more rapidly than bottle-fermented wines. The nitrogen content per liter of wine was 9.6 mg. for the bottle-fermented and 6.2 for the tank-fermented.

When the same cuvée was used for tank and bottle fermentation (Janke and Röhr, 1960B), there was a significant difference between the wines after 42 days as measured by the carbon dioxide release test, 29–45, average 34, for 28 tank-fermented bottles and 23–35, average 30.6, for 34 bottle-fermented bottles. The average carbon dioxide release test value for tank-fermented bottles stored for 18 months decreased to 31.0, while that for bottle-fermented bottles disgorged after 18 months was 26.0. After 250 to 380 days, the nitrogen by the ultrafiltration test was 6.2 mg. per liter for the tank-fermented wine and 8.2 for the bottle-fermented. Janke and Röhr concluded that the difference between tank- and bottle-fermented wines lay in the influence of yeast autolysis. They asked the question of whether an improvement in quality of the tank-fermented wines could be obtained by influencing yeast autolysis.

The decrease and then increase in total nitrogen and in the amounts of the amino acids are well-illustrated by the data of Bergner and Wagner (1965)—all in mg. per liter:

		Days from Addition of Yeast					
	Cuvée	1[1]	3[1]	21[1]	21[2]	180[3]	395[3]
Total N	855.2	785.9	766.3	768.3	792.2	805.5	837.7
Alanine	27.8	9.7	7.6	7.6	12.8	14.0	21.6
Arginine	38.2	24.3	23.5	23.7	27.2	30.4	33.6
Aspartic acid	28.2	4.8	3.4	3.8	4.6	8.0	18.8
Cystine	6.6	5.9	5.5	6.0	5.9	5.1	5.5
Glutamic acid	65.6	15.5	10.3	10.9	11.3	16.0	25.7
Glycine	23.0	11.3	11.5	11.6	14.1	19.4	21.9
Histidine	19.4	18.1	17.1	18.9	20.4	22.6	25.4
Leucine + isoleucine	23.2	6.7	4.8	4.9	6.6	10.9	14.4
Lysine	6.0	5.3	4.3	4.8	5.2	10.3	40.5
Phenylalanine	11.8	5.3	4.8	5.1	5.8	9.0	9.7
Proline	296.0	286.0	282.0	280.0	306.0	350.0	420.0
Serine	15.0	3.1	3.4	3.7	4.0	6.5	9.8
Threonine	7.4	5.4	6.0	6.2	5.6	5.6	5.7
Tryptophane	14.6	12.8	14.1	16.5	14.0	14.4	14.8
Valine	31.2	5.9	4.5	4.8	6.6	8.3	14.2

[1] Tank fermentation.
[2] Bottled tank wine after fining, filtering, and liquoring.
[3] Bottle fermented and aged on the yeast.

The increases in proline, lysine, glutamic acid, leucine and isoleucine, phenylalanine, serine and valine are especially notable in the bottle-aged wine. Thus, it is not the fermentation in the bottle which differentiates tank- and bottle-fermented wines, but the period of time the bottle-fermented wine remains in contact with the yeast. The oxygen introduced in bottling tank-fermented and in handling and bottling transfer wines also introduces a difference.

CARBONATION

Carbonated wines are those charged with carbon dioxide artificially instead of by fermentation. Several different methods of carbonating are in use. Probably the best method is that of carbonating in bulk at low temperature. In this system the wine is cooled in a brine-jacketed tank to near the freezing point and is charged at about 24°F. It is allowed to stand to come to equilibrium with the gas and is then bottled cold. It is advisable to pass the charged wine through a filter and bottle under pressure of the gas. The wine should have a pressure of about 75 lbs. per sq. in. at 50°F. Like champagne, it should be served cold.

One French-made carbonator consists of four heavy bottles covered with strong wire netting. The wine is chilled and filled into these charging bottles and impregnated with carbon dioxide. These charging bottles are then connected to champagne bottles; these are filled by the pressure of the gas and corked at once. Two bottles are charged and filled at a time, while the other two are absorbing the gas.

Various high-pressure water carbonators of the types used for soda water can be used if made of stainless steel or other completely corrosion-resistant metal, but unless the wine is chilled to near the freezing point, loss by frothing will be very severe and corking difficult. At low temperatures, the solubility of the gas in the wine greatly increases, and its pressure is correspondingly less. Miller (1959) has shown that if the wine is first placed under a slight vacuum to deaerate it and then slowly carbonated that the carbon dioxide will be better absorbed and that the charge will not be rapidly lost when the bottle is opened, i.e., will discharge carbon dioxide for a longer period of time. His process is protected by a patent. For the theory see Miller (1964, 1966).

Carbonated wines are much less costly to prepare than are champagnes and other wines fermented in the bottle; nevertheless, are pleasing in character if made of wine of good quality. Most Californian wines should be acidified with citric acid before carbonating, as consumer preference seems to be for carbonated wines of rather high acidity. Also some sugar should be added. On this account, the wines used should be of relatively high alcohol content to minimize danger of fermentation in the bottle.

The practical problems of low level carbonation of wines were considered by Rossi, Jr. and Thoukis (1960). They observed that a wine carbonated to a given pressure at a high temperature contained less carbon dioxide than if carbonated at low temperatures. For this type of carbonation they also showed higher carbon dioxide at low soluble solids content (0.236 gm. per 100 ml. at 3.5° Brix versus 0.219 at 11.2, 0.208 at 16.9, 0.192 at 22.7 and 0.179 at 27.80). Alcohol had only a small effect with a decreasing solubility from 11.9 per cent alcohol to 19.5 (0.257 gm. per 100 ml. versus 0.241). They recommended use of gauge pressure as a means of controlling the carbon dioxide content of the wine. One must make allowances for the influence of various factors on carbon dioxide solubility. Nevertheless, they found it possible to carbonate two wines to contain the same amount of carbon dioxide even though their gauge pressure was slightly different. The relation is apparently a straight-line function in this range:

Gauge Pressure, Lb./In.²	Carbon Dioxide, Gm./100 Ml.
8	0.174
12	0.212
16	0.249
20	0.286

The data of Etienne and Mathers (1956) gives the equilibrium head pressures at 60°F. containing the indicated amounts of carbon dioxide. Their data differ from that of Rossi and Thoukis (1960) because the latter's carbonator gave less than 100 per cent efficiency of carbon dioxide dispersion at the carbonator pressures used.

The work of Deinhardt (1961) indicates that accurate data on the solubility of carbon dioxide in wine are not available. Subtraction of about 1.5 atm. from the solubility of carbon dioxide in ten per cent alcohol gives an approximately correct value. See also Fig. 104. He (1965) states that no general solubility coefficient for carbon dioxide is possible because of the number of variables. He presented data showing the carbon dioxide content at various pressures and temperatures—values which are lower than those usually reported. The chart of Rentschler (1965) at ten per cent alcohol is also useful but gives a lower pressure for the same amount of dissolved carbon dioxide than Deinhardt's values. The table of Miller (1958) is useful for pressures up to 25 lb. per sq. in. for the carbon dioxide content at 50° to 70°F.

The troublesome problem of distinguishing between carbonated wines and those produced by tank- or bottle-fermentation was studied by Liotta (1956). He opened the bottles and left them open for seven days at 40°F. At this time carbonated wines contained less than 0.23 gm. per 100 ml. of carbon dioxide (0.15 to 0.22 in eight samples) while those fermented in the bottle had over that amount (0.27 to 0.54 gm. in 13 examples). Further data would be desirable.

BIBLIOGRAPHY

AGABAL'YANTS, G. G. 1954. Khimiko-Tekhologicheskii Kontrol' Proizvodstva Sovetskogo Shampanskogo (Chemical and Technological Control of Soviet Champagne Production). Pishchepromizdat, Moscow.

AMERINE, M. A. 1959. Continuous flow production of still and sparkling wine. Wines and Vines 40, No. 6, 41–42.

AMERINE, M. A. 1963. Continuous fermentation of wines. Wines and Vines *40*, No. 6, 41–42.

AMERINE, M. A. 1965. Laboratory Procedures for Enologists. Associated Students Store, Davis.

AMERINE, M. A., and JOSLYN, M. A. 1951. Table Wines. The Technology of Their Production in California. University of California Press, Berkeley and Los Angeles.

AMERINE, M. A., and MONAGHAN, M. 1950. California sparkling wines. Wines and Vines *31*, No. 8, 25–27; No. 9, 52–54.

BERGNER, K. G., and WAGNER, H. 1965. Die freien Aminosäuren während der Flaschen- und Tankgärung von Sekt. Mitt. Rebe u. Wein, Serie A (Klosterneuburg) *15*, 181–198.

BO, M. J. 1965. The transfer methods. Wine Institute, Tech. Advis. Committee, June 7, 1965.

BROUSSILOVSKI, S. 1959. Modification of the continuous sparkling wine process (transl.) Vinodelie i Vinogradarstvo S.S.S.R. *19*, No. 3, 12–26.

CARPENÈ, A. 1959. Della tecnica dei vini spumanti. Riv. viticolt. e enol. (Conegliano) *12*, 179–189.

CHAPPAZ, G. 1951. Le Vignoble et le Vin de Champagne. Louis Larmat, Paris.

DEIBNER, L. 1957. Potentiel oxydoréducteur des vins: son importance, sa signification; tendances actuelles de la technique de sa mesure. Ind. agr. aliment. (Paris) *74*, 273–283.

DEINHARDT, H. 1961. Löslichkeit von Kohlensäure im Wein. Deut. Wein-Ztg. *97*, 68, 70, 72.

DEINHARDT, H. 1965. Die Löslichkeit von Kohlensäure im Wein und Sekt. Weinberg u. Keller *12*, 428–434.

DE ROSA, T. 1964. Tecnica dei Vini Spumanti. Tipografia Editrice F. Scarpis. Conegliano, Italy.

DRBOGLAV, U. 1940. Variation of dissolved oxygen and of the oxidation-reduction potential in the course of fermentation by the Chaussepied procedure. Vinodelie i Vinogradarstvo S.S.S.R. No. 2, 3.

ETIENNE, A. D., and MATHERS, A. P. 1956. Laboratory carbonation of wine. J. Assoc. Off. Agr. Chemists *39*, 844–848.

FILIPPOV, B. A. 1963. Poluchenie fermentnykh kontsentratov i ikh primenenie (Production of enzyme concentrates and their use). Vinodelie i Vinogradarstvo S.S.S.R. *23*, No. 2, 11–14.

FRANÇOT, P. 1945. Acide total et acidité fixé réele des moûts et des vins de Champagne. Bull. office intern. vin *18* (167/170), 114–118.

FRANÇOT, P. 1950. Champagne et qualité par le pressurage. Vigneron Champenois *71*, 250–255, 273–283, 342–351, 371–382, 406–416.

FRANÇOT, P., and GEOFFROY, P. 1951. Les pectines et les gommes dans les moûts et les vins de Champagne. Vigneron Champenois *72*, 54–59.

FROLOV-BAGREEV, A. 1948. Sovetskoe Shampanskoe. (Soviet sparkling wine; technology of production of sparkling wines). Pishchepromizdat, Moscow.

GEISS, W. 1959. Technische Fortschritte bei der Sektherstellung. Deut. Wein-Ztg. *95*, 616, 618, 620, 622, 624.

HEMPHILL, A. J. 1965. The traditional method of champagne production. Wine Institute, Tech. Advis. Committee, June 7, 1965.

HERZOG, G. 1954. Die deutschen Sektkellereien, ihre Entwicklung und ihre Bedeutung für den deutschen Weinbau. Daniel Meininger, Neustadt a.d. Weinstrasse.

JANKE, A., and RÖHR, M. 1960A. Über Schaumweine und deren Untersuchung. I. Objektive Teste zur Beurteilung von Schaumweinen. Mitt. Rebe u. Wein, Serie A (Klosterneuburg) 10, 111–123.

JANKE, A., and RÖHR, M. 1960B. Ibid. II. Über einem kontrollierten Vergleichsversuch Tankgärverfahren/Flaschengärverfahren. Ibid. 10, 210–217.

KIELHÖFER, E., and WÜRDIG, G. 1963. Die Oxydationsvorgänge im Wein. 6. Die Sauerstoffaufnahme durch den Sekt bei der Sektbereitung nach dem Grossraumgärverfahren. Ibid. 13, 18–35.

KISHKOVSKIĬ, Z. N. 1963. Aminokislotnyĭ sostav nekotorykh vin (Amino acid compounds in various wines). Vinodelie i Vinogradarstvo S.S.S.R. 23, No. 1, 13–15.

KOCH, K. 1923. Deutsche Sektindustrie. Zabern, G.m.b.H., Mainz.

KUNKEE, R. E., and OUGH, C. S. 1966. Multiplication and fermentation of Saccharomyces cerevisiae under carbon dioxide pressure in wine. Appl. Microbiol. 14, 643–648.

LIOTTA, C. 1956. Interim report concerning experiments on naturally fermented and artificially carbonated wines. Internal Revenue Service, Washington, 21174.

MANCEAU, E. 1929. Vinification Champenoise. Chez l'Auteur, Épernay.

MERZHANIAN, A. A. 1963. Nekotorye fizicheskie usloviia rozliva shampanskogo (Some physical conditions in transfer of sparkling wines). Vinodelie i Vinogradarstvo S.S.S.R. 23, No. 8, 3–8.

MILLER, F. J. 1958. Carbon Dioxide in Water, in Wine, in Beer and in Other Beverages. Oakland.

MILLER, F. J. 1959. Carbon dioxide in wine. Wines and Vines 40, No. 8, 32.

MILLER, F. J. 1964. Carbon dioxide stability in beverages. Food Technol. 18, 60–63.

MILLER, F. J. 1966. Viewpoint: quality carbonation of wine. Wines and Vines 47, No. 6, 49–50.

PACOTTET, P., and GUITTONNEAU, L. 1930. Vins de Champagne et Vins Mousseux. J.-B. Baillière et Fils, Paris.

PAUL, F. 1960. Chemische Untersuchungen an Schaumweinen I. II. Der Gehalt an schwefeliger Säure. Mitt. Rebe u. Wein, Serie A (Klosterneuburg) 10, 138–155, 238–247.

POSTEL, W. 1970. Kohlensäurebestimmung und Kohlensäuregehalt in Wein, Perlwein und Schaumwein. Deut. Lebensm.-Rundsch. 66, 185–190.

PROTIN, R. 1960. Personal communication. Office International du Vin, Paris.

RENTSCHLER, H. 1965. Die Löslichkeit von Kohlensäure in Wein in Abhängigkeit von Temperatur und Druck. Schweiz. Z. Obst- u. Weinbau 74, 662–663.

RODOPULO, A. K. 1966. Biokhimiya Shampanskogo Proizvodstva. "Pishchevaya Promyshlennost," Moscow.

ROSSI, E. A., JR., and THOUKIS, G. 1960. Low-level carbonation of still wines. Am. J. Enol. Vitic. 11, 35–45

Rossi, E. A., Jr. 1965. Sparkling wine production by Charmat process. Wine Institute, Tech. Advis. Committee, June 7, 1965.

Schanderl, H. 1938. Kellerwirtschaftliche Fragen zur Schaumweinbereitung. Wein u. Rebe 20, 1–8.

Schanderl, H. 1943. Eine vergleichende Studie über Champagner- und Schaumweinbereitung. Ibid. 25, 74–82.

Schanderl, H. 1959. Die Mikrobiologie des Mostes und Weines. Eugen Ulmer, Stuttgart.

Schanderl, H. 1965A. Über die Entstehung von Hefefett bei der Schaumweingärung. Mitt. Rebe u. Wein, Serie A (Klosterneuburg) 14, 13–20.

Schanderl, H. 1965B. Der Einfluss von Kationenaustausch des Grundweines auf Sektgärungen. Jahresbericht Hessische Lehr- u. Forschungsanstalt Wein-, Obst- u. Garbenbau, Geisenheim 1965, 18–19.

Schanderl, H., and Staudenmayer, T. 1964. Über den Einfluss der schwefligen Säure auf die Acetaldehydebildung verschiedenen Schaumweingärungen. Ibid. 14, 267–281.

Simon, A. L. 1962. Champagne: with a Chapter on American Champagne by Robert J. Misch. McGraw-Hill Book Co., New York.

Stephan, E. 1964. Polyäthylenstopfen für Wein- und Sektflaschen. Weinberg u. Keller 11, 447–450.

Tarantola, C. 1937. La preparazione dell' "Asti Spumante" con fermentazione a bassa temperatura. Ann. staz. enol. sper. Asti ser. 2 2, 315–321.

Tschenn, C. 1934. Champagnization by the Charmat process. Fruit Prods. J. 13, 334–336.

U. S. Internal Revenue Service. 1956. The determination of carbon dioxide in wine. Washington, D. C., IRS-14791.

U. S. Internal Revenue Service. 1961. Part 240.531 of Title 26, Code of Federal Regulations. U. S. Govt. Print. Office, Washington.

Vogt, E. 1963. Der Wein, seine Bereitung, Behandlung und Untersuchung. 4 ed. Verlag Eugen Ulmer, Stuttgart.

Weinmann, J., and Telle, L. F. 1929. Manual du Travail des Vins Mousseux. Hirt et Cie., Reims.

CHAPTER 12

Wine Making in Eastern United States[1]

The most important grape growing areas east of the Rocky Mountains are the Finger Lakes region of New York State, the western area of New York bordering on Lake Erie, and the Niagara River and the southern shores of Lake Ontario. This latter region extends into Canada on the Niagara Peninsula between Lake Ontario and Lake Erie and around the western end of Lake Ontario. Also to be included in the grape belt are parts of southern Michigan, northern Ohio, and a section of northern Pennsylvania bordering on Lake Erie. In the eastern part of New York State, there is a grape producing area in sections of the Hudson Valley. In New Jersey there is an area in the south central part of the state where grapes are grown, and some grapes are produced in Maryland. Grapes are also grown in Missouri and to a limited extent in many other states.

VARIETIES

The grapes grown in these areas are the so-called labrusca grapes, with some Scuppernong in the southern states. These are native American grapes, the most common varieties of which are Elvira, Delaware, Concord, Niagara, Ives Seedling, and Catawba. These grapes are generally winter-hardy, productive, and resistant to the attacks of fungus diseases and phylloxera. The pulp of the berry is not firmly attached to the skin (thus the origin of the term "slip skin"), and the seeds are rather difficult to separate from the pulp. The juice of these grapes is lower in sugar content and of higher acidity than the V. vinifera grapes grown in California. New wine varieties of grapes are being developed from the crossing of V. vinifera species with native American or labrusca species. Known as French hybrids, several of these have been planted in the Finger Lakes wine growing sections, in Canada, and in Maryland and have proved quite successful for wine production. In recent years, the growing and use of these French hybrids has increased considerably.

According to the New York Crop Reporting Service, in 1965 about 125,000 tons of grapes grown in New York State were purchased by wineries and juice processing plants. The Concord variety makes up the bulk of the New York grapes processed in the state. Other leading varieties are Ca-

[1] The authors gratefully acknowledge the assistance of Mr. Theodore E. Carl of Hammondsport, New York, in the writing of this chapter.

488

tawba, Delaware, Elvira, Ives Seedling, Niagara, French hybrids, and Fredonia. The Concord is also utilized by juice processing plants. However, its use in wine making has increased appreciably in recent years due to public acceptance of the types of wines in which this variety is used. For further information on the varieties, see Hedrick (1908, 1945), Munson (1909), and Wagner (1956, 1965).

In the New York Finger Lakes area, and other grape growing areas of the state, the grapes reach maturity during a 6 to 8 week period, starting usually about the middle of September and lasting until the last week in October and sometimes into early November. It is of utmost importance in producing top quality wine that the grapes be harvested at the peak of their maturity and be processed at the wineries as quickly as possible after they are picked.

Courtesy of Taylor Wine Co.

FIG. 114.   HARVESTING GRAPES IN NEW YORK VINEYARD

Fortunately, the grapes used in wine making ripen at various times during the harvesting season. Thus Delaware, Elvira, and Fredonia ripen early, followed by Niagara, Dutchess, Concord, and Ives Seedling; Catawba reaching maturity last. Many of the eastern wineries own considerable acreage of grapes tended to by their own vineyard personnel, but none of the wineries grows enough fruit to meet their annual requirements, so must depend on independent grape growers. Close cooperation is maintained between the wineries and the independent grower throughout the year.

WINE PRODUCTION

At the approach of the harvesting season winery representatives pay more frequent visits to the vineyards of the area and make field tests of the grapes to ascertain the degree of ripeness of the various varieties and to estimate the tonnage of grapes to be expected from each vineyard. As full maturity develops in individual varieties, field representatives gather samples and bring them to the laboratory at the wineries where more complete analyses are conducted. When it is determined that the grapes are ready for harvesting, a picking and delivery schedule is set up with the grower so that the grapes arrive at the wineries as soon as possible after picking, and that quantities are in such amounts that can be pressed the day of arrival, Fig. 114.

Prior to the start of the crushing and pressing operation, all winery equipment is thoroughly cleaned and operationally checked so that the work will proceed smoothly and efficiently when the grapes begin to arrive at the weighing platform.

The grapes are picked into specially designed picking boxes or into the conventional bushel baskets for transportation to the wineries, Fig. 115. As the loads of grapes arrive at the winery they are inspected and weighed

Courtesy of Taylor Wine Co.

FIG. 115. LAKESIDE VINEYARD IN NEW YORK

prior to being fed to the stemmer and crusher. Here the stems are removed and the grapes crushed to a semi-liquid consistency in which condition they are sent to the presses or to the fermenter.

Presses

There are several types of presses used in the eastern wineries. In most of the wineries the hydraulic rack and cloth press is being used, Fig. 116. However, several wineries are using cylindrical presses, such as the Willmes and the Vaslin types (see p. 253).

In the rack and cloth hydraulic presses fairly open weave nylon press cloths are now in general use to enclose the crushed grapes (called cheeses). The build up of the press consists of series of wooden press racks between which the crushed grapes are deposited in these press cloths. The press cloth is placed on a rack and after the crushed grapes are deposited on the cloth, the ends are folded over in order to enclose them in the cloth. Then another rack is placed on top and again some crushed grapes are deposited on another cloth. This process is repeated until a press set up is completed. A complete press set up will usually consist of 15 to 18 of such cloth-enclosed sacks of crushed grapes or cheeses. As the press is being built up the free-run juice is drained off and in some instances kept separate from the juice subsequently obtained

Courtesy of Gold Seal Vineyards

FIG. 116. RACK AND CLOTH PRESSES IN NEW YORK WINERY

when pressure is applied. When the press set up is complete the filled racks are moved over the hydraulic press where a pressure up to 2000 to 2500 lbs. per sq. in. is applied.

The amount of grapes in a fully loaded press will vary depending on the size of the press. Some hydraulic presses can handle up to five tons of grapes in one build up. The press racks are from 3 to 5 feet square and the corresponding press cloths somewhat larger to enable the crushed grapes to be entirely enclosed in the cloths between the racks. Prior to the time that the crushed grapes are deposited on the cloths a small amount of diatomaceous earth or paper pulp is added to the crushed grapes. Also added at this time is a small amount of a pectic-splitting enzyme in order to obtain juice of fairly good clarity.

For the past several seasons,, two of the largest wineries in the Finger Lakes area have been using the cylindrical type Willmes presses (p. 252). The users of this type of press report highly satisfactory results both in cold pressing and hot pressing of all varieties of labrusca-type grapes. Although this type of press can be loaded fairly fast (3 or 4 minutes), the best results were obtained by loading at a slower rate of about twelve minutes. Even though upward of five tons can be used, best results were obtained with a load of approximately 3.75 tons. The pressing cycle in this type of press averages about 50 minutes. Another type of cylindrical press is equipped with metal end plates that are slowly moved toward each other after the press is loaded, thus expressing the juice.

As in the hydraulic press, it is important to use filter aid such as paper pulp and pectic-splitting enzymes to obtain best results. The chief advantage of these cylindrical types of presses is the saving of labor.

Pretreatment

There are several methods for preparing the grapes for the fermentation tubs and casks. In white wines the varietal grapes used are cold pressed as they come from the stemmer and crusher.

For red wines, two methods are being used. In the more popular method, known as hot pressing, the stemmed and crushed grapes are heated either in kettles or through heat exchangers to a temperature of 140° to 150°F. prior to loading of the press.

Juice from the presses flows into an accurately metered series of press tanks, usually glass lined containers, from which uniform samples of the juice are obtained. These are tested immediately for degree Balling and total acidity so that the necessary amelioration can be calculated and directions given into which fermenters the juice is to be pumped.

The other method still in vogue at some wineries is known as fermenting on the skin. In this procedure the bottom of each fermenter to be used is equipped with an inverted perforated box, around which is piled clean straw. The straw is weighted down with bricks. The grapes to be used are crushed but not stemmed and deposited in the previously prepared fermenters. About two and one quarter tons of crushed grapes for each 1000-gallon capacity of the fermenters is the quantity generally used. The grapes should be weighed in order to estimate the quantity of juice they represent. Samples of free-run juice are drawn off at intervals to get the average degree Balling of the juice in order to calculate amelioration prior to fermentation. The grapes are pressed towards the latter stages of fermentation.

Amelioration

The matter of degree of amelioration of respective juices is a decision the wine maker must make and is dependent on the type of wine for which the particular juice is destined to be used. For practically all varieties of grapes grown in eastern United States, the total acid of the juice is sufficiently high to permit full amelioration of 35 per cent of the resulting product. However, judgment must be used in determining the degree of amelioration the individual wine maker uses. Some of the more delicately flavored grapes, such as the Delaware and Dutchess, should receive little or no amelioration, especially when they are to be used for champagne production. Other juices, if they are destined for eventual use in dessert wines, may advantageously be ameliorated close to the permissible limits. Thus, we see that no set rule has been set for degree of amelioration.

In cold pressing of grapes, the average yield will approximate 170 to 175 gallons per ton. In hot pressing a yield close to 190 gallons of juice per ton is attained. The degree Balling of the various juices obtained from the eastern labrusca grapes varies from approximately 14 to 21. Thus we see that amelioration is necessary in most cases to produce wines of the desired alcoholic content. For those wines which are to be used for champagne and sparkling wines, a fermented wine of eleven per cent alcohol is needed. For table wines an alcoholic content of 12.5 per cent is desired and for dessert wines not over 13 per cent alcohol prior to fortification with wine spirits, plus the desired sugar, is the aim.

Dividing the alcohol percentage wanted by the factor 0.57 gives the degree Balling the ameliorated juice should be prior to fermentation. Thus if a wine of 12.5 per cent alcohol is desired the ameliorated juice should have a degree Balling of approximately 22.

Some wineries have their own pet formula for the calculation of amelioration. Some use section 240.978 of Federal Wine Regulations (U. S. Internal Revenue Service, 1970 or U. S. Laws, 1954) which gives a table showing the pounds of dextrose or cane or beet sugar required to raise 1

TABLE 41

AMOUNTS OF DEXTROSE OR SUCROSE REQUIRED PER GALLON TO INCREASE THE SOLUBLE
SOLIDS OF JUICE TO 23° BALLING[1]

Balling of Juice	Dextrose	Resultant Gallonage	Cane or Beet Sugar	Resultant Gallonage
Degree	Lbs.		Lbs.	
0	2.8206	1.2203	2.4877	1.1836
1	2.7084	1.2115	2.3887	1.1765
2	2.5955	1.2027	2.2890	1.1692
3	2.4815	1.1939	2.1886	1.1647
4	2.3589	1.1841	2.0804	1.1536
5	2.2511	1.1759	1.9853	1.1434
6	2.1343	1.1668	1.8823	1.1392
7	2.0168	1.1577	1.7787	1.1316
8	1.8984	1.1485	1.6743	1.1239
9	1.7788	1.1391	1.5688	1.1161
10	1.6584	1.1297	1.4626	1.1083
11	1.5370	1.1203	1.3556	1.1004
12	1.4145	1.1107	1.2475	1.0924
13	1.2852	1.1004	1.1335	1.0838
14	1.1335	1.0877	1.0291	1.0763
15	1.0414	1.0815	0.9184	1.0681
16	0.9149	1.0716	0.8069	1.0598
17	0.7875	1.0617	0.6945	1.0515
18	0.6590	1.0516	0.5812	1.0442
19	0.5294	1.0415	0.4669	1.0346
20	0.3986	1.0312	0.3516	1.0261
21	0.2668	1.0209	0.2353	1.0174
22	0.1340	1.0105	0.1182	1.0088

[1] Source of data: U. S. Internal Revenue Service (1961) or U. S. Laws (1954).

gallon of grape juice to 23° Balling and the resultant gallonage, Table 41.
Figures for fractional Balling readings are readily arrived at by interpolation. In some wineries the old rule of thumb method is employed based upon 1 lb. of cane sugar dissolved in enough water to make 1 gallon results in a Balling reading of 12°.

When dextrose sugar is used instead of cane sugar allowance must be made for the 8 per cent water of crystallization in the dextrose sugar, unless anhydrous dextrose is used. In recent years the use of liquid sugar has become increasingly popular. This form of invert sugar is a syrup of about 76.5° Balling, weighs about 11.5 lbs. to the gallon, and each gallon contains the equivalent of approximately 9 lbs. of cane sugar, calculated on a dry basis. The use of liquid sugar results in a considerable saving in time and labor.

Containers

White oak casks, redwood, and cypress fermenters are in quite general use in the eastern wineries. Recently coated iron and stainless steel tanks have come to be quite popular. These containers are used both as fermenters and storage tanks. To the juices as they come from the presses is

Courtesy of Taylor Wine Co.

FIG. 117. SHERRY BAKING TANKS IN NEW YORK

Note oxygen cylinders.

added about 75 p.p.m. of sulfur dioxide to retard the action of the undesirable yeasts and other microorganisms. After the necessary amount of amelioration (sugar or sugar and water solution) is added, a pure culture yeast is pumped in to initiate fermentation. The various containers are only filled to about 75 per cent of capacity to prevent overflowing from effects of the initial violent fermentation. The ratio of water to sugar in the amelioration solution will necessarily vary according to the total acidity of the juice being processed.

Temperature Control

In the eastern United States the temperatures prevalent during the harvesting season are relatively cool. Hence the juice being processed will

Courtesy of Widmer Wine Co.

FIG. 118.   AGING SHERRY ON ROOF OF NEW YORK WINERY

have a temperature of from 40° to 60°F.   There will, of course, be exceptions if the weather becomes exceptionally warm or cold, but in general the above holds true.   When fermentation is conducted in relatively small containers, that is, casks or tubs under 5000 gallon capacities, there is little danger of fermentation temperatures rising above 85°F.   However, where larger fermenters are employed, it is necessary to employ cooling devices to keep the fermentation temperatures below the critical point. This may be accomplished by passing the fermenting wine through tubular heat exchangers using water as the cooling medium.   In some cases fermenters are equipped with cooling coils to keep the temperature of the fermenting juice under control.

When hot pressing is used for extraction of color, it is necessary to cool the juice to 60° or 65°F. before the fermentation starts.   Should some fermentations result in excessive foaming, the foam can be made to subside with an anti-foam agent.   Only a small amount, about 1 oz. per 1000 gallons of fermenting juice, will suffice.

Post-Fermentation Care

After the initial very active fermentation quiets down to a more orderly action, the fermenters are filled almost to capacity, usually equipped with water seals, and fermentation allowed to continue to completion.   In 2 to 3 weeks the various fermentations should be completed and racking or filtering may be started.   The sooner the fermented juice is separated from the lees or sediment the better the quality of the new wine. However, some wineries may wish to delay racking in order to encourage a malo-lactic fermentation. Rice (1965) demonstrated a malo-lactic fermentation in 28 of 41 New York red wines and in 15 of 55 white wines. There was a marked difference between wineries in the incidence of the malo-lactic fermentation. He isolated three types of bacteria: a heterofermentative rod, a homofermentative rod, and a homofermentative coccus.

While filtering is more satisfactory in removing the new wine from the lees, few wineries have the filtering capacity to conduct this procedure with all of their new wines. Those wines that are not filtered undergo a series of rackings to partially separate the new wine from the heavy lees. The wines are held according to variety after racking or filtering for later selection in preparing blends. Those to be used in dessert wines for fortification with grape brandy to the desired alcoholic content may also be sweetened to the desired level of market acceptability.

At present no eastern wineries produce their own grape brandy for fortification. It is necessary to obtain these wine spirits from California. The spirits are usually about 189° proof and are transported in metal drums or in tank cars. Only grape or raisin brandy is permitted by the government for the fortification of grape wine. The calculations given in Chapter 6 should be noted.

FINISHING

After fermentation is completed and the wines have been either filtered or racked the wine makers make their selections and note the quantities to be used in the various blends. Each winery has its trade secret for the particular blends used in preparing their commercial types. However, it is not divulging such secrets in mentioning that in white table wines blends of Delaware, Catawba, Dutchess, and Elvira are used for rhine, chablis, and sauterne. Other white varieties may also be utilized as supplementary wines. In red table wines, hot-pressed Concord, Fredonia and Ives Seedling are used for burgundies and claret, and these may be supplemented by others such as Baco, Seibel, and similar varieties. Gradation in coloring may be obtained in blending reds and whites to arrive at types lighter in color than the deep red of a burgundy. For dessert wines various varieties are used. In reds such as port, Concord and Niagara may be employed. As the acidity of eastern wines is quite high it is a general practice to blend in up to 25 per cent of California wines to obtain wines of the desired acidity. No more than 25 per cent California wines may be used for blending, unless the eastern wines are permitted to lose their geographical identity. They must be labeled as "American" wines if less than 75 per cent come from a given region.

Clarification

When the various blends are made and conform to their respective specification as to composition, color, flavor, and aroma they are clarified and treated for stability. The general types of fining agents used are tannin and gelatin, bentonite, Sparkolloid, casein, or combinations of these. Some wineries flash-pasteurize their blends in a closed system while others do not. All wineries make a general practice of refrigerating their blends at 26°F. for table wines and at 19°F. for dessert wines. They are held at these colder temperatures for 10 days to 2 weeks after which they are filtered to remove the excess cream of tartar thrown out during refrigeration and are kept at a uniform cool temperature until such time as they are prepared for bottling with a finished polishing filtration. Some work is now being done to eliminate the refrigeration with the use of ion exchange columns for removal of excess cream of tartar and the initial results appear quite promising. It is the aim of most wineries to hold finishing blends several months in casks or tanks prior to bottling. These wines are examined periodically and tested for stability.

At the time of the polishing filtration for bottling, some wine makers make a practice of adding small amounts of sulfur dioxide to retard any oxidation that may occur due to the oxygen in the headspace of the bottle. Each day's bottling is generally coded with the date of bottling and samples of each bottling are kept for about a year for reference purposes.

TYPES

Some eastern wineries make a practice of marketing certain varietal wines. Formerly red Concord wine was not considered a very acceptable wine as such. During the past ten years a highly sweetened Concord wine, both fortified and unfortified has proven quite popular and has been produced and sold very successfully throughout the United States. Other varietal eastern wines, usually of the table wine type, have been produced and successfully marketed. These include Delaware, Elvira, Niagara, Seibel and others.

Very few vintage wines are produced by eastern wineries. This is probably because most wineries try to keep on hand varietal wines of several year's vintages to blend together in order to maintain uniformity. A number of New York wineries specialize in sparkling wine production—some blended to a low anthranilate odor (p. 112) while others are distinctively "eastern."

The favorable position of New York and other "eastern" sparkling wines (49 per cent in 1964) is attributed by Goldman (1965) to their "eastern" or labrusca flavor. He also claims low yield, rocky well-drained soils, cool climate, and low pH, high acid, high extract musts, and use of sucrose as positive factors. No data whatsoever are offered to substantiate these claims.

Eastern sherry wines are in the main produced by a method or modification of the method patented by Tressler (1939A,B). This method consists of heating a fortified labrusca wine such as Concord, Niagara, Elvira, Catawba, or blends of these for 4 to 6 weeks at approximately 140°F., Fig. 117. Oxygen from tanks is released slowly into the wine during heating under very slight pressure, through alundum or unglazed porcelain diffusers. Air under pressure may also be employed. Since the pores of the diffusers are very small, the oxygen entering the wine is in the form of extremely fine bubbles. Thus, a small volume of oxygen gives a relatively large surface in constant contact with the wine and greatly increases the rate of oxidation. The oxygen leaving the top of the tank carries in it, in the form of vapor, some alcohol and esters. Hence, a trap is provided at the top of the tank to recover these volatile materials and return them to the wine. The trap contains cold wine, of the type being heated, in which the vapors being carried by the oxygen are readily condensed. Various methods may be employed in maintaining the temperature of the wine under process. Hot water coils, thermostatically controlled, have proven very satisfactory. It is believed essential that the acidity of the sherry baking stock be 0.5 per cent or lower calculated as tartaric acid, as higher acidity seems to mask the sherry flavor being developed by baking. Calcium carbonate is being successfully used to reduce the acidity to the desired level. The wine being baked is examined daily and sensory testing is at present the criterion upon which the completion of treatment is based. Upon completion of baking the wine is cooled, fined, and filtered and held for several months or longer before being used in preparing finished blends.

In a study of the Tressler process Mattick and Robinson (1960) reported that the volatile carbonyl, volatile and total acidity and esters increased during the baking process. The pH decreased from 3.52 to 3.22 in one case. No such decrease is noted in the baking of California sherries. They attributed this increase in the total acidity and decrease in pH to the effect of a non-enzymatic browning system which releases a carboxyl group.

A modification of the aforementioned process is being successfully used in preparing a tawny port. Port stock of the bright ruby red color of port wine is heated to 120°F. for a period of about ten days while bubbling oxygen through the wine. It is necessary to regulate the time and temperature so that the oxygen treatment is terminated before a sherry flavor is developed. The oxygen treatment reduces the labrusca (foxy) flavor of the wine.

Another method of producing eastern sherries is by what is known as the weathering process. The sherry stock, made with labrusca grapes, is produced by fermentation and fortification. After clarification and filtering oak sherry barrels are filled with this stock and exposed to the weather for four years. One large eastern winery conducts this process on the roof of the winery, Fig. 118. The buildings on the roofs of which the method is used are specially constructed to carry the extra load of the full barrels, four high. On these roofs, there is constructed a framework of special cast iron stands, steel channel supports and cross support. The steel is covered with wood boards, bolted to the channels so that the barrels rest on wood instead of steel. The first row of barrels is placed on this and the other three tiers rest on 2 by 4 in. wooden supports.

The barrels are completely filled, then a half gallon drawn out to allow for expansion and the barrels sealed with long bungs. Normally the shrinkage and losses during the four year aging period does not exceed 18 per cent. As the sherry stock is taken off the roofs it is blended, clarified, refrigerated, and filtered, and then this four year old sherry is blended with older sherries removed in previous years.

While this is not the so-called solera system (p. 415) this winery maintains a constant blend of stock taken from the barrels after four years with the older sherry. The average life of the barrels so exposed is about 12 years; in some instances 16 to 20 years. The iron hoops of the barrels are painted before filling to extend the life of the barrels. While this sherry method is time consuming and costly it does produce an excellent product.

BIBLIOGRAPHY

GOLDMAN, M. 1965. Sparkling wine production in New York. Wine Institute, Tech. Advis. Committee, June 7, 1965.

HEDRICK, U. P. 1908. The Grapes of New York. J. B. Lyon Co., Albany. (New York Department of Agriculture.)

HEDRICK, U. P. 1945. Grapes and Wines from Home Vineyards. Oxford University Press, New York.

MATTICK, L. R., and ROBINSON, W. B. 1960. Changes in volatile constituents during the making of sherry wine by the Tressler process. Food Technol. *14*, 30–33.

MUNSON, T. V. 1909. Foundations of American Grape Culture. Denison, Texas.

RICE, A. C. 1965. The malo-lactic fermentation in New York State wines. Am. J. Enol Vitic. *16*, 62–68.

TRESSLER, D. K. 1939A. Wine process. U.S. Pat. 2,181,838. Nov. 22.

TRESSLER, D. K. 1939B. Wine process. U.S. Pat. 2,181,839. Nov. 28.

WAGNER, P. M. 1956. American Wines and Wine-Making. Alfred A. Knopf, New York.

WAGNER, P. M. 1965. A Wine-Grower's Guide. 2 ed. Alfred A. Knopf, New York.

U. S. INTERNAL REVENUE SERVICE. 1970. Wine; Part 240 of Title 26, Code of Federal Regulations. U. S. Govt. Print. Office, Washington. (U. S. Treasury Dept., IRS Publication No. 146 (Rev. 7–70.) Chapter 51. Title 26, United States Code 1. Washington.

U. S. LAWS. 1954. Internal Revenue Code of 1954, as amended. Sub-title E, Chapter 51. Title 26, United States Code 1. Washington.

CHAPTER 13

Special Natural Wines: Vermouth and Flavored Wines

Vermouth is a 15 to 21 per cent alcohol wine flavored with a characteristic mixture of herbs and spices, some of which impart an aromatic flavor and odor and others a bitter flavor. Two classes are recognized in the trade, the sweet or Italian-type vermouth and the dry or French type. Dubonnet, Byrrh, Bonal, and Cap Corse are flavored wines that are usually classed with vermouth and will also be discussed in this chapter. In addition, there are on the market several wines that are lightly flavored with certain herbs, spices, fruit juices, essences, aromatics, and other natural flavorings. They have attained considerable popularity, such as Thunderbird, Silver Satin, etc. Many formulas for the preparation of each type exist. According to Joslyn and Amerine (1964), the Italian or sweet vermouth contains from 15 to 17 per cent of alcohol by volume and 12 to 19 per cent of reducing sugar; and the French or dry vermouth usually contains about 18 per cent of alcohol and about 4 per cent of reducing sugar. The quantity of herbs and spices used in making the dry vermouth is less per unit of vermouth than for the sweet; customarily about 0.5 to 0.75 oz. per gallon of the dry and 0.75 to 1 oz. per gallon of the sweet. While vermouth is served principally "straight" in European countries it is used in America principally in mixed drinks such as Martini and Manhattan cocktails. Some is served mixed with sherry as a "sherry cocktail."

Origin

The name is probably derived from "Wermut," the German word for wormwood, a frequent ingredient of vermouth. The "w" in German is pronounced like "v" and "u" as "oo"; hence the natural tendency to change the German spelling in English. The German word is probably based on the alleged beneficial properties of wines containing wormwood. The addition of wormwood to wine appears to date from early Roman and probably early Greek times, although the production of vermouth itself in Italy did not begin until the eighteenth century. The quality and type of vermouth depend upon the quality and nature of the base wine and on the kind, quality, and amounts of the various herbs used. According to Valaer (1950) the formulas for the European-made vermouths are closely guarded secrets, whereas there is less secrecy among the American producers. However, Valaer occupied a privileged position in the Internal Revenue Service. Few producers are willing to divulge their vermouth formulas.

Before passage of the 18th Amendment, only a limited amount of vermouth was produced in the United States; most of that then on the market came from Italy and France. After repeal of the amendment the demand greatly increased and production in America rose accordingly. According to Valaer (1950) California produced about 2,000,000 gallons of vermouth in 1945. New York State is also an important producer of vermouth. Table 42 gives the production for the United States from 1948 to 1970.

TABLE 42

PRODUCTION STATISTICS FOR VERMOUTH AND FLAVORED WINES IN THE UNITED STATES

Fiscal Year	Number of Producers	Production	Number of Producers	Production
		Vermouth		Flavored Wines
1948–1952	181	2,332,100	13[1]	219,440
1953–1957	144	3,345,480	16	451,755
1958–1962	137	4,223,738	53	11,354,169
1963–1967	121	4,996,735	65	16,234,986
1968	100	5,318,075	68	16,251,607
1969	94	5,727,851	70	18,329,177
1970	92	5,503,715	57	27,978,261

Source: Annual reports of U. S. Treasury Department.
[1] Average of 1949–1952.

In 1964 California produced 3,336,626 gallons in 72 establishments and New York State produced 1,629,463 gallons in 22 establishments. The imports of vermouth totaled 4,190,288 gallons in 1964, of which Italy supplied 3,285,092 gallons and France, 877,545 gallons. Other countries supplied only small amounts. Importation from South America, principally Argentina, was of considerable importance during World War II, owing to lack of imports from Italy and France; but it is now of very minor importance. Much of the South American vermouth is made by branches of the European producers or according to their formulas.

Flavored wines, euphemistically and legally called "Special Natural Wines," have come on the market in the past fifteen years in considerable quantities. These are not vermouths and they do not resemble the usual aperitif wines very closely, although classed as such. They represent a new type of wine. They usually contain the same amount of alcohol as dessert wines, 18 to 19 per cent by volume, and are sweeter than dry vermouth but not so sweet as Italian-style sweet vermouth. The natural flavors used for flavoring these wines must be approved by the Alcohol, Tobacco and Firearms Division of the Internal Revenue Service. The flavoring is often mild. Small amounts are also made in other states. These products sell at only slightly higher prices than dessert wines. They are served usually "straight," often with ice ("on the rocks"), rather than as an ingredient of mixed drinks; in that respect differing from vermouth. Recently an increasingly large percentage of the special natural wines have had less than 14 per cent alcohol, some with noticeable carbonation. These "pop" wines are most popular with young people. The regular types often contain citrus or exotic tropical-fruit types of flavors. Analysis of three brands purchased in 1959 were as follows:

Sample	Alcohol	Total Acid as Tartaric	Balling	Color
	Per cent by Vol.	Gm./100 ml.	Degree	
1	20.4	0.66	5.2	Very light
2	20.5	0.65	5.6	Very light
3	20.1	0.66	5.1	Amber

Legal Requirements

Before June, 1936, vermouth made in the United States paid three taxes: (1) that on the wine at the regular rates, (2) a rectification tax of 30 cents per gallon, and (3) a tax on the finished product. Likewise, production of vermouth in wineries was illegal until 1936. Under the provisions of the Liquor Tax Administration Act of 1936 vermouth pays a single tax only, the withdrawal tax, provided it is made by a bonded winery from fortified wine without addition of additional alcohol during manufacture of the vermouth itself. The product must have, according to the regulations, the taste, aroma, and other characteristics generally attributed to vermouth. If vermouth is used in making a cordial it must then pay an additional rectification tax. Distilled spirits may not be added to the previously fortified dessert wine or to the vermouth without payment of a rectifier's tax. However, according to Valaer (1950), the producer may add an essence made with tax-paid brandy. Such essence (brandy extract of herbs) may be made by the vermouth producer or obtained from a manufacturer; but it must be made with tax-paid spirits (usually brandy) or spirits withdrawn tax free. If essence is used it must be declared in the formula. The base wine may be sweetened with grape concentrate or sucrose. See also Bianchini (1940) and Fessler and Jacoby (1949).

Formerly the room or building in which vermouth was made had to be completely separated from the other winery premises; but this requirement now no longer applies and the vermouth may be made in any tank on bonded winery premises. After manufacture the vermouth may be transferred to and stored in any department of the bonded winery. A formula showing the ingredients used, details of process of manufacture, and the alcohol content of the finished product must be filed with the Assistant Regional Commissioner of the Alcohol, Tobacco and Firearms Division of the Internal Revenue Service and the producer must obtain approval before manufacture of vermouth is undertaken. A natural wine must be used in making vermouth or the flavored special natural wines, but such wine may be made with the usual permitted cellar practices.

Production of vermouth in the United States is under the supervision of the Commissioner of Internal Revenue and according to such regulations as he may prescribe. Regulations of the U. S. Treasury Department, Internal Revenue Service (1970) contain the various legal requirements that apply in the production of vermouth (see also pp. 735–736).

A number of botanicals, flavoring substances and natural substances long used in wines have been the subject of new regulations over the last several years. Section 121.90 (a) of the Food Additives Regulations (21 CFR 121) disapproved the use in wines of: *Aloe perryi, A. barba densis, A. ferox*, (and hybrids of this species with *A. africana* and *A. spicata*), *Rocella fuciformis*, boldo leaves (*Peumus boldus*), bryony (*Bryonia alba*), *Acorus calamus*, goldenshower senna (*Cassia fistula*), *Guarea rusbyi, Myosotis* sp., *Phyllitis scolopendrium*, lungwort (*Sticta pulmonaria*), *Spirea ulmaria, Filipendula ulmaria*, yellow melilolt (*Melilotus officinalis*), soapbark extract or China bark extract (*Quillaja saponaria*), red sandalwood (*Ptercarpus santalinus*), starwort (*Aletris farinosa*), *Tanacetum vulgare*, and *Juglans* sp. Calamus may no longer be used.

There appeared to be tacit permission to continue use of these botanicals in vermouth production until more data could be obtained as to their physiological effects. This situation was clarified by publication of a notice in the Federal Register by the Food and Drug Administration (1966) proposing to amend Sec. 112.1163 (b) of the Food Additives Regulations, 21 CFR 121 and later authorized. The amendment permits the use of the previously banned species. In addition, it changed the expression of a stated thujone limitation for wormwood (*Artemisia* sp.), white cedar (*Thuja occidentalis*), oak moss (*Evernia prunastic*), tansy (*Tanacetum vulgare*), and yarrow (*Achillea millefolium*) to thujone-free. The thujone content is to be determined by an analytical method sensitive to at least ten parts per million. The method of the Association of Official Analytical Chemists (1970) or equivalent must be used, e.g. the gas chromatography one of Usseglio-Tomasset (1966). He found 0 to 0.36 and 0 to 0.12 mg. per liter of α- and β-thujone in vermouths.

Herbs and Spices

The herbs and spices used in vermouth are furnished in dry form and represent different parts of various plants such as the seeds, wood, leaves, bark, or roots (see Table 43). Until World War II practically all of the herbs used for vermouth production in the United States were imported, but during the War successful attempts were made to obtain some of the

TABLE 43

SCIENTIFIC, ENGLISH, ITALIAN, AND FRENCH NAMES AND THE PLANT PART USED, OF THE HERBS REQUIRED IN THE MAKING OF VERMOUTH AND RELATED WINES[1]

Common Commercial[2]	Scientific name	Italian[2]	French[2]	Portion of Plant Commonly Used
Allspice	Pimenta dioica or P. officinalis	Pépe garofanato	Piment, tout-épice	Berry
Aloe (socotrine)	Aloë perry[3]	Aloë ordinario	Aloès lucide socotrin	Plant
Angelica	Angelica archangelica	Angelica	Angélique	Root (occasionally seed)
Angostura	Cuspar. febrifuga or galipea	Fave tonke, angustura	Angusture	Bark
Anise	Pimpinella anisum	Anace, anacio	Anis, anis vert	Seed
Benzoin, gum benzoin tree	Styrax benzoin	Benzoino	Benzoin	Gum
Bitter almond	Prunus amygdalus	Mandorle amare	Amande amère	Peel of fruit
Bitter orange[9]	Citrus aurantium var. amara	Arancio amaro	Orange ramer, bigaradier	Seed
Blessed thistle	Cnicus benedictus	Cardo beneditto, larito	Chardon bénit	Aerial portion + seeds
Calamus, sweet flag	Acorus calamus	Acoro aromatico	Acore aromatique	Root
Calumba[7]	Jateorhiza columbo	Columba	Colombo	Root
Cascarilla	Croton eleuteria	Cascariglia, china aromatica	Cascarille	Bark
Cinchona	Cinchona calisaya	China	Quinquina	Bark
Cinnamon	Cinnamomum zeylanicum	Cannella aromatica, etc.	Cannellier de Ceylon	Bark
Clammy sage, common clary	Salvia sclarea	Salvia sclarea, etc.	Sauge sclarée	Flowers and leaves
Clove	Syzygium aromaticum	Garofano	Girofle des moluques[4]	Flower
Coca	Erythroxylon coca	Coca	Coca	Leaves
Common horehound	Marrubium vulgare	Marrobbio	Marrube	Aerial port on
Common hyssop	Hyssopus officinalis	Issopo	Hyssope	Flowering plant
Coriander	Coriandrum sativum	Coriandolo	Coriandre	Seed
Dittany of Crete	Amaracus dictamnus	Dittamo cretico, origano di Creta	Dictane de Crète	Aerial portion + flowers
Elder	Sambucus nigra	Sambuco	Sureau	Flowers (also leaves)
Elecampane, common inula	Inula helenium	Enula campana	Aunée	Root
European centaury	Erythraea centaurium	Centaurea minore	Petite centaurée	Plant
European meadowsweet[5]	Filipendula ulmaria	Ulmaria	Reine des prés	Root
Fennel	Foeniculum vulgare	Finocchio	Fenouil	Seed
Fenugreek	Trigonella foenum-graecum	Fieno greco	Fénugrec	Seed
Fraxinella, gasplant	Dictamnus albus	Dittamo	Dictame	Root
Galangal, galingale	Alpinia officinarum	Galanga minore	Galanga mineur	Root
Gentian	Gentiana lutea	Genziana maggiore	Grand gentiane	Root
Germander	Teucrium chamaedrys	Camendrio, querciola	Germandrée, petite chêne	Plant
Ginger	Zingiber officinale	Zenzero	Gingembre	Root
Hart's tongue	Phyllitis scolopendrium	Lingua cervina	Scolopendre	Plant
Hop	Humulus lupulus	Luppolo	Houblon	Aerial portion + flowers
Lemon balm, common balm	Melissa officinalis	Melissa, cedronella	Mélisse	Flowering plant
Lesser cardamom	Elettaria cardamomum	Cardamomo	Cardamome mineur[4]	Dried fruit
Lung wort, sage of Bethlehem	Pulmonaria officinalis or P. saccharata	Polmonaria	Pulmonaire	Aerial portion + flowers
Lungwort lichen, lung moss	Sticta polmonacea	Lichene pulmonario	?	Plant (a lichen)
Marjoram	Origanum vulgare	Origano	Origan	Aerial portion + flowers
Masterwort, hog's fennel	Peucedanum ostruthium	Imperatoria	Impératoire	Root
Nutmeg, and mace	Myristica fragrans	Noce moscata, macia	Muscadier, noix muscade	Seed
Orris, Florentine iris	Iris germanica var. florentina	Iride fiorentina, giaggiolo	Iris de Florence	Root
Pomegranate	Punica granatum	Melegrano, granato	Grenadier	Bark of root
Quassia	Quassia amara	Quassio, legnuo qassio	Quassia	Wood

English	Latin	Italian	French	Part used
Quinine fungus	Fomes officinalis	Agarico bianco	Agaric blanc	Plant
Rhubarb	Rheum rhaponticum	Rabarbaro	Rhubarbe	Root
Roman camomile	Anthemis nobilis	Camomilla odorosa	Camomille romaine	Flowers
Roman wormwood	Artemisia pontica	Assenzio pontico[6]	Absinthe pontique (petite absinthe)	Plant
Rosemary, old man	Rosmarinus officinalis	Rosmarino	Rosmarin	Flowering plant
Saffron, crocus	Crocus sativus	Zafferano	Safran	Portion of flower
Sage	Salvia officinalis	Salvia	Sauge	Aerial portion + flowers
Savory (summer)	Satureja hortensis	Cerea, santoreggio	Sarriette	Aerial portion of plant
Speedwell	Veronica officinalis	Veronica	Véronique mâle, thé d'Europe	Plant ?
Star anise	Illicium verum	Anacio stellato	Anis étiole, badiane	Seed
Sweet marjoram	Marjorana hortensis	Maggiorana	Marjolaine, amaracus	Aerial portion + flowers
Thyme, garden thyme[8]	Thymus vulgaris	Timo	Thym	Leaf
Valerian	Valeriana officinalis	Valeriana minore	Valériane, herbe aux chats	Root
Vanilla	Vanilla fragrans	Vaniglia	Vanillier légume[4]	Bean
Wormwood	Artemesia absinthium	Assenzio maggiore	Grande absinthe, absinthe amère	Plant
Yarrow	Achillea millefolium	Achillea	Achillée	Plant
Zedoary, setwell, curcum	Curcuma zedoaria	Zeodoaria	Zedoaire	Root

[1] Source of data: Joslyn and Amerine, 1964.
[2] Many local synonyms and divergent spellings have been omitted; for additional names in each language see: Bedevain, A. Illustrated polyglottic dictionary of plant names. Argus and Papazian Presses, Cairo, Egypt. 1936. Hoare, A. An Italian dictionary. Cambridge University Press, Cambridge, England. 1925.
[3] Aloë vera and A. feros are other aloes which are sometimes used.
[4] Preferred.
[5] Possibly same as the commercial "Queen of the Meadows" (Eupatorum purpurum).
[6] Assenzio gentile is the same as or a similar wormwood cultivated primarily in the Piedmont district of Italy. Artemesia vallesiaca (assenzio gentile alpino) is usually confused with A. pontica. For a discussion of the various wormwoods and their uses see: Mattirolo (1915) and Balzac (1915).
[7] Also spelled colombo, columbo, and calumbo.
[8] Thymus serpyllum (timo serpillo, Italian) also used.
[9] The peel of sweet oranges is also used.

TABLE 44

COMPOSITION OF DRY AND SWEET VERMOUTH[1]

Source	Number of Samples	Alcohol Per cent			Extract Gm./100 Ml.			Total Acid Gm./100 Ml.			Tannin Gm./100 Ml.		
		Min.	Max.	Avg.	Min.	Max.	Avg.	Min.	Max.	Avg.	Min.	Max.	Avg.
Dry													
France (a)	6	17.4	19.3	18.3	3.7	6.1	4.8	0.55	0.66	0.61	0.05	0.08	0.07
United States (a)	77	15.0	22.0	17.7	1.4	7.9	3.8	0.31	0.66	0.50	0.03	0.07	0.04
Sweet													
Italy (a)	20	15.5	17.1	16.1	14.9	20.7	18.6	0.36	0.52	0.28	0.058	0.110	...
Italy (b)	10	13.7	16.9	15.7	14.0	17.2	15.6	0.36	0.52	0.45	0.05	0.11	0.08
United States	100	14.0	21.0	17.1	10.0	19.0	13.8	0.26	0.63	0.45	0.03	0.10	0.06

[1] Sources of data: (a) Valaer (1950) and (b) Rizzo (1957).

herbs from plants growing wild and to grow some of the others in this country. Considerable quantities of these are now grown in the United States, although most of the herbs and spices now used are imported. Some species are obtained from the tropics and others from the Near East, but most from European countries such as Italy, France, and Belgium.

Information on the classification of the more important herbs and spices used in vermouth production is given by Pilone (1954) as bitter, aromatic, or bitter-aromatic. Bitter plants include aloe, angelica, blessed thistle, cinchona, European centaury, germander, lungwort, lungmoss, quassia, and rhubarb. Aromatic plants are anise, bitter almond, cardamom cinnamon, clove, coriander, dittany of Crete, galingale, marjoram, nutmeg, Roman, camomile, rosemary, summer savory, thyme, tonka bean, and vanilla bean. The bitter-aromatic plants include allspice, elder, elecampane, gentian, juniper, bitter orange, sweet orange, saffron, sage, sweet flag, speedwell, wormwood (common), wormwood (gentile), wormwood (pontico), and yarrow.

The major flavoring constituents of the herbs and spices used in vermouth manufacture have been given by Brévans (1920) as follows:

1. Hydrocarbons (such as styrol, cymene, pinene, and other terpenes)
2. Aldehydes (such as citral, citronellal, furfural, benzoic aldehyde, vanillin, cinnamaldehyde)
3. Ketones (such as methyl heptenone, carvone, luparone, thujone)
4. Lactones (such as alantolactone)
5. Oxides (such as cineole or eucalyptol)
6. Phenols and phenol derivatives (such as luparol, thymol, cadinone, caryophyllene)
7. Alcohols, particularly terpenic alcohols (such as calamenol, citronellol, borneol, anethol, eugenol, terpineol, safrol)
8. Alkaloids (such as quinine, cusparine, absotin)
9. Glucosides (such as absinthin, gratiolin, quassin, aloin)
10. Saccharides (such as gentinose)
11. Tannins
12. Coloring matters
13. Gums and pectins
14. Resins (such as humulon)
15. Esters (such as amyl valerianate)
16. Simple acids (such as citric)
17. Complex acids (such as angelic, alantolic)

A comprehensive list of the plants used in vermouth production and their scientific, English, Italian, and French names has been compiled by Joslyn and Amerine (1964). Since vermouth formulas often use the Italian or French instead of the English or scientific names, Joslyn and Amerine's table of synonyms is reproduced here as Table 43.

An even more complete list has been published by Lazarus (1965). In some cases the scientific names of his list differ from those in Table 43. These differences probably arise from changing taxonomic classifications of botanists rather than to the different herbs. See also Morini (1955), Ottavio and Garina-Canina (1930), Scurti and Tacchini (1916), Twining Laboratories (1941) and Valvassori (1954).

The herbs and spices are usually purchased in dried form. Therefore, quality will be affected by the care given them in harvesting and storage. They should be purchased only from a reliable supplier who furnishes products of the highest quality. Specimens of the same variety of plant grown under different climatic or cultural conditions may differ markedly in character and quality. The longer the dried products are stored before use, the poorer will be their flavor and aroma, as these depend to a great extent on volatile compounds that slowly evaporate during storage. Furthermore staling of the flavor through oxidation and other chemical reactions occur during storage. For these reasons, the dried herbs and spices should be as fresh as possible. During prolonged storage, insects may infest the dried products and render them completely unfit for use in vermouth. If the moisture content of the storage room or of the dried products during storage is too high, molding is apt to occur with more or less damage to quality. Fumigation at suitable intervals with methyl bromide or other effective fumigant is advisable to control insects if the products are to be stored for an appreciable period. If they are in tightly sealed containers such as friction top cans, jars, or moisture proof plastic bags, observation must be made occasionally to make certain that moisture has not distilled from the product and condensed on the walls of the package or on the product causing a local rise in moisture content with resultant spoilage by mold. Vermouth producers should carefully inspect all herbs offered for sale before purchase.

It is preferable to purchase the dried plant materials in the whole form, as they can be examined more satisfactorily than if powdered or in granular form. When the whole plant is available it is easier to determine whether the material is from an old or new crop. Also, the storage life of the powdered and granular products is shorter than that of the whole materials because volatilization of flavor and aroma is more rapid from ground material.

There seems to be an increasing use of fluid and solid extracts, concretes, absolutes, oils, gums, balms, resins, oleoresins, waxes, and distillates in the production of vermouth. These may be used in amounts not to exceed the amount reasonably required to accomplish their intended physical, nutritional or other technical effect. Microscopic detection of impurities in or falsification of *Artemesia absinthium* with other *Artemesia* or with *Achillea* is described by Griebel (1955).

Methods of Flavoring Base Wine

A variety of procedures for extraction of flavors and their addition to the wine have been employed.

Direct Extraction.—The simplest method of flavoring the base wine for vermouth is by placing weighed amounts of the herbs and spices in the wine and leaving them until the wine has absorbed the desired flavors and aromas. The plant materials may be finely ground or in granular form to hasten extraction. However, some producers believe that undesirable flavoring and odorous constituents are more apt to be taken up by the wine if the herbs and spices are in powdered form. During extraction the wine is usually circulated or stirred at frequent intervals. The wine may be heated to 140°F., or applied at room temperature, extraction naturally being more rapid at the higher temperature. The extraction period is usually two weeks or longer if the wine is not heated. The extraction tank should be covered to minimize excessive loss of volatile flavors and aromas. The herbs and spices may be placed in cloth bags and these suspended in the wine. After the first extraction fresh base wine may be used for a second and even a third extraction. Partial extraction is preferable to the complete because the latter may dissolve substances of undesirable flavor or aroma. The spent materials should not be pressed to secure the residual flavoring and aromatic substances because this will extract objectionable bitter flavors.

Concentrates.—Instead of directly flavoring a large lot of wine in the above manner it is more common to prepare a smaller volume of more concentrated extract. This is often done by placing the herbs and spices in a special vessel outside the extraction tank and circulating the wine by pump from the tank through the herbs in the extraction vessel until most of the desired substances have been extracted. According to Pilone (1954) the wine is usually heated during extraction. This extract may then be used to flavor a relatively large volume of base wine.

For sweet (Italian style) vermouth, according to Joslyn and Amerine (1964), 0.5 to 1 oz. of mixed dry flavoring materials per gallon of base wine is sufficient to give the best flavor. At much higher concentrations the vermouth will be too strong in flavor. These amounts are for each gallon of the final vermouth, regardless of the method of flavoring (direct or by addition of extract). For dry (French style) vermouth the amount is less, about 0.5 oz. of the herb and spice mixture per gallon of wine. One kilogram per hectoliter (100 liters) is equivalent to 1.27 ozs. per gallon.

Hot water has also been used to prepare a concentrated extract used in flavoring the base wine for vermouth. Water extracts different substances from the herbs and spices than does alcohol or wine. If the herbs and spices are softened by a short immersion in hot water it is said they may then be more readily extracted with wine or brandy (Joslyn and Amerine 1964).

Jacoby (1948) has suggested that a "library" may be made up by placing a weighed amount of each herb and spice in a bottle, such as a fifth-gallon bottle, and filling with the base wine. After standing for a month or more with frequent shaking, measured portions of these extracts can be used to flavor a measured small volume of base wine (such as 1000 ml.). By varying the amounts of each extract a vermouth of the desired flavor and aroma can theoretically be approximated. On the basis of such laboratory scale tests one should be able to make up a commercial quantity of vermouth.

Other Extraction Methods.—Brandy or alcohol extracts are available from reputable manufacturers of essences and flavoring materials. These may be used alone to flavor a commercial lot of base wine for vermouth, or they are more often used in small amounts to balance or "round out" the flavor of a lot of base wine previously flavored by direct extraction of the herbs and spices or one that has been flavored by the addition of concentrated wine extract. In this manner vermouths produced at different times can be matched fairly closely.

Joslyn and Amerine (1964) have stated that in Turin, Italy, an alcoholic extract is preferred. Six kilograms of the herbs are allowed to infuse for eight days in 10 liters of 85 per cent alcohol. This alcoholic extract is mixed with 18 liters of alcohol and 7 liters of white wine. The combined liquids are then distilled to 18 liters residual volume. This residue is cooled and allowed to stand 15 days with frequent stirring. It is used at the rate of 1.5 to 2 liters per hectoliter of base wine.

According to Valaer (1950), a method at one time used by a large American producer of vermouth for preparing an extract consisted in macerating a mixture of herbs in sherry material at 140°F., cooling and allowing to stand for 3 to 6 weeks. The wine was then removed, the herbs covered with hot wine, and allowed to stand ten days. This wine was blended with the first extract. The blend was used to flavor base wine for vermouth. In our opinion the use of a baked sherry as a base does not produce vermouth of highest quality.

Valaer states that in 1950 the use of commercial extracts was common. The extracts were used according to the manufacturers' directions. A small amount of quinine may sometimes be included in the extract or essence in addition to that extracted from the cinchona bark of many vermouth formulas. The amount of material extracted from the herbs and spices is small and affects the basic composition of the wine only slightly.

Valaer (1950) states that the Federal Regulations allow a maximum of one-tenth of one per cent of thujone extracted from wormwood. Kasakova (1958) has recommended that for making vermouth in Russia the herbs be extracted first with a wine and brandy mixture of 50 per cent alcohol content for 10 days, then with wine for 5 days. A moderate amount of heating can be employed according to this investigator.

Bo and Filice (1948) give the following as the preferred method of flavoring sweet vermouth. Based on preliminary laboratory experiments the herbs and spices each in the proper amount are weighed and mixed. About five per cent of the base wine is heated to 140°F. and pumped into the extraction tank and the dry flavoring materials are then added and the tank tightly closed. After 24 hours the remainder of the wine is added at cellar temperature and left with circulation once daily for seven days. The wine is then separated from the herbs and spices and filtered. The sugar content is increased to the desired level by addition of sucrose.

While foreign manufacturers are reported to have discovered how to extract the maximum flavor from herbs and spices this does not have appeared to be the case in this country, otherwise so many systems of extraction would not be employed. On the other hand, different herbs and spices may require different extraction systems, but no systematic studies have been made upon them.

ITALIAN-TYPE (SWEET) VERMOUTH

Sweet vermouth is produced in Italy, Spain, Argentina, and other countries as well as in the United States. At one time, most of the sweet vermouth consumed in the United States was imported but in 1959, the volume of that produced in this country was nearly one and one-half times that of the imported. For a description of the Italian industry see Rossati (1934), Cotone (1922) and others. Typical analyses are given in Table 44.

Italian Methods

A typical Italian vermouth is that of Martini and Rossi. It is dark amber in color, with a light muscat, sweet nutty flavor and a well-developed and pleasing fragrance. It has a generous and warming taste, and a slightly bitter but agreeable aftertaste. According to Rizzo (1957) and Walter (1956) vermouth made in Italy must contain at least 15.5 per cent of alcohol and 13 per cent or more of reducing sugar. American vermouths are higher in alcohol and usually somewhat lower in sugar than the Italian.

Formerly the preferred base wine in Italy was a fortified wine with a muscat flavor, such as that of the Muscat blanc produced from grapes grown in Piedmont of northern Italy. Nowadays other white wines are used. Among these are those of southern Italy that are more neutral in flavor than those of Piedmont. The vermouth made from these wines is said to age more quickly and to be easier to clarify. In Turin the base wine is usually flavored with an alcohol extract of various herbs and spices. Those most commonly used are, according to Joslyn and Amerine (1964), wormwood, coriander, bitter orange peel, Roman wormwood, cinchona, European centaury, calamus, elder flowers, angelica, orris, gentian cinnamon, cloves, nutmeg, and cardamon. See Table 43 for the Italian, French, English, and botanical names of these plants. Sweetening is done with sucrose or liquid invert sugar of over 60° Brix. Caramel is reported by various authorities to be added to vermouth in Italy to give or reinforce the customary dark color of their sweet vermouths. It is strange, therefore, that Valaer (1950) did not find caramel in any imported sweet vermouth samples analyzed by him.

In France, Joslyn and Amerine (1964) state the base wine was usually flavored by direct maceration of the herbs and spices rather than by the addition of an alcohol extract (Turin method). About 0.5 to 1 oz. of the mixed herbs per gallon are allowed to macerate in the wine for one or two weeks, with stirring or pumping over once a day. The wine is tasted periodically during extraction and at the first sign of any excessive bitterness or "herbaceous" character the wine is drawn off and filtered. However, Ferrarese (1951) states that essences and extracts are more often used now than direct extraction of the herbs in wine.

Aging and Finishing

In Italy and France the wine used for manufacture of vermouth is reputed to be at least one year of age. After flavoring the vermouth is aged about 4.5 years or longer, according to Valaer (1950). In both France and Italy, he states, the length of time between infusion of the herbs and spices and final bottling is usually 3 to 5 years. The new vermouth is refrigerated to cold stabilize it. It is then filtered and aged. It is again filtered before bottling. In our opinion, such long aging lowers the quality of the vermouth and we doubt if such is the present practice.

California Methods

The base wine used for making sweet vermouth in California is a fortified sweet wine of light color such as a new angelica or white port. It should contain enough muscatel to impart a recognizable muscat flavor, but this is by no means general industry practice. Red port wine is also permitted at present as a base wine for manufacture of vermouth. The base wine should be analyzed for copper and iron content and any excess

TABLE 45

HERB MIXTURES IN SWEET VERMOUTH FORMULAS[1]

Herbs	Amount Used Per Hectoliter (100 Liters) of Wine Base							
	No. 1 Grams	No. 2 Grams	No. 3 Grams	No. 4 Grams	No. 5 Grams	No. 6 Grams	No. 7 Grams	No. 8 Grams
Angelica	..	60	6	44	30	..	36	..
Bitter orange peel	..	250	50	..	58	60	..	50
Blessed thistle	..	135	..	..	..	60	100	..
Calamus	22	150	40	86	..	60	96	80
Cinchona	..	150	30	..	..	500	80	80
Cinnamon	22	100	15	..	72	..	..	50
Clammy sage	33	..	..	60	60	100	..	..
Clove	22	50	2	36	24	..	20	20
Coriander	112	500	100	76	84	25	76	70
Elder	..	200	..	90	90	100	..	..
Elecampane	..	125	50	80	70	500	..	50
European centaury	..	135	12	..	..	60	..	40
Galingale	..	50	..	..	..	100	..	40
Gentian	..	..	50	..	..	100	..	..
Germander	..	125	..	..	..	100	..	..
Lesser cardamon	..	..	12	..	..	..	..	..
Mace	..	..	6	..	56	..	..	..
Marjoram	..	..	..	70	70	..	84	..
Nutmeg	17	50	..	..	80	25	70	..
Orris	..	250	..	60	..	..	..	..
Quassia	..	30	..	..	..	..	..	50
Roman wormwood	50	..	..	..	..	60	..	..
Saffron	..	..	..	10	10	..	2	2
Wormwood	56	124	..	200	240	..	180	180

Additional constituents:
No. 1, 56 grams of thyme; 167 grams sweet marjoram; 50 grams angostura; 67 grams savory.
No. 3, 6 grams allspice.
No. 4, 16 grams anise; 50 grams lemon balm; 60 grams sweet marjoram; 76 grams masterwort; 50 grams zedoary.
No. 5, 12 grams Roman camomile; 64 grams masterwort; 80 grams hops.
No. 6, 25 grams angostura; 25 grams yarrow.
No. 7, 66 grams sage; 70 grams hop flowers.
No. 8, 70 grams zedoary; 40 grams quinine fungus; 30 grams each benzoin and sage; 70 grams common hyssop; 16 grams star anise; 80 grams germander.
[1] Sources of data:
Bennet 1935, Cotone (1922), Dober (1927), Hopkins (1921), Marescalchi (1943), Rizzo (1957), and Sebastian (1909).

of either metal removed by fining with Cufex or given other permissible treatment. Copper is especially likely to cause clouding of the bottled product. If the wine is too low in sugar, grape concentrate or sucrose in the form of a syrup of not less than 60° Balling may be used to sweeten vermouth in California. In other states dry sucrose may be used. The total amount of water may not exceed 10 per cent of the volume of the vermouth. Citric acid may be used if the total acidity is too low. The alcohol content must be high enough to allow for dilution when extracts low in alcohol are employed for flavoring. The final alcohol content of the sweet vermouth is usually in the neighborhood of 17 per cent, the total extract (total soluble solids) about 13 to 14 per cent, total acidity expressed as tartaric about 0.45 per cent, and tannin about 0.04 per cent. Caramel syrup is added if the color is not dark enough. Jacoby (1948) has recommended that grape concentrate darkened by heating in the open to a boiling point of 238° to 240°F. be used instead of caramel to darken the color. At present American consumers do not demand as deep a color in sweet vermouth as formerly. Tannic acid may be added if the tannin content is too low. Jacoby (1948) has stated that pectinous materials may cause slow filtration but can be removed by treatment with a pectic enzyme as described elsewhere. This should be confirmed by laboratory tests in each case (see p. 315). See also Cavalli (1946).

Joslyn and Amerine (1964) state that pasteurization, refrigeration, and filtration are usually sufficient to stabilize the vermouth. Persistent cloudiness may develop (Luckow 1937) on refrigeration if licorice or catechu are used. If these are used they should be extracted separately, the extract diluted, cooled, allowed to settle, and then filtered before addition to the wine base. Joslyn and Amerine (1964) state that prolonged aging is not desirable because of possible loss of aroma by volatilization and oxidation. Jacoby (1948) recommends that the vermouth be aged about three months before filtration. As previously stated, American vermouths are not aged so long as the European. No good experiments in this country are known to the authors as to the quality of vermouth after various aging periods. Economic demands more than quality considerations may dictate practice. This is particularly true with our dry vermouth where a very mild herb character and nearly water-white color are common owing to the use of this wine in cocktails.

Formulas.—One of the formulas given in Table 45 can be used as a starting point and the vermouth then balanced or adjusted to the desired flavor and aroma by addition of a small amount of a commercial essence or extract or by modifying the amounts of the ingredients. Following the table the amounts of various additional herbs and spices required for each formula are given. The table contains formulas for sweet vermouth (see Table 46 for the dry vermouth formulas). According to Joslyn and Amerine (1964) none of the formulas gives products that closely approach the imported vermouths in flavor and aroma. However, according to Fessler (1959) and others familiar with American methods, producers no longer attempt to duplicate the imported vermouths, but aim to manufacture a product that is uniform in character from year to year and that possesses a pleasing but rather distinctive flavor and aroma. The present demand is for dry vermouth of relatively light flavor; that is, one that is not heavily flavored with herbs and spices. However, sweet vermouth should be more highly flavored.

Finishing.—Pilone (1954) strongly recommends that the pH be adjusted to a sufficiently low level to prevent spoilage and that the sulfur dioxide content be sufficiently high for the same reason. We have seen sweet vermouth made in California that had been spoiled by *Lactobacillus trichodes* ("the hair bacillus"). It is easily controlled by maintaining a total sulfur dioxide content of above 75 p.p.m.

FRENCH-TYPE (DRY) VERMOUTH

Dry vermouths are usually not only much lower in sugar content and lighter in color than the sweet, but also are often higher in alcohol content and sometimes more bitter in flavor. A typical analysis of a popular French dry vermouth, that of Noilly Prat of Marseille, is, according to Joslyn and Amerine (1964), alcohol 18 per cent by volume, reducing sugar 4 per cent, total acidity, as tartaric, 0.65 gm. per 100 ml. and volatile acidity as acetic, 0.053 gm. per 100 ml. It is more difficult to produce a dry vermouth that closely resembles the imported than to produce a sweet vermouth that approximates the imported (see also Valaer's analyses given in Table 44).

European Methods

It will be noted from the formulas for a dry vermouth given in Table 46, that they call for much larger amounts of wormwood and bitter orange peel than do those for sweet vermouth. Note also that in formula 3 for dry vermouth aloe, a bitter herb, is recommended as an additional ingredient. In France, according to Sichel (1945), a white wine of the Herault region is preferred and may be blended with white wine made from the Grenache variety of grapes grown elsewhere. The wine must be sound, of light color and one of moderate acidity is preferred. It is fortified with good quality high proof brandy to about 18 per cent alcohol content. Schoonmaker and Marvel (1935) state that the wine to be used in France for dry vermouth production is aged in butts in the open until it acquires a flavor similar to that of an unbaked dry sherry. This practice is no longer prevalent.

Valaer (1950) states that a fewer number of herbs and spices are used in the French than in the Italian vermouth and a smaller quantity of these flavoring materials per unit of wine is customary, about 0.5 oz. per gallon. He reports that one method in use in France is the following:

The herbs are placed in the extraction tank and covered with fortified wine of about 18 per cent alcohol content and left for 30 to 40 days. The wine is then drawn off and the extraction repeated several times with fresh wine. The extracts are combined and base wine is added in sufficient amount to dilute the flavor the desired amount. The blended vermouth is then refrigerated and filtered. *Mistelle,* grape juice preserved with alcohol, or *muté,* grape juice preserved with sulfur dioxide, is added to give the desired amount of reducing sugar. In the formulas for dry vermouth given in Table 46 the lack of coriander, cinnamon, and clove as well as inclusion of large amounts of wormwood should be noted. One of the formulas given in the table may be used as a starting point

TABLE 46

HERB MIXTURES IN DRY VERMOUTH FORMULAS[1]

Herbs	Amount Used per Hectoliter (100 Liters) of Wine Base				
	No. 1	No. 2	No. 3	No. 4	No. 5
	Grams	Grams	Grams	Grams	Grams
Angelica	..	60	..	75	..
Bitter orange peel	1000	350	200	75	400
Blessed thistle	300	125	200	150	500
Calamus	..	150	..	150	..
Cinchona	..	..	200	..	750
Cinnamon	10	..	..	..	..
Clammy sage	..	..	..	..	..
Elder	..	..	50	200	..
Elecampane	..	..	..	150	..
European centaury	800	150	50	150	..
Gentian	..	..	..	75	..
Germander	..	50	50	150	..
Lesser cardamon	100	..	..	..	..
Marjoram	..	..	100	..	..
Nutmeg	10	..	..	75	..
Orris	100	..	160	..	400
Quassia	..	15	..	..	..
Roman wormwood	..	..	200	..	..
Wormwood	1000	35	200	150	1000

Additional constituents:
No. 1, 250 grams Roman camomile; 5 grams socotrine aloe; 40 ml. of an infusion of raspberries; some muscat wine or elder flowers.
No. 2, 25 grams vanilla extract; 125 grams speedwell; 50 grams rosemary; 25 grams Chinese rhubarb.
No. 3, 200 grams each of speedwell and lungwort; 24 grams Chinese rhubarb.
No. 4, 200 grams of peach pits.
No. 5, 450 grams lungwort; 300 grams elder flowers.
[1] Sources of data: Same as for sweet vermouth formulas (see Table 45).

and modified by changing the proportions of the ingredients or by the addition of small amounts of essence until the desired flavor is obtained.

California Methods

Joslyn and Amerine (1964) state that most California wine makers prefer to use a neutral sauterne-type wine as the base for dry vermouth. It is usually made by fortifying a lot of sauterne low in sulfur dioxide content to 24 per cent alcohol content and then mixing the fortified wine with a sauterne of 12 to 14 per cent alcohol content to give a blend containing 18 to 18.5 per cent of alcohol. The dry vermouths made at present in America are very pale in color and rather lightly flavored. If the color of the wine is darker than desired it is treated with decolorizing carbon. However, the federal regulations require that the color not be reduced below

0.5 Lovibond. By careful production practices it is possible to produce wine lighter than 0.5 Lovibond in color. Carbon should not be used in vermouth itself, but only in the wine, because carbon absorbs the herb flavoring and aromatic compounds.

Pilone (1954) emphasizes that the wine be made from grapes that are well balanced in acidity and sugar content and that produce wines that are not subject to oxidative deterioration in color and flavor. Joslyn and Amerine (1964) state that better American dry vermouth would be produced if a wine of higher natural acidity were used. Casein fining will reduce the color of vermouth without removing an appreciable amount of flavor or aroma. Gelatin fining can be employed to remove excess tannin. The wine should be fortified with neutral, high proof brandy. Pilone recommends that a sherry not be used in the base wine as its cooked taste will mask the flavor of the vermouth. Uniformity of the final product is essential. Usually a young wine is used, as aging darkens the color and develops an aged flavor. This may tend to mask the flavor of a high quality dry vermouth. Pilone (1954) states that it may be advisable to ferment the base wine to dryness, i.e., very low sugar content and to sweeten with sucrose (cane or beet sugar), as experience shows that sucrose "brings out" and does not mask the flavor and aroma of vermouth as much as does grape concentrate or *mistelle*.

Caramel is usually not needed in dry vermouth as the color of the wine is usually deep enough; and, in fact, often too deep. For the same reason dry vermouth for the present market should not be aged very long, but finished and bottled young. This is in contrast with French practice, in which the dry vermouth may be aged three years before bottling. In producing a dry vermouth in California an extract or spice and herb essence prepared in one of the manners previously described may be used to flavor the base wine instead of direct maceration of the herbs in the base wine. Joslyn and Amerine (1964) state that a water extract is preferable for flavoring French vermouth, although this is seldom used at present. Dry vermouth should not be of low total acidity and is usually 0.10 to 0.15 per cent higher in total acidity than is sweet vermouth. Dry vermouth may be made up according to one of the formulas given in Table 46 and balanced by the addition of the required amount of a commercial extract or essence to give a vermouth of the desired flavor and aroma. However, the use of such extract or essence must appear in the formula approved by the Internal Revenue Service. As with the sweet vermouth the pH value and sulfur dioxide content should be at such levels that spoilage by *L. trichodes* is prevented (see Chapter 16 on bacterial spoilage).

Maintaining the light color of dry vermouth is essential for the American market. Wright (1960) recommended using as little herbs as possible without adversely affecting the flavor, storage at 35°F., bottling at or above 60°F. to reduce oxygen solubility, and a sulfur dioxide level of 100 mg. per liter or greater. Vermouths stored for four months at 68° or 86°F. were definitely inferior to those held at 35°F.

According to Halász (1958) Hungarian vermouth is made with the following herbs (per hectoliter, 26.4 gallons): wormwood, 100–150 gm.; European centaury, 70 gm.; bitter orange peel, 35 gm.; lemon juice, 17 gm.; rhyzome (*Rhizoma calmi*), 17 gm.; cinnamon, 17 gm.; clove, 8 gm.; coriander, 8 gm.; sweet mustard meal (*Sinapsis alba*), 130 gm.; bitter mustard meal (*Sinapsis nigra*), 70 gm.; calamus (*Acorus calamus*), 17 gm.; and star anise, 8 gm. *Sinapsis alba* is white mustard and *S. nigra* is the black.

Composition of Vermouth

Analyses of imported and domestic vermouths by Valaer (1950) and by Rizzo (1957) are given in Table 44.

NON-VERMOUTH TYPES

According to Valaer (1950), Federal Regulations state that aperitif wine is a grape wine containing grape spirit or added alcohol and having an alcohol content of not less than 15 per cent by volume. It is flavored with herbs, spices, fruit juices, natural aromatic flavoring materials natural essences or other natural materials and processed in such manner that the final product possesses a distinctive flavor, and may be distinguished from natural wine not so treated. Retsina wine produced by the addition of resin may enjoy the same privileges under the regulations as do aperitif wines and like the latter may be made on bonded wine premises.

Dubonnet is now made in the United States by the French formula and is probably the most important of the European-type aperitif wines. Others made in Europe and imported in rather small amounts are Byrrh, Campari, Bonal, Amer Picon and Cap Corse, all of which are made with red wine and St. Raphaël, made with white wine. The aperitif wines are often more bitter than vermouth but are usually flavored with a smaller number of herbs and spices. See Latronico (1947) on other flavored wines.

Garino-Canina (1934) gives the composition of two well-known aperitif wines as follows:

	Byrrh	Dubonnet
Alcohol, volume per cent	18.1	16.2
Extract, gm. per 100 ml.	13.7	18.8
Total acid, gm. per 100 ml.	0.49	0.47
pH value	3.30	3.42
Alkaloid, gm. per 100 ml.	0.005	0.095
Tannin, gm. per 100 ml.	0.12	0.15

Aperitif wines containing quinine, and so labeled, are made in Europe and South America, but have not proven popular in the United States. They are quite bitter. Methods of determining the quinine, an alkaloid, have been developed by Garelik (1953), and by Bonastre (1955). Some formulas recommend as much as 25 gm. of cinchona bark (the usual source of quinine) per gallon of wine but present federal regulations limit them to not more than 83 mg. per liter of total cinchona alkaloids in the finished beverage. Vanilla, angostura, and cinnamon are listed in some formulas. The wines are slightly sweet and quite bitter and are popular in France, when served either "straight" or with soda.

Special Natural Wines

Under the provisions of Public Law 85–859 of September 2, 1958, a new type of wine was provided for—special natural. These are products produced by the use of approved formulas with a natural wine base (including heavy-bodied blending wine). Natural herbs, spices, fruit juices, aromatics, essences, and other natural flavorings may be used in such quantities as to enable such products to be distinguished from any natural wine not so treated. The regulations are that sugar or liquid sugar, water and caramel may be employed. Since sugar may not be used to produce a "California" wine they are designated as "American" wine.

These new types of wines have had a spectacular acceptance by the American market. They have all been labeled with proprietary names such as Thunderbird, Silver Satin, Pagan Pink, Golden Spur, Key Largo, Bali Hai, Spanada, and Eden Roc, among many. Not all the new types, however, have achieved lasting popularity. Several, after a momentary popularity have disappeared. A few have gained consumer acceptance in some areas but not in others. Some of these wines are made with wine that is very light in color, but several are amber in color. The composition of three different brands of these wines is given earlier in this chapter. (See p. 504.)

The most interesting aspect of these wine types is their difference from traditional types. They are obviously intended to enlarge the basis of wine sales by attracting the non-wine drinking public. This seems to have been achieved as shown by the rapid increase in sales of special natural wines, much of which is under 14 per cent alcohol (Table 42 and p. 504). It is believed that they have increased consumption not only of special natural wines but also of the traditional non-flavored types.

Several flavor houses supply a variety of natural flavors for producing these types of wines.

BIBLIOGRAPHY

BALZAC, F. 1915. Le artemisie dei Vermouths e dei Génépis. Ann. R. Accad. Agr. Torino 58, 279–303.

BENNET, H. 1935. The Chemical Formulary. Vol. II. D. Van Nostrand Co., New York.

BIANCHINI, L. N. 1940. Vermouth. Problems confronting its manufacture in America. Wine Review 8, No 12, 20, 21.

BO, M. J., and FILICE, M. J. 1948. Gold medal sweet vermouth. Wines and Vines 29 (8), 27–29.

BONASTRE, J. 1955. Evaluation de la quinine des quinquinas asperitifs par chromatographie sur papier. Ann. fals et. fraudes 48, 109–113.

BRÉVANS, J. de. 1920. Le Fabrication des Liqueurs. 4 ed. J.-B. Baillière et Fils, Paris.

CAVALLI, M. 1946. Practical notes on vermouth production. Wines and Vines 27, No. 5, 23, 25–27.

COTONE, D. A. 1922. Vino Vermouth ed i Suoi Componenti. Casa Editrice F. Marescalchi, Casale Monferrato.

DOBER , W. 1927. Formulario para la Fabricación de Licores por Destilación y sin Destilación. Casa Editorial Araluse, Barcelona.

FERRARESE, M. 1951. Enologia Practica Moderna. Ulrico Hoepli, Milan.

FESSLER, J. H. 1959. Personal communication.

FESSLER, J. H., and JACOBY, O. F. 1949. Vermouth. Its production and future. Wines and Vines 30, No. 12, 15–17.

FOOD AND DRUG ADMINISTRATION. 1965. Food additives regulations. Washington. 21 Code of Federal Regulations, section 121.90(a).

GARELIK, A. 1953. Analisis de vinos quinados. Anales nacl. direc. quím. 6, No. 11, 20–21.

GARINO-CANINA, E. 1934. Vini aperitivi francesi. Annuar. R. staz. enol. sper. Asti 1, 223–233.

GRIEBEL, C. 1955. Gemahlene Wermutkräuter Z. Lebensm. -Untersuch u. -Forsch. 100, 270–274.

HALÁSZ, Z. 1958. Voyage Autour des Vins Hongrois. Corvina, Budapest.

HOPKINS, A. A. 1921. The Scientific American Cyclopedia of Formulas. Scientific American Pub. Co., New York.

JACOBY, O. F. 1948. Developing the vermouth formula. Wines and Vines 29, No. 4, 73–75.

JOSLYN, M. A., and AMERINE, M. A. 1964. Dessert, Appetizer and Related Flavored Wines. University of California, Division of Agricultural Sciences, Berkeley.

KASAKOVA, E. 1958. Preparing spices for the production of vermouth (transl.) Izvest. Vysshikh. Ucheb. Zavadenii Tekhnol. 1, 109–112. (Chem. Abs. 53, 8532, 1959.)

LATRONICO, N. 1947. I Vini Medicinali, dalle Antiche Formule alle Preparazioni Moderne. 2 ed. Casa Editrice Bertuzzi, Milan.

LAZARUS, J. R. 1965. Final botanical bulletin. Wine Institute Bull. 1360-L, 1–8.

LUCKOW, C. 1937. Trübung in Wermut Bitter. Wein u. Rebe 19, 11–13.

MARESCALCHI, A. 1943. Manuale del Enologo e del Cantiniere. Casa Editrice Fratelli Marescalchi, Casale Monferrato.

MATTIROLO, O. 1915. Sulla coltivazione e sul valore delle "Artemisie" usate nella fabricazione dei Vermouths. Ann. R. Accad. Agr. Torino 58, 225–277.
MORINI, P. 1955. Le piante officinali nella industria dei liquori. Riv. Ital. Essenze Prof. 37, 16–19.
OTTAVIO, O., and GARINO-CANINA, E. 1930. Vini di Lusso. 8th Edition. Casa Editrice Fratelli Ottavi, Casale Monferrato.
PILONE, F. J. 1954. Production of vermouth. Am. J. Enol. 5, 30–46.
RIZZO, F. 1957. La Fabricazione del Vermouth. Edizione Agricole, Bologna.
ROSSATI, G. 1934. Sweet wines of Italy. Calif. Grape Grower 15, No. 6, 24–25.
SCHOONMAKER, F., and MARVEL, T. 1935. The Complete Wine Book. Simon and Schuster, New York.
SCURTI, F., and TACCHINI, R. 1916. Sulla composizione del vermouth piemontese. Staz. Sper. Agr. Ital. 49, 299–313. (Also R. staz. chim. agr. Torino 6, 147–161, 1914–1916.)
SÉBASTIAN, V. 1909. Traité Pratique de la Préparation des Vins de Luxe. Coulet et Fils, Montpellier.
SICHEL, H. O. 1945. Vermouth. Its production and future. Wines and Vines 26, No 3, 22–25.
TWINING LABORATORIES. 1941. Herbs for vermouth production. Wines and Vines 22, No. 9, 28, 30.
U. S. INTERNAL REVENUE SERVICE. 1970. Wine. Part 240 of Title 26, Code of Federal Regulations. U. S. Govt. Print. Office, Washington. (U. S. Treasury Dept., IRS Publication No. 146 (rev. 7–70).
USSEGLIO-TOMASSET, L. 1966. La determinazione dell'α e β-Tujone nelle bevande alcoliche aromatizzate. Riv. viticolt. e enol. (Conegliano) 19, 3–24.
VALAER, P. 1950. The Wines of the World. Abelard Press, New York.
VALVASSORI, S. 1954. Le piante officinalli nell' industria dei vermut e degli aperitivi. Riv. Ital. Essenze Prof. 36, 639–643.
WALTER, E. 1956. Wermut Wein. Carl Knoppke Grüner Verlag, Berlin.
WRIGHT, D. 1960. Factors affecting the color of dry vermouth. Am. J. Enol. Vitic. 11, 30–34.

CHAPTER 14

Fruit Wines

Considerable wine is now made in the Pacific Coast states and in British Columbia from apples, berries, and plums. Also some sweetened Concord grape wine similar in composition to berry wines is made on the Pacific Coast and in several Eastern states.

In England and in several European continental countries apple wine (hard cider) is produced in important quantities. In fact, the cider of Normandy is nearly as famous as French Burgundy or Roquefort cheese. Berry wines are made in several European countries, particularly in Switzerland, Germany, and the Scandinavian countries. See Baumann (1959), Charley (1953, 1954), Charley and Harrison (1939), Cruess et al. (1935), Dupaigne (1959), Gachot (1955, 1957), Jacobsen (1934), Koch (1956), Kroemer and Krumholz (1932), Lüthi (1953), Mehlitz (1951), Schanderl and Koch (1957), Valaer (1950A, 1950B), Villforth (1954), and Yang (1953).

CIDER AND APPLE WINE

In Great Britain the term "cider" means apple wine, hard cider, or fermented apple juice and nothing else. Unfortunately in the United States it may designate either unfermented apple juice, or the fermented, hence is ambiguous. In France the fermented juice of the apple is *cidre* and in Germany it is *Apfelwein*. For general information, see Alwood (1903), Alwood et al. (1904), Arengo-Jones (1941), Barker (1911A, 1911B, 1937), Braskat and Quinn (1940), Caldwell (1928), Charley (1937, 1953), Clague and Fellers (1936), Cruess and Celmer (1938), Davis (1933), Gore (1914), Martinez et al. (1958), Smock and Neubert (1950), Tschenn (1934), and Warcollier (1909, 1928).

Statistics

According to Anon (1965), France produced in 1963 over 250 million gallons of cider, of which a considerable proportion was distilled for apple brandy such as Calvados. Charley (1937) reported that England at the time produced about 20 to 25 million gallons and Germany about 6 million gallons per year. According to Kroemer and Krumholz (1932) there was produced in Switzerland at that time about 12,000,000 gallons of apple cider per year. Cider and other fruit wines are also made in most other European countries and in Canada. The U. S. Treasury Department has reported 21.5 millions of bushels of apples and over 1,750,000 gallons of cider were used for making commercial apple wine in the United States or a total of about 3,475,000 gallons in a single year. This total does not include the hard cider made in the home.

Apples for Cider in Europe

In Switzerland and Germany many of the apple and pear trees are not grown in orchards as in America and Canada, but are found as border trees or are scattered through the pastures, along the roadside or in back yards. In England the trees are usually grown in orchards with grass forming a sod between and under the trees. The trees are usually headed quite high. In England, Switzerland, and France a large proportion of the apple crop is of varieties grown expressly for the production of cider rather than for table use. Such varieties are usually high in sugar content, of medium to low fixed acidity and higher in tannin content than table apples.

Composition of Cider Apples

Many analyses of apples used for cider production in various countries have been published and while all of these cannot be reviewed here the data given in Table 47 will illustrate fairly well the range in composition that has been observed. Certain varieties are grown in France, Switzerland, and England for cider making, whereas in the United States, Germany, and Canada table varieties are usually employed.

It will be seen that some of the French cider varieties are higher in sugar content than the apples used in the other countries listed in the table and both the French and British cider apples are higher in tannin content than the apples analyzed from the United States, Germany, and Canada.

TABLE 47

COMPOSITION OF APPLES USED FOR CIDER PRODUCTION

Variety	Region Grown	Sugar		Total Acid	Tannin	Source
		Degrees Balling	or Per cent	Gm./100 Ml.	Gm./100 Ml.	
Cider apples, avg. 4 varieties	Normandy	17.5°		0.39	0.26	Alwood (1903)
Cider apples, avg.	England	13.7°		0.27	0.32	Charley (1937)
St. Laurent[1]	Virginia		16.5	0.27	0.24	Caldwell (1928)
Bramlot[1]	Virginia		19.05	0.22	0.53	Caldwell (1928)
Omont[1]	Virginia		14.2	0.33	0.27	Caldwell (1928)
Bidan[1]	Virginia		14.9	0.14	0.20	Caldwell (1928)
Several varieties, mostly table, avg.	Germany		14.4	0.73	0.07	Kroemer and Krumholz (1932)
Several varieties, mostly table, avg.	Oregon		11.2	0.70	...	Yang and Wiegand (1949)
8 varieties, mostly table, 1933 and 1944, avg.	New England		12.3	0.50	0.06	Clague and Fellers (1936)

[1] French cider apple varieties.

French Methods

According to Kroemer and Krumholz (1932) and Charley (1937) cider is made in France about as follows: the apples are stored in bins for a few days to develop aroma. They are then washed, sorted to remove rotten fruit, crushed and pressed in a rack and cloth press. In some plants, according to Charley, the crushed apples are not pressed at once but are allowed to stand for 3 to 24 hours to develop color and flavor before pressing. The crushed fruit is allowed to drain during this period of maceration. It is then pressed. The maceration greatly improves the "pressability" of the crushed apples. To the juice is added sulfur dioxide or metabisulfite to give 50 to 100 mg. of sulfur dioxide per liter (50 to 100 p.p.m.). It is then allowed to cool to 32° to 46°F. and settle until fairly clear through the action of natural pectic enzymes. This practice is termed "keeving." The juice is then racked and allowed to ferment at 40° to 50°F. Fermentation is slow at this temperature, but it is believed that a low temperature during fermentation is essential for the production of cider of best quality. Temperature during the apple season is low and the cider producers have no means of controlling it.

The pomace is often mixed with water, allowed to stand several hours, and is then pressed. Sugar and sulfur dioxide are usually added and the "juice" fermented to give a product of rather low quality called *cidre marchand*. The resulting pomace may be watered and pressed a second time to give *petite cidre*.

After the primary fermentation is completed the cider is drawn off from the yeast lees and below the cap, "*chapeau brun*." It then undergoes a slow secondary fermentation for several months in casks at about 40°F. It is then racked, bottled, and develops some carbon dioxide pressure in the bottle. Procedure varies considerably, however. For example, Charley reports that in some cases some of the juice is fermented completely. It is then filtered and blended with sweeter cider or with unfermented juice preserved at about 32°F.

Pure yeast starters may be used in the production of French ciders in some plants, but, according to Charley, natural fermentation is the more common procedure. Sparkling cider is made by the bottle fermentation procedure or by the Charmat bulk fermentation process as described for sparkling wines in Chapter 11.

Swiss Methods

The apples are carefully sorted, washed, crushed or disintegrated, and pressed. Pectic enzymes are often added to the juice to hasten and improve clearing of the cider during and after fermentation. See Kertesz (1930) and Kilbuck *et al.* (1949).

The most recent information on the production of apple wine from Switzerland (Joslyn 1959) indicates that the pressed apple juice is sulfited to 100 p.p.m. and fermented with a pure yeast culture. The fermentation takes about two months and a malo-lactic fermentation occurs before the alcoholic fermentation is completed. The new wine is stored under carbon dioxide. When needed it is sweetened with apple juice concentrate, filtered, carbonated, pasteurized (usually), and bottled.

German Methods

German apples used for production of cider, according to Kroemer and Krumholz (1932), Schanderl and Koch (1957), and Wilhelm (1957), are, as previously stated, on the average of lower sugar content and higher acidity than those of Normandy and England.

The apples are washed, sorted, and crushed and then pressed at once without maceration. Juice expressed from pears of high tannin content is sometimes added to apple juice deficient in tannin. If the acidity of the juice is below 0.6 gm. per 100 ml. Schanderl and Koch (1957) recommend the addition of lactic acid to increase the acidity to that level. They recommend the addition of potassium metabisulfite and advocate the use of selected yeast, such as Steinberg or Winningen. Often the juice is centrifuged before fermentation to clarify it partially and remove much of the undesirable bacteria and wild yeasts.

At 59°F, the usual cellar temperature in the Rhine district, fermentation is rather slow, but should be completed in 4 to 6 weeks. If the new wine darkens on exposure a small amount of sulfur dioxide or metabisulfite may be added. A secondary fermentation of 4 to 6 weeks usually ensues. During the last stages of the primary fermentation and during the secondary fermentation the cask must be equipped with a fermentation bung to prevent acetification. Schanderl and Koch (1957) state that the final alcohol content should be at least 5.5 per cent by volume. Wilhelm (1957) gives similar instructions for making apple wine in Germany.

Schanderl and Koch, and also Kroemer and Krumholz, state that a dessert apple wine is also made in Germany in one of two ways. The cider may be fortified with high proof brandy; or a cider of high alcohol content may be made by fermentation of sweetened, pasteurized juice to which is added about 20 gm. per hectoliter of ammonium phosphate as a yeast food. A selected yeast of high alcohol forming power is used. The sugar is not all added at once, but in three portions during fermentation, a modification of the syruped fermentation method.

Vogt (1963) in making apple and pear wine recommended washing and crushing the fruit, adding 50 p.p.m. of sulfur dioxide and 10 per cent water and pressing after several hours. The press juice is then sugared to the desired degree. Pure yeast cultures of cold-acclimated yeasts are recommended. Nitrogen, as ammonium chloride or phosphate, must be added. European apple wines contained 5.6 to 7.3 per cent alcohol.

English Methods

Charley and Harrison (1939) have described the usual procedure of making cider in England as follows. As the cider apples are always shaken from the trees, it is necessary as in France to wash them thoroughly before crushing. Also, they are sorted to remove rotten fruit not previously separated from the sound fruit by flotation in water. The apples are grated or hammer milled and pressed at once in a rack and cloth hydraulic press. Maceration and keeving are no longer practiced, except in a few isolated cases.

Fermentation is allowed to proceed naturally in most plants without the use of pure cultures of yeast. It is usually fermented to a specific gravity of 1.008 to 1.005. Racking from the yeast sediment slows down the fermentation and in addition the cider may be centrifuged to remove most of the yeast. The cider is usually stored in concrete tanks lined with a suitable coating. The usual precautions must be taken to prevent acetification during storage.

Before delivery to retail establishments the cider is usually sweetened by the addition of boiled cane or beet sugar syrup, then filtered through pulp or plate and frame filters using a filter aid. The filtered cider is then usually sterilized by germ proof filtration by Seitz EK filter or other suitable filter before bottling.

If a naturally sweet hard cider is to be made the fermentation is allowed to proceed to a specific gravity of 1.025 to 1.030, approximately 5° to 7.5° Balling. It is filtered or centrifuged to arrest fermentation. The clarified cider is then stored in wooden casks or other suitable containers until needed for consumption when it is again filtered, carbonated and bottled.

Increasingly large quantities of surplus table and cooking apples are used in England for production of cider. Their juices ferment very rapidly. Charley and Harrison (1939) state that only cider varieties of apples should be used for making dry cider, as the dessert and cooking varieties give dry cider of harsh flavor. Considerable sparkling cider is also made by the Charmat process.

Californian Methods

If apple juice is allowed to ferment naturally and nothing is done to alter or preserve it and it contains not more than eight per cent of alcohol by volume, it may be sold tax-free. Filtration, pasteurization, use of pectic enzymes, or other customary cellar operations used in wine making are considered to make the product taxable. Consequently, practically all commercially made hard cider and apple wine made in this country pays the regular wine tax. On the other hand, much partially fermented apple juice is made on the farm or in the home without payment of a tax.

In the United States the Federal Alcohol Regulations divide apple wines into several classes, namely, those containing not more than 14 per cent of alcohol by volume; those containing 14 to 21 per cent; and those containing 21 to 24 per cent. If above 24 per cent alcohol, the product is termed distilled spirit.

Apparently the labeling of fermented apple juice is not uniform. Samples labeled "hard cider" on sale in California ranged from 11 per cent to 13.5 per cent alcohol content by volume and a sample labeled "apple wine" contained 20.0 per cent. "Hard cider," as produced in California, is not fortified and apparently may have up to 14 per cent alcohol. Federal regulations define apple wine as "the product of the normal alcoholic fermentation of the juice of sound ripe apples, with or without the addition of cane, beet or dextrose sugar for the purpose of perfecting the produce according to standards, but without the addition or abstraction of other substances, except as may occur in the usual cellar treatment." Brandy may be added under proper permit and other conditions and under the supervision of a gauger of the Internal Revenue Service.

Eventually, producers of hard cider and apple wine and the trade will probably establish standards of identity for hard cider and apple wine.

The apples used in California and elsewhere in the United States are those grown for table or culinary use. Of the varieties available in commercial quantities on the Pacific Coast, Winesap is one of the best in composition and fermentation characteristics. It is grown chiefly in the State of Washington. The Northern Spy, Rome Beauty, Gravenstein, Stayman Winesap, Yellow Newtown, McIntosh, Spitzenberg, Jonathan, Roxbury, and other varieties of pronounced flavor and medium acidity are satisfactory. In California the Gravenstein is of excellent flavor and desirable acidity. It is available in midsummer to early fall. The Newtown (Yellow Newtown) is a late fall apple of excellent keeping quality and available in abundance. Its juice is rather mild in flavor and of medium acidity. It should be blended with a more flavorful and acid variety such as the Winesap.

The Delicious, now grown extensively in the Pacific Northwest, is of poor quality both for unfermented juice and for cider because of its low acidity. If it is used at all for cider its juice should be blended with that of a variety of higher acidity such as the Winesap or Northern Spy. It is common practice to mix two or more varieties for cider production.

Cruess and Celmer (1938) reported on experimental production of

Courtesy of Martinelli Apple Products Co.

FIG. 119.   WASHING APPLES IN CALIFORNIA CIDER PLANT

hard cider from California apples.   They found that the addition of sulfur dioxide or metabisulfite, a starter of pure wine yeast and a pectic enzyme were very desirable.   Cruess and Montgomery (1934) studied the naturally occurring yeasts from cider fermentations and the use of selected cultures in cider making.

Only fruit that is sound and free of rot and worm damage should be used for cider.   The apples are thoroughly washed, Fig. 119, and then sorted.   It is reported by apple juice producers that spray removal is no longer an important problem since other insecticides (i.e. Guthion) have replaced lead arsenate for control of codling moth and most of these new agents disappear from the fruit before it is picked.

The washed and sorted sound apples are prepared for pressing by passage through a grater or hammer mill.   The latter is now much the more common.   The pressing of the hammer milled apples gives a higher yield of juice because of the more thorough grinding by the mill.   The grated or hammer milled fruit is pressed in a rack and cloth press, Fig. 120.   Press cloths of nylon are stronger than cotton cloths and are more easily washed, more easily separated from the press cake, and more durable than cotton, though more costly.

In most plants in the Pacific Coast states, the freshly expressed juice, goes directly into the fermenters, although one cider producer transports the juice from the mill by tank truck about 50 miles to his fermentation cellar.   In plants in which the juice goes directly from the press to the fer-

Courtesy of Martinelli Apple Products Co.

Fig. 120. Rack and Cloth Presses in California Cider Plant

menters a small amount of sulfur dioxide or bisulfite is added to give about 100 to 125 p.p.m. of sulfur dioxide. If the juice is to be held overnight to permit settling and clearing with use of a pectic enzyme, somewhat more sulfur dioxide is used in order to delay fermentation. The sulfur dioxide also aids in preventing undue oxidation and browning and inhibits wild yeasts and bacteria.

In one case there is added 1 lb. of sulfur dioxide gas from a cylinder of liquid sulfur dioxide and 2 lbs. of a so-called "5 to 1" or 1 lb. of a "10 to 1" pectic enzyme to each 1000 gallons of juice. The juice is allowed to stand overnight, is then filtered and transferred to the fermentation cellar. Spontaneous fermentation may begin during settling. Dextrose is added so that after fermentation is completed the cider will have about 13 per cent of alcohol by volume. The juice is fermented rapidly. When fermentation is completed or has proceeded to the desired point, cane or beet sugar is added to give about 10° Balling. The cider is usually clarified with bentonite. It is then filtered and bottled.

In another plant the apples are washed, sorted, hammer milled and pressed in rack and cloth presses. Two pounds of metabisulfite are added per 1000 gallons and a starter of champagne, Ay, variety of wine yeast is added. Sufficient sugar is added to give a hard cider of about 12 to 13 per cent alcohol after fermentation to dryness is completed. The juice is fermented in covered redwood tanks of two sizes of about 900 and 3000 gallon capacity respectively. During the final stage of fermentation, traps consisting of one-gallon bottles of water for the smaller tanks and five-gallon bottles for the larger are employed. A rubber hose or plastic tube leads from the tank through the tank bung and into the bottle of water. When fermentation is complete and the yeast has settled the cider is racked, filter aid is added and the product is filtered brilliantly clear. The cider is sweetened to 9° to 10° Balling, flash pasteurized, bottled hot in crown cap bottles and the bottles cooled on a continuous conveyor under sprays of water.

In most cases no pectic enzyme is employed but to juice of varieties which yield a cider that is very difficult to filter a pectic enzyme is added. According to Fessler (1959), much hard cider is made from apple concentrate. The final product is darker in color and less fruity in flavor than that made from the fresh fruit. Apple essence can be added for flavor and excess color can be removed with decolorizing carbon.

At present California plants use the term "hard cider" for the unfortified apple wine and the term "apple wine" for the fortified product. In the Pacific Northwest, according to Yang (1959) much of the cider is fortified to about 20 per cent alcohol content. A California fortified apple wine was found to contain 20.5 per cent alcohol by volume, 0.34 gm. total acid as malic per 100 ml., 0.015 gm. volatile acid per 100 ml. and was of 6.5° Balling.

If clouding due to excess copper or iron is encountered, it is customary to treat the cider with Cufex or ion exchange as described in Chapters 6 and 15. At present, there is considerable difficulty with this problem, except where stainless steel equipment is used.

Oregon and Washington Methods

The procedures outlined are more or less typical of the practice in other western plants, but methods vary somewhat in the different plants in the Pacific Coast states. According to Yang and Wiegand (1949) water is not added to apple juice to be made into hard cider. They recommend that not all of the sugar used in amelioration be added at one time, but that it be added in several portions; the first before fermentation and the remainder in 2 or 3 lots during fermentation.

They found that addition of urea, while it greatly increased the rate of fermentation of ameliorated berry juices, did not appear to be of great benefit in the fermentation of the apple juice used by them. The effect of temperature, however, was pronounced. Apple juice sweetened and fermented five days with champagne yeast at 76°, 86°, and 98°F. contained 17.3, 14.95, and 6.2 per cent alcohol by volume; indicating that the lowest of the three temperatures was the most favorable. Seven strains of wine yeast were compared in fermentation at 76°F.; champagne yeast gave the best results. For information on the yeast flora of apples and ciders, see Pearce and Baker (1939) and Legakis (1961).

Clark *et al.* (1954) at McGill University in Montreal, Canada, found that the fermentation rate of apple juice varied more or less directly in proportion to the amount of yeast extract added.

Yang and Wiegand (1949) give the average composition of Pacific Northwest hard cider at the time of their report as: alcohol 12.8 per cent by volume; Balling 4.6°; total acidity as malic 0.41; volatile acid 0.105 and total sulfur dioxide 96 p.p.m. Analysis of three California 1959 hard ciders gave alcohol 11.10, 13.6, and 11.6 per cent; Balling (or Brix) 9.0°, 7.4°, and 7.0°; total acidity as malic 0.48, 0.47, and 0.35; and volatile acidity 0.045, 0.06, and 0.015 gm. per 100 ml.

SPARKLING APPLE WINE

For many years fermented apple wines have been carbonated or tank- or bottle-fermented in England to produce a sparkling cider. Sparkling ciders are also common in Switzerland and Germany and may occasionally be found on the market in other European countries. Before the war Tressler *et al.* (1941) described a tank process for New York apple wines. Atkinson *et al.* (1959) have given an outline of the carbonation process being used commercially in British Columbia. Pectinase is added, the whole agitated after one hour and then allowed to settle. A clear juice is obtained by rough filtering. This is ameliorated to 16 per cent solids with sucrose, and fermented at 77°F. When the refractometer reading indicates 8.9 per cent soluble solids (in about four days) the wine is cooled to 29°F. to stop fermentation at 8.2 per cent (approximately 5 per cent alcohol). The cold wine is polish-filtered and carbonated at about 35 lbs. pressure. It is held in the bottling tank at 29° to 32°F. until filled into 28-oz. soft drink vinyl-spotted crown-cap bottles. Finally, it is bottle-pasteurized to obtain a center temperature of 145° to 150°F. and immediately cooled, labeled, and stored at a cool temperature until distributed.

Brown *et al.* (1959) reported that the best apples for the above process were those of firm ripe fruit which were used after a minimum storage period. Delicious blended with Jonathan made the best cider.

Recently slightly sparkling apple wines have become very popular in this country. They have excellent apple aroma, probably owing to addition of apple flavor essence.

THE FREEZING METHOD

Hard cider of high alcohol content was made at one time in British Columbia by the freezing process. Hard cider made in conventional manner was filtered, frozen to a slushy consistency and the concentrated cider and ice crystals were then separated by draining by the Monti process. The final alcohol content was about 18 to 20 per cent by volume. The concentrated hard cider was aged, filtered, and bottled. It was of pleasing flavor and suitable for use as a dessert wine. The ice crystals and concentrated hard cider could be separated also by basket centrifuge (Gore 1914), or the Linde-Krause method as described by Charley (1937) could be used. This latter process consists in freezing the product on the outside of a slowly revolving, refrigerated drum. Ice is removed from the drum by a scraper and the lower part of the drum dips into a tank of the product which becomes concentrated by freezing water on the drum.

OTHER FRUIT WINES

Cherries, plums, and several varieties of berries are used in Europe and in America for the production of wines of various types. Special varieties of pears are also used in Europe for this purpose. In the Pacific Coast states, particularly, berry wines are made in considerable quantities and are increasing in popularity. In Germany berry wines are well known. See Henry (1936) and Osterwalder (1948) for data on berry wines.

Berry Wines in Europe

Both table and dessert wines are made from various berries in Europe. The methods described by Schanderl and Koch (1957) for preparing both types of wine from red currants will illustrate the customary procedures. The red currants have about 2.4 per cent acid content, expressed as tartaric. Therefore, considerable dilution of the juice with water is necessary in order to produce a palatable wine. The juice has about 6 per cent of sugar. If a wine of 8 per cent alcohol by volume is desired there is added to each liter of juice 2 liters of water and 345 gm. of sugar; if 10 per cent of alcohol is desired, 445 gm. of sugar are used. More water should not be used as the resulting wine will be too "dilute" in flavor. If a dessert wine of 16 per cent alcohol is to be made, 1 liter of juice, 2 liters of water and 735 gm. of sugar are used; or 1 liter of juice, 1.4 liters of water and 570 gm. of sugar. Schanderl and Koch also give the proportions of the three materials to make dessert wines of other alcohol content.

In making both the table wine and the dessert wine, a starter of pure yeast is added. For rapid clarification of the wine, addition of a pectic enzyme is beneficial; for example, about 1 gm. per liter of Pectinol-O or other enzyme of like activity. The addition of 10 to 15 gm. of potassium metabisulfite per hectoliter (100 liters) is recommended.

The directions given by Schanderl and Koch (1957) for other berry wines are similar to those for red currant wine. They suggest that only enough water be used to reduce the acidity to 0.8 per cent as tartaric.

Fermentation is conducted with a starter of 2 to 5 per cent by volume of a powerful wine yeast such as Steinberg. Aging, filtration, etc. are conducted as outlined for apple cider. Berry wines should not be aged too long as they then lose color and flavor. Usually they are sweetened to balance properly sugar and acidity and to "bring out" the berry flavor. Germ-proof filtration or pasteurization is recommended for the bottled berry table wines.

The instructions given by Wilhelm (1957) for the making of berry wines in Germany are similar to those of Schanderl and Koch.

Cherry Wines in Europe

Schanderl and Koch (1957) recommend sour cherries in preference to the sweet for making wine as the acidity of the latter is too low. A blend of the two or a blend of currant and a table variety of cherries may be used. In crushing the cherries a few of the pits, but not too many, should be broken in order to enhance the flavor of the wine; but not more than 10 per cent of the pits should be broken or too much prussic acid may be liberated from the bitter kernels.

A cherry dessert wine rather than a table wine is recommended by Schanderl and Koch, who give the amounts of sugar required for each liter of juice plus a liter of water to give dessert wines of various alcohol contents ranging from 12 to 17 per cent. For one of 16 per cent alcohol the amount is 430 gm. to each liter of juice. The sugar is dissolved in water. Like berry wines the cherry wine should not be aged very long. Sugar may be added before bottling to give the desired degree of sweetness. Germ-proof filtration or pasteurization may be used to preserve the bottled wine. The use of a small amount of potassium metabisulfite is advisable before fermentation. The use of a pectic enzyme to hasten and improve clarification is desirable.

Plum Wines in Europe

Schanderl and Koch (1957) recommend that to the crushed plums or sour prunes a liter of water be added for each pound of crushed fruit. Sugar and a starter of yeast are added. The mixture is allowed to ferment for 8 to 10 days before pressing, as it is practically impossible to press the fruit before fermentation. Addition of a pectic enzyme before fermentation greatly facilitates pressing, increases the yield of juice and hastens clearing of the wine. Additional sugar may be added to the partially fermented juice; the amount will vary according to whether a table or a dessert wine is to be made. Aging, filtration, bottling, and preservation are similar to these operations for berry wines.

Berry Wines in Pacific Coast States

As previously stated, the amelioration of berries used for wine production is permitted.

Yang and Wiegand (1949) give the average values shown in Table 48 for sugar and acid content of several fruits and berries used in Oregon for production of fruit wines.

TABLE 48

AVERAGE SUGAR AND ACID CONTENTS OF SEVERAL FRUITS USED IN WINE MAKING IN THE PACIFIC NORTHWEST[1]

Fruit	Total Sugar	Total Acid
	Per cent	Per cent
Apple	11.2	0.70 as malic
Blackberry	7.2	1.20 as citric
Cherry	8.5	1.00 as malic
Currant	6.4	2.10 as citric
Loganberry	6.9	2.00 as citric
Plum	12.0	0.90 as malic
Raspberry	6.8	1.60 as citric

[1] Source of data: Yang and Wiegand (1949).

In order to insure the production of high quality fruit and berry wines, Yang (1955) recommended harvesting the fruit at optimum maturity. Since blackberries have higher pigment concentration towards the end of the season and this leads to pigment deposits in the bottle, it would be, presumably, better to pick blackberries before full maturity. He also preferred berries from nonirrigated plantings. Confirmatory data would be welcome. Stillman (1955) states that maturity, sugar and acid content, variety, and whether the fruit has been held in cold storage are factors. Fruit held in cold storage apparently produces lesser quality wine.

Analyses of Oregon and California berry wines were made at the University of California with the results shown in Table 49.

Yang and Wiegand (1949) have reported the analyses of Pacific Northwest fruit wines as as shown in Table 50.

Yang et al. (1950) reporting on the effect of the use of a pectic enzyme, Pectinol M, at the rate of one pound per ton of fruit, have given the data presented in Table 51. The enzyme was added before fermentation. Evidently the use of the enzyme increased the yields materially. Amelioration included addition of water and sugar as permitted by state regulations of Oregon and Washington.

TABLE 49

COMPOSITION OF SAMPLES OF OREGON AND CALIFORNIA BERRY WINES OF 1958 CROP

Fruit and Where Made	Balling	Total Acidity as Malic	Volatile Acidity	Alcohol
	Degree	Gm./100 Ml.	Gm./100 Ml.	Per cent/Vol.
Loganberry, Oregon	11.0	0.74	0.060	11.6
Loganberry, California	11.5	0.78	0.040	12.5
Blackberry, Oregon	12.0	0.79	0.065	12.5
Red currant, California	10.0	0.84	0.070	12.3
Red currant, Oregon	15.5	0.74	0.060	12.4
Elderberry, California	9.5	0.46	0.030	13.7
Raspberry, California	12.5	0.97	0.060	11.9
Strawberry, California	13.0	0.62	0.030	13.3
Strawberry, California	8.0	0.74	0.119	13.7
Boysenberry, California	12.0	0.91	0.042	12.4

TABLE 50

TYPICAL COMPOSITION OF FRUIT WINES OF THE PACIFIC NORTHWEST[1]

Wine	Alcohol	Balling	Total acid	Vol. acid	Total SO$_2$
	Per cent/Vol.	Degree	Gm./100 Ml.	Gm./100 Ml.	P.P.M.
Apple	12.8	4.6	0.411	0.105	96
Blackberry	12.2	8.2	0.890	0.069	103
Cherry	12.3	6.8	0.534	0.102	113
Currant	13.0	9.1	1.000	0.051	87
Loganberry	12.6	8.0	0.870	0.074	64
Plum (fortified)	19.8	11.9	0.790	0.088	70
Raspberry	12.0	8.8	0.903	0.060	75

[1] Source of data: Yang and Wiegand (1949).

TABLE 51

EFFECT OF PECTIC ENZYME ON YIELD OF JUICE[1]

Treatment	Loganberry	Blackberry	Currant	Concord Grape
		Gallons Per Ton		
Enzyme treated	195	200	193	182
Untreated	180	183	183	163
Per cent increase	7.69	8.5	5.18	10.44
Yield after amelioration:				
Enzyme treated	512	317	509	270
Untreated	475	300	480	224
Per cent increase	7.22	5.36	5.7	17.04

[1] Source of data: Yang et al. (1950).

Yang and Wiegand (1949) state that apple juice, plums, and cherries produced in the Pacific Northwest ferment satisfactorily without the addition of nitrogenous yeast food (urea or ammonium phosphate), but that such addition is necessary for rapid and complete fermentation of ameliorated (diluted and sweetened) berry juices. Their data on the effect of added urea are given in Table 52.

TABLE 52

EFFECT OF ADDED UREA ON FERMENTATION OF VARIOUS JUICES AT 76°F. BY CHAMPAGNE YEAST[1]

Amount of Urea Added	Alcohol Volume Per cent after 5 Days Fermentation						
	Apple	Blackberry	Cherry	Currant	Loganberry	Plum	Raspberry
Per cent							
0	17.00	5.90	16.60	7.90	9.20	14.20	8.70
0.05	17.10	8.30	16.55	10.25	12.50	14.00	12.50
0.10	17.30	8.80	16.45	10.70	13.00	13.80	12.70

[1] Source of data: Yang and Wiegand (1949).

Addition of urea did not increase the rate of fermentation of apple, cherry, and plum juices appreciably but increased the rate markedly of blackberry, currant, loganberry, and raspberry juices. Apparently addition of 0.05 per cent of urea was about as effective as 0.10 per cent.

As previously stated for fermentation of apple juice, Yang and Wiegand found that 96°F. was unfavorable for fermentation by champagne yeast of all of the juices tested, but that 76°F. was more favorable than 86°F. only for apple, cherry, and plum juices, while 86°F. gave more rapid fermentation than 76°F. of blackberry, currant, and other fruit juice.

In a small grower's plant in Oregon visited in 1958, the berries were lightly crushed, allowed to ferment for two days, pressed, the juice ameliorated with water and sugar and allowed to ferment in 50-gallon barrels. The wine was then filtered and bottled. No pure yeast or sulfur dioxide were used.

In a large western plant visited in 1958, the fresh berries were coarsely crushed by fruit pulper with a 0.5 in. screen of stainless steel; water, sugar, a small amount of metabisulfite and a yeast starter were added, the berries were fermented a short time, pressed in a rack and cloth press, and the juice fermented in covered wooden tanks. Additional sugar was added during fermentation. The fermented wine was allowed to settle, was racked, filtered, and aged a short time in well-filled, sealed redwood tanks. It was then sweetened with sugar, filtered, flash-pasteurized to 140°F., filled hot into bottles by automatic vacuum type filling machine, bottles sealed with screw caps, and cased hot without cooling. The bottles were filled almost completely so that on cooling only a small headspace devoid of oxygen results. Frozen berries used during the off season are thawed but not crushed before fermentation.

Yang (1959), states that in the Pacific Northwest berries are not usually crushed before fermentation; that fermentation lasts from 7 to 14 days depending on the temperature; about 100 p.p.m. of sulfur dioxide or an equivalent amount of metabisulfite is added before fermentation;

about one-fourth of the total amount of sugar is added before fermentation and the remainder during fermentation; pure yeast is used in most plants; that amelioration with water and sugar may be made before, during, or after fermentation; that the use of pectic enzymes is not universal but that they are used in some plants; and that the alcohol content of the new wine before final sweetening is 12 to 14 per cent by volume. Addition of sugar after fermentation reduces the alcohol content about one per cent owing to the dilution effect of the added sugar.

In adding the sugar it should first be dissolved in a small amount of wine or water to give a heavy syrup, as the syrup can be mixed with the wine more readily than can the dry sugar. The latter is inclined to sink to the bottom of the mixing tank and to dissolve very slowly.

In a western plant visited in 1959, frozen berries are generally used. They are allowed to thaw and are fermented without crushing after addition of a yeast starter, water, sulfur dioxide, and dextrose sugar. The aim is to attain about 13 per cent of alcohol. A cap forms during fermentation and a large yield of free-run is obtained before pressing. The wine is rough filtered and is sweetened to 10° to 13° Balling with sucrose. After settling and aging in covered tanks the wine is racked and again filtered. It is flash pasteurized, bottled hot in screw top bottles, and cooled before labeling and casing. Sweetening before aging preserves flavor and color but the sweetened wine must be stored under refrigeration to prevent re-fermentation. Strawberry wine is difficult to filter. Addition of a pectic enzyme would be desirable with this variety.

Cherry and Plum Wines in Pacific Coast States

Sour cherries are preferred to the sweet dessert varieties because of higher acidity and richer flavor. Pectic enzymes should be used in the fermentation of both fruits. In the Northwest the "Oregon prune" (Fellenburg), a sour variety often canned or frozen as "purple plum," is used to some extent in making a fortified wine.

Cherries and plums or sour prunes may be coarsely crushed, ameliorated with water and sugar, sulfur dioxide, or metabisulfite added to give 100 to 125 p.p.m. of sulfur dioxide, a starter of pure yeast added and the crushed fruit fermented. A pectic enzyme such as Pectinol O or A or M, at the rate of 1 lb. per 1000 lbs. of fruit, or Pectizyme or other pectic enzyme should be added. After several days fermentation the fruit can be pressed in a rack and cloth apple press and the juice fermented to completion.

Cherry wine is treated about as previously described for berry wines. Plum or sour prune wine is usually fortified to about 20 per cent alcohol by volume and sweetened with sucrose to about 10° to 12° Balling.

At present, insofar as the authors are aware, no plum or prune wine is made in California.

Pomegranate Wine

A commercial pomegranate wine recently made in California had the following composition: alcohol 11.9 per cent by volume, Balling degree 11.5, total acid as citric 0.85 gm. per 100 ml. and volatile acid 0.07 gm. per 100 ml.

If crushed before pressing an extremely astringent juice unsuited to wine making results.   If, however, the whole fruit is pressed without preliminary crushing a juice is obtained that is suitable for making a claret type dry wine or a sweetened unfortified or fortified dessert wine. .

Cruess *et al.* (1935) have given the following directions based on pilot scale experiments: press the whole fruit without crushing.   Add sugar to 22° to 23° Balling and 2 lbs. of metabisulfite to each 1000 gallons of juice. Ferment with a starter of wine yeast.   Age and finish in the same manner as red grape wine.

If a sweet table wine is desired add sugar to 8° to 10° Balling after aging.   Flash pasteurize at 140°F.; bottle hot and seal; cool bottles in sprays of cold water.

A port-like wine can be made by fortifying the sweetened wine to about 20 per cent alcohol.

From Concord Grapes

In addition to the wines made from Concord grapes by the "orthodox" methods described in Chapter 12, considerable sweet table wine similar in composition to berry wines is made in the Pacific Northwest, California, and in the eastern United States.   One such wine made in California had the following composition: alcohol content 13.7 per cent by volume, total acidity as tartaric 0.66 gm. per 100 ml., volatile acidity 0.100 gm. per 100 ml., and Balling 12°.   One from an Oregon plant had: alcohol 12.5 per cent by volume, 0.60 gm. total acid per 100 ml., volatile acidity 0.050 gm. per 100 ml. and was of 12° Balling.   One from New York State had: 13.9 per cent alcohol, 0.60 gm. per 100 ml. of total acid, 0.070 gm. per 100 ml. of volatile acid and was 17° Balling.

Much of such wine is made directly from the grapes, but some also is made from Concord grape concentrate and from the fresh or frozen juice. In an eastern state one method of producing a sweetened Concord wine is about as follows: the grapes are crushed and stemmed in a plant near the vineyards; heated to extract the color; pressed to give a juice of deep red color; cooled, and a pectic enzyme is added.   The juice is transported by tank truck to the winery, which is located at a considerable distance.   At the winery sugar and water are added and the juice fermented with a yeast starter. The finished wine is sweetened by the addition of sugar and stirred vigorously mechanically until the sugar is dissolved. A filter aid is added and the wine heated to about 165°F., filtered hot and filled hot into bottles. These are sealed hot and cooled artificially. Some wine is stored unsweetened for use after the grape season has ended.

Pineapple Wine

Insofar as the authors are aware, pineapple wine is not made in the United States commercially, although it has been made in the home. In Hawaii and the Philippines alcohol is made from pineapple waste for the production of distilled vinegar.

In the laboratory Hohl and Cruess (unpublished data) have observed that canned pineapple juice and the fresh juice of Mexican grown pineapple ferments rapidly with wine yeast and that on aging and clarification a pleasing dry wine of rather low alcohol content results. As the natural juice is of only 12° to 15° Balling the addition of sugar to give 22° to 23° Balling would be desirable in order to give a wine of 12 to 13 per cent alcohol by volume. Such a wine could be sweetened and preserved by pasteurization as described earlier in this chapter for hard cider and berry wines. Also, the wine could be fortified and sweetened to give a dessert wine.

The waste cores, trimmings, and peel scrapings from pineapple canning could be crushed and pressed for wine making. If the whole fruit is used it should be peeled by Ginaca machine as for canning as the peel imparts a somewhat disagreeable taste to the juice. The addition of a small amount of tannin improves the flavor of the wine.

Pear Wine

In France, Switzerland, and Germany special varieties of pears of high tannin content, as previously mentioned, are grown and used for making perry, a cider-like fermented pear beverage; or the juice is blended with apple juice before fermentation. In Oregon waste peels and cores from pear canning are disintegrated, fermented, and distilled for production of pear brandy and vodka. For the latter product the distillate must be highly rectified to give a neutral spirit of about 95 per cent alcohol and practically free of fruit flavor or odor.

Bartlett pears were made into wine experimentally at the University of California as follows: the fruit was used while still firm ripe, because it was found that crushed pears of table ripeness cannot be successfully pressed. The pears were grated in an orchard size apple grater and pressed in a rack and cloth press. The juice was of 14° Balling and approximately 0.25 per cent acidity as malic. Sugar was added to increase the Balling to 21° and sufficient citric acid was then added to increase the total acidity to 0.5 per cent; also about 100 p.p.m. of sulfur dioxide and a starter of pure wine yeast were used. Fermentation to dryness was rapid. The wine was allowed to settle in glass containers; was racked and aged in glass with oak chips. It was clarified with bentonite after final racking. The final product was dry and fairly palatable. A pectic enzyme should be used as the wine is difficult to filter or fine. The dry wine could be sweetened and pasteurized before bottling as is apple hard cider.

Wine from Oranges

A number of years ago a fortified sweet dessert orange wine was made commercially in southern California. The wine was dark amber in color and resembled angelica wine in composition. See Von Loesecke *et al.* (1936) for the Florida experiments; Joslyn and Marsh (1934), and Cruess (1914) and Cruess *et al.* (1935) for the California experiments with orange wine.

It was found that the Navel orange as grown in California gave a juice and a wine that soon became bitter, but the juice and wine made from the Valencia variety did not show this defect. In Florida several varieties were used successfully by Von Loesecke *et al.* (1936).

Orange wines darken rapidly and develop a harsh, stale taste unless a fairly high level of sulfur dioxide is maintained. The fruit should be thoroughly ripe, but not over-ripe, as the wine then is apt to have a stale flavor. Although the juice can be extracted by crushing the fruit and pressing in a rack and cloth press or by use of a continuous screw press, the juice then contains so much essential oil from the peel that it ferments very slowly, as the orange oil is toxic to yeast. The juice is best extracted by the usual juice equipment in which the oranges are cut in half by machine and reamed mechanically in a Brown or F.M.C. juice extractor. However, a rotary juice extractor such as is used in Florida or a Citro-Mat extractor, both of which obtain the juice by pressure, can be used if the juice is centrifuged to remove most of the esssential oil.

The oranges should be sorted to remove rotten and other unfit fruit. They should then be washed thoroughly. For efficient juice extraction the fruit should be graded into three sizes as the machines are usually built to work best on fruit of fairly uniform size.

To the fresh juice should be added about 150 p.p.m. of sulfur dioxide or an equivalent amount of bisulfite or metabisulfite. Sugar dissolved in a small amount of juice should be added to increase the Balling degree to 22° to 23°, and a starter of wine yeast should be used. About 0.1 per cent of Pectinol-O or an equivalent amount of other pectic enzyme such as Pektizyme should be added, as untreated orange wine does not clear satisfactorily and is difficult to filter.

Fermentation of orange juice is rapid, as it is an excellent culture medium for yeast. It should be fermented as previously described for apple juice and to dryness. Sugar may then be added to about 10° Balling; sulfur dioxide added to about 200 p.p.m. of total sulfur dioxide, the wine filtered, pasteurized at 140° to 145°F., bottled hot and the bottles cooled in sprays of water as described for apple and berry wines.

Or the wine, after addition of sugar, may be fortified to 20 per cent alcohol, aged, given an addition of sulfur dioxide as for the table wines, filtered and bottled without pasteurization. A small amount of terpeneless orange oil or orange extract may be added before filtration to impart an orange flavor. Wines of 18 per cent alcohol content were made experimentally at the University of California by adding sugar in 3 to 4 lots during fermentation, a modification of the syruped method of fermentation previously outlined for grape wines (p. 451).

Von Loesecke et al. (1936) made an orange cordial by distilling orange wine to give an orange brandy, adding sugar to the brandy and diluting with distilled water to about 33 per cent alcohol content and about 37 per cent sugar. A small amount of cold pressed orange oil was added; the cordial was then aged, and finally filtered before bottling. In making cordials the regulations of the Internal Revenue Service must be followed.

Grapefruit Wine

Grapefruit may be used in the same manner as oranges for the production of table wine, dessert wine, and cordials. The wines are somewhat bitter. If the wine is too high in acidity, as is sometimes the case, a calculated amount of potassium carbonate may be added, or the calculated amount of calcium carbonate may be added and the mixture heated to 150° to 160°F. to hasten the reaction and to make the calcium citrate less soluble; filtering hot, and cooling. Ion-exchange treatment may also be used to reduce the acidity.

Wine from Dried Fruits

Dried figs and dates can be made into a fair wine as follows: to the dried, shredded fruit in a vat or open barrel, add 3 to 4 lb. of boiling hot water to each pound of fruit or about 10 gal. to each 25 pounds of fruit. The water should contain about 0.6 per cent of citric acid (about 0.5 pound per 10 gallons). Let cool, and then add about 150 p.p.m. of sulfur dioxide. Add a starter of pure yeast.

As shredding or grinding the dried fruit before adding the water is difficult, a better procedure is us follows. Pass the fruit, with the proper amount of hot water, through a Rietz disintegrator and pump the resulting slurry of ground fruit and water through a cooler into a fermenting vat. Add the required acid (0.6 per cent citric acid) and 100 to 150 p.p.m. sulfur dioxide and pure yeast. Ferment until most of the sugar is fermented. Draw off the free-run, and bag filter the pomace, or press it in a rack and cloth press, adding, if needed, infusorial earth filter aid, such as Hyflo Super-Cel. Analyze the wine for sugar and alcohol content. Add sufficient dextrose or sucrose to give, on complete fermentation, about 12 per cent of alcohol. When fermentation is complete, treat as any other white table wine.

Raisins should be passed through raisin seeder rolls with fingers removed, to cut the raisins. From this point handle in the same manner as previously described for figs and dates. Raisins contain about 60 per cent sugar, hence somewhat less water than that recommended for figs and dates may be used. Another method is soaking the raisins in water until plump. They may then be crushed and pressed, as are fresh grapes. The cold water in which they are soaked should contain about 150 p.p.m. of sulfur dioxide.

Dried apricots and peaches are not very satisfactory for making wine as they are too "solid" or "pulpy" and the extract too gummy.

Swiss Research on Fruit Juice Fermentation

At Wädenswil, Lüthi (1953) conducted an interesting investigation on the fermentation of pear and other fruit juices. Often the fermentation of pear juice is very slow or may cease before completion. He states that lack of nitrogenous yeast nutrients or of certain growth factors is usually the cause of such unsatisfactory fermentation.

The addition of 200 mg. per liter of ammonium sulfate to pear juice markedly improved its fermentation but the addition of peptone gave a still greater effect. The addition of thiamin and biotin gave an important increase in the rate of fermentation. However, addition of ammonium sulfate with the thiamin and biotin gave a still greater increase in the rate of fermentation. In apple juice the ammonium sulfate and peptone exerted some favorable effect, but thiamin, 4 mg. per liter, gave a much greater positive effect. The addition of certain amino acids as sources of nitrogenous nutrients increased the rate of fermentation.

It was found that high tannin content of some pear juices retarded fermentation. Fining with gelatin removed the excess tannin and normal fermentation ensued. It was also found that heating the juice for 35 minutes to a moderate temperature (122°F. or above) caused a marked improvement in fermentation of the juice. Lüthi reports that mesoinositol, pantothenic acid and "Adermin" also exerted a favorable effect on the fermentation of pear juice.

HONEY WINE (MEAD)

While honey is not usually considered a fruit product, much of it comes from the flowers of fruit trees and wine is made from honey in a manner similar to that used in making fruit wines. There is considerable demand for instructions for producing honey wine on a small scale. For these reasons honey wine is included in this chapter. Mead is more or less a synonym for honey wine and dates back to prebiblical times.

Filipello and Marsh (1934) found that the addition of a nitrogenous yeast food to the diluted honey was necessary for successful fermentation and that phosphate was also very beneficial. A honey of mild flavor is recommended in preference to honeys of very strong flavor. The addition of acid was also found very desirable, as the non-acidified product is almost neutral in reaction.

On the basis of Filipello and Marsh's experiments as well as the instructions given by Wilhelm (1957) the following method is suggested for producing a dry table wine from honey. A sound honey of pleasing and rather mild flavor should be used. It is diluted with water to about 22° Balling. To each liter of diluted honey is added 5 gm. of citric acid, 1.5 gm. of diammonium monohydrogen phosphate ($(NH_4)_2HPO_4$), 1 gm. of potassium bitartrate (cream of tartar) and 0.25 gm. each of magnesium chloride and calcium chloride. These can be dissolved in a small amount of the diluted honey by heating and stirring and this solution then added to and mixed with the main volume of diluted product. The addition of about 100 p.p.m. of sulfur dioxide or about 200 p.p.m. of potassium metabisulfite or sodium bisulfite, corresponding to about 1.25 ozs. of sulfur dioxide or 2.5 ozs. of metabisulfite or sulfite per 100 gallons of diluted honey is recommended.

A starter of 2 to 3 per cent by volume of pure wine yeast starter, such as burgundy, champagne, or other good variety must be added. This can be grown in pasteurized diluted honey prepared as above or in pasteurized grape or other fruit juice. See Chapter 6 for directions for preparing yeast starters. During the final stages of fermentation the cask or tank should be fitted with a fermentation bung in order to prevent acetification.

The new wine is allowed to settle for several weeks and is racked. Filter aid is added and the wine is filtered, aged a few months in completely filled, tightly sealed casks or tanks, racked, polish filtered, and bottled. It is suitable for use on the table.

It may be sweetened to 5° to 10° Balling by addition of honey or sugar, filtered, flash pasteurized at 140° to 145°F., bottled hot and the bottles cooled in sprays of water.

The sweetened wine may be fortified to 18 to 20 per cent alcohol by addition of high proof brandy as outlined in the chapters on dessert wines. Another method of producing a fortified sweet honey wine consists in adding brandy to the partially fermented product. Fortification must be done under supervision of the Internal Revenue Service. Instead of filtering the wine it may be clarified with bentonite in the same manner as white grape wine (see Chapter 6). For data on fruit liqueurs, see Reittersmann (1952).

BIBLIOGRAPHY

ALWOOD, W. B. 1903. A study of cider making in France, Germany and England. U. S. Dept. Agr., Bur. Chem. Bull. 71.

ALWOOD, W. B., DAVIDSON, R. J., and MONCURE, W. A. P. 1904. The composition of apples and cider. U. S. Dept. Agr. Bur. Chem. Bull. 88.

ANON. 1965. France, Minist. de l'Agric., Statistique agricole 1964: 243.

ARENGO-JONES, R. W. 1941. The preparation of fermented ciders. Fruit Prods. J. 20, 300–309, 321.

ATKINSON, F. E., BOWEN, J. F., and MACGREGOR, D. R. 1959. A rapid method for production of a sparkling apple wine. Food Technol. 13, 673–675.

BARKER, B. T. B. 1911A. Processes of cider making. J. Bd. Agr. (London) 18, 501–511.

BARKER, B. T. B. 1911B. The principles and practices of cider making. J. Inst. Brew. 17, 425–441.

BARKER, B. T. B. 1937. Cider apple production. Great Britain Minist. Agr. and Fisheries Bull. 104.

BAUMANN, J. 1959. Handbuch des Süssmosters. Eugen Ulmer, Stuttgart.

BOWEN, J. F., MACGREGOR, D. R., and ATKINSON, F. E. 1959. Effect of variety and maturity on quality of apple wine. Food Technol. 13, 676–679.

BRASKAT, N., and QUINN, H. A. 1940. Apple wine. Wine Review 8, No. 2, 6–9, 26, 27.

CALDWELL, J. S. 1928. Chemical composition of American grown French cider apples. J. Agr. Res. 36, 391–406.

CHARLEY, V. L. S. 1937. Notes on cider making practices in Europe. Long Ashton Research Station Annual Report 1937, 160–170.

CHARLEY, V. L. S. 1953. The Cider Factory. Plant and Layout. Leonard Hill, London.

CHARLEY, V. L. S. 1954. Principles and Practices of Cider Making. Leonard Hill, London.

CHARLEY, V. L. S., and HARRISON, T. H. 1939. Fruit juices and related products. Imp. Bur. Hort. and Plantation Crops, East Malling, Kent, Tech. Communication 11, 1–104.

CLAGUE, J. A., and FELLERS, C. R. 1936. Apple cider and cider products. Mass. Agr. Expt. Sta. Bull. 336.

CLARK, D. S., WALLACE, R. H., and DAVID, J. J. 1954. Factors affecting the fermentation of apple juice. Appl. Microbiol. 2, 334–348.

CRUESS, W. V. 1914. Utilization of waste oranges. Calif. Agr. Expt. Sta. Bull. 244.

CRUESS, W. V., and CELMER, R. 1938. Utilization of surplus apples. Fruit Prods. J. 17, 325, 356; 18, 4, 43, 79.

CRUESS, W. V., MARSH, G. L., and MENDELS, S. 1935. Fruit wines. Ibid. 14, 295–298.

CRUESS, W. V., and MONTGOMERY, L. M. 1934. A study of cider fermentation. Ibid. 14, 107–109.

DAVIS, M. B. 1933. The manufacture of sweet and fermented cider by the closed curvée method. Ibid. 12, 294–298

DUPAIGNE, P. 1959. L'Analyse des Jus de Fruits. Masson et Cie., Paris.

FESSLER, J. H. 1959. Personal communication.

FESSLER, J. H. PARSONS, J., and NASLEDOV, S. 1949. Sterile filtration. Proc. Am. Soc. Enol. 1949, 52–68. (See also Wines and Vines 30, No. 6, 24; No. 9, 67 and Wine Review 17, No. 5, 14–16; No. 6, 9–11, 1949.)

FILIPELLO, F., and MARSH, G. L. 1934. Honey wine. Fruit Prods. J. 14, 40–42, 61.

GACHOT, H. 1955. Manuel des Jus de Fruits. 2 ed. P. H. Heitz, Strasbourg.

GACHOT H. 1957. Dictionnaire Technique de l'Industrie des Jus de Fruits. Français-Anglais-Allemand. Fruit-Union Suisse, Zoug, Switzerland.

GORE, H. C. 1914. Apple syrup and concentrated cider. U. S. Dept. Agr. Year Book 1914, 233–245.

HENRY, B. S. 1936. Studies of yeasts and the fermentation of fruits and berries of Washington. Univ. Washington Bull. Published by the Secretary of State, State of Washington.

JACOBSEN, E. 1934. Obstweine, Fruchtsäfte und Süssmoste. Braunschweigische Konservenzeitung, Braunschweig, Germany.

JOSLYN, M. A. 1959. Private communication. Berkeley, Calif.

JOSLYN, M. A., and AMERINE, M. A. 1964. Dessert, Appetizer and Other Flavored Wines. University of California, Division of Agricultural Sciences, Berkeley.

JOSLYN, M. A., and MARSH, G. L. 1934. Suggestions for making orange wine. Fruits Prods. J. 13, 307, 315.

KERTESZ, Z. I. 1930. New method for enzymic clarification of unfermented apple juice. N. Y. Agr. Expt. Sta. Bull. 589.

KILBUCK, J. H., NUSSENBAUM, F., and CRUESS, W. V. 1949. Pectic enzymes. Investigations on their use in wine making. Wines and Vines 30, No. 8, 23–25.

KOCH, J. 1956. Neuzeitliche Erkentnisse auf dem Gebiet der Süssmostherstellung. 2 ed. Verlag Sigurd Horn, Frankfurt.

KROEMER, K., and KRUMHOLZ, G. 1932. Obst- und Beerenwein. Dr. Serger und Hempel, Braunschweig, Germany.

LEGAKIS, P. A. 1961. A contribution to the study of the yeast flora of apples and apple wine. Athens.

LÜTHI, H. 1953. Gärführung und Behandlung der Obstweine im Kleinbetrieb. 2 ed. Verlag Huber and Co., A. G. Frauenfeld.

MARTINEZ, D. V., CONTÉS, I. H., and MARQUEZ, J. G. 1958. Elaboración de sidra. Ensayos de fermentación usando enzymas pectolificas y sulfuroso. Rev. cienc. appl. 63, 229–303.

MEHLITZ, A. 1951. Süssmost, Fachbuch der gewerbsmässigen Süssmosterzeugnung. 7 ed. Dr. Serger and Hempel, Braunschweig, Germany.

OSTERWALDER, A. 1948. Vom Mäuselgeschmack der Weine, Obst- und Beerenwein; eine Erwiderung. Schweiz. Z. Obst- u. Weinbau 57, 429–431.

PEARCE, B., and BAKER, P. 1939. The yeast flora of bottled ciders. J. Agr. Sci. 3, 55–79.

REITTERSMANN, R. 1952. Die Frucht-Liköre, mit besonderer Berücksichtigung der Fruchtsaft- und Fruchtsirup-Herstellung. 2 ed. Carl Knoppke Grüner Verlag und Vertrieb, Berlin.

SCHANDERL, H., and KOCH, J. 1957. Die Fruchtweinbereitung. Eugen Ulmer, Stuttgart, Germany.

SMOCK, R. M., and NEUBERT, A. M. 1950. Apples and Apple Products. Interscience Publishers, New York and London.

STILLMAN, J. S. 1955. Fruit and berry wine production in California. Am. J. Enol. 6, 32–35.

TSCHENEN, C. 1934. Modern cider manufacture in France. Fruit Prods. J. 14, 111–113, 118.

TRESSLER, D. K., CELMER, R. F., and BEAVENS, E. A. 1941. Bulk fermentation process for sparkling cider. Ind. Eng. Chem. 33, 1027–1032.

U. S. INTERNAL REVENUE SERVICE. 1955. Wine; Part 240 of Title 26 (1954). Code of Federal Regulations. U. S. Govt. Print. Office, Washington. (U. S. Treasury Dept., IRS Pub. 146.)

VALAER, P. J. 1950A. Blackberry and other fruit wines, their methods of production and analysis. Alcohol Tax Unit, Bur. Internal Revenue. Mimeo. Circ.

VALAER, P. J. 1950B. Wines of the World. Abelard Press, New York.

VILLFORTH, F. 1954. Die Bereitung und Behandlung von Obstmost und Obstwein. Eugen Ulmer, Stuttgart.

VOGT, E. 1963. Der Wein, seine Bereitung, Behandlung und Untersuchung. 4 ed. Verlag Eugen Ulmer, Stuttgart.

VON LOESECKE, H. W., MOTTERN, H. H., and PULLEY, G. N. 1936. Wines, brandies and cordials from citrus fruits. Ind. Eng. Chem. 28, 1224–1229.

WARCOLLIER, G. 1909. Pomologie et Cidrerie. J.-B. Baillière et Fils, Paris.

WARCOLLIER, G. 1928. La Cidrerie. J.-B. Baillière et Fils, Paris.

WILHELM, C. F. 1957. Fruchtweine, Obst- und Beerenweine. Carl Knoppke Grüner Verlag, Berlin.

YANG, H. Y. 1953. Fruit wines. Requisites for successful fermentation. J. Agr. Food Chem. 1, 331–333.

YANG, H. Y. 1955. Selection of fruits and berries in wine production. Am. J. Enol. 6, No. 2, 32–35.

YANG, H. Y. 1959. Personal communication.

YANG, H. Y., and WIEGAND, E. H. 1949. Production of fruit wines in the Pacific Northwest. Fruit Prods. J. 29, 8–12, 27, 29.

YANG, H. Y., THOMAS G. E., and WIEGAND, E. H. 1950. The application of pectic enzymes to berry and Concord wines. Wines and Vines 31, No. 4, 77–78.

WINE INSTITUTE. 1971. Fruit and fruit speciality wine type specifications. Wine Institute, San Francisco. June 14, 1971.

CHAPTER 15

Non-Bacterial Spoilage

In addition to spoilage by microorganisms, wines are subject to various types of clouding resulting from metallic contamination, protein precipitation or, occasionally, to oxidation of certain organic constituents. Crystalline deposits of cream of tartar or calcium tartrate may also occur. Haziness, cloudiness or a sediment indicate a defective wine to many consumers, although the affected wine may be fundamentally sound. However, a wine may be aged too long and it then exhibits breaking of the color, and deposition of a sediment, even though it is free of bacterial spoilage or excess metallic contamination.

NON-METALLIC DETERIORATION

In this section we shall consider non-metallic conditions which favor darkening, primarily in white wines.

Darkening of Color

With age, wine in barrels or tanks darkens in color naturally or may change in color. One is not alarmed if old port or burgundy becomes slightly tawny or brownish in color. However, an old Riesling or muscatel may have lost its original pale-yellow color and changed to a brownish or light-amber color. Bottled white dry table wines of normal age should not be amber in color. Red table or dessert wines 3 to 5 years of age should be bright in tint and little color should have been deposited.

Berg has defined wine stability as the attainment of a state or condition such that the wine will not *for some definite period* exhibit undesirable physical or organoleptic changes. To give specific meaning to this definition, the duration of the stable condition, the undesirable changes, and the conditions to which the wine will be subjected should be specified. In other words, stability is a relative term. The undesirable changes that denote instability, as listed by Berg and Akiyoshi (1956) are: (1) browning or darkening of the color, (2) haziness,[1] (3) cloudiness, (4) deposits, and (5) undesirable taste or odor. In this section we shall discuss the first item.

Amerine (1953) and Berg and Akiyoshi (1956) have discussed a number of factors of importance in the browning of white wines. An important one is temperature. The latter determined the rates of darkening at

---

[1] By haziness we mean a very slight cloudiness.

548

four temperatures by measuring the optical density of the wines. The rate of darkening increased as the temperature of storage increased. They obtained evidence that there are substances that react at different rates at low and at high temperatures. Variation in the proportions of these substances may account, they suggest, in part for the great variation in rate of increase of browning in different wines with rise in temperature. In these experiments the oxygen supply was 600 ml. per liter, a very generous amount.

It is very probable that browning not due to oxidation also occurs. One such darkening reaction for sweet wines may be that between amino acids and hexose sugars, the Maillard reaction. Mackinney and Temmer (1948) studied the darkening of dried fruits. They concluded that decomposition products of sugars in dried fruits, fruit concentrates, jellies and other concentrated fruit products are involved in the darkening reaction, in addition to the reactions between hexose sugars and amino acids. Stadtman (1948) in addition to furfural and hydroxymethylfurfural found at least 13 other carbonyl compounds in the blackened syrup extracted with ethyl acetate from darkened dried apricots. Addition of furfural to apricot syrup greatly increased its rate of darkening. The resulting dark compounds were indistinguishable from those produced in the natural browning of the fruit. He concludes that certain carbonyl compounds may be involved in the darkening of dried fruits and other concentrated fruit products.

Weast and Mackinney (1941) found that the purified black compound extracted from darkened dried apricots contained 3.26 per cent nitrogen. They produced black compounds with properties very similar to those of the black compound of darkened dried apricots by reaction between glutamic acid or aspartic acid and levulose or dextrose, levulose reacting more rapidly. Since wines contain amino acids and the hexose sugars levulose and dextrose, it is possible that the Maillard reaction occurs during the darkening of certain wines, particularly those high in sugars. See also Haas *et al.* (1948) and Haas and Stadtman (1949).

Berg and Akiyoshi (1956) state that varietal effect is the most important factor in the darkening of white wines and that other factors merely modify its influence. Wines of the varieties Emerald Riesling, Palomino, and Pinot blanc were found to darken especially easily. This observation has been verified by winery experience.

Enzymic Oxidation

They found, as Hussein and Cruess (1940) had earlier, that enzymic darkening of commercial white California wines is not of great importance. However, the rapid browning of fresh grape juice is due to enzymic oxidation. In experiments reported by Cruess (1948) and by Berg and Akiyoshi (1956), pasteurization of white California table wines at a high enough temperature to inactivate oxidase did not noticeably reduce the rate of browning. See also Pilone (1953).

In certain European wine producing regions summer rains are frequent and, as a consequence, the fungus *Botrytis cinerea* often develops extensively on grapes and secretes a polyphenoloxidase. If not inactivated, it will, under proper conditions, cause browning of white wines. Occasionally it has been observed that wines made from very moldy California grapes in California are subject to oxidasic browning.

Oxidasic browning of wines made from botrytis-infected grapes can be prevented by heating the must or new wine to a high enough temperature for a sufficient time to inactivate the enzyme. Laborde (1907) recommended 185°F. for 15 seconds and Pacottet (1926) 158° to 176°F. for five minutes. It appears that 1 to 2 minutes at 180°F. would be sufficient. A common method of preventing undue darkening by the polyphenoloxidase is to maintain a fairly high level of free sulfur dioxide. More sulfur dioxide is required for a high-sugar sweet wine, such as a sauterne, than for a dry table wine owing to the combining of sulfur dioxide with the sugar and the reduction of the free sulfur dioxide content.

Removal of Excess Color

Excess color can be removed by fining with casein or by use of activated carbon. Ibarra and Cruess (1948) and O'Neal *et al.* (1950) found casein fining a convenient and effective means of reducing the color of dark white wines. They reported casein to affect the flavor of the wine less than did the activated carbon used by them in comparative experiments. Special carbons may be used to remove excess color from wine as in the production of pale sherries and white ports, but legal restrictions must be taken into account. This treatment is discussed further in Chapter 9. Special ion exchange resins can also be used for this purpose.

De Villiers (1961) and Cantarelli (1962) recommended use of nylon paste to improve the color of white wines, to remove browning precursors, to increase resistance to browning, and to reduce anthocyanogen and tannin content. Fuller and Berg (1965) recommended nylon in preference to casein because of its greater protection against browning and absence of an adverse effect on wine quality. They emphasized the necessity for laboratory trials in view of Caputi, Jr. and Peterson's finding (1965) that in some cases nylon treatment can increase browning. Nitrogen stripping, carbon dioxide blanketing, and addition of sulfur dioxide or sometimes of ascorbic acid all have their place in the handling of these wines.

Oxidasic Casse

In severe cases oxidasic casse due to polyphenoloxidase from molds may cause clouding in addition to darkening. Its presence may be detected as follows: allow a half-filled, loosely corked bottle of the wine to stand for 3 or 4 days, heat another sample to 185° to 190°F. for 3 or 4 minutes in a thin-walled flask and cool it at once under the tap. If it becomes cloudy during heating, filter it. Let it stand in a half-filled bottle beside the untreated sample for 3 to 4 days. If the untreated sample darkens severely and the heated sample does not, the presence of an active oxidase is indicated. If both samples become cloudy, iron casse is indicated. If neither sample clouds or darkens, the wine may have neither form of casse or may have such a high sulfur dioxide content that one or both forms of casse are held in check temporarily.

Berg and Akiyoshi (1956) found that California white wines that had been heated to destroy oxidase darkened more rapidly on exposure to air than the unheated—indicating that the heating had resulted in the production of precursors that materially increased the rate of browning. They also observed that white wine to which sulfur dioxide had been added darkened in color at 113°F. when the free sulfur dioxide had dropped to a low level, 0 to 40 p.p.m. *These observations suggest that unnecessary pasteurization of white wines should be avoided.*

Other Factors in Browning

In Berg and Akiyoshi's experiments, addition of grape-seed tannin decreased the rate of browning, whereas synthetic tannic acid increased it. Small amounts of soluble copper and iron increased the rate of darkening, but their effect was additive rather than synergistic. Iron was a more active catalyst than copper in the presence of dissolved oxygen.

Added citric acid at the rate of 2 lbs. per 100 gallons (about 2 to 4 gm. per liter) exerted an inhibitory effect on browning, because of its ability to form non-pigmented compounds with iron.

Darkening of sherry during heating is probably due to oxidation and caramelization of sugars. One or more of the browning reactions discussed by Weast and Mackinney (1941), and by Mackinney and Temmer (1948) in the browning of dried fruits may occur during sherry baking. Heitz *et al.* (1951) have made a study of the changes that occur during the baking of sherry. See also p. 399.

Protein Clouding

Protein clouding is mainly a problem of white wines. Where the pH of the wine is near to the isoelectric point of the wine proteins, greater precipitation will occur. This may also occur during blending. Fermentation results in precipitation of proteins, more of Koch's (1963) fraction II than I. Lowering the pH of the must increases the precipitation (Du Plessis 1964). Proteins are lost during aging. They can be removed by heating or bentonite fining with the former removing more of fraction I than II and the latter removing equal amounts of the two fractions. See Kean and Marsh (1956A, 1956B) and Koch and Sajak (1959). Böhringer and Dölle (1959) reported the eight amino acids primarily involved in clouding are: aspartic acid, isoleucine, leucine, methionine, phenylalanine, threonine, tyrosine and valine. Wines containing aspartic acid and threonine were more stable. Wucherpfennig and Franke (1967) found that bentonite-treated German musts produced protein-stable wines.

Koch's test (1963) for successful removal of protein was to add 5 per cent of saturated ammonium sulfate to a sample of the wine and heat at 113°F. for nine hours. The sample was then placed in water at 33°F. for 15 minutes. The wine was considered protein-stable if there was no precipitation. A practical test for protein stability was proposed by Berg and Akiyoshi (1961). To 10 ml. of wine, 1 ml. of 55 per cent trichloroacetic acid was added and the tube placed in boiling water for two minutes. The sample was allowed to cool to room temperature and the degree of clouding determined in a Coleman Model 9 Nepho-Colorimeter. Complete absence of haze or amorphous deposit classified the wine as protein stable. Moretti and Berg (1965) found four major protein fractions with one being much more heat labile than the others. Protein stability in wines is apparently a function of the ratio of the amount of this fraction to the combined amount of the other fractions.

METALLIC DETERIORATION

The more serious non-bacterial defects of wine are due to excess metals. See Amerine and Joslyn (1970), Ash (1935), Draper and Thompson (1955), Filipello (1947), Mrak et al. (1937), and Walter (1951).

White Casse

The common form of casse in California wines is due to formation of a white precipitate or cloud of ferric phosphate. Iron casse, consisting of a greenish or bluish precipitate of iron tannate, is very rare in California.

As Amerine and Joslyn (1951) have pointed out, the formation of iron clouds in wine depends upon a number of factors: the concentration of iron, the nature of the predominant acid and its concentration, the pH value, the oxidation-reduction potential, the concentration of phosphates and the kind of tannin and its concentration. "White casse" is due to ferric phosphate. Ribéreau-Gayon (1930, 1933) found that iron phosphate casse can only form in the range of pH 2.9 to 3.6. Marsh (1940) confirmed his findings with California wines. Many of our wines have pH values above 3.6 and hence are not subject to white casse. Iron is present in the ferrous (Fe^{++}) and ferric (Fe^{+++}) forms. Normally the ferrous predominates over the ferric. On aeration ferrous is converted to ferric and ferric phosphate may then form and cause clouding—if other conditions, such as pH value, etc. are favorable. Berg (1953B) found the maximum iron content for stability to be 5 p.p.m. The wine usually contains more than sufficient phosphate to form a haze or cloud with the iron, if other conditions are favorable. Amerine (1958) quoting from European reports gives the phosphate content for 77 French wines as follows: minimum, 0.039 gm.; maximum, 0.60 gm. per liter; and the average, 0.262 gm. of phosphate per liter; for 534 Italian wines the values were 0.070, 0.637, and 0.236 gm. per liter; and for 456 wines of Portugal the values were 0.080, 0.900, and 0.36. Jaulmes (1951) states that if the phosphate content exceeds 0.50 gm. per liter, it is an indication of sophistication, that is, of the addition of phosphate.

Jaulmes (1951) states that French wines normally contain 5 to 30 mg. per liter of iron. Amerine (1958) has given the following data on iron content of wines: 720 California wines had a minimum of 0 mg. per liter, a maximum of 35 with an average of 4.89; 38 samples of French wines showed 3.5, 26.0, and 8.81 mg. of Fe per liter for the minimum, maximum, and average values; and for 630 samples of Swiss wines the values were 2.1, 26.0, and 5.5 mg. per liter. A California wine with no more than about 4 mg. per liter of iron usually represents a wine that has been treated to remove iron.

Ribéreau-Gayon (1933) made a very extensive study of the conditions under which iron casse forms. He studied the role of redox potential, pH value, state of oxidation of the iron, iron concentration, enzymes, and other factors. Even if the iron concentration is fairly high casse will not form unless other conditions are proper. Iron forms complex ions with citrate ion in which form it no longer reacts as ferric or ferrous ion and, on that account, addition of citric acid to susceptible wines will usually prevent ferric phosphate casse. He reported that Bouffard as early as 1887 advocated the addition of citric acid in order to prevent clouding due to iron and found it much more effective than tartaric acid for this purpose. Amerine and Joslyn (1951) state that addition of 1 lb. of citric acid per 1000 gal. of wine is usually sufficient. See also Genevois (1935).

Blue casse (iron tannate cloud) is uncommon in California. It occurs in white wines occasionally, but only after addition of tannin or tannic acid. In red wines it may result in a blue cloud and later a blue deposit. Amerine and Joslyn (1951) state that aeration may convert the ferrous to the ferric condition. If followed by fining and filtration this usually results in a clear, stable wine. Many California wines become brown and vapid in taste by such a treatment. The removal of iron and copper from wine by use of ferrocyanide or Cufex or by other methods is discussed in a later section in this chapter.

Sources of Iron

Some wine makers have the impression that the natural iron content of grapes is sufficient to cause iron casse. However, research indicates that much (to most) of the excess iron present in grapes disappears during fermentation. Thus, Byrne et al. (1936) found that the iron content of musts of 57 samples of grapes grown in various districts in California ranged from 1.5 to 23 p.p.m. Probably much of the iron came from dust on the grapes. The average iron content of the must was 9 p.p.m. Sixteen of the musts were fermented in glass, and the iron content of the resulting wines averaged only 1.8 p.p.m. The iron content of 55 samples of commercially made wines ranged from 1.0 to 35 p.p.m., with an average of 5.4 p.p.m.

Thaler and Mühlberger (1956) found 10 to 25 p.p.m. of iron in seven German musts, average 17 p.p.m., but only 0.5 to 12 p.p.m. in the clarified musts. Thoukis and Amerine (1956) found that 47.5 to 70 per cent of the iron was lost from small volumes of must during fermentation, on a laboratory scale and that most of this was held by the yeast. Marsh (1959A) has pointed out that these small scale fermentations are subject to error unless the wine is removed from the fermentation flask immediately after fermentation. Otherwise air will enter, convert the ferrous to ferric ion and much of the iron will be precipitated as ferric phosphate, etc. Schanderl (1959) found a marked decrease in the iron content of German musts during fermentation; the yeast contained most of the iron that had disappeared from the must. Capt (1957) in Switzerland concluded on the basis of analysis of 608 wines that equipment was the main cause of excessive iron content. In nearly all cases addition of citric acid would protect the wines against ferric casse. He concluded that 8 p.p.m. of iron was the critical concentration for Swiss wines to which no citric acid is added. Wines made in glass are reported to contain only 1.0 to 4.5 p.p.m. of iron compared to wines made commercially from the same grapes which contain 5 to 39 p.p.m. of iron. The increased use of stainless steel equipment has further reduced the iron content of California wines.

Vitagliano (1956) found that the iron content of wines of southern Italy stored in concrete tanks was six times that of wines stored in wood. He also observed that the use of continuous presses constructed of steel increased the iron content appreciably.

Genevois (1933) has reviewed most of the research of Ribéreau-Gayon and others of the Bordeaux school of enologists on the iron problem of French wines. The review includes such points as how iron causes clouding, the effect of redox potentials, and formation of iron complexes in wine. He found that iron as part of a citric complex ion travelled to the anode in electrophoresis experiments, indicating that it was part of a negatively charged anion.

Capt and Michod (1951) found certain filter pads to be an important source of iron in Swiss wines. Saywell (1935) made a similar observation in California and various winery chemists in this state have found that some of the filter pads in use shortly after repeal contained excessive amounts of iron. However, modern filter pads are treated by the manufacturer to remove all or most of the wine-soluble iron and calcium. Capt (1957) has stated that gelatin and isinglass used in the fining of white wines may also increase the iron content appreciably. The evidence, therefore, would indicate that excessive iron content in wine comes from the equipment rather than from the grapes.

Equipment

One method of minimizing the iron content (and copper content as well) of wine is by use of equipment made of corrosion-resistant materials. Metals are used very generally in wineries not only in crushers, pumps, filters, pasteurizers, pipe lines, refrigerating equipment, and bottling machinery but also for storage tanks, tank cars, tank trucks, pipe fittings, and hose fittings. For transfer, wineries have used Pyrex glass piping; vinegar factories hard rubber and plastic piping, filters, and pumps. Mrak et al. (1937) conducted experiments in three California wineries and in the laboratory on the corrosion of various metals and alloys by musts and wines. They found Inconel alloy, aluminum alloy No. 76, and stainless steel to be the most resistant of the metals tested. In the wineries corrosion was most severe at the crushers.

Searle et al. (1934) studied the corrosion of seven corrosion-resistant metals and alloys by wines made from V. labrusca grapes. They concluded that Inconel alloy is adequate for all winery uses and that nickel, Monel metal alloy, 18-8 stainless steel, aluminum, and copper were adequate for most purposes, except in equipment in which the relation between liquid volume and area of exposed metal is unfavorable. (Copper has since been found undesirable for most purposes in the winery.) Shortly after repeal it was not yet recognized that copper was the principal cause of clouding of California wines. Much of the clouding diagnosed as due to iron was caused by copper. Aluminum pitted badly and should probably not be used. Also, according to Marsh (1959A), aluminum may reduce sulfur dioxide to hydrogen sulfide and may reduce the color of white wines to an almost water white condition. One large California winery had to replace aluminum equipment on that account. However, certain aluminum alloys may be satisfactory.

Joslyn and Lukton (1953) point out that although stainless steel is very resistant to attack by wine it cannot be used for both the shaft and the bearing in a pump because of binding. Therefore, while the stainless steel part of the pump will be corrosion resistant, the bearing made of another metal may corrode. Modern wineries have come a long way toward replacing copper, brass, and iron with stainless steel.

Joslyn and Lukton (1953) have suggested that hard chrome plating might be utilized to coat certain winery equipment. They have reported on rather extensive laboratory scale experiments with brass, bronze, copper, stainless steel, hot-rolled steel, cast iron, and cold-rolled steel strips plated with chromium. Rossi, Jr. (1951) has also conducted similar experiments. While results were not entirely satisfactory there was no chromium pick-up by the wine, and with improved plating the method may have possibilities. However, Marsh (1959B) recommends the use of stainless steel and states that the industry in California is following that practice rather than the one of chromium plating. See also Ploderl and Weyman (1957).

Copper Casse

Occasionally white wines containing sulfur dioxide and a small amount of dissolved copper, when stored in sealed bottles, develop a haze or cloud that eventually settles out as a reddish brown precipitate. The haziness or deposit occurs only in the absence of oxygen and ferric iron and redissolves readily upon exposure of the wine to air or upon addition of hydrogen peroxide. Storage of the bottled wine in sunlight hastens formation of the cloudiness (copper casse): light acting in a reducing manner in this case. As Joslyn and Lukton (1953) as well as Kean and Marsh (1956A) point out, the copper casse problem greatly increased during and shortly after World War II. This was due to the replacement of much of the iron equipment with copper in California wineries in order to get away from the iron casse problem and the great increase in the bottling of wine. See also Rentschler and Tanner (1951).

Ribéreau-Gayon (1933, 1935) believed at one time that the cloud consisted of cupric sulfide. The following reactions explain on this basis the formation of copper casse:

(1) $Cu^{++} + RH \rightarrow Cu^+ + R + H^+$

(2) $6Cu^+ + 6H^+ + SO_2 \rightarrow 6Cu^{++} + H_2S + 2H_2O$

(3) $Cu^{++} + H_2S \rightarrow CuS + 2H^+$

(4) $CuS + $ electrolytes $ + $ colloids $\rightarrow$ flocculation

(5) $6RH + SO_2 = 6R + H_2S + 2H_2O$

On exposure to air or addition of hydrogen peroxide he suggested that the following reaction occurred: $CuS + 2O_2 \rightarrow CuSO_4$. He did not believe that copper ions were directly involved in reduction of the sulfur dioxide but that a reducing agent of unknown composition reduces cupric ions to cuprous, and these in turn reduce sulfur dioxide to hydrogen sulfide.

Kean and Marsh (1956A) reported that copper casse is high in nitrogen and low in sulfur content and that the nitrogen represents protein nitrogen rather than amino nitrogen, although the nitrogen content of wines is principally in the form of amino acids. The protein content is very low; nevertheless, under California conditions there is sufficient to take part in formation of copper casse. In one case the protein content of a sauterne wine was only 1 mg. per liter, yet copper casse, with a sediment containing 49.6 per cent of protein, developed. The total nitrogen content of this wine was 312 mg. per liter. Joslyn and Lukton (1956) obtained similar results.

Kean and Marsh confirmed by chromatographic technique that the nitrogen of the copper casse cloud is proteinaceous or polypeptid in character. By means of experiments with synthetic wines containing a hydrolysate of lactalbumin of low protein and high amino acid content, they found that sulfur dioxide and copper were necessary for formation of a completely reversible cloud (forming under reducing conditions and disappearing under oxidizing conditions). No casse appeared when amino acids were the only source of nitrogen. Sulfur dioxide always catalyzed clouding in sunlight. A completely irreversible cloud formed in the absence of copper and sulfur dioxide and a partially reversible cloud formed if copper was present and sulfur dioxide absent. They concluded that what is referred to as copper casse is usually a combination of several "clouds," namely, protein-tannin, copper-protein, and a copper-sulfur complex (probably copper sulfide).

Joslyn and Lukton (1956) concluded on the basis of X-ray data taken on purified copper casse that both cuprous and cupric sulfide were present. At that time there was some doubt as to whether the sulfur of the copper sulfide came from the reduction of sulfur dioxide or from cleavage of the disulfide bonds in protein. Peterson et al. (1958) used a sulfite containing radioactive sulfur and concluded that in the light the copper complex is formed by reduction of sulfite with subsequent formation of insoluble cupric sulfide and the flocculation by protein. In the dark some denaturation of protein by sulfite occurs, resulting in a copper-protein complex capable of yielding sulfate-S on oxidation.

In the above investigations protein was determined by precipitation with trichloracetic acid followed by a micro-Kjeldahl determination of the nitrogen.

Removal of Iron and Copper

About fifty years ago W. Möslinger in Germany found that excess iron in wine could be removed by addition of ferrocyanide. Meyer in 1910 described this treatment of wine and stated that it should be followed by addition of zinc sulfate and tannin. Later the use of zinc salts in the treatment of wine was prohibited in Germany. Heide (1933) has given an extensive and detailed report on the use of potassium ferrocyanide in Germany for the removal of excess iron from wine. This treatment of wine is known as blue fining, or "Blauschönung" in German. He states that at that time its use was permitted in Germany, Yugoslavia, and Austria under strict governmental supervision. It is in common use in Germany at present. It is not officially permitted in the United States and both the California and Federal authorities concerned require that wine must contain less than 1 p.p.m. of cyanide (a decomposition product of ferrocyanide), as shown by the Hubach test. However, a ferrocyanide-containing complex known as Cufex is permitted in the United States. This compound is subject to the same limitation (p. 742).

Until recently the use of ferrocyanide was prohibited in France, but it may now be used under specified conditions. For an early French report, see Ribéreau-Gayon (1934). Wall's (1932) study is also valuable. Calcium phytate, sodium sulfide, and charcoal can be used in France in the treatment of wine under the control of designated chemists. Properly used, ferrocyanide removes not only excess iron but also copper and protein and does not adversely affect the flavor and bouquet of the wine.

Heide (1933) stated that a simple iron and copper determination cannot be used as a guide for the amount of potassium ferrocyanide required; for the reason that some of the ferrocyanide is used in precipitating organic colloids, including protein. He recommended that a series of practical tests be made with measured volumes of the wine and 0.5 per cent ferrocyanide solution followed by measured volumes of tannin and gelatin solutions, allowing them to settle, filtering and testing for excess ferrocyanide by addition of dilute ferric potassium sulfate and a little hydrochloric acid. Any such tests should be made on the wine immediately after removal of the sample from the storage tank, because in standing much of the ferrous iron may be oxidized to the ferric condition and be precipitated.

The complicated and not completely resolved chemistry of the reaction of ferrocyanide and iron has been studied by Bonastre (1959). He showed that the presence of an organic fining agent, isinglass, markedly reduced the efficiency of the ferrocyanide. The removal of iron is greater in dilute solutions even when the ratio of ferrocyanide/iron is constant. The reaction is slow, lasting up to seven days. Castino (1965) recommended adding 50 mg. per liter of ascorbic acid to bring all the iron to the ferrous state and thus increase the efficiency of blue fining. The wine should have a pH of about 3.4 for best results.

An addition of ferrocyanide that will remove most of the iron usually removes all of the copper. Fessler (1952) has recommended that the copper be completely removed, although Lherme (1931–1932) has stated that Bordeaux wines can tolerate 0.5 mg. of copper per liter and Amerine and Joslyn (1951) gave 0.3 mg. per liter as the maximum tolerance for California wines. Marsh (1959A) suspects that European wines of very low protein content tolerate more copper than many California wines. Insofar as we are aware, the first publication in this country on use of ferrocyanide for the removal of iron from grape products was that of Brown (1932). It led to its experimental use for wine in California.

Ramage (1938, 1941) proposed the use of ferrous-ferricyanide complexes for the removal of iron and other metallic impurities from wine. The preparation, (essentially a Prussian blue) was precipitated in the presence of excess soluble ferricyanide, either alone or in combination with silica gel, activated carbon or cellulose. Zeolite, also, was first treated with an iron solution then with ferricyanide to form an insoluble coat of Prussian blue. He obtained patents in 1938 and in 1941.

In 1951 and 1952 a test on the use of a new preparation known as the "Fessler compound" for removal of copper and iron from wine was made in six California wineries. Marsh (1952) who cooperated with the California Department of Public Health and Fessler in conducting the experiments, reported that over 100,000 gallons of wine were treated. All of the copper was removed by the treatment, and although ten times the required amount of the Fessler compound was used experimentally no cyanogenetic residues were found by the Hubach test. Later the Fessler compound was given the trade name of Cufex. As described by Fessler (1952) it is a mixture of salts that are brownish in color and disperse easily in wine. Marsh reports that it reacts instantly with the copper in the wine and settles quickly. He states that the lees or sediment is small in volume and that the flavor and bouquet of the wine are not damaged. The preparation is now sold in the form of a cream. It is included in the list of permissible chemicals for use in wine. It is also allowed by Federal and State of California regulation agencies, but under the limitation that the treated wine shall contain no insoluble residue in excess of 1 p.p.m. and no soluble residue; in other words, it must be used at the wine producer's risk. Nevertheless, it is in common use.

Joslyn and Lukton (1953) reported that in their investigation of iron and copper turbidities in wines, they made a Prussian blue preparation by adding a ferric chloride solution to potassium ferrocyanide in an amount equal to about 50 per cent excess of that required to precipitate the iron. The precipitate was washed several times with water and dried. It was ground in a mortar and mixed with about 10 per cent by weight of infusorial earth filter-aid to increase the particle size and to facilitate settling and filtration. When washed well with warm water, this preparation left no excess ferrocyanide in the wine treated with it. Joslyn and Lukton suggest that a coagulated protein, bentonite, cellulose, or other inert substance might be used as a carrier for their preparation, essentially Prussian blue.

The usual test for residual cyanide in wine is the Hubach (1948) test (see pp. 717–718). When ferrocyanide or a special preparation such as Cufex has been used in wine to remove copper and iron, special care should be taken in order that all of the precipitate is removed from the wine by close filtration. Berg (1953A, 1953B) has given precautions that should be observed. Among them are the following: Only clear wines should be treated. The treated wine should be allowed to stand overnight. In precoating the filter, use filtered wine or water. Care must be taken to remove all of the entrapped air from filter presses. Low pressure and a constant, medium flow rate should be maintained during filtration. This will require the use of a vari-speed drive pump. The filtration should be stopped when the pressure rises beyond 50 lbs. Add pink filter-aid at such rate that a constant flow rate is maintained. After each filtration flush out with water all hoses, the filter, and other equipment used. Finally, flush out with a dilute alkali solution followed by water. Additional directions are given for handling screen and plate and frame filters in Berg's articles.

Phytates and phytic acid have been suggested for removal of iron and copper from wine. Phytic acid is a product obtained from corn, and phytates are obtainable from corn products refining companies. Joslyn et al. (1953) report that calcium phytate and phytic acid removed some of the iron from wine, but none of the copper. Auerbach and DeSoto (1955), confirming the earlier research of Cohee and Steffen (1949) of the Corn Products Refining Co., also have reported that Aferrin removed up to 88 per cent of the iron from dry white wine but none of the copper. Calcium phytate increased the calcium content of the wine appreciably and might contribute to calcium instability in wines of moderately high natural calcium content (see also p. 562). Auerbach and DeSoto found Aferrin to be principally magnesium phytate.

Joslyn and Lukton (1953) tried a number of ion exchange resins, both cation and anion types, for removal of copper and iron from wine, but report that none of the resins was a suitable substitute for ferrocyanide. They observed slight to moderate reduction in copper and iron content, but insufficient to be of practical value. They, therefore, are not in agreement with Pecheur (1957) who has stated that cation exchange resins will reduce the copper content of wine sufficiently to prevent copper casse. Rankine (1955B) found that ion exchange resins had little effect on the copper content of Australian wines. However, as Marsh (1959A) has indicated, lowering of the pH value of the wine sufficiently will make removal of heavy metals, particularly iron, by certain exchange resins effective. This relationship has been demonstrated by Pato (1959). Joslyn and Lukton state that it is possible that an ion exchange resin with specific high capacity for copper can be developed. They point out that the various ferrocyanide complexes made by them, as well as commercially by others, are in effect exchange resins.

A large number of compounds were tested by Joslyn and Lukton (1953) as to their effect in removing copper and iron from wine, but none except ferrocyanide, Prussian blue ferrocyanide complex and rubeanic acid reduced the wine's content of these elements appreciably. The substances tested included chlorophyll, tannic acid, diatomaceous earth, bauxite, cupferron, phytates, and hemoglobin. However, they report that further investigation should be made of the applicability of sulfhydryl compounds, such as cysteine and thioglycollic acid, ascorbic acid under certain conditions and proteins rich in sulfur containing amino acids.

The sequestering effect of EDTA (ethylenediaminetetraacetate) also known as Versene and Sequestrene) has been studied. Krum and Fellers (1952) reported that eight parts per million of Sequestrene per part of metal in the wine produced clarification, but they did not indicate whether elimination of copper casse was caused by the added Sequestrene or by exposure of the wine to air (oxidation). In experiments made by Joslyn and Lukton (1953) it was found that iron in wine is apparently tightly bound by Versene and no longer reacts with ferrocyanide or thiocyanate. They quote Fessler (1952) as reporting that copper in wines to which Versene has been added continues to form copper casse but no longer responds to ferrocyanide fining. In Joslyn and Lukton's experiments Versene was effective in preventing copper casse in many, but not in all, cases.

Rubeanic acid was found by Joslyn and Lukton (1953) to be very effective in removing copper, but less effective in removing iron from wine. Rubeanic acid is dithiooxamide. The precipitation of copper proceeds slowly enough to insure formation of particles of relatively large size; consequently, separation of the black copper rubeanate can be readily accomplished by filtration or decantation. A disadvantage of its use is that it must be dissolved in a small amount of alcohol before it is added to the wine, and this would require approval by State and Federal regulatory agencies. Also, its relatively high cost at present is another limiting factor.

Joslyn and Lukton (1953) point out that since proteins and polypeptides, particularly those rich in sulfur-containing amino acids, are involved in copper casse formation, their complete removal from the wine and the avoidance of their increase by yeast autolysis might prevent copper casse even in wines containing considerable copper. As previously mentioned, fining with bentonite is one simple method of removing protein from wine. Use of gelatin with the bentonite should be avoided because it increases the protein content of the wine and thereby increases its susceptibility to copper casse.

Iron casse (white casse) in California wines is, as mentioned earlier, due to formation of ferric phosphate. Also, as previously stated, the addition of citric acid, about one pound per thousand gallons, by formation of complex ferric-citrate ions will usually prevent its appearance. If the iron content of the wine is reduced sufficiently by blue fining or the use of a ferrocyanide-Prussian-blue, complex formation of white casse can be prevented even if citric acid is not added. However, addition of this acid is much the simpler of the two methods.

Calcium Tartrate Instability

A very troublesome cause of instability in California wines has been the deposition of calcium tartrate crystals after bottling. As Berg (1957) has stated, refrigeration as now used by commercial wineries for removal of excess tartrates by formation of potassium bitartrate and calcium tartrate crystals usually does not remove enough of the calcium tartrate to prevent later deposition on prolonged standing after bottling.

Amerine (1958) has given the calcium content of 101 samples of California wines as follows: 6 mg. per liter minimum; 117 mg. maximum, and 52 mg. average; and for 70 French wines, 36 mg. per liter minimum, 112 mg. maximum, and 91 mg. average. He, as well as other enologists, state that excess calcium gets into the wine from plastering (see p. 410), from storage or fermentation in concrete tanks, from filter pads, and from fining materials. Crawford (1951) found 1 to 15 per cent of calcium in the asbestos fiber used in the filtration of his plant's wines. He concluded that much of the crystalline deposit from some of the bottled wine examined in his laboratory was calcium oxalate. Cambitzi (1947) observed that on long standing some of the dextro-rotatory tartaric acid of wines changes into the racemic form. The calcium salt of the racemic tartaric acid is soluble only to the extent of 30 mg. per liter, whereas, 230 mg. per liter of the calcium salt of dextro-tartaric acid is soluble. Cambitzi (1947) states that at ordinary cellar temperature enough of the racemate is formed to exceed its solubility. Crawford (1951) observed calcium tartrate deposits in wines ranging from 50 to 120 p.p.m. of calcium, crystallization taking from 4 to 7 months to become apparent.

DeSoto and Warkentin (1955) found that the pH value of sherry is a critical factor in the formation of calcium tartrate deposits. Thus, sherry of pH 3.4 held in solution a maximum of 128 p.p.m. of calcium, one of pH 3.6 held 98 p.p.m.; pH 3.8 held 63 p.p.m.; pH 4.0, 51 p.p.m. and wine of pH 4.2, only 41 p.p.m. Commercial wines of pH 3.5 to 3.70 and 80 to 117 p.p.m. showed no calcium deposits on long storage in the bottle, but in wines of pH 3.80 to 3.85 and 73 to 78 p.p.m. of calcium tartrate deposits developed. They recommend that the pH value of sherry be adjusted to 3.5 to 3.7, depending on its calcium content.

Crawford (1951) reported that when the calcium content of the wine was reduced to 30 p.p.m. by treatment with a cation exchange resin, no calcium tartrate deposit formed in two years' storage of the bottled wine. Garoglio (1957), Kielhöfer (1957), Pecheur (1957), Dickinson and Stoneman (1958), Rankine (1955B), S. Schanderl (1957), and others have found that proper treatment of wine with cation resins lowers the calcium content below the level required for formation of crystalline deposits in bottled wine. The use of ion exchange resins is discussed further in the next section.

The customary method of removal of excess calcium tartrate is by refrigeration of the wine to near its freezing point for a period of about two weeks. After refrigeration the wine is filtered cold to prevent redissolving of the crystals of tartrates. The wine maker hopes that the treated wine will remain stable insofar as subsequent deposition of tartrates is concerned. However, experience has shown that the treated wine on long standing in the bottle may show a deposit of calcium tartrate. Refrigeration is covered more fully elsewhere (p. 291). Brown's (1953) recommendation of calcium malate has not been adopted. Berg and Keefer (1958–1959) calculated that calcium tartrate is more soluble in wine than in alcohol-water solutions. They have also calculated the solubility products of saturated solutions of potassium acid tartrate (ionic strength 0.038) for temperatures between 24.8° and 68°F. They were as follows ($\times$ 10^{-6}):

Tempera-ture	Alcohol, Per Cent by Volume					
°F.	10	12	14	16	18	20
24.8	25.6	20.3	16.2	12.9	10.3	8.2
32.0	36.0	29.0	23.2	18.5	14.8	11.8
41.0	56.0	45.0	36.0	28.9	23.2	18.6
50.0	89.3	72.9	59.7	48.9	40.0	32.9
59.0	128.0	108.0	91.0	76.9	64.8	54.6
68.0	197.0	164.0	136.0	113.0	94.0	77.9

The concentration product (CP) is calculated from the product of mols per liter of potassium times mols per liter of total tartrate (in the form of acid tartrate). Tables are given for calculating the latter. This product is then compared with the solubility product given above for the proper temperature and alcohol content to determine if the wine will be stable.

For saturated solutions of calcium tartrate the solubility product constants for the same temperatures and per cent alcohol were as follows ($\times 10^{-8}$):

Tempera-ture	Alcohol, Per Cent by Volume					
°F.	10	12	14	16	18	20
24.8	32.3	24.0	17.7	13.1	9.7	7.1
32.0	41.5	30.4	22.4	16.5	12.2	9.0
41.0	55.4	41.0	30.5	22.7	16.9	12.6
50.0	74.8	55.8	41.8	21.3	23.5	17.7
59.0	102.0	76.6	57.7	43.5	32.8	24.8
68.0	137.5	104.0	78.3	59.2	45.0	34.1

The concentration product (CP) is calculated from the product of mols per liter of calcium times mols per liter of total tartrate (in the form of tartrate). Tables are given for calculating the total tartrate in the form of tartrate at different pH and alcohol contents. The amounts of calcium reported in normal wines varies from 0.03 to 0.21 gm. per liter. There is less in wines than in the musts from which they were made. Wines of less than 0.07 gm. per liter are generally considered safe from calcium tartrate deposition but this depends on the pH as indicated above.

Potassium Bitartrate Instability

Wine when new is supersaturated with potassium bitartrate, cream of tartar, and unless the excess is removed in some manner deposits of it are apt to form in the bottled wine. Although such crystallization does not constitute spoiling of the wine, the consumer is apt to consider it a serious defect.

The variables influencing tartrate stability have been studied in many laboratories, Berg (1957, 1960) and Marsh (1959B). Among the factors which have been shown to be important are alcohol, acids, cations, anions, pH, pigments, and various complexing compounds. Pilone and Berg (1965) showed that the changes in potassium and tartrate content during storage or after ion-exchange or charcoal treatment could not be explained solely on the basis of a simple reaction between the two ions. In red wines resolubilization of potassium acid tartrate occurred. This they attributed to polyphenol-tartrate reactions. They also suggested potassium-colloidal pigment reactions. In white wines solubilization of tartrates was attributed to the binding power of proteins for tartaric acid.

Berg and Keefer (1958–1959) calculated the relative stability of potassium and calcium tartrates in wines of various alcohol contents under different conditions of time and temperature. They gave tables for using concentration products (CP) to calculate tartrate stability:

CP = (mol./l. K) $\times$ (mol./l. total tartrate) $\times$ (% acid tartrate ion) and CP = (mol./l. Ca) $\times$ (mol./l. total tartrate) $\times$ (% tartrate ion)

On the basis of extensive commercial tests, De Soto and Yamada (1963) suggested the following maximum concentration product levels for potassium acid tartrate and calcium tartrate for various types of California wines:

Wine Type	Potassium Acid Tartrate ($\times 10^5$)		Calcium Tartrate ($\times 10^8$)	
	Highest Level Found	Suggested Safe Level	Highest Level Found	Suggested Safe Level
White table	18.5	16.5	230	200
Red table	34.7	30.0	590	400
Pale dry sherry	14.6	10.0	170	90
Sherry	15.0	17.1	202	125
Cream sherry	15.0	10.0	171	120
Muscatel	18.0	17.5	310	250
White port	11.0	10.5	175	155
Port	23.3	20.0	410	275
Dry vermouth	7.0	6.0	69.5	50

While these levels appear safe for most wines, not all of the factors influencing tartrate stability are known. Furthermore, these levels were determined for one winery and presumably might be different for another winery under different plant and climatic conditions. A detailed study of 34 white Bordeaux table wines showed that sulfate was the most important factor in stability, other than potassium or tartrate, according to Peynaud et al. (1964). Other significant correlations between mineral content and stability are noted but the authors conclude that more data are needed. While refrigeration or ion-exchange are used to achieve tartrate stability in this country metatartaric acid is widely used in France, see Scazzola (1956), Ribéreau-Gayon and Peynaud (1960–1961) and Weger (1957). Its effect is not permanent and it is not recommended for use in this country.

Koch and Schiller (1964) found little effect of pH on the rate of crystallization of potassium acid tartrate. The tartrate concentration had less effect on rate of crystallization than the potassium content. Reduced temperature, of course, speeded up the precipitation rate but with a constant supersaturation the opposite was observed. Presence of magnesium, calcium, and ferrous iron speeded up crystallization, but sodium slowed it down.

It is of interest to note that in California sherry, pale dry sherry and cream sherry, De Soto and Yamada (1963) found 50 to 90 per cent oxalate in the deposits.

Cold Stability Test

The usual test for cold stability is conducted as follows according to Warkentin (1952): chill a sample of the wine to 18°F. for 96 hours, observe, let stand 24 hours at room temperature, and observe again. Any deposit formed at 18°F. should redissolve in 24 hours at room temperature. He did not get very good correlation between shelf life and the cold stability test and suggests that the chilling period for stabilization be extended to 30 days to approximate winter conditions in some markets. While such tests, if extended long enough, could provide the necessary information, the winery rarely has the time available. As De Soto and Yamada (1963) correctly point out, it is often difficult to interpret crystalline precipitation because of the presence of other interfering materials. Also, laboratory tests often fail to duplicate in-plant conditions and this may change the stability.

Other Metals

Lead may be present in wines made from grapes that have been sprayed with lead compounds. It may also get into the wine from the lead foil capsule used on some bottles of wine, the lead migrating through the cork into the wine (Ferré and Jaulmes 1948). The legal limit in Germany is 0.35 mg. per liter. Several European investigators have found considerably more than this amount in samples of European wines. Insofar as the authors are aware, no study of the lead content of Californian wines has been made. Lead sprays are not used in this state on grape vines. See also Greenblau and Westhuyzen (1957), Hickenbotham (1954), and Rankine (1955A).

Insofar as the authors know, magnesium is not a cause of instability in wines, as its salts are more soluble than those of calcium. The sodium content of wines is of interest in connection with low sodium diets and in the use of sodium ion-exchange resins. Excessive amounts may adversely affect the flavor. Amerine (1958) has summarized the data on the sodium content of wines of various wine producing regions as shown in Table 53. No reports of cloudiness due to excessive sodium have been published.

TABLE 53

SODIUM CONTENT OF VARIOUS TYPES OF WINES[1]

Region	Type	No. of Samples	Minimum	Maximum	Average
			Mg./Liter	Mg./Liter	Mg./Liter
Algeria	Table	8	51	162	118
California	Table and dessert	146	26	400	85
California	Table	155	10	172	55
California	Dessert	104	15	253	71
France	Various	28	30	125	62
Germany	Table	187	5	43	15
Miscellaneous	Dessert	24	19	443	167
Portugal	Miscellaneous	33	30	87	58
Spain	Table	4	80	343	221
Switzerland	"	11	23	65	41

[1] Source of data: Amerine, 1958.

Amerine (1958) states that the normal tin content of wine is less than one mg. per liter. One of us (W. V. C.) has observed a white wine that became cloudy because of its excessive content of tin. Protein precipitation occurs when wine containing tin is heated. See also Kielhöfer and Aumann (1955).

The zinc content of French wines made from grapes that have not been sprayed with a zinc spray is low, less than one mg. per liter, according to Ney (1948). Amerine noted that much higher concentrations have been reported by some European investigators. It may enter the wine from zinc-coated utensils. Also, at one time zinc sulfate was added with ferrocyanide in blue fining, and there is evidence that residual zinc will remain in the wine after blue fining. Zinc salts are poisonous, and wine should be free or nearly so of zinc.

Cadmium should not be used as a lining for wine containers since cadmium pick-up occurs and the wines are toxic.

Wines are naturally low in aluminum, but may dissolve it from aluminum equipment. If excessive amounts are dissolved, they may cause clouding, or the aluminum may reduce sulfur dioxide to hydrogen sulfide. Thaler and Mühlberger (1956) found a maximum of 1.52 mg. and a minimum of 0.30 mg. of aluminum per liter in 103 Swiss musts. If aluminum bronze or aluminum is used in contact with wine, the producer should make certain that the wine does not dissolve sufficient aluminum to cause clouding or damage to the flavor.

Aluminum picking containers are successfully used in Germany, according to Eschnauer (1963B). They must be properly constructed and lined. Of the small aluminum pick-up, over 70 per cent is lost during fermentation. However, Eschnauer (1963A), cautions against undue aluminum pick-up, clearly undesirable changes being caused by amounts of over ten mg. per liter. Aluminum haze is rare in California since equipment containing this metal is seldom used. In Australia Rankine (1962) showed that a maximum of 5 mg. per liter could be tolerated in dry white table and white dessert wines. The maximum haze occurred at pH 3.8.

Arsenic-containing insecticides in grape production may lead to public health problems. In some European countries arsenical sprays are illegal and they are not used on grapes in California.

DETERMINATION OF CAUSES OF CLOUDING OR DEPOSITS

In many cases it is difficult to identify the cause of non-bacterial clouding or defects. The following key (partially adapted from Tanner and Vetsch, 1956) should be helpful.

Group Classification by Microscopic Examination.—Group A is mostly crystals and group B is mostly amorphous.

	Group A		
	Potassium Bitartrate	Calcium Tartrate	Calcium Oxalate
	Screening tests		
Silver mirror reaction	Positive	Positive	Negative
Flame color with magnesia rod without cobalt glass	. . .	Brick red flame	Brick red flame
Flame color with magnesia rod with cobalt glass	Red flame	. . .	. . .
	Confirmatory tests		
Microscopic appearance	Prisms	Prisms	Small cubic crystals
Chilling			
pH 3.6	Crystals form	. . .	. . .
pH 6.0	. . .	Crystals form	. . .
Oxalic acid	Crystals may form	Crystals always form	Crystals may form
Solubility of precipitate	0.492 gm./100 ml. H_2O at 68 °F.	0.0322 gm./100 ml. H_2O at 68 °F.	0.00067 gm./100 ml. H_2O at 55 °F.
Chromatography of precipitate	Positive	Positive	Negative

GROUP B

Group B-1		
Copper Sulfide	Copper-Proteinate	Ferric Phosphate
Screening tests		
Hydrogen peroxide Turbidity disappears	Turbidity remains	Turbidity remains
Burning precipitate Doesn't burn	Burns partly	Doesn't burn
Potassium ferrocyanide		
Without HCl Red coloration	Red coloration	No change
With HCl		Blue coloration
Confirmatory tests		
Sulfur demonstration Positive	Usually positive	Negative
Flame color with Green	Green	...
magnesia rod without		
cobalt glass		
Biuret test Negative	Positive	Negative
Nitrogen demonstration Negative	Positive	Negative
Copper test Positive	Positive	Negative
Iron test Negative	Negative	Positive

GROUP B-2		
Protein	Protein-Tannate	Pigment-Tannin
Screening tests		
Conc. sulfuric with Carbonizes	Carbonizes—may	Red coloration later
gentle warming	become red	becoming dark red to
		black
Silver mirror reaction Negative	May be positive	Positive
Nitrogen demonstration Positive	May be positive	Negative
Confirmatory tests		
Biuret test Positive	May be positive	Negative
Sulfur demonstration Usually positive	May be positive	Negative

Centrifuge sufficient wine to give a few milliliters of sediment. Save centrifuged wine for additional tests. Wash sediment with 5–10 ml. of 95 per cent ethanol, re-centrifuge and decant.

Equipment and Reagents Required:—centrifuge, centrifuge tubes, microscope, Bunsen burner, filter funnels, filter paper, sodium fusion tubes, standard test tubes and pipettes, cobalt glass 5 x 5 cm. in size and 3 to 4 mm. thick, magnesium oxide rods (copper free), stainless steel spatula and silver coin (grease-free), Whatman No. 1 filter paper and small chromatography tube, cation exchange resin (IR-120 or Duolite C-3 regenerated with 5 per cent hydrochloric acid and thoroughly washed with distilled water to remove all traces of hydrochloric acid), ferrous ammonium sulfate crystals, sodium metal (keep under kerosene; *do not* allow sodium to contact water), ethyl alcohol (95 per cent by volume), concentrated sulfuric acid, hydrogen peroxide (30 per cent and 3 per cent), hydrochloric acid (concentrated and 10 per cent), methyl alcohol, saturated oxalic acid solution, organic phase of n-butanol-formic acid-water (10:2:15 v/v/v), potassium ferrocyanide (0.5 per cent), silver mirror reagent (keeps well if stored in a brown bottle, mix 50 ml. $N/10$ silver nitrate solution with 5 ml. 10 per cent sodium hydroxide solution, add concentrated ammonium hydroxide drop by drop until silver hydroxide precipitate has dissolved, prevent the reagent from drying as there is danger of explosion when it is dry), biuret reagent (to 50 ml. of 40 per cent sodium hydroxide solution add one per cent copper sulfate solution, drop by drop, with constant stirring, until the mixture assumes a deep blue color. This reagent is quite stable (if kept in a brown bottle), copper test reagents and iron test reagents for Marsh procedure, solution of 0.04 per cent chlorophenol red in 95 per cent alcohol with pH adjusted to 10, sodium hydroxide (50 per cent), and pine shavings.

Group A

(1) Silver mirror reaction: Dissolve some of the precipitate in hot water in a test tube. Add three "kitchen knife tips" of cation exchange resin, shaking after each addition. Filter into a test tube, add 5 ml. silver mirror reagent, and then heat lightly for five minutes over an open flame. The colloidal silver that is produced is deposited on the test tube walls forming a shining mirror. This is a positive test for both tartaric acid and tannins.

(2) Flame color with magnesia rod: Heat the end of a magnesia rod (magnesium oxide) red hot and dip for an instant into the wet precipitate. Heat again for a short time in the hot part of the Bunsen burner and again dip into the precipitate. Repeat this procedure until the magnesia rod is loaded. Then place the loaded end of the rod in the outer part of the flame. A brick red flame without the cobalt glass is a positive test for calcium. A beautiful rose flame looking through the cobalt glass is a positive test for potassium.

(3) Chilling: Adjust pH of the centrifuged wine with either concentrated hydrochloric acid or 50 per cent sodium hydroxide solution and then chill in a test tube. Crystal formation at pH 3.6 is a positive test for potassium bitartrate. Crystal formation at pH 6.0 is a positive test for calcium tartrate.

(4) Oxalic acid: To centrifuged wine add oxalic acid. Crystal formation indicates presence of calcium. Confirmation is obtained by adding a few drops of concentrated sulfuric acid to precipitate which will dissolve. Then add excess methyl alcohol and heat gently—precipitate will reappear.

(5) Chromatography of precipitate: Dissolve precipitate in hot water—if not soluble add concentrated hydrochloric acid. Run through a cation exchange column in the hydrogen form. Spot effluent (the equivalent of 0.04 to 0.05 ml. of wine) on paper and develop with n-butanol-formic acid-water (10:2:15 v/v/v) using the organic phase (supernatant) as the developing solution. Dry paper at room temperature until odor of developing solution disappears. Spray paper with 0.04 per cent chlorophenol red. Compare with known tartaric acid spot.

(6) Kielhöfer and Würdig (1961) found calcium saccharate responsible for crystalline deposits in some German wines. Saccharic acid is apparently produced from the galacturonic acid present in grapes attacked by *Botrytis cinerea*. It has not been reported in California. If negative tests are obtained for tartaric and oxalic acids the crystalline deposit can be checked for the presence of saccharic acid by means of the pyrrole reaction. Wash the crystalline deposit with

water and alcohol and dry by suction. Put in 1 ml. of water and add a little ammonia to dissolve. Evaporate a few drops to dryness. Place pine shavings moistened with hydrochloric acid over the deposit. Now heat. The rising fumes color the pine shavings an intense red violet if saccharic acid is present. Tartaric acid colors the pine shavings only a faint red.

Group B

(1) Add several ml. of 10 per cent hydrochloric acid to 20 ml. of wine.

Group B-1

(1) Add a few drops of 30 per cent hydrogen peroxide to 20 ml. of wine. See table on p. 569 for interpretation of results.

(2) Burning precipitate: Place a small amount of precipitate on a fine, stainless steel spatula, and heat very carefully to complete dryness with a small luminous flame placed several cm from the material. Then bring spatula close to flame and continue to heat.

(3) Potassium ferrocyanide: Add several ml. of 0.5 per cent potassium ferrocyanide to 20 ml. of wine. Red color development is a positive test for copper. Add several ml. of 10 per cent hydrochloric acid. Blue color development is a positive test for iron.

(4) Sulfur demonstration: Place sediment in a soft glass test tube (6 mm. diameter x 7 cm. length), add one drop of 30 per cent hydrogen peroxide and carefully dry over a luminous flame. Dry a piece of sodium metal on blotting paper, cut on all sides to produce a piece several cc. in size, and drop into the test tube. Using a wooden clamp hold the test tube in a flame until the contents are completely charred, and then drop test tube into another tube containing 3 ml. of water. The small test tube shatters and its contents are dissolved in the water. Place one to two drops of the liquid on a defatted silver coin. Formation of a black discoloration shows the presence of sulfur.

(5) Flame color with magnesia rod without cobalt glass: See 2 under Group A. A green flame is confirmation of the presence of copper.

(6) Biuret test: To the sediment in water add biuret reagent, a drop at a time with mixing, until the solution assumes a violet color. This is a positive test for protein.

(7) Nitrogen demonstration: Filter liquid left over from the sodium fusion (see 4 under Group B-1). Add three small ferrous ammonium sulfate crystals, boil for a short time, cool, and add 1 ml. of 10 per cent hydrochloric acid. Blue coloration proves presence of nitrogen.

(8) Copper test: Determine copper content of the sediment using the Marsh procedure (see Chapter 19).

(9) Iron test: Determine iron content of the sediment using the Marsh procedure see Chapter 19).

Group B-2

(1) Concentrated sulfuric with gentle warming: Add 1 ml. of concentrated sulfuric acid to sediment and gently warm. Carbonization indicates the presence of protein. A red coloration later becoming dark-red to black is evidence of the presence of pigment and tannin.

(2) Silver mirror reaction: See 1 under Group A.

(3) Nitrogen demonstration: See 7 under Group B-1.
(4) Biuret test: See 6 under Group B-1.
(5) Sulfur demonstration: See 4 under Group B-1. Proteins usually give a positive reaction.

BIBLIOGRAPHY

AMERINE, M. A. 1953. Influence of variety, maturity, and processing on clarity and stability of wines. Proc. Am. Soc. Enol. *1953*, 16–29.

AMERINE, M. A. 1958. Composition of wines. II. Inorganic constituents. Advances Food Research *8*, 133–225.

AMERINE, M. A., and JOSLYN, M. A. 1951. Table Wines: the Technology of Their Production in California. Univ. Calif. Press, Berkeley and Los Angeles.

ASH, C. S. 1935. Metals in wineries. Ind. Eng. Chem. *27*, 1243–1244.

AUERBACH, R. C., and DESOTO, R. 1955. Phytates for removal of metals in wine. Wine Institute, Tech. Advis. Committee, August 5, 1955.

BERG, H. W. 1953A. Special wine filtration procedures recommended for use following Cufex fining of wines. Wine Institute, Tech. Advis. Committee, July 30, 1953.

BERG, H. W. 1953B. Wine stabilization factors. Proc. Am. Soc. Enol. *1953*, 91–116.

BERG, H. W. 1957. Use of ion exchange resins for the stabilization of tartrates. Wine Institute, Tech. Advis. Committee, May 13, 1957.

BERG, H. W. 1960. Stabilization studies on Spanish sherry and on factors influencing KHT precipitation. Am. J. Enol. Vitic. *11*, 123–128.

BERG, H. W., and AKIYOSHI, M. 1956. Some factors involved in browning of white wines. Am. J. Enol. *7*, 1–8.

BERG, H. W., and AKIYOSHI, M. 1961. Determination of protein stability in wine. Am. J. Enol. Vitic. *12*, 107–110.

BERG, H. W., and KEEFER, R. M. 1958–1959. Analytical determination of tartrate stability in wine. Am. J. Enol. *9*, 180–193; *10*, 105–109.

BÖHRINGER, P., and DÖLLE, H. 1959. Über die Eiweisstrübungen hervorrufenden Eiweissarten des Weines. Z. Lebensm.-Untersuch. u. -Forsch. *111*, 121–136.

BONASTRE, J. 1959. Contribution à l'étude des matières minérales dans les produits végétaux. Application au vin. Ann. technol. agr. *8*, 377–446.

BROWN, E. M. 1953. Calcium malate instead of refrigeration. Wine Institute, Tech. Advis. Committee, July 24, 1953.

BROWN, J. G. 1932. A note on the removal of iron from grape juice by means of potassium ferrocyanide. Fruit Prods. J. *11*, 274–275.

BYRNE, J., SAYWELL, L. G., and CRUESS, W. V. 1936. The iron content of grapes and wine. Anal. Chem. *9*, 83–84.

CAMBITZI, A. 1947. The formation of racemic calcium tartrate in wines. Analyst *72*, 542–543.

CANTARELLI, C. 1962. I trattamenti con resine poliammidiche in enologia. Atti accad. Ital. vite vino *14*, 219–249.

CAPT, E. 1957. Un enquête sur la teneur en fer des vins de la suisse romande. Annuaire agr. suisse *58*, 801–808.

CAPT, E., and MICHOD, J. 1951. Recherches sur la presence de fer dans les matières filtrantes en relation avec les risques de casse blanche. *Ibid.* Annuaire agr. suisse *52*, 887–896.

CAPUTI, JR., A., and PETERSON, R. G. 1965. The browning problem in wines. Am. J. Enol. Vitic. 16, 9–13.

CASTINO, M. 1965. L'azione riducente dell'acido ascorbico nella demetallizzazione dei vini con ferrocianuro potassico. Ann. accad. ital. vite vino 17, 143–151.

COHEE, R. F., and STEFFEN, G. 1949. Takes heavy metals out of acid food. Food Inds. 21, 1746–1748, 1895.

CRAWFORD, C. 1951. Calcium in dessert wine. Proc. Am. Soc. Enol. 1951, 76–79.

CRUESS, W. V. 1948. The darkening of white wine. Fruit Prod. J. 28, 4–5.

DE SOTO, R., and WARKENTIN, H. 1955. Influence of pH and total acidity on calcium tolerance of sherry wine. Food Research 20, 301–309.

DE SOTO, R. T., and YAMADA, H. 1963. Relationship of solubility products to long range tartrate stability. Am. J. Enol. Vitic. 14, 43–51.

DE VILLIERS, J. P. 1961. The control of browning of white table wines. Ibid. 12, 25–30.

DICKINSON, B. N., and STONEMAN, C. F. 1958. Stabilization of wines by ion exchange. Chemical Process Co., Mimeo. Circ. Redwood City, California.

DRAPER, W., and THOMPSON, J. L. 1955. Cloudiness in wines. Chemistry in Canada 78, No. 8, 35–38.

DU PLESSIS, C. S. 1964. The ion exchange treatment (H cycle) of white grape juice prior to fermentation. II. The effect upon wine quality. S. Afr. Agr. Sci. 7, 3–15.

ESCHNAUER, H. 1963A. Aluminiumtrübungen im Wein. Vitis 4, 57–61.

ESCHNAUER, H. 1963B. Bewährung der Aluminium-Herbstbütten. Wein-Wissen. 18, 613–619.

FERRÉ, L., and JAULMES, P. 1948. Les capsules en étain plombifère, cause de la presence de plomb dans les vins. Compt. rend. acad. agr. France 34, 864–865.

FESSLER, J. H. 1952. Development of the Fessler compound. Wines and Vines 33, No. 7, 15.

FILIPELLO, F. 1947. Treatment of metallic clouding. Wines and Vines 28 (9), 23.

FULLER, W. L., and BERG, H. W. 1965. Treatment of white wine with nylon 66. Am. J. Enol. Vitic. 16, 212–218.

GAROGLIO, P. G. 1957. Contributo Sperimentali allo Studio delle Possibili Applicazione Enologiche delle Resine Scambiatrici di Ioni. Instituo di Industrie Agrarie, Università de Firenze, Firenze.

GENEVOIS, L. 1933. Recherches récentes sur les complexes du fer. Ann. brass. et dist. 31, 188–192, 205–208.

GENEVOIS, L. 1935. A propos des complexes du fer dans les vins. Bull. soc. chim. France (5) 2, 1594–1596.

GREENBLAU, N., and WESTHUYZEN, J. P. van der. 1957. Lead contamination of wines, spirits, and foods. S. African Ind. Chemist 11, 150–153.

HAAS, V., and STADTMAN, F. H. 1949. Use of ion-exchange resins to identify compounds involved in browning. Ind. Eng. Chem. 41, 983, 986.

HAAS, V., STADTMAN, E. R., STADTMAN, F. H., and MACKINNEY, G. M. 1948. Deterioration of dried fruits. I. The effect of sugars and of furfurals. J. Am. Chem. Soc. 70, 3576–3578.

HEIDE, C. VON DER. 1933. Die Blauschönung. Wein u. Rebe 14, 325–335, 348–359, 400–408; 15, 5–19, 35–44.

HEITZ, J., ROESSLER, E. B., AMERINE, M. A., and BAKER, G. A. 1951. A study of certain factors affecting the composition of California sherry during baking. Food Research 16, 192–200.

HICKINBOTHAM, A. R. 1954. The lead content of beverages. Australian Brewing Wine J. 72, No. 8, 20.

HUBACH, C. E. 1948. Detection of cyanides and ferrocyanides in wines. Anal. Chem. 20, 1115–1116.

HUSSEIN, A. A., and CRUESS, W. V. 1940. A note on the enzymatic darkening of wine. Fruit Prods. J. 19, 271–272.

IBARRA, M., and CRUESS, W. V. 1948. Observations on removal of excess color from wine. Wine Review 16, No. 6, 14–15.

JAULMES, P. 1951. Analyse des Vins. 2 ed. Libraire Poulain, Montpellier.

JOSLYN, M. A., and LUKTON, A. 1953. Prevention of copper and iron turbidities in wine. Hilgardia 22, 451–533.

JOSLYN, M. A., and LUKTON, A. 1956. Mechanism of copper casse formation in white wines. I. Relation of changes in redox potential to copper casse. Food Research 21, 384–396.

JOSLYN, M. A., LUKTON, A., and CANE, A. 1953. The removal of excess copper and iron from wine. Food Technol. 7, 20–29.

KEAN, C. E., and MARSH, G. L. 1956A. Investigation of copper complexes causing cloudiness in wines. I. Chemical composition. Food Research 21, 441–447.

KEAN, C. E., and MARSH, G. L. 1956B. Investigation of copper complexes causing cloudiness in wines. II. Bentonite treatment of wines. Food Technol. 10, 355–359.

KIELHÖFER, E. 1957. Die Weinentsäuerung mittels Ionenaustaucher Vergleich zu der Entsäuerung mit kohlensäurem Kalk. Weinberg u. Keller 4, 136–145.

KIELHÖFER, E., and AUMANN, H. 1955. Das Verhalten von Zinn gegenüber Wein. Mitt. Rebe u. Wein, Serie A (Klosterneuburg) 5, 127–135.

KIELHÖFER, E., and WÜRDIG, G. 1961. Kristalltrübungen in Wein durch das Kalzalz einer bisher unbekannten Säure des Weines. Deut. Wein-Ztg. 97, 478–480.

KOCH, J. 1963. Protéines des vins blancs. Traitements des precipitations protéiques par chauffage et à l'aide de la bentonite. Ann. technol. agr., numero hors ser. I, 12, 297–313.

KOCH, J., and SAJAK, E. 1959. A review and some studies on grape protein. Am. J. Enol. Vitic. 10, 114–123.

KOCH, J., and SCHILLER, H. 1964. Kinetik der Kristallisation von Weinstein. Z. Lebensm.-Untersuch. u. -Forsch. 124, 180–183.

KRUM, J. K., and FELLERS, C. R. 1952. Clarification of wine by a sequestering agent. Food Technol. 6, 103–106.

LABORDE, J. 1907. Cours d'Oenologie. L. Mulo, Paris; Feret & Fils, Bordeaux.

LHERME, G. 1931–32. La teneur en cuivre des vins de la Gironde (récolte 1931). Proc. verb. séan soc. sci. phys. nat. Bordeaux 1931–32, 119–121.

MACKINNEY, G. M., and TEMMER, O. 1948. The deterioration of dried fruit. IV. Spectrophotometric and polarographic studies. J. Am. Chem. Soc. 70, 3586–3590.

MARSH, G. L. 1940. Metals in wine. Wine Review 8, No. 9, 12–13; No. 10, 24–29.

MARSH, G. L. 1952. New compound ends metal clouding. A report on the Fessler compound. Wines and Vines 33, No. 6, 19–21.

MARSH, G. L. 1959a. Personal communication. Davis, Calif.

MARSH, G. L. 1959b. Refrigeration in wine making. Am. Soc. Refrig. Eng. Data Book, Vol. I, Chap. 10.

MORETTI, R. H., and BERG, H. W. 1965. Variability among wines to protein clouding. Am. J. Enol. Vitic. 16, 69–78.

MRAK, E. M., CASH, L., and CAUDRON, D. C. 1937. Effects of certain metals and alloys on claret and sauterne-type wines made from vinifera grapes. Food Research 2, 539–547.

NEY, M. 1948. Dosage rapide du zinc. Ann. fals. et fraudes 41, 533–537.

O'NEAL, R., MEIS, L., and CRUESS, W. V. 1950. Observations on the fining of wines with casein. Food Technol. 5, 64–68.

PACOTTET, P. 1926. Vinification. J. B. Baillière et Fils, Paris.

PATO, C. M. 1959. Effect of pH on the removal of iron and copper from wine with ion exchange resins. Am. J. Enol. and Vitic. 10, 51–55.

PECHEUR, P. (Translated by H. C. Stollenwerk). 1957. Ion exchange in wines by percolation through continuous columns. Wine Institute, Tech. Advis. Committee, December 6, 1957.

PETERSON, R. G., JOSLYN, M. A., and DURBIN, P. W. 1958. Mechanism of copper casse formation in white table wine. III. Source of the sulfur in the sediment. Food Research 23, 518–524.

PEYNAUD, E., GUIMBERTEAU, G., and BLOUIN, J. 1964. Die Löslichkeitsgleichgewichte von Kalzium und Kalium in Wein. Mitt. Rebe u. Wein, Serie A (Klosterneuburg) 14, 176–186.

PILONE, B., and BERG, H. W. 1965. Some factors affecting tartrate stability in wine. Am. J. Enol. Vitic. 16, 195–211.

PILONE, F. J. 1953. The role of pasteurization in the stabilization and clarification of wines. Proc. Am. Soc. Enol. 1953, 77–84.

PLODERL, F., and WEYMAN, W. E. 1957. Corrosion resistant coatings-properties and uses. Am. J. Enol. 8, 135–138.

RAMAGE, W. D. 1938. Process for clarification and removal of iron from beverages. U. S. Pat. No. 2,128,432.

RAMAGE, W. D. 1941. Process for removal of metallic impurities from wines and other beverages. U. S. Pat. 2,258,216.

RANKINE, B. C. 1955A. Lead content of some Australian wines. J. Sci. Food Agr. 6, 576–579.

RANKINE, B. C. 1955B. Treatment of wine with ion-exchange resins. Australian J. Appl. Sci. 6, 529–540.

RANKINE, B. 1962. Aluminum haze in wine. Australian Wine, Brewing, Spirit Rev. 80, No. 9, 14, 16.

RENTSCHLER, H., and TANNER, H. 1951. Über die Kupfersulfittrübung von Weissweinen und Süssmosten. Schweiz. Z. Obst- u. Weinbau 60, 298–301.

RIBÉREAU-GAYON, J. 1930. La fer et le cuivre dans les vins blancs. Ann. fals. et fraudes 23, 535–544.

RIBÉREAU-GAYON, J. 1933. Contribution à l'Étude des Oxydations et Réductions dan les Vins. 2 ed. Delmas, Bordeaux, France.

RIBÉREAU-GAYON, J. 1934. Grands vins blancs français et traitement au ferrocyanure (collage bleu). Compt. rend. acad. agr. France 20, 538–543.
RIBÉREAU-GAYON, J. 1935. Le cuivre des moûts et des vins. Ann. fals. et fraudes 28, 349–360.
RIBÉREAU-GAYON, J., and PEYNAUD, E. 1960–1961. Traité d'Oenologie. 2 vol. Librairie Polytechnique Ch. Béranger, Paris.
ROSSI, E. A., JR. 1951. Report on chrome plating. Proc. Am. Soc. Enol. 1951, 191–200.
SAYWELL, L. G. 1935. Effects of filter aids and filter materials on wine composition. Ind. Eng. Chem. 27, 1245–1250.
SCAZZOLA, E. 1956. De l'utilization de l'acide metatartrique. Ann. fals. et fraudes 49, 159–163.
SCHANDERL, H. 1959. Die Mikrobiologie des Mostes und des Weins. Eugen Ulmer, Stuttgart.
SCHANDERL, S. 1957. The use of cation exchange resins in the prevention of tartrate crystal precipitation after bottling of wine. Wine Institute, Tech. Advis. Committee, May 13, 1957.
SEARLE, H. E., LaQUE, F. L., and DOHROW, R. H. 1934. Metals and wines. Ind. Eng. Chem. 26, 617–627.
STADTMAN, F. H. 1948. The chemical deterioration of dried fruit during storage. III. Chromatographic separation of carbonyl compounds as 2, 4-dinitrophenylhydrazones. J. Am. Chem. Soc. 70, 3583–3585.
TANNER, H., and VETSCH, U. 1956. How to characterize cloudiness in beverages. Am. J. Enol. 7, 145–146.
THALER, H., and MÜHLBERGER, F. H. 1956. Der Aluminum Gehalt von Pfälzer Traubenmost und Wein. Z. Lebensm.-Untersuch. u -Forsch. 103, 97–108.
THOUKIS, G., and AMERINE, M. A. 1956. The fate of copper and iron during fermentation of grape musts. Am. J. Enol. 7, 62–68.
VITAGLIANO, M. 1956. I constituenti minerali del vino. II. Il ferro. Ann. sper. agrar. (Rome) 10, 659–668.
WAAL, H. L. 1932. The heavy-metal content of South African wines and the treatment of wine with potassium ferrocyanide. Ann. Univ. Stellenbosch Ser. A. 10, 1–50.
WALTER, E. 1951. Die Einwirkung von Metallen auf alkoholische Flüssigkeiten. Alkohol-Ind. 64, 235–237.
WARKENTIN, H. 1952. Shelf life versus stability results. Wine Institute, Tech. Advis. Committee. Dec. 12, 1952.
WEAST, C. A., and MACKINNEY, G. M. 1941. Nonenzymatic darkening of fruits and fruit products. Ind. Eng. Chem. 33, 1408–1412.
WEGER, B. 1957. Die Verhinderung des Weinsteinausfalles durch Metaweinsäure. Mitt. Rebe u. Wein, Serie A (Klosterneuburg) 7, 246–248.
WUCHERPFENNIG, K., and FRANK, I. 1967. Zur Frage der Eiweissstabilisierung von Wein durch eine Bentonitbehandlung des Mostes. Wein-Wissen. 22, 213–226.

CHAPTER 16

Bacterial Spoilage

The bacteria that can develop in wine are of two types in respect to their oxygen requirements. The acetic acid bacteria require oxygen for growth and acetification, whereas the lactic acid bacteria grow best under conditions of reduced oxygen content, that is, they are microaerophilic. In modern winery practice, the lactic acid bacteria are much more important as wine spoilage organisms than the acetic bacteria. For a general discussion see Castelli (1959), Cruess (1943), Maestro Palo (1952). Niehaus (1930), Schanderl (1959), and Verona and Florenzano (1956).

ACETIC SPOILAGE

During Red Fermentation

Acetification may occur in the pomace of the cap that forms on open vats of fermenting crushed red grapes, unless the pomace is punched down regularly or the fermenting must is pumped over the cap frequently in small open tanks or the tank is covered and kept under an atmosphere of carbon dioxide. Air supply is usually adequate for vinegar bacteria to develop and to convert alcohol to acetic acid. Use of moderate amounts of sulfur dioxide, 125 to 150 p.p.m., in the crushed grapes will usually minimize or prevent acetification. See especially Cruess (1912) and Quinn (1940).

During Muscat Fermentation

During the first few years following Repeal, considerable spoilage of muscat musts occurred in the San Joaquin Valley of California during fermentation in periods of unusually hot weather. The grapes, frequently over-ripe or harvested late in the season, were crushed at 95° to 100°F. and the musts allowed to ferment naturally without use of sulfur dioxide or cooling. At such elevated temperatures the wine yeast is sluggish in growth and usually ceases multiplication at 105°F. At this temperature some acetic and lactic bacteria are still active. It was thought at one time that lactic bacteria were the principal cause of spoilage, since they were observed in large numbers under the microscope in samples of the spoiled wine and grew abundantly in ten-gallon lots of muscat juice allowed to ferment naturally in the laboratory at 85°F. However, research by Vaughn (1938) proved that vinegar bacteria growing in association with

577

the yeast was the chief cause of the observed spoilage. As the yeast produced alcohol the bacteria oxidized it to acetic acid. When the population of acetic acid bacteria or the temperature rose sufficiently, yeast activity ceased and the bacteria then oxidized the dextrose of the must to gluconic acid, $CH_2OH(CHOH)_4COOH$, and some of the accumulated acetic acid to carbon dioxide and water. Therefore, both the volatile acid and the fixed acid rose. The spoiled must had a "sweet-sour" and usually a mousy flavor, which is also an indication of the activity of certain lactic acid bacteria responsible for wine spoilage. Vaughn (1938) found that acetic bacteria in this type of spoilage under winery conditions to be an unusual strain of *Acetobacter.*

During Storage

If wine of less than 15 per cent alcohol is stored in casks or tanks that are not completely filled and tightly sealed against entrance of air, the wine will often become vinegar sour. Prevention consists in keeping casks and tanks well filled and sealed at all times.

Of Flor Wine

Bobadilla (1943) recommended that wine to be used in the production of flor sherry in Spain contain at least 14.5 per cent alcohol. Cruess (1937), however, found experimentally that acetification sometimes occurred rapidly in dry wine at 14.7 per cent alcohol under California conditions and recommended that wine for flor sherry production be brought to 15.5 per cent alcohol before inoculating with flor yeast. Vaughn (1955) states that the maximum alcohol tolerance of most acetic bacteria lies between 14 and 15 per cent; but he also states that species and strains of *Acetobacter* exist which cannot develop at above 10 per cent alcohol.

California Wines

Vaughn (1955) has encountered only two species of *Acetobacter* capable of causing acetification in California wines. These are *A. aceti* and *A. oxydans.* However, he has frequently isolated *A. xylinum* from grapes and must and *A. melanogenum, A. suboxydans,* and *A. roseum* infrequently. He believes that they are of little importance in the spoilage of California wines.

A. oxydans, according to Vaughn (1955), has a lower optimum temperature than *A. aceti,* namely about 68°F. compared to 86° to 95°F. for *A. aceti.* In Hoyer's media ethyl alcohol is oxidized completely to carbon dioxide and water by *A. aceti,* whereas *A. oxydans* fails to grow in this medium. These properties are valuable in differentiating the two species.

Morphology.—The acetic bacteria are small, usually about 0.5 × 1.0 μ (microns) and are non-motile. They occur frequently in pairs or in chains, and may or may not be surrounded by a zoögloeal sheath. However, as Vaughn (1942) and others found, involution forms occur under certain conditions. These may be long filaments or other distorted forms.

Acetic bacteria that occur in hard cider usually form a heavy, leathery film, called "vinegar mother," but in wines of 12 to 14 per cent alcohol the vinegar bacteria are usually found throughout the wine and without formation of typical "mother," probably because the species which form "mother" cannot grow in this range of alcohol content.

In the Midi of France, Dupuy (1957A) reported 32 per cent of the *Acetobacter* of wines were *A. paradoxum*, 24 per cent *A. rancens*, 19 per cent *A. ascendens*, 19 per cent *A. mesoxydans*. *A. suboxydans* was seldom found. Dupuy makes the special point that the acetic acid bacterial flora of wines is different than that of vinegar. Apparently the *A. mesoxydans* is the same as *A. aceti*. The classification used by Dupuy was that of Frateur (1950).

Aside from oxygen, Dupuy (1957B) reported pH and per cent alcohol were the most important factors influencing the growth of *Acetobacter*. He found little growth at pH 3.2 or 13 per cent alcohol. Sulfur dioxide was most effective as an antiseptic. Other factors had little influence on growth of *Acetobacter*: sugar, glycerol, tannin, blue fining, or addition or elimination of minor elements.

Pomace and Stuck Wines

Pomace rapidly acetifies after pressing and should be disposed of as quickly as possible. Also, it is an excellent breeding place for vinegar flies, drosophila, which carry vinegar bacteria from the pomace to fermenting crushed grapes or other exposed wine or must surfaces. At present most wineries dispose of the pomace daily. Stuck wines are very susceptible to spoilage by vinegar bacteria if in partially filled tanks or casks. Addition of sulfur dioxide to maintain a level above 125 p.p.m. and prompt refermentation of the stuck wine are recommended (see Chapter 6 for further information on stuck wines). Vinegar production is presented in Chapter 18.

Volatile Acidity

The volatile acid content of wine is a good indication of its soundness. Wines that are high in volatile acid usually smell vinegar-sour. The present California regulations provide that white table and dessert wines must not have a volatile acidity above 0.11 gm. per 100 ml. calculated as acetic and exclusive of sulfur dioxide. The limit for red wines is 0.120 gm. per 100 ml. The Federal limits are somewhat higher, namely, 0.120 and 0.140 respectively. The principal reaction in acetification is:

$$C_2H_5OH + O_2 \rightarrow CH_3COOH + H_2O$$

However, Peynaud (1936, 1937) has shown that much of the spoiled odor of vinegar-sour wines is due to ethyl acetate, an ester formed by acetic bacteria:

$$C_2H_5OH + CH_3COOH \rightarrow CH_3COOC_2H_5 + H_2O$$

Vaughn (1955) states that acetic bacteria can oxidize glycerol, citric acid, malic acid, and tartaric acid *in vitro,* but there is no evidence that they attack these compounds in wine, probably because of their preference for alcohol.

Deacidification

While the total acidity of a wine can be reduced by the addition of any permissible alkaline substance, the volatile acidity, acetic acid chiefly, is not reduced. If a wine slightly exceeds the legal limit in volatile acidity and is sound in other respects, it may be blended with wine of low volatile acidity. However, if the volatile acidity is very high, the wine may be only fit for distillation or for making into vinegar.

It was found by Pasteur (1864) and confirmed subsequently by Cruess (1948) and others that certain film yeasts (Spanish flor yeasts and French Chalon yeasts) can oxidize acetic acid in wine to carbon dioxide and water. Insofar as the authors know, flor yeast has not been used commercially for this purpose.

SPOILAGE BY LACTIC BACTERIA[1]

The most common acid-tolerant bacteria responsible for wine spoilage are those that produce lactic acid. They are found as short and long rods and spheres (sometimes slightly elongated), very often in chains. Many different species of *Lactobacillaceae* have been found in wine, but the most common are those of the genera *Lactobacillus, Leuconostoc,* and *Pediococcus.* See Orla-Jensen (1919), Pederson (1957), Shimwell (1941), Snell (1946) and Wood *et al.* (1940).

---

[1] The authors are greatly indebted to Prof. R. H. Vaughn for much of the information presented in this chapter.

Not all lactic acid bacteria are necessarily spoilage bacteria. As early as 1900, Koch pointed out that many sound wines contain bacteria. In fact, p. 584, modern enological practice often utilizes them. Lüthi (1957) has emphasized that in most cases it is not a single species which causes spoilage but several growing symbiotically.

Both the appearance and flavor of the wine may be altered by lactic acid bacteria. When gently shaken in a test tube or bottle, the wine will have a silky-cloudy appearance. This characteristic of streaming or "silkiness," according to Amerine and Joslyn (1951), is caused by alignment of the rod bacteria in chains. A wine spoiled by lactic bacteria usually has a disagreeable smell, often mousy, and a flocculent or pulverulent sediment. As Vaughn (1955) has pointed out, acetic acid bacteria also can produce a mousy smell in musts. Lactic bacteria inhibit growth of S. cerevisiae, probably because they produce L-ornithine, Biodron (1969).

Historical

Pasteur was one of the first to study the lactic spoilage of wines in the period 1861 to 1870. He recognized four types of spoilage; namely, (1) acetification, (2) the spoilage known as *tourne* and *pousse*, (3) slimy wine spoilage, and (4) the bitterness disease (*amertume*) of wines. In the lactic spoilage termed *pousse* gas is formed and many enologists considered it separate and distinct from *tourne*. Pasteur, however, considered *pousse* merely a gassy type of *tourne*.

Pasteur and other early investigators were handicapped by having no means of making pure cultures. Koch's pure culture technique (1881) was soon widely applied by various microbiologists in the study of wine spoilage organisms. While it is still customary to speak of bacterial spoilage of wines as "diseases," Vaughn (1955) rightfully objects because the organisms concerned are saprophytes and wine is inanimate. Spoilage is a more appropriate term.

At one time enologists thought that each form of spoilage or bacterial transformation was caused by a specific organism and it was customary to speak of *tourne* (Nickles, 1862) bacteria, *pousse* bacteria, *malo-lactic* bacteria, and *mannite* bacteria; whereas it is now recognized that each of these conditions can be produced by several species of bacteria. Vaughn suggests that the words *tourne, pousse,* and others be used to designate wine conditions rather than the microorganisms concerned. There is still much confusion among enologists in respect to wine spoilage terminology.

At one time, as a result of the research of Carles (1891), Gayon and Dubourg (1894, 1901) and Laborde (1904) mannitol production in wines by bacterial action on levulose was considered as due to the activity of a short rod bacterium termed by them *ferment mannitique* and thought to be quite distinct from the bacteria causing *tourne* or *pousse*. We now know that a considerable number of species of lactic acid bacteria are heterofermentative and form mannitol. *Lactobacillus brevis, L. hilgardii,* and others as well as *Leuconostoc mesenteroides,* form mannitol from levulose. The term mannitic bacteria (*ferment mannitique*) is no longer valid.

Tartrate Decomposition

Similarly, although several European investigators claimed that tartaric acid, and still others that glycerol, underwent decomposition in *tourne* spoilage with production of propionic acid, Vaughn (1955) states that the latter view is untenable because the lactic acid bacteria do not produce propionic acid from any of the major fermentable constituents of wine. Some enologists state that *tourne* spoilage is characterized by decomposition of tartrate; but in view of the recent research of Fornachon (1943), Fornachon *et al.* (1940, 1949), Olsen (1948), and Vaughn *et al.* (1949) in which only one strain of the bacteria isolated from spoiled wine was able to decompose tartrates in wine or culture media, it would appear that, insofar as Californian and Australian conditions are concerned, tartrate decomposition is not a good criterion of *tourne* spoilage. Berry and Vaughn (1952), however, obtained from spoiled red wine and from lees tartrate-fermenting cultures of *L. plantarum* that, after careful training for alcohol tolerance, could be grown in wines enriched with yeast autolysate. The major end products of tartrate decomposition were lactic acid and carbon dioxide (Krumperman *et al.* 1953). See also Cruess (1935) and d'Estivaux (1935).

Both types of spoilage were very prevalent in California wineries during the first two years following repeal of the 18th amendment. Because of the inexperience of the winemakers of that period, much wine was made without use of sulfur dioxide or cooling. This form of spoilage is now very rare in California wineries.

Swiss Research.—The research of Müller-Thurgau and Osterwalder in Switzerland (1912, 1918, 1919) was the first serious attempt to clarify the previously confused situation applying to the bacterial spoilage of wine. They made pure cultures of wine spoilage bacteria by Koch's methods and conducted well-planned and exhaustive studies of the pure cultures. For example, they recognized four species of bacteria capable of producing mannitol from levulose and, therefore, that the *ferment mannitique* of Gayon and Dubourg is only one of a group of heterofermentative *Lactobacilli* that form mannitol from levulose.

An important result of their investigations was the finding that malic acid is fermented not only by cocci but also by many rod-shaped lactobacilli. Therefore, enologists should not speak of the malo-lactic bacterium as a single species. They also isolated and studied an organism named by them as *Bacterium tartarophthorum*, which decomposed tartrate with the formation of carbon dioxide and acetic acid, and decomposed glycerol with the production of acetic, lactic, and propionic acids. These findings made obsolete the old theory of Duclaux (1898–1901) and Sémichon (1905) that propionic acid is formed in the bacterial decomposition of tartrate. Vaughn (1955) suggests that *B. tartarophthorum* may be a species of the heterofermentative *Lactobacilli*.

Arena (1936) in Argentina confirmed much of the research of Müller-Thurgau and Osterwalder. In addition he found a spoilage organism that he named *Bacterium acidovorax*. It decomposed tartrate. Vaughn (1955) suggests that it may be a homofermentative *Lactobacillus*. Ribéreau-Gayon (1938, 1946) and also Ribéreau-Gayon and Peynaud (1938) confirmed much of the Swiss investigators' findings in respect to fermentation of malic acid. The research of Vaughn (1955) and of Fornachon (1936, 1943, 1957) and their associates has done a great deal to clarify and extend our knowledge of the spoilage of wines by lactic bacteria.

Homofermentative Versus Heterofermentative Lactobacilli

The homofermentative lactic acid bacteria convert the hexose sugars dextrose and levulose into lactic acid chiefly without formation of appreciable amounts of carbon dioxide or acetic acid, whereas the heterofermentative species produce not only lactic acid from dextrose but also carbon dioxide, acetic acid, alcohol, and glycerol. They also reduce considerable amounts of levulose to mannitol. Many strains of both species can ferment malic and citric acids in wine, although some strains prefer malic acid. Some strains that prefer citric (Vaughn, 1955) apparently cannot attack malic acid at all. Both species are classed as facultative aerobes, although they prefer slightly anaerobic conditions and are classified as microaerophiles. In the light of modern knowledge certain strains of heterofermentative lactic acid bacteria can cause all four types of bacterial spoilage or transformation of wine; namely, *tourne, pousse,* mannitol formation, and malo-lactic fermentation.

Leuconostoc

Like the heterofermentative rod shaped *Lactobacilli, Leuconostoc* forms lactic acid, acetic acid, carbon dioxide, and ethyl alcohol from dextrose and, in addition, form mannitol from levulose. *Leuc. mesenteroides* is a spherical (coccus) form that is a very important producer of lactic acid in the fermentation of sauerkraut and pickles. It may cause ropiness or gelation in fruit wines and in grape wines containing sucrose, because of the formation of dextrans (polysaccharides). It is more frequently encountered in European wines of low alcohol content than in the wines of California which usually contain twelve per cent or more of alcohol.

In some cases the cells are short ellipsoidal rather than spherical. One of us (W. V. C.) has encountered a few slimy (gelatinous), new, white California table wines in which cocci in long chains were abundant, but the species was not identified. Its alcohol tolerance is 10 to 14 per cent, and it is a facultative aerobe.

Malo-Lactic Fermentation

A considerable portion of the fixed acidity of wine is due to malic acid. In cool wine producing regions, such as Switzerland, the Rheingau of Germany and certain sections of France, the wines are unpleasantly high in total acidity. It is customary in these regions to leave the wines on the yeast lees longer than is customary in warmer regions to promote the growth of bacteria that convert malic acid into lactic acid and carbon dioxide. The total acidity of the wine may be reduced as much as one-third by this fermentation. It may be caused by certain micrococci described by Müller-Thurgau and Osterwalder or by rod forms of lactic bacteria. The resulting wine, particularly when new, is slightly sparkling (*pétillant*). As the bacteria concerned are sensitive to sulfur dioxide, the wines are made with a minimum addition of sulfur dioxide or bisulfite.

Sulfur dioxide not only increases the time until the malo-lactic fermentation starts but also increases the duration of this fermentation. They grow under a wide range of pH, but are retarded at pH's of below 3.2, and at temperatures from 50° to 98.6°F. The malo-lactic fermentation may require special catalysts for growth but these are still unknown. Schanderl (1954), for example, believes that there is a symbiosis between the bacteria and the yeasts. A good review of the malo-lactic problem was presented by Fell (1961). He noted that the problem of the source of energy for the malo-lactic fermentation has not been solved. (The reaction is believed to be endothermic but this is not known.) The three possibilities are: from fermentation of hydrocarbon, from decomposition of malic acid to carbon dioxide and from decomposition of nitrogenous materials.

In many sections of California and in other warm grape growing regions, the malo-lactic fermentation is frequently undesirable as it results in reduction in the total acidity. Racking and the addition of sulfur dioxide in adequate amounts will usually control this form of spoilage. French producers of the Bordeaux and Burgundy area believe that the high quality of their red wines is due in part to malo-lactic fermentation. As indicated above it is considered essential for high acid German, Swiss, and other northern European wines.

Suverkrop and Tchelistcheff (1949) observed malo-lactic fermentation in red wines of the Napa Valley in California. Vaughn and Tchelistcheff (1957) have reported on the malo-lactic fermentation in California wines. Amerine (1950) observed the formation of large amounts of lactic acid in new wines accompanied by a corresponding decrease in malic acid. Vaughn (1959) and Ingraham et al. (1960) have also studied this fermentation in California wines. Amerine (1950) has emphasized that a malo-lactic fermentation should be prevented in California wines that are already too low in total acidity. He also noted that gas production in tanks of new wine with rising temperature in early spring often may be due to a malo-lactic fermentation rather than fermentation of residual sugar by yeast.

The classification of the bacteria associated with decarboxylation of malic acid is still difficult and often confusing. As Fornachon (1943) has noted, it is normal for newly isolated cultures of the lactic acid bacteria to differ from the presently classified species. Barre and Galzy (1960) also found this to be true, and similar conclusions were reached by Bidan (1956) and Dupuy (1957).

Recently, Ingraham et al. (1960) have conducted an extensive investigation of the bacteria isolated from California wines and capable of attacking malic acid in wines. They report that there are at least five distinct types of lactic acid bacteria, representing four genera, which occur in California wines and are capable of destroying malic acid. In addition to destroying malic acid, the bacteria affect the flavor of the wine by production of minor end products of metabolism. Control of malo-lactic fermentation, therefore, might offer an opportunity for improvement in the flavor of dry wines. This possibility might outweigh the undesirable property of these organisms, previously mentioned, of reducing the fixed acidity of California wines. Homofermentative cocci and heterofermentative cocci were found among the 47 strains studied. Most of the rod forms were heterofermentative and were identified as *Lactobacillus hilgardii* and as *L. brevis;* the homofermentative rods were of *L. plantarum,* one of *L. brevis* and two of *L. delbrueckii* species. Of the cocci, ten isolates were identified as *Leuconostoc mesenteroides,* and twelve isolates as species of *Pediococcus.* The former are heterofermentative and the latter, homofermentative. See also pp. 285–287.

A complete survey of the lactic acid bacteria involved in the malo-lactic fermentation of wines was given by Radler (1962). The following heterofermentative rods have been isolated from table wines: *Lactobacillus fermenti* (the *Bacillus gayoni* and *B. intermedium* of Müller-Thurgau and

Osterwalder), *L. brevis, L. buchneri* (formerly *B. mannitopoeum*) and *L. pastorianus.* In dessert wines *L. trichodes* and *L. hilgardii* have been reported. The homofermentative rod types include: *L. plantarum, L. casei* and *L. delbrueckii.* The heterofermentative *cocci* are *Leuconostoc mesenteroides, Leuc. dextranicum* and *Leuc. citrovorum.* The only homofermentative coccus verified by Radler was *Pediococcus cerevisiae.*

Almost every unbottled dry wine sample, red or white, examined by Ingraham *et al.* (1960) contained lactic bacteria capable of decomposing malic acid. It would seem, therefore, that the bacteria are of widespread occurrence in California wines and if a wine producer should desire to have a malo-lactic fermentation in his dry wine, it would not be necessary to inoculate artificially. As Fornachon (1957) has pointed out, low pH, high sulfur dioxide and high alcohol contents, and early racking delay or prevent malo-lactic fermentation. Early racking prevents extensive autolysis of the yeast in the lees and thus reduces the amount of products of autolysis that can be used as growth factors by the bacteria.

Kunkee *et al.* (1965) also found a high incidence of malo-lactic fermentation in wines from Southern California—67 per cent of the whites, 80 of the rosés and 78 of the reds. Wines which had undergone a malo-lactic fermentation tended to be high in acetoin. Six of the nine wines with high acetoin had 4 p.p.m. or greater of diacetyl.

Adams (1964) reported very general occurrence of a malo-lactic fermentation in Canadian wines. However, he determined this on the basis of the presence of lactic acid and not on the disappearance of malic acid.

Differences in the sensory characteristics of wines fermented with several strains of bacteria were demonstrated by Pilone and Kunkee (1965). However, the panel used could not consistently rank wines with and without a malo-lactic fermentation.

The heterofermentative cocci isolated by Ingraham *et al.* (1960) were readily identified as *Leuconostoc,* but it was difficult to classify the homofermentative cocci because a medium in which these organisms will develop for study of the various sugar reactions has not been developed. However, since they were Gram-positive, catalase-negative, lactic acid-producing, and occur singly or in pairs and tetrads, they have been tentatively placed in the genus *Pediococcus.*

As Vaughn (1955) points out, lactic bacteria from pickles, sauerkraut, green olives, and other sources can be trained to grow in and spoil wine; therefore, the concept that wine spoilage *Lactobacilli* are found only in wine is erroneous.

Further data on the enzyme systems of lactic acid bacteria (*Lactobacillus plantarum*) were reported by Flesch and Holbach (1965). Three enzymes were studied: malic dehydrogenase (which catalyzes the reversible oxidation of malic acid to oxaloacetic acid), "malic" enzyme (which catalyzes the reversible decarboxylation of malic acid to pyruvic acid), and oxaloacetic decarboxylase (which catalyzes the reversible decarboxylation of oxaloacetic acid to pyruvic acid). Flesch and Holbach (1965) reported that the latter two enzymes were distinctly different based on Michaelis constants, p-chloromercuribenzoate inhibition, and effect of avidin. Malic dehydrogenase is apparently not very active in wines since its pH optimum is much too high. The conclusion to date is that malic acid is decarboxylated directly to pyruvic acid rather than being dehydrogenated to oxaloacetic acid and then decarboxylated. For the reactions see Korkes et al. (1950) and p. 285.

It is now clear that a variety of bacterial phenomena which are associated with decarboxylation of malic acid are in many cases desirable enological practices. On the other hand, those bacterial activities which involve degradation of tartaric acid or glycerol (usually associated with *tourne* and propionic acid) are harmful to the quality of wines. For bacteria attacking citric acid see Charpentié et al. (1951).

Species in Table Wine

The homofermentative and heterofermentative groups of *Lactobacilli* have been defined briefly in previous sections. *Lactobacillus plantarum* was the only homofermentative species isolated from spoiled California

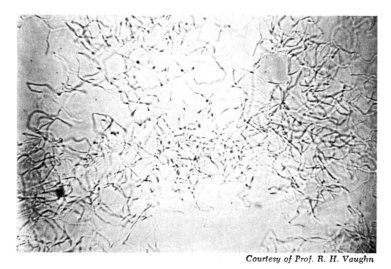

Courtesy of Prof. R. H. Vaughn

Fig. 121.   *Lactobacillus trichodes*

Not stained

wines by Vaughn and associates, Vaughn (1955) and Vaughn and Douglas (1938). On the other hand five different species of heterofermentative lactobacilli have been found in such wines; namely, *L. brevis, L. fermenti, L. buchneri, L. hilgardii,* and *L. trichodes,* Fig. 121. *L. plantarum* is readily differentiated from the heterofermentative species by its lack of carbon dioxide production from dextrose and its inability to form mannitol from levulose. It is, however, much more difficult to differentiate most of the various species of heterofermentative *Lactobacilli.* The fermentation of various pentoses and temperature relationships have been the criteria used most frequently for this purpose. *L. plantarum* forms long, slender rods, is Gram-positive, and does not form catalase. It does not attack alcohol and forms lactic acid in its fermentation of dextrose and levulose.

L. hilgardii was first described by Douglas and Cruess (1936A). It was later studied more extensively by Vaughn, *et al.* (1949). The original type culture of Douglas and Cruess unfortunately was lost, but ten new isolates considered to be identical with the type species were studied. These were compared with various species of heterofermentative *Lactobacilli.* On the basis of these comparisons, it was decided that *L. hilgardii* is a valid species, although it closely resembles *L. fermenti.* Vaughn (1955) places *L. hilgardii* next in importance to *L. plantarum* and *L. brevis* as a spoilage organism of California table wines.

From the new description of the organism by Vaughn *et al.* (1949) the following characteristics have been taken. Under the microscope the rodlike cells are single or in short chains, and filament formation is frequent. The cell size is 0.5–0.8 μ × 2.0–4.0 μ. The optimum temperature range is 86°F to 95°F. It ferments dextrose slowly, levulose rapidly, and does not ferment mannose, glycerol, or tartaric acid. It forms mannitol in addition to lactic acid, carbon dioxide, acetic acid, and alcohol. Its tolerance for alcohol is 15 to 18 per cent by volume. It produces a mousy type of smell in wine. It grows very slowly in culture media and in wine in contrast with certain other *Lactobacilli* such as *L. brevis.* These characteristics are given in order to illustrate the points usually investigated in establishing the identity of lactic bacteria isolated from spoiled wine. Müller-Thurgau and Osterwalder (1912, 1918, 1919) have described and named several lactic bacteria from wines including *L. gracilis, L. intermedius, L. gayoni;* and strains F, G, K, and P of *L. mannitopoeus.* From 450 bottled dry wines Du Plessis and Van Zyl (1963) recovered a variety of Gram-positive, catalase-negative, microaerophilic, non-motile, non-capsulated, nonsporeforming, non-nitrate reducing and non-dextran producing bacteria. Twenty-one were of 2 types of *Lactobacillus leichmannii* and 16 of *Pediococcus cerevisiae,* 2 of *L. buchneri,* 15 of *L. hilgardii,* 3 of *L. brevis* and 4 were unidentified isolates of *Lactobacillus.* Space will not permit the listing of properties of these and certain other *Lactobacilli* of wine described by various investigators in America and in other wine-producing regions (see Pederson (1938), Breed *et al.* (1957), Fornachon (1943), Vaughn *et al.* (1949), and Ingraham *et al.* (1960) for further information).

Dittrich and Kerner (1964) clearly established that the lactic sour odor of spoiled German wines was due to high diacetyl: a typical odor at 0.9 mg. per liter with some badly spoiled wines having 4.3 mg. per liter. Normal wines had 0.2 to 0.4 mg. per liter. To remove diacetyl a short refermentation (1 per cent sugar) is recommended. The reduction products are acetoin and then 2,3-butylene glycol. Some reduction of volatile acidity also occurs if the refermentation is carefully made.

Spoilage of Fortified Wines

In California, Australia, and South Africa fortified wines usually contain 19 to 20 per cent of alcohol and, therefore, bacteria that are able to grow in such wines must have an exceptionally high tolerance for alcohol. Fevrier (1926) isolated a long rod bacillus from South African wines of 20 per cent alcohol content. It possessed high heat resistance, withstanding 176°F. for 15 minutes. Niehaus (1932) found a thread-like bacillus in South African wines that grew readily in wines containing 18 per cent of alcohol and formed mannitol from levulose. It was probably the same organism described by Fornachon *et al.* (1949) as *L. trichodes.*

Fornachon (1943) has made an extensive study of the bacteria of spoiled Australian wines. He isolated them from spoiled fortified wines and from the lees of such wines. The one hundred and ten strains investigated were all heterofermentative species. These were divided into five groups or types. Type I, was probably *Lactobacillus trichodes,* Fig. 121. While they differ somewhat from the published properties of the organism, Fornachon's Types III and IV appeared to be varieties of or closely resemble *L. buchneri* of Henneberg (1926) and Pederson (1938); and similarly, Types II and V resembled *L. fermenti* of Beijerinck. Type I tolerated higher alcohol concentration than Types II to V and was the species most often causing spoilage of wines of 20 per cent or higher alcohol content. He states that the bacteria are widely distributed and probably occur in all Australian wineries. Therefore, a wine which remains sound does so because it is not susceptible to bacterial attack. None of the strains were able to cause serious spoilage in wines which contained only traces of fermentable sugar. According to Fornachon spoilage of Australian fortified wines is characterized by an increase in the volatile and fixed acidities and by production of mannitol and carbon dioxide.

Dupuy (1957) isolated a new *Lactobacillus* from a muscat dessert wine. It resembled Fornachon's Type II. The wines were gassy, of high viscosity (*graisseux*), high in ammonia, mannitol, and volatile acidity and contained no malic acid. The material causing the increased viscosity was a polyoside which gave on hydrolysis 90 per cent reducing sugars. See Kayser and Manceau (1909) for an early report of this type of spoilage, which was prevalent at that time.

All of Fornachon's cultures were quite sensitive to sulfur dioxide and failed to grow in wines containing 75 to 80 p.p.m. of total sulfur dioxide; at 100 the bacteria were killed. Growth was prevented at pH 3.6 or lower, and one means of control is acidification of the must or wine. He found, however, that acidification to pH 3.6 of wines of exceptionally high pH value often caused them to be too sour in taste. Type I required accessory growth factors from yeast autolysis for growth. Autolysis is favored by warm temperature and prolonged storage of the new wine on the lees and is more rapid in wines of high pH. Pasteurization at 158°F. for 60 seconds killed the bacteria and 149°F. for 15 minutes was also effective. He emphasizes the necessity of heating all portions of a given wine to pasteurizing temperature. The temperature of destruction probably depends to a great extent on the alcohol content and pH value of the wine. Oak tannin and Merck's reagent tannin prevented growth of Type I when 1 gm. per liter was added and only a trace of growth occurred when 0.5 gm. was added.

Germ-proof filtration, as Fornachon has indicated, can be used to rid a wine of lactic bacteria, although it is less easily applied effectively than pasteurization. Fornachon points out that lactic spoilage of wine often occurs during alcoholic fermentation, but that his Type I is unable to grow in must owing to the absence of growth accessory substances. However, Types II to V grow in must and might cause spoilage before fortification. Type I of Fornachon was somewhat more resistant to alcohol than Types II to V, and he states that many wines which would undergo spoilage at 18 to 19 per cent of alcohol might remain sound if fortified to 20 per cent alcohol. He concluded that the total nitrogen content of the wine is not a reliable indication of the susceptibility of a wine to attack. However, among the accessory growth factors from yeast autolysis there may be certain compounds that promote growth of his Type I.

During the early post-Repeal period in California, one of us (W. V. C.) and Saywell received many samples of fortified wines of 18 to 20.5 per cent alcohol containing a flocculent sediment which under the high power of the microscope appeared as a mass of tangled filaments, hence the name "hair bacillus" given it in the wineries and wine trade. It was also known as Fresno "mold" since the macroscopical appearance of the sediment is mold-like. Douglas and Cruess (1936B,C) reported briefly on this spoilage finding it very susceptible to sulfur dioxide, as 50 p.p.m. prevented its growth in sherry. Douglas and McClung (1937) described the organism and its culture characteristics.

Fornachon et al. (1949) have made an exhaustive study of this bacillus and have named it *Lactobacillus trichodes*, a new species. Briefly, its cultural characteristics are as follows. Unless autolysed yeast extract is added it fails to grow in the customary laboratory culture media. Rods are 0.4 to 0.6 by 2 to 4 μ; they occur in pairs or chains with a marked tendency to grow into very long, thread-like chains and filaments, they are Gram-positive in young cultures, and are microaerophilic. Acid is formed in dextrose and levulose media, and sometimes a small amount is formed in sucrose and maltose media. It fails to attack arabinose, xylose, galactose, lactose, raffinose, glycerol, mannitol, malic acid, citric acid, and tartaric acid and is catalase-negative. Lactic acid, acetic acid, carbon dioxide, and alcohol are the chief products from dextrose. In addition to these, mannitol is formed from levulose. The optimum temperature for growth in wine is 68° to 77°F. It grows well at 20 per cent alcohol and some strains grow at 21 per cent. The optimum pH range is 4.5 to 5.5 and it does not grow below pH 3.5 or above 5.8. It has been isolated from Spanish sherry and Italian vermouth.

Until recently *L. trichodes* was the only identified organism associated with the spoilage of fortified dessert wines in California. Gini (1959) has isolated members of the genera *Bacillus* and *Pediococcus* from spoiled dessert wines. Six strains were recovered from spoiled dessert wines and nineteen from winery production and storage equipment. He states: "*Bacilli* and *Pediococci* have been associated with spoilage of California dessert wines for the first time." He found that the spores were quite heat resistant and would probably survive the pasteurization customarily given wines.

Gini and Vaughn (1962) were unable to isolate *Lactobacillus* from California dessert wines. They did isolate seven strains of *Bacillus* from spoiled dessert wines or from winery equipment: *B. coagulans, B. subtilis, B. circulans, B. macerans, B. pumilis, B. sphaericus,* and *B. pantothenticus*. The cultural characteristics of the strains were not always normal. Spores of these were found to be very resistant to heat. They were capable of utilizing *l*-malic acid as an energy source (but not potassium bitartrate). When reinoculated into wines, the growth was not the same as in original wines. They also reported four strains of Gram-positive cocci, identified as *Pediococcus cerevisiae*. For further information on bacterial spoilage of dessert wines see Joslyn and Amerine (1964) and Radler (1962).

BITTER WINES

Bitterness in wines has been mentioned by several French investigators, including Pasteur (1873), Duclaux (1898–1901), and Voisenet (1910, 1918). Voisenet, who ascribed the condition to bacterial action, thought the responsible organism was *Bacillus amaracrylus*. He found that it forms acrolein from glycerol. Vaughn (1955) states that it is identical to *B. polymyxa*, but that the exact cause of the bitter taste is not clear. Pasteur (1873) sterilized 100 bottles of red Burgundy wine and left a similar set unheated. All of the unheated samples became cloudy and finally bitter; all of the pasteurized samples remained clear and free of bitterness. Müller-Thurgau and Osterwalder suggest that the bitter taste is due to compounds of tannin; the ethyl ester of gallic acid is intensely bitter. The authors have not encountered this spoilage of wine in California.

SPOILAGE BY YEASTS

In the past table wines have undergone clouding and fermentation in the bottle by wine yeasts and clouding of dry table wines has also occurred frequently in recent years. Less frequent has been the clouding of fortified dessert wines by alcohol-tolerant yeast.

In California

Baker (1936) isolated five cultures of yeast from cloudy California sauterne-type wine but did not identify the species definitely. Phaff and Douglas (1944) obtained the species *Saccharomyces bisporus* var. *bisporus* from cloudy dessert wines.

Scheffer and Mrak (1951) isolated 14 cultures of yeasts from bottled dry wines which were cloudy or showed a yeast sediment. These were commercial wines that were brilliantly clear when bottled. The yeasts were identified as *Saccharomyces chevalieri*, *S. uvarum*, *S. bayanus*, *S. cerevisiae*, *Pichia membranaefaciens* and *Candida rugosa*. Various properties of the yeasts were studied including morphology, spore formation, alcohol production, tolerance to sulfur dioxide in wine, and alcohol tolerance. Several formed high amounts of alcohol, 18.05 to 18.5 per cent. All were quite resistant to sulfur dioxide, growing readily at 200 p.p.m. The two cultures of *S. chevalieri* closely resembled the Spanish flor yeasts, tending to confirm the belief of several wine producers that flor yeasts have caused clouding of bottled wine. See also Castor (1952) and Mrak and McClung (1940).

In South Africa

Van der Walt and Van Kerken (1958) and Van Kerken (1963) examined many samples of cloudy wines from South African wineries. They identified *Brettanomyces* sp. in about 50 per cent of the samples, *S. uvarum* was recovered from 18 per cent, *S. bayanus* from 18 per cent, *S. cerevisiae* from 15 per cent, and *Pichia membranaefaciens* from 13 per cent. The very high incidence of *Brettanomyces* is unusual—much higher than from wines of the Gironde region of France (Peynaud and Domercq 1953).

Control

Yeast growth in bottled wine depends on pH, alcohol content, sulfur dioxide content, temperature, nitrogen content (macro- and micronutrients), and a source of infection, according to Van Kerken (1963). Dubourg (1897) reported viable yeasts in wines bottled 88 years.

Control of this type of spoilage can be accomplished in one of several ways: by germ-proof filtration, use of sulfurous acid or DEPC or by pasteurization. Of these methods, that of germ-proof filtration affects the flavor and bouquet of the wine least. The aged clear wine is sterile filtered into sterile bottles that are then closed with sterile caps or corks (p. 304). DEPC has little effect on the odor when properly used.

Unfortified fruit wines are pasteurized in California and Oregon wineries by flash heating to 145° to 165°F. and bottling hot. In one such plant the wine is bottled at 165°F., the bottles closed with crown caps and the filled bottles cooled at once in sprays of water. One California winery pasteurizes grape wine at about 145°F. in a heat interchanger type pasteurizer, cools it continuously, and bottles it at about 110°F. It is probable that the death temperature of yeasts in wine is lower than in fruit juices, owing to the alcohol content of the wine.

Sweet sauterne type wines have been preserved with addition of sulfurous acid, but this method has been found to be unreliable, even when high concentrations of sulfurous acid are used. Federal regulations set a maximum limit of 350 p.p.m. More than this amount can be added to the wine before bottling if the bottled wine is allowed to rest several months before marketing as the sulfur dioxide gradually decreases after bottling. However, such high amounts of sulfur dioxide greatly reduce the quality of the product.

DETERMINATION OF CAUSES OF MICROBIAL SPOILAGE

It is outside the score of this text to include all of the tests to determine which microorganism is involved. The following procedure will differentiate the major groups.

Centrifuge sufficient wine to give a few milliliters of sediment. Save the centrifuged wine for additional tests. Wash sediment with 5–10 ml. of water and re-centrifuge and decant. Follow the tests in this table:

DETERMINATION OF CAUSES OF MICROBIAL SPOILAGE

	Yeast	Acetic Acid Bacteria	Bacteria	
			Bacilli	Lactic Acid Bacteria
Visual appearance	Fine haze or precipitate or film; wine may be gassy	Thick gray film on surface	Fine haze or precipitate or silky, streaming cloud when shaken. Wine may be dull	Wine may be slightly gassy
Odor	Not characteristic	Vinegary (acetic acid and ethyl lactate)		Often mousy or saurkraut
Microscopic appearance	Greater than 4–5 μ	Ellipsoidal or rods	Less than 4–5 μ Rods	Less than 4–5 μ Rods or cocci (like tangled mass of hair = *Lactobacillus trichodes*)
Growth on Basic medium[1]	+	+	+	+ (Ferments malate to lactate = malo-lactic bacteria)
Basic medium + cycloheximide[2]	0 or trace	0 or +	+	+
Catalase test[3]	...	+	0 or +	+
Spore formation	0 or +	–	+	–
Calcium carbonate plates[4]	...	Clearing	No clearing	No clearing

Source of data: Tanner and Vetsch (1956) and personal observations of authors.

[1] Basic medium: The basic culture medium contains 2.0 gm. per 100 ml. of Bacto tryptone, 0.5 of Bacto peptone, 0.5 of Bacto yeast extract, 0.3 of dextrose, 0.2 of lactose, 0.1 of liver extract (Wilson), 0.1 ml. of 5 per cent aqueous Tween 80, 100 ml. of diluted and filtered S & W tomato juice, and 2.0 gm. agar. To prepare tomato juice, dilute one can (0.355 liters) of S & W tomato juice to 1500 ml. with distilled water. Filter through Whatman No. 1 paper using a Büchner funnel and Super Cel filter aid. To prepare the basic medium dissolve solid ingredients in 50 ml. of the diluted tomato juice by heating. Avoid scorching by frequent agitation of the flask. When mixture appears homogeneous add remainder of the diluted tomato juice and cool. Adjust pH to 5.5 with concentrated hydrochloric acid, add the agar, mix, cover flask and autoclave 15 minutes at 15 lbs.

[2] If cycloheximide ("Actidione") is desired, add 1 ml. containing 10 mg. of cycloheximide to each 100 ml. of medium prior to autoclaving.

[3] Basic medium with cycloheximide: Add a drop of 3 per cent hydrogen peroxide to colonies. If gas is evolved the organism is catalase positive.

[4] Basic medium with cycloheximide minus the dextrose and lactose and containing 2 per cent calcium carbonate and 3 per cent calcium carbonate and 3 per cent ethyl alcohol (the ethanol is added after autoclaving): If acetic bacteria grow they will cause clearing of this cloudy medium around the colonies.

BIBLIOGRAPHY

ADAMS, A. M. 1964. Malo-lactic fermentations in Ontario wines. Rept. Hort. Exper. Stat. and Prod. Lab. *1964*, 108–111.

AMERINE, M. A. 1950. The acids of California grapes and wines. I. Lactic acid. Food Technol. *4*, 177–181.

AMERINE, M. A. and JOSLYN, M. A. 1970. Table wines: The Technology of Their Production. 2 ed. Univ. California Press, Berkeley and Los Angeles.

ARENA, A. 1936. Alteraciones bacterianas de vinos argentinos. Rev. Agr. Vet. (Buenos 'Aires) *8*, 155–320.

BAKER, E. E. 1936. Bottle pasteurization of sauterne. Wine Review *4*, No. 7, 16–18.

BARRE, P., and GALZY, P. 1960. Étude d'une nouvelle bactérie malolactique. Ann. technol. agr. *9*, 331–343.

BERRY, J. M., and VAUGHN, R. H. 1952. Decomposition of tartrates by lactobacilli. Proc. Am. Soc. Enol. *1952*, 135–138.

BIDAN, P. 1956. Sur quelques bactéries isolées de vins en fermentation malolactique. Ann. technol. agr. *5*, 597–617.

BOBADILLA, G. F. DE. 1943. Aplicaciones industriales de las levaduras de flor. Agricultura (Revista Agropecuaria) *12*, No. 133, 203–207.

BOIDRON, A. M. 1969. Contribution à l'étude de l'antagonisme entre les levures et les bactéries. Bordeaux. Thèse.

BREED, R. S., MURRAY, E. G. D., and HITCHINS, A. P. 1957. Bergey's Manual of Determinative Bacteriology, 7 ed. Williams and Wilkins, Baltimore.

CARLES, P. 1891. Sur la caractéristique des vins figue. Compt. rend. *112*, 811–812.

CASTELLI, T. 1959. Introduzione alla Microbiologia Enologica. Tipografia Setti e Figlio, Milan.

CASTOR, J. G. B. 1952. Yeast spoilage of wines. Proc. Am. Soc. Enol. *1952*, 139–160.

CHARPENTIÉ, Y., RIBÉREAU-GAYON, J., and PEYNAUD, E. 1951. Sur la fermentation de l'acide citrique par les bactéries malo-lactiques. Bull. soc. chim. biol. *33*, 1369–1378.

CRUESS, W. V. 1912. Effect of sulfurous acid on fermentation organisms. Ind. Eng. Chem. *4*, 581–585.

CRUESS, W. V. 1935. Control of tourne. Fruit Prods. J. *14*, 359–360.

CRUESS, W. V. 1937. Observation of '36 season on volatile acid formation in muscat fermentations. Fruit Prods. J. *16*, 198–200, 219.

CRUESS, W. V. 1943. The role of micro-organisms and enzymes in wine making. Advances in Enzymol. *3*, 349–386.

CRUESS, W. V. 1948. Investigations of the flor sherry process. Calif. Agr. Expt. Sta. Bull. *710*.

DITTRICH, H. H., and KERNER, E. 1964. Diacetyl als Weinfehler. Ursache und Beseitigung. Wein-Wissen. *19*, 528–535.

DOUGLAS, H. C., and CRUESS, W. V. 1936A. A lactobacillus from California wine: *Lactobacillus hilgardii*. Food Research *1*, 113–119.

DOUGLAS, H. C., and CRUESS, W. V. 1936B. A note on the spoilage of sweet wine. Fruit Prods. J. *15*, 310.

DOUGLAS, H. C., and CRUESS, W. V. 1936C. Sweet wine treatment. Wine Review *6*, No. 12, 9–10.

Douglas, H. C., and McClung, L. S. 1937. Characteristics of an organism causing spoilage in fortified sweet wines. Food Research 2, 471–475.

d'Estivaux. 1935. Sur un développement intense du microbe de la tourne dans un milieu très alcoolique. Ann. fals. et fraudes 28, 288–291.

Doubourg, E. 1897. Contribution à l'étude des levures de vin. Rev. vitic. 8, 468–472.

Duclaux, E. 1898–1901. Traité de Microbiologie. 4 v. Masson, Paris.

Du Plessis, L. de W., and Van Zyl, J. A. 1963. The microbiology of South African winemaking. IV. The taxonomy and incidence of lactic acid bacteria from dry wines. S. African J. Agr. Sci. 6, 261–273.

Dupuy, P. 1957. Une nouvelle altération bactérienne dans les vins de liqueur. Ann. technol. agr. 6, 93–102.

Dupuy, P. 1957A. Les Acetobacter du vin. Identification de quelques souches. Ibid. 6, 217–233.

Dupuy, P. 1957B. Les facteurs du développement de l'acescence dans le vin. Ibid. 6, 391–407.

Fell, G. 1961. Étude sur la fermentation malolactique du vin et les possibilités de la provoquer par ensemencement. Land. Jahr. Schweiz 75, 249–264.

Fevrier, F. 1926. A bacterial disease of wine. J. Dept. Agr. Union of South Africa 12, 120–122.

Flesch, P., and Holbach, B. 1965. Zum Abbau der L-Äpfelsäure durch Milchsäurebakterien. I. Über die Malat-abbauenden Enzyme des Bakterium "L" unter besonderer Berücksichtigung der Oxalessigsäure-Decarboxylase. Arch. Microbiol. 51, 401–413.

Fornachon, J. C. M. 1936. A bacterium causing "disease" in fortified wines. Australian J. Expt. Biol. and Med. Sci. 14, 214–222.

Fornachon, J. C. M. 1943. Bacterial Spoilage of Fortified Wines. Australian Wine Board, Adelaide.

Fornachon, J. C. M. 1957. The occurrence of malo-lactic fermentation in Australian wines. Australian J. Appl. Sci. 8, 120–129.

Fornachon, J. C. M., Douglas, H. C., and Vaughn, R. H. 1940. The pH requirements of some heterofermentative species of Lactobacillus. J. Bact. 40, 644–655.

Fornachon, J. C. M., Douglas, H. C., and Vaughn, R. H. 1949. Lactobacillus trichodes nov. spec., a bacterium causing spoilage in appetizer and dessert wines. Hilgardia 19, 129–132.

Frateur, J. 1950. Essai sur la systématique des Acetobacter. La Cellule 53, 287–392.

Gayon, V., and Dubourg, E. 1894. Sur les vins mannités. Ann. inst. Pasteur 8, 108–116.

Gayon, V., and Dubourg, E. 1901. Nouvelles recherches sur la ferment mannitique. Ibid. 15, 526–569.

Gini, B. 1959. Characteristics of some bacteria associated with the spoilage of dessert wines. Thesis for M.A. degree in Microbiology, Univ. Calif., Davis, California.

Gini, B. and Vaughn, R. H. 1962. Characteristics of some bacteria associated with spoilage of California dessert wines. Am. J. Enol. Vitic. 13, 20–31.

Henneberg, W. 1926. Handbuch der Gärungs-Bakteriologie. 2 v. Paul Parey, Berlin.

INGRAHAM, J. L., VAUGHN, R. H., and Cooke, G. M. 1960. Studies on the malo-lactic organisms isolated from California wines. Am. J. Enol. Vitic. *11*, 1–4.

JOSLYN, M. A., and AMERINE, M. A. 1964. Dessert, Appetizer and Related Flavored Wines. University of California, Division of Agricultural Sciences, Berkeley.

KAYSER, E., and MANCEAU, E. 1909. Les Ferments de la Graisse des Vins. Henri Villers, Épernay.

KOCH, A. 1900. Ueber die Ursachen des Verschwindens der Säure bei Gärung und Lagerung des Weines. Weinbau u. Weinhandel *18*, 395–396, 407–408, 417–419.

KOCH, R. 1881. Zur Züchtung von pathogenen Mikro-organismen. Kaiserl. Gesundheitsampte *1*, 4–48.

KORKES, S., DEL CAMPELLO, A., and OCHOA, S. 1950. Biosynthesis of dicarboxylic acids by carbon dioxide fixation. IV. Isolation and properties of an adaptive "malic" enzyme from *Lactobacillus arabinosus*. J. Biol. Chem. *187*, 891–905.

KRUMPERMAN, P. H., BERRY, J. M. and VAUGHN, R. H. 1953. Utilization of tartrate by *Lactobacillus plantarum*. Bacteriol. Proc. *1953*, 24.

KUNKEE, R. E., PILONE, G. J., and COMBS, R. E. 1965. The occurrence of malo-lactic fermentation in Southern California wines. Am. J. Enol. Vitic. *16*, 219–223.

LABORDE, J. 1904. Sur le ferment de la maladie des vins poussés et tournés. Compt. rend. *138*, 228–231.

LÜTHI, H. 1957. Symbiotic problems relating to bacterial deterioration of wines. Am. J. Enol. *8*, 176–181.

MAESTRO PALÓ, F. 1952. Defectos y Enfermedades de los Vinos. Tip. "La Académica," Zaragoza.

MRAK, E. M., and McCLUNG, L. S. 1940. Yeasts occurring on grapes and in grape products in California. J. Bact. *40*, 395–407.

MÜLLER-THURGAU, H., and OSTERWALDER, A. 1912. Die Bakterien im Wein und Obstwein und die dadurch verursachten Veränderungen. Zentr. Bakteriol. Parasitenk. Abt. II *36*, 129–338.

MÜLLER-THURGAU, H., and OSTERWALDER, A. 1918. Weitere Beiträge zur Kenntnis der Mannitbakterien im Wein. *Ibid.* 48, 1–35.

MÜLLER-THURGAU, H., and OSTERWALDER, A. 1919. Ueber die durch bakterien verursachte Zersetzung von Weinsäure und Glyzerin im Wein. Land. Jahr. Schweiz. *33*, 313–371.

NICKLES, J. 1862. Sur le vin tourné. Compt. rend. *54*, 1219–1220.

NIEHAUS, C. J. 1930. The principal South African wine diseases. Farming in South Africa 4, 475–476, 521–522, 526.

NIEHAUS, C. J. 1932. Mannitic bacteria in South African sweet wines. Farming in South Africa 4, 443–444.

OLSEN, E. 1948. Studies of bacteria in Danish fruit wines. Antonie van Leeuwenhoek J. Microbiol. Serol. *14*, 1–28.

ORLA-JENSEN, S. 1919. The lactic acid bacteria. Kgl. Danske Videnskab. Selskabs. Skritter Naturvidenskab. Math. Afdel 5, No. 8, 81–196.

PASTEUR, L. 1864. Étude sur les vins. Compt. rend. *58*, 142–150.

PASTEUR, L. 1873. Études sur le Vinaigre et sur le Vin. *In* Oeuvres de Pasteur. III. Masson et Cie., Paris. 1924.

PEDERSON, C. S. 1938. Lactic acid producing bacteria in fermentation and food spoilage. Food Research *3*, 317–321.

PEDERSON, C. S. 1957. Genus I: *Lactobacillus* Beijerinck. *In* "Bergey's Manual of Determinative Bacteriology," 7th ed., 542–552. Williams and Wilkins Co, Baltimore.

PEYNAUD, E. 1936. L'acetate d'ethyl dans les vins atteints d'acescence. Ann. ferment. *2*, 367–384.

PEYNAUD, E. 1937. Études sur les phénomènes d'estérification dans les vins. Rev. viticult. *86*, 209–215, 227–231, 248–253, 299–301, 394–396, 420–423, 440–444, 472–475; *87*, 49–52, 113–116, 185–188, 242–249, 278–285, 297–301, 344–350, 362–364, 383–385.

PEYNAUD, E., and DOMERCQ, S. 1953. Études des levures de la Gironde. Ann. technol. agr. *4*, 265–300.

PHAFF, H. J., and DOUGLAS, H. C. 1944. A note on yeasts occurring in dessert wines. Fruit Prods. J. *23*, 332–334.

PILONE, G. J., and KUNKEE, R. E. 1965. Sensory characterization of wines fermented with several malo-lactic strains of bacteria. Am. J. Enol. Vitic. *16*, 224–230.

QUINN, D. G. 1940. Sulfur dioxide: Its use in the winery. J. Dept. Agr. Victoria *38*, 200–204.

RADLER, F. 1962. Über die Milchsäurebakterien des Weines und den biologischen Säureabbau. I. Systematik und chemische Grundlagen. Vitis *3*, 144–176.

RIBÉREAU-GAYON, J. 1938. Les bactéries du vin et les transformations qu'elles produisent. Bull. Assoc. chim. de sucr. et de distill. de France et des colon. *55*, 601–656.

RIBÉREAU-GAYON, J. 1946. Sur la fermentation de l'acide malique dans les grands vins rouges. Bull. off. intern. vin *19*, No. 182, 26–29.

RIBÉREAU-GAYON, J., and PEYNAUD, E. 1938. Bilan de la fermentation malolactique. Ann. ferment. *4*, 559–569.

SCHANDERL, H. 1954. Über die Rolle des Schwefelwasserstoffs und des molekularen Schwefels bei dem Metabioseverhältnis zwischen Weinhefen und Säuerabbaubakterien. Naturwiss. *41*, 284.

SCHANDERL, H. 1959. Die Mikrobiologie des Mostes und Weines. Eugen Ulmer, Stuttgart.

SCHEFFER, W. R., and MRAK, E. M. 1951. Characteristics of yeast causing clouding of dry white wines. Mycopathol. et Mycol. Appl. *5*, 236–249.

SÉMICHON, L. 1905. Maladies des vins. Librairie Coulet, Montpellier.

SHIMWELL, J. L. 1941. The lactic bacteria of beer. Wallerstein Labs. Communs. *4*, 41–48.

SNELL, E. E. 1946. The nutritional requirements of the lactic acid bacteria and their application to biochemical research. J. Bact. *50*, 373–382.

SUVERKROP, B., and TCHELISTCHEFF, A. 1949. Malo-lactic fermentation in California wines. Wines and Vines *30*, No. 7, 19–23.

TANNER, H., and VETSCH, U. 1956. How to characterize cloudiness in beverages. Am. J. Enol. *7*, 145–146.

VAN DER WALT, J. P., and VAN KERKEN, A. E. 1958. The wine yeasts of the Cape. I. A taxonomical survey of the yeasts causing turbidity in South African table wines. Wine Industry Research Group, Stellenbosch, South African Council for Scientific and Industrial Research, Pretoria.

VAN KERKEN, A. E. 1963. Contribution to the ecology of yeasts occurring in wine. University of the Orange Free State, Pretoria. Mimeo.

VAUGHN, R. H. 1938. Some effects of association and competition on *Acetobacter*. J. Bact. *36*, 357–367.

VAUGHN, R. H. 1942. The acetic bacteria. Wallerstein Labs. Communs. *5*, 5–26.

VAUGHN, R. H. 1955. Bacterial spoilage of wines. Advances Food Research *6*, 67–108.

VAUGHN, R. H. 1959. Personal communication; Davis, Calif.

VAUGHN, R. H., and DOUGLAS, H. C. 1938. Some lactobacilli encountered in abnormal musts. J. Bact. *36*, 318–319.

VAUGHN, R. H., DOUGLAS, H. C., and FORNACHON, J. C. M. 1949. The taxonomy of *Lactobacillus hilgardii* and related heterofermentative lactobacilli. Hilgardia *19*, 133–139.

VAUGHN, R. H., and TCHELISTCHEFF, A. 1957. Studies on the malic acid fermentation of California table wines. Am. J. Enol. *8*, 74–79.

VERONA, O., and FLORENZANO, G. 1956. Microbiologia Applicata all'Industria Enologica. Edizioni Agricole, Bologna.

VOISENET, E. 1910. Nouvelles recherches sur les vins amers et la fermentation acrylique de la glycerine. Compt. rend. *151*, 518–520.

VOISENET, E. 1918. Sur une bacterie de l'eau vegetant dans les vins amers capable de deshydrater la glycérine. Glycero-reaction. Ann. inst. Pasteur. *32*, 476–510.

WOOD, H. G., GEIGER, C., and WERKMAN, C. H. 1940. Nutritive requirements of the heterofermentative lactic acid bacteria. Iowa State Coll. J. Sci. *14*, 367–378.

CHAPTER 17

Brandy Production

Throughout the world since at least the Middle Ages wine has been distilled to concentrate the alcohol to a higher percentage than occurred in the original wine.[1] These wine distillates have been called *aqua vini, eaux-de-vie, Weinbrand,* Cognac, *Branntwein, aguardiente, aquavit,* and in English-speaking countries, brandy. For general information on brandy, see Amerine and Winkler (1938), Büttner (1938), Chaminade (1930), Dujardin (1955), Hartmann (1955), Hirsch (1936), Joslyn and Amerine (1941), Ricciardelli (1909), Rocques (1913), U. S. Internal Revenue Service (1955), Valaer (1939), and Xandri (1958).

DEFINITIONS

In the United States, with which this book is primarily concerned, spirits distilled from wine are classified as follows (U. S. Internal Revenue Service 1955):

Grape brandy or brandy is distilled at not exceeding 170 degrees of proof solely from the juice or mash of whole, sound, ripe fruit, or from natural wine, specially sweetened natural wine having a volatile acidity, calculated as acetic acid and exclusive of sulphur dioxide, not in excess of 0.20 gm. per 100 cu. cm. with or without the addition (to juice or wine only) of not more than 20 per cent by weight of the pomace of such juice or wine, or 30 per cent by volume of the lees of such wine or both (calculated prior to the addition of water to facilitate fermentation or distillation). This is qualified in another section of the regulations which provides that brandy may not be produced from "distillates containing one-half of 1 per cent or more of aldehydes or 1 per cent or more of fusel oil."

Brandy derived from raisins or from raisin wine shall be branded "Raisin Brandy" . . .

Brandy distilled from the lees of natural wine, specially sweetened natural wine, or standard agricultural wine made from dried fruit, which are run into the still, shall be branded "Lees Brandy," qualified by the name of the fruit from which such wine and lees are derived (e.g., Grape Lees Brandy).

Brandy distilled from the skin and pulp of sound, ripe fruit which are run into the still, after the withdrawal of the juice or wine therefrom, shall be branded "Pomace Brandy" or "Marc Brandy," qualified by the name of the fruit from

---

[1] The Chinese probably discovered distillation at a very early period according to Simmonds (1919). Needham (1954), however, doubts this. Alchemists were distilling wine in the thirteenth century and Shakespeare refers to it in Othello (Act II, Scene 3). "O thou invisible spirit of wine, if thou hast no name to be known by, let us call thee devil." See Egloff and Lowry (1929) for further information on ancient methods of distillation.

which derived (e.g., "Grape Pomace Brandy"). Grape pomace brandy may be also designated as "Grappa" or "Grappa Brandy."

Brandy distilled at more than 170 degrees of proof and less than 190 degrees of proof, shall be branded in the same manner as if distilled at a lower proof except that the designation shall be qualified by the word "Neutral," e.g., "Neutral Brandy" . . .

Brandy which in whole or in part is treated with wood chips throughout percolation or otherwise, during distillation or storage, shall be further marked, either by branding or stenciling with the words "treated with oak chips."

Provision is also made in the regulations for "residue brandy" and "substandard brandy."

Neutral spirits are defined as follows:

All spirits distilled from fruit at or above 190 degrees of proof shall be branded "Neutral Spirits—Fruit." In the case of fruit neutral spirits produced for use in wine production, the words Neutral Spirits—Fruit branded on the package shall be followed by the name of the fruit from which produced, in the following form Neutral Spirits—Fruit—Grape.

"Wine spirits" shall mean brandy, as defined (elsewhere) distilled at 140 degrees of proof or more and not reduced with water from distillation proof.

In practice, two types of spirits distilled from wine are actually found on the market. Wine spirits or as we shall say "fortifying brandy" are spirits distilled from wine at a proof of 140° or more and sold as such. Brandies for beverage purposes may be distilled only at a proof of 140° to 170° and are reduced to a lower proof before and after aging. For further notes on legal restrictions see Chapter 19.

Alcohol Content

The alcohol concentration of distilled spirits is expressed differently in various countries. In Germany per cent alcohol by weight (gm. per 100 gm.) is used. In France per cent by volume (ml. per 100 ml.) at 59°F. is official (p. 602). In other countries per cent by volume is most often determined at 68°F.

In England and the United States proof as commonly used by the definition varies in the two countries. In the United States the official definition is as follows: " 'proof' shall mean the ethyl alcohol content of a liquid at 60°F., stated as twice the per cent ethyl alcohol by volume." In addition " 'proof spirits' shall mean that alcoholic liquor which contains 50 per cent of ethyl alcohol by volume at 60°F. and which has a specific gravity of 0.93418 in air at 60°F. referred to water at 60°F. as unity." From this "proof gallon" is defined as "the alcohol equivalent of a United States gallon at 60°F., containing 50 per cent of ethyl alcohol by volume."

In England proof is measured by Sike's alcohol hydrometer so that "proof spirit" contains 49.28 per cent alcohol by weight or 57.10 per cent

TABLE 54

ALCOHOL STRENGTHS BY DIFFERENT SYSTEMS[1]

Italy, Austria, Russia, U. S.	United States	Great Britain	France Belgium	Germany	Specific Gravity	Cartier[2]
Per cent by Vol. 60°F.	Proof 60°F.	Proof 60°F.	Per cent by Vol. 59°F.	Per cent by Wt. 59°F.	60°F.	59°F.
0.0	0.0	100 u.p.[3]	0.0	0.0	1.0000	10.0
5.0	10.0	91.2 u.p.	4.9	4.0	0.9928	10.9
10.0	20.0	82.4 u.p.	9.9	8.1	0.9866	11.8
15.0	30.0	73.8 u.p.	14.8	12.2	0.9810	12.5
20.0	40.0	65.2 u.p.	19.8	16.3	0.9759	13.2
30.0	60.0	47.6 u.p.	29.8	24.7	0.9653	14.7
40.0	80.0	30.1 u.p.	39.9	33.4	0.9517	16.6
50.0	100.0	12.5 u.p.	49.8	42.7	0.9342	19.2
57.1	114.2	Proof	56.9	49.3	0.9197	21.4
60.0	120.0	5.0 o.p.[4]	59.8	52.1	0.9133	22.4
70.0	140.0	21.7 o.p.	69.9	62.7	0.8899	26.3

[1] Souce of data: Simmonds (1919); Rentschler and Braun (1950).
[2] Now used only in Switzerland.
[3] Under proof.
[4] Over proof.

by volume at 60°F. For alcohol percentages below "proof spirit" the proof is expressed as "under proof" and above 57.10 per cent as "over proof." The approximate alcoholic strength by different systems is summarized in Table 54. These values are not always interchangeable owing to the use of slightly different values for the specific gravity of alcohol and to varying calibration temperatures.

BRANDY TYPES

Brandy is produced from wine in many parts of France. Some of it is for industrial use. A small amount is used for fortifying dessert wines. That produced for beverage purposes may be divided into the following classes: Cognac, Armagnac, eaux-de-vie, and eaux-de-vie de marc. Brandy is also produced in most of the wine-producing countries.

Cognac

This brandy can be produced in France only in the Departments of Charente and Charente Maritime (with a small acreage in Deux Sèvres and Dordogne). The right to the name is limited by law by the United States, Germany, Cuba, Denmark, Italy, Switzerland, etc., to brandy produced in France in this region. Production is very variable. In the years between 1933 and 1962, brandy equivalent to a minimum of 639,962 and a maximum of 8,982,310 gallons of pure alcohol (average 3,256,704) were made per year. The low production occurred in 1945 owing to a severe spring frost. Sales also vary from year to year as the figures for the years from 1933 to 1962 show (as gallons of pure alcohol):

	Minimum	Maximum	Average
France	342,408	2,284,207[1]	884,875
Export[2]	188,589[3]	3,674,273	1,746,820

Source of data: Lafon *et al.* (1964).
[1] Includes some W.W. II shipments to Germany.
[2] Includes shipments of wines fortified to 22 per cent alcohol.
[3] Low values are for 1943–1944.

The vineyard acreage (162,168 in 1962) of the departments is subdivided into the districts of Grande Champagne 11.8 per cent, Petite Champagne 11.7, Borderies, 3.8, Fin Bois 33, Bons Bois 28.8, and Bois Ordinaires 10.9. All are entitled to produce wine which, when distilled, may be labeled Cognac. The soils of these regions differ in their calcium carbonate content. The prices paid for wines or brandies from the first two districts is always higher than that of the others. Cognacs produced from these two districts are also entitled to the appellation "fine champagne."

The two predominant varieties are Saint Émilion (also called Trebbiano in Italy or Ugni blanc in the south of France) and Folle Blanche. Because of its greater resistance to botrytis the Saint Émilion has gradually replaced the Folle Blanche. Variety *per se* is usually *not* a critical factor in brandy quality. Their cool climate limits ripening so that the wines for distillation have a relatively low alcohol content. Lafon *et al.* (1964), from 1936 to 1961, found the alcohol varied from 7.1 to 12.0 per cent with an average for the 26 years of 9.2. Between 1900 and 1920 the average was 7.9 per cent. The years with the higher alcohol content were generally of lesser quality! The grapes are pressed immediately after crushing as fermentation on the skins produces less desirable wines for distillation. Moldy grapes constitute an especially difficult problem in certain years and besides removing the fruit with more rot special care in pressing, settling, etc. is taken in these seasons. Lafon *et al.* (1964) stress the following quality factors: no late vineyard sulfuring, no botrytis on the fruit, high must fixed acidity, clean fermentation, little press wine, low alcohol, removal of seeds and dry stems, low wine volatile acidity, and storage of the wine in absence of air.

Distillation starts immediately after the vintage and continues until all the newly fermented wine is distilled. All authorities emphasize the use of clean wine which has been stored for as short a time as possible, and which must not be oxidized. Only direct-fired pot stills of 150- to 500-liter capacity are employed (p. 619). The new wine (with its lees, but with not more than 8 per cent of added lees) is placed in the still and brought

Fig. 122. Harvesting Scene in Cognac Vineyard

to boiling. The distillation continues until the vapor contains negligible alcohol. The distillation takes eight or more hours and the main distillate contains about 24 to 32 per cent alcohol. A tails fraction may be separated. The still is then emptied, refilled with fresh wine and also often the "tails" of the previous distillation, and a second distillation made. A third distillation is also made. The three main distillates are finally combined and then redistilled. This last distillation takes longer than the original distillations—14 or more hours. About 1 to 2 per cent heads are separated. The main distillate averages 58 to 60 per cent alcohol. A tail fraction is also separated. Continuous tasting and use of an alcohol hydrometer are practiced to control the amount of each fraction. Lafon *et al.* (1964) note that individual distillers modify the process in various details, particularly in years of moldy grapes. In some cases the product of the second distillation is reduced to 26 to 28 per cent with water and redistilled.

The new brandy is placed in new Limousin or Tronçais oak. The oak is well dried before being made into casks. The casks are washed several times with water and once with brandy. Before too much tannin is extracted, the brandy is transferred to used casks or tanks. Brandy usually acquires its best quality after 15 to 20 years in the wood. In some cases, this improvement may continue to 40 or even 50 years, but not longer. Older brandies are kept in glass.

The important production quality factors are the method of double distillation and especially its careful execution, and the aging of the brandy in *hard* oak casks. Hennig and Burkhardt (1962) reported a different chromatographic pattern in Cognac compared to German brandies, particularly of higher tannin content (especially of ellagic and gallic acids) and less caramel and sugar. Longer aging in oak containers appeared to be responsible for the differences. For further information on Cognac see Anon. (1947), Chaminade (1930), Delamain (1935), Hartmann (1955), Jackson (1928), Prioton (1929), and Ravaz (1900).

For formulas for making imitation cognac see Xandri (1958). None of these recipes produces an artificial cognac worthy of commercial production in our opinion. Nevertheless, there does seem to be opportunity for flavored brandy in the hand of a skillful and patient distiller.

Armagnac

This brandy is produced in a delimited area in the southwest of France, mainly in the department of Gers. The western portion is called Bas-Armagnac, the central portion Ténarèze, and the eastern Haut-Armagnac.

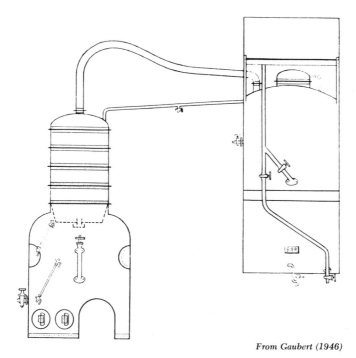

From Gaubert (1946)

FIG. 123.   ARMAGNAC-TYPE OF STILL

The products of these districts are not, however, distinguishable on a quality basis as are those of the Cognac sub-districts. The influence of soil conditions must be small. However, Armagnac producers claim to find differences in the quality produced on the different soil types. The climate is cool and is influenced by the proximity of the Atlantic.

Phylloxera caused a change in the varieties planted in this region. The Saint Émilion, as in Cognac, is very important. Folle Blanche (there called Picpoul or Piquepoult) has been nearly abandoned and a direct-producer hybrid, Baco 22A, is extensively planted because of its resistance to mildew and anthracnose. Some red grapes are used for wine for distilling.

The composition of Armagnac's produced from three varieties have been studied by Flanzy and Jouret (1963) using gas chromatography. The brandy of Folle Blanche was richer in a wider range of esters than those of Saint-Émilion or of Baco 22A. Sensory examination showed the Folle Blanche had a better bouquet. No ethyl laurate was found, possibly due to the method of distillation used for Armagnac. They were unable to detect differences in the higher alcohol content of brandies made from the three varieties.

The new wines are distilled in semicontinuous stills of a special design, Fig. 123. The stripping column has only 5 or 6 plates. The heat is supplied by fire so that some destructive distillation does occur. The proof of distillation is very low, not exceeding 126°. The brandy is aged in native Gascon oak casks of not over 110 gallons. While some Armagnac brandy is aged for 20 or more years much is sold after only 5 to 8 years' aging. Generally Armagnac is drier than Cognac and the odor less distinctive. See Gaubert (1946) and Flanzy and Lamazou-Betbeder (1938).

Other Regions

Many other eaux-de-vie are produced in France, particularly in the south where continuous stills are used. Pomace brandy (eaux-de-vie de marc) occasionally is made in Burgundy, Champagne, and elsewhere. Pot stills are used and the brandy is often aged in glass or paraffined barrels as it is usually colorless. The aroma is very pungent and one must acquire a taste for it. Flanzy and Lamazou-Betbeder (1938) have shown that marc brandies are very high in their coefficient of non-alcohols (acid plus aldehyde plus esters plus higher alcohols), and especially in aldehydes (indicating that the pomace is not fresh).

Other Countries

Brandy is made in Germany (often partially from French wine), Italy, Greece, Russia, Bulgaria (Fig. 124), and Spain and elsewhere. Limited

FIG. 124. DISTILLERY IN LIASKOVETS, BULGARIA

amounts from Germany, Greece, and Spain are exported to this country. Greek brandies are often sweet, some are flavored, and many are distilled from raisin (currant) wine. Spanish brandy has at least the merit of being reasonably uniform (owing to the use of fractional blending systems, p. 415) but they also are often sweet, and the younger types are hot to the taste. The Spanish brandy industry originated in the region of Jerez de la Frontera during the Moslem occupation according to Xandri (1958) and much of the finest Spanish brandy for local use or for export still comes from this region. Some very interesting brandies are also produced in the Montilla district south of Cordova. The modern industry dates from the late nineteenth century. Details of the Spanish regulations are also given by Xandri (1958). Originally direct-fired pot stills were used but an Armagnac-type still is now employed. Both new and used oak casks are used for aging. The commercial products vary from 5 to 25 years of age with 80° to 90° proof. Spain also uses wine spirits to produce anise-flavored liqueurs. Italian brandy is also imported into this country. Some appears to be flavored.

We have tested several good Russian brandies, but some are quite hot to the taste. They are producing a series of qualities of brandies (p. 50). The brandies from Mexico (and in Mexico) have not been of superior

Courtesy of K.W.V.

Fig. 125. Distillery in South Africa

Note wine being delivered in tank trucks

quality and some were excessively flavored with "oil of cognac." Elena (1941) has given a revealing description of the state of the Argentinean brandy industry. Both pot and continuous stills are employed. She found that many of the products were made with neutral alcohol and simply flavored and sold without aging.

South Africa has made a major effort to improve the quality of its brandy by use of pot stills and adequate aging, Fig. 125. The result is that the South African brandies which we have tasted have been of very pleasant character but are more neutral than those of Cognac, possibly because of the nature of the wood used in aging them.

Peru has long been a producer of brandy. At present these brandies can hardly be called quality products. Muscat and other wines are distilled and the brandy aged in paraffined containers. It does not, therefore, darken with aging. It is called pisco[2] and the samples we have tasted have been hot and hardly worthy of its nineteenth century reputation. Pisco punch, a long drink made with pisco brandy, was popular in California before Prohibition.

California

Brandy has been produced in this state since the Mission days. In the pre-prohibition period a number of producers distilled wines to produce beverage brandy, some of which achieved a good reputation. Both pot

---

[2] From the Pisco Indians of the Ica Valley who made pottery which, when lined with beeswax, was used to store, age, and transport the brandy, according to Carranza (1939). The port of Pisco got its name from the brandy jars, not *vice versa*.

and continuous stills were employed but aging was almost always in new fifty-gallon, American oak barrels. These were aged for 3 to 10 or 15 years. American regulations made blending difficult but some fairly distinctive types were produced. Grappa, or pomace brandy, was also produced in limited quantities.

Following Prohibition, the pot stills were gradually abandoned and at present nearly all California brandy is produced in continuous column stills. The crop control program of 1938 included compulsory distillation so that a very large amount of brandy was placed in barrels. These brandies were most useful to the industry during W.W. II when other alcoholic beverages were in short supply. Consumption of California brandy has continued to increase since the war. For more complete data see Table 55.

TABLE 55

CALIFORNIA BRANDY AND SPIRITS PRODUCTION AND END-OF-YEAR INVENTORIES

Fiscal Years 1959–60 to 1964–65, Inclusive
(Thousands of Tax Gallons[1])

Year (July 1–June 30)	Production[2]	Spirits for Addition to Wine[3]	End-of-Year Inventory[2,4]
1959–60	7,974	35,903	12,962
1961–62	5,738	30,968	15,580
1963–64	9,921	38,312	17,223
1965–66	15,980	42,836	24,039
1967–68	13,004	30,120	31,015
1969–70	12,961	38,288	34,996
1970–71	9,875	Not Available	31,759

Source of data: Prepared by Wine Institute from reports of Internal Revenue Service, U.S. Treasury Department.
[1] Same as proof gallons.
[2] Segregations into beverage and non-beverage and grape and non-grape are not available. Almost entirely grape brandy, mostly for use as beverage brandy.
[3] Does not include brandy used for fortification.
[4] In bonded storage at Distilled Spirits Plants in California. Does not include tax-paid stocks of rectifiers, wholesalers and retailers; stocks of foreign brandy in custom bonded warehouses; and small quantities temporarily stored in wineries. Almost entirely grape beverage brandy.

Four general types of beverage brandy are presently produced in California. Brandies aged in bond at above 100° proof for four or more years and bottled at not under 100° proof are entitled to be "bottled-in-bond." The other two types of brandy are not readily distinguished from each other. They usually are 80° in proof. One type may have up to two per cent flavoring material added. Finally some grappa or pomace brandy is produced. Very little fruit brandy has been made in this state since W.W. II.

While our bonded brandies and unflavored and flavored brandies are justifiably popular and have a distinctive quality in highballs there is need for development of a smoother brandy for consumption straight. Neutral sweet brandy is not the answer to this problem, in our opinion (see Table 56 for U. S. brandy production and consumption data).

TABLE 56

BEVERAGE BRANDY ENTERING DISTRIBUTION CHANNELS[1,2]

(In Thousands of Proof Gallons)

Based on Calendar Years	Brandy Distribution in the United States			Gallons, per Capita
	U. S. Produced	Foreign	Total	
1955–1959	3139	1445	4584	0.050
1960–1964	4584	1952	6536	0.068
1965–1969	7379	2245	9624	0.096
1970[3]	8852	2674	11526	0.111

[1] Sources: Prepared by Wine Institute from reports of U. S. Treasury Department, Internal Revenue Service, and U. S. Department of Commerce, Bureau of the Census.
[2] For population of age 21 years and over.
[3] Preliminary.

COMPONENTS OF BRANDY

The chief constituent of brandy is, of course, ethyl alcohol. But many other volatile compounds are present in grapes or are formed during alcoholic fermentation of grape must (see Chapters 2 and 6). Since these distill with and are not completely separated from the alcohol during distillation they appear in larger or smaller amounts in the distillate. Other components are formed during aging or are extracted from the wood. Finally, some are added to beverage brandy during processing. For further data see Joslyn and Amerine (1964) and Marsh (1935).

Ethyl Alcohol

Ethanol, C_2H_5OH, is completely miscible with water and forms a constant boiling point mixture with it at 96.0 per cent alcohol by weight (Horsley 1952). It is a clear, colorless, inflammable liquid with a density of 0.7939 at 100 per cent alcohol or at 200° proof. It is a good solvent for essential oils, esters, tannins, various organic acids, and certain other organic compounds. It is, therefore, a very important industrial solvent.

Other Alcohols

Grapes of high pectin content, particularly if moldy, may yield considerable methyl alcohol (wood alcohol). A small amount may be present in the brandy, as methyl alcohol has physical properties similar to those of ethyl alcohol. Valaer (1939) reported traces to 0.188 per cent (average 0.048) of methanol in 114 samples of California commercial brandy (average proof 103.4°). It is apt to be higher in the brandy if the pomace is present during distillation. Tolu Libero (1962) reported 0.039 to 2.86 per cent methanol (average 1.65) in 37 uncut Piedmont pomace brandies (average 63.5 per cent alcohol).

Maïorov (1958), in pot still distillation of press wine, reported slightly more methanol in the tails than in the main cut and suggested that by taking off a large tail cut much of the methanol could be eliminated—hardly a feasible procedure. Just how methanol could accumulate in the tails is not clear.

The fusel oil of brandy is made up of higher alcohols. Their total content is usually less than 0.3 per cent. They constitute a part of the flavor of brandies. Valaer reports that amyl alcohol is the principal higher alcohol in the California product. Extensive analysis of fusel oils in California have been made by Webb *et al.* (1952) and Ikeda *et al.* (1956). Their analyses are summarized as follows (weight per cent):

Component	Thompson Seedless	Emperor	Muscat of Alexandria	Mixed Varieties
1-Propanol	0.66	5.14	1.07	4.1
2-Butanol	0.00[1]	0.40	0.00	4.9
2-Methyl-1-propanol	6.52	9.77	5.20	18.3
1-Butanol	0.95	0.55	0.65	1.9
2-Methyl-1-butanol	15.31	14.00	15.02	9.6
3-Methyl-1-butanol	67.89	61.38	72.73	54.0
1-Hexanol	1.40	1.14	1.49	1.5
β-Phenethyl alcohol	Trace	?[2]	Trace	0.0
Acetate ester	Trace	0.00	0.00	. . .
Residue (mainly esters)	7.25	7.61	3.85	5.6

[1] May have been removed during washing process.
[2] Distillation discontinued before boiling point of component.

The presence of 2-propanol in wine has been reported by Genevois and Lafon (1958) and others but it is apparently most often absent. For a review of the origin and composition of fusel oils, see Brau (1957B), Genevois and Lafon (1957), Thoukis (1958), Ingraham and Guymon (1960), Baraud (1961), and Pfenninger (1963).

The composition of a fusel oil from the distillation of wine made from Muscat of Alexandria raisins was studied by Kepner and Webb (1961). They separated a fraction (15 per cent) with a boiling range higher than 3-methyl-1-butanol. This fraction contained ethyl caprate (25 per cent), ethyl laurate (13), ethyl caprylate (13), 2-phenethyl acetate (12), isoamyl caprate (4), ethyl palmitate (3), isoamyl laurate (3), ethyl pelargonate (2), isoamyl capryate (2), ethyl myristate (1.5) and small amounts of ethyl pentadecanoate, *n*-propyl caprylate, isobutyl caprylate, isoamyl caproate, *act*-amyl caprylate, *act.*-amyl caprate, *act.*-amyl laurate and traces of *act.*-amyl caproate, acetic, caproic, caprylic, capric and isovaleric acids and 4 per cent of 1-hexanol. Probably present were *n*-hexyl acetate, ethyl caproate, isobutyl caprate, ethyl heptanoate, isoamyl myristate, *act.*-amyl myristate, isobutyric acid, heptanoic acid, pelargonic acid, a heptanoate ester and a pelargonate ester. Similar results on the esters and other compounds in Cognac are given by Baraud (1961).

Charro and Simal (1964) have also identified ethyl formate, acetaldehyde, acetal, ethyl acetate, methanol, 2-butanol, 1-propanol and 3-methyl-1-butanol in Spanish brandies. Pomace brandies were especially high in 1-propanol.

The total fusel oil of various brandies analyzed by Valaer (1939) was as follows (gm. per hectoliter):

Source	Number of Sample	Proof	Minimum	Maximum	Average
California	114	103.7	14.1	250.0[1]	90.7
California	12	92.3[2]	14.1	77.4	48.5
Cognac	20	84.6	89.8	127.0	103.9
Armagnac	4	84.8	91.5	96.8	94.4
Greek	25	89.1	10.6	121.4	58.0

[1] One sample of 385 omitted.
[2] Apparent proof.

Riffart and Diemair (1944) found Cognacs higher in higher alcohols than other European brandies.

The fusel oils are of higher boiling points than ethyl alcohol and can be separated from it to a large degree during distillation. They tend to collect on certain plates of the distillation column (p. 626). While they are more toxic than ethyl alcohol they are present in brandy in such low concentrations that they cause no danger to the health of the average brandy consumer.

Aldehydes

Aldehydes, chiefly acetaldehyde, are present in small amounts in brandy. Propanal, butyraldehyde, and heptanal have been reported. During distillation and aging some acetaldehyde is produced by the oxidation of ethyl alcohol:

$$C_2H_5OH + 1/2O_2 \rightarrow CH_3CHO + H_2O$$

This reaction is hastened by charcoal or aeration. Alcohol and acetaldehyde react slowly to form acetal, a compound of rather pronounced odor. Furfural is mainly formed during distillation. The free aldehyde content of French Cognacs is reported by Procopio (1958) to be 38 to 112 mg. per liter. The range for Italian brandies was 30 to 116. The acetal in French Cognacs varied from 26.5 to 77.5 mg. per liter and in young Italian brandies, from 27 to 165, in old 18 to 112. The per cent of the total that is combined varies generally from 17 to 28 per cent. The aldehyde and furfural content of various brandies analyzed by Valaer (1939) were as follows (gm. per hectoliter):

Source	Number of Sample	Proof	Aldehydes			Furfural		
			Mini-mum	Maxi-mum	Aver-age	Mini-mum	Maxi-mum	Aver-age
California	114	103.7	1.4	24.0	10.7	Trace	5.0[1]	1.7
California	12	92.3[2]	2.3	14.0	7.9	0.4	4.0	1.8
Cognac	20	84.6	6.3	14.0	8.6	1.0	3.0	1.3
Armagnac	4	84.8	8.7	9.5	9.1	0.6	1.0	0.7
Greek	25	89.1	4.0	23.6	13.8	Trace	2.4	1.0

[1] One sample with 48 omitted.
[2] Apparent proof.

Egorov and Borisova (1957) found eight or more aromatic aldehydes in Russian brandy, including vanillin, coniferyl and syringinyl aldehydes, and p-hydroxybenzaldehyde—all apparently from the oak containers. In authentic young Cognacs, Ronkainen et al. (1962) reported these plus iso-butyraldehyde, isovaleraldehyde (or act.-valeraldehyde), methylglyoxal and glyoxal. These are undoubtedly of importance to the character of the brandy.

Esters

During distillation and aging alcohol reacts with acids to form small amounts of esters such as ethyl acetate:

$$C_2H_5OH + CH_3COOH \rightleftarrows CH_3COOC_2H_5 + H_2O$$

Many other esters are also formed during fermentation, distillation, and aging (p. 208). They may be responsible for some of the flavor of the brandy.

Among the esters of brandy, ethyl acetate is the most common. Esters of propyl and butyl alcohols have also been reported and in small concentrations are not disagreeable. Valaer found amyl acetate in French but not in California brandy (see, however, p. 611). There is some evidence that during aging the volatile ester content increases at the expense of the non-volatile. The minimum ester content of brandies investigated by Valaer (1939) are summarized below (gm. per hectoliter as ethyl acetate):

Source	Number of Samples	Proof	Minimum	Maximum	Average
California	114	103.7	20.2	18.4	68.9
California	12	92.3[1]	17.6	77.4[2]	48.5
Cognac	20	84.6	36.1	58.1	44.3
Armagnac	4	84.8	49.3	59.8	52.8
Greek	25	89.1	7.9	79.2	40.5

[1] Apparent proof.
[2] One sample with 374 omitted.

Other Constituents

Wine contains acetic and lactic acids and small amounts distill into the brandy—usually less than 100 mg. per liter of 100° proof brandy. If spoiled wine is distilled propionic and butyric acids may be found in the distillate. The total and volatile acid contents of various brandies analyzed by Valaer (1939) were as follows (gm. per hectoliter as acetic):

Source	Number of Samples	Proof	Total Acid			Volatile Acid		
			Mini-mum	Maxi-mum	Aver-age	Mini-mum	Maxi-mum	Aver-age
California	114	103.7	4.8	101.0	54.8	4.8	88.0	42.9
California	12	92.3[1]	21.6	86.4	57.0	19.2	64.8	57.2
Cognac	20	84.6	26.4	110.4	51.5	21.0	72.0	34.2
Armagnac	4	84.8	62.4	67.2	64.0	37.8	45.6	41.9
Greek	25	89.1	21.6	103.2	51.9	6.0	70.8	33.8

[1] Apparent proof.

Brandy made from muscat wines often has considerable muscat aroma. When young wines are distilled they usually foam owing to the rapid loss of carbon dioxide. The foam-producing compounds have not been identified, according to Amerine et al. (1942).

Sulfur dioxide, if present in the wine, will distill with the alcohol and be present in the brandy. High proof brandy which is high in sulfur dioxide will dissolve iron and other metals from pumps, pipe lines, and metal storage tanks; therefore, such brandy should not be stored in metal tanks. In oak the sulfur dioxide oxidizes to sulfuric acid, an undesirable constituent of beverage brandy. Therefore, it is desirable to control fermentation of must for distilling for beverage brandy by other means than by sulfur dioxide. By special venting of the still, much of the sulfur dioxide can be removed during distillation but, even so, the quality of the brandy suffers.

Ammonia and various nitrogenous degradation products have been reported in distillates. Sulfur from dusts applied to the vines and grapes may be reduced to hydrogen sulfide during fermentation. This may react with alcohols to form mercaptans, compounds of very disagreeable ("skunk") odor and flavor. Such wines should be treated before distilling or used only for the production of fortifying brandy. Acrolein is highly toxic, is irritating to the eyes and nose and has a foul horseradish odor. Rosenthaler and Vegezzi (1955) reported small amounts in Swiss fruit brandies but seldom in brandy distilled from wine or pomace. The amount decreases but does not disappear in storage. It was completely removed by redistillation in a multicolumn still.

Occasionally, brandy has an excessive copper or iron content. Australian brandies contain 0.7 to 12 mg. per liter of copper (average 3.4), according to Rankine (1961A). He reported that it can be removed from unaged brandy by treatment with cation-exchange (but not by anion-exchange).

Rankine (1961B) found 0.01 to 0.06 mg. per liter of lead (average 0.029) in 37 Australian brandies.

Measures of Quality

A minimum non-alcohol content of 280 has been established in France for beverage brandy. The non-alcohol content is the sum of the acidity (as acetic), esters (as ethyl acetate), aldehydes (as acetaldehyde), higher alcohols (as isobutyl) and furfural—all as gm. per hectoliter of 100 per cent alcohol. Maltabar (1952) suggests the following chemical standards for brandy: (a) a higher acohol/ester ratio of two to one, (b) a non-alcohol content of not less than 300, (c) a high oxidation coefficient (amounts of acetal and aldehyde), and (d) a minimum amount of vanillin and coloring substances. Similar standards for Cognac were given by Rocques (1913).

De Vries (1958) determined the approximate amount of volatile minor constituents in spirits by measuring the absorption at 218 mμ. He also determined the fusel oil content. The results were divided as follows:

Group	Fusel Oil mg./100 ml.	Absorption 218 mμ
1	≤ 0.30	≤ 0.050
2	$> 0.30 - \leq 0.50$	$> 0.050 - \leq 0.085$
3	$> 0.50 - \leq 1.00$	$> 0.085 - \leq 0.125$
4	> 1.00	> 0.125

A total of 719 samples were then divided into two quality groups by sensory tests. For the more neutral brandies there was a coefficient of correlation of 0.971 between the analytical and sensory data. For samples of high flavor the correlation was less but the over-all correlation for the 719 samples was 0.870. See also Mergerand and Thellier (1946).

DISTILLATION

As the temperature of a liquid is raised the mean kinetic energy of its molecules increases and the number and velocity of the molecules escaping from the surface of the liquid become greater—thus increasing the vapor pressure. When the vapor pressure of the liquid equals that of the external (atmospheric) pressure on the liquid surface the liquid "boils." Different substances require varying degrees of heat to raise their temperature one degree, i.e., their specific heat varies—that of alcohol is only about 0.6 compared to water at 1.0. The heat required to change the substance from the liquid state to the vapor state is known as the heat of vaporization. It is approximately the same for substances of similar molecular weights.

In a mixture of gases the pressure exerted by each gas is independent of the pressures of the other gases (Dalton's law). The vapor pressure of a liquid is reduced in proportion to the mol percentage of the dissolved solute (Raoult's law). When the solute is non-volatile the total pressure of the solvent is reduced; if volatile, the partial pressure of the solvent is lowered. Furthermore, the vapor pressure of the solute is proportional to the mol fraction of the solute in the solution (Henry's law).

The liquid-vapor system of alcohol and water follows the above laws and particularly the phase rule which states that for a given system the number of components (c) plus 2, minus the number of phases (P) is equal to the number of variables (V) which must be fixed for the system to be in equilibrium, without altering the original number of phases present. Pressure, temperature, and concentration are the variables. If two of the variables are specified the value of the third is fixed. Thus, in the usual distilling apparatus the pressure is constant and temperature and concentration are interdependent. At constant pressure there is a definite boiling temperature for each concentration of alcohol and water.

The vapor leaving a water alcohol boiling mixture contains a higher percentage of alcohol than the original liquid. This is the basis for the separation of alcohol and water by fractional distillation. The nature of the mixture and the method of distillation also affect the degree of separation. Furthermore, binary mixtures may form maximum or minimum boiling point mixtures and thus prevent separation of the two components at lower or higher temperatures. The alcohol-water system has a minimum boiling point at 97.4 per cent alcohol so that separation of the two components above a boiling point of 172.6°F. is impossible at atmospheric pressure. (At reduced pressures the alcohol content of the constant boiling point mixture is higher.)

The ratio between the percentage alcohol in the vapor and that in the liquid is called the Sorel or k value. It varies according to the alcoholic strength of the liquid as shown in Table 57. For more complete and slightly different k values see Joslyn and Amerine (1941). For further discussion of distillation see Barron (1944), Gay (1935), Guymon (1949A), Hanson (1948), Hausbrand (1925), Klimovskiĭ and Stabnikov (1950), Lafon et al. (1964), Mariller (1948), Meloni (1952–1958), Monier-Williams (1922), Robinson and Gilliland (1950), Simmonds (1919), Villa (1946), Walker et al. (1937), Willkie and Prochaska (1943), Wüstenfeld and Haeseler (1964) and Young (1922).

TABLE 57

SOREL'S VALUES FOR THE RATIO k FOR DIFFERENT SUBSTANCES[1]

Alcohol in Boiling Liquid Volume Per cent	For Amyl Alcohol[2] (B. pt. 132°) Ratio	For Ethyl Formate (B. pt. 54.3°) Ratio	For Methyl Acetate (B. pt. 56°) Ratio	For Ethyl Acetate (B. pt. 77.1°) Ratio	For Ethyl Isobutyrate (B. pt. 110°) Ratio	For Ethyl Isovalerate (B. pt. 134.3°) Ratio	For Isoamyl Acetate (B. pt. 137°) Ratio	For Isoamyl Isovalerate (B. pt. 196°) Ratio	For Ethyl Alcohol (B. pt. 78°) Ratio
95	0.23	5.1	3.8	2.1	0.95	0.8	0.55	0.30	1.006
90	0.30	5.8	4.1	2.4	1.1	0.9	0.6	0.35	1.02
85	0.32	6.5	4.3	2.7	1.2	1.1	0.7	0.40	1.05
80	0.34	7.2	4.6	2.9	1.4	1.3	0.8	0.50	1.08
75	0.44	7.8	5.0	3.2	1.8	1.5	0.9	0.65	1.12
70	0.54	8.5	5.4	3.6	2.3	1.7	1.1	0.82	1.17
65	0.65	9.4	5.9	3.9	2.9	1.9	1.4	1.05	1.23
60	0.80	10.4	6.4	4.3	4.2	2.3	1.7	1.30	1.30
55	0.98	12.0	7.0	4.9	...	...	2.2	...	1.39
50	1.20	...	7.9	5.8	...	...	2.8	...	1.50
45	1.50	...	9.0	7.1	...	...	3.5	...	1.63
40	1.92	...	10.5	8.6	...	...	...	...	1.80
35	2.45	...	12.5	10.5	...	...	...	...	2.02
30	3.00	...	...	12.6	...	...	...	...	2.40
25	5.55	...	...	15.2	...	...	...	...	2.70
20	...	...	...	18.0	...	...	...	...	3.30
15	...	...	...	21.5	...	...	...	...	4.10
10	...	...	...	29.0	...	...	...	...	5.10

[1] Source of data: Sorel (1899) cited by Monier-Williams (1922).
[2] From fermentation.

Courtesy of Goguet, Cognac

FIG. 126.   TYPICAL COGNAC DISTILLING SCENE

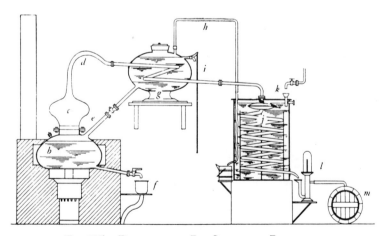

FIG. 127.   DIAGRAM OF A POT STILL WITH PREHEATER

Pot *b*, preheater *g*, worm condenser *j*

Pot Stills

Originally the wine was simply placed in a closed pot with an outlet line leading to a suitable vapor-condensing apparatus. Heat was applied and the alcohol concentration of the vapor at any given moment will be in equilibrium with the alcohol concentration of the liquid in the pot. Since the alcohol concentration of the liquid was gradually reduced the alcohol concentration of the vapor decreased correspondingly. Today this simple system is employed only for Cognac, Fig. 126. A diagram of such a still is found in Fig. 127. Attention is called to the economy introduced by using the wine to be distilled to partially cool the vapors. This, of course, warms the wine and reduces the amount of heat required to bring it to the boiling point when heated in the pot. Some pot stills have simple or complex rectifying columns.

In the first distillation of Cognac (see p. 604) Lafon *et al.* (1964) find the non-alcohol components distill early in the distillation when the per cent alcohol in the distillate is above 50 per cent, except for the higher alcohols which continue to be carried over in appreciable amounts until the per cent alcohol reaches about 30 per cent. Furfural, however, only appears when the alcohol drops to about 40 per cent and continues to distill down to 25 percent.

In the second distillation the curves are similar but the product varies

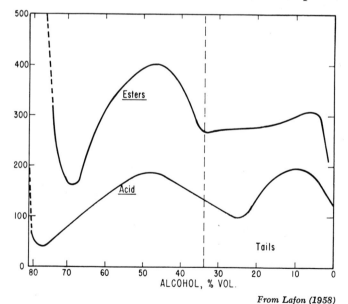

From Lafon (1958)

Fig. 128. Esters and Acids in the Product During Cognac
Distillation

because of the separation of the three fractions. This is shown in Figs. 128 and 129. Note that the aldehydes are primarily in the heads, while the esters which are also found in the heads continue to pass over, particularly in the tails. The higher alcohols appear in the highest amounts in the heads and in rapidly decreasing amounts in the tails. In contrast, the amount of volatile acids in the distillate increases as the distillation continues. Furfural passes over in very small amounts throughout the second distillation. Rapid heating of the pot increases the rate of distillation of the volatile acids and esters up to 65 per cent and may cause a secondary undesirable odor to appear in the tails. A slow distillation gives a higher quality product with less of the undesirable secondary odor. Redistillation of the tails results in lesser amounts of volatile acids and less volatile esters and improves the product. Removing more heads improves the brandy made from poor wine but reduces the quality of that made from

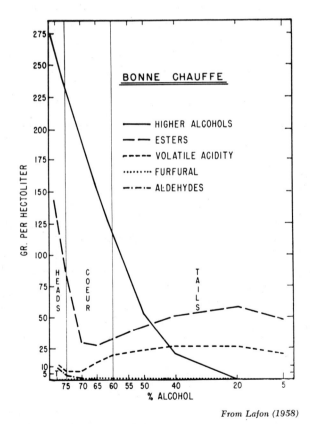

From Lafon (1958)

FIG. 129. DISTILLATION OF VARIOUS CONSTITUENTS DURING
THE SECOND DISTILLATION

good wine. When the wine is good, the odor of the tails is less undesirable than that of the heads.

Lafon *et al.* (1964) attribute an important role to the copper of the pot stills. Organic copper compounds of butyric, caproic, caprylic, capric, and lauric acids are apparently formed during heating and are distilled. These acids have a very disagreeable odor but the copper fixes these as their salts are insoluble. They found that products distilled in glass stills were less desirable than those distilled in copper stills. They recommend cleaning pot stills every eight days.

Lafon and Couillaud (1953) reported low copper in Cognacs, usually less than 3 mg. per liter. Some copper is dissolved during distillation. Some of this is precipitated during aging, but, as the acidity increases during aging, there is a redissolution of copper from the precipitate. Young Cognacs contained 0.5 mg. per liter while very old Cognacs had 3 to 4 mg. per liter. With copper bottling equipment, copper pick-up may occur.

While the actual complexing of copper and phytate in brandy is not clear, Cordonnier (1954) found sodium phytate a useful means of removing copper from brandy, especially if calcium was present to insure the formation of a calcium-copper phytate complex. When more than 6 mg. per liter of copper was present, the efficiency of removal of copper was much less.

Lafon *et al.* (1960) found normal Cognacs to have less than 0.2 mg. per liter of lead. Old brandy and brandy stored in crystal bottles or in bottles stored on their side with lead foil capsules were higher in lead, up to 1.2 mg. per liter or more.

Guymon (1949A) found little analytical difference between pot- and column-distilled brandies from the same wine but noted that they were readily distinguishable by sensory testing. Furthermore, it is unlikely that the slow pot still procedure would have survived in the Cognac region if it did not contribute to the character of the brandy.

When pot stills are used for producing grappa, either fresh or aged pomace may be used. Fresh pomace produces a less distinctive product but the odor of grappa from aged pomace is too strong for many consumers. If aged pomace is used the oxidized-acetic surface layer of the pomace pile should not be employed. Vegezzi *et al.* (1951) have shown that methyl alcohol is present in pomace brandy and may exceed the legal limit if the pomace is pressed too tightly. It is customary in California to redistill the pot-still product in a continuous still.

Column Stills

A continuous still is a sort of series of interconnected pot stills. Their continuous operation is more efficient than that of pot stills.

The modern column still (Figs. 130 and 131) is a cylindrical shell divided into sections by a series of plates. The plates are perforated or have openings covered by bubble caps (about 10 per cent of their area is open) to allow passage of vapor. Nowadays, perforated or sieve plates are used in the lower stripping section of the column since they permit using distilling material with a higher percentage of suspended solids. Bubble cap plates with down pipes are used in the upper (rectifying) section of the column.

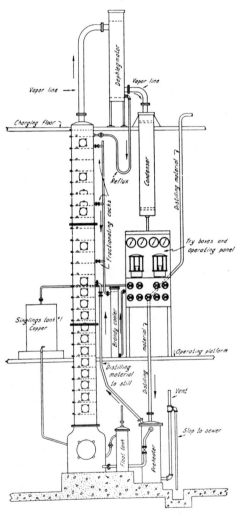

FIG. 130. DIAGRAM OF SIMPLE MODERN COLUMN STILL

The plates in the column are spaced 18 to 30 in. apart. If the plates are close together the vapor velocity must be kept low. If the vapor velocity is too great mechanical carry-over of liquid will occur in the column. Barron (1944) recommends that, as a general rule, the plates should be spaced a distance apart in inches equal to ten times the vapor velocity in feet per second. Thus, for a vapor velocity of 2.4 feet per second the plates should be 24 in. apart. In practice columns are operated at velocities 25 to 50 per cent greater than this. For a calculation of the number of plates required and other principles of still design, see Hanson (1948).

Heat is supplied by a stream sparger at the bottom of the column. Down pipes between plates provide for return of liquid from one plate to another. The down pipes are located on opposite sides of the still for alternate plates so that the liquid passes across the plate before entering the next down pipe. The upper part of the down pipe extends above the

Courtesy of N. Nedeltchev

Fig. 131. Column Stills in Suhindol, Bulgaria

plate so as to allow a liquid layer of 1 to 2 in. on the plate. The lower end of the down pipe is inserted in a cup on the lower plate to form a liquid seal.

Wine is introduced at some intermediate plate in the column. The ascending steam vapor prevents the liquid from falling through the perforations on the plate. There is a layer of liquid on each plate—the overflow passing to the next lower plate through the down pipe. The vapor leaving the boiling layer of liquid on the plate passes through perforations of the plate above and condenses in the liquid layer on that plate. Some of the liquid is evaporated by the heat released by the condensation of the incoming vapor and passes on to the next higher plate. Alcohol has a higher vapor pressure than water and thus evaporates from each plate more easily than water. The alcohol concentration thus increases from plate to plate. The alcohol concentration on each plate of the stripping section remains essentially the same (once the still is in balance) since it continuously receives a fresh feed supply from the plate above.

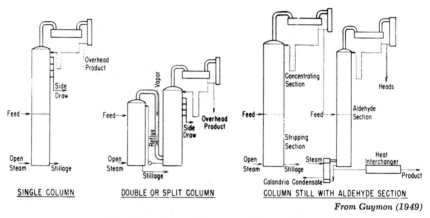

From Guymon (1949)

FIG. 132. VARIOUS TYPES OF COLUMN STILLS

To conserve heat the hot dealcoholized liquid which accumulates at the base of the still is discharged through a heat exchanger which warms the incoming wine. Some columns, particularly the fractionating section, are insulated (lagged) to avoid heat loss. Insulation is also useful with small columns to secure better control.

Three different types of column stills are shown in Fig. 132. The single column and double or split column stills may be operated either with an overhead product or side draw. The column still with an aldehyde section is particularly useful in producing neutral fortifying spirits. Recently, some rather complicated stills have been built which produce a rather

Courtesy of Mont La Salle Vineyards

FIG. 133. CONTROL PANEL FOR TWO 4-COLUMN STILLS

neutral product at below 170° proof. The complexity of their control panel is indicated in Fig. 133.

Condensers

Whatever system of distillation is employed, the alcohol-containing vapor must be condensed back to a liquid. Condensers serve two functions: conversion of vapor to liquid and cooling the resultant liquid to room temperature. The second step removes only a small amount of the total heat but requires greater condenser area since there is a slower heat transfer through cooling surfaces with liquids on both sides. The transfer of heat between liquid and vapor is by the film of stationary liquid on the water side and the film of stationary vapor on the vapor side. Vapor films are thinner; hence, heat transfer is more rapid for an apparatus condensing a vapor than for the same apparatus cooling a liquid. The heat transfer coefficient may be increased by increasing the velocity of the cooling water through the tubes or by using condensers of special design.

The vapor from the top of the column still passes through a dephlegmator and condenser. A portion of the vapor condenses in the first and is returned to the column as the reflux. The condenser may also return a reflux to the column and the remainder be taken off as heads. The actual product in this case is removed as a side stream from the upper plates in the column. Guymon (1948) has shown that a side stream take-off results in less esters and aldehydes in the product. This was true either for production of fortifying brandy at 186° to 189° proof or of beverage brandy at 164° to 167° proof.

Fusel Oil Removal

Separation of alcohol and water is not the only problem of distillation. Various desirable and undesirable congeners must be retained or removed —at least partially. Separation of the higher alcohols, particularly from fortifying brandy, is an especially important problem. The higher alcohols (p. 610) are only slightly soluble in water. Their boiling points are higher than that of water but they have a high relative volatility with steam and are thus distilled upward in the column. As they reach plates of higher alcohol content they become soluble; their volatility is then normal and they tend to return down the column. The result is that they concentrate in the region of the still where the increase in alcohol percentage is greatest—at about 135° proof or at a boiling point of about 183°F. This can be seen in the data of Table 58.

The best recent data on the composition of plate samples are those of Guymon (1960). He showed that, to be meaningful, the distilling material must be normal, the column in balance, and the balance must not be upset by sampling. A 54-in. diameter commercial column was used. The higher alcohols concentrated on plates nearest in apparent proof to 135°. The observed plate temperature was 185°F. When the column is used to produce commercial brandy at 170° or less proof, the highest higher alcohol content on a plate was about 0.5 per cent. This is due to the fact that much of the higher alcohols pass over into the product. He showed that higher alcohols cannot be separated by dilution with water and passage through a decanter if the proof of distillation is 170° or less. Some reduction in higher alcohols can occur when a "low oils" cut is made one or two plates below that used for product removal. Even when distilling at 185° to 190° proof not all the higher alcohols are removed. Isobutyl is the chief higher alcohol present in the product in such cases. When distilling at a high proof to obtain the most neutral brandy, Guymon recommended taking off a side stream from a plate 5 to 10 plates from the top. This permits removal of low boiling point aldehydes and esters in a head cut.

In the distillation of fortifying brandy the concentration of fusel oil in the column is sufficient so that it exceeds its solubility at about 135° proof. It is possible to draw a fraction from this plate which will be very high in

TABLE 58

ANALYSES OF CUTS FROM INDIVIDUAL PLATES OF A COLUMN STILL[1]

Plate	Initial Boiling Temperature °F.	Proof Degrees	Acidity Per cent	Extract P.p.m.	As'[1] P.p.m.	Esters P.p.m.	Aldehydes[2] P.p.m.	Furfural P.p.m.	Higher Alcohols P.p.m.
4	174.6	187.1	0.0024	26	14	422.4	17.6	Nil	440.0
7	175.4	183.5	0.0036	14	2	264.0	22.0	Trace	2,288.0
10	176.8	171.3	0.014	24	2	1,108.8	30.8	12.5	15,100.8
12	178.9	163.3	0.029	26	0	2,164.8	44.0	29.0	27,209.6
14	183.0	134.6	0.139	78	20	8,430.4	79.2	54.0	65,560.0
16	198.9	19.3	0.420	342	134	11,897.6	44.0	15.0	8,304.0
18	206.0	7.9	0.216	796	170	3,555.2	30.8	Trace	1,056.0
20	206.3	7.6	0.102	274	116	844.8	17.6	Trace	704.0
22	206.4	7.4	0.047	202	44	352.0	13.2	Trace	528.0
24	206.4	7.4	0.035	150	6	281.6	13.2	Trace	352.0
26	206.6	7.3	0.030	140	2	211.2	13.2	Nil	528.0
28	206.7	7.2	0.034	152	38	211.2	13.2	Nil	274.0
30	206.6	7.4	0.041	154	58	299.2	8.8	Nil	440.0
32	206.3	9.6	0.264	13,928	1944	211.2	8.8	Trace	352.0

[1] Source of data: Wilkins and Walling (1939).
[2] Includes furfural.

higher alcohols. Most continuous column stills now have fusel oil decanters, Fig. 134. In their simplest form these consist of a try box into which the fusel oil is introduced at the top through a pipe. Inside this pipe is a smaller perforated water pipe. The water is thus intimately mixed with the incoming fusel oil. The mixture then flows through perforated screens and falls to the liquid surface in the try box.

Guymon (1958) has presented complete data on the principles of separation of fusel oils (higher alcohols) during distillation. Dilution ratios of 2 to 2.7 would improve fusel oil recovery by decantation. He recommended that a minimum of four contiguous plates be connected to provide

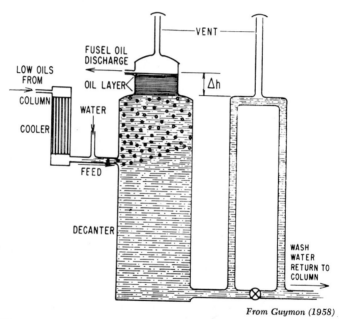

From Guymon (1958)

FIG. 134. SCHEMATIC ARRANGEMENT OF A FUSEL OIL DECANTER

for drawing off of the fusel oils. Temperature indicators should be installed on one or more of these plates. Experience should then determine the best plates for fusel oil removal. As he says, "Flow meters should be provided for the "low oils" cut and the dilution water lines."

A vertical draw-off pipe extends twelve inches from the bottom of the try box. It is completely enclosed in another tube which has an opening several inches below the top of the draw-off pipe. This allows continuous withdrawal of the water-alcohol mixture back to the still while maintaining a constant liquid level in the try box.

Fusel oil draw-off is accomplished through another vertical pipe which extends several inches above the water alcohol draw-off pipe. When visual observation shows a layer of fusel oil on top of the water-alcohol, water is then introduced through a third pipe and the liquid level raised so as to allow the fusel oil layer to flow out the fusel oil draw-off pipe.

In the production of beverage brandy, where the product has only about 160° proof, the plate with 135° proof is only one or two plates lower on the column than the plate with 160° proof. The higher alcohol content of the distillate is sufficiently high so that accumulation on the 135° proof plate sufficient to permit draw-off seldom, if ever, occurs. Reduction of the fusel oil content of the distillate is still possible if a fraction is taken from the appropriate plate and later redistilled.

Guymon (1949A) found little difference in composition of brandies distilled at 165° to 170° proof compared to 170° to 180° proof except a reduction of fusel oil in the latter. Since this is generally considered desirable he recommended that the maximum legal proof distillation for beverage brandy be raised from 170° to 180° proof. Brandies for aging should not have over 125 mg. per 100 ml. (at 100° proof) of higher alcohols, in his opinion. This suggestion has not been acted on.

Aldehyde Removal

Removal of aldehydes is also desirable. This can be done by use of an aldehyde column. Guymon and Nakagiri (1955) and Guymon and Pool (1957) have shown that the most rational use of this high aldehyde product is by introducing it into rapidly fermenting musts. Most of the aldehydes should, therefore, be utilized for alcohol production (see, however, p. 612). Guymon (1949A) recommended that brandies for aging contain no more than 3 mg. per 100 ml. of aldehydes or 50 of esters.

Automatic Control

Most modern column stills have automatic controls so as to produce a uniform product. These consist of an actuating element on bulb which electrically or mechanically actuates a diaphragm valve. A continuous recorder is a part of the system. The usual controls include steam supply to the base of the stripping column, on the feed, on the product flow, and on the flow of water to the dephlegmator.

Even when the manual control is employed, better uniformity in the product can be achieved by providing thermometers and temperature recorders. The thermometer bulb should be placed in the plates directly above the feed. Thermometers in the plate of product draw and a manometer or pressure gauge are also useful. Rotameters to indicate feed and product rates as well as reflux rate, heads and fusel oil fractions and water flow also help maintain control. Stillage testers are desirable to prevent loss of alcohol from the bottom of the still in the still slop.

Brau (1957A) has given a description of several different types of automatic control systems. He found quantity-control systems were inadequate since they are not capable of detecting and correcting changes in composition in the column. In his system (two column) a control system based on altering the rate of feed proved best. Other types of control are also employed.

Periodically stills must be cleaned to remove sediment. If wines containing sulfur dioxide are employed much corrosion may occur and the bubble caps or sieve plates may not function properly.

Metzner Stills

A still, Fig. 135, to handle undisintegrated pomace has been introduced into the California industry (Metzner 1945). Basically this still mechanically moves the pomace through several levels of the still and a moderate rectification occurs so that a product of about 20 per cent alcohol is produced. This low wine is then diluted and redistilled in a regular column still. The recovery of alcohol from the pomace is nearly 100 per cent and justifies the double distillation. Several modifications have been built. Another type of pomace dealcoholizing process involving use of a slight vacuum has been proposed by Bachmann (1957).

FIG. 135. METZNER STILL FOR POMACE

Vacuum Distillation

Flanzy and Lamazou-Betbeder (1938) found vacuum distillation produced an especially desirable brandy but with a coefficient of non-alcohols of below 280. Since French law requires beverage brandies to have a coefficient of at least 280 this eliminated them from the beverage brandy market, which they considered unfair. Guymon has made interesting and promising experiments with vacuum distillation at the Enology Laboratory at Davis, California. Large vacuum stills are, of course, expensive. Rakcsányi (1958) in Hungary has also made successful experiments with vacuum distillation.

Fire and Explosion Hazards

The distillery premises should be of fireproof materials. Smoking or open fires, such as blow torches, should not be permitted near the still. Recently-emptied brandy barrels contain a highly explosive mixture of alcohol and air. A cigarette spark can cause a fatal explosion of such barrels.

Distilling Material

Berti (1949) has emphasized the importance of using sound grapes for producing distilling material even for fortifying brandy. He writes, "The use of moldy, partially fermented, and otherwise rotten grapes, cannot be excused ... [and] we should prohibit the crushing of poor grapes by law, if necessary."

It is generally believed that wines of high total acidity produce the best beverage brandy. Maltabar (1952) harvested grapes at four stages of maturity. No aging or sensory tests were made but using the ratio of higher alcohol/volatile esters it was concluded that the best brandy was made from mature grapes. The Russian brandy experts believe that a higher alcohol/volatile ester ratio of two to one makes the best brandy. In this study, wines from early-harvested grapes (14 per cent sugar, 1.2 per cent titratable acidity) produced brandies with ratios of 1.52 to 1.62 while wines of mature grapes (22 to 23 per cent sugar, 0.5 to 0.6 per cent titratable acidity) produced brandies with ratios of 2.29 to 3.34. Of course, such an experiment does not prove that a low acid wine is desirable. An experiment with moderately ripe grapes or wines with the acidity modified would be desirable.

Berti (1949) recommended addition of 50 p.p.m. of sulfur dioxide to the must. Certainly as little sulfur dioxide as possible should be used as is necessary to secure a clean fermentation. Sulfur dioxide distills over and produces brandy of high fixed acid and of reduced olfactory quality. Where pomace wash is used for distilling material the alcohol content will be low and contamination and undesirable microorganism growth may occur. Very early distillation should always be employed for such material. Wines of high volatile acidity produce poor brandy.

Generally the best wines for distillation are clean white wines. It is believed that the best beverage brandy should be made only from wine. Pomace wash wines should be used for production of fortifying brandy.

Raisins and raisin seed wash water have also been used successfully to produce fortifying brandy. The raisins must be thoroughly soaked in water and may then be passed through a hammer mill to secure their complete disintegration. Pomace is also frequently ground in a hammer mill to secure complete disintegration of sugar-containing materials that have escaped solution and fermentation. Ground raisins or pomace material after fermentation must be kept constantly agitated. It is then pumped to special column stills which are capable of handling liquids with such a high percentage of suspended solids. This type of distilling material should, of course, be used only for the production of fortifying brandy.

Fortifying Brandy

"High proof" is produced in California at 185° to 189° proof. This should give a neutral spirit but the data of Berti (1949) show that, at least at the time of his study, considerable variation in composition occurred Table 59.

TABLE 59

COMPOSITION OF FORTIFYING BRANDY[1]
(Mg. per Liter)

Constituent	Number of Samples	Minimum	Maximum	Average
Fusel oil				
Colorimetric	42	84	2510[2]	572
AOAC	21	141	1038	270
Aldehyde	36	0	480	70
Esters	7	190	740	500
Total acidity	7	20	80	50
pH	6	3.3	6.6	...

[1] Source of data: Berti (1949).
[2] One sample of 6000 mg. per liter omitted.

Pool and Heitz (1950) reported that generally fortifying brandies of high fusel oil (over 600 mg. per liter), high aldehyde (over 200 mg. per liter), and of poor sensory quality produced poor dessert wines. Guymon and Amerine (1952) confirmed this. Filipello (1951) reported a negative coefficient of correlation of $r = -0.480$ between fusel oil content and wine quality, but noted exceptions. Webb (1951) recommended neutral fortifying brandy for production of early-maturing dessert wines, but fortifying brandy for slower maturing wines should, he states, be produced from lower-proof brandy.

The quality of high proof alcohol is frequently determined by permanganate titration—the time required for decoloration of the permanganate being directly proportional to the quality. Tamburrini *et al.* (1955) showed that acids and aldehydes most affected the test. Esters and higher alcohols were of minor importance.

DISTILLERY SLOP DISPOSAL

The disposal of the dealcoholized solution from the still constitutes one of the major problems of the wine industry. This results from its high percentage of material in solution or suspension and the difficulty in decomposing this material. The oxygen requirements for its complete decomposition are very great. According to York (1958) and MacMillan *et al.* (1959) the BOD[3] may amount to 1500 to 5000 p.p.m. for ordinary stillage and 7000 to 50,000 p.p.m. for lees stillage—very high values indeed. For this reason the distillery slop may not be run into streams since it constitutes a hazard to fish. If it is run onto the land and is not speedily evaporated its decomposition results in volatile and obnoxious odors which constitute a public nuisance. Not only are the odors unpleasant for neighbors but they give a poor impression to prospective clients who visit the winery. Even though Joslyn and Amerine strongly condemned this nuisance in 1941 there are still undesirable operations.

City Sewage

Many wineries are located in or near cities and can use the city sewage disposal system. This is very satisfactory where the city system is large enough to handle this very seasonal input. Even where the city system can handle it, the disposal district may charge a special fee.

The alternative of building a sewage disposal plant for the exclusive use of the winery has so far not been found economically feasible. However, city systems might find the distillery waste a more attractive product if more of the suspended material were removed. Several California wineries have tried flocculation and sedimentation systems but none have proven practicable. If such a system is contemplated, the services of a sanitation expert should be retained.

Field Disposal

This is the most common system presently used in California, and, at present, the only feasible one. Where the winery is located in an area

---

[3] Biological oxygen demand.

with plenty of sandy land for disposal of the distillery slop, it makes an admirable system; particularly when there is sufficient sunshine to assure rapid evaporation. Successful operation of this system requires ponds with dividing ridges not more than one foot high. Each pond should be large enough to hold, at a depth of not more than six inches, the stillage output over a period of twenty-four hours. This requires an area of one acre for each 100,000 gallons. The ponds are filled in succession, one each day. Thus, each pond is filling one day and drying six. After the ponds have been filled with stillage three or four times the soil, after thorough drying of the cake on the bottom of the ponds, is loosened with a disc.

Deep ponding should not be used as objectionable odors will be produced by gas-forming bacteria.

AGING

Most distilled spirits intended for sale as a beverage, except grappa, vodka, and gin, are aged in wood following distillation. The improvement in the character and quality of the product is, of course, the reason for this aging process. The harsh burning taste and unpleasant odor of newly-distilled spirits are ameliorated by this aging and certain new and desirable odors and flavors develop from the aging.

Preparation for Aging

As it comes from the still at 170° proof, or less, the brandy must be further diluted to about 110° for aging. Usually burnt sugar or caramel syrup is added before the water for dilution. The usual amount of caramel is four ounces per 50-gallon barrel. Only iron-free caramel which is completely soluble in 110°-proof brandy should be employed. Following dilution, the brandy is placed in weighed 50-gallon barrels—preferably new, according to most industry authorities, Fig. 136. However, some brandy has been aged in reused whiskey barrels. Brown (1938) recommends that dry oak be used in making the barrels as new oak has a higher moisture percentage and retards aging. The barrels are not treated before use as the soakage allowance would not be permitted. Teodorescu et al. (1958) recommended aging brandies in 130-gallon oak casks. Casks which had been used for storage of wine or brandy were preferred.

Changes During Aging

Dzhanpoladyan and Petrosyan (1957) believe the aging process begins with the extraction of phenolic compounds from the wood, followed by their oxidation by atmospheric oxygen to peroxides and participation of the peroxides in subsequent reactions. Lignin was shown to decrease dur-

Courtesy of Wine Institute

FIG. 136. BRANDY AGING IN OAK BARRELS IN CALIFORNIA
WINERY

ing aging and it is considered to play an especially important role as vanillin is one of its oxidation products.

Guymon (1949B) has classified the changes occurring during aging as follows:

1. Physical
   a. Losses by evaporation or soaking
   b. Changes due to concentration by evaporation or to dissolution of substances from the wood
2. Chemical
   a. Oxidation of original or extracted constituents
   b. Reaction between original and oxidation product or dissolved substances

The factors which influence these changes were given as:

1. Initial composition—as affected by raw material, fermentation and distillation
   a. Per cent alcohol

    b. Fixed acid content
    c. Sulfur dioxide, hydrogen sulfide, etc.
2. Length of aging period
3. Cooperage
    a. Size and type: surface to volume ratio
    b. Porosity and wood thickness
    c. Composition of wood (dryness, tannin content, etc.)
    d. Condition: new or reused, pretreatment, etc.
4. Environment
    a. Temperature and variations in temperature
    b. Relative humidity
    c. Vapor pressure of alcohol in warehouse
    d. Air circulation and replacement
    e. Agitation

The changes occurring in the brandy in a plain new barrel during a four year period were measured by Valaer (1939) and may be summarized as follows (except for proof, pH, and color, as gm. per hectoliter, not calculated to proof; acidity as acetic, esters as ethyl acetate, fusel oil as a mixture of isoamyl and isobutyl alcohol, and aldehyde as acetaldehyde):

Age	Proof	pH	Total Acidity	Esters	Fusel Oil	Aldehyde	Furfural	Solids	Color in 0.5 Lovibond
0	100.3	5.35	8.4	40.5	79.2	2.0	0.5	66	2.5
1	102.8	3.96	62.4	58.1	85.3	7.9	1.4	172	10.0
2	103.4	3.93	69.6	59.8	88.9	7.8	1.4	194	10.5
3	104.6	3.91	76.8	66.6	102.0	9.8	2.0	214	...
4	105.1	3.90	79.2	71.3	104.3	11.2	2.0	230	13.5

Note the increase in acidity, esters, fusel oil, aldehyde, furfural, solids, and color. This results from the concentration effect of evaporation losses. The increase in alcohol is due to the greater loss of water compared to alcohol under the low-humidity conditions in California warehouses. There are obviously some increases which result from chemical and physical changes. The increase in aldehydes and acids is probably largely chemical. The increase in acidity accounts for the decrease in pH. The increase in color and solids results from solution of substances from the wood. The changes when the brandy is stored in reused cooperage are much smaller.

    Tolbert *et al.* (1943) found that brandy stored in small cooperage extracts more tannin than from large cooperage, even taking into account evaporation losses. However, more tannin is extracted per square centimeter of exposed surface from larger than small containers.

    In new Bulgarian brandies the pH varied from 4.5 to 5.0. The heads were higher (6.2) than the tails (3.1). After aging in the wood the pH was 4.1 to 4.8, decreasing with time. The development of a "cognac" flavor was best at a lower pH, according to Litchev (1959).

Guymon (1949A) has demonstrated that for proofs of distillation from 120° to 186° the changes in esters in the brandy during aging are essentially parallel. The distillation of wines high in volatile acids results in brandies of high ester content. Distillation of wines containing sulfur dioxide yields brandies of high fixed acid and high aldehyde content. They darken with age and have a characteristic and unpleasant odor. He also showed that the rate of increase of chemical substances and the per cent loss is proportionately larger for the smaller containers.

The best temperature and humidity of storage is not known. If the temperature is too high there will be excessive losses of alcohol. If too dry, there will be excessive losses of water and the proof of the brandy will rise. A cool (below 70°F.) and even temperature with moderate humidity seems best but definitive evidence is lacking.

The government allows a certain loss from barrels for each period of storage. This increases from 1 proof gallon at 2 months' storage to 5 proof gallons at 18 months, 8 gallons at 36 months, and 13.0 at up to 80 months.

Rapid Aging

Various mechanical, physical, and chemical procedures have been used to age brandy more rapidly. Mechanical vibration (even by long ocean transport), variable temperatures, ultrasonics, adsorption (charcoal), ion exchangers, ultra-violet and infra-red have all been tried. Ozone, peroxide, permanganate, electrolysis and metallic and biological catalyzers have also been used. Tolbert and Amerine (1943) reported improvements in certain brandies using activated charcoal, particularly in reducing excessive tannin. Dekov and Tsakov (1957) reported favorable effects of storing 140° proof brandy in five-liter oak barrels for 15 days at temperatures which varied from 102.2° to 167°F. No statistical data were given. The best that can be said is that some of the results have been encouraging. The economics of the treatment and unprejudiced sensory examination of the products have not always been adequately considered. Further work could be profitably done.

The Russian literature recommends using oak chips (treated with alkali or untreated) in the aging of brandy. Oxidation of tannin substances during aging was responsible for the darkening of color. Ethanolysis of lignin and hydrolysis of hemicellulose also occurs. Ethanolysis of lignin results after oxidation in formation of aldehydes of the vanillin type. Optimum results were secured by treating oak chips with 0.063–0.075 N alkali at 50° to 60°F. for two days, according to Skurikhin (1960). He recommended keeping the brandy with the treated oak chips at 68° to 77°F. for six to eight months with periodic introduction of oxygen (15 to 20 mg. per liter). This was considered the equivalent of three to five years' aging in the wood. Otsuka and Imai (1964) also reported extraction of syringic- and vanillin-like compounds as well as gallic acid from oak chips.

Lashki (1963) found that lack of oxygen during storage slowed the rate of aging but that too much oxygen resulted in loss of bouquet. Finished bottled brandy should contain no more than 3 to 5 mg. of oxygen per liter. The legal aspects if such processes were used in this country would also have to be clarified.

Pro and Etienne (1959) have shown that distilled spirits produced before 1954 can be dated with reasonable accuracy from their tritium contents. After 1954 the tritium content of the atmosphere was affected by hydrogen bomb explosions. Further, it is not possible to determine accurately the age of spirits which have been diluted with post-bomb water.

Removal from Storage

Brandy may be removed from storage at any time. If less than four years of age it may not be bottled in bond, that it, it may not be bottled at 100°-proof with a revenue stamp giving the dates of distillation and bottling. Most brandies are reduced to 80° proof for sale. Some are flavored to give them a distinctive character. This flavoring is, of course, the trade secret of each producer. It usually consists of some sweetening agent with a variety of flavoring materials added. We have not been impressed with the wine-flavored brandies that we have tasted. As a matter of fact, some of the flavored brandies are too sweet and too obviously treated for our taste.

When young brandies are cut they often throw a sediment of caramel or of oak extractives. Chilling, settling, and filtration have been reported, p. 294, useful to prevent this sediment getting into the bottle.

Brandies of more than four years' age often, but not always, are simply cut to 100°-proof, chilled, filtered, and bottled. Under present regulations the tax is paid on the content of the containers as they are removed from storage and this need not be before the twentieth year.

Rectification and Purification

If the brandy is purified or treated after distillation in any but the manner specified in the regulations, a special rectification tax must be paid and the treatment done in a separate building.

But, after approval of the Internal Revenue Service is secured, it is permissible to treat the brandy continuously during distillation by passing it through oak shavings, or treating with an oxidizing agent to improve flavor or to remove sulfur dioxide or other impurities.

Blending

Blending would be beneficial to uniformity of quality. Present regulations permit some blending under specified conditions. In other cases blending may be called rectification and involve additional taxes.

No experiments have been performed in this country with fractional blending systems for brandy but they have been very successfully used for brandy in Spain. Extensive changes in the regulations would be necessary but it might make possible the production of more uniform and higher quality brandies than is possible under present regulations. The calculations for sherry (p. 417) could be applied to determine the average age of the product.

FRUIT BRANDY

Apple brandy or applejack was an important commercial product of colonial and nineteenth century America. At present there is a small but regular production of apple brandy. Similar brandy produced in the Normandy district of France is sold as Calvados. The method of production has been described by Valaer (1939). The classic American process included a double pot-still distillation of the hard cider. In the first distillation a product of 60° proof was produced. This was then redistilled to 110°–130° proof with appropriate head and tail cuts. Continuous column stills are now often used. We find some American apple brandies to be aged for too short a period in the wood. Every effort should be made to use fresh, mold-free, ripe apples to secure a clean fermentation, and to distill after clarification. Only the juice should be fermented to keep the methanol content of the product as low as possible.

The work of Margerand and Thellier (1946) suggests that chemical standards are necessary to prevent inferior Calvados reaching the market in France. These included amount of esters and higher alcohols and their ratio and sum, the ratio of total acidity to aldehydes and their sum.

There have been sporadic attempts to make pear, fig, and prune brandy in this state. The use of waste fruit of poor quality usually dissipated any chance of success. For methods of preparing cherry, plum and other fruit brandies see Büttner (1938). There appears to be some commercial demand for small quantities of fruit brandies in California.

The sensory examination of brandy is more difficult than that of wines because of their high alcohol content. Rocques (1913) recommends diluting the brandy with lukewarm water (*not* distilled), covering the glass with a watch glass, shaking, and then smelling. Four distinct observations may be made: the odor of the straight brandy, the odor of the diluted brandy, the taste of the straight brandy, and the taste of the diluted brandy. Also, the glass containing the straight brandy may be emptied and the odor observed after a few minutes.

For methods of analysis of brandy, see pp. 720–724.

BIBLIOGRAPHY

AMERINE, M. A., MARTINI, L. P., and DEMATTEI, W. 1942. Foaming properties of wine, method and preliminary results. Ind. Eng. Chem. *34*, 152–157.

AMERINE, M. A. and WINKLER, A. J. 1938. Brandy. Wines and Vines *19*, No. 10, 1.

ANON. 1947. Cognac et Sa Region. Ses Grandes Eaux-de-Vie. Bordeaux et le Sud-Ouest. Éditions Delmas, Bordeaux.

BACHMANN, J. A. 1957. Pomace dealcoholizing process. Wine Institute, Tech. Adv. Committee, Dec. 6, 1957. This is covered by U. S. Pat. 2,690,-019.

BARAUD, J. 1961. Étude quantitative, par chromatographie en phase vapeur, des alcools et esters de la fermentation alcoolique. Bull. soc. chim. France [5] *1961*, 1874–1877.

BARRON, H. 1944. Distillation of Alcohol. Joseph E. Seagram and Sons, Louisville, Kentucky.

BERTI, L. A. 1949. Problems of the production of distilling material and fortifying brandy. Proc. Wine Tech. Conference, Davis *1949*, 129–134.

BRAU, H. M. 1957A. Automatic Controls in Continuous Alcoholic Distillation. Univ. Puerto Rico, Agr. Expt. Sta., Río Piedras, Tech. Paper *18*.

BRAU, H. M. 1957B. Review of the Origin and Composition of Fusel Oil. *Ibid.* Technical Paper *17*.

BROWN, E. M. 1938. The production of brandy. Wine Review *6*, No. 12, 8–10, 34.

BÜTTNER, G. 1938. Branntweine. *In* Bleyer, E. Alkoholische Genussmittel. Julius Springer, Berlin, pp. 538–718.

CARRANZA, F. 1939. Licores de Peru. Bull. soc. quím. Peru *5*, 3–27.

CHAMINADE, R. 1930. La Production et le Commerce des Eaux-De-Vie de Vin. Librairie J.-B. Baillière et Fils, Paris.

CHARRO ARIAS, A., and SIMAL LOZANO, J. 1964. Application de la chromatographie en phase vapeur à l'analyse des eaux-de-vie espagnoles. IV Congrès d'Expertise Chimique, Athenes, special no., 375–390.

CORDONNIER, R. 1954. L' élimination du cuivre dans les eaux-de-vie par les phytates de calcium et de sodium. Ann. technol. agr. *3*, 179–191.

DEKOV, L., and TSAKOV, D. 1957. Thermal treatment of brandy (transl.). Sadovodstvo, Vinogradarstvo i Vinodelie Moldavii *12*, No. 1, 45–57.

DELAMAIN, R. 1935. Histoire du Cognac. Librairie Stock, Paris.

DE VRIES, M. J. 1958. Spektrofotometriese ontleding van wyspiritus. South Africa J. Agr. Sci. *1*, 195–202.

DUJARDIN, J. 1955. Recherches Retrospectives sur l'Art de la Distillation. Dujardin-Salleron, Paris.

DZHANPOLADYAN, L. M., and PETROSYAN, Ts. L. 1957. Okislitel'nye reaktsii pri sozrevanii kon'yachnykh spirtov (Oxidation reactions during the aging of brandy). Biokhim. Vinodeliya *5*, 46–53.

EGLOFF, G., and LOWRY, C. D., JR. 1929. Distillation methods, ancient and modern. Ind. Eng. Chem. *21*, 920–923.

EGOROV, I. A., and BORISOVA, N. B. 1957. Aromaticheskie al'degidy kon'yachnogo spirta (The aromatic aldehydes of brandy). Biokhim. Vinodeliya 5, 27–37.

ELENA MARTINEZ, J. 1941. El Cognac, Consideraeiones Sobre el Estado Actual de su Fabricación en el Pais. Imprenta de la Universidad, Buenos Aires.

FILIPELLO, F. 1951. Correlation of fortifying brandy with wine quality. Proc. Am. Soc. Enol. 1951, 154–156.

FLANZY, M., and JOURET, C. 1963. Contribution à l'étude des eaux-de-vie d'Armagnac par chromatographie en phase gazeuse. Ann. technol. agr. 12, 39–50.

FLANZY, M., and LAMAZOU-BETBEDER, M. 1938. Sur la composition des eaux-de-vie de la region languedocienne. Ibid. 1, 106–119.

GAUBERT, I. 1946. Armagnac, Terre Gasconne. Édition Havas, Paris.

GAY, M. 1935. Distillation et Rectification. Librairie J.-B. Baillière et Fils, Paris.

GENEVOIS, L., and LAFON, M. 1957. Origine des huiles de fusel dans la fermentation alcoolique. Chem. Ind. (Paris) 78, 323–326.

GENEVOIS, L., and LAFON, M. 1958. Dosage de l'isopropanol et du butanol secondaire dans les boissons fermentés. Chem. Anal. 40, 156–158.

GUYMON, J. F. 1948. Principles of still operation. Proc. Wine Tech. Conference, Davis, 1948, 64–73.

GUYMON, J. F. 1949A. Composition of brandy, investigation of the influence of distillation practices upon the composition of brandies. Wines and Vines 30, No. 10, 21–24.

GUYMON, J. F. 1949B. Factors effecting physical and chemical changes in beverage brandy during aging. Proc. Wine Tech. Conference, Davis 1949, 135–146.

GUYMON, J. F. 1958. Principles of fusel oil separation and decantation. Am. J. Enol. Vitic. 9, 64–73.

GUYMON, J. F. 1960. The composition of plate samples from distilling columns with particular reference to the distribution of higher alcohol. Ibid. 11, 105–112.

GUYMON, J. F., and AMERINE, M. A. 1952. Tasting of experimental dessert wines produced with brandies of different qualities. Wines and Vines 33, No. 9, 19.

GUYMON, J. F., and NAKAGIRI, J. A. 1955. Utilization of heads by addition to alcoholic fermentations. Am. J. Enol. 6, No. 4, 12–25.

GUYMON, J. F. and POOL, A. 1957. Some results of processing heads by fermentation. Ibid. 8, 68–73.

HANSON, D. N. 1948. Principles of still design. Proc. Wine Tech. Conference, Davis, 1948, 46–63.

HARTMANN, G. 1955. Cognac, Armagnac, Weinbrand. Carl Knoppke Grüner Verlag und Vertrieb, Berlin.

HAUSBRAND, E. 1925. Principles and Practice of Industrial Distillation. John Wiley and Sons, Inc., New York.

HENNIG, K., and BURKHARDT, R. 1962. Chromatographische Trennung von Eichenholzauszügen und deren Nachweis in Weinbränden. Weinberg u. Keller 9, 223–231.

HIRSCH, I. 1936. Manufacture of Whiskey, Brandy and Cordials. Avi Publishing Co., Westport, Conn.

HORSLEY, L. H. 1952. Azeotropic Data. American Chemical Society, Washington.

IKEDA, R. M., WEBB, A. D., and KEPNER, R. E. 1956. Comparative analysis of fusel oil from Thompson Seedless, Emperor, and Muscat of Alexandria wines. J. Agr. Food Chem. 4, 355–363.

INGRAHAM, J. L., and GUYMON, J. E. 1960. The formation of aliphatic alcohols by mutant strains of Saccharomyces cerevisiae. Arch. Biochem. Biophys. 88, 157–166.

JACKSON, G. H. 1928 . The Medicinal Value of French Brandy. Thérien Frères, Montreal.

JOSLYN, M. A., and AMERINE, M. A. 1941. Commercial production of brandies. California Agr. Expt. Sta. Bull. 652.

JOSLYN, M. A., and AMERINE, M. A. 1964. Dessert, Appetizer and Related Flavored Wines. University of California, Division of Agricultural Sciences, Berkeley.

KEPNER, R. E., and WEBB, A. D. 1961. Components of muscat raisin fusel oil. Am. J. Enol. Vitic. 12, 159–174.

KLIMOVSKIĬ, D. N., and STABNIKOV, V. N. 1950. Tekhnologiya Spirtovogo Proizvidstva (Technology of Spirit Production). Pishchepromizdat, Moscow.

LAFON, J., and COUILLAUD, P. 1953. Sur la présence du cuivre dans les eaux-de-vie de Cognac. Ann. technol. agr. 1, 41–50.

LAFON, J., COUILLAUD, P., CAUMEIL, M., and MARCHE, M. 1960. Teneur en plomb des eaux-de-vie de Cognac. Ibid. 9, 109–116.

LAFON, R., LAFON, J., and COUILLAUD, P. 1964. Le Cognac; Sa Distillation. J.-B. Baillière et Fils, Paris.

LASHKI, A. D. 1963. Izmenenie sostavnykh komponentov spirtov raznykh vozrastov pri ikh vyderzhke (Changes in the components of brandies of different ages). Biokhim. Vinodeliya 7, 173–188.

LITCHEV, V. 1959. The pH in wine brandy (transl.) Nauch. Trud. Tekh. Inst. Vina. i Vino. Promishlenosti 3, 155–166.

MACMILLAN, J. D., YORK, G. K., and VAUGHN, R. H. 1959. B.O.D. vs C.O.D. methods of determining brandy stillage purification. Am. J. Enol. Vitic. 10, 199–205.

MAĬOROV, V. S. 1958. Faktory, obuslovlivayushchie nakoplenie metanola v vyzhimochnykh spirtakh (Factors affecting methanol separation from press wine). Vinodelie i Vinogradarstvo S.S.S.R. 18, No. 8, 7–11

MALTABAR, V. M. 1952. Ovliyanii khimicheskogo sostava vinomaterialov na kachestvo kon'yachnykh spirtov (The effect of chemical composition of raw wine materials on the quality of brandy.) Ibid. 12, No. 6, 22–26.

MARGERAND, P., and THELLIER, R. 1946. Introduction à l'étude analytique et organoleptiques des eaux-de-vie. Rev. viticult. 92, 387–392.

MARILLER, C. 1948. Manuel du Distillateur. 3 ed. J.-B. Ballière, Paris.

MARSH, G. L. 1965. Composition of brandy. Fruit Products J. 15, 42–43.

MELONI, G. 1952–1958. L'Industria dell'Alcole. Editore Ulrico Hoepli, Milan. 3 v. V. I. Alcolometria. 1952; v. II. Processi e Impianti di Produzione e Trasformazione. Le Materie Prime—Le Acquaviti. 1953; v. III. Processi e Impianti di Produzione e Trasformazione. Spiriti, Alcole Assoluto, Alcoli Sintetici. 1958.

METZNER, E. K. 1945. Grape pomace. A source of alcohol and tartrates. Chem. Met. Eng. 52, No. 10, 102–103.

MONIER-WILLIAMS, G. W. 1922. Power Alcohol. Frowde and Hodder and Stoughton, London.

NEEDHAM, J. 1954. Science and Civilization in China. University Press, Cambridge, Vol. 1.

OTSUKA, K., and IMAI, S. 1964. Studies on the mechanism of aging of distilled spirits. I. On phenolic compounds from oak wooden chips. Agr. Biol. Chem. 28, 356–362.

PFENNINGER, H. 1963. Gaschromatographische Untersuchungen von Fuselölen aus verschiedenen Gärprodukten. III. Ergebnisse der gaschromatographischen Untersuchung von Fuselölen aus verschiedenen Gärprodukten. Z. Lebensm.-Untersuch. u. -Forsch. 120, 117–126.

POOL, A., and HEITZ, J. E. 1950. Correlation of fortifying brandy with wine quality. Proc. Am. Soc. Enol. 1950, 101–109.

PRIOTON, H. 1929. La Culture de la Vigne dans les Charentes et la Production du Cognac. Librairie J.-B. Baillière et Fils, Paris.

PRO, M.-J., and ETIENNE, A. D. 1959. Dating distilled spirits. J. Assoc. Offic. Agr. Chem. 42, 386–392.

PROCOPIO, M. 1958. Studio sulle acqueviti di vino aldeidi e acetati. Riv. viticolt. e enol. (Conegliano) 11, 253–260.

RAKCSÁNYI, L. 1958. Égetett szeszesitalok készitése vákuumlepárlással (Production of brandy by vacuum distillation). Kísérlet. Közlem, 52, 31–77.

RANKINE, B. C. 1961A. Factors influencing uptake of copper from brandy by ion-exchange resins. J. Sci. Food Agr. 12, 188–194.

RANKINE, B. C. 1961B. Lead content of Australian brandies. Ibid. 12, 194–196.

RAVAZ, L. 1900. Le Pays du Cognac. Louis Coquemard, Angoulême.

RENTSCHLER, H., and BRAUN, F. 1950. Über die Bestimmung des Alkoholgehaltes in Getränken. Schweiz. Z. Obst- u. Weinbau 59, 223–226.

RICCIARDELLI, N. 1909. I Cognacs Italiani. Libreria Editrice Concetto Battiato di Francesco Battiato, Catania.

RIFFART, H., and DIEMAIR, W. 1944. Beitrag zur Untersuchung von Brennwein. Z. Lebensm.-Untersuch. u. -Forsch. 87, 61–64.

ROBINSON, C. S., and GILLILAND, E. R. 1950. The Elements of Fractional Distillation. McGraw-Hill Book Co., New York.

ROCQUES, X. 1913. Eaux-De-Vie. Librairie Polytechnique Ch. Béranger, Paris.

RONKAINEN, P., SALO, T., and SUOMALAINEN, H. 1962. Carbonylverbindungen der Weindestillate und deren Veränderungen im Verlaufe der Reifeprozesse. Z. Lebensm.-Untersuch. u. -Forsch. 117, 281–289.

ROSENTHALER, L., and VEGEZZI, G. 1955. Acrolein in Spirituosen. Ibid. 102, 117–123.

SIMMONDS, C. 1919. Alcohol, Its Production, Properties, Chemistry, and Industrial Applications. Macmillan and Co., London.

SKURIKHIN, I. M. 1960. Khimizm protsessov sozrevaniya kon'yachnykh spiritov v emalirovannykh tsisternakh (Chemical processes of treating brandy in metal tanks). Trudy konferentsii po biokhimii vinodeliya 1960, 179–190.

SOREL, E. 1899. Distillation et Rectification Industrielle. G. Carré et Cie., Paris.

TAMBURRINI, V., PALLADINI, F., and DARD, E. 1955. Caratteristiche di alcoli buon gusto del commercio e considerazioni sul saggio merceologico di resistenza al permanganate in relazioni alle loro impurezze. Riv. viticolt. e enol. (Conegliano) 8, 53–65.

TEODORESCU, S. C., ILIESCU, L. V., and IONESCU, A. I. 1958. Evolution de la composition chimique des eaux-de-vie au cours du vieillissement. Anal. Inst. Cercet. Agron. 26, 115–140.

THOUKIS, G. 1958. The mechanism of isoamyl alcohol formation using tracer techniques. Am. J. Enol. 9, 161–167.

TOLBERT, N. E., and AMERINE, M. A. 1943. Charcoal treatment of brandies. Ind. Eng. Chem. 35, 1078–1082.

TOLBERT, N. E., AMERINE, M. A., and GUYMON, J. F. 1943. Studies with brandy. II. Tannin. Food Research 8, 231–236.

TOLU LIBERO, A. 1962. Il metanolo nelle acqueviti di vinaccia. Ann. Fac. Sci. Agr. Univ. Torino 1, 199–202.

U. S. INTERNAL REVENUE SERVICE. 1955. Brandy Production. IRS Publication No. 157, U. S. Govt. Print. Off., Washington. (See also Federal brandy regulations, 26CFR (1954) part 221, effective January 1, 1955, New York, etc., Commerce Clearing House, Inc., 11001–11097, 11121–11139, 1114–11161, 11201–11225, 11251–11268 p.)

VALAER, P. 1939. Brandy. Ind. Eng. Chem. 31, 339–353.

VEGEZZI, G., HALLER, P., and WANGER, O. 1951. Le problème de l'eau-de-vie de marc de raisin. Mitt. Gebiete Lebensm. Hyg. 42, 316–341.

VILLA, Q. 1946. Elementi di Calcolo sulla Distillazione Frazionata. Editore Ulrico Hoepli, Milano.

WALKER, W. H., LEWIS, W. K., McADAMS, H. H., and GILLILAND, E. R. 1937. Principles of Chemical Engineering. 3 ed. McGraw-Hill Book Co., New York.

WEBB, A. D. 1951. Flavor factors in fortifying brandy. Proc. Am. Soc. Enol. 1951, 148–153.

WEBB, A. D., KEPNER, R. E., and IKEDA, R. M. 1952. Composition of a typical grape brandy fusel oil. Anal. Chem. 24, 1944–1949.

WILKINS, E. A., and WALLING, M. E. 1939. Quality brandy through controlled distillation. Wine Review 7, No. 9, 7–9, 27.

WILLKIE, H. G., and PROCHASKA, J. A. 1943. Fundamentals of Distillery Practice. Joseph E. Seagram and Sons, Louisville, Ky.

WÜSTENFELD, H., and HAESELER, G. 1964. Trinkbranntweine und Liköre. Verlag Paul Parey, Berlin.

XANDRI TAGÜENA, J. M. 1958. Elaboración de Aguardientes Simples, Compuestos y Licores. Salvat Editores, S. A., Barcelona.

YORK, G. K. 1958. Winery waste disposal. Wine Institute, Tech. Adv. Committee, May 26, 1958.

YOUNG, S. 1922. Distillation Principles and Practices. Macmillan Co., London and New York.

Note: For Federal brandy regulations, see pp. 754–760.

CHAPTER 18

Winery By-Products

In California during W. W. II, because of the interruption of imports, calcium tartrate was made from the tartrate and tartaric acid occurring in pomace and in stillage. Also, for a few years the pomace from several large dessert wineries was dehydrated for use in mixed stock feeds and some oil was made from the seeds separated from the pomace. At the present time, 1966, the recovery of tartrates from pomace and stillage has practically ceased, owing to the resumption of imports of tartrates. The production of other oils, such as cottonseed, corn, and soy bean oil, since the war has made the use of grape seeds for oil recovery economically unattractive. The dehydration of pomace for use in stock feeds has declined to a negligible volume in recent years. Both tartrates and wine grape seed oil are still made commercially in Europe. See Aries (1957).

A more favorable report on the use of by-products comes from Agostini (1964) in South Africa. There the pomace is used for alcohol, tartrates, seeds as cattle feed, for production of methane and as a fertilizer.

Conditions may arise that will make it profitable or in the national interest to resume tartrate production from American winery wastes. The production of concentrates, tannin, grape juice, and wine vinegar will be presented briefly, since from the winery's standpoint they are by-products rather than primary products.

TARTRATES

According to Marsh (1943A) the annual peace-time production at that time of tartaric acid in America was about 9,000,000 lbs. and cream of tartar production amounted to approximately 5,000,000 lbs. These were made by commercial factories from cream of tartar and calcium tartrate supplied by the wine industry. Before the war about 90 per cent of the crude tartrates used in America came from wine-producing countries of the Mediterranean area. South America provided most of the remainder. During W.W. II most of these imports were cut off; hence California's wine industry was called upon to furnish much of the deficit.

While tartaric acid can be made synthetically by the Vaghounney and other methods, evidently costs have been too high to compete successfully with the natural tartrates from wine making. Tartrates occur naturally in winery pomace, still slops from brandy distillation, in the lees that settle in wine tanks, and in the wine stone or argols that separate, as a crystalline coating of almost pure cream of tartar, on the walls and bottoms of wine

645

storage tanks. The principal tartrate compound in these accumulations is potassium bitartrate (cream of tartar). Cream of tartar also separates in the sediment in tanks of filtered wine undergoing refrigeration; in this case it is of high purity. This source of bitartrate will decrease as use of ion exchange resins increases. The largest potential sources of tartrates in California wineries are unwashed pomace from wineries producing dry table wines and from distilling material, or still slops, from dessert wine wineries.

Tartrate Content of Grapes

Marsh (1943A, 1943B) points out that previously published data give only the tartrate content of the juice of the grape which is considerably lower than of the whole grape. He finds that ripe *V. vinifera* varieties of grapes grown in California range from 0.8 to 1.2 per cent in total tartrate content, expressed as cream of tartar. Over 90 per cent of the total acidity of must is due to the malic and tartaric acids. As grapes ripen the malic acid, Amerine and Winkler (1942), decreases relatively more rapidly than the tartaric (see p. 82). Thus, early in the season they found that only 25 to 40 per cent of the fixed acidity was due to tartaric acid, but that late in the season it accounted for 45 to 81 per cent. However, the ratio of tartaric to malic varied markedly with the variety.

Tartrates from Table Wine Wineries

Most of the wineries of France, Italy, and other European and North African countries produce only unfortified table wines, and much of the pomace is not utilized for distillation for brandy recovery. This pomace could supply a tremendous amount of tartrates if there were a market. Normally, the lees and argols are more than sufficient to supply the world markets. In the United States, the lees and argols are not sufficient to supply this country's needs for tartrates, and it would be necessary to utilize the pomace and still slops for tartrate recovery in order to provide an important fraction of our needs.

California normally crushes over 2,000,000 tons of grapes for wine, of which only about 20 per cent or less are used for dry wine making. The reason for segregating dry wine pomace from the sweet in our discussion is that dessert winery pomace is washed thoroughly with water to prepare distilling material for high proof brandy production. Therefore, the dessert wine pomace contains little tartrates.

Pomace from dry red wine making is richer in tartrates than pomace from dry white wine making, because much cream of tartar separates during the fermentation of red must on the skins; whereas, white grapes are nearly always pressed before fermentation and there is no fermentation on the skins. Marsh reports that samples of red wine pomace from the 1941 and 1942 vintages contained 11.1 to 16.1 per cent of tartrate on a dry weight basis, and white wine pomace, 4.2 to 11.1 per cent.

The average yields of pomace per ton of grapes in dry wine making observed by one of the authors (Cruess) in 1912 and 1913 at the Swett winery were 17.1 per cent or 342 lbs. per ton for dry red wine and 17.25 per cent or 345 lbs. per ton for dry white wine. However, normally, reds yield less than white grapes. Bioletti (1914) gave 345 lbs. per ton as the average yield of pomace in red wine making and 391 lbs. in dry white wine making. These values are for basket press pomace—with a continuous screw press they are probably somewhat lower. It was found that dry wine pomace from a basket press ranged from 56.2 to 68.5 per cent liquid and averaged 63.6 per cent; 7 to 8 per cent of the liquid was alcohol.

Storage of Pomace

In the rush of the vintage it is usually not practicable to extract tartrates from the pomace as rapidly as it accumulates. In most cases it was formerly stored and processed after the vintage. It was merely placed in as deep and compact a pile as possible. Stems must be separated from the skins at the time of crushing because they prevent compacting of the pomace and cause air pockets. Mold then grows in the pomace and destroys the tartrates. If all the stems have been removed and the pomace is well compacted, mold grows only in the outer 6 to 10 in. of the pomace pile. The lower the ratio of surface to volume, the less is the loss due to mold action. Marsh reports that the tartrates below this outer moldy layer keep well for several years. The pomace and stems are now removed daily from the winery premises and spread in fields or vineyards to dry. On this account they would have to be utilized at once for by-products. See also Celmer (1943), Cherski (1943), Halperin (1946), Matchett et al. (1944), and Vaughn and Marsh (1945).

Extraction of Tartrate from the Pomace

Much of the tartrate is present as small crystals of cream of tartar adhering to the skins. As the cream of tartar is soluble in hot water there is no need to use acidified water in large scale operations. For small operations where steam is not available, Marsh states that extraction in the cold with dilute acid may be justified as it greatly hastens solution.

Marsh and Guadagni (1942) report that cold acid extraction was about four times as rapid as cold water extraction and yielded much more tartrate because solution was nearly complete. In a typical experiment one cold acid treatment extracted 60 per cent of the tartrate present; this was followed by cold water extraction which dissolved practically all of the remaining tartrate. Two hours' treatment with 2 per cent hydrochloric acid or 5 hours with 1 per cent was suggested.

Continuous or batch extraction can be used. In the continuous method, the pomace is conveyed through a tank of hot water into which water continuously flows, and from which extract flows continuously. However, Marsh states that extraction is probably poor; also corrosion of metal equipment, such as chain conveyors, etc., is rapid, and the extract is very cloudy. He prefers batch extraction in which the pomace is first mixed with 3 parts of water to 1 of pomace, heated to 140° to 212°F., drained, heated again with two parts of water to one of pomace, and the drained pomace is then pressed. The press extract will be muddy and can be settled separately to rid it of coarse suspended matter. The Metzner continuous pomace still also yields a hot water extract of cream of tartar.

Pomace can also be extracted by the beet diffusion battery principle, in which pomace is placed in several tanks in series, p. 254, using hot water extraction. The extract from tank number one is used to extract the pomace in number two and so on, so that each lot of pomace is extracted 3 or 4 times, the last extraction being with water, after which the pomace may be pressed. The diffusion battery procedure gives an extract relatively free of suspended solids.

The hot extract may be cleared by filtration, Fig. 137, or fining, if too cloudy, but settling is usually sufficient. The liquid from the first extract or from pot distillation is rich in cream of tartar, much of which can be recovered by crystallization on cooling and standing several days. Crystallization is slow. To prevent molding and losses of tartrates by other organisms, the solution should be sulfited by adding sulfur dioxide to 150 to

FIG. 137. LARGE FILTER PRESS FOR FILTRATION OF TARTRATE
SOLUTIONS

200 p.p.m.   In most plants the extracts were combined, then treated with calcium hydroxide and chloride to recover the tartrates as calcium tartrate. Table 60 illustrates the percentages of potassium tartrate extracted at various water-to-pomace ratios.

TABLE 60

PERCENTAGES OF CREAM OF TARTAR, $KHC_4H_4O_6$, EXTRACTED AT VARIOUS WATER-TO-POMACE RATIOS[1]

Kind of Pomace	Water : Pomace	Concentration of $KHC_4H_4O_6$ in First Extract	Extracted by First Extraction
	ratio	Gm./100 Ml.	per cent
Unfermented white	1:1	1.50	36.5
Unfermented white	2:1	1.00	65.0
Unfermented white	3:1	0.74	78.0
Fermented red	1:1	3.00	29.5
Fermented red	2:1	2.20	56.0
Fermented red	3:1	1.35	62.7
Fermented red	4:1	1.08	72.5

[1] Sources of data: Marsh 1943a.

For hot water extraction of pomace without the use of acid, Marsh and Guadagni (1942) make the following recommendations:

(1) If the concentration of tartrate in the pomace is 4 per cent or higher use 3 parts of water to 1 part of pomace by weight; if below 4 per cent the ratio is 2 to 1.   The first extract will contain 13 to 16 gm. of potassium acid tartrate per liter.   Partially fill the tank with the calculated amount of water and heat to near the boiling point.

(2) Shovel or convey the calculated amount of pomace into the tank and allow to stand 15 minutes, continuing the heating.

(3) Drain off the free-run liquid and pump it to precipitating tanks.

(4) Cover the pomace with the required amount of water, never more than 2 to 1 by weight of the original pomace.   Heat 30 minutes.

(5) Drain off and pump to precipitating tank.

(6) Remove the pomace from the extraction tank and press it in a continuous press.   Pump the liquid to a settling tank.   Settle well.   Rack and pump to the precipitating tank.

For cold acid extraction they recommended the following procedure:

(1) Partially fill the tank with a known weight of pomace.

(2) Add the required volume of one per cent hydrochloric acid solution (3:1 or 2:1 by weight depending on the cream of tartar content of the pomace). Leave five hours without agitation.   To make one per cent hydrochloric acid solution, mix 261 lbs. or 84 gallons of 20° Baumé hydrochloric acid with 1000 gallons of water.

(3) Drain off the free run to the precipitating tank, by gravity if possible as the acid solution is very corrosive to pumps and other metal equipment.

(4) Cover the pomace with the required amount of water (2:1 or less).   Let stand 16 hours.

(5) Drain off the free run and combine it with the first extract in the precipitating tank.

(6) Remove and press the pomace and transfer the liquid to settling tank. Let settle. Draw off the clear liquid and combine with other extracts. Discard the lees sediment.

Precipitation of Calcium Tartrate

Since crystallization of cream of tartar from solution is so slow and incomplete, it is much more satisfactory to recover tartrate as calcium tartrate. However, careful chemical control is essential. High purity in the finished product is necessary for a satisfactory financial return. Careless operation can very greatly reduce the value of the product because of impurities.

Calcium tartrate is relatively insoluble in water—0.053 gm. per 100 ml. at 68°F. or 0.219 gm. per 100 ml. at 185°F. However, various substances in solution affect its solubility. Thus, calcium tartrate is several times more soluble at pH 7 in the pomace extract than in plain water. The pH value affects its solubility markedly. Because of that fact special care must be taken in the handling of tartrate extracts made by extraction of pomace with dilute hydrochloric acid, as the pH value is much lower than that of hot water extracts of pomace.

Contrary to previous general belief, Marsh points out that no single calcium compound such as lime, $Ca(OH)_2$ or calcium carbonate, $CaCO_3$, will precipitate more than 50 per cent of the tartrate. However, a combination of salts, such as calcium chloride and neutralization with calcium hydroxide or other alkali, will give nearly complete precipitation. The reactions are:

$$2KHC_4H_4O_6 + Ca(OH)_2 \rightarrow CaC_4H_4O_6 + K_2C_4H_4O_6 + 2H_2O$$
$$2K_2C_4H_4O_6 + CaCl_2 \rightarrow CaC_4H_4O_6 + 2KCl$$

In pure water solution, the highest yield is obtained at pH 6.8 to 7.2 with a slight excess of calcium chloride. Too high or too low a pH value, or too great an excess of calcium chloride, will decrease the yield. In pomace extracts the highest purity occurs at pH 4.5 rather than at pH 7.0. One reason is that colloids present in the extract flocculate out at higher pH values. Their isoelectric point, above which they flocculate completely, is pH 6.2. The colloids in this case will contaminate the tartrate precipitate. Also elevating the pH value much above 4.5 renders the extract very susceptible to bacterial decomposition.

Marsh advises addition of the calculated amounts of lime and calcium chloride, based on chemical analysis of the extract, in order to obtain the maximum yield of calcium tartrate of the highest purity. The usual procedure has been to add an excess of calcium hydroxide as indicated by litmus paper. The litmus paper should be replaced with indicators covering the range pH 4 to 5. There is then less overshooting with calcium hydroxide with resultant high impurities.

Marsh calculates the proper amounts of calcium hydroxide and chloride for maximum precipitation of calcium tartrate at pH 4.5 by determining the tartrate content by a modified Halenke and Möslinger (1895) procedure (see also Amerine 1970) and the total acidity. One-fourth of the difference between the standard alkali solution needed for neutralization, and that required to neutralize the potassium bitartrate, is calculated in terms of calcium hydroxide for the volume of material to be treated. This determines the amount of calcium hydroxide to raise the pH approximately one pH unit. The amounts of calcium chloride and calcium hydroxide required to precipitate the tartrates stoichiometrically can be calculated from the two chemical reactions given above and the tartrates present, as determined by the Halenke and Möslinger procedure. The total amount of calcium hydroxide needed is the sum of that required to raise the pH value and that needed for precipitation of potassium bitartrate, as based on the first chemical reaction of the two given above. In order to provide the proper excess of calcium chloride, 1.15 times the amount calculated according to the second reaction given above should be added.

The calculated amounts of calcium hydroxide and chloride should be weighed out and dissolved and slurried together with water in the same tank, or prepared separately and added simultaneously, because, as Marsh states, the change in pH value will be quite different if they are added separately. See also Genevois (1934).

Marsh and Guadagni (1942) gave the following example to illustrate the method of calculating the total amount of calcium ions needed for precipitating a given concentration of potassium bitartrate. Let KHTa represent potassium bitartrate. Suppose the extract were to contain 1.5 gm. of bitartrate per 100 ml. and a pH value of 3.5.

Then,

$$\frac{\text{Grams KHTa per 100 ml.} \times 3785}{454} = \text{lbs. KHTa per 100 gallons, or } 1.5 \times$$
$$8.35 = 12.53 \text{ lbs. KHTa per 100 gallons.}$$

The theoretical amount of calcium required for precipitation then becomes

$$\frac{\text{lbs. KHTa per 100 gallons} \times 40}{188} = \text{lbs. calcium required for precipitation}$$

per 100 gallons, of extract, or $12.53 \times 0.213 = 2.67$ lbs. calcium per 100 gallons.

For precipitation according to the two reactions previously given one-half of the calcium would be furnished by calcium hydroxide and one-half by calcium chloride. This amount of calcium chloride is multiplied by 1.15 and sufficient excess calcium hydroxide is added to raise the pH value one unit, i.e., to pH 4.5.

A simpler, empirical, yet fairly satisfactory, method of calculating the proportions of calcium hydroxide and chloride to be used is that formerly used by one large wine company. Total acidity expressed as tartaric acid is divided by 0.20 and the quotient is multiplied by 4 and 6. The results are the amounts of calcium hydroxide and chloride in pounds needed per 1000 gallons of slop or extract.

During and after addition of the calcium chloride and hydroxide the liquid in the precipitating tank is mixed by pumping until uniform in physical and chemical condition. If successful the precipitate will be heavy and settle rapidly. The supernatant liquid is racked off and discarded. The calcium tartrate precipitate is resuspended in water by pumping, and settled in order to remove impurities of low specific gravity. This is repeated one or more times. The addition of 200 p.p.m. of sulfur dioxide to the wash water is recommended in order to prevent bacterial spoilage during washing.

The compacted tartrate is then dried on trays in a forced draft dehydrator, such as a prune dehydrator, or in a steam-jacketed metal cylinder about 3.5 feet in diameter and about 12 to 15 feet long equipped with a revolving agitator, or in other suitable drier. The steam-jacketed cylinder drier has proven very satisfactory. Some wineries successfully dried the tartrate in the sun on concrete slabs. The tartrate must be dried to low moisture content, below 5 per cent, in order to prevent spoilage by microorganisms.

Recovery of Tartrates from Lees

The lees, which settle in storage tanks after fermentation or fortification are rich in cream of tartar and alcohol. The usual practice is to dilute the lees with about an equal volume of water, distill to recover alcohol, settle hot to get rid of most of the suspended matter, cool and allow to stand several days for crystallization of cream of tartar, and then rack, wash and dry the crystals. The racked liquid is then treated with calcium chloride and hydroxide as previously described, to recover the remaining tartrate as calcium tartrate. Or the step of crystallization of cream of tartar can be omitted and all of the tartrate recovered as calcium tartrate. The tartrates can also be recovered from lees by centrifuging in a continuous centrifuge and drying the tartrates so recovered. At present prices this process does not appear feasible.

Argols

The "wine stone" that forms on the walls and floors of wine tanks and the crystals that separate during the refrigeration of wine are almost pure cream of tartar and can be sold in that form. "Wine stone" adheres tightly to the walls of the tank. Formerly, it was chipped off laboriously by hand or by air chisel. "Wine stone" can be flaked off the walls of concrete wine tanks by applying a steam jet to the surface. At present, it is often dissolved by applying strong sodium hydroxide solution to the surface. Soluble Rochelle salt, $NaKC_4H_4O_6$, is formed.

The solution can be acidified to pH 3.5 with hydrochloric acid, which converts the Rochelle salt to cream of tartar and sodium bitartrate. The cream of tartar then crystallizes out. Any tartrate remaining in solution is precipitated as calcium tartrate by addition of calcium hydroxide and chloride.

Tartrates from Dessert Wine Pomace

The pomace from dessert wine making is usually washed twice or three times with water and the resulting wash or distilling material is distilled for production of brandy, mostly 180° to 190° proof fortifying brandy. The pomace is then pressed. The leaching of the pomace for brandy manufacture removes most of the cream of tartar. Marsh (1943A), therefore, states that treatment of this pomace for tartrate recovery is usually uneconomical.

Tartrate Recovery from Distilling Material and Still Slops

In the production of dessert wines, most of the cream of tartar present in the pomace is dissolved by leaching of the pomace for distilling material. Hence, most of the tartrate from dessert winery wastes is in the still slops or distilling material. Precipitation of calcium tartrate can be made before or after distillation. Marsh prefers precipitation after distillation; that is, in the still slops rather than in the distilling material. A purer tartrate is obtained by precipitation after distillation as settling is better. Also there is less danger of spoilage by microorganisms. If the pH is brought to too high a value in the distilling material before distillation that may adversely affect the quality of the beverage brandy distilled from it. Also the chemicals used for precipitating the tartrates may damage the still.

The tartrate content of distilling material and still slops varies greatly— Marsh reporting a range from 1.25 gm. to 7.25 gm. per liter. The limiting minimum concentration is about 0.25 gm. per 100 ml. or about 0.02 lb. per gallon.

The slop from the still should be cooled to below 122°F. and allowed to settle in tanks of 30,000 gallons or larger. Or the slop is clarified with bentonite. If the waste sediment is to be disposed of on the land by intermittent irrigation, bentonite should not be used as it tends to clog the soil and thus interfere with percolation of the liquid into the soil.

The clarified liquid is racked and pumped to a tank for precipitation of tartrates with calcium chloride and hydroxide (see p. 651). If the slop has been bentonited or filtered it is not essential to control the pH value as closely as in the unclarified liquid. The loss in bentonite clarification is from 15 to 20 per cent. It is possible that an Oliver continuous filter could be used if sufficient Hyflo or other coarse infusorial filter-aid was added. As in making calcium tartrate from pomace extract, the calcium tartrate precipitate from the slop is settled, washed with water, and then dried to below five per cent moisture.

There are no data on the recovery of tartrates from slops where disintegrated pomace is distilled. With our present facilities and procedures this appears to be impossible.

Microbiological Decomposition of Tartrates

Early in the production of calcium tartrate in California, during W.W. II, alarming losses through bacterial action were encountered. Vaughn and Marsh (1943) state that the first case brought to their attention was caused by thermophilic bacteria growing in hot liquors at 132° to 158°F. The responsible organism was isolated by Vaughn from samples of calcium tartrate from all wine districts of the state. Gas and bad odors and considerable butyric acid were produced. The organism is a *Clostridium* but its species was not established. Maintenance of temperature below 122°F. and use of 150 to 200 p.p.m. of sulfur dioxide are good preventive measures.

Mesophilic bacteria (those growing at temperatures below 113°F.) also have caused serious losses of tartrates. Those isolated from spoilage cases were facultative aerobes and Gram-negative. Members of the coli-aerogenes group were common. Strict aerobes are probably of little importance. Berry and Vaughn (1952), Tabachnick and Vaughn (1948), and Mercer and Vaughn (1951) have reported on bacteria that decompose tartrates.

The *Aerobacter aerogenes* types of bacteria of the coli-aerogenes group were the most important mesophilic destroyers of tartrates. They grow at a pH value of 4.5, or somewhat lower, to pH 7.3. Below pH 4.5 tartrate destruction is retarded. The simplest method of control is to hold the pH value at not above 4.5 and to add 175 to 250 p.p.m. of sulfur dioxide. Other antiseptics are less suitable because of off-odors and off-flavors or other objections. Some of the *Aerobacter* cultures destroyed all the tartrates in a 1 per cent solution in two days.

Vaughn and Marsh (1943) offer the following recommendations for minimizing losses due to microorganisms:

(1) Dry the tartrates below 5 per cent moisture to prevent mold growth in potassium bitartrate and bacteria or mold in calcium tartrate.

(2) Make all calcium tartrate precipitations at a controlled pH of 4.5.

(3) Conduct washing of the precipitated calcium tartrate rapidly, using, if necessary, about 200 p.p.m. of sulfur dioxide in the wash water.

(4) If decomposition appears at any stage of the process use sulfur dioxide.

(5) Observe sanitary precautions to reduce infection to a minimum. For example, do not allow stagnating pools of water to accumulate on the floors to be tracked by workmen into the recovery plant. Examine the water supply and treat it if it is contaminated with spoilage bacteria. Refuse piles of wash sludge should not be left near the plant. Clean sumps, pipe lines, pumps, etc., thoroughly after each use.

(6) The writers would offer the additional suggestion that if or when spoilage develops in a tank of liquor undergoing precipitation or settling, the tank itself be very thoroughly sterilized with a 0.5 to 1.0 per cent solution of sodium bisulfite, acidified with half its concentration of hydrochloric or sulfuric acid, before further use. The large amount of organic matter present on the walls and floor of the tank renders the use of dilute chlorine solutions ineffective.

OIL AND TANNIN FROM GRAPE SEEDS

Until W.W. II pomace from California wineries was not widely utilized, although some had been dehydrated for use as stock feed, and some had been spread in the vineyards to improve soil texture. It has relatively little fertilizing value.

Aside from the tartrates, the readily recoverable principal by-product from winery pomace is the oil from the seeds. In Europe and Australia tannin is also recovered from the seeds and skins, but in California most of the pomace is washed several times with water for the production of distilling material for high proof brandy.

Some edible oil was made from wine grape seeds in the nineteenth century by drying, grinding, and pressing the seeds. The practice died out when lower priced oils came into general use.

A few years before W.W. I grape-seed oil production was resumed and during that war, because of lack of transportation for oil-bearing materials from the tropics, it was greatly expanded in Europe. Solvent extraction of oils also greatly stimulated this industry at that time. During this period

(Rabak and Shrader, 1921; Klinger, 1921) the production of grape-seed oil by pressing of oil from washed, dried raisin seeds was established in Fresno, California and continued until about 1960.

Since 1930 the struggles for self-sufficiency have caused retention of grape-seed oil production in Europe as a food oil. It has also been used in paints and in soap making (Bonnet 1924).

Seed Content of Pomace

Cruess and Weast (1939) reported seed contents of several wine pomaces (on the wet basis) from about 20 to 30 per cent. Rabak and Shrader (1921) gave the seed content of pomace from grape juice manufacture as 20 per cent. Bonnet (1924) reported that French winery pomace contained on the wet basis (65 to 70 per cent moisture) about 22.5 per cent of seeds. However, the European pomace is chiefly from table wine wineries in which the pomace is not washed for alcohol recovery; in California about 80 per cent of the pomace comes from dessert wine wineries in which the pomace is washed several times with water, resulting in a considerable increase in per cent seed content. Examination in 1942 of pomaces from several large dessert wine establishments gave seed contents of 25.7 to about 27 per cent on the wet basis, or about 43.6 to 45.7 per cent on the dry basis. The seeds were lower in moisture content, 34 to 36 per cent, than the accompanying skins and pulp, which contained 50 to 55 per cent.

Available Tonnage.—The normal average annual crush of wine grapes in California is about 2,000,000 tons. Assuming that 40 per cent of all grapes crushed represents seedless grapes, there would be about 1,200,000 tons of seed-bearing varieties yielding about 12 per cent of pomace. If the pomace contains about 25 per cent of seeds, this is equivalent to about 36,-000 tons, on the wet basis, or about 19,080 tons of seeds on a moisture-free basis. At an average recoverable oil content of 12 per cent this would yield about 2290 tons or 575,892 gal. of oil. Compared with the production of most other oils, this is not an important volume, and in normal times would be of no great significance. See also Valebregue (1943).

Oil Content of Seeds

Cruess and Weast (1939) found the oil content of wine-grape seeds (dry basis) to range from about 11 to 15 per cent. In a later investigation it varied for eight samples between 12.8 and 22.2 per cent, most of the samples being below 16 per cent. The sample with the highest oil content consisted of seeds from a muscat grape pomace thoroughly washed for recovery of sugar. It is not wise to estimate an average of above 12 per cent of oil on the dry basis, recoverable by commercial solvent extraction, since some wine-grape varieties have heavy seed coats, relatively small kernels, and a considerable number of blank seeds.

Preservation of Pomace and Seeds

At Fresno, California, raisin seeds after drying keep very well stored in bins. One sample of oil, extracted by pressing seeds stored two years, contained only 1.03 per cent free fatty acid. Where the pomace is allowed to stand in piles it keeps well for several months, except for the outer 12 to 15 in., although the free fatty acid of the seed oil does increase considerably. A sample from the interior of a pile of pomace from Lodi, California, taken about four months after the close of the wine-making season, gave a seed oil that contained 7.8 per cent free fatty acid; oil from seeds from the same pomace allowed to stand for two months and become moldy showed 15.9 per cent free fatty acid; and oil from seeds from the same pomace, allowed to mold an additional two months, showed 32.8 per cent free.

Also, the seeds should be stored in a dry condition to minimize microbial activity and heating up as the following instance appears to indicate. A portion of a large lot of muscat seeds of slightly too high moisture content (8.3 per cent) warmed up during storage, probably because of an excessive rate of oxidation. The oil from these seeds contained 3.7 per cent fatty acid; that from seeds that had not heated up (from same bin) contained only 1.03 per cent free fatty acid.

Separation of Seeds from Pomace and Drying

In small scale tests the seeds were separated from the dried pomace by screening and winnowing after drying. An ordinary wheat or barley seed cleaner or a clipper cleaner for peas would probably do a satisfactory job. The seeds should be promptly dried in rotary, direct gas-fired drum driers.

Solvent Extraction *versus* Pressing

A comparison was made of the oil from raisin seeds pressed commercially and that from the same lot of seeds extracted with gasoline. The free fatty acid contents of the two oils were 2.3 and 2.4 per cent; the Lovibond colors were 40 Y, 1.6 R, and 43 Y, 2 R, 0.5 B, respectively. In other words, the free fatty acid contents were similar and the solvent-extracted oil was slightly deeper in color.

In laboratory tests extraction by gasoline was somewhat more rapid where the seeds contained about 10 per cent of moisture than at higher or lower moisture contents. The solvent and the medium finely ground seeds reached equilibrium as to oil content in about 30 minutes' contact. If ground too finely the mass is difficult to handle in the extractor.

In Argentina, oils obtained by pressing and by solvent extraction are refined and used as edible oils. In Italy the refined oil is blended with natural oil for table and culinary use. Marx and Cruess (1943) refined a small sample of the grape-seed oil by neutralizing the free fatty acid and by deodorizing with steam in vacuo. However, the grape-seed oil takes up oxygen on prolonged exposure to air, becoming odoriferous and gummy. Hence, if used as an edible oil, it would be desirable to package it to exclude oxygen.

Composition of the Oil

Jamieson and Mackinney (1935) examined California raisin-seed oil, and Rabak (1921) Concord grape-seed oil. Early analytical reports indicated the presence of hydroxylated fatty acids, but Kaufmann and Sprick's (1938) data on the fatty acids and tests by Marx and Cruess indicate that the oils do not acetylate and are therefore probably free of hydroxyl groups. The iodine number of the University's samples ranged from 122 to 131, which should place the oil in the semi-drying class, although Jamieson (1943) classifies it as a drying oil. The saponification number of our samples ranged from 188 to 194, similar to that of many other oils.

Jamieson and Mackinney (1935) reported 2.1 per cent linolenic acid in the acids from saponification of raisin-seed oil. The data of Marx and Cruess, by the A.O.A.C. lead-salt-ether procedure, indicated that about 54 per cent of the total fatty acids is linoleic and about 31 per cent oleic. The ratio of oleic to linoleic was calculated from the iodine values; consequently it is probably only approximate. Flanzy and Flanzy (1959) reported 61.6 to 71.4 per cent linoleic acid, 13.8 to 28.2 per cent oleic acid and 10.2 to 14.8 per cent saturated acids in four samples of grape-seed oil. Similar results were obtained by Prévot and Cabeza (1962). The unsaponifiable matter was low (0.3 to 1.21 per cent). Crystals obtained from the acetylated nonsaponifiable fraction melted at 264.9°F., indicating the presence of sitosterol. Others have also reported this compound. Silvestre (1953) reported tocopherols in grape seed oil. Flanzy and Dubois (1964) reported 0.05 to 0.07 per cent in the oil of seeds of Carignane and Mourastel and 0.026 per cent in a commercial oil. According to Dubois (1964A), they are the principal natural polyphenolic anti-oxidants of the grape-seed oil. There is thus a marked decrease in tocopherols at temperatures above 149°F. A synergistic effect on the anti-oxidant property of tocopherols appears to be exercised by phospholipides, Dubois (1964B).

Egorov and Borisova (1955) isolated protocatechualdehyde, vanillin, cinnamaldehyde and possibly coniferyl aldehyde from grape seeds.

In general, grape-seed oil resembles soybean oil in make-up and behavior. It has given good results in paint tests when mixed with 75 per cent of linseed oil. The oil absorbed one-half as much oxygen in film tests as did linseed oil (7.5 and 15 per cent, respectively).

Tannin

In France, Australia, and Italy, tannin is extracted from grape seeds for use in wine making. However, in the seeds used in our studies (from dessert-wine wineries) there were only very small amounts of tannin (less than 0.3 per cent). In seeds from an unwashed unfermented white dry-wine pomace it was over 3 per cent as judged by extraction with 60 per cent alcohol. If seeds from unfermented pomace were collected separately, and the oil solvent-extracted by gasoline, tannin could be extracted with alcohol or acetone from the residue. This does not seem very practicable under present conditions. Also, the use of dark brown colored grape-seed tannin in wine making is not legal in the United States (U. S. Internal Revenue Service 1943).

Disposal of Residue

The extracted, ground seeds are steam-distilled to recover the solvent. However, there would probably be enough high-boiling petroleum residue to render the meal unpalatable to livestock. Nevertheless, if dehydrated to low moisture content, it might find some use in that direction, although it is very high in crude fiber and would, therefore, require mixing with feeds of lower crude-fiber content. Probably its best disposition is to spread it rather sparingly on the soil and plow it under.

On the other hand, if the seeds were decorticated (hulled) and only the kernels used for oil extraction by pressing, a valuable press cake for feeding would result. This is, however, more easily said than done.

With the return of normal supplies of other oils since the war, one seriously doubts whether wine-grape-seed oil production will attain much importance.

USE OF POMACE FOR STOCK FEED

Several large wineries and others have dehydrated winery pomace to low moisture content and ground it for use in feeding live stock, particularly dairy cows. The principal defect of winery pomace for use as stock feed is its very high crude fiber content, largely the indigestable hulls of the seeds. Therefore, it cannot be fed safely as the sole feed, but at best as a supplemental feed. One dairyman mixed it with bran in preparing a wet mash.

The analysis on the tags attached to bags of one producer's dried ground pomace was: crude protein not less than 11.08 per cent; crude fat not less than 6 per cent; crude fiber not over 40 per cent; and crude ash not over 8 per cent. Other crude fiber determinations reported by commercial chemists showed an apparent crude fiber content below 30 per cent. Six dried pomace samples from dessert wineries of the Lodi area showed moisture contents from 2.6 to 8.1 per cent; ash 4.7 to 8.1 per cent; oil 3.7 to 6.4 per cent; crude protein 11 to 12.7 per cent; crude fiber 31.3 to 40.9 per cent; reducing sugars 0.40 to 1.4 per cent; and 7.4 to 7.9 per cent "starch" (on acid hydrolysis). Sixteen other samples showed crude fiber of 26.2 to 38.8 per cent and oil 3.3 to 7.4 per cent; the averages being oil 4.52 per cent and crude fiber 34.02 per cent. The composition of 160 samples of dehydrated grape pomace meal[1] ranged from 3.26 per cent to 9.59 per cent in moisture content, 5.01 to 9.64 per cent in ash content, 12.05 to 14.88 per cent in protein content, 5.63 to 8.97 per cent in fat content and 17.74 to 34.99 per cent in fiber content. The averages were: moisture 5.10 per cent, ash 6.42 per cent, protein 13.45 per cent, fat 7.35 per cent, and fiber 26.94 per cent. Analyses[1] of four samples of washed, dried seeds gave an average crude fiber content of 53 per cent.

Sémichon (1907) in France called attention to the value of grape pomace as a stock feed. The French considered the dried pomace of about the same feeding value as meadow hay; but experiments by Folger (1940) indicated that it is no better than good quality wheat straw in feeding value. Nevertheless, several dairymen have mixed the ground dried pomace with molasses and used it as a supplementary feed. See Latreto (1953).

Rotary, direct-fired drum driers are used for drying the pomace. The usual drum resembles a cement kiln and is about 6 to 8 feet in diameter and about 60 to 70 feet long. It is inclined, the pomace entry port being at the higher end and exit port at the lower. A gas or crude oil burner throws a generous flame into the upper end of the drier and a large fan draws a blast of air that mixes with the products of combustion and carries the spent gases and moisture vapor out the cooler end of the drier. The wet pomace drops into the hot air and combustion gases zone at the furnace end of the tunnel; the estimated temperature at this point is above 1000°F. Evaporation is very rapid and cools the pomace, preventing much scorching; although some skins dry instantly and then scorch.

The bone-dry pomace passes through a hammer mill which grinds it to a meal. The meal may or may not then be admixed continuously and mechanically with a small amount of molasses to improve its palatability and carbohydrate content.

The dried, ground pomace must be low in moisture (preferably not about 6 per cent), otherwise it will be subject to spoilage. On the basis of

---

[1] Data furnished by the Roma Wine Co., Fresno, California.

63 per cent moisture content—the average for samples analyzed in 1938 and 1939—a ton of fresh pomace would yield about 775 lbs. of dried pomace of 5 per cent moisture content; a ton of pomace of 50 per cent moisture would yield about 1050 lbs. of dry pomace of 5 per cent moisture. Agostini (1964) reported pomace may be improved as a cattle feed if lime is added to raise the pH.

USE OF POMACE AND STILLAGE AS FERTILIZERS

Jacob and Proebstring (1937) found that winery pomace has about the same ultimate fertilizing value as barnyard manure, although it becomes available more slowly. They reported 1.5 to 2.5 per cent nitrogen, about 0.5 per cent phosphorus and 1.5 to 2.5 per cent of potassium on a dry-weight basis. It also improves the physical texture of heavy soils. Pirrone (1958) preferred composting before spreading.

They found that very heavy applications of still slops created a temporary toxic condition in the soil; sometimes killing plants. Seepage along the hard pan from a settling basin has killed vines at a considerable distance from the basin. Evidently toxic substances are formed during early stages of decomposition. That the toxicity is temporary is shown by the fact that after old slop settling basins have dried and stood several months, growth of grass and weeds in the basin is very luxuriant during the ensuing spring. Probably if the slops were put through a sewage treating system, such as a trickle filter, and were limed to recover tartrate before sewage treatment, the effluent would be useful and safe in irrigation if not applied in excessive amounts.

DISPOSAL OF DISTILLERY SLOPS AND STEMS

Distillery slops disposal is a serious problem. Past practice has been to run the slops into basins, each perhaps a quarter of an acre in extent. While one is filling, the slops in several others are evaporating and sinking into the soil and subsoil. Highly offensive odors develop and certain insects propagate by the millions in the standing liquid. Often nearby residents complain of the stench.

The disposal of distillery slops by intermittent irrigation is much preferable to the basin method and is discussed in Chapter 6. For determination of tartrates in slops and stems see Amerine (1965), Marsh (1942), and Marsh and Vaughn (1944).

Stems.—The utilization and disposal of stems have been discussed previously (see p. 249).

Amerine and Bailey (1960) found the reducing sugar content of the main stem of the cluster to be 0.08 to 0.70 gm. per 100 gm., while that in the side stems varied from 0.15 to 0.40 gm. Sucrose in the main stem fluctuated from 0.04 to 1.4 gm. per 100 gm. and from 0.12 to 0.197 in the side stems. Starch in the main stem amounted to 2.37 to 7.09 gm. and from 1.94 to 5.20 in the branches. Their results indicate that appreciable amounts of fermentable carbohydrate can be recovered from the stems.

Schreffler (1954) has reported on a method of handling waste stems from a large winery by which distilling material is obtained and a previous cost of disposal of $75 to $100 a day avoided. The stems are disintegrated in a Rietz hammer mill, Fig. 63. Water is added automatically during disintegration. The ground stems are drained and the resulting liquid is used in extracting pomace for distilling material. An average of 16.3 proof gallons of brandy was obtained per ton of stems; or about 0.5 proof gallon per ton of grapes crushed.

WINE VINEGAR

Considerable wine vinegar is made in California. One large plant was devoted solely to this product and several wineries and vinegar plants make moderate amounts of vinegar from wine. Red wine vinegar is more in demand than the white.

If table wine is exposed to the air, various species of acetic bacteria develop and convert the alcohol into acetic acid; that is they cause acetification. As defined in the Food, Drug and Cosmetic Act, grape vinegar or wine vinegar is made by the alcoholic and subsequent acetous (acetic) fermentation of the juice of grapes and must contain at 68°F. more than 1 gm. of grape solids, more than 0.13 gm. of grape ash and at least 4 gm. of acetic acid per 100 ml. Vinegar made from diluted distilled alcohol from any source, such as brandy made from wine, must be called spirit vinegar or distilled vinegar. The vinegar bacteria have been described in Chapter 16 and by Vaughn (1942).

Slow Methods of Acetification

Acetification is an oxidation process, essentially according to the reaction:

$$C_2H_5OH + O_2 \rightarrow CH_3CO_2H + H_2O$$

There are three general methods of vinegar making or acetification in commercial use, namely, the slow process, the generator and the submerged culture tank process. For more detailed discussion see Carpentieri (1947), Maestro (1952), Mitchell (1926), and Pacottet and Guittonneau (1926).

In the slow process barrels of wine are left partially filled with the bung open until the wine changes to vinegar of its own accord. An abundant supply of air is necessary. The bung hole should be plugged with cotton or covered with fine screen to exclude vinegar flies. If the wine becomes covered with a film yeast acetification may be very slow and much alcohol wasted by the film yeast. If the alcohol content of the wine is too high acetification will also be slow. Lactic bacteria may then develop and damage the flavor of the vinegar.

A better slow process is that known as the "Orleans" system. The barrels are filled about three-fourths full and holes are bored in both ends of the barrel slightly about the surface of the liquid. The bunghole is left open and all openings are screened. The wine should be diluted to ten per cent alcohol if necessary. To the wine is added from one-fourth to one-fifth its volume of new wine vinegar to serve as an inoculum and to raise the acetic acid content sufficiently to prevent the growth of film yeast. A temperature of 70° to 85°F. should be maintained. Acetification will usually be complete within three months. One-fourth to one-third of the vinegar is drawn off and replaced with wine of about ten per cent alcohol. Normally thereafter from one-fourth to one-third of the contents of the barrels may be drawn off and replaced with wine 3 or 4 times a year. The Orleans process results in aging as well as acetification and therefore usually produces a vinegar of superior flavor and general quality.

Generator Process

The rate of acetification is proportional to the oxygen supply. Therefore, if the surface to volume ratio is increased the rate is correspondingly increased. The generator process makes use of this principle. The "old style" vinegar generator consists of a cylindrical wooden tank, 48 to 60 inches in diameter and about 10 to 14 feet in height, divided into three compartments. The central compartment occupies most of the volume and is filled with beechwood shavings, pieces of coke, corn cobs, rattan, or other suitable material. The uppermost compartment has a perforated head over which the incoming wine is distributed by a tilting trough or by sprinkler head. The lowermost compartment is a receiving chamber for the acetified liquid.

The wine trickles slowly downward over the filling material on which the vinegar bacteria develop. Usually an equal volume of vinegar is added to the wine before it enters the generator. One passage through the generator will then usually complete the acetification. The generator operates more satisfactorily on such a mixture than on wine only.

The modern vinegar generator is usually of the recirculating type. It consists of a much larger tank than the old style generator. The bottom compartment is large and may hold several thousand gallons of wine or other vinegar stock. The liquid is delivered by pump from the lower compartment to the sprinkling device in the uppermost compartment. The liquid trickles downward over the coke or shavings into the lower compartment from which it is pumped continuously to the distributor. Acetification is rapid. When it is completed a fresh lot of wine replaces about two-thirds of that in the generator. Some cooling of the liquid is usually necessary as the acetification is an exothermic reaction. In this generator, and in the old style generators as well, considerable alcohol is lost by evaporation, by oxidation to carbon dioxide and water and by utilization by the bacteria for growth.

Tank Process

Vinegar making by the submerged acetification process is now coming into commercial use. It has been described by Joslyn (1955). In this method air in the form of very fine bubbles is passed through the vinegar stock (wine in this instance). Vinegar bacteria growing in the liquid conduct rapid acetification. The process is efficient and rapid; but the bacteria must be in contact with the air bubbles *continuously*, as they die rapidly if the air supply is cut off. Joslyn (1955) states that the latest Frings generators are of this type. There is very little loss of alcohol. Several California wineries have vinegar generators of this type.

Aging

Freshly-made vinegar is often harsh in taste and odor. On aging for several months in well-filled barrels or tanks it becomes more mellow in flavor. Aging is in part due to the formation of esters.

Vinegar is often clarified by fining, in much the same manner as wine. Bentonite is the usual clarifying agent, although casein or gelatin plus tannin can also be used. If the vinegar is reasonably clear, filtration alone may be sufficient. The filter should be made of stainless steel, or hard rubber, or other material that will not be attacked by the acetic acid (see Chapter 7). Considerable clouding of vinegar because of excess copper or iron content has occurred. Fining with "Cufex" or other agent may be necessary in such cases as described in Chapters 6 and 15.

Vinegar is usually given a final polishing filtration to render it brilliantly clear. It may be flash-pasteurized and bottled hot to kill vinegar bacteria and thus prevent their growth and clouding of the bottled product. Addition of about 150 p.p.m. of sulfur dioxide at the time of bottling may be made instead of pasteurization. For further information see Cruess (1958), Joslyn (1955), Mitchell (1926), Saywell (1934), or Smock and Neubert (1950).

CONCENTRATE

While the principal use for grape concentrate in California has been to sweeten dessert wines, there is a potential demand for concentrate of high quality for other purposes. It is used for blending with other concentrates, particularly frozen pack Concord grape, and orange, and other frozen concentrates. These may be processed into jellies, beverages, bakery products, etc. For data on the European industry see Mensio (1929).

Discontinuous Process

In making a white concentrate the free-run fresh juice should be treated overnight with a pectic enzyme as described in Chapter 6, filtered and concentrated in a modern, low-temperature vacuum concentrator. A small amount, about 125 p.p.m. of sulfur dioxide should be added to the crushed grapes in order to prevent undue browning of the juice. With high acid grapes some favor detartrating with calcium carbonate prior to concentration. Clarification by fining with bentonite is also practiced.

To make a red juice for concentrate the crushed and stemmed grapes are heated to about 140°F. but not above 145°F. because of damage to flavor at higher temperatures. Heating can be done in large stainless steel kettles as in the making of Concord juice in the eastern United States, or may be done in lined or stainless metallic tanks by continuously drawing off the free-run juice, heating it in a heat interchanger (continuous-type pasteurizer), such as the plate type pasteurizer used for wine pasteurization, and recirculating the heated juice over the crushed grapes. This is continued until the crushed grapes and juice reach 140°F. The free-run is drawn off and the grapes pressed in a basket, Willmes, or rack-and-cloth press. The juices may be mixed and should then be cooled by a heat interchanger with water cooled plates or tubes to near room temperature. The juice may be treated overnight with a pectic enzyme and filtered. Pectic enzyme treatment greatly facilitates filtration of the juice and prevents jellying of the concentrate. Bentonite fining is also recommended. In most cases the pomace is not pressed but is used for making distilling material.

Continuous Process

A continuous method of extraction of juice and color from red grapes in commercial use in a California winery has been described by Nury (1957). The stemmed, crushed grapes are pumped continuously through a heat exchanger in which they are heated for a short time (about two minutes) to 190° to 200°F. They then pass through a second heat exchanger in which they are cooled to about 100°F. A solution of a pectic enzyme is added continuously to the stream of cooled must. The juice is allowed to drain from the skins and seeds in special tanks and is then screened to remove suspended materials (fines). The drained pomace is pressed in a continuous press. The juice may then be filtered or clarified if a clear concentrate is desired. Nury reports that concentrate made by this procedure is much superior in color and flavor to that made from juice extracted by the discontinuous heat extraction process. Berg (1950) and Berg and Marsh (1950) have also described a similar procedure for extraction of color and juice from grapes for the production of red wine.

Cream of tartar slowly separates from grape concentrate and its removal is a difficult problem. Consequently the excess should be removed before concentration by cooling the juice to near its freezing point, storing it at or below 32°F. for about two weeks and filtering it cold. Even this treatment does not remove all of the excess cream of tartar. A better pretreat-

Courtesy of Valley Foundry and Machine Works, Inc.

FIG. 138. SIXTY-INCH DIAMETER STAINLESS STEEL VACUUM PAN WITH STEAM JET VACUUM PUMP AND BAROMETRIC CONDENSER

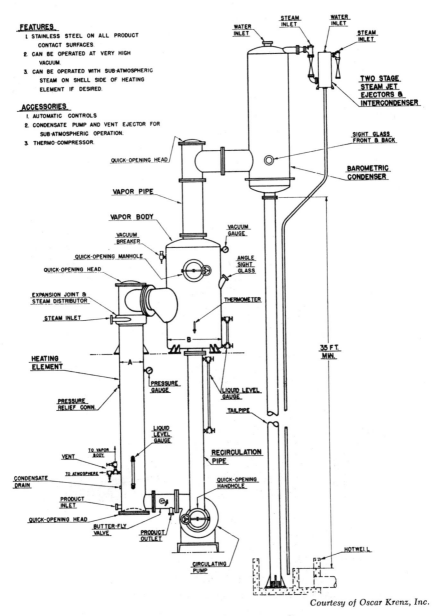

FEATURES
1. STAINLESS STEEL ON ALL PRODUCT CONTACT SURFACES.
2. CAN BE OPERATED AT VERY HIGH VACUUM.
3. CAN BE OPERATED WITH SUB-ATMOSPHERIC STEAM ON SHELL SIDE OF HEATING ELEMENT IF DESIRED.

ACCESSORIES
1. AUTOMATIC CONTROLS
2. CONDENSATE PUMP AND VENT EJECTOR FOR SUB-ATMOSPHERIC OPERATION.
3. THERMO-COMPRESSOR.

WATER INLET
STEAM INLET
WATER INLET
STEAM INLET

TWO STAGE STEAM JET EJECTORS & INTERCONDENSER

SIGHT GLASS FRONT & BACK

BAROMETRIC CONDENSER

QUICK-OPENING HEAD

VAPOR PIPE

VAPOR BODY

VACUUM BREAKER

VACUUM GAUGE

QUICK-OPENING MANHOLE

ANGLE SIGHT GLASS

QUICK-OPENING HEAD

EXPANSION JOINT & STEAM DISTRIBUTOR

STEAM INLET

THERMOMETER

HEATING ELEMENT

35 FT. MIN.

A

B

PRESSURE GAUGE

LIQUID LEVEL GAUGE

PRESSURE RELIEF CONN.

LIQUID LEVEL GAUGE

TAIL PIPE

VENT

TO VAPOR BODY

RECIRCULATION PIPE

TO ATMOSPHERE

CONDENSATE DRAIN

QUICK-OPENING HANDHOLE

PRODUCT INLET

QUICK-OPENING HEAD

BUTTER-FLY VALVE

PRODUCT OUTLET

CIRCULATING PUMP

HOTWELL

Courtesy of Oscar Krenz, Inc.

FIG. 139.   MODERN FORCED CIRCULATION CONCENTRATOR

ment is that with a cation ion exchange resin as outlined in Chapters 6 and 15. The cation resin in the sodium form rather than the hydrogen should be used. It replaces much of the potassium of the cream of tartar with sodium, the resulting sodium bitartrate being soluble in the concentrate. One large company is treating all of its juice to be used for concentrate in this manner.

The clear stabilized juice is now ready for concentration by vacuum pan. In order to prevent heat damage a low temperature and high vacuum should be used during concentration. A stainless steel vacuum pan, Figs. 138 and 139, with a continuous outside heating unit is preferred. The juice is flash-heated and enters the vacuum pan as a spray as the pan is under very high vacuum. The juice and concentrate are at not above 120°F. in the pan, usually at about 110°F. All metal equipment that comes in contact with the juice should be of corrosion-resistant metal or alloy.

Courtesy of Vie-Del Grape Products Co.

Fig. 140. Continuous Vacuum Concentrator

Types of Concentrators

Orange juice is concentrated in Florida and California in vacuum concentrating units of two types at temperatures of 60°F. and lower. In one type the concentrator is of triple effect, falling film design. Water at 90°F. is used as the heating medium in the first effect. Water vapor from the first effect heats the second effect and vapor from it heats the third effect. The water used in heating drops to 80°F. in the first effect, after which it is returned to the jacket of the compressor used in compressing the vapor of the refrigerant, Freon. The liquefied Freon is used to cool water to 37°F. for use in the barometric condenser of the vacuum pan. The vacuum in the first effect is 29.125 in., in the second 29.44 in. and in the third 29.64 in. The temperature of the final orange concentrate is about 50°F. This is known as the Kelly-Howard or Carrier-Howard concentrator. It has been known for some time that grape concentrates produced at temperatures of below 100°F. have a fresh grape flavor and a greenish color. Matalas *et al.* (1965A) compared three concentrates produced at 69° to 71°F., 92°F., and 132°F. They found that the initial color of the product was proportional to the temperature.

In another type of vacuum concentrator ammonia is used as the heating medium. It is a multistage type and is a single effect in operation; that is all units of the concentrator are under the same degree of vacuum. The three stages are heated by warm ammonia gas direct from a compressor. The ammonia gas or vapor gives up its heat of condensation to the three boiling chambers in which the juice is being concentrated. Juice at room temperature flows under high vacuum into stage one and concentrate is pumped continuously from stage 3 at about 50°F. The liquefied ammonia is used to cool and condense the water vapor from the juice and is in turn vaporized. It then goes to a compressor and is compressed. From the compressor it flows at 105°F. to begin the cycle again. A two stage steam ejector removes uncondensible gases and maintains a very high vacuum in the concentrator. Multiple-effect evaporating equipment has been used by the sugar industry for a number of years. Nowlin (1963) has calculated that triple-effect evaporators would not be economical for the seasonal operations of the grape industry. However, double-effect installations appear economical. He estimated savings of about $5000 per season for a 500 gallons-per-hour capacity evaporator. See Beisel (1954), Cruess (1958), Heid (1943) and Heid and Kelly (1953) for further description of these two types of low temperature vacuum concentrators. See also Cross and Gemmill (1948), Kelly (1949), and Walker and Patterson (1955).

The degree of concentration will depend upon whether the grape concentrate is to be used soon, or is to be stored for several months. If it is to be used within a few weeks it may be concentrated to only 68° Balling; if it is to be held at room temperature for several months it may be concentrated to 72 to 74° Balling to prevent or minimize damage by fermentation. However at concentrations above 68° Balling there is serious danger of crystallization of dextrose (grape sugar) which may become so extensive as to convert the concentrate into a solid or pasty mass.

Konlechner and Haushofer (1959) were apparently the first to point out that quality concentrates must be stored at low temperatures ($32°F.$) for $60°-70°$ Brix concentrate and at $23°F.$ for $40°-65°$ Brix concentrate. Matalas *et al.* (1965B) also reported undesirable darkening of color when concentrate was stored at $86°F.$ The effect was greater the higher the temperature used for concentrating. The harmful effect was reflected in poorer quality wines produced from such reconstituted concentrates. They recommended storage of high quality concentrate at or near $32°F.$

Dimotaki-Kourakou and Kandilis (1964) added 1.5 to 2.5 per cent of concentrate to flour and successfully made bread from it.

Flavor Recovery

In concentrating under vacuum the juice boils and most of the volatile flavor constituents are lost unless special methods are used for their recovery. In several California fruit concentrate plants the vapor from the vacuum pan is fractionally condensed, the most volatile fraction being at a very low temperature. This fraction containing most of the volatile flavor constituents may be added back to the concentrate.

Another method described by Milleville (1944) consists in momentarily flash heating the juice to above its boiling point in a closed system and then passing it in the form of a spray into a chamber in which it flash boils and is cooled quickly to below the heat-damage temperature. About 30 per cent of the juice is vaporized. The vapor is fractionally condensed in such a manner that most of the volatile flavor constituents are held in a distillate equal to only about 1/150 of the volume of the original juice. The cooled juice, now stripped of its volatile constituents, is concentrated in a low temperature vacuum pan. The concentrated volatile constituents fraction may be blended with the concentrated juice. It may be blended with Concord grape concentrate, the blend diluted to $50°$ to $52°$ Balling and preserved by freezing. For use as a beverage one part of the concentrate by volume is mixed with three parts of water. For household use the concentrate of $50°$ to $52°$ Balling is packed in 6 oz. cans.

Plate type evaporators and essence recovery systems are now available. They are reported to be more economical in their use of steam. Other advantages of the plate type evaporator are the rapid start-up (compared to traditional tubular calandria), their adjustable capacity (by adding or removing plates), ease of shutdown and cleaning, and low liquid hold-up.

Recovery of the methyl anthranilate in grape concentrate production is more difficult since this ester is not very volatile. It is necessary to strip 25 to 30 per cent of the incoming juice even to attain 50 per cent recovery. In the traditional tubular calandria the essence-bearing vapors from the first effect are concentrated in a vapor feed column. With the plate type evaporators, the unit is arranged as a triple effect evaporator. The first effect evaporates about 25 per cent of the incoming juice and thus acts as a stripping evaporator. The available heat of the vapor is recovered as the vapor condenses in the steam chest of the second effect. The weak essence condensate is then fed to the liquid feed column. For a description of a highly versatile unit, see Anon. (1966).

For shipment to jelly makers or other large users the concentrate of 68° to 74° Balling may be packed in enamel-lined 30-lb. tins or in plastic lined metal drums. There is a growing demand for red grape concentrate for blending with Concord grape concentrate and for use in fruit punch syrup blends. Some interest is also reported in the use of grape concentrate for home wine making.

Use of Raisins

Occasionally in Europe, especially in years of short crops, raisins may be used to produce wines. While the general chemical characteristics of these wines appear normal, they usually have a distinct caramel odor and, unless especially treated, a darker color. They also show, according to Ournac and Flanzy (1962) a yellow-green fluorescent spot at Rf 0.5 instead of the normal fluorescent blue spot. For the use of raisins to produce syrups see Musco *et al.* (1954).

JUICES

While most fruit juices are considered primary products rather than by-products, some fruit wine producers and some vinegar factories also make unfermented fruit juices. At least one large winery in California produces unfermented grape juice commercially. See Cruess (1958) or Tressler and Joslyn (1954), for further information. European methods are described by Mehlitz (1951), Koch (1950, 1951), and Baumann and Schliessmann (1960).

Grape Juice

While Concord (*Vitis labrusca*) is used almost exclusively for making grape juice in this country, various varieties of V. *vinifera* are used in Europe. Certain direct-producing hybrids gave higher quality grape juice than that of Chasselas doré or Müller-Thurgau in the study of Huglin and Schwartz (1960). The best hybrids were Kuhlman 191-1, Landot 244, and Seyve-Villard 5276.

The grape juice industry of France depends to a large extent on desulfiting *muté* (highly sulfited grape juice). Flanzy and André (1959) constructed a continuous vacuum desulfiter operating at 112°F. If grape juice undergoes some fermentation, the aldehyde-bisulfite complex will be formed. This compound distills unchanged, according to Deibner and Benard (1954–1955).

Red grape juice can be made by crushing and stemming, followed by heating the crushed grapes to 140° to 150°F. to extract the color; cooling; treatment with a sodium cation exchange resin as described in Chapter 15, to prevent separation of tartrates in the bottled product; treatment with a pectic enzyme overnight; filtering; flash pasteurizing to 185° to 190°F.; bottling hot; sealing and cooling the bottled product in sprays of water. Most plants, however, still rely upon removal of excess cream of tartar and calcium tartrate by storage of the juice under refrigeration for several months. The ion exchange method is much less costly and much more effective.

Commercial pectolytic enzyme preparations sometimes are helpful in fruit and grape juice clarification and in the clarity of the wines but the results usually cannot be correlated with the methyl esterase (PE) or polygalacturonase (PG, whether of the endo- or exo-type) content of the enzyme, according to Joslyn et al. (1952), Berg (1959), and Marteau et al. (1963). The latter also found no direct correlation between speed of clarification and amount of methanol produced. Natural clarification of grape juices appears to be limited by their low endo-PG activity. The commercial preparations, on the other hand, appear to have a large excess of endo-PG activity and their efficiency seems limited by their PE activity.

Flanzy and André (1959) have studied the problem of desulfitation of muté to produce grape juice or for concentration. To reduce the sulfur dioxide to 100 mg. per liter, a vacuum of 200 mm. of mercury and a temperature of at least 122°F. was necessary. At greater vacuum more sulfur dioxide can be removed. More sulfur dioxide is, of course, removed at a low pH than at a high.

Kern (1964) showed that grape juices have a greater tendency to form hydroxymethylfurfural (hmf) than those of apples, oranges or black currants. Flash pasteurization at 189°F. for two minutes produces only traces of hmf. He set the level for quality reduction at 100 mg. per liter. To produce this amount grape juice had to be heated at 203°F. for $2^{1}/_{2}$ hours. However, a sensory difference is produced by heating for 30 minutes, even though only 4 mg. per liter is produced in this period. He believes that undesirable sensory differences are due to chemical changes induced by hmf or by changes in other components. In Kern's work with fruit juice (apple?), fermentation removed the hydroxymethylfurfural (hmf). No hmf was found in fresh grapes by Flanzy and Collon (1962B). It was found in grape juices heated at 176°F. for more than five minutes, in desulfited grape juice that had been stored three years, and in grape concentrate. Flanzy and Collon (1962A) consider the presence of hmf in grape juice to be evidence of poor handling techniques. Probably other compounds are also present.

The efficiency of pressure versus vacuum filtration of grape juice was studied by Harris (1964) but the latter is less versatile. He showed that pressure filtration is more costly, but, if used during the period when a winery is not using its pressure filtration equipment for wines, might be more desirable. He recommended enzyme treatment and relatively high temperature pressure filtration. The original paper should be consulted for details since his data admittedly apply to only a single grape juice under specified plant conditions. Costs of grape juice filtration appear to be about 1¢ per gallon. Garoglio and Stella (1964) also found DEPC useful in preparing nonfermentable grape juice. The technique was to filter and then add 25 mg. per liter of sulfur dioxide and 500–1000 mg. per liter of DEPC. In our opinion 500 mg. per liter of DEPC is an excessively high level for grape juice.

Berry Juices

Berry juices have been prepared by coarsely crushing, heating to 175° to 180°F. to extract the color; pressing hot; cooling; treatment with a pectic enzyme overnight; filtering; adding water and sugar in such proportions that a palatable beverage is obtained; flash pasteurizing and bottling or canning as described for apple and grape juices. Loganberries, Youngberries, sour varieties of blackberries, and red currants give very attractive beverages.

In European countries, particularly in Germany, Switzerland, Holland, and England, the Boehi (also called the Seitz-Boehi) cold process is used, particularly for apple juice. The juice is usually depectinized with a pectic enzyme and filtered brilliantly clear. It is then chilled; heavily charged with carbon dioxide and preserved by carbon dioxide and refrigeration in glass-lined steel tanks until it is to be bottled. It is then filtered through sterile germ-proof filter pads under aseptic conditions into sterile bottles and the bottles sealed with sterile closures. No heating is employed. Preservation in the bottle depends on removal of all yeast and mold cells by germ-proof filtration. Usually the bottled product is carbonated.

At present the best apple juices are produced by use of aroma concentrates and by flash pasteurization of the clear juice according to Wucherpfennig and Bretthauer (1964). Storage of opalescent juice, sterile filtration without enzyme inactivation and storage under carbon dioxide pressure (Boehi-process) are less satisfactory. See Tressler and Joslyn (1954) or Mehlitz (1951) for details.

BIBLIOGRAPHY

AGOSTINI, A. 1964. Utilization of by-products of vines and wines. Wynboer 32, No. 395, 13–16.

AMERINE, M. A. 1970. Laboratory Procedures for Enology. Associated Students Book Store, Davis.

AMERINE, M. A., and BAILEY, C. 1960. Carbohydrate content of various parts of the grape cluster. Am. J. Enol. 10, 196–198.

AMERINE, M. A., and WINKLER, A. J. 1942. Maturity studies with California grapes. II. The titratable acidity, pH and organic acid content. Am. Soc. Hort. Sci. 40, 313–324.

ANON. 1966. Grape and apple processing. Food Technol. 20, 49.

ARIES, R. S. 1957. Tartrates. Encyclopedia of Chemistry, G. L. Clark (Editor) Reinhold Pub. Co., New York.

BAUMANN, J., and SCHLIESSMANN, C. 1960. Gärunglose Obst- und Beerenverwertung. Gesundheitswerte und Herstellung von Obst-, Beeren- und Traubensüssmosten. Eugen Ulmer, Stuttgart.

BEISEL, C. G. 1954. Vacuum concentration of fruit and vegetable juices. In The Chemistry and Technology of Fruit and Vegetable Production by D. K. Tressler and M. A. Joslyn. The Avi Publishing Company, New York.

BERG, H. W. 1950. Heat treatment of musts. Wines and Vines 36, No. 6, 24–26.

BERG, H. W. 1959. The effect of several fungal pectic enzyme preparations on grape musts and wines. Am. J. Enol. Vitic. 10, 130–134.

BERG, H. W., and MARSH, G. L. 1950. Heat treatment of musts. Wines and Vines 31, No. 7, 23–24; No. 8, 29–30.

BERRY, J. M., and VAUGHN, R. H. 1952. Decomposition of tartrates by lactobacilli. Proc. Am. Soc. Enol. 1952, 135–139.

BIOLETTI, F. T. 1914. Winery directions. Calif. Agr. Expt. Sta. Cir. 119.

BONNET, J. 1924. L'Olivier et les Produits de l'Olivier. J.-B. Baillière, Paris.

CARPENTIERI, F. 1947. L'Aceto. 7 ed. Ottavi, Casale Monferrato.

CELMER, R. F. 1943. Research on tartrates. Wine Review 11, No. 4, 12–13.

CHERSKI, E. 1943. Recovery of tartrates. Wines and Vines 24, No. 1, 19–20.

CROSS, J. A., and GEMMILL, A. V. 1948. Revolutionary evaporator raises quality and lowers costs. Food Inds. 20, 1421–23.

CRUESS, W. V. 1958. Commercial Fruit and Vegetable Products, 4 ed. McGraw-Hill Book Company, New York.

CRUESS, W. V., and WEAST, C. A. 1939. The utilization of pomace and still slops Wine Review 7, No. 2, 10–13, 27–28.

DEIBNER, L., and BENARD, P. 1954–1955. Recherches sur la séparation de l'acide acétaldéhyde sulfureux contenu dans les boissons alcooliques. Ind. agr. aliment. (Paris) 71, 973–978; 72, 13–18.

DIMOTAKI-KOURAKOU, V., and KANDILIS, J. 1964. Methode de constation de l'emploi du moût de raisin concentre dans la panification de la farine de ble. IV Congrès d'Expertise Chimique, Athenes, special no., 411–416.

DUBOIS, P. 1964A. Autoxydation des huiles de pèpins de raisin. I. Rôle des tocophérols. Ann. technol. agr. 13, 97–103.

DUBOIS, P. 1964B. Ibid. II. Présence d'un synergiste des tocophérols. Ibid. 13, 105–108.

EGOROV, I. A., and BORISOVA, N. B. 1955. Issledovanie aromaticheskikh al'chegidov semyan vinograda (Aromatic aldehydes in grape seeds). Vinodelie i Vinogradarstvo S.S.S.R. 15, No. 7, 36–38.

FLANZY, M., and ANDRÉ, P. 1959. Desulfitation des jus de raisin. Ann. technol. agr. 8, 171–192.

FLANZY, M., and COLLON, Y. 1962A. Sur la présence de l'hydroxyméthylfurfural dans certains jus de raisin. Ibid. 11, 227–233.

FLANZY, M., and COLLON, Y. 1962B. Sur l'origine de l'hydroxyméthylfurfural de certains jus de raisin. Ibid. 11, 271–273.

FLANZY, M., and DUBOIS, P. 1964. Étude du dosage des tocophérols totaux. Application à l'huile de pépins de raisin. Ibid. 13, 67–75.

FLANZY, J., and FLANZY, M. 1959. Note sur la valeur de l'huile de pépins de raisin en acides gras essentiels. Ibid. 8, 107–111.

FOLGER, A. H. 1940. The digestibility of ground prunes, winery pomace, avocado meal, asparagus butts, and fenugreek meal. Calif. Agr. Expt. Sta. Bull. 635.

GAROGLIO, P. G., and STELLA, C. 1964. Recerche sull'impiego in enologia dell'estere dietilico dell'acido pirocarbonico (DEPC). Riv. viticolt. e enol. (Conegliano) 17, 422–453.

GENEVOIS, L. 1934. La solubilité des tartrates de potassium et de calcium dans les solutions alcooliques acides, les moûts et les vins. Ann. brass. et dist. 32, 310–315, 326–328, 337–343.

HALENKE, A., and MÖSLINGER, W. 1895. Beiträge zur Analyse von Most und Wein. Z. analyt. Chem. 34, 263–293.

HALPERIN, Z. 1946. Tartrates recovered from winery wastes. Chemurgic Digest 4, 91–95.

HARRIS, M. B. 1964. Grape juice clarification by filtration. Am. J. Enol. Vitic. 15, 54–62.

HEID, J. L. 1943. Concentrating citrus juices by the vacuum method. Food Inds. 15, 7–8.

HEID, J. L., and KELLY, E. J. 1953. The concentration and dehydration of citrus juices. Canner 116, No. 5, 9–13; No. 6, 13–15.

HUGLIN, P., and SCHWARTZ, J. 1960. Essai d'obtention et de dégustation de jus de raisin à partir d'hybrides-producteurs. Ann. technol. agr. 9, 53–65.

JACOB, H. E., and PROEBSTRING, E. L. 1937. Grape pomace as a vineyard and orchard fertilizer. Wine and Vines 18, No. 10, 22–23.

JAMIESON, G. S. 1943. Vegetable Fats and Oils. Chem. Catalog Co., New York.

JAMIESON, G. S., and MACKINNEY, R. S. 1935. California raisin seed oil. Oil and Soap 12, 241–243.

JOSLYN, M. A. 1955. Vinegar. Encyclopedia of Technology. Interscience Encyclopedia, Inc., New York. Vol. 14, 675–686.

JOSLYN, M. A., MIST, S., and LAMBERT, E. 1952. The clarification of apple juice by fungal pectic enzyme preparations. Food Technol. 6, 133–139.

KAUFMANN, H. P., and SPRICK, M. 1938. Deutsche Trauben Kernelöle. Fette u. Seifen 45, 288–290.

KELLY, E. J. 1949. New low-temperature evaporator doubles plant production. Food Inds. 21, 1386–1389.

KERN, A. 1964. Die Bedeutung des Hydroxymethylfurfurols als Qualitätsmerkmal für Fruchtsäfte und Konzentrate. International Fruchtsaft-Union, Berichte wissensch.-techn. Kommission 5, 203–214.

KLINGER, E. 1921. Grape seed oil. Analyst 46, 138–141.

Koch, J. 1950. Über die Herstellung von Süssmost nach dem Böhi-Verfahren. Ind. Obst-Gemüseverwert. 35, 248–251.

Koch, J. 1951. Neuzeitliche Erkenntnisse auf dem Gebiet der Süssmostherstellung. Joh. Wagner & Söhne, Frankfurt/Main.

Konlechner, H., and Haushofer, H. 1959. Konzentrieren von Traubenmost. Mitt. Rebe. u. Wein, Serie A (Klosterneuburg) 9, 161–217.

Latreto, R. 1953. New method of developing fertilizer and compost values in winery pomace. Wine Institute, Tech. Advis. Committee, Mar. 9, 1953.

Maestro Paló, F. 1952. Vinagre. 2 ed. Semper, Zaragoza.

Marsh, G. L. 1942. Method of determining tartrate and calculations of the amounts of precipitants required for its recovery. Wine Institute, San Francisco. Mimeo. Circ.

Marsh, G. L. 1943A. Recovery of tartrates from winery wastes. Proc. Inst. Food Technol. 1943, 183–195.

Marsh, G. L. 1943B. Tartrate recovery from the dessert winery. Wines and Vines 24, No. 11, 14–16.

Marsh, G. L., and Guadagni, D. 1942. Extraction and recovery of tartrates from pomace of table wines. Excerpts from a report to Wine Institute, San Francisco.

Marsh, G. L., and Vaughn, R. H. 1944. Slop disposal system based on tartrate recovery. Wines and Vines 25, No. 6, 15–19.

Marteau, G., Scheur, J., and Olivieri, C. 1963. Le rôle des enzymes pectolytiques du raisin ou de préparations commerciales dans le processus de la clarification des jus. Ann. technol. agr. 12, 155–176.

Marx, C., and Cruess, W. V. 1943. Oil from wine grape seeds. Proc. Inst. Food Technol. 1943, 196–201.

Matalas, L., Marsh, G. L., and Ough, C. S. 1965A. The effect of concentration conditions and storage temperatures on grape juice concentrate. Am. J. Enol. Vitic. 16, 129–135.

Matalas, L., Marsh, G. L., and Ough, C. S. 1956B. The use of reconstituted grape concentrate for dry table wine production. Ibid. 16, 136–143.

Matchett, J. R., Legault, R. R., Ninimo, C. C., and Notter, C. K. 1944. Tartrates from grape wastes. Ind. Eng. Chem. 36, 851–857.

Mehlitz, A. 1951. Süssmost, Fachbuch der gewerbsmässigen Süssmosterzuegung. Drs. Serger and Hempel, Braunschweig, Germany.

Mensio, C. 1929. I Mosti Concentrati. Fratelli Ottavi, Casale Monferrato.

Mercer, W. A., and Vaughn, R. H. 1951. The characteristics of some thermophilic, tartrate-fermenting anaerobes. J. Bact. 62, 27–37.

Milleville, H. P. 1944. Recovery of natural apple flavors, Fruit Prods. J. 24, 48–51.

Mitchell, C. A. 1926. Vinegar, its Manufacture and Examination. 2 ed. Chas. Griffin and Co., Ltd., London.

Musco, D., Yanase, K., and Lee, L. J. 1954. Results of University of California studies on quality of syrups made from low-grade raisins. Food Packer 35, No. 12, 27–35

Nowlin, R. L. 1963. The economics of multiple-effect evaporation for production of grape juice concentrate. Am. J. Enol. Vitic. 14, 80–85.

Nury, M. S. 1957. Continuous color and juice extraction of grapes. Wine Institute, Tech. Advis. Committee, Dec. 6, 1957.

OURNAC, A., and FLANZY, M. 1962. Essais de caractérisation des vins de raisins secs. Ann. technol. agr. *11*, 33–43.

PACOTTET, P. and GUITTONNEAU, L. 1926. Eaux-de-Vie et Vinaigres. J. -B. Baillière et Fils, Paris.

PIRRONE, A. F. 1958. Composting of pomace piles. Wine Institute, Tech. Advis. Committee, May 26, 1958.

PRÉVOT, A., and CABEZA, F. 1962. Note sur la composition de quelques corps gras peu communs par chromatographie en phase gazeuse. Rev. Franc. Corps Gras [9], *3*, 149–152.

RABAK, F. 1921. Grape seed oil. Ind. Eng. Chem. *13*, 919–923.

RABAK, F., and SHRADER, J. H. 1921. Commercial utilization of grape pomace and stems from the grape juice industry. U. S. Dept. Agr. Dept. Bull. *952*.

SAYWELL, L. G. 1934. Clarification of vinegar. Ind. Eng. Chem. *26*, 981–982.

SÉMICHON, L. 1907. Dried grape marc as a feed for farm animals. Compt. rend. Cong. Soc. Aliment. Ration. Betail. *12*, 144–150.

SCHREFFLER, C. 1954. Recovery of sugar from grape stems. Wine Institute, Tech. Advis. Committee, Dec. 3, 1954.

SILVESTRE, J. 1953. Contribution à l'étude des tocophérols du pépin de raisin. Thèse, Faculté de Pharmacie, Toulouse.

SMOCK, R. M., and NEUBERT, A. M. 1950. Apples and Apple Products. Interscience Publishers, Inc., New York and London.

TABACHNICK, J., and VAUGHN, R. H. 1948. Characteristics of tartrate-fermenting species of *Clostridium*. J. Bact. *56*, 435–443.

TRESSLER, D. K., and JOSLYN, M. A. 1954. Fruit and Vegetable Juice Production. Avi Publishing Co., Westport, Conn.

U. S. INTERNAL REVENUE SERVICE. 1943. Circular No. 14-607, 14th District, San Francisco, Dec. 14, 1943.

VALEBREGUE, G. 1943. The production of oil from grape seeds. Wines and Vines *24*, No. 11, 24.

VAUGHN, R. H. 1942. The acetic bacteria. Wallerstein Labs. Commun. *5*, 5–27.

VAUGHN, R. H., and MARSH, G. L. 1943. Bacterial decomposition of crude calcium tartrate during the process of recovery from grape residues. J. Bact. *45*, 35–36.

VAUGHN, R. H., and MARSH, G. L. 1945. The disposal of winery waste. Wine Review *13*, No. 11, 8–11.

WALKER, L. H., and PATTERSON, D. C. 1955. A laboratory fruit-essence recovery unit. Food Technol. *9*, 87–90.

WUCHERPFENNIG, K., and BRETTHAUER, G. 1964. Beitrag zur Veränderung in Apfelsäften während der Lagerung. International Fruchtsaft-Union, Berichte wissensch.- techn. Kommission *5*, 105–130.

CHAPTER 19

Evaluation of Wines and Brandies

Examination of wines in the laboratory is a necessary and regular practice in all wineries and may include tasting and other sensory observations, microscopical examination, fining tests, and determination of such constituents as alcohol, total acidity, volatile acidity, sugar, extract, tannin, sulfur dioxide, and depth of color. These observations and analyses may be made for one or more of the following and other purposes; namely, to ascertain whether a wine is sound, to check the sensory quality of wines to be bought or to be sold, to aid in blending, to ascertain whether the fermentation of a dry wine is complete, and to guide the wine maker in ameliorating a wine, that is, for example, in deciding whether or not to add tartaric or citric acid, or tannin, or grape concentrate, etc.

SENSORY EXAMINATION

This is an important, although often neglected, cellar operation. Every winery should have on its staff at least one person who is responsible for collecting and evaluating the records of the sensory examination of its wines. He, or preferably a panel of tasters, should have a keen palate, discriminating judgment, know wines types, and be able, with reasonable accuracy, to classify the cellar's wines. Because a wine is white and dry is not sufficient reason for calling it a chablis! The tasters should know the characteristic flavor and bouquet of the types of wine which the winery produces. It is questionable whether familiarity with European types is of much value to California producers (or those of other non-European countries, for that matter). The climatic conditions, varieties, and processes used all differ so markedly that there is little resemblance between the wines (even when produced from the same varieties). This does not mean that our producers may not profitably taste European types. But they *should* develop their own standards of identity and quality. These may or may not resemble European wine types (see Chapter 1).

Troost (1965) stresses three different objectives of sensory evaluation of wines: (1) in the care of the wines at the winery, (2) for quality evaluation, and (3) by governmental food authorities. In the first case chemical analysis should be used to supplement the sensory data. As long as qualified personnel and adequate laboratory data (particularly stability tests) are available no difficult problems should arise. In the second case Troost (1965) especially calls attention to the difficulty when wines of different

678

regions or seasons are compared. He also emphasizes the psychological factors which influence tasters, particularly information as to source or price. In this case analytical data are of little value. Wines with the same analysis may have very different tastes and odors. As Troost notes, quality and market success are not necessarily related. In the third case (not used in this country), the tasters are asked to judge the relative merit of a group of wines in relation to normal conditions. Is the wine deserving of a "Spätlese?" Is the year a bad, good or excellent one? Analytical data are useful in reaching a decision, particularly for abnormal wines.

In spite of the wealth of information available on how to conduct sensory examination of wines Ough (1959) reported very haphazard practices in the California wine industry. The fact that only 25 per cent of the California wineries answered his questionnaire would indicate widespread indifference to critical sensory examination of wine in the industry.

Sensory examination may be for one or more of several purposes, namely, (a) to classify the wine as to type (as established by winery policy and practicability), (b) to detect incipient bacterial activity, (c) to evaluate the desirability or undesirability of constituents such as sugar, tannin, total acidity, for the wine in question, (d) to suggest necessary cellar treatment, (e) to decide whether the wine is "bottle ripe," and (f) to establish the quality of the wine.

Successful tasters should have good sense of differentiation of color, odor and flavor, and, as well, a good memory for these wine characteristics. The results of Filipello (1957A, B) as summarized by Filipello and Berg (1959) demonstrated that experienced judges were significantly better in wine quality evaluations compared to inexperienced judges. However, use of a reference sample was essential for both groups. Filipello also preferred attitude-rating scales to numerical scoring scales. Tasting should be done in a clean, neat, well-lighted room free of pronounced odors or distracting sounds.

Tasting Glasses

For all general tasting an 8 to 10 oz. tulip-shaped thin-walled glass is best. Silver cups may be useful for evaluating red colors but they are useless for critical tasting. Special glasses with very narrow openings are useful for judging aroma and bouquet but the large tulip-shaped glass is generally sufficient.

Appearance

The appearance of a wine will often tell the experienced taster much about its condition. White wines that have become brown are usually oxidized and overaged in odor, or so low in sulfur dioxide that oxidation has occurred. Or, a brown color in a white wine may mean great age; or, in a Madeira, normal color.

A silky, "wavy" sheen in a hazy or cloudy white or red dry wine accompanied by a characteristic odor is unmistakable evidence of bacterial spoilage. Once observed, this condition can always be recognized if seen again. Fortunately, it is now very rarely found in California.

If red wine is high in acid, it will have a bright red color. The depth of color is important in indicating its type. Also, the age of red wine is indicated by the tint; the older the wine the more the red color shifts toward the brown or brownish red. Old port is apt to be tawny in color; young port red or purplish red. Angelica and muscatel should be light gold or gold-amber in color; Madeira is light amber to brown. Chablis and Riesling should be pale yellow, sauterne more so. Sherry may range from very pale to a dark amber, depending on type (see pp. 144–145).

Ough and Berg (1959) showed that extremely small differences in color, as determined from tristimulus data, could be differentiated by their panel. A fluorescent light (Sylvania, 40 watt, cool white standard with white reflector) was significantly better for identifying small differences compared to daylight or incandescent light (a special 500 watt incandescent globe with a heavy blue filter). There was a one blend preference shift under fluorescent light compared to the other two. Orange tints were especially disliked under fluorescent light.

Odor

After visual inspection, the bouquet and odor of the wine are noted. The age of the wine greatly affects the bouquet and, with experience, the taster can tell much about the age of a wine by its bouquet. Even more important, slight vinegar souring or lactic souring can be detected, if present. Excess sulfur dioxide content or the presence of hydrogen sulfide can also be easily recognized.

Certain varieties of grapes impart characteristic aromas to wine; among the vinifera varieties e.g. muscat, Sémillon, Sauvignon blanc, White Riesling, and Traminer; and among the labrusca-type varieties, the Catawba, Delaware and Concord. Tasters should distinguish between bouquet and aroma. They designate as bouquet the odors developed by wine in normal aging through esterification, oxidation, etc., and aroma as the odor derived from the fresh grapes. There are also odors not due to either aroma of the grape or to aging: e.g. sulfur dioxide or hydrogen sulfide.

Taste

Following olfactory examination one proceeds to the evaluation of the taste. The four aspects of taste are sour, sweet, salty, and bitter. All of these have importance in wine tasting, though the salty taste is seldom encountered and is of least importance. The sour or acid taste is of value for all wine types, particularly table wines. A low acidity gives wines of a flat or insipid taste. Sweetness is, of course, most important for sweet table and dessert wines, but is also especially critical for sparkling wines. Red wines all have some bitter taste. The goal is a slight but not persistent astringent taste. Pangborn *et al.* (1964), using twelve highly trained judges, showed that increasing acidity interfered with sweetness perception and intensity. Caffeine reduced response to sweetness but bitterness perception was slightly enhanced by sucrose.

Flavor

Flavor is made up, in part, of bouquet and aroma, and in part by taste evident chiefly to the tongue. This may be the "over-all" impression of the wine. It is also completed by the after-taste—the sensory notes which linger on the palate after the wine is tasted or swallowed.

Tasting should be supplemented by chemical analysis if the tasting is of importance in connection with cellar treatment or purchase or sale of wine. Also tasting of a wine and subsequent checking with the analysis improves the taster's ability to judge wines and to detect incipient spoilage. It is advisable, as part of one's training in tasting, to taste and judge the same wines on several different dates in a blind tasting of several wines each time. By keeping notes on such tastings and comparing them, skill and confidence are increased. Wines for such tastings cannot be kept in a refrigerator since they will change when stored in less than full containers. The wines should be served at the same temperature, glasses, etc. for such comparisons.

Tasting is of great importance in blending, in deciding when a wine is ready to bottle or ship, and in deciding what cellar treatment is needed—if the taster knows his job.

Difference Tasting

In many cases it is desirable to determine if a sensory difference exists between two wines. If the difference is a *known* chemical difference the paired test is usually used. In this test the taster is presented two coded glasses containing the wines. A panel (or an individual) successfully differentiating the two wines a certain number of times establishes a certain probability of difference between the wines (Table 61).

Where the difference is a qualitative one a triangular test is commonly used. In this the two wines are poured into three coded glasses—one into two glasses and one into the other. If the wines are A and B six orders of presentation are possible: AAB, ABA, BAA, BBA, BAB, ABB. A panel (or an individual) identifying the odd glass a certain percentage of the time establishes a certain probability of a difference between the wines— Table 62. For further information see Amerine *et al.* (1959B, 1965).

TABLE 61

SIGNIFICANCE IN PAIRED TASTE TESTS[1] ($p = \frac{1}{2}$)

Number of Tasters or Tastings	Minimum Correct Judgments to Establish Significant Differentiation (one-tailed test) Probability Level[2]			Minimum Agreeing Judgments Necessary to Establish Significant Preference (two-tailed test) Probability Level[2]		
	0.05	0.01	0.001	0.05	0.01	0.001
7	7	7	..	7	.	..
8	7	8	..	8	8	..
9	8	9	..	8	9	..
10	9	10	10	9	10	11
11	9	10	11	10	11	11
12	10	11	12	10	11	12
13	10	12	13	11	12	13
14	11	12	13	12	13	14
15	12	13	14	12	13	14
16	12	14	15	13	14	15
17	13	14	16	13	15	16
18	13	15	16	14	15	17
19	14	15	17	15	16	17
20	15	16	18	15	17	18
21	15	17	18	16	17	19
22	16	17	19	17	18	19
23	16	18	20	17	19	20
24	17	19	20	18	19	21
25	18	19	21	18	20	21
30	20	22	24	21	23	25
35	23	25	27	24	26	28
40	26	28	31	27	29	31
45	29	31	34	30	32	34
50	32	34	37	33	35	37
60	37	40	43	39	41	44
70	43	46	49	44	47	50
80	48	51	55	50	52	56
90	54	57	61	55	58	61
100	59	63	66	61	64	67

[1] Source of data: Amerine *et al.* (1959B).
[2] $p = 0.05$ indicates that the odds are only 1 in 20 that this result is due to chance; $p = 0.01$ indicates a chance of only 1 in 100; and $p = 0.001$, 1 in 1000.

Scoring Wines Numerically

It is customary to assign a numerical score to each wine tasted in many wineries. With experience, and when one is in practice, it is possible to assign a fairly accurate score off-hand, after noting the appearance, bouquet and aroma, and the flavor of the wine. A score card such as the following may be used:

```
 (1)  Clarity and freedom from sediment . . . . . . . . . . . .   2
 (2)  Color (depth and tint and appropriateness, for type) . . . . .   2
 (3)  Aroma and bouquet . . . . . . . . . . . . . . . . . . .   4
 (4)  Freedom from acetic odor . . . . . . . . . . . . . . . .   2
 (5)  Total acid to the taste . . . . . . . . . . . . . . . . .   2
 (6)  Tannin (astringency) . . . . . . . . . . . . . . . . . .   2
 (7)  Extract (body) . . . . . . . . . . . . . . . . . . . . .   1
 (8)  Sugar . . . . . . . . . . . . . . . . . . . . . . . . .   1
 (9)  General flavor  . . . . . . . . . . . . . . . . . . . . .   2
(10)  Over-all  impression . . . . . . . . . . . . . . . . . . .   2
                                                                  ――
                                                                  20
```

Admittedly, this is an arbitrary score card, but it will aid in distinguishing wines of different quality. Where one has several wines scored by the same taster a number of times or by the various tasters it is possible to determine the probability that the average scores differ significantly from each other. See Amerine and Roessler (1952) or Amerine *et al.* (1959B, 1965) for the appropriate statistical procedures. Score cards should not have more than 20 steps and 10 is often sufficient. With a 20 step scale wines of 13 or more points may be considered commercially acceptable and with 17 points or over to constitute a quality product.

Use of an anchor or reference sample improved performance in comparison with a straight score card in some cases and not in others in the experiments of Baker *et al.* (1965).

TABLE 62

SIGNIFICANCE IN TRIANGULAR TASTE TESTS[1]

Number of Judges or Judgments	Minimum Correct Judgments to Establish Significant Differentiation ($p = 1/3$) Probability Level			Number of Judges or Judgments	Minimum Correct Judgments to Establish Significant Differentiation ($p = 1/3$) Probability Level		
	0.05	0.01	0.001		0.05	0.01	0.001
5	4	5	5	21	12	13	15
6	5	6	6	22	12	14	15
7	5	6	7	23	13	14	16
8	6	7	8	24	13	14	16
9	6	7	8	25	13	15	17
10	7	8	9	30	16	17	19
11	7	8	9	35	18	19	21
12	8	9	10	40	20	22	24
13	8	9	10	45	22	24	26
14	9	10	11	50	24	26	28
15	9	10	12	60	28	30	33
16	10	11	12	70	32	34	37
17	10	11	13	80	35	38	41
18	10	12	13	90	39	42	45
19	11	12	14	100	43	46	49
20	11	13	14	200	80	84	89

[1] Source of data: Roessler *et al.* (1948).

Hedonic and Flavor Profile

Another procedure for differentiating wines is the use of attitude rating scales such as hedonic score cards. The taster simply rates the wine on a scale of pleasantness or unpleasantness. A typical seven-step scale is:

1. Like very much
2. Like moderately
3. Like slightly
4. Neither like or dislike
5. Dislike slightly
6. Dislike moderately
7. Dislike very much

The steps can then be converted to scores, 1 to 7, and averaged and the averages treated statistically. For modifications of this see Amerine *et al.* (1959B, 1965).

A descriptive system using panel tasting has found commercial use for a number of food products. It has not yet been applied in its original form to wines but the descriptive score cards are similar in intent. See Amerine *et al.* (1959B) for a score card with suggested descriptive words. Rank-order procedures (Amerine *et al.*, 1965) were praised by Paul (1967) when the ranking was made on specified characteristics.

Frequency of Tasting

One thorough sensory examination by a panel is worth several superficial tastings. Normally a tasting every six months is sufficient. Previous results should not be available to the panel before or during tasting. Discussions after the results have been recorded however are often very useful. The tasting room should be quiet and individual tasting booths are very much to be desired for critical work. The panel members should be given time off from their regular duties and motivation by praise or extra compensation has been found valuable.

MICROSCOPICAL EXAMINATION

Microscopical examination will usually indicate whether or not fermenting must or wine contains spoilage organisms.

Musts

Usually no microscopical examination is made of fermenting musts unless a fermentation sticks or unless the volatile acidity of the new wines is abnormally high, indicating the presence of bacteria in the fermentations. If, however, the volatile acidity of the newly fermented wines is running abnormally high, microscopical examination of the original musts is advisable. A sample of the must from a vat or tank may be taken by bottle to the laboratory. There a drop or two of the fermenting liquid is placed on a clean microscope slide. A clean cover glass is placed on this drop of liquid and pressed down gently. The slide is placed under the high dry power of the microscope and the material between the cover glass and slide is brought into focus. See p. 587 and 594 for identification of the cause of the spoilage.

In a properly operated fermentation cellar, the fermenting musts and new wines should be relatively free of spoilage microorganisms. Most of them are very sensitive to sulfur dioxide and maintenance of as little as 100 p.p.m. of sulfur dioxide during fermentation will prevent their development. There is no excuse for their presence in excessive numbers.

Examination of Yeast Starters

Most large wineries grow starters of pure yeast in sterilized must or in must treated with sulfur dioxide and use the starter for inoculating crushed grapes or white musts (p. 259). In order to make certain that the starter is relatively free of contamination with *Acetobacter* sp., *Kloeckera* sp., *Pichia* sp., *Lactobacilli*, etc., the starter should be examined microscopically. Examination of a drop of the fermenting must with the high dry power of the microscope on a slide under a cover glass will indicate whether or not the starter is relatively free of these or other undesirable organisms. It will not show whether the original pure wine yeast culture consists of a single strain of the desired strain of yeasts since these strains so closely resemble each other that they cannot easily be differentiated under the microscope.

Wines

Microscopical examination of table wines during aging should be made at regular intervals, usually once every six months and fortified wines at least once a year. If the wine is heavily infected with bacteria, these can be seen by merely mounting a drop of the wine on a slide and examining it under the high dry power of the microscope. Usually, however, it is necessary to place a few ml. of the wine in a centrifuge tube and centrifuge it for several minutes. A physician's blood centrifuge, hand operated or motor driven, is very satisfactory for centrifuging wines for microscopical examination. The supernatant liquid is poured off and a drop of the sediment is mounted on a slide and examined without staining; or, if preferred, the drop may be dried and stained as follows:

Place a drop of the sediment on a slide. Pass the slide quickly above a small flame of a Bunsen burner in such manner that the liquid is evaporated but the dry material is not scorched. The slide should be heated only sufficiently so that it can be barely borne on the palm of the hand. When the sample has dried, apply a drop of dilute methylene blue or carbon fuchsin bacterial stain, prepared as described in any laboratory manual of bacteriology. Hold the slide well above the flame a few seconds to heat the stain to steaming. Let stand 30 to 60 seconds. Pour off the stain. Rinse under a tap of cold water. Dry the slide well above the flame and examine under the high dry objective of the microscope or under oil immersion.

The microscope will usually show the presence of lactic bacteria long before they have noticeably injured the wine. In fortified wines, the usual bacteria are of the "hair bacillus" (p. 590) type, that is, long chains of slender rods. For an excellent book on use of the microscope in the wine laboratory see Castelli (1969).

FIG. 141. HYDROMETERS FOR WINERY USE

From left to right: 0°–8° Balling with enclosed thermometer,
0°–30°, 12°–18°, 18°–24°, −5°–+5°

CHEMICAL ANALYSIS OF WINES

While sensory tests are indispensable chemical analyses are equally important. For most constituents they are paramount.

Recent suggested changes in methods of analyses at the international level are summarized by Anon. (1955), Jaulmes (1959), Joslyn and Amerine (1964), Amerine (1970), and Amerine and Joslyn (1970).

For general instructions on wine analyses, see Amerine (1965), Anon. (1953), Association of Official Analytical Chemists (1970), Beythien and Diemair (1957), Dujardin *et al.* (1938), Heide and Schmitthenner (1922), Hennig (1962), Joslyn (1970), and Vogt (1958).

Hydrometers

Hydrometers are used in the winery to measure the soluble solids content of fresh grape must or the fermenting must, the alcohol content of the distillate in the laboratory determination of alcohol in wines, the apparent sugar content of fortified dessert wines, and for other purposes. Those used in American wineries are of three types, namely, Balling (or Brix) hydrometers which indicate dissolved solids expressed as sucrose in 100 gm. of solution, alcohol hydrometers, which are calibrated directly in per cent alcohol, and specific gravity hydrometers, Fig. 141. The last-named

TABLE 63

SPECIFIC GRAVITY AT 60°F. CORRESPONDING TO READINGS OF THE BALLING HYDROMETER[1]
(Assuming specific gravity of water at 60°F. as unity)

Balling	Specific Gravity	Balling	Specific Gravity	Balling	Specific Gravity
Degrees		Degrees		Degrees	
0.00	1.0000	10.0	1.03933	20.0	1.0814
0.50	1.0019	10.5	1.0414	20.5	1.0836
1.00	1.0038	11.0	1.0434	21.0	1.0859
1.50	1.00575	11.5	1.0454	21.5	1.0881
2.00	1.0077	12.0	1.04746	22.0	1.0903
2.50	1.00966	12.5	1.0495	22.5	1.0926
3.00	1.01163	13.0	1.05153	23.0	1.0949
3.50	1.01356	13.5	1.05356	23.5	1.0971
4.00	1.0155	14.0	1.05556	24.0	1.0994
4.50	1.0174	14.5	1.05753	24.5	1.1017
5.00	1.01926	15.0	1.05943	25.0	1.1040
5.50	1.0212	15.5	1.06163	25.5	1.1063
6.00	1.02323	16.0	1.06386	26.0	1.1086
6.50	1.0252	16.5	1.0660	26.5	1.1109
7.00	1.02706	17.0	1.06803	27.0	1.1133
7.50	1.02906	17.5	1.0701	27.5	1.1155
8.00	1.0313	18.0	1.07233	28.0	1.1180
8.50	1.03336	18.5	1.07456	28.5	1.1203
9.00	1.03523	19.0	1.0769	29.0	1.1227
9.50	1.0372	19.5	1.07926	29.5	1.1251
				30.0	1.1274

[1] Source of data: U. S. Internal Revenue Service (1962).

is sometimes used in determining alcohol content of wines by distillation. Also, it is used very generally in European hard cider establishments in making determinations for which we would use a Balling or Brix hydrometer. Many special-purpose hydrometers are also occasionally used.

A hydrometer consists of a hollow cylindrical glass bulb weighted at the lower end with shot or mercury and attached to a long, narrow stem containing a graduated scale on white paper. The hydrometer sinks in a liquid until the weight of the displaced liquid equals that of the hydrometer. Therefore, it sinks further in a liquid of low density than in one of high density. The Brix and Balling hydrometers are identical in respect to the meaning of degrees Brix and degrees Balling; thus a pure sugar solution containing 20 gm. of sucrose per 100 gm. of liquid will read 20° Brix or 20° Balling. Both read 0° in distilled water at the temperature of calibration.

All hydrometers are based on specific gravity. Specific gravity of liquids may be explained as follows: pure water at standard temperature has a specific gravity of 1.000; in other words, it is the standard reference liquid in specific gravity measurements. Sugar solutions are heavier (of greater specific gravity) than water whereas alcohol solutions are lighter (of lower specific gravity) than water. Density and specific gravity, insofar as wines and musts are concerned, are more or less synonymous.

If one knows the weight of a measured volume of liquid, he can calculate its specific gravity from the formula $S = W/V$, where S is the specific gravity, W the weight of the liquid, and V its volume. Once the specific gravity of a must is known, its Balling (or Brix) degree can be found from tables such as those published in books on food analysis (see Table 63). Similarly, mixtures of pure alcohol and water vary in specific gravity with alcohol content, the tables are available showing alcohol per cent versus specific gravity (see Table 64).

Temperature greatly affects specific gravity; hence it must be determined simultaneously with the hydrometer reading. Temperature correction tables are available in books on food analysis such as the Methods of Analysis of the AOAC (1965). See also Tables 64 and 65. See Jaulmes and Marignan (1953), Anon. (1963), and Jaulmes and Brun (1963B) for details on temperature and volume corrections.

In using the Balling hydrometer the following procedure is followed. The sample of must or wine is poured into a hydrometer cylinder, which may be of glass, metal, or rubber, about 1.5 in. in diameter and about 15 in. high. In filling the cylinder tilt it to an angle of about 45 degrees and pour the liquid down the side of the cylinder in order that froth and bubbles do not form. Bubbles are apt to cling to the hydrometer and cause serious error. Insert the hydrometer and twirl it gently with the fingers to disengage bubbles and to assure a proper resting point.

TABLE 64

Proof	Alcohol Per cent by vol.	Alcohol Per cent by wt.	Alcohol Gm. per 100 cc.	Specific Gravity[1]
0.0	0.00	0.00	0.00	1.00000
1.0	0.50	0.40	0.40	0.99923
2.0	1.00	0.79	0.79	0.99849
3.0	1.50	1.19	1.19	0.99775
4.0	2.00	1.59	1.59	0.99701
5.0	2.50	1.99	1.98	0.99629
6.0	3.00	2.39	2.38	0.99557
7.0	3.50	2.80	2.78	0.99487
8.0	4.00	3.20	3.18	0.99417
9.0	4.50	3.60	3.58	0.99349
10.0	5.00	4.00	3.97	0.99281
11.0	5.50	4.40	4.37	0.99215
12.0	6.00	4.80	4.76	0.99149
13.0	6.50	5.21	5.16	0.99085
14.0	7.00	5.61	5.56	0.99021
15.0	7.50	6.02	5.96	0.98959
16.0	8.00	6.42	6.35	0.98897
17.0	8.50	6.83	6.75	0.98837
18.0	9.00	7.23	7.14	0.98777
19.0	9.50	7.64	7.54	0.98719
20.0	10.00	8.04	7.93	0.98660
21.0	10.50	8.45	8.33	0.98603
22.0	11.00	8.86	8.73	0.98546
23.0	11.50	9.27	9.13	0.98491
24.0	12.00	9.67	9.52	0.98435
25.0	12.50	10.08	9.92	0.98381
26.0	13.00	10.49	10.31	0.98326
27.0	13.50	10.90	10.71	0.98273
28.0	14.00	11.31	11.11	0.98219
29.0	14.50	11.72	11.51	0.98167
30.0	15.00	12.13	11.90	0.98114
31.0	15.50	12.54	12.30	0.98063
32.0	16.00	12.95	12.69	0.98011
33.0	16.50	13.37	13.09	0.97960
34.0	17.00	13.78	13.49	0.97909
35.0	17.50	14.19	13.89	0.97859
36.0	18.00	14.60	14.28	0.97808
37.0	18.50	15.02	14.68	0.97758
38.0	19.00	15.43	15.08	0.97708
39.0	19.50	15.84	15.47	0.97658
40.0	20.00	16.26	15.87	0.97608
41.0	20.50	16.67	16.26	0.97558
42.0	21.00	17.09	16.66	0.97507
43.0	21.50	17.51	17.06	0.97457
44.0	22.00	17.92	17.46	0.97406
45.0	22.50	18.34	17.86	0.97355

Source of data: Hodgman (1964).
[1] Referred to water at the same temp. Multiply by 0.99808 to convert to specific gravity referred to water at 4°C.

When the hydrometer has come to rest, read the indicated degree Balling at the bottom of the meniscus, that is at the general level of the surface of the liquid but not at the top of the meniscus. The meniscus is the surface of the liquid that climbs up the stem of the hydrometer because of surface tension. In other words, place the eye on a level with the general surface. The difference between the top of the meniscus and the general surface can result in an appreciable error.

Insert a thermometer in the liquid and note the temperature. Also note from the printing on the hydrometer its standard or temperature of calibration. By means of Table 65 or 66 make the necessary addition to the observed reading for temperatures above the standard and subtract if the temperature is below the standard. The table can be used even if the hydrometer is calibrated for different standard temperature than that of the table 68°F. as the following examples show.

Example 1.–For a hydrometer calibrated at 68°F. (20°C.) the observed Balling was 21.3° at a temperature of 77°F. (25°C.). The necessary correction is found as follows: the nearest degree Balling is 20° in the table. Follow down the 20° Balling column to 77.0°F. (25°C.) and note the correction which is 0.34. Then 21.3 + 0.3 = 21.6° Balling. Interpolation

TABLE 65

CORRECTIONS FOR BRIX OR BALLING HYDROMETERS[1] CALIBRATED AT 68°F. (20°C.)

Temperature of Solution		Observed Percentage of Sugar						
°C.	°F.	0	5	10	15	20	25	30
Below Calibration					Subtract			
15	59.0	0.20	0.22	0.24	0.26	0.28	0.30	0.32
15.56	60.0	0.18	0.20	0.22	0.24	0.26	0.28	0.29
16	60.8	0.17	0.18	0.20	0.22	0.23	0.25	0.26
17	62.6	0.13	0.14	0.15	0.16	0.18	0.19	0.20
18	64.4	0.09	0.10	0.11	0.12	0.13	0.13	0.14
19	66.2	0.05	0.05	0.06	0.06	0.06	0.07	0.07
Above Calibration					Add			
21	69.8	0.04	0.05	0.06	0.06	0.07	0.07	0.07
22	71.6	0.10	0.10	0.11	0.12	0.13	0.14	0.14
23	73.4	0.16	0.16	0.17	0.17	0.20	0.21	0.21
24	75.2	0.21	0.22	0.23	0.24	0.27	0.28	0.29
25	77.0	0.27	0.28	0.30	0.31	0.34	0.35	0.36
26	78.8	0.33	0.34	0.36	0.37	0.40	0.42	0.44
27	80.6	0.40	0.41	0.42	0.44	0.48	0.52	0.52
28	82.4	0.46	0.47	0.49	0.51	0.56	0.58	0.60
29	84.2	0.54	0.55	0.56	0.59	0.63	0.66	0.68
30	86.0	0.61	0.62	0.63	0.66	0.71	0.73	0.76
35	95.0	0.99	1.01	1.02	1.06	1.13	1.16	1.18

[1] Source of data: Association of Official Agricultural Chemists (1965).

TABLE 66

CORRECTIONS FOR HYDROMETERS IN DESSERT WINES AT 20 PER CENT ALCOHOL[1]

Temperature		Observed Balling					
°C.	°F.	0	2.5	5.0	10.0	12.5	15.0
		Subtract					
15	59.0	0.43	0.46	0.49	0.53	0.55	0.57
16	60.8	0.34	0.35	0.39	0.41	0.43	0.44
17	62.6	0.26	0.27	0.27	0.29	0.30	0.31
18	64.4	0.17	0.17	0.19	0.21	0.23	0.25
19	66.2	0.09	0.09	0.09	0.09	0.10	0.11
20	68.0	Add					
21	69.8	0.08	0.08	0.08	0.08	0.09	0.10
22	71.6	0.20	0.17	0.19	0.21	0.23	0.25
23	73.4	0.25	0.27	0.29	0.29	0.30	0.31
24	75.2	0.35	0.37	0.39	0.41	0.43	0.44
25	77.0	0.43	0.45	0.49	0.49	0.51	0.54

[1] Source of data: Jaulmes (1951).

between intermediate per cent sugar and temperatures may be made for even more exact corrections.

Example 2.—If the hydrometer is calibrated for 60° (15.5°C.) and the observed temperature is 79°F. (26.1°C.), then subtract 60 from 79, and 19°F. is the temperature correction to be made. Then 68°F., standard temperature of table, plus 19°F., 68 + 19°F. = 87°F., and the correction will be the same for your hydrometer as it would be for a 68°F. standard hydrometer read at 87°F. The table does not show 87°F., the nearest value being 86°F. But you can see from the table that each change of 1°F. in the table causes about 0.04° Balling (or Brix) change in reading. Then the correction is 0.71 + 0.04 = 0.75; and the corrected Balling or Brix degree is 21.3 + 0.75 = 22.05° Balling. Since the hydrometer is usually only read to 0.1° this is rounded off to 22.1°.

Extrapolation in similar manner can be made for other temperatures that may be slightly off the table or between those given in the table.

Table 63 will be found useful in showing the relation between specific gravity and degree Balling. This table is particularly useful in determining the dealcoholized extract content of wines.

Arnold (1957) confirmed the value of the refractometer for determination of approximate sugar content. Since the sugar values determined did not agree with the true values, a correction table and a temperature correction were developed. Generally in this country the refractometer is checked against a standard sugar solution and adjusted accordingly.

It has long been recognized that soluble solids measurements on grape musts are influenced by the presence of solid materials. Cooke (1964) showed that the hydrometer readings of unfiltered musts were 0.4° to 0.7° Brix higher than those of the refractometer. He emphasizes that an empirical correction of the refractometric readings is needed owing to the fact that the refractive index of dextrose and levulose is less than that of sucrose upon which the refractometer scale is based. This correction amounts to +0.3 for Brix readings of 15.0 to 15.5, +0.4 for Brix readings of 15.6 to 20.2, +0.5 for Brix readings of 20.3 to 24.7, and +0.6 for Brix readings of 24.8 to 29.3.

Acidity

The total acidity, volatile acidity, and pH of musts and wines are important in their rational handling and all wineries should have facilities for their rapid and accurate determination. For certain legal purposes and to follow changes during the malo-lactic fermentation the fixed acidity may be useful. This is usually obtained by calculation from the total and volatile acid determinations. A knowledge of the individual fixed acids, particularly tartaric, malic and lactic, is occasionally desirable.

The determination of the tartrate content by precipitation of potassium bitartrate was first used by Pasteur and has been modified by Nègre et al. (1958) and others. They proposed two bitartrate procedures which resulted in excellent recovery: (1) reducing 50 ml. of must (or wine) to 7 ml. and adding a 3.5 pH buffer and filtering after 4 days, and (2) using 20 ml. of must (or wine) adding alcohol to 16.5 per cent and a 3.8 pH buffer and proceeding as before. The first procedure was recommended. They showed that the presence of malic acid reduced the speed of precipitation of potassium bitartrate. Some entrainment of potassium malate occurs, but this is compensated by the solubility of potassium bitartrate. Sulfates and phosphates did not interfere unduly. Their procedure was comparable to precipitation of calcium racemate, and much more rapid.

There are numerous procedures for the determination of malic acid in musts and wines. See Koch and Bretthauer (1951) and Matchett et al. (1944). Peynaud and Blouin (1965) have compared five procedures (chemical, chromatographic, enzymatic, manometric, and microbiological). They recommend the microbiological procedure of Peynaud and Lafon-Lafourcade (1965). The enzymatic method of Mayer and Busch (1963) appears more precise, however, the report of Poux (1969) that L-malate dehydrogenase has some effect on tartaric acid casts doubt on this procedure. For details see Amerine (1970).

The total acidity includes the fixed and non-volatile acids. It is commonly measured in this country by titration, with phenolphthalein as the indicator. However, in large wineries potentiometric titration to a given pH, usually 8.4 is more rational. Titrimeters or even automatic titrimeters are very useful for this purpose. For the theory, see Koch and Schiffner (1957).

Have on hand 0.1 N sodium hydroxide, several 250 ml. Erlenmeyer flasks, a burette, a gas burner or hot plate, distilled water, 1 per cent phenolphthalein solution in 90 to 95 per cent alcohol (previously neutralized with sodium hydroxide), a 5 ml. pipette, and ring stand or other burette support. In a 500 ml. or larger flask boil several hundred ml. of distilled water. Pipette 5 ml. of the white must or wine into a 250-ml. Erlenmeyer flask. Add about 75 ml. of boiling water and five drops of phenolphthalein. Read the level of the 0.1 N sodium hydroxide in the burette. Slowly add to the sample sodium hydroxide until finally one drop gives a pink color that will last a minute or longer. Read the burette again. The ml. of alkali used times 0.150 equals the total acidity expressed as tartaric acid per 100 ml. If the standard alkali is not exactly 0.1 N, multiply the result by 10 times its actual normality. For example, if it is not 0.1 N, but is 0.12 N and 5.1 ml. of the alkali were used in the titration. Then 5.1 $\times$ 0.150 $\times$ 10 $\times$ 0.12 = 0.75 gm. apparent total acid per 100 ml. as tartaric acid. There should be always on hand some exactly 0.1 N hydrochloric or sulfuric acid with which to check the normality of the sodium hydroxide from time to time as it will decrease in strength with age.

For red wine, pipette 5 ml. into a 250-ml. Erlenmeyer flask. Add 100 ml. of boiling distilled water. Titrate with alkali to a bluish or blue-green color. Then add 5 drops of phenolphthalein and continue the titration to a pink end point.

If a titrimeter is used titrate to a pH of 8.4.

Volatile Acidity

The volatile acidity is a measure of the soundness of fermentation of a new wine and the keeping quality of older wines. An appreciable rise in the volatile acidity in a wine during storage indicates bacterial spoilage and usually the wine needs immediate pasteurization, or addition of 100 to 150 p.p.m. of sulfur dioxide or both. Small amounts of acetic acid are formed in normal alcoholic fermentation but sound, new wine should show less than 0.05 gm. of volatile acidity per 100 ml. and a sound aged wine less than 0.08. The present California legal maximum limits of volatile acidity are 0.110 gm. per 100 ml. for white wines and 0.120 gm. for red wines, exclusive of sulfur dioxide. Jaulmes (1959) proposed a limit of 250 mg. per liter for ethyl acetate in wines. This seems high to us. See Jaulmes et al. (1964) for a procedure for sorbic acid which partially distills as a volatile acid.

Have on hand a Horvet, Fig. 142, or other suitable volatile acid still (preferably the Cash modification, Fig. 143) consisting of an outer round bottom 1000 ml. wide-mouthed boiling flask, or a 1000 ml. wide-mouthed Erlenmeyer flask, an inner cylindrical tube fitted inside the boiling flask through a wide stopper (see Fig. 142) and connected to a vertically set Liebig condenser as shown in the illustration. Have on hand also a 10 ml. pipette, 0.025 N sodium hydroxide (or a solution of standardized alkali of from 0.01 to 0.05 normality), a burette stand, phenolphthalein indicator, heater for boiling flask, and cold water connec-

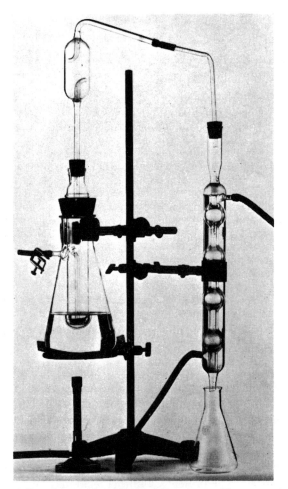

Fig. 142.   Simple Laboratory Setup for Volatile Acid
Determination

tion to condenser.   Set up the still as shown in the figure.   Start cold water
flowing through the condenser jacket.

Place 500 to 600 ml. of distilled water in the boiling flask and remove the
clamp from the short rubber tubing at side of flask.   Heat the water to boiling
for 2 to 3 minutes.   Reduce the heat.   Place a 250-ml. Erlenmeyer flask under
the outlet of the condenser.   Previously mark the 100 ml. level on this flask.   Introduce 10 ml. of wine by pipette into the inner tube.   Insert the stopper connecting it to the condenser.   Increase the heat and bring the water to boiling
and when boiling vigorously replace the clamp, thus closing the rubber tubing at
the side of the flask.   Continue boiling until 100 ml. of liquid distills over into
the 250-ml. flask.   Open the clamp on the side piece of rubber tubing so that
the wine will not suck back into the boiling flask and turn off the flame.

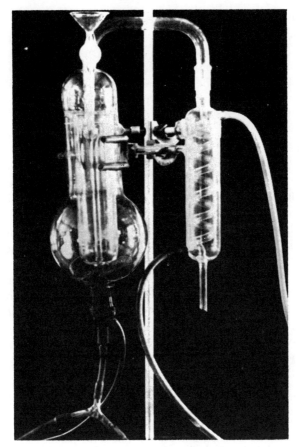

FIG. 143.   CASH VOLATILE ACID APPARATUS

Note electrical heating coil

To the distillate in the Erlenmeyer flask add 3 to 4 drops of phenolphthalein indicator and titrate to a definite pink color with the 0.025 N sodium hydroxide. Then, ml. 0.025 N sodium hydroxide × 0.015 equals grams volatile acid expressed as acetic per 100 ml.   For example, if 2.5 ml. of 0.025 N sodium hydroxide are used the grams of volatile acidity per 100 ml. expressed as acetic acid equals 2.5 × 0.015 or 0.037.   If the normality of the alkali is not 0.025 N multiply the actual normality by 10 and multiply by the above result.

Fixed Acidity and pH

⌈The total acidity less the volatile is called the fixed acidity.⌉ While there is some difficulty in expressing each exactly, the term has utility in indicating changes in the total non-volatile acid components.   Since the total acidity is usually expressed as tartaric acid, it is necessary to convert the volatile acidity (as acetic) to its equivalent as tartaric before making the subtraction. The volatile acidity × 1.25 will make the conversion.

The pH should be determined in a pH meter, not colorimetrically. The directions accompanying the meter should be followed carefully. A saturated solution of potassium acid tartrate (pH 3.57 at 68°F.) is used for standardization.

Alcohol

Alcohol can be determined by ebullioscope, or by specific gravity of the distillate from a measured volume of wine, or by chemical means by dichromate titration of the distillate from a measured volume of wine. For a comparison of procedures see Joslyn et al. (1937).

The ebullioscope method is based on the regular variation in the boiling point of mixtures of water and alcohol. Many of the ebullioscopes in use in wineries are of the Dujardin-Salleron type, Fig. 144. They are nickel-plated copper and consist of a small boiling chamber, a standard Centigrade thermometer, the bulb of which is inserted into the boiling chamber, a metal reflux condenser, a small alcohol lamp, a measuring cyclinder and a special slide rule, that has a special adjustable scale showing the relation between boiling point and alcohol of the sample. Similiar instruments are now produced in this country.

In using the ebullioscope for dry wine proceed as follows:

Place 25 ml. of distilled water in the previously rinsed boiling chamber. Insert the thermometer. Screw the reflux condenser in place but do not fill with water. Fill the alcohol lamp with 95 per cent denatured alcohol or use a micro gas burner. Light the burner and place it under the boiling spout of the ebullioscope. Heat the water to boiling and continue boiling until the height of the mercury column in the thermometer remains constant. In California wine making areas this will usually be about 212°F. (100°C.). Set the slide rule so that 0.0 per cent alcohol is opposite this temperature. The boiling point of water should be re-run once or twice per day, especially if the barometric pressure is changing rapidly.

Now empty the ebullioscope and rinse it with a few ml. of the wine sample. Discard the rinsings and pipette or measure with a cylinder 50 ml. of the wine sample into the boiling chamber. Insert the thermometer and screw the reflux condenser in place. Fill the latter with cold water. Light the alcohol lamp (or gas burner) and place it below the boiling chamber. Heat until the boiling point on the thermometer becomes constant. Read the temperature. Remove the flame. On the slide rule read off the per cent of alcohol opposite the observed boiling point of the wine. There are two alcohol scales on the slide rule; use the one which is labeled for wine. When used at maximum efficiency the ebullioscope should give values within 0.25 per cent above or below the true per cent alcohol content. With fermenting musts or sweet wines it is customary to accurately dilute the sample in a volumetric flask so that the extract content is

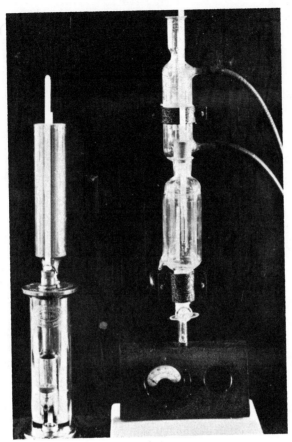

Fig. 144. Metal and Glass Ebullioscopes

Note rheostat for control of rate of heating with the latter

five per cent or less. The results must then be multiplied by the appropriate dilution factor.

More accurate results for alcohol are obtained by distilling the wine and using the distillate in the ebullioscope. An accuracy of ±0.15 per cent is possible by this procedure. The scale on the slide rule for alcohol is used in this case.

In using the ebullioscope for wines of low alcohol content care should be taken that the condenser has adequate cooling capacity. Itoga (1958) attempted to use the Tag Twin ebulliometer for beer but noted uniformly low results due to alcohol losses from the condenser.

To determine the alcohol by hydrometry proceed as follows:

Set up a small distilling apparatus consisting of a 500-ml. or 800-ml. round bottom Kjeldahl flask and connect it to a vertical condenser, both attached to a

heavy ring stand.   Place a gas burner or electric hot plate beneath the flask.
Place a 100 ml. volumetric flask under the outlet of the condenser.
   Pipette 100 ml. of wine into the distilling flask and add 50 ml. of distilled
water.   A better procedure is to fill a volumetric flask with the wine and bring it
to temperature and volume.   Then pour the contents of the flask into the distilling flask and rinse the flask three times with 15 ml. of water, adding the rinsings
to the distilling flask.   Use this volumetric flask to receive the distillate.   If the
wine is high in volatile acidity (above 0.10 per cent) neutralize the wine with N
sodium hydroxide to a pH of 7.   Start cold water flowing through condenser.
Heat the sample to boiling and boil until about 96 to 98 ml. of distillate collects
in the volumetric flask.   Using distilled water, bring the contents of the flask
to volume at the original temperature of the wine.   Then bring the contents
of the flask to a temperature as near to that of the calibration temperature of the
alcohol hydrometer as possible—usually 60°F.
   Transfer the distillate to a hydrometer cylinder and insert a clean dry alcohol
hydrometer.   Read the indicated alcohol content very quickly, yet accurately,
before the liquid can change appreciably in temperature.   Also take its temperature.   Make a correction by use of the temperature correction in Table 67.

   For slightly more accurate results one may use a pycnometer.   A pycnometer is a small (50 ml. usually), thin-walled bottle fitted with ground
glass stopper and accurate thermometer.   A rapid technique for use of the
pycnometer has been by Jaulmes and Brun (1963A).   The procedure is based on accurately measuring the temperature of the pycnometer
(made from specified glass) rather than bringing the pycnometer and its
contents to a specified temperature.   They prefer a pycnometer of Pyrex
glass and a thermometer calibrated to read to 0.02°C.

   Weigh the pycnometer when dry and empty, using an analytical balance and
weigh to 0.1 mg.   Fill with distilled water a degree or two below the standard
temperature, usually 60°F. (15.5°C.).   Insert the thermometer.   Bring the contents to exactly the standard temperature—in this example 60°F.   Wipe the pycnometer dry with a soft cloth and put the ground glass cover of the overflow
tube in place.   Weigh again very accurately.   These two weighings need be
done only once for a given pycnometer.   Thereafter one need only weigh the
pycnometer filled with the alcoholic distillate of a wine sample.
   Now empty the pycnometer.   Prepare the wine distillate as indicated above,
taking care to bring the contents to volume at the same temperature as used for
the original wine.   Rinse the pycnometer with a little of the distillate.   Cool the
distillate in the pycnometer to a little below the standard temperature.   Insert
and seat the thermometer.   Allow the contents to warm up to exactly the standard temperature—in this example 60°F. (15.5°C.).   Wipe the pycnometer dry
with a clean soft cloth.   Put the overflow tube's cap in place and weight accurately.
   Then calculate specific gravity of distillate as follows:

$$\frac{\text{Wt. of pycnometer with distillate} - \text{wt. of empty pycnometer}}{\text{Wt. of pycnometer with water} - \text{wt. of empty pycnometer}}$$

$$= \text{specific gravity of distillate}$$

TABLE 67

CORRECTIONS OF ALCOHOL HYDROMETERS CALIBRATED AT 60°F, IN PER CENT BY VOLUME OF ALCOHOL,[1] WHEN USED AT TEMPERATURES ABOVE OR BELOW 60°F.

Observed Alcohol Content	Add at			To or from the Observed — Subtract at															
Per cent	57°F.	58°F.	59°F.	61°F.	62°F.	63°F.	64°F.	65°F.	66°F.	67°F.	68°F.	69°F.	70°F.	72°F.	74°F.	76°F.	78°F.	80°F.
1	0.14	0.10	0.05	0.05	0.10	0.16	0.22	0.28	0.34	0.41	0.48	0.55	0.62	0.77	0.93	..	..	..
2	0.14	0.10	0.05	0.05	0.11	0.17	0.23	0.29	0.35	0.42	0.48	0.56	0.63	0.78	0.94	1.10	1.28	1.46
3	0.14	0.10	0.05	0.06	0.12	0.18	0.24	0.30	0.36	0.43	0.50	0.57	0.64	0.80	0.96	1.13	1.31	1.50
4	0.14	0.10	0.05	0.06	0.12	0.19	0.25	0.32	0.38	0.45	0.52	0.59	0.67	0.83	1.00	1.17	1.35	1.54
5	0.15	0.10	0.05	0.07	0.13	0.20	0.26	0.33	0.40	0.47	0.54	0.62	0.70	0.86	1.03	1.21	1.40	1.60
6	0.17	0.11	0.06	0.07	0.14	0.20	0.27	0.34	0.42	0.50	0.57	0.66	0.74	0.90	1.09	1.27	1.46	1.66
7	0.18	0.12	0.06	0.07	0.14	0.21	0.29	0.36	0.44	0.52	0.60	0.68	0.77	0.94	1.13	1.32	1.52	1.73
8	0.19	0.13	0.06	0.08	0.16	0.23	0.31	0.39	0.47	0.55	0.64	0.73	0.81	0.99	1.18	1.38	1.59	1.80
9	0.21	0.14	0.07	0.08	0.16	0.24	0.32	0.41	0.50	0.58	0.67	0.76	0.86	1.04	1.25	1.46	1.67	1.89
10	0.23	0.16	0.08	0.08	0.17	0.25	0.34	0.43	0.52	0.61	0.71	0.80	0.90	1.10	1.32	1.54	1.76	1.99
11	0.25	0.16	0.08	0.09	0.18	0.27	0.37	0.46	0.56	0.65	0.75	0.85	0.96	1.16	1.39	1.61	1.84	2.09
12	0.27	0.18	0.09	0.10	0.20	0.29	0.39	0.49	0.59	0.70	0.80	0.91	1.02	1.23	1.46	1.70	1.94	2.20
13	0.29	0.19	0.10	0.10	0.21	0.31	0.42	0.52	0.63	0.74	0.85	0.97	1.08	1.31	1.55	1.80	2.05	2.31
14	0.32	0.21	0.11	0.11	0.22	0.32	0.44	0.55	0.66	0.78	0.91	1.02	1.14	1.39	1.65	1.91	2.17	2.44
15	0.35	0.23	0.12	0.12	0.24	0.35	0.48	0.60	0.71	0.84	0.97	1.10	1.23	1.50	1.76	2.03	2.30	2.58
16	0.37	0.24	0.12	0.13	0.26	0.38	0.52	0.65	0.77	0.90	1.03	1.17	1.31	1.60	1.88	2.16	2.44	2.72
17	0.40	0.26	0.13	0.14	0.27	0.41	0.54	0.68	0.82	0.96	1.10	1.25	1.40	1.70	1.99	2.28	2.58	2.87
18	0.44	0.29	0.14	0.14	0.29	0.44	0.58	0.73	0.88	1.03	1.18	1.33	1.49	1.80	2.10	2.41	2.72	3.02
19	0.47	0.32	0.16	0.15	0.30	0.46	0.62	0.78	0.94	1.10	1.26	1.42	1.58	1.90	2.22	2.54	2.86	3.17
20	0.51	0.34	0.17	0.16	0.32	0.49	0.66	0.82	0.98	1.15	1.33	1.48	1.65	2.00	2.32	2.65	2.98	3.33
21	0.53	0.35	0.18	0.17	0.34	0.51	0.68	0.85	1.02	1.20	1.38	1.54	1.72	2.06	2.41	2.76	3.10	3.45
22	0.56	0.38	0.19	0.17	0.36	0.53	0.71	0.90	1.07	1.25	1.44	1.61	1.78	2.13	2.48	2.84	3.20	3.56
23	0.58	0.40	0.20	0.18	0.37	0.55	0.74	0.92	1.11	1.30	1.49	1.66	1.84	2.20	2.56	2.93	3.30	3.67
24	0.60	0.40	0.20	0.18	0.38	0.56	0.77	0.96	1.16	1.35	1.54	1.72	1.91	2.27	2.65	3.03	3.40	3.78

[1] Source of data: U. S. Internal Revenue Service (1962).

For example: (a), wt. of empty pycnometer = 12.8541 gm.; (b), wt. of pycnometer + water = 62.7937 g.; (c), wt. of pycnometer + distillate = 61.9451 gm.; (d), then (61.9451 − 12.8541)/(62.7937 − 12.8541) = (49.0910/49.9396) = 0.9832, the specific gravity of the distillate.

From a standard alcohol table for 60°F. (or from Table 64) find the corresponding alcohol content; in this case 13.1 per cent by volume. The alcohol of wines is always expressed in volume per cent that is, in ml. of alcohol per 100 ml. of sample. To transform it to approximate per cent by weight multiply it by specific gravity of absolute alcohol, 0.7938.

The alcohol content of the distillate can also be determined chemically by oxidizing an aliquot with a known volume of standard dichromate solution and titrating the excess dichromate with standard ferrous ammonium sulfate. As this method requires much experience in chemical analysis and is, therefore, somewhat beyond the scope of this book, those who wish to use the method should consult Amerine (1965), Fessler (1941), Guymon and Crowell (1959) or Jaulmes and Mestres (1958). The latter determined the specific conditions for the stoichiometrical conversion of ethanol to acetic acid. The sulfuric acid must be less than 40 per cent of the volume. The speed of oxidation is inversely proportional to the cube of the sulfuric acid concentration. If 20 per cent sulfuric acid (7 N) is used the reaction is complete in less than 30 minutes in the cold. Careful attention must be paid to the details of the reaction.

Zimmermann (1963) reported that dichromate results were 0.24 per cent higher in alcohol than the results of densimetric procedures, while dichromate and pycnometric results were identical. This result he showed to be fortuitous because of a compensation of errors (due to a highly volatile component other than alcohol which is eliminated by aerating the fresh distillates). The volatile acidity and sulfur dioxide content of wines depress the pycnometer and hydrometer results but have little influence on the dichromate results. About 40 per cent of the remaining difference between pycnometer and dichromate results appears to be due to a substance which depresses the pycnometer results but does not effect those of the dichromate procedure. Under these circumstances, Zimmermann argues that the dichromate results more accurately reflect the true alcohol content of the wine. This may be true under very precise laboratory controls.

The dichromate procedure was adapted for semi-automatic operation by Morrison and Edwards (1963). They point out particularly the need to use primary-standard potassium dichromate, high quality distilled water, accurately calibrated volumetric glassware, and a standard ethanol-water solution as a daily check on the analyst and the apparatus. They indicate that the 95 per cent confidence limit for the standard deviation is ±0.12.

Extract of Dealcoholized Sample

The extract of a wine is the alcohol-free soluble solids and is made up mainly of cream of tartar, malic, lactic, and succinic acids, glycerol, tannin, protein, and other nitrogenous compounds, and sugar. In low acid (high pH) wines there may be considerable neutral potassium tartrate. In sweet wines sugar predominates over the other constituents in concentration. There are several methods of determining extract.

One simple procedure is to take the Balling (or Brix) degree of the dealcoholized sample, from the alcohol determination, which has been brought to the original volume and temperature. A hydrometer graduated in 0.1° Balling (or Brix) is used. Or, if no such residue is available pipette 100 ml. of wine into a 250-ml. beaker. Evaporate on a hot plate or steam bath to 20 ml. or slightly less, taking care to prevent splattering or burning. Transfer to a 100-ml. volumetric flask. Cool the flask and sample in cold water to the temperature of calibration of the flask. Bring to volume with distilled water and mix well. Pour into a hydrometer cylinder and float a Balling hydrometer in it. Hydrometers calibrated for ±5° Balling or 0° to 8° or 8° to 16° are used. Note the temperature and make the appropriate correction according to Table 65. The reading will be in gm. per 100 gm. Multiply by the specific gravity to report in terms of gm. per 100 ml. The extract should then be reported as "soluble solids by hydrometer."

The extract can also be determined as follows: pipette 25 ml. of dry table wine or 10 ml. of sweet dessert wine or sweet sauterne into a flat-bottomed, weighed evaporating dish about 2.5 in. in diameter. Evaporate to a syrupy consistency on a steam bath. Transfer to a vacuum drying oven and dry at 158°- F. (70°C.) at 28 to 29 in. of vacuum for not less than six hours. Cool in a desiccator and weigh. Subtract the weight of the evaporating dish and multiply this value by 4 or by 10, depending on whether 25 ml. or 10 ml. of wine were taken. The extract content determined by this procedure is subject to losses of volatile constituents. The results are, therefore, empirical and should always be reported as "extract in vacuo."

The extract may also be approximately determined by calculation from the alcohol content and specific gravity of the wine as follows:

Determine the specific gravity of the wine by an accurate specific gravity hydrometer, a Westphal balance, or an accurate Balling or Brix hydrometer and convert this reading to specific gravity from Table 63. This must be done at the standard temperature of the hydrometer, usually 60°F. (15.5°C.). Determine the alcohol content by any of the methods previously described and find the corresponding specific gravity of an alcohol solution of this alcohol content from the table of alcohol per cent and specific gravity (see Table 64). Subtract the specific gravity of the alcohol from the specific gravity of the wine; add 1 for the specific gravity of water and the result will be the specific gravity of the alcohol-free wine.

Convert this specific gravity to Balling from Table 63. This will be the extract content of the wine in gm. per 100 gm. Multiply by the specific gravity to get the extract in terms of gm. per 100 ml.

The following example will illustrate the method: Balling of the wine 6.0° which is equal to 1.0232 specific gravity (from Table 63). Its alcohol is 12.0 per cent. The specific gravity of 12.0 per cent alcohol is 0.98435. Subtract this value from the specific gravity of the wine: 1.0232 − 0.98435 = 0.03885. Add 1.0 to give 1.03885, the specific gravity of the dealcoholized wine, which corresponds to 9.90° Balling (from Table 63) and is the extract content of the wine in gm. per 100 gm. of wine. The hydrometer or Westphal balance readings must be made very accurately and at the standard temperature, or else the values for extract will be worthless. The extract as gm. per 100 ml. will be 9.90 × 1.0373 or 10.3.

The per cent soluble solids of musts and dealcoholized wines may also be determined by the Abbé refractometer, Fig. 145.

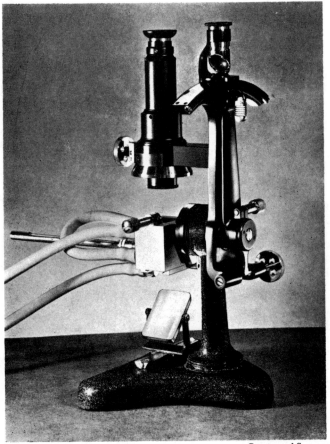

FIG. 145. ABBÉ REFRACTOMETER

Reducing Sugars

For a sweet dessert wine it is rarely necessary to determine the sugar content chemically since the Balling degree of the wine or, at most, the extract determination is usually sufficient. The sugar content of dry table wines, however, is very important since it indicates whether or not fermentation is complete. For dry sherries the sugar content determined chemically is also often of legal importance. There are many methods of determining sugar in beverages and foods. Dextrose and levulose, the natural sugars of wine, reduce the cupric copper of copper salts in alkaline solution to cuprous copper on heating. The cuprous copper separates as red cuprous oxide. The amount formed is proportional to the amount of sugar present. The cuprous oxide can be collected by filtration, dried, and weighed. But such a procedure is slow, and laborious. Hence, practically all sugar determinations in the winery are made by one of the approved volumetric methods. Of these, the Lane and Eynon method (described below) is one of the most convenient and satisfactory.

Have on hand a 50-ml. burette, glass filter funnel about 3 in. in diameter, filter paper of rapid filtering quality about 6 to 8 in. in diameter, several 250- or 300-ml. Pyrex Erlenmeyer flasks, a wooden flask tongs to hold the Erlenmeyer flask during titration, a burette stand and clamp, tripod and wire gauze on which to heat the flask, two 50-ml. pipettes, two 25-ml. pipettes, a 10-ml. pipette, a 100-ml. volumetric flask, a 500-ml. volumetric flask, and a Bunsen burner.

The following solutions and reagents are needed: decolorizing charcoal such as Darco, Norit, or Nuchar; infusorial earth filter aid such as Hyflo Super-Cel; Fehling's copper sulfate solution, made by dissolving 34.639 gm. of copper sulfate ($CuSO_4 \cdot 5H_2O$) in distilled water and diluting to 500 ml. in a volumetric flask; Fehling's alkaline tartrate solution, made by dissolving 173 gm. of Rochelle salts (sodium potassium tartrate) and 50 gm. of C.P. sodium hydroxide (free of carbonate) in distilled water and diluting to 500 ml. and then filtering if necessary; methylene blue solution, made by dissolving one gm. of methylene blue in water and diluting to 100 ml.; standard dextrose solution made by dissolving exactly 0.5 gm. of Reagent A.C.S. anhydrous dextrose in 100 ml. of distilled water. The solution is not stable and must be made up fresh as required.

Prepare the wine sample as follows: to 50 ml. of the wine in an Erlenmeyer flask add 2 or 3 teaspoonfuls of decolorizing charcoal. Shake several times and add a teaspoon of Hyflo Super-Cel, or similar filter aid, and shake. Filter through a folded filter paper in a glass funnel. If the filtrate contains charcoal, filter a second time. The filtrate should be water-white and clear. This treatment removes tannin, coloring matter, and certain other copper-reducing substances.

Standardize the Soxhlet solution as follows: using a separate pipette for each solution, pipette 50 ml. of Fehling's copper sulfate solution and 50 ml. of the alkaline tartrate into an Erlenmeyer flask and mix well. It should be clear and deep blue. The mixed Fehling solution should be made up in the quantities dictated by the number of analyses to be prepared in a 3 or 4 hour period. Pipette

10 ml. of the mixed Fehling solution into a narrow-mouth, 250-ml. Erlenmeyer flask. Add 40 ml. of distilled water. Fill a burette with the standard 0.5 per cent dextrose solution. Place the flask on a wire gauze on a tripod. Add 4 to 5 ml. of 0.5 per cent dextrose solution from the burette, taking a reading before adding. Place a flame under the flask and heat to boiling. Boil 15 to 20 seconds holding the flask with wooden tongs and gently moving the flask to avoid bumping. Now add 2 to 3 ml. more of dextrose solution. Again boil 15 to 20 seconds. Add about 5 to 6 drops of the methylene blue indicator. Keep the liquid in the flask boiling and slowly add from the burette 0.5 per cent dextrose solution, boiling 3 to 4 seconds after each addition, until one drop changes the color from blue to a full brick red.

Repeat this titration adding about 90 per cent of the necessary dextrose solution immediately. Then, after the solution boils, titrate to the end point as above. It must not take longer than two minutes after the solution begins to boil, after the first addition of dextrose solution, until the end point is reached. This gives the dextrose equivalent of the Fehling solution. Call it "a."

Place in another Erlenmeyer flask 10 ml. of the mixed solution, 40 ml. of distilled water, and 10 ml. by pipette of your decolorized wine. Heat to boiling. Boil 20 to 30 seconds. Add methylene blue indicator, as before. Then add dropwise from the burette, a little at a time, standard dextrose solution, boiling a few seconds after each addition until one drop bleaches the blue color to a full red color. Call the ml. of dextrose used "b." If the 10 ml. of wine "uses up" the 10 ml. of Fehling solution as shown by complete disappearance of all the blue color before adding any dextrose then the wine must be diluted before use. Try diluting 25 ml. of the decolorized wine to 100 ml. in a volumetric flask with distilled water. Then repeat the titration using 10 ml. of this diluted wine and finishing the titration with the dextrose solution. If still too high in sugar, try diluting 10 ml. to 100 ml.

Calculation.—Suppose 9.6 ml. of the 0.5 per cent dextrose were needed for titrating the 10 ml. of Fehling solution; that is, "a" = 9.6 ml. Titrating in the presence of 10 ml. of wine, 4.3 ml. of dextrose solution were required; that is, "b" = 4.3 ml. Then $a - b$ = ml. of dextrose solution equal to the reducing sugar in 10 ml. of wine, or 9.6 − 4.3 = 5.3 ml. and 5.3 × 0.005 = 0.0265 gm. sugar in 10 ml. of wine. Or in 100 ml. of wine it is 10 × 0.0265 = 0.265 gm. (reported as 0.27). If the wine had to be diluted then the result must be multiplied by the dilution factor.

With sweet wines first dilute the wine to below 0.50 gm. sugar per 100 ml., preferably to about 0.25 to 0.30 gm. per 100 ml. by means of an accurate pipette and volumetric flask. For muscatel, port, and angelica this is a dilution of about 25:1 or of 10 ml. diluted to 250 ml. with distilled water. Then decolorize this diluted material and proceed as with the dry wine. Multiply the final result by the dilution factor, in this case 25. For the drier sherries dilution of 10:1 will usually be sufficient.

For the gravimetric method of sugar determination and for other volumetric methods see Association of Official Analytical Chemists (1970) and Amerine (1970). Most wine chemists prefer the Lane-Eynon method, because of its simplicity and dependability.

Robirds and Rossi, Jr. (1966) pointed out that the Lane-Eynon method does not account for all of the levulose present in grape juice. Because of this, it accounts for only about 96 per cent of the total sugars. They recommended the Luff-Schoorl copper reagent which is reduced equally by dextrose and levulose. The difference between the methods is negligible for solutions of low sugar content but for musts it is appreciable. For wineries which calculate winery efficiency from must sugar analysis it will be worthwhile to use the Luff-Schoorl reagent or to correct the values obtained by the Lane-Eynon procedure.

Balling-Alcohol-Extract Chart

In Fig. 146 is given a chart by which one may readily find the approximate extract of a wine if its alcohol content and Balling degree are known; or if the extract and alcohol are known, the approximate Balling degree can be found from the chart. Also the sugar content of sweet dessert wines can be roughly estimated by first finding the extract content from the chart and then, for white dessert wines subtracting 2.2 from the extract and for port, subtracting 2.5. The remainder is the approximate sugar content.

An example or two will make the use of the chart clearer, e.g., a sample of tokay dessert wine has 19.4 per cent alcohol and its Balling is 4.5°. What is its extract content and approximate sugar content? First lay a ruler or straight edge across the chart with the upper edge resting on 4.5° Balling and at 19.4 on the alcohol line on the chart. It will cross the extract line at 10.5, and this will be the extract content of the wine. Its approximate sugar content will be 10.5 −2.2 or approximately 8.3 gm. per 100 ml.

Suppose that a sherry has 3.7 per cent sugar by the Lane-Eynon method and has 19.6 per cent alcohol. What is its Balling degree? Add 2.2 to the sugar content giving 5.9 which is its extract content. Place the ruler on 5.9 extract and 19.6 per cent alcohol, and the Balling degree from the chart will be seen to be minus 0.5.

Determination of Sulfur Dioxide

Distillation.—The keeping quality of wines of all kinds is dependent in large measure on their sulfur dioxide content. That of white dry table wines should not fall below 100 p.p.m. and of fortified wines below 75 p.p.m. during storage in tanks or casks. Another reason for accurate determination of the sulfur dioxide content, is the legal maximum for both total and free in many countries and states (p. 751). Total sulfur dioxide may be determined either by the distillation method or by the Ripper method. The distillation method outlined below is the more accurate.

The following equipment is needed: an 800-ml. or 600-ml. Kjeldahl distillation flask, Liebig condenser with rubber tubing connections, ring stand and clamps to hold the flask and condenser, Kjeldahl distillation trap, 500-ml. Erlenmeyer flask to receive the distillate, 50-ml. burette, 5- and 50-ml. pipettes, calcium chloride tube or piece of glass tubing attached to end of condenser to

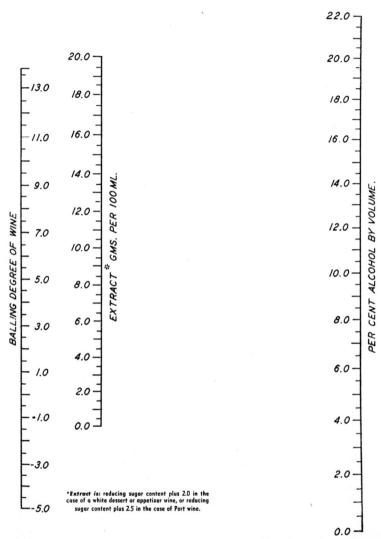

*Extract is: reducing sugar content plus 2.0 in the case of a white dessert or appetizer wine, or reducing sugar content plus 2.5 in the case of Port wine.

Prepared by G. L. Marsh for Wine Institute

FIG. 146.   NOMOGRAPH BETWEEN BALLING OF WINE, EXTRACT, AND ALCOHOL PER CENT OF DESSERT WINES

To use lay ruler connecting the two known values and then read off the value of the unknown

deliver the distillate into the iodine solution in the Erlenmeyer flask, a gas flame or electric heater and ring to hold the flask above the burner. The following reagents are needed: concentrated hydrochloric acid, 0.1 N iodine solution, 0.1 N thiosulfate solution, saturated solution of sodium bicarbonate, and 1 per cent freshly-made starch solution, made by boiling 1 gm. of corn starch in water and diluting to 100 ml. The 0.1 N iodine and thiosulfate can be purchased from any chemical supply house, or can be made up as directed in any text book on quantitative chemical analysis. The iodine solution is made by dissolving 12.70 gm. of Reagent A.C.S. iodine and 25 gm. of Reagent A.C.S. potassium iodide in a little distilled water and diluting to 1000 ml. in a volumetric flask. It must always be standardized just before use. Thiosulfate is likewise not stable and should be restandardized every few months.

Proceed as follows: pipette 50 ml. of wine and 200 ml. of distilled water into the distillation flask and 25 ml. of iodine and 25 ml. of water into the 500-ml. Erlenmeyer flask. Mark this flask at 200 ml. Place the latter beneath the outlet of the condenser with the outlet tube dipping into the solution. In order to avoid loss of iodine it is desirable to set the Erlenmeyer flask in a large beaker or small pan containing ice water and ice.

Pipette 10 ml. of the bicarbonate solution and 5 ml. of the concentrated hydrochloric acid into the 50 ml. of wine in the distillation flask and connect the flask to the condenser. Start water flowing through condenser jacket. Heat the distillation flask and wine with a gas burner or electric heater to boiling and distill 150 ml. of the sample into the iodine solution in about 45 minutes. Remove the iodine flask; rinse off the calcium chloride tube with water.

Add 0.1 N thiosulfate from the burette to the iodine solution until the color fades to a light yellow. Then add 5 ml. of starch indicator solution and continue the titration until the color just changes from blue to colorless. Call the ml. of the thiosulfate used "b."

Check the normality of the iodine solution as follows: place 50 ml. of distilled water and by pipette 25 ml. of iodine in a 500-ml. Erlenmeyer flask. Add a few drops of starch solution and titrate to colorless with 0.1 N thiosulfate. Call the ml. used "a." Suppose that 9.4 ml. 0.1 N thiosulfate is required to neutralize 25 ml. of the iodine solution, this is "a." Suppose that 7.1 ml. of 0.1 N thiosulfate were needed to neutralize the iodine in the distillate, this is "b."

Then $(a - b) \times 3.2 \times 20 =$ mg. sulfur dioxide per liter; or $(9.4 - 7.1) \times 3.2 \times 20 = 2.3 \times 3.2 \times 20 = 147.2$ mg. sulfur dioxide per liter.

Ripper Method for Total Sulfur Dioxide.—This is a volumetric method based on direct titration of the sulfur dioxide in the wine after hydrolysis of the combined sulfur dioxide by strong alkali. It is not so accurate as the distillation method previously described.

The following apparatus is needed: 10, 25, and 50 ml. pipettes, one 50 ml. burette, and one 30 ml. Erlenmeyer flask; and the following reagents: 10 per cent sodium hydroxide solution, dilute sulfuric acid consisting of 100 ml. of concentrated sulfuric acid added to 300 ml. of distilled water, freshly made 0.02 N iodine solution made by diluting 0.1 N iodine 5:1 as needed, one per cent starch solution made by boiling 1 gm. of starch in 100 ml. of water three minutes, and 0.1 N thiosulfate solution.

Proceed as follows: check the normality of the 0.02 N iodine solution by pipetting 25 ml. into 50 ml. of distilled water in a 300 cc. Erlenmeyer flask.

Add 10 ml. of the dilute sulfuric acid and a few drops of starch solution. From a burette add exactly 0.1 N thiosulfate until one drop finally destroys the blue color. The normality of the iodine solution is then obtained by the following calculation: (ml. thiosulfate $\times$ 0.10)/25 = normality of iodine. For example, suppose 4.9 ml. of thiosulfate were used. Then (4.9 $\times$ 0.10)/25 = 0.49/25 = 0.0196 N.

Now pipette 20 ml. of the wine into a 300 ml. Erlenmeyer flask. Add 25 ml. of 10 per cent sodium hydroxide. Mix, stopper, and allow to stand exactly 15 minutes. Then add ten ml. of the dilute sulfuric acid solution and five ml. of starch indicator solution. Titrate immediately to a permanent blue color with the 0.02 N iodine.

The calculation is based on the fact that 1 ml. of exactly 0.1 N iodine $\times$ 32 $\times$ normality of iodine = mg. of sulfur dioxide. Suppose 2.41 ml. of the approximately 0.02 N iodine were used. If its exact normality is 0.0196 then 2.41 $\times$ 32 $\times$ 0.0196 $\times$ 1000/20 = 75.6 mg. per liter.

Ripper Method for Free Sulfur Dioxide.—It is the free sulfur dioxide that one tastes in a freshly-sulfured wine or in a heavily sulfured older sauterne. However, during aging in the cask or bottle much of the free sulfur dioxide is fixed and is much less perceptible.

To 50 ml. of wine add 10 ml. of 3:1 sulfuric acid (the 1 volume of sulfuric to 3 of water used in the total sulfur dioxide determination; 3:1 by weight is about equal to 4:1 by volume for sulfuric acid solutions). Quickly add a few drops of starch indicator and titrate to the first persistent blue color with 0.02 N iodine. In this case 32 $\times$ 20 $\times$ cc. iodine used $\times$ normality of iodine = p.p.m. of free sulfur dioxide.

Tannin and Coloring Matter

The tannin content of wine is of importance because it affects the flavor, color, and stability of many wines. The usual method, Neubauer-Loewenthal, for tannin content includes the coloring matter. Essentially it consists in titrating a sample of the dealcoholized wine before and after decolorizing with carbon. For details see Nègre (1942–1943).

Smit et al. (1955) showed that the Loewenthal procedure gave high results compared to the Pro method for catechol and chlorogenic acid, and low results for catechin, quercetin and commercial tannin preparations (but not for pure tannic acid).

The Neubauer-Loewenthal Method.—Have on hand 0.1 N oxalic acid solution consisting of 5.305 gm. of pure oxalic acid dissolved in water and diluted to exactly a liter, standard potassium permanganate solution, made by dissolving 1.33 gm. of potassium permanganate in water and diluting to a liter, indigo indicator solution, made by dissolving 6 gm. of sodium indigotinsulfonate (indigo carmine) in 500 ml. of distilled water by heating, cooling, adding 50 ml. concentrated sulfuric acid, making to a liter and filtering. A decolorizing carbon free of permanganate reducing matter is also required. The following equipment is needed: burette with stand and clamps, glass funnel and filter paper, 20 ml.

and 10 ml. pipettes, 2000 ml. porcelain dish, 300 ml. evaporating dish, 100 ml. volumetric flask, stirring rod, 250 or 300 ml. Erlenmeyer flask.

The procedure is as follows: dealcoholize 100 ml. of wine by diluting to 150 ml. with water and evaporating to about 50 ml. on a water bath and transfer to a 100 ml. volumetric flask and bring to temperature and volume; or, use the extract from the alcohol distillation and bring to volume and temperature in a 100 ml. volumetric flask; mix well. Pipette five ml. of the dealcoholized sample to 500 ml. of distilled water in a liter Erlenmeyer flask. Add exactly 10 ml. of the indigo indicator. Pipette in the standard permanganate solution from a pipette 1 ml. at a time, until the blue changes to green, then one drop at a time until a golden yellow color is reached. Thoroughly stir the solution with a glass stirring rod or an electrical stirrer throughout the titration. Designate the ml. of permanganate used as "a."

To 40 or 50 ml. of the dealcoholized sample (at its original volume) add a spoonful or two of decolorizing carbon (Nuchar WW, for example). Shake thoroughly and let stand about five minutes. Add a little Hyflo Super-Cel or other infusorial earth and filter through a hard filter paper. The filtrate must be water-white and perfectly clear. Titrate 5 ml. of the decolorized sample diluted as before and with the same amount of indigo carmine. Record the ml. of permanganate used as "b."

Then $a - b = c$, the number of ml. of permanganate required for oxidation of the tannin and coloring matter in 5 ml. of wine. Also, $20 \times c \times$ normality of permanganate$/0.1 \times 0.00416$ equals the tannin and coloring matter in grams per 100 ml. of wine.

The permanganate solution is not very stable, particularly if stored in the light. It is therefore necessary to ascertain its normality occasionally by titration against a 0.1 N oxalic acid solution.

Tannin.—The tannin method of Pro, (1952) is rapid and accurate:

Prepare Folin-Dennis reagent by adding 100 gm. of sodium tungstate (Na_2-$WO_4 \cdot 2H_2O$), 20 gm. of phosphomolybdic acid and 50 ml. of phosphoric acid to 750 ml. of water, reflux two hours and dilute to 1 liter. Also prepare a saturated solution of sodium carbonate by adding 35 gm. of anhydrous sodium carbonate to 100 ml. of water at about 176°F. (80°C.). Allow to cool overnight and seed with a few crystals of sodium carbonate ($Na_2CO_3 \cdot H_2O$). Also prepare daily a standard tannic acid solution by dissolving 100 mg. of tannic acid in a liter water.

Pipette 1 ml. of wine into a Nessler tube containing 80 ml. of water. Add 5 ml. of the Folin-Dennis reagent and 10 ml. of the sodium carbonate solution and shake well and make to the mark. After 30 minutes compare the color to that developed with standard tannic acid solutions prepared in the same way. Standards containing 0.0 to 2.4 ml. of the standard solution are useful. Singleton and Rossi, Jr. (1965) used a modified Folin-Ciocalteu reagent with gallic acid for the standard and obtained better results.

Color

Color assay is of importance in blending and standardizing wine types. The tint and depth of color of red wines are difficult to measure accurately, except with costly spectrophotometric equipment. However, it now appears that such procedures are necessary for color standardization in large wineries according to recent papers by Crawford *et al.* (1958) and Amerine *et al.* (1959A). Abridged colorimeters give data which are only satisfactory for approximate color standardization. See Mackinney and Chichester (1954) and Winkler and Amerine (1938).

For red wines the Dujardin-Salleron *vino colorimeter* is sometimes useful. It consists of color discs mounted on a cardboard strip which indicates the tint at a standard depth of color. Winkler and Amerine (1938) used certain dyes for preparing solutions of standard color. These were then compared in a Dubosc colorimeter. The Lovibond Tintometer is sometimes used for measuring the color of beers and vegetable oils. By proper selection of slides it can also be used for wines, both white and red. It consists of small glass slides, somewhat smaller than microscope slides, made of colored glass, the usual colors being red, yellow, and blue, each color being represented by a long range of slides ranging in depth of color from very light to very deep. The sample is placed in one tube of the comparator and distilled water in the other. Slides are stacked beneath the water side of the comparator, various combinations being tried until the color is matched. The slides are then added up to get the tint and depth of color. Unfortunately the proper slides are not generally available.

A photoelectric colorimeter can be used to measure depth of color of the predominant tint.

Villforth (1958) has suggested a simplified color index. He determined the optical density at 420, 450, 470, 490, 530, 550, 570, 590, 620, 670, 720, and 750 nm using appropriate filters in a photoelectric photometer. The sum of the optical densities at 420–490 he added as blue, at 530–550 as green, at 570–620 as yellow, and at 670–750 as red. The blue sum $\times 100/$ the total gave the per cent blue, the green sum $\times 100/$ the total gave the per cent green, the yellow sum $\times 100/$ the total gave the per cent yellow, and the red sum $\times 100/$ the total gave the per cent red. The intensity of color was measured by determining the absorption (A) at 1 mm. with a red filter (RG_2). The color value (D) equals 100-A. Typical data for five German red wines were as follows:

Variety	Year	Color Value	Color Components			
			Blue	Green	Yellow	Red
			Per cent	Per cent	Per cent	Per cent
Limberger	1948	32.7	29.8	14.8	25.9	29.5
Trollinger	1948	45.2	28.0	14.5	26.2	30.5
Pinot Noir	1952	29.5	30.3	14.8	25.9	29.0
Red Wine[1]	1955	60.9	24.6	11.6	27.0	36.8
Red Wine[2]	1955	34.8	29.6	14.7	26.1	29.6

[1] From France.
[2] From Italy.

A simpler method involves the use of a photoelectric colorimeter equipped with three tristimulus filters. By making one transmission measurement with each filter, it is possible to specify a color in the same numerical values obtained with a spectrophotometer. However, because color filters cannot be found which perfectly duplicate the desired tristimulus functions, such instruments can accurately measure the difference in chromaticity coordinates between a standard and a sample only if the difference is not large and if the standard and sample do not differ widely in spectral characteristics.

Sudraud (1958) stresses the fact that the brilliance and dominant wave length are the two most important factors in the specification of color of red wines. He recommends, therefore, specifying the color of red wines by the ratio of the optical density at 420/520 nm and the sum of the optical densities at 420 and 520 nm.

Pataky (1965) has emphasized the importance of pH in the spectrophotometric determination of anthocyans. He recommended a pH of 0.8 and establishment of the pH by pH meter rather than with buffers. He doubts if there is a simple equilibrium of the type oxonium (colored)⇌leucobase (colorless) because there is no evidence of an isobestic point. Because of the high optical density in alkaline media and the fact that malvidin appears to be the only pigment that fluoresces, Pataky believes that it is possible to develop a purely physical procedure for its determination.

Berg (1963) presented data indicating the presence of two types of pigments: one pH-responsive and the other non-responsive to pH change. This would invalidate spectrophotometric measurement at a given pH as a means of determination of anthocyans in wine.

However, the wine maker is chiefly interested in making blends that will match previous blends for given brands of his wine. Perhaps it is his "Special Reserve Claret." The simplest procedure, then, is to take a sample of a previous blend that he has set aside for the purpose, and fill a test tube or small bottle with it. Then from the cellar obtain samples of the wines he proposes to use in the new blend. Next measure and blend various amounts of each and compare with his standard blend until a match is obtained. A Duboscq colorimeter may profitably be used for making this comparison. For more recent information on spectrophotometric standards for wine color see Crawford et al. (1958) and Amerine et al. (1959A).

A major drawback to the above method for matching blends is that the reference samples change in color with time. Spectrophotometric determination of color provides a permanent standard, but requires a number of measurements and a rather lengthy calculation. To simplify color matching of blends, Berg et al. (1964) developed charts from which, with spectrophotometric readings at 420 and 520 mμ, the dominant wave-length of luminous-transmittance differences necessary for discrimination are read directly.

Aldehydes

A measure of the aldehyde content of sherries is of value to the wine maker and is sometimes of importance for other types of wine. It is even more important in brandies than in sherries.

This is essentially the direct bisulfite procedure of Jaulmes and Espezel (1935) as modified by Guymon and Crowell (1963). See Kielhöfer and Aumann (1958) and Amerine (1965).

The equipment and reagents required include 10- and 50-ml. pipettes, 1 liter Erlenmeyer flask (marked at 370 ml.), 500-ml. Kjeldahl flask, 500-ml. graduated cylinder, capillary tubes or boiling chips, condenser, calcium chloride tube, source of heat, 10- or 25-ml. burette, saturated borax ($Na_2B_4O_7 \cdot H_2O$) 0.2% starch indicator solution, 0.1 N iodine, 0.050 N iodine, and solutions A, B, C, and D. Solution A is made by mixing 15 gm. potassium metabisulfite, $K_2S_2O_5$, 70 ml. concentrated hydrochloric acid and diluting to 1000 ml. with water; solution B by dissolving 200 gm. trisodium phosphate, Na_3PO_4, and 4.5 gm. disodium ethylenediamine tetraacetate (EDTA) in water and diluting to 1000 ml.; solution C by diluting 250 ml. concentrated hydrochloric acid to 1000 ml. with water; and solution D by mixing 100 gm. boric acid, H_3BO_3, with 170 gm. sodium hydroxide and diluting to 1000 ml. with water.

Pipette 50 ml. of wine into the Kjeldahl flask, add 50 ml. of the saturated solution of borax, boiling chips and connect to condenser. Add 300 ml. of boiled water and 10 ml. each of solution A and solution B to the Erlenmeyer flask. Use calcium chloride tube as an adapter and set so that it just dips into this solution. Distill 50 ml. into the Erlenmeyer flask, stopper, swirl to mix and let stand 15 minutes. Add 10 ml. solution C and 10 ml. of starch solution, swirl to mix and add 0.1 N iodine to just destroy the excess bisulfite and bring the solution to a light blue end point. Add 10 ml. solution D and titrate liberated bisulfite ion with 0.050 N iodine solution to the same light blue end point with continuous swirling. Calculate aldehydes as follows:

$$\text{mg. acetaldehyde per 100 ml.} = \text{ml. I}_3^- \times N \times 22 \times 100/50$$

The above procedure determines only free aldehydes. For table wines (12 per cent alcohol), the amount of aldehyde present as acetal is negligible. For dessert wines (20 per cent alcohol), and essentially free of bisulfite, the amount of acetal present usually amounts to only two to three per cent of the free aldehyde.

Iron Determination

G. L. Marsh (Joslyn and Amerine, 1964) gives the following method of determining the iron content of wines (see also Marsh and Nobusada, 1938):

"Total iron in wines is most easily and accurately determined by the procedure developed by Saywell and Cunningham (1937). The method involves wet-ashing and the development of a colored complex which ferrous iron forms with o-phenanthroline.

"Pipette 2 ml. of wine into 25 × 150 mm. Pyrex test tubes previously marked at 10 ml. Evaporate to dryness, cool, and add 1 ml. of concentrated sulfuric acid. Heat over a flame under a hood with care until the contents of the tube are completely liquefied. Allow to cool, and then add 0.5 ml. of 70 per cent perchloric acid. Heat *continuously* until partial clarification has occurred, set aside to cool, and then add 0.5 ml. of perchloric acid. Continue the digestion until the sample is clear and *until all the excess perchloric acid has been evaporated off*. At this stage set the tubes aside to cool. *Caution:* the digestion should be conducted behind a shatterproof glass, because perchloric acid occasionally explodes during heating.

"Add 2 ml. of distilled water and a small piece (0.5 cm. square) of Congo red paper. Then add 1 ml. of a 10 per cent aqueous solution of hydroxylamine hydrochloride and 1 ml. of a 0.1 per cent solution of o-phenanthroline in 50 per cent alcohol. Titrate to the color change (blue to a light red) of the Congo red paper with concentrated ammonium hydroxide and set aside to cool. Then make to 10 ml. with distilled water and transfer to standardized test tubes for comparison against a series of standards or to colorimeter tubes for comparison by photoelectric photometers.

"Prepare a standard stock solution of iron to contain 1 mg. iron per ml. Prepare from this standard stock solution, a series of solutions containing known concentrations (in parts per million of iron). Run these solutions through the procedure given above for the unknown, using all the reagents and following directions closely. Transfer to standard-diameter test tubes and cork tightly for use as a series of standards. These standards are stable for long periods and the procedure outlined automatically corrects for the iron in the reagents. In like manner, the solutions can be used to establish a curve for use with a photoelectric colorimeter. In this case, however, a blank containing water instead of an iron solution but containing all the reagents must be prepared. Use this blank to set the instrument to zero reading."

The standard iron solution is prepared as follows: weigh out 7.022 gm. of ferrous ammonium sulfate; dissolve it in 500 ml. of distilled water to which 5 ml. of concentrated hydrochloric acid has been added. Transfer to a liter volumetric flask and make to volume with distilled water.

Copper Determination

Copper sometimes causes clouding of white table wines and when the clouding of such wines occurs it is important to know whether or not it is due to traces of copper and, if due to copper, how much copper is present in order that the proper amount of Cufex or other permissible precipitant can be used. For a sensitive method using an ashed sample, see Hennig and Lay (1964).

The Marsh method is as follows (see Joslyn and Amerine, 1964): pipette 10 ml. of wine into a 25 × 150 mm. Pyrex test tube. Add 1 ml. of hydrochloric-citric acid reagent, shake, and then add 2 ml. of 5 N ammonium hydroxide (333 ml. concentrated ammonium hydroxide per liter), and again shake. Then add 1 ml. of a 1 per cent aqueous solution of sodium diethyldithiocarbamate, shake and set aside for a minute or so before adding 10 ml. of amyl acetate. Follow-with 5 ml. of absolute methyl alcohol.

"Place the palm of the hand over the top of the test tube and shake vigorously for at least 30 seconds. Set aside and allow the two phases to separate. When separation is complete, draw off[1] the aqueous phase by inserting a length of glass tubing to the bottom of the test tube and apply suction. Then dry the organic phase by adding anhydrous sodium sulfate, powdered, from the tip of a spatula and shaking, adding only a sufficient amount to accomplish the purpose. It should be added while holding the tube at an angle and at the same time rotating the tube for the purpose of drying the moisture film adhering to the walls. Transfer the dried organic phase to clean dry test tubes for color comparison against a set of standards or to the colorimeter tubes of the Duboscq or any of the new photoelectric colorimeters.

"The absolute methyl alcohol which is added to the reaction mixture serves two purposes. It markedly reduces the tendency of the two phases to emulsify and thereby aids in a quick and clean separation of the aqueous and organic phases. More important, however, is its second purpose. Coulson shows that the intensity of the color which is extractable by amyl acetate from the aqueous phase is dependent upon the pH value of the aqueous phase. At pH 8.0 to 8.5, maximum color intensity is developed and great care must be exercised in adjusting the pH value if accurate values are to be obtained. This is common to most colorimetric procedures and Coulson's method differs little from most others in this respect. It was found in developing the procedure outlined above that when methyl alcohol was added to tubes containing samples adjusted to varying pH values, no difference in color intensity of the extracted colored solution could be detected. Without methyl alcohol, the color intensity of the extracted colored solution was dependent upon the pH value of the aqueous phase. With methyl alcohol present the pH value of the aqueous phase can vary over rather wide limits with no effect on the color intensity.

"Standard copper solution for this procedure is best prepared from Merck copper metal (reagent quality) so as to contain 0.50 mg. of copper per ml. Solutions for the preparation of the series of standards are prepared by pipetting 1, 2, 3, 4, 5, 6, 8, and 10 ml. of the above stock solution into separate liter volumetric flasks, adding 150 ml. of 95 per cent ethyl alcohol and making each up to volume with distilled water. These solutions then contain 0.5, 1.0, 1.5, 2.0, 2.5, 3.0, 4.0, and 5.0 p.p.m. of copper, respectively.

"Pipette 10 ml. of each solution into separate 25 × 150 mm. test tubes and proceed as directed for the unknown. The solutions so obtained can be used as a series of standards or can be used to establish standard curves for use with photoelectric photometers."

Ester Determination

Joslyn and Amerine (1941) state that the ester content of wine can be determined by the method generally used for brandy and whisky.

---

[1] A soda-glass stopcock, drawn to a capillary on one side and connected to a liter filter flask through rubber tubing on the other side, serves the purpose excellently. Connect the filter flask to a water aspirator or vacuum pump.

Pipette exactly 100 ml. of brandy (or wine) and about 35 ml. of water into a 500-ml. distillation flask. Distill slowly nearly 200 ml. into a 200-ml. volumetric flask. The last 50 ml. should be distilled at a maximum heat to assure distillation of all of the furfural. The receiving tube from the condenser should reach well into the receiving flask. Electric heat is preferable to gas, because local overheating may result when gas is used and some furfural may be produced. Bring the distillate to volume at the temperature of calibration. Take 100 ml. of the distillate in a 500-ml. round-bottom flask and neutralize the free acid present with 0.1 N sodium hydroxide, using phenolphthalein as an indicator. This titration is sometimes considered to represent the volatile acids present, but not all the volatile acids distill by this procedure and this therefore represents only a minimum value for the volatile acids. Then add a measured excess amount of 0.1 N sodium hydroxide, usually 25 ml. Connect the flask to a reflux condenser and boil for one hour. Cool the flask and add 25 ml. of 0.1 N hydrochloric acid. Titrate to a pink endpoint with 0.1 N sodium hydroxide. The ml. of 0.1 N alkali added minus the ml. of 0.1 N hydrochloric acid used for the final titration gives the ml. of 0.1 N alkali required to saponify the esters present. The number of ml. required multiplied by 8.8 gives the mg. of ester as ethyl acetate in 100 ml. of spirits (or wine). An occasional blank using water in place of distillate should be run and the necessary correction applied. Tobie (1941) has shown that aldehydes do not materially interfere with the ester determination when this procedure is used. They do apparently interfere when the saponification is allowed to take place at room temperatures over a 24-hour period.

A better procedure given by Amerine (1965) is as follows: pipette 100 ml. of wine and 25 ml. of water into a 250-ml. round-bottom distillation flask. Connect to a condenser and distill 105 ml. directly into an anion ion-exchanger column.[2] Collect the liquid issuing through the column in another 250 ml. distillation flask. Exactly neutralize with 0.1 N sodium hydroxide (carbonate-free) to a phenolphthalein end point. Then add 5 ml. of 0.1 N sodium hydroxide and reflux one hour. Cool and back titrate with 0.1 N hydrochloric acid. Calculate the ester content as mg. of ethyl acetate per liter as above.

Hydroxymethylfurfural

When sugars such as levulose are heated in acid solution they may be dehydrated and yield hydroxymethylfurfural. Its presence is thus a good test of heat treatment of dessert wines. Grape concentrate as usually produced is also high in this substance. Fiehe's solution is used for its semiquantitative measurement. The procedure is that of Amerine (1948).

Needed are 2- and 10-ml. pipettes, 125-ml. separatory funnels, 100-ml. evaporating dish, 30 per cent hydrochloric acid, freshly-prepared Fiehe's solution (0.1 gm. resorcinol in 10 ml. of concentrated hydrochloric acid), freshly purified anhydrous ether (prepared by washing the ether twice with water, once with cleaning solution, again with water, and then with 10 per cent sodium hydroxide, finally with water, and filter through ashless filter paper).

---

[2] The column is prepared ahead of time by soaking an anion exchange resin in water over night. Wash into the column and keep covered with water. Drop in 100 ml. of two per cent freshly prepared sodium hydroxide and leave one hour. Pass water through the column until it is alkali-free to phenolphthalein.

Pipette 10 ml. of wine and 10 ml. of the ether into a 125-ml. separatory funnel. Shake, allow the layers to separate and draw off the wine into another funnel. Add 10 ml. more ether to the wine and shake. Discard the wine and combine the two ether extracts in the evaporating dish. Allow the ether to evaporate at room temperature. Wash down the sides of the dish with 5 ml. of the hydrochloric acid, add 2 ml. of Fiehe's solution. The presence of hydroxymethylfurfural is indicated by a slight pink color. Greater concentrations will give a full red color. A rough estimate of the amount is made from trace to +, ++, and +++.

Carbon Dioxide

Since the enactment by Congress of Public Law 85-859 (85th Congress, H. R. 7125, September 2, 1958) which classifies wines containing 0.256 gm. of carbon dioxide per 100 ml. or less as still wines, an accurate method for determining carbon dioxide is obviously important. This was later raised to 0.277; see U. S. Internal Revenue Service (1961). The standard procedure will obviously be that of the regulatory agency concerned as given by Pro *et al.* (1959) or U. S. Internal Revenue Service (1959). Their procedure is classified as a vacuum method and is especially applicable to concentrations of 0.150 to 0.400 gm. of carbon dioxide per 100 ml. It is given

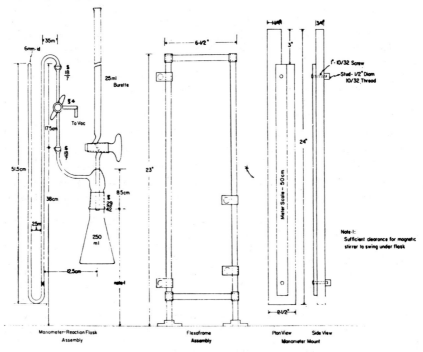

FIG. 147. APPARATUS FOR DETERMINATION OF CARBON DIOXIDE

in Amerine (1970). See also Caputi, *et al.* (1970), Hennig and Lay (1962), Paronetto (1953), and Postel (1970).

Another procedure approved for determining carbon dioxide in wines is the titrimetric procedure (Anon. 1959). The following reagents are required: phosphoric acid (85 per cent, reagent grade), hydrogen peroxide (10 per cent), sodium or potassium bicarbonate (reagent grade dried 24 hours over sulfuric acid before use), sodium hydroxide (made by dissolving 500 gm. of sodium hydroxide in 500 ml. of distilled water and filtering after 24 hours). From this 0.25 N sodium hydroxide is prepared. This is standardized against potassium acid phthalate daily using 5 ml. of barium chloride. The indicator is one gm. of phenolphthalein plus 0.5 gm. of thymolphthalein in 100 ml. of 95 per cent alcohol. The hydrochloric acid (about 0.25 N) is standardized against the 0.25 N sodium hydroxide. The barium chloride is prepared by dissolving 60–65 gm. of $BaCl_2 \cdot H_2O$ in a liter of water and neutralizing to phenolphthalein.

The procedure is as follows: chill the unopened bottle in an ice-salt bath which is less than 32°F. for one hour. Open the bottle and add 1.5 ml. of 50 per cent sodium hydroxide per 100 ml. of wine. Set up the apparatus as shown in Anon. (1959). The receivers should be set in water so as to be below 80°F. Pipette 20 ml. of standard sodium hydroxide in the first and second receivers and 10 ml. of hydroxide and 10 ml. of barium chloride into the third.

Now pipette 50 ml. of the cold alkaline wine into the distilling flask and 3 ml. of 10 per cent hydrogen peroxide. Add boiling chips (not marble). Attach a vacuum line to the last receiver and slowly increase the vacuum to a maximum when bubbling practically ceases. Add about 5 ml. of the phosphoric acid to the dropping funnel and allow 3 ml. to enter the distilling flask. Gradually increase the heat under the distilling flask as the bubbling slows down and until a few ml. of liquid distil and the top of the receiver is warm. Close the line between the first trap and the distilling flask. Return to atmospheric conditions and transfer the contents of the first two receivers, including the spargers, into a titration flask (and the third also if barium carbonate precipitates.) Add 50 ml. of barium chloride to the titration flask and titrate with hydrochloric acid.

Then, ml. N base consumed by $CO_2 = (N$ NaOH × ml. NaOH) − (N HCl × ml. HCl) and carbon dioxide in 100 ml. wine = 0.022 × ml. N NaOH × 2. Samples should be run in duplicate and compared with recovery from simulated samples prepared from sodium or potassium bicarbonate.

Modified Hubach Test

The apparatus, Fig. 148, consists of an aeration tube, condenser, and glass flanges for the test tube, assembled in that order. It is of importance that all connections be made air tight so that the only possible path for air is into the liquid in the aeration tube, and out by way of the condenser, and through the test paper held in the flanges. Side leaks of air markedly reduce the sensitivity of the test.

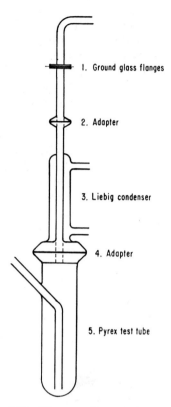

1. Ground glass flanges

2. Adapter

3. Liebig condenser

4. Adapter

5. Pyrex test tube

FIG. 148.   MODIFIED HUBACH APPARATUS
FOR CYANIDE AND FERROCYANIDE

Immerse a sheet of Whatman No. 50 filter paper in a solution of ferrous sulfate (5 gm. $FeSO_4 \cdot 7H_2O$ and one drop of 1:1 sulfuric acid in 50 ml. of water) for 5 minutes.   Remove the filter paper from the solution, suspend it by means of a clamp and allow it to dry in the air.   When dry, immerse the paper in alcoholic sodium hydroxide solution (10 ml. saturated sodium hydroxide solution made to 100 ml. with 95 per cent ethyl alcohol).   When the paper is thoroughly wet in the alcoholic sodium hydroxide solution, remove and again allow to air dry.   The paper should have a light green color or, at most, a light tan color. The paper is now ready for use and can be cut into circles or squares to fit the flange.   The paper should be stored in a cool dark place in a tightly-closed amber bottle containing calcium chloride.

To prepare the wine sample for testing neutralize 20 ml. of the wine with 6 N sodium hydroxide solution and add one drop in excess.   Evaporate over a steam bath to 5 ml. to remove alcohol.   To test the wine for cyanides, scrub the apparatus with air until dry and place the test paper between the flanges and tighten the flanges securely.   Turn on the water to the condenser.   Wash the evaporated wine sample into the test tube through the aeration tube with 10 ml. of water and acidify with several drops of 1:1 sulfuric acid solution.   Dilute to approximately 20 ml. with distilled water. Add 10 mg. of cuprous chloride to the solution in the aeration tube. Quantities in excess of 15 mg. must be avoided. Turn on the vacuum and connect the test tube to the condenser. Add 1 ml. of the sulfuric acid solution through the air inlet tube and draw air through the solution. Adjust the rate of flow so that air just ceases to bubble through the solution and begins to form a continuous stream. Immerse the test tube in a beaker of hot water to just above the sample liquid level. (The water temperature must not be below 176° or exceed 194°F.) Aerate the sample for ten minutes. Remove the test paper and place it in a 1:3 hydrochloric acid solution in a clean, white evaporating dish. Leave the paper in the dish until white. The appearance of a blue stain in the center of the test paper indicates the presence of cyanide or of a soluble or insoluble ferro or ferricyanide compound. As little as 0.05 to 0.1 p.p.m. of hydrogen cyanide or its equivalent in the ferro- or ferricyanide will give a positive test. It is recommended that a blank be run after each positive test. Test papers showing faint or questionable stains should be confirmed by two or more checks.[3] See Edge (1958), Gettler and Goldbaum (1947) and Hubach (1948).

Other Determinations

Modern winery operation may require a knowledge of other metals than copper and iron, especially of calcium, potassium and sodium.

Jouret and Poux (1961a) reported that simply diluting wines 1:25 or 1:50 made it possible to determine potassium directly in the flame photometer with an error of ±3 per cent in the usual wine and ±5 per cent in the most unfavorable case. They especially did not recommend ashing as there was often a loss, apparently due to volatilization, during ashing. The chief interference is from sulfates and phosphates. For determining sodium by flame photometry, Jouret and Poux (1961b) recommend diluting 1:10 or 1:25. Both sulfates and phosphate cause low sodium results so they recommend adding 0.01 to 0.3 milliequivalent of sodium per liter to the diluted samples. Of course, sulfate and phosphate could be removed by use of anion-exchange. In using flame photometry for potassium, sodium and calcium in fruit juices, Ditz (1965) emphasized the importance of preparing the standard curves containing normal amounts of the other cations as well as sugar and citric acid. Because·of the severe inhibitory effect of phosphate on calcium emissivity (Dean, 1960), it is essential that phosphate be added to both the standard solutions and wine samples if reliable results are to be obtained. As lactate ion also inhibits calcium emissivity, a more satisfactory method for calcium (and magnesium) determination in wine is the colorimetric procedure of Iwano and Sawanobori (1962). See also Amerine (1970), Amerine and Joslyn (1970), Amerine and Kishaba (1952), Amerine et al. (1953), Diemair and Gundermann (1959), Jaulmes (1951), Pro and Mathers (1954), and Ribéreau-Gayon

---

[3] The assistance of Prof. George Marsh and Mr. Min Akiyoshi in preparing this section is gratefully acknowledged.

and Peynaud (1958). Semi-micro methods for metals are given by Bonastre (1959).

Atomic absorption spectrophotometry is now the preferred method for determining cations. Caputi, Jr. and Ueda (1967) used it for copper and iron and Meranger and Somers (1968) for heavy metals. Bergner and Lang (1971) give precise directions for determining iron, copper, zinc, manganese, and cadmium by this procedure.

The problem of the precise determination of the redox potential of wines has been extensively studied by Deibner (1953, 1956, 1957). Among the many variables which must be controlled are preparation of electrodes, number of electrodes (Deibner recommends four), and time to reach a limiting value (measurements should be made at 10 to 15 minute intervals and continued, often for 1 to $2^1/_2$ hours, until the change is less than 0.2 mV per minute). Deibner and Mourgues (1964) showed a decreased potential as the temperature was increased. They recommended measuring the potential at 20°C. (68°F.) in millivolts with a simultaneous determination of the pH. The redox potential, rH, may also be calculated. They also recommended no agitation or circulation of the wine during the determination (in contrast to Deibner, 1956) even in the absence of all aeration. See also Ough and Amerine (1959).

BRANDY

Because of their high alcohol content accurate analyses of brandies are more difficult to attain than with wines. The high coefficient of cubical expansion may introduce volumetric errors. Alcohol itself may interfere in the reaction or modify the end point. The procedures given here generally follow those of the Association of Official Analytical Chemists (1970). For a method of determining esters, see p. 714. For a discussion of brandy analysis, see Guymon (1965), and Soumalainen et al. (1968).

Apparent Proof

Float an appropriate hydrometer in the brandy. The usual hydrometers used by government agents are for 80° to 100° proof, 100° to 140°, 130° to 170°, or 160° to 206°. These are calibrated in 0.5 per cent subdivisions at 60°F. It is possible to estimate to 0.1°. Measure the temperature and make the appropriate correction from Table 68.

Schoeneman (1959) has shown that distilled spirits can be proofed more accurately at room temperature. If it is necessary to proof spirits at a temperature different than room temperature, the temperature gradient between the spirits and the room should not be greater than 10°F. Schoeneman recommends in proofing operations that the hydrometer,

TABLE 68

APPROXIMATE TEMPERATURE CORRECTION TABLE FOR ALCOHOL HYDROMETERS[1]

(Calibrated at 60°F.)

Proof	Average Correction per °F.			
Reading	51°–59°F.	61°–70°F.	71°–80°F.	81°90°F.
	Add	Subtract	Subtract	Subtract
10	0.08	0.13	0.16	0.19
20	0.12	0.16	0.20	0.23
30	0.20	0.23	0.25	0.26
40	0.29	0.30	0.30	0.30
50	0.37	0.35	0.35	0.35
60	0.42	0.39	0.38	0.38
70	0.41	0.40	0.41	0.41
80	0.40	0.40	0.41	0.41
90	0.38	0.39	0.39	0.40
100	0.37	0.38	0.38	0.39
110	0.36	0.36	0.37	0.38
120	0.34	0.35	0.36	0.36
130	0.33	0.34	0.35	0.35
140	0.32	0.33	0.34	0.34
150	0.31	0.32	0.32	0.33
160	0.29	0.31	0.31	0.32
170	0.28	0.29	0.29	0.30
180	0.25	0.26	0.27	0.28
190	0.21	0.22	0.24	0.25
200	. . .	0.17	0.18	0.20

[1] Source of data: U. S. Internal Revenue Service (1962).

thermometer, cylinder, and sample should be allowed to come to room temperature. Then after the first set of hydrometer and thermometer readings, the analyst should remove and dry the hydrometer, re-invert the cylinder and contents (with thermometer left in place) several times to again bring about complete thermal equilibrium throughout the system, re-temper the hydrometer, dry the stem, and again take readings.

True Proof

An approximation of the true proof can be obtained by correcting the apparent proof for the effect of the extract. Determine the extract as indicated on p. 722 and for every 100 mg. of extract per 100 ml. add 0.4° proof. This procedure is applicable to brandies containing not more than 600 mg. of extract per 100 ml.

The pycnometer procedure requires a water bath, an accurate analytical balance, and a distillation apparatus. Fill a 100 ml. glass-stoppered volumetric flask, and bring to 60° or 68°F. in the water bath. Correct to the exact volume and transfer to a 500 ml. distillation flask. Rinse three times using a total of 25 ml. of water. Place the volumetric flask so that the adapter just extends into the bulb. Surround the volumetric flask with ice. Distill about 96 ml. in not less than 30 or more than 60 minutes. Rinse off the adapter. The water at the outlet of the condenser should not be less than 77°F. Place in the water bath and bring to volume and temperature (after mixing). Use a filter paper to dry the neck of the volumetric flask. Dry the outside and weigh. The volumetric flask should previously have been weighed dry and empty and filled with water at 60° or 68°F. The specific gravity in air equals weight of sample divided by the weight of water. The alcohol percentage at 60°F. corresponding to the specific gravity is given in Table 67. A more complete table is given by the Association of Official Analytical Chemists (1970).

The true proof can also be obtained on the distillate by the use of the proper hydrometer or with the immersion refractometer.

Extract

Clean a platinum crucible or a porcelain evaporating dish and dry at 230°F. Cool in a desiccator and weigh. Transfer the residue from the alcohol determination to the crucible or dish. Rinse out three times with a total of 25 ml. of 50 per cent alcohol. (Of course, the original brandy may also be used as the sample.) Evaporate nearly to dryness on a steam bath, then heat 30 minutes in a drying oven at 212°F. Cool in a desiccator and weigh.

Acidity

Neutralize about 250 ml. of boiled distilled water in a large porcelain evaporating dish. Use 2 ml. of 1 per cent phenolphthalein in neutral alcohol as an indicator. Now add 25 ml. of brandy and titrate with 0.1 N sodium hydroxide using a 10 ml. burette calibrated in 0.05 ml. With aged brandies the end point is more to an orange rather than pink. Calculate the total acidity as mg. acetic per 100 ml. ($N \times$ ml. sodium hydroxide $\times$ 60 $\times$ 100/25.)

The fixed acidity is determined by evaporation of 25 or 50 ml. of brandy in a platinum or porcelain dish to dryness on a steam bath. Then dry in an oven for 30 minutes at 212°F. Dissolve the residue with several portions (25 to 50 ml. in all) of neutral alcohol (of about the same proof as the sample) transferring to a large porcelain dish. Add 250 ml. of boiled, distilled, neutralized water. Titrate with 0.1 N sodium hydroxide and calculate as above.

The volatile acidity is obtained by the difference between the total and fixed acidities. For problems in the determination of the pH and total acidity of brandy see Koch et al. (1965).

Fusel Oil

The procedure is that of Guymon and Nakagiri (1952). Dissolve 0.05 gm. of p-dimethylaminobenzaldehyde in 100 ml. concentrated sulfuric acid. (Prepare daily.) Prepare fusel oil standards by mixing four volumes of isoamyl alcohol and one volume of isobutyl alcohol. (The alcohols should be redistilled and a middle cut used for the standards.) Then weigh 1.0 gm. of this mixture and dilute to 1000 ml. with water. Finally, pipette 0, 5, 10, 25, 35 ml. of this solution into 100 ml. volumetric

TABLE 69

PERCENTAGES BY VOLUME AT 60°F. CORRESPONDING TO SPECIFIC GRAVITIES AT VARIOUS TEMPERATURES[1]

Apparent Specific Gravity	$\frac{60°}{60°}$	$\frac{68°}{68°}$	Apparent Specific Gravity	$\frac{60°}{60°}$	$\frac{68°}{68°}$
0.9532	39.04	37.69	0.9389	47.52	46.18
0.9525	39.49	38.14	0.9380	48.00	46.67
0.9517	40.01	38.65	0.9371	48.48	47.15
0.9509	40.52	39.16	0.9361	49.01	47.68
0.9501	41.02	39.67	0.9351	49.52	48.21
0.9493	41.52	40.16	0.9341	50.04	48.73
0.9485	42.01	40.65	0.9332	50.50	49.19
0.9477	42.49	41.14	0.9322	51.01	49.70
0.9468	43.04	41.68	0.9312	51.51	50.21
0.9460	43.51	42.15	0.9302	52.01	50.71
0.9451	44.04	42.60	0.9292	52.51	51.21
0.9443	44.50	43.15	0.9282	53.00	51.70
0.9434	45.02	43.67	0.9272	53.50	52.20
0.9425	45.53	44.18	0.9261	54.03	52.74
0.9416	46.04	44.69	0.9251	54.52	53.22
0.9408	46.48	45.14	0.9241	55.00	53.71
0.9398	47.03	45.69			

[1] Source of data: Association of Official Agricultural Chemists (1965).

flasks, add 7 ml. of 95 per cent neutral ethanol, and dilute to volume with water.

The distillate from the ester determination (p. 714) may be used for fusel oil analysis following an appropriate dilution, generally 1 to 5. If high concentrations of acetaldehyde are present, they must be removed by oxidation with silver oxide.

Pipette 1 ml. samples of standards and diluted brandy distillates into 25 × 150 mm. Pyrex test tubes and place in an ice bath. With the bottom of the test tube submerged in the ice water, add 20 ml. of ice-cold p-dimethylaminobenzaldehyde in sulfuric acid with a free flowing pipette. Care should be taken to agitate the contents of the tube as the first few ml. are run in. Mix and keep in the ice bath until all samples are prepared. Cover the tops of all the tubes with aluminum foil. Transfer the tubes to a boiling water bath for 20 minutes. After 20 minutes, return the tubes to the ice bath for 3 to 5 minutes. Finally, bring the contents of the tubes to room temperature and determine the transmittancy in a colorimeter at 520 mμ against concentrated sulfuric acid. Read the fusel oil content from a standard curve of concentration versus transmittancy as mg. fusel oil per 100 ml.

Aldehydes

The reagents are the same as those given under aldehyde determination in wines on page 712.

To 300 ml. of boiled distilled water, add 10 ml. of solution A and 50 ml. of brandy distillate of about 50 per cent alcohol content. Stopper, mix, and allow to stand 15 minutes. Add 10 ml. of solution B, mix, and let stand another 15 minutes. Then, add 10 ml. of solution C, 10 ml. of starch solution, mix, and titrate to a faint blue end point with ca. 0.1 N iodine solution. Now add 10 ml. of solution D and titrate to the same blue end point with 0.05 N iodine. Total aldehydes as mg. acetaldehyde per 100 ml. equals ml. iodine $\times N \times 22.4 \times 100$/ml. sample. This procedure gives total aldehyde. For free aldehydes use the procedure given on page 712. See also Guymon and Nakagiri (1957).

Furfural

The furfural content of wine is of minor importance and is seldom determined. However, it is of importance in the analysis of brandy; and is given here for those who may wish to assay the furfural content of brandy. The following procedure is taken from Joslyn and Amerine (1941).

"The basis for this method is the color developed by furfural in the presence of aniline and hydrochloric acid.

"Prepare a standard furfural solution by weighing out 1 gm. of redistilled furfural and diluting to 100 ml. with 95 per cent alcohol. This solution is fairly stable. Also prepare a dilute furfural solution using 1 ml. of the standard and diluting to 100 ml. with 50 per cent alcohol. One ml. of this latter solution contains 0.1 mg. of furfural. The aniline used must be as nearly colorless as possible. It can be prepared by redistillation.

"An aliquot of the distillate prepared for the ester determination may be used for this procedure. Dilute 10 to 20 ml. of this distillate to 50 ml. with 50 per cent alcohol in a large test tube. Also dilute 0.5, 1, 2, 3, and 4 ml. of the dilute furfural standard with 50 per cent alcohol to 50 ml. in large test tubes. Add two ml. of colorless aniline and 0.5 ml. of hydrochloric acid (sp. gr. 1.125) to all the tubes. Mix and leave in a water bath at about 60°F. for 15 minutes. Compare the color in the unknown with that of the standards, either directly or with one of the knowns in a color comparator. A photoelectric color comparator may be used advantageously."

BIBLIOGRAPHY

United States

AMERINE, M. A. 1948. Hydroxymethylfurfural in California wines. Food Research 13, 264–269.

AMERINE, M. A. 1970. Laboratory Procedures for Enology. Associated Students Store, Davis.

AMERINE, M. A., and JOSLYN, M. A. 1970. Table Wines; the Technology of Their Production. University of California Press, Berkeley and Los Angeles.

AMERINE, M. A., and KISHABA, T. T. 1952. Use of the flame photometer for determining the sodium, potassium and calcium content of wine. Proc. Am. Soc. Enol. 1952, 77–86.

AMERINE, M. A., and ROESSLER, E. B. 1952. Techniques and problems in the organoleptic examination of wines. Ibid. 1952, 97–115.

AMERINE, M. A., OUGH, C. S., and BAILEY, C. B. 1959A. Color values of California wines. Food Technol. 13, 170–175.

AMERINE, M. A., PANGBORN, R. M., and ROESSLER, E. B. 1965. Principles of Sensory Evaluation of Food. Academic Press, New York.

AMERINE, M. A., ROESSLER, E. B., and FILIPELLO, F. 1959B. Modern sensory methods of evaluating wine. Hilgardia 28, 477–567.

AMERINE, M. A., THOUKIS, G., and VIDAL-BARRAQUER MARFÁ, R. 1953. Further data on the sodium content of wines. Proc. Am. Soc. Enol. 1953, 157–166.

ANON. 1955. Convention internationale pour l'unification des méthodes d'analyse et d'appréciation des vins. Bull. office intern. vin 28 (291), 22–34. (See also Ann. ferment. 1, 310–319.)

ANON. 1959. The titrimetric method of measuring carbon dioxide in wine. Wines and Vines 40, No. 9, 29.

ANON. 1963. Arrêté du 24 juin 1963 relatif aux méthodes officielles d'analyses des vins et des moûts. Paris, Journaux Officiels. Journal officiel N° 63–154, 1037 (4551–4587), 20 September 1963.

ANON. 1970. Méthode de dosage des constituants des vins et des moûts. Bull. Office Inter. Vin 43, No. 473–474, 772–798.

ARNOLD, A. 1957. Beiträge zur refraktometrischen Methode der Mostgewichtsbestimmung. Vitis 1, 109–120.

ASSOCIATION OF OFFICIAL ANALYTICAL CHEMISTS. 1970. Official Methods of Analysis of the Association of Official Analytical Chemists. 11 ed. Washington, D. C.

BAKER, G. A., OUGH, C. S., and AMERINE, M. A. 1965. Scoring vs. comparative rating of sensory quality of wines. J. Food Sci. 30, 1055–1062.

BERG, H. W. 1963. Stabilisation des anthocyannes. Comportement de la couleur dans les vins rouges. Ann. technol. agr., 12, numéro hors-série 1, 247–261.

BERG, H. W., OUGH, C. S. and CHICHESTER, C. O. 1964. The prediction of perceptibility of luminous-transmittance and dominant wave-length differences among red wines by spectrophotometric measurements. J. Food Sci. 29, 661–667.

BERGNER, K. G., and LANG, B. 1971. Zur Bestimmung von Eisen, Kupfer, Zink, Mangan und Cadmium in Traubenmost und Wein mit Hilfe der Atomabsorptionsspektrophotometrie. Deut. Lebensm.-Rundsch. 67, 121–124.

BEYTHIEN, A., and DIEMAIR, W. 1963. Laboratoriumsbuch für den Lebensmittelchemiker. 8 ed. Verlag von Theodor Steinkopff, Dresden und Leipzig. The German AOAC for wines, brandy, etc. Later editions should be consulted.

BONASTRE, J. 1959. Contribution à l'étude des matières minérales dans les produits végétaux application au vin. Ann. technol. agr. 8, 377–446.

CAPUTI, JR., A., and UEDA, M. 1967. The determination of copper and iron in wine by absorption spectrophotometry. Am. J. Enol. Vitic. 18, 66–70.

CAPUTI, JR., A., UEDA, M., WALTER, P., and BROWN, T. 1970. Titrimetric determination of carbon dioxide in wine. Am. J. Enol. Vitic. 21, 140–144.

CASTELLI, T. 1969. Il vino al microscopio. L. Scialpi, Rome.

COOKE, G. M. 1964. Effect of grape pulp upon soluble solids determinations. Am. J. Enol. Vitic. 15, 11–16.

CRAWFORD, C., BOUTHILET, R. J., and CAPUTI, A., JR. 1958. Color standards for white wines. Am. J. Enol. 9, 194–201.

DEAN, J. A. 1960. Flame Photometry. McGraw-Hill Book Co., New York.

DEIBNER, L. 1953. Quelques dispositifs spéciaux facilitant les mesures poten-tiométriques dans les vins à l'abri de l'air. Ann. fals. et fraudes 46, 111–122.

DEIBNER, L. 1956. Recherches sur les techniques de mesure du potentiel d'oxydoréduction dans les jus de raisin et les vins. Détermination de ce potentiel dans quelques jus de raisin et quelques vins. Ann. technol. agr. 5, 31–67.

DEIBNER, L. 1957. Potentiel oxydoréducteur des vins: ' son importance, sa signification; tendances actuelles de la technique de sa mesure. Ind. agr. alim (Paris) 74, 273–283.

DEIBNER, L., and MOURGUES, J. 1964. Influence de quelques facteurs sur les résultats de mesures du potentiel oxydoréducteur des vins. Ann. technol. agr. 13, 31–43.

DIEMAIR, W., and GUNDERMANN, E. 1959. Zur Kalium und Natriumbestim-mung in Wein. Z. Lebensm.-Untersuch. u. -Forsch. 109, 469–474.

DITZ, E. 1965. Contribution au dosage des jus de fruits. Détermination du phosphore, du potassium, du sodium et du calcium. Ann. technol. agr. 14, 67–78.

DUJARDIN, J., DUJARDIN, L., and DUJARDIN, R. 1938. Notice sur les Instru-ments de Précision Appliqués à l'Oenologie. Dujardin-Salleron, Paris.

EDGE, R. A. 1958. The detection of cyanides and ferrocyanides in wines. S. African J. Agr. Sci. 1, 337.

FESSLER, J. H. 1941. Alcohol determination by dichromate method. Wines and Vines 22, No. 4, 17–18.

FILIPELLO, F. 1957. Organoleptic wine-quality evaluation. II. Performance of judges. Food Technol. 11, 51–53.

FILIPELLO, F., and BERG, H. W. 1959. The present status of consumer tests on wine. Am. J. Enol. Vitic. 10, 8–12.

GETTLER, A. O., and GOLDBAUM, L. 1947. Detection and estimation of micro-quantities of cyanide. Anal. Chem. 19, 270–271.

GUYMON, J. F. 1965. Analytical Procedures for Brandy. Department of Viti-culture and Enology, Univ. California, Davis.

GUYMON, J. F., and CROWELL, E. A. 1959. The chemical determination of al-cohol in wines and stillage by dichromate. J. Assoc. Off. Agr. Chem. 42, 393–398.

GUYMON, J. F., and CROWELL, E. A. 1963. Determination of aldehydes in wines and spirits by the direct bisulfite method. Ibid. 46, 276–284.

GUYMON, J. F., and NAKAGIRI, J. 1952. Methods for the determinations of fusel oil. Proc. Am. Soc. Enol. 1952, 117–134.

GUYMON, J. F., and NAKAGIRI, J. 1957. The bisulfite determination of free and combined aldehydes in distilled spirits. J. Assoc. Off. Agr. Chem. 40, 561–575.

HEIDE, C. VON DER, and SCHMITTHENNER, F. 1922. Der Wein. F. Vieweg und Sohn, Braunschweig.

HENNIG, K. 1962. Chemische Untersuchungsmethoden für Weinbereiter und Süssmosthersteller. 5 ed. Verlag Eugen Ulmer, Stuttgart.

HENNIG, K., and LAY, A. 1962. Die Bestimmung der Kohlensäure in Wein, Perlwein und Schaumwein. Weinberg u. Keller 9, 202–205.

HENNIG, K., and LAY, A. 1964. Kolorimetrische Bestimmung von Kupfer im Wein mit Oxalsäure-bis-(cyclohexylidenhydrazid) "Cuprizon." Ibid. 11, 585–588.

HODGMAN, C. D. 1964. Handbook of Chemistry and Physics. 45 ed. The Chemical Rubber Co., Cleveland. (See latest edition.)

HORAK, W., FREY, A., and GUNTHER, G. 1968. Untersuchungen der Branntweine und Sprite. *In* Diemair, W. *ed.* Alkoholische Genussmittel. Springer Verlag, Berlin. (See p. 654–719.)

HUBACH, C. E. 1948. Detection of cyanides and ferrocyanides in wines. Anal. Chem. 20, 1115–1116.

ITOGA, I. 1958. Results of the test of "Tag Twin Ebulliometer" ethanol determining apparatus. Rep. Research Lab. Kirin Brewery Co. 1, 57–59.

IWANO, S., and SAWANOBORI, H. 1962. Titration of calcium and magnesium in wine with ethylenediamine tetraacetate. Am. J. Enol. Vitic. 13, 54–57.

JAULMES, P. 1951. Analyse des Vins. 2 ed. Librairie Coulet, Dubois et Poulain, Montpellier.

JAULMES, P. 1959. La sous-commission pour l'unification des méthodes d'analyse des vins de l'Office International de la Vigne et du Vin. Ann. fals. et fraudes 52, 215–220.

JAULMES, P., and BRUN, S. 1963A. La mesure pycnometrique de la masse volumique de la densité et du degré alcoolique des vins. Ann. fals et. expert. chim. 56, 129–142.

JAULMES, P., and BRUN, S. 1963B. Les nouvelles tables de corrections de température pour le masse volumetrique des moûts, vins, vins doux, etc. *Ibid.* 56, 143–178.

JAULMES, P., and ESPEZEL, P. 1935. Le dosage de l'acetaldehyde dans les vins et les spiritueux. *Ibid.* 28, 325–335.

JAULMES, P., and MARIGNAN, R. 1953. Conséquences de l'adoption de la témpérature de référence de 20° pour la definition du degre alcoolique des vins et des spiritueux. *Ibid.* 46, 208–212.

JAULMES, P., and MESTRES, R. 1958. Dosage de alcools par oxydation. Chim. anal. 40, 413–424.

JAULMES, P., MESTRES, R., and MANDROU, B. 1964. Le dosage de l'acide sorbique dans le vins. *Ibid.* 57, 119–122.

JOSLYN, M. A. 1970. Methods in Food Analysis: Physical, Chemical, and Instrumental Methods of Analysis. Academic Press, New York.

JOSLYN, M. A. 1950. Methods in Food Analysis, Applied to Plant Products. Academic Press, Inc., New York.

JOSLYN, M. A., and AMERINE, M. A. 1941. Commercial production of brandy. Calif. Agr. Expt. Sta. Bull. 652.

JOSLYN, M. A., and AMERINE, M. A. 1964. Dessert, Appetizer and Related Flavored Wines. University of California, Division of Agricultural Sciences, Berkeley.

JOSLYN, M. A., MARSH, G. L., and FESSLER, J. 1937. A comparison of several physical methods for the determination of the alcohol content of wine. J. Assoc. Off. Agr. Chem. 20, 116–130.

JOURET, C., and POUX, C. 1961A. Étude d'une technique de dosage du potassium par spectrophotométrie de flamme dans les vins et les moûts. Ann. technol. agr. 10, 351–359.

JOURET, C., and POUX, C. 1961B. Note sur les teneurs en potassium, sodium et chlore des vignes des terrains salés. *Ibid.* 10, 369–374.

KIELHÖFER, E., and AUMANN, H. 1958. Die Aldehydbestimmung im Wein. Z. Lebensm.-Untersuch. u. -Forsch. 107, 406–413.

KOCH, J., and BRETTHAUER, G. 1951. Über eine zuverlässige Methode zur Bestimmung der Milchsäure in Süssmost und Wein. Z. anal. Chem. 132, 346–356.

KOCH, J., and SCHIFFNER, F. 1957. Die Bestimmung der Gesamtsäure in Fruchtsäften und -weinen. Z. Lebensm.-Untersuch. u. -Forsch. 106, 119–122.

KOCH, J., HESS, D., and SCHILLER, H. 1965. Zur Analytik von Weinbrand. I. Bestimmung des pH-Wertes und der Gesamtsäure. Ibid. 126, 275–281.

MACKINNEY, G., and CHICHESTER, C. O. 1954. The color problem in foods. Adv. Food Research 5, 301–351.

MARSH, G. L., and NOBUSADA, K. 1938. Iron determination methods. Wine Review 6, No. 9, 20–21.

MATCHETT, J. R., LEGAULT, R. R., NIMMO, C. C., and NOTTER, G. K. 1944. Tartrates from grape wastes. Ind. Eng. Chem. 36, 851–857.

MAYER, K., and BUSCH, I. 1963. Über eine enzymatische Äpfelsäure-bestimmung in Wein und Traubensaft. Mitt. Gebiete Lebens. u. Hyg., 45, 60–65.

MERANGER, J. C., and SOMERS, E. 1968. Determination of heavy metals in wines by atomic absorption spectrophotometry. J. Assoc. Off. Anal. Chem. 51, 922–925.

MORRISON, R. L., and EDWARDS, T. E. 1963. Semi-automatic determination of ethanol in wine by the micro-dichromate method. Am. J. Enol. Vitic. 14, 185–193.

NÈGRE, E. 1942–1943. Les matières tannoïdes et la composition des vins. Bull. office intern. vin 15, No. 154, 20–52; 16, No. 155, 25–56.

NÈGRE, E., DUGAL, A., and EVESQUE, J. M. 1958. Dosage de l'acide tartrique sous forme de bitartarte de potassium dans les moûts et les vins. Ann. technol. agr. 7, 31–101.

OUGH, C. S. 1959. A survey of commercial practices in sensory examination of wines. Am. J. Enol. Vitic. 10, 191–195.

OUGH, C. S., and AMERINE, M. A. 1959. Dissolved oxygen determination in wine. Food Research 24, 744–748.

OUGH, C. S., and BERG, H. W. 1959. Studies on various light sources concerning the evaluation and differentiation of red wine color. Am. J. Enol. Vitic. 10, 159–163.

PANGBORN, R. M., OUGH, C. S., and CHRISP, R. B. 1964. Taste interrelationship of sucrose, tartaric acid, and caffeine in white table wine. Am. J. Enol. Vitic. 15, 154–161.

PARONETTO, L. 1953. Dosaggio della CO_2 in peso nei vini spumanti. Riv. viticolt. e enol. (Conegliano) 6, 143–147.

PATAKY, M. B. 1965. Sur les particularités du dosage spectrophotométrique des anthocyannes. Ann. technol. agr. 14, 79–85.

PAUL, F. 1967. Die "Rangziffern-Methode," ein einfache Möglichkeit für den organoleptischen Vergleich zweier oder mehrerer Proben. Mitt. Rebe Wein, Obstbau Früchtever. (Klosterneuburg) 17, 280–288.

PEYNAUD, E., and BLOUIN, J. 1965. Comparaison de quelques méthodes de dosage de l'acide L-malique. Ann. technol. agr. 14, 61–66.

PEYNAUD, E., and LAFON-LAFOURCADE, S. 1965. Étude d'un dosage simple de l'acide malique appliqué aux vins à l'aide de Schizosaccharomyces pombe. Ibid. 14, 49–59.

POSTEL, W. 1970. Kohlensäurebestimmung und Kohlensäuregehalt in Wein. Deut. Lebensm.-Rundsch. 66, 185–190.

POUX, C. 1969. Dosage enzymatique de l'acide L(−) malique. Ann. technol. agr. 18, 359–366.

PRO, M. J. 1952. Report on the spectrophotometric determination of tannin in wines and whiskies. J. Assoc. Off. Agr. Chem. 35, 255–257.

PRO, M. J., ETIENNE, A., and FEENY, F. 1959. Vacuum system for the determination of carbon dioxide. Internal Revenue Service, Washington, D. C. See also J. Assoc. Off. Agr. Chem. 42, 679–683.

PRO, M. J., and MATHERS, A. P. 1954. Metallic elements in wine by flame photometry. J. Assoc. Off. Agr. Chemists. 37, 945–960.

RIBÉREAU-GAYON, J., and PEYNAUD, E. 1958. Analyse et Contrôle des Vins. 2 ed. Librairie Polytechnique Ch. Béranger, Paris.

ROBIRDS, F. M., and ROSSI, E. A., JR. 1966. Non-sugar solids in various varieties of California grapes. Am. J. Enol. Vitic. 17, 31–37.

ROESSLER, E. B., WARREN, J., and GUYMON, J. F. 1948. Significance in triangular taste tests. Food Research 13, 503–505.

SAYWELL, J. G., and CUNNINGHAM, B. B. 1937. Determination of iron. Colorimetric o-phenanthroline method. Ind. Eng. Chem., Anal. Ed. 9, 67–69.

SCHOENEMAN, R. L. 1959. Report on distilled spirits. J. Assoc. Off. Agr. Chemists 42, 327–329.

SINGLETON, V. L., and ROSSI, JR., J. A. 1965. Colorimetry of total phenolics with phosphomolybdic-phosphotungstic acid reagents. Am. J. Enol. Vitic. 16, 144–158.

SMIT, C. J. B., JOSLYN, M. A., and LUKTON, A. 1955. Determination of tannins and related polyphenols in foods; comparison of Loewenthal and Pro methods. Anal. Chem. 27, 1159–1162.

SOUMALAINEN, H., KAUPPILA, O. A. P., NYKÄNEN, L., and PEETONEN, R. J. 1968. Branntweine. In Diemair, W. ed. Alkoholische Genussmittel, Springer Verlag, Berlin. (See p. 496–653.)

SUDRAUD, P. 1958. Interpretation des courbes d'absorption des vins rouges. Ann. technol. agr. 7, 203–208.

TOBIE, W. C. 1941. Improved methods of distilled-liquor analyses. Food Research 6, 15–19.

TROOST, T. 1965. Unter welchen Voraussetzungen lässt eine organoleptische Weinprüfung in Zusammenspiel mit einer Weinanalyse ein Höchstmass an Zuverlässigkeit erwarten? Deut. Weinbau 20, 262–264.

U. S. INTERNAL REVENUE SERVICE. 1959. Carbon dioxide test procedures. Office of the Commissioner of Internal Revenue, Industry Cir. 59–47.

U. S. INTERNAL REVENUE SERVICE. 1970A. Part 240.531 of Title 26, Code of Federal Regulations. U. S. Govt. Print. Office, Washington, D. C.

U. S. INTERNAL REVENUE SERVICE. 1970B. Gauging Manual Embracing Instructions and Tables for Determining the Quantity of Distilled Spirits by Proof and Weight. U. S. Govt. Print Office, Washington, D. C. (U. S. Treasury Dept., IRS Publication No. 455).

VILLFORTH F. 1958. Studien zum Farbwert und zur Farbenanalyse von Rotweinen. Wein-Wissen. 1958, 1–8.

VOGT, E. 1958. Weinchemie und Weinanalyse. 2 ed. Eugen Ulmer, Stuttgart.

WINKLER, A. J., and AMERINE, M. A. 1938. Color in California wines. I and II. Food Research 3, 429–447.

ZIMMERMANN, H. W. 1963. Studies on the dichromate method of alcohol determination. Am. J. Enol. Vitic. 14, 205–213.

Other Countries[4]

France[5]

ANON. 1963. Textes d'intérêt général, répression des fraudes. Méthodes officielles d'analyses des vins et des moûts (Arrêté du 24 juin 1963). Journaux Officiels, Paris.

Germany[6]

FRANCK, R., and JUNGE, C. 1970. Weinanalytik. Untersuchung von Wein und ähnlichen alkoholischen Erzeugnissen sowie von Fruchtsäften nach der allgemeinen Verwaltungsvorschrift und den Vorschriften des Internationalen Amtes für Rebe und Wein. Verlag Carl Heymanns, Köln. (Not official).
HESS, D., and KOPPE, F. 1968. Wein II: Weinanalytik. *In* Diemair, W. Alkoholische Genussmittel, Springer Verlag, Berlin. (See p. 311–495.)

Italy

ANON. 1958. Metodi Ufficiali Analisi per Materie che Interassano l'Agricoltura. II (part I). Mosti, Vini, Birre, Aceti, Sostanze Tartariche, Materie Tanniche. Librerie dello Stato, Rome.

Portugal

ANON. 1963. Métodos Oficiais para a Análise de Vinhos, Vinagres e Azeites. Ministério do Comércio, Indústria e Agricultura, Direcção Geral da Acção Social Agrária, Lisbon.
AZEVEDO, M. P. DE. 1948. O. Auxiliar do Analista. 2 ed. Edição do Instituto do Vinho do Pôrto, Pôrto. (Not official).

Russia

AGABAL'ĨANTS, G. G. *ed.* 1969. Khimiko-tekhnologicheskii kontrol vinodeliĩã. Pischepromizdat, Moscow. (Not official.)

Spain

ANON. 1956. Analisis de Vinos. Metodos Oficiales para los Laboratorios Dependientes del Ministerio de Agricultura. Ministerio de Agricultura, Madrid.

Switzerland

SCHWEIZ. VEREIN ANALYTISCHER CHEMIKER. 1937. Schweizerisches Lebensmittel buch. 4 ed. Zimmermann & Cie, Berne (wines p. 287–310).

---

[4] These are official or semi-official procedures.
[5] See Anon. (1963) on p. 725.
[6] See also Beythien and Diemair (1963) on p. 725.

CHAPTER 20

Legal Restrictions on Wine Making

Assyrian records indicate that legal controls on wine making are several thousand years old. The regulations seem to have been made with the idea of preventing adulteration or sophistication of commercial wines. To prevent dilution of wine in the Middle Ages, taverns were forbidden to have water. This concept is present in the laws of many countries at present. In Italy, for example, law 176 of August 4, 1954, provides a minimum fine of 200,000 lira for use of prohibited non-grape products in wine making. During Roman and later times wines became a source of revenue. Various legal restrictions were set up to prevent wines from being diluted or otherwise reduced in quality with consequent loss in sales and reduction in the state's revenue. This aspect is still inherent in many of the regulations of the U. S. Internal Revenue Service. The importance of this is indicated by the large volume of sales of alcoholic beverages in this country, Table 70. The federal revenue from the sale of alcoholic beverages amounted to 3.7 billion dollars in 1964!

Another concept, developed particularly in England, was that alcoholic beverages were a luxury product and should be especially taxed to produce additional revenue for the state. This idea is very much in evidence in modern British and American taxes on alcoholic beverages. It is not absent from the French and Italian tax structure. In the nineteenth and twentieth centuries taxes also took on a puritanical aspect as a means of controlling alcoholism or of securing conformity in behavior.

Finally, in the late nineteenth century the development of public health regulations for foods began and many of these were applied to wines. This aspect of legal control is still being developed. Wiley's (1906) tour to Europe specifically considered the public health aspects of wine production in certain wine and brandy regions in France and elsewhere.

Where a certain region has developed a particularly desirable reputation for the quality of its wines, the growers may attempt to prevent other areas from using their geographical appellation for their wines. Many countries, particularly France, thus protect their most famous regional wine names. Certain restrictions may also be placed on the producers as to varieties, production, minimum alcohol in addition to the geographical origin of the wine (p. 5). An interesting attempt to establish a regional appellation was the California law (p. 751) protecting "Central Coast Counties Dry Wine." Although their wines have a reputation for quality it is doubtful that a regional name could become established unless it represented a distinctive type. This is probably why varietal appellations have achieved public recognition to a much greater extent than regional appellations in California.

The 21st amendment to the U. S. Constitution repealed the 18th amendment and control of alcoholic beverages was returned to the states. The states have thus enacted 50 diverse legal and tax structures under which wines may be made and sold. The Wine Institute of California has evolved a suggested uniform wine law for the states. There is some uniformity in state regulations owing to this model law. At present, although wine can be legally made or sold in all states, there are many areas in some states which by local option laws are dry or which seriously obstruct the sale of wine.

TABLE 70

UNITED STATES PER CAPITA CONSUMPTION OF ALCOHOLIC BEVERAGES
(in Thousands for Totals)

Calendar Years Average	Population[1]	All Wine	Per Capita	Malt Beverages[2]	Per Capita	Distilled Spirits[3]	Per Capita
1900–1904	79,127	...	0.38	...	17.32	...	1.39
1905–1909	87,057	...	0.46	...	19.96	...	1.47
1910–1914	95,590	...	0.52	...	20.77	...	1.48
1915–1919	102,699	...	0.54	...	15.62	...	1.19
1935–1939	128,967	63,285	0.49	1,519,521	11.78	121,738	0.94
1940–1944	133,225	100,121	0.75	1,971,855	14.80	161,121	1.21
1945–1949	142,148	117,162	0.82	2,555,883	17.98	188,665	1.33
1950–1954	155,977	137,493	0.88	2,589,912	16.60	190,321	1.22
1955–1959	171,126	151,593	0.89	2,621,886	15.32	213,558	1.25
1960–1964	185,778	172,922	0.93	2,839,867	15.29	252,978	1.36
1965–1969	197,875	206,707	1.04	3,329,714	16.80	326,738	1.65

Source: Private communications, Wine Institute (1959, 1966, 1971).
[1] Population 1955–1969, inclusive, taken from "1970 Statistical Abstract of the United States."
[2] Data for 1955–1961, inclusive, taken from "1963 Brewers Almanac." 1962–1964, inclusive, data from U. S. Brewers Association, Inc. 1965–1969 from "1970 Brewers Almanac."
[3] Data for 1955–1969, inclusive, taken from "1969 Annual Statistical Review of Distilled Spirits Industry."

Only the most important California and Federal regulations can be reviewed. The Federal and State laws are often changed and, although we believe those presented here are correct as of the date of going to press, small and large changes in the regulations can be anticipated. For those who wish to go into wine production in this country in the future we recommend that they consult the local regulatory agencies as well as the nearest regional office of Internal Revenue Service, Alcohol, Tobacco and Firearms Division. Regional offices are located in Atlanta, Chicago, Cincinnati, Dallas, New York, Philadelphia, and San Francisco. The head office is, of course, in Washington, D. C. For California producers the legal staff of the Wine Institute in San Francisco is a valuable source of information and advice. There are also a number of consultants in this state who specialize in wine regulations.

WINES—FEDERAL

The statutory basis upon which all of the Internal Revenue Service regulations relating to the production of distilled spirits, wine, and beer are issued in the United States Internal Revenue Code of 1954, as amended, Sub-title E, Chapter 51, Title 26, United States Code 1; see U. S. Laws (1954, 1958, 1965). Similarly, regulations relating to the advertising of wine and distilled spirits and related matters are based on the Federal Alcohol Administration Act of 1935, as amended, 49 Stat. 977; see U. S. Federal Alcohol Administration (1937), U. S. Internal Revenue Service (1961A, 1961B, 1961C), and Udell (1968).

Definitions.—It is not our intention here to give a comprehensive discussion of State and Federal regulations but only to indicate the major problems involved. No one should contemplate operating a winery without carefully studying the above regulations. Consultation with officers of the Internal Revenue Service or with lawyers or professionals who specialize in interpreting these regulations is also advised.

Wine must contain not less than 7 nor over 24 per cent alcohol. Grape wine is defined (U. S. Internal Revenue Service, 1961A) as "wine produced by the normal alcoholic fermentation of the juice of sound, ripe grapes (including restored or unrestored pure condensed grape must), with or without the addition, after fermentation, of pure condensed grape must, and with or without added fortifying grape spirits or alcohol, but without other addition or abstraction except as may occur in cellar treatment: *Provided,* That the product may be ameliorated before, during or after fermentation by either of the following methods:

(i) By adding, separately or in combination, dry sugar, or such an amount of sugar and water solution as will not increase the volume of the resulting product more than 35 per cent; but in no event shall any product so ameliorated have an alcohol content, derived by fermentation, of more than 13 per cent by volume, or a natural acid content, if water has been added, of less than 5 parts per thousand, or a total solids content of more than 22 grams per 100 cubic centimeters.

(ii) By adding, separately or in combination, not more than 20 per cent by weight of dry sugar, or not more than 10 per cent by weight of water.

(iii) In the case of domestic wine, in accordance with section 5383 of the Internal Revenue Code.

The maximum volatile acidity, calculated as acetic acid and exclusive of sulphur dioxide, shall not be, for natural red wine, more than 0.14 gram, and for other grape wine, more than 0.12 gram, per 100 cubic centimeters (20°C.). Grape wine deriving its characteristic color or lack of color from the presence or absence of the red coloring matter of the skins, juice, or pulp of grapes may be designated as "red wine," "pink (or rose) wine," "amber wine," or "white wine" as the case may be. Any grape wine containing no added grape brandy or alcohol may be further designated as "natural."

(2) "Table wine" is grape wine having an alcoholic content not in excess of 14 per cent by volume. Such wine may also be designated as "light wine," "red table wine," etc., as the case may be.

(3) "Dessert wine" is grape wine having an alcoholic content in excess of 14 per cent but not in excess of 24 per cent by volume. Dessert wine having the taste, aroma and characteristics generally attributed to sherry and an alcoholic content, derived in part from added grape brandy or alcohol, of not less than 17 per cent by volume, may be designated as "sherry." Dessert wines having the taste, aroma and characteristics generally attributed to angelica, madeira, muscatel and port and an alcoholic content, derived in part from added grape brandy or alcohol, of not less than 18 per cent by volume, may be designated as "angelica," "madeira," "muscatel," or "port" respectively. Dessert wines having the taste, aroma, and characteristics generally attributed to any of the above products and an alcoholic content, derived in part from added grape brandy or alcohol, in excess of 14 per cent by volume but, in the case of sherry, less than 17 per cent, or, in other cases, less than 18 per cent by volume, may be designated as "light sherry," "light angelica," "light madeira," "light muscatel" or "light port," respectively."

The definition elsewhere in the Code of Federal Regulations (U. S. Internal Revenue Service 1970A) differs somewhat. It defines natural grape wine as:

"the product of the juice of sound, ripe grapes, made with cellar treatment authorized by this part and having a total solids content subject to limitations stated in this subpart, but the total solids content of the wine shall in no case exceed 21 per cent by weight.

"In the production of natural grape wine without the use of sugar, no materials may be added to the juice or crushed grapes at the time of starting fermentation, except:

"(a) Water to reduce the juice to not less than 22 degrees (Brix) of total solids;

"(b) Yeast, or yeast cultures grown in grape juice, to any extent desired; or

"(c) Yeast foods, sterilizing agents, or other fermentation adjuncts under the provisions of subpart zz of this part."

It is in this definition of natural grape wine that practices in eastern and western United States differ radically. Under California climatic conditions grapes almost always ripen sufficiently to produce ten or more per cent alcohol and the acid content of the juice of our grapes is very rarely excessive. The opposite conditions prevail in grapes grown in eastern states. The regulations as applied to California permit use of a minimum amount of water at the time of crushing to flush equipment if the density of the juice is not reduced below 22° Balling or by more than one degree.

Outside of California, on the other hand, dry sugar or a sugar-water solution is commonly added: the latter when the acid content of the grape juice is high. The volume of ameliorating material (sugar and water) may not exceed 35 per cent of the total volume. Water, dry sugar or invert sugar solutions are used. This amelioration must not reduce the acidity of the finished wine below 0.5 per cent (calculated as tartaric acid). The same limitations apply to natural fruit wines. The pertinent regulation regarding amelioration (U. S. Internal Revenue Service, 1970A) are as follows:

Sec. 5383. Amelioration and Sweetening Limitations for Natural Grape Wines. (a) SWEETENING OF GRAPE WINES.—Any natural grape wine may be sweetened after fermentation and before taxpayment with pure dry sugar or liquid sugar if the total solids content of the finished wine does not exceed 12 per cent of the weight of the wine and the alcoholic content of the finished wine after sweetening is not more than 14 per cent by volume; except that the use under this subsection of liquid sugar shall be limited so that the resultant volume will not exceed the volume which could result from the maximum authorized use of pure dry sugar only.

[¶ 23860]

(b) HIGH ACID WINES.—

(1) AMELIORATION.—Before, during, and after fermentation ameliorating materials consisting of pure dry sugar or liquid sugar, water, or a combination of·sugar and water, may be added to natural grape wines of a winemaker's own production when such wines are made from juice having a natural fixed acid content of more than five parts per thousand (calculated before fermentation and as tartaric acid). Ameliorating material so added shall not reduce the natural fixed acid content of the·juice to less than five parts per thousand, nor exceed 35 per cent of the volume of juice (calculated exclusive of pulp), and ameliorating material combined.

(2) SWEETENING. — Any wine produced under this subsection may be sweetened by the producer thereof, after amelioration and fermentation, with pure dry sugar or liquid sugar if the total solids content of the finished wine does not exceed (A) 17 per cent by weight if the alcoholic content is more than 14 per cent volume, or (B) 21 per cent by weight if the alcoholic content is not more than 14 per cent by volume. The use under this paragraph of liquid sugar shall be limited to cases where the resultant volume does not exceed the volume which could result from the maximum authorized use of pure dry sugar only.

(3) WINE SPIRITS.—Wine spirits may be added (whether or not wine spirits were previously added) to wine produced under this subsection only if the wine contains not more than 14 per cent of alcohol by volume derived from fermentation.

[Sec. 5383 as amended by Act of June 21, 1965, P. L. 89-44, 79 Stat. 136, effective Jan. 1, 1966; Act of Oct. 22, 1968, P. L. 90-619, § 3, 82 Stat. 1236, effective Feb. 1, 1969.]

Citrus and fruit wines are similarly defined; only the definitions for fruit wine will be given (U. S. Internal Revenue Service 1961A):

(i) "Fruit wine" is wine (other than grape wine or citrus wine) produced by the normal alcoholic fermentation of the juice of sound, ripe fruit (including restored or unrestored pure condensed fruit must), with or without the addition, after fermentation, of pure condensed fruit must, and with or without added fruit brandy or alcohol, but without other addition or abstraction except as may occur in cellar treatment: *Provided*, That a domestic product may be ameliorated or sweetened in accordance with the provisions of section 5384 of the Internal Revenue Code and any product other than domestic may be ameliorated before, during, or after fermentation by adding, separately or in combination, dry sugar, or such an amount of sugar and water solution as will increase the volume of the resulting product, in the case of wines produced from loganberries, currants, or gooseberries, having a normal acidity of 20 parts or more per thousand, not more than 60 per cent, and in the case of other fruit wines, not more than 35 per cent, but in no event shall any product so ameliorated have an alcoholic content, derived by fermentation, of more than 13 per cent by volume, or a natural acid content, if water has been added, of less than 5 parts per thousand, or a total solids content of more than 22 grams per 100 cubic centimeters.

(ii) The maximum volatile acidity, calculated as acetic acid and exclusive of sulphur dioxide, shall not be, for natural fruit wine, more than 0.14 gram, and for other fruit wine, more than 0.12 gram, per 100 cubic centimeters (20°C.).

(iii) Any fruit wine containing no added brandy or alcohol may be further designated as "natural."

(2) "Berry wine" is fruit wine produced from berries.

(3) "Fruit table wine" or "berry table wine" is fruit or berry wine having an alcoholic content not in excess of 14 per cent by volume. Such wine may also be designated "light fruit wine," or "light berry wine."

(4) "Fruit dessert wine" or "berry dessert wine" is fruit or berry wine having an alcoholic content in excess of 14 per cent but not in excess of 24 per cent by volume.

"(5) Fruit wine derived wholly (except for sugar, water, or added alcohol) from one kind of fruit shall be designated by the word 'wine' qualified by the name of such fruit, e.g., 'peach wine,' 'blackberry wine.' Fruit wine not derived wholly from one kind of fruit shall be designated as 'fruit wine' or 'berry wine,' as the case may be, qualified by a truthful and adequate statement of composition appearing in direct conjunction therewith. Fruit wines which are derived wholly (except for sugar, water, or added alcohol) from apples or pears may be designated 'cider' and 'perry,' respectively, and shall be so designated if lacking in vinous taste, aroma, and characteristics. Fruit wine rendered effervescent by carbon dioxide resulting solely from the secondary fermentation of the wine within a closed container, tank, or bottle shall be further designated as 'sparkling'; and fruit wine rendered effervescent by carbon dioxide otherwise derived shall be further designated as 'carbonated.'"

The definition in U. S. Internal Revenue Service (1970A) or U. S. Laws (1954) for fruit wine differs from that of U. S. Federal Alcohol Administration (1937). Fruit wine is not specified as a fermented product and an upper limit of 21 per cent by weight of total solids is imposed.

Other types of wine which are provided for are "light" wine (alcohol not over 14 per cent), "natural" wine (fortifying spirits or alcohol may be added), raisin wine, retsina wine, sake (rice wine), etc.

The definition of vermouth is as follows (U. S. Internal Revenue Service 1961A):

" 'Vermouth' is a type of aperitif wine compounded from grape wine, having the taste, aroma, and characteristics generally attributed to vermouth, and shall be so designated."

Not less than 80 per cent of the volume of the finished product must be natural wine.

"Special natural wine" has been defined in Section 5386 of the Internal Revenue Code (U. S. Laws 1954)as follows:

"(a) In General.—Special natural wines are the products made, pursuant to a formula approved under this section, from a base of natural wine (including heavy-bodied blending wine) exclusively, with the addition, before, during or after fermentation, of natural herbs, spices, fruit juices, aromatics, essences, and other natural flavorings in such quantities or proportions as to enable such products to be distinguished from any natural wine not so treated, and with or without carbon dioxide naturally or artificially added, and with or without the addition, separately or in combination, of pure dry sugar or a solution of pure dry sugar and water, or caramel. No added wine spirits or alcohol or other spirits shall be used in any wine under this section except as may be contained in the natural wine (including heavy-bodied blending wine) used as a base, or except as may be necessary in the production of approved essences or similar approved flavorings. The Brix degree of any solution of pure dry sugar and water used may be limited by regulations prescribed by the Secretary or his delegate in accordance with good commercial practice.

"(b) Cellar Treatment.—Special natural wines may be cellar treated under the provisions of section 5382 (a) and (c).

A formula giving a complete list of the ingredients (Form 698-Supplemental) must be filed and the process of production stated in detail.

In addition to complying with Federal regulations, wines made in California must also comply with State regulations. Though Federal regulations authorize the production of natural grape wine with the use of sugar, Section 17010 (a) of the California Standards of Identity and Quality for Wine (Title 17, Chapter 5, Sub-Chapter 2 of the California Administrative Code; see California (1969) expressly forbids the use of sugar. This section thus prohibits the production of special natural wines sweetened with sugar. However, Section 17010 (a) (2) permits the use of sugar in the production of carbonated and special natural wines, and Section 17010 (a) (1) permits the use of sugar in the production of sparkling wine (where sugar or liquid sugar may be used only in the traditional secondary fermentation and dosage) if produced in accordance with a formula approved by the Alcohol, Tobacco and Firearms Division of the Internal Revenue Service. Sugar, sugar-water solutions and liquid sugar would be permissible components of the essence used in producing special natural wines in the volume indicated in the approved formula.

Other types of wine defined in U. S. Internal Revenue Service (1970A) include high-fermentation, heavy-bodied blending, Spanish-type blending, distilling material, and spoiled wine, and specially sweetened natural wine. High fermentation wine is a wine made within the restrictions for natural wines, see U. S. Internal Revenue Service (1970A) paragraphs 240.483 and 240.365 or 240.405, except that the alcohol content after complete fermentation or complete fermentation and sweetening is more than 14 per cent and that wine spirits may not be added. "High fermentation wine is not a natural wine or a standard[1] wine" but it may be produced, stored, and handled on standard wine premises.

Heavy-bodied blending wine and Spanish-type blending wines fall under similar regulatory provisions—they are not to be sold as beverage wine. The former has a total solids in excess of 21 per cent. The latter is made with caramelized grape concentrate. These wines are used by whisky and other blenders whose products need their sugar, flavor or color.

Distilling material is wine produced without sugar, but unlimited water can be employed. However, any natural wine may be used providing its residual sugar is not fermented. Lees, filter wash, unmarketable special natural wine (under conditions specified in Section 240.632 of U. S. Internal Revenue Service (1970A) and other wine residues may be used as distilling material. They are reported as wine on Form 702 (p. 741) but can only be used for distilling purposes.

Vinegar stock also permits unlimited use of water, either at the time of fermentation, or preferably, after fermentation is nearly completed. If water is added to such wine it is transferred to the vinegar stock inventory at the time of adding water. Spoiled wine is standard wine which has become sub-standard. Wines of over a certain percentage volatile acidity fall in this class. Wine regulations Sections 240.545 through 240.550 (U. S. Internal Revenue Service (1970A) or U. S. Laws (1954)) contain a specific provision for "experimental" wine. This permits colleges and universities to produce and receive wine with a minimum of forms, bonds, etc., free of tax for experimental or research purposes, but not for consumption or sale.

Sparkling or artificially carbonated wines are described in some detail. Two general types of effervescent wine are provided for: artificially carbonated and fermented. The former are seldom produced at present. Where the wine is produced by fermentation in a closed container (tank or bottle) the use of carbon dioxide gas, even for transfer of the wine, is not permitted. Both types of wine are limited to a maximum of 14 per cent alcohol. The producer of effervescent wine must submit a detailed

---

[1] Standard wine includes natural wine, specially sweetened natural wine, special natural wine, and standard agricultural wine.

statement of the process to be employed to the Director, Alcohol, Tobacco and Firearms Division on Form 698-Supplemental. For fermented effervescent wines this must include a description of the tank or bottle process used. The specific type definitions are given in U. S. Internal Revenue Service (1961A). Champagne is defined as a "sparkling light wine which derives its effervescence solely from secondary fermentation of the wine within containers of not greater than one gallon capacity and which possesses the taste, aroma and other characteristics attributed to champagne as made in the Champagne district of France." Sparkling wines made in larger containers but otherwise conforming to the above standard must be designated as "sparkling wine" and may, in addition be designated as "champagne-style," "champagne type," "American champagne bulk process," etc.

The regulations of U. S. Federal Alcohol Administration (1937) also define grape-type (varietal) wines—the varietal name may be used as the type designation of a grape wine if the wine derives its predominant taste, aroma, and characteristics, and at least 51 per cent of its volume from that variety of grape. An explanatory statement as to the significance of the varietal appellation is permitted on the label. There may be some laxity in enforcement of the 51 per cent minimum as applied to imported wines. While foreign appellations of origin frequently limit the varieties permitted, they seldom specify a single variety. An appellation of origin for a "Medoc," therefore, does not guarantee that a wine contains *any* Cabernet Sauvignon, though it may.

These regulations also define generic, semi-generic and non-generic designations of geographical origin. Vermouth and sake are considered generic appellations. Semi-generic names listed in the regulations include angelica,[2] burgundy, claret,[3] chablis, champagne, chianti, malaga, marsala, madeira, moselle, port, rhine wine (syn. hock), sauterne, haut sauterne, sherry, and tokay.[4] In using these for any except the region where the name originated the proper geographical origin must be stated: thus "American," "New York," or "California" port.

Names of geographical significance may be used only if they are known to the consumer and trade as the designation of a specific wine of a particular place or region, distinguishable from all other wines. Names such as American, California, Lake Erie Islands, Napa Valley, New York State,

---

[2] An error as the type is of California origin and has no geographical significance as far as we can determine, see p. 141.

[3] Also an error. Claret is not used in France as a geographical appellation. In England claret is commonly used as a type name for the red wines from Bordeaux.

[4] The spellings and capitalization are not as in the regulations but conform to good practice.

French, Spanish are not distinctive designation of specific types. But, Bordeaux, Médoc, St. Julien, Margaux, Barsac, Bourgogne, Grand Chablis, Hermitage, Tavel, Loire, Anjou, Alsatian, Vouvray, Mosel, Swiss and others are. A wine is entitled to a geographical appellation if (1) at least 75 per cent of the volume is derived from fruit both grown and fermented in the place or region indicated by such appellation, (2) it has been fully manufactured and finished within such place or region, and (3) it conforms to the requirements of the laws and regulations of such place or region governing the composition, method of manufacture, and designation of wines for home consumption (i.e., in the named region). However, cellar treatment outside the place or region of origin is permitted. The regional requirement in (1), (2) and (3) above should be rigidly enforced for all wines.

Permits, Notices, Bonds, etc.

To establish a bonded wine cellar application for a basic permit (under the Federal Alcohol Administration Act and the regulations pursuant thereto in Part 1, Title 27 of the Code of Federal Regulations) is made. Internal Revenue Service Form 698 must be filed in triplicate with the appropriate assistant regional commissioner to operate the winery. The operating name, ownership, location of and description of premises and equipment, etc. is required in Form 698. A bond for winery operation is filed on Internal Revenue Service Form 700 and in addition on Form 2053 for payment of taxes by return. Various other kinds of bonds may be required and detailed provisions for termination of bond, etc., are given in U. S. Internal Revenue Service (1970A) or U. S. Laws (1954). An accurate plot of the premises in a specific form is prescribed.

The regulations (U. S. Federal Alcohol Administration 1937) provide in substance that before a vintage date can be used on a label, the wine must have been bottled by the person who crushed the grapes, fermented, and cellar-treated the wine. Also there must be an appropriate appellation of origin. Further, the wine must be produced from grapes gathered in the same calendar year and in the same viticultural area. These provisions prevent a California wine maker from buying wines fermented by others of the same vintage year for blending and even prevent him from topping tanks with wine not made by him in the specific vintage year. Obviously some small percentage tolerance should be permitted. However, foreign vintage wines need only be labeled and produced in accordance with the laws and regulation of the country of origin but this fact must be attested to by a certificate issued by a duly authorized official of the country of origin of the wine. In many cases foreign regulations are much less restrictive than those of this country.

When changes in ownership, location, etc., are made certain specific reports are required.

Construction and Equipment

Bonded wine cellars must be located, constructed and equipped in accordance with pertinent federal regulations, and, in addition, are subject to approval by the assistant regional commissioner. The intent of the regulations is that the wines' potential revenue must be protected and that the wines not be difficult to inspect by authorized personnel. A government office for the exclusive use of Internal Revenue Service officers must be provided. However, small wineries usually simply designate the winery office or laboratory as the official office for government personnel. A government cabinet for safeguarding government seals, keys, etc., is also necessary.

As far as tanks are concerned these must be arranged so as to permit ready examination. The capacity of all tanks and other containers on a bonded winery premise must be accurately determined by the proprietor, including capacity per inch of depth for tanks of uniform dimensions or for each inch of depth for tanks of irregular dimensions. Subpart XX of U. S. Internal Revenue Service (1970A) or U. S. Laws (1954) gives rules for determining capacity. The tanks must be marked with permanent serial number and the capacity in wine gallons. Tanks of uniform dimensions will also be marked as noted above with the capacity per inch of depth. Also, it must be marked to indicate its current use, i.e., "Fermenting Tank" or "Fermenter," "Intermediate Storage Tank," "Wine Spirits Addition Tank," etc. Abbreviations are permitted and the use signs may be changed. Some tanks have to be permanently marked to show their use—"Vermouth Processing Tank," "Grape Concentrate Storage Tank," etc. Containers of 60 gallons' capacity or less need not have a permanent serial number but their capacity must be given. Wine spirits storage tanks have to be of metal and tanks in which wine spirits are to be placed must be provided with facilities for locking or other secure fastening or sealing. They must also have floats or other devices to indicate actual contents.

Finally, the proprietor must provide at his own expense a measuring rod or steel tape, scales, and measures for weighing materials received or used in the production of wine (except that when used immediately upon receipt a shipper's weight or public weighmaster certificate may be accepted). When wine or wine spirits are tax paid by weight a set of 50 lb. cast iron test weights conforming to Class C requirements of the National Bureau of Standards will be needed. The weights may not be required when an accurate scale is provided.

Production

Many of the restrictions in production have been considered in the definition of the various types of wines. The process of adding wine spirits however is so important that it deserves special comment. The proprietor must advise the assistant regional commissioner of the intent to use wine spirits in sufficient time so that an Internal Revenue officer can be assigned.

The wine to be fortified is placed in approved tanks. The volume and alcohol content of the wine and of the wine spirits to be added are accurately determined. Internal Revenue Service Form 275 is prepared in triplicate and one copy delivered to the Internal Revenue officer. The wine spirits must be gauged and Form 2629 completed and attached to Form 275.

Following addition of wine spirits the proprietor must thoroughly agitate the mixture and following stirring take three pint samples—two for the Internal Revenue officer. The other is immediately tested for alcohol and the per cent entered on Form 275. The alcohol content must not exceed 24. The total volume is entered on Form 702. It is of interest to note that concentrate or fresh grape juice may be fortified in the manner just described.

Baking of wine is permitted on bonded wine cellar premises. A record must be maintained showing the serial number of the tank, the date the wine was placed in the tank, the quantity, the alcohol content of the wine, and the dates when baking started and was completed, as well as the date on which the wine was removed from the tank and the quantity and alcohol content of the baked wine. In case baking is done in barrels the records may be maintained on the basis of groups of barrels. Sun baking is permitted provided the area is secure and on bonded premises.

Flor sherry producers have special permission to add wine spirits at two different times. Producers of Spanish type and flor sherry may also add calcium sulfate (gypsum) providing the finished wine contains no more than 2 gm. of gypsum[5] per liter of wine.

At present the primary restriction on the use of grape concentrate in producing natural grape wine is that the finished wine contain not more than 21 per cent, by weight, of total solids. Fruit concentrates of the same kind of fruit may be used for natural fruit wines in the same way.

Storage and Finishing

Wine may be stored on the bonded premises in tanks, casks, barrels, cased or uncased bottles, or in any other approved containers. If ferment-

---

[5] Undoubtedly an error. Should be potassium sulfate.

ing or storage tanks previously used for one class of wine are to be used for wine of another class they must be carefully cleaned to avoid contamination. The regulations specifically call attention to the necessity of cleaning or treating tanks which have contained special natural wine before using for another wine.. They could also have noted the necessity of thorough cleaning of tanks used for vermouth and of the necessity of removing tartrates before placing fruit wines in the tanks.

The materials which may be used in normal cellar practices are specified in the regulation as follows:

Material	Use	Reference or Limitation[6]
Acetic acid	To correct natural deficiencies in grape wine.	The use of acetic acid shall not exceed 0.4 gallon of the equivalent of 100 per cent pure acetic acid per 1,000 gallons of grape wine, and such acid shall not be added in a solution of less than 50 per cent strength. Acetic acid in finished red grape wine shall not exceed 0.14 gram per 100 cubic centimeters or 0.12 gram per 100 cubic centimeters in other finished grape wine. § 240.364. 21 CFR 121.101(d) (8).
Actiferm (Roviferm)	Fermentation adjunct.	The amount used shall not exceed 2 pounds per 1000 gallons of wine. GRAS.
Activated carbon	To assist precipitation during fermentation.	§§ 240.361, 240.366, 240.401, 240.405. GRAS.
	To clarify and purify wine.	GRAS.[7]
	To remove excess color in white wine.	§ 240.527. GRAS.[7]
Aferrin	To reduce trace metals from wine.	No insoluble or soluble residue in excess of one part per million shall remain in the finished wine, and the basic character of the wine shall not be changed by such treatment. GRAS.
AMA special gelatine solution	To clarify wine	GRAS.[7]
Antifoam "A"; Antifoam AF emulsion; Antifoam C	Defoaming agent in production of wine.	The residual silicone content in the wine shall not exceed 10 parts per million. 21 CFR 121.1099.
Ascorbic acid Iso-ascorbic acid (Erythorbic acid)	To prevent darkening of color and deterioration of flavor in wines and wine materials, and the over oxidation of vermouth and other wines.	May be added to fruit, grapes, berries, and other materials used in wine production, to the juice of such materials, or to the wine, within limitations which do not alter the class or type of the wine. Its use need not be shown on labels. 21 CFR 121.101(d) (2).
Atmos 300	Antifoaming agent.	No soluble residue in excess of 25 parts per million shall remain in the finished wine. GRAS.[7]
Bentonite (Wyoming Clay)	To clarify wine.	21 CFR 121.101(d) (8).

Material	Use	Reference or Limitation[6]
Bentonite compound (Bentonite, activated carbon, copper sulfate)	To clarify and stabilize wine.	Copper added in the form of copper sulfate shall not exceed 0.5 part per million of copper with a residual level not in excess of 0.2 part per million of copper. GRAS.[7]
Bentonite slurry	To clarify wine.	Not more than 2 gallons of water shall be added to each pound of Bentonite used. The total quantity of water shall not exceed 1% of the volume of wine treated. GRAS[7]
Bone charcoal	—do—	GRAS.[7]
Calcium carbonate	To reduce the excess natural acids in high acid wine.	The natural or fixed acids shall not be reduced below five parts per 1,000. 21 CFR 121.101(d) (8).
Calcium sulfate (Gypsum)	Production of Spanish type or Flor sherry wine.	§ 240.385. Finished wine shall not contain more than 2 grams of calcium (potassium?) sulfate per 1,000 ml. of wine. GRAS.[7]
Carbon	To clarify and purify wine.	GRAS.[7]
Carbon dioxide, CO_2	To stabilize and preserve wine.	§§ 240.531 through 240.535. 21 CFR 121.101(d) (8).
Casein	To clarify wine.	GRAS.[7]
Citric acid	To increase the acidity of wine.	§§ 240.364, 240.404. 21 CFR 121.101(d) (8).
	To stabilize grape wine.	§§ 240.526, 240.539. 21 CFR 121.101(d) (8).
Combustion product gas	To maintain pressure during filtering and bottling of sparkling wines.	The carbon dioxide content of the combustion gas shall not exceed 1%. 21 CFR 121.1060.
	To stabilize wine and prevent oxidation in still wines.	§ 240.531. 21 CFR 121.1060.
Compressed air	Aeration of sherry wine.	The use of compressed air shall not cause changes in the wine other than those occurring during the usual storage in wooden cooperage over a period of time. GRAS.[7]
Copper sulfate	To clarify and stabilize grape wine.	Copper added in the form of copper sulfate shall not exceed 0.5 part per million of copper with a residual level not in excess of 0.2 part per million of copper. GRAS.[7]
Cufex	To remove trace metal from wine.	No insoluble or soluble residue in excess of one part per million shall remain in finished wine. Basic character of the wine shall not be changed by such treatment. GRAS.[7]
Defoaming agents (polyoxyethylene-40-monostearate and silicon dioxide) (sorbic acid, carboxy methyl cellulose, dimethyl polysiloxane, polyoxyethylene (40) monostearate, and sorbitan monostearate)	Defoaming agent	Defoaming agents which are 100 per cent active may be used in amounts not exceeding 0.15 pound per 1,000 gallons of wine. Defoaming agents which are 30 per cent active may be used in amounts not exceeding 0.5 pound per 1,000 gallons of wine. Silicon dioxide shall be completely removed by filtration. 21 CFR 121.1099, 121.101(d) (2), 121.101(d) (8).

Material	Use	Reference or Limitation[6]
Diammonium phosphate	Yeast food in distilling material.	The amount used shall not exceed 10 pounds per 1,000 gallons of distilling material. 21 CFR 121.101(d) (8).
Diethyl pyrocarbonate	To preserve wine.	The amount used shall not exceed 200 parts per million. 21 CFR 121.1117. (see p. 193)
Eggs (albumen or yolks)	To clarify wine.	GRAS.[7]
Freon C-318 (octafluorocyclobutane)	Propellant in aerosol containers of vermouth.	Only a minute amount of the gas shall remain in the dispensed vermouth. 21 CFR 121.1065.
Fulgur (aluminum silicate and albumin)	To clarify wine.	The amount used shall not exceed 6.6 pounds per 1,000 gallons of wine. GRAS.[7]
Fumaric acid	To stabilize grape wine and to correct natural deficiencies in grape and fruit wine.	The amount used shall not exceed 25 pounds per 1,000 gallons of wine. The fumaric acid content of the finished wine shall not exceed 0.3 per cent. §§ 240.364, 240.404. 21 CFR 121.1130.
Gelatin	To clarify wine.	GRAS.[7]
Glycine (amino acetic acid)	Yeast food in fermentation of wines.	The amount used shall not exceed 2 pounds per 1,000 gallons of wine. GRAS.[7]
Granular cork	To treat wines stored in redwood and concrete tanks.	The amount used shall not exceed 10 pounds per 1,000 gallons of wine. GRAS.[7]
Gum arabic	To clarify and stabilize wine.	The amount used shall not exceed 2 pounds per 1,000 gallons of wine. 21 CFR 121.101(d) (7).
Gypsum (see calcium sulfate)		
Hydrogen peroxide	To reduce aldehydes in distilling material.	The amount used shall not exceed 200 parts per million. GRAS.[7]
	To facilitate secondary fermentation in production of sparkling wine.	The amount used shall not exceed 3 parts per million. The finished product shall not contain any hydrogen peroxide. GRAS.[7]
Ion exchange resins	Treatment of wine.	Anion, cation, and non-ionic resins, except those anionic resins in the mineral acid state, may be used in batch or continuous column processes as total or partial treatment of wine, provided that after complete treatment:

1. The basic character of the wine has not been altered.
2. The color of the wine has not been reduced to less than that normally contained in such wine.
3. The inorganic anions in the wine have not been increased by more than 10 mg. per liter.
4. The metallic cation concentration in the wine has not been reduced to less than 300 mg. per liter.
5. The natural or fixed acid in grape wine has not been reduced below 4 parts per thousand for

Material	Use	Reference or Limitation[6]
		red table wines, 3 parts per thousand for white table wines, or 2.5 parts per thousand for all other grape wines; and the natural or fixed acid in wine, other than grape wine, has not been reduced below 4.0 parts per thousand. 6. The pH of the wine has not been reduced below pH 3 nor increased above pH 4.5. 7. The resins used have not imparted to the wine any material or characteristic (incidental to the resin treatment) which may be prohibited under any other section of the regulations in this part. Conditioning and/or regenerating agents consisting of water, fruit acids common to the wine being treated, and inorganic acids, salts and/or bases may be employed, provided the conditioned or regenerated resin is rinsed with water until the resin and container are essentially free from unreacted (excess) conditioning or regenerating agents prior to the introduction of the wine. Tartaric acid may not be used in treating wines other than grape. 21 CFR 121.1148.
Isinglass	To clarify wine.	GRAS.[7]
Lactic acid	To stabilize wine and correct natural deficiencies in wine.	§§ 240.364, 240.404, 240.526. 21 CFR 121.101(d) (8).
Malic acid	To increase acidity of wine.	§§ 240.364, 240.404. 21 CFR 121.101(d) (8).
Mineral oil	On surface of wine in storage tanks to prevent the access of air to the wine.	The oil shall not remain in the finished wine when marketed. 21 CFR 121.1146.
Nitrogen gas	To maintain pressure during filtering and bottling of sparkling wine. To prevent oxidation of wine.	The gas shall not remain in sparkling or still wine. 21 CFR 121.101(d) (8).
Oak chips (charred)	To treat Spanish type blending sherry.	The finished product, after addition of oak chips, shall have the flavor and color of Spanish type blending sherry commonly obtained by storage of sherry wine in properly treated used charred oak whisky barrels. GRAS.[7]
Oak chips (uncharred and untreated)	To treat wines	21 CFR 121.1163
Oak chip sawdust (uncharred and untreated)	To treat wines.	21 CFR 121.1163.
Oxygen	In baking or maturing wine.	May be used provided it does not cause changes in the wine other than those occurring during the

Material	Use	Reference or Limitation[6]
		usual storage in wooden cooperage over a period of time. Application must be filed. GRAS.[7]
Pectolytic enzymes	To clarify and stabilize wine, and to facilitate separation of the juice from the fruit.	21 CFR Part 121. The pectolytic enzymes shall be derived from nontoxic strains of *Aspergillus niger*. GRAS.[7]
Phosphates	To start secondary fermentation in manufacturing champagne and sparkling wines.	Small quantity only shall be used. (The use of ammonium phosphate, ammonium sulphate, or potassium acid phosphate as yeast food in the production of still wine is not permitted.) GRAS.[7]
Polyvinylpolypyrrolidone (PVPP)	To clarify and stabilize wine.	The amount used shall not exceed 6 pounds per 1,000 gallons of wine. Material shall be removed during filtration. 21 CFR 121.1110.
Potassium metabisulphite	Sterilizing and preserving wine.	The sulphur content of the finished wine shall not exceed the limits prescribed in 27 CFR Part 4. 21 CFR 121.101(d) (2).
Potassium salt of sorbic acid	As a sterilizing and preservative agent and to inhibit mold growth and secondary fermentations.	Not more than 0.1% of sorbic acid or salts thereof shall be used in wine or in materials for the production of wine. 21 CFR 121.101(d) (2).
Promine-D	To clarify and stabilize wine.	The amount used shall not exceed 1.5 pounds per 1,000 gallons of wine. Water used in process shall not exceed 0.5 per cent of wine treated. GRAS.[7]
Protovac PV-7916	To clarify wine.	The amount used shall not exceed 2 pounds per 1,000 gallons of wine. GRAS.[7]
Roviferm (see Actiferm)		
Sodium bisulfite	As a sterilizing or preserving agent.	§ 240.523. 21 CFR 121.101(d) (2).
Sodium carbonate	To reduce excess natural acidity in wine.	Natural or fixed acids shall not be reduced below 5 parts per thousand. § 240.523. 21 CFR 121.101(d) (8).
Sodium caseinate	To clarify wine.	§ 240.523. 21 CFR 121.101(d) (8).
Sodium metabisulphite	Sterilizing and preserving wine.	§ 240.523. 21 CFR 121.101(d) (2).
Sodium salt of sorbic acid	As a sterilizing and preservative agent and to inhibit mold growth and secondary fermentations.	Not more than 0.1% of the sorbic acid or salts thereof shall be used in wine or in materials for the production of wine. 21 CFR 121.101(d) (2).
Sorbic acid	As a sterilizing and preservative agent and to inhibit mold growth and secondary fermentations.	Not more than 0.1% of the sorbic acid or salts thereof shall be used in wine or in materials for the production of wine. 21 CFR 121.101(d) (2).
Sparkaloid No. 1	To clarify wine.	GRAS.[7]
Sparkaloid No. 2	To clarify wine.	GRAS.[7]
Sulphur dioxide	Sterilizing and preserving wine.	§ 240.523, 27 CFR Part 4. 21 CFR 121.101(d) (2).
Sulfuric acid	To effect a favorable yeast development in distilling material.	§ 240.486. 21 CFR 121.101(d) (8).

Material	Use	Reference or Limitation[6]
Takamine cellulase 4,000	To clarify wine.	The amount used shall not exceed 5 pounds per 1,000 gallons of wine. The enzymes shall be derived from nontoxic strains of *Aspergillus niger*. GRAS.[7]
Tannin	Clarifying grape wine.	§ 240.525. GRAS.[7]
Tansul clays Nos. 7, 710, and 711	To clarify wine.	The amount used shall not exceed 10 pounds per 1,000 gallons of wine. GRAS.[7]
Tartaric acid	To increase acidity of grape wine.	§ 240.364. 21 CFR 121.101(d) (8).
Uni-Loid Type 43B (pure U.S.P. agar agar and standard supercel)	To clarify and stabilize wine.	The amount used shall not exceed 2 pounds per 1,000 gallons of wine. GRAS.[7]
Urea	To facilitate fermentation of wine.	The amount used shall not exceed 2 pounds per 1,000 gallons of wine. GRAS.[7]
Veltol (maltol)	As a stabilizing and smoothing agent.	The amount used shall not exceed 250 parts per million. 21 CFR 121.1164.
Wine clarifier (containing pure U.S.P. agar agar and standard supercel)	To clarify wine.	The amount used shall not exceed 2 pounds per 1,000 gallons of wine. GRAS.[7]
Wine clarifier (Clarivine B) (containing locust bean gum, carragheen, alginate, bentonite, agar agar, and diatomaceous earth)	To clarify wine	The amount used shall not exceed 2 pounds per 1,000 gallons of wine. GRAS.[7]
Yeastex	To facilitate fermentation.	The amount used shall not exceed 2 pounds per 1,000 gallons of wine. GRAS.[7]
Yeastex 61	To facilitate fermentation.	The amount used shall not exceed 2 pounds per 1,000 gallons of wine. GRAS.[7]

Citric acid is limited to 5.8 lbs. per 1000 gallons of wine for the purpose of stabilization. In another section this and tartaric or malic acid may be employed to correct natural deficiencies, providing the finished wine does not exceed 0.8 per cent fixed acid (calculated as tartaric). Obviously the latter section is much more liberal and is the one under which the wineries operate.

Lactic acid may be used under the limitations imposed by Sections 240.364, 240.404 and 240.526, 26 CFR to correct natural deficiencies and to stabilize. Section 240.1051, 26 CFR (U. S. Internal Revenue Service, 1970A) permits the addition of not over 25 lbs. of fumaric acid per 1000

[6] See section 240.1051 (U. S. Internal Revenue Service, 1970A) or Treasury Decision 6475, effective July 1, 1960, as amended by Treasury Decision 7031, effective May 1, 1970.
[7] GRAS means "generally recognized as safe."

gallons of wine to correct natural deficiencies provided it constitutes not over 0.3 per cent by weight of the finished wine. Under Section 240.1015, 26 CFR acetic acid may be used to correct natural deficiencies, provided the addition does not exceed 0.4 gallons of 100 per cent acetic acid per 1000 gallons of wine, and provided the acetic acid is not added in a solution of less than 50 per cent. The acetic acid content may not exceed 0.14 gm. per 100 cc. in red wine or 0.12 gm. per 100 cc. in all other finished grape wines.

In using tannin, finished white wines shall not contain more than 0.08 gm. of tannin per 100 ml. after clarification and red wines more than 0.3. Only tannins which do not color the wines may be used.

Filter aids such as inert fibers, pulps, earths, or similar materials can be used without limit provided they do not alter the character of the wine. With regard to sulfur dioxide, Section 4.22 of U. S. Internal Revenue Service (1961A) limits the total sulfur dioxide in the finished wine to not more than 350 parts per million. Records need not be maintained for the use of inert fining agents, oxygen, filter aids or sulfur dioxide.

The removal of excessive color from white wines is provided for but treated and untreated samples of the wine and of the activated carbon or other material used must be submitted to the assistant regional commissioner. A written statement of the reasons for desiring to treat the wine, the quantity, kind or type of wine to be treated, the kind and quantity of the material to be used, and the proposed process must be submitted. "If the chemical analysis of the samples shows that the proposed treatment will remove only the excess color and will not remove any of the usual natural color or other characteristics of the wine the assistant regional commissioner will authorize the treatment of the wine in question. If the chemical analysis shows that the proposed treatment will remove the natural characteristics of the wine the assistant regional commissioner will disapprove the application. A separate application with representative samples must be submitted for each lot of wine it is desired to treat."

Obviously this regulation is subject to interpretation of "usual natural color or other characteristics." A minimum color level of 0.6 Lovibond reading is presently specified. Up to nine pounds of charcoal per 1000 gallons is permitted without submitting samples.

For additional information on permitted additives and treatments in other countries see Paronetto (1963), Cerutti (1963) and Office International de la Vigne et du Vin (1964). The latter also gives the tolerance limits for impurities in permitted additives.

Containers for Removal

Wine may be removed from bond in casks, barrels, kegs, tanks, tank trucks, railroad tank cars, tank ships, barges, deep tanks of vessels, in cases (when bottled) of any desired size, in uncased demijohns (or bottles) of two gallons or more capacity, and by pipeline. Movement of wine between non-contiguous portions of a bonded wine cellar is not considered a removal of wine. Serial numbers must be used on all containers used for removal except on cases which may be marked with the date of fill in lieu of a serial number. There are detailed provisions for certain other exceptions. Requirements for masks, labels, and tags and for their destruction are also given.

The alcohol content must be stated in all cases and must definitely show the taxable grade of the wine. The wine gallon content is also required. In the case of bottles they must be filled as nearly as possible to conform to the amount shown on the label or blown in the bottle.

Labeling Bottled Wine

The label must show: (a) the brand name; (b) the name and address of the bottler, or the name, registry number, and state where the premises of the bottler are located; (c) the kind of wine (class and type); (d) the alcohol content by volume (except "Table" or "Light Wine" may be so designated in lieu of alcohol content); and (e) the net contents of the bottle, unless legibly blown into the bottle. If there is no brand name the name of the bottler may take the place of a brand name.

A certificate of label approval (Form 1649) or certificate of exemption from label approval (Form 1650) must be obtained for all bottled wines for distribution or sale. Relabeling is possible when approval is requested.

Tax Payment

The tax on wine is to be determined at the time of removal from bonded wine cellar premises (or transfer to a tax paid room on the premises) for consumption or sale. The tax is paid with Form 2050 which is filed semimonthly at prescribed times. Considerable penalties are provided for failure to pay the tax or to file the return at the time required.

The present taxes are: (a) on still wine containing not more than 14 per cent alcohol by volume, 17 cents per wine gallon; (b) on still wine containing more than 14 per cent and not exceeding 21 per cent, 67 cents; (c) on still wine containing more than 21 per cent and not exceeding 24 per cent $2.25; (d) on champagne and other sparkling wine, $3.40; and (e) on artificially carbonated wine, $2.40.

Records and Reports

The basic form is the monthly 702 which reports all bonded wine cellar operations. Instructions for filling in this form are given on the form or issued with them. The necessary information to properly complete this form is obtained from wine cellar records.

Form 2050 is used when wine subject to tax is removed from a bonded wine cellar. Provision for reporting previous errors is made. Form 2052 is used to prepay the tax. Form 702-C is a detailed report made on the inventory of a bonded wine cellar at the close of business on June 30 and December 31 of each year. Forms 275 and 2629 are used when wine spirits are used in the production of wine. Form 2054 is used as a wine fermentation record for still wines. Amelioration is recorded on this form. Form 2056 is a record of still wine made with excess water. Form 2057 gives the details of the production of effervescent wine. Form 2058 does the same for special natural wines. Form 2061 is a record of wine received on or removed from bond.

Records must be kept of sugar received and used, of other materials received and used, of wines eligible for varietal or vintage designations, of acids used, of wine baked, etc. All prescribed returns reports and records must be retained for a period of three years (or up to three years longer if the assistant regional commissioner so requires). Records must be kept at the bonded wine cellar and be available for inspection by Internal Revenue officers at any reasonable hour.

Miscellaneous.—The addition to and retention in still wines of small amounts of carbon dioxide has been permitted since July 1, 1959. The maximum is 0.277 gm. per 100 ml. of wine with a tolerance of 0.009 based on good commercial practices. Notice of intention to add carbon dioxide is required, with information on the equipment and process to be employed and the kinds of wine to be treated. Strict penalties are provided for misrepresenting this wine as sparkling wine.

In 1959, Treasury Decision No. 6395 redefined the term "own production" so that addition of wine spirits, amelioration or both could be done at one or several bonded wineries affiliated or owned or controlled by the same proprietor located within a state. The Treasury Decision also provided for increase in the amount of amelioration permitted with fruit wines of 23° to 25° Balling.[8] In 1970, Treasury Decision No. 7031 amended the regulations to permit the addition of grape wine spirits to natural grape wine in a bonded cellar, the proprietor of which produces natural wine by fermentation, and which is located in the same state as the bonded wine cellar where the natural wine was produced. Invert sugar or liquid sugar of not less than 60° Balling may be used in amelioration of the juice or wine produced from fruit other than grapes, and in special natural wine.

Finally, all unmerchantable wine may be returned to bond so as to recover the tax. This applies to United States or foreign wine.

Federal law (¶1798(2) of the Tariff Act of 1930) formerly permitted a

---

[8] Brix is given in the regulations. It is equivalent to Balling.

United States resident returning from a trip abroad to bring in not over one wine gallon of alcoholic beverages duty free, if for his own use and not intended for sale. In 1965, this was reduced to one-fifth.

A regulation prohibits the use of the term "unfortified" on labels for wine, U. S. Internal Revenue Service (1958). For regulations on vinegar, procedures, tax-paid bottling rooms, gauging, and volatile fruit-flavor concentrates, see U. S. Internal Revenue Service (1955A, 1955B, 1962, 1970B, 1963).

Food and Drug Administration

Under the Food Additives Amendment of 1958 many substances which are presently added to wine may come to the attention of the Food and Drug Administration. However, under a grandfather clause materials which had been authorized for use prior to January 1, 1958 were considered safe until March 5, 1960. Studies on the safety of Aferrin, polyvinyl-polypyrrolidone (PVPP), pectinol and pectizyme have resulted in their approval by the Food and Drug Administration. In the future new materials will have to have the approval of the Food and Drug Administration prior to use and producers will have to satisfy this agency as to their safety for human consumption. The present GRAS (generally recognized as safe) list is currently under review.

CALIFORNIA—WINES

The main California regulations are in Title 17 of the California Administrative Code, section 17,000–17,135. They have been published in a special pamphlet hereafter referred to as California (1954). Obviously these regulations apply primarily to California but they may also apply in states or countries which provide for recognition of local regulations. Further regulations may be found in the California Alcohol Beverage Control Act effective September, 11, 1957 (hereafter referred to as California 1965).

Definitions

The present California (1970) standards of identity and quality for wine produced in California or elsewhere is as follows:

(a) The standards herein established are minimum standards for wine of the several classes and types defined.

(b) *Prohibited Wine.* Wine derived from raisins, dried grapes, dried berries, and other dried fruit, and imitation or substandard wine, shall not be produced, imported, or sold in this state except for distillation into wine spirits or for industrial or nonbeverage purposes.

(c) *Cellar Treatment.* Cellar treatment shall conform to the methods and materials authorized for treatment of wine by the Alcohol, Tobacco and Firearms Division of the Internal Revenue Service as well as the California Pure

Foods Act and the Federal Food, Drug, and Cosmetic Act and the regulations adopted thereunder. In case of conflict between Federal and State laws or regulations the California law or regulation shall take precedence.

(d) *Appellations of Origin.* Wines of any defined class or type, which are labeled or advertised under an appellation of origin such as "Spanish," "New York," "Ohio," "Finger Lakes," "California," etc., shall meet the requirements of the standards herein prescribed applicable to such wines and shall, in addition, contain the minimum percentage of alcohol and conform as to composition in all other respects with all standards of identity, quality and purity applicable to wines of such classes, or types marketed for consumption in the place or region of origin.

For wines produced in California the following provisions apply:

(a) *Sugar Use.* No sugar, or material containing sugar, other than pure condensed grape must, and no water in excess of the minimum amount necessary to facilitate normal fermentation, may be used in the production or cellar treatment of any grape wine except:

(1) In the production of sparkling wine (where sugar or liquid sugar may only be used in the traditional secondary fermentation and dosage),

(2) Carbonated and special natural wine; provided, however, that sparkling and carbonated wine or the residuum thereof may be reconverted into still wine, and such wine and special natural wine or the residuum thereof may be distilled into wine spirits if the unfermented sugar has not been refermented.

(3) Natural grape wine produced outside of the State of California with the use of sugar pursuant to applicable federal regulations may be blended with grape wine produced in California pursuant to these regulations only for the purpose of producing sparkling wine and carbonated wine. The resultant blend shall not be entitled to the appellation of origin "California" or any geographical subdivision thereof.

(b) *Alcohol Content.* (1) The alcohol content of the following specified wines shall be as follows:

(A) Any type of red grape table wine—not less than 10.5 per cent alcohol by volume;

(B) Any type of white, rose, or pink grape table wine not less than 10.0 per cent alcohol by volume;

(C) Any type of grape dessert wine (except sherry) not less than 18.0 per cent alcohol by volume:

(D) Any type of sherry—not less than 17.0 percent alcohol by volume.

(2) The foregoing minimum alcoholic content requirements, stated in Subsection (1), shall not apply to the following:

(A) *Special natural wine.* The alcohol content shall be stated on the label of any special natural red wine which is less than 10.5 per cent alcohol by volume or any special natural white wine which is less than 10.0 percent alcohol by volume.

(B) Sacramental wine which possesses such alcohol content as required by ecclesiastical codes.

(C) The production of wine or wine products rendered unfit for beverage use pursuant to applicable federal laws and regulations.

(3) The minimum alcohol content requirements of this section may be waived when the wine is produced solely to conform to the laws and regulations of another state, district, territory, possession, or foreign country, whose

laws or regulations prohibit or otherwise restrict the sale of wine conforming to the aforementioned minimum alcoholic content including, but not limited to, restrictions by reason of tax classification or distribution restriction. Waivers will be granted only upon the furnishing of such evidence as may be required to support the fact of such prohibition or restriction, and such waiver is effective only if such wine is actually shipped thereto. Such wine shall not be entitled to the appellation of origin "California" or any geographical subdivision thereof.

(c) *Sweetness Limitation.* (1) The Brix saccharometer test, using a saccharometer calibrated at 20°C. and made in the presence of the alcohol content provided herein shall be:

(A) Not less than 5.5 degrees for Angelica, Muscatel, Port and White Port.

(B) Not less than 3.5 degrees for Tokay (as a dessert wine).

(2) The reducing sugar content (per 100 milliliters at 20°C. and calculated as dextrose for sherries shall be as follows:

	Minimum	Maximum
Dry Sherry	0.0 gram	2.5 grams
Sherry	2.5 grams	4.0 grams
Sweet, Golden, Cream or Mellow Sherry	4.0 grams	

(d) *Fixed Acidity.* The minimum titratable fixed acidity per 100 milliliters at 20°C. for grape wine (except wine used solely for blending, medicinal or industrial purposes) calculated as tartaric acid, shall be as follows:

red table wine	0.4 gram
white table wine	0.3 gram
all other wine	0.25 gram

The maximum volatile acidity, calculated as acetic acid and exclusive of sulfur dioxide, is 0.12 gm. per 100 cc.[9] for red table wines and 0.11 gm. for other wines. The California limit for sulfur dioxide is 350 parts per million. For wines bearing the appellation of origin "California" or of any geographical subdivision thereof the following limitations apply:

(1) 100 per cent of its volume is derived from fruit grown and juice therefrom fermented within the State of California, and

(2) It has been fully produced and finished within the State of California, and

(3) It conforms to the requirements of these regulations; provided, that no wine shall be entitled to an appellation of origin in violation of Section 25236 or Section 25237 of the California Alcoholic Beverage Control Act.

Vintage wines must be produced from grapes produced in and fermented in the same year and area as identified on the label or as in the advertisement of such wine. This latter requirement is interesting as it apparently imposes a production standard on the producer as well as his distributors.

The California definitions for vermouth, champagne, champagne style

---

[9] cc. not ml. are specified.

or champagne-bulk process, carbonated wines, berry, citrus and fruit wines generally follow Federal regulations and will not be repeated here.

California regulations limit cellar treatment but do provide for use of neutral potassium tartrate or calcium carbonate, acidifying agents such as tartaric acid "produced from grapes," or commercial malic or citric acid, sulfur dioxide "where required to insure the soundness and stability of the wine, and blending processes and treatments, such as electrolysis, where desirable or necessary to improve the quality of the finished product. No definitions of what constitutes improvement are given. In fact the following paragraph specifically recognizes that new processes may be recognized as proper. Monochloroacetic acid or other chemical preservatives, except sulfur dioxide and its compounds may not be used in wines in this state. Recently this has been modified to permit sorbic acid and sorbate and DEPC.

Labeling

The California regulations do not differ fundamentally from the federal rules except in so far as the definitions above are concerned, including the fact that federal label approval is required. There is one curious permissive section: blends of foreign and United States wines require reference to the exact percentage of foreign wine. So far as we know this blending privilege has not been utilized.

Labeling may not be false or misleading, it may not disparage competitor's products (surely potentially difficult to avoid), may not be indecent or obscene, may not imply municipal, state or federal approval of the product (even if licenses, registry numbers or permits are required, all of which do imply approval of the respective agencies), may not carry a statement, design, device, a representation relative to the armed forces or the flag, may not imply fortification (an ostrich-like requirement which should be forthwith repealed), and finally may not imply that the wine is old if it is not.

The most recent California regulations prohibit sale of wines which bear labels with:

(1) A type or brand designation which implies mixtures of wines for which standards of identity have been established in this Article;

(2) A type or brand designation which resembles an established wine type name such as Angelica, Madeira, Marsala, Muscatel, Port, Tokay, White Port, Sherry, Sauterne, Claret, Burgundy, etc.

If the wine is sold in distinctive containers the following limitation applies:

The sale of wine in containers which have blown, branded, or burned therein the name or other distinguishing mark of any person engaged in business as a

wine grower, wine blender, importer, rectifier, or bottler, or any person different from the person whose name is required to appear on the brand label, is
hereby prohibited.

Miscellaneous Requirements.—Advertising not in conformity to regulations is prohibited. Prohibited statements on labels may likewise not be
used in advertising. Brands may not be confused in advertising. Again
this offers some interesting possibilities as far as present practice is concerned.

Wine growers may supply display materials to retailers with certain
specified exceptions and limitations, California (1969A). The intent of
the restrictions is to prevent giving retailers premiums, gifts, or free goods.

Wineries are subject to all the requirements of the Health and Safety
Code, the Food Sanitation Act, and all rules and regulations prescribed
in the California (1970) regulations. Furthermore these specifically state
that "all containers, pipelines and other equipment of whatever description shall be thoroughly cleansed in conformity with established sanitary
practices for foodstuffs and beverages, before such containers, pipelines
and other equipment are used for, or in any other manner come into contact with, wine." This section of the California Administrative Code is, of
course, admirable.

Finally, producers, bottlers, wholesalers, and retailers of wine are required to furnish samples for analyses and the wine may be seized and disposed of if in violation of these regulations.

Permits and Notices

Various licenses are *annually* required by the Alcoholic Beverage Control Act, California (1969A): wine growers', 200–5000 gallons, $22.00,
over 5000 to 20,000, $44.00, over 20,000 to 100,000, $82.50, over 100,000 to
200,000, $110.00, over 200,000 to 1,000,000, $165.00, and for each 1,000,-
000 gallons or fraction thereof over 1,000,000, $110.00; wine rectifiers,
$276.00; wine brokers', $56.00, beer and wine importers, no fee, beer and
wine wholesalers, $56.00, retail package off-sale beer and wine, $24.00, on-
sale beer and wine, $168.00; on-sale beer and wine for trains, $16.00, on-
sale beer and wine for boat, $56.00, and on-sale beer and wine for air-
planes, $16.00. General license fees will be given under brandy (p. 761).
Applications for license must be on prescribed forms which require certain
information on ownership and location. If the applicant has been convicted of a felony it may be grounds for denial of his application.

Wine growers and retailers have the privilege of selling wine and
brandy to consumers without any limitation per sale for consumption off
the premises. A wine grower's license is issued to those who operate a
winery or bonded wine cellar under Internal Revenue Service regulations.

Taxes

The taxes on wines are given in the California Alcoholic Beverage Tax Law (California, 1971). On still wines of not over 14 per cent alcohol (by volume) the tax is one cent per wine gallon. For still wines over 14 per cent it is 2¢ per gallon. On all types of sparkling wine it is 30¢ per gallon but on sparkling hard cider it is 2¢.

California has a mandatory price posting and fair trading for retail sales off the premises (with certain exceptions). Pocket flasks of less than 0.2 gallon capacity may not be used for wine in this state (California, 1970).

Wine prepared for market in California when placed in a container suitable for transportation, whether exported from the state or not, is subject to a special tax for market promotion by the Wine Advisory Board. This amounts to 1¢ per gallon for table wines and 1¹/₂¢ for dessert wines. Concentrate, distilling material, grape juice, and wine for bond-to-bond transfer within the state are exempt from the tax. See California, Bureau of Marketing (1969B).

Other States

The rules and regulations of other states generally closely follow those of the federal government, particularly the permission to use sugar for amelioration of musts and wines. Mention should be made of the limitation of alcohol in Michigan to 16 per cent. This ostrich-like regulation is an anachronism in modern wine practice and obviously works great hardships on non-Michigan producers without promoting temperance.

For a general introduction to the state regulations see Anon. (1941) and Distilled Spirits Institute (1969).

BRANDY—FEDERAL

The basic Federal regulations are contained in U.S. Internal Revenue Service (1960, 1961B, 1968). Federal liquor laws have also been summarized by Udell (1968). Until recently legal source material with reference to brandy was somewhat confused. Chapter 51 of the Internal Revenue Code containing the basic law with respect to all alcoholic beverages was extensively amended by the Excise Tax Technical Changes Act of 1958, Public Law 85-859, 85th Congress, H.R. 7125, September 2, 1958), effective July 1, 1959 (U. S. Laws, 1954, 1958). In many instances, the statutory amendments require implementation by regulation issued by the Secretary of the Treasury. Lack of time precluded a complete revision of all of the Internal Revenue Service Regulations that were affected by the amendments to the Internal Revenue Code. The Internal Revenue Service, under these circumstances, issued amendments implementing only those amended sections of the Internal Revenue Code that were absolutely necessary to be in effect as of July 1. These regulations are now contained in new Part 201 of 26 CFR. Most regulations with respect to distilled spirits are, therefore, in one part rather than in four or five parts.

Treasury Decision No. 6395 confirms that new law (PL 85-859) does eliminate the 30¢ blending tax on the blending in bond of beverage brandy two years or more old. Proprietors also may now blend brandies distilled by different distillers. Section 5373(c) of the Internal Revenue Code was amended to permit the return of distillates containing aldehydes from the distilled spirits plant to an adjacent bonded wine cellar for addition to distilling material. U. S. Laws (1958, 1965) also made some progress in codifying the distilled spirits regulations.

Definitions. —Legal definitions of distiller, distillers, distillery premises, heads, and tails, etc., are given in U. S. Laws (1954). It is worthwhile giving certain legal definitions. Proof means the ethyl alcohol content of a liquid at 60°F., stated as twice the per cent of ethyl alcohol by volume. Proof gallon means the alcoholic equivalent of a U. S. gallon at 60°F. containing 50 per cent of ethyl alcohol by volume. Proof spirits means an alcoholic liquor which contains 50 per cent of ethyl alcohol by volume at 60°F. and which has a specific gravity of 0.93418 in air at 60°F. referred to water at 60°F. as unity. Wine spirits means brandy, as later defined, distilled at 140 degrees of proof or more and not reduced with water from distillation proof.

Brandy as such is defined as spirits distilled at less than 190° proof. If distilled at not over 170° proof solely from wine with a volatile acidity of less than 0.20 gm. per 100 ml. (exclusive of sulfur dioxide) and with not more than 20 per cent by weight of pomace or 30 per cent of lees is classed as fruit brandy. Depending on the raw material it may be labeled as "grape brandy" or "brandy," "peach brandy," "apple brandy" etc. If more than one fruit is used it must be labeled "fruit brandy . . . % grapes and . . . % blackberries" or as appropriate.

Dried fruit brandy, raisin brandy, dried peach, apple, etc., brandy, lees brandy, pomace brandy (which may also be labeled as marc brandy, grape brandy, or grappa), residue brandy, etc., are also defined in the regulations.

If distilled at 190° proof or over the spirits are known as "neutral spirits —fruit—grape" (or other fruit if appropriate).

Location and Construction

Distilled spirits plants may not be located in a dwelling house, on board a vessel or boat, on premises where beer, wines, or vinegar are produced, or where sugars or syrups are refined or where any other business is carried on—with certain specified exceptions.

The distillery buildings must be securely constructed and must be completely separated from contiguous buildings not on distillery premises again subject to stated exceptions. There are provisions for foundations, floors, walls, roofs, doors, windows, shutters, skylights, ventilators, drains, etc.

A brandy deposit room was formerly provided for unless all the brandy is removed from the distillery during the regular working hours of the same day on which it is drawn from the receiving tanks. All the doors of the brandy deposit room were provided with locks. This is no longer needed since spirits may now be left in the receiving tanks if the tanks are indicated on the plat as being used for this purpose. A filled-package room and a fermenting room may be required in certain cases.

A government office is obligatory, except that the government office on contiguous premises may be used (see p. 740). A government cabinet is also necessary.

A conspicuous sign, not less than three inches in height of lettering, must be placed outside and in front of the distillery indicating the name of the distiller, the distilled spirits plant number (fruit distillery), and the character of the business, or businesses, conducted on its premises.

Equipment

Where brandy or heads or tails are drawn into packages at the distillery the distiller must provide suitable and accurate scales. Weighing tanks of a specific design and construction are also required where brandy is recovered from a distillery by pipeline. Test weights are required—again unless they are provided on contiguous premises (p. 740). However, volumetric methods of measurement are now permitted and are used more often than weighing.

Locks on furnace doors, and steam and fuel lines must be provided for. Also distilling material measuring and storage tanks are required. In some cases fermenters and washwater receiving tanks are required.

Stills must be of substantial construction and must have a clear space of one foot around them. Locks are necessary. The doubler or worm tanks must be elevated not less than 1 ft. from the floor.

All tanks used as receptacles for brandy between the outlet of the first condenser or worm and the receiving tanks must be constructed of metal unless enclosed within a securely constructed room equipped for locking with a government lock. All tanks must be constructed with a suitable measuring device. Where such tanks are of irregular dimensions a table showing capacity of the tank for each inch of depth is needed. The tanks must be clearly labeled as to use, serial number and capacity in gallons. Distilled water tanks need not be equipped with locks. The "heads and tails" tanks must be labeled with serial number and the capacity in gallons.

The try boxes must be provided and so constructed as to permit reading the proof of the brandy as well as the temperature. These too, of course, must be equipped for locking with a government lock.

Singlings tanks may be used and sumps or chargers into which they may be run—again the inlets, outlets, and other openings must be provided for closing and securing with government locks. Receiving tanks of a size so that the receiving and singling tanks can hold a three days run are needed when the distillery is of such a size as to require frequent attendance of a storekeeper-gauger. Otherwise the receiving tanks should be large enough so that a visit of an internal revenue officer more than twice a month to gauge the brandy is not needed.

Special requirements for pipelines, sealing flanges, sealing unions, etc., are made. The pipelines must be painted blue for the conveyance of spirits (green for denaturants or denatured spirits). These colors may not be used for any other pipelines. Additional markings for other pipelines may be required.

Documents.—To establish a distilled spirits plant application for registration notice and, for the basic distiller's permit must be made on form 2607 to the assistant regional commissioner. If the operation is not covered by a Federal Alcohol Administration basic permit then an operating permit is necessary. The lot or tract of land on which the distillery is situated is described on form 2607. The continuity of the distillery premises must be unbroken, except that the premises may be divided by a public street or highway. The buildings and rooms must be accurately described. The estimated maximum number of proof gallons of brandy that will be distilled in 15 days, or are in transit to the premises, must be stated. This estimated maximum volume is to be based on maximum capacity of the stills and the use of maximum alcoholic strength of the distilling material. Likewise, the maximum volume of each kind of material intended for distilling each day must be stated.

Technical provisions concerning ownership, alternating ownerships, bonds, certificate of title, corporate documents, changes in ownership, list of stockholders, power of attorney, registry of still, plat, and plans, changes in premises or equipment in construction or use, and statement of process are also given in the regulations.

Special note should be made of the detailed requirements concerning the plat and plans. These include very specific drawings at specified scales, definition of contiguous premises, floor plans, elevational flow diagrams, etc.

Following filing of Form 2607 and receipt of notice, plat, plans, bond (Form 2601), and consent (Form 1602) the assistant regional commissioner will assign an inspector to examine the premises, buildings, apparatus and equipment to determine whether they conform with the proprietor's description. Corrections may be made during the inspection. The assistant regional commissioner will also ascertain whether an individual, firm, partnership, corporation controlling or actively participating in the business has been convicted of, or has compromised, any fraudulent noncompliance with any provision of any law of the United States relating to internal revenue or customs taxation of distilled spirits, wines, or fermented malt liquors or of any felony in the same connection.

If all documents are in order and the inspector's report is favorable a notice of registry is issued and a distilled spirits plant number is assigned.

Operation

To commence operations the proprietor files Form 2610 with the assistant regional commissioner specifying the date. Storekeeper-gaugers are assigned at the start of operations but normally are not on constant duty. The government agents remove and apply locks as required.

Materials received for distillation are entered on Form 2730. This form requires that the volume and alcohol content of the distilling material be known. If water is added to permit more economical distillation the volume and alcohol percentage is determined after addition of the water. The government inspector may verify the accuracy from time to time. An approved ebullioscope is used for the alcohol determination though other procedures may be approved. No chemicals or other materials, such as essences, flavors, coloring matter, etc., which are volatile and would remain incorporated in the brandy may be added to the distilling material. Tracer amounts of rare non-toxic metals may be added.

The regulations provide that the process of distillation must be a continuous one, i.e., that the brandy passes through continuous, closed stills, pipes, and vessels from the time the vapors rise in the first still until the finished brandy is deposited in the receiving tanks. However, during this process the distiller may carry the product through as many distilling operations as he may desire. The collection of heads and tails for the purpose of redistillation is not considered a break in the continuity of the distilling process.

On written application chemicals separated during distillation may be removed as the proprietor wishes and the assistant regional commissioner permits. Chemicals separated during distillation may be refermented or added to the distilling material.

Distilled water and carbon dioxide may be produced on distillery premises. Redistillation is possible on approval of application. Form 236 is used following approval. Burnt sugar or caramel, not containing any substantial quantity of sugar, may be added but this must be done prior to the time the brandy is gauged for removal from the distillery.

Tax-free samples of unfinished brandies in limited but reasonable amounts may be removed by the operator. They may be used only for organoleptic and laboratory analysis. The regulations impose certain other limitations on this privilege.

Other Regulations.—Brandy may be removed to Internal Revenue bonded warehouses—usually for aging in wooden containers as beverage brandy—to bonded wine cellars for fortification, or for exportation. Very detailed regulations on gauging for removal (Forms 2629 and 2630) are given. If to be used in winery for fortification of wine, Form 257 is used. Only spirits of 140° proof or over may be used in wine production.

The tax on all brandy becomes attached to brandy as soon as it is produced but may not be paid until removed from bond. It is a first lien on distilled spirits. The present tax is $10.50 per proof gallon. Taxes are determined when spirits are withdrawn from bond. They are paid by return on Form 2521 if prepaid and on Form 2522 if deferred.

Formerly there were several provisions whereby treating or handling brandy in a certain way resulted in payment of a rectification tax. At present few California brandies are subject to a rectification tax (U. S. Laws 1965, see action 805, subsection k).

If operations are to be suspended for 30 days or more or if operations are to be resumed, Form 2610 is filed. Provision for locking furnace doors, etc., is made.

The basic record of distillery operations is Form 2730. This is filled in daily, is kept at the distillery as a permanent record. One copy is forwarded to the assistant regional commissioner monthly. Form 2629 is used for the storekeeper-gaugers reports for the quantity of brandy produced. When tax-paid distilled spirits are received, stored or sold in bulk, Forms 338 or 2731 are used. These are daily reports. A list of the forms and records is given in U. S. Laws (1954).

STATE REGULATIONS

A summary of state laws and regulations relating to distilled spirit has been made by the Distilled Spirits Institute (1964). This study reveals how illogical and restrictive many of these state rules are. They range from preventing sale of miniatures (or imposing excessive taxes on them), to forbidding advertising in Sunday newspapers. The 17 monopoly states (where liquor is bought and sold mainly through a government agency) are usually the least favorable to the sale of alcoholic beverages though Georgia, which is not a monopoly state, has its share of weird laws affecting alcoholic beverages.

California

There are several definitions and regulations affecting brandy production in this state. California (1970) and (1969A) contain the main provisions.

Brandy is defined essentially as in the Federal regulations in California (1970). Geographical appellations are protected so that Cognac may be used only for grape brandy distilled in the Cognac region of France. Armagnac, Greek brandy, Pisco brandy, etc., are also considered names of distinctive types and may not be used for California-produced brandy.

In labeling distilled spirits California (1970) prohibits false or untrue statements. Specifically prohibited statements are "Furnished to His Majesty, the King of _____," "Due to our method of storage, this product ages in half the time," "Distilled from a scientifically controlled fermentation under laboratory control," etc. Statements disparaging a competitor's products are also prohibited. Statements such as "Contains no neutral spirits or alcohol," "Matured naturally—not heat treated," "Contains no headaches," are also illegal. Obscene or indecent statements, designs, devices, or representation are not permitted. Statements likely to mislead the consumer such as "From 20 to 30 scientific determinations are required for each bottle tested," "Analyzed by state laboratories and found to be pure and free from deleterious ingredients," "Tasted and approved" and "signed by_____Research Institute," etc., are also prohibited. Producers may not use statements such as "Guaranteed to consumer by _____," "Warranted to be the best product in its price range," "Guaranteed to be 10 years old," etc. "Pure," "double distilled," curative or therapeutic statements may not be used. Flags, seals, coats of armor, crests or other insignia which might be construed as relating to the armed forces of the United States or the American flag may not be employed.

Certificates of age and origin are required for all brandy sold in California—whether imported or domestic. Brandy may be sold only in 1 gallon, 0.5 gallon, 1 qt, 0.8 qt, 1 pt, 0.8 pt, and 0.5 pt liquor bottles. Similar Federal restrictions on labeling, advertising and standards of fill are given in U. S. Internal Revenue Service (1961B).

Finally, California (1954) sets a maximum tolerance of 0.35 per cent by volume for methanol.

The California Alcoholic Beverage Control Act (California 1969A) also imposes certain restrictions on brandy sale. The producer is known as a brandy manufacturer. The annual license fees are as follows: brandy manufacturer, $168.00; still, $12.00; rectifier, $276.00, brandy imported, no fee; distilled spirits or brandy wholesalers, $276.00, retail package off-sale general, $200.00, on-sale general, $580.00 (in cities of 40,000 population or over), $412.00 (for cities of 20,000 to 40,000), and $360.00 (for all other localities), on-sale general license for seasonal, $145.00, $103.00, and $90.00 (for cities as above), etc.

Restrictions in issuing licenses for on-sale of brandy are as for wine in California (p. 753). Distilled spirits sold at retail must be sold at fair trade and at the prices posted.

The Alcoholic Beverage Tax Law of California (California 1969A), gives the detailed provisions for collecting this tax. A surety bond is prescribed equivalent to twice the estimated monthly tax. The excise tax is $2.00 per wine gallon for distilled spirits of 100° proof or less. Brandy for fortification is not so taxed. The tax is due monthly.

BIBLIOGRAPHY

United States Regulations

ANON. 1941. State Liquor Legislation. Prepared by the Marketing Laws Survey. U. S. Govt. Print. Office, Washington, D. C.

CALIFORNIA. 1969A. Alcoholic Beverages Control Act, Business and Professions Code, Division 9 and Related Statutes. Calif. State Print. Office, Sacramento.

CALIFORNIA. Bureau of Marketing. 1969B. Marketing Order for Wine, as Amended, Effective July 1. Mimeo. Circ. Sacramento.

CALIFORNIA. 1970. Regulations Establishing Standards of Identity, Quality, Purity, Sanitation, Labeling, and Advertising of Wine. California Administrative Code, Title 17, Chapter 5, Article 14, Sections 17000–17105. California State Printing Office, Sacramento.

CALIFORNIA. 1971. California Excise Tax Laws, Part 14. California State Print. Office, Sacramento.

CERUTTI, G. 1963. Manuale degli Additivi Alimentari. Et/As Kompass, Milan.

DISTILLED SPIRITS INSTITUTE. 1969. Summary of State Laws and Regulations Related to Distilled Spirits. 17 ed. Distilled Spirits Institute, Washington, D. C. (See also later editions.)

OFFICE INTERNATIONAL DE LA VIGNE ET DU VIN. 1964. Codex Oenologique International. Vol. 1. Paris.

PARONETTO, L. 1963. Ausiliari Fisici Chimici Biologici in Enologia. Enostampa Editrice, Verona.

UDELL, G. G. 1968. Liquor Laws. U. S. Govt. Print. Office, Washington.

U. S. FEDERAL ALCOHOL ADMINISTRATION. 1937. Federal Alcohol Administration Act of 1935, as Amended, 49 Stat. 977. U. S. Govt. Print. Office, Washington, D. C.

U. S. INTERNAL REVENUE SERVICE. 1955A. Production of Vinegar by the Vaporizing Process. Part 195 of Title 26, Code of Federal Regulations. U. S. Govt. Print. Office, Washington, D. C. (U. S. Treasury Dept. IRS Publication No. 197).

U. S. INTERNAL REVENUE SERVICE. 1955B. Statement of Procedural Rules. Part 601 of Title 26, Code of Federal Regulations. U. S. Govt. Print. Office, Washington, D. C.

U. S. Internal Revenue Service. 1958. Use of the Terms, "Unfortified," or "Fortified," on Labels for Wine. U. S. Treasury Decisions 6319, C. B. 1958-2, pp. 1023, 23 F. R. 7698.

U. S. Internal Revenue Service. 1960. Liquor Dealers Regulations. Part 194 of Title 26, Code of Federal Regulations. U. S. Govt. Print. Office, Washington, D. C. (U. S. Treasury Dept., IRS Publication No. 195 (Rev. 9-60)).

U. S. Internal Revenue Service. 1961A. FAA Regulations No. 4 Relating to the Labeling and Advertising of Wine. Part 4 of Title 27, Code of Federal Regulations. U. S. Govt. Print. Office, Washington, D. C. (U. S. Treasury Dept., IRS Publication No. 449 (2-61)).

U. S. Internal Revenue Service. 1961B. FAA Regulation No. 5 Relating to the Labeling and Advertising of Distilled Spirits. Part 4 of Title 27, Code of Federal Regulations. U. S. Govt. Print. Office, Washington, D. C. (U. S. Treasury Dept., IRS Publication No. 449 (2-61)).

U. S. Internal Revenue Service. 1961C. FAA Regulation No. 6 Relating to Inducements Furnished to Retailers under the Provision of the Federal Alcohol Administration Act, Part 6 of the Title 27, Code of Federal Regulations. U. S. Govt. Print. Office, Washington, D. C. (U. S. Treasury Dept., IRS Publication No. 449 (2-61)).

U. S. Internal Revenue Service. 1962. Tax Paid Wine Bottling Houses. Part 231, Title 26, Code of Federal Regulations. U. S. Govt. Print. Office, Washington, D. C. (U. S. Treasury Dept., IRS Publication 202).

U. S. Internal Revenue Service. 1968. Distilled Spirits Plants Regulations. Part 201 of Title 26, Code of Federal Regulations. U. S. Govt. Print. Office, Washington, D. C. (U. S. Treasury Dept., IRS Publication No. 440 (1-68)).

U. S. Internal Revenue Service. 1969. Production of Volatile Fruit-Flavor Concentrates. Part 198 of Title 26, Code of Federal Regulations. U. S. Govt. Print. Office, Washington, D. C. (U. S. Treasury Dept., IRS Publication No. 189 (8-69)).

U. S. Internal Revenue Service. 1970A. Wine. Part 240 of Title 26, Code of Federal Regulations. U. S. Govt. Print. Office, Washington, D. C. (U. S. Treasury Dept., IRS Publication No. 146 (Rev. 7-70)). This is the most important U. S. document on wines.

U. S. Internal Revenue Service. 1970B. Gauging Manual, Embracing Instructions and Tables for Determining the Quantity of Distilled Spirits by Proof and Weight. U. S. Govt. Print. Office, Washington, D. C. (U. S. Treasury Dept., IRS Publication No. 455).

U. S. Laws. 1954. Internal Revenue Code of 1954, as amended. Sub-title E, Chapter 51. Title 26, United States Code 1. Washington, D. C.

U. S. Laws. 1958. Excise Tax Technical Changes Act of 1958, Public Law 85-859, 85th Congress, H. R. 7125, September 2. Washington, D. C.

U. S. Laws. 1965. Excise Tax Reduction Act of 1965. Public Law 89-44. Title VIII. Miscellaneous structural changes. p. 26 (This amends the Internal Revenue Code of 1954, paragraph 23, 370A).

Wiley, H. W. 1906. Foreign Trade Practices in the Manufacture and Exportation of Alcoholic Beverages and Canned Goods. Government Print. Office, Washington, D. C. (U. S. Dept. Agr., Bureau of Chem., Bull. 102).

Other Countries

General

No attempt will be made here to discuss the legal restrictions on wine and brandy production of foreign countries. Those of France and Germany, for example, are very voluminous. A few suggestions for research in this field are given in the following references.

BAMES, E. 1938. Ausländische Gesetzgebung über Alkoholische Genussmittel. *In* Bleyer, E. Alkoholische Genussmittel. Julius Springer, Berlin. pp. 760–797.

HOT, A. 1938. Les Appellations d'Origine en France et à l'Étranger. Éditions de "La Journée Vinicole, Montpellier.

FOOD AND AGRICULTURE ORGANIZATION. 1952–date. Food and Agricultural Legislation. Rome. 4 times a year.

OFFICE INTERNATIONAL DE LA VIGNE ET DU VIN. 1965. Mémento de L'O.I.V. Édition de 1965. Paris. (This and preceding editions (entitled Annuaire) have excellent summaries of the legislation of many countries. The monthly Bulletin of this organization should also be consulted for current information.

France

AUBOUIN, J.-M. 1950. Le Statut du Nom de Cognac et à l'Étranger. Bordeaux.

BLANCHET, B. 1960. Code au Vin et Textes Viti-Vinicoles. Édition de "La Journée Vinicole," Montpellier.

COMBES, D. 1957. La Fraude et le Code du Vin. Causse, Graille, Castelnau, Montpellier.

DAVID, J. 1938. Éléments d'Appréciation de la Nouvelle Législation Viticole des Appellations d'Origine Contrôlées. Les Éditions du Cuvier, J. Guillermet, Villefranche en Beaujolais.

DEAGE, P., and MAGNET, M. 1959. Le Vin et le Droit. 2 ed. Éditions de "La Journée Vinicole," Montpellier.

LEROY, J. 1931. Le Vin. Réglementation de la Production et du Commerce Vinicoles. J. -B. Baillière & Fils, Paris.

MARFAING, N. 1940. Contrôle de la Production de l'Alcool en France Les Éditions Domat-Montchrestien, Paris.

QUITTANSON, C., CIAIS, A., and VANHOUTTE, R. 1949–1965. La Protection des Appellation D'Origine des Vins et Eaux-de-Vie et le Commerce des Vins; Législation et Jurisprudence Suivies des Documents Officiels et de Tableaux Analysant Toutes les Appellations Contrôlées Réglementées. 3 vol. "La Journée Vinicole," Montpellier.

RIBÉREAU-GAYON, J., and PEYNAUD, E. 1958. Analyse et Contrôle des Vins. 2 ed. Libraire Polytechnique Ch. Béranger, Paris and Liège.

RIVERTON, C. 1940. Petite Traité de Législation Française en Matière Viti-Vinicole. Librairie J.-B. Baillière & Fils, Paris.

ROZIER, J. 1957. Le Code du Vin; Production, Commerce, Infractions, Fiscalité. Librairies Techniques, Paris.

VIVEZ, J. 1956. Appellations d'Origine. Librairies Techniques, Paris.

Germany and Austria

ANON. 1969. Das neue deutsche Weingesetz. Gesetz über Wein, Dessert-wein, Schaumwein, weinhaltige Getränke und Branntwein aus Wein. Zeitschriftenverlag Bilz. und Fraund, Wiesbaden.

BERGNER, K. G. 1968. Hinweise für die lebensmittelrechtliche Beurteilung. *In* Diemair, W. Alkoholische Genussmittel. Springer-Verlag, Berlin. (See p. 720–728.)

BÜRKLIN, A. 1934. Rechtliche Probleme in Weingeschäft. J. Kruse & Söhne, Bruchsal in Baden.

GALLOIS, H. 1954. Handelsbräuche und allgemeine Verkehrssitte im Deutschen Weinhandel. D. Meininger, Neustadt a.d. Weinstrasse.

GOLDSCHMIDT, E. 1951. Deutschlands Weinbauorte und Weinbergslagen. 6 ed. Verlag der Deutschen Wein-Zeitung, Mainz. (See pp. 4–14.)

HIERONIMI, H. 1958. Weingesetz. 2 ed. Verlag C. H. Beck, München und Berlin. Ergänzungsband. 1967.

HIERONIMI, H. 1959. Lebensmittelgesetz. 2 ed. Verlag C. H. Beck, München und Berlin.

HOLTHÖFER, H. 1938A. Deutsche Gesetzbung über Branntwein. *In* Bleyer, E. Alkoholische Genussmittel. Julius Springer, Berlin. (See pp. 719–759.)

HOLTHÖFER, H. 1938B. Deutsche Gesetzebung über Wein. *In* Bleyer, B. Alkoholische Genussmittel. Julius Springer, Berlin.

HOLTHÖFER, H., JUCKENACK, A. and NÜSE, K.-H. 1959. Das Lebensmittelgesetz und sonstiges Deutsches Lebensmittelrecht. I. Carl Heymanns Verlag, Berlin-Köln.

HOLTHÖFER, H., and NÜSE, K.-H. 1959. Das Weingesetz. 2 ed. Carl Heymanns Verlag, Berlin-Köln. Ergänzungsband. 1967.

KOCH, H.-J. 1955. Probleme des Weingesetzes unter Berücksichtigung von Reformfragen. Verlag Daniel Meininger, Neustadt.

KOCH, H.-J. 1970. Das Weingesetz. Verlag Daniel Meininger, Neustadt a.d. Weinstrasse.

KRAMER, O. 1954. Kellerwirtschaftliches Lexikon. Druck und Verlag: D. Meininger, Neustadt a.d. Weinstrasse.

PLATZ, R. 1956. Der weingesetzliche Ratgeber für den Kleinhandel. 2 ed. D. Meininger, Neustadt a.d. Weinstrasse.

REINER, H. 1957. Die Bestimmugen über Spirituosen und Fruchtsäfte im Sinne des Oesterreichischen Lebensmittelbuches. 2 ed. Verlag Hans Mally, Wien.

RIEGER, R. 1950. Die Weinfälschung im Strafrecht. D. Meininger, Neustadt a.d. Weinstrasse.

Italy

ANON. 1967. Codice degli alcoli, delle acqueviti e dei liquori. 2 ed. Agenda Vinicola, Rome.

PUECHER-PASSAVALLI, P. 1955. Prontuario della Legislazione sugli Alimenti, Prodotti Agrari, Sostanze de Uso Agrario. Ministero dell'Agricoltura, Roma.

RABAGLIETTI, G. 1958. Codice della Legislazione Sugli Alimenti, Bevande, Sostanze e Prodotti Agrari. Casa Editrice Spel, Bologna.

SCIALPI, L. 1961. Codice del Vino. Legislazione, Guirisprudenza Circolari e Risoluzioni Ministeriali. Luigi Scialpi Editore, Rome.

SCIALPI, L. 1965. Agenda Vinicola. 7 ed. Luigi Scialpi Editore, Roma. (Also contains much statistical information.)

768   THE TECHNOLOGY OF WINE MAKING

Spain

ANON. 1933. Estatuto del Vino. Revista de Alcoholes, Azúcares e Industrias Derivadas, Madrid.

ANON. 1955. Reglamento del Impuesto sobre el Alcohol Aprobado por Decreto de 22 de Octubre de 1954. Madrid.

RIVERO PEREDA, S., and FERNÁNDEZ DE CORDOBA COLLADO, D. 1946. Legislación Vitivinícola. Lar, S.L., Madrid.

Switzerland

BENVEGNIN, L., CAPT, E., and PIGUET, G. 1951. Traité de Vinification 2 ed. Librairie Payot, Lausanne. (See pp. 518–525.)

Index[1]

A

Acetal, 112–113, 207, 283, 430, 433, 712
  in brandy, 612, 615
Acetaldehyde, see *Aldehyde*
Acetic acid (volatile acidity), 24, 114,
    208–210, 579–580, 611
  addition of, 743–749
  as acylating acid, 104
  bacteria, see *Acetobacter* sp.
  determination of, 209, 319, 375, 693–
    695
  distillation of, 620
  effect of amino acids and ammonia on
    formation, 204, 209–210
  effect of pressure on formation, 198
  effect of sugar on formation, 184, 209
  effect of sulfur dioxide, 191, 257
  effect of temperature on formation, 196,
    198, 266
  effect on yeasts, 186
  excessive, 41, 55, 167, 209–210, 286,
    366, 399, 424, 577–578
  fermentation of, 183, 209–210, 421–423
  formation, 204, 209–210, 282, 284, 399,
    429
  in brandy, 614, 619–620
  in distilling material, 632
  in fruit and berry wines, 532, 536
  in grapes, 112
  in Madeira, 41
  in musts, 684
  in pressure-fermented wines, 386
  in sherry, 417, 431, 433
  in vinegar, 177
  in wine, 231–232, 431–433, 499, 516,
    532
  limits, 26, 65, 208–210, 580, 693, 733,
    736, 743, 749, 752
  odor, 680
  of distilling materials, 600
  oxidation by yeasts, 580
  production, 167, 169, 184, 191, 211,
    213, 286, 693
  utilization by yeasts, 183, 209–210
Acetification, 279, 367, 373, 386, 418,
    420, 544, 577–580, 662–664
Acetobacter sp., 154, 206, 259, 371, 450–
    451, 577–580, 594, 663–664, 685
  aceti, 578–579
  aerogenes, 654
  ascendens, 579
  effect of alcohol, 578

melanogenum, 578
mesoxydans, 579
  metabolism of, 580
oxydans, 578–579
paradoxum, 579
rancens, 579
roseum, 578
suboxydans, 578–579
xylinum, 578
Acetoin, 114, 196, 205–206, 231, 287,
    418, 426, 430, 586, 589
Acetone, 112
  see also *n-Propyl, alcohol*
Acetylmethylcarbinol, see *Acetoin*
Acidity, addition of, 358
  correction of, 268, 385, 392, 396–397,
    492, 497, 499, 514, 526, 533–534,
    541–542, 544
  determination of, 91, 319, 374, 692–693
  during maturation, 79, 81–83, 86, 89,
    96
  effect of *Botrytis* on, 12
  effect on color and tannin extraction,
    369
  effect on fermentation, 185–186
  effect on sucrose threshold, 215
  effect of sulfur dioxide on, 257
  fixed, 210–214, 257, 299, 422–423, 603,
    692, 695–696, 722, 754
  in brandy, 614, 619–620, 627, 636–637,
    722
  limits, 140–144, 147–149, 754
  of fruits and berries, 524, 531–533,
    535–536, 539–540
  of herbs, 508
  of shermat, 406
  of sparkling wine base, 460, 464
  of vermouth, 518
  removal, 214
  threshold, 211–212
  total (brandy), 614, 619, 627, 632
  total (Champagne), 14
  total (fruit and berry wine), 532, 536
  total (and malo-lactic fermentation),
    19
  total (musts), 9, 10, 33, 37, 58, 79, 99,
    103, 118–119, 122–123, 128, 357–
    358, 382
  total (sherry), 417, 431–433, 499
  total (vermouth), 507, 514, 516
  total (wine), 7–8, 26, 121, 128, 139,
    232, 299, 372, 430–431, 519

---

[1] Only the common English names of the numerous herbs given in Chapter 13, when available, have been listed here. See pp. 502–519 for their scientific and French and Italian names.

M

Maccabeo, 55
Mace, see *Nutmeg and mace*
Madeira, 41–42, 123, 208, 210, 282, 391, 440, 452, 680
    in the U.S., 143, 452, 734, 738, 755
Magarach, 49
Magnesium, 19, 115, 211, 229, 566–567
    effect on tartrate precipitation, 566
    in fermentation, 179–180, 187, 544
    phytate, 551
    removal, 296–297, 299
Maillard reaction, 549
Malaga, grape, 124, 392
    wine, 31, 208, 440
    in the U.S., 143, 147, 452, 739
Malathion, 335
Malbec, 9, 58–59, 103
Malic acid and malates, 9, 83, 98–99, 114, 120, 210, 229, 285, 646, 701
    addition, 746, 755
    and *Botrytis*, 77, 156
    and malo-lactic fermentation, 19, 28, 213, 229, 372, 426, 458, 582–583, 587, 591
    determination, 692
    effect of pressing, 251
    enzyme, 283, 587, 692
    fermentation by yeasts, 164, 213, 254
    intracellular fermentation of, 374
    of wines, 232
    oxidation of, 580
    pKs of, 211
    relative sourness, 211–212
    threshold, 211
Malic enzymes, 587
Malmsey, 41
Malo-lactic fermentation, 213–214, 284–287, 357, 362, 369, 372, 374, 455, 457–458, 583–589, 692
    and alcoholic fermentation, 261
    and racking, 279
    and sulfur dioxide, 191, 193, 257, 375
    effect on amino acids, 218–219
    effect on casse, 229
    in apple wine, 526
    in California, 286–287
    inducing, 286
    in Europe, 8, 10, 19, 21, 24, 27–28, 37
    in New York, 497
    reactions during, 285
Malta, 2
Maltose, 97
    fermentation of, 165
Malvasia, 28
    bianca, 449
Malvidin, 85, 103–106, 109, 222–223, 711
Malvin, 104, 222–223
Malvoisie, 124
Malvon, 104
Manganese, 115, 229–239, 720
    removal, 316

Manhattan (cocktail), 502
Mannitol, 206, 266, 582–583, 588–591
    bacteria forming, 581–582, 588–599
Mannose, 588
Mantuo Castellano, 408
Mantuo de Pilas, 408
Manzanilla, 35, 409, 416, 421
Maraština, 48
Marjoram, 506, 508, 514, 517
    sweet, 507, 514
Marsala, 25, 28, 119
    in the U. S., 143, 440, 452, 739, 755
Martini (cocktail), 138, 502
Maryland, 488
Masterwort, 506, 514
Mataro, 120, 124, 440
Maturity, changes during, 76–86
    factors effecting, 117–123
    for grapes for sparkling wine, 462–463
    measurement of, 86–94, 358
    time of, 489
Mavro, 51
Mavrud, 47
Mead, see *Honey*
Médoc, 9–10, 739, 740
    see also *Bordeaux*
Melibiose, 97, 163
Melon, 17
Mercaptans, 188, 226–227, 614
Mereshnik, 47
Merlot, 9, 27, 47–48, 58–59, 83, 97, 103–104, 257
Mesoinositol, see *Inositol, meso*
Mesoxalic acid, 114
Metabisulfite, see *Sulfur dioxide*
Metals, corrosion resistant, 554–556
Metatartaric acid, 566
Methane, from sewage, 345
Methanol, see *Methyl alcohol*
Methionine, 100–102, 218–219
    and protein instability, 552
    sulfone, 101
Methyl, acetate, 112–113, 617
    alcohol, 112–114, 202, 217, 222, 254, 610–612, 672, 763
    anthranilate, 60, 84–85, 112–113, 148, 392, 498, 670
    esterase, 672
    esters, 202
    pentosans, 216
2-Methyl-1-butanol, see *act.-Amyl alcohol*
3-Methyl-1-butanol, see *Isoamyl alcohol*
3-Methyl-2-butanol, 202
2-Methyl-3-buten-2-ol, 113
2-Methyl-2,3-dihydroxybutyric acid, 214
    (*also* 3-methyl)
Methylglyoxal, 613
2-Methyl-1-propanol, see *Isobutyl, alcohol*
2-Methyl-2-propanol, see *tert-Butyl alcohol*
α-Methylmalic acid, see *Citramalic acid*
Methylpentose, 216